T3-BNT-540

EVALUAT

Review Annual

Jonathan A. Morell, *Oakridge National Laboratory*
Jeri R. Nowakowski, *Northern Illinois University*
Robert G. Orwin, *United States General Accounting Office*
Robert Perloff, *University of Pittsburgh*
David B. Pillemer, *Wellesley College*
Charles Reichardt, *University of Denver*
Lee Sechrest, *University of Arizona*
William R. Shadish, Jr., *Memphis State University*
Nick L. Smith, *Syracuse University*
Bruce D. Spencer, *Northwestern University*
Robert E. Stake, *University of Illinois*
Daniel L. Stufflebeam, *Western Michigan University*
William M.K. Trochim, *Cornell University*
Carol H. Weiss, *Harvard University*
Joseph S. Wholey, *University of Southern California*
Paul M. Wortman, *University of Michigan*
William H. Yeaton, *University of Michigan*

Evaluation Studies

Evaluation Studies
Review Annual
Volume 11   1986

Edited by
David S. Cordray
and
Mark W. Lipsey

SAGE PUBLICATIONS
Newbury Park   Beverly Hills   London   New Delhi

WE DEDICATE THIS VOLUME TO
THE NEXT GENERATION:
ERIN,
LOREN,
and
MARISA

For information address:

SAGE Publications, Inc.
2111 West Hillcrest Drive
Newbury Park, California 91320

SAGE Publications Inc.
275 South Beverly Drive
Beverly Hills
California 90212

SAGE Publications Ltd.
28 Banner Street
London EC1Y 8QE
England

SAGE PUBLICATIONS India Pvt. Ltd.
M-32 Market
Greater Kailash I
New Delhi 110 048 India

Printed in the United States of America
International Standard Book Number 0-8039-2599-9
International Standard Series Number 0364-7390
Library of Congress Catalog Card No. 76-15865

FIRST PRINTING

CONTENTS

PART I

PROGRAM EVALUATION AND PROGRAM RESEARCH:
AN OVERVIEW

SECTION 1
Introduction

1

Evaluation Studies for 1986

Program Evaluation and Program Research

David S. Cordray and Mark W. Lipsey

Progress within the field of evaluation studies is often described somewhat anthropomorphically. For example, Conner, Altman and Jackson (1984) characterize evaluation of the 1960s as resembling the "fast developing childhood years"; by the 1980s it was said to have weathered the turbulent "early adolescent years" and was moving toward "adulthood." Others (e.g., Campbell, 1984; Scriven, 1984) view its development from a sociology of science perspective, seeing its pervasive turmoil as a natural part of the emergence and establishment of a new field.

Although the analogy offered by Conner et al. is intuitively appealing, it might be taken to imply that the roots for evaluation are established firmly (i.e., the genetic material is laid down) and a fully developed field of evaluation studies will unfold if given enough time, a forum to resolve disputes and gentle guidance. The sociology of science perspective suggests a more cantankerous process. In fact, Scriven (1984) views the controversies in the field as "a sign of ferment . . . and the seriousness of the methodological problems which evaluation encounters" (p. 49). To some, development means rejecting old conceptions and methods. This position implies that serious progress in evaluation is not the result of an orderly sequence of successive refinements but a complete paradigm shift. Indeed, from the tone of some writers, our contemporary "late-adolescent" field of evaluation might profit from a brief stint in an "evaluation reformatory," prior to taking on the responsibilities of a mature, adult profession. One thing is clear, the field of evaluation studies has grown at a brisk pace. It is also safe to say that not everyone is pleased with its developmental progress.

Currently, debates about the prospects for the field abound. As such, it is hard to bring a comprehensive picture of evaluation studies into focus. Part of this difficulty is due to the great diversity of practice that is labeled *evaluation*. Also contributing to the confusion is the propensity of evaluation theorists to attempt to encompass this diversity in a single overarching framework. Despite countless attempts, however, we still find that the fit between the frameworks and practice is not quite right. It seems that each effort to provide a framework for describing the "proper" role of methods, procedures, and philosophy in evaluation invariably includes too much or too little by some other reasonable standard. Our objective for this volume of the *Annual* is to provide a review of the range of issues and topics that characterize the field. Failing to resist the temptation, we also provide a framework for organizing the diversity of perspectives in the field. However, rather than imposing one overarching framework, we have taken a different approach and wish to argue for subdividing the field of evaluation studies into at least two distinct, if overlapping, specialty areas.

PROGRAM EVALUATION AND PROGRAM RESEARCH

A review of this volume's table of contents reveals our principal organizational scheme and the thematic perspective it embodies. We believe that recent trends, debates, and actual evaluation practices are best viewed as reflecting either mixtures or confrontations between two distinct approaches. We refer to these two approaches as *program evaluation* and *program research*. To provide some definition of these phrases, we offer the following short parable of the nature and history of evaluation studies.

There is little doubt that the dominant paradigm in evaluation studies today is that of applied social science, in particular, the quantitative-comparative experimental paradigm. The evidence is everywhere apparent. The evaluation methods most frequently employed use quantitative measures, some sort of control or comparison group (or offer apologies for the lack thereof), and the logic of the experiment with its focus on the dependent variable "effects" of the program or treatment independent variable. Moreover, most evaluation practitioners were themselves trained as social scientists—psychologists, sociologists, educators, and so forth—and the jargon and concepts of those disciplines pervade the evaluation field.

The roots of the applied social science paradigm in evaluation studies can be traced to two seedbeds. In education, the frame was set in the 1940s by Ralph Tyler's achievement-of-objectives approach, in which educational objectives were defined and formal testing was used to determine students' attainment of those objectives (see Guba & Lincoln, Part I, this volume). More generally, the seminal work of Campbell and Stanley (1966) gave the field an indelible imprint of (quasi-) experimentation.

Whatever the conceptual and methodological merits of the applied science paradigm for evaluation study, it carried with it some features that attracted immediate criticism on philosophical grounds, and other features that proved unsettling in actual practice, leading to additional criticism on practical grounds. Indeed, the surest way to know that the applied science paradigm is dominant in the evaluation field is to observe the vigor and pungency of criticism directed toward it. Few critics would waste the ammunition required to sally forth and deliver a full broadside unless they believed they were facing the armada of the ruling empire.

Among the features carried as baggage by the applied social science paradigm, three elements are most noteworthy. First, the positivistic heritage of social science endowed it with a descriptive "value-free" ideology that left no apparent room for the value judgment implied by the notion of "evaluating" a program. Second, social science is conducted from a particular point of view, that of the "objective" researcher. The perspectives of the major players in a program situation, and the meaning a program might have for them, could, at best, be represented dryly (and indirectly) as "data." Third, the social science approach to inquiry has primarily to do with the development and testing of knowledge, not the advising of decision makers. The process is difficult to implement, inherently slow, and proceeds with painstaking care and conservatism. From a practical standpoint, it takes too long to produce answers, and the questions it addresses are not necessarily those of interest to decision makers.

It was, of course, just these characteristics of the applied social science paradigm that attracted criticism of its appropriateness for evaluation study. The result has been debate and controversy and, most important, the proliferation of alternate views (if not defined "paradigms") of how evaluation should be conducted. Among those alternate views we would count Cronbach's reforms (1980), Eisner's Connoisseurship Model (1979), stakeholder evaluation (Gold, 1981), naturalistic evaluation (Guba & Lincoln, 1981), valid evaluation (House, 1980), utilization-focused evaluation (Patton, 1978), Scriven's goal-free evaluation (1973), responsive evaluation (Stake, 1975), CIPP (Stufflebeam, 1971), adversarial evaluation (Wolf, 1979), as well as others no doubt familiar to the reader.

The details of these various alternate perspectives, although important, are not our present concern. What does concern us is to try to mark and bound the ground these critics have wrested from the dominant applied social science paradigm. Collectively, they define an evaluation practice that puts its principal emphasis on valuing and judging a social program, assessing its meaning for recipients and sponsors, being responsive to context and politics, and, above all, providing timely, useful information to decision makers (whether they be program sponsors or managers, stakeholders, policymakers, or consumers themselves).

The distinguishing features of this composite orientation are that it is preeminently practical and it is evaluative. It is this orientation that we wish to call *practical program evaluation* or, in shorthand, simply *program evaluation.* Program evaluation thus represents essentially a service-oriented, practical mode of inquiry that primarily has evaluative intent. Typical questions include "How good is a program?" "Was it worth doing?" "How can it be made better?" The hub around which this approach revolves is the practical information needs of evaluation clients and, particularly, their need for a credible judgment of a program's value. Its methods have no priority of their own but are selected to serve the defined practical purposes. The methods are thus eclectic, tailored to particular demands and circumstances, and may often be informal or "subjective" by social science research standards.

What remains, then, of the applied social science paradigm in evaluation studies after the assault of the critics? These advocates of alternative approaches have hoisted their own flag over the field and declared victory. The defenders of applied social science, however, have stuck to their guns—unwilling to concede that their approach cannot be timely, useful, and evaluative, they have scrambled for ways to make their paradigm more responsive and useful. Their defense is strongest just where the alternatives are weakest—in the scientific values that give credibility to the results of inquiry.

It is here that our parable of evaluation history departs most from what we take to be conventional views on the subject. We agree with the critics who have claimed for their approaches the virtues of responsiveness, utility, and valuation. But we do not agree with the further implication that the applied social science paradigm is thus an inappropriate approach to the study of social programs. Conversely, although we agree that the applied social science approach produces valid and important knowledge about social programs, we do not agree that the social science paradigm can generally produce timely evaluative information of practical use to decision makers and consumers. In short, we believe that both the program evaluation approach (as we have dubbed it) and the applied social science approach are left holding important ground after the fray. We argue, however, that they are not holding the same ground and, furthermore, that distinguishing these separate terrains is crucial to the identity of evaluation studies as a specialty field and to resolving its fiercest current controversies.

The issue turns on the question of what is left of the applied social science perspective if you grant the general points of the critics, that is, that it is not timely, responsive, evaluative, useful to stakeholders, and so on. Contrary to the imperialistic tone of much recent discourse that attempts to sweep the science paradigm from the field, we believe that there is much of value left to the social science approach after these concessions. Indeed, we think that such concessions serve to free applied social science for a reorientation toward a very important and much neglected role in the field of evaluation studies.

We wish to use the term *program research* to describe an applied social science study of social programs with no pretensions to be evaluative, responsive, or useful (at least in the short term). Such study encompasses inquiries directed at questions such as—"How does a program work, that is, by what psychological, sociological, and organizational process?" "What are the effects of the program on a selected range of dependent variables?" "What mediates those effects?" "How general are the relationships?" Although evaluative statements might be derived from program research studies, the focus is on establishing cause-and-effect relationships, constructs, and linkages among constructs. At the primary study level, program research should direct attention at theory, implementation, presenting social problems, and the processes that connect the intervention with changes in social conditions. At the synthesis level (e.g., meta-analysis), concern should focus on the conceptual generalizations that can be derived from examining multiple realizations of programs, different intervention strategies, client by treatment interactions, and the context within which interventions operate. Program research, therefore, is a rather academic inquiry distinguishable from other areas of social science only by its target topic—social intervention—and its attention to those independent variables that are subject to manipulation by policymakers (see Rossi & Wright, Part I, this volume).

We grant that this portrait of what we are calling program research is somewhat extreme, relative to contemporary practice. We can cite few examples of research on social programs that are as unconcerned with utility and evaluation as suggested here or, conversely, as concerned with theory and generalization as we suggest. Our point is that such research, even in more extreme form, need make no apologies—it performs essential functions that are not fulfilled by what we have called program evaluation nor by other specialty areas in social science. Before moving on to some of the details that contrast the program evaluation and the program research perspective, we want to elaborate on some of the neglected functions of program research.

The principle function of program research is to develop valid, generalizable knowledge about intervention, the social problems on which intervention is targeted, and the social system within which intervention is implemented. Although of limited immediate applicability, the long-term utility of a cumulation of such knowledge almost needs no defense. Such information would be of great benefit in the design of social programs and policy, permitting inferences about the best approaches to particular kinds of problems, the manner in which interventions should be organized, the kinds of variables upon which success generally depends, and a host of other such practical matters of program or policy design and implementation. In this mode, program research, over the long run, becomes a wellspring of ideas and advice for innovation in social policy.

A second contribution of program research is in the area of program diagnosis and improvement—determining the likely causes of program or policy failure (e.g., faulty theory) and identifying ways to rectify them. Scriven, in this volume (Part I, Section 3) makes the point, appropriate to the program evaluation perspective, that the evaluators' task is to evaluate, not simply to suggest how improvements should be made. He illustrates his point with the case of product evaluation. An evaluator might show that a dishwashing detergent failed to get the dishes clean, but would be unable to indicate how it should be improved— that would be the job of the chemist, engineer, and others who understood the theory of the product. We would stand Scriven's point on its head and ask, Who plays the role of the chemist or engineer for social programs? Who is it that understands the principles of their operation and has the capability of improving their design? These matters have been neglected by the traditional social science researcher and go beyond the expertise of most program administrators and policymakers. Although agreeing with Scriven that the program evaluator need not have this knowledge, we would maintain that the program researcher should. Moreover, effective collaboration between program evaluator and program researcher, as well as collaboration between product tester and product engineer, can only produce better products, that is, social programs and policy.

Finally, we think program research, as we have described it, gives essential guidance to the program evaluator. Properly developed, program research can provide a conceptual frame that identifies variables likely to be important in typical programs, informs the assessment of implicit program theory, alerts the evaluator to relationships that are likely to hold in program circumstances, and generally helps the evaluator focus his or her efforts in an effective way. More strongly, we would argue that every evaluator approaches the evaluation task with some theory or conceptual frame about how programs work and what issues are important. We think evaluation practice will be improved if such theories and frames are explicit and subject to testing.

We thus argue that program evaluation and program research have legitimate, but different, functions within the field of evaluation studies. In its extreme form the differences in function can be stated succinctly: The former establishes the presence of merit within an intervention, action, or entity; the latter illuminates the mechanisms and causes of the features judged meritorious.

In practice, we recognize substantial overlap between these approaches—an evaluative inquiry necessarily includes some analysis and description of program process, causal mechanism, theory, outcome, and so forth. Similarly, a research inquiry yields results that lead more or less naturally to an evaluative judgment (e.g., certain desirable effects were or were not attained; performance was "better" under regimen A than regimen B) and practical advice for decision makers. Nonetheless, we see differences of purpose, emphasis, and method sufficiently large to justify this distinction as an organizational scheme for the recent literature in the field and, indeed, as a basis for the field's conception of its own activities and purposes.

The primary implication of this scheme is that, by distinguishing between evaluation study and research study of social programs, careful consideration must be given to the alignment of purpose and method in the study of a social program. From the program evaluation perspective, much of the current difficulty and controversy stems from the widespread use of the experimental paradigm as the methodological frame within which studies are set. Because that methodology is not inherently well suited to the purpose of providing timely, evaluative information for practical short-term, numerous compromises must be made. The result, all too often, is neither man nor beast. As social science research, it looks shoddy (poor design, measures, sampling, and so on). As evaluation it is cumbersome, slow, detached from participant's intuitions and experience, and descriptive rather than evaluative. Distinguishing evaluation purposes from research purposes, as so many commentators have noted, legitimates the development and use of a great variety of less formal or, if you will, less "scientific" methods appropriate to the evaluation tasks. In this regard, we find the recent upsurge of interest in qualitative and naturalistic methods to be healthy and appropriate. And, although the validity of such methods certainly warrants concern within the context of their use, we do not think it is appropriate to compare them with experimental research methodology and criticize their rigor. We rightfully use different tools with different properties for different purposes—it is being clear on the properties and the purposes that presents the challenge.

From the research perspective, the implications are similar but reverse. What requires legitimation here is not the methodology, which is only too well established, but the purpose—the idea of studying social programs in order to have a better understanding of them and to build a knowledge base that continuously improves that understanding. To saddle research with the burden of being responsive, evaluative, timely, useful, and so on, is to cross purposes in ways that will generally yield either poor research or poor evaluation (or, worse, both). In particular, burdening research with short-term practical concerns misdirects it from the matters of theory and concept that should be its primary concern. The result has been a great deal of research in the methodological sense but remarkable underdevelopment of such concepts as program theory, organizational theory, strength and integrity of treatment, implementation process, and so forth, as they apply to social programs. We see some assertion of the research perspective in the recent literature, especially with regard to the role of theory in program study. Generally, however, research seems to be on the defensive, more condemned than exhalted. We see this as a symptom of the field's confusion about method and purpose rather than the making of a revolution to overthrow a dominant paradigm.

Careful consideration of method and purpose also highlights those fortuitous circumstances when the evaluation perspective and the research perspective converge. For example, demonstration programs being tried out in advance of full implementation are frequently ideal candidates for social experimentation in which rigorous social science methodology is applied to produce just the kind of assessment of effects that interest policymakers. A similar convergence may occur in program development—the creation and testing of techniques and treatments to refine them and establish their efficacy for subsequent program use. In situations such as these not only does "research" methodology suit "evaluation" purposes, but "evaluation" methodology may also suit "research" purposes. That is, the formal social science research conducted in such circumstances can frequently be enhanced and augmented by informal and qualitative techniques that contribute significantly to full understanding of the program and its context.

With these images and implications in mind, we turn now to a closer look at the distinction between program evaluation and program research and their different attributes and purposes.

PROGRAM EVALUATION AND
PROGRAM RESEARCH:
FURTHER DISTINCTIONS

In monitoring the development and progress of the field, several metaobjec-
tives, performance indicators, or dimensions have been proposed in the past
decade. We highlight four somewhat interrelated attributes as a way of detailing
the distinction between program research and program evaluation. The first
three attributes—utility, knowledge-building, and institutionalization—are
taken from Cook's (1978) assessment of the field in the late 1970s. From Scriven's
chapter (Part I, Section 3) we add the notion of a logical methodology for
evaluation. Including additional facets of each attribute, we identify seven
concepts on which the perspectives can be distinguished. These are summarized
in Table 1.1.

A priority among evaluation theorists and practitioners is the utility of
evaluation studies. Following Chelimsky (1983), three facets can be specified:
timeliness, technical adequacy, and responsiveness. The latter can actually be
thought of in two ways; responsiveness to the requests of the client for
information *or* to the context. An evaluation that is responsive to the program
context would faithfully record what transpired (and changed) within a program
and its ecology. Normally, this requires a flexible methodology that can be easily
adapted to a dynamic setting.

Knowledge-building has also been touted as the primary rationale for engaging
in evaluation activities. As used here, knowledge-building is broadly conceived
to include gains in generalized understanding of the social problems, the
"theories of action" embedded in program structure, and methodological
insights.

A much overlooked aspect of evaluation studies is its own identity as a
discipline. One aspect of identity includes institutionalization. This refers to
outward signs of a separable and durable profession or discipline.

Scriven's call for a *logical methodology of evaluation,* highlights the most
distinctive function of the field—the rendering of an evaluative judgment of
merit or worth. More to the point, a comprehensive evaluation perspective
should contain a logic for translating *information* into a judgment of merit or
worth. Conceptually, it is unappealing simply to define evaluation as a collection
of research methodologies, tools, and tactics.

In Table 1.1 we identify what we see as the stereotypical emphasis of program
research and program evaluation for each of these concepts. The entries show
some points of convergence and substantial differences in emphasis across the
two perspectives. It should be recognized that there is considerable variation
within each perspective; some approaches exhibit more of one attribute than
suggested in the table and others exhibit less. However, to bring the major
distinctions into relief, we emphasize the *pattern* of entries to highlight the
fundamental trade-offs across these concepts for program evaluation and
program research.

TABLE 1

Relative Emphasis of Program Evaluation and Program
Research Perspectives on Key Dimensions

	Perspective	
	PROGRAM EVALUATION	PROGRAM RESEARCH
I. UTILIZATION		
o Timeliness	HIGH	LOW
o Responsivenss		
(a) Context	HIGH	MODERATE
(b) Stakeholders	HIGH	LOW
o Technical Quality	RELATIVE	RELATIVELY ABSOLUTE
II. KNOWLEDGE-BUILDING	LOW	HIGH
III. LOGICAL EVALUATION METHODOLOGY	YES	NO
IV. INSTITUTIONALIZATION	HIGH	HIGH

NOTE: This table is intended as a schematic representation of the two perspectives. In practice, these distinctions are more continuous than is depicted here.

Responsiveness

The program evaluation perspective, in large measure, places a premium on delivering information that is responsive to the context within which programs operate *and* to decision makers and stakeholders. On the other hand, program research places a lower priority on responsiveness to information demands of the decision maker. Recent interest in theory, client by treatment interactions, and program implementation imply, however, that program context cannot be ignored in the research perspective. That is, to be useful, program research must be at least modestly attentive and responsive to the program context. After all, simply determining that a program did not achieve its intended effects (a likely result; see Cordray & Sonnefeld, 1985) gives little information upon which understanding or corrective actions could be based. Nonetheless, in Table 1.1, we indicate that program research is only modestly responsive to the context because this form of inquiry is generally limited to assessing, quantitatively, relatively static features of the program. Compared to other methods, say the anthropological methods described by Dorr-Bremm (Part II, Section 5), much less evidence is typically derived on the dynamic nature of the program. We do not mean to imply that program research could not use qualitative forms of inquiry; in fact, qualitative and quantitative inquiry blend very nicely as methods for describing the program context and for estimating numerical impact, respectively. In the recent literature, however, we found no study reporting such a mixture.

Timeliness

The issue of timeliness, although intuitively appealing, is conceptually quite messy. The now timeworn image of untimely delivery of the evaluation report "just as the train is pulling away from the station" seems to be fading. Within practical program evaluation, practices have been focused toward the delivery of intermediate products and establishing close working relationships (e.g., Cronbach et al., 1980, and the chapters in Part II, Section I) as insurance against unforeseeable delays that render the evaluation report useless. In many instances, timely evaluation can be characterized as a flow of information rather than the delivery of a discrete product.

For program research involving primary data collection, timeliness is better thought of as elapsed time—that is, the amount of time before results will be available. In this regard, program research is mixed. At the primary level, the time needed to perform a comprehensive "theory-driven" evaluation (see Chen & Rossi, 1983; Wang & Walberg, this volume) can be substantial. If the substantive area is uncharted or in its early phases of development, conducting needs assessments or evaluability assessments, searching prior literature for evidence on exogenous variables that are related to theory-relevant outcomes, conducting pilot tests, assessing measurement sensitivity, and so on add to overall elapsed time.

Extended elapsed time should not be taken as justification for not engaging in program research, however. To the extent that decision makers/clients are made aware of these extended time requirements, elapsed time may not be a problem. After all, timeliness is a relative concept that merely depends on the match between someone's expectations and actual performance; when the match is poor, the evaluation is untimely. Further, the potential long-run utility and timeliness of a study should also be considered within the context of a research synthesis framework. That is, the investment in time and expense for primary studies can be partially recovered through research synthesis. When time is of the essence, research synthesis may be the only way that a policymaker's schedules can be accommodated (see Light, this volume, for an example). For this scenario to work, a stockpile of high-quality program research is necessary.

Studies under the experimental paradigm that have attempted, nonetheless, to serve timely evaluative functions have generally made a relatively poor showing. Reviews of the methodological underpinnings of such studies indicate that many are seriously flawed (see Lipsey et al., Part I, Section 3). There are many reasons for this state of affairs. Some of these relate to the external pressures (e.g., short time frames or unreasonable deadlines); other reasons are more damaging to the reputation of the field (e.g., the studies were not competently performed). Given the difficulty of conducting applied research within program settings, it seems to us that timeliness (in the short run) should be deemphasized for program research. Responsiveness to the context should be emphasized but responsiveness to the particular demands of the stakeholder, although a desirable objective, should not drive decisions on what is assessed or how. The exceptions to this claim would be those cases in which researchers and stakeholders had common research objectives, for example, social policy experiments and research synthesis.

Technical Adequacy

By *technical adequacy* we mean the extent to which information that is collected is both credible and sufficient to answer the questions implied by the purposes of the study. In practice, credibility and sufficiency are open to endless interpretation and argument. This is especially true within the program evaluation perspective with its great diversity of tools, tactics, and approaches. As such, we characterize the issue of technical adequacy as *relative* for program evaluation and *relatively absolute* for program research. The reason for this is simple. Within program evaluation, the diversity of questions, issues, and program circumstances requires the analyst to be flexible. There are no hard and fast rules for how evaluations are to be conducted. Thus the technical adequacy of the chosen strategy must be examined relative to the available resources, desired level of precision, and ultimate purpose for collecting the information in the first place. On the other hand, we have labeled concerns about technical adequacy within the program research perspective as *relatively absolute*. That is, statistical theory and validity concepts (e.g., Cook & Campbell, 1979) serve as a fairly well-established set of guidelines for examining the technical evidence supporting different forms of inference. Naturally, in practice, there are limits to such standards (Berk, 1982).

To make this distinction concrete, consider the following examples. It is well recognized that post hoc stratification of client groups to ascertain whether or not specifiable subgroups experienced differential outcomes cannot be justified by conventional statistical standards (see Leamer, 1978, for some exceptions). But, if the purpose of such an analysis is to probe the data for information about how a program might be retargeted, such procedures are, relative to this specific purpose, defensible. In contrast, for establishing cause-and-effect linkages, such post hoc stratification incorporates well-known selectivity biases and even advanced statistical procedures will not guarantee an unequivocal result. In the first example, judgments of technical adequacy need to be tempered relative to the stated exploratory purpose of the analysis. In the second case, the technical issues are well known and judgments of technical adequacy are relatively absolute.

The principal point of this discussion is that the practical program evaluation perspective contains many more "degrees of freedom" in selecting or devising methods for meeting the needs of clients and stakeholders. When trade-offs become necessary, therefore, technical quality considerations can be adjusted. The program research perspective has fewer degrees of freedom in this regard. Despite claims such as "in the practical realities of applied research, methodological trade-offs are inevitable and will rarely meet textbook standards," we argue that these realities ought to be considered and if they yield a poor match with the experimental methods then the purposes of the study ought to be renegotiated and some other form of assessment should be considered.

Knowledge-Building

In terms of purpose, knowledge-building as an objective for the field is another primary distinguishing characteristic that separates the two perspectives. In practical program evaluation, with its client-focused orientation, knowledge-building is a circumscribed activity dealing narrowly with the particular program at hand. Theory can be brought to bear in the inquiry, but it is typically limited to the use of theoretical knowledge as a way of guiding the inquiry; that is, it represents an application of theory, not a test of theoretical propositions. In some cases, for example, Weinholtz and Freidman (Part II, Section 5), application gives rise to theoretical insights that could be subjected to further testing. Knowledge-building, in the sense of developing and testing generalized conceptions of interventions, causal relationships underlying the change process, and so on is a fundamental characteristic of the program research perspective. Here, the inquiry is oriented toward advancement of theory or conceptual generalization regarding processes underlying social interventions using the particular intervention study as an instance of a broader class.

Several additional points regarding theoretical knowledge merit further consideration. Theories vary in their application to program research as well as their testability within a program setting. Grand theories of human nature are unlikely to be useful in program development or testable in the program research context. Rather, each of the successful applications we have seen have been restricted to smaller-scale theories or empirically examined models based on economic, psychological, sociological, and organizational principles.

Special requirements for theory testing. The difficulty of theory testing within a program context should not be underestimated. For delicate theoretical models, noisy program environments pose a substantial challenge. An adequate assessment of the theoretical basis for an intervention requires answering several preliminary questions—"Was the treatment implemented adequately to trigger the process implied by the model?" "Were the methods (measures and design) sufficiently well implemented (e.g., technically sound, sensitive, and unbiased)?" To answer these questions, two forms of evidence are needed.

The first is exclusionary evidence. This entails demonstrating that effects (positive or negative) were not an artifact of the research methods used or uncontrolled circumstantial factors. This is a familiar concept, that is, testing and, to the extent possible, *ruling out* rival explanations. The second form of evidence is inclusionary, meaning evidence that supports a claim. For example, it has to be demonstrated that the purported theoretical mechanisms were installed with sufficient integrity and strength to have triggered the causal chain of events implied by the theory. That is, we have to *rule in* the treatment as a plausible cause. Additionally, it is also necessary to provide evidence on the integrity of the research process. That is, the inclusion of evidence that demonstrates the sensitivity of measures, designs, and analysis tactics.

To substantiate a claim that a theory does not work, moreover, requires evidence that any null results are not due to program failure (i.e., the treatment was not implemented adequately) and not due to method failures (i.e., the design and measures were too insensitive to detect the true effect). These questions are not easily answered. As a result, although we think incorporating theory into the program research process is a significant step forward, enthusiatic optimism is unwarranted. To avoid additional frustration, this ought to be used only when conditions are optimal.

Theory-guided program research. A more realistic and modest position for program research might be termed *theory-guided* inquiry, as opposed to *theory-driven.* Some prior research and theory can be helpful in identifying aspects of a causal linkage. For example, Crano and Meese (1984), arguing from an information processing model, tested whether the participants' comprehension of a complex treatment influenced the overall success of the program. Similarly, the research on motivation for treatment reviewed by Miller (Part III, Section 3) provides a basis for examining behavior that is maladaptive (e.g., failure to comply with the treatment regimen) within treatment environments.

Epistemology. At a more abstract level, the distinction between program evaluation and program research (at least with respect to extreme points of view on this continuum) can be described from an epistemological point of view. Guba and Lincoln (Part I, Section 2) regard programs as pluralistic constructions, inextricably connected to the values of the separate observers. As such, there is not a single reality that can be objectively identified, measured, and tested as a basis for assessment. This poses considerable difficulty for the program research perspective with its emphasis on conceptual generalizations. Implicit within the measurement, design, and analysis aspects of the methods implied by program research is a belief that programs contain objectively identifiable characteristics that are separate from the construals of involved observers.

There is little question that programs have identifiable features that can be described and measured. The difference between the two perspectives is a matter of the values that different observers assign to these features. The program research perspective examines one set of "facts" about the tangible aspects of an intervention (client flow, treatment delivery, changes in status on variables of interest, and so on). The program evaluation perspective may examine a different range of "facts," as seen from many points of view. Each has a legitimate epistemological basis depending on the purposes of the inquiry.

Logical Evaluation Methodology

Scriven (Part I, Section 2) makes an elegant and simple point about contemporary evaluation—if evaluation is a distinctive form of inquiry, there must be a logical methodology (more accurately, a set of logical methodologies) for connecting a statement of value, worth, or utility of a program with the evidence that is gathered. The notion of valuational interpretation is so fundamental that the Joint Committee on Standards for Educational Evaluation (1980) has designated it as one of their principal standards of conduct. (Note that such a standard was not included in the Program Evaluation Standards issued by the Evaluation *Research* Society; see Stufflebeam, 1982.) As guidelines for implementing this standard, the Joint Committee suggested the following: (1) considering alternative bases for interpreting findings (e.g., project objectives, democratic ideals, assessed needs of a consumer group); (2) deliberations on who will make valuational interpretations (e.g., the client, audience, evaluator, some combination of these); and (3) considering alternative techniques that might be used to assign value meanings to collected information (e.g., different teams writing advocacy reports, adversarial hearings, or specifically charging the evaluator to arrive at such a judgment).

Guba and Lincoln's proposal (Part I, Section 2) to achieve this end characterizes the role of evaluator as someone who systematically describes the value positions of all relevant stakeholders and serves as a negotiator. Scriven's position is more direct; judgments of merit are a natural part of human cognition and easily rendered by observers. The role of a professional discipline is to understand the basis for these judgments, be explicit about the values they embody, and minimize the harmful consequences of the methods used to formalize a summative judgment of merit.

The program evaluation perspective has, therefore, made some progress in developing a logical methodology for valuing worth. There are, indeed, several methods (e.g., Delphi, priority sort, and needs assessment) that are quite explicit about how program results can be linked to value judgments about the merit of the program. Nonetheless, Scriven's point is well taken and considerably more work is needed on this central program evaluation issue.

For program research, the issue of valuational interpretation is complex. On procedural grounds, program research, with its emphasis on technical, analytical assessment does not directly yield a judgment about the worth of a program, except in a relative, comparative sense. That is, reliance on quantitative indicators, allocation to conditions, and "summative" assessment through statistical significance testing yields, at most, a judgment of relative performance, that is, program X produced a statistically significant decrease in behavior Y. In some cases, the procedures yield the basis for a claim about merit, that is, the intervention is *better* than no intervention. This, however, is a limited view of the merits of the program. Who is to say that decreasing behavior Y is a worthwhile outcome? How much of a reduction is meaningful? Is it more meaningful to reduce behavior Y than Z? Are conditions substantially *better* now than they were without the treatment? And are they better for all recipients? The program research perspective, as an *evaluation* perspective, is more descriptive/analytical in these regards than it is evaluative. As such, program research is better suited to understanding the causes of merit than it is at providing a direct assessment of the presence or absence of merit.

Indeed, for all intents and purposes, it appears that proponents of a research-oriented perspective have abdicated their role in valuational interpretation, tacitly leaving this phase of the evaluation process to the client or stakeholder. In their discussion of social policy experimentation, for example, Berk et al. (Part

III, Section 4) do not use the term *evaluation* at all. When the term is used (e.g., Wortman, 1983), it is equated with assessment.

There are ways that social experimentation and research synthesis can be augmented to make the linkage between research and valuing programs clearer. For example, coupling monetary indicators of cost and benefits pushes the experimental perspective closer to a basis for judging worth, but in a limited sense. Prerelease reviews of program research evidence by all stakeholders may also help to assure that different perspectives on the value of a program are represented. And, simultaneous, independent analyses of data by different researchers represent another means of broadening the basis for evaluative judgments about programs. We found no recent instances of such practices, however.

Institutionalization

As indicated earlier, institutionalization refers to outward signs of a separate and durable profession or discipline. Such signs would include the presence of professional associations (e.g., the American Evaluation Association—recently formed through the merger of the Evaluation Research Society and the Evaluation Network), standards of conduct (ERS Program Evaluation Standards, 1982; Joint Committee on Educational Evaluation Standards, 1980), publications (journals and books), practitioners, clients, sources of revenue, and so forth. As shown in Table 1.1, institutionalization is an important aspect of each perspective.

For a professional discipline, institutionalization has survival value in the sense that structural arrangements (e.g., conferences, publications, networks) provide outlets for exchanging ideas, capitalizing on professional wisdom, and an accumulation of experience. There are several very clear signs that the field of evaluation studies has become more institutionalized in some regards over the past decade *and* less so in others. In this section we focus on the latter.

To date, evaluation studies have been predominantly driven by external forces. These include, for example, legislative mandates, user/client requests, and pressures for public accountability. Although contributing to the rapid development of the field, these external forces have also left evaluation vulnerable to the ebbs and flows of the political process. That is, we have seen that evaluation can become unfashionable as quickly as it became fashionable. The consequences of this dependency have been both good and bad. External pressures have been good in the sense that rapid developments in methods and perspectives emerged as practitioners and theorists attempted to meet the needs of users and clients. They have been bad for evaluation practices in the sense that external forces have pressured the field into valuing unidimensional attributes (e.g., immediate utilization versus technical/statistical quality) as a criterion for success and continued existence. Further, there has been little systematic thinking about what our portfolio of activities ought to look like to maximize short- and long-run benefits for evaluation as a field.

Deinstitutionalization of Evaluation

Today we see several signs suggesting that evaluation, as a field, is becoming "deinstitutionalized." For over a decade, the funding for evaluation and other applied social research has been on a downhill path (Rossi & Wright, Part I, Section 2; Wortman, 1975). Although few need to be reminded, this trend has accelerated and sets a context for the various themes that appear in the recent literature (e.g., the need for timely, user-focused, quick response evaluations). In the main, the consequences of operating within a constrained fiscal environment have been negative. The products of the "golden era" of evaluation (e.g., large-scale, national evaluations) have, for the most part, been issued and few new ones are in the pipeline. The persistence of this trend has resulted in evaluation specialists taking a more proactive approach to the problem by identifying alternative methods and sources of support, including private foundations (see Smith, 1985a) and the private sector. The prospects for the latter appear limited (Cook, 1984). The picture at the federal level, where much evaluation work originates, reveals several trends threatening the institutional support for evaluation (as a field) and the character of its products.

Legislative changes. Several important changes in the organization of social programs have contributed to these declines. The conversion of numerous categorical grants into block grants created a fundamental change in the administration of federal nondefense programs. This, in turn, has influenced the level and types of mandates for evaluation. Other legislation (e.g., the Deficit Reduction Act of 1984, and the Paperwork Reduction Act of 1980), has had its own separate influences on the conduct of evaluation. The Balanced Budget and Emergency Deficit Control Act of 1985 (Gramm-Rudman and Hollings) promises to tighten our collective belts one more notch.

Changes in fiscal resources for evaluation. The diversity of evaluation practice (e.g., federal, state, and local) makes it impossible to provide a precise assessment of changes in fiscal resources. There are partial indicators that reveal continued losses, however. For example, according to Chelimsky (1986), federal evaluations conducted in the Department of Education declined considerably between 1980 and 1984. Specifically, the Office of Planning Budget and Evaluation (OPBE) showed a 62% decline in fiscal measures (in 1980 constant dollars) for program evaluation activities. On the other hand, the federal investment in education remained relatively stable. Further, the reduction in fiscal resources, of course, resulted in the production of many fewer studies. Whereas OPBE reported conducting 114 studies in 1980, by 1984 that number had been reduced to 11 evaluation studies. Moreover, evaluations were not the only activities reduced within the Department of Education. Similar reductions were seen for research conducted in (or sponsored by) the National Institute of Education and for statistical activities undertaken by the National Center for Education Statistics.

Changes in statistical information. This deinstitutionalization is also seen in other aspects of government operations. In terms of fiscal resources for major statistical activity, the Congressional Research Service (1984) reported that 1984 levels were 8% (inflation adjusted) less than they were in 1980; personnel declined by 12% over the same period. Of course, each of the eight major statistical systems they examined were differentially affected. On balance, however, there were "more losers than winners" (Pearson, 1984). Prospects for 1986 appear even more grim (Congressional Research Service, 1985).

The adjustments that agencies have made to accommodate these funding reductions have some important implications for evaluation specialists. Some statistical series were eliminated altogether. Whether or not these were "important" activities that will be missed is not answered by the available reports. Others were eliminated and then restored, creating temporary gaps in the series. In other cases, series have been permanently altered (e.g., the interval was lengthened, sample sizes lowered, and geographic or demographic information reduced). Pearson (1984) also reports the termination or "scaling down" of validation studies designed to assess and provide input into further developments. How damaging these changes will be for sophisticated analyses is unknown at this time. It is clear that some alterations will pose considerable challenges.

The above suggests that just as the field of evaluation studies has begun to solidify its intellectual foundations, monetary resources—the fuel of the profession—have diminished. More fundamental for evaluation studies is the change in program structure instigated by recent legislation. The creation of block grants, for example, decentralizes program administration. Vague guidelines on evaluation also leave decisions of whether or not to evaluate and how to conduct these assessments up to the discretion of state and local authorities. It seems likely that evaluation studies will become even more oriented to providing timely information to meet specific and immediate client needs—threatening the knowledge-building objective that has served as a principal focus for at least some members of the profession. Several questions need to be raised. How can the field optimize diverse objectives in light of these fundamental changes? How can practices be altered to achieve a balance among these objectives? What is the role of academic-based researchers in developing and preserving our knowledge base?

PROSPECTS AND STRATEGIES
FOR THE FUTURE

Rossi and Wright (Part I, Section 2) begin their review of contemporary evaluation with good and bad news. Our discussion reinforces their assessment. That is, although the technical and intellectual foundations for evaluation have been greatly strengthened in the last decade, the financial viability of the field is on shaky ground. The trends in fiscal resources suggest that increased investments in comprehensive evaluation studies—either those advocated by Rossi and Wright, or the labor intensive ones described by Guba and Lincoln—are unlikely in the near future. Further, ongoing studies may be scaled down as efforts to reduce the current national deficit comes into full swing. As a case in point, Johnson (1985) provides a detailed accounting of how and why several longitudinal case studies of the impact of handicapped-education programs were truncated long before their scheduled termination. Undoubtedly, similar untold stories exist.

Although there may be new domains that could and should be explored under the rubric of evaluation (e.g., personnel evaluations), "folding up our tents" and moving to new pastures may be unwise if we are concerned about the long-run survival of evaluation studies as a field. The obvious question is, What courses of action exist that could push evaluation studies toward its goals and allow us to weather the cold winds of Washington? Program research, in contrast to program evaluation, is somewhat less vulnerable to political winds and whims, in part because of its more academic base. The coming years, therefore, may be a good time for increased emphasis on neglected research issues that are important to the field. In the next section we highlight three areas where we think important work can be done: research synthesis, secondary analysis, and systematic assessments of evaluative judgment processes.

Research Synthesis

Literature reviews are a normal part of any field. In recent years, the application of quantitative procedures for summarizing research and evaluation findings has gained considerable popularity, amidst occasional and vigorous objections from some quarters. Debates now have subsided and attention is being directed at expanding its applicability (e.g., Berger, Part III, Section 5; Finsterbusch, 1984; Hunter, Schmidt, & Jackson, 1982). Further, a spate of recent articles have been directed at overcoming obstacles (e.g., reporting deficiencies) and guidelines for sound synthesis practices. An additional sign of maturity is revealed by the appearance of several recent texts (e.g., Cooper, 1984; Light & Pillemer, 1984; Rosenthal, 1984) that have nicely organized and consolidated the diversity of meta-analysis practices suggested over the past decade. These books promise to contribute greatly to the popularity and appropriate use of research synthesis tactics.

Research synthesis also comes along at a propitious moment in the development of the field. Within the program research perspective, it serves as a means of systematically "summing-up" prior efforts that, to an unaided eye, may appear to contain little resemblance to a body of knowledge. With regard to substantive knowledge, several recent reviews illustrate how we can gain a better understanding of the diversity of effects, across studies, as well as plausible reasons for them. For example, Shadish and Reis (1984) provided an illuminating review of the available evidence in the area of maternal health; Wortman and Yeaton (in press) did the same for quality-of-life changes associated with medical interventions; and Betsey, Hollister, and Papageorgiou (1985) did a heroic job of summarizing studies emanating from the Youth Employment and Demonstration Projects Act. These syntheses reveal what is known about the effects of interventions and they glaringly point out gaps in knowledge thus serving as a rational basis for the development of subsequent programs and investigations. Although periodic assessments of what we know to date ought to be a routine part of a professional discipline, this has only recently become a valued activity within evaluation studies. The "timeout" we are currently experiencing, if used to take stock of what we know, should serve the field well when interest in new programs and studies reemerges as a priority.

Moreover, research synthesis is not limited to simply the accumulation of substantive knowledge about programs and their impact. There are at least three new directions for research synthesis that can be encouraged. These include, accumulation of nonexperimental evaluation evidence, syntheses of research and evaluation practices, and assessments of evaluation methods (i.e., meta-evaluation).

Synthesis of nonexperimental evaluative evidence. Until recently, research synthesis has been focused primarily on the aggregation of quantitative study outcomes, limiting the accumulation process to quantitative comparison group studies. Several promising reconceptualizations of synthesis have been developed that expand its purview. For example, Hunter, Schmidt, and Jackson (1982) provide a technical framework and logic for aggregating correlational evidence. This opens several doors for improving the sensitivity and sophistication of structural models of the sort described by Chen and Rossi (1983). Another bright spot in this area is the work by Berger (Part III, Section 5) and Finsterbusch (1984) who take a sizeable step forward by demonstrating how case studies can be cumulated. The untapped studies in this pool of evidence expands the data base for program research enormously and, as a consequence, expands the number and type of questions that can be addressed.

Synthesis of evaluation practices. Systematic examination of prior applied research and evaluations can be used to shape and sharpen evaluation policy (Boruch, 1985). It can also be used as a way of gaining insights into the inferential costs associated with employing incomplete and weak experimental designs (Lipsey et al., Part I, Section 3) and as a basis for improving the planning process for subsequent studies.

In practice, we think that more attention to the microfeatures of prior evaluations is warranted. Numerous reviews of the methodological under-pinnings of prior evaluation have enumerated general pitfalls in prior assessments but have stopped short of providing the kind of information that would be necessary to take corrective action. For example, the reasons why designs are underpowered (statistically) needs to be carefully probed. We may be using estimates of effect sizes that are unrealistically large, operating in environments that have lower than expected client flows or higher than expected attrition, or measurement insensitivity (Lipsey, 1983) might be the major determinant. To avoid making similar mistakes in future studies, these features need to be systematically examined. The prior literature is remarkedly informative in these regards and is easily available for careful synthesis (see Cordray & Sonnefeld, 1985).

Assessments of evaluation practices. The methodological ingenuity exhibited by evaluation specialists has been truly remarkable. After more than two decades of evaluation activity we have generated a considerable stockpile of studies. These range from novel applications of tools, tactics, and strategies to complex analyses of mediational mechanisms that document if, how, and why an intervention worked. Without trying to dampen this enthusiasm, we think it is wise for a profession to periodically step back and subject its creations and adaptations to systematic review. Within the program research perspective this is typically referred to as *meta-evaluation.* The notion quite naturally extends to other forms of evaluative practices and, indeed, several methodological assessments of evaluation methods were located as part of our review of the recent literature.

The review of stakeholder evaluation methods by Mark and Shotland (Part I, Section 3) represents one such assessment. Others include, for instance, Rog's (1985) review of 57 evaluability assessments conducted between 1972 and 1984. In this case, Rog augmented her review of actual studies with a survey of individuals responsible for the studies to ascertain how the evaluability assessment was conducted, funded, and used. Smith's (1985b) review of adversarial and committee-based evaluation procedures is another example of how we might systematically assess strengths and weaknesses of these forms of evaluation. The diversity of practices leaves open numerous additional opportunities for conducting these kinds of meta-evaluations.

Several improvements in practices at the primary study level will be necessary if research synthesis is to attain its full potential. In particular, the quality of documentation and reporting of results within primary studies will have to improve. At present, reporting deficiencies ranging from failure to disclose evaluation studies altogether (i.e., the file-drawer problem) to insufficient reporting of evidence seriously hinder the synthesis process. The papers by Pollard and associates, and the chapter by Levine (Part II, Section 2) should serve as guidance for correcting this situation. To maximize utility of primary studies within a program research perspective, documentation will require greater attention to contextual factors (see Blalock, 1984 and Part III, Section 1), program theory, and mediational mechanisms that link program activities to outcomes and strengths and weaknesses of methods underlying the assessment. In this way, the program research specialist can begin to isolate factors that influence programs, recipients, and results.

Secondary Analysis

The second tactic that we wish to highlight as an interim solution to the current evaluation drought is suitably labeled *secondary analysis,* that is, reanalysis of existing data. Whereas research synthesis typically uses *reported* evidence from prior research, evaluations, and other statistical information-gathering activities, secondary analysis takes this a step further by examining and remanipulating microdata from primary studies (or statistical systems). There are at least two general reasons—one pragmatic and the other scientific—for advocating secondary analysis. Namely, secondary analysis can be cost effective and it provides a mechanism for verifying results and stimulating the development of methodologies.

Cost-effective use of data. As noted in Fienberg, Martin, and Straf (1985), rarely does a single study exhaust the information value of a data collection effort. That is, new questions can be answered with extant data or established phenomena can be reexamined from different perspectives; and usually at a fraction of the cost of collecting new data. Within the past couple of years, several volumes have appeared on this topic. Stewart (1984) provides discussions of the availability of government- and nongovernment-sponsored data bases, along with helpful criteria for establishing the usability of secondary data sources. Bowering's (1984) edited collection, among other things, catalogues large-scale data bases, provides thoughtful tips on data preparation, and offers several good illustrations of the use of large-scale data bases sponsored by the federal government.

Verification and development. Experienced researchers are fully aware of the multitude of decisions and judgment calls that take place in transforming data into evidence. Data do not always conform to the salient features of statistical models, and in some cases a "proper" statistical model may not be readily identifiable. As such, what is reported is often several steps removed from the actual data. To gain a comprehensive understanding of the evidence that is presented in primary studies it is often necessary to obtain the actual microdata, critically review the procedures that were used, and reanalyze the data to determine the influence of various decision rules (Boruch, Wortman & Cordray, 1981). In this instance, secondary analysis allows us to verify the robustness of analytical procedures and serves as a corrective mechanism by positing (and testing) more appropriate statistical methodologies. Bloom (1984) provides a clear example of how secondary analysis can be used to test and to develop an alternative statistical model in evaluations of manpower training programs. Murnane et al. (1985) reanalyzed the High School and Beyond data base to ascertain how selectivity bias influences estimates of the relative effectiveness of public and private schools. Here, two prior studies show conflicting results. In both of these examples, the reanalyses resulted in refinements over the "standard" statistical practices.

Issues in secondary analysis. Enthusiasm for secondary analysis can be easily tempered by considering the myriad of obstacles imposed by professional (e.g., proprietary rights, unwillingness to release data), institutional (e.g., lack of policies and guidelines, legal constraints), and practical (e.g., documentation) considerations. These are discussed in depth by the Committee on National Statistics (Fienberg, Martin, & Straf, 1985). The Committee also provides several recommendations that may relax these constraints. However, the problems seem to be most difficult to resolve for data that is not collected under federal sponsorship. Access to primary data, then, will be contingent on professional courtesy and goodwill.

Research on Judgments:
The Evaluator as Subject

The last topic we wish to draw attention to concerns the need for systematic research on the nature and process of evaluative judgments. The models of evaluation described in several chapters (e.g., Guba & Lincoln; Scriven) demonstrate that human judgment is a key aspect of evaluation practice. Guba and Lincoln's conception of the evaluator as negotiator is likely to require expertise in group decision making and judgments. Scriven argues that evaluators should be more directly involved in rendering judgments of merit. Beyond our intuitions, what do we know about the factors that influence, distort, or limit human abilities to carry out these functions? With few exceptions (e.g., Grizzle & Witte's, 1984, work using social judgment theory), little attention has been directed at how evaluative judgments are made, either collectively or individually. The conceptual push toward a more judgment-based approach to evaluation makes this a prime area for investigation. In other words, the evaluator needs to be the subject of the assessment.

The complexity of human cognition and the evaluation process makes it difficult to speculate on what would be the most profitable entry point into such an inquiry. However, several recent reviews provide hints at sensible places to begin. For instance, Showers and Cantor's (1985) review of research on "motivated social cognition" is certainly relevant. Here the issues are, for example, how individuals interpret situations and what factors influence how we reflect on the past. Of particular relevance to the evaluation specialty might be topics on the role of expertise, expert strategies, and other cognitive dimensions that facilitate (or impede) the acquisition of information or the interpretation of communications and actions within applied settings. Pitz and Sachs (1984) focus more directly on the features of the judgment processes and application of theory and research to "live" settings. Viable areas for additional research, as it pertains to the program evaluation task, include models of judgment, bases for inferences, mechanisms for coping with conflict, integration and trade-offs, as well as behavioral strategies for judgment and choice.

Space does not permit extensive discussions of these "frontier" areas. We have attempted to characterize evaluation studies within a broad context and then make some prognostic forecasts on new areas or old ones that look like they fit well within given fiscal trends. Our final assessment of the field takes a different perspective. Whereas the preceding pages have highlighted trends and promising practices appearing in the literature, in the final section we step back from the available literature and ask the question—"What is missing?"

WHAT IS MISSING?

The experience of editing this volume has left us with a mixture of enlightenment and frustration. We are newly impressed with the breadth, diversity, and ingenuity of the field of evaluation studies and gratified that such a relatively small specialty field can produce so much good work. We hope the contributions selected for this volume serve well our intention to display that good work.

At the same time, we are struck by what seem to be conspicuous gaps and omissions among the topics on which those in the evaluation field choose to discourse. As we framed the issues and topic categories in evaluation studies, we became aware that this volume should have five parts, not the three shown in the Table of Contents. We would like to end this introductory chapter by describing the missing Parts IV and V of this volume for which an insufficient quantity of suitable contributions could be found. This may simply be peevishness on our part, but we hope that our remarks might stimulate some of our compatriots in evaluation studies to turn their attention to these topics.

Part IV: Trade-offs

Part IV of this volume was to deal with the trade-offs inherent in the field of evaluation studies. We hoped to find discussions or examples that illustrated the advantages and disadvantages of various tactical or strategic choices in evaluation study. As we have argued earlier, the program evaluation and program research approaches have complementary strengths and weaknesses—choosing one necessitates a choice about which functions to maximize. Similarly, choices about what aspects of a program to focus on, what methods and techniques to use, how to organize and report the study, and so on, all involve setting priorities among competing considerations.

We think the field badly needs to begin sorting through its tactics and strategies to clarify the relative advantages and disadvantages of each and the nature of the situations to which each best applies. More to the point, we think careful analysis is needed of the various functions and purposes of evaluation studies and the extent to which they are served by the various tactics and strategies available to the evaluator. Much of the recent controversy in evaluation has amounted to one author or another attempting to sweep the whole field with a particular stipulation of evaluation's purpose and the methodology implied by that purpose. Moreover, much of recent evaluation practice has amounted to imposing a particular methodological strategy on the evaluation situation without close attention to whether or not the purposes served best by those methods were in fact appropriate to the situation.

All evaluation situations are not created equal, and what is needed in the way of inquiry and the purposes that inquiry may serve can vary greatly from one situation to another. The practical professional issue for the evaluator is how to analyze the situation, indentify appropriate objectives for the evaluation study, and select the most relevant methods of inquiry. Some very good work was done years ago by Wholey and his colleagues, which should have served as the beginning of sustained attention to this issue (e.g., Wholey, Nay, & Schmidt, 1975; Wholey, 1977). Wholey's concept of "evaluability assessment" opened up the possibility of making explicit the kinds of considerations that go into deciding if a program can be evaluated and, if so, how it should be done (see Rog, 1985, for a review of prior evaluability assessments).

More recently, Bryson and Cullen (1984) conducted an interesting simulation study using evaluation trainees. They presented various scenarios involving different evaluation goals and project phases and asked their respondents to choose appropriate evaluation tactics and procedures. They found that the preferred tactics did change as the evaluation situation changed. This particular study was only a paper and pencil simulation and did not use experienced evaluators, making the results somewhat difficult to interpret. The underlying issue, however, is an important one deserving of much more thought and investigation.

We were thus disappointed not to be able to locate a significant body of recent work that pursues the promising earlier work and helps evaluators sort through the claims of the competing paradigms whose skirmishes are evident everywhere. Most important, we think the lack of careful work and vigorous discussion of this issue is the root cause of an embarassing amount of inappropriate and shoddy program evaluation research.

Part V: Evaluation and Valuing

A candidate for Part V of this volume perhaps falls in the realm of "too much to hope for" at this stage in the development of evaluation studies as a professional specialty. Yet, it seems to us a topic too fundamental to be deferred. As frequently pointed out in this volume, it is now widely argued and widely acknowledged that evaluation has to do intrinsically with values and value judgments. The discussion, however, seems to be arrested at the point of defining the evaluator's responsibilities for, first, ethical conduct and, second, for providing explicit evaluative judgment on the programs studied. What we find largely missing in these discussions is encounter with the fact that all such case-by-case valuing, of necessity, derives from some broader framework of values—a philosophy or logic if you will—about which ends the profession should serve (Scriven, Part I, Section 2, provides a notable exception).

Some illustrations might clarify this point. In product testing, such as that conducted by Consumer's Union, evaluation is based on two explicit sets of standards—the functional and general. Functional standards have to do with how well the product performs its primary purposes—how clean the detergent gets the dishes, how well the stereo equipment reproduces sound, and so forth. General standards consist of a small set of value dimensions applicable to virtually all products; for example, safety, relative cost, durability, and workmanship. The realm of social programs presents an analogous situation. One set of criteria for program evaluation has to do with the functions they are expected to perform, and much has been written about identifying the objectives and goals of programs. What, however, are the general criteria that we wish to apply to social programs? Implicitly, evaluators work with some set of humanitarian and democratic values, but careful explication and analysis of those values are rare. Consider the seemingly simple assumption that a program should benefit its target clientele. Shapiro shows, in the article reprinted in this volume (Part II, Section 4), that judging such benefits raises complex issues. Do we mean benefit for the greatest number of persons? the most even distribution of benefits? more benefit for those with the greatest need? Radically different valuation of the same program can be made depending on which position is adopted. Similar points could be made about "effectiveness," "efficiency," "cost-effectiveness," "accessibility," or any other of the general criteria evaluators commonly use for judging programs.

From another perspective, we all recognize that at some level social programs are (or should be) attempts to improve the quality of life in the society. Implicit in the concept "quality of life" are images of the "good society" and the "good life" along with certain procedural assumptions, for example, that organized social action is worthwhile. Evaluators must have a stance on these issues to have any independent basis for criticizing or judging social programs. The alternative is simply to adopt unquestioningly the values inherent in each program situation. Some might argue for such relativism. Guba and Lincoln (Part I, this volume) seem to, for example. But what are the boundaries to such relativism—do we give the same credence to the Ku Klux Klan as we do to other stakeholders in a desegregation program (Mark & Shotland, Part I, Section 3)? These matters are worthy of more sustained analysis, discussion, and (inevitably) debate within the evaluation profession.

We should note that there have been some brave attempts, in recent years, to attend to these issues. The volume by House (1983) on "Philosophy of Evaluation," for example, opens a discussion that deserves vigorous follow-up. On a different tack, the special issue edited by Smith (1985c) on ethical issues touches on some of the themes we raise here, although it is more concerned with standards of professional practice. The most striking feature of both these contributions, however, is how atypical they are. That, we think, reveals a serious deficiency in the program evaluation literature.

Final Note

We would like to close on an optimistic note. There has been much recent gloom and doom expressed in the evaluation profession, based largely on cutbacks in social programs and the resulting effects on the employment of evaluators. This bears on the economic viability of the profession and is, indeed, a serious matter. Relatively independent, however, is the intellectual viability of the field. Our experience editing this volume reaffirms that many lively minds are grappling with the issues inherent in this complex field. Evaluation may live for a while like an ascetic yoga master, moving toward enlightenment but not especially well fed, until when the political climate is more receptive to its wisdom. That there is wisdom, we have no doubt.

REFERENCES

Berk, R. A. (1982). Where angels fear to tread and why. *New directions for program evaluation: Standards for evaluation practice, 15*, 59-66.

Betsey, C. L., Hollister, R. G., Jr., & Papageorgiou, M. R. (Eds.). (1985). *Youth employment and training programs: The YEDPA years.* Washington, DC: National Academy Press.

Blalock H. M. (1984). Contextual-effect models: Theoretical and methodological Issues. *Annual Review of Sociology, 10,* 353-372.

Bloom, H. S. (1984). Estimating the effect of job-training programs, using longitudinal data: Ashenfelter's findings reconsidered. *The Journal of Human Resources, XIX* (4), 544-556.

Boruch, R. F. (1985). Implications of the youth employment experience for improving applied research and evaluation policy. In C. Betsey, R. G. Hollister, Jr. & M. R. Papageorgiou (Eds.), *Youth employment and training programs: The YEDPA years.* Washington, DC: National Academy Press.

Boruch, R. F., Wortman, P. M., Cordray, D. S. (Eds.). (1981). *Reanalyzing program evaluations: Policies and practices for secondary analysis of social and educational programs.* San Francisco, CA: Jossey-Bass.

Bowering, D. J. (Ed.). (1984). *New directions for program evaluation: Secondary Analysis of available data bases, No. 22.* San Francisco, CA: Jossey Bass.

Bryson, J. M., & Cullen J. W. (1984). A contigent approach to strategy and tactics in formative and summative evaluations. *Evaluation and Program Planning, 7,* 267-290.

Campbell, D. T. (1984) Can we be scientific in applied social science? R. F. Conner, D. G. Altman & C. Jackson (Eds.), *Evaluation studies review annual, Vol. 9* (pp. 26-48). Beverly Hills, CA: Sage.

Campbell, D. T., & Stanley, J. C. (1966). *Experimental and Quasi-experimental Designs for Research.* Chicago: Rand McNally.

Chelimsky, E. (1986, February 19). *Statement before the Select Education Subcommittee, Committee on Education and Labor, House of Representatives.* Washington D.C.

Chen, H-T., & Rossi, P. H. (1983). Evaluating with sense: The theory driven approach. *Evaluation Review, 7,* 283-302.

Congressional Research Service. (1984). *The federal statistical system 1980 to 1985* (Report prepared for the Congressional Research Service by Baseline Data Corporation). Washington, D.C.: Government Printing Office.

Congressional Research Service. (1985). *An update on the status of major statistical agencies: Fiscal year 1986.* Washington, D.C.: Government Printing Office.

Conner, R., Altman, D. G., & Jackson, C. (1984). 1984: A brave new world for evaluation? In R. Conner, D. G. Altman, & C. Jackson (Eds.), *Evaluation studies review annual, Vol. 9* (pp. 239-252). Beverly Hills, CA: Sage Publications.

Cook, T. D. (1978). Utilization, knowledge-building, and institutionalization: Three criteria by which evaluation research can be evaluated. In T. D. Cook & Associates (Eds.), *Evaluation studies review annual, Vol. 3.* Beverly Hills, CA: Sage Publications.

Cook, T. D. (1984). Opportunities for evaluation in the next few years. In R. F. Conner, D. G. Altman, & C. Jackson (Eds.), *Evaluation studies review annual, Vol. 9* (pp. 726-752). Beverly Hills, CA: Sage Publications.

Cook, T. D., & Campbell, D. T. (1979). *Quasi-experimentation: Design and analysis issues for field settings.* Chicago, IL: Rand McNally.

Cooper, H. M. (1984). *The integrative research review: A systematic approach.* Beverly Hills, CA: Sage Publications.

Cordray, D. S., & Sonnefeld, L. J. (1985). Quantitative synthesis; An actuarial base for planning impact evaluations. *New directions for program evaluation: Utilizing prior research in evaluation planning, 27,* 29-48.

Crano, W. D., & Messé, L. A. (1985) Assessing and redressing comprehension artifacts in social intervention research. *Evaluation Review, 9*(2), 144-172.

Cronbach, L. J., Ambron, S. R., Dornbusch, S. M., Hess, R. D., Hornik, R. C., Phillips, D. C., Walker, D. F., & Weiner, S. S. (1980). *Toward reform of program evaluation.* San Francisco, CA: Jossey-Bass.

Eisner, E. W. (1979) *The educational imagination.* New York: Macmillan.

Evaluation Research Society Standards Committee. (1982). Standards for program evaluation. *New Directions for Program Evaluation: Standards for Evaluation Practice, 15,* 7-19.

Fienberg, S. E., Martin, M. E., & Straf, M. L. (Eds.). (1985). *Sharing research data.* Washington, DC: National Academy Press.

Finsterbusch, K. (1984). *Statistical Summary of 52 AID Projects: Lessons on Project Effectiveness.* College Park, MD: University of Maryland Press.

Gold, N. (1981). *The stakeholder approach for educational program evaluation.* Washington, DC: National Institute of Education.

Grizzle, G. A., & Witte, A. D. (1984). Evaluating multidimensional performance: A social judgment theory approach. *Evaluation Review, 8*(6), 777-800.

Guba, E. G., & Lincoln, Y. S. (1981). *Effective evaluation: Improving the usefulness of evaluation results through responsive and naturalistic approaches.* San Francisco, CA: Jossey-Bass.

House, E. R. (1980). *Evaluating with validity.* Beverly Hills, CA: Sage.

House, E. R. (Ed.). (1983). Philosophy of evaluation. *New Directions for Program Evaluation, 19.* San Francisco: Jossey-Bass.

Hunter, J. E., Schmidt, F. L., & Jackson, G. B. (1982). *Meta-analysis: Cumulating research findings across studies.* Beverly Hills, CA: Sage.

Johnson, E. L. (1985). Struck down in their prime: The truncation of five federal longitudinal qualitative impact evaluations. *Evaluation Review, 9*(1), 13-20.

Joint Committee on Standards for Educational Evaluation. (1980). *Standards for evaluation of educational programs, products, and materials.* New York, NY: McGraw-Hill.

Leamer, E. E. (1978). *Specification searches: Ad hoc inference with non-experimental data.* New York, NY: John Wiley.

Light, R. J., & Pillemer, D. B. (1984). *Summing up: The science of reviewing research.* Cambridge, MA: Harvard University Press.

Murname, R. J., Newstead, S., & Olsen, R. J. (1985). Comparing public and private schools: The puzzling role of selectivity bias. *Journal of Business and Economic Statistics, 3*(1), 23-35.

Patton, M. Q. (1978) *Utilization-focused evaluation.* Beverly Hills, CA: Sage.

Pearson, R. W. (1984) The changing fortunes of the U.S. statistical system, 1980-1985. *Review of Public Data Use, 12,* 245-269.

Pitz, G. F., & Sachs, N. J. (1984) Judgment and decision: Theory and application. *Annual Review of Psychology, 35,* 139-163.

Rog, D. J. (1985). *A methodological analysis of evaluability assessment.* Unpublished doctoral dissertation, Vanderbilt University, Department of Psychology, TN.

Rosenthal, R. (1984). *Meta-analytic procedures for social research.* Beverly Hills, CA: Sage.

Scriven, M. (1973). Goal-free evaluation. In House, E. R. (Ed.), *School evaluation: The politics and process.* Berkeley, CA: McCutchan.

Scriven, M. (1984). Evaluation ideologies. In R. F. Conner, D. G. Altman, & C. Jackson (Eds.) *Evaluation studies review annual, Vol. 9* (pp. 49-80). Beverly Hills, CA: Sage Publications.

Scheirer, M. A., & Rezmovic, E. L. (1983). Measuring the degree of program implementation: A methodological review. *Evaluation Review, 7,* 599-633.

Shadish, W. R., Jr., & Reis, J. (1984). A review of studies of the effectiveness of programs to improve pregnancy outcomes. *Evaluation Review, 8*(6), 747-776.

Showers, C., & Cantor, N. (1985). Social cognition: A look at motivated strategies. *Annual Review of Psychology, 36,* 275-306.

Smith, N. (1985a). Founaation support of evaluation. *Evaluation Review, 9*(2), 215-239.

Smith, N. (1985b). *Adversary and committee hearings as evaluation methods. Evaluation Review, 9*(6), 735-750.

Smith, N. (Ed.). (1985c). Special Issue of *Evaluation and program planning,* vol. 8.

Stake, R. E. (Ed.). (1975). *Evaluating the arts in education: A responsive approach.* Columbus, OH: Merrill.

Stewart, D. W. (1984). *Secondary research: Information sources and methods.* Beverly Hills, CA: Sage.

Stufflebeam, D. L., Foley, W. J., Gephart, W. J., Guba, E. G., Hammond, L. R., Merriman, H. O., & Provus, M. M. (1971). *Educational evaluation and decision-making.* Itasca, IL: Peacock.

Stufflebeam, D. (1982). A next step: Discussion to consider unifying the ERS and Joint Committee standards. In P. H. Rossi (Ed.), *New directions for program evaluation: Standards for evaluation practice, No. 15,* (pp. 27-36). San Francisco, CA: Jossey-Bass

Wholey, J. S., Nay, J. N., & Schmidt, R. E. (1975). Evaluation: Where is it really needed? *Evaluation Magazine, 2*(2), 89-93.

Wholey, J. S. (1977). Evaluability assessment. In Rutman, L. (Ed.), *Evaluation research methods: A basic guide* (pp. 41-56). Beverly Hills, CA: Sage.

Wolf, R. L. (1979). The use of judicial evaluation methods in the formulation of educational policy. *Educational Evaluation and Policy Analysis, 1,* 19-20.

Wortman, P. M. (1983). Evaluation research: A methodological perspective. *Annual Review of Psychology, 34,* 246-260.

Wortman, P. M. (1975). Evaluation research: A psychological perspective. *American Psychologist, 30,* 562-575.

Wortman, P. M., & Yeaton, W. H. (in press). Cumulating quality of life results in controlled trials of coronary artery bypass graft surgery. *Controlled Clinical Trials.*

SECTION 2
Points of View on History and Recent Development

We begin with two quite different perspectives on the history and recent development of evaluation studies. These perspectives reveal themes and contrasts of such fundamental importance that they not only make a proper beginning for this volume but foreshadow topics that recur throughout and provide much of this volume's organizational framework.

In the first chapter of this section, Rossi and Wright take an "applied social research" perspective on evaluation studies. From this perspective, evaluation is the "estimation of the net impacts or effects of social programs." The seminal works in this tradition are those developing experimentation and quasi-experimentation for application to field settings. The prototypical evaluation study in applied social research is the "social experiment" in which a control group methodology is used to assess the effects of a social innovation.

In the second chapter, Guba and Lincoln take a very different perspective on evaluation study, one that emphasizes the judging or valuing inherent in the concept of evaluation. Rather than assessing net *effects* of a program, their focus is on assessing the net *worth* of a program. This perspective has its roots in the works of Stake and Scriven and has developed in the form of a variety of models centered on the judgment process that should be used by the evaluator. These models generally incorporate the notion of different stakeholders in a program whose concerns are pertinent to that judgment. Guba and Lincoln themselves make a distinctive contribution to this approach by calling attention to the value pluralism of different stakeholder groups and drawing the implications for the role of the evaluator as a mediator in a pluralistic value negotiation rather than as the sole judge of the program.

Despite the substantial differences between these perspectives, there are two important areas of agreement that should not be overlooked. First, both Rossi and Wright, and Guba and Lincoln, recognize the dominance of the experimental "positivistic" paradigm in contemporary evaluation studies. More striking, both sets of authors identify problems and failures of that paradigm. Their respective identification and analysis of those problems, however, differ as greatly as do their perspectives on the field.

Rossi and Wright call attention to the "parade of close-to-zero effects" that resulted from the major experimental and quasi-experimental investigations of social programs during the last two decades. They point out that the Campellian framework, with its emphasis on distinguishing true program effects from artifacts, provides little guidance for handling situations where no effects are found at all. The recent developments in evaluation of greatest interest to Rossi and Wright, therefore, are those that enlarge the experimental paradigm in various useful ways.

Chief among those enlargements is the differentiation of the experimental paradigm beyond the simple independent variable, dependent variable formulations characteristic of much of the earlier work. Greater attention to a priori theory is called for as is greater exploration and specification of what is inside the "black box" that represents the independent (program) variable in experimental design. Also pertinent is the increased attention evaluators are giving to the matter of program implementation as a prerequisite for program effects and the rise of the "comprehensive evaluation" that includes needs assessement, implementation research, and program monitoring along with impact assessment. This broadened view of the experimental paradigm in evaluation blends seamlessly with the general study of social problems, as Rossi and Wright note, with evaluation studies being that facet of social problem research that deals with variables policymakers can control.

Guba and Lincoln, in contrast, delineate an entirely different set of problems with the experimental paradigm in evaluation studies. First, its "positivistic" heritage stipulates that it is value neutral and thus permits abdication of the central responsibility of evaluation to judge or value a program. Even in the "third generation" form of the experimental paradigm, in which evaluation judgment is based on whether or not certain program "effects" are attained, Guba and Lincoln find fatal flaws. In particular, that paradigm imposes the dominance of the researcher's judgmental perspective upon a program of multiple stakeholders with multiple value perspectives. They find it necessary to reject any approach that gives special authority to the researcher's perspective in favor of a view that emphasizes the discovery and mediation of pluralistic stakeholder perspectives. This shift in emphasis renders inappropriate most of the tools of the experimental paradigm and brings to the fore the method of "naturalistic inquiry" in which more qualitative and participatory approaches are taken to the evaluation situation.

Thus, whereas Rossi and Wright report and suggest a variety of reforms to the experimental paradigm, Guba and Lincoln find it necessary to reject the paradigm in favor of a radically different conception of evaluation study.

These two chapters press upon us some distinctions too compelling to be ignored. At the broadest level, we see another instance of the recurring clash between what William James called the "toughminded" and the "tenderminded" or, if you will, between the objective and the subjective as orientations in the social sciences. More pointedly, however, we are asked to consider the fundamental purposes and functions of evaluation. What is the nature and necessity of having evaluative judgment rendered about a social program and by whom should it be done? Is program evaluation always an enterprise in service to all program stakeholders, and are the values of all stakeholders to be treated equally? What is the proper role in evaluation of "facts" about the psychosocial mechanisms through which a program works and the measurable effects it has? Is there any special authority inherent in the researcher's studied perspective or should research aim only to illuminate stakeholder perspectives? And, most fundamental, what epistemological stance do we want to take regarding the program reality we study? Is it a single or a multiple reality; primarily a matter of pluralistic social construction or something with objectively identifiable characteristics separate from the construal of involved observers?

We are also pressed to ask if these are either-or questions, watershed issues that put an evaluator into one ideological camp or another with little common ground between. In this regard, we have to notice that the images of social programs and the purposes of evaluation brought up in these two chapters differ in crucial details. Rossi and Wright, for example, talk mostly of proposed new programs mounted on a demonstration basis; Guba and Lincoln seem to have in mind established programs with entrenched stakeholders. We might also ask about the applicability of these differing perspectives to large-scale versus small-scale programs, politically charged contexts versus those marked by consensus on program goals, studies concerned with the specifics of contexts versus those concerned with the generalizable aspects of programs, evaluation needed for timely service of decision-makers' needs versus that contributing to longer-range learning about program and policy options, stable well-defined programs versus those with fluid or ambiguous goals, and so on. We might even note that Rossi and Wright speak from a sociological perspective encompassing a variety of social service programs whereas Guba and Lincoln speak from the perspective of educational programs. Are there inherent differences in these (and other) types of programs that direct the evaluator to different approaches?

The contemporary challenge to the field of evaluation studies is to sort through the purposes and functions of evaluation and examine the critical differences that distinguish various evaluation circumstances in order to seek a better alignment of method with purpose. We are doubtful that this matter can be resolved categorically on the basis of adherence to a single all-purpose approach, whether it is "social science" or "naturalistic inquiry." We think integration will come to the field of evaluation studies by way of explicated understanding of the appropriate match between evaluation circumstances and the what, when, and where of evaluation methodology rather than through the triumph of one philosophical position or another.

Without making any pretense of resolving the fundamental issues raised by the two provocative chapters in this first section, we devote the remainder of this volume to exploring aspects of the contrasting perspectives they present so well.

2

Evaluation Research

An Assessment

Peter H. Rossi and James D. Wright

Abstract

This paper reviews the past 25 years of applied social research, with an emphasis on evaluation research, whose intent is the estimation of the net impacts or effects of social programs. The 1960s and early 1970s represent the "Golden Age" of evaluation, an age that ended with the Reagan Administration. During this period, the evaluation field was dominated by the randomized, controlled experimental paradigm. Accordingly, several of the major field experiments of the era are reviewed in some detail. Recently, various alternatives to this paradigm have been advanced; they too are discussed.

The key lesson from the Golden Age is that the expected effects of social programs hover near zero, a devastating discovery for the social reformers of the time. Some reasons why this is the case are presented. One important consequence of this experience has been the development of so-called comprehensive evaluations, studies aimed at discerning not only *if* programs have effects, but also *why*. A second consequence has been the recognition of the importance of implementation research in overall evaluations.

INTRODUCTION

To assess the state of evaluation research at this time (1984) is to uncover a set of distressing paradoxes and a mixture of good and bad news. First, the bad news: Activity in the field has crested and is currently undergoing a decline as budget cutbacks in human service and entitlement programs force parallel

Reproduced, with permission, from the Annual Review of Sociology, Volume 10, © 1984 by Annual Review Inc.

reductions in evaluation activities, especially at the federal level. Ironically, these cutbacks have arrived just when the evaluation research field is beginning to reach a high level of intellectual accomplishment, that is, just as the best evaluation research of the prosperous decades is being published. New developments in techniques and methodology have appeared that promise to raise the overall quality not only of evaluations but of many other areas of social science research as well. Evaluation researchers have learned how to conduct field experiments successfully and how to analyze the resulting complicated data sets, and they have also started to provide solutions to some of the most serious validity problems of nonexperimental research.

An additional irony is that the social science disciplines within the universities are beginning to pay more attention to applied social research generally and to evaluation research particularly. The recent cutbacks in university growth have made the placement of new MAs and PhDs in academic settings increasingly problematic. More and more graduate departments are seeking to place their students in positions where they will do applied research. The irony is that opportunities for applied work have also declined to the point where disappointments are clearly in the cards for both these departments and their graduates (Manderscheid & Greenwald 1983).

This article reviews these developments and others and provides an assessment of the future prospects—both intellectual and professional—for this applied field.

AFTER THE BOOM CAME THE BUST

Evaluation research came into prominence as an applied social scientific activity during the Great Society programs of the mid-1960s. The distinctive feature of the past 25 years is the explicit recognition among policymakers and public administrators that evaluations could be conducted systematically using social scientific research methods and could produce results that had more use and validity than the judgmental approaches used previously. During the Great Society era, Congress authorized many new programs, and systematic evaluations were mandated in several of the more important pieces of legislation.[1]

The new administrative agencies set up to implement many of these programs were partially staffed by social scientists who had strong interests in applied work. The entire gamut of the social scientific disciplines was in-

---

[1] Especially important were the evaluations mandated in the 1964 Elementary and Secondary School Education Act (McLaughlin 1975), in the Housing and Urban Development budget authorization of 1970 calling for the experimental evaluation of a proposed housing allowance program (Struyck & Bendick 1981), and in the enabling legislation for the Department of Labor's Comprehensive Employment Training Program (Rossi et al 1980).

volved. Economists had a strong foothold in the Office of Economic Opportunity; sociologists, psychologists, and educators were ensconced in the Office of Education (later the Department of Education); the Department of Health, Education, and Welfare (now Health and Human Services) was big enough to accommodate members of all of the social scientific disciplines in critical positions; and the Department of Labor's Manpower Research Division was also generous, providing opportunities for all.

The interdisciplinary character of this new social scientific activity was especially noteworthy. Economists, sociologists, psychologists, and educational researchers often found themselves bidding on the same contracts in competition with each other, a process that facilitated the transfer of knowledge, craft lore, and mutual respect across disciplinary boundaries. Research firms and institutes previously dominated by one discipline broadened their outlooks by hiring professionals from other social sciences, mainly in order to increase their competitive edge. Interdisciplinary professional societies were also founded, e.g. the Evaluation Research Society[2] and the Evaluation Network.

University-based social scientific researchers were slow to take advantage of the new opportunities for research funding, even though the topics involved were often of central interest, a reflection of the indifference (even hostility) to applied work that has characterized the academic social science departments until very recently (Raizen & Rossi 1981, Rossi & Wright 1983, Rossi et al 1978). Private entrepreneurs, however, were quicker to notice and exploit the new emphasis on evaluation. Some existing firms that had not been particularly interested in the social sciences opened subsidiaries that could compete for social research contracts (e.g. Westinghouse). Others greatly expanded their social science research sections (e.g. The Rand Corporation). In addition, literally hundreds of new firms appeared on the scene, a handful of which became spectacular successes during the "golden years" (e.g. Abt Associates).[3]

By the middle of the 1970s, some 500–600 private firms existed primarily to bid on contracts for applied social research. As in other areas of corporate activity, a few firms garnered the majority of the available funds. For example,

[2]A tabulation of the primary disciplines of the members of the Evaluation Research Society (Evaluation Research Society 1979) nicely illustrates the interdisciplinary character of the evaluation research field. Herewith, the breakdown of membership by field: psychology 47%; sociology 10%; economics 4%; political science 6%; education 15%; and other 18%.

[3]Some of the spectacular successes of those prosperous times, of course, have been greatly diminished by the reverses of today's harder times. At its height, Abt Associates employed more PhDs in the social sciences than any one of the Boston area universities and more than most combinations of universities. In the past few years, its PhD workforce has been reduced by almost 50%.

in the period 1975–1980, 6 large research firms received over 60% of the evaluation funds expended by the Department of Education (Raizen & Rossi 1981).

An additional large number of firms sprang up to bid on contracts for evaluation and other applied social research activities at the state and local levels. These research opportunities were neither as well funded as those on the federal level nor were the tasks as intellectually or technically challenging. There was (and continues to be) enough evaluation "business" on the state and local levels, however, to provide the essential "bread and butter" for a very large number of small-scale job shops.

Some of the existing university-based research institutes with histories of large-scale social research also prospered during this period. The National Opinion Research Center at the University of Chicago and the Survey Research Center at the University of Michigan both grew enormously in size. Their staffs eventually came to dwarf most academic departments in the relevant fields. New academic research organizations also were started to take advantage of the funding opportunities offered through the grant and contract mechanism.

A corresponding growth took place on the conceptual side of evaluation research. The publication in 1966 of Donald T. Campbell and Julian Stanley's seminal work on research designs useful in the evaluation of educational programs created an entirely new vocabulary for the taxonomy of research designs and for the discussion of validity issues. It also made the randomized, controlled experimental paradigm the method of choice for causal analyses. Both of these emphases came to dominate large portions of the evaluation field for the next decade.

Evaluation research was initially seen as, quintessentially, the assessment of programs' net effects. Correspondingly, the main problem in designing evaluation research was to specify appropriate *ceteris paribus* conditions that would permit valid estimates of these net effects. Within this framework, the randomized, controlled experiment became the ruling paradigm for evaluation research. The conceptual foundations had been developed many decades earlier, and this approach had been the ruling research paradigm in both psychology and biology for many years. The special contribution made during the period under current review was that the paradigm was taken out of the laboratory and into the field, and it was combined with the sample survey in studies designed to test the effects of the proposed programs. To many social scientists of a technocratic bent, the randomized field experiment promised to replace our bumbling trial-and-error approaches to forging social policy with a more self-consciously rational "experimenting society" (Campbell 1969).

By the early 1970s, an impressive number of large-scale field experiments had been funded and started. These experiments covered a wide variety of topics: income maintenance plans intended to replace the existing welfare benefits system; housing allowances that might stimulate the market to produce better housing for the poor; health insurance plans that would not create perverse medical-care price effects; and so on through a veritable laundry list of field experiments. Ironically, most of them were designed and run by economists, members of a field not noted for its tradition of experimental work.

The realization quickly emerged, however, that randomized, controlled experiments could only be done correctly under very limited circumstances and that the demand for evaluation covered many programs that simply could not be assessed in this way. Not only were there frequent ethical and legal limitations to randomization, but many existing programs that had full (or almost full) coverage of their intended beneficiary populations could not be assessed using controlled experiments because there was no way to create appropriate control groups. It also turned out that field experiments took a long time—3 to 5 years or more—from design to final report, a delay that was simply intolerable given the much shorter time horizons of most policymakers and public administrators.

Campbell & Stanley (1966) had provided one possible solution to this dilemma by coining the term quasi-experiments and using it to cover evaluation research designs that do not rely on randomization to form controls. Although they explicitly recognized the inferior validity of data generated in this way, they also discussed the conditions under which valid causal inferences could be drawn from evaluation studies using such designs. Their treatment of quasi-experimental research designs certainly stimulated the use of such designs in evaluation studies, sometimes under conditions that Campbell & Stanley explicitly stated were potentially fatal. Indeed, the vast majority of the evaluations that have been carried out have been quasi-experiments, rather than randomized, "true" experiments, mainly because the latter have proven difficult, if not impossible, to implement in real world settings.

But even quasi-experimental designs have their limitations. For one thing, while not as expensive or time consuming as "true" experiments, a well-conducted quasi-experiment may demand more funds, time, and talent than are available. Another problem is that many of the more sophisticated quasi-experimental designs (in particular, interrupted time series designs) require long time series of data—ideally, series that contain a long run of observations prior to the introduction of a policy intervention and that continue for several years after that. Concerning the first, the necessary data often do not exist; and, concerning the second, the old problem of timeliness reappears. A final problem, of course—one Campbell & Stanley discussed in detail—is that there are potential threats to the validity of *any* quasi-experimental design. In using such designs, one always runs some risk of mistaking various artifacts for true program effects. Hence, quasi-experiments are almost always vulnerable to critical attack: witness the rancorous controversies surrounding some of the major educational evaluations (e.g. McLaughlin 1975, Mosteller & Moynihan 1972, Rossi & Wright 1982).

Due to the many evident problems of both experimental and quasi-experimental approaches to evaluation research, the need for methods of evaluation that were timely, relatively inexpensive, and responsive to many program administrators' and officials' fears that evaluations would somehow "do them in" quickly became apparent. This statement applies especially to evaluations that were mandated by Congress and that the program agencies themselves were supposed to conduct. Indeed, Congress—coupling its new-found enthusiasm for evaluations with a seriously flawed understanding of the time, talent and funding needed to carry out evaluations of even minimum quality—often imposed evaluation tasks on program agencies that far exceeded the agencies' research capacities and then provided funds that were grossly inadequate to accomplish them.

The need for evaluations that could be carried out by technically unsophisticated persons and that would be timely and useful to program administrators fueled a strong interest in qualitative approaches to evaluation research (Patton 1980, Scriven 1977, Guba & Lincoln 1981, House 1980). Qualitative research methods have always had some following in all of the social sciences, especially in sociology. Their special attraction in sociology is their presumed ability to stay close to reality and to promote an understanding of social processes through intimate familiarity with field conditions. In addition, for evaluation purposes, qualitative methods seemed to have the attractive triple advantages of being inexpensive, timely, and responsive to administrators' needs.

These approaches were especially attractive to program sponsors and operators because they appeared to be flexible enough to cope with social programs that, once implemented, tend to vary sharply from one locale to another not only in their goals but also in the benefits and services that are actually delivered. The goals for some broad-spectrum programs (e.g. Model Cities) were not clearly defined by Congress or the administering agencies. Each operating agency thus defined its own goals and often changed them frequently (Kaplan 1973, Williams 1980). The appeal, at least initially, of qualitative approaches to evaluation is that they apparently had the potential to be sensitive to the nuances of ill defined and constantly evolving program goals.

The great boom in evaluation ended in 1981 when the Reagan administration began to dismantle the social programs that had been developed over the previous 20 years. The extensive manpower research program of the Department of Labor was reduced to almost nothing and there were similar (although less drastic) cuts in the Departments of Health and Human Services, Education, and Agriculture, among others. The immediate consequence was a drastic reduction in the amount of federal money available for applied social research.

Ironically, the Reagan cutbacks occurred just as more and more academic departments began to discover that there was a nonacademic market for newly minted PhDs. Openings for evaluation researchers were a large component of this market. The American Sociological Association held an extremely well-attended conference in Washington, D.C. in 1981 (Freeman et al 1983) on the appropriate training for careers in applied sociology. Many graduate departments throughout the country began programs to train applied researchers of all kinds, and there was an evident interest among at least some prominent sociologists. Indeed, both Presidents of the American Sociological Association in 1980 and 1981 devoted their presidential addresses to applied work (Rossi 1981, Whyte 1982).

THE INTELLECTUAL HARVEST OF THE GOLDEN YEARS OF EVALUATION

The frenzied growth of evaluation research during the 1960s and 1970s produced a real increment in our knowledge about the relevant social problems and a decided increase in the technical sophistication of research in the social sciences. Both of these developments have already had some impact on the social sciences and will be increasingly valuable to our fields in the future.

The Large-Scale Field Experiments of the "Golden Age"

Perhaps the most impressive substantive and technical achievements of the entire Golden Age were those of the large-scale field experiments. Most of these experiments were initially funded by the Office of Economic Opportunity and, upon the demise of that agency, by the Department of Health, Education, and Welfare.

On the technical side, these experiments combined both sample survey techniques and classical experimental designs. Experimental and control groups were created by sampling open communities and then randomly allocating sampled households to experimental and control groups. Interviews with experimental and control households were then undertaken, using traditional sample survey techniques to measure responses to the experimental treatments. Looked upon as surveys, these experiments were long-term panels with repeated measurements of the major dependent (i.e. outcome) variables. Measures were taken as often as once a month in some of the experiments and extended over periods of up to five years. Viewed as experiments, the studies were factorial ones in which important parameters of the treatments were systematically varied.

Perhaps the best-known of the field experiments during the Golden Age were those designed to test various forms of the "negative income tax" (NIT) as a means of maintaining a reasonable income floor for poor households. All told, there were five such experiments in the United States and one in Canada.

Although the five experiments each tested slightly different negative income tax plans at different sites, they all had one objective in common, namely, to measure the experimental households' labor force response to income maintenance treatments.

The policy question at issue when these experiments were initiated was whether transfer payments would give poor families an incentive either to stop working altogether or to withdraw from the labor market to some degree. As Senator John Stennis of Mississippi put it in a debate on the floor of the Senate, "Who will want to iron our shirts?" This question also coincided with an important issue in microeconomics, namely, the shape of the function that describes the so-called work-leisure tradeoff—that is, the point where individuals' earnings do not motivate them sufficiently to work so that leisure becomes the more attractive option.

Theoretically, the amount of work disincentive generated by the negative income tax would depend on the tax rate applied to earnings and the levels of guaranteed payment offered. All the plans therefore tested a variety of tax-rate/ guarantee-level alternatives in an effort to find the optimal plan, i.e. the combination of guarantee level and tax rate that would provide sufficient income while minimizing the work disincentive effects.

The five experiments were all located in different parts of the country and addressed slightly different populations with slightly different treatment plans. The first experiment (Kershaw & Fair 1975, Watts & Rees 1976, Rossi & Lyall 1974) was sited in three cities in New Jersey and one in Pennsylvania. It ran for three years and addressed a population of intact urban households. A second experiment was run simultaneously and addressed a rural population (Bawden & Harrar 1978). This experiment was sited in rural countries in Wisconsin and North Carolina.

A third experiment took place in Gary, Indiana (Moffitt 1979), and was addressed largely to poor, black, single-parent families. Treatments paralleled those in the other experiments in terms of payments but also included various social services (counselling, job training, child care, etc.). Extraordinary difficulties arose in administering this experiment, in particular in actually delivering the promised social services and in persuading the experimental families eligible for such services to take them.

The final two experiments (Robins et al 1980) were started well before the New Jersey–Pennsylvania experiments were completed and analyzed, but they benefited greatly from some of the experiences and shortcomings of their predecessors. They had larger samples of families, addressed a population that was more representative of the likely target population of a real income maintenance policy, ran for longer periods, and had more varied treatments. The two experiments were sited in Seattle and Denver, had treatments that ran for five years, and provided job training services as well as transfer payments.

All five experiments showed a small reduction (about 5%) in work effort as an effect of the payments, with the impact varying slightly with the applicable tax rate. Additional effects of a noneconomic nature were also found. In the Seattle-Denver experiments, for example, payments apparently provided an incentive for households to break up: Since the separating adults could each receive payments, the guaranteed income apparently provided the kind of fiscal independence from the marital tie to enable women to terminate unsatisfactory marriages more easily.

The 5 experiments taken together provide an excellent basis for designing a national income maintenance program—were such a policy ever to become politically feasible. As luck would have it, however, no such policy changes appear in the offing; Congressional and Presidential interest in such programs peaked in the early 1970s, well before any of the experiments were completed.

For a time in the mid-1970s, it looked as if each of the major federal departments concerned with social programs had to have at least one major field experiment under way. The Department of Housing and Urban Development ran its Housing Allowance Experiments, the Department of Labor ran the Transitional Aid to Released Prisoners (TARP) experiment as well as the Supported Work Experiment, and the Department of Justice funded experiments on increased police patrolling.[4]

The Housing Allowance experiments (Struyk & Bendick 1981, Bradbury & Downs 1981, Friedman & Weinberg 1983) used a treatment consisting of payments to poor families calculated on the basis of income and local housing costs. Some of the experimental treatments made the payments dependent on income alone. Others were conditional on the households' occupying housing that met certain public health standards, and still others had payments that were proportional to rents. Two sets of experiments were commissioned, one (sited in Pittsburgh and Phoenix) directed at measuring the effects of payments on the demand for housing and the other (sited in Green Bay, Wisconsin, and South Bend, Indiana) measuring the effects of payments on housing supply. All were directed at poor households.

The Demand Experiment was intended to estimate the effect of housing allowance payments on the consumption of housing, based on the reasoning that the subsidies would enable poor households to purchase better housing on the open market. The Supply Experiment was predicated on the suspicion that increasing the money people have to spend on housing may simply lead

---

[4]Conspicuous by its absence from this roster of federal agencies that sponsored field experiments is the Department of Education. The educational evaluations of this era relied not on field experiments but on quasi-experimental designs. The only major field experiment in education—contract learning—was financed and supervised by the Office of Economic Opportunity (Gramlich & Koshel 1975).

housing suppliers to raise housing costs. In the Supply Experiments, payments were offered to all income-eligible households in the two cities, just as if the program had actually been enacted. The housing suppliers' response to the payments were monitored over a three-year period through surveys of housing units in those cities.

The two experiments demonstrated that households participated at very low rates when payments were made contingent upon occupying housing that met the standards used. Furthermore, there was considerable evidence that households used the payments as if they were general increments to income, rather than to increase the quality of their housing. Nor did suppliers in the two Supply Experiment sites increase the prices of their housing stock. The data produced by these experiments provide excellent longitudinal information on the housing behavior of poor families. They allow us to estimate ethnic discrimination on the housing market, show the relationships between housing consumption and household composition and size, and supply much information on other critical topics.[5]

The Department of Labor's TARP experiments (Rossi et al 1980) also used money as the form of intervention. The social problem involved was the unacceptably high recidivism rates among released prisoners. The treatment consisted of being eligible for limited amounts of unemployment compensation payments, presumably to aid felons in the transition from prison life to gainful, legitimate employment and a law-abiding existence.

Four thousand prisoners released from the Georgia and Texas state prisons during 1977 participated in the experiment and were randomly assigned upon release either to one of the experimental groups or to one of the several control groups. Those in the experimental groups became eligible for either 3 or 6 months of minimum unemployment compensation payments, which were administered through the Employment Security offices of the two states in question. Periodic interviews with the released prisoners provided data on postrelease employment, and the computerized arrest records of the state provided data on postrelease arrests. In addition, earnings subject to Social Security taxes were obtained from Social Security Administration tapes.

The payments administered in the experiment had no effect on postrelease arrest rates (Rossi et al 1980). A further (and somewhat controversial) analysis of the data (Zeisel 1983, Rossi et al 1983) suggested, however, that the payments had beneficial effects but that they were masked by an unanticipated (and strong) work disincentive effect. Payments, that is, tended to decrease recidivism directly, but because they created a work disincentive, they also led to an increase in unemployment and thus, indirectly, to a rise in recidivism.

---

[5]The data tapes from both experiments have been released for public use and are available through Abt Associates.

Other large-scale field experiments were undertaken during the Golden Age aimed at estimating the effects of various levels of subsidized medical insurance on the consumption of medical care (Newhouse et al 1980), the provision of work in the rehabilitation of ex-felons, drug addicts, and released mental health patients (Manpower Demonstration Research Corporation Board of Directors 1980), and the effects of alternative police patrol practices on crime rates (Kelling et al 1974), as well as the effects of alternative treatments of offenders accused of spouse abuse (Sherman & Berk, unpublished work, 1983).

A great deal was learned during the Golden Age about the limitations of field experiments in the evaluation of social programs. First of all, the successful experiments all dealt with *proposed* changes in social programs. Randomized, controlled experiments appear to be politically and logistically feasible only when the program being tested is one that policymakers might consider for future enactment and implementation. Existing, ongoing social programs usually do not present the conditions necessary for randomization, and even if they did, policymakers typically would not allow randomized treatments in any case. Second, the successfully executed experiments are almost invariably those that dispense a robust treatment, usually income payments. Attempts to deliver human services under the conditions of a controlled experiment have generally not been successful. Third, maintaining the integrity of a randomized, controlled experiment over the long periods of time necessary for a treatment to take effect is extremely difficult. Due to the time spans involved, there is often considerable missing data because subjects drop out of the experiment, migrate to places out of easy reach, or otherwise evade cooperation with researchers. Finally, field experiments are expensive both in terms of funds needed and time. The latter is a particularly fatal shortcoming, if one is interested in influencing policy.

The Emergence of Alternatives to the Experimental Paradigm

One of the most important lessons to be learned from all the evaluations initiated during the Golden Age is that it is extremely difficult to design programs that produce noticeable effects in any desired direction. In retrospect, a reasonable summary of the findings is that the expected value of the effect of any program hovers around zero. This conclusion was devastating to the social reformers who had hoped that the Great Society programs would make appreciable (or at least detectable) gains in bettering the lot of the poor and redressing the ills of society.

In part, the disappointment over the poor showing of most social programs was generated by overly optimistic expectations about their likely effects. Dramatic changes from the small treatment dosages of most programs were simply not in the cards. For example, the funds allocated under the Elementary and Secondary School Act of 1965 (McLaughlin 1975) to elementary schools to enrich the education of the poor on the bottom line amounted to less than $25 per pupil per year. In the aggregate, the funds appeared to be very generous, adding billions of dollars to the federal budget, but they were much less impressive when viewed as increments to per capita pupil expenditures.

In addition, the difficulties of delivering programs as designed were not fully appreciated. It was easy enough (in those days of apparent prosperity) to declare that most chronically ill mental patients would be better off outside the mental hospitals and thus to fund a program of community-based treatment centers. But it was another matter altogether to set up organizations on the local level that would be able to deliver the needed treatments with the care and attention to individual differences that, according to the philosophy behind the program, were required for full effectiveness.

Problems of appropriate implementation were especially intractable in programs involving the delivery of human services. Both public and private human service agencies quickly became remarkably adept at the grantsmanship game, devising projects on paper that could be funded under the numerous programs that were available. They then used the monies so obtained to fund business as usual instead of the innovations that the programs were designed to foster. For example, some school systems classified English-dominant students as bilingual in order to qualify for subsidies under the federally funded bilingual education program (American Institutes for Research 1977). Another example was the Push-Excel program designed to spur the aspirations of disadvantaged high school students. It was found, upon evaluation, to be largely nonexistent in the schools where it had supposedly been installed (American Institutes of Research 1980).

The intellectual consequence of this steady parade of close-to-zero effects was a closer examination of the methods used. The Campbell & Stanley (1966) volume was based on a presumption that turned out to be largely unwarranted: The authors believed that evaluations would typically yield data that appeared to show that the programs were effective. Hence the major methodological problem in program evaluation research would be that various artifacts of design and method would be mistaken for true program effects; thus, the authors explicate the "threats to internal validity" arising out of the defects in the research design in great detail. Very little attention was paid to the more common problem actually encountered—that of zero effects.

The resulting critical reappraisal of the dominant experimental paradigm took three forms: first, a general rejection of the experimental paradigm itself and its presumed "positivistic" intellectual roots in favor of more qualitative approaches; second, a rejection specifically of the "black box" experimental paradigm that Campbell & Stanley implicitly advanced and its replacement by an orientation that stressed the importance of a priori theory in evaluation; and, third, the development of a concern for designing social programs so that they will or can be implemented in accordance with the policymakers' original intentions. Each of these three themes is taken up in detail below.

The preference for qualitative over experimental approaches is rooted in a belief that social programs tend to develop their goals as they proceed; thus, to saddle them with evaluations that stress a priori goals does an injustice to the evolving nature of most programs. Advocates of this position (e.g. House 1980, Patton 1980, Scriven 1977, Weiss & Rein 1972, Guba & Lincoln 1981, Deutscher 1977) tend to be concerned mainly with educational evaluations and to have participated in the evaluation of small-scale local projects. According to this viewpoint, many potentially innovative social projects are funded with vague goals that are supposed to be achieved using unspecified procedures. An experimental approach that demands fixed procedures and unchanging goals simply does not work in the "real world" where both goals and procedures are continually being changed in an effort to find something that appears to work.

Unquestionably, the qualitative approach to evaluation has some merit, especially in dealing with the development phase of programs and projects when changes in procedures are desirable. The approach is also congenial to program and project managers who often believe that qualitative evaluations are better suited to their needs. Finally, qualitative approaches to the evaluation of small-scale projects also tend to be relatively inexpensive.

It is, however, equally clear that qualitative evaluations have their limits as well. However inexpensive they may be for single, small-scale projects, they are very expensive and not very sensible approaches to the evaluation of fully developed programs that have quite specific goals. Qualitative evaluations are very labor intensive and cannot be used on very many sites except at considerable cost. Furthermore, qualitative approaches rarely provide estimates of the effects that are either very precise or free and clear of possible confounding factors. Indeed, the only large-scale programs to which qualitative approaches were applied had vaguely stated goals, e.g. Model Cities (Kaplan 1973) and revenue sharing (Nathan et al 1981). In these evaluations, the findings were composed more of descriptions of program operations than of assessments of program effects.

Another attack on the experimental paradigm, especially on its black box version, has been made by those who believe that experimental evaluations will be more useful if the program being evaluated is examined theoretically and the experimental design is tailored to the results of the theoretical analysis (Chen & Rossi 1983, Cronbach 1982, Watts & Skidmore 1981). A black box experiment is one in which the treatment is regarded as an undifferentiated unit—i.e. a black box—about whose components nothing is known. Thus, a manpower training program might be composed of a curriculum, selection and training procedures, classroom activities, on-the-job experience, perhaps a placement project, and several other elements. A black box evaluation of such a program would treat the entire program as an undifferentiated unit by, for example, comparing the employment success of those who had been in the program and those who were in a control group. Black box experimental evaluations such as the one just described can provide unbiased estimates of net effects but, because the treatment is regarded as a unit, would normally provide no information on why the treatment either did or did not work.

According to the "theory-driven" approach, theoretical analyses should be undertaken beforehand to provide a basis for the design of sensible evaluation experiments. Thus, the manpower training program just described might be evaluated using a factorial experiment that systematically varied theoretically important components of the program—e.g. curriculum or placement methods. The outcome of such an evaluation will be more useful, say its proponents, because the design will enable researchers to judge the effectiveness of various program components and combinations of components; hence, it will serve as a basis for devising a new, more effective program in the future.

The third major reaction to the "no effects" problem was to shift attention away from estimating the net effects and toward creating programs that are likely to be (or are capable of being) implemented in accordance with their design. For some researchers, this shift has meant paying more attention to the problems of implementation (Pressman & Wildavsky 1973, Williams & Elmore 1976, Williams et al 1982, W. S. Pierce 1981, Hamilton 1979). For them the issue has been to learn, primarily through descriptive research, under which conditions agencies will carry out programs as directed. For others (Fairweather & Tornatzky 1977, Tornatzky et al 1980, Davidson et al 1981), the problem was defined as how to design experiments that would test alternative ways for operating agencies to implement programs in the field. Perhaps the most elaborate research program of all along these lines was carried out by Fairweather and his associates (Fairweather & Tornatzky 1977) who conducted a series of related experiments over a 15-year period. They attempted to devise an effective and implementable program for returning mental health patients to their communities while allowing those patients to lead more effective lives.

Another kind of implementation endeavor is exemplified by the administrative "experiment" that was conducted along with the Housing Allowance studies. Eight cities were funded to conduct Housing Allowance programs with the expectation that each would implement the program differently in accordance with local political structures and local market conditions. A central contractor was supposed to track and later analyze these demonstrations in order to extract generalizations on the best way to implement a housing allowance program (Hamilton 1979).

Fixing Up Nonexperimental Designs

The discussion so far has been fairly narrowly focused on randomized experimental designs for impact assessment because (a) the technically most successful impact assessments were carried out using that design and therefore (b) the randomized, controlled experimental paradigm has dominated the evaluation scene for the last two decades. As detailed above, however, there are good reasons at least to modify the experimental paradigm, chief among them being that for most social programs evaluation must perforce use nonexperimental methods.

There are many reasons why randomized experimental designs cannot be used in some evaluation studies. First, ongoing programs that cover most or all of their intended target populations simply do not admit of believable controls. For example, an estimated 5–10% of the persons eligible for Old Age and Survivors Insurance (Social Security) benefits have not applied for them. These nonapplicants cannot realistically serve as controls for estimating the effects of social security benefits, however, because the self-selection factors are undoubtedly strong. Comparing persons receiving social security benefits with those who are eligible but, for whatever reasons, have not applied for them violates the *ceteris paribus* condition.

Second, some programs, such as Head Start, fail to reach significantly large proportions of the eligible population—perhaps as much as 25% in the Head Start example. These children are not reached by the Head Start program because parents have not allowed their children to enroll or because the school systems involved have too few poor children to support Head Start projects. Clearly, strong self-selection factors are at work, and hence, contrasting Head Start participants with eligible nonparticipants would not hold constant important differences between the two groups.

Finally, it would be ethically unthinkable to use randomization in the evaluation of some programs. For example, a definitive way of estimating the relative effectiveness of private and public high schools would be to assign adolescents to one or the other randomly and observe the outcome over an extended period of time. Obviously, there is no way that either policymakers or parents would allow such an evaluation to take place.

Thus, many of the evaluation studies of the past two decades have employed something other than classical randomized experimental designs. Unfortunately, these evaluations have not been technically successful on the whole. Each of the major nonexperimental evaluations has been shrouded in controversy—controversy that arises out of the political implications of the findings but that often centers on the technical inadequacies of the designs employed. Thus, Coleman's (1966) attempt to sort out schools' effects on achievement by analyzing a cross-sectional survey of thousands of students from hundreds of high schools was criticized mainly because of the statistical models he used

(Mosteller & Moynihan 1972). Similarly, an evaluation (Westinghouse Learning Corporation 1969) of the long-lasting effects of participation in Head Start came under fire (Campbell & Erlbacher 1970) because the researchers compared youngsters who had attended Head Start preschools with "comparable" children who had not. According to the study's critics, confounding self-selection factors were undoubtedly at work that made the two groups incomparable in important respects.

The problem of administrative or self-selection of program participants and nonparticipants is at the heart of nonexperimental evaluation designs' vulnerability to criticism. To illustrate this point, we can consider Coleman and his associates' (1982) recent study of academic achievement in public and private (mostly Catholic) high schools. The critical comparisons in such a study are clearly plagued by self-selection factors: whether a child attends the Catholic parochial high schools or the public high schools cannot by any stretch of the imagination be considered a random choice. Parents often make the choice alone, although they sometimes consult the child; they make their educational decisions on the basis of factors such as their anticipated income, their commitment to their religious group and its ideology, their assessments of their child's intellectual capabilities, the relative reputations of the local high schools, and so on. Nor are parents and child the only forces involved. Parochial high schools exercise judgment about whom they want to admit, selecting students on the basis of factors like their previous educational experience, the kind of curriculum the child or parents want, and the child's reputation as a behavioral problem. Some of these factors are probably related to high school achievement; the extent to which these factors independently affect such achievement would confound any *simple* comparisons between the achievement scores of parochial and public high school students.

Obviously, one way out of the problem is to hold constant statistically those factors relating both to achievement and to school choice. The difficulties of doing so, however, are also obvious. First, it is necessary to specify the relevant factors correctly, a task that is usually difficult because of the absence of empirically grounded theory to aid in that specification. Secondly, if the element of choice is one of those factors (as in this example), it *cannot* be held constant since choice exists for one group but not for the other; in the present case, that is, non-Catholics would not have the option of sending their children to parochial schools. [See Rossi & Wright (1982) for a more detailed critique of Coleman along these lines.]

A potentially fruitful solution to this problem has recently been suggested by the econometricians (Goldberger 1980, Barnow et al 1980, Berk & Ray 1982). They propose that researchers construct explicit models of the decision process and incorporate these models into structural equation systems as a means of holding constant the self-selection process. Although these proposals are somewhat more attractive than the usual approach of adding independent variables to a regression equation, they are still largely irrelevant because the appropriate decision models cannot be constructed except in special circumstances.

Another important development in the methodology used in nonexperimental evaluations has been the application of time series models to the assessment of the net effects of large-scale programs. [These models were originally developed in economic forecasting (Pindyck & Rubinfeld 1976) and subsequently applied specifically to evaluation problems (McCleary & Hay 1980, Cook & Campbell 1979).] First suggested by Campbell & Stanley (1966) as "interrupted time series" designs, the application of time series models has made it possible to assess the impact of new large-scale programs or the effects of modifying existing ones without recourse to classical randomized experiments. This approach is limited to programs that have long time series of data on their outcomes available and whose onset can be definitely located in time as, for example, with the enactment of new legislation.

Among the best-known interrupted time series evaluations are the various assessments of the Massachusetts Bartley-Fox gun law (G. L. Pierce & Bowers 1979, Deutsch & Alt 1977, Hay & McCleary 1979). This law imposed a mandatory penalty for carrying guns without a license, with the objective of reducing the use of guns in crimes. Using time series models, the researchers modeled the trends in gun-related crimes before the Bartley-Fox law went into effect and compared the resulting projections with the trends observed after the law was enacted. The findings suggest that the law led to only a slight reduction in the use of guns in crimes. The time series models used (Box-Jenkins models) are composed of a family of frameworks, each differing from the other in its assumptions about the kinds of time-dependent processes at work. To some degree, the choice among models is a judgment call, a condition that has led to polemical exchanges among independent researchers about the law's true effects (e.g. Hay & McCleary 1979, Deutsch 1979).

The two developments just discussed have implications for sociology that go considerably beyond evaluation research per se. The conceptualization of the self-selection problem in evaluation research has direct applications to most sociological research that relies on cross-sectional studies. The data analysis problems encountered are identical, so solutions developed in the evaluation field have immediate applications in the many sociological studies in which self-selection issues complicate the interpretation of findings.

Time series of critical data are available on many of the substantive areas of interest to sociologists. Aggregate data on crime rates go back almost 50 years; unemployment rates have been available on a monthly basis for almost 40 years; and so on. The time series models developed by econometricians for prediction purposes will undoubtedly prove to be generally useful in the study of social trends, possibly even more so as social indicators of all sorts become more widely and regularly available.

Expanding the Scope of Evaluation

One final reaction to the repeated findings of zero or small effects has been the expansion of the scope of evaluation research to include topics other than the estimation of the net impact. Many of the analyses of the "zero-effects" programs, for example, suggested that the apparent lack of impact might well have been due to inadequate program design in the first place, to faulty implementation of the program, to misunderstandings of the participants' actual needs, or to insufficient development of program concepts prior to implementation, among other factors. Concerns such as these make it quite apparent that a useful evaluation has to answer many questions other than simply, Did the program work? Knowing that a program failed to achieve its ends is certainly useful information, but knowing why it failed is, undeniably, more useful.

Concern about why zero or few effects were consistently found has accordingly led to a considerable expansion of the scope of evaluation studies. Indeed, in the late 1970s and early 1980s several prominent evaluation researchers began to call for "comprehensive evaluations" as the prototype for evaluation research activities [e.g. Bernstein & Freeman (1975), Rossi & Freeman (1982), Cronbach et al (1980).] A comprehensive evaluation of a social program includes the following components: (*a*) research and development work to aid in the design of social programs (including basic research on the relevant social processes involved); (*b*) needs assessment studies where data are gathered on the incidence, prevalence, and distribution in social and physical space of the social problem involved; (*c*) implementation research to explore alternative ways of delivering programs to ascertain which are most cost efficient and/or achieve the greatest impacts; (*d*) program monitoring research to explore the issue of how well social programs, once enacted, are actually implemented; and (*e*) impact assessment, the traditional concern of evaluation research.

Comprehensive evaluations in this sense are, of course, possible only under very limited circumstances, mainly in the prospective evaluation of proposed programs. Few, if any, real examples of comprehensive evaluations can be found, although Fairweather & Tornatzky's (1977) research program comes the closest to meeting all the criteria. Despite the rarity of actual examples, the concept of a comprehensive evaluation is useful because it focuses attention upon several critical issues in our understanding of social programs and their success or failure (Rossi 1978).

Many programs apparently fail because they are poorly conceptualized:

Either the nature of the social problem to which they are addressed is misunderstood, or the true nature of the proposed treatment is not appreciated. Thus, it would be a mistake to start up a program to reduce the welfare dependency of unmarried mothers by training them for jobs that pay less than the welfare payments. Or, it would be equally foolish to use prison guards as group therapy leaders in prisons. (See Rossi 1978 for additional examples.) The first two elements of a comprehensive evaluation draw attention to these issues.

In addition, a social program has to embody an appropriate understanding of the nature and distribution of the targeted social problem and the relevant beneficiaries of the proposed program. Therefore, programs to reduce crime rates must take into account that most of the crimes reviewed in our criminal courts are ones from which economic gain can be obtained. Such programs also have to be based on the understanding that the criminal justice system is usually activated by citizen action in the form of reports of crimes committed and that available prison space acts as an operational constraint for criminal justice programs. A crime reduction program that is insensitive to these basic facts about crime and criminal justice is necessarily doomed to failure.

The nature of the treatment being applied can also be misunderstood. The housing allowance experiments described earlier found that housing allowances had no effect on the quality of housing consumed, despite the apparent fact that poor families were being given monies to enhance the quality of their housing. What the designers of the policy failed to appreciate was that the recipients would treat these payments as increments to general income, not as funds "set aside" to be spent for a specific purpose (Struyk & Bendick 1981).

Yet another problem, perhaps an obvious one in retrospect, arises with the design and delivery of programs that address nonexistent needs. For example, the Disaster Relief Act of 1974 (PL 93–288) contained provisions whereby federal monies would be made available to aid communities' "economic recovery" in the aftermath of a disaster. The assumption was that communities would suffer severe economic disabilities as a result of the disasters, ones sufficiently serious and long lasting that federal monies would be warranted. Subsequent research (e.g. Friesema et al 1979, Wright et al 1979) suggested, however, that this assumption is incorrect and, indeed, that after a disaster many communities experienced something of a "boom" instead. This example illustrates the utility of needs assessment research as part of a comprehensive evaluation.

Research addressed to an appropriate understanding of the social problem at issue can be comprised of a wide variety of technical approaches, ranging from experiments through surveys. Essentially, such research is no different in form from basic disciplinary work. Indeed, the necessity to work with variables that are potentially under policymakers' control is perhaps the only salient difference between basic and applied social research.

Research on program implementation is primarily research in public administration. Although good examples are rare, in principle it is no more difficult to test several alternative ways of delivering a program than to test several alternative programs: indeed the two problems are formally identical. That implementation issues are often critical is widely recognized (Williams & Elmore 1976, Pressman & Wildavsky 1973, W. S. Pierce 1981), but the importance of research on the issues involved has not received the attention it deserves.

THE FUTURE OF EVALUATION RESEARCH

In the political climate imposed by the current Reagan administration, evaluation research has suffered a decline in fiscal support. As one of the present authors commented elsewhere (Rossi 1983), it is conceivable that financial support for evaluation research will eventually be restored as conservatives discover that they too need the information obtained by such research. Indeed, there are signs of growing support for evaluations during this fiscal year (1984). Some of the private-sector evaluation research firms have begun to rebuild their decimated staffs, and the flow of "requests for proposals" from the federal agencies seems to be stronger this year than it has been in any year since 1980.

Evaluation research appears to have become part of the tools of government, especially on the federal level. Therefore, there will probably be a continuing need for personnel well-trained in the social sciences to staff the research projects that will be undertaken, and sociologists may continue to find employment in evaluation research.

We also anticipate that basic research will continue to benefit from the substantive and technical advances made by applied researchers as the latter attempt to tackle even more complicated applied research tasks. There is no doubt that much technical and substantive knowledge flows the other way as well. A discipline that does not have an applied side loses a certain richness of theory and method. An applied field that loses touch with its basic discipline also runs a risk of parochialism and overly narrow attention to policymakers' definitions of social problems and their most feasible solutions.

Literature Cited

American Institutes for Research. 1977. *Evaluation of the Impact of the EASA Title 7 Spanish/English Bilingual Education Program.* Vols. 1–3. Palo Alto, Calif: Am. Inst. Res.

American Institutes for Research. 1980. *The National Evaluation of the PUSH for Excellence Project.* Washington DC: Am. Inst. Res.

Barnow, B. S., Cain, G. G., Goldberger, A. S. 1980. Issues in the analysis of selectivity bias. In *Evaluation Studies Review Annual*, ed. E. Stormsdorfer, D. Farkas, 5:43–59. Beverly Hills, Calif: Sage

Bawden, D. L., Harrar, W. S., eds. 1978. *Rural Income Maintenance Experiment: Final Report.* 6 vols. Madison, Wis: Inst. Res. Poverty

Berk, R. A., Ray, S. C. 1982. Selection biases in sociological data. *Soc. Sci. Res.* 11(4): 352–98

Bernstein, I., Freeman, H. 1975. *Academic and Entrepreneurial Research.* New York: Russell Sage Found.

Bradbury, K., Downs, A., eds. 1981. *Do Housing Allowances Work?* Washington DC: Brookings Inst.

Campbell, D. T. 1969. Reforms as experiments. *Am. Psychol.* 24:409–29

Campbell, D. T., Erlebacher, A. 1970. How regression artifacts in quasi-experiments can mistakenly make compensatory education look harmful. In *The Disadvantaged Child,* ed. J. Helmuth, pp. 185–210. New York: Brunner-Mazel

Campbell, D. T., Stanley, J. C. 1966. *Experimental and Quasi-Experimental Designs for Research.* Skokie, Ill: Rand McNally

Chen, H., Rossi, P. H. 1983. Evaluating with sense: The theory driven approach. *Eval. Rev.* 7(3):283–302

Coleman, J. C. 1966. *Equality of Educational Opportunity.* Washington DC: USGPO

Coleman, J. C., Hoffer, T., Kilgore, S. 1982. *High School Achievement: Public, Catholic and Private Schools Compared.* New York: Basic

Cook, T. D., Campbell, D. T. 1979. *Quasi-Experimentation: Design and Analysis Issues for Field Settings.* Chicago: Rand McNally

Cronbach, L. J. 1982. *Designing Evaluations of Educational and Social Programs.* San Francisco: Jossey-Bass

Cronbach, L. J., Ambron, S. R., Dornbusch, S. M., Hess, R. D., Hornik, R. C., Phillips, D. C. 1980. *Toward Reform of Program Evaluation.* San Francisco: Jossey-Bass

Davidson, W. S., et al. 1981. *Evaluation Strategies in Criminal Justice.* New York: Pergamon

Deutsch, S. J. 1979. Lies, damned lies and statistics: A rejoinder to the comment by Hay and McCleary. *Eval. Q.* 3(2):315–28

Deutsch, S. J., Alt, F. B. 1977. The effect of Massachusetts' gun control law on gun-related crimes in the city of Boston. *Eval. Q.* 1(3):543–67

Deutscher, I. 1977. Toward Avoiding the Goal Trap in Evaluation Research. In *Readings in Evaluation Research,* ed. F. G. Caro, pp. 108–23. New York: Russell Sage Found.

Evaluation Research Society. 1979. *Membership Directory.* Columbus, Ohio: Eval. Res. Soc.

Fairweather, G. W., Tornatzky, L. G. 1977. *Experimental Methods for Social Policy Research.* New York: Pergamon

Freeman, H., Dynes, R., Rossi, P. H., Whyte, W. F., eds. 1983. *Applied Sociology.* San Francisco: Jossey-Bass

Friedman, J., Weinberg, D., eds. 1983. *The Great Housing Experiment.* Beverley Hills, Calif: Sage

Friesema, H. P., Caporaso, J., Goldstein, G., Lineberry, R., McCleary, R. 1979. *Aftermath.* Beverly Hills, Calif: Sage

Goldberger, A. S. 1980. Linear regression after selection. *J. Economet.* 15(2):357–66

Gramlich, E. M., Koshel, P. P. 1975. *Educational Performance Contracting: An Evaluation of an Experiment.* Washington DC: Brookings Inst.

Guba, E. G., Lincoln, Y. S. 1981. *Effective Evaluation.* San Francisco: Jossey-Bass

Hamilton, W. L. 1979. *A Social Experiment in Program Administration: The Housing Allowance Administrative Agency Experiment.* Cambridge, Mass: Abt

Hay, R. Jr., McCleary, R. A. 1979. Box-Tiao time series models for impact assessment: A comment on the recent work of Deutsch and Alt. *Eval. Q.* 3(2):277–314

House, E. 1980. *Evaluating With Validity.* Beverly Hills, Calif: Sage

Kaplan, M. 1973. *Urban Planning in the 1960's: A Design for Irrelevancy.* New York: Praeger

Kelling, G. L., Pate, T., Dieckman, D., Brown, C. E. 1974. *The Kansas City Preventive Patrol Experiment: A Technical Report.* Washington DC: Police Found.

Kershaw, D., Fair, J. 1975. *The New Jersey–Pennsylvania Income Maintenance Experiment.* Vol. I. New York: Academic

Manderscheid, R. W., Greenwald, M. 1983. Trends in employment of sociologists. In *Applied Sociology,* ed. H. E. Freeman, R. R. Dynes, P. H. Rossi, W. F. Whyte, pp. 51–63. San Francisco: Jossey-Bass

Manpower Demonstration Research Corporation Board of Directors. 1980. *Summary and Findings of the National Supported Work Demonstration.* Cambridge, Mass: Ballinger

McCleary, R., Hay, R. A. Jr. 1980. *Applied Time Series Analysis.* Beverly Hills, Calif: Sage

McLaughlin, M. W. 1975. *Evaluation and Reform: The Elementary and Secondary Education Act of 1965.* Cambridge, Mass: Ballinger

Moffitt, R. A. 1979. The labor supply response in the Gary experiment. *J. Hum. Resour.* 14(4):477–87

Mosteller, F., Moynihan, D. P., eds. 1972. *On Equality of Educational Opportunity.* New York: Vintage

Nathan, R., Cook, R. F., Rawlins, V. L. 1981. *Public Service Employment: A Field Evaluation.* Washington DC: Brookings Inst.

Newhouse, J. P., Rolph, J. E., Mori, B., Murphy, M. 1980. The effects of deductibles on the demand for medical care services. *J. Am. Stat. Assoc.* 75(371):525–33

Patton, M. 1980. *Qualitative Evaluation Methods.* Beverly Hills, Calif: Sage

Pierce, W. S. 1981. *Bureaucratic Failure and Public Expenditures.* New York: Academic

Pierce, G. L., Bowers, W. J. 1979. *The Impact of the Bartley-Fox Gun Law on Crime in Massachusetts.* Boston: Cent. Appl. Soc. Res., Northeastern Univ.

Pindyck, R. S., Rubinfeld, D. L. 1976. *Econometric Models and Economic Forecasts.* New York: McGraw-Hill

Pressman, J., Wildavsky, A. 1973. *Implementation.* Berkeley: Univ. Calif. Press

Raizen, S., Rossi, P. H. 1981. *Program Evaluation In Education.* Washington DC: Nat. Acad. Sci. - Nat. Res. Counc.

Robins, P. K., Spiegelman, R. G., Weiner, S., Bell, J. G., eds. 1980. *A Guaranteed Annual Income: Evidence from a Social Experiment.* New York: Academic

Rossi, P. H. 1978. Issues in the evaluation of human services delivery. *Eval. Q.* 2(3):573–99

Rossi, P. H. 1981. Presidential address: The challenge and opportunities of applied social research. *Am. Sociol. Rev.* 45(6):889–904

Rossi, P. H. 1983. Pussycats, Weasels, or Percherons? Current Prospects for the Social Sciences under the Reagan Regime. *Eval. News* 40(1):12–27

Rossi, P. H., Berk, R. A., Lenihan, K. 1980. *Money, Work and Crime.* New York: Academic

Rossi, P. H., Berk, R. A., Lenihan, K. 1983. Saying it wrong with figures. *Am. J. Sociol.* 88(2):390–93

Rossi, P. H., Freeman, H. E. 1982. *Evaluation: A Systematic Approach.* Beverly Hills, Calif: Sage. 2nd ed.

Rossi, P. H., Lyall, K. 1974. *Reforming Public Welfare.* New York: Russell Sage Found.

Rossi, P. H., Wright, J. D. 1982. Best schools—Better discipline or better students? *Am. J. Educ.* 91(1):79–89

Rossi, P. H., Wright, J. D. 1983. Applied social science. *Contemp. Sociol.* 12(2):148–51

Rossi, P. H., Wright, J. D., Wright, S. R. 1978. The theory and practice of applied social research. *Eval. Q.* 2(2):171–91

Scriven, M. 1977. *Evaluation Thesaurus.* Inverness, Calif: Edgepress. 3rd ed.

Struyk, R. J., Bendick, M. Jr. 1981. *Housing Vouchers for the Poor.* Washington DC: Urb. Inst.

Tornatzky, L., Fergus, E., Avellar, J., Fairweather, G., Fleischer, M. 1980. *Innovation and Social Process: A National Experiment in Implementing Social Technology.* New York: Pergamon

Watts, H. W., Rees, A. 1976. *The New Jersey Income-Maintenance Experiment,* Vols. 2, 3. New York: Academic

Watts, H. W., Skidmore, F. 1981. A critical review of the program as social experiment. See Bradbury & Downs 1981, pp. 33–65.

Weiss, R., Rein, M. 1970. The evaluation of broad-aimed programs: Experimental design, its difficulties, and an alternative. *Admin. Sci. Q.* 15(1):97–109

Westinghouse Learning Corporatic '^69. *The Impact of Head Start.* Athei   )hio: Westinghouse Learn. Corp. & Ohio Univ.

Whyte, W. F. 1982. Presidential address: Social questions for solving human problem... *Am. Sociol. Rev.* 47(1):1–13

Williams, W. 1980. *Government by Agency: Lessons from the Social Program Grants-in-Aid Experience.* New York: Academic

Williams, W., Elmore, R. F. 1976. *Social Program Implementation.* New York: Academic

Williams, W., Elmore, R., Hall, J., Jung, R., Kirst, M., Machmanus, S. 1982. *Studying Implementation: Methodological and Substantive Issues.* New York: Chatham

Wright, J. D., Rossi, P. H., Wright, S. R., Weber-Burdin, E. 1979. *After the Clean-Up: Long Range Effects of Natural Disasters.* Beverly Hills, Calif: Sage

Zeisel, H. 1983. Evaluation of an experiment. *Am. J. Sociol.* 88(2):378–89

3

The Countenances of Fourth-Generation Evaluation: Description, Judgment, and Negotiation[1]

Egon G. Guba and Yvonna S. Lincoln

The history of evaluation has been characterized by dramatic change. The melange of evaluation models, principles, and advice that has emerged over more than a half century can be ordered and classified in many different ways (see, for example, Stake, 1973; House, 1978; Stufflebeam & Webster, 1980; Guba & Lincoln, 1981). What appears in this chapter is yet another construction, arbitrary to be sure, but one that may nevertheless cast some light on how the field of evaluation came to be what it is today, and, more important, how it is becoming what it is likely to be tomorrow.

It is our thesis that evaluation has moved through three generations of development and is currently entering the fourth generation. We shall describe these four generations, delineate the fundamental principles that underlie the fourth, and show how both the concept of evaluation and the role of the evaluator are accordingly shifting.

The Four Generations of Evaluation

The first generation of evaluation began to form in the early part of this century, but received a particular stimulus with the sudden availability of intelligence, aptitude, and achievement tests following World War I. This generation of evaluation may be characterized as *technical,* and the evaluator's role as that of *technician.* During this period evaluation meant little more than measurement— determining the status of individual pupils or groups of pupils with respect to

AUTHORS' NOTE: We are indebted to our classes in program evaluation at Indiana University and the University of Kansas whose students helped us to evolve the principles developed in this chapter in a systematic fashion. Their constant challenges to our thinking were instrumental in developing and refining our ideas. We also acknowldege a debt to Judy Meloy, graduate student at Indiana University, who assisted in sorting out the many ideas thrown into the hopper by our classroom students, and who read and commented on the draft. This selection has been excerpted from a chapter to appear in *Politics of Education,* edited by Dennis Palumbo.

norms that had been established for certain standardized tests. Pupils were seen as the "raw material" to be "processed" in the "school plant" presided over, appropriately enough, by the school "superintendent." The industrial metaphor is no accident because this period of American history is well described as the era of scientific management, as Eisner (1969) and others have shown. Evaluation was seen as a means of determining whether or not pupils measured up to the "specifications" that the school had set—largely college-preparatory specifications. That this technical sense of evaluation persists today cannot be doubted, as evidenced, for example, by the frequent practice of requiring pupils to pass such tests as part of their high school graduation or college admission procedures; by the use of such tests scores in many states to rank schools and even individual teachers for effectiveness; and by the continued publication of texts that use the phrase *measurement and evaluation* in their titles (see, for example, Gronlund, 1985).

By the late 1920s the secondary schools of America were experiencing an influx of types of students who had earlier rarely gone beyond elementary levels; these students exhibited needs and aspirations that could not be met adequately by the prevailing college-preparatory curricula. Many of these students saw the secondary school as an opportunity to acquire the skills needed to rise above the social and economic status of their parents, but the schools were ill equipped to provide such teaching. Moreover, efforts to devise curricula that were more appropriate were defeated before they could receive a fair trial, because the secondary schools were inextricably locked into the Carnegie unit system. The chief obstacles in the path of altering this requirement were, not surprisingly, colleges and universities, which feared that if the Carnegie unit was abolished as the basis for accumulating secondary school credits, they would be forced to accept high school graduates who were ill prepared to cope with their standard curricula.

The Eight Year Study launched in 1933 was intended to determine the validity of that position. Thirty public and private secondary schools were given license to develop more responsive curricula with the understanding that their graduates would be admitted to cooperating colleges without necessarily having met normal Carnegie requirements. The purpose of the Eight Year Study was to demonstrate that students who were trained by these unorthodox curricula would nevertheless be able to succeed in college. The time period of eight years was selected to permit at least one cohort of such students to complete four full years each of secondary school and college work.

An immediate problem confronting the designers of the study was to devise a means for assessing whether the developing new curricula were working as intended—it would not be a fair test if students failed in college because the secondary curricula were inadequate. By a serendipitous occurrence, Ralph W. Tyler, a member of the Bureau of Educational Research at Ohio State University, the campus at which the Eight Year Study was headquartered, had for several years been working with selected Ohio State faculty to develop tests that would measure whether or not the students had learned what the professors had wanted them to learn. These desired learning outcomes were labeled *objectives.* Tyler was engaged to carry out the same kind of work with Eight Year Study schools, but with one important variation from conventional evaluation (measurement): The purpose of the studies would be to refine the developing curricula and make sure they were working. Program evaluation was born.

As the participant secondary schools began devising their new curricula, Tyler collected information about the extent of achievement of their defined objectives by the pupils in their programs. This information, together with an analysis of the patterns of strengths and weaknesses that emerged, was then utilized to guide refinements and revisions—a process we today would be inclined to call *formative* evaluation, except that the results were not available until *after* rather than *during* a trial. This process was reiterated until the curriculum was found to produce an appropriate level of achievement.

Thus was born second-generation evaluation, an approach that was characterized by *description* of patterns of strength and weakness with respect to certain stated objectives. The role of the evaluator came to be that of *describer,* although the earlier technical aspects of the role were also retained. Measurement was no longer treated as the equivalent of evaluation but was redefined as one of several tools that might be used in its service. When the five-volume results of the Eight Year Study were published in 1942, the third volume, which reported on the evaluation activities of the project (Smith & Tyler, 1942), drew widespread attention. Like Lord Byron, Tyler awoke one morning to find himself famous, the acknowledged leader of a new group of curriculum evaluators. Later he was to be recognized as the "Father of Evaluation" (Joint Committee, 1981).

But the objectives-oriented descriptive approach had some serious flaws, although they were not very noticeable until the post-Sputnik period, when it proved inadequate to the task of evaluating the federal government's response to the (purported) deficiencies of American education that had allowed the Russians to gain a march in space exploration: the course content improvement programs of the National Science Foundation (BSCS Biology, Project CHEM, PSSC Physics, and SMSG Mathematics) and of the then Office of Education (Project English and Project Social Studies). Because it was essentially descriptive in nature, second-generation Tylerian evaluation neglected, at least explicitly, an equally important matter, referred to by Robert E. Stake in his now-classic 1967 paper as the *other* countenance or face of evaluation: *judgment.* Stake noted:

> The countenance of evaluation beheld by the educator is not the same one beheld by the specialist in evaluation. The specialist sees himself as a "describer", one who describes aptitudes and environment and accomplishments. The teacher and the school administrator, on the other hand, expect an evaluator to grade something or someone as to merit. Moreover, they expect that he will judge things against external standards, on criteria perhaps little related to the local school's resources.

Neither sees evaluation broadly enough. *Both* description and judgment are essential—in fact, they are the two basic acts of evaluation. (Worthen & Sanders, 1973, p. 109)

The call to include judgment in the act of evaluation marked the emergence of third-generation evaluation, a generation in which evaluation was characterized by efforts to reach *judgments,* and in which the evaluator assumed the role of *judge,* while retaining the earlier technical and descriptive functions as well. This call, widely echoed in the profession, notably by Michael Scriven (1967), exposed several problems that had not been dealt with adequately in the earlier generations. First, it required that objectives *themselves* be taken as problematic; goals no less than performance were to be subject to evaluation. As a wag pointed out, something not worth doing at all is certainly not worth doing well. Further, judgment requires, as Stake pointed out, *standards* against which the judgment can be made. But the inclusion in a scientific and therefore putatively value-free enterprise such as evaluation of standards that must by definition of the genre be value-laden was repugnant to most evaluators. Finally, if there is to be judgment, there must be a judge. Evaluators did not feel competent to act in that capacity, felt it presumptuous to do so, and feared the political vulnerability to which it exposed them. Nevertheless, they were urged to accept that obligation, largely on the ground that among all possible judge-candidates, the evaluators were without doubt the most objective (Scriven, 1967).

In the final analysis the call to judgment could not be ignored, and evaluators soon rose to the challenge. A bevy of new evaluation models sprang up in 1967 and thereafter: neo-Tylerian models including Stake's own Countenance Model (1967) and the Discrepancy Evaluation Model (Provus, 1971); decision-oriented models such as CIPP (Stufflebeam et. al., 1971); effects-oriented models such as the Goal-Free Model (Scriven, 1973); neomeasurement models in the guise of societal experimentation (Campbell, 1969; Rossi & Williams, 1972; Boruch, 1974; Rivlin & Timpane, 1975); and models that were directly judgmental, such as the Connoisseurship Model (Eisner, 1979). All of these post-1967 models agreed on one point, however: Judgment was an integral part of evaluation. All urged, more or less explicitly, that the *evaluator* be the judge. There were differences in the extent to which evaluators were represented as appropriate judges, ranging from the tentativeness of decision-oriented models whose proponents hesitated to advocate an aggressive judgmental role because that seemingly co-opted the very decision makers whom the evaluations were ostensibly to serve, to the assertiveness of the judgmental models in which the evaluator was chosen precisely because of his or her connoisseurship qualities, which assured that the judgment could be trusted. Nevertheless, it seems fair to say that during the decade and more following 1967, judgment became the hallmark of third-generation evaluation.

The fourth generation is currently emerging, as a new class of models takes its place on the evaluation scene. Commonly called *responsive,* these models take as their point of focus not objectives, decisions, effects, or similar organizers but the *claims, concerns, and issues* put forth by members of a *variety* of *stakeholding audiences,* that is, audiences who are in some sense involved with the evaluand (the entity being evaluated) and hence are put at risk by the evaluation. Such audiences include *agents* (e.g., developers, funders, implementers), *beneficiaries* (e.g., target groups, potential adopters), and *victims* (e.g., excluded target groups, potential beneficiaries of opportunities forgone by the decision to implement the particular evaluand) (Guba & Lincoln, 1981). The principles undergirding these responsive models may be noted to a greater or lesser degree in responsive evaluation (Stake, 1975), naturalistic evaluation (Guba & Lincoln, 1981), illuminative evaluation (Parlett & Hamilton, 1972), utilization-focused evaluation (Patton, 1978), and adversarial evaluation (Wolf, 1979).

Fourth-generation models share one highly consequential belief: that of value-pluralism. Judgments must be made in terms of standards that derive from particular value postures. The judgments affect various stakeholding audiences, all of whom are at some degree of risk in the evaluation. But there is no assurance that the various audiences *share* the value position that undergirds any particular set of standards; indeed, the evidence of the past 15 years is that American culture (and probably every other advanced culture) is characterized by value-pluralism. Thus it is more than merely possible that different stakeholder values might lead to *conflicting* judgments even *in the face of the same* "factual" evidence.[3] But if one group, say, finds an evaluand effective and appropriate, while another, on the same evidence, finds it ineffective and inappropriate, what is to be done at the point of action? Clearly the evaluator cannot arrogate to himself or herself the making of a judgment that would so obviously infringe the rights of certain of the stakeholders. Worse, such an act of evaluator judgment would *dishonor* the values of the infringed group(s), and *exploit the power* of the evaluation to override their self-perceived interests. The evaluator therefore cannot ethically undertake to render judgments; what he or she must do instead is to act as mediator in a negotiation process. The theme of *negotiation* is the hallmark of fourth-generation evaluation, and the role of *negotiator and change agent* of the fourth-generation evaluator. We believe that these concepts will shape evaluation practice for the foreseeable future. It is the purpose of this chapter to explicate the form of that shaping.

FUNDAMENTAL PRINCIPLES
GUIDING FOURTH-GENERATION EVALUATORS

We begin the task of explicating fourth-generation evaluation by outlining certain principles that guide evaluators practicing in this mode. These principles are generated from a consideration of five more or less axiomatic concepts that we shall take up in turn: value-pluralism, stakeholder constructions, fairness, merit and worth, and negotiation. In two later sections we shall show how these principles coalesce to redefine evaluation and the role of the evaluator.

(1) The concept of value-pluralism. Four-generation evaluation is the first that

explicitly recognizes and deals with the possibility of value-pluralism. The earlier generations tended to assume value consensus, even if only implicitly. It makes no sense, for example, to evaluate by objectives unless one implicitly assumes that the objectives are agreed to by all; indeed, it is difficult to imagine how objectives could be formulated in the first place without such agreement. In practice, disagreements are often papered over through the statement of grandiose and/or ambiguous objectives, so as not to generate resistance or lose constituencies. But in the end such a maneuver is self-defeating, because the evaluator *must* render the objectives into a specific form so as to be able to assess objectives/performance discrepancies. The evaluator "takes the heat" for the failure of the legislating parties to come to prior agreement. In similar fashion one cannot imagine a decision-oriented evaluation without assuming agreement on the criteria by which decision options are to be assessed. Nor can one do a goal-free evaluation without assuming consensus on some needs assessment against which the effects can be tested, particularly because needs themselves are value based (Guba & Lincoln, 1982a). The connoisseurship model assumes agreement with the values to be brought to bear by the connoisseur. And so on.

Fourth-generation evaluators open the door to a consideration of value differences, but in doing so they introduce two complications—one methodological and one substantive. Methodologically, they relinquish some control over the evaluation as a process. They must include different value positions in a consideration of what is to be studied, how, with what reports, and the like. They are consequently no longer able to provide a priori assurance to clients and stakeholders that the evaluation will be useful, because they are not in a position to determine ahead of time whether or not consensus, even if only at the level of practical accommodation, will be possible. Substantively, they must now include *political elements* among those that will be taken account of in the evaluation. The evaluation becomes a political act as well as an investigatory process. Different political positions will have to be recognized and accommodated. Hence, fourth-generation evaluators operate according to the following principles:

Principle 1:   Conflict rather than consensus must be the expected condition in any evaluation taking account of value differences.

Principle 2:   The technical/descriptive/judgmental processes that have completely characterized evaluation practice in the past cannot alone deal with partisan discord; some means must be invoked to reach an accommodation among different value postures.

Principle 3:   The parties holding different value postures must themselves be involved if there is to be any hope of accommodation.

(2) The concept of stakeholder constructions. Fourth-generation evaluation is rooted in a relativist ontology. The position of positivist science is that there exists an objective reality that goes on about its business independently of the interest that human beings may exhibit in it.[4] Compelling evidence is building up

in the "hard" and life sciences such as physics and biology to suggest that this view is no longer tenable (Lincoln & Guba, 1985). Instead, the concept of a single objective reality onto which inquiry can converge by continuous and systematic effort is being replaced by the concept that reality is *multiple* and*constructed* in form, so that inquiry continuously diverges (the more you know, the more of the unknown you contact) (Lincoln & Guba, 1985). These constructions are made by persons, and it is in the minds of persons that one finds them, not "out there."

Fourth-generation evaluation also takes issue with positivism's epistemological position: That what there is to be known can be known objectively by an inquirer who is able to stand "outside" of it. Evaluations focus the attention of participants and stimulate them to synthesize, crystallize, and coalesce their ideas to form, create, and expand their realities. The evaluator thus becomes a major agent in the construction of the realities that define the evaluand, make claims for it, and raise concerns and issues about it. In a very real sense evaluations *create* reality rather than objectively discover it. But they do so in relation to the contexts in which the evaluands are found (including the expectations for the evaluand in relation to that context) and to the particular value patterns that are held by the various constructing stakeholders. Contexts and values thus play a vital role in reality definition. It is value differences that account for the different constructions made by different stakeholders in some given context (although the latter will also be constructed differently by the various parties), but the fact of differing constructions is usually hidden from the stakeholders themselves, who are prone to be aware only of that one admitted by their own values. Fourth-generation evaluation thus also operates according to these next principles:

Principle 4:   The evaluator is at times a *learner* who must learn what the constructions of stakeholders are, while recognizing that the very act of learning them helps to create those constructions.

Principle 5:   The evaluator is at times a *teacher* who communicates the constructions of other stakeholders to each stakeholding audience, and in the process, clarifies the value positions that account for them.

(3) The concept of fairness. The fourth-generation evaluator, recognizing that different stakeholders may base their judgments on very different value patterns, is concerned that no one of them be given unfair preference in the evaluation. There is, finally, no meta-criterion that can be used to distinguish more worthy from less worthy values (although for some purposes it may be possible to order values hierarchically); equity demands that the constructions, claims, concerns, and issues that stem from each value pattern be solicited and honored. The evaluator must project an *emic* (Pike, 1954), that is, an insider's view for *each* audience, and be prepared to accept it at face value unless and until that audience itself determines to change it.[5]

It may be taken as axiomatic that evaluation equitably carried out will inevitably upset the prevailing balance of power. Evaluation produces information, and information *is* power. To deny information to some groups is to disenfranchise them. Those holding power may argue for selective dispersal of information on such apparently sound grounds as efficiency, minimization of conflict, personal accountability, or even a "higher social good," but, as Cronbach (1980) points out in the 19th of his 95 theses bearing on evaluation:

> An open society becomes a closed society when only the officials know what is going on. Insofar as information is a source of power, evaluations carried out to inform a policymaker have a disenfranchising effect. [p. 4].

Thus the fourth-generation evaluator adds the following principles to his or her repertoire:

Principle 6:   The evaluator is ethically bound to solicit the constructions, claims, concerns, and issues of all identifiable stakeholders, and to clarify the values that undergird them.

Principle 7:   Equity demands that the evaluator honor all constructions, claims, concerns, and issues by collecting information that is responsive to them (for example, validates or invalidates them) without regard to their source audience, and to disseminate that information so that it is equally accessible to all.

Principle 8:   The evaluator must collect information in ways that expose "facts" useful both to protagonists as well as to antagonists of an evaluand.

Principle 9:   The evaluator must release findings continuously and openly so as to provide ample opportunity for the assessment of their credibility from all constructed points of view and for their rebuttal should that be the desire of some audience(s).

(4) The concepts of merit and worth. Both merit and worth are aspects of value, which it is the purpose of evaluation to assess, but they are very different from one another (Guba & Lincoln, 1981). Merit depends on *intrinsic* characteristics of the evaluand, those characteristics that the evaluand would retain regardless of the circumstances under which it is used. Thus we may speak of the temper of the steel or the flexibility of the handle of an axe; the scholarliness and writings of a professor; or the internal consistency, modernity, continuity, sequence, and integration of a curriculum. Worth, on the other hand, is an *extrinsic* assessment, which depends heavily on the context of use. Thus the worth of an axe may depend on the nature of the tree to be cut down or on the expertise of the cutter who uses it; the worth of a professor to an employing institution may depend on his or her ability to teach high-demand courses, set a good role model, or attract outside funding; and the worth of a curriculum may depend on its utility for teaching particular target groups in particular socio-economic and cultural contexts when used by teachers with particular training and experience. Merit may be assessed through an examination of the evaluand in relative isolation, while worth can only be assessed in terms of its ability to meet

needs-in-context. Values have a "double dip" here: They are the basis for defining the needs whose fulfillment may be the purpose of the evaluand (although sometimes needs are met as a serendipitous side effect of an evaluand intended for some other purpose), as well as for setting the standards useful for determining how well the needs are "in fact" met. The possibilities for value conflict are thus noticeably exacerbated.

In light of these considerations the fourth-generation evaluator adds these three principles to the repertoire of guidelines:

Principle 10: While merit can be assessed in isolation, worth can be assessed only in relation to particular needs-in-context. Change the context and you change both needs and worth.

Principle 11: The evaluator cannot carry out an assessment either of needs or worth except with field-based methods that take full account of the local context.

Principle 12: Transferability of assessments of needs and/or of worth from one context to another depends on the *empirical* similarity of sending and receiving contexts.

(5) The concept of negotiated process and outcomes. Once the concept of value-pluralism is admitted and the criterion of fairness is invoked, it becomes plain that fair judgments can be reached only through negotiation, if at all. The basis for negotiation is collaboration—the inclusion of stakeholders in the evaluation process itself. Most past evaluations have been *exogenous,* that is, with control vested entirely in the hands of the professional evaluator. A few evaluations are *endogenous,* that is, with control vested in the hands of the audience(s), particularly if an evaluation is carried out by a single audience for its own purposes, such as a group of teachers who evaluate the discipline practices in their own building for the sake of improving their available time-on-task. But what is called for in light of the fourth-generation position is *full collaboration,* in the sense that evaluator(s) and stakeholder(s) or their representatives are *continuously* involved.[6]

The concept of collaboration has both a strong sense and a weak sense. In the weak sense, stakeholders are given an opportunity to react to findings and to the evaluator's constructions thereof. Such "member checks" (Lincoln & Guba, 1985) have both validational and ethical utility. It is of little use to impute a construction to an audience if that audience cannot identify its own position therein. Moreover, to persist in that erroneous construction is to exploit and to enervate the audience that it putatively represents.

In the strong sense, which the fourth-generation evaluator advocates, stake-holding audiences are given the opportunity to provide inputs *at every stage* of the evaluation: the charge, the goal, the design, the data collection and analysis instruments and methods, the interpretation, and so on. Clearly soliciting and incorporating what are likely to be very divergent views will require an intensive *political* effort from the evaluator. Further, the strong sense of collaboration requires that the inputs that are preferred be *honored* so far as possible, limited only by competing inputs provided by other legitimate stakeholders (Torbert, 1981; Rowan, 1981). Again the political acumen of the evaluator is likely to be severely taxed. The evaluator will soon lose credibility if inputs, once sought, are apparently ignored; yet the inclusion of these divergent views into anything resembling a viable course of action requires extreme political dexterity, persuasiveness, compromise, and let it be noted, integrity.

The collaborative approach adds several more principles to the evaluator's repertoire of guidelines:

Principle 13: Stakeholders must be given an opportunity to react to findings for both validational and ethical reasons, to satisfy the weak sense of the collaboration requirement.

Principle 14: The evaluator must involve all stakeholders (or their representatives) at all points in the evaluation process, soliciting and honoring their inputs even on what might be called the more technical decisions that must be made.

Principle 15: Stakeholders (or their representatives) must be engaged in a negotiation process to determine what course of action should be taken in light of their findings. This stakeholder group, not the evaluator alone, should act as judges in making recommendations. The evaluator rather acts as mediator of the process.

Principle 16: The evaluator must allow for the possibility of continuing disagreements among the stakeholders. The goal of the negotiation process is not so much consensus as understanding.

Principle 17   The evaluator should act as mediator and change agent in these negotiations, encouraging follow through in relation to whatever may be decided by the parties and acting as monitor to assess the extent to which follow through occurs. The evaluator's role thus extends well beyond the point of reporting findings.

THE CHANGING MEANING OF EVALUATION

The evaluation guided by the concepts and principles outlined in the preceding section is clearly very different from more traditional forms. Indeed, we may point to eight distinctive features of this fourth-generation form, a version based not on measurement (first-generation), description (second-generation), or judgment (third-generation), but on negotiation.

(1) Evaluation is a social-political process. As Cronbach's (1980: 13) 11th thesis asserts, "A theory of evaluation must be as much a theory of political interaction as it is a theory of how to determine facts." Because of its intimate involvement with value issues, evaluation inevitably serves a political agenda and becomes a tool of political advocacy. Consequently any individual or group with a stake in the evaluand (i.e., put at risk by the evaluation) has a right to provide

input based on its own value position, to have that input honored, and to be consulted in any decision making that results. Evaluation acts to produce change,and any given change may be construed as relatively more or less desirable by different stakeholders. Value differences that result in different constructions cannot be resolved on rational bases alone, but only through political negotiation. Failure to provide the opportunity for such negotiation is tantamount to disenfranchisement.

(2) Evaluation is a learning/teaching process. No basis for negotiation can exist in the absence of information about the value positions held and judgments made by various stakeholding audiences. Evaluation must be conducted initially as a learning encounter, in which these different value positions and judgments are exposed. Later evaluation becomes a teaching encounter in which the positions of each of the audiences are clarified for and made more understandable to the others. Evaluation is not intended to capture an evaluand "as it really is" but rather to explore how it is constructed by many different groups. Evaluation not only teaches stakeholders about the positions of others but also how to ask better questions of one another.

(3) Evaluation is a continuous, recursive, and divergent process. Traditional evaluators have often treated evaluations as discrete, closed-ended, and convergent events. But the evolving conception of evaluation sees them as continuous, open-ended, and divergent. In this sense evaluations are never completed (although they may end for arbitrary reasons such as depletion of funds or time), but feed on themselves to yield ever-enlarging understandings. As the inputs from one audience are "taught" to another, questions emerge from the second audience that can profitably be put to the first. Thus the process is recursive as well. When the number of significant audiences numbers more than two or three (as is almost always the case), the number of recursions that can profitably be undertaken becomes quite large, usually greater than available time and resources will permit the evaluator to explore. The number of new questions enlarges in a virtually exponential ratio as compared to the number of old questions that have been answered.

(4) Evaluation is a process that creates "reality." According to the evolving conception, reality does not exist in objective form but is constructed by those persons who claim to "know" it. It is never the case that such constructions are either complete or immutable. The act of evaluation is an intervention that brings stakeholders face-to-face with their own constructions as well as those of others, and this intervention may lead to changes as stakeholders comprehend additional elements to consider, or as they revise their formulations in accordance with the apparently more sophisticated or informed constructions of others. Among the things that are constructed is the evaluand itself; the evaluand may *change* during the process of evaluation, as may the values brought to bear on it and the judgments made of it. Evaluation thus does not "discover" reality but fosters its creation.

(5) Evaluation is an emergent process. Traditional evaluation approaches require that a design for an evaluation be specified beforehand and then, once accepted, be followed in undeviating form except for circumstances that are beyond the evaluator's control, for example, history, maturation, or mortality effects. But the evolving concept of evaluation suggests that evaluation designs *cannot* be very completely specified a priori, but must evolve as the evaluation proceeds. Because neither the constructions of stakeholders nor the value positions on which they are based are likely to be known beforehand, the opening phases of an evaluation must be devoted to learning about them. Further, these constructions cannot be known for all time, for the very act of evaluation is apt to change them. Structure emerges only as the evaluation unfolds; the "design" can be completely described only retrospectively.

(6) Evaluation is a process with unpredictable outcomes. Traditional evaluation is predictable at least to the extent that one can say, depending on the model being followed, that the outcomes will be information about the extent of congruence of performance with objectives, information about decision alternatives, information about effects, and the like. But the new evaluation cannot project even possible outcomes until at least stakeholders' claims, concerns, and issues have been explored, and even these may change as the process unfolds. There is no "correct" or "objective" outcome. Even when ended, evaluations represent at best constructions, values and beliefs at some particular point in time and do not necessarily represent what the future state is likely to be or what the past state has been.

(7) Evaluation is a collaborative process. Judgments remain an essential part of fourth-generation evaluations, but those judgments must not be made solely by the evaluator or the client. If different value postures can lead to quite different judgments even on the basis of the *same* evidence, then negotiation among the holders of those different values cannot be avoided if the evaluation is to be fair and nonexploitative. Further, the stakeholders must not be confronted with a *fait accompli,* in which only those options delineated by the evaluator or client remain open to choice. Finally, different stakeholders must be afforded the opportunity to provide inputs to the evaluation process at its every stage—and not only substantive or informational inputs but *methodological* ones as well. The stakeholders and the evaluator must jointly—collaboratively—be in control of the *entire* procedure.[7] Negotiation based on options that emerge from activities controlled solely by the evaluator, or by the evaluator and the client, is patently unfair, as though the issues to be discussed by General Motors and the United Auto Workers were to be limited solely to those that General Motors elected to put on the table. The proper outcome of a collaborative evaluation is less a technical report than an *agenda for negotiation.*

(8) The agenda for negotiation is best displayed in a case study format, with items requiring negotiation being spelled out in relation to the particulars of the case. A case study can be explicit about contextual and value factors, and can

provide each audience the opportunity to experience the evaluand from a variety of constructed viewpoints. Further, the development of the case can be handled in such a way as to explicate and clarify the items about which further negotiation is needed, as well as to spell out those items about which there seems to be substantial agreement. The case provides a basis for a discussion that the several audiences will recognize as authentic, representing as it must the emic views of each of them; it provides a "slice of life" with its fullest ramifications. It tends to force display of all elements rather than only selected ones, reducing the likelihood that information can be withheld, and, concomitantly, the fear that it has been.

The eight characteristics of fourth-generation evaluation—its social-political nature; its learning/teaching posture; its continuous, recursive form; its reality-creating dynamic; its unfolding design; the relative unpredictability of its outcomes; its collaborative quality; its case study reporting format—describe a kind of evaluation dramatically different from earlier generation forms. And as a result, the role of the evaluator practicing this new form is also dramatically different.

THE CHANGING ROLE OF THE EVALUATOR

Traditional conceptions of evaluation gave rise, historically, to different definitions of the role of the evaluator, beginning with *technician* (first-generation measurement-oriented evaluation), moving through *describer* (second-generation objectives-oriented evaluation), and thence to *judge* (third-generation judgmentally oriented evaluation). Fourth-generation evaluation retains all of these roles, albeit in markedly different form, and adds several others: *collaborator, learner/teacher, reality shaper,* and *mediator and change agent.* Looking first at the retained but redefined role aspects:

(1) The evaluator retains certain technician functions but these are given a new form: the *human instrument and analyst.* The evaluator was traditionally seen as a person knowledgeable about the important variables that the profession was instrumentally capable of assessing, one who had a high level of familiarity with available standardized and normed instruments (paper-and-pencil and brass), one who knew the details of valid, reliable, and objective data collection and analysis (usually statistical), and one who was competent to write a technical report that would receive high marks from his or her professional peers. But in fourth-generation evaluation the focus of activity has shifted from objectives, decisions, effects, and other similar organizers to the claims, concerns, and issues raised by stakeholders, and these are often unpredictable a priori. Hence advance selection or development of instruments is largely impossible. Further, even when discovered, these claims, concerns, and issues may not be possible of assessment by existing instruments or by instruments that might be conventionally developed; they may, for example, be cultural or political in nature. While the fourth-generation evaluator should without doubt be well informed about

conventional instruments, he or she must perceive the *self* as the most immediately available and useful form of instrumentation. If claims, concerns, and issues must be assessed before an evaluation can begin (in the usual sense), the assessment instrument must be highly adaptable and reprogrammable, so that it can ferret out the most salient and relevant matters (that is, salient and relevant with respect to the evaluand) and progressively focus on them through *continuous* data processing. If many of the claims, concerns, and issues do not deal simply with technical questions (e.g., "Will turning over ownership of prisons to profit-making firms improve corrections in America?") but include social, political, religious, cultural, aesthetic, and other nontechnical matters (e.g., "Does workfare exploit the poor?"), then the evaluator may well find that the continued use of the self-as-instrument and the self-as-analyst is essential if these matters are to be usefully explored. Clearly "normal" designs, data collection devices, and data analytic techniques will not serve well.

(2) The evaluator retains certain describing functions but exercises them all in an *illuminative and historical mode* rather than in an objective scientific mode. The evaluator describes (reconstructs) constructions and the value positions on which those constructions are based, recognizing that these have no objective reality and are subject to change on a moment-to-moment basis. Often these descriptions (reconstructions) have more value as history than as science, as Cronbach (1975) has pointed out. The purpose of these descriptions (reconstructions) is not to *fix* an image but to *illuminate* a scene, in such a way that the evaluator himself or herself, the client, and all other stakeholding audiences can come to a greater appreciation and better understanding of the constructions that are being entertained.

(3) The evaluator understands the need for judgments in evaluation but eschews the role of judge; instead, the evaluator becomes the *mediator of the judgmental process.* This process is a *political* one. Value-pluralism leads inevitably to judgmental pluralism. Action cannot be taken unless and until some compromise is reached among these variable judgments, or unless one or a few actors are sufficently powerful that they can control the decision process—not an unusual but certainly an immoral state of affairs. The evaluator is in a position to serve as orchestrator because he or she has continuously interacted with the several stakeholder groups and, if the process has been carried out in terms of the earlier-described principles, has gained their trust. The fourth-generation evaluator is the agent most qualified and able to act as mediator.

Turning now to the emergent role aspects:

(4) The evaluator conducts the evaluation from a *collaborative* rather than a controlling posture. We have noted the fact that unless stakeholders have the ability to provide inputs into all aspects of an evaluation, they are in the end presented with nothing more than a *fait accompli*, a choice only among the options provided by those more privileged. Of course to act collaboratively, the evaluator must necessarily *give up some of the control* that has not only been vouchsafed in traditional approaches but that has been insisted upon in the name

of validity, reliability, and objectivity. Control is of the essence in standard designs; without it the inquirer cannot guarantee, it is said, the integrity of the findings. Giving up control thus has more far-reaching consequences than simply a reduction of personal autonomy and power; it seems to fly in the face of conventional principles for sound design. Yet without an extension of control to include stakeholders (or their representatives), the evaluation is an empty political vessel. Evaluations of the conventional sort are, not surprisingly, given short shrift in the political decision-making arena.

(5) The evaluator plays the roles of both *learner and teacher*. Initially the evaluator strikes a very open posture, soliciting information about constructions and values, as well as claims, concerns, and issues, which he or she does not yet comprehend, could not have predicted, or about which he or she cannot ask very penetrating questions. That the evaluator is a learner is apparent to all. But after a time, as the learning leads to insights and understandings (that is, when the evaluator finds it possible to make some initial constructions of his or her own), the evaluator can share those not only with the audience from which they were derived (for the purpose, among others, of verifying their credibility),but with other audiences, whom he or she can now presume to *teach*. In practice, the learner/teacher roles are intertwined; at no stage does the evaluator not continue to learn, and at no stage is he or she not in a position to do some teaching (as, for example, engaging in consciousness raising when dealing with an audience relatively unsophisticated about the evaluand).

(6) The evaluator is part and parcel a *reality shaper*. While the constructions that emerge from various stakeholding groups may initially reflect only *their* values, the evaluator, in teaching those constructions to others, inevitably infuses them with his or her own reconstructions. Further, as we have noted, initial constructions of stakeholders are themselves subject to change as that audience interacts with the evaluator, and through the evaluator, with other stakeholders. Thus evaluators and audiences literally produce the outcomes of the evaluation by their continuous interrelationship. Insofar as the responsibility of the evaluator extends to clarifying and refining the evaluand, such an outcome may be viewed as a major benefit of fourth-generation evaluation. More informed constructions that take the perspectives of other audiences into account are clearly preferable to partial, imperfectly informed constructions.

(7) The evaluator is inevitably a *mediator and change agent*. It is the bane— and shame—of traditional evaluations that they are little used. That should not surprise us, for in conventional evaluations, many stakeholders will *not* find information that they consider germane to their own interests, while the information that *is* provided may represent a single value position that is repugnant to those of other persuasions. But when the output of an evaluation is not a technical report with a series of conclusions and recommendations that (tend to) represent the evaluator's judgments, but a case study that includes an *agenda for negotiation* to be mediated by the evaluator, then the evaluator becomes a change agent and the evaluation "findings" (constructions, value

positions, and data relevant to stated claims, concerns, and issues) serve as a powerful means to agreeing on needed change.

We may end this section with a few observations about the characteristics that a fourth-generation evaluator must display to be effective. The new evaluator appreciates diversity, respects the rights of individuals to hold different values and to make different constructions, and welcomes the opportunity to air and to clarify these differences. The new evaluator must possess the personal qualities of honesty, respect, and courtesy, and like Caesar's wife, his or her integrity must be above suspicion. Without that the evaluator loses the ingredient without which no fourth-generation evaluation can be conducted successfully: trust. There can be no question of the new evaluator's professional competence either; training and experience that include not only technical skills but social, political, and interpersonal skills as well must be clearly demonstrable. The new evaluator must have a high tolerance for ambiguity and a high frustration threshhold. The new evaluation is a lonely activity, for one must remain sufficiently aloof to avoid charges of undue influence by one or another stakeholder group. The new evaluator must be aware of the possibility that he or she is being used by clients or other powerful groups, as well as of the fact that stakeholders may, individually or in groups, engage in lies, deceptions, fronts, and cover-ups. Finally, the new evaluator must be ready to be personally changed by the evaluative process, to revise his or her own constructions as understanding and sophistication increase. To be willing to change does not imply a loss of objectivity but a gain in fairness.

POSTSCRIPT

The major purpose of this chapter has been to suggest that a fourth-generation mode of evaluation is emerging whose hallmark is negotiation. We have identified certain concepts and principles that undergird this new mode, and have tried to show how the concept of evaluation, as well as the role of the evaluator, would change accordingly. Certain constraints that tend to inhibit the orderly development of these changes were identified. Finally, we have suggested a number of meta-criteria that might be appropriate to judging exemplars of this evolving style of evaluation.

This chapter is *not* a call for an either-or allegiance. We have been accused of divisiveness (we think incorrectly) in other matters, for example, in insisting on a clear choice between positivist and postpositivist paradigms to guide inquiry, while arguing that mix-and-match strategies or ecumenical embraces are not tenable (Guba & Lincoln, in preparation, *a*). But that is not the issue here. Fourth-generation evaluation is neither a competitor nor a replacement for earlier forms; instead, it subsumes them, while moving the evaluation process to higher levels of sophistication and utility.

But fourth-generation evaluation cannot become a fully functioning reality unless two conditions are met. It must, first, achieve acceptance and legitimation in the evaluation community. Clients cannot be expected to embrace it while it remains a dubious choice among evaluation "experts." Indeed, one can confidently assert that the lack of legitimation will be used by unscrupulous clients as a reason for rejecting it, and the power sharing that it implies. Second, it must be implemented by practitioners who are properly trained in its methods and socialized to its values. The evaluation training programs currently offered by the universities of this country are not adequate to this task. New programs must be developed and installed. That too requires a prior achievement of acceptance, for no university will offer a program that is treated derisively by the very faculty who must teach it. We beg the indulgence of our colleagues to examine this new evaluation, and if it is determined to have *both* merit and worth, to join us in working for its wide dissemination and implementation.

NOTES

1. *Pace,* Stake.

2. The authors are aware that this section is based almost exclusively on the evolution of evaluation in one arena: education. We are not in a position to judge whether or not similar developments took place in other arenas such as criminal justice, health, and the like. But regardless of what particular evolutionary patterns might have been, it does not seem to us open to dispute that technical, descriptive, and judgmental activities also have been typical in these other arenas and that all will seriously need consider the role of negotiation in evaluation over the next few years.

3. We are aware that what is taken to be factual depends in part on the values of the apprehender. Science is *not* value free, and hence facts are themselves value laden. For an extended treatment of this topic see Lincoln and Guba, 1985.

4. The more traditional position is now frequently discounted as "naive realism;" postpositivists who continue in this tradition are more likely to label themselves "critical realists" (see Hesse, 1980; Cook & Campbell, 1979).

5. The evaluator must also construct some view; that view may properly be termed "etic."

6. The process described here should not be confused with *transactional* evaluation (Rippey, 1973), which focuses upon changes in the organization in which evaluation is taking place rather than on the evaluand and the findings regarding it per se.

7. The kind of control that can be asserted over an inquiry is discussed in detail in Guba and Lincoln, in preparation, *b.* It is only the positivist paradigm that insists on complete inquirer control as a precondition for disciplined inquiry.

REFERENCES

Boruch, R. F. (1974). Bibliography: illustrated randomized field experiments for program planning and evaluation. *Evaluation, 2,* 83-87.

Campbell, D. T. (1969). Reforms as experiments. *American Psychologist, 24,* 409-429.

Cook, T. D. & Campbell, D. T. (1979). *Quasi-experimentation: Design and analysis issues for field settings.* Chicago, IL: Rand McNally.

Cronbach, L. J. (1975). Beyond the two disciplines of scientific psychology. *American Psychologist, 30,* 116-127.

Cronbach, L. J. (1980). Toward reform of program evaluation. San Francisco, CA: Jossey-Bass.

Eisner, E. W. (1960). Instructional and expressive objectives: their formulation and use in curriculum. *AERA Monograph Series in Curriculum Evaluation, No. 3.* Chicago, IL: Rand, McNally.

Eisner, E. W. (1979). *The educational imagination.* New York: Macmillan.

Gronlund, N. E. (1985). *Measurement and evaluation in teaching.* New York: Macmillan.

Guba, E. G. (1981). Criteria for assessing the trustworthiness of naturalistic inquiries. *Educational Communication and Technology Journal, 29,* 75-92.

Guba, E. G. & Lincoln, Y. S. (1981). *Effective evaluation.* San Francisco, CA: Jossey-Bass.

Guba, E. G. & Lincoln, Y. S. (1982a). The place of values in needs assessment. *Educational Evaluation and Policy Analysis, 4,* 311-320.

Guba, E. G. & Lincoln, Y. S. (1982b). Epistemological and methodological bases of naturalistic inquiry. *Educational Communication and Technology Journal, 30,* 233-252.

Guba, E. G. & Lincoln, Y. S. (In preparation, *a*). Do inquiry paradigms imply inquiry methodologies?

Guba, E. G. & Lincoln, Y. S. (In preparation, *b*). Types of inquiry defined by choice of an insider or outsider stance and inquirer or respondent control. (working title)

Hesse, M. (1980). *Revolutions and reconstructions in the philosophy of science.* Bloomington: Indiana University Press.

House, E. R. (1978). Assumptions underlying evaluation models. *Educational Researcher, 7,* 4-12.

Joint Committee (1981). *Standards for evaluations of educational programs, projects, and materials.* New York: McGraw-Hill.

Lincoln, Y. S. (1985). The ERS Standards for program evaluation: guidance for a fledgling profession. *Evaluation and Program Planning, 8,* 251-253.

Lincoln, Y. S. & Guba, E. G. (1985). *Naturalistic inquiry.* Beverly Hills, CA: Sage.

Morgan, G. (Ed.). (1983). *Beyond method: Strategies for social research.* Beverly Hills, CA: Sage.

Parlett, M. & Hamilton, D. (1972). *Evaluation as illumination: A new approach to the study of innovatory programs.* Edinburgh Scotland: Centre for Research in the Educational Sciences, University of Edinburgh, Occasional Paper no. 9.

Patton, M. Q. (1978). *Utilization-focused evaluation.* Beverly Hills, CA: Sage.

Pike, K. (1954). *Language in relation to a unified theory of the structure of human behavior, Vol. 1.* Glendale, CA: Institute of Linguistics.

Provus, M. (1971). *Discrepancy evaluation.* Berkeley, CA: McCutchan.

Rippey, R. M. (1973). *Studies in transactional evaluation.* Berkeley, CA: McCutchan.

Rivlin, A. M. & Timpane, P. M. (Eds.). (1975). *Planned variation in education.* Washington, DC: Brookings Institution.

Rossi, P. H. (Ed.). (1982). *Standards for evaluation practice. No. 15, New directions for program evaluation.* San Francisco, CA: Jossey-Bass.

Rossi, P. H. & Williams, W. (Eds.). (1972). *Evaluating social action programs: Theory, practice, and politics.* New York: Seminar.

Rowan, J. (1981). A dialectical paradigm for research. In Reason, P. & Rowan, J. (Eds.). *Human inquiry: A sourcebook of new paradigm research.* (Chap. 9) New York: John Wiley.

Scriven, M. (1967). The methodology of evaluation. *AERA Monograph Series in Curriculum Evaluation, No. 1.* Chicago, IL: Rand, McNally.

Scriven, M. (1973). Goal-free evaluation. In House, E. R. (Ed.). *School evaluation: The politics and process.* Berkeley, CA: McCutchan.

Sims, D. (1981). From ethogeny to endogeny: How participants in research projects can end up doing action research on their own awareness. In P. Reason & Rowan, J. (Eds.). *Human inquiry: A sourcebook of new paradigm research* (Chap. 32). New York: John Wiley.

Smith, E. R. & Tyler, R. W. (1942). *Appraising and recording student progress.* New York: Harper.

Stake, R. E. (1967). The countenance of educational evaluation. *Teachers College Record, 68,* 523-540.

Stake, R. E. (1973). *Program evaluation, particularly responsive evaluation.* Presented at the Conference on New Trends in Evaluation, Goteborg, Sweden.

Stake, R. E. (1975). *Evaluating the arts in education.* Columbus, OH: Merrill.

Stufflebeam, D. L. & Webster, W. J. (1980). An analysis of alternative approaches to evaluation. *Educational Evaluation and Policy Analysis, 2,* 5-19.

Stufflebeam, D. L., *et al.* (1971). *Educational evaluation and decision-making.* Itasca, IL: Peacock.

Torbert, W. R. (1981). Why educational research has been so uneducational: The case for a new model of social science based on collaborative inquiry. In Reason, P. & Rowan, J. (Eds.) *Human inquiry: A sourcebook of new paradigm research* (Chap. 11). New York: John Wiley.

Wolf, R. L. (1979). The use of judicial evaluation methods in the formulation of educational policy. *Educational Evaluation and Policy Analysis, 1,* 19-28.

Worthen, B. R. & Sanders, J. R. (1973). *Educational evaluation: Theory and practice.* Columbus, OH: Jones.

SECTION 3
Critical Perspectives

If the 1960s and early 1970s are characterized as the "golden era of experimentation and large scale evaluations," the past decade is probably best thought of as an era of reconceptualization—one that has spawned several alternatives to the classic social science paradigm. The chapters in the preceding section attest to the vigorousness of this period. As a by-product, efforts to operationalize or refine these models have resulted in an exponential growth in the amount of literature on methods, tactics, and evaluative tools. Indeed, rising to the challenges of conducting evaluation studies, theorists and practitioners have shown a remarkable ability to devise, adapt, and exploit a broad spectrum of methodological tools and tactics. Methodological inventiveness has been encouraged on all fronts.

Recent literature hints that an era of reassessment may be on the horizon. That is, given the conceptual and methodological diversity in the field and the stockpile of experience gained from trying new methods, it is time to take a critical look at how the field of evaluation studies is shaping up as a distinct field of inquiry and to ask whether or not the methods that appear relevant to the evaluative function perform as advertised. Of course, questions such as these leveled at the experimental paradigm are what initiated the era of reconceptualization. Considerably less independent appraisal has been directed at new conceptions of evaluation and the many nontraditional tools, techniques, and tactics they generated. The chapters in this section illustrate some of the recent critical commentary and assessments of evaluation and research practices.

Critical commentary comes in a variety of forms. It can range from appraisals of the field (e.g., Guba & Lincoln; Rossi & Wright, section 2, Part 1) to assessments of individual studies or methods, with various levels of effort in between (e.g., Carr-Hill, 1985). The first chapter in this section, by Michael Scriven, examines current evaluation theory and practice from a broad perspective, offering several dimensions from which to judge conceptions of evaluation. The next two chapters are appraisals of the methods embodied within two major conceptions of evaluation. Mark and Shotland systematically examine the processes underlying stakeholder-based evaluations. Lipsey, Crosse, Dunkle, Pollard, and Stobart review the conceptual and methodological underpinnings of prior evaluations that follow the experimental paradigm. The last chapter by Gilsinan and Volpe concerns the role of critical commentary within the field.

Scriven's essay is unique in the sense that he views current conceptualizations of evaluation from outside what we would conventionally view as its main purview (e.g., product, personnel, and curriculum evaluation). Although the chapter contains several important messages, of particular note is his analysis of how definitions of evaluation within several major conceptualizations place restrictions on the nature and scope of the field. These are often ignored, leaving the uninitiated reader with a partial view of evaluation. For example, restricting evaluation to descriptive (i.e., formative evaluation) statements strips evaluation of its distinctive function—deriving a summative judgment of merit. Further, the formative-only brand of evaluation is likely to inappropriately focus attention on ways of improving conditions when what that is needed is a summative statement of whether or not an intervention had any merit. After all, why would we want to improve the operation of a program that has no merit (by anyone's standards)? Similarly, defining evaluation as exclusively focused on assessing social programs removes from consideration a host of other tasks or areas that are legitimate evaluative domains, involving judgments of quality, merit, or worth (e.g., personnel or product evaluation). Within Scriven's logic of evaluation, its purpose is to establish the existence of merit. Under this notion, an evaluation perspective that *merely* describes a program, monitors its client flow, or checks to see if stated objectives were reached is not a complete definition of evaluation as a field. The critical feature is a summative judgment of merit.

Restrictions on the nature and scope of evaluation can be traced to an avoidance of topical areas and methods that naturally require value judgments. Although we make these judgments regularly, they are studiously avoided in many conceptualizations of evaluation. Scriven's position is that we should not narrow our conception of evaluation simply to avoid the discomfort associated with value judgments; rather, as a profession, our work should focus on limiting harmful effects and on establishing the validity of precedures used to derive evaluative claims. This brings us to the set of issues represented in the chapters by Mark and Shotland, and Lipsey et al.

These chapters have been singled out because they represent the critical appraisal we think is necessary in the field (Cook, 1984, makes a similar point). Several other appraisals also appeared in the last year that are worth mentioning. For example, Smith (1985) tackles many of the same issues as Mark and Shotland but focuses on the assumptions and evidence surrounding the viability of adversarial and committee-based models of evaluation. Champion (1984), speaking from a manager's perspective, encourages far greater attention to the guiding assumptions underlying how evaluation studies are conducted. He also echoes Scriven in calling for more "evaluation" in our evaluations.

A pivotal aspect of the program evaluation perspective advocated by Guba and Lincoln is the involvement of all relevant stakeholders in the evaluation process. Because the perspective and values of the researcher, evaluator, program manager, or the decision maker can claim no special standing in judging the worth or merit of a program, the only equitable solution is to assure that all positions are presented. The logic of this position is clear, especially for interventions that are controversial. Logic aside, at an operational level, the procedures ought to be routinely assessed to determine whether or not such schemes work as planned. Mark and Shotland's analysis of the influence of values in stakeholder-based evaluation reveals the potential for unintentional (and intentional) harmful consequences. They note that differential power, legitimacy, knowledge, and leverage can undermine the principal rationale for the stakeholder perspective.

The chapter by Lipsey et al. represents a critical appraisal of key conceptual and methodological underpinnings of recently published evaluations. First, their analysis reaffirms the general impression of the experimental paradigm as the dominant perspective within evaluation (at least among those that are published). It also reveals several conceptual and methodological shortcomings, reaffirming Rossi and Wright's call for further refinements.

Consistent with the views of other commentators for practical, technical, temporal, and logistical reasons, Lipsey et al. conclude that the experimental paradigm is not an all purpose evaluation design. That does not mean it should be discarded. Rather, it is particularly useful for exploring casual linkages and theoretical propositions embodied within interventions. On the other hand, the machinery needed for high-quality experimentation is not likely to fit within the temporal and practical constraints of normal program evaluation. This leaves several critical questions unanswered. When are conditions "right" for this brand of assessment? How should they be financed? How are the results of carefully executed experimental assessments linked to judgments of merit described by Scriven? We leave the answers to these questions to subsequent sections of this volume.

For completeness, the final chapter in this section addresses the role of critical commentary within evaluation studies. Gilsinan and Volpe argue that, to some extent, presentational style and the use of faulty benchmarks in criticizing the practices of others may lead to a belief that there is a crisis in evaluation studies when, in fact, there is not. To the extent that perpetuating the myth of a crisis leads policymakers to become suspicious of evaluations, of the profession expansion may become more difficult. They recommend that evaluation specialists adopt a more positive stance in communicating and critiquing the fruits of our labors.

The chapters in this section attempt to be balanced in their presentations; nevertheless they are appropriately critical. As a profession we have an obligation to assure that the knowledge steming from evaluations is not biased due to methodological failings and conceptual incompleteness. Excessive criticism should be avoided, along with uncritical application of methods and perspectives. This is a fine line to traverse.

REFERENCES

Carr-Hill, R. A. (1985). The evaluation of health care. *Social Science and Medicine, 21*(4), 367-375.

Champion, H. (1984). Physician heal thyself: One public manager's view of program evaluation. *Evaluation News, (4),* 29-40.

Cook, T. D. (1984). Opportunities for evaluation in the next few years. In R. F. Conner, D. G. Altman, & C. Jackson (Eds.). *Evaluation studies review annual, Volume 9* (pp. 726-752). Beverly Hills, CA: Sage.

Lipton, J. P., & Hershaft, A. H. (1985). *On the widespread acceptance of dubious medical findings.* Unpublished manuscript, University of Arizona.

Smith, N. (1985). Aversary and committee hearings as evaluation methods. *Evaluation Review, 9*(6), 735-750.

4

New Frontiers of Evaluation
Michael Scriven

PREFACE

I should really begin by saying that the new frontiers of evaluation are of course all to be found in Western Australia, which the local license plates somewhat pejoratively and optimistically describe as "Home of the America's Cup." At the very least, I do bring you greetings from The Evaluation Association. Please note that I am not bringing you greetings from the Evaluation Association of Western Australia or even the Evaluation Association of Australia; as far as I know, there are no such bodies. I am bringing greetings from The Evaluation Association. Out there, we don't fool around. There was, for example, some suggestion in Parliament that we should rechristen the America's Cup, "the Australia's Cup," regardless of the fact that it happens to be named after a historic racing yacht, and when it comes to an evaluation association, why we just called it *The* Evaluation Association. You might think that was a little pretentious for a group that musters about 20 on a good Friday afternoon, which is when we meet— itself a statistically rare event (though of course a historic one). But it was just that irregularity that meant we couldn't resist the acronym of something called The Evaluation Association; and so, on certain Friday

AUTHOR'S NOTE: This paper was the invited keynote speech at the joint meeting of the Evaluation Network, Evaluation Research Society, and the Canadian Evaluation Association, Toronto, October 1985.

afternoons, the answering machines all over Perth say, "Sorry, gone to TEA." In any case, if you rather fancy the name, on the trivial grounds of size and international membership, we are prepared to negotiate about a merger—on our terms, of course, as the New York Yacht Club used to say.

In any case, I *do* bring you greetings from TEA, especially from its founder and chairman, Ralph Straton, director of the Center for Program Evaluation at Murdoch University; and from its godfather, whose only contribution was to its christening—an event occurring well after its birth—and who stands before you now, about to begin the serious part of this article.

INTRODUCTION

It is a topological necessity that any area expanding as fast as evaluation must be creating new frontiers at a great rate. Of course, the expansion might just be in one part of the host territory of potential applications, say in the area of routine program evaluation. That would be what we might call quantitative expansion, a mere increase in the number but not the types of evaluation that are being done. It seems clear that something more than that is happening—there is expansion into new areas, areas that present qualitatively different problems. The examples I have chosen to illustrate this kind of expansion are of course a rather personal selection, but perhaps they will be enough to demonstrate the range of applications that are sitting there waiting to be developed more seriously and systematically. At least my list involves a variety of topics, so that if you find one or two to be uninteresting, others may intrigue you. On the last page or two you will find some discussion of topics I wanted to cover but could only define here. They may be more interesting than any I do cover.

I have tried to show that they are relevant to the present state of the art by using some references to the latest anthology of recent evaluation studies and some recent and well-known books. But I should warn you in advance that I devote much of the space to the first topic, which is work on the "foundations frontier" where the concern is with clarifying the nature of evaluation itself. This is partly, no doubt, because of my own strong interest in it, but I think also because of its continued importance in developing a sense of identity for the field. Certainly it haunts me perpetually, and I think I have one or two new ways to approach parts of it. Reactions to them (or to any other part of the paper)—formal or informal, favorable or critical—would be most welcome.

LOGICAL FRONTIERS: THE NATURE
AND HISTORY OF EVALUATION

Evaluation, like technology or psychology or philosophy, is a subject with a very long history and a much shorter consciousness. People have *engaged in* technology and psychology and philosophy for much longer than they have had the *concepts* of technology or psychology or philosophy.

Saying that philosophy—to use that example—began long before it was conscious of itself means that humans have speculated in more or less explicit ways about the nature of the world or of their species or about their own limitations and differences from other animals much longer than they have speculated about the nature of that kind of speculation. Doing something is less of a strain on our conceptual resources than discussing in an explicit and critical way what it is one is doing. The latter activity requires a whole new set of metaconcepts to describe the concepts used at the first level. And, of course, it isn't necessary to get to the metalevel in order to make some important progress. Moreover, metadiscussions often lead to fruitless "speculation for its own sake," and come to be regarded with disdain by practitioners of the subject itself. In evaluation—which is still finding its feet, conceptually speaking—there must, for a while, continue to be a good deal of dependence on methodological sophistication; but that is not to say that practitioners will acknowledge this. Sometimes they do, sometimes not; and when they do, they may mean something quite limited by the term "methodology."

The latest volume of the *Evaluation Studies Review Annual* (volume 10), for example, contains 728 pages devoted to the theme of large-scale multisite evaluations of big social programs, and is edited by people from the field studies end of the spectrum from methodologists to practitioners. Nevertheless, it has a substantial section on methodology, something you will not find in recent volumes of annual reviews of sociology and of psychology, significantly to the detriment of the latter subjects. But then, it must be said in their defense, they have paid their methodological dues over the years.

For the most part, the methodological issues that relate to the theme of this volume are, as you might expect, mainly matters of what one might call specific or technical methodology in contrast to general or logical methodology. All the same, there are discussions of some key foundational issues like the difference—and needed interface between—qualitative and quantitative studies, the presuppositions of meta-analysis, the crucial generalizability problem in looking at demonstrations or experimental runs of big programs, and the problem of designing studies that will have useful validity, while still being "timely" in the fast-moving political context; and—an example to which we'll return—the evaluative burden of the significance test.

Careful study of the volume reveals the dependence of a number of the contributions on other crucial methodological issues that are not addressed in the methodology section, partly—one might surmise—because they don't look much like the *traditional social science* kind of methodology, given that the editors view evaluation research as a fairly modest extension of traditional social science. Problems of this kind would include: the measurement of quality of life in evaluating hospice and other medical programs, a topic that cannot be handled without getting into some serious philosophical issues for which no social science training is going to provide answers; the demonstration of causation in isolated case studies, where the methodology of history is the only current source of the solutions; the problem of identifying opportunity costs in a *systematic* way, something that economists have yet to address; how to identify and report on unethical program practices when doing evaluation of a program; how to incorporate or how to exclude personnel evaluation and practices from the evaluation of programs; and so on.

The most serious omission of all, to my mind, is the failure to address the absolutely central weakness in current evaluation methodology—the fact that evaluation, as currently conceived by most of its practitioners, can only lead to descriptive conclusions, not to evaluative ones. To call that a weakness is somewhat euphemistic—it is more like a terminal disease. We'll come back to it later. But first, a moment's further thought about the need, if any, to get into the logical methodology of evaluation.

In the case of technology, physics, and psychology, very considerable achievements were notched up before the subjects became self-conscious, autonomous entities, talking about their own nature and methods. It's worth remembering that full autonomy came remarkably late; even in the period after World War II, physics was still referred to in many British Commonwealth universities as "natural philosophy" and psychology was not only officially called "mental philosophy" but was administratively and intellectually simply part of many philosophy departments. The emancipation of technology from many science faculties, interestingly enough, is still in that same embryonic and simple-minded state where its independence is denied, and its role minimized. This is one reason for the foundation of institutes of technology where the necessary autonomy is possible, even with some—albeit diminishing—cost in status. I suggest the same underestimation of status and rights applies with respect to the dependence of evaluation on social science.

Although great progress was possible in all these subjects without emancipation and self-consciousness, some major steps forward in these subjects were made, and indeed could *only* be made, when they became independent and began to look at their own nature in a comprehensive and critical way. Einstein only came to look at the foundations of physics, as he said, because the fundamental philosophical questions raised by Ernst Mach suggested that the traditional foundations were logically unsound. His reformulation of the foundations led, as we all know, to major practical as well as conceptual results. Psychology, to take a second example, had to work out its own special combination of empirical and conceptual methods before it could see that the Wundtian or Freudian or Jamesian or Pavlovian approaches were seriously limited; great developments—admittedly along with some further idiosyncrasies—emerged in the ensuing decades. The emancipation of evaluation, both from philosophy and from the social sciences, is probably even more essential to its own future development. In what does this kind of emancipation consist?

In these days of specialization, we sometimes talk as if the description "doing philosophy" (or psychology, etc.) actually *means* talking in a self-conscious way about philosophical issues *as* philosophical issues, that is, as views associated with one or another school of philosophy or distinguished philosopher of the past. But it is mere academic snobbery to refuse to classify as philosophy those discussions by serious people, who happen not to have had academic training, of the origins of the universe or the authority deserved by ethical principles. They are doing philosophy, and doing it in the way that provides the primary justification for the entire subject, which only sprang up in order to assist in the quests embodied in such pre-academic discussions.

It is particularly impertinent to dismiss the pre-academic activity—or some large slice of it—as "not part of the area." If the academic subject has any merit other than contemplating its own navel, it will lie in the ability to *improve* not exclude, the deliberations of any nonacademic who is concerned with the same issues, not define it out of existence. And that should be our touchstone for work on the "logic of evaluation." What is to count as "the same issue" begins with the use of the same term—"evaluation." Although it is perfectly possible that program evaluation is special in several ways, that is obviously something that should lead one *not* to use the general term "evaluation" for the subfield. Moreover, if one's alleged reason for only discussing program evaluation is that one feels modest about one's competence in other areas, then one cannot argue that program evaluation is either typical of all evaluation *or* distinctive, as that has to be shown, not assumed, and you have just disqualified yourself from being able to show it.

This advice has more teeth than might appear at first sight because the territorial imperative has very strong attractions to the academic. Under the guise of modesty about our competence, we move rapidly toward excluding some vast section of the subject from consideration and hence from legitimacy. As part of this (largely unconscious) campaign, we introduce jargon and generalizations that only make sense in our little slice of the territory, which of course strengthens our hold on it by providing informal tribal membership markers to generate a peer-group with mutual recognition and support, and by making the "outsider"—who in fact came first—feel lost and incompetent. Evaluators are a little more subtle about this than sociologists and psychologists, because they have had to adapt to dealing with nontechnical clients and audiences who are not much impressed by technical jargon. But we still do it, and we do it in a very gross way when we define or act as if evaluation is the study and practice of program evaluation. It's one thing to restrict a discussion or a book to that part of evaluation—in fact, it's perfectly sensible to do that—but it's something entirely different to assert that that is all there is to evaluation. The practitioners have long been doing evaluation on the personnel scene, in the product area and in assessing proposals, to mention just three of a dozen well-established practices. Not only is the exclusion of these areas intellectually objectionable in terms of any defensible epistemological taxonomy, it is extremely serious in terms of weakening the competence of the program evaluator, because it turns out that a number of techniques from the other fields are extremely important to program evaluation, and even worse, it turns out that study of those techniques reveals serious errors in the way in which program evaluation is usually done.

So it seems clear that we should not accept the view that evaluation, or evaluation research, is restricted in the way that Rossi and Freeman, speaking for many social scientists, would restrict it. They *define* it as concerned only with the study of "social intervention programs" using "social research methodologies" (1982). This is rather like defining statistics as a subject that studies the effects of crop treatments using Fisherian designs. In both cases, it can be argued that the subject first reared its academic head in the context mentioned, but the idea that it should be restricted to that area in the future is not only narrow-minded and socially costly, but totally disdainful of most previous practice as opposed to academic sanctification. If social scientists had spent more time thinking about the kind of product evaluation on which they based many of their own most important consumer purchases, we might have been spared the long period in which it was, and still is, supposed that checking programs to see if they met their goals was the main aim and only proper concern of evaluation. "Discrepancy evaluation" became not just one school/model of evaluation but a *Zeitgeist,* a paradigm, a dominant conception. It was, in fact, a perfectly good model of *something*— namely *monitoring*—that is, checking on compliance with contractual commitments. That's a long way short of program evaluation, however, and it's a measure of the narrow vision of the times that the discrepancy model was so well received.

Had anyone suggested that this is the proper way to do product evaluation we would have detected immediately the anti-consumer and indeed anti-scientific bias in the approach. You don't evaluate cars by seeing if they turned out the way the design team or the board of directors intended, but in terms of whether they meet the needs of consumers.

But because we had broken the ties to the areas of evaluation other than program evaluation, it did not occur to most program evaluators to look for, or worry about, differences in the way in which program evaluation and product evaluation were done. They had defined such differences into irrelevancies. This is a familiar event in the history of science, of course, but it's always hard to see oneself in a historical perspective. Yet it is important to try, because it helps us avoid some of the worst blunders. The justification for calling this topic one of the "new frontiers in evaluation" is that we still have a good deal to learn about the nature of what we are doing as we develop evaluation.

Similar lessons to those that product evaluation can teach are easily learned from looking at what goes on in personnel evaluation and half a dozen other areas. It is probably true that these areas are more alien to someone with the evaluator's usual social science background than to program evaluators. But sticking one's head in the sands of social science is no way to expand one's horizons. It's much better to take a wide-ranging look at long-established careful practice before one starts legislating about the limits of a subject, especially if you finish up staking out the entire turf, defining it narrowly, and claiming it as your own. Besides, there is the inescapable truth that evaluating programs, particularly if one is interested in improving them, sometimes involves personnel evaluation. For one of the improvements that one must sometimes recommend is a change in the personnel. The same essential involvement sometimes occurs with product evaluation, as drug programs, for example, require one to look at the materials used; and so on.

A case can be made that the emergence of evaluation as an autonomous discipline actually occurred in the context of curriculum evaluation, not social program evaluation. In fact, we will be arguing that many practitioners and most of the leaders in the latter area are still not practicing an autonomous discipline at all; whereas evaluators in the educational area are, in general, very conscious of the autonomy. I believe that one reason for this is that educational practitioners were less tied to the so-called empiricist, or value-free, tradition in the social sciences, having for long cohabited schools of education with philosophers and historians of education, to whom values held less or no threat. In any case, it is clear that one can hardly evaluate curricula without sometimes having to make two kinds of value judgments—one about the validity (merit) of the content and one about its moral legitimacy. With the latter we find the sticking point for many of the relatively liberated educational evaluators. The ethical domain is often avoided by professional curriculum evaluators, instead of being done professionally. Getting into value judgments is one thing, they seem to feel, but getting into moral value judgments is going a bit too far. Here again we find ourselves looking at a short-term, ill-thought-out policy based on an incomplete perspective of evaluation. For, how could one claim to do curriculum evaluation that was acceptable to any framework of professional ethics if one accepted all moral teaching as equally legitimate? Similarly, one could hardly do program evaluation without looking at personnel policies within the program; would not unjust policies—perhaps extremes of gender discrimination—constitute grounds for downgrading or even condemning a program? Once the nose of the values camel gets into the tent, you can't keep the ethical hump out. Practice makes that obvious, and the attempt to build a wall around program evaluation can't keep the camel out, because there are already tunnels between program evaluation and the camel compound—the tunnels of personnel and content connections.

The historical span of evaluation practice is impressive. For as long as humans have done philosophy (and perhaps longer), they have done evaluation; that is, they have evaluated things and people and places.

A great deal of critical evaluation was involved in the transition from the tools and production techniques of the Old Stone Age to the Neolithic ones. The completely counterintuitive conclusion had to be established that the best way to achieve the best results in chipping flint was to use tools that were *softer* than flint, tools of bone and wood. It took good strong credible evaluation to demonstrate that, and it's not surprising that it took a long time to sink in. In the same way, evaluation, in the twenty-odd years of its semiautonomous existence, has had to establish several difficult and, to many people, counterintuitive conclusions, such as the very possibility of objectifying evaluative conclusions, the crucial difference between formative and summative evaluation (and their independent legitimacy), and the need to go beyond goal achievement in designing evaluations.

More recently, and going beyond the area of program evaluation, we are running into difficulty with native intuitions when some of us, speaking—we think—as professional evaluators, deny that the best way to evaluate teaching is to look at it. In fact, we argue, it is invalid and unethical to base summative teacher evaluation on classroom visits. To make such counterintuitive claims at all, and to make them plausible to others, absolutely requires one to invest time on the methodological side. For evaluation, as for psychology and technology, the metastudy is thus essential to making many of the major steps in its progress. More remains to be done on this frontier, and indeed a good deal needs to be done in consolidating even such points as those just mentioned (which need to be incorporated into law as quickly as possible).

It must be said that the general understanding of the kind of methodological point of which we have just given an example is still very shallow. At least Rossi et al., for all their limitation of evaluation to social reform programs, think that it is sometimes appropriate to draw evaluative conclusions about a program. It is surprising how many people fail to realize that the Cronbach et al. book (*Towards Reform of Program Evaluation*) is built on the rejection of this possibility. They criticize Rossi for allowing it, and set up a definition of evaluation that excludes *by definition* any kind of summative evaluation. That is an extraordinary blunder to have made, given the amount of discussion that has gone on in the field; that it could be made by a group of workers with some acquaintance with the area indicates how poorly the foundations are being grasped and perhaps presented. For Cronbach, that tough-minded master of conceptual distinctions, to have made such a mistake (and indeed to have made a virtue of it), is precisely as if he had said there can be no such thing as legitimate inferential statistics, and as if he had written a text in which statistics is defined as consisting only of descriptive statistics.

Notice that what was happening was not that the authors defined the subtopic in which they were interested and on which they proposed to focus, as formative evaluation. That would be legitimate enough. What they did, by contrast, was to argue repeatedly that "the other side of evaluation"—the summative side—was improper, misconceived, and to be excluded from the proper purview of the subject. In fact, their definition excludes evaluative consideration of any completed program, as perhaps it must as that is the most obvious context of legitimate summative program evaluation. Summative evaluation is, after all, simply the kind of conclusion that audit agencies or congressional committees or political scientists will express after examining an unsuccessful program effort in a certain area. (And, of course, it is the kind of conclusion that fills every issue of *Consumer Reports.*)

We have seen a good deal of discussion of summative program evaluation lately, in the two books by Murray and Schwarz, which present alternative and conflicting evaluations of the massive social interventions of recent decades. These books are referred to by Aiken and Kehrer in their introduction to the current volume of *Evaluation Studies* as examples that illustrate the importance of the evaluation of large-scale programs. I heartily agree, and indeed I think one could argue that this kind of effort at summative evaluation is *more* important than any formative evaluation of current programs; it has a huge influence on future policy and hence on the welfare of millions of people. In the same way, reflective analysis on the war in Vietnam is probably more important to the future of this and other countries than formative evaluation of the campaigns as they occurred.

You might suppose that this shows it was really formative evaluation. But this kind of reflective evaluation is not aimed at *improving* future efforts of the same kind. In fact, it is often aimed at *avoiding* any such efforts; alternatively, at repeating them. This is what summative product evaluation is all about—assisting the decision of what to buy or not buy—and summative program evaluation is no different. The primary point of these efforts, as of much of the historian's work, is to draw conclusions about the worth or merit of the war and of the way it was conducted. It is a contortion to suppose that this means an effort is being made to improve the conduct of future wars. The Cronbach definition, however, excludes this kind of effort from evaluation: "By the term *evaluation* we mean systematic examination of events occurring in and consequent on a contemporary program—an examination conducted to assist in improving this program and other programs having the same general purpose'' (p. 14).

The question naturally arises why those authors should reject summative evaluation. One view would be that a crucial failure of nerve is involved, because to do summative evaluation confronts one somewhat more directly with the necessity to come to evaluative conclusions; and, if one's heritage is the value-free doctrine about the nature of the social sciences, this will be an unwelcome posture. Of course, it's the posture that defines evaluation, but ingenious rationalizations can lead one to think one is beyond the reach of the dictionary's power. Apart from sacrilege, or perhaps underlying it, there is the simple distaste for judging others—we make exceptions for politicians and students—that has certainly produced an early retirement in the case of one distinguished erstwhile program evaluator. Perhaps the root cause of that diffidence is self-protective (as in "judge not that ye be not judged," the biblical advice most frequently ignored by the Bible), perhaps other-protective, perhaps just a distaste for bitter disputes; failure of evaluative nerve is easy to understand.

One can think of the suggestions so far considered as representing successive restrictions of evaluation's territory in order to strengthen the hold over it, a picture consistent with the Failure-of-Nerve view. If we represent the whole range of evaluation as practiced for centuries by a line the width of the page, then the restriction to social program evaluation cuts out more than half of it. What's left includes both formative and summative evaluation, and Cronbach is now proposing that we drop half of that. The part that is being thrown out at each stage is in square brackets.

The Subject Matter Restriction

| Social programs (Rossi & Freeman) | [Personnel, producers, proposals, plans, etc.] |

The Function Restriction

| Formative (Chronbach et al.) | [Summative] |

In contrast with the Failure-of-Nerve view would be the Lust for Power theory, according to which the attraction of the formative-only approach is that it puts the evaluator into a kind of program co-authoring/codirecting role, much more attractive to today's academic than the ivory tower or "detached observer" role. It should be noted, however, that there is some risk of cooption and a guarantee of lost externality if one goes this way, which is inconsistent with what I take to be the primary responsibility of evaluation.

But I think a more charitable view is appropriate, here as in consideration of Cronbach's earlier and equally bizarre view that evaluation should not be comparative. I am sure that he was then looking for a way to avoid *inappropriate* or *excessive* interstudent comparisons, which he rightly saw as detrimental to the welfare of students.

In this view, the territory of evaluation would be further restricted. As we're running out of room to give a description of what remains in the promised land, I'll use a symbol to indicate the continued flight:

The Modality Restriction

    [comparative]

But it isn't useful to redefine concepts in order to avoid inappropriate uses of them, and the fact is that comparative evaluation of students is the only sensible way to select for admissions, or most jobs and scholarships, so one can hardly toss it out entirely. One must instead work on validating it and limiting its harmful effects. And so it is here. Evaluation must be summative as well as formative, because in this world we have to make decisions about whether to get or forgo, admire or condemn, whole packages of attributes, in situations where we have no power to improve them, and indeed in situations where no one any longer has that power. It makes no difference whether the packages are programs or products or people; there is no escaping the logic of this argument.

I am sure that the restrictive definition just quoted was put forward in the worthy cause of encouraging constructive rather than merely negative criticism. That puts a better face on it than the much earlier assertion of a more extreme version of the point by the research officer of the AFT, when he said that only formative evaluation was legitimate. He could be accused of having some bias in this matter of attacking summative evaluation as summative evaluation is what leads to dismissal and disciplinary action.

It appeals to the pious in all of us to say that one should not produce criticism if one is not willing to offer suggestions for improvement. Nevertheless, it qualifies as a blunder among professionals to make this recommendation, let alone make it into a definition of evaluation; and it is a particularly unfortunate kind of blunder because it is completely inconsistent with many of the best practices in practical evaluation, the field that we are supposed to be analyzing, or at least the one from which one would suppose one might learn something inasmuch as it has been around a couple of millenia longer than program evaluation. We next take up a contemporary example in more detail, as it is absolutely crucial to understand the independence and the importance of summative evaluation, and because it leads on to another point that has been discussed even less.

It is obvious that much of the product evaluation done by *Consumer Reports* is enormously useful, scientifically sound, and purely summative. If they report that a particular detergent does a less good job at cleaning soiled dishes or clothes than another, they do not offer suggestions to the industrial chemists as to how to improve the formulation, because they lack the expertise to do so. Indeed, no one may have that expertise, it may require further research to establish it. And that research is research into causal questions, not evaluative ones. The evaluation *established the existence* of superior merit, it has nothing to do with *establishing the causation* of the superiority. Track and field events establish the relative merit, on the day, of the competitors; no one protests the results on the grounds that the judges made no suggestions as to how the losers could improve, or as to the balance of genetic versus environmental factors that accounted for the winner's achievement. People are frequently and correctly evaluated as seriously ill by doctors who cannot explain the origin or mechanism of the causative disease, let alone cure it. Teachers can, in many circumstances, be correctly evaluated as incompetent by students who have not only no idea as to how to fix the problem but sometimes and equally correctly believe that it cannot be fixed. Similarly, students give wrong answers on multiple-choice questions and managers run social programs badly and people design reading programs that don't work, and it's really rather important to say so if you can prove so, even if you come to no conclusions as to the reasons for the failure. Bad is bad and good is good and it is the job of evaluators to decide which is which. And there are many occasions when they should say which is which, whether or not they have explanations and remediations.

Unfortunately, it panders to our sense of omniscience to be encouraged in the belief that we know how to fix what we find to be bad, and/or know what made it bad. But it is a simple methodological point that the resources for explanation and remediation are dependent on subject-matter expertise, whereas the resources for evaluation of relative merit only require competence in studying the effects on consumers, doing cost-analysis, and so on. Or perhaps we are too easily seduced because many of us are teachers, or parents, and teachers, like parents, are commonly required to be both evaluators and remediators. But the roles are logically separate and often best segregated in practice, even for teachers; in many other situations, they are necessarily separated—examiners are not remediators, pharmacists are not evaluators.

There are many circumstances—not all—in which we can determine the merit or lack of merit of a teacher by inspecting the learning gains achieved by his or her students compared to those of comparable students in the classes of other teachers in the same or very similar schools. This is likely to give us no basis at all for suggestions as to how the teacher might improve, but will give us grounds that the Ninth Circuit Court of Appeals (if I remember the title correctly) has ruled are adequate for dismissal from the public schools. Although common sense and ethics jointly endorse the view that one should try to find ways to improve a teacher before dismissing him, the bottom line is that he should be dismissed whether or not he can be remediated, because the schools are there for the benefit of students and society, not of teachers.

Thus the view expressed by the AFT director of research—that summative evaluation of teaching is never valid though formative sometimes is—would render all teachers immune to negative personnel action. But the view is self-contradictory because if one can ever evaluate teaching validly, for whatever purposes, one can evaluate it validly for summative purposes. The harder part of evaluation is to do useful formative evaluation, because it involves no less and sometimes more than summative evaluation. The letter grade on the Registrar's records is often exactly what is needed for summative evaluation, but it won't do much of a job for helping the student improve.

However, this is not true for the reason suggested by Cronbach's objections to summative evaluation, namely that one has to produce remediation recommendations in order to do useful formative evaluation. Here, in fact, we find that the Cronbach school, while restricting the traditional territory of evaluation, is also recommending an extension beyond it in another dimension. To understand the nature of the point that really is involved, one has to look more closely at a distinction that has not received much attention, the distinction between remediation and explanation, or causation.

Even if you can correctly identify the factors in a product, person, or program that have caused a poor overall performance, it is completely wrong to suppose either that this leads easily or always or nearly always to recommendations for remedy, or even that it will point us in the right direction. Discovering the cause of AIDS, as several researchers have recently been at pains to stress, may do absolutely nothing for the sufferer—or the physician or the researcher looking for a cure. Because it sometimes does something, we don't mind someone spending some time in that line of research. But it is always expensive to search for causes, and in a time of limited resources it is often much better strategy to search for cures, even if one does not understand the mechanism of the cure or of the disease itself. And, contrary to much popular and even scientific opinion, there are a number of systematic ways to make that kind of search, as cancer researchers often testify. Many of medicine's most useful contributions to human welfare involve treatments for which we have nothing that qualifies as an explanation rather than a mere description of process—obvious examples include aspirin and lithium. The academic kudos and the Nobel prizes tend to go with the discovery of causes, following the high-status patterns of the pure sciences; but the benefits to humanity go with the discovery of cures. Evaluation, one might say, should be benefit-oriented, not explanation-oriented.

It would be helpful to have more studies of the way in which evaluation reports segue from their evaluative conclusions to their recommendations with or without hypotheses about causation. Because we are all rather unclear about the difference, we tend to slide onto this client-demanded kind of conclusion by using some assumptions that have not been made explicit and are often hard to justify when they are made explicit. In the clinical context, practitioners are generally more careful; when a clinical psychologist does an evaluation of a patient or case, this by no means guarantees an explanation or a prescription (remediation recommendation).

So far, then, we have argued against three proposed restrictions and one proposed expansion of the domain of evaluation. We now come to the most extraordinary suggestion of all.

The fundamental methodological weakness of current program evaluation, as well exemplified in *Evaluation Studies,* can be summed up in the words of one of the contributors: "Evaluators generally contend that it is their task to measure the impact of a policy on society ... and that it is the role of others to make appropriate normative, political and philosophical judgments" (Schneider & Darcy, p. 599; this view is not being ascribed to them). On this view, the conclusions of evaluative research should not be evaluative conclusions, and in fact evaluation research is not evaluative!

The Ultimate Restriction

 [Evaluative evaluations]

I think it is fair to say that this is still the modal view among people working on evaluation studies, not only in social program evaluation. It is, however, not only paradoxical but socially disastrous; it is the continuation of the logically absurd and socially irresponsible doctrine of value-free social science, and the worst symptom of our field's continued ignorance of the ABCs of evaluation methodology. In our diagram, we can think of it as the situation in which the remaining territory simply consists of the helicopter itself, representing the artefactual version of evaluation that we have introduced. There is virtually nothing left in the way of actual evaluative territory to which it is taking us.

I say "virtually" because there are one or two cases where the description implies an evaluation without anyone having to spell it out. Sometimes I think that Bob Stake's current view is that this is the only proper role for evaluation. In my view, as many mistakes are made in the step from a full description of a program and its effects to the proper evaluative conclusion as in all the rest of evaluation put together. It is here that the evaluator has one of the profession's most important roles to play—and it is arguable that it is the only one that is distinctive of the profession.

I hasten to add that the reason science is not value free has nothing at all to do with the reason usually given, originally by supporters of the radical left, namely that scientists have personal or political values and these enter into their selection of problems to study and into the way they interpret and use the results. So they do; but the first and third of these ways in which values operate are licit but irrelevant to the claim that values have no place *within* science because they refer to the pre-scientific process of career selection and the post-scientific business of applications. The second is simply one form of bias and should be excluded. So, neither example counts against the legitimacy of the value-free doctrine, which was only about sound, internal, scientific practice. To refute this view, one must show that sound scientific practice must, or often can, support evaluative conclusions that are also part of science. It's pretty easy to show this, by looking at the way that scientists evaluate experimental designs, theories, data sources, contributions to the literature, instruments, and arguments. This shows that there is no essential logical gap between the subject matter of science and evaluations; it doesn't show that the particular subspecies of ethical value judgments can legitimately be supported by scientific arguments, but they make up a very small part of the evaluations that are undertaken or should be undertaken by evaluators. We'll skip the further argument required to establish that point.

The correct formulation of the role of values in evaluation research is to say that the evaluator *must* draw evaluative conclusions (otherwise they are doing less than their job); that these conclusions *must not* be drawn from the evaluator's personal values (whether or not those values coincide with the ones used); that the conclusions must be shown (or be capable of being shown) to follow from objectively determined, demonstrably relevant, and comprehensive facts by way of logically sound inferences; and that these conclusions will sometimes not reflect all of the values that will correctly enter into implementation decisions. Typically the values will come from the best available needs assessments and from whatever other sound scientific, legal, lexical, and logical arguments and evidence that bear on the issue. This is the way that product evaluation gets to evaluative conclusions, and this is the way that engineers happily set up what they call quality control systems, and this is how doctors have managed to draw conclusions about proper and improper treatments for several millenia (not at all the same as treatment aimed to produce the results the patient wants), all without (necessarily) violating any logical, scientific, or, for that matter, ethical code of proper conduct.

The view that social research cannot do what the older and more respectable fields have done for so long, and that it should instead merely report on impacts, in purely descriptive language, is what might be called the "lackey" view of evaluation research, and describes something that should have gone out with the sixties. Lackeys are "liveried retainers," in Webster's words, but even the livery of statistics and economics does not make up for the flunky role. Evaluators are not decision makers, indeed; but it is a crude confusion to think that only the decision makers are entitled to *evaluate*. Only they are entitled to *decide*, which is another matter entirely. The evaluator, on the other hand, is not just entitled but required to evaluate.

In the practice of medicine, it is the patient who—with few exceptions—decides, but that doesn't restrict the doctor to description or simply to telling the patient how to achieve the ends the patient values (e.g., suicide, murder). Prescription is as old as the practice of medicine, as proper and as evaluative.

Of course, even those who espouse the lackey view when in the pulpit tend to let their common sense get the better of them when they get down to business. The very social scientists who proclaim to their introductory courses that science cannot legitimate value claims quickly proceed to assert, to the same audience, that certain experimental designs are invalid and others inappropriate, that certain texts or articles or research projects or answers by students to examination questions are flawed—or outstanding. To their colleagues, and in writing, they are prepared to utter evaluations of researchers and programs and proposals—and, of course, graduate programs. All of these claims are evaluative and, very often, scientifically well based. It is completely bizarre that their authors should imagine that drawing such conclusions is any different from concluding that certain social programs are failures, others flawed, and yet others remarkably successful and cost-effective. The cynical explanation is that they want to keep out of the heat in the kitchen so badly that they are willing to accept gross inconsistencies between their official world view and their common practice—but what a sorry picture that paints of the profession. Throughout any anthology of evaluation material one finds the inevitable and sensible intrusion of common sense in the form of careful use of conclusions involving evaluative terms like "improvement in patient care" or "better police protection." It is surely time to end the hypocrisy and inconsistency by thinking out more carefully our view of the nature of evaluation.

It is time to return to the distinction between formative and summative evaluation, and relate it to the distinctions between evaluation, explanation or causation, and remediation or recommendations. People in the field often think formative evaluation must by its nature include recommendations for improvement. That is certainly false. All that it must include by its nature is a report that: (1) is prepared while there is still time and resources for the improvement of whatever is evaluated; (2) is given to those who have the power to bring about such improvements; and (3) provides assistance to the development process, while remaining within the legitimate range of evaluation. Of course, this report is often reached by a process that can be most helpful (or destructive) to the program being evaluated; but if that process is interactive, it does involve some risk of contamination by cooption.

There are some important examples where formative evaluation is best done by merely simulating summative evaluation in an "early-warning" context. If you go beyond this, as is often helpful, you do not have to move into the territory of causal explanations or remediation recommendations. There is an important area of what might be called **analytical** evaluation, which is still clearly evaluative. Analytical evaluation contrasts with **holistic** evaluation—the single overall grade or rank, arrived at without going through any process of allocating and then assembling subratings/rankings.

Analytical evaluation can be of two kinds: dimensional *evaluation* and component *evaluation*. (It is often—and wrongly, so we have been arguing—thought also to include causal analysis.) In *dimensional* evaluation, the report involves not just an overall conclusion but reports of performance along a set of dimensions of merit; for example, a computer can be evaluated in terms of throughput speed, task-size capacity, and range of processing capabilities. (Note that there is no one-to-one correlation between those dimensions and the components of the computer.) The dimensions may be evaluative in themselves, or—as in this case—descriptive but with evaluative implications in the context of this overall evaluation; or a mix, as in the case of the scoring of Olympic diving. The dimensions in the computer example, and in many other uses of dimensional evaluation, are useful because they are the payoff dimensions for the user. The overall conclusion, in both types of analytical evaluation, is reached after, in the light of, and preferably by systematic inference from the subratings.

Haven't I just legitimated descriptive program evaluation, which surely provides reporting on dimensions that are "descriptive, but with evaluative implications in . . . . [this] . . . . context"? No, for two reasons: First, because in dimensional evaluation there are normally ratings (evaluations) on each of the dimensions, not just numbers (unless you want to take a chance on the client's competence at interpreting the numbers). For example, one might remark that the Macintosh has outstanding task size capacity among current microcomputers rather than merely saying "it can directly address 16MB." Second, whichever way one goes on that decision, one big evaluative step still remains—integrating the factor ratings into an overall rating, a step that requires you to justify factor weightings and an integration function. Leaving that to the client, in all but trivial cases, guarantees disaster; and in the trivial cases, what's needed is not an evaluation but a simple answer to one or more factual questions. That's a lackey function for an evaluator, though not a dispensable or trivial function in itself. (Note that in any evaluation that requires grading rather than ranking, the overall evaluation has to be done in terms of a framework of several cutting scores—that is, between adequate and superior, or between inadequate and marginal).

Component evaluation, which is often much harder—for one reason, there are often more components than dimensions—*does* identify the merits of the separate components. An additional problem is that it usually has a much harder job establishing how those merits are to contribute to overall merit. However, it has the nice feature that one can often change defective components, which gives us an easier step toward remediation. (The step is less simple than might appear because of interactive effects; hence, replacing a weak component with a better one may lead to reduced overall performance, a common problem in short-wave radio and computer servicing.) The scoring of the Olympic decathlon is an example of component evaluation, and it has the nice feature that we can make up our own combinatorial formula. In program evaluation we cannot make arbitrary decisions of that kind, and instead have to relate the formula/weightings to the needs of the impacted population.

Either of these types of dimensional evaluation is almost certain to be more helpful in the formative context than a mere holistic rating; in fact, they are often more useful in summative contexts where they serve to justify or explain a rating rather than point the way to improvement. But remember that the holistic rating: (1) may be the only kind you *can* get; (2) will certainly be much easier and cheaper to get and to validate; and (3) is all you need for many summative purposes, such as the purposes of a prospective purchaser. Furthermore, we know from some well-documented cases that: (4) the validity of holistic evaluations may be greater than the validity of either species of analytic evaluation—an important, and at first sight, counterintuitive result.

We could now do with some further studies of how to make the best use, and where to make the best use, of component and dimensional evaluation as formative evaluation. The applications to teacher evaluation, for example, are, I think, quite important; the applications to technology assessment and software evaluation are also interesting.

As one begins to look at the new thrusts toward teacher evaluation, one sees a curious mix of dimensional and component evaluation, and one realizes the importance of the missing element in most approaches, the element whose peculiar power and elusiveness explains why holistic evaluation can be more valid than analytical. The missing element is the combinatorial procedure, the algorithm for getting from the parts to the whole, from the ratings on dimensions or of components, to an overall rating. Absent a precise formula, there is a great deal of intercase and interjudge variation in the way the elements are weighted and interacted. It is possible in teacher evaluation to identify a set of dimensions that can plausibly be said to be exhaustive, each of which can be given quite strict and highly plausible interactive weights. These might be quality of content taught, amount learned, professionality of the teaching/counseling/committeework process—which would include setting appropriate homework, assignments, and tests, and correcting/marking them appropriately—and the ethicality of all conduct. This is harder with components, though there are some lines of attack on the problem; clearly, it is not possible if the components are elements of the teacher's classroom style in view of the weak evidence on style payoff. The approach I like best here begins with a functional analysis of the teacher's complete job description (de facto if not *de jure*), including keeping records, interviewing parents, meeting with the curriculum committee, writing reports, preparing and delivering classes, meeting with students, and so on. We need much more work on the practical implementation of such schemas.

So much for some examples of needed work on the frontiers of evaluation. Back to the distinction between the practice of evaluation and the long-delayed emergence of the study of evaluation methodology.

One kind of metastudy of something that is related to evaluation has been around for a long time. Indeed, for about as long as we have had something called philosophy, we have had theories of value and more recently the subject of axiology as well as ethics. What was lacking was a theory of *evaluation,* a methodological analysis of the practical process of evaluating things. There were some glimmerings of it in Aristotle, and no doubt by others of that or earlier periods in other cultures; but those preliminary speculations soon led philosophers to the much grander subject of ethics. Even the application of ethics to practical ethical problems, which are a very small subset of the problems of evaluation, was extremely rare until the seventies. It was quite an effort to get a course on Practical Ethics into even the Berkeley philosophy curriculum—even after the riots of the sixties. But it is now entirely fashionable and extremely desirable that such courses are standard fare, that specialized versions of them on medical ethics or the ethics of journalism or environmental action are quite common, and that many journals exist (and more are springing up) that are devoted entirely to such matters. But all this was slow in coming about.

It seems to me that it was really the 1950s before Urmson's paper "On Grading" showed any significant new interest in the practical subject of evaluation among any of the power groups of twentieth-century philosophy (in his case the so-called ordinary language philosophers). But, once again, the old temptation to go on to higher things proved too strong and the development of the self-styled "good reasons" theories of ethics took over. Nevertheless, that name, good reasons, was meant to and does remind us that the influence of the practical had not completely evaporated, which was important because ethics had rarely been closely related to practical reasoning up to that point— the utilitarians and the casuists deserve mention as exceptions. It took until the 1970s to get that interest translated into serious and sustained attention to practical ethical problems. And it was still a long way from practical nonethical evaluation.

Most of the work in ethics in the fifties, sixties, and seventies from other schools of philosophy was totally remote from commonsense evaluative reasoning. One thinks of Sartre and existentialism, of situation ethics, of deontic logic, and so on. Some of these approaches were actually intended to represent the logic of practical reasoning, but the results had no effect on practical evaluative reasoning simply because they flew in the face of the common sense of the practical people doing that reasoning. This is the kind of mistake that is repeated by the Cronbach et al. work, which is, in effect, telling medical researchers that reports of outcome studies on ineffective cancer cures are not evaluations. They would only qualify as evaluations if they contained suggestions for making the quack medicine work.

Perhaps some of you are thinking that program evaluation is essentially different from product evaluation, and the formative-only thesis is more defensible in the latter case. But why on earth can't one report that a remedial reading program claiming spectacular results simply doesn't work in East Palo Alto, without having any suggestions as to how it could be improved? There are quack programs just as there are quack medicines, and it is very unattractive to deny that evaluators are doing their job properly in so reporting.

Urmson's work on grading begins by looking at the way in which apples are graded, an approach consistent with the then-current emphasis on ordinary language analysis that characterized his school of philosophy. But no one ever graded apples differently as a result of Urmson's discussion. And it never crossed the mind of Oxford dons like Urmson to look at how students were graded, as a subject for critical study, although they did that kind of grading all the time. The fact is that there was, and is, more philosophical meat and educational drink—not to mention scandal—in the latter subject than in the grading of apples—but of course it comes very close to home. The bizarre notion of grading on a curve, for example, used—by psychologists in particular—as a way to avoid having to make any value judgments about the real quality of student work, would have deserved some comment. The complex interaction of the comparative and absolute dimensions of merit that lies behind the tutor's comments needs unpacking. The hidden weightings of various dimensions of academic merit that lay behind the award of honors at Oxford would have made a most interesting conceptual study, before it became a matter for empirical research. But no one did any of this.

Therein lies the big difference between the philosophy of value—all there was to value theory as it was until the emergence of evaluation as we think of it today—and evaluation methodology. Evaluation methodology makes a difference in the way that evaluation is done or clearly should be done. If it doesn't come up with those practical recommendations, spelled out in detail, it is rightly regarded as no more than philosophical musings. Now, I have a good deal of interest in philosophical musings, but they are not the kind of thing you want to have interfere with the way in which you perform practical tasks. And most of those who practice philosophical musing have little interest in those applications.

So it took us a long time to get around to the serious analysis of the practical processes of evaluation. When we did so, we discovered that they were in shoddy shape indeed; the standing models of evaluation in education, such as the way in which schools were accredited or teachers assessed, were laughable, and even the ways in which grant applications were rated—in the hard sciences as well as the social sciences—was a paradigm of unscientific method.

Of course, the period of self-consciousness in philosophy is a couple of thousand years, whereas in evaluation it is a couple of decades. Even after a couple of millenia, philosophy can hardly be said to have reached any general agreement about its own nature and proper methodology, so it might be unreasonable to expect there to be any general agreement about those matters in the case of evaluation. Still, we could do better than we are doing given that we—unlike philosophy—have many examples of other disciplines to guide us.

In spite of that kind of bad news, what I have so far described might be called a generally optimistic view of how it took evaluation so long to emerge as a discipline in its own right. The optimistic view is the view that the delay occurred because when people started looking at the logic of evaluation they were quickly lured onward to the study of grand things like virtue and "the good life" and moral right and wrong. But there is a darker side to our reactions to evaluation, and I believe we have only begun to scratch the surface of it with the recent work on implementation and the passing remark or two above about the Failure of Nerve problem. Study of that darker side must focus on what I call valuephobia, the irrational fear of evaluation.

PSYCHOLOGICAL FRONTIERS: VALUEPHOBIA

There is nothing in the least irrational about fearing evaluation in itself, if it impinges on areas of one's own work, and in particular fearing the way in which much evaluation is done, especially personnel evaluation. It is decidedly sensible to fear that one's own best efforts may be denigrated on the basis of some totally inadequate sample of one's work, such as is provided by classroom visits that never amount to more than a half percent sample quantitatively (and that a biased sample), interpreted on the basis of some currently fashionable and dubiously generalized research about teaching styles. But there is an irrational fear of evaluation, valuephobia, and it is something quite different from that sensible negative reaction.

It is even quite different from what we might call anti-social attitudes to evaluation, such as the successful attempt by business interests in the 1940s to get Consumers Union on the Attorney General's list of subversive organizations, or the systematic refusal by newspapers to accept their advertisements for a decade or more. That reaction by those who were successfully exploiting an uncritical public is also rational in the short-range sense that excludes ethical considerations. Not acceptable by the society, for good reasons; a sign of impropriety and lack of ethics, indeed—but not of phobia. And one might even allow that the unprofessional attitude of attempting to prevent evaluation of one's own work, whether or not it is valid, is understandable and merely improper rather than irrational. After all, the possibility of serious criticism is an unattractive one. But then, so is going to the dentist, and we correctly regard it as irrational to avoid such visits entirely.

We notice valuephobia at work when we start hearing intelligent professionals producing arguments for the impossibility of, let us say, teacher or administrator evaluation; arguments that are clearly absurd by their own intellectual standards. The all-time classics of this genre are the most general ones—the set of arguments used by social scientists to support the dogma of value-free social science, arguments that were simply contradicted by their own practices in the best of their own journals, classrooms, and laboratories, where they continually and appropriately evaluated the work of others, and the instruments, designs, findings, and data of their own profession. Now both of these cases involve irrational behavior—in particular, the classic phenomenon of denial, the denial of what is obvious to others, for reasons of internal psychic harmony. Looking seriously at the psychodynamics of this process is essential if our work on implementation is not to suffer from the assumption that rational argumentation is the relevant mode.

THE PERSONNEL EVALUATION FRONTIER: EVALUATING PROFESSIONALS

Professionals in general, and professional academics in particular, cannot appeal to incompetence or ignorance as an excuse for holding beliefs that could be exposed as absurd by the application of some intelligence. This is why one must conclude that valuephobia is at work if their response to requests for evidence that they are doing good teaching (or administration)—and where it needs to be improved—is to say that evaluating such matters is impossible. That answer to an analogous question—for example, "What makes you think that your experimental design and procedures will lead to an answer to the question you are investigating, and where could it be improved?"—might well be grounds for failing one of their own doctoral students. The brain power that the faculty member puts into learning how to evaluate experimental designs would have had no more trouble with evaluating teaching or administration. But such an area for evaluation has been studiously avoided. Why, because it comes too close to home?

Of those academics who do not deny the impossibility of teacher evaluation, some from the social sciences will offer evidence for their merit as a teacher that fails to pass any test of scientific evidence ever mentioned in one of their own introductory or graduate courses—for example, they may quote ratings from an alumni questionnaire with a 20% response rate, or from a questionnaire that had to be signed by graduate students still working on their degree. Why this blindness?

Is it really blindness? Can we really evaluate teaching? The question is not whether complete and comprehensive evaluation is possible, though in fact there is no barrier to doing this rather well. The question is whether evaluation is possible in important, independent subareas, because, if even that much is possible, these are areas where improvement or achievement can be demonstrated and progress initiated. And systematic objective evaluation is extremely easy in many subareas—a good example is the area of setting competent tests and other assignments, marking them in a professionally acceptable way, and providing pedagogically useful feedback on them.

Few teachers, from kindergarten to postgraduate, have ever had their tests and scoring keys looked at against minimum standards of professional competence, if indeed they have ever heard of such standards; and those that have been looked at present a very depressing picture. The multiple-choice questions are overcued or ambiguous or could be answered by students on the first day; the essay questions are obscure, cover the area poorly, are graded by standards that vary as more answers are read; there is no scoring key or it is applied inconsistently or not explained to the students when materials are returned; the test booklets are marked serially instead of in parallel, the student's name is on the front cover; the feedback is simply evaluative, not remedial; the grades are too uniform, or misleadingly high, or inconsistently or indefensibly assembled from the subscores; no item pool is developed and no item analysis is done to identify weak questions, and so on.

Similar unimpeachable minimum requirements can be set in a dozen other areas of professional competence, particularly including: (1) the use of student and/or peer feedback to improve instruction; (2) systematic reading of and note-taking on new materials dealing with the content and pedagogy of the subject matter; and (3) the use of planned variation to explore alternative approaches and materials for improved results; this would certainly involve pre-tests and some type of control group, either longitudinal or concurrent. The conventional entry in this list is in fact the least defensible—the requirement of lesson plans (as opposed to a list of topics).

It's hard to argue that any of these aspects of professional teaching performance are impossible to evaluate or irrelevant or unimportant, yet there are almost no examples of teacher evaluation procedures in which they figure explicitly. Instead we find the new pre-college systems focusing on classroom visits that not only violate every tenet of sampling theory (too small, nonrandom, reactive, biased observer, etc.) but can only look at what is essentially irrelevant in all but the most bizarre cases, namely teaching style. This is ritualistic evaluation at its worst, the bait-and-switch technique of substituting something worthless for what is advertised to the community as a serious accountability. The classroom visit approach is most notable for its failure to look systematically at the two most obvious principal factors—the quality of the content presented, and the amount of learning inspired by the teacher. Instead, someone in the worst possible position to make unbiased judgments of any kind is required to make judgments that are by their nature incapable of any validity. Of course, such approaches do not begin or continue without strong support, and we should be conscious of several sources of support. From the principal's point of view, the visit from the Almighty approach has: (1) the great practical attraction of not requiring very much time—though more than in the past—compared to the unknown alternatives; (2) the attraction of pandering to fantasied omniscience; (3) the chance to work off a few grudges; and (4) the chance to further a favored teaching style. The fifth source of support is, I fear, the educational researcher who brings the Effective Teaching Practices checklist to the party. And of course, the public—and possibly the central administration—supports the idea of looking at the teaching because they don't know any better and do know that something needs to be done.

The role of the educational researcher here is of particular interest because she or he is a worker at the frontier, yet not trained as an evaluator. That's not a distinction that researchers view with awe, and so it is of some interest to demonstrate that it leads to support for a use of research results that is totally invalid. Invalid personnel evaluation is not just a matter of scientific error, it is a matter of injustice to humans—it is immoral, and sometimes also illegal. The error in this case is the use of statistical indicators as summative criteria.

We all know that we aren't supposed to use skin color (gender, religious affiliation, etc.) as a criterion in personnel evaluation, and many of us could give some kind of ethical justification for the prohibition in addition to the legal consideration. Still, I've run into administrators that feel this prohibition requires them to throw away some evidence they should be able to use, for example, because of the known correlation between criminality and skin color. They are perfectly willing to allow the possibility that correlation is a by-product of racial discrimination in the past and hence in some sense not the fault of the victims; and they agree that taking account of it leads to a vicious cycle of continued discrimination. Nevertheless, they argue that their primary responsibility is to their taxpayers and existing employees/students/parents and not to reform our society; and given this, they should be able to use any indicators that improve the probability of good selection of candidates and hence performance of duties.

I find that few of their peers are able to say why this argument is scientifically incorrect, even if they won't follow where it leads for ethical/social/legal reasons. One of the ways they put their ethical objections is in terms of language like this: "You can't condemn someone for what others (with one shared characteristic) have done." That's an important part of the ethical issue, though of course it doesn't address some other parts of it such as the problem of the self-fulfilling prophecy. But let's begin our discussion of improper "research-based" teacher evaluation by making it clear that the reason just quoted would completely rule out the use of any statistical indicators of teaching merit. Yet every one of these administrators is happy to use such indicators. The correlation between high eye contact (or whatever style variable "research" has favored) and good teaching is rarely better than that between skin color and crime, yet they will use the one and not the other.

Perhaps that is because there is no long history of oppression of teachers with low eye contact. But there's no long history of oppression of teachers who are Christian Scientists and yet the same administrators would almost certainly refuse to reject a candidate for a science teaching position who is a Christian Scientist just because more Christian Scientists reject the atomic theory—which is officially condemned by that church—than do people of other religious persuasions (a research-based fact). They would ask the candidate exactly where she or he stood on the matter and perhaps look at references from previous supervisors—exactly the correct procedure. Yet they sanctify the educational research on teaching style by making it exempt from these correct procedures! And they are, of course, supported in this by the high-status educational researchers who hold the big contracts to provide states with "scientific" methods of teacher evaluation. (Note that exactly the same line of argument applies to the use of "research-based" indicators of administrative merit such as the use of "shared decision-making procedures" (the so-called democratic style of administration, management by objectives, etc.).

One must begin by getting clear about the limits on the scientific inferences here. It is only possible to infer that a black is more likely to commit a crime than a white if *all* that you—as the administrator responsible for making the selection—know about either is their skin color. But if that *is* all you know about your candidates for a job, then we should certainly dismiss *you*. If what you know includes something about prior track record in similar positions, academic qualifications, and so on, as it obviously should, then of course you are no longer dealing with someone who is simply a random sample from the whole population of blacks and whites. In that case, the only relevant statistic is the incidence of crime in that more specifically defined population, a statistic that you don't have. In fact, if you have the kind of detail about the candidate that we expect you to get in order to make a reasonable decision, it will almost certainly be too specific for any known statistic to apply. Certainly, skin color has no incremental validity once you know even a little about a candidate. Now, that's why it is scientifically incorrect to use the statistical argument; and because it is scientifically incorrect, the ethical/legal prohibition is not taking anything useful away.

Statistical correlations between certain characteristics and meritorious (or poor) performance can never make those characteristics into legitimate criteria of merit. Criteria of merit must have logical or legal connections with the job for which they are said to indicate merit. They must meet the requirement of being necessary for good teaching. (Components do not in general have that kind of connection; so if you want to do analytic evaluation for summative purposes, only dimensional evaluation and not component evaluation is usually legitimate.) Statistical correlates of merit are for this reason only to be regarded as secondary indicators of merit; and the argument here is that you can't use secondary indicators in summative personnel evaluation. (Nor can you use goal achievement as a criterion for the merit of a program, though it is a criterion for "success," narrowly conceived, and it can sometimes be relevant to report it, as long as the real criteria are directly addressed.)

And that's why the "research-based" evidence on teaching style cannot be used legitimately to make personnel decisions about teachers. The evidence you should have obtained and could have obtained about the teacher's actual achievements in producing valuable learning while using proper procedures (e.g., avoiding the use of cruel and unusual punishments) automatically supervenes over the indirect evidence of statistical indicators. If you didn't get that evidence, we fire you; if you did, you can't use the secondary indicators. They only apply if you are dealing with someone who has been drawn as a random sample from the teacher population. That isn't even true when you appoint someone to a probationary appointment as they have had prior (supervised) teaching experience, and that's what you should get evidence about. No one was ever hired to have eye contact; and so they can never be legitimately fired because they didn't have it.

[I leave to the reader the exercise of identifying the (somewhat surprising) consequences of this view for the use of tests in selection for college admissions, given that the tests are "merely statistical indicators" of college success. Or are they?]

Spelling out in a little more detail the four legitimate dimensions (criteria) of teacher merit previously mentioned—the only ones I can think of—we have to include: the quality of the content taught (does the teacher really know the subject well enough to provide sound and illuminating answers to any questions that the best student could legitimately ask about the actual or required curriculum content); the success in imparting and/or inspiring learning (which includes learning the value of learning, of systematic inquiry, cooperation, etc.—that is, learning is not restricted to the cognitive domain); the mastery of professional skills (how to set valid tests, deal with the nonclassroom duties, etc.); and the adherence to ethical standards (avoiding racism or favoritism, etc.). Hence teacher competency tests are an appropriate component of teacher evaluation, because competence is a necessary condition for being a good teacher. Of course, careful study of performance improvement by the students is also a necessary part of any comprehensive system of teacher evaluation, but complete systems are not necessary for all personnel action, only for favorable action and for improvement recommendations.

The performance issue here is not the absolute level of the students' work because that is due to many factors outside the teacher's control; but the performance against what is possible for each student, on which the best guidance is usually the performance of comparable students taught by the most successful teachers in the same or comparable schools or districts. Strictly, this only gives you ratings for comparative merit; but it can be supplemented so as to give a plausible rating of absolute merit (the only kind on which personnel decisions can be based.) Failure on either of these criteria—as on the ethical or professional ones—would constitute completely adequate grounds for dismissal, because they are necessary conditions, which means you cannot trade off weaknesses on one against strengths on another. Unions and teachers often complain about minimum competency tests on the grounds that they don't cover everything that's relevant to good teaching. They don't have to.

On the other hand, you cannot give someone a reward for good teaching unless you can show that you are using a set of criteria that is not only separately necessary, but collectively complete. Otherwise you may be unfair to someone else whose overall performance is better because of outstanding performance on some dimension you have omitted. I believe the four mentioned are jointly complete as well as separately necessary.

To these four criteria should be added the consideration of worth as opposed to merit. Worth is the extent to which—and areas in which—the candidate possesses those qualifications that are of particular importance to the employer (suitability). A great Latin teacher should not be hired over a good math teacher when you need a math teacher—hence, teacher evaluation is not just a matter of looking at merit as a teacher. This point is often denied by unions who argue that no one should be dismissed on the grounds of redundancy, because the occurrence of that is not the fault of the teacher. Exhausting the goldfields of the Klondike was not the fault of the miners, either, but it doesn't follow that someone should have paid them to continue to live there without work or for that matter for building highways that nobody needed.

Versatility is perhaps the most overlooked worth factor, and should be written into job descriptions as a standard desideratum, because changing curricula and student demand are often best handled by moving personnel resources around, rather than by dismissal and new hires (or by moving people to positions for which they are unqualified).

Is all that research on the style variables that characterize good teachers wasted? Not at all; it has a useful role in formative evaluation as follows. If you have demonstrated that a teacher is doing badly, using the proper criteria, then the "anthology of successful styles" built up by researchers provides a valuable resource for suggestions as to practices the teacher might consider adding to his or her current repertoire in the quest for improvement.

Contrast this with the use that led to the resignation of a brilliant math teacher in a school district I visited recently. After years of turning out an extraordinarily high proportion of students who scored very high on the math achievement tests (compared to those from the same school in other subjects), many of whom went on to college as math majors, his class was recently visited by the team armed with the new state instruments. He was called in front of the committee after the visit and reprimanded for unsatisfactory performance; the visitors substantiated their evaluation by pointing to five areas where "validated" indicators showed he was deficient—such as failure to spend time setting out the lesson plan on the board and explaining it in detail, low eye contact, and so on. Now, it is statistically certain that many of the best teachers have a style that results in low scores on many validated indicators—otherwise the correlations would be nearer to one—and attempts to treat their style as if they can adjust each component of it without detrimental overall effects are stupid. *No criticisms of teachers based on their failure to perform well on validated indicators are valid unless it has first been shown that the teacher is a poor teacher, using the proper criteria.* The sooner we stop putting the indicators cart ahead of the success horse the faster we'll get improvement in teaching.

I'll close this section by saying that the worst current abuse in personnel evaluation is probably none of those mentioned so far, but the excessive weighting of personality characteristics that should be almost irrelevant ("unsuitable" is a favorite euphemism for threat here, instead of being a well-reasoned evaluation of someone with qualifications ill-matched to institutional needs).

I hope enough has now been said to suggest that personnel evaluation is a frontier where much exploration and building remains to be done—and to suggest that our late start with a logically sound approach to the area may be due to valuephobia rather than indolence. After all, even if researchers discover that there is a high correlation between success at the marathon and favoring a vegetarian diet, we would severely criticize a coach who weighted diet at all against track record; yet we have plunged into the analogous mistake with teacher evaluation. Gross blunders of this kind require explanation, and the best explanation seems to be that this area increases anxiety enough to weaken our critical faculties.

And if your primary interests are in program evaluation, remember, you can't do much formative program evaluation without doing personnel evaluation.

SCALING AND MEASUREMENT FRONTIERS: EVALUATIVE VALIDITY

In this section, I suggest a new approach to conceptualizing values, in the hope that it may undercut what may be the last rational objection to the recognition that evaluations have equal rights with any other scientific constructs.

We are all familiar with the notion of construct validity in the methodology of psychological tests and measurement. It is roughly the extent to which a test measures the concept that it is said to measure; it is established probabilistically by showing a network of correlations between test scores and other indicators of the presence of the construct in question. It is normally contrasted with, for example, the notions of concurrent and predictive validity. Messick, Ross, and I have independently argued that in fact the latter are just special instances of the former.

Referring to another distinction in the literature that also came from Meehl's pen, this time in collaboration with MacCorquodale instead of Cronbach, one can take the matter further and argue that all so-called intervening variables—variables that are introduced at first as mere abbreviations for functions of other variables—that acquire any scientific currency become in fact hypothetical constructs, entities like electrons or aptitudes whose presence can only be indirectly demonstrated or inferred from the results of tests. Those tests then become tests with a certain construct validity for the presence of these theoretical constructs. (This all gets simpler in a moment.)

Construct validity thus becomes a central notion in the lexicon of scientific inference. I want to suggest that value, worth, quality, and merit are simply constructs from observable variables, just as aptitudes and achievements and motivation and anxiety are. A test of Spanish competence (at a certain level) or typing skill (at a certain speed) is never 100% valid, however carefully administered, but it can get to usefully high levels if we look carefully at variables describing the conditions of administration, and so forth. No observations can establish the merit of a program beyond all possibility of error—but enough of them, made carefully and systematically enough on enough variables, establish it beyond reasonable doubt. Understanding the concept of typing skill—that is, understanding the construct—and understanding the typical problems of testing and sampling, enables us to say exactly what array of checks and balances must be gone through to make plausible the inference from raw scores to conclusions about ability.

Contrary to the hopes of the radical behaviorists and the operationists, who wanted to define all scientific concepts directly in terms of observables (that is, make them all intervening variables), we have come to settle for the view that they all have "surplus meaning" over and above whatever observational implications they connote. It is not something metaphysical in the sense of obscure and untestable; it is something rich, flexible, and essential for the operation of science. And that precisely defines the status of the evaluative concepts. A good watch is one that tells time accurately, is shockproof, not cumbersome, legible, and probably some other things, too. But if I show that all of these properties apply to a watch, I have established a prima facie case for its merit; I have made it plausible to say that it is a good watch in just the same way that I can show that certain test results obtained from a test administered in a certain way make it plausible to conclude that a subject understands the process of long division.

Validity is, of course, itself an evaluative term, just as right and wrong in scoring the arithmetic test are evaluative. That is, testing is built on evaluation and is just a higher-level evaluation. This repeats the way in which so-called observations such as "observing that the subject did not read the answers from a neighbor's test form," are in fact themselves inferences from yet simpler observations or sense impressions. In the history of epistemology, this led philosophers to the search for the ultimate units of knowledge, the sensations (perhaps) about which one could not possibly be wrong. The clear consensus is that there are no such things; there are varying degrees of certainty about various kinds of claims, but no empirical claims on which all other knowledge can be built. The pyramidical structure of knowledge is an illusion.

Instead we have come to realize that knowledge has a netlike structure in which all parts are connected to all other parts more or less directly. When we find discrepancies between our predictions/inferences from one part of the net—and our observations—themselves dependent on other parts of the net—we have to go back and look for the most appropriate adjustments to be made in the elements of the net. Perhaps we shall have to change theoretical axioms, perhaps reject some previous observations, perhaps rethink some inference or assumption. The net is thus not divided into the certain and the speculative, and indeed it is not even divided sharply into observable elements and theoretical elements; which is which depends as much on the context of the investigation as it does on some intrinsic property.

In fact, the net is not even divisible into factual and value elements because concepts like true and false, applied, let us say, to the answers given by a subject to test questions or to scientific explanations, are not sharply distinct from correct and incorrect, right and wrong, valid and invalid, sound and unsound, good and bad, proper and improper. It is of the essence of knowledge that the factual is connected with the evaluative because the distinction between knowledge and mistaken belief is itself evaluative.

Value claims—evaluations—are thus built into our knowledge network. None are ultimate, none are sharply distinct from factual claims, just as no factual claims are ultimate and none are sharply distinguishable from theoretical ones. All form an essential part of the epistemological net of concepts in which our knowledge is embedded. Thus all are supportable in principle by a mixture of factual claims and other value claims; and value claims are refutable in the same way as all other claims, theoretical or observational. If you claim this is a well-built house and I show you the wood-rot damage due to carelessly allowing water into the structure while it was being constructed, I am giving evidence against a claim just as I could against any "purely factual" claim. This process of establishing a prima facie conclusion is the key process in arguing about the existence of the position, or the guilt of the accused; it is the essential process in scientific and legal reasoning and it long antedates—indeed, it underpins—statistical inference.

The only distinction one can make between factual and value claims is that value claims are only rarely at the level of "basic observations." But they are often only one step up. And in evaluating a student's response to an arithmetic question, it is hard to argue that there is anything wrong with the claim that one can *see* that the answer is wrong, that is, that the value is observable. Perhaps one might add that values are *in some ways* a little nearer to being methodological constructs rather than empirical ones; in this sense they resemble constructs like cause, factor, consequence, correlate, or experimental design, rather than economy, electron, or ecosystem. These constructs are, of course, even more essential to science than an equal number of substantive constructs because they are so pervasive.

The bottom line is that there is nothing more arbitrary about evaluations than about factual or methodological claims—which is not to say there is nothing more to them than an abbreviation for a list of observations. They have to be supported in the same way as claims about any not directly observable entities or properties. They are observation generators just as theoretical claims are observation generators; both are essential to making it possible to think, for without either we would be lost in the chaos of unchecked and unorganized observations. Worse, we could not even form the concepts that we need in order to formulate the observations. Evaluations, like theoretical constructs of the more familiar kind, are key elements in the economy of the mind, idea banks from which solid cash can be obtained, but far more active than a pile of ingots.

The value of programs, the merit of teachers, the quality of products are simply theoretical constructs that can be indefinitely unpacked into factual implications, tied into the net of our concepts and needs and environment, and used like any other constructs in the practical or intellectual world. It is not possible to have accepted the role of empirical constructs in science and have any arguments against the role of value constructs.

SUNDRIES

I had many other topics on my list of frontier areas but there's only space to mention some of them, perhaps providing enough to inspire you to do some more of the brushcutting. I'll begin with an example from the scaling/measurement area.

1. *"Step-ranking."* I'd like to propose a modest elaboration of our scaling resources to cope with certain demands from practical evaluation. The four existing evaluative predicates are ranking, grading, scoring, and apportioning. In designing any evaluation, we need to determine in advance which of these the client needs because a completely different evaluation design/resources/time line, and so on is required for each of them. I have recently discovered a need for a hybrid and I describe it briefly; it may be ill-conceived, or already documented; in either case I would appreciate enlightenment. The need arises when you must select something, but may not be able to afford the best. You need to know how large the intervals are to lower-cost entries. Ranking tells us nothing about the intervals between candidates; grading requires that we establish cutting scores; scoring tells us nothing about the utility of a difference of one unit, and apportioning is only relevant to cases where one can divide the spoils. Step-ranking goes like this; first we define a series of merit steps down from the best candidate in terms of what we might call the unit of a minimum substantial difference of merit (msd). On this ladder we place the entrants as follows; in group 1, to which we assign step-rank 1, we place all entries that are less than one msd from the best entry. In group 2, we place all entries that are only one msd from the best, if any. In group 3 . . . Unlike ranking, we do not increase the rank number to include the number of entries of higher rank; in this respect, step-ranking is like grading; and we may increase the rank number even when there are no intermediate entries. Unlike grading, we do not make any judgment about the absolute merit of any entry or about how large the differences have to be to amount to a categorical difference of merit; entries with rank 1 may be bad or good, and those with rank 10 may still be just as bad or good. Unlike scoring, we require that the unit be not just any merit increment, but the minimum significant one (which might be the equivalent of half a point or twenty points); and that it must be constant (many point scoring systems award the first points more easily than later ones, some do the opposite). The advantage of step-ranking is that the entity that is ranked second may be step-ranked fifth, which tells us that a large tradeoff is involved

in going down to the runner-up; conversely, one that is ranked fifth may be step-ranked first.

2. *Converting the concepts of statistics, tests, and measurement into evaluatively useful concepts.* The previous example bears on this, but there are many more. The great scandal, of course, concerns the concept of significance where statistical significance was and still is regarded as having some evaluative status, instead of being an occasionally necessary condition for opening a discussion. The *Sesame Street* evaluation is perhaps the *locus classicus* of this mistake. Even the discussion previously referenced in *Evaluation Studies* does not consider the way in which the relative utility of the alternative hypotheses, as well as their antecedent probabilities must be considered when deciding what "significance level" to regard as significant. Too often we see texts in which it is said that criterion-referenced tests (CRTs) are more useful for this or that, without any reference to the value of the criterion behavior. CRTs have no value unless what they identify has value—and a good many of them in the reading area, where their use is perhaps most widespread, are vitiated by this point. For example, CRTs that identify performance on a scale whose value is totally dependent upon the validity of a particular theory about how to teach reading are not obviously useful.

3. *Software evaluation.* I have recently reviewed a large number of systems of software evaluation and find them to exhibit many faults, particularly including the tendency to use overlapping criteria without realizing that this double-weights some criteria (documentation is often included as a separate dimension from ease of learning, but of course the documentation is largely responsible for good or bad ratings on ease of learning); the failure to ensure completeness (e.g., by omitting content validity); the frequent inclusion of fashionable secondary indicators (e.g., use of dynamic graphics, which are expensive and often pointless); the requirement that every entry be scored on every dimension (instead of scoring on the "killer" dimensions first—those on which most are likely to fail—thereby saving as much as 75% of the resources available for the evaluation).

4. *Evaluation in education.* But the general point all this raises is more interesting than the specific example. We need to develop criteria for sets of evaluative criteria, just as long ago we developed criteria for axiom sets. Some are provided above, but there are a good many more (and some refinements to those are needed—for example there are circumstances in which criteria should overlap), and I think it would be a helpful part of general education to teach people something

about systematic evaluation. In particular, it seems well past time to get some very substantial material about evaluation into the science and technology curricula. It is arguably the most important single methodological concept in science or technology, and is omitted from all the concept lists that I know.

5. *The evaluation of information.* We are all on the verge of drowning in a sea of information—witness the length of this paper—and yet there are few efforts to tackle the problem at a very general level. This will require not just abstracting services, already well done in some areas, but evaluation services refined to the point where one can avoid reading the abstracts of poor articles and books. There are obvious risks, and partial attempts at this through the present reviewing process, but we lack systematic discussion. Evaluators should be in the forefront of planning here, and perhaps a session on the evaluation of information and information sources would be in order at a subsequent meeting.

6. It is time to take this down to the airport for the midnight flight, and still I have not got to the problem of applying evaluation techniques to a complete state educational system, the problem of upgrading technology assessment, and certain interesting features of common procedures for evaluating funding proposals. We are fortunate to be involved in an area with so many frontiers.

5

Stakeholder-Based Evaluation
and Value Judgments

Melvin M. Mark and R. Lance Shotland

The nature of values in stakeholder-based evaluations is discussed. One key value judgment involves the selection of stakeholder groups for participation. In the first major section of this article, the role of values in such selection is emphasized by considering two dimensions on which stakeholder groups may vary—power and legitimacy. It is shown that the selection of stakeholder groups can be based on a rationale for stakeholder-based evaluation; however, the choice of a rationale for stakeholder participation is itself a value judgment, implicitly or explicitly. Further, in implementing a rationale, value judgments are required, particularly if the rationale involves empowerment and democratization. In a second section, the consequences of stakeholder participation are discussed. Although numerous commentaries imply positive effects, much is not known, such as the type or level of stakeholder involvement required for effective participation. Further, stakeholder participation may serve as a means of preempting criticism by stakeholders, or may be a form of pseudoempowerment. Ironically, the evaluator may autocratically designate which groups participate in a process meant to empower democratically. Finally, some suggestions are made about how evaluators might better deal with the value judgments inherent in stakeholder-based evaluations, and, more generally, how stakeholder-based approaches to evaluation might be improved.

*E*valuation, in theory and in practice, increasingly acknowledges and accommodates the existence of multiple groups interested in evaluation results. The need to incorporate in an evaluation the interests of multiple groups has been acknowledged by evaluators with markedly different perspectives (e.g., Cook,

AUTHORS' NOTE: *We wish to thank Jennifer Greene, Janet Weiss, and an anonymous reviewer for their comments on a previous version of this article. Correspondence should be addressed to Melvin M. Mark, Department of Psychology, Pennsylvania State University, University Park, PA 16802.*

EVALUATION REVIEW, Vol. 9 No. 5, October 1985 605-626
© 1985 Sage Publications, Inc.

1985; Cronbach et al., 1980; Guba and Lincoln, 1981; Patton, 1980), using a variety of terms such as "constituency analysis," "pluralism," and the "policy setting community." The term "stakeholders" is frequently used in such discussions, and we employ it here to refer to the distinct groups interested in the results of an evaluation, either because they are directly affected by or involved in program activities, or because they must make a decision about the program or about a similar program at other locations or times (Gold, 1983; Guba and Lincoln, 1981).

Discussions of the role of stakeholder groups almost uniformly recommend that, if it is feasible, multiple stakeholder groups' perspectives should be incorporated in the definition of evaluation goals and the selection of outcome measures (e.g., Cook, 1985; Cronbach et al., 1980; Patton, 1980; Weiss, 1983a). Additional mechanisms for stakeholder involvement in the evaluation are sometimes incorporated, including the periodic feedback of interim results to participating groups, the dissemination of final evaluation results to stakeholders, and even the reporting of stakeholders' interpretations of evaluation results (Patton, 1980; Weiss, 1983a). A range of activities are thus available for stakeholder participation, and in the present article we define "stakeholder-based evaluations" broadly: the term here refers to evaluations that involve stakeholder groups, other than sponsors, in the formulation of evaluation questions and in any other evaluation activities.[1]

Although early presentations of stakeholder approaches uncritically focused on the promise of stakeholder-based evaluation, more recent discussions have considered possible technical difficulties (e.g., Cohen, 1983; Weiss, 1983a, 1983b). For example, it has been noted that: stakeholders may not be able to specify their information needs clearly; the multiple information demands of various stakeholder groups may exceed the research capacities of an evaluation; and some stakeholders may see little value in central evaluation goals, for example, service deliverers may see summative evaluation as superfluous because their direct experience has convinced them that the program is effective (Cohen, 1983; Weiss, 1983a, 1983b).

The present article focuses on another basic problem that has received inadequate attention in the literature on stakeholder-based evaluation (but see Guba and Lincoln, 1981): the role of values in stakeholder approaches, particularly in the selection of stakeholder groups for participation in the evaluation. Although technical issues are important, the basic issue in stakeholder-based evaluation—

choosing stakeholder groups for participation—involves primarily a value judgment, rather than a technical one (and, further, it is a value judgment that may have implications for technical decisions in the evaluation).

In particular, the decision about *whose questions* will guide an evaluation can be seen as essentially an issue of values (Krathwohl, 1980: 40). That is, if a particular stakeholder group is allowed to participate effectively, *its* value preferences will determine the focus of the evaluation. In principle, this ability to determine the focus of an evaluation is a valuable resource: "Knowledge is power." Social experiments "are, or can be, a strong source of political power. Other things being equal, those who can show with data that a policy opinion works are in a better position than those who must make their case from *a priori* reasoning" (Warwick, 1978: 270).

ARE VALUES MORE PROMINENT
IN STAKEHOLDER-BASED EVALUATIONS?

One response to our focus on values and stakeholder participation is to ask whether value issues arise in stakeholder-based evaluations to a greater degree than they do in evaluations that ignore stakeholders. Clearly values are involved in all evaluations—indeed, even in the decision to conduct an evaluation. One might suggest then that the value concerns in stakeholder-based evaluations are no different from those in other evaluations.

We contend that this is not the case; that is, we believe that stakeholder-based evaluations, although sharing many value concerns with nonstakeholder approaches, also raise some unique value questions for evaluators. In particular, in stakeholder approaches the evaluator's tasks include deciding *whose* questions to address. In contrast, in nonstakeholder approaches, this critical value judgment (and others) are taken as falling outside of the responsibility of the evaluator. It is simply assumed that the evaluation will address those questions that the sponsor desires to have addressed (see the concept of evaluator as servant of the experimenting society in Campbell, 1975).

This nonstakeholder approach can be criticized by saying that "to leave the definition of the ethical situation to the sponsor of a program would be to abdicate one's moral judgment" (Kelman and Warwick, 1978: 6). However, one could alternatively contend that in nonstakeholder evaluations in the public sector, one is "abdicating one's moral judgment" to the elected and appointed officials whose official responsibilities include representing the people.[2] Thus evaluators could claim that they were allowing questions to be formulated by those who have the legitimate, socially based responsibility to do so. We believe this was the position of most early evaluators. In recent years, however, most evaluators have come to believe that public representatives may not adequately define the scope of questions for policy debate, given the pluralistic nature of society and social decision making (Cook, 1985; Cronbach et al., 1980; Lindblom and Cohen, 1979). Such a realization has been one of the major forces leading toward stakeholder-based evaluation.

And with the movement toward stakeholder-based evaluation comes additional value concerns. In particular comes the task about which this article deals: the selection of stakeholders for participation.

PERCEIVED POWER AND LEGITIMACY AS CRITERIA IN THE SELECTION OF STAKEHOLDER GROUPS

At issue in stakeholder-based evaluation is *which* stakeholder groups' values will control the evaluation. Practical constraints generally keep the evaluator from attempting to answer all the questions that might be of interest to each stakeholder group. In some cases this may not be a problem, because the evaluation audience is limited or there is consensus among stakeholders about what is important (Boruch and Shadish, 1983). More commonly, different stakeholder groups will be interested in different questions (Boruch and Shadish, 1983; Cook, 1984; Cronbach et al., 1980; Shadish et al., 1982). In the face of practical resource constraints, the evaluator must choose to focus on particular questions, and in doing so decide *which* stakeholders groups' questions to address. (Although in fact the issue will generally be "How many and which specific ones of which groups' questions will be included?" we will, for the sake of simplicity, speak about which groups are included.)

Insight can be gained as to how evaluators choose stakeholder groups by classifying groups along two dimensions, the perceived power and the perceived legitimacy of the group's interests. Although these are continuous dimensions, for the sake of simplicity our discussion will treat them as dichotomous. Power refers here to the ability to influence policy decisions involving the program being evaluated. Thus, funding agencies are high in power. Organized stakeholders with formal lobbying power (e.g., unionized teachers) will also typically have high power, whereas service recipients who have no formal organization (e.g., students) will typically be low in power. Legitimacy of the group's interest refers to the perception that the stakeholder group's interest in the program and in program effects is socially acceptable. This judgment is likely made in terms of the theory and philosophy underlying the program. Thus, rapists will be seen as low in legitimacy when changes in rape laws are evaluated, whereas in the same evaluation rape victims' interests will be seen as legitimate. The typology is represented in Table 1.

Although our presentation treats power and legitimacy as independent dimensions, they are probably correlated in reality—that is, power is likely to confer the perception of legitimacy. Therefore, the four cells in Table 1 may differ in their frequency of occurrence, for example, the high power, low legitimacy cell may be relatively infrequent. Further, it should be clear that power and legitimacy are not inherent characteristics of stakeholder groups, but are *as perceived,* which may depend on the perspective of the viewer. In particular, judgments about power and legitimacy will be influenced by (1) the evaluator's characteristics (e.g., the evaluator's political philosophy), (2) the evaluator's role relative to various stakeholders (e.g., is one stakeholder paying for the evaluation?), and (3) the purpose of the evaluation (e.g., is the purpose external accountability, in which case an external audience might be seen as most powerful, or internal program improvement in which case program staff might be seen as most powerful?). Although the relativistic nature of judgments of power and legitimacy is important in any particular case, it is still useful and possible to examine the role of these two factors in the selection of stakeholder groups in general.

THE RATIONALE FOR STAKEHOLDER PARTICIPATION AND THE SELECTION OF STAKEHOLDER GROUPS

It is possible to relate the value judgment involved in stakeholder selection to the purpose, goal, or rationale for conducting a stakeholder-based evaluation. Different rationales may imply alter-

TABLE 1
A Typology of Stakeholder Groups, with Illustrative Examples

| | | Perceived Power | |
		Low	High

Perceived Legitimacy of Interests	High	Clients
		Social Service
		   recipients
			Traditional decision makers
			Service deliverers with
			   organizational
			   lobbying power

	Low	Rapists in studies of
		   rape law reform
		   (e.g., Marsh et al.)
		Ku Klux Klan in
		   studies of
		   desegregation
			Teachers in performance
			   contracting studies
			
			Absentee owners in studies
			   of old age homes

native rules for choosing among stakeholder groups that differ in terms of power and legitimacy.

There are at least three rationales for involving stakeholders in evaluation. One rationale is that involving shakeholders in evaluation planning will increase *utilization*. Increased utilization, it is presumed, will arise because the questions important to stakeholders will be identified and addressed, and because the process of stakeholder participation will lead stakeholders to become committed to the evaluation (Gold, 1983; Weiss, 1983a). To the extent that the rationale for stakeholder participation is to increase utilization, stakeholder selection logically should be based on the power of stakeholder groups. This position is implicit in Cronbach et al's. (1980) model of question selection, which indicates that the evaluator should select those questions with high leverage.[3] A question is high in leverage if providing an answer to it is likely to affect policy decisions. Leverage is therefore greater for those questions of interest to high-power stakeholders.

A second, closely related rationale for stakeholder-based evaluations involves the desire to accurately *represent the decision making process*. Early evaluation efforts were apparently guided by a model that assumed the existence of *a* "decision maker" (see Lindblom and Cohen, 1979, for documentation). More recently, evaluators have realized that decisions are made more out of political accommodation than from a single decision maker's command, and that in fact "decisions" are often not single unitary choices, but rather the accumulation of numerous choices by multiple parties (e.g., Cronbach et al., 1980; Lindblom and Cohen, 1979). In other words, earlier evaluation efforts were based on the presumption that some decision maker's information needs defined "the right questions" for evaluation. More recent approaches recognize that the multiple groups involved in decisions have different "right questions" that may be addressed in evaluation. Such recognition leads to the notion that multiple parties' concerns should be represented in an evaluation—to a stakeholder perspective (Cook, 1985). Logically, the best way to represent the decision-making process is to weight stakeholder groups according to their expected ability to influence that process. Thus, this rationale also suggests that one should select stakeholder groups based on their power.

Selecting stakeholder groups based on their power seems incongruous with most discussions of stakeholder-based evaluation. This is because the movement toward stakeholder-based evaluations is motivated, in part, by considerations other than utilization and the accurate representation of the decision making process. Most notable is a desire for justice in evaluation and for the empowerment of stakeholder groups. Critics have contended that evaluations generally fail to address the concerns of less powerful groups, such as the recipients of social service programs (House, 1976, 1980; Weiss, 1983a). Stakeholder-based evaluation is offered as a direct remedy to this problem, by including low-power groups in evaluation planning and practice. Thus, another rationale for stakeholder-based evaluations is that they serve as a mechanism of *empowerment.* In other words, this rationale is that stakeholder analysis leads to the "democratization" of decision making, or in Hirschman's (1970) terminology, gives less powerful stakeholders "voice."

The difficulty that arises with this empowerment rationale, however, is that it is unclear how the goals of justice and democratization should best be met in practice. Does justice require equal participation of all stakeholder groups? Does a positive relationship between power and voice in the evaluation lead to an unjust evaluation, even though it may enhance utilization? Should voice be distributed inversely with power to compensate for existing power differences among stakeholders? Our belief is that an exclusive commitment to an empowerment rationale does indeed imply giving greatest voice to the least powerful.

Another question arises in attempting to operationalize the empowerment rationale. Should groups that are low in perceived legitimacy be given voice? For example, is justice served or disserved if we give rapists voice in an evaluation of rape laws? As another example, should one include as a stakeholder group businesses whose primary interest is profit (e.g., absentee corporations that run old age homes, where substandard care may mean huge profit)? Simply put, should empowerment apply equally to all interested groups or only to those whose interests are judged to be legitimate? Our assumption is that most evaluators seeking to achieve empowerment will agree with the position of Laue and Cormick (1978: 222) who, in describing their ethical principles for community interventions, state:

> While empowerment of the powerless is a premier value in our system, intervenors should not lend their skills to empowering groups who do not hold the values of empowerment, freedom and justice for all people . . . [our] value[s] . . . do *not* call for intervention activities that will further empower racists, sexists, fascists, militarists, or religious bigots.

Similarly, in the case of evaluation, the evaluator is unlikely to choose to extend power to a group whose very interests in the program are seen as illegitimate. In sum, the empowerment rationale would seem to imply the selection of low-power, high-legitimacy stakeholder groups. However, we are less confident about the implications of the empowerment rationale than of the two other rationales already discussed.

The preceding discussion of three rationales illustrates that the selection of stakeholder groups involves not just technical questions, but also basic value judgments. The use of a particular rationale can provide a basis for selecting stakeholder groups (e.g., the utilization rationale implies selecting stakeholders high in power). However, the choice of a particular rationale is itself a value judgment, implicitly or explicitly: Is utilization more or less important than empowerment? Further, value judgments must be made in implementing any rationale, particulary that one involving empowerment and democratization. As shown in the following section, such value questions remain preeminent when stakeholder selection is based on a mixture of rationales.

LOW-POWER, LOW-LEGITIMACY STAKEHOLDERS

The role of values in selecting stakeholder groups can further be explicated by focusing on a special case, that of stakeholder groups who are low in both power and perceived legitimacy, and by contrasting this cell of Table 1 with other cells. Perhaps the best example of a stakeholder group that has neither power nor legitimate interests would be rapists in the case of an evaluation of rape law reform. Another example might be the Ku Klux Klan in studies of desegregation. Our analysis suggests that such groups are unlikely to be included in stakeholder-based evaluations. If stakeholder selection is based solely on either of the first two rationales described above (utilization or a desire to represent the decision-making process), such groups are likely to be excluded because they are low in power. If stakeholder selection is based on the empowerment rationale, such groups are likely to be excluded because their low legitimacy makes them seem undeserving of empowerment. Further, if stakeholder selection is based on a mixture of rationales—as it is likely to be—low-power, low-legitimacy groups will be excluded because they do not meet the criteria for inclusion of any of the three rationales.

Although we have not empirically tested the hypothesis that low-power, low-legitimacy groups generally will be excluded from stakeholder-based evaluations, the extant evidence seems compatible. For example, in a major study of rape law reform (Marsh et al., 1982), rapists were not included among the many stakeholder groups consulted—even though rapists' stake in the effects of the new law are as strong and direct as those of any other stakeholder groups.[4] Nor are the Ku Klux Klan or other racist groups considered in Cook's (1984) analysis of stakeholders in desegregation.

From one perspective, excluding low-power, low-legitimacy groups is appropriate: Doing so should not adversely affect utilization or the decision-making process, and the illegitimacy of their interests may mean that they are not entitled to voice in the evaluation. However, this perspective (and other justifications for excluding low-power, low-legitimacy stakeholders) is clearly based on value judgments. Further, from another perspective the exclusion of low-power, low-legitimacy groups raises serious questions. Is it appropriate for such groups to be excluded if groups that are low in legitimacy but *high* in power are included? For example, is it proper to exclude rapists from participation in an evaluation of rape law reform because they are low in power, but to include in an evaluation of old age home policy the politically powerful absentee owners who are interested only in profit? Should power be a sufficient condition to override the illegitimacy of a stakeholder group's concerns? The answer, it would seem, depends on the relative importance placed upon the factors of power and legitimacy, which derives in turn from the relative importance of the three rationales—a question of values.

Even if there were consensus that low legitimacy groups should be excluded regardless of power—an apparently reasonable position—other value issues would arise. Who determines that a particular stakeholder group's interests are low in legitimacy, and by what mechanism? To what extent are judgments about legitimacy based on the biases of the person making the judgment? Evaluators may prefer not to deal with such issues, but they must unless they choose to involve all identified stakeholder groups equally, regardless of the groups' legitimacy—a strategy that itself clearly involves a value judgment.

THE CONSEQUENCES OF
STAKEHOLDER PARTICIPATION

One reaction to the observation that certain stakeholder groups are likely to be included in evaluations and others excluded is "So what? Does stakeholder participation cause any difference in the conduct or use of evaluations?" One might argue that it does not—that stakeholder participation is a form of window dressing, that powerless stakeholder groups may lack the ability to contribute to the planning of an evaluation (Murray, 1983), and that stakeholder participation thus is unlikely to have any salutary effect on the evaluation. Further, research in organizations indicates that employee ownership does not inherently lead to greater employee participation in decision making (Long, 1981); by analogy it might be argued that stakeholder involvement does not inherently lead to stakeholder influence. Such a position would indicate that our concern for the values involved in selecting stakeholders is specious, in that the value issue is inconsequential if stakeholder involvement has no effect.

Unfortunately, there are no systematic comparative studies that examine whether stakeholder participation makes a difference in the way an evaluation is conducted or used. There are, however, numerous critical commentaries on specific evaluations suggesting that stakeholder participation *would have* made a difference. For example, Rossi et al. (1978) point out that the primary research focus of the New Jersey-Pennsylvania Income Maintenance Project would likely have been different if the researchers had consulted various stakeholders, such as the poor, employers, and social workers. As another example, House et al. (1978) suggest that the Follow Through evaluation would have focused on different outcome measures if different local (model) sponsors' values had controlled the evaluation.

Similar contentions can and have been made about numerous specific evaluations. Further, some commentators have made the same point—not for a specific evaluation, but for entire policy areas. Shadish et al. (1982) describe the distinct interests of different stakeholder groups in evaluations of community care for mental patients. Cook (1984) reviews the apparent concerns of different stakeholder groups in studies of desegregation. In these and other cases, it is clear that many commentators *believe* that the distinct perspectives of different stakeholder groups—if allowed to control an evaluation's focus—would lead to different research questions being investigated.

All of this is not to argue that stakeholder participation inevitably and in all cases changes the focus of an evaluation. Nor is it to say what level of stakeholder participation is required. Consider the National Institute of Education-sponsored evaluations of the Cities-in-Schools and Push/Excel programs, which were based on the ideal of extensive interaction between evaluators and stakeholders (Bryk, 1983). Commentaries about those evaluations suggest that the extensive stakeholder participation did not affect the evaluation questions (apparently because the evaluators anticipated the information preferences of the stakeholders); however, the stakeholder involvement did seem to facilitate conditions that are thought (Leviton and Hughes, 1981) to enhance the utilization of results (Farrar and House, 1983: 44-46; Murray, 1983; Stake, 1983: 29).

In short, although evidence that meets rigorous standards of internal validity may not exist, it is easy to conclude—as many commentators have—that evaluation questions typically will change depending on which stakeholder groups' values are represented in an evaluation. However, it is not clear under what conditions stakeholder participation will and will not make a difference in an evaluator's focus or in its utilization. Nor has it clearly been specified what type or level of stakeholder involvement is required.

STAKEHOLDER INPUT AS A
MECHANISM FOR AVOIDING CRITICISM

The preceding discussion implies that stakeholders have at least the potential for deriving positive benefit from being involved in evaluation: Knowledge is power. We should also consider the possibility, however, that participation in an evaluation comes at a cost, and we should explore the ethical implications of this possibility. Some discussions of stakeholder participation in evaluation suggest that potential criticism of an evaluation can be avoided by including the critics' concerns in the planning of the evaluation (see, for example, Joint Committee on Standards for Educational Evaluation, 1981: 56-59). This strategy seems most likely to be undertaken when the potentially critical stakeholders have some power to influence decisions about the program. As an example, according to this approach it would be important to include welfare workers as a stakeholder group in an evaluation of direct transfer payments.

From one perspective, the inclusion of critical stakeholder groups can be useful to an evaluation by leading it to ask more of the "right questions." For example, the evaluation may be more likely to measure possible negative side effects of the treatment, or to focus on possible inefficiencies of the program, and thus one may obtain a more complete and accurate understanding of a program and its effects.

However, inclusion of potential critics as stakeholders can also be viewed more critically as a form of cooptation, or as an attempt to "pull the legs out from under" potential criticism. As an example, imagine a pilot evaluation of some new educational technology that threatens teachers' jobs. By measuring the affective outcomes that interest teachers, the evaluator can address empirically the teachers' potential criticism that the new technology has harmful effects on affective development. Given the apparently low frequency of effects in social programs—particularly in the case of certain kinds of relationships, such as the effect of social service programs on affect—including measures of affect in the evaluation probably renders impotent the teachers' potential criticism. It is important to remember that just as "knowledge is power," so too the absence of knowledge can be an effective tool of power (as indicated by the common argument that action should be deferred "pending further study"). Thus, by anticipating the criticism of stakeholder groups opposed to a program, stakeholder-based evaluations may reduce their power, rather than empower them.

This result may seem appropriate, if it means that factually inaccurate arguments are rendered powerless in policy deliberations. However, important questions of values arise. If a stakeholder group's potential criticism is addressed in an evaluation, does fairness demand some minimal level of research quality, that is, some minimal level of power to detect an effect on a valid measure or set of measures? Is a form of "truth in advertising" required? Should a stakeholder group's participation be solicited without "informed consent" that null findings can reduce their power to influence decisions about the program? We hope the answers to these questions are evident.

PSEUDOEMPOWERMENT AND ITS POSSIBLE EFFECTS

Implicit in most discussions of stakeholder-based evaluation is the notion that giving stakeholder groups a voice in evaluation is a positive value. An alternative perspective is that such participation is actually a form of pseudoempowerment. Pseudoempowerment may result for either of two reasons.

First, the evaluator, through a variety of techniques, may guide stakeholder activities so that the unique preferences of the stakeholder groups are not advanced, but rather stakeholder participation is directed (i.e., controlled) by the evaluator. Among the techniques through which this might occur is the selection of cooperative stakeholder representatives for participation; the appeal to the evaluator's superior technical skills, substantive knowledge, or relevant experience; and persuasion and subtle guidance by a socially skilled evaluator (see the discussion of cooptation in Witte, 1980).

Second, pseudoempowerment may result because participation in evaluation may not give stakeholders power to control issues that are truly important to them (see Witte, 1980, on structural impotence). As Weiss (1983b) points out, to give stakeholders a voice in evaluations is to share power in what may not be the stakeholders' primary concern. For many groups "it is the program and its future that concern them, not information about the program" (Weiss, 1983b: 92). That is, stakeholder-based evaluations may give low-power stakeholder groups a voice in evaluation, but not in the programmatic issues that are of greater concern. Thus stakeholder-based evaluations can be viewed as a meager method of democratization, particularly if, as is frequently suggested, the results of evaluations often are of little use to stakeholders.

Even if stakeholder-based evaluations provide pseudoempowerment rather than voice about important programmatic issues, they may still have broader effects on stakeholders. It is possible that the perceived "voice" given stakeholders will be like a "high procedural justice" manipulation, and will therefore increase stakeholders' satisfaction with the program in particular and with the political process more generally (Greenberg and Folger, 1983; Thibaut and Walker, 1975; Tyler and Caine, 1981). Viewed cynically, this possible effect of stakeholder-based evaluation could be seen as a means of social control, rather than empowerment, by which the powerful appease the less powerful by giving the appearance of control without relinquishing any actual power. Obviously, the way one views such an effect is a value judgment.

Of course, granting stakeholders voice in an evaluation may not increase stakeholders' satisfaction levels. In fact, it is possible that the opposite effect might occur. Expectations for power could increase, or political mobilization could intensify, or stakeholders could perceive that they are being given a "sham" voice with no real control—all of which could lead to resentment and dissatisfaction (Greenberg and Folger, 1983). Unfortunately, current theory does not specify precisely the conditions under which voice will lead to less, rather than more, staisfaction.

Whatever the effects, the image of stakeholder participation as pseudoempowerment raises questions about values. Is voice in an evaluation a meaningful form of participation? Alternatively, is it a subtle means of social control? When is participation meaningful to and useful for stakeholders? And should not such questions concern evaluators?

A FUNDAMENTAL IRONY

Finally, it should be noted that the empowerment rationale, in which stakeholder-based evaluation is used to distribute power, involves a fundamental irony. This might be labeled "autocratic power sharing." That is, empowerment proceeds "top-down" from the evaluator to the stakeholder groups that are supposedly being empowered. It is tempting to suggest that stakeholder-based evaluation replaces the model of evaluator as "philosopher-king" with a model of evaluator as "benevolent dictator." And, of course, underlying this irony is an issue of values: On what basis should evaluators intervene in the political process by allocating the power that information holds? Is evaluation an appropriate or useful forum for the overtly political goal of empowerment?

TOWARD RECOMMENDATIONS

In this article we have raised a number of questions about value concerns in stakeholder-based evaluations. Unfortunately, there are often expectations that those who raise questions should also attempt to answer them. Thus in this section we shall deal with the following questions: What are the implications of the previously discussed value concerns for the conduct of stakeholder-based evaluations? What are evaluators to do given the value issues we have raised?

One perhaps pessimistic appraisal is that evaluators can do little more about these value concerns than to recognize them. In other words, perhaps the best evaluators can do is to be honest and explicit, both with themselves and with others, about the value choices underlying their actions. In this way, evaluators and evaluation users might better recognize what is "evaluation" and what is "value judgment," pure and simple. This position can be seen as a call to ferret out and to be explicit about the value assumptions underlying evaluation (Guba and Lincoln, 1981: 306). There have been recent admonitions for the evaluator to take the role of teacher and for evaluation to serve as illumination (e.g., Cronbach et al., 1980); in a pluralistic social setting this can best occur when both teacher and student recognize the value bases for the source of the illumination.

However, it can alternatively be argued that evaluators can do more than simply acknowledge the value bases of an evaluation. According to this perspective, evaluators can consciously explore the rationale for stakeholder participation during the planning phase of an evaluation. They can then tailor both the selection of stakeholder groups for participation and the nature of stakeholder participation to the rationale for including stakeholders in the evaluation.

Toward that goal, we can offer some recommendations about the consequences of the three rationales described earlier. These recommendations are tentative, and subject to future confirmation.

(1) If stakeholder participation is based on a desire to increase the likelihood of utilization (a) it is logical to include powerful stakeholders, as noted earlier, and (b) it may be desirable to involve stakeholders extensively, as in the NIE-sponsored evaluations. The latter recommendation is based first on the observation that such extensive participation seemed in the NIE evaluations to make participant stakeholders more receptive to evaluations findings (Murray, 1983), and second on the belief that extensive participation should stimulate various psychological mechanisms that lead to commitment (Brickman, forthcoming). It should be noted, however, that such ex-

tensive participation on the part of stakeholders may have disadvantages, among them that: stakeholders may not understand the technical limitations of evaluation, and may become frustrated if the evaluation cannot accomplish their goals; the evaluator may need to spend considerable time interacting with stakeholders, including attempts to educate them about the potential and limits of evaluation; and the evaluator may become committed to the stakeholders' goals, which may lead to compromises in the scientific integrity of the evaluation (Gold, 1983; Murray, 1983; Weiss, 1983a).

(2) If stakeholder participation is based on a desire to adequately represent the decision process, which involves asking the questions of relevance to the different groups that may influence decisions, (a) it is logical to select stakeholders based on power, as noted earlier, but (b) it may not require the extensive level of stakeholder participation suggested by the utilization rationale.[5] In fact, it is not completely clear that extensive stakeholder participation will generally lead to substantial changes in question formulation, as compared to minimal stakeholder interaction with a sensitive evaluator who attempts to anticipate stakeholders' information needs and who examines relevant literature.

(3) If stakeholder participation is based on a desire to increase the empowerment of deserving groups, it would seem that low-power stakeholders should be selected and it seems appropriate to omit groups with illegitimate interests, as discussed previously. However, given concerns about pseudoempowerment, one might seriously question whether participation in evaluation is a meaningful method of empowerment. It would seem more meaningful to empower participation in program formulation and modification. Although this is generally outside the scope of evaluators, one recently proposed model for the evaluation of social programs lends itself well to such a goal. Campbell (1984) has proposed a "contagious cross-validation model" of program evaluation. In this model, funding is given to local programs focusing on common problems. Evaluation of the more successful of the independently constructed local programs would be followed by dissemination and subsequent reevaluation, providing cross-validation and evidence about the program's transferability. In principle, stakeholders could be incorporated into Campbell's (1984) model. That is, each local program might involve a different stakeholder group in the program *design*. In this way more meaningful empowerment might occur. Campbell's (1984) model is particularly useful for policy areas in which multiple stakeholder

groups exist with competing interests, which may be difficult to resolve in a single program setting. Further, this approach may help solve a problem we have not discussed in the present article which is, "Who speaks for a particular stakeholder group?" In the contagious cross-validation model, different local programs could involve different types of representatives of a particular stakeholder group.

Of course, this concept of stakeholder participation in program formulation has some very serious practical constraints. Foremost is the need for generous funding of a new approach to social problem solving. Another is the procedure by which meaningful stakeholder participation is ensured (see next section). In short, this proposed model may at present be both impractical and unlikely, but it may represent one of the few ways in which evaluation can actually contribute meaningfully to empowerment.

Again, of course, these recommendations should be considered tentative and may be modified by future experience. In addition, our recommendations could also be expanded in at least two ways. First, we have given little attention to other factors such as uncertainty and cost (Cronbach et al., 1980) that may influence stakeholder group selection; a more complete statement of stakeholder selection can readily be made by adding such factors to our recommendations. Second, we have not discussed the possibility of using different rationales for different aspects of stakeholder participation (e.g., one rationale for stakeholder involvement in question formulation and another for stakeholder receipt of interim and final evaluation results). Neither of these expansions should change the nature of the value issues we have raised.

Further, we have not discussed the implication of other possible rationales for conducting stakeholder-based evaluations, such as "one person (or one dollar), one vote in the evaluation." Although we believe we have considered implications of three major rationales for stakeholder-based evaluation, we also strongly do not believe we have provided the final word on the value choices involved in stakeholder approaches. To do so would require a comprehensive moral theory of evaluation.

ENHANCING STAKEHOLDERS' EFFECTIVENESS

One serious obstacle to successful stakeholder-based evaluation may be the difficulty of ensuring that stakeholders are effective collaborators in evaluation. For example, stakeholders are sometimes seen as lacking the skills or knowledge necessary to make a contribution (Murray, 1983). Yet stakeholders must be independent contributors if we are to avoid pseudoempowerment and to gain additional understanding from stakeholder participation. The literatures on industrial democracy and organizational development provide some suggestions for techniques that increase the likelihood that participation will be meaningful. Although we cannot review these literatures in detail here, some of their implications for stakeholder evaluation can be noted briefly.

One lesson is the importance of time—typically a scarce commodity in evaluation. Time is needed for stakeholders to develop trust in the evaluator and evaluation process, and to acquire the skills requisite for effective participation (Kanter, 1983; Witte, 1980). The needed skills are of two kinds: technical (e.g., concerning economic or methodological constraints on evaluation), and social (e.g., the process of group decision making; O'Toole, 1981). The evaluator can aid in the development of such skills through facilitating access to relevant information, allowing an adequate time for learning, using appropriate small groups techniques, using several special-purpose committees, each with a limited range of responsibilities, and being empathetic in interactions with stakeholders (Witte, 1980). It may also be useful to employ stakeholder group members who have acquired relevant social science background.

Other structural and task variables may also enhance stakeholder participation. Although special-task committees may be helpful, rigid segmentation should probably be avoided (Kanter, 1983). Tasks can be structured so that some visible results occur early, and the evaluator should clearly attend to stakeholder input. The evaluator should specify to stakeholders the possible range of evaluation activities; that is, ground rules and boundaries should be established (Kanter, 1983). The evaluator should not assume that stakeholders wish to focus on "big issues," but should be open to focus on smaller issues of day-to-day program operation. Nor should the evaluator expect that stakeholders will contribute significantly to technical and methodological decisions (Kanter, 1983). Finally, attempts should be made to create a "local culture" supportive of participation (O'Toole, 1981).

These suggestions do not exhaust the recommendations that can be borrowed from the literatures on organizational development and industrial democracy. Nor does following these and other suggestions guarantee success. It is clear that the task of mutual education, which evaluator and stakeholder must accomplish for highly meaningful participation, is not easy. Further development of methods to accomplish this goal is clearly called for.

Given the apparent difficulty of ensuring stakeholder participation, one might also question whether extensive stakeholder involvement is an appropriate goal for most evaluations. It might be argued that modest stakeholder participation is generally appropriate for identifying evaluation questions, but that empowerment or other benefits might not accrue from more extensive participation in many cases. Identifying those conditions under which benefits will accrue from more extensive involvement is another important task for advocates of stakeholder-based evaluation—and it is not clear that these conditions include simply the existence of powerless groups whom the evaluator is attempting to empower. In short, enhancing the effectiveness of stakeholder participation requires not only the use of techniques that strengthen stakeholders' ability to participate, it also requires a clear and reasonable sense of what can be accomplished with what type and level of stakeholder participation, under what conditions.

CONCLUSION

We have attempted to point out the central role of values in stakeholder-based evaluations. Our discussion should not be taken as an indictment of such approaches. Most evaluations are still conducted from the singular perspective of the evaluation sponsor. This approach is also based on a value position; one which may be more difficult to justify to the extent that the rationales that underlie stakeholder-based evaluation are valid.

Our intention is simply to describe the role of values in stakeholder-based evaluation, and to suggest the need for evaluators to give further consideration to this issue. The value judgments involved in selecting stakeholder groups may ordinarily be made without thoughtful analysis of their implications; and the social science expertise of evaluators may not be suitable training or appropriate qualification for making such judgments in any case. One can hope for a comprehensive moral philosophy of evaluation that can guide judgments such as the selection of stakeholder groups. In the absence of such, we can at least attempt to be mindful of the value judgments involved in selecting stakeholder groups for participation, and to be explicit about the rationale used for their selection. The need for value judgments should of course not stand as an impediment to action—only as an impediment to action that is not carefully considered.

NOTES

1. To avoid confusion, it should be noted that our conception of stakeholder-based evaluations therefore includes, but is broader (i.e., less specific) than, the stakeholder-based evaluation model sponsored by the National Institute of Education and discussed in Bryk (1983).

2. For evaluations that are privately sponsored, one could contend that responsibility for defining questions lies with the sponsor, under the same economic principles that govern business exchanges.

3. Cronbach et al. (1980) also discuss uncertainty and cost as determinants of question selection.

4. It should be noted, however, that Marsh et al. (1982) did ask other stakeholders (judges, prosecutors, and defense attorneys) whether they believed the new law violated defendants' constitutional rights.

5. Of course, implicit in the "decision-making" rationale is the belief (or desire) that more adequate representation of the decision-making process will ultimately increase utilization. However, this rationale is based on the notion that better, more complete, or more relevant information will lead to utilization; the utilization rationale suggests seeking other mechanisms to enhance utilization, such as stakeholder commitment, as a result of stakeholder participation.

REFERENCES

BORUCH, R. F. and W. R. SHADISH, Jr. (1983) "Design issues in community intervention research," pp. 73-98 in E. Seidman (ed.) Handbook of Social Intervention. Beverly Hills, CA: Sage.
BRICKMAN, P. [ed.] (forthcoming) Commitment, Conflict, and Caring. Englewood Cliffs, NJ: Prentice-Hall.
BRYK, A. S. [ed.] (1983) Stakeholder-Based Evaluation. San Francisco: Jossey-Bass.
CAMPBELL, D. T. (1984) "Can we be scientific in applied social science?" in R. Conner et al. (eds.) Evaluation Studies Review Annual (vol. 9). Beverly Hills, CA: Sage.
———(1975) The social scientist as methodological servant of the experimenting society," in S. S. Nagel (ed.) Policy Studies in the Social Sciences. Lexington, MA: D. C. Heath.
COHEN, D. K. (1983) "Evaluation and reform," pp. 73-81: in A. Bryk (ed.) Stakeholder-Based Evaluation. San Francisco: Jossey-Bass.
COOK, T. D. (1985) "Post-positivist critical multiplism," pp. 21-62 in R. L. Shotland and

M. M. Mark (eds.) Social Science and Social Policy. Beverly Hills, CA: Sage.
——(1984) "The philosophy and politics of quasi-experimental research: the case of desegregation." Unpublished manuscript, Northwestern University.
CRONBACH, L., S. AMBRON, S. DORNBUSCH, R. HESS, R. HORNIK, D. PHILLIPS, D. WALKER, AND S. WEINER (1980). Toward Reform of Program Evaluation. San Francisco: Jossey-Bass.
FARRAR, E. and E. R. HOUSE (1983) "The evaluation of Push/Excel: a case study," pp. 31-57 in A. S. Bryk (ed.) Stakeholder-Based Evaluation. San Francisco: Jossey-Bass.
GOLD, N. (1983) "Stakeholders and program evaluations: characterizations and reflections," pp. 63-72 in A. Bryk (ed.) Stakeholder-Based Evaluation. San Francisco: Jossey-Bass.
GREENBERG, J. and R. FOLGER (1983) "Procedural justice, participation, and the fair process effect in groups and organizations," pp. 235-256 in P. B. Paulus (ed.) Basic group processes. New York: Springer-Verlag.
GUBA, E. and Y. S. LINCOLN (1981) Effective Evaluation. San Francisco: Jossey-Bass.
HIRSCHMAN, A. O. (1970) Exit, Voice, and Loyalty: Responses to Decline in Firms, Organizations, and States. Cambridge, MA: Harvard Univ. Press.
HOUSE, E. R. (1980) Evaluating with Validity. Beverly Hills, CA: Sage.
——(1976) "Justice in evaluation," in G. V. Glass (ed.) Evaluation Studies Review Annual (Vol. 1). Beverly Hills, CA: Sage.
——G. V GLASS, L. D. McLEAN, and D. F. WALKER (1978) "No simple answer: critique of the Follow Through evaluation." Harvard Educ. Rev. 48, 1: 128-160.
Joint Committee on Standards for Educational Evaluation (1981) Standards for Evaluations of Educational Programs, Projects, and Materials. New York: McGraw-Hill.
KANTER, R. M. (1983) The Change Masters. New York: Simon & Schuster.
KELMAN, H. C. and D. WARWICK (1978) "The ethics of social interventions: Goals, means, and consequences," pp. 3-33 in G. Bermant et al. (eds.) The Ethics of Social Intervention. Washington, DC: Hemisphere.
KRATHWOHL, D. R. (1980) "The myth of value-free evaluation." Educ. Evaluation and Policy Analysis 2: 37-45.
LAUE, J. and G. CORMICK (1978) "The ethics of intervention in community disputes," pp. 205-232 in G. Bermant et al. (eds.) The Ethics of Social Intervention. Washington, DC: Hemisphere.
LEVITON, L. C. and E.F.X. HUGHES (1981) "Research on the utilization of evaluations: a review and synthesis." Evaluation Rev. 5: 525-548.
LINDBLOM, C. E. and D. K. COHEN (1979) Usable Knowledge. New Haven, CT: Yale Univ. Press.
LONG, R. J. (1981) "The effects of formal employee participation in ownership and decision making on perceived and desired patterns of organizational influence: a longitudinal study." Human Relations 34: 847-876.
MARSH, J. C., A. GEIST, and N. CAPLAN (1982) Rape and the Limits of Law Reform. Boston: Auburn House.
MURRAY, C. A. (1983) "Stakeholders as deck chairs," pp. 59-61 in A. S. Bryk (ed.) Stakeholder-Based Evaluation. San Francisco: Jossey-Bass.

O'TOOLE, J. (1981) Making America Work: Productivity and Responsibility. New York: Continuum.

PATTON, M. Q. (1980) Qualitative Evaluation Methods. Beverly Hills, CA: Sage.

ROSSI, P. H., M. BOECKMANN and R. A. BERK (1978) "Some ethical implications of the New Jersey-Pennsylvania income maintenance experiment," pp. 245-266 in G. Bermant et al. (ed.) The Ethics of Social Intervention. Washington, DC: Hemisphere.

SHADISH, W. R., S. THOMAS, and R. R. BOOTZIN (1982) "Criteria for success in deinstitutionalization: perceptions of nursing homes by different interest groups." Amer. J. of Community Psychology 10: 553-566.

STAKE, R. E. (1983) "Stakeholder influence in the evaluation of Cities-in-Schools," pp. 15-30 in A. S. Bryk (ed.) Stakeholder-Based Evaluation. San Francisco: Jossey-Bass.

THIBAUT, J. W., and L. WALKER (1975) Procedural Justice: A Psychological Analysis. Hillsdale, NJ: Erlbaum.

TYLER, T. R. and A. CAINE (1981) "The influence of outcomes and procedures upon satisfaction with formal leaders." J. of Personality and Social Psychology 41: 642-655.

WARWICK, D. P. (1978) "Ethical guidelines for social experiments," pp. 267-288 in G. Bermant el al. (eds.) The Ethics of Social Intervention. Washington, DC: Hemisphere.

WEISS, C. (1983a) "The stakeholder approach to evaluation: origins and promise," pp. 3-14 in A. Bryk (ed.) Stakeholder-Based Evaluation. San Francisco: Jossey-Bass.

————(1983b) "Toward the future of stakeholder approaches in evaluation," pp. 83-96 in A. Bryk (ed.), Stakeholder-Based Evaluation. San Francisco: Jossey-Bass.

WITTE, J. F. (1980) Democracy, Authority, and Alienation in Work: Worker's Participation in an American Corporation. Chicago: Univ. of Chicago Press.

Melvin M. Mark is Associate Professor of Psychology at Pennsylvania State University. He is co-editor (with Lance Shotland) of Social Science and Social Policy *(Sage, 1985), co-editor of* Evaluation Studies Review Annual *(vol. 3) and author of several chapters and articles on methodological issues in evaluation and applied social science. In addition to his interests in the use of social science theory and research in policy processes, Dr. Mark's research focuses on relative deprivation and the social psychology of justice.*

R. Lance Shotland is Professor of Psychology at Pennsylvania State University. His interests include the interphase between social science and social policy, methodology, evaluation research, bystander behavior, and crime control. In addition to his other publications he is co-editor of Social Science and Social Policy *(with Melvin Mark), co-author of* Television and Antisocial Behavior *(with Stanley Milgram), and author of* University Communications Networks: The Small World Method.

6

Evaluation
The State of the Art and the Sorry State of the Science
Mark W. Lipsey, Scott Crosse, Jan Dunkle,
John Pollard, and Gordon Stobart

*A representative sample of studies drawn from the published
program evaluation literature is systematically examined.
Weak designs, low statistical power, ad hoc measurement, and
neglect of treatment implementation and program theory
characterize the state of the art in program evaluation.
Program evaluation research under the experimental paradigm
requires better planning and execution.*

The dominant methodological approach to program evaluation research
today is based on the experimental paradigm, that is quantitative
measurement of dependent variables with controlled designs to establish
cause-and-effect relationships. Though the universal appropriateness of this
paradigm for program evaluation has been vigorously disputed in some
quarters, most of the studies actually conducted and publicly disseminated
under the program evaluation label nonetheless embody at least the
rudiments of experimental design. The telltale signs of quantitative
measurement, some attempt at control or baseline groups, and cause-and-
effect thinking are present even when there is otherwise little resemblance to
the classical randomized experiment.

It is also widely acknowledged that program evaluation is often poorly
done within the experimental paradigm. It has been commonplace for
reviews of selected program evaluation research to sharply criticize the
methodology of the studies examined. For example, Bernstein and Freeman
(1975) reviewed 236 federally sponsored evaluation studies and concluded
that at least half the studies that evaluated impact were "deficient either in

From Lipsey et al., "Evaluation: The State of the Art and the Sorry State of the Science," *New
Directions for Program Evaluation*, 1985, 27, 7-28. Copyright 1985 by Jossey-Bass Inc., Publishers.

design, sampling, or validity of measures" (p. 97). A similar conclusion was reached by Gordon and Morse (1975) after close examination of a sample of 93 program evaluation studies published in sociological journals.

The difficulty of doing good experimental work under program evaluation circumstances can be attributed to at least two rather different factors. First, as has often been noted, there are numerous practical difficulties inherent in the matching of good research design to practical program circumstances. Weiss (1972) described the program context as "intrinsically inhospitable" to the methods of social science. Secondly, social scientists for the most part are not very well trained to do methodologically exacting research under field conditions. Applied research has been a neglected stepchild in many of the social science disciplines that confer higher prestige on theoretical work and basic research. Ironically, the more that evaluation researchers learn about appropriate application of experimental methodology in program evaluation settings, the more difficult the research becomes. Thoughtful evaluation researchers struggling to understand the complex phenomena of social programs with the available tools have increasingly differentiated the range of substantive and methodological concerns with which, to be cogent, the research must deal.

Key Aspects of Program Evaluation Research. Our purpose here is to review and assess current practice in program evaluation research under the experimental paradigm with special attention to some relatively neglected issues that have only recently become prominent in the literature. In order to provide a framework for this task, we have attempted to extract the most important methodological and conceptual imperatives from the metaliterature in program evaluation research, that is, the literature discussing how program evaluation should be done. The result is five factors that, once articulated, take on the character of common sense. Their essential role in program evaluation is readily apparent and neglect of them makes program evaluation under the experimental paradigm difficult to interpret.

Research Design. Only reaffirmation is required on this topic since design issues are the oldest and most thoroughly discussed of the methodological concerns that face evaluation researchers. At issue, of course, is valid identification of the cause-and-effect linkages central to the experimental paradigm. Proper research design is required to determine if a particular effect is actually produced by a particular intervention and to separate the effect of the intervention from other happenstances that have similar effects. A valid determination of causal links requires that the research design include proper controls. Campbell has been the most influential advocate for the use of randomized control groups in such research and has systematized the concept of quasi-experiments as approximations to controlled experiments (Campbell and Stanley, 1966; Cook and Campbell, 1979). From the present perspective, the striking thing about this topic is the great volume of literature and methodological advice available and the general awareness of the pertinent issues among evaluation researchers. By comparison, other important methodological issues have been sorely neglected.

Statistical Power. Statistical power is the probability of a statistically significant result on a dependent measure when there is, in fact, a real effect produced by the treatment. Power is an important matter in program evaluation research for at least two reasons. First, there is good reason to believe that statistical power is often quite low for research done under field conditions. Boruch and Gomez (1979) have shown that the inconsistent treatment delivery and increased measurement error likely in the field degrade statistical power by multiplicative factors. Moreover, such research is often done under practical constraints that limit the available sample size, which in itself limits power. Second, statistical power is important in program evaluation because of its close relationship to Type II error, the probability of accepting the null hypothesis of no treatment effect when, in fact, it is false. While Type I error receives predominant concern in theoretical research, it can be argued that Type II error is of equal or greater importance in practical research. Such error means that the research finds no effect for a program or treatment that is genuinely effective. In the political context of program evaluation research, a null result will almost certainly be interpreted as program failure and may produce practical difficulties for the program, that is, diminished support from sponsors or funders, staff demoralization, reputational injury, and so forth. Research with low statistical power thus has the potential for falsely branding a program as a failure when, in fact, the problem is the inability of the research to detect an effect, not the inability of the program to produce one.

Measurement. It is fundamental that, without outcome measures that are sensitive to potential program effects, adequate assessment of those effects cannot be made. Measurement sensitivity is a somewhat unfamiliar term for applied researchers (see Aiken, 1977), but it has the advantage of encompassing the traditional issues of reliability and validity while emphasizing the ultimate responsiveness of the measures to the effects of interest. Dependent measures can fail to respond to underlying treatment effects because they: (1) lack validity (do not measure the construct on which change occurs), (2) lack reliability (contain so much measurement error that change variance is obscured), or (3) lack sensitivity (do not respond proportionately to changes on the construct of interest) (see Carver, 1974). Lipsey (1983) demonstrated the interplay of validity, reliability, and sensitivity in the measurement of surrogate treatment effects deliberately constructed to simulate large differences. The results indicated that inadequate measurement easily obscures important treatment effects under program evaluation circumstances. Measurement issues are thus closely related to statistical power since they influence the apparent effect size that in turn, is one of the major determinants of statistical power (Sechrest and Yeaton, 1981; 1982).

Treatment Implementation. It is a truism that a treatment that is not actually implemented and delivered cannot have effects. Moreover, even if implemented, a trivial or inappropriate treatment relative to the problem it addresses will not have effects either. Sechrest and his collaborators (Sechrest and Redner, 1979; Sechrest and others 1979; Yeaton and Sechrest, 1981) have taken the lead in specifying the treatment characteristics necessary to reasonably expect an effect. In their language, a treatment must have adequate strength and integrity. That is, it must, in principle, be sufficiently powerful to alter the condition being treated and it must be fully delivered according to the intended regimen. Methodologically, some independent check is required on the integrity of the treatment implementation as well as a conceptual framework that plausibly links the nature and level of the treatment to the expected effects as measured. Dilution of the treatment as implemented, through low dosage, weak or inconsistent delivery, and so forth, causes a sharp drop in the effects that can be expected and, consequently, in the likelihood that an evaluation study will detect positive effects (Boruch and Gomez, 1979).

Program Theory. It is becoming increasingly apparent that adequate program evaluation cannot be done by representing treatments as black box processes, either present or absent in a specific case but otherwise working through unspecified mechanisms. An insight of the evaluability assessment concept (Rutman, 1980; Wholey, 1977) is the recognition that a program is as much a conceptual construction as an organizational one. In its essence, a program consists of a set of rational linkages between program activities and expected outcomes abstracted from the particular behaviors in which program personnel happen to engage. If there is not at least an implicit program model in the conceptual sense, there is virtually no program to evaluate and no basis for determining what effects it could be expected to have or the circumstances to which it might generalize. Chen and Rossi (1981, 1983) describe the virtues of designing program evaluation around specifiable program theory. Among those virtues are: (1) the methodological advantages of identifying likely program effects that may not be stated in program goals, (that is, being able to look in the right place for effects), (2) defining intermediate or intervening effects that may signal at least partial success in advance of a longer term outcome, and (3) anticipating and managing obfuscatory variance from interactions of participant characteristics with treatment processes.

Sources of Null Results. Another way to state the various key aspects of program evaluation research is to analyze the sources of potential null results, that is evaluation results that show no program effects and thus, at least provisionally, conclude that the programs being evaluated failed to produce the intended effects (see Weiss, 1972). Null results can be produced by:

1. *Methods·failure.* The research design may not be adequate to properly isolate the effects produced by the treatment. Statistical power may be inadequate. Outcome measures may be insensitive to treatment effects or the wrong measures may be taken. These and related problems represent a failure of the research, not necessarily a failure of the program being evaluated. They must be ruled out before any further statements can be made with confidence about the impact of the program itself.

2. *Implementation failure.* The treatment may not be delivered in sufficient dosage or coverage to have an effect. This might result through failure to deliver the full treatment as intended to all targeted recipients or through application of a potentially effective treatment in a dosage too weak to have results. Problems such as these represent program failure, but at a largely operational level that may have little bearing on the validity of the program concept itself.

3. *Theory failure.* The program concept may be wrong or misleading. Program activities may not, in fact, produce the effects expected even when they are implemented as intended. Program concepts may fail miserably and be discarded as part of trial and error learning about social intervention, or they may fail partially and be the basis for modification or reform that produces more promising approaches.

Current Practice: Some Descriptive Data

Forceful articulation of the essential features of adequate program evaluation under the experimental paradigm has occurred relatively recently. Moreover, it has only been since about the mid-1970s that program evaluation research has emerged as a distinct specialty field with its own training programs, textbooks, professional organizations, and codified standards for evaluation research practice. This increased disciplinary integrity and self-awareness should result in a steadily improving quality of work. It is illuminating, therefore, to assess recent program evaluation practice within the experimental paradigm against the five key research considerations described above.

The authors of this chapter and those who assisted them (known collectively as the Program Evaluation Research Group) have been engaged in an ongoing project to identify, sample, and describe published evaluation studies of recent vintage. Data from that project can be used to characterize current practice with regard to research design, statistical power, measurement sensitivity, treatment implementation, and program theory. We will first describe the general nature of that project and then review the pertinent findings.

Methods and Procedures. Using a broad and thorough search strategy, program evaluation studies listed in the 1978–1980 volumes of *Psychological Abstracts, Sociological Abstracts,* and *The Current Index to Journals in Education* were first identified and compiled into a master bibliography. A study was identified as program evaluation if it met two criteria: (1) that there be a distinct program or policy designed and implemented to accomplish some social purpose, and (2) that the study present a more or less systematic assessment of at least some of the accomplishments of that program. In other words, there had to be a program and there had to be some sort of evaluation of it.

The bibliography of 617 items that resulted was stratified by general program area (for example, mental health, education) and a random sample of 205 references was drawn proportionately across the strata. A sustained attempt was then made to locate and photocopy each sampled article. To date, 198 of the sampled articles have been obtained, 97 percent of the total. Of those, 30 were judged not to meet the criteria for program evaluation research when the full report was examined and these were eliminated from the sample.

Each of the remaining 168 reports was then read by one of the members of the Program Evaluation Research Group, all of whom were familiar with program evaluation research, and the characteristics of the research were coded onto a form that assessed program context, treatment implementation, measurement, design, program outcome, author conclusions, overall quality, and related matters (a total of 148 variables). This coding form had been developed after examining the schemes used by other researchers (Gordon and Morse, 1975) and thoroughly discussing the issues among the members of the Program Evaluation Research Group. It was pilot tested on a sample of ten of the articles and minor adjustments in wording and format were made. An assessment of the reliability of the coding was made by having a second coder recode 18 of the reports drawn randomly. The mean agreement between coders over the 148 variables and the 18 articles at that point was 85 percent. The coding categories producing the largest coder disagreements were subsequently reviewed, redefined after discussion, and all studies were recoded on those items using the clarified definitions. Seven of the 168 articles coded reported two different evaluation research studies, each of which was coded separately, making a total of 175 studies in the analysis.

Results. We note first the dominance of the experimental paradigm and its variations in the methodological approach taken by the studies in our sample (see Table 1). Recall that our definition of what constituted program evaluation research was liberal, with no specification of appropriate methodology. Indeed, we particularly wanted to represent qualitative and unconventional approaches. Despite that inclusive sampling, more than two-thirds of the research designs were of a quantitative-comparative sort,

Table 1. Methodological Approach Taken in the Total Sample of Studies

	Number of Studies	Proportion of Total
Quantitative-Comparative		
Randomized experiments	33	
Quasi-experiments	69	
Prepost comparisons	20	
Subtotal	122	.70
Other		
Comparison against goals/history	18	
No performance baseline	17	
Qualitative	18	
Subtotal	53	.30
TOTAL	175	

modeled more or less on one of the now notorious Campbell and Stanley (1966) designs. The remaining studies were characterized by relative neglect of the internal validity issues that so concerned Campbell and Stanley. Many of them were qualitative outright or, if they presented quantitative information, made no attempt to construct a comparison baseline or judge cause-and-effect issues, that is, compared quantitative information against administratively set goals or previous program performance.

Whether the author was affiliated with an academic institution had no relationship with the type of design utilized nor did program area (for example, mental health, education). However, the relationship of the evaluator to the program was significantly associated with the type of design (Chi-square (9, $N = 175$) = 25.30, $p < .01$). The pattern of relationships indicated that when the evaluator had been the designer of the program, the evaluation was much more likely to utilize a stronger experimental design. Also, the type of design was related to the timing with which the evaluation was instigated (Chi-square (12, $N = 175$) = 35.49, $p < .01$). Those evaluations begun after the program had been established for any length of time were more likely to be weaker quasi-experimental designs.

What follows is a close examination of the characteristics of the subset of 122 studies that approached the program evaluation research task with quantitative-comparative methodology, that is, the experimental paradigm. We will look in turn at each of the five components—research design, statistical power, measurement sensitivity, treatment implementation, and program theory—espoused above as essential aspects of adequate evaluation research under that paradigm.

Research design. Most of the research designs employed in the sample of program evaluation studies conducted under the experimental paradigm

Table 2. Characteristics of the Research Design for Studies
Using the Experimental Paradigm (N=122)

	Number of Studies	Proportion of Total
Type of Design		
Randomized experiment	33	.27
Quasi-experiment	69	.57
Regression-discontinuity	1	.01
Time series	10	.08
Nonequivalent comparison	58	.48
Prepost "nonexperiment"	20	.16
Convergent Designs		
Single design alone	68	.56
Single design with supplement	40	.33
Multiple design, treatment variations	2	.02
Multiple design, same treatment	11	.09
Other	1	.01

were quasi-experimental comparisons (see Table 2). Among the quasi-experimental designs, most were nonequivalent comparisons, by far the weakest and most difficult to analyze and interpret (see Reichardt, 1979). Altogether, the weaker design categories (nonequivalent and prepost comparisons) were used in almost two-thirds of the studies; the remaining one-third were randomized experiments or stronger quasi-experimental designs (regression-discontinuity or time-series). Furthermore, most of the studies relied on only a single design and comparison, possibly with some noncomparative supplementary data collection (a client satisfaction survey). Only 11 percent used multiple designs to try to demonstrate convergent results or examine treatment variations.

Statistical Power. Only nine of the 122 quantitative-comparative studies included any mention of the statistical power of the research design and analysis that was employed to investigate program effects. The massive silence on this issue cannot, however, be interpreted to mean that statistical power was not a relevant question. On the contrary, even under generous assumptions power appeared to be quite low for the preponderance of studies. Table 3 reports the percentile distribution of the comparison group sample size for the studies reviewed and the associated statistical power under assumptions of different effect sizes, two-group t-test comparison, and conventional .05 alpha levels. Statistical power is presented in Table 3 as beta, the probability of obtaining statistical significance given that there was a true effect of specified magnitude. The effect size categories suggested by Cohen (1977) as representing "small" (1 percent of variance), "medium" (6 percent), and "large" (14 percent) effects in social science research were used to provide a range for the potential effects under investigation.

Table 3. Distribution of Comparison Group Sample Size
and Associated Statistical Power for Studies
Using the Experimental Paradigm (Alpha = .05)

Sample Size Percentile	Sample Size	Statistical Power for Assumed Effect Sizes (% Variance)		
		"Small" 1 percent	"Medium" 6 percent	"Large" 14 percent
10	7	.07	.15	.31
20	11	.07	.20	.43
30	17	.09	.29	.62
40	27	.11	.43	.82
50	39	.14	.58	.94
60	59	.19	.76	.99
70	90	.26	.91	>.99
80	116	.33	.96	>.99
90	209	.53	>.99	
100	3735	>.99	>.99	>.99
Expected proportion of significant results if there were true effects in all studies		.28	.63	.81

(beta = .80 and beta = .95 step indicators shown at right of "Large" column)

Cohen suggested beta = .80 as a reasonable level for statistical power in general social science research, that is, a .20 chance of Type II error along with the conventional .05 chance of Type I error. As noted earlier, a case can be made that Type II errors in program evaluation are much more serious than in nonapplied research and statistical power levels should accordingly be kept higher, perhaps as high as .95.

Table 3 shows that by either standard the statistical power of the evaluation studies published in recent literature fell far short. For detection of relatively small effects or, equivalently, larger effects in high noise environments, more than 90 percent of the statistical comparisons reported fell short of the desirable power level. Sixty percent of the comparisons had less than one chance in five of detecting a small effect. Even for effects of medium size, statistical power fell below the recommended .80 level for more than 60 percent of the studies. In short, most of the evaluation studies represented in this sample had very limited ability to detect program effects on the order of magnitude that social programs are most likely to produce under field conditions.

Given the demonstrably low statistical power of the comparisons made in the recent program evaluation literature, we would expect a high proportion of null results. We coded each study in our sample to indicate whether the majority of the treatment vs. control comparisons reported showed statistically significant effects or null effects. Overall, 63 percent of the studies reported a majority of statistically significant effects and the remaining 37 percent reported a majority of null effects. Curiously, these are about the proportions we would expect under the available power levels if every program did in fact have an effect of medium size. Since universal program effectiveness of that order of magnitude seems somewhat unlikely, we presume that other factors are influencing the results. Two factors capable of upwardly biasing the proportion of positive results come readily to mind. First, since the sample represented published studies, there is the possibility of publication bias—null results are less likely to be published, whether because of the reluctance of authors or of journal editors. Second, recall that a large number of the studies in this sample used quasi-experimental designs rather than randomized experiments. In many applications, quasi-experiments have been shown to exaggerate program effects in comparison to more carefully controlled experiments (Light, 1983). The evaluation studies of interest here, therefore, most likely show some unknown mix of understatement of program effects because of low statistical power and overstatement of effects because of frequent use of quasi-experimental designs and bias against publishing null results.

Measurement. A variety of types of dependent measures were used in the sampled evaluation studies, with psychometric tests and survey questionnaire items most frequent (see Table 4). Fewer than half of the studies used a dependent measure without alteration that had been used previously in other research; almost 40 percent of the studies used one or more measures that had been developed ad hoc for the evaluation with no reported pretesting or validation. Most striking was the general failure to report or demonstrate that the fundamental properties of the measures used were adequate for evaluation purposes. More than 70 percent of the studies made no mention of the reliability of any of the measures, 81 percent made no mention of the validity of the measures, and 93 percent made no mention of the sensitivity of the measures to the expected program effects.

On the other hand, the use of multiple dependent measures to broaden the coverage of outcome variables was quite common. Nearly all of the studies (90 percent) used more than one dependent measure and many of those had multiple follow-up measures at various stages after treatment. About one-third of the studies used multiple measures of the same outcome construct to produce some measurement triangulation on important

Table 4. Characteristics of the Dependent Measures in Studies Using the Experimental Paradigm

	Number of Studies	Proportion of Total
Type of at Least One Measure Used		
Psychometric	48	.39
Criterion referenced	21	.17
Survey item	52	.43
Judgment rating	27	.22
Behavioral observation	25	.20
Records or reports	38	.31
Qualitative	8	.07
Source of at Least One Dependent Measure		
Developed/Used by others	54	.44
Adapted from others	18	.15
Developed ad hoc, pretested	33	.27
Developed ad hoc, not pretested	48	.39
Measurement Properties Described or Demonstrated		
Reliability	33	.27
Validity	23	.19
Sensitivity	8	.07
Use of Multiple Measures		
Multiple dependent measures	110	.90
Analyzed individually	100	.82
Multivariate analysis	10	.08
Construct triangulation	41	.34

Note: There were multiple responses allowed on the items in this table so the total in each case exceeds 122. The proportion column reports the proportion of the 122 studies with each response.

variables. Very few of the studies, however, provided a multivariate analysis of the multiple measures, making it difficult to tell the extent of their overlap or redundancy. Results were typically reported individually for each of a series of measures that were probably not truly independent.

Treatment Implementation. The question of interest with regard to the sample of program evaluation studies under examination here is whether the implementation of treatment was monitored and reported in sufficient detail to document its strength and integrity in each respective application. The importance of this matter is greater to the extent that the treatments were complex and administered on a variety of occasions. Under such circumstances, there is considerable opportunity for variation or dilution in

Table 5. Complexity of Treatment in Studies Using the Experimental Paradigm

	Number of Studies	Proportion of Total
Simple, administered only once	4	.03
Simple, administered on multiple occasions	21	.17
Complex, administered only once	5	.04
Complex, administered on multiple occasions	92	.75

the actual treatment application from case to case. For example, if the treatment consists only of a one-time administration of a standard drug dosage, we need only know the proportion of the target group to whom the dose was given to ensure adequate treatment implementation. If the treatment is more variable and administered over multiple occasions, such as in psychotherapy, much more information is required to establish that the treatment as delivered maintained adequate strength and integrity.

Table 5 reports the categorization of the studies sampled according to the potential variability of treatment. For each program, a judgment was made with regard, first, to the complexity of the treatment, that is, how much room there was for variation from one application to another, and, second, whether it was administered on more than one occasion. Three-fourths of the studies involved treatments that were judged to be both complex and multiply administered—the very circumstance that can permit great variation in the actual amount of treatment delivered to individual recipients.

Given the possibility of great variation in the delivery of treatment in the typical program, information regarding the level and extent of treatment implementation for the sampled studies is quite pertinent. To code what type of information was reported, we dimensionalized treatment into the following five factors: (1) how many clients received it, (2) the proportion of clients who dropped out before treatment was complete, (3) the amount of treatment received (hours of contact), (4) the duration or timing of the treatment (once a week, ten week period), and, (5) the elements or components of the treatment (methadone, counseling, home visits). For each factor, we further distinguished between the reporting of facts, that is, observations and measures of what actually occurred, and the reporting of treatment format, that is, statements about the treatment plan or intent without reference to how well it was actually fulfilled. For example, a program described as weekly counseling sessions over a ten week period is reporting a treatment plan or format. But, a statement that clients received an average of 11.3 hours of counseling each over an average of 8.7 sessions reports factual information about the treatment implementation.

Table 6 presents the data regarding what was reported on each of the

Table 6. Treatment Implementation Information in Studies Using the Experimental Paradigm

Information Reported	Number of Studies	Proportion of Total
Number of Clients		
Facts	89	.75
Format only	8	.07
Neither	22	.19
Attrition from Treatment		
Facts	43	.36
Format only	4	.03
Neither	72	.61
Amount/Intensity of Treatment		
Facts	32	.27
Format only	44	.37
Neither	43	.36
Duration/Timing of Treatment		
Facts	41	.34
Format only	46	.39
Neither	32	.27
Elements/Components of Treatment		
Facts	33	.28
Format only	42	.35
Neither	44	.37

Note: N=119; information unavailable for three studies.

five treatment factors for those evaluation studies in the sample. The only item reported factually for a majority of the studies was the number of clients served by the program. Well less than half of the studies reported factual information regarding attrition from treatment, amount of treatment, duration or timing of treatment, or the components of treatment. Format information was provided somewhat more frequently, with the exception of attrition, but that still left sizeable proportions of the sample that reported neither format nor facts on these factors.

Another way to depict how the evaluation studies in the sample handled the possibility of variability in the delivery of treatment to the targeted recipients is to describe the nature of the independent variable that was actually entered into the design and analysis. The independent variable, of course, represents the treatment level, usually a dichotomy encoding the treatment group vs. control group contrast. Such a dichotomy, however, assumes that each member of the treatment group received the same treatment and each member of the control group received none. If variability

Table 7. Representation of the Treatment as an Independent Variable in Studies Using the Experimental Paradigm

	Number of Studies	Proportion of Total
Categorical	103	.84
Group variable, one group	24	.20
Group variable, multiple groups	79	.65
Differentiated	19	.16
Metric treatment variable	8	.07
Multivariate representation	11	.09

in treatment delivery is expected, the independent variable can be measured in metric form, that is, varying over a continuum of values, or even represented in multivariate form combining various separately measured treatment dimensions. As Table 7 shows, the treatment variable in the sample of studies was generally defined categorically with no further differentiation of the actual amount of treatment received. Only 16 percent of the sampled studies used a more differentiated metric or multivariate representation of the treatment variable.

Program Theory. As Table 5 showed, almost none of the evaluations in our sample of studies investigated the relatively unvarying, one-shot type of intervention. Most of the treatments were complex and multifaceted (psychotherapy, math curriculum). Individuals receiving the treatment probably encountered a variety of experiences and uniform treatment effects would not be expected across all individuals. Furthermore, most of the treatments included in this analysis were extended in time, requiring multiple administrations to complete the program and thus introducing issues of sequencing effects, temporal variation of treatment, and potential interaction effects across the series of treatment events. From this perspective, the issue of program theory is quite relevant—most of the programs actually evaluated did not provide simple structured treatments that could be expected to work through readily apparent mechanisms.

While program theory has received increasing emphasis in the literature (Chen and Rossi, 1981, 1983), we know of no well-developed classification scheme that defines the nature and form of program theory that can be expected in evaluation studies. Our first task, therefore, was to derive inductively, from our own sample of evaluation studies, some framework for recognizing and differentiating types of program theory.

We found that four characteristics of the program description helped discriminate between different levels of theoretical sophistication. One such characteristic was the degree of explication of the intervention, that is, how well the individual program elements making up the intervention were described. The second issue was whether the program was described primarily in terms of operations and procedures, intervention strategies and philosophies, or general constructs and concepts. A third characteristic was the extent to which there was a delineation of the causal sequences relating program elements—whether the elements of intervention and outcome were related to each other in some sort of causal sequence or simply listed in more or less disconnected fashion. Finally, we found it important to note whether the program description invoked concepts specific to the particular program context or if it was placed in a larger conceptual/theoretical context.

What emerged from our application of these distinctions was a classification scheme for program theory comprised of the following categories and subcategories:

Nontheoretical

Black Box Treatments. Virtually no information on the program was provided other than a descriptive label. No rationale was given as to why the intervention should work or what elements combined to form the intervention. Example: Crisis counseling was provided to all treatment participants.

Sub-Theoretical

Program Strategy. Studies describing programs in this category reported a treatment strategy that was framed largely in terms of operational or service goals with little reference to the outcomes expected for clients. The program was structured around some quality of service standards and separable program components, but presented no explanation of how providing service at that standard would produce the desired impact. Example: The crisis counseling consisted of an attempt to reach the family quickly, a focus on and support of the battered spouse, and appropriate referral for followup treatment.

Program Principles. Studies judged to fall into this category presented general statements about the treatment and the assumed effects but no explanation of the details or the reasons why the treatment was believed to produce the expected effects. The program appeared, therefore, to be based on a belief or principle that was itself neither analyzed nor demonstrated. Example: Crisis counseling was provided to raise self-esteem and improve family communication.

Theoretical

Hypothesis Testing. In this category, programs framed their efforts in terms of specific formulations linking elements of the program to desired outcomes. However, the framework was somewhat ad hoc, of limited scope, and applicable primarily to the

Table 8. Theory Types Found in Studies Using the
Experimental Paradigm

	Number of Studies		Proportion of Total
Nontheoretical			
Black-box	23		.19
Subtheoretical	55		.46
Program strategy		29	.24
Program principles		26	.22
Theoretical	35		.29
Hypothesis testing		24	.20
Integrated theory		11	.09
Unclassified	6		.05

Note: N=119; information unavailable for three studies.

specific program under investigation. It was represented most clearly by studies that did hypothesis testing on the particular independent and dependent variables measured in the evaluation. Example: Testing whether support to the battered spouse raised self-esteem scores, lowered willingness to tolerate physical abuse, and so on.

Integrated Theory. Program descriptions classified in this category provided an a priori theory within which the specific formulation of program elements, rationale, and causal linkages was embedded. The program theory was more general than the specific application represented by the program under investigation and was derived from some source other than the experience or folk wisdom of the program personnel or the evaluation researchers. Example: Social learning theory as a basis for developing techniques of assertiveness training for battered spouses.

With this classification scheme in hand, we were able to provide some review of the level of program theory reflected in our sample of evaluation studies. Table 8 presents the classification of the studies into the theory types defined above. Note, however, that the results indicate the level at which program theory was described in published evaluation studies. Whether those descriptions represented the actual level of theoretical thinking embodied in the program cannot be determined from our data.

As Table 8 indicates, approximately two-thirds of the sample of studies failed to reflect a theoretical basis any higher than what we called "Sub-theoretical." Fewer than one out of ten of the studies were judged to provide an "integrated theory" to describe the program and nearly one in five presented "black boxes." Moreover, the lack of theory development appeared to be widespread throughout the evaluation community. For example, whether the primary author of the evaluation had an academic affiliation made no difference (Chi-square (4, $N = 108$) = 4.72, $p > .30$), nor did program area (for example, mental health, education) show any relation to level of program theory (Chi-square (16, $N = 90$) = 13.94, $p > .60$).

Conclusions

The experimental paradigm, dominant in evaluation research, is primarily concerned with investigating the causal relationships between programs viewed as social interventions and their effects on recipients. Proper assessment of such relationships requires a research design capable of isolating any true causal effects, adequate statistical power to detect real effects, measures sensitive to those effects, an actual and relatively complete implementation of the treatment so that whatever effects are possible will in fact be produced, and some information about, or at least investigation of, the mechanism by which the effects are produced.

The conclusion emerging from analysis of the present sample of evaluation studies is that evaluation research under the experimental paradigm is largely conducted at a level of marginal methodological and conceptual quality. Inferentially weak designs predominated, and the reliability, validity, and sensitivity of dependent measures were rarely demonstrated. Lack of statistical power compromised many studies, even if otherwise well designed, and precluded confident statements about program effects. Moreover, while most of the programs evaluated involved relatively complex treatments administered over multiple occasions, little information regarding the extent of treatment implementation was integrated into the analysis or even reported as background. Additionally, these complex treatments were generally described in such superficial and atheoretical form that little understanding could be gleaned of the rationale linking the chosen treatment to the expected results. The net result of these various deficiencies is a program evaluation literature with many of the trappings of scientific study and little of the substance.

One limitation of the present review is that it considered only published studies even though it is likely that the majority of program evaluation research is not formally published. We would suppose, for example, that the unpublished literature contains a lower proportion of experimental and quasi-experimental studies than found in our sample. On that basis, one might judge the experimental paradigm to be less dominant in evaluation research than we have claimed. The selection of such work for publication, however, suggests to us that it is widely viewed as the best work and thus represents a dominant image of evaluation research among practitioners even if not the most common mode. Furthermore, given disproportionate publication of evaluation studies under the experimental paradigm, we think it very unlikely that unpublished studies under that paradigm hold to higher methodological and conceptual standards than those selected by researchers, reviewers, and editors for publication. Our sample, with all its shortcomings, therefore, most probably represents higher standards than generally practiced in evaluation research.

To conclude that most evaluation research is methodologically weak only reaffirms what other reviewers have discovered about less recent work (for example, Bernstein and Freeman, 1975; Gordon and Morse, 1975). The important issue is whether methodologically deficient work in evaluation research is benign in its consequences. Collectively, evaluation research under the experimental paradigm represents our best knowledge about the effects of social programs. Does its low quality distort that knowledge or misrepresent those programs?

The effect of the methodological and conceptual problems described in this review is to render the conclusions of evaluation research highly equivocal. The widespread use of inferentially weak (nonrandomized) research designs is most likely to overestimate rather than underestimate treatment effects (for example, Light, 1983; Wortman and Yeaton, 1983), though clearly that is not always the case (see, Campbell and Erlebacher, 1970). The result of the other factors—measurement insensitivity, low statistical power, inconsistent or incomplete treatment implementation, and lack of understanding of the causal mechanism embodied in the treatment— however, is to lower the estimation of treatment effects; collectively these factors can easily render worthwhile program effects undetectable.

It is tempting to look at these two countervailing sets of factors and hope that they cancel each other out to yield program evaluation conclusions in reasonable accordance with the actual effects of the programs studied. Where judgments about individual programs are concerned, however, no such benign result is likely. Rather, a large and unknown error component is added to the results which only confounds interpretation. Statistically positive outcomes may therefore be spurious, especially if based on weak designs. Perhaps more troubling, statistically null outcomes seem likely to result all too easily from low power, insensitive measures, and weak or incomplete treatment implementation, leaving it uncertain whether it is the program or the research that has failed.

The matter of statistically null results from program evaluation research deserves our close attention. Within the context of social programs and the policymaking that influences them, a null research finding is not merely an academic matter. Few program developers will greet with enthusiasm the claim that their program has no demonstrable effects nor will such programs readily escape the stigma that follows. Their funding, community and political support, and even survival may be negatively affected along with the morale of the program personnel themselves. Perhaps even more serious, the cumulation of erroneous evaluation studies can misdirect public policy and undermine support for whole categories of program initiatives that may in fact be genuinely effective (see Prather and Gibson, 1977).

Finally, we have to consider the long range implications for the evaluation research profession itself. How long will it be possible to engage routinely in weak, narrow research that potentially misrepresents program effects and still maintain credibility with the policy community? As policymakers and program administrators come to learn the limitations and deficiencies of evaluation research as now practiced under the experimental paradigm, their reaction may well be to condemn the whole approach, even when it is well done. Neither social programs, policymakers, nor evaluation researchers themselves are well served by the present ubiquity of feeble implementations of diluted versions of the experimental paradigm.

The lesson we draw from our analysis is that it is time to acknowledge that, despite its current widespread use, the experimental paradigm is not an all-purpose program evaluation methodology. Research under that paradigm requires special circumstances, resources, skills, and a time frame that permits appropriate attention to the details of design, measurement, treatment implementation, and program theory. The exacting nature of this kind of program evaluation research may, in fact, require that it become a largely academic endeavor. The usual demands for evaluation results that are timely and useful within the program setting may preclude the careful, systematic investigation of measures, treatments, and causes necessary to do good research under the experimental paradigm. Furthermore, the history of the most carefully conducted social intervention experiments (for instance, the negative income tax experiments) indicates that even after the evaluation results are reported they must be probed, criticized, and amended by the research community before their validity can be confidently judged.

This is not another polemic against use of the experimental paradigm in program evaluation nor a justification for some allegedly all-purpose alternate approach. It is rather an attempt to take seriously the requirements for valid experimental research under field conditions and avoid the embarrassment of invalid results when those requirements are not met. Our recipe for improving evaluation practice, therefore, is this: Do experimental research under circumstances where causal effects are a paramount issue and the methodological and conceptual requirements for good research can be met. Nothing will improve our general understanding of social programs and the principles of intervention in the social ecology faster than vigorous, causal, theoretically thoughtful, and methodologically sound experimental research. However, in circumstances where causal issues are not paramount or where it is not possible to do good experimental research, some alternative approach outside the experimental paradigm should be chosen in contrast to the current practice of conducting an impoverished, potentially misleading, and intrinsically uninterpretable version of experimental research.

This is not the place to discuss in detail the alternatives to the experimental paradigm that are available, but impressive cases have been made for the insight and understanding of social programs that can be gained through such approaches as studying program process, case flow, service delivery, and so forth in a program monitoring or information system mode (Attkisson and others, 1978), naturalistic observational and survey studies (Guba and Lincoln, 1981), and other such rational-empirical investigations (Cronbach, and others, 1980; Glass and Ellett, 1980; Scriven, 1974). These approaches are generally superior to the experimental paradigm for answering a broad range of important questions about social programs, many of which cannot be handled well within the experimental paradigm.

Eventually, it may be wise to distinguish between program research, which will draw on the power of the experimental paradigm for careful explication of the causal links and theoretical propositions embodied in social programs, and program evaluation, which will use less restrictive approaches to provide prompt, useful information to policy makers and program administrators about the specific programs with which they are concerned. By its very nature, program research may not be amenable to routine application under circumstances where answers are needed quickly or where support for extensive programmatic research is not feasible. And, by its nature, program evaluation may not be capable of answering the ultimate causal question, "Does this social intervention produce the intended effects?" The challenge to the evaluation profession is to know the difference between these approaches and their domains of applicability.

References

Aiken, L. R., "Note on Sensitivity: A Neglected Psychometric Concept." *Perceptual and Motor Skills,* 1977, *45,* 1330.

Attkisson, C. C., Hargreaves, W. A., Horowitz, M. J., and Sorensen, J. E. (Eds.). *Evaluation of Human Service Programs.* New York: Academic Press, 1978.

Bernstein, I. N., and Freeman, H. E. *Academic and Entrepreneurial Research.* New York: Russell Sage, 1975.

Boruch, R. F., and Gomez, H. "Measuring Impact: Power Theory in Social Program Evaluation." In L. Datta and R. A. Perloff (Eds.), *Improving Evaluations.* Beverly Hills, Calif.: Sage, 1979.

Campbell, D. T., and Erlebacher, A. E. "How Regression Artifacts in Quasi-Experimental Evaluations Can Mistakenly Make Compensatory Education Look Harmful." In J. Hellmuth (Ed.), *Compensatory Education: A National Debate.* (Vol. 3). *Disadvantaged Child.* New York: Brunner/Mazel, 1970.

Campbell, D. T., and Stanley, J. C. *Experimental and Quasi-Experimental Designs for Research.* Chicago: Rand McNally, 1966.

Carver, R. P. "Two Dimensions of Tests: Psychometric and Edumetric." *American Psychologist,* 1974, *29,* 512–518.

Chen, H-T., and Rossi, P. H. "The Multi-Goal, Theory-Driven Approach to Evaluation: A Model Linking Basic and Applied Social Science." In H. E. Freeman and M. A. Solomon (Eds.), *Evaluation Studies Review Annual.* (Vol. 6). Beverly Hills, Calif.: Sage, 1981.

Chen, H-T., and Rossi, P. H. "Evaluating with Sense: The Theory-Driven Approach. *Evaluation Review,* 1983, *7,* 283–302.

Cohen, J. *Statistical Power Analysis for the Behavioral Sciences.* New York: Academic Press, 1977.

Cook, T. D., and Campbell, D. T. *Quasi-Experimentation: Design and Analysis Issues for Field Settings.* Chicago: Rand McNally, 1979.

Cronbach, L. J., and Associates. *Toward Reform of Program Evaluation: Aims, Methods, and Institutional Arrangement.* San Francisco: Jossey-Bass, 1980.

Glass, G. V., and Ellett, F. S. "Evaluation Research." *Annual Review of Psychology,* 1980, *31,* 211–228.

Gordon, G., and Morse, E. V. "Evaluation Research." In A. Inkeles, J. Coleman, and N. Smelser (Eds.), *Annual Review of Sociology.* Palo Alto, Calif.: Annual Reviews, 1975.

Guba, E. G., and Lincoln, Y. S. *Effective Evaluation.* San Francisco: Jossey-Bass, 1981.

Light, R. J. "Introduction." In R. J. Light (Ed.), *Evaluation Studies Review Annual.* (Vol. 8). Beverly Hills, Calif.: Sage, 1983.

Lipsey, M. W. "A Scheme for Assessing Measurement Sensitivity in Program Evaluation and Other Applied Research." *Psychological Bulletin,* 1983, *94,* 152–165.

Prather, J. E., and Gibson, F. K. "The Failure of Social Programs." *Public Administration Review,* 1977, *37,* 556–564.

Reichardt, C. S. "The Statistical Analysis of Data from Nonequivalent Group Designs." In T. D. Cook and D. T. Campbell, *Quasi-Experimentation: Design and Analysis Issues for Field Settings.* Chicago: Rand McNally, 1979.

Rutman, L. *Planning Useful Evaluations: Evaluability Assessment.* Beverly Hills, Calif.: Sage, 1980.

Scriven, M. "Evaluation Perspectives and Procedures." In W. J. Popham (Ed.), *Evaluation in Education: Current Applications.* Berkeley, Calif.: McCutchan, 1974.

Sechrest, L., and Redner, R. *Strength and Integrity of Treatments in Evaluation Studies. Evaluation Reports:* Washington, D.C.: National Criminal Justice Reference Service, 1979.

Sechrest, L., West, S. G., Phillips, M. A., Redner, R., and Yeaton, W. H. "Some Neglected Problems in Evaluation Research: Strength and Integrity of Treatments." In L. Sechrest, S. G. West, M. A. Phillips, R. Redner, and W. H. Yeaton (Eds.), *"Evaluation Studies Review Annual.* (Vol. 4). Beverly Hills, Calif.: Sage, 1979.

Sechrest, L., and Yeaton, W. H. "Empirical Bases for Estimating Effect Size." In R. F. Boruch, P. M. Wortman, and D. S. Cordray (Eds.), *Reanalyzing Program Evaluations.* San Francisco: Jossey-Bass, 1981.

Sechrest, L., and Yeaton, W. H. "Magnitudes of Experimental Effects in Social Science Research." *Evaluation Review,* 1982, *6,* 579–600.

Weiss, C. H. *Evaluation Research: Methods of Assessing Program Effectiveness.* Englewood Cliffs, N.J.: Prentice Hall, 1972.

Wholey, J. S. "Evaluability Assessment." In L. Rutman (Ed.), *Evaluation Research Methods: A Basic Guide.* Beverly Hills, Calif.: Sage, 1977.

Wortman, P. M., and Yeaton, W. H. "Synthesis of Results in Controlled Trials of Coronary Artery Bypass Graft Surgery." In R. J. Light (Ed.), *Evaluation Studies Review Annual.* (Vol. 8). Beverly Hills, Calif.: Sage, 1983.

Yeaton, W. H., and Sechrest, L. "Critical Dimensions in the Choice and Maintenance of Successful Treatments: Strength, Integrity, and Effectiveness. *Journal of Consulting and Clinical Psychology,* 1981, *49,* 156–167.

Mark W. Lipsey is professor of psychology at Claremont Graduate School. He has conducted evaluations of juvenile delinquency treatment and a variety of other human service programs. His recent work focuses on methodological issues in program evaluation.

Scott Crosse is an evaluator in the Program Evaluation and Methodology Division at the U.S. General Accounting Office, Washington, D.C. He is also a doctoral candidate in the Department of Psychology at Claremont Graduate School. (The statements and opinions expressed in this chapter do not represent official U.S. General Accounting Office policy.)

Jan Dunkle is staff development coordinator for Charter Oak Hospital, a medical care facility in Covina, California. She is also a doctoral candidate in the Psychology Program at Claremont Graduate School.

John Pollard is a doctoral candidate in the psychology program at Claremont Graduate School. He has conducted research on counseling services and is currently interested in evaluation methodology and program theory.

Gordon Stobart is a doctoral candidate in the psychology program at Claremont Graduate School. He has recently completed a study of the social interaction of mainstreamed learning disabled children in the public schools.

7

Do Not Cry Wolf Until You Are Sure
The Manufactured Crises in Evaluation Research
James F. Gilsinan and L. Carl Volpe

ABSTRACT

This article argues that the so-called crisis in evaluation is phenomenological rather than empirical. That is, our statements about evaluation, the presentational strategies used to define our expertise, and the ceremonies surrounding the dissemination of results are more problematic than what it is we actually do. If we can avoid calling attention to imaginary wolves, people might well listen when we do have something to say.

Introduction

The story of the boy who cried wolf once too often provides an uncomfortable example of what manufactured crises can do to those who rely on them for care, concern, and attention. There are short-term gains, but in the long run the too frequent and premature sounding of an alarm creates a situation ripe for disaster. Nobody pays attention when there is something truly urgent and important to convey. Evaluation may be well on its way toward creating just such a situation for itself.

In this article, the phrase "crying wolf" refers to the increasing propensity for describing problems of evaluation research in terms that suggest the field has reached a crucial stage or turning point. Such crisis literature demands choices that will seemingly dictate either future directions for evaluation research or, indeed, whether there will be a future. To facilitate these decisions, the literature will often present two or more clearly distinguished options and then argue for a particular one. The correct choice will solve the specific problem under consideration while the incorrect choice will severely hamper

---

* To whom all correspondence should be addressed.

0032–2678/84/$ 03.00 © 1984 Elsevier Science Publishers B.V.

Originally published in *Policy Sciences* Vol. 17 (1984) pp. 179-191. Reprinted by permission of Elsevier Science Publishers B.V., Amsterdam.

the field. Examples of crying wolf can be found in discussions pertaining to methodology (Weiss and Rein, 1969; Guba, 1978; Palumbo and Nachmias, 1983), to programmatic efficacy (Prather and Gibson, 1977; Hackler, 1978), and to the appropriate relationship among evaluators, policymakers, and administrators (Cronbach and Associates, 1980; Chelimsky, 1982). This last body of literature is primarily concerned with the utilization of evaluation results by those in authority.

While much of this literature has been useful in defining the problems and prospects of the evaluation enterprise, taken as a whole it portrays a field "undergoing an identity crisis . . . Instead of a dominant paradigm, several alternative approaches to evaluation have emerged and skepticism about its potential contributions to public policy has been raised" (Palumbo and Nachmias, 1983: 67).

This article rejects the notion that evaluation is in an objective state of crisis. It argues instead that our statements about evaluation, the presentational strategies used to define our expertise, and the ceremonies surrounding the dissemination of results are more problematic than what it is we actually do. In short, the "crisis" is an artifact of how we think about and discuss the evaluation enterprise. Confusing these phenomenological issues with objective ones can create the following problems.

First, debates tend to become stagnant and unresolved since there is no clear agreement on the exact nature of the problem to be solved. Second, as both problem definitions and solutions multiply, the field presents outsiders with an image of disorganization and confusion. Literally too much talk about crisis can create crisis. Finally, there is the temptation to adopt solutions that will incorporate as many divergent opinions as possible. This dialectical response can result in inappropriate strategies for carrying out evaluations. This of course will lead to even further perceptions of crisis.

If debates about the field are to bear fruit, those involved need to pay more attention to the way we conceptualize and define our activities, and less attention to the activities themselves. In this way, the strategies of evaluation can be more cogently applied to the world of the policymaker and program manager. If we can avoid calling attention to imaginary wolves, people might well listen when we do have something to say.

Current Debates: A Metaphor Is Not A Fact

Metaphor is a useful device for capturing certain elements of a phenomenon. However, when metaphor, an artifact of human reflection, is taken as fact, it confuses rather than enlightens. In the words of Schuman (1982), a person will then tend "to trip and fall right on his artifact." This certainly seems to be occurring in the field of evaluation. Much of the current discussion and debate is based on a particular metaphor of science. "Science is like a logical recipe for discovering truth." Unfortunately, this metaphor is taken as an actual description of how science gets accomplished. Its unreflective adoption by evaluators can be found lurking in a wide variety of evaluation literature. Historical accounts of the field, methodological debates, strategies to increase utilization of research results, and judgments about the appropriateness of quantitative or qualitative data seem to take this particular image of science for granted. It is this metaphorical hegemony that fuels talk of crisis and what increasingly seems to be unproductive debate.

House (1982), in a brief history of social science, unintentionally both describes the main elements of this metaphor and illustrates the problems with its acceptance as fact. He argues that early practitioners of social science based their new discipline on the natural science model. He connects this image of science with medieval epistemology. Both sought or assumed a single, underlying reality. Within this context, elimination of competing explanations is a necessary, worthwhile endeavor. Further, generalization is a hallmark of this model of science (as it had been in medieval scholasticism). Juxtaposed to this is what House terms humanistic evaluation methods, which can capture elements of a program not available through the scientific mode of investigation. House's concern with the inability of certain techniques to capture certain elements of a program are well taken. To suggest that the scientific mode of investigation is the culprit however, and to deny scientific status to humanistic methods throws out the baby with the bath water. It confuses metaphor with fact. Metaphor's strength, its ability to highlight certain aspects of a phenomenon, becomes an extreme liability if those aspects are taken to be a complete and exhaustive description. The scientific process is neither as simple nor as rigidly deductive and straightforward as House suggests. It can therefore encompass a wider variety of techniques and methods than House allows. Yet, it is this oversimplification that seems to form the background against which the concern about rigorous methods for field investigation and other issues germane to evaluation are debated.

Field research, by definition, is assumed to differ significantly from laboratory procedures. Thus, in the attempt to develop credible results, applied empiricists have sought to make the quasi-experimental method approximate the idealized situation of the laboratory. This strategy, since its inception, has been highly problematic. In a field situation all of the extraneous variables are neither held constant nor allowed to vary randomly. This has obvious implications for the validity of results obtained through a quasi-experimental design. When Campbell and Stanley (1966) systematically examined quasi-experimental methods, they identified seven threats to validity. When the work was expanded by Cook and Campbell (1979), the list was itself expanded to forty-two possible threats to validity. Moreover, Cook and Campbell state in an early section of their book that it is incumbent on the researcher to identify all of the threats to the experiment and interpret the results in light of these possible threats. Clearly, a discussion of all of the threats to validity within the context of evaluation research would undermine the integrity of the results as well as the ability of the researcher to gain the confidence of his policy audience.

Numerous authors have commented on the need to bring the worlds of the researcher and the policy actor closer together in order to increase the use of evaluation findings (Caplan, 1979; Chelimsky, 1982; Lindblom and Cohen, 1979). Yet, researchers have typically responded to utilization problems by attempting to increase the technical sophistication of the quasi-experimental method. This has had the ironic effect of further distancing the world of the research from that of the policymaker. Chelimsky suggests that, indeed, it is an overcommitment to the traditional scientific model that causes evaluators to both concentrate on improving the technical sophistication of their efforts and be less concerned about user needs than they should be:

> But these particular characteristics truth for truth's sake, dependence upon earlier research, focus on other researchers as the essential research user, and autonomy in the conduct of the work have a natural, but perhaps unintended, side-effect. Because they focus so heavily upon the research (or upon the evaluation) and because every emphasis also implies some deprivation (as every economist knows, there are no free lunches), these characteristics lead inevitably to at least some indifference on the researcher's part in the use or application of research findings *when the users are not researchers* (Chelimsky, 1982: 22 23; italics in the original).

The difficulties in applying an idealized version of laboratory experiments to the field have led some qualitative methodologists to reject certain of the basic assumptions attributed to the natural science paradigm, notably concern with generalization and a search for single cause and effect sequences. Qualitative evaluations tend to be largely descriptive in orientation. Policymakers and program operators are somewhat suspicious of such an approach, since it may not immediately suggest what variables can be manipulated to bring about a desired result. There is an irony in this. Policy practitioners seem enamored of the scientific method, yet research on policy organizations indicates that administrators and members of legislative bodies often make the most use of anecdotal data (Deal and Kennedy, 1982; Meltsner and Bellavita, 1983; Nakamura and Smallwood, 1980).

The paradoxical nature of the use of qualitative data and the preference of the policy community for quantitative data provide some evaluation reformers with a seemingly obvious and cogent solution to the question of appropriate methods. To quote Reichardt and Cook (1979: 11):

> Treating the method-types as incompatible obviously encourages researchers to use only one or the other when it may be a combination of the two that is best suited to research needs. It also paralyzes any attempt at reconciling the differences between the opposing sides of the debate over method-types. For these reasons, the conceptualization of the method-types as antagonistic may well be leading astray current methodological debate and practice. It is our view that the paradigmatic perspective which promotes this incompatibility between method-types is in error.

The assumption that method-types are nonparadigmatic is a beguiling alternative to the debate between quantitative and qualitative researchers. This position can only be maintained, however, by overlooking a number of key issues. First, qualitative and quantitative methods assume different things about the nature of social reality (Gilsinan, 1973; Wilson, 1970). Second, these different assumptions result in specifically different questions about organizational phenomena and in different ways of assessing program outcomes (Palumbo and Nachmias, 1983). Third, different assumptions, questions, and assessment routines result in different professional commitments and practice (Cronbach, 1980; Carton and Harmon, 1981). Last, given all of these differences, it is unclear whether the types of information generated by the two approaches are in fact so easily reconcilable. A case study by M. G. Trend (1979) in the same volume as the Reichardt and Cook article demonstrates the difficulties of assuming that different methods will yield a neat dovetailing of information. Moreover, Trend (1979: 68–69) states:

> Different analyses, each based upon a different form of information, should be kept separate until late in the analytic game. Alternative explanations should be allowed to "mature" and gain adherents and defenders. Then, the stories should be compared. If the accounts mesh, this provides an independent test of the validity of the research. If they do not, the areas of disagreement will provide points at which further analytical leverage can be exerted.

Although Trend suggests that a synthesis of competing explanations should eventually be attempted, he makes clear that qualitative and quantitative methods should maintain their separate identities (i.e., paradigmatic anchors) if analysis is to be as strong as possible. Synthesis should be at the level of competing, case-by-case explanations, not paradigms. This approach is of course less parsimonious and more conflict-ridden than either abandoning or melding paradigms. But, at least in its literature about itself, the evaluation community seems uncomfortable with ambiguity, conflict, and the general lack of robust findings. Such things are not the stuff of science, or so we have been led to believe by confusing our metaphor of science with its actuality. Thus, we perceive crises where none may exist, and in the process face the real danger of "falling on our artifact."

The Different Worlds We Live In

The phenomenological predicament described above is not entirely of our own making. The model of natural science that we sometimes unconsciously adopt is one that has served science well in its battle for legitimacy. Science has itself tended to idealize its processes when seeking to establish and expand its domains of influence. Such idealization involves moving from metaphor to myth (Sarbin, 1972; Edelman, 1977). The phrase "science is like a logical recipe for discovering truth," becomes, "science *is* a logical recipe for discovering *truth*."

The anthropologist Claude Levi-Strauss (1963) notes that myths allow individuals to live with the inherent contradictions of social life. Robert Merton (1973) argues from the sociological perspective that social institutions are a composite of "potentially conflicting pairs of norms." Merton goes on to argue that the social organization of science does not escape such ambivalence. Thomas F. Gieryn (1983) provides compelling evidence for this observation in a review of three scientific controversies. He concludes by specifying the several antinomies his examples illustrate:

> . . . scientific knowledge is at once theoretical and empirical, pure and applied, objective and subjective, exact and estimative, democratic (open for all to confirm) and elitist (experts alone confirm), limitless and limited (to certain domains of knowledge) (Gieryn, 1983: 792).

The myth of science has functioned to hide these antinomies, and, as Gieryn shows, thereby contributed to its success when threatened or challenged by competing systems.

Evaluation, of course, shares these antinomies by virtue of its imaging the procedures of science. But since it is specifically applied in orientation, its practice highlights a particular set of opposing impulses. Concern about theory and method underscores the tension between knowledge and utility. Worry about whether or how results of our efforts get used by those in decisionmaking positions raises the issue of the entrepreneurial role versus the scientist role. Questions of program efficacy highlight the tension between the roles of diagnostician and judge. Unfortunately, our current myth of science, its history, and its methods have hindered our ability to constructively deal with the antinomies of our practice, both those we have inherited and those unique to evaluation. We have become unwitting victims of the mythology of science. We need to reconsider this myth to more creatively deal with the issues that confront us. This is particularly true if we are to be successful in convincing others of the legitimacy of our enterprise. These points can be illustrated by a brief analysis of how the laboratory actually functions in scientific research.

Weick (1969) developed the notion of an enacted environment. Within any environment, individuals pay attention to only a select number of elements in the total milieu and thereby develop a selected context for their action. In this way individuals literally create their own environments within organizations. By applying this concept to the actual process of conducting laboratory experiments, one can avoid an overly idealized view of how "pure" research gets done.

Laboratory research occurs in an enacted environment. The researcher, in an effort to isolate a causal sequence, attempts to control and eliminate all alternative sources of explanation for an observed effect. This is done, of course, through explicit random variation or control. Indeed, as Binder and Geis (1983) remark, the amount of control exercised over extraneous variables defines the laboratory. What is generally not acknowledged in the archival literature is the iterative process within each experiment. The laboratory and thus the final experiment is literally created through repetitive testing as the researcher successfully isolates and eliminates confounding variables. In some cases each iteration is a new pilot test, in other cases, changes in the procedure may occur after one subject is tested. Put another way, the researcher progressively pays attention to elements in the environment that must be controlled to obtain the conditions of a successful experiment.

The nature of the publication rituals within laboratory-oriented sciences, however, clouds the enacted components of such experiments and contributes to the myth which extols the elegance and simplicity of the scientific method. The published article gives a simple precise description of the final experiment, identifying relevant variables which led to the result, i.e., the successful experiment. The process of creating the experiment, of eliminating the numerous extraneous variables, and most important, the iterative process, are glossed. One result of this practice is that laboratory techniques appear more successful than they are, and the techniques appear simpler to apply than is actually the case. The myth is further perpetuated by the bias against publishing negative results in the professional journals.

Since the culture of natural science dictates that much of its activity takes place in private, through controls exercised by the laboratory scientist, its antinomies are often hidden from public view. Science appears more objective and exact, in short "purer," than it actually is. Such appearances are beguiling - both to the general public and to the social science evaluation community. Science provides a method for discovering a single truth, a method for successfully eliminating alternative hypotheses, a method for establishing expert judgments about programs and their effects. When the reality of field research falls dismally short of expectations, we then criticize how we do what we do, rather than how we conceptualize and talk about what we do. Natural scientists and evaluative scientists do very similar things. What differ are the presentational strategies of the two groups. As a result, we live in phenomenologically different worlds, ours appearing more subjective, estimative, contaminated, sloppy and soft.

Three crucial points contained in the above argument must be underscored. First, our world is contaminated, sloppy, subjective, and soft, but so is the world of traditional science. Second, their world is occasionally capable of exacting, objective, "pure" findings, but so is ours. Finally, antinomies are not resolved. They exist side by side. The trick is developing appropriate repertoires for the circumstances in which we find ourselves. This means stressing one or the other of a conflicting pair of elements in response to the context of activity.

Implications of Phenomenological Reform

We have seen that the dissemination ceremonies of laboratory science gloss the iterative nature of the process. As a consequence, more knowledge appears to be generated from this process than is actually the case. But, is the pursuit of knowledge a primary goal for evaluators?

Meltsner and Bellavita (1983) note the distinction between data, information, and knowledge. Data are simply observations about phenomena. Information is data that are meaningful to an administrator or researcher because they suggests a next likely step in a progression toward a goal. Knowledge lays out all of the previously verified steps to a given end. Most of what the laboratory scientist discovers is in the nature of data and information. Most of what he or she reports is in the nature of knowledge. The policy evaluator also discovers mostly data and information. But unlike his laboratory counterpart, the culture of evaluation dictates that data and information be publicly reported and discussed directly.

Social policy is fundamentally a political phenomenon directed by normative decisionmaking. There are no "ultimate truths" for social policy, only prevailing perceptions. Answers to social problems, right or wrong, come from the political process. The social scientist working in this arena has an obligation to contribute to informed public debate (Cronbach and Associates, 1980). This can be done by isolating and specifying alternative explanations of issues under examination: providing data and information.

As the iterative process refines the basic science experiment, the iterative process is also used for developing social policy. Within this framework, Cook and Campbell's argument that threats to validity must be articulated by the social policy evaluator takes on a somewhat different meaning. The evaluator must observe and describe alternative explanations, recognize their importance, and not make apologies for being unable to eliminate them. Rather, he or she can describe the likely consequences of alternative explanations for problem definition, program interventions, and ameliorations, given particular policy contexts. Articulation of alternative explanations in this manner makes for a more credible evaluation, a better informed policy actor and direction for the next iteration.

Such an approach has consequences for the question of the efficacy of social programs. The evaluator should be less concerned about whether his or her study will ultimately determine if the program is successful. Attention should be refocused to how results of a study can be effectively presented to contribute to the larger debate, since public debate is the only true forum for determining if the social policy is consistent with current norms.

Most program evaluations provide information about the next most likely or reasonable step. Both evaluators and policy actors err when they attempt to equate such information with knowledge. Normative questions, those that seek information, can never be answered with ultimate answers, those that provide knowledge. When this is attempted, questions of program efficacy assume a greater degree of significance than is warranted and the policy actor becomes an unwilling victim of the misapplication of the scientific method.

All too often, the policy actor assumes that evaluation studies will provide unambiguous knowledge because the evaluator has promised scientific results. This expectation is reasonable since the perception of the scientific method is that it will generate clear results. What is not made clear to the policy actor, and perhaps what is denied or unrecognized by the evaluator, is that science is a process of trial, error, and retrial. The evaluator, though, rarely has the luxury of conducting multiple pilot studies in order to identify the interrelationships among variables. As a result, the evaluation researcher is faced with perhaps a single opportunity to design and implement an experimental study under less than ideal conditions. Given the expectations associated with scientific research, however, this severely truncated procedure is expected to produce results that are decisive and readily usable. When the results are presented, they invariably reflect empirical uncertainty and talk of absolute truth is expeditiously obfuscated.

Policy actors operate in their day-to-day environments without relying on unambiguous knowledge. In fact they seem to operate much as the laboratory scientist. Caplan (1979) notes that upper level executives do use social science, particularly its methodology. The use is overwhelmingly instrumental, that is, applied in the solution of day-to-day problems. Progressive control of relevant variables based on progressively accumulated information is, of course, the enacted laboratory. The point here is that most evaluations of social programs simply require an extension of the activity that administrators engage in on a daily basis, the progressive accumulation of information to guide the implementation of the next step. From this perspective, social programs simultaneously perform two functions. They are a step toward a solution to a problem and a way to accumulate better information (Nakamura and Smallwood, 1980).

The above discussion sheds some light on the apparently contradictory demands of program executives for quantitative data and their seeming neglect of these data in favor of more qualitative presentations. The anecdote is the primary means used by policy-makers and implementors to turn data into information. The anecdote also is used suasively to present information as knowledge. The frustration sometimes engendered in evaluators due to tendencies of policy actors to go beyond the data in their interpreta-tions is due to the former's lack of understanding of the importance of the anecdote. The real dilemma for evaluators is not the apparent contradiction between requests for quantitative procedures and qualitative results. Instead, the evaluator faces the quan-dary of how to provide the full range of stories about a program, avoiding the temptation to use only the single anecdote that gives the appearance of knowledge, when one really has only information or data. Statistical presentations too often give the impression of a single story. This is particularly true of less complex statistical procedures (e.g., means, standard deviations, and simple measures of association). Ironically, however, the more complex and nuanced the statistical data, the more the administrator is tempted to "get to the heart of the matter." These data, too, then encourage the administrator to embellish the exactitude of quantitative results to form a suasive anecdote (Gilsinan, 1984). This issue, rather than whether quantitative or qualitative methods are most appropriate, needs the attention of research practitioners. Both methods can be useful, but quantitative methods become dysfunctional when they give the impression that an authoritative, single story is possible in a multi-story environment. Using each method independently within a single evaluation, as described above, can check this tendency.

The propensity of the policy practitioner to rely on a single story to make a point is understandable. But the evaluator and the policy analyst can also provide a valuable service by suggesting alternative ways of thinking about an issue and, more specifically, the impact of a programmatic intervention. The latter is particularly important given the current national policy environment.

The issue of the efficacy versus the nonefficacy of social programs has itself become a focus of concern for both evaluators and policymakers. This concern underscores the importance of dealing creatively with the antinomies of our practice and being conscious of how we use and report evaluation findings.

In criminal justice the works of Lipton et al. (1975), Fishman (1977), and Lerman (1975), using experimental and quasi-experimental methods, seemingly have demon-strated the nonefficacy of various delinquency and corrections programs. Similarly, negative results have been reported for social interventions in education, mental health, and organizational performance (Prather and Gibson, 1977). The "nothing works" argument has in turn led to pleas to abandon the experimental method in such evaluation projects, since it can lead to dangerously reactionary social policies (Hackler, 1978).

In much of this literature, the evaluators have seemingly chosen to emphasize the role of judge over that of diagnostician. Thus, results are reported as unambiguous findings (i.e., as knowledge) and not as information. The role of diagnostician demands a different form of presentation, one that encourages program administrators and policy-makers to move away from viewing programs in a summative (either it works or it does not) context. Ironically, the role of diagnostician can also move evaluators closer to establishing the basis for social knowledge. This creative balancing or use of the tension between knowledge and utility, judge and diagnostician, demands the integration of social science theory and program evaluation.

Glaser (1980) maintains that theoretically anchoring program evaluations consider-ably lessens the problems of sampling, program application bias, and the theoretical irrelevance of findings. According to Glaser, such problems all too often lead to the false conclusion that social programs are relatively meaningless. Of course, the preponder-ance of negative findings does not endear evaluators to those responsible for these programs.

As noted, though, the image of natural science that informs much of the current debates about the field of evaluation assumes a single underlying reality. Given this metaphor of science, elimination of alternative hypotheses through a deductive method is an appropriate way to proceed. Social science, however, cannot assume a single reality, nor are its theories sufficiently well developed to permit a simple deductive approach in program evaluation. Certainly, construct validity cannot be assumed.

Two approaches to theory based evaluation have been suggested that avoid the problems inherent in a traditional logico-deductive procedure. Only in very small, highly structured demonstrations would the traditional strategy be appropriate. Most large scale demonstrations are, however, simply too complex for such an approach.

Glaser uses an after-the-fact procedure in his re-analysis of evaluations of delinquency treatment programs. Generating hypotheses from traditional criminological theory, he demonstrates that programs had differential impacts on theoretically distinct subcatego-ries of delinquents in the directions predicted by the theory. This re-analysis demon-strates two important points. First, the so-called nonefficacy of social programs may in fact be due to the use of administratively derived rather than theoretically derived categories of the target population. All delinquents are not alike. Treating them as an undifferentiated group may cause a cancelling out of programmatic gains by losses. Certain theoretical categories of delinquents may improve because of a program inter-vention. Other types may be made worse by such an intervention. A nontheoretically differentiated population will, however, show no overall change, since the gains in one group will be cancelled out by the losses in the other group. Second, a post hoc application of theory lessens the inherent problems with construct validity that plague a priori applications in large-scale demonstrations. This procedure, then, might be most useful in reviews of programmatic effects by policy area. Thus, analyses similiar to Glaser's might be carried out to reassess programs in mental health, education, and so on. Such analyses might considerably alter the perception that nothing works.

Chen and Rossi's (1981) "multi-goal, theory driven" strategy for evaluation represents a second approach to using theory in an evaluative context. This application can bring greater structure to what has been termed "goal free" evaluation (Scriven, 1972). It can also be used in an a priori fashion to generate lists of possible outcomes for a program. The authors emphasize the advantages of such an approach for both utilitarian and theoretical concerns:

> Certainly both social science and policy are better served by the ability of the completed evaluation to decide among competing understandings of the social problems or treatments involved. Hence, all the outcomes deemed possible by social science theory and knowledge should constitute the pool out of which outcomes are to be selected for evaluation testing (Chen and Rossi, 1981: 46).

Theory used in the ways described above can provide the policymaker with alternative viewpoints, a method for systematically exploring unintended program consequences, and even better theoretical categories for the development of more sophisticated theory.

Summary

The national policy scene provides an instructive lesson in presentational styles for those concerned with evaluation. President Reagan's critics seem unable to diminish his public image. Pointing out substantive problems with his policies and his fairly numerous misstatements of fact do not appear to affect voters' perceptions of him as an aggressive, competent leader. Style rather than substance has clothed him in what one critic has described as a "Teflon coated" suit. Nothing bad sticks. This provides an obvious contrast with his predecessor, whose style apparently conveyed the image of a president beleaguered and unable to cope with the demands of the job.

Evaluators must pay attention to presentational styles, both when they present specific project findings and when they critique the practice of their profession. Otherwise, policymakers and others who are the consumers of our products may come to believe that we cannot in fact accomplish the tasks we have set for ourselves. The current national policy environment is particularly dangerous for those inclined to cry wolf, i.e., define evaluation research as being in a state of crisis. As Freeman and Solomon (1981) note, existing federal budget policies together with an administration suspicious of social science research, of which evaluation is considered a part, do not bode well for professional expansion. This is particularly true if we ourselves raise doubts about the validity of our professional practice.

We have argued that such doubts are in large part derived from overcommitment to a particular description of how science gets done. As a result, we tend to present our findings measured against a faulty benchmark. In fact both evaluative and normal science fall short of this image. Publication rituals in traditional science, however, gloss the antinomies of the actual process of gaining knowledge. Therefore, in our public presentations we need to accentuate the positive and the possible. Judicious use of social science theory can help in searching out the former and in structuring our discussion of the latter. And, as we discuss the state of the field, we should perhaps adopt the sentiments expressed by the renowned physicist, Peter Carruthers:

There are basically two kinds of scientists. Some believe we will solve all the riddles, and that our understanding will converge. Others experience the fact that every time you understand one thing, 10 more questions pop up. Tempermentally, I've always belonged to that second group. I don't believe there's an end point at which all science is aimed. You have to be happy with the joy of insight, and hopefully sharing it with your colleagues. Science is not the pursuit of this undefinable thing called truth. It's more the process of understanding than the product. The paradox is that we always know more as we expand the frontier of uncertainty (quoted in *The New York Times Magazine,* May 6, 1984, p. 62).

Following Carruthers, we in evaluation might profitably adopt a new metaphor to conceptualize what it is we do – "science is like an adventure." Such a metaphor will allow us to be comfortable with confusion and cease seeing wolves where none exist.

References

Binder, Arnold and Gilbert Geis (1983). *Methods of Research in Criminology and Criminal Justice.* New York: McGraw-Hill.

Campbell, D. T. and J. C. Stanley (1966). *Experimental and Quasi-Experimental Designs for Research.* Skokie, IL: Rand McNally.

Caplan, Nathan (1979). "The two-communities theory and knowledge utilization," *American Behavioral Scientist* 22: 459–470.

Carton, Bayard L. and Michael Harmon (1981). "Action theory in practice: toward theory without conspiracy," *Public Administration Review* 41: 535–541.

Chelimsky, Eleanor (1982). "Making evaluations relevant to congressional needs," *GAO Review* 17: 22–27.

Cook, T. D. and D. T. Campbell (1979). *Quasi-Experimentation: Design and Analysis Issues for Field Settings.* Skokie, IL: Rand McNally.

Chen, Huey-Tsyh and Peter H. Rossi (1981). "The multi-goal, theory driven approach to evaluation: a model linking basic and applied social science," in H. E. Freeman and M. A. Solomon (eds.), *Evaluation Studies Review Annual,* vol. 6. Beverly Hills: Sage.

Cronbach, Lee J. and Associates (1980). *Toward Reform of Program Evaluation.* San Francisco: Jossey-Bass.

Deal, Terrence E. and Allan A. Kennedy (1982). *Corporate Cultures: The Rites and Rituals of Corporate Life.* Reading, MA: Addison-Wesley.

Edelman, Murray (1977). *Political Language: Words That Succeed and Policies That Fail.* New York: Academic Press.

Fishman, R. (1977). "An evaluation of criminal recidivism in projects providing rehabilitation and diversion services in New York City," *Journal of Criminal Law and Criminology* 68: 283–305.

Freeman, Howard E. and Marian A. Solomon (1981). "Introduction: evaluation and the uncertain '80's," in H. E. Freeman and M. A. Solomon (eds.), *Evaluation Studies Review Annual,* vol. 6. Beverly Hills: Sage.

Gieryn, Thomas F. (1983). "Boundary-work and the demarcation of science from non-science," *American Sociological Review* 48: 781–795.

Gilsinan, James F. (1973). "Ethnomethodology and symbolic interaction: a comparison," *The Rocky Mountain Social Science Journal* 10: 73–83.

Gilsinan, James F. (1984). "Information and knowledge development potential: the public vs. private sector jobs demonstration project," *Evaluation Review* 8: 371–388.

Glaser, Daniel (1980). "The interplay of theory, issues, policy, and data," in Klein and Teilmann (eds.), *Handbook of Criminal Justice Evaluation.* Beverly Hills: Sage.

Guba, Egon (1978). *Toward A Methodology of Naturalistic Inquiry In Educational Evaluation.* Los Angeles: Center for the Study of Evaluation, U. of Calif.

Hackler, J. C. (1978). *The Prevention of Crime: The Great Stumble Forward.* Toronto: Methuen.

House, E. R. (1982). "Introduction: scientific and humanistic evaluations," in E. R. House (ed.), *Evaluation Studies Review Annual.* Beverly Hills: Sage.

Lerman, P. (1975). *Community Treatment and Social Control.* Chicago: Univ. of Chicago Press.

Levi-Strauss, Claude (1963). *Structural Anthropology.* New York: Basic Books.

Lindblom, Charles E. and David Cohen (1979). *Useable Knowledge*. New Haven: Yale University Press.

Lipton, D., R. Martinson and J. Wilks (1975). *The Effectiveness of Correctional Treatment*. New York: Prager.

Meltsner A. J. and C. Bellavita (1983). *The Policy Organization*. Beverly Hills: Sage.

Merton, Robert (1973). *The Sociology of Science*. Chicago: Univ. of Chicago Press.

Nakamura, R. T. and F. Smallwood (1980). *The Politics of Policy Implementation*. New York: Basic Books.

Palumbo, Dennis J. and David Nachmias (1983). "The preconditions for successful evaluation: is there an ideal paradigm?" *Policy Sciences* 16: 67–79.

Prather, James E. and Frank K. Gibson (1977). "The failure of social programs," *Public Administration Review* 37: 556–563.

Reichardt, Charles S. and Thomas D. Cook (1979). "Beyond qualitative vs. quantitative methods," in T. D. Cook and C. S. Reichardt (eds.), *Qualitative and Quantitative Methods in Evaluation Research*. Beverly Hills: Sage.

Sarbin, Theodore R. (1972). "Schizophrenia is a myth, born of a metaphor, meaningless," *Psychology Today* 6: 18–27.

Schuman, H. (1982). "Artifacts are in the mind of the beholder," *American Sociologist* 17: 21–8.

Scriven, M. (1972). "Pros and cons about goal-free evaluation," *Evaluation Comment* 3: 1–4.

Trend, M. G. (1979). "On the reconciliation of qualitative and quantitative analyses: a case study," in T. D. Cook and C. S. Reichardt (eds.), *Qualitative and Quantitative Methods in Evaluation Research*. Beverly Hills: Sage.

Weick, Karl (1969). *The Social Psychology of Organizing*. Reading, MA: Addison-Wesley.

Weiss, Robert and Martin Rein (1969). "The evaluation of broad-aim programs: a cautionary case and a moral," *Annals of the American Academy of Political and Social Science* 385: 133–142.

Wilson, Thomas P. (1970). "Normative and interpretive paradigms in sociology," in Jack D. Douglas (ed.), *Understanding Everyday Life*. Chicago: Aldine.

PART II

PRACTICAL PROGRAM EVALUATION

In Part II and Part III of this volume we draw a distinction between *program evaluation* and *program research* to recognize the dual role of evaluation studies as practical evaluative information for decision makers and as research that illuminates the nature of planned social intervention. By program evaluation we mean those inquiries that primarily have evaluative intent, that is, ask of a program "how good is it?" and emphasize the practical matter of providing timely, useful information to decision makers, stakeholders, and consumers. In contrast, we use the phrase program research to designate inquiries oriented more toward analytic-descriptive questions of a program, that is, "how does it work?"

Part III will be concerned with the program research perspective. In Part II, which follows, we turn our attention to the program evaluation perspective. Our notion of this orientation is that it emphasizes the practical need to come to a balanced judgment of the social value of a program in the context of its purposes, politics, environment, and alternatives. This orientation has several distinctive features that have been widely discussed in the evaluation literature. Chief among these is the centering of the inquiry on the matter of evaluation, that is, rendering a judgment as to the merit and worth of the program (see Guba & Lincoln; Scriven, Part I of this volume). Another distinctive feature of this orientation is its situational responsiveness. It is intended to serve the needs and concerns of decision makers, stakeholders, and consumers in a manner that is timely, comprehensible, intuitively valid, and relevant. It follows that such evaluation inquiry is preeminently practical. The ultimate criteria of its success are whether or not it has been helpful and, more particularly, whether or not it has actually been used by those stakeholders it seeks to serve.

In this view, program evaluation is much like the product testing conducted and reported by Consumer's Union. The purpose of such testing is to provide a comparative judgment of the quality and value of the products examined, evaluated according to criteria specific to their functions in addition to a few general dimensions such as safety, cost, durability, and so forth. No attempt is made to develop any overarching theory or generalization about the nature of detergents and automobiles, only to provide practical information to the consumer who may purchase and use such products and, perhaps, to the manufacturer who makes them. Moreover, the testing methodology is very eclectic. Much of it is improvised for the particular situation at hand (e.g., dropping suitcases down stairs to test their durability). Mixed in as appropriate, however, are more formal techniques from social science and statistical theory, for example, sampling and confidence limits.

The applicable methods of inquiry for program evaluation, like those for product evaluation, are both constrained and diversified by the practical objectives of the endeavor. On the one hand, the need for timeliness and responsiveness militates against those research methods that require substantial preparation and extended periods of data collection and analysis before yielding results. Work in the program evaluation orientation thus often reflects a reluctance, even an animosity, toward experimental design and other such techniques from the repertoire of quantitative methods in the social sciences. Under this influence, there has been a burgeoning interest in qualitative techniques—observation, ethnography, naturalistic inquiry, and the like— because of the relative ease and speed with which they produce information and the close contact they maintain with stakeholders, decision makers, clients, and so on.

On the other hand, the centering of inquiry on evaluative judgment in this orientation defines a purpose for which there is no established methodology, leaving the evaluator free to use all reasonable means of collecting and analyzing information. This permits an eclectic strategy in which a variety of methodological tools can be pressed into service or, indeed, invented as required by the particular evaluation situation of interest. The program evaluation orientation, therefore, does not cleave to any particular methodological paradigm and may use, as needed, a great variety of concepts and techniques. Some of these represent recognizable categories, for example, survey research, demographic analysis, participant observation, cost-benefit analysis, historical analysis, tests and measures, legal analysis, case studies and so on, while others are improvisations born of the mating of evaluators' ingenuity and program circumstances.

Professional life, like personal life, abounds in choices of the "either A or B" sort and rarely offers those of the "both A and B" sort. Breaking out of established methodological paradigms in order to be responsive and evaluative requires the sacrifice of some otherwise desirable features of evaluation study. For example, critics working within the established paradigms have been quick to point out that the largely qualitative inquiry often favored in the program evaluation orientation lacks the structured, repeatable procedures central to scientific validity and thus is vulnerable to error, idiosyncracy, and excessive subjectivity in its results. Less well remarked, but equally germane, is the trade-off between generalizability and responsiveness to context. Whatever its methodology, the program evaluation orientation is inherently a case study of the particulars of a given situation that does not easily support identification of concepts, variables, or relationships that might also characterize other such situations.

Trade-offs such as these force distinctions and choices upon the field of evaluation studies. No one approach seems capable of serving all purposes and responding to all demands of this multifaceted enterprise. Any orientation will have its strengths and weaknesses. In the chapters of Part II that follow we have tried to select those that represent different aspects of the program evaluation perspective in a proactive and exemplary way, but without suppressing the inherent conflicts and problems.

These chapters are organized into five sections. The first section consists of several general chapters that discuss the nature and prospects of evaluation oriented toward practical program concerns. The second section presents useful practical advice for evaluators on such topics as advising decision makers, documentation during the research process, and legal issues. The next is a section that presents a sample of recent chapters reflecting the methodological eclecticism and ingenuity of the program evaluation practitioner. Here is a potpouri of useful tools, techniques, and ideas. The fourth section deals with the troublesome matter of valuing program benefits, with special attention to cost-benefit analysis. Because of its distinctive role in the practical program evaluation orientation, the final section is devoted to recent discussions of qualitative inquiry and the issues it faces.

SECTION 1
Evaluation and Practical Utility

If evaluation is to be used it must be useful. This simple, almost tautotogical truism triggers several cogitations. For what is evaluation to be used for . . . and by_whom? What, then, makes it useful for those purposes and what makes it actually get used?

The chapters in this section provide a common set of answers to these questions. A chief function of evaluation is its use to improve programs; in particular, to improve program management. It should, therefore, be used by program managers and decision makers and will prove useful if it aids them in their respective tasks. To actually get used it must be relevant, credible, understandable, and timely. The starting point for designing an evaluation, therefore, is an analysis of the information needs of managers and decision makers and the strategies likely to be effective in obtaining and presenting that information.

The details of this view provide us with a framework for defining evaluation as a practical activity serving the specific needs of a client organization. The three chapters that follow not only give a ringing endorsement of that definition but make a cogent case for the organizational and social benefits that result.

In the first chapter, Wholey addresses the role of evaluation in managing government programs in times of fiscal stress. His analysis focuses on the leadership functions that must be performed by the managers of such programs if they are to be successful. Wholey finds that each of the key leadership functions falls into close alignment with the functions of evaluation and the skills of evaluators. The stage is thus set for evaluation to play a constructive role in program management by providing practical assistance to managers in their struggle to maintain and improve programs under budgetary duress.

McClintock's ambitious chapter also centers on the role of evaluation in serving program managers, but focuses on the concept of formative evaluation to represent the interaction of evaluator and program improvement. McClintock sketches a framework or "theory" of formative evaluation that highlights three essential elements. First is the need to incorporate program theory, that is, some explicit model of how the program works, into the evaluation. Second is an accurate conceptualization of the organizational dynamics of the program including, especially, how organizational change comes about and how information is used in program decision making. The third element is a broad set of empirical procedures and a basis for determining which are appropriate for the setting and issues at hand. Along the way to erecting this framework McClintock treats us to various insights about the benefits of uncertainty, evolutionary theory, and the constructive role of the "methodological fool."

The last chapter of this section, by Brown, Newman, and Rivers, deals head-on with the decision-making process in social programs. Their view is that evaluators must understand the decision-making context if they want their work to be used when program decisions are made. Because understanding is enhanced by having some descriptive framework to apply, Brown et al. offer two models of decision-making situations—the conflict model and the social model. These models are complementary and, when integrated, lead to a variety of carefully charted implications for evaluators faced with making input within different decision contexts.

Collectively, these three chapters provide the basis for a theory of evaluation practice. This theory takes as its focal issue the interaction of the evaluator and the program decision-maker and then begins to specify the tactics, circumstances, and contexts, that will influence whether or not the interaction is constructive. The ultimate criterion for the success of the interaction is whether or not the information produced by the evaluation is used effectively for program management and program improvement. An interesting test of whether or not this theory's emphasis on evaluator-decision-maker interaction is misplaced could be mounted by examining a varied set of actual evaluation studies to determine which were used in program management. If the studies were classified according to their approach (e.g., "interactive" versus detached "scientific"), we might expect to find that those approached interactively were frequently used. Just such a study was conducted by Rafter (1984) using a set of evaluation studies commissioned by the Wisconsin State Legislature. Rafter found that studies taking the interactive approach were indeed more frequently used by policy-makers than those taking the scientific approach. The "hybrid" approach combining both interactive and scientific components, however, attained the highest utilization scores. We thus not only have the basis for a theory of evaluation practice, but some supportive evidence as well—evidence that gratifyingly also shows the value of the "scientific" underpinnings of evaluation.

REFERENCES

Rafter, D. O. (1984). Three approaches to evaluation research. *Knowledge: Creation, Diffusion, Utilization, 6*(2), 165-185.

8

Managing for High Performance
The Role of Evaluation
Joseph S. Wholey

I would like to explore roles that evaluators can play in helping those who lead government organizations in times of fiscal stress. I will suggest that evaluators' talents are likely to be of greater value as governments are called upon to do more with less. I will provide examples to support this suggestion. If we can do our own work efficiently, evaluation can have greater positive impact in these interesting times.

From Joseph S. Wholey, "Managing for High Performance: The Role of Evaluation," *Evaluation News*, 1985, 6(1), 40-50. Copyright 1985 by Sage Publications, Inc.

Let me first be explicit about the assumptions that underlie my message. I believe, and for today I ask you to assume, that

(1) in our increasingly complex, increasingly interdependent society, we need effective government agencies and programs;

(2) government performance too often leaves a great deal to be desired;

(3) we will continue to have a highly complex political system, a system in which resources and powers will be shared among three levels of government (federal, state, and local) and among three branches of government (executive, legislative, and judicial);

(4) for at least the balance of this century, the public will continue both to demand more effective government action and to sharply restrict the resources available to government; and

(5) effective government management will be more necessary and more difficult than ever before.

We could explore all of these assumptions at some length. Instead, I would like to discuss just the first of these assumptions and to add an assumption about the talents and expertise that evaluators could bring to bear. Put simply, I will argue that the pressures for efficient, effective government increase the demand for services that evaluators know how to provide. Government leaders need us; we can help them.

If our government is to solve complex problems within tight financial constraints, we will need government managers who can perform four key leadership functions:

● defining expected government performance by establishing and communicating clear objectives and performance indicators for government agencies and programs;

● assessing agency/program performance, and within program performance, variations in terms of those objectives and performance indicators;

● credibly communicating the value of an agency's or program's activities to those who control needed resources, and

● stimulating improvements in the performance of government agencies and programs.

What I find interesting is that evaluators appear to have talents needed by government managers who are attempting to perform these key leadership functions. I state this as a last assumption:

(6) Evaluators have the talents—the knowledge, skills, and abilities—that government managers need to solve many of their most important leadership problems. Among these are skills in working with policymakers and managers to identify relevant program objectives;

the ability to produce valid, reliable information on program outcomes; the ability to draw credible conclusions regarding program
effectiveness and cost-effectiveness; and ability to document variations in performance within and among programs.

What is new, it seems to me, is the likelihood that competition for
scarce resources will increase the value of the talents that evaluators
have had to offer all along. Government leaders are showing an increasing interest in credible information on what government programs are
accomplishing—and an increasing tendency to use such information
when making difficult policy, program, and budgeting decisions. Therefore, evaluators are in a position to help government managers guide,
defend, and improve their programs at a time when managers face
increasingly tough competition for scarce resources.

Over the past several years, I have been impressed by many instances
in which evaluators have helped managers to clarify program objectives
and priorities, to communicate the value of program activities to skeptical others, and to stimulate needed improvements in program performance. I would like to share some of those examples with you.

ESTABLISHING AND COMMUNICATING PERFORMANCE EXPECTATIONS FOR GOVERNMENT AGENCIES AND PROGRAMS

A first task for performance-oriented government managers is to
establish and communicate clear expectations for the outcomes to be
achieved by government agencies and programs. In the American political system, government often promises more than it can deliver in
attempting to reach agreement on policies or programs. Whether the
program concerns protection of air quality, deinstitutionalization of
mental patients, or procurement of weapons systems, policymakers tend
to focus on problems and needs. They tend not to focus on the specific
chains of program activities, short-term outcomes, and longer-term
outcomes that will be needed to translate resource allocations into
progress toward policy goals. Faced with ambitious, competing goals,
government managers often seem to be placed in "no win" situations.
Performance-oriented government managers need to find ways to translate policy goals into ambitious but realistic input, process, and outcome
objectives in terms of which programs will be implemented and results
demonstrated.

In some cases, government managers will move on their own to
operationalize policy goals. In the Community Health Centers pro-

grams, for example, federal managers, staff, and grantees worked for four years to identify appropriate program objectives and performance indicators. Although their "priority output" objectives emphasized health services delivery and efficiency, they also included outcome objectives like that of immunizing 90% of the two-year-olds receiving health services (Wholey, 1983). In the Harlem Valley Psychiatric Center, line and staff organizations translated deinstitutionalization and community mental health care goals into ambitious but realistic objectives. These included rapid reduction of the inpatient census, development of community-based services, and high-quality care for all patients in the hospital and in the community (Wholey, 1983; Levine, 1980).

Given the pressures that they face, most government managers will need a good deal of help to operationalize policy goals. Evaluators can help government managers to identify and sort through policy goals, test possible program objectives against past performance, and clarify the types of program performance information that could be produced. Evaluators can help government managers to establish priorities among program objectives by helping to create systems for monitoring and evaluating program performance and by helping managers communicate how the resulting information will be used.

In a Tennessee Health Department prenatal care program, for example, evaluators helped managers to agree on priority objectives. These related to the proportion of health department patients initiating prenatal care in their first trimester of pregnancy and the proportion of low-birth-weight infants born to health department patients (Wholey, 1983). In the National Institute of Mental Health Community Support Program, evaluators helped managers to clarify an overly ambitious goal that had called for development of systems of "comprehensive, coordinated, community-based care" for chronically mentally ill people including those returning to the community from state mental hospitals. Those in charge of the program decided to drop the unrealistic objective of "nationwide" development of community support systems and to get evaluators' help in developing the specific performance indicators needed to operationalize the remaining program objectives (Wholey, 1983).

In these programs and others, the key initial leadership task is to determine what services outcomes can realistically be expected given the resources available. Then policy goals must be translated into specific input, process, and outcome objectives and indicators in terms of which programs can be managed and program results demonstrated. We evaluators can help managers in this important work.

ASSESSING GOVERNMENT PERFORMANCE
AND VARIATIONS IN PERFORMANCE

A second task for performance-oriented government managers is to assess the outcomes of the policies and programs for which they have implementation and operational responsibilities. Government managers tend to lack valid, reliable, credible, communicable information on the performance and, in particular, outcomes of the programs for which they are responsible. Accounting systems may provide data on agency expenditures (though often not on "program" expenditures); management information systems may provide data on clients served and on services delivered; but most of the available program outcome data tends to be anecdotal and of uncertain validity and reliability. Consequently they find these low in credibility. Government leaders need credible information on program outcomes. Only in this way can they communicate the value of program activities to those who control resources and stimulate higher performance in decentralized programs.

Over the past several years, I have been impressed by a number of government managers who developed monitoring and evaluation systems that provided valid, reliable, credible evidence on the extent to which intended program results were achieved. In the Community Health Centers program mentioned earlier, for example, the bureau chief monitored grantee and regional performance in terms of service delivery, efficiency, and outcome targets. The bureau allocated additional staff and grant funds to high-performing regions. Regional offices then allocated additional funds to high-performing grantees (Wholey, 1983).

The director of the Harlem Valley Psychiatric Center used at least seven different monitoring and evaluation systems to assess line and staff performance in a large operating agency. "Line" units were assessed in terms of such indicators as number of inpatients, quality of inpatient service, length of stay, number of inpatients eligible for placement versus number actually placed in community settings, quality and appropriateness of placements in the community, number of discharged patients followed in the community, and current status of discharged patients. "Staff" units were assessed in terms of their responsiveness in providing needed service. Data on the performance of line and staff units were used in identifying problems, in initiating corrective actions, and in reallocating resources. The performance of all units was well publicized throughout, as well as beyond, the center (Wholey, 1983).

In many situations, evaluators can help government managers by providing valid, reliable, credible, communicable information on resources expended, services delivered, and outcomes achieved. This information complements and supplements the large amount of program performance information already available to knowledgeable government managers. Three types of evaluation information are of possible interest to government managers:

(1) Quantitative data that systematically monitor important outcomes both within and among programs and over time: To produce quantitative data on important program outcomes, evaluators may have to develop new measurement schemes to summarize and communicate information "buried" in case records. In other instances, evaluators may have to use sample surveys to get behavioral and attitudinal data on program quality or program results.

(2) Quantitative data that systematically evaluate program results in comparison to the results of other programs: To produce evaluation data estimating the effectiveness, cost-effectiveness ratios, or net benefits (benefits minus costs) of program activities, the evaluators may also have to collect data on appropriate comparison groups or to conduct interrupted time-series analyses comparing trends in outcomes before and after program operations.

(3) Qualitative (narrative) data from observations or open-ended interviews documenting program operations or program outcomes for specific operating units or specific clients.

In each situation, the question will be whether improvements in the quantity or quality of program performance information will outweigh the cost and time required to obtain and use the information.

Of course there are many examples in which evaluators have assisted managers by providing credible, communicable information on program performance. For the Tennessee Health Department prenatal care program mentioned earlier, evaluators provided useful information by comparing the birth weights of infants born to health department patients with the birth weights of infants born to other low-income women who had been receiving food stamps and WIC nutrition vouchers but had not received prenatal program services (Wholey & Wholey, 1981, 1982).

For the Job Corps, evaluators carried out a three-year longitudinal evaluation to determine whether the relatively expensive Job Corps program produced better results than the results achieved for comparable groups of disadvantaged youth served by other programs. In their Job Corps evaluation, researchers estimated Job Corps program costs, resulting changes in client outcomes such as earnings and criminal behavior, and the total dollar value of each of the program effects (Mallar et al., 1980, 1982).

For the WIC nutrition program, researchers developed a large-scale evaluation program that allowed them to estimate the effectiveness of the program. For example, they estimated the effectiveness of the WIC program in reducing the proportion of low-birth-weight infants among infants born to low-income women. Most of the WIC evaluations relied on comparison groups; a few of the WIC evaluations used randomly assigned experimental and control groups (U.S. General Accounting Office, 1984). There is evidence that the WIC program improves nutrition, increases infants' birth weight, improves children's growth and development, and saves health dollars in the long run (Wholey, 1984).

For each of these programs, the evaluators' evidence on program effectiveness proved to be important in policy decisions on the future of the program. In each of these cases and in many others, the key initial step was to focus on specific process and outcome objectives in terms of which aspect of program performance could be credibly assessed. Managers and evaluators will often find themselves using multiple performance indicators because the programs typically have multiple objectives. Evidence on intraprogram performance variations will often be useful, as will information tracking changes in program performance over time.

CREDIBLY COMMUNICATING THE VALUE
OF GOVERNMENT ACTIVITIES

A third task of performance-oriented government managers is to credibly communicate the value of government activities. This is done to ensure that needed resources will be available for future program activities. In many instances, government managers have difficulty demonstrating what results flow from government programs. The anecdotal evidence that is sufficient for internal program management may be insufficient for credible communication with higher policy levels or with important publics. Here again, evaluators can be helpful. At all levels of government, I have seen programs of demonstrated effectiveness withstand pressures to eliminate programs or to reduce spending. At the same time, other programs (programs generally recognized as ineffective) have been sharply reduced or eliminated.

Congressional responses to the Reagan administration's human resources program budget proposals are very interesting in this regard. In 1981 and 1982, although Congress agreed to make substantial reductions in employment and training programs, food and nutrition programs, and health and mental health programs, Congress maintained several programs whose effectiveness had been demonstrated.

Funding for the Job Corps was maintained in the face of administration proposals for sharp reductions. Evaluations had shown that Job Corps benefits outweigh the program's high costs (Mallar et al., 1980, 1982). Senator Orrin Hatch, Chairman of the Senate Committee on Labor and Human Resources, used those evaluations to help convince fellow conservatives that the program should be maintained (Congressional Record, 1981).

Evidence of program effectiveness played a part in congressional decisions to keep the WIC program separate from the maternal and child health block grant, to minimize proposed program cuts in FY 1982, and to expand the WIC program in subsequent years. The principal investigators in WIC evaluation studies have testified at many congressional hearings on legislation and appropriations.

Evidence of program effectiveness also played a part in congressional decisions to continue the Community Support Program for the chronically mentally ill. There was evidence from federal, state, and local evaluations that participating states had redirected their service delivery systems to focus on the needs of chronically mentally ill adults. Data also showed that Community Support Program funds had helped to mobilize state and local funding for programs for the chronically mentally ill (Katz, 1981) and Community Support Program clients had less need for hospitalization as a result of the program (Congressional Record, 1983). Although the Reagan administration made no effort to get appropriations for the program in FY 1982 or 1983 (on the ground that states could fund such activities through the Alcohol, Drug Abuse, and Mental Health block grant), Congress decided to maintain the Community Support Program as a categorical federal program. For each of the programs cited here, it proved worthwhile for government leaders to agree on realistic objectives, to systematically assess program performance, and to use that information to communicate the value of program activities.

Credible information on program performance has also influenced policy and budget decisions at state and local levels. At a time when other state programs were being cut back in Tennessee, there were data that demonstrated that Tennessee's 19-county prenatal care program had been associated with reductions in numbers of low-birth-weight infants. This proved helpful in executive branch decisions to maintain the program and expand it statewide after a five-year federal grant expired (Smith, 1984). When many local programs were being cut back in

Arlington, Virginia, funds were appropriated to maintain a successful robbery prevention program after a federal grant expired; to maintain a successful auto tag enforcement program; to maintain a successful police take-home patrol car program; and to maintain an effective child abuse prevention program after a federal grant expired (Wholey, 1978).

STIMULATING IMPROVEMENTS IN THE PERFORMANCE OF GOVERNMENT AGENCIES AND PROGRAMS

A fourth task for government managers is the stimulation of improvements in the performance of the agencies and programs for which they are responsible.

In government, intangible incentives (for example, public recognition for jobs well done) are among the most important motivators. Removal of constraints and delegation of authority are other incentives that motivate managers. In some cases, modest increments of discretionary funds have been used to stimulate and reward effective organizational performance. The federal office of Child Support Enforcement has long used both intangible and financial incentives to motivate better state performance in getting absent fathers to contribute to the support of their children. Many of those children would otherwise be on welfare. The Office of Child Support Enforcement tracks the success of each state child support enforcement agency on several performance indicators and recognizes high performance on selected indicators in their newsletter. It has also held award ceremonies honoring states whose performance was outstanding.

I noted earlier that the Federal Bureau of Community Health Services has stimulated Community Health Center's program performance by allocating staff and grant funds on the basis of regional and grantee performance on priority output indicators. The Harlem Valley Psychiatric Center has used tangible and intangible incentives to stimulate improved performance by line and staff units.

A number of government agencies have encouraged efficiency by allowing subordinate units to keep—and reallocate—a portion of any savings achieved in a given fiscal year. Instead of "losing" the amounts by which they underspent their budgets, subordinate units were allowed to carry 50% of any savings over into the next fiscal year (Wholey, 1983).

I am very interested in seeing what policymakers and high-level managers can do to stimulate performance-oriented management and improved performance in the agencies and programs over which they have influence. In the Virginia Board of Social Service, for example, we are beginning to explore how we might create incentive systems that will stimulate and reward high performance as well as improved performance by local welfare agencies. At the same time, we are seeking to minimize disincentives that inhibit better performance by local agencies. Central to any such system will be agreement on outcome objectives, agreement on outcome indicators, and development of outcome monitoring systems that will provide information on performance variation among local agencies.

CONCLUSIONS

Government managers need help. Evaluators can play positive, constructive roles by:

(1) helping government managers establish and communicate clear objectives and performance indicators for government agencies and programs;

(2) helping managers assess agency and program performance and within-program variations in performance in terms of identified objectives and performance indicators:

(3) helping managers to communicate the value of agency and program activities to those who control needed resources; and

(4) helping managers to stimulate improvements in the performance of government agencies and programs.

We can do this useful work without losing our objectivity and credibility by concentrating on:

(1) outcome monitoring, focusing on important intermediate outcome objectives;

(2) evaluations of program effectiveness, cost-effectiveness, and net benefits using comparison-group and interrupted time-series designs; and

(3) qualitative (narrative) evaluations· documenting program activities and outcomes.

In future years, government policymakers and managers will have to allocate scarce resources among competing projects and programs. If we evaluators can do our work efficiently (we face declining resources too), our work is more likely than ever to be used at both a management and a policy level. Today's "New Frontier" for evaluators will be work aimed at the development of the incentives needed to produce better government management and better government services in an environment offering scarce resources. I look forward to working with you as evaluators in a time of challenge!

REFERENCES

Congressional Record. (1981). Washington, DC: Government Printing Office. February 26, 1981, pp. s1600-s1601.

U. S. Congress, House Committee on Appropriations (1983). *Departments of Labor, Health, and Human Services, Education and Related Agencies Appropriations for 1984, Part III: Health.* Hearings: 98th Congress, First Session 1983 (pp. 725-726). Washington, DC: Government Printing Office.

Katz, J. (1981). *Report on the NIMH Community Support Program (CSP).* Rockville, MD: U.S. Department of Health and Human Services.

Levine, M. (1980). *From state hospital to psychiatric center.* Lexington, MA: D. C. Heath.

Mallar et al. (1980, 1982). *Evaluation of the economic impact of the Job Corps Program: Second follow-up report and third follow-up report.* Princeton, NJ: Princeton University Press.

Smith, J. D. (1984). *Defining and improving performance: Tennessee's prenatal program.* Paper delivered at the Joint Meeting of the Evaluation Research Society and the Evaluation Network, San Francisco, CA.

United States General Accounting Office. (1984). *WIC evaluations provide some favorable but no conclusive evidence on the effects expected in the special supplemental program for women, infants, and children.* Washington, DC: GAO/PEMD 84-4.

Wholey, J. S. (1978). *Zero-based budgeting and program evaluation.* Lexington, MA: D.C. Heath.

Wholey, J. S. (1983). *Evaluation and effective public management.* Boston, MA: Little, Brown, Co.

Wholey, J. S. (1984). Executive agency retrenchment. In M. Gregory & J. Palmer (Eds.), *Federal budget policy in the 1900s.* Washington, DC: Urban Institute Press.

Wholey, J. S., & Wholey, M. S. (1981). *Evaluation of TIOP and related prenatal care programs: Interim report.* Arlington, VA: Wholey Associates.

Wholey, J. S., & Wholey, M. S. (1982). *Toward improving the outcomes of pregnancy: Implications for the statewide programs.* Arlington, VA: Wholey Associates.

9

Toward a Theory of Formative Program Evaluation

Charles McClintock

The design of formative program evaluation and its practice by in-house evaluators require systematic attention to program theory, decision and action contexts in which evaluation is to be used, and empirical procedures.

Political and bureaucratic conditions typically dictate incremental program modification rather than termination. Under these circumstances, formative studies are more useful than summative studies for discovering and assessing possible program improvements. While much has been written about how to enhance the use of evaluation results for program improvement, evaluation theory has not yet formalized a constructive accommodation among the methodological, social psychological, and political forces that surround a formative evaluation process. This chapter presents a framework to conceptualize the design of formative evaluation studies and the development of in-house program evaluation functions.

The term *formative evaluation* is used here to mean the systematic use of empirical procedures for appraisal and analysis of programs as a way of providing ongoing information to influence decision making and action on policy, resource allocation, and program operations.

There are three implications of the emphasis on decision making and action. First, the intention here is to identify with other recent efforts that focus on evaluation for program improvement (for example, Patton, 1978; Cronbach and Associates, 1980). While these efforts are relatively new, historically there have been several major statements emphasizing the program-improvement function of evaluation (Cronbach, 1963) or the links between

From Charles McClintock, "Toward a Theory of Formative Program Evaluation," pp. 77-95 in D. Deshler (Ed.) *Evaluation for Program Improvement*. New Directions for Continuing Education, No. 24. Copyright 1984 by Jossey-Bass. Reprinted by permission.

evaluation and decision making (Stufflebeam and others, 1971). Cronbach's recent prescriptions for reform of program evaluation clearly recognize that evaluation does not affect programs in a direct manner; rather, it affects decision making and action related to programs (Cronbach and Associates, 1980). Thus, a theory of formative evaluation should include attention to the dynamics of various organizational phenomena, such as development and change, information use, and decision making.

The second implication of the emphasis on decision making and action is that those who perform evaluations must be able to observe programs over time and in context before they can be responsive to the information needs of the program's various constituencies (Stake, 1975). Thus, more attention should be given to internal evaluators and the ways in which methodological requirements are reconciled with organizational demands (Kennedy, 1983).

Finally, with respect to the third implication, the present definition conceives of formative evaluation as a decision-support system for management at all levels of the organization (Keen and Morton, 1978). In this sense, formative evaluation is similar to institutional research (Knapp, 1982) or internal audit (Millington, 1983). An important function of these two activities is to identify and analyze options for management, at various levels, that will improve program performance or help management conform to resource and accountability requirements. The identification of program options is a crucial objective of formative evaluation, since maintaining variety in an organization's functioning is so important to the organization's capacity for adaptability and its ability to overcome bureaucratic resistance to change (Pondy, 1977; McClintock, 1979).

Toward a Theory of Formative Evaluation

The Need for a Focus on Formative Evaluation. In developing a theory of formative evaluation, it is necessary for evaluators to expand and integrate their knowledge of empirical methods and organizational behavior. Within the field of program evaluation and related areas, there has been steady growth in a wide variety of activities that can be placed under the heading of formative evaluation. A partial list would include process studies, program and performance monitoring, management information systems, action research, decision-support systems, program and management audits, institutional research, and accountability reviews. While these activities may not always be used in formative ways—that is, to have an ongoing effect on decision making and action—they are consistent in concept with that purpose. The variety of perspectives in this list, however, illustrates the need for a broad conception of empirical methods and organizational contexts.

Why is there a need for special focus on the methods of formative evaluation? From the perspective of evaluators, the reasons are mainly historical. Suchman's (1967) distinction between program evaluation and evaluative research formalized an already present emphasis on the methodological aspects of the evaluation process and, in particular, on the summative study of program outcomes. These emphases constituted the "theory" of program evaluation, which was based largely on laboratory research methods and paid little systematic attention to the political and organizational contexts of evaluation or to the relationships among evaluation, planning, and decision making. While it is common today to consider carefully how evaluations are used as part of program and policy development (Patton, 1978; Cronbach and Associates, 1980), much more still needs to be known about how to design internal formative evaluation systems. Freeman and Solomon (1979), for example, discuss the need for evaluation methods that can be used systematically to monitor program processes and performance and that can produce data for program managers in a timely manner. Their agenda for evaluators in the 1980s is summed as follows: "If there is one area of urgent study to be pressed in the forthcoming decade, it is the design, testing, and implementation of uniform procedures in various fields to obtain process data and to have the means to analyze it rapidly so that feedback to program managers is feasible while the information is still relevant" (1979, p. 261).

From the perspective of policy makers and program managers, there is a need for formative evaluation that maintains methodological rigor and is also responsive to different political perspectives, decision processes, and time frames (Zweig, 1981; Weiss and Weiss, 1981). Nevertheless, as Knapp (1982) showed in his study of offices of institutional research in higher education settings, there is often confusion and conflict among evaluators and decision makers about the relationship of evaluation and research to planning and policy making. Wildavsky (1972) suggests that the tension between internal evaluators and management may be inherent, since they are in competition for control of information. Kennedy's (1983) study of in-house evaluators within school districts illustrates the variety of ways in which evaluators must accommodate organizational demands to maintain their status and function. Thus, it is clear that it takes considerable political, technical, and interpersonal skill, as well as carefully thought-out organizational arrangements, to make a formative evaluation unit a viable enterprise.

Formative Evaluation and the Concept of Uncertainty. To define formative evaluation as a source of information for decision making and action implies the operation of a rational model of behavior. In this model, feedback serves as a control mechanism to reduce uncertainty about program performance and changes in the environment. Other perspectives on the evaluation and feedback function, however, stress the need to increase uncertainty and variability in program functioning as a way of counteracting certain effects of bureaucracy (Pondy, 1977; McClintock, 1979).

The perspective presented here defines high-quality formative evaluation as simultaneously increasing and decreasing uncertainty with respect to different aspects of the program. This prescription for formative evaluation is based partly on a national study of state government-level human service agencies (McClintock and Reilinger, 1980). Respondents identified two areas of uncertainty as possibly affected by planning and evaluation activities. One had to do with the structural arrangements for programs (including organizational, social, and political factors), and the other focused on the operational aspects of program performance.

Structural uncertainty includes questions about roles and interrelationships among groups involved with program management and delivery. Thus, for example, we can ask whether program structures and support services should be centralized or decentralized; what the interorganizational arrangements should be among service providers at local, state, and federal levels; what the mix should be between public and private-sector involvement; and how clients should be included in the process of planning and program development. Other questions concern the roles that can be played by different groups (legislators, administrators, service providers) and how they should be coordinated, the goals and resource allocation plan for programs, and the processes that will establish and review resource priorities and goals.

Performance uncertainty, as opposed to structural uncertainty, is primarily concerned with questions about the need for and effects of programs. Often these questions focus on very basic unknowns about the nature and extent of client needs, resource distribution, and program activities. Thus, we find ourselves wondering how many clients with what characteristics are being served where and by whom, where the resources are going, what program alternatives are being tried, what the effects of those alternatives are, and what the projected future needs are.

Figure 1 describes the qualities of those evaluators whose efforts produce different results with respect to structural and performance uncertainty.

Figure 1. Evaluator Qualities as a Function of Evaluation Results

Uncertainty About Program Structure

		Low	High
Uncertainty About Program Performance	High	Useless Evaluator	Risky Evaluator
	Low	Foolish Methodologist	Methodological "Fool"

As argued here, the most desirable cell in Figure 1 is the cell that results in low performance uncertainty and high structural uncertainty, and this objective places two different demands on the formative evaluator. When reducing uncertainty about program performance, the evaluator functions (in the traditional manner) as a technician or a methodologist. When uncertainty about program structure is increased, the evaluator functions like the medieval fool, a character who was permitted to make humorous, bizarre, or dangerous suggestions that stimulated creativity and catharsis in others. To improve effectiveness, there must be information about program performance, on the one hand, and alternative strategies and structures for program delivery, on the other. Combining these kinds of information will maximize the program's potential for effectiveness and adaptability in changing environments. Thus, it may be preferable to have formative evaluators who are methodological "fools" rather than foolish methodologists.

To summarize, a theory of formative evaluation must be based on broad knowledge of empirical methods and organizational dynamics. The theory must simultaneously provide information about program performance and raise questions about program structure. A conceptual framework for moving toward such a theory is presented below. It considers three areas of theory and knowledge that can be used to guide evaluation design and practice: program theory, the decision and action contexts of formative evaluation, and empirical procedures. Within each of these areas, attention will be given to the issues of study design and the evaluation function's organization and practice. While program evaluation can be done by agents who are either externally or internally related to the organization (or a combination of both), the focus here will be on internally based formative evaluation efforts. It is hoped that this conceptual framework will serve as the foundation for moving toward a broadly based theory of formative evaluation.

Conceptual Framework for the Design of Program Evaluation

The basic rationale for program evaluation is that its findings are to be used in some decision or action context with respect to particular programs. Evaluation becomes one component of the feedback and control process for program functioning. It is obvious, therefore, that evaluation is more than a set of empirical methods governed solely by the standards of social science. Judgments of the quality of program evaluation must also be based on criteria that are meaningful both to the immediate users and to the larger systems in which the program is embedded. Many recent major treatments of program evaluation make it clear that criteria concerning program characteristics and constituents are crucial to the evaluation's design and conduct (Patton, 1978; Cronbach and Associates, 1980).

Program evaluation consists of a set of empirical procedures applied to a particular program area (education, health and social welfare programs, administrative and support services). These procedures generate information that is used in decision and action contexts. It follows, then, that a conceptual framework for the design of evaluations must include systematic attention to procedures and program area. Evaluation theory and practice have been based traditionally on preferences for certain empirical procedures. The present conceptual framework considers methods last, since design and measurement decisions should be based on prior considerations of program theory and decision and action contexts.

Program Theory. A major source of relatively specific guidance for evaluation design and measurement procedures must be the particular substantive domain of the program. For example, the design of an evaluation of adult education programs should take into account material from developmental research, family sociology, and theories of education and learning. Chen and Rossi (1980) argue that a theory-driven approach to program evaluation is likely to identify a wide range of possible effects. Evaluation designs that are based on program-related theory will therefore be more useful for program improvement. Others, such as Schwarz (1980), have pointed to the absence of adequate program theory as one of the main impediments to good evaluation design. Rockart (1979) has used a similar argument regarding profit-making organizations. Each author suggests that planning and evaluation systems should be designed around key activities and outcomes that can be manipulated to achieve the intended program objectives. It is important to be as explicit as possible about the model of a program; as Schwarz (1980) argues, many implicit models in human services have been detrimental to an understanding of the programs because the models have simplistically attributed much greater effects to programs than were actually feasible. While one approach to the problem of simplistic models would be ridding ourselves of inflated language in the policy and evaluation literature (for example, the term *impact* connotes greater effects than can usually be realized), a more pragmatic approach would be incorporating modeling techniques for problems and programs into the design of evaluation studies. In this way, we would be able to assess the soundness of a program model as part of the evaluation process.

Many modeling techniques are based on participants' perceptions of situations (Weick, 1979, pp. 72–88). Sometimes called *causal maps,* diagrams of situational factors and their interrelationships to describe a problem or a program's operation can be helpful in several ways. They can make goals, constraints, causes, and effects explicit. Causal maps can also focus attention on which variables produce stability and change and which ones can be controlled or influenced to some degree. Comparison of causal maps from different individuals or subgroups involved in a program (clients, front-line staff, management, legislators) can reveal implementation problems as well as new concepts for program design. If causal maps could be quantified, then it would be possible to simulate long-range effects of different program structures and operations mathematically.

How are maps of a program or an organization developed? One

approach is to conduct an evaluability assessment of the program. This method was described by Jung (1982) as a process of specifying the logical model of the program, as derived from policy documents and from interviews of knowledgeable subjects, and then comparing what was planned with what actually exists. As part of the process, diagrams or maps are developed of how program inputs are connected to the processes of program design and delivery, which in turn are expected to produce outputs with measurable characteristics. Analysis of discrepancies between intended and actual program components and specification of the indicators of those components create a more useful evaluation design. It is also very likely that identifying discrepancies and indicators will itself have a useful evaluative function, in that program managers and staff can begin to build more realistic and consensual perceptions of the program and its central components.

Another approach to program mapping is based on brainstorming techniques (Trochim and Linton, 1983). In this method, program staff or clients are asked to list any entity that comes to mind in thinking about program goals, activities, constituents, and so on. These entities are then grouped by program participants into more general concepts, which can be interrelated verbally, pictorially, or mathematically. This method has the virtue of starting from a relatively unstructured point, so that a conceptual framework for an evaluation study that will address a broad range of program participants' concerns can be developed. In this sense, this method is similar in purpose (but not in method) to goal-free evaluation (Scriven, 1974) and to Delphi techniques for program development (Delbecq and Van de Ven, 1971).

There are also more elaborate approaches to causal mapping (Hall, 1978). With these methods, one can specify reciprocal causalities among program variables and identify the type of relationship that exists between any two variables. Weick (1979, pp. 72–88) has described the issues involved in interpreting causal maps. These issues can become quite complex, as can those that concern predicting the behavior of social systems on the basis of causal maps.

Clarifying program models and developing causal maps will have two probable results. First, the evaluator can be more systematic in focusing data-collection activities on the identified components of the program model, and so content and construct validity should be improved. Second, evaluation designs can be developed that are appropriate to the program or to current knowledge about the program model. Experimental designs may be more useful when models are well specified, while exploratory strategies may contribute more when theory is weak (Maynard-Moody and McClintock, 1981). The process of assessing program models is likely to constitute a useful evaluative exercise in itself.

Decision and Action Contexts. The second component of this conceptual framework for evaluation design and practice consists of theory and knowledge about decision and action contexts. Conceptualizations of decision or action contexts are usually more abstract or general than theory and knowledge pertaining to a particular program. There are several possible perspectives on context that might be applied to the design and practice of program evaluation. These include the context of community decision making (Aiken and Alford, 1970), the context of legislative policy development (Zweig, 1981), and the context of organizational behavior (Wergin, 1976). Our present focus is on in-house formative evaluation, and so we shall analyze decision and action contexts from an organizational perspective. Context concepts should be generalizable across various program areas. Thus, they are particularly important for evaluation systems within complex organizations that have heterogeneous programs. This discussion of organizational perspective, as related to formative evaluation, will focus on change and development within organizations and on processes of information use and decision making.

Organizational Change and Development. This discussion of organizational change and development draws on concepts from the fields of social evolution, cybernetics, and change-agent consulting. In social evolution, as in biological evolution, three processes operate to produce change: variation, selection, and retention (Aldrich, 1979). From this perspective, program evaluation is viewed as part of the selection process; that is, evaluation is a source of information useful for identifying and selecting changes that will improve the program. The selection process is similar to the feedback and control functions described in systems theory and cybernetics. One important quality of an effective feedback and control is the principle of *requisite variety*. Requisite variety refers to a control function's ability to register sufficient variety in the system under observation so that feedback maintaining an adaptive relationship between the system and its environment can be provided. Therefore, a crucial function of formative evaluation is to provide rich descriptive detail about the state of the program.

Pondy (1977) has discussed the need in program evaluation for descriptive variety, which he relates to the difference between goal-oriented summative evaluation and discovery-oriented formative evaluation. Because summative evaluation narrows the information-gathering function to a few questions about goal attainment or effects, it is of only limited help as a feedback mechanism with respect to the variety of program conditions and constituent perspectives that affect program performance. In contrast, the discovery-oriented approach to formative evaluation is similar to a detailed assessment of constituent information needs and decision processes. In this sense, formative evaluation resembles the assessment procedures used in designing organizational information systems (Yourdon, 1976).

Several evaluation models are consistent with the principles of requisite variety and discovery. Stufflebeam and others (1971) describe a decision-oriented model that contains a systematic method for assessing program context, inputs, processes, and products and for relating this information to a wide range of possible selection needs. The responsive evaluation model described by Stake (1975), as well as Guba and Lincoln's (1981) naturalistic inquiry method, also attempts to reflect perspectives and information on a wide variety of the issues, concerns, and individuals related to the program being studied. Gold (1981) has described an evaluation strategy called the *stakeholder approach*. This strategy attempts to improve use of evaluation findings by involving stakeholders in the design process. Stakeholders are individuals whose lives are affected by the program and whose decisions affect the program. These strategies for the design and practice of formative evaluation should be effective selection processes, since they will be able to identify information needs, concerns, and decision requirements for different program constituents and components.

As a selection mechanism, formative evaluation helps to reduce uncertainty about program performance. Because evaluation should also increase structural uncertainty, it contributes to the variation process that is part of evolution. Thus, the evaluator takes the role of a change agent. While there are many change-agent techniques for facilitating program design and development, there are relatively few examples of how methods for creating program alternatives can be integrated into evaluation design and decision making (Leavitt, 1976). Some guidance for creating novel program design alternatives can be found in Weick's (1977) discussion of wordplay exercises and in the prescriptions of Hedburg and others (1976) for self-designing organizations. In both cases, the authors propose principles and techniques that organizations can use for maintaining adaptability in unpredictable environments.

In addition to the technical aspects of program design and development, there are many psychological and political issues that emphasize the formative evaluator's role as educator, consultant, and change agent. To overcome resistance, the formative evaluator must carefully and thoroughly diagnose the situation and involve the client in the diagnosis and change processes. These two tasks are similar to the methods of action research, in which clients' motivations for using findings and for change are activated through their involvement in the evaluation design and its implementation (Passmore and Friedlander, 1982).

As a change agent, the formative evaluator must balance difficult role demands and be careful not to assume responsibility for advocating a particular change. Although Scriven (1967) has argued that, given a set of needs, the evaluator should make judgments about which program features are best, other writers have documented ethical dilemmas and practical disasters that result when the evaluator becomes an advocate (Adams, 1983). Nevertheless, it is crucial that the formative evaluator identify and assess options for program improvement and thus contribute to the variation process in organizational change and development.

The literature on organizational development and change is highly varied, with many themes besides the ones discussed here (Goodman and Associates, 1982). In the design of formative evaluation, however, special attention should be paid to the ways in which evaluation can provide descriptive detail of program operations and stimulate variation in design options. Involving constituent groups in evaluation design and implementation appears to be a central requirement of such descriptions.

Information Use and Decision Making. Decision and action contexts also involve another very significant design concern: the use of information in decision making for program development (Patton, 1978). There is growing awareness that evaluation should be linked to policy development, management, and service delivery. Still, there needs to be more understanding of how to create this connection (Beyer and Trice, 1982). Weiss and Bucuvalas (1980) have identified five factors that influence the use of information (such as that produced by evaluation) in decision making and action: perceived relevance of information, perceived research quality of information, conformity of information to the user's prior expectations, action feasibility, and challenge to the status quo. These five factors have in common a focus on the relationship between the content and the form of the information provided and the information needs and values of the users. Others have argued that evaluation's usefulness has been limited by the lack of this very relationship between information and needs (Cox, 1977; Patton, 1978). Part of the problem, then, is to identify the information needs of evaluation users accurately enough so that appropriate evaluation activities can be designed. As discussed earlier, one approach to identifying information needs is to draw on particular models or theories related to the program being evaluated. Another approach, which could be applied to many different programs, is to develop a framework for identifying the information and decision-making needs of evaluation users. Knowledge of these needs should lead to clearer expectations about the kinds of evaluation information that would be useful for decision making and action.

It is often difficult to obtain accurate descriptions of information needs from individuals. In a national study of human service agencies within state government, the producers and the users of planning and evaluation, were asked to describe their information needs and how these related to various kinds of decision making (McClintock and Reilinger, 1980). Among both groups of respondents there was a strong bias in favor of a "rational choice" model. This model is one in which organizational goals and market needs are determined, the costs and benefits of alternative courses of action are calculated, and benefit-maximizing choice is made, and these results are evaluated for a new round of choices.

It is clear that this model is misleading (McGowan, 1976), but it still pervades much evaluation thinking and practice. Feldman and March (1982) have argued that adherence to rational models despite realities is driven largely by political and normative pressures that require the appearance of accountable, rational decision making. Especially in the public sector, organizations are expected to portray orderly and responsible procedures for allocating funds and coordinating activities efficiently, regardless of whether these images are real (Meyer and Rowan, 1977). When it comes to program evaluation, therefore, decision makers claim to value the scientific integrity of the process more than they value other, more practical aspects (Weiss and Weiss, 1981).

Feldman and March (1982) suggest that pressures toward rationality lead information users habitually to request large amounts of scientifically credible information without giving much thought to its actual usefulness for decision making. Thus, information users are often at least as culpable as the producers in perpetuating the illusion that decision making follows the rational model of information gathering and choice. As a result, little progress is made in understanding the ways in which different kinds of information actually are used in a variety of decision-making situations.

One impediment to better formative evaluation design is the absence of generalizable diagnostic methods for assessing information needs. Evaluability assessment procedures represent a step in the right direction, in that they are intended to demonstrate whether a program's goals and implementation processes are developed and clear enough to permit meaningful evaluation. Similarly, Rousseau (1983) has described a framework for systems analysis that can be used to assess the information needs related to program inputs, causal processes, outputs, and feedback or control processes, but Rousseau did not present specific diagnostic instruments and procedures. We still need to develop generic methods that can give formative evaluators a means of assessing information needs at the level of organizational subunits or programs.

Another perspective on information needs in organizations draws on the concept of developmental and problem cycles. Tichy (1980) argues that organizations have three ongoing decision dilemmas, which vary over time and require different information and action resolutions. These three problem areas are the design of technology for production of goods and services, the question of how to allocate power and resources, and the values and beliefs that will dominate the social atmosphere of the organization. In the perspective presented here, the problem of designing formative evaluation becomes primarily a matter of assessing the decision needs associated with cycles when uncertainty is high.

The design of formative evaluations must also focus on how information is used. Three types of use have been identified in the literature (Leviton and Hughes, 1981): instrumental use, which is action-oriented and focuses on short-term issues of program design and problem solving; conceptual use, which has a more indirect educational value and whose effects are broad and, in Weiss's (1979) terms, more like enlightenment; and symbolic or persuasive use, whose focus is primarily political and whose objective is to defend or attack programs or policies. Several points are noteworthy in considering these distinctions. They can be helpful as probes for getting users to specify the content and format of their information needs as they relate to different types of use. Also, as reported in Beyer and Trice's (1982) review, the research literature indicates that conceptual and symbolic/persuasive uses are much more common than instrumental use. There are several reasons why instrumental use may be low, including the fact that there are many determinants of development decisions other than information from program evaluation. Given specialization in program areas and jobs, a particular piece of information may be relevant to only a few individuals. It may also be difficult to identify instrumental use because of the diffuseness inherent in many decision situations.

While symbolic/persuasive use is thought to be quite common, it may also be underreported, since it is less socially acceptable to claim primarily political purposes in using evaluation. Nevertheless, Zweig's (1981) discussion of legislative decision making urges that program evaluation information be used with other forms of policy-relevant considerations for persuasive purposes. Also, symbolic/persuasive use may be seen as more justifiable in post-choice situations, when decisions are being implemented.

Given all these varieties of information use, what are the processes by which it is used? Beyer and Trice (1982) make distinctions among behaviors and phases in the information-use process, distinctions relevant to the problem of identifying information needs. They identify two phases of use: adopting the choice indicated by the information and then implementing that choice. Each phase can have different users and different information needs. For example, there is a need in the adoption phase for sensing and search behaviors, which will yield information that contains many alternatives and points of view. Argyris and Schön (1977) describe this process as an important component of organizational learning and suggest its necessity for producing information that permits questioning of the assumptions that underlie a program's purposes and methods of operation. Keen and Morton (1978), arguing that the dimensions of many decisions are amorphous, suggest that *decision support system* is a more appropriate term than *management information system* as a description of the role information plays in the adoption phase. The information provided in a decision support system should be able to accommodate varied decision styles, as well as the changing requirements of unstructured choice processes. The information itself may be routinely collected monitoring data, but it should be capable of being manipulated and collated in various ways to address the numerous questions that may be posed during the adoption phase.

In the implementation phase, information needs may be more routine. During this phase, monitoring activities become important as means of tracking implementation of the choices that have been adopted. Thus, routinely gathered information may be needed for purposes of external accountability or internal control. It is also possible that, during either the adoption or the implementation phase, users may need information that helps them understand program processes and explain program achievements, especially if users' primary interest is program improvement. This kind of formative use of information may require evaluation strategies that stress qualitative information and are designed to gather data in successive waves of interaction with program staff and constituents (Stake, 1975).

To review, it has been suggested that the design of formative evaluations should include methods that assess the information needs of the users. This task can be difficult because of normative pressures to describe a supposedly rational process. One method of encouraging the needs-assessment process is to probe for different types of information use during the adoption and implementation phases of the decision-making cycle. Information needs may relate to questions about underlying assumptions and methods of program operation or to routine monitoring data for purposes of external accountability and internal control.

Empirical Procedures. Evaluation design has traditionally focused on methodological and technical matters related to the empirical procedures for evaluation—that is, on research and sample design, measurement procedures, and analysis techniques. Empirical procedures should include qualitative and quantitative techniques, especially in evaluations of human services programs, where a mixture of measurement approaches is usually necessary to represent context, inputs, processes, and effects of programs (Reichardt and Cook, 1979). The selection of specific empirical procedures for evaluation relies on basic epistemological assumptions and arguments that govern not only choices for the procurement and analysis of evidence but also choices for the testing of inferences drawn from evidence (Glaser and Straus, 1967; Cook and Campbell, 1979). Techniques related to sampling, measurement, and data collection are also important. For instance, an evaluator designing a study may draw on the general theory and technology of testing (Cronbach, 1970), survey research (Warwick and Lininger, 1975), observational methods (Weick, in press), analysis of documents (Webb and others, 1966), or cost analysis (Levin, 1983).

The range of choice for empirical procedures has widened considerably over the past ten years, although it is not yet clear how free evaluators feel to use less conventional methods. Smith's (1981a) work on metaphors for evaluation has challenged evaluators to conceptualize their methods in ways that, in some instances, are radically different from the framework of Cook and Campbell. While evaluation may be more of an art than a science, selecting evaluation methods by the standards of artistic truth (Gephart, 1981) is often problematic. The difficulty with nontraditional methods, or methods that draw on the humanities more than on the sciences, is partly that evaluators are not trained to use them. But even if evaluators had broader exposure to methods of inquiry and analysis, the expectations of evaluation users are strongly disposed toward traditional approaches drawn from the social sciences (Weiss and Weiss, 1981). Often users want a study that appears scientifically sound so that they can reinforce the perception of rationality in decision making (Feldman and March, 1982).

It is up to evaluators to demonstrate that nontraditional methods can test the inferences drawn from evidence, rigorously and in ways that include or go beyond issues of internal, external, construct, and statistical validity (Cook and Campbell, 1979). The standards for evaluating logic and evidence can be drawn from a variety of areas, including law (Levine, 1974), philosophy (Gowin, 1981), photography (Becker, 1979), or naturalistic inquiry (Guba and Lincoln, 1981). Similarly, causal inquiry can take many forms in addition to those derived from an experimental framework. Examples would include the modus operandi strategy derived from methods of criminal investigation (Scriven, 1976) and the ethogenic approach, which is based on analysis of ordinary language and was developed from the Oxford school of philosophy (Harre, 1977). In addition, Smith (1981b), claiming that most questions in evaluation and policy research are not causal, has outlined a list of questions and appropriate methods for noncausal inquiry. These questions are very pertinent to formative evaluation, since they deal with such issues related to ongoing decision making as cost, description of daily events, and distribution of services. In all cases, however, it is important for evaluators to test the inferences drawn from evidence and to state explicitly which validity rules are being used.

Another especially useful method for internally based evaluation efforts is time-series analysis. In ongoing programs, issues of internal validity typically cannot be controlled by the use of comparison groups, and so longitudinal designs become a reasonable alternative. Creating a time series from existing organizational records or by means of other program monitoring methods is an attractive concept but also an empirical procedure that may pose inferential difficulties. Among these are limitations in comparing observations and changes in meaning over time, statistical problems involving a short time series, and ambiguity concerning the onset of the intervention being evaluated. Straw and others (1982) discuss these issues with respect to designs for time series that use archival data, and they suggest ways of strengthening these methods by adding primary data collection and by exploring alternative causal explanations for the findings.

In time series, designs require some form of regular program monitoring. There is recognition of the technological and political challenges of program monitoring (Grant, 1978), but evaluators have not associated themselves enough with the empirical methods for monitoring. Evaluators will need to assert their rights to monitor and examine program records in much the same way as auditors do now. In fact, there is a remarkable convergence between statements of professional purposes made by internal auditors and those made by program evaluators. It is likely that these two groups have much to learn from each other: Auditors can teach evaluators about program monitoring and ways to organize monitoring internally, and evaluators can teach auditors about a broad range of empirical procedures and epistemologies.

To accommodate the total possible variety of decision settings and needs, it is both possible and necessary that formative evaluators should broaden their choice of methods. Rather than merely broadening the array of alternatives, however, it is important to assess the program and decision settings carefully so that methods appropriate to settings can be selected. For the selection of evaluation methods, Maynard-Moody and McClintock (1981) propose a contingency framework based on the degree of uncertainty that characterizes program goals and causal processes. Cronbach and Associates (1980) present a two-variable scheme for making data-collection choices, which cross-tabulates types of evaluation users and their information needs with the degree to which the program is an established or an experimental entity. Questions about program characteristics and contexts of decision making must be considered in choices of empirical procedures. As these examples show, these questions can be addressed systematically.

The burgeoning variety of empirical procedures open to formative evaluators places a burden on their training. Since no single person can expect to be fully competent to perform the whole range of empirical tasks, it is necessary to organize the formative evaluation function so that it can incorporate a variety of skills and perspectives on empirical procedures and organizations. This objective could be achieved by the deliberate creation of an interdisciplinary staff or by way of contracts for the services of individuals who have the required skills (Millington, 1983).

Conclusion

The traditional and primary sources of guidance for evaluation design have been theory and knowledge pertaining to empirical procedures and their underlying assumptions. Empirical procedures are centrally concerned about the validity of inferences drawn from evidence, but these judgments also can be based on validity criteria drawn from other fields—law, philosophy, education, psychology, and so on. Moreover, the broader range of methodological choices available to evaluators today requires attention to program and decision characteristics as a guide to matching methods and settings appropriately.

A theory of formative evaluation should include systematic attention to issues of performance uncertainty, structural uncertainty, program theory, decision and action contexts, and empirical procedures. This conceptual framework is summarized in Figure 2. Careful attention to each of the issues outlined in this framework should make it possible to design formative evaluations that not only reflect varied program charcteristics, but also are responsive to constituents' information needs and to epistemological concerns about the quality of inferences derived from evaluation findings.

Figure 2. A Conceptual Framework for
the Design of Formative Evaluation

Purpose of Formative Evaluation: To reduce uncertainty about program performance and increase uncertainty about program structure.

The design of formative evaluation is

Based on assessment of   Which results in

Program theory, including
- Social science theory   Specified problem/program models
- Evaluability assessment   Measurement and design procedures
- Causal mapping   that are appropriate to the program

Decision/action context, including
- Processes of organizational   Identification of program options
  development and change
- Use of information   Identification of information needs

Empirical procedures, including
- Mixed methods/epistemologies   Selection of procedures based on
                                                   methodological and program
                                                   characteristics
- Time series/monitoring designs   Specified criteria for assessing the
                                                   quality of inferences

References

Adams, K. A. "Knowing When to 'Hold' 'Em and When to 'Fold' 'Em: Ethical Problems in the Role of the Internal Evaluator." Paper presented at the annual conference of the Evaluation Research Society, Montreal, April 1983.

Aiken, M., and Alford, R. R. "Community Structure and Innovation: The Case of Urban Renewal." *American Sociological Review*, 1970, *3*, 650–665.

Aldrich, H. E. *Organizations and Environment.* Englewood Cliffs, N.J.: Prentice-Hall, 1979.

Argyris, C., and Schön, D. A. *Organizational Learning: A Theory of Action Perspectives.* Reading, Mass.: Addison-Wesley, 1977.

Becker, H. "Do Photographs Tell The Truth?" In T. D. Cook and C. S. Reichardt (Eds.), *Qualitative and Quantitative Methods in Evaluation Research.* Beverly Hills, Calif.: Sage, 1979.

Beyer, J. M., and Trice, H. M. "The Utilization Process: A Conceptual Framework for Synthesis of Empirical Findings." *Administrative Science Quarterly*, 1982, *27*, 591–622.

Chen, H., and Rossi, P. H. "The Multi-Goal Theory-Driven Approach to Evaluation: A Model Linking Basic and Applied Social Sciences." *Social Forces*, 1980, *59*, 106–122.

Cook, T. D., and Campbell, D. T. *Quasi-Experimentation: Design and Analysis Issues for Field Settings.* Chicago: Rand McNally, 1979.

Cox, G. B. "Managerial Style: Implications for the Utilization of Program Evaluation Information." *Evaluation Quarterly*, 1977, *1*, 499–508.

Cronbach, L. J. "Course Improvement Through Evaluation." *Teachers College Record*, 1963, *64*, 672–683.

Cronbach, L. J. *Essentials of Psychological Testing.* New York: Harper and Row, 1970.

Cronbach, L. J., and Associates. *Toward Reform of Program Evaluation.* San Francisco: Jossey-Bass, 1980.

Delbecq, A. L., and Van de Ven, A. H. "Problem Analysis and Program Design: Nominal Group Process Technique." *Journal of Applied Behavioral Science,* 1971, *7,* 466–492.

Feldman, M. S., and March, J. G. "Information in Organizations as Signal and Symbol." *Administrative Science Quarterly,* 1982, *26,* 71–186.

Freeman, H. E., and Solomon, M. A. "The Next Decade in Evaluation Research." *Evaluation and Program Planning,* 1979, *2,* 255–262.

Gephart, W. J. "Watercolor Painting." In N. L. Smith (Ed.), *New Techniques for Evaluation.* Beverly, Hills, Calif.: Sage, 1981.

Glaser, B. G., and Straus, A. L. *The Discovery of Grounded Theory.* Chicago: Aldine, 1967.

Gold, N. *The Stakeholder Approach for Educational Program Evaluation.* Washington, D.C.: National Institute of Education, 1981.

Goodman, P. S., and Associates. *Change in Organization.* San Francisco: Jossey-Bass, 1982.

Gowin, D. B. "Philosophy." In N. L. Smith (Ed.), *Metaphors for Evaluation: Sources of New Methods.* Beverly Hills, Calif.: Sage, 1981.

Grant, D. L. (Ed.). *Monitoring Ongoing Programs.* New Directions for Program Evaluation, no. 3. San Francisco: Jossey-Bass, 1978.

Guba, E. G., and Lincoln, Y. S. *Effective Evaluation: Improving the Usefulness of Evaluation Results Through Responsive and Naturalistic Approaches.* San Francisco: Jossey-Bass, 1981.

Hall, R. I. "Simple Techniques for Constructing Explanatory Models of Complex Systems for Policy Analysis." *Dynamica,* 1978, *4,* 101–114.

Harre, R. "The Ethogenic Approach: Theory and Practice." In L. Berkowitz (Ed.), *Advances in Experimental Social Psychology.* New York: Academic Press, 1977.

Hedburg, B. L. T., Nystrom, P., and Starbuck, W. H. "Camping on Seesaws: Prescriptions for a Self-Assessing Organization." *Administrative Science Quarterly,* 1976, *21,* 41–65.

Jung, S. M. "Evaluability Assessment: A Two-Year Retrospective." Palo Alto, Calif.: American Institute for Research, 1982.

Keen, P. G. W., and Morton, M. S. *Decision Support Systems: An Organizational Perspective.* Reading, Mass.: Addison-Wesley, 1978.

Kennedy, M. M. "The Role of In-House Evaluator." *Evaluation Review,* 1983, *7,* 519–541.

Knapp, M. S. *Organizational Expertise: Building and Sustaining an Institutional Research and Planning Capability in College Administration.* Menlo Park, Calif.: SRI International, 1982.

Leavitt, H. J. "On the Design Part of Organizational Design." In R. H. Kilmann, L. R. Pondy, and D. P. Slevan (Eds.), *The Management of Organizational Design: Strategies and Implementation.* New York: North Holland, 1976.

Levin, H. M. *Cost Effectiveness: A Primer.* Beverly Hills, Calif.: Sage, 1983.

Levine, M. "Scientific Method and the Adversary Model: Some Preliminary Thoughts." *American Psychologist,* 1974, *29,* 661–677.

Leviton, C. C., and Hughes, E. F. "Research on the Utilization of Evaluation: A Review and Synthesis." *Evaluation Review,* 1981, *5,* 525–548.

McClintock, C. *Program Evaluation as Sense Making: An Approach for the 1980s.* Ithaca: N.Y.: Department of Human Service Studies, Cornell University, 1979.

McClintock, C., and Reilinger, E. "The Best-Laid Plans: Theory and Practice in Social Service Planning." *The Urban and Social Change Review,* 1980, *13,* 21–28.

McGowan, E. F. "Rational Fantasies." *Policy Sciences,* 1976, *7,* 439–454.

Maynard-Moody, S., and McClintock, C. "Square Pegs in Round Holes: Program

Evaluation and Organizational Uncertainty." *Policy Studies Journal*, 1981, *9* (5), 644–666.

Meyer, J. W., and Rowan, B. "Institutionalized Organizations: Formal Structure as Myth and Ceremony." *American Journal of Sociology*, 1977, *82*, 440–463.

Millington, P. S. "Internal Audit as Evaluation." Paper presented at Evaluation '83, Chicago, October 1983.

Passmore, W., and Friedlander, R. "An Action–Research Program for Increasing Employee Involvement in Problem Solving." *Administrative Science Quarterly*, 1982, *27*, 343–362.

Patton, M. Q. *Utilization-Focused Evaluation.* Beverly Hills, Calif.: Sage, 1978.

Pondy, L. R. "Two Faces of Evaluation." In H. W. Melton and D. J. H. Watson (Eds.), *Interdisciplinary Dimensions of Accounting for Social Goals and Social Organizations.* Columbus, Ohio: Grid, 1977.

Reichardt, C. S., and Cook, T. D. "Beyond Qualitative Versus Quantitative Methods." In T. D. Cook and C. S. Reichardt (Eds.), *Qualitative and Quantitative Methods in Evaluation Research.* Beverly Hills, Calif.: Sage, 1979.

Rockart, J. F. "Chief Executives Define Their Own Data Needs." *Harvard Business Review*, 1979, *57*, 81–93.

Rousseau, D. M. "Technology and Organization: A Constructive Review and Analytic Framework." In S. E. Seashore, E. E. Lawler, P. H. Mirvis, and C. Cammann (Eds.), *Assessing Organizational Change.* New York: Wiley, 1983.

Schwarz, P. A. "Program Devaluation: Can the Experiment Reform?" In E. H. Loveland (Ed.), *Measuring the Hard-to-Measure.* New Directions for Program Evaluation, no. 6. San Francisco: Jossey-Bass, 1980.

Scriven, M. "The Methodology of Evaluation." In R. W. Tyler, R. M. Gagné, and M. Scriven (Eds.), *Perspectives on Curriculum Evaluation.* AERA Monograph Issues on Curriculum Evaluation, no. 1. Chicago: Rand McNally, 1967.

Scriven, M. "Evaluation Perspectives and Procedures." In W. J. Popham (Ed.), *Evaluation in Education: Current Applications.* Berkeley, Calif.: McCutchan, 1974.

Scriven, M. "Maximizing the Power of Causal Investigation: The Modus Operandi Method." In G. V. Glass (Ed.), *Evaluation Studies Review Annual.* Beverly Hills, Calif.: Sage, 1976.

Smith, N. L. (Ed.). *Metaphors for Evaluation: Sources of New Methods.* Beverly Hills, Calif: Sage, 1981a.

Smith, N. L. "Noncausal Inquiry in Evaluation." *Educational Researcher*, 1981b, *10*, 23.

Stake, R. E. (Ed.). *Evaluating the Arts in Education: A Responsive Approach.* Columbus, Ohio: Merrill, 1975.

Straw, R. B., Fitzgerald, N. M., Cook, T. D., and Thomas, S. V. "Using Routine Monitoring Data to Identify Effects and Their Causes." In G. Forehand (Ed.), *Applications of Time Series Analysis to Evaluation.* New Directions for Program Evaluation, no. 16. San Francisco: Jossey-Bass, 1982.

Stufflebeam, D. L., Foley, W. J., Gephart, W. J., Guba, E. G., Hammond, L. R., Merriman, H. O., and Provus, M. M. *Educational Evaluation and Decision Making.* Itasca, Ill.: Peacock, 1971.

Suchman, E. A. *Evaluative Research: Principles and Practice in Public Service and Social Action Programs.* New York: Russell Sage Foundation, 1967.

Tichy, N. M. "Problem Cycles in Organizations and the Management of Change." In J. R. Kimberly and R. H. Miles (Eds.), *The Organizational Life Cycle.* San Francisco: Jossey-Bass, 1980.

Trochim, W., and Linton, R. "Structured Conceptualizations: Framing the Evaluation Question." Ithaca, N.Y.: Department of Human Service Studies, Cornell University, 1983.

Warwick, D. P., and Lininger, C. A. *The Sample Survey: Theory and Practice.* New York: McGraw-Hill, 1975.

Webb, E. J., Campbell, D. T., Schwartz, R. D., and Sechrest, L. *Unobtrusive Measures: Nonreactive Research in the Social Sciences.* Chicago: Rand McNally, 1966.

Weick, K. E. "Repunctuating the Problem." In P. S. Goodman and J. M. Pennings (Eds.), *New Perspectives in Organizational Effectiveness.* San Francisco: Jossey-Bass, 1977.

Weick, K. E. *The Social Psychology of Organizing.* Reading, Mass.: Addison-Wesley, 1979.

Weick, K. "Systematic Observational Methods." In G. Lindzey and E. Aronson (Eds.), *The Handbook of Social Psychology.* Reading, Mass.: Addison-Wesley, in press.

Weiss, C. H. "The Many Meanings of Research Utilization." *Public Administration Review,* 1979, *39,* 426–431.

Weiss, C. H., and Bucuvalas, M. "Truth Tests and Utility Tests: Decision Makers' Frames of Reference for Social Science Research." *American Sociological Review,* 1980, *45,* 302–313.

Weiss, J. A., and Weiss, C. H. "Social Scientists and Decision Makers Look at the Usefulness of Mental Health Research." *American Psychologist,* 1981, *36,* 837–847.

Wergin, J. "The Evaluation of Organizational Policy Making: A Political Model." *Review of Educational Research,* 1976, *46,* 75–115.

Wildavsky, A. "The Self-Evaluating Organization." *Public Administration Review,* 1972, *32,* 509–520.

Yourdan, E. *Structured Design.* New York: Yourdan, 1976.

Zweig, F. M. "On Educating the Congress for Evaluation." In F. Zweig and K. M. Marvin (Eds.), *Educating Policy Makers for Evaluation.* Beverly Hills, Calif.: Sage, 1981.

Charles McClintock is assistant dean for educational programs and policy and director of institutional studies in the College of Human Ecology at Cornell University, where he also teaches organizational behavior and program evaluation.

10

A Decisionmaking Context Model
for Enhancing Evaluation Utilization

Robert D. Brown, Dianna L. Newman, and Linda S. Rivers

A major reason for performing evaluations is to provide useful information that will assist administrators, advisory boards, and program developers and planners in making decisions. Researchers and theoreticians have focused extensively in recent years on examining the concept of use and factors influencing use of evaluation information. There have been discussions about the definition of use (Braskamp & Brown, 1980), how to measure use (Weiss, 1982), use and policymaking (Caplan, 1977), and different kinds of use (Leviton & Hughes, 1981). There has also been research on the applicability of communication theory to understanding evaluation use (Newman, Brown, & Braskamp, 1980) and the relationship of personalogical variables, such as locus of control, to acceptance and use of evaluative information (Newman, Brown, & Rivers, 1983). Researchers and practitioners alike now know more about how the characteristics of the evaluator (Braskamp, Brown, & Newman, 1980), the evaluation report (Thompson, Brown, & Furgason, 1981), and the decisionmaker (Newman, Brown, & Littman, 1979) are related to how evaluative information is used. These efforts have been helpful, but there is at least one missing element: the characteristics

of the decision context. How do various decision contexts affect use of evaluation information?

The importance of understanding decisionmaking in evaluation has been recognized for some time (Provus, 1969; Stufflebeam et al., 1971). Stufflebeam et al. (1971) confronted the importance of the decision context when they suggested there were four types of decisions: neomobilistic, incremental, homestasic, and metamorphic. There have been few efforts, however, to examine systematically the possible effect different decision contexts have on the use of evaluation information. Many evaluation models that adhere to a decisionmaking framework present a series of steps in program design and implementation that include decision points made with evaluative input. The decisionmaking process is usually characterized as a linear step-by-step process with flow charts indicating when and what information is needed for the next decision in program development. These schemas may be useful for ensuring the timeliness of information, but they do not illuminate the process itself (Attkisson, Brown, & Hargreaves, 1978; Schulberg & Jerrell, 1979).

If the evaluator is concerned about the

From Brown et al., "A Decisionmaking Context Model for Enhancing Evaluation Utilization," *Educational Evaluation and Policy Analysis*, 1984, 6, 383-400. Copyright 1984, American Educational Research Association, Washington, DC.

usefulness of the information provided, as well as the timeliness, his or her role expands from being a technical provider of information to that of being a consultant. An effective consultant needs to understand the decisionmaking context.

The decision context includes internal influences, such as pressures to maintain or improve status and to make the right decision. External influences include time limitations, financial constraints, and interpersonal and organizational concerns. These interact in a complex fashion to make up a decision context. The evaluator must be able to make judgments about the specific decisionmaking context he or she is operating in to answer such questions as (a) Why am I being asked to do this evaluation? (b) What kinds of information does this organization want? And, importantly, (c) What kinds of data are the decisionmakers most likely to utilize? To answer these questions, the evaluator needs to understand individual decisionmakers and organizations and the unique circumstances that influence how decisions are made. Evaluators have not always demonstrated this awareness (DeYoung & Conner, 1982).

This paper discusses two models that hold promise for helping evaluators understand and cope with different decision contexts: the Conflict Model (Janis & Mann, 1977) and the Social Process Model (Vroom & Yago, 1974). This paper describes the basic tenets of the two models to give the evaluator a theoretical base. At appropriate points, these tenets are related to decisionmaking in an evaluation setting. Finally, implications for using a decisionmaking model in evaluations are explored and specific guidelines for using a model in evaluation settings are outlined.

The Conflict Model

Janis and Mann (1977) sought to determine how intrapersonal factors influence decisionmaking. Their Conflict Model of decisionmaking suggests that the degree of conflict faced by the decisionmaker affects the decisionmaking process and the quality of the decision. Conflict is described as the presence of simultaneous opposing tendencies within the individual to accept or reject a specific course of action. The intensity of the conflict varies depending on (a) perceived magnitude of potential loss for the decisionmaker, (b) amount of time available to make the decision, and (c) whether a "right" choice or solution is thought to be possible.

Loss to the decisionmaker can include diminishing utilitarian values (e.g., loss of money or job), lessening of social approval (e.g., peer recognition or status group membership, or a reduction in self-approval, e.g., self-perception as a "wise" decisionmaker or as a person with good judgment). Variations in the magnitude of perceived potential loss in any one or combination of these perceptions affects the intensity of the conflict and the nature of the decisionmaking process. Potential loss of job or status is a powerful source of stress, but the impact of loss of peer recognition or self-esteem based on being a good decisionmaker should not be underestimated.

The amount of time available to find a solution is another factor affecting the degree of stress and conflict present in decisionmaking. Severe time limitations usually heighten tension and lead to behaviors different from those made when time is viewed as unlimited.

The availability of a correct or best solution is an important determinant of stress. If the decisionmaker perceives there is a correct answer that can be determined if the proper kinds of information are available, his or her behavior and the amount of stress will differ from when there is supposedly no best answer. If there is a "correct" answer, there must be "wrong" answers, and no decisionmaker wants to be wrong.

Variations in any one of the three variables—perceived personal loss, amount of time available, and possibility of a correct solution—affect an individual's decisionmaking behavior. The variables also interact with each other to produce different effects. Janis and Mann (1977) postulate different behaviors in situations with a variety of combinations of personal loss, time limits, and the availability of satisfactory solutions leading to vigilance, hypervigilance, procrastination, or shifting responsibility. Depending on variations and interactions in perceived personal risk, availability of a correct solution, and time limitations, the decision-maker is more or less likely to (a) explore alternative courses of action, (b) conduct an intensive search for new information, (c) assimilate new information, (d) pay attention to expert judgments, and (e) plan for implementation of a decision. In general, the vigilant and hypervigilant engage in more of these activities than either the procrastinator or the shifter of responsibility. The vigilant decisionmaker, however, will be less frenetic and more effective.

These postulates were derived for personal decisionmaking, and they have rather strong inherent face validity. (Think about the last time you purchased a car.) A decision about whether or not to implement a new sex education program fits into the conflict model quite well. If there is a time limitation (a school board member wants to discuss it at the next meeting), the principal is likely to seek advice from others but perhaps at a hurried pace, asking questions about one or two specific alternatives. If the principal believes there is only one program that will appeal to board members (availability of a solution) and there is fear of rejection or lessening of self-approval through proposing a "bad idea" (personal risk), his or her information demands will differ from if there was no time limitation or no fear of rejection.

The Social Model

Vroom and his associates (Vroom, 1976; Vroom & Yago, 1974; Vroom & Yetton, 1973) view decisionmaking primarily from a social perspective. They sought to determine whether good decisionmakers operate the same in every decision setting. Vroom suggests that approaches to decisionmaking are and should be influenced by the nature of the particular situation. He posits that there is no one preferred style for all individuals or for all situations. Like Janis and Mann (1977), Vroom suggests that time limitations affect decisionmaking style. He adds variables, however, for further consideration. Although these variables are not completely distinct from Janis and Mann's views, they merit attention. Vroom's factors include (a) quality or rationality of the decision, (b) acceptance or commitment of subordinates to implement the decision, and (c) whether or not the problem is structured.

The quality of the decision can be affected by several dimensions of the problem. A decision is characterized as one of low quality if the expected value of the alternative outcomes is equal and if there appears to be no technical or rational method for choosing among alternatives. A high quality context, on the other hand, is one in which a correct decision will yield better results and it is possible to decide rationally or with the assistance of technology. Deciding how to allocate scarce resources or making decisions that are not easily reversible are examples of high quality decision contexts. Quality can be considered similarly to Janis and Mann's (1977) factor of the availability of a correct solution.

An important criterion for determining who should be consulted and involved in a decision is whether acceptance of the decision by subordinates is necessary for successful implementation to occur. Some examples of questions of concern include the following: For what kinds of decisions should staff be consulted? For what decisions should staff be consulted, but not asked to vote on or make the decision? What kinds of decisions should staff be allowed to vote on and have the vote be the final decision? Questions about staff decisionmaking are receiving increasing attention in both industry and education (Hare, 1980; Hoy & Miskel, 1978; Larson, 1980; Meadows, 1980).

Face validity for this model might be less evident for individual personal decisionmaking than it would be for persons in an administrative position. Vroom and Yago (1974), however, report empirical evidence they believe supports the model as being descriptive of strategies used by decisionmakers. Most persons who have been in administrative positions have probably been faced with several of the contexts described by Vroom and found that even though they wish to be democratic, there are instances in which subordinates prefer that the decision be made by the administrator. There are also situations when staff want to be intimately involved in the process and to have a direct say in the decision.

Evaluators are generally conscious of trying to determine who the decisionmakers are in an evaluation context. This model suggests that knowing who is affected by the potential decisions is also important, and these people may be an important data source.

Implications for Evaluators

Decision Contexts

Both the conflict and social models have implicit implications for evaluation. The situations they portray and resultant decisionmaker behaviors have ramifications for whether and how evaluation information is used. They also suggest a variety of consulting roles and behaviors that will enhance utilization and an evaluator's effectiveness.

For illustrative purposes, four combinations of risk, time constraints, and availability of a solution are described, along with implications for evaluators, such as involving staff and influencing the extent of data collected and presented (see Table I).

1. *No risk, no time limit, no one solution.* In this situation, the decisionmaker faces no potential loss and as a result is indifferent. Because there is nothing to lose, the decisionmaker is unlikely to be

TABLE I

Possible Decisionmaker Behaviors and Evaluator Concerns for Selected Decision Contexts

Decision context	Decisionmaker behaviors	Evaluator concerns
No risk, no time limitation, no one solution	Indifferent to evaluation in general. Little interest in new information. No concern for exploring program options or implementing changes as a result of evaluation.	Must motivate self-interest of decisionmaker in value and uses of evaluation. Might seek input from staff who may see more value in formative evaluation. Should guard against recommendations being ignored or slavishly followed without serious study.
High risk, time limits, no one solution	Will try to avoid decision through procrastination or passing decision on to someone else. Is likely to want only information that supports biases and to avoid all information that questions these biases.	May be asked to assume the decisionmaker role. Must guard against information being slanted toward biases. Should be sensitive to staff and decisionmaker identification with program. Might consider role as a conflict reducer.
High risk, time limitation, solution possible	Will fluctuate between high and low interest in new information. Will have difficulty in discriminating between relevant and nonrelevant information and is unlikely to distinguish most valid sources of data. Most receptive to information supporting biases.	Need to focus on establishing priorities of information needs and relate data to specific decision. Should avoid overcollection of data and overanalysis. Need to concentrate on succinct data reporting. May not be time for extensive surveys of staff or others, but quick assessment might be possible.
High risk, no time limitation, solution possible	Will be open to new program options and thorough review of program objectives and analysis of evaluation information. Will spend time assessing value of information provided—its validity and reliability. Open to staff concerns.	Comprehensive evaluation possible. Effort should be made to ensure that instruments are reliable and valid. Consider involving staff in evaluation process.

biased when presented with new information. If a program change is an expected outcome of an evaluation, this decisionmaker will be open to reviewing current policies to determine those that are applicable. For the most part, however, this decisionmaker is unlikely to be greatly concerned about studying program objectives, looking at potentially new policies, obtaining evaluation information, or planning for implementation for any resulting recommendations.

This situation confronts the evaluator with several basic questions. Should an evaluation be conducted at all? If the decisionmaker is unconcerned, he or she is unlikely to give attention to the evaluation process or the results. If the evaluation is conducted, how extensive should it be? Will a minimal effort, perhaps focusing on key selected variables, be sufficient? A narrow, well-focused evaluation might be one solution.

The evaluator might consider different strategies for getting the decisionmaker involved. Perhaps if there are no risks there could be positive gains for the decisionmaker if the correct information is collected. The evaluator might focus on how the decisionmaker's position could be enhanced or how the program might be improved by the evaluation. An evaluation effort aimed at determining ways to improve the program might be especially appealing to the decisionmaker. Some research findings suggest that educating decisionmakers about how evaluation can be helpful increases their interest in an evaluation's usefulness (Brown, Newman, & Rivers, 1980).

In this situation, it is possible that the evaluator will be asked for his or her recommendations. This is especially likely if there are no other evaluation audiences with special interests or concerns. The evaluator will have to be on guard that the recommendations are not followed slavishly and without deliberation because of indifference. If the decision affects staff or subordinates, or if their support is needed, it is possible the staff might become the evaluator's major source for determining information needs. Involving the staff in the evaluation design may also increase the possibility that the results will be used. The

decisionmaker may be awakened from indifference when the staff show interest.

2. *High risk, time limited, no one solution.* In this situation the decisionmaker faces a risk of high personal loss with a definite timeline. This situation could lead to several alternative decisionmaker behaviors affecting an evaluation effort. One possible response is delay. Another is to attempt to shift responsibility to someone else. Still another possibility is that an evaluation would not be commissioned by the decisionmaker, or at least not directly.

If an evaluation is conducted, the procrastinator is going to be most responsive to positive feedback that contains opinions and findings supporting the decisionmaker's biases. The evaluator must be particularly alert to misuse of information, incomplete quotes, and other abuses. Perhaps the decisionmaker may attempt to shift the responsibility to the evaluator. A question such as, "What do you think we should do?" might not reflect the decisionmaker's faith in the judgment of the evaluator; rather, it may be an attempt to set him or her up as the scapegoat for tough decisions that have to be made now or for future blame if recommendations are followed and prove ineffective. One potential role for the evaluator is to assist the decisionmaker in identifying, labeling, and examining the kinds and sources of information that could be most damaging. This would probably be a more fruitful approach if the evaluator is involved early in the program development stages. The evaluator may have to take the initiative and also assume a transactional role (Rippey, 1973), assisting the decisionmaker by determining sources of resistance and hostility. Rippey suggests that evaluators probably would not want to engage in conflict resolution unless they are members of the program staff.

If a decisionmaker is facing high personal risk, he or she is unlikely to relegate the decision to staff unless shifting responsibility will reduce the personal risk. It might be possible that making the decision a collective one will diffuse the personal risk. If so, a staff decision could be a viable option. This would be especially true if the potential loss is in self-esteem and not loss of job or money. The evaluator might serve a useful role in this context by suggesting ways to obtain staff suggestions through questionnaires, interviews, or town meetings.

3. *High risk, time limited, solution possible.* The decisionmaker who fears personal loss, is under a timeline, and believes there is a right solution, will want many kinds of information. Not all of the requested information will be relevant. It may not be unique for an evaluator to be confronted with a decisionmaker who aggressively wants more information, but this does not guarantee the information will be used any more effectively or appropriately than in the previously described situations. In this situation, the evaluator can expect great fluctuations in the decisionmaker's behavior. At times he or she will demand all kinds of information from a multitude of sources. At other times, the same decisionmaker will be so overwhelmed with the available information that no new information is welcomed. The attention of the decisionmaker will flit from one bit of information to another. The result is continued confusion and indecision.

Good consulting skills are vital for an evaluator's success in this situation. The evaluator will have to actively assist the decisionmaker in determining what information is pertinent and what is not. If time is limited, priorities will have to be placed on data collection processes. The evaluator will have to tread a fine line. A danger to be avoided is reinforcing the decisionmaker's frenzy through data collection processes that result in lengthy questionnaires and massive amounts of data. To avoid this pitfall it is necessary that sufficient breadth of coverage be provided to include the decisionmaker's concerns that might arise after the data are collected. This requires a highly skilled evaluator. Especially in this situation, the evaluator must be a good synthesizer of information. He or she must present information clearly and demonstrate concrete ties between decisions that have to be made and the information collected.

4. *High risk, no time limitation, solution possible.* This decision context exists when conflict is present and a correct solution is possible, but there is no time limitation. According to Janis and Mann,

this is the optimal decisionmaking context. The decisionmaker is likely to be open to new information and willing to explore alternative program options and objectives. Of all the decision contexts, this one finds the decisionmaker least likely to be biased. With a correct solution possible and no time limitations, the decisionmaker is more likely to spend time scrutinizing the validity and reliability of the evaluation information. He or she will be concerned about how changes will be implemented as well as whether or not they need to be made.

At first, this appears to be the ideal decision context for the evaluator. The responsibilities and consulting skills of the evaluator are needed, however, as much in this context as they are in any of the other three. In this situation, the chances for a thorough evaluation and the potential usefulness of the evaluation information are both high. The evaluator needs to be concerned about the needs of the staff who will be implementing any revisions in the program. The staff should probably be involved at the beginning of the evaluation process, helping to define issues, determine information needs, and sort out information resources. Special care must be given to developing and selecting technically good evaluation instruments.

More combinations of the context factors of risk, time, and solution are possible, but the four provided in Table I should provide sufficient illustrations of the implications for evaluators.

Questions for Evaluation Consultants

The evaluator also must be able to discern what classification or category best fits his or her current evaluation context. To do this the evaluator must be able to analyze the situation and the decisionmaker's concerns. Suggested questions to help make this determination are presented in Appendix A.

Conclusion

Neither the descriptions in Table I nor the questions in Appendix A are intended to be exhaustive; rather, they illustrate evaluation contexts, possible decisionmaker behavior, and potential evaluator concerns and actions. The value of the

---

APPENDIX A

Check List of Questions for Evaluation Consultants To Determine Potential Conflict and Loss

Extent of Potential Conflict
1. Does the client believe there are serious risks if some change is not made in the program?
2. Does the client believe there are serious risks if some change is made in the program?
3. Is it possible that there is a *best* course of action for the client?
4. Does the client believe there is sufficient time to conduct an extensive evaluation?
5. Is staff support vital in the successful implementation of the program changes?
6. What constituencies (e.g., staff) are affected by potential program change?

Sources of Potential Loss for the Client
1. Can the client lose his or her job as a result of program decisions based on evaluation?
2. Can the client lose group status as a result of program decisions based on evaluation?
3. Can the client lose self-esteem as a result of program decisions based on evaluation?
4. Can the client lose power within the organization as a result of evaluation?
5. Is it possible that morale will suffer within the organization as a result of decisions based on evaluation?
6. Can significant amounts of funding for the organization be lost as a result of program decisions based on evaluation?

---

suggestions and guidelines for evaluators who are working with decisionmakers depends on the validity of the decisionmaking paradigms and their applicability to evaluation contexts. As good theories often do, the Janis and Mann conflict model and the Vroom social perspective model make good sense. They fit well with experiences of administrators making decisions as well as those of individuals who must make choices. Initial empirical simulation studies employing these models to investigate decisionmaking in evaluations support the effect of time and risk in decisionmaking by school boards and administrators (Newman, Brown, Rivers, & Glock, 1983) and in group decisionmaking by educators (Pflum & Brown, 1984).

Evaluations are not always used for decisionmaking if decisionmaking is thought of as an entirely formal and rational process leading to a decision based on a direct one-to-one relationship with the evaluation information. With broadened definitions of information use and decisionmaking, however, researchers can search out the subtleties. The models illustrated in this paper can serve as a stimulus for further research and a temporary heuristic for practitioners.

References

ATTKISSON, C. C., BROWN, T. R., & HARGREAVES, W. A. (1978). Roles and functions of evaluation in human service programs. In C. C. Attkisson, M. Horowitz, & J. E. Sorenson (Eds.), *Evaluation of human service programs*. New York: Academic Press.

BRASKAMP, L. A., & BROWN, R. D. (Eds.). (1980). *Utilization of evaluative information*. San Francisco: Jossey-Bass.

BRASKAMP, L. A., BROWN, R. D., & NEWMAN, D. L. (1980). Credibility of a local educational program evaluation report: Author source and client characteristics. *American Educational Research Journal, 15*, 441–450.

CAPLAN, N. (1977). Social research and national policy: What gets used by whom for what purposes and with what effect. In M. Guttentag (Ed.), *Evaluation studies review annual*. Beverly Hills, CA: Sage.

DeYOUNG, D. J., & CONNER, R. F. (1982). Evaluation preconceptions about organizational decisionmaking: Rational versus incremental perspectives. *Evaluation Review, 6*(3), 431–440.

HARE, P. A. (1980). Consensus vs. laboratory vote. *Small Group Behavior, 11*(2), 131–144.

HOY, W. K., & MISKEL, C. (1978). *Educational administration theory, research, and practice*. New York: Random House.

JANIS, I. L., & MANN, L. (1977). *Decision-making*. New York: Free Press.

LARSON, S. H. (1980). The behavioral side of productive meetings. *Personnel Journal, 59*(4), 292–295.

LEVITON, L. A., & HUGHES, E. F. X. (1981). Research on utilization of evaluations: A review and synthesis. *Evaluation Review, 5*(4), 525–548.

MEADOWS, J. S. (1980). Organic structure, satisfaction and personality. *Human Relations, 33*(6), 383–392.

NEWMAN, D. L., BROWN, R. D., & BRASKAMP, L. A. (1980). Communication theory as a paradigm for studying evaluation use. In L. A. Braskamp & R. D. Brown (Eds.), *Utilization of evaluative information*. San Francisco: Jossey-Bass.

NEWMAN, D. L., BROWN, R. D., & LITTMAN, M. (1979). Evaluator report and audience characteristics which influence the impact of evaluation reports: Does who says what to whom make a difference? *CEDR Quarterly, 12*, 14–18.

NEWMAN, D. L., BROWN, R. D., & RIVERS, L. S. (1983).

Locus of control and evaluation use: Does sense of control affect information needs and decision-making? *Studies in Educational Evaluation, 9,* 77–88.

NEWMAN, D., BROWN, R., RIVERS, L., & GLOCK, R. (1983). School boards' and administrators' use of evaluation information: Influencing factors. *Evaluation Review, 7*(1), 110–125.

PFLUM, G., & BROWN, R. D. (1984). The effect of conflict, quality, and time on small group information use and behavior in evaluative decision-making situations. *Evaluation and Program Planning, 7,* 35–43.

PROVUS, M. M. (1969). Evaluation of ongoing programs in the public school system. In R. T. Tyler (Ed.), *Educational evaluation: New roles, new means.* The Sixty-eighth Yearbook of the National Society for the Study of Education, Part II. Chicago: University of Chicago Press.

RIPPEY, R. M. (Ed.). (1973). *Studies in transactional evaluation.* Berkeley, CA: McCutchan.

SCHULBERG, H. C., & JERRELL, J. M. (1979). *The evaluation and management.* Beverly Hills, CA: Sage.

STUFFLEBEAM, D. L., FOLEY, W. J., GEPHART, W., GUBA, E. G., HAMMOND, R. L., MERRIMAN, H. O., & PROVUS, M. M. (1971). *Educational evaluation and decision-making in education.* Bloomington, IN: Phi Delta Kappan National Study Committee on Education.

THOMPSON, P., BROWN, R. D., & FURGASON, J. (1981). The impact of evaluation audiences: Jargon and data do make a difference. *Evaluation Review, 5*(2), 269–279.

VROOM, V. H. (1976). Can leaders learn to lead? *Organizational Dynamics, 3,* 17–28.

VROOM, V. H., & YAGO, A. G. (1974). Decision-making as a social process: Normative and descriptive models of leader behavior. *Decision Sciences, 5,* 743–768.

VROOM, V. H., & YETTON, P. W. (1973). *Leadership and decision-making.* Pittsburgh: University of Pittsburgh Press.

WEISS, C. H. (1982). Measuring the use of evaluations. In E. House (Ed.), *Evaluation studies review annual* (Vol. 7, pp. 129–146). Beverly Hills, CA: Sage.

Authors

ROBERT D. BROWN, Professor, Teachers College, University of Nebraska, Lincoln, NE 68588-0440. *Specializations:* Utilization of evaluation information.

DIANNA L. NEWMAN, Assistant Professor, Applied Behavioral Sciences, Oklahoma State University, Stillwater, OK 74074. *Specializations:* Evaluation, statistics.

LINDA S. RIVERS, Counselor, Counseling Center, University of Nebraska, Lincoln, NE 68588. *Specializations:* Evaluation, child development.

SECTION 2
Practical Advice

Program evaluation, viewed as a profession that offers services to various client programs and their constituents is necessarily concerned with many aspects of professional practice that go beyond those intrinsic to the research function. Chief among these aspects are relationships with clients and the evaluator's obligation to be an effective, accountable, and responsible consultant.

The three chapters in this section offer eminently useful advice on crucial facets of professional practice in program evaluation. Collectively, they serve to heighten our awareness of the need for high professional standards in the field and the nature of the required standards. Not incidentally, these chapters also remind us of the hard work entailed if we are to thoroughly understand the issues with which we deal, openly document and verify our findings, and stay well within accepted ethical and legal boundaries in our dealings with the various persons and programs involved in our work.

The first chapter, by Verdier, represents a former insider's view of how congressional decision-making actually occurs and, most important, what is required of a researcher/analyst who wishes to influence that decision making. At first glance, this chapter may seem somewhat narrow and inappropriate. It is written for economists with reference to congressional decision making at the federal level. Verdier's analysis, however, loses none of its insight, accuracy, usefulness, or good humor when read with the label "evaluator" substituted for "economist" and when applied to any level of program or policy decision making other than congressional.

In the second chapter of this section, Pollard, Cooper, and Griffin focus on a rather different, and much neglected, aspect of evaluation practice—documentation. They observe that documentation is the primary tangible product of evaluation study and that, in many ways, it provides the framework for thinking through the evaluation plan and management. Most important, perhaps, is the role of documentation in maintaining accountability in the evaluation. It is through documentation that the evaluator demonstrates that careful work was done, shows how the results were obtained and verified, and makes explicit the connection between evidence and advice. Good documentation thus reflects good evaluation management, high scientific standards, and the attention to detail expected of professionals. Pollard et al. make a particularly useful contribution by carefully charting the various phases of an evaluation project and the types of documentation appropriate to each.

The final note struck in this section is both sobering and revealing. As evaluation matures toward full professional standing and intimate involvement in inherently political program contexts, increased awareness of applicable legal standards will be essential to effective, responsible practice. As Thurston, Ory, Mayberry, and Braskamp observe in their chapter, evaluation practice potentially is subject to many legal challenges—the surprise is that so few cases have been reported. Their careful review of the areas of legal theory most applicable to program evaluation covers defamation, breach of contract, malpractice, and confidentiality of sources. The moral of this chapter is that it is a foolish evaluator who proceeds without awareness of the legal implications of virtually every phase of the evaluation. As evaluators increasingly adopt a consultant role and move away from the role of value-neutral researcher, increased challenge seems inevitable. Even without such challenge, a responsible professional practices within applicable legal standards and with awareness of those standards. Equally important is the protection that evaluators can find in legal theory if they are cognizant of the relevant issues when negotiating contracts, collecting information, and publicizing evaluation results.

Much of the history and literature of program evaluation has focused on the research function—collecting, analyzing, and interpreting data. The lesson we draw from the chapters in this section is that equal attention is needed for issues of professional practice. Managing evaluation, advising clients effectively, maintaing professional and legal standards, documenting activities and evidence, and other such matters are as central, as important, and as complex as research design, measurement, and statistics. We should give such topics the attention they deserve.

11

Advising Congressional Decision-Makers
Guidelines for Economists
James M. Verdier

Abstract

Economists have less influence on congressional decision-making than they might because they do not make a sufficient effort to learn how issues look from the politicians' point of view. Politics and economics are inextricably connected in congressional decision-making. For those economists who are willing to try to bridge the gap between economists and politicians, the article suggests ten guidelines: (1) learn about the history of the issue; (2) find out who will be making the decision; (3) timing is critical; (4) learn everyone's interests and arguments; (5) it's OK to think like an economist, but don't write like one; (6) keep it simple; (7) congressmen care more about distribution than efficiency; (8) take implementation and administration into account; (9) emphasize a few crucial and striking numbers; and (10) read the newspapers.

A substantial literature has grown up lamenting the failure of policymakers to make use of sound economic analysis,[1] and advising economists on how best to have an impact on policy decisions.[2] The justification for adding yet another piece to this body of work is that most such efforts reflect (as does this one) a relatively limited perspective. Economic analysis is used, misused, or not used in a variety of different contexts. Lessons drawn from one may be less applicable in others. If enough efforts are made to pull together useful guidelines from a variety of contexts, however, more generally applicable principles may ultimately emerge. Samuel Johnson, who had little patience with dullards, dismissed such continual accretion as an "epidemical conspiracy for the destruction of paper."[3] For those of us who are slower of wit, however, there may be no better way to proceed.

   This article focuses on providing economic advice to congressional policymakers. Following ancient tradition, the guidelines it offers number ten in all. Before getting to the guidelines, however, some preliminary discussion of the role of economists in congressional decision-making may be helpful.[4]

From James M. Verdier, "Advising Congressional Decision-Makers: Guidelines for Economists," *Journal of Policy Analysis and Management.* Copyright 1984 by the Association for Public Policy Analysis and Management. Reprinted by permission of John Wiley & Sons, Inc.

ECONOMISTS IN
CONGRESSIONAL
DECISION-MAKING

Economists are sometimes dismayed and chagrined by how little impact the "economic merits" of an issue seem to have on congressional decisions. Congressmen appear to pay much more attention to the views of constituents, organized interest groups, congressional colleagues, the president, and the media than they do to those of economists. This should not be surprising. The Congress was designed to be a representative body, and each economist has only one vote. To get beyond their "one person, one vote" allocation of influence, economists must overcome two problems.

The Access Problem

Congressional decision-makers suffer from an almost unmanageable information overload; government agencies, trade associations, lobbyists, newspapers, journals, magazines, think tanks, academics, people they meet at cocktail parties, old cronies, and an endless stream of petitioners all deluge them with information.

The time congressmen have to absorb all of this is extremely limited. A 1977 study found that the average congressman worked an 11-hour day, but spent only about 11 minutes of that time reading in the office.[5] This does not include reading at home in the evening and on weekends, or reading done "on the run." It probably also does not include newspapers, which congressmen consume voraciously. But it does include the kind of information economists are most likely to produce: journal articles, studies, and reports.

Given these constraints, most economic analysis reaches congressmen indirectly and through a variety of filters. One is congressional staff, both those that are personal to each congressman and those that are attached to congressional committees. While the degree of economic understanding among staff members varies enormously, a number of those who serve the tax, budget, banking, and other committees with major economic responsibilities have extensive backgrounds in economics. Their time is extremely limited, however. Something that takes a week is a long-term project. They act mainly as distillers and transmitters of economic advice that comes from other sources, and specialize in "quick and dirty" analysis.

Congressional support agencies, such as the Congressional Budget Office (CBO) and the Congressional Research Service (CRS), have large numbers of professional economists on their staffs, but these economists have less direct access to congressional policymakers than committee and personal staffs. They do some original economic analysis, but they act primarily as translators, converting analysis that is done elsewhere into a form that is usable by congressmen and their staffs.[6] More time may be available, however. Some projects at the CBO may take as long as six months or a year.

Outside economists can sometimes reach congressmen and senators directly through testimony at hearings or in occasional private meetings if they are especially well-connected. Even in such cases, however, there is likely to be more staff in attendance than senators or congressmen.[7]

The Two-Cultures Problem Politicians are at least as different from economists as literary intellectuals are from scientists.[8] Politicians inhabit a world in which they must constantly bargain for outcomes that never wholly satisfy them or anyone else. Economists find this messy, hard to understand, and irrational. Decision-making should be orderly. It ought to be possible to specify goals, even if they are multiple and conflicting, and then measure the effectiveness of various ways of achieving those goals and the tradeoffs involved when they conflict.

Politicians, on the other hand, see the world as too subtle and complex to be captured in a mathematical model. Many of the things they think are important cannot be measured quantitatively. And besides, many of the bargains and truce lines they must negotiate would never hold up if all the tradeoffs and conflicting goals were made explicit.

Economists care more about the long run, despite what Keynes told them. Politicians care more about the here and now and years divisible by two, four, and six. A policy that might have beneficial effects in the long run, like decontrol of natural gas, will be unattractive to politicians if it causes hardship and disruption for their constituents in the short term.

Many economists find this politicians' world uncongenial and are reluctant to try to bridge the cultural gap. But some, believing that economic decision-making is too important to be left solely to politicians, may be willing to make the effort.[9]

The first step toward understanding the politicians' world is to realize that politics and substance are almost inextricably connected. The politician wants to know—simultaneously—whether an idea makes sense on its economic merits and whether it can get political support. If it does not make sense on the merits, the politician who pursues it risks looking foolish or feckless; and if it cannot muster political support, it is usually not worth pursuing, at least not now.

Economists tend to view political considerations as external constraints that are taken into account, if at all, only at the end of the analysis. If the optimum economic solution cannot be achieved because of these constraints, the economist may have some fallback or second-best solutions. But they are not deliberately designed to be any better politically; they are just next-best solutions from an economic point of view.

For the politician, political considerations are not just a constraint; they may present opportunities as well. A proposal cast in one form may face insurmountable political obstacles, but in a somewhat different form, or in a different context, it may have a better chance. As an abstract proposition, taxing Social Security benefits has little or no political support. In the context of the need to find ways to prevent the Social Security trust fund from going bankrupt, however, taxing half the benefits for recipients with higher incomes turned out to have substantial appeal.[10] Cutting back tax-free veterans' disability payments for those with higher incomes has no support in the congressional veterans committees; achieving the equivalent effect by subjecting those benefits to taxation might have a better chance in the tax-writing committees.

To prepare themselves to take part in this continual movement back and forth between politics and economics, economists who advise political decision-makers should try to learn as much as they can about the political context in which the decision will be made. They should know who will be in favor of a decision, who will be against it, and why, and they should have some general awareness of the strengths and weaknesses of the contending forces.

Economists will never be as good at political analysis as politicians are. Leon Keyserling, the Chairman of President Truman's Council of Economic Advisers, is said to have told Truman once that he should do something because it was good politics. Truman's response was: "Don't try to teach your grandmother to suck eggs."[11]

Given the difficulty of fully understanding the politicians' world, it is legitimate to ask whether it is a good use of economists' time even to attempt it. Especially in a congressional support agency like CBO or on a committee staff, where supervisors are available to take care of the politics, shouldn't staff economists stick to economics, with just enough political guidance from their supervisors to keep them from getting too far off the track? While this sounds good in theory, politics and economics are so intimately tied together in congressional decision-making that the option is not really available. Political supervisors simply cannot do enough handholding to adequately protect the innocent economist.

Nevertheless, economists ought not regard themselves as interchangeable with politicians. To be sure, economists have political and social values and goals, just as everyone else does. But their claim to extra influence over congressional decision-making rests on their professional economic expertise. That expertise may enable them to measure the effects of a policy on the distribution of income, but it does not enable them to say whether that effect is good or bad. That is the politicians' job.

Economists who serve political decision-makers therefore should be, in Charles Schultze's term, "partisan efficiency advocates,"[12] concerned centrally with costs, efficiency, and the like. Economists may seek a broader role than this, and many do, but it is something beyond economics that must arm them for it.

For those who adhere to that modest admonition, and even for those who do not, the following guidelines may help to bridge the cultural gap between economists and politicians, and enable economic analysts to gain better access to the congressional decision-making process

GUIDELINES

Learn About the History of the Issue

There are almost no new issues. Most issues the Congress deals with have come up before in one way or another. Learning the history of an issue can help the analyst understand both the economics and the politics of its current incarnation.

To begin with, going back to the history of past attempts to deal with an issue can give the analyst a short course in the arguments on both sides. Many of those arguments may no longer be valid. Experience, greater understanding, new research, economic or demographic changes, new countervailing pressures, and the like may have undermined them. Other arguments may have been strengthened by new developments and the passage of time.

The politics may also have changed. Prior consideration of an issue may have been dominated by individuals or groups who no longer have the same influence, or who are no longer around. In the past, their influence may have prevented issues from receiving the serious attention and analysis that can sometimes change perceptions and decisions. Their absence or diminished influence may pave the way for economic analysis to have a major impact.

The context of the issue may also have changed. Something that slipped through with little serious analysis in a time of seemingly unlimited resources may be open to serious scrutiny when priorities have changed or budgetary resources have become more limited.

In a recent account of President Carter's attempts at welfare reform, Laurence E. Lynn, Jr. and David deF. Whitman provide an instructive description of the problems that can arise when the economic and political analysis of an issue proceeds on separate, largely unintegrated tracks. The authors trace part of the difficulty to a failure to learn from history:

> Achieving comprehensive welfare reform was first and foremost a political problem—which even a casual reading of welfare reform history would have made clear. The basic issues that made Congress reluctant to adopt the kind of reform that Carter appeared to favor were philosophical and value-laden more than they were analytic or technical. Yet little real political discussion affecting the policymaking process occurred at the top levels of the Carter administration. . . .
>
> Carter did not receive, nor apparently did he request, any memos on the history of previous reform attempts.[13]

Find Out Who Will Be Making the Decision

Decision-making in the Congress is multilayered and overlapping. As a result, there are multiple access points for those who are seeking to influence decisions. Most of the major decisions in an area are effectively made by the committees that have jurisdiction over the area. In some areas, such as taxation, it is clear which committee has jurisdiction, but in others, such as energy or the environment, there are a number of committees and subcommittees that may have at least a piece of the issue. Each issue also goes through layers of consideration: subcommittee, full committee, floor, House–Senate conference, and back to the floor for final approval. Some issues must be dealt with first by the authorization committees, which establish the framework for a program, and then by appropriations committees, which set annual spending levels. Finally, the House and Senate budget committees, which set overall spending and tax levels, may require changes in programs falling within the primary jurisdiction of other committees.

Analysts for congressional support agencies must be highly sensitive to jurisdictional issues. Ideally, the analyst's work should be done for the committee that has the best "handle" on the issue: the clearest jurisdictional claim and the greatest influence on the ultimate outcome. This is not always possible, of course. The committee with the best handle may see analysis as a threat to its control over the issue, as indeed it often is. Analysis can open up conflicts that have been papered over, expose tradeoffs that have been obscured, and raise options that have been ignored. This opens up the decision-making process to often unwelcome "outside" influences.

Some other committee with influence over the issue may welcome the analysis, however, often for the same reasons that the committee with the best handle is leery of it. The analyst should avoid becoming directly involved in these contests: When elephants are fighting, ants get crushed. Analysts should be aware of these considerations, however, and do as much of their work as possible for the committees that have clear jurisdiction over the issue involved.

The role of analysis varies, depending on the nature of the issue and the number of people involved. On some obscure and complicated issues affecting only a few people, the effective decision may be made by committee staff at an early stage, and simply ratified at each subsequent stage. On issues that become more visible and controversial, and that affect large numbers of people, decisions may be made, unmade, and modified dozens of times as more and more decision-makers become actively involved.

On low-visibility, tightly held issues, economic analysis can have an impact if it gets to the few people who are effectively involved in time for them to use it, and in a form they can understand. If the analyst does not have access to those people, or misses the opportunity to influence the decision by providing information that is too late or unintelligible, the opportunity may be lost for good.

On highly visible and controversial issues with many players, the economic analyst has many more opportunities to become involved. With many people and many diverse interests trying to affect the decision, at least some of them will want to use the information and analysis that economists develop in order to support their own positions. Again, however, analysis that comes early in the process can usually have much more impact than that which comes later. At the early stages, people's minds are more open, and they have not become locked in by commitments to

interested parties. Economic analysis at this stage can help frame
the terms of the debate and structure the options that are presented. At later stages, politics tends to dominate analysis. Economic analysis is then used the way a drunk uses a lamp post, for
support rather than illumination.

Two analyses done in recent years by the Congressional Budget
Office illustrate these differences. A report done in 1980 on the
use by states of tax-exempt bonds to finance student loans involved a fairly narrow and obscure issue that only a few people
understood.[14] In addition, only a few hundred million dollars in
tax revenue was involved. The final decision was essentially
worked out at the subcommittee staff level, with the CBO staff
person who wrote the report playing a major role. On the other
hand, a 1979 report on the use of tax-exempt bonds to finance
single-family housing involved a highly visible and controversial
issue and many billions of dollars.[15] While the report came very
early in the debate, and indeed had a great deal to do with putting
the issue on the congressional agenda and structuring the terms
of the debate, the legislation finally adopted was shaped by
hundreds of different hands.

Timing Is Critical As the preceding discussion suggests, timing can be critical in determining whether economic analysis has an impact. Issues have
a certain rhythm in the Congress. They may take months or years
to develop, but then move through the whole legislative process
in days or weeks. The five-cent-a-gallon gas tax and highway
construction bill approved in December 1982 is one example.
Transportation Secretary Drew Lewis had been quietly gathering
support for it for more than a year, but it was only after the unemployment rate began to soar toward record levels that the lame-
duck Congress, fresh from the November elections and eager to do
something about unemployment, seized on the gas tax and
highway measure and passed it as a "jobs bill." Another example
is the major change in hospital reimbursement under Medicare
enacted in early 1983 as part of the major Social Security financing compromise. This complex cost control measure would
normally have taken months or years to be approved; but once it
was tied to the fast-moving and more controversial Social Security
compromise, it moved through Congress in less than a month.[16]
On the other hand, once the Congress has acted on an issue, it is
not likely to want to take it up again for at least another few years.
Where a truce is involved, as is usually the case, the truce is expected to last for a decent interval.

If an issue seems to be developing too fast for credible economic
analysis to be done in time, analysts are best advised to stay out
of it unless they have a direct line to decision-makers who are
willing to rely on "quick and dirty" economic analysis. This puts
a premium on predicting well in advance what issues are likely to
develop, so that the data and the analysis can be ready when the
issue is.

On rare occasions, an analyst's work can create an issue, and thereby control the timing. More often, issues have a momentum of their own. For an issue to find its way onto the congressional agenda, there must be both a problem and some possible solutions. If there are no solutions, there is no problem as far as Congress is concerned. The signs of a developing problem are often found in newspaper and magazine articles describing some unsatisfactory situation—abuses, horror stories, and heart-rending tales. Television news stories, books, government and private reports, congressional mail, bills, speeches, articles in the *Congressional Record*, learned journal articles, conversations with cab drivers— all these provide evidence of developing problems.

The political context can change quickly. Problems that seem to have no solution one year may be readily dealt with in the next. By the same token, solutions that seem to be "greased" and ready to put in place may be undone by unexpected events.

Perhaps the only simple lesson that can be drawn from this is that the analyst should expect to be wrong a certain percentage of the time in predicting when issues will develop. Always be prepared to put aside or scrub an analytic project if an issue seems to be going nowhere. But never throw anything away. Issues almost always come back.

Learn Everyone's Interests and Arguments

Once an issue moves onto the congressional agenda, the arguments of the interested parties set the terms of the debate, and their underlying interests determine the outlines of any possible solution.

These interested parties include the major actors within the Congress and the executive branch, as well as outside interest groups and others who are seeking to influence the debate. The work done by congressional support agencies is often filtered through these interested parties. While this means that the analyst's work is sometimes "distorted" by one side or the other, the adversarial process on the Hill usually serves to counter most distortions. And in the process, the staffs on all sides, if not the congressmen themselves, are forced to read the analyst's work carefully.

The analyst who is familiar with the arguments and interests of all the parties will know which arguments are likely to have the most impact and which options will be taken most seriously. Options and arguments that are taken seriously in the economic literature may not be relevant if no current or prospective interested party is likely to find them compelling or useful. On the other hand, simple economic analysis or readily available data may be all that is needed to shoot down an argument or an option. But unless the analyst knows this option or argument is being taken seriously, an opportunity may be lost.

The analyst should never forget that congressional decisions are made by real people with distinct backgrounds, personalities, interests, goals, and ambitions. Their decision on any one issue is affected and sometimes determined by factors that may seem completely unrelated to the analyst—personal friendships, committee jurisdictional considerations, political ambitions, the need to pick up votes on another issue, and so forth. Congressional staff people will often provide this information if the analyst knows enough to ask.

As discussed earlier, analysis can have a greater impact if it is done before people are locked into positions. The analyst should therefore search out all potential interested parties as early as possible in the analysis and get from them all of the statements, position papers, background papers, and the like that they have on the issue.

Differences in the willingness of interested parties to supply data to an analyst may have a major impact on the kind of analysis that can be done. For many legislative issues, there are just no good data available. For the outside academic, this means either that it is not a researchable problem, or that heroic assumptions and ingenuity must be employed to make up for the inadequacy of the data.

For the analyst who is perceived by outsiders as having good access to congressional decision-makers, however, interested parties may be quite willing to provide otherwise inaccessable data. Even if there are no good data, the "conventional wisdom" of people working in the area can provide valuable insights into what is going on. In CBO's work in the tax-exempt bond area, for example, an enormous amount was learned about the workings of the tax-exempt bond market and new trends in tax-exempt financing from discussions with investment bankers, underwriters, bond counsel, and state and local officials who were involved with tax-exempt bonds on a day-to-day basis.

This is the kind of research that economists often dismiss as "casual empiricism." While the economist may find such grubbing about in the ambiguities of the real world uncongenial, politicians rely a great deal on this kind of evidence. Furthermore, a trained economist should be able to evaluate this information more reliably than the politician, so looking at it carefully and critically can be a good way of helping to keep politicians from being misled.

It's OK to Think Like an Economist, But Don't Write Like One The economics profession puts its highest premium on explaining how a piece of analysis is done, and how conclusions (if any) were reached. The Congress doesn't care. Congressmen want to know what you know, not how you know it. Analysts can think the issue through in their own minds in whatever way they find most congenial, but they should write it up the way politicians and their staffs think:

- What is the decision that has to be made and when?
- What is the underlying problem the decision will address?
- What are the options for dealing with the problem, and how much of it will each option deal with?

Start with the conclusions, and then tell only enough about how they were reached so that an audience of noneconomists can be confident that the conclusions follow logically and are supported by reliable evidence.

Avoid jargon, use short sentences and simple Anglo-Saxon words, and never ever use an equation. Use lots of illustrative examples. They can help explain complicated proposals and make abstract discussions more vivid and accessible.

Keep It Simple Congressmen must be able to explain their decisions to their constituents. Even if congressmen have a fairly good understanding of economics themselves, analysis that is too complicated to explain to the uninitiated is not much help. A tariff on imported oil, for example, increases the price that must be paid for imported oil in the U.S. It is possible to explain that such a tariff may also allow the prices of domestically produced oil and gas to go up. But when you try to explain that the amount by which the price will go up also depends on the state of supply and demand in world oil markets, and on monetary policy in the United States, almost everyone is lost. No one can understand it unless they carry around in their heads little models of how all these interactions work, and most ordinary people do not.

If these extra complexities are truly important to the decision, however, the analyst has to persist. With enough thought and imagination, it may be possible to convey the essence of the analysis in ways that politicians can understand and explain to their constituents. Some of the more complex second- and third-order effects may be easier to appreciate if they can be illustrated with examples of how actual people and industries would be affected.

But the analyst should not push this too far. Many of the complexities that it is possible to spin out are based on theoretical models that are so conjectural, debatable, and unsupported by data that analysts should not really expect policymakers to make decisions based on them. A little analysis of supply and demand, opportunity costs, and incentives at the margin can go a long way.

Congressmen Care More About Distribution Than Efficiency Congressmen want to know what the effects of a policy will be on their constituents. They generally do not care about whether a program is inefficient unless that inefficiency can be demonstrated to have a direct and obvious impact on people whose support they need. Some types of inefficiency are harder to explain than others. Allocative inefficiency—the loss to the economy that results when government subsidizes some activities at the expense of others that may be more productive—is usually a lost cause. It generally does not bother congressmen that, for example, the current income tax may impose an "excess burden" or "welfare loss" on the economy as compared with a consumption tax, or that the current tax treatment of business depreciation may lead to an inefficient allocation of investment. Those effects, if they exist, are too obscure for most congressmen to worry about.

Inefficiency in the mechanisms by which subsidies are delivered is usually easier to explain. Most congressmen on the tax committees understand, for example, that tax-exempt bonds are not the most efficient way of delivering subsidies to state and local governments, since a large portion of the federal subsidy is diverted to bond purchasers in high tax brackets, bond counsel, investment bankers, and other intermediaries. They may not count such inefficiency as important; but at least they are likely to understand it.

More important than efficiency is the initial distributional effects of a policy, especially those that are direct and observable. Economists have argued for years that decontrol of natural gas would produce efficiency gains and lower prices, but politicians' concern with the initial distributional effects for a long time stood in the way. It still does; but the favorable experience with decontrol of oil prices and the gradually increasing impact of economists' arguments has brought decontrol of natural gas much closer.

Take Implementation and Administration into Account
Economists sometimes give short shrift to possible problems of implementation and administration. In this, however, they are little different from most congressional politicians. Congressmen tend to leave problems of this kind to the executive to work out; economists tend to assume them away.

Control of air and water pollution is a good example. Congressmen, most of them being lawyers, favor a regulatory approach: Pollution shall be limited to a specified amount, with fines and other penalties for those who exceed the limits. Details are left to the executive branch or state and local governments. Economists, by contrast, favor incentives. Taxes or effluent charges should be imposed on each unit of pollution emitted, so both society and the polluter can readily calculate how much pollution can be afforded. A neat and economically efficient solution. Either approach, however, requires some method of measuring both the amount of pollution emitted from millions of sources and the harm done by the pollution. The ability to actually perform such measurements has lagged far behind the inventive analytic work done in formulating the principles for controlling pollution.

Difficulties of implementation and administration result frequently from congressmen's attempts to deal with all the special cases they think their constituents will complain about. The more special categories and rules that are set up, however, the harder laws are to administer. Economists tend to worry not at all about these hard cases. As a result, they continually find their neat and orderly program proposals rendered less effective or even made unworkable by the baroque features politicians add to them. Giving some thought to these potential problems in advance should enable economists to tell what kinds of proposals might be loaded down in this way, so they can warn politicians of the implementation problems that might result, or think of some other approach that produces fewer special cases.

Emphasize a Few Crucial and Striking Numbers Congressmen love numbers, but not in the same way economists do. Congressmen look for a single striking number that can encapsulate an issue and can be used to explain and justify their position. They have little use for endless columns and rows of unassimilated data. One good number can be worth pages of analysis. As an example of the kind of numbers politicians like, take the testimony Joseph W. Barr, Secretary of the Treasury in the latter part of the Johnson administration, delivered to the Joint Economic Committee in January 1969. When he pointed out that 155 taxpayers with incomes over $200,000, including 21 with incomes over $1,000,000, paid no federal income taxes for 1967, he touched off a furor that led to major tax changes in the Tax Reform Act of 1969.

Economists, however, often undermine the usefulness of their analysis for politicians by trying to cover too much. They list all possible effects and repercussions of a policy, instead of concentrating on the most likely major effects and trying to quantify them as well as possible. They tend to hedge every statement and every number. But life is uncertain; politicians need economists' best guesses.

Economists tend to weigh gains and losses solely by their monetary value, rather than by the number of persons helped and hurt. They forget that politicians weigh losses more heavily than gains. (A policy that hurts five people and helps five people, says the sage, produces five enemies and five ingrates.)

Several CBO reports offer examples of simple numbers that illustrated crucial points in the analysis. These numbers are often difficult to accumulate or calculate, but they are usually worth the effort. A 1977 study on real estate tax shelters estimated that less than 12% of the total $1.3 billion revenue loss from real estate tax shelters would go to subsidize low- and moderate-income rental housing in fiscal year 1978, with the rest going to middle- and upper-income rental housing and office buildings, shopping centers, and other commercial buildings.[17] A 1981 study of the tax treatment of homeownership estimated that less than 40% of homeowners benefitted from the home mortgage interest deduction in 1978, with the rest either having no mortgage or using the standard deduction.[18]

Read the Newspapers Congressmen and senators get a very large share of their information from newspapers. They read a number of newspapers every day (including state and local papers), along with a variety of magazines and periodicals. An analyst, to be effective, must know the world as his audience sees it. He must also know how much his audience knows about a particular subject, and thus how much does not have to be explained. Reading the newspapers is a good way to find out what congressmen are likely to be interested in, and how much they know about issues.

The major national newspapers, magazines, and journals that are widely read in Washington are the *Washington Post, New York*

Times, Wall Street Journal, Time, Newsweek, and specialized publications such as *Congressional Quarterly* and the *National Journal.*
These contain much of the information on the political context of
issues that analysts need to know in order to be effective. The
early signs of emerging issues, in-depth articles on the political
forces surrounding an issue, personality and background profiles
of major participants, capsule summaries of the major arguments
being made, and a host of other tidbits and insights can be gleaned
from these sources.

The specialized trade press, however, sometimes has critical odd
bits to offer as well. A June 1983 article in the trade press on the
prospects for President Reagan's enterprise zone proposal, for example, contained the following item buried deep in the story:

> [The House Ways and Means Committee] staff member said the com-
> mittee has no intention of holding a hearing on the enterprise zone bill,
> since passage of such a measure would be akin to giving Reagan "75
> media events" by allowing him to announce the zones between the date
> of enactment and election day in 1984.[19]

When this strong political argument is added to the public and
private doubts that many in Congress have about the economic
merits of enterprise zones, it should be clear to the analyst that
devoting further resources to the study of enterprise zones need
not have a high priority.

For those who want to go the extra mile, the *Congressional Record* can be an invaluable source. Early signs of emerging issues
can be detected in the bills that are introduced and the statements
their sponsors make about them. Committee hearings, which are
noted in a digest in the back, are a good early-warning device,
although issues are usually fairly far along by the time hearings
are held on them. The witnesses' prepared statements can be a
good summary of the arguments on both sides of an issue.
Speeches and articles inserted in the *Record* show what issues congressmen are interested in and what impresses them. The floor
debate on legislation indicates what arguments are used most frequently on particular issues. The *Record* will also often contain
discussion of future legislative plans, which can help the analyst
anticipate what is coming.

AN EXAMPLE A recent CBO study of small-issue industrial revenue bonds provides an example of how several of these guidelines are applied in
practice.[20] Industrial revenue bonds have been issued by states
and localities since the 1930s to finance factories and other projects for private industry. Because the bonds are issued by state
and local governments, the interest on them is tax exempt. The
interest rate can therefore be lower, and the saving is then passed
on to the private user for whom the bonds have been issued. These
bonds proliferated rapidly in the 1960s until Congress imposed

limits on them in 1968. A number of exceptions were permitted, however, including one for "small issues," defined then as issues of less then $5 million.

This history suggested that the Congress was willing to allow some tax-exempt financing for private industry, but would step in if the volume got out of hand. (Learn about the history of the issue.) In the late 1970s evidence began to show up that small-issue IRBs were being used much more heavily than published figures suggested, and that many of the uses were far different from those the Congress had in mind in 1968. This came in the form of newspaper and magazine articles, "how-to-do-it" articles in the trade press, ads for seminars and conferences, and anecdotal evidence from lawyers, promoters, and local officials. (Read the newspapers.)

CBO was asked by the House Ways and Means Committee, which had jurisdiction over the issue, to investigate the extent of the problem and suggest some possible options for congressional action. (Find out who will be making the decision.) This required an exhaustive and time-consuming survey of state records of the use of industrial revenue bonds since only sketchy data were kept at the national level. There was little danger that the CBO study would be overtaken by events, however, since the Congress would not want to deal with the issue until the extent of the problem was known, and it would not be known until the CBO study was completed. (Timing is critical.)

The CBO study revealed that the use of these bonds had grown sharply, rising from $1.3 billion in 1975 to more than $8 billion in 1980, five or six times higher than previous estimates. (Emphasize a few crucial and striking numbers.) In addition, they were being used for purposes that Congress had never anticipated, such as the financing of country clubs, ski resorts, corporate planes, chains of McDonalds and K-Marts, and even a topless go-go bar and dirty book store in Philadelphia.

The states and localities were ambivalent about possible limits on the use of industrial revenue bonds. Most viewed them as an extremely attractive tool for attracting industry and promoting job creation, but many also realized that large-scale issuance of such bonds could drive up tax-exempt interest rates and squeeze out some tax-exempt bond issues for more traditional public purposes such as schools, roads, sewers, and public buildings. Many established local businesses also resented the competition from IRB-financed new businesses, and objected strongly to their local governments. Even those state and local officials who were skeptical about small-issue IRBs and who realized that they would be difficult to curb without federal action (since any state acting alone would be vulnerable to competition from other states) were nonetheless uneasy about federal restrictions. They valued the autonomy and freedom from federal interference that the tax-exempt bond tool gave them, and were reluctant to see more precedents for further federal control.

The interest of the Congress was primarily to control the burgeoning federal revenue loss, but there was also a desire on the part of many in Congress to prevent bonds from being used to finance golf courses, massage parlors, and the like. These varying interests suggested that options that limited the overall volume and cut out the most questionable uses, while maintaining as much state and local autonomy as possible, would have the best chance of adoption. (Learn everyone's interests and arguments.)

The CBO paper suggested the following options for limiting small-issue IRBs:

- target IRBs to smaller businesses;
- target IRBs to distressed areas;
- eliminate IRBs for commercial projects;
- set a limit on state IRB sales;
- limit tax exemption to general obligation bonds;
- require federal, state, or local matching funds; and
- eliminate small issues completely.

The first three options would have intruded fairly substantially on state and local decisions on the proper uses of IRBs. Moreover, it was not clear that limitations of this kind would significantly reduce the overall volume of IRBs. Finally, such limits could be very difficult to administer. (Take implementation and administration into account.) The next two options would have substantially cut back on the volume of IRBs, while leaving the decision on the types of projects to support almost entirely to state and local governments and voters. The first of these "hands-off" options would put a cap on the total amount of IRBs that could be issued in any state, while the second would have allowed IRBs to be issued only if they were backed by the full faith and credit of the issuing locality. These so-called "general obligation" bonds normally must be approved by the voters in a referendum, putting a substantial check on any questionable projects. Requiring matching funds was also a relatively hands-off way of assuring that a reasonable public purpose was being served. The last option—eliminating IRBs completely—would have achieved completely the goals of curbing the revenue loss and questionable uses, but at the expense of a substantial intrusion on state and local autonomy.

When the Congress finally took action to limit small-issue IRBs in the Tax Equity and Fiscal Responsibility Act of 1982, it followed mainly the hands-off approach, but included some bans on specific uses.[21] The major features included:

- a requirement that there be a public hearing and approval by an elected public official or legislative body—or, alternatively, a voter referendum—before IRBs can be issued;
- a limit on the amount of accelerated depreciation deductions that can be taken on projects financed with IRBs (called the

"anti-double-dip" rule because it prevented two major tax breaks from being combined in a single project); and
- limits on the use of IRBs for retail food and beverage services, automobile sales or service, or the provision of recreation or entertainment, and an outright ban on the use of IRBs for

any private or commercial golf course, country club, massage parlor, tennis club, skating facility (including roller skating, skateboard, and ice skating), racquet sports facility (including any handball or racquetball court), hot tub facility, suntan facility, or racetrack.[22]

Finally, the Congress provided that no small-issue IRBs could be issued after 1986, with the expectation that the whole question of IRBs would be reviewed again before that time, using information gathered in the meantime under new reporting requirements in the 1982 Act.

The effects of these new limits on IRB volume were expected to be relatively modest, reducing projected volume of new issues by no more than 15%. The truce line drawn in 1982 lasted for only a short time, however. The House Ways and Means Committee held hearings in June 1983 to explore further ways of limiting IRB volume, and in October reported a bill that would have limited the annual volume of IRB issues in each state to an amount equal to $150 times the state's population.[23] The bill faced heavy opposition from governors, mayors, and local officials, however, and the House voted just before adjourning in November not to take it up.[24]

An instructive feature of the debate over small-issue IRBs is how modest a role considerations of economic efficiency played. Scarcely any one mentioned the possibility that IRBs were distorting the allocation of resources by encouraging investment that, on the margin, was less productive than alternative investments. The inefficiency of tax-exempt bonds as a subsidy delivery mechanism received somewhat more attention, but mainly because the subsidy was being diverted to people whom congressmen didn't especially want to help: investment bankers and other promoters of tax-exempt "deals." The Congress was much more concerned about who was being helped by the bonds and who was being hurt by them, such as merchants faced with competition from bond-subsidized shopping centers. (Congressmen care more about distribution than efficiency.)

CONCLUSION

Economic analysis is rarely determinative in congressional decision-making. But the economic analyst need not be stymied by politics. It can present opportunities as well as constraints. The guidelines set out here will not, by themselves, make analysts as good at politics as politicians are. But they can help the analyst understand more fully the complex interplay of economics and politics. The key to their successful application, however, is one of attitude. The analyst must believe that politics and politicians play a legitimate role in economic decision-making. He or she must believe that it is important not only that decisions be made with the fullest possible understanding of their economic ramifications, but also that, in a democracy, elected officials are entitled to take political considerations into account as well. That may sound elementary, but there are many frustrated analysts on Capitol Hill who do not really believe it, and many satisfied and effective ones who do.

I am very grateful for the valuable comments and suggestions I received on earlier versions of this article from the staff of the Tax Analysis Division of the Congressional Budget Office and from John W. Ellwood, Robert W. Hartman, Robert D. Reischauer, Allen Schick, James W. Wetzler, and two anonymous reviewers.

JAMES M. VERDIER served for 15 years in various staff positions in the U.S. Congress, most recently as assistant director for Tax Analysis in the Congressional Budget Office, and he is now a lecturer in Public Policy at the John F. Kennedy School of Government at Harvard University.

NOTES

1. See, for example, Weiss, Carol H., "Improving the Linkage Between Social Research and Public Policy," in *Knowledge and Policy: The Uncertain Connection*, Laurence E. Lynn, Jr., Ed. (Washington, DC: National Academy of Sciences, 1978), pp. 23–81; and Haveman, Robert H., "Policy Analysis and the Congress: An Economist's View," *Policy Analysis*, 2(2) (Spring 1976): 235–250.
2. See, for example, Enthoven, Alain C., "Ten Practical Principles for Policy and Program Analysis," in *Benefit–Cost and Policy Analysis Annual, 1974*, Richard Zeckhauser, Ed. (Chicago: Aldine, 1975), pp. 456–465; Behn, Robert D., "Policy Analysis and Policy Politics," *Policy Analysis*, 7(2) (Spring 1981): 199–226; Leman, Christopher K., and Nelson, Robert H., "Ten Commandments for Policy Economists," *Journal of Policy Analysis and Management*, 1(1) (Fall 1981): 97–117; Stein, Herbert, "The Chief Executive as Chief Economist," in *Essays in Contemporary Economic Problems, 1981–1982 Edition* (Washington, DC: American Enterprise Institute, 1981), pp. 53–78; Meltsner, Arnold J., *Policy Analysts in the Bureaucracy* (Berkeley, CA: University of California Press, 1976).
3. Quoted in Bate, W. Jackson, *Samuel Johnson* (New York: Harcourt Brace Jovanovich, 1977), p. 491.
4. This article deals almost entirely with microeconomic issues. For an excellent discussion of the role of economists in congressional decision-making on macroeconomic issues (budget, fiscal, and monetary policy), see Reischauer, Robert D., "Getting, Using, and Misusing Economic Information," in *Making Economic Policy in Congress*, Allen Schick, Ed. (Washington, DC: American Enterprise Institute, 1984), pp. 38–68.
5. *Final Report of the Commission on Administrative Review*, H. Doc. No. 95-272, 95th Cong., 1st Sess. (1977), Vol. 1, pp. 630–634.
6. James Sundquist, in an excellent 1978 article, discusses the need for this kind of "research brokerage" in the Congress. See "Research Brokerage: The Weak Link," in Lynn, Ed., *Knowledge and Policy*, pp. 126–144.

7. For a good recent discussion of congressional staffs, see Malbin, Michael J., *Unelected Representatives* (New York, Basic Books, 1980).
8. Compare Snow, C. P., *The Two Cultures and the Scientific Revolution* (Cambridge: Cambridge University Press, 1959).
9. For other discussions of the differences between political and analytic decision-making, see Schultze, Charles L., *The Politics and Economics of Public Spending* (Washington, DC: The Brookings Institution, 1968), pp. 35–76; and Wildavsky, Aaron, *Speaking Truth to Power* (Boston: Little Brown, 1979).
10. The Social Security Amendments of 1983 (P.L. 98-21, Sec. 121) subjected up to half of Social Security benefits to tax for single persons with incomes over $25,000 and couples with incomes over $32,000.
11. Quoted in Stein, note 2, p. 73.
12. Schultze, *The Politics and Economics of Public Spending*, p. 96.
13. Lynn, Laurence E., Jr., and Whitman, David deF., *The President As Policymaker: Jimmy Carter and Welfare Reform* (Philadelphia: Temple University Press, 1981), pp. 263–264, 266.
14. CBO, *State Profits on Tax-Exempt Student Loan Bonds: Analysis and Options* (March 1980).
15. CBO, *Tax-Exempt Bonds for Single-Family Housing* (April 1979).
16. For details of the gas tax bill, see 1982 *Congressional Quarterly Almanac*, pp. 317–330, and for the Medicare changes, see *Congressional Quarterly Weekly Report*, "Major Change in Medicare Hospital Payment System Is on Fast Track in Congress," pp. 455–457 (March 5, 1983); and *National Journal*, "Who Says Congress Can't Move Fast? Just Ask Hospitals About Medicare," pp. 704–707 (April 2, 1983).
17. CBO, *Real Estate Tax Shelter Subsidies and Direct Subsidy Alternatives* (May 1977), p. 38.
18. CBO, *The Tax Treatment of Homeownership: Issues and Options* (September 1981), p. 10.
19. *Housing and Development Reporter* (Washington, DC: Bureau of National Affairs, Inc.), "Senate Panel Puts Enterprise Zone, Mortgage Bond Bills in Withholding Amendment," pp. 7–8 (June 6, 1983).
20. CBO, *Small Issue Industrial Revenue Bonds* (April 1981; revised September 1981).
21. Public Law 92-248, Sections 214–216, 219 (September 3, 1982).
22. Section 214(e).
23. H.R. 4170, the Tax Reform Act of 1983, Title VII, reported on October 21, 1983.
24. *Congressional Quarterly Weekly Report* (November 19, 1983), p. 2409.

12

Documentation in Evaluation Research
Managerial and Scientific Requirements

William E. Pollard, Alfred C. Cooper, and Deborah H. Griffin

ABSTRACT

Documentation in evaluation research consists of written material, in human- or machine-readable form, pertaining to the plans, activities, and results of the project. It is argued here that good documentation is essential for effective management of evaluations, and for responsible reporting of the research procedures and findings. Documentation relating to electronic data processing activity is especially important. The purpose of this paper is to stimulate consideration and discussion of documentation, and to emphasize its importance in evaluation research. The role of documentation in the planning and control functions of project management is reviewed, and the importance of documentation in the assessment of research quality with respect to objectivity, validity, and replicability is discussed. Reasons for poor documentation are considered. An outline of documentation required in different phases of research projects is provided, and recommendations for improving the quality of documentation are presented.

The purpose of this paper is to stimulate consideration and discussion of documentation, and to emphasize its importance in evaluation research. By documentation we mean written material, in human- or machine-readable form, that pertains to the plans, activities, and results of the project. This includes material necessary for internal project operations, as well as deliverables in written form that satisfy external reporting requirements. Documentation thus includes a wide variety of material ranging from project correspondence and minutes of meetings to final reports and descriptions of archived data files. Indeed, documentation constitutes the major tangible product of the evaluation. We argue that good documentation is essential for effective management of evaluation projects and for responsible scientific reporting of research procedures and findings. Investigators in charge of evaluation studies are responsible for efficiently

achieving project objectives and for meeting standards of the scientific community for objectivity, validity, and replicability; a well-planned, comprehensive documentation system is a key factor in meeting these responsibilities.

There is a considerable range in the scope of evaluations, and documentation requirements will differ accordingly. A small client satisfaction study carried out by one person over a period of a few days in an outpatient health facility may require only a few pages of documentation. On the other hand, a nationwide longitudinal study of educational development involving the collection of survey and testing data on a very large sample of students could require thousands of pages of documentation. Whatever the features of a particular study may be, evaluators need to give some consideration to what kinds of documents they will need in conducting their research projects. Good doc-

254 EVALUATION STUDIES REVIEW ANNUAL

umentation will not just happen—it requires planning. Documentation will accumulate whether it is planned or not; planning enables one to control this to meet project needs.

Unfortunately, essential elements of documentation are often handled haphazardly or ignored altogether. Although there is an extensive literature on practical issues in the design of evaluations and the analysis of data, documentation is seldom addressed. Problems with inadequate documentation, especially in the area of computerized data analysis, are increasingly being recognized, however; many of the difficulties encountered in the secondary analysis of evaluations, for example, are seen to relate to the lack of documentation (Hedrick, Boruch, & Ross, 1978; Linsenmeier, Wortman, & Hendricks, 1981).

In this paper, we examine the role of documentation in project management and scientific reporting. Al- though documentation in evaluation research has not been given much attention until rather recently, the topic of documentation has been treated extensively in the data processing literature. Much of this literature pertains to software and system development cycles, and may seem somewhat removed from the needs of evaluators. Yet, writers in this area have given considerable thought to the use of documentation in managing complex development projects and producing a usable product, and we draw on this literature, as well as the evaluation and general social science research literature, in our discussion. In the following sections, the need for good documentation is discussed; reasons for poor documentation are considered; the necessary elements in a comprehensive system of documentation are described, along with references to the literature in this area; and recommendations for improving the quality of documentation are discussed.

MANAGERIAL REQUIREMENTS

Project management involves the judicious application of project resources to achieving project objectives. Managers are responsible for planning how these objectives are to be achieved and for controlling the project according to plan. Internal documentation is necessary for a number of reasons in carrying out both the planning and control functions.

First, the very process of writing down plans and decisions is important because it encourages, if not forces, thorough consideration and articulation. Few of us would deny the value of such written materials, yet as Brooks (1975, p. 111) points out in his discussion of project management, there is often a tendency to jump from general planning meetings and discussions into the tasks at hand. He goes on to argue that

> writing the decisions down is essential. Only when one writes do the gaps appear and the inconsistencies protrude. The act of writing turns out to require hundreds of mini-decisions, and it is the existence of these that distinguishes clear, exact policies from fuzzy ones.

Burrill and Ellsworth (1980, p. 50) note that such planning documents have value in preventing the "seat-of-the-pants" management style.

Second, good documentation is necessary for clear communication on what the project objectives are, what decisions were made, what actions were taken, and what was achieved. This is especially important for communication in large projects between different task groups working simultaneously and between groups working at different points in time. For example, interviewing operations may have terminated by the time that the statistical analysts perform their tasks, yet detailed information on interviewing operations and problems encountered by the interviewers in the field can be critical in properly interpreting results.

Documentation of the planning process and the decisions that were made is very important. This process may involve a number of meetings over a period of time with a changing cast of characters due to schedule conflicts, presence of consultants, and so on. Unless decisions, and the reasoning behind them, are recorded and made available in the form of minutes and working papers, large amounts of time can be wasted in bringing everyone up to date and in rehashing issues that should have been resolved. Because planning typically involves highly paid consultants and professional staff, such waste of time can be costly.

Third, it is essential for management review of project activity and facilitating management control. A number of writers concerned with management of data processing operations argue that a system of documentation should be established in conjunction with specification of project objectives and assignment of responsibility (Enger, 1976a, 1976b; Gaydasch, 1982; Gray & London, 1969; Jancura, 1977; Metzger, 1981). Documentation can be required at specific project control points to assure that desired actions have been taken and proscribed actions avoided. As Gray and London (1969) point out, project control becomes a built-in function of the documentation, thus freeing the manager from a policing role.

Fourth, documentation is important in minimizing the disruptive effects of staff turnover. In a review of applied research projects, Weiss (1973, p. 53) was struck by "the tremendous instability of evaluation staffs." She writes:

> Part-time directors were the rule rather than the exception. Turnover in evaluation staff at all levels was phenomenal. It was not uncommon for a 3-year study to have had three or four different directors and three complete turnovers in research associates.

Unfortunately, information that isn't recorded in writing leaves the project when staff members leave. This problem can be especially acute in university-based projects employing students, because staff attrition is virtually built in by the educational cycle. However, simply having the information written is not the full solution to this problem if the written material is prepared in some idiosyncratic style and/or filed in a disorganized manner; a well-organized documentation system is necessary for continuity of operation. It provides the necessary material for orientation and training of new staff. In some instances, replacement staff may need to be trained; in other instances, different types of personnel may be hired in the various project phases and training will be required. Green (1974/1977, p. 188) points out that in data processing operations, good documentation is the most practical means for training people in new jobs.

Fifth, it is necessary for efficient report writing. If planned in advance and prepared according to a standardized format, interim documents describing completion of various tasks can be assembled with little modification in progress reports and final reports, either in the main body or in appendixes. The report writing effort can thus be spread out over time, helping to minimize last-minute scrambles and overruns. Also, the material is written while the issues and details are fresh in the writer's mind. This saves time that is often spent in trying to reconstruct what happened in the past and prevents loss of information due to lapse in memory.

Sixth, documentation provides an important historical record for planning future projects. A record of what was planned and what actually took place, along with relevant cost and staffing information, can be useful in designing future studies and avoiding problems encountered in the past.

Finally, it is necessary for controlling paperwork. This might seem surprising because documentation is often seen as involving "too much paperwork." Metzger (1981, p. 47) writes:

> I think one important cause of our so often getting buried under paper is that we don't take the time to define the documents we want to use on the project. As a result, whenever a project member needs to write something, he dreams up his own format and suddenly there is a new kind of document to file and keep track of. We probably need a little chaos in the world to keep us from growing too dull, but there are many better places to allow for the chaos; let's keep it out of the documentation system.

By carefully planning the kinds of documents that will be needed and how they will be used, the production of unnecessary paperwork can be minimized and the benefit from the documentation that is produced can be maximized.

SCIENTIFIC REQUIREMENTS

The virtue of scientific inquiry lies in its disciplined, objective approach to collecting and analyzing data, and to making valid inferences regarding the phenomena of interest. Documentation describing the investigation is extremely important because it is the basis for evaluating the scientific adequacy of the research. It is the responsibility of the investigator to provide a clear description and record of the design and its rationale, the data collection process and the data obtained, the processing and analysis of the data, and the findings and logic of the conclusions. Good documentation is basic to quality assessment in all of these areas; however, there are three respects in which good documentation is of special value in evaluation research.

First, it is necessary for assessing the objectivity of the investigation. This takes on special importance in evaluation research because evaluation is advocated primarily on the grounds of being a systematic, objective means of obtaining information for debate and decision making regarding public policy. Publicly funded evaluations should be documented in such a way that the procedures and results are auditable and available to interested constituencies. In discussing documentation standards in program evaluation, Robbin (1981, p. 86) writes:

> As public policy makers become increasingly dependent on statistical data, it is critical that standards for data quality be established. Such standards must reflect the principle that statistical data represent objective and verifiable evidence that is unambiguously described so that analysis or evaluation based upon this evidence can be effectively reviewed, criticized, and replicated.

Hedrick, Boruch, and Ross (1978, p. 274) make a similar point in their discussion of secondary analysis of evaluations, recommending that "all data, documentation, and logs stemming from federally supported research used in policy, especially program evaluations, must be made available to the community of analysts." They make this argument on scientific, public interest, and economic grounds, along with the grounds of protecting the public and the scientific community from fraud. The latter point is worth noting, given recent widely discussed cases of scientific fraud (Broad & Wade, 1982). If the production of adequate documentation is required throughout the project, and is reviewed on a routine basis, it becomes considerably more difficult to fabricate or alter data without serious inconsistencies appearing.

Second, it is necessary for assessing the validity of the inferences drawn from the data. Making causal inferences in evaluation studies requires a great deal of care. Evaluations are typically carried out in field settings, where experimental control is considerably less than in laboratory settings, and the quality of the design and the measurement procedures can be degraded by a variety of random and systematic factors. This can limit the kinds of inferences that can be made. Furthermore, many evaluations employ quasi-experimental designs which, depending on contextual factors, may require some strong assumptions to rule out plausible rival explanations of observed effects. Given these circumstances, any interpretation of the data requires fairly detailed information about the nature of the investigation. In the absence of good documentation, validity may be difficult to assess.

Third, it is essential for carrying out reanalysis and replication, and interpreting comparisons with the original findings. These activities have a bearing on assessing objectivity and validity, as well as extending or modifying the original findings, and there have been increasing calls for both reanalyses and replications of evaluations. Yet, without adequate documentation regarding how the study was actually implemented and

how the analyses were carried out, successful reanalysis and replication can be difficult, if not impossible.

These points may seem obvious. Yet, Mosteller, Gilbert, and McPeek (1980) in a review of 152 published clinical trials on cancer, found widespread deficiencies in the published documents regarding important procedural and statistical issues including randomization, statistical method, blindness, power, sample size, survival, and informed consent. Obviously not all details can be included in a journal article; however, attempts to obtain additional detailed information from the original investigators are often unproductive as pointed out by Wolins (1962) and by Boruch, Cordray, and Wortman (1981) and their discussion of problems in secondary analysis. Keep in mind also that the papers considered by Mosteller and his colleagues had been subjected to review and had been published. As Schmandt (1978) notes, much policy research is not subjected to the traditional quality control system of the scientific disciplines; one might therefore expect even more problems with documentation and the assessment of scientific adequacy in this area.

REASONS FOR POOR DOCUMENTATION

Unfortunately, as most writers concerned with documentation note, high quality documentation is rare. If good documentation does indeed have the benefits just discussed, why is it so often ignored? Part of the problem is what Sonquist and Dunkelberg (1977, p. 405) describe as the "almost irresistable tendency to get on with the analysis and not to keep written records of what was done and in what sequence." It is often seen as a chore by technical staff—Weinberg (1971, p. 262) comments on documentation being the "castor oil" of computer programming. The problem is that the benefits are often not realized until some later point in time; in addition, much of the documentation may be for the benefit of persons other than the writer. In their discussion of data archives, Mosteller, Gilbert,

and McPeek (1980, p. 56) describe an all-too-common scenario:

> By the time a research project is completed, the analysis finished, and publications prepared, not infrequently the investigators' attention has turned elsewhere, technical assistants are tired of the project, the grant overextended, and preserving the data gets short shrift. The original data, if not thrown out, are likely to be packed helter-skelter in a box in the far corner of the storeroom. Even an important, well-funded project is likely to end with the data tapes unmarked or preserved in such a way that it is difficult to tell the original materials from edited versions or those produced for special analyses.

Clearly, if documentation is not planned and supported by project management from the beginning, it will not be done.

TYPES OF DOCUMENTATION REQUIRED

In this section, an overview is provided of the document types required in different phases of evaluation studies. The purpose of this section is to provide a framework for thinking about and anticipating the kinds of documentation one would use in conducting evaluations. As was mentioned earlier, documentation needs will vary from project to project and there is no single outline of document types that will fit every project. Yet, even though the relative emphasis on, and level of detail of, the different types of documentation may vary across projects, the functions they serve will have to be addressed. Discussion of detailed formats and specifications for the various document

types is beyond the scope of this paper; however, references to sources discussing those details are provided at the end of this section.

In considering this material one should keep in mind the importance of documentation planning. Some decision by project management is required regarding the document types and level of detail necessary for project management and scientific reporting. Most writers in this area emphasize that a documentation plan needs to be developed in the early stages of a project; it is very unlikely that adequate documentation will be developed without planning. One aspect of this planning is to define the types of documents that will be necessary. A second aspect is to define the procedures and resources for document production. A third, and very important, aspect is to define a system for documentation management. Many of the writers cited in this discussion recommend designating a documentation manager to handle this. This person would be responsible for monitoring documentation and its completion, filing it for easy retrieval, and controlling revisions and additions.

The types of documents to be discussed are shown in Table 1. They are arranged in terms of project phases. Most evaluation projects involve a general planning phase, a design phase, a data collection phase, a data processing and analysis phase, and a summary and interpretation phase. These are in rough chronological order, although there is often overlap. In addition to

---

TABLE 1
TYPES OF DOCUMENTATION

Planning Documents
    Project phase plan
    Organization plan
    Documentation and reporting plan

Design Documents
    Detailed design plan
    Working papers

Data Collection Documents
    Data collection/field administration plan
    Data collection reports
    Editing and coding documents
    Data collection forms
    Data entry documents
    Working papers

Data Processing and Analysis Documents
    Data processing plan
    Data cleaning and validation report
    Data file documents
    File index system
    Data dictionary
    Processing summaries
    Program library
    Printed output
    Summary tables
    Working papers

Interpretation and Summary Documents
    Interim and final reports
    Executive summaries
    Press releases
    Project history
    Archival data file

General Project Documents
    Accounting records and cost reports
    Personnel files
    Contracts and agreements
    General project correspondence
    Project proposal
    Project library
    Index to project documentation

---

documentation for each of these project phases, some general administrative and reference documentation is required throughout the project; this is also shown in Table 1.

Planning Documents

These documents provide the reference point for all project activities. In the *project phase plan*, the objectives and tasks to be accomplished for each phase are spelled out. For example, the tasks in the design phase include defining the variables of interest, selecting measuring instruments, identifying populations to be studied, and so on. The phase plan should include a calendar with timelines for the major tasks within each phase, showing projected completion dates. The *organization plan* defines staffing, responsibilities, and flow of work. The *documentation and reporting plan* defines the documents to be produced for internal and external use; who will use them for what purpose; standardized formats; responsibilities for production, review, and maintenance; and the schedule for document production. A filing system and index for all documentation should be outlined as part of this plan.

Design Documents

The major document here is the *detailed design plan*. In this document, the relationship of the design to the general study objectives is spelled out. The variables of interest are defined, measuring instruments are selected, specific populations to be studied are identified, the sampling plan with the necessary sample size is specified, and the types of statistical analyses to be performed are described. For some projects, this may be very similar to material included in an initial project proposal; more often, however, the proposal will be less specific than the detailed design. This document provides the basis for planning the field administration and data analysis operations. In addition to the detailed design, various *working papers* including memos, consultants' recommendations, minutes, and proposals will be generated in this phase. A file of these papers should be maintained because they can be useful in reconstructing decisions when questions arise. Ideally, the rationale for the various aspects of the design should be covered in the detailed design document; however, unforeseen problems may sometimes require rethinking certain issues, and a review of the working papers can be of value.

Data Collection Documents

Given the data specifications in the detailed design document, the *data collection/field administration plan* contains a description of how these data will be obtained. Included here are plans for selection and training of data collection staff, contacting respondents or subjects, scheduling and monitoring data collection, and maintaining quality control. The types of *data collection reports* will vary considerably depending upon the nature of the study and the data requirements—the operations necessary to obtain data from medical records, for example, will be quite different from those necessary to obtain data from surveys involving personal interviews. Included here might be training reports; quality control reports (such as those describing abstractor or interviewer reliability measures); reports on problems encountered in data collection and their resolution; and other documents such as training manuals, data collection assignments and schedules, and supervisor reports on data collection staff. Also included in the data collection documents are those pertaining to editing, and if necessary, coding of the raw data. The *editing and coding documents* consist of instructions, logs and records of what was done, and summary reports including discussion of data quality along with problems encountered in editing and coding and their solutions. Specific editing and coding actions should be indicated on the original *data collection forms*; these forms should be bound together and filed. *Data entry documents* include instructions to keypunchers and the coded data sheets. Again, any *working papers* should be retained along with the data collection documents.

Data Processing and Analysis Documents
The quality of documentation in the area of electronic data processing is critical; the level of detail and complexity is such that inadequate documentation can lead to considerable inefficiency, if not serious errors which are costly and time-consuming to correct. The *data processing plan* contains a description of the processing steps necessary for data cleaning and validation, file construction, and statistical analysis. The overall organization and sequence of these steps should be spelled out. Input and output specifications and a description of what is to be done should be part of the write-up of each step. Cleaning and validation operations involve checks for illegal codes and for inconsistencies among codes for different variables. A *data cleaning and validation report* on these operations should include a description of all errors encountered and actions taken, plus summary statistics on data quality. File construction operations may involve the rearrangement and transformation of data and the creation of derived variables. The resulting data files need to be described in *data file documents* in terms of identifiers, medium, contents, format, creation date and author, and backup files. Documentation for all files should be referenced in a central *file index system*. A *data dictionary* should be maintained with an entry for each variable. Each entry should contain a unique variable name, a variable number, aliases used in different computer runs, the source, file locations, legitimate codes, and any descriptive statistics that would aid understanding. In carrying out the statistical analy-sis, *processing summaries* should be prepared following each run or series of related runs. The summaries should include information on input files, program parameters (along with references to the programs used), output files, steps taken to verify correct execution, along with a written description of what was done. The *program library* should include manuals for canned programs and full descriptions of programs developed by project staff along with the source files. The descriptions of programs developed in-house should include a verbal overview, input and output specifications, parameters to be specified by the user, a flow chart, and a listing with liberal use of comment statements. The *printed output* should reference the appropriate run summary so that the input files and parameters, such as those for treating missing values, and so on, are clear. The output should be indexed and maintained in a central location, although to facilitate study of the results, duplicates copies of the output may sometimes be necessary. *Summary tables* should be prepared in a standardized format and should reference the printed output from which the contents were obtained. Any *working papers* should be maintained along with these documents.

Interpretation and Summary Documents
The usual documents prepared in this phase include *interim and final reports*, *executive summaries*, and *press releases*, if any. The *project history* is for the investigator's use in planning future projects. It contains a summary of important project events, along with a discussion of problems encountered and their solutions. A comparison between what was planned and what actually occurred should be included. This comparison should involve time, staffing, resources, and budget considerations. If the data are to be fully available for review, an *archival data file* must be prepared. The file must be accompanied by all the information necessary for a secondary analyst to use and interpret the data. If the documentation discussed in this section has been adequately prepared, the material needed to accompany the archival data file can be easily assembled.

General Project Documents
This category includes various administrative and reference documents that are not phase-specific. Included here are *accounting records* and *cost reports*, *personnel files*, *contracts and agreements*, *general project correspondence*, the *project proposal*, the *project library* of books and reprints with an index system, and an *index to project documentation*.

There are a number of publications that the reader may wish to consult for more detailed information on the planning and preparation of documentation. Sonquist and Dunkelberg (1977) provide a comprehensive discussion of the different types of documentation necessary in survey research. They give special attention to documentation of data files and data processing, and they provide samples of various document types. Assenzo and Lamborn (1981) review the kinds of documentation needed in clinical trials; and Mosteller, Gilbert, and McPeek (1980) make a number of specific recommendations for improvement in this area. Fiedler (1978) provides an overview of documentation necessary in field research; and Rogson (1975) outlines the types of documentation that will be produced in different phases of large studies. David, Gates, and Miller (1974) discuss their experiences in documenting a large archive of microeconomic data. Lefferts (1983) discusses the reporting program in grants management. Roistacher (1980) provides a detailed style manual for documenting data files, and

Robbin (1981) draws on this material in providing specific guidelines for documenting data files in evaluation and policy research. Certain books in the data processing literature provide useful guidelines for developing documentation (Enger, 1976a, 1976b; Gaydasch, 1982; Gray & London, 1969; Kindred, 1973; Metzger, 1981; U.S. Department of Commerce, 1976). Most of these references contain discussion of the use of documentation for managerial purposes. Metzger (1981) is especially useful in this respect; there is much discussion of documentation in planning and of the use of documentation to control projects and to assure the quality of the results. The discussion is accompanied by format outlines for a wide variety of document types.

RECOMMENDATIONS FOR IMPROVING DOCUMENTATION

Given that good documentation is required for managerial and scientific purposes, what could be done to improve the quality of documentation? The first recommendation is a rather straightforward one, directed toward persons in charge of evaluation research projects, and is one that we have touched on already — documentation needs should be carefully considered by project management in the planning phase of the project. This means spelling out what documents will be needed for what purposes, who will produce them, when they will be produced, what format will be appropriate, how they will be maintained, and so on. If it is left for undesignated project staff members to do whenever they happen to feel like it, in whatever format and degree of detail they choose, and to file according to some system known only to them, it will be of limited valued. A slapdash system may be adequate if there is no staff turnover, if no problems arise requiring review of plans and operations, if all staff know exactly what they need to accomplish by what date, if everyone involved has excellent memories and no other tasks to distract them, and so on. However, such a fortuitous combination of circumstances will be rather rare in most evaluation studies. Furthermore, the documentation that is produced will be of limited value for purposes of outside review and reanalysis. Producing documentation does require time and money, and project management will need to decide what documentation will be necessary. The point here is that this should be an informed decision. In planning the project, it is essential that the costs and benefits of documentation be considered in deciding what will be necessary for managerial and scientific purposes. In some instances this may require additional staff, technical assistance, and other resources, especially in technical areas of data base management and data processing, and this needs to be built into the project budget request.

Such planning would be greatly facilitated by the availability of models from which to work. A second recommendation, directed toward specialists in project management and data base management, is that standards and guidelines for documentation be developed and disseminated. It is a waste of time and effort for every project to have to reinvent the wheel in setting up a documentation system. Additional work, along the lines of that cited in the previous section, would be of great value in documentation planning. Furthermore, proposed standards should be tested — reports of experiences in using specific standards would be valuable. Information on what worked well and what did not, on costs, on effort required, and so on would greatly aid subsequent users. Practicing evaluators could contribute significantly in this regard.

A third, more general, recommendation is that documentation for data processing be given more attention in the training of evaluators. Many evaluators gain experience with data analysis and data file management during training, and in subsequent professional positions are often involved in directly supervising data processing for research projects. Unfortunately, documentation is seldom given much attention during training. As a result, many evaluators learn to live with inadequate, ad hoc systems. Training in planning and preparing adequate documentation could very easily be combined with training in data analysis and file management. The availability of standards and guidelines, as discussed previously, would be of great value for training purposes.

A fourth, and final, recommendation is that more attention should be given to project management in the training of evaluators and in discussions in the evaluation literature. In their treatment of the management of survey research projects, Sonquist and Dunkelberg (1977, p. 460) write, "keeping administrative control of the highly complex project that a survey can be is probably the most underexplained topic (relative to its importance) in survey research methodology texts." As St. Pierre (1982, 1983) notes, the situation is not much different in the field of evaluation; he writes (1983, p. 1), "while the technical science or art of conducting field-based evaluations has advanced steadily over the past decades, the management of pro-

gram evaluation has received little attention." We have argued that documentation is an essential ingredient in effective project management. Increased attention to research management could lead to better production and use of documentation, and, ultimately, to improved scientific reporting.

REFERENCES

ASSENZO, J. R., & LAMBORN, K. R., (1981). Documenting the results of a study. In C. R. Buncher & J. Y. Tsay (Eds.), *Statistics in the pharmaceutical industry* (pp. 251-299). New York: Marcel Dekker, Inc.

BORUCH, R. F., CORDRAY, D. S., & WORTMAN, P. M. (1981). Secondary analysis: Why, how, and when. In R. F. Boruch, D. S. Cordray, & P. M. Wortman (Eds.), *Reanalyzing program evaluations: Policies and practices for secondary analysis of social and educational programs* (pp. 1-20). San Francisco: Jossey-Bass.

BROAD, W., & WADE, N. (1982). *Betrayers of the truth.* New York: Simon and Schuster.

BROOKS, F. P., JR. (1975). *The mythical man-month: Essays on software engineering.* Reading, MA: Addison-Wesley.

BURRILL, C. W., & ELLSWORTH, L. W. (1980). *Modern Project management: Foundations for quality and productivity.* Tenafly, NJ: Burrill-Ellsworth Associates, Inc.

DAVID, M. H., GATES, W. A., & MILLER, R. F. (1974). *Linkage and retrieval of microeconomic data: A strategy for data development and use. A report on the Wisconsin assets and income archives.* Lexington, MA: Lexington Books, D. C. Heath and Co.

ENGER, N. L. (1976a). *Documentation standards for computer systems.* Fairfax Station, VA: Technology Press.

ENGER, N. L. (1976b). *Management standards for developing information systems.* New York: AMACOM.

FIEDLER, J. (1978). *Field research: A manual for logistics and management of scientific studies in natural settings.* San Francisco: Jossey-Bass.

GAYDASCH, A., JR. (1982). *Principles of EDP management.* Reston, VA: Reston Publishing Co., Inc.

GRAY, M., & LONDON, K. (1969). *Documentation standards.* Princeton, NJ: Brandon/Systems Press.

GREEN, J. D. (1977). Systems documentation, internal control, and the auditor's responsibilities. In E. G. Jancura (Ed.), *Computers: Auditing and control* (pp. 186-192). New York: Petrocelli/ Charter. (Reprinted from *The CPA Journal,* 1974, July, 25-28).

HEDRICK, T. E., BORUCH, R. F., & ROSS, J. (1978). On ensuring the availability of evaluative data for secondary analysis. *Policy Sciences, 9,* 259-280.

JANCURA, E. G. (Ed.). (1977). *Computers: Auditing and control.* New York: Petrocelli/Charter.

KINDRED, A. R. (1973). Documentation and manuals. In *Data*

systems and management: An introduction to systems analysis and design. Englewood Cliffs, NJ: Prentice-Hall.

LEFFERTS, R. (1983). *The basic handbook of grants management.* New York: Basic Books.

LINSENMEIER, J. A. W., WORTMAN, P. M., & HENDRICKS, M. (1981). Need for better documentation: Problems in a reanalysis of teacher bias. In R. F. Boruch, P. M. Wortman, & D. S. Cordray (Eds.), *Reanalyzing program evaluations: Policies and practices for secondary analysis of social and educational programs* (pp. 68-83). San Francisco: Jossey-Bass.

METZGER, P. W. (1981). *Managing a programming project.* Englewood Cliffs, NJ: Prentice-Hall.

MOSTELLER, F., GILBERT, J. P., & McPEEK, B. (1980). Reporting standards and research strategies for controlled trials: Agenda for the editor. *Controlled Clinical Trials, 1,* 37-58.

ROBBIN, A. (1981). Technical guidelines for preparing and documenting data. In R. F. Boruch, P. M. Wortman, & D. S. Cordray (Eds.), *Reanalyzing program evaluations: Policies and practices for secondary analysis of social and educational programs* (pp. 84-143). San Francisco: Jossey-Bass.

ROGSON, M. M. (1975). *Documentation in massive social science experiments* (Rand Paper Series P-5494). Paper presented at 83rd Annual Convention of the American Psychological Association, Chicago, August 30-September 3, 1975.

ROISTACHER, R. C. (1980). *A style manual for machine-readable data files and their documentation.* Washington, DC: U. S. Department of Justice.

SCHMANDT, J. (1978). Scientific research and policy analysis. *Science, 201,* 869.

SONQUIST, J. A., & DUNKELBERG, W. C. (1977). *Survey and opinion research: Procedures for processing and analysis.* Englewood Cliffs, NJ: Prentice-Hall, Inc.

ST. PIERRE, R. G. (1982). Management of federally funded evaluation research: Building evaluation teams. *Evaluation Review, 6,* 94-113.

ST. PIERRE, R. G. (1983). Editor's notes. In R. G. St. Pierre (Ed.), *Management and organization of program evaluation* (pp. 1-3). New Directions for Program Evaluation, No. 18. San Francisco: Jossey-Bass.

U. S. DEPARTMENT OF COMMERCE, NATIONAL BUREAU OF STANDARDS. (1976). *Guidelines for documentation of computer programs and automated data systems.* (Federal Information

Processing Standards Publication 38) Washington, DC: U. S. Government Printing Office.

WEINBERG, G. M. (1971). *The psychology of computer programming.* New York: Van Nostrand Reinhold Co.

WEISS, C. H. (1973). Between the cup and the lip . . . *Evaluation, 1,* 49–55.

WOLINS, L. (1962). Responsibility for raw data. *American Psychologist, 17,* 657–658

13

Legal and Professional Standards in Program Evaluation

Paul W. Thurston, John C. Ory, Paul W. Mayberry, and Larry A. Braskamp

There are several legal considerations that program evaluators need to be aware of, although there are few specific examples of large awards or settlements by a jury in a case involving program evaluation. In fact, the dearth of actual reported appellate court decisions involving some type of legal challenge to a particular program evaluation is rather surprising. It is hard to know why so few cases have been reported. Possibly evaluators tend to be uncritical, and therefore there is no reason to sue. Or, evaluators may be so cautious and/or professionally competent that there are no grounds for legal action challenging the evaluation. Whatever the reasons, there are several legal issues inherent in program evaluation that evaluators need to understand. Because sound evaluation practice closely tracks legal conduct, an examination of legal considerations should be instructive in shaping program evaluations. To the extent the evaluator understands the legal boundaries involved in the profession, the evaluator will be in a much stronger position to make critical judgments without fear of legal vulnerability.

This article will briefly describe four legal considerations involved in program evaluation: defamation, contract, evaluation malpractice, and confidentiality of sources. Before describing these general areas, we must make two cautionary statements. First, the general areas of law described in this paper are simplified considerably. There are details that go beyond what is described here, and consequently any specific problems that arise should prompt the evaluator to consult with legal counsel for more specific advice. Second, these areas of the law tend to be matters of state law, and therefore variations exist from one state to another. For purposes of this article, these differences largely are ignored.

Defamation

Defamation is one specific area of tort law and it is a general rubric that covers two specific types of law: libel, which refers to written or more permanent forms of defamation, and slander, which refers to spoken or transitory forms of defamation. To better understand defamation in a general sense, we will identify first the prima facie case that needs to be proven by the plantiff, and then the defenses that are available to the defendant (Prosser, 1971).

The Prima Facie Case

Defamatory language. The first element in the prima facie case is that there must be defamatory language, language that injures one's reputation, made by the defendant. To say precisely what language is defamatory is impossible because this is a factual determination usually made by the jury. But considering the four types of characterizations that are considered slander per se should be instructive.

From Thurston et al., "Legal and Professional Standards in Program Evaluation," *Educational Evaluation and Policy Analysis*, 1984, 6, 15-26. Copyright 1984, American Educational Research Association, Washington, DC.

(Slander per se simply means that if one of the four following characterizations of a person is made by a defendant, this will amount to actionable slander without the plaintiff having to show the extent and monetary value of actual injury to reputation or professional standing.) The four types of characterizations are (1) to declare the unchastity of a woman, (2) to allege that someone is guilty of a crime involving moral turpitude, (3) to allege that a person has venereal disease or leprosy, and (4) to characterize a person in such a way that it adversely reflects the plantiff's abilities in his or her business, trade, or profession. To satisfy this fourth type, the statement or accusation must refer to something that the plaintiff does professionally. For example, Prosser (1971) describes several cases in which the statements made about a certain profession were found to be slanderous per se. These include

> saying of a physician that he is a butcher and the speaker would not have him for a dog, of an attorney that he is a shyster, of a school teacher that he has been guilty of improper conduct as to his pupils, of a clergyman that he is the subject of scandalous rumors, of a chauffeur that he is habitually drinking, of a merchant that his credit is bad or that he sells adulterated goods, of a public officer that he has accepted a bribe or has used his office for corrupt purposes, or that he is a communist, or of any of these that he is dishonest, incompetent, or insane— since these things obviously discredit him in his chosen calling. (Prosser, 1971, p. 758)

The second element of the prima facie case is that the defamatory language must be "of or concerning" the plaintiff. This means that the language must identify the plaintiff to a reasonable reader, listener, or viewer. There are two central aspects of this element that often make it difficult to satisfy. First, even though the statement may have no specific or clear reference to a particular person, there may be sufficient extrinsic facts in the statement that would lead a reasonable person to connect the plaintiff with the defamatory meaning. If this is possible, it is merely a question of fact for the jury to determine whether they, as reasonable persons, could imply that the plain meaning of the language refers to the particular plaintiff. The second aspect of this element is to determine whether or not a person or a few persons belong to a group sufficiently small so that the entire group may be defamed. In other words, is a group sufficiently large so that individual members of that group are not defamed? For example, statements that "politicians are dishonest" or "farmers are liars" are not defamatory because they do not specifically identify a small enough group to be actionable. There is no precise guideline on what the maximum size of a group is before it moves out of the actionable category, but as a general rule of thumb, if a group is larger than 20 or 25, the court would probably not hold a statement made about the particular group actionable to one member of that group.

The third element of the prima facie case is that the defendant publicizes the defamatory language to a third person. Simple statements of defamation made by the defendant to the plaintiff do not satisfy this publication requirement. On the other hand, if the statement is overheard by a third party, or the publication is made to a third party without the plaintiff being present, the publication requirement is satisfied.

The fourth element is that there must be damage to the plaintiff's reputation. The amount of damage necessary can vary. For example, in the slander per se categories described above, no actual damages need to be shown. So, if an evaluator is heard to say that a teacher takes indecent liberty with his students the teacher does not need to show the extent of damage in lost earnings or mental pain or suffering to recover. Still, such evidence would be persuasive in enhancing the damages awarded. This is in contrast to other allegations of slander where the plaintiff must be able to show some actual injury to recover against the defendant. While showing actual injury is not necessary to successfully justify the prima facie case of defamation, the level of the award that one hopes to recover is closely related to the amount of damages that one can show. In the slander per se categories described above, in which defamation results in no actual damages, punitive damages are available. Punitive damages are severe enough to financially burden the defendant, thereby motivating him or her to behave properly in the future and discouraging other potential defamers.

One other element may be considered part of the prima facie case, although occasionally it is described as a defense. Because of constitutional first amendment considerations, the status of the plaintiff as well as the fault of the defendant must be considered in determining liability. Two general rules apply in this area. First, if the statement or article is about a public official or public figure, then the defendant is liable for general damages only if malice can be shown on the part of the defendant. Absent malice, the publisher is not liable for a defamatory statement made about a public figure.

A public official or public figure may be of either a general or limited status. One may be a general public official or public figure by either achieving such pervasive fame or notoriety that he or she becomes a public figure for all purposes (e.g., sports celebrity Reggie Jackson, movie star Burt Reynolds, or President and Mrs. Reagan). Their status as public figures extends to reports of their social and personal activities as well as their professional activities. This is distinguished from the limited public figure who injects him or herself into a particular public controversy. Here the public figure status is limited to only that activity for which he or she has projected himself into the public light (*Walston vs. Readers Digest Assoc.*, 1979).[1] This limited public figure status would include such a high-level government employee as a dean of a state college as long as the statements pertain to professional behavior (*Byers vs. Southeastern Newspapers Corp.*, 1982).[2]

If the statement is made about a public figure or a public official, then the defendant is liable only if the statement was made with malice. One way of showing malice is if the defendant had actual knowledge of the untruthfulness of the statement. An example would be a parent making statements before the school board about a teacher that the parent knew were false. (*Nodar vs. Galbreath*, 1983).[3] A second way to prove malice is if the defendant had serious doubts about the truthfulness of the statement, but proceeded in a reckless fashion to make the statement without checking its veracity. The professional standards can play an important role here in establishing the standard of good practice, and therefore provide guidance as to what amounts to reckless practice.

The second general rule is that if the statement is made about a private person, then the general standard of negligence will apply to the defendant. The damages here are limited to the actual injury of the plaintiff, although these damages may be shown to be impairment of reputation or standing in the community, personal humiliation and mental anguish and suffering, as well as actual monetary loss from business-related activities.

Defenses to Defamation

If the plaintiff has satisfactorily pleaded and proved the elements in the prima facie case, the defendant can claim one of several defenses. The defenses include consent, truth, qualified privilege, and absolute privilege.

Consent, as it suggests, indicates that the defendant said or wrote something with the plaintiff's approval. As one would expect, central in any consent defense is whether or not the alleged consent actually encompasses the alleged defamatory statement. For example, there may have been a consent for an interview, but there was not consent to say certain things that went beyond the scope of that interview.

Truth is a defense to defamation. A statement made about a plaintiff may be damaging and harmful, but if the defendant can prove the statement to be truthful, the truth of the matter will bar the plaintiff from successfully suing the defendant. However, the burden of proof is on the defendant.

There are many absolute privileges that protect the maker of any statement. These

---

[1] *Walston vs. Readers Digest Association*, 443 U.S. 157 (1979)

[2] *Byers vs. Southeastern Newspapers Corporation*, 228 S.E. 2d 698 (Ga. App. 1982)

[3] *Nodar vs. Galbreath*, 429 So. 2d 715 (Fla. App. 4 Dist., 1983)

privileges include judicial, legislative, and executive statements that are made during reasonable exercise of those governmental activities. Some states provide by statute an absolute privilege for public officials who are properly discharging an official duty. This protection can provide grounds for summary dismissal of a defamation suit brought by a professor against a dean for removing him or her from the department chairmanship (*Small* vs. *McRae*, 1982).[4] Another example of an absolute privilege is the communication between spouses. The policy behind the absolute privilege is that the cost of limiting free and open discussion by certain people outweighs the individual defamatory costs that are involved, and therefore a defamation interest is secondary to the public policy interest in supporting certain types of information.

There are many qualified privileges which, in certain circumstances, the defendant can use to dispel the claimed defamation. Once again the defendant bears the burden of proof. One qualified privilege is someone who acts in the public interest. For example, a citizen may report to the public (i.e., the police), in good faith, a crime believed to have been committed. It may turn out, on further investigation, that a crime was not in fact committed, but the citizen nonetheless would be protected. A second type of qualified immunity is fair comment and criticism. This involves a reviewer's critique of something of public interest, such as a play, an art show, or a book. The production of these works legitimately raises the opportunity for comment and criticism, which members of the general public would like to hear, and liability for defamatory statements made in the reviews would dampen their vitality and robustness. This seems applicable to program evaluations, but because there is no case law in which this defense has been recognized, it is premature to put too much reliance on it. The third qualified privilege is in statements that are made to protect the interest of the publisher. For example, a person can make reasonable statements to defend his or her own rep-

utation, including an allegation that the accuser is a liar. The statement must be within the scope of what the person can reasonably show. Finally, the interest of another person can be the basis for a qualified privilege. For example, a warning made by a father to his daughter not to marry a suitor because he is worthless is protected. To enjoy this qualified privilege, it is important that the maker of the statement have a legitimate connection with the person to whom the statement is made. In all these qualified privileges, a central issue is whether or not the statement that is the basis of the alleged defamation stays within the scope of the qualified privilege.

Contracts

Contracts is a major area of law, and it can be an important way to define the obligations and responsibilities of various parties involved in the program evaluation process. Two or more parties may agree to conduct an evaluation that obligates each party to some responsibility or detriment as an exchange for a benefit sought. This agreement will be enforceable in court as long as no defenses exist to void the agreement.

The agreement between the parties is characterized in contract law by a number of phrases: mutual assent, a meeting of the minds, and offer and acceptance. Stripped to its essentials this means that the parties have agreed to something at the same time. This agreement is measured by an objective standard of what the apparent intention was which was manifested to the other party. The subjective intention of the parties is irrelevant. Also, certainty and definiteness must be part of the essential terms of the agreement. For a program evaluation contract the minimal essential terms would seem to include (a) identity of the parties and the type of evaluation desired, (b) price to be paid, (c) time of payment and completion of evaluation, and (d) nature of program to be evaluated. Certainly there are many additional details about the evaluation and the program that ought to be included in the contract, but without these basic terms the contract is considered unformed. When a contract is formed be-

[4] *Small* vs. *McRae*, 651 P. 2d 982 (Mont. 1982)

cause of the existence of these essential elements but a disagreement develops over a missing term, custom and usage and professional standards can play a vital function in supplying the missing term.

Custom and usage can be related specifically to relationships between these two parties in earlier program evaluations or they may relate to a general practice in the field that the parties ought to be familiar with. To the extent that there is a gap in the contract over an item for which professional standards exist, these standards can substitute. Where custom and usage and professional standards are consistent, there is a strong argument for using this as the meaning of the missing term. Where they are inconsistent, courts will probably treat custom and usage, particularly where there is a previous relationship between the parties, as more important than professional standards.

For a contract to be enforceable, there must be a bargained-for change in legal position between the parties, known as "consideration" in legal parlance. This "consideration" involves a bargained-for exchange between the parties for something that has legal value. Most commonly this is satisfied by noting that the party has incurred a detriment either by performing an act or making a promise to act in the future. The subtleties of legal analysis that might develop in this area are unlikely to occur in program evaluation contracts.

Defenses to a contract generally fall under two broad categories: legal incapacity of one of the parties to enter into the contract and evidence that the parties did not in fact form a contract. Legal incapacity can exist where one of the parties is a minor, is mentally incapable of understanding the nature and significance of the contract, or is intoxicated. It can also be unenforceable if it can be shown that there was not willing agreement to the contract either because of duress and coercion or fraud in the contract negotiations stage.

The primary defense to a valid formation of a contract involves mistakes the parties made. Where both parties were mistaken about an essential element of the contract, then the contract is deemed not formed. Where only one of the parties

is mistaken about the facts relating to the agreement, the mistake will not prevent formation of the contract. Yet this potentially harsh rule is softened by the rule that will not allow the nonmistaken party to take advantage of the other party's mistake if the nonmistaken party is or should have been aware of the error. Finally, certain contracts are illegal as a matter of public policy and will not be enforced.

Even though there is apparently more interest in the use of contracts for program evaluation in the past few years (House & Care, 1979; Stake, 1976; Wright & Worthen, 1975; Sieber, Note 1) there have been no reported cases involving judicial action challenging the performance of a program evaluation pursuant to a breach of contract action. Three areas of contract law merit special attention because of their implications for an enforceable program evaluation contract: the parole evidence rule, third-party interest in the contract, and the measure of damages.

An oral agreement can be as enforceable as a written contract, although it has the obvious shortcoming of being difficult to demonstrate what precisely the parties agreed to. If a written contract exists there is a general rule—the parole evidence rule—that says that all contemporaneous oral agreements adding to or altering the written agreement are inoperative. Basically this says that the written agreement will control. Still, because the meaning of the written agreement may be unclear, information that sheds light on the intent of the parties at the time of the agreement will be important and probably allowed into evidence.

This suggests that parties to a contract must be thoughtful about expressing all the terms of a contract in writing when any writing exists. Inevitably, though, the contract will not include language on a particular matter that might later be the point of disagreement. The parties could make a general statement that past dealings between the parties or acceptable practice as described by the standards would control when there is no language to the contrary.

A second area of interest is the right of third parties in enforcing the contract. Consider, for example, an evaluation contract between the federal government and an evaluator to assess a particular public school program. One term of the contract specifies that all subjects interviewed will be kept anonymous, but when the evaluation report is published, the identity of one parent who was critical of the program is clear from the context. Does this person have any basis for protection under the contract? In this hypothetical situation the success of the individual in getting redress will depend on whether he or she is characterized as an incidental beneficiary, and therefore not protected by the contract, or an intended beneficiary. Here the parent is probably an incidental beneficiary and therefore enjoys no protection under the terms of the contract. The question of the appropriate characterization of third parties can arise in a variety of cases and can be important in determining the enforceable scope of an agreement.

Litigation of contractual disputes is primarily a matter of obtaining financial redress for breach of contract that has caused financial hardship. It is difficult to apply this economic measure of damages to the program evaluation context. Contract law distinguishes between compensatory and consequential damages. Compensatory damages intend, so far as money can do this, to put the nonbreaching party in as close to the position he or she would have been in had the contract been performed. Consequential damages allow for additional losses to be claimed if they resulted from the breach as long as a reasonable person could have foreseen that such losses would occur from such a breach at the time of entry into the contract. Both parties must have been aware of the special circumstances at the time of the contract.

In trying to apply these principles to the program evaluation context, assume that the evaluator has made a critical assessment of a program and that the assessment has been made using techniques that go beyond the methodologies specified in the evaluation agreement. At a fundamental level it is difficult to demonstrate what economic implications there are for a program that has been critically reviewed. Beyond this, the agreement does not specify that the evaluation will be positive. The plaintiff,

therefore, will need to show that there is a connection between the use of unspecified techniques—the breach of contract—and the overall critical evaluation. There is no area for consequential damages here because there was no understanding at the time of the making of the contract about what foreseeable future losses could result from a particular breach in methodology.

The difficulty of showing damages is probably the most important reason that contracts in program evaluation do not move to litigation. Both the commercial insignificance of many educational programs and the difficulty of showing a relationship between the alleged breach and a financial loss explain how hard it is to show damages. Because punitive damages are not awarded in contracts, there is no reason to allege breach of contract unless some monetary damages can be demonstrated.

Evaluation Malpractice

Evaluation malpractice, like its more firmly established counterpart, medical malpractice, is based on the tort theory of negligence (Prosser, 1971). Generally stated, malpractice is the failure of one party to perform at a reasonably acceptable level in a relationship with a second party, where the second party presumes a certain level of professional services to be performed. For example, medical malpractice can be shown when a physician sews up a patient with the sponges still in the stomach cavity and medical experts testify that this is contrary to standard medical practice. Consequently the practicing physician can be held liable for damages to the patient resulting from this improper operation. A central question in medical malpractice cases is determining what level of care could reasonably be expected from the doctor. For example, the standard of professional care from a specialist like a surgeon or ophthalmologist would be greater than one would expect from a general practitioner. The level of care one can reasonably expect from the doctor also could vary from one region of the country to another.

Because of the professional relationship that exists in evaluation, evaluators could be held to a certain standard of performance. To the extent there is an agreed-upon level of acceptable practice in evaluation, which is probably best identified in the professional standards, this practice can become the standard to which evaluators' conduct can be compared. Although there are no reported appellate level cases of evaluation malpractice in the program evaluation area, it is a possibility, particularly with increased publication and acceptance of professional standards. The major focus of inquiry, then, would be whether or not the evaluator's practice has differed sufficiently from accepted professional standards to amount to a breach of duty.

The difficulty of employing evaluation malpractice theory as a basis for recovery under negligence is that the injury will most likely be to someone's reputation. Because reputation is protected under defamation it is likely that analysis will shift to this legal arena. Professional standards will be important, therefore, because they identify a recognized code of behavior for evaluators and provide a benchmark for measuring the extent to which other behavior is reckless or malicious.

Confidentiality of Sources

Although confidentiality of sources is not a specific area of law, as are defamation and contracts, there is a general notion that privacy ought to be protected. The difficulty is that privacy is an elusive concept, and how far it is protected depends on what other competing interests are involved. In program evaluation, confidentiality of sources most commonly involves two different claims: the privacy or anonymity of sources used by the evaluator that is compromised, and the protection of sources when a judge needs information for a related judicial action. In the first situation, sources think they are providing information that will be kept confidential, and when they discover that it has not been—either through personal or contextual identification—they must rely on some particular legal theory such as defamation or breach of contract to assert a claim. The particular factual circumstances will be critical in assessing the merits of any one of these legal claims for confidentiality. Breach of contract or

negligence founded upon an evaluation malpractice theory are the two best avenues to proceed for a redress of this type of breach of confidentiality.

The second and less frequent type of confidentiality issue involves the extent to which an evaluation can guarantee confidentiality of sources when a judge wants to know the identity of certain persons so he or she can pursue a related judicial matter. This recently has received considerable attention because of cases in which faculty members sought to maintain their confidentiality on a campus vote involving a tenure decision of a female colleague (Dinnan, 1980; Gray, 1983; Middleton, 1980),[5] and newspaper reporters have sought to protect the confidentiality of their sources when prosecuting attorneys have sought identification of these sources to present evidence to a grand jury. Once a matter comes before a court, the First Amendment will not protect the sources of newspaper reporters, and consequently how can the First Amendment protect the confidentiality of an evaluator's sources? Therefore, although there are no reported cases on this point, the evaluator probably cannot guarantee confidentiality to sources short of being willing to go to jail in contempt of court when asked by the judge to identify such sources.

These four legal considerations provide background information that is relevant to program evaluators. We next present two hypothetical problems to illustrate some of the implications of these considerations. Both problems attempt to highlight several of the potentially troublesome legal aspects of program evaluation. Finally, we present several suggestions for evaluation practice.

Hypothetical Evaluation Problem #1

A college professor believes that he has been defamed by remarks in an evaluation report on an innovative curriculum project sponsored by the federal government. The evaluator:

A. expresses the opinion in the report that the professor appears to be "totally

---

[5] *In re Dinnan*, 625 F. 2d 1146 (5th Cir. 1980); *In re Dinnan*, 661 F. 2d 426 (5th Cir. 1981) and *Gray vs. Board of Higher Education, City of New York*, 692 F. 2d 901 (2d Cir. 1982).

inept as a teacher" and explains how the professor has been known to ask for favors from his students in return for higher grades;

B. provides copies of the report to the sponsoring agency as well as to the dean and board of trustees; the evaluator also refers to the professor's ineptness as a teacher in a letter to the editor of the local newspaper;

C. directly quotes other faculty to say, "This guy couldn't teach if his life depended on it," and "I could never imagine asking one of my students to mow my lawn for extra credit; I guess it doesn't bother him."

The first hypothetical problem focuses on potential defamation. There are two statements that seem to injure the professor's professional reputation and would be a basis for defamation without having to show actual damages. The comment that the professor is "totally inept as a teacher" certainly adversely reflects on the professor's ability in his profession, whereas the charge that the professor has been known to ask for favors from his students in return for higher grades is a serious charge questioning the moral fitness of the faculty member. This allegation simply charges the faculty member with practicing "academic extortion," a charge that fundamentally challenges the faculty member's professional integrity. Although the hypothetical problem is sparse on factual information, the charges seem sufficiently damaging to support a prima facie case of defamation. These are injurious statements made publicly about the faculty member. Assumedly the faculty member is personally named in the report or easily identifiable by information provided. The publication requirement is satisfied by issuance of the evaluation report. Although the prima facie case can be proven, the evaluator may ultimately win—not have to pay any damages—because the evaluator may be able to prove the truthfulness of the charges. But the burden will have shifted to the evaluator, who will need to satisfy the jury about the truthfulness of the statements to be vindicated.

What significance does the use of "opinion" and "appears" have in insulating the evaluator from liability? Couching a statement in terms of an opinion does not automatically protect the maker of the statement from liability for defamation. There are circumstances in which an opinion is appropriate and can be provided without having to fear that everything involved in the statement can be proven. One example of this is a recommendation by a blue ribbon panel about the program. The statement of opinion must be true, in other words actually believed by the maker, and also within the scope of the maker's position. The evaluator's opinion must be based on evidence obtained in the evaluation. Insufficient information is provided to know what evidence was used to arrive at this conclusion of teaching incompetence. Although these data will be important in determining the legitimacy of the conclusion reached, it will not, in itself, protect the evaluator from liability. The evaluator has not shown, and probably cannot show, the high level of personal expertise he possesses as an evaluator of teaching that might allow him to make such a strongly worded opinion.

The fact that the professor "appears" to be totally inept is potentially important in softening the characterization. Yet is is curious because in this context it seems to be contradictory. A charge of "total ineptness" is hard to soften. So, although the limiting language of "appearance" does not soften the defamatory language in the hypothetical problem, there are other circumstances in which this might be important in limiting the impact of what is alleged to be defamatory.

The evaluator quotes other faculty to support the general contention of total ineptness. This use of quotes deserves some attention. First, it is important to distinguish why quotes are reported. They are being used here to support the truthfulness of the general claim of ineptness where otherwise they conceivably might be used very differently to report the perceptions of other faculty members about the professor's teaching. Even if the second strategy is being used, the evaluator needs to be careful in reporting the quotations. As a general rule, the repeater of a defamatory statement is as liable as the originator of the statement. This is done to protect victims from rumor spreaders. Consequently, evaluators need to be conscious of the potentially defamatory content of statements they are quoting.

The second quote, of allowing students to mow the lawn for extra credit, is not necessarily defamatory. It does raise an allegation of fact, something that can and should be verified by independent sources. Beyond this it is important to see the context of the quote.

The fact that the faculty member's work is sponsored by federal money, combined with the likelihood that the faculty member is employed at a public university, is irrelevant to whether he is a public figure. It would take an unusual set of circumstances to claim that the professor had cast himself into the public arena through the research work so that the higher malice standard would apply (*Hutchinson vs. Proxmire*, 1979).[6]

A potential qualified privilege exists for the evaluator. The availability of the privilege will depend greatly on the identity of the evaluator and the scope of the publication. The problem provides no helpful information about the evaluator's identity. If the evaluator was a member of the university staff or was employed by a campus administrator to evaluate the program and report on this professor's performance, it would be a much better candidate for qualified privilege than if the evaluator was private and had no link with the institution. Still the privilege might have been protected if the publication of the information had been restricted to the dean and possibly even the report to the sponsoring agency and the board of trustees. But when the critical remarks are communicated in a letter to the newspaper, any possibility of a qualified privilege defense is lost, at least as to the specific contents of the letter. The existence of a qualified privilege is affected by where or to whom the statement is made. For example, under certain circumstances an evaluator would be privileged to communicate certain information about a professor to a dean or trustee—someone with responsibility over the employment of the faculty member—and not

_____
[6] *Hutchinson vs. Proxmire*, 443 U.S. 111 (1979)

privileged to make the information available to the newspaper. The location of the statement will be important in determining the appropriate scope of the qualified privilege.

Hypothetical Evaluation Problem #2

The evaluator of a federally funded program promises confidentiality to those individuals willing to participate in evaluation interviews. During one interview, the evaluator learns that one of the top administrators is skimming funds for personal gain.

A. The head administrator is seeking legal action to force the evaluator to either identify the embezzler and the informant or to release her tape recordings and field notes.

B. At the same time, several interviewees are employing legal counsel because the quotations presented in the report (although not attributed to anyone in particular) can be easily traced to their source.

C. Months after the report is submitted to the local program administrator, the evaluator happens to see a copy of "her" report to the national office. To her dismay much of the original report has been rewritten to include only positive findings. The evaluator is seeking legal advice for some recourse.

The second hypothetical problem raises questions about the ownership of the evaluation report, violations against promises of confidentiality, and the potential for a malpractice suit. The question of authorship and control of the evaluation report could have been avoided with a clear and comprehensively written contract between the evaluator and client. Additional information is needed to know the relationship between the evaluation agency and the program being administered. If the evaluation agency is large enough, it would not be uncommon to have several people working on a project and have the final report written by someone else. The contract between the evaluation agency and the program being evaluated will be critical in describing the authority of the different interests in reviewing and writing the reports. If this contractual relationship is honored, the evaluation agency can protect its final report by copyrighting it. Violations could then be met through the provisions of the federal copyright laws.

A question of confidentiality is raised when the evaluator learns of an embezzling administrator. This is a classic example of the qualified privilege protecting one who is making a statement in the public interest. This qualified privilege shields the evaluator from liability if she reports her belief about embezzlement to the police even if it subsequently turns out to be inaccurate.

The head administrator does not have the legal authority to force the evaluator to identify the embezzler, although the administrator can go to the criminal authorities who can request this information. If the evaluator refuses to give the information to the criminal authorities, the judge can hold the evaluator in contempt of court. Punishment for being in contempt is imprisonment. Because reporters do not have constitutional authority to protect their sources when criminal prosecution is involved, it is unlikely that evaluators can protect their sources in a similar circumstance. In addition, when states pass shield laws to protect newspaper sources, evaluators are not likely to be included. Consequently, promises of anonymity cannot always be kept unless the evaluator is willing to go to jail while sitting out a contempt of court citation.

When sources are aggrieved because anonymity has not been honored as claimed by the interviewees, the two most important considerations are the contract between the evaluator and sources and the extent of injuries suffered by the source. If the contract does not provide a basis for remedy, it is possible to allege negligence on the evaluator's behavior. This would have some chance for success if the evaluator violated acceptable standards of practice and an injury to the source occurred.

Potential for malpractice suits brought against the evaluator in this hypothetical problem will depend largely on the professional acceptability of the design and/or methodology employed in the evaluation. This will involve a battle of evaluation experts, and the existence of professional standards will be important in shaping this argument. The professional standards established by the Joint Committee on Standards for Educational Evaluation (JTC, 1981) and the Evaluation Research Society (ERS, Note 2) could be used by the court in the same manner that the Standards for Educational and Psychological Tests (APA, AERA, NCME, 1974) and Equal Employment Opportunity Commission (EEOC, 1966) Guidelines on Employment Testing have been used for questions of testing practice. Both sets of testing standards have been used by the court in numerous judicial decisions as criteria for professional testing practice (Bersoff, 1981).

Suggestions

In this last section, we present four major suggestions for evaluation practice, which are based on the legal issues discussed in this paper as well as the standards published by the ERS and the JTC.[7]

1. Evaluators should be able to substantiate the truth of potentially defamatory comments, charges, or allegations expressed in the evaluation report that are attributed to themselves or to others (as in the use of quotations).

The evaluator must prove the truthfulness of his or her statements, especially in cases of defamation. Data should be available that corroborate quotes and generalizations made in the evaluation report. For example, allegations of fact should be verified by independent sources if possible. The evaluator should separate and identify facts from opinion and descriptions from interpretations especially for those situations where opinions need not be proven (as in expert appraisal). Evaluators may attempt to "soften" potentially defamatory opinions or comments by using words such as "appears to be," "most likely is," or "seems to be." Evaluators also may choose to exclude from the report any potentially defamatory comments made by others regardless of the extent of their truthfulness, because, as stated earlier, the repeater of a defamatory statement is as liable as the originator of the statement.

---

[7] For a discussion of how the professional standards on evaluation relate to legal aspects of evaluation, see Braskamp and Mayberry (Note 3).

2. Evaluation contracts should be written comprehensively to include mention of:
—which audiences have the right to know of and/or access to the evaluation results;
—which party, the client or the evaluator, has final editing rights of the evaluation report; and
—which party, the client or the evaluator, has access to and ownership of the evaluation report, data, field notes, and tape recordings.

Evaluators are encouraged to specify in a written contract as many details as necessary regarding access and ownership rights to the evaluative information. To whom is the final report submitted? Can the report be published in a professional journal without client approval? Does the client have the right to review the field notes or tape recordings of the evaluator? A written contract provides a legal basis for any postevaluation problem. Evaluators also may choose to copyright their version of the final report to legally "guarantee" final editing rights.

Evaluators should be aware that restrictions on access to evaluative information, as specified in a contract, do not apply to court requests. The court can insist on all evaluative information as evidence in a judicial hearing. The court may limit access to the information through a closed session or protective order; yet the fact remains that the evaluator must release all the requested information at the risk of being in contempt of court.

3a. Evaluators should make it clear to all informants that promises of anonymity and confidentiality are limited by the reach of the court.

3b. Evaluators should maintain all promises of anonymity and confidentiality within the limitations of court acquisition of information.

Written or verbal agreements with informants should specify that promises of anonymity and confidentiality are limited to the needs of the court. If viewed as necessary information, the court can require evaluators to identify their sources. To date, there are no precedents to suggest that evaluators have constitutional authority to protect their sources, nor are they included in locally developed shield laws.

Within these limitations of court acquisition, evaluators should still maintain all promises of anonymity and confidentiality. Failure to do so when agreed upon in advance through a verbal or written contract may hold the evaluator liable for a charge of negligence or possible breach of contract.

4. Evaluators should document all phases of the evaluation including details about its purpose(s), design, procedures, and findings to allow for an external professional review.

A charge of malpractice or negligence would accuse an evaluator of violating professionally acceptable practices in evaluation. Substantiation of these charges would depend most likely on evidence indicating that the procedures followed by the evaluator did not follow professional standards of behavior. Most often in cases like this, external experts are asked to give their professional opinions. Experts are likely to use existing standards in the profession, such as ERS and JTC. For this comparison to be made, evaluators must keep complete records of their data collection methods, sampling plans, and statistical analyses. Whether or not an evaluator has followed "acceptable practice" will always be difficult to determine, yet the information necessary to determine this should always be available.

Reference Notes

1. SIEBER, J. Negotiating a program evaluation contract. Mimeo.
2. Evaluation Research Society. Standards for program evaluation. Mimeo. October 1981.
3. BRASKAMP, L. A., & MAYBERRY, P. W. A comparison of two sets of standards. Paper presented at the annual meeting of the Evaluation Research Society, Baltimore, Md., October 1982.

References

American Psychological Association, American Educational Research Association, and National Council on Measurement in Education. Standards for educational and psychological tests. Washington, D.C.: American Psychological Association, 1974.
BERSOFF, D. Testing and the law. American Psychologist, 1981, 36, 1047–1056.
Equal Employment Opportunity Commission. Guidelines on employee selection procedures. Washington, D.C.: Author, August 24, 1966.
GRAY, J. Confidentiality of faculty peer review in the tenure process. West's Education Law Reporter, 1983, 11(1), 11–29.

HOUSE, E. R., & CARE, N. S. Fair evaluation agreement. *Educational Theory,* 1979, *29*(3), 159–169.

MIDDLETON, L. Academic freedom vs. affirmative action: Georgia professor jailed in tenure dispute. *Chronicle of Higher Education,* September 2, 1980. p. 1.

PROSSER, W. *Handbook of the law of torts* (4th ed). St. Paul, Minn.: West Publishing, 1971.

STAKE, R. E. *Evaluating educational programmes: The need and the response.* Paris: Organization for Economic Cooperation and Development, 1976.

The Joint Committee on Standards for Educational Evaluation. *Standards for evaluations of educational programs, projects, and materials.* New York: McGraw Hill, 1981.

WRIGHT, J. W., & WORTHEN, B. R. *Standards and procedures for development and implementation of an evaluation contract.* Portland, Ore.: Northwest Regional Educational Laboratory, October 1975.

Authors

PAUL W. THURSTON, Associate Professor, University of Illinois, 334 Education, 1310 S. 6th Street, Champaign, IL 61820. *Specializations:* School law, Personnel administration.

JOHN C. ORY, Coordinator of Exam Services/Associate Professor in Ed. Psych., Measurement and Research Division, Office of Instructional Resources, University of Illinois, 307 Engineering Hall, Urbana, IL 61801. *Specializations:* Evaluation Methodology, Applied Measurement.

PAUL W. MAYBERRY, Doctoral Student, University of Illinois, 1308 W. Green, 307 Engineering Hall. *Specializations:* Applied Measurement, Statistics.

LARRY A. BRASKAMP, Head, Measurement and Research Division, University of Illinois, 1308 W. Green, 307 Engineering Hall, Urbana, IL 61801. *Specializations:* Uses of evaluation, adult motivation.

SECTION 3
Practical Tools, Techniques, and Tactics

The sheer ingenuity of the program evaluation profession is perhaps nowhere more evident than in the creative variety of practical schemes, techniques, and tactics that evaluators come up with to accomplish their various purposes in the diverse situations in which they find themselves. More clever approaches and procedures have been reported in the evaluation literature in the past year or so than can possibly be reproduced in this volume. We have had to content ourselves, therefore, with selecting for this section only a few chapters that we think represent good contributions on relatively neglected topics. Before introducing those chapters, we will give a brief description of some of the many others that offer interesting practical ideas to the evaluator.

One category of good ideas might be labeled *approaches* to evaluation, that is, ways of structuring the evaluation around the presenting issues and contextual constraints of the evaluation situation. An interesting example is Bickman's (1985) use of program "components" as the focus of evaluation rather than entire programs. Faced with numerous complex, varying, and multisite programs in a statewide system of services to preschool children, Bickman recognized that most were variations and combinations of a smaller set of identifiable program components, for example, a family intervention component. By concentrating on program components rather than programs, a coherent evaluation approach was designed despite the great diversity among programs. A similar spirit is evidenced by Bland, Ullian, and Froberg (1984), but from the perspective of the internal evaluator in medical education. They call their approach "user-centered evaluation" and structure it around the concept of maximizing the usefulness of the evaluation data to the host organization.

In a more restricted domain, two recent papers (Faley & Sundstrom, 1985; Ford & Wroten, 1984) attempt to define an approach to the evaluation of personnel training programs that goes beyond pre-post measures and "happiness ratings." The strategy presented in these papers is to focus on the content of a training program in relation to the broader functions it serves. These papers demonstrate methods for linking training with dimensions of job performance and training needs assessment in ways that support both program evaluation and program improvement.

The idea of linking evaluation with needs assessment is an attractive one that raises a question about recent work on needs assessment as a significant program evaluation tool. After vigorous developmental work some years ago, we find comparatively little literature on this topic within the last year or two. An integrative book by Witkin (1984) emphasizing needs assessment for educational programs is a noteworthy exception as is the attempt by Deaux and Callaghan (1984) to compare the results of a statewide telephone survey approach with use of key informants.

A topic that is beginning to receive considerable attention is the development and use of computerized decision support system (DSS) for administrative decision making. DSS is reputed to be the next generation of management information system (MIS), distinguished primarily by inclusion of functions for selecting and manipulating data, simulating and modeling decision contexts, and optimizing specified model parameters. Like MIS, evaluators are likely to encounter and use DSS in a variety of ways—making input to their development, using data results they produce, evaluating their utility, and so forth. O'Sullivan (1985) provides a useful introduction and overview for evaluators. Henderson and Schilling (1985) discuss the use of DSS in the public sector, drawing on examples from a community mental health system. Less general, but in a related vein, Burstein (1984) analyzes the potential for better use of existing data bases in improving educational programs and Williams and Bank (1984) report an interesting assessment of the instructional information systems in school districts.

With or without computer automation, ways to collect and display relevant evaluation data are topics of perennial interest to evaluators. The recent literature reports a number of clever contributions in this area. Huber and Gay (1984) describe the use of educational technology to obtain information useful to the formative evaluation of the educational programs that use that technology. Focusing on the individual classroom, Kerr, Kent, and Lam (1985) report on an instrument they call the Interactive Teaching Map that can be used to measure the degree of implementation of educational programs designed to influence teaching strategies.

Another interesting instrument of more general applicability was developed in the context of personnel selection to measure service orientation, "the disposition to be helpful, thoughtful, considerate, and cooperative" (Hogan, Hogan, & Busch, 1984). It appears to have good potential for evaluative use in service organizations. Kelly (1985) provides evaluators with a comprehensive overview of the associative group analysis method, a technique based on word associations that can be used to measure changes in conceptual development and belief systems. A different focus is taken by Baker and Perkins (1984) who describe how to obtain information about "program maturity," a parameter that describes program status rather than the status of persons.

The first two chapters reprinted in the following pages take up a still different theme. Both describe procedures the evaluator can use early in the evaluation process to identify the salient goals, priorities, and perspectives of various program stakeholders. There has been perhaps too little work devoted to the development of tools for use at this crucial beginning phase of program evaluation. Although not a complete solution, these two chapters present useful systematic approaches to determining the intrinsic program values and objectives that should guide the evaluative inquiry. In the first chapter, Garard and Hausman present a general technique they call the priority sort. It consists of an adaptation of Q-sort methodology to the task of assessing the relative importance, or changes in perceived importance, of such items as program objectives, planning priorities, desirable program content, and so forth. In the second chapter, Fazio presents an application of Delphi technique to similar purposes. Its advantages are the high level of participation and intellectual engagement required of respondents and the relative anonymity they are permitted in dealing with conflict and attempting to reach consensus.

The third chapter reprinted in this section also deals with measurement instruments, but of a more conventional sort. In that chapter, Williams focuses on the problem of identifying and selecting a standardized measure for application in a particular site. Using the example of job satisfaction measures, she demonstrates how a small-scale field test of candidate measures can be used to choose the instrument most applicable to the purpose and population of interest. An interesting companion piece to the Williams chapter, which is not reprinted here, is Mazzeo and Seeley's (1984) presentation of generalizability theory as a framework for evaluating medical measurement instruments.

The final chapter in this section presents a good example of constructive improvisation at the data analysis stage of an evaluation. Rog and Bickman call their strategy *the feedback research approach.* It consists of structuring data collection to include descriptive information about the nature of the problem as well as about the outcome of treatment, then mounting selective post hoc analyses to further differentiate and probe the evaluation results on the outcome measures. Their example shows that this approach is especially useful as a guide for program redesign when null results are obtained on the primary outcome variables (see also Russell et al., 1984, for a somewhat similar approach).

Collectively, the papers reviewed and reprinted in this section show an impressive vitality and responsiveness to the complex contexts within which program evaluation is done. In grappling with the many practical problems that face them in designing an evaluation, evaluators have proven to be most resourceful in developing tools and techniques to serve their purposes.

REFERENCES

Baker, R., & Perkins, D. U. (1984). Program maturity and cost analysis in the evaluation of primary prevention programs. *Journal of Community Psychology, 12,* 31-42.

Bickman, L. (1985). Improving established statewide programs: A component theory of evaluation. *Evaluation Review, 9*(2), 189-208.

Bland, D. J., Ullian, J. A., & Froberg, D. G. (1984). User-centered evaluation. *Evaluation and the Health Professions, 7*(1), 53-63.

Burstein, L. (1984). The use of existing data bases in program evaluation and school improvement. *Educational Evaluation and Policy Analysis, 6*(3), 307-318.

Deaux, E., & Callaghan, J. W., (1984). Estimating statewide health-risk behavior. *Evaluation Review, 8*(4), 467-492.

Faley, R. H., & Sundstrom, E. (1985). Content representativeness: An empirical method of evaluation. *Journal of Applied Psychology, 70*(3), 567-571.

Ford, J. K., & Wroten, S. P. (1984). Introducing new methods for conducting training evaluation and for linking training evaluation to program design. *Personnel Psychology, 37,*651-665.

Henderson, J. C., & Schilling, D. A. (1985). Design and implementation of decision support systems in the public sector. *MIS Quarterly, 9*(2), 157-169.

Hogan, J., Hogan, R., & Busch, C. M. (1984). How to measure service orientation. *Journal of Applied Psychology, 69*(1), 167-173.

Huber, V. L., & Gay, G. (1984). Users of educational technology for formative evaluation. In D. Deshler (Ed.). *Evaluation for program improvement. New Directions for Continuing Education, v. 24.*

Kelly, R. M. (1985). The associative group analysis method and evaluation research. *Evaluation Review, 9*(1), 35-50.

Kerr, D. M., Kent, L., & Lam, T.C.M. (1985). Measuring program implementation with a classroom observation instrument: The interactive teaching map. *Evaluation Review, 9*(4), 461-482.

Mazzeo, J., & Seeley, G. W. (1984). A general framework for evaluating the reliability of medical measurement systems. *Evaluation and the Health Professions, 7*(4), 379-341.

O'Sullivan, E. (1985). Decision support systems: An introduction for program evaluators. *Evaluation Review, 9*(1), 84-92.

Russell, C. S., Atilano, R. B., Anderson, S. A., Jurich, A. P., & Bergen, L. P. (1984). Intervention strategies: Predicting family therapy outcome. *Journal of Marital and Family Therapy, 10*(3), 241-251.

Williams, R. C., & Bank, A. (1984). Assessing instructional information systems in two districts: The search for impact. *Educational Evaluation and Policy Analysis, 6*(3), 267-282.

Witkin, B. R. (1984). *Assessing needs in educational and social programs.* San Francisco, CA: Jossey-Bass.

14

The Priority Sort
An Empirical Approach to Program Planning and Evaluation
Judith Garrard and William Hausman

The purpose of this paper is to describe a methodology, the Priority Sort, that is applicable to individual and group decision-making on the basis of a large number (N > 20) of items or objectives. The use of the Priority Sort results in quantitative data that can be used for purposes of program planning and evaluation. Since the set of items to be used in a Priority Sort can be unique to the program being planned or evaluated, procedures for estimating the validity and reliability are discussed. This methodology is a viable approach to systematically identifying the priorities of a large number of items, and its practicality, together with the quantifiable nature of the data that result, make the Priority Sort a useful addition to the methodological repertoire of the planner, evaluator, and researcher.

With the nationwide agony of budget cuts in the health professions and the resulting necessity to eliminate many programs and reduce the size and scope of those successful enough not to be cut, the decision maker is faced with the nearly impossible task of simultaneously considering the value and merit of a large number of programs and making hard decisions about which to eliminate and which to reduce. Such decisions require objective data which have been gathered on a systematic basis. Such decisions must take into account the values of the individuals and groups committed to the various programs. Such decisions are nearly impossible if approximately 20 or more programs or variables must be considered simultaneously. What is needed is a methodology that:

1) consists of a systematic approach to data gathering that is easily understood by decision makers and subjects;
2) is capable of quantitatively summarizing qualitative information, such as values and attitudes, about programs;
3) is applicable to individual and group decision making;
4) is capable of being applied to a large number (N > 100) of programs or variables; and
5) results in quantifiable data that can be used objectively and simultaneously to compare a large number of programs or variables with each other.

The purpose of this paper is to describe just such a method — the Priority Sort. This approach can be used for program planning and evaluation in which there is individual and/or group decision making about a large number of items, which results in quantitative data about the relative importance of the items. This approach will be discussed in the context of the following four sections: 1) methodology; 2) data analysis; 3) comparisons with other decision-making techniques; and 4) applications to planning and evaluation.

METHODOLOGY

The Priority Sort was developed over a five-year period by the authors and was used initially in making decisions about educational objectives in the education of mental health professionals and was further used extensively in a comparative study* of the similarities and differences in educational objectives in psychiatry, psychiatric nursing, and social work. Despite the focus on education in our work, we regard the Priority Sort as a *general* methodological technique that

Dr. Garrard is Associate Professor, School of Public Health, and Department of Psychiatry, University of Minnesota Medical School. Dr. Hausman is Professor, Department of Psychiatry, University of Minnesota Medical School. Requests for reprints should be addressed to Dr. Garrard, Box 197 Mayo, Program in Health Education, School of Public Health, University of Minnesota, Minneapolis, MN 55455.

*Project #1 T24 MH15430 funded by the Experimental and Special Projects Section of the Division of Manpower and Training, NIMH; William Hausman, M.D., Principal Investigator; Judith Garrard, Ph.D., Co-Principal Investigator and Project Director

From Judith Garrard and William Hausman, "The Priority Sort: An Empirical Approach to Program Planning and Evaluation," *The American Journal of Social Psychiatry*, 1985, 5(5), 29-36.

can be used in a variety of areas and disciplines for purposes of research, as well as in planning and evaluation activities. Thus, in this paper, our description of the technique will be at a general level; whereas, examples of application will be in mental health education.

The emphasis upon a "large" number of variables or programs (N > 20) should be noted. Previous research by Guilford[1] has shown that humans can simultaneously process a maximum of 20 items, but rarely more. The necessity to rank order items, such as programs or goals, requires that all such items be processed simultaneously. Thus, if more than 20 must be considered, then the decision maker is faced with a humanly impossible task, and a method for breaking the task down into manageable subtasks must be used. This is possible with the Priority Sort. The reader should also note that if the number of items to be considered is less than 20, other techniques such as a simple rank ordering would be more appropriate.

Description of the Priority Sort

In performing a Priority Sort, the subject (whether an individual or a group) is given a deck of 120–200 cards consisting of one item or objective per card (examples of items given in Table 1 are educational objectives in psychiatry). The instructions are to assign each objective to one of 10 levels of priority from "highest" to "lowest," with an equal number of cards at each level. Logistically, if the sorter is an individual, a deck of 3" × 5" index cards is used; if a group is performing the task, then the deck consists of cards that are 8" × 12", thus permitting the use of larger print. With a group, only one deck is used, and the group members must decide among themselves the decision rules they will use in assigning each objective to a priority level. Actually when the sorting instructions are given to a group, no mention is made of decision rules; thus the group has to either let a system evolve as they proceed with the task or confront the need directly and establish some rules. The rationale behind this strategy is twofold: 1) It is assumed that the system for decision making that emerges will more closely approximate the working system used in the larger context of the sorters' department or organization; whereas, a system imposed on the group (e.g., a majority vote) will pose an artificial constraint. 2) The sorting task itself forces participants to make decisions about the items in the deck; by not giving group decision rules, the task also forces them to recognize the *need* to decide how to decide about the content of the deck.

Methodological Antecedents

The Priority Sort is an extension of the Q-sort technique that was first described by William Stephenson,[2] and used for many years in personality and psycho-

TABLE 1

Examples of Items Used in a Priority Sort
(Examples are Educational Objectives
in Psychiatry)

001	Psychoanalytic theories of personality
002	Personality development
003	Intelligence, thinking and problem solving
004	Psychology of sex and gender
005	Psychology of aggression
006	Developmental tasks of adolescence
007	Small group processes
008	Family systems
009	Human ethology and methology
010	Dying and bereavement
011	Psychology of aging
012	Moral development
013	Psychology of learning
014	Social development
015	Language development
016	Existential theories of personality structure
017	Cognitive development
018	Psychology of perception
019	Physical and motor development
020	Cognitive and learning theory contributions to personality theory
021	Theories of personality organization
022	Psychological correlates of sleep stages
023	Biological processes in learning and memory
024	Biochemical and genetic principles of the synapse and neurotransmitters

therapy research. Basically, the Q-sort is a method for rating a large number (N > 20) of stimulus items. In its original, psychological context, the Q-sort technique required the subject to assign each card in a standardized deck to one of several numerical categories. Each card contained a personality descriptor (e.g., "I am calm most of the time"), and the categories usually ranged from one to ten on a continuum from "most like me" to "least like me." The Q-sort was widely used for about 15 years beginning in the mid 1950s, but for reasons that are not entirely clear in the literature, began to decline in popularity by the late 1960s. During the period of its most extensive use, the technique was also the subject of intensive study by psychometricians and methodologists, with the result that the psychometric literature on this subject is very comprehensive. In reviewing this literature from 1952 to the present, it is clear that the elegance of this technique lies in the ease with which instructions for its use can be understood by subjects in most settings, together with a large number of methodological variations available to the researcher, characteristics which make it a very versatile instrument. Included in some of the variations are decisions about the number of items, the number of categories into which the items are sorted, the kind of theoretical structure underlying the items, the conditions under which the sorting takes place, the distribution of the items across the categories, and the kinds of statistical analyses that are appropriate.

Similarities and Differences

The Priority Sort is identical to the Q-sort technique in the use of the sorting task and in the underlying psychometric theory; however, this extension of the Q-sort represents a radical departure from its traditional use as an instrument for psychological assessment. We have chosen to call this extension by another name, the Priority Sort, in order to emphasize a new set of applications and expectations about its use in program planning and evaluation. Several of the differences between the new applications of the Priority Sort and the traditional uses of the Q-sort technique can be summarized as follows:

The most obvious difference between the two approaches lies in the application of the results of the sorting task. Rather than the traditional use as an instrument for assessing personality traits, this extension can be applied at the macro level to problems such as corporate decision making. An example would be the making of decisions about which of a large number of academic programs across the health sciences must be reduced or eliminated. Broadly speaking, this kind of decision making occurs in any organization in which resources must be allocated on the basis of a large number of variables or programs with input to the decision by many individuals or groups. Differences between the Priority Sort and the Q-sort are also evident at the micro level when decisions about program goals or objectives within a program must be made. For example, an appropriate use of the Priority Sort would be to summarize the priorities of a large number of individuals or groups about a large number of program goals or objectives. These uses at the macro and micro levels of an organization require basic changes in instructions for the sorting task of the Q-sort. For example, consideration must be given to the inclusion or exclusion of decision rules. In examining the Q-sort literature, no report can be found that deals with this kind of use or these kinds of modifications of the basic task.

A second difference between the two approaches is the use of the Priority Sort to make decisions about course or curriculum content based on quantitative comparisons. Heretofore, comparisons of educational objectives have been based on prose summaries, and statistical comparisons have not been possible; however, with the use of the Priority Sort with educational objectives as the items in the deck to be sorted, quantitative and statistical comparisons can be made between curricula or courses between departments within the same discipline across universities, of the same department at different points in time, etc. Such a use of the sorting technique has not been reported previously in the Q-sort literature; however, the use of the Priority Sort to compare priorities of educational objectives in psychiatric education has recently been reported.[3]

A third difference between the Q-sort and the Priority Sort is the application of the latter to group decision making. In some of the studies with the Q-sort technique, the use of mean ratings computed across several individuals is described, but nowhere in this literature is mention made of a single decision being made by a group. In permitting the sorting task to be done on a group basis as in the Priority Sort, instructions for the task must reflect consideration of group dynamics and interactions.

In summary these two approaches differ basically in that the Q-sort technique was originally designed as a research tool and used primarily in psychological studies; whereas, the Priority Sort is not only a research tool but is also one that can be used for planning and evaluation in a variety of settings.

Validity

Are we measuring what we think we are measuring? In applying this question to the Priority Sort, we focused mainly on the validity of the deck of items used in the sorting task. Three types of validity have been discussed in the psychological and educational literature: content (the representativeness or sampling adequacy of the content); criterion-related (comparisons with one or more external variables or criteria known to measure the attribute under study), and construct (what factors or constructs account for the variance in test performance (i.e., how can individual differences in the data be explained?).[4] Of the three major types of validity, our concern was primarily with that of content validity. For example, was the deck of items a representative sample of the range of issues or the domain being considered? Thus the content validity of the Priority Sort (and the Q-sort) is deck-specific and must be established each time a new set of items is generated.

In our work with mental health education, we generated four decks of educational objectives, one each in psychiatry, psychiatric nursing, social work, and consumer concerns about mental health. The content validity of each deck (N = 140–170 items each) was examined by means of a standardized set of procedures that we called a Content Sort. Subjects, who were experts in their respective fields, were tested individually using a deck of cards arranged randomly, with one objective per card. Instructions for the Content Sort consisted of the following, using a deck of objectives in Psychiatry as an example:

The purpose of this task is to improve this set of educational objectives by making it as representative of residency training programs in psychiatry as possible. Examine each objective and put together the cards that go together . . . Label each of the resulting clusters of cards . . . Now examine the clusters and tell me if any clusters are missing . . . Next, examine the objectives within each cluster and tell me which items or objectives, if any, need clarification, or should be merged or eliminated or added. There are no right or wrong ways to do this sorting and what we are especially interested in is your perception of how knowledge is organized and how this set of objectives can be improved.

Using the Content Sort we tested a total of 106 subjects on a nationwide basis and the results of these testings were used to modify and improve each deck of objectives on an iterative basis. In general, the Content Sort appears to be a viable approach to establishing the content validity of the deck of items used in the Priority Sorting task.

Reliability

In examining the reliability of the Priority Sort, we were most concerned with consistency or stability of the results of the sorting task across time.[4] The psychological conditions under which the individual and group Priority Sorts are performed are different; therefore, separate estimates of reliability were needed for each. In considering the reliability of the *individual* Priority Sort, we can examine the psychometric literature on the Q-sort technique. Research on the reliability of the Q-sort method was reported by Frank,[5] who found that the test-retest correlation coefficients ranged from .93 to .97 (10 subjects were used in this study, and the instrument was a personality test consisting of 100 stimulus items). There appears to be general agreement in the literature with Frank's conclusion that the method results in reliable data.

Comparative studies of the reliability of the Q-sort technique have not been reported in which either the number of items or the level of specificity of the items has been systematically varied. We suspect that these two variables plus two others, the content of the items and the expertise of the sorter, contribute to moderate variations in reliability estimates. Such empirical research has yet to be done and offers a fruitful area of investigation in the future. Because of these potential sources of variation, the reliability of the Priority Sort (and the Q-sort) is deck-specific and should be reported for each deck of items used.

There is no Q-sort analogy to the *group* Priority Sort since no studies have been reported in which the Q-sort was used by a group of individuals to make a decision about each item in the deck. In those cases where the researcher was interested in examining Q-sort data from more than one person, the sorting task was performed on an individual basis and the data summarized across subjects.[6]

In our research project in mental health education, we are currently in the process of designing test-retest studies to examine the reliability of the individual and group Priority Sorts using different decks of objectives. Given the strong positive correlations reported previously for the Q-sort technique, we anticipate that the reliability of the individual Priority Sort will also be high, despite differences in the decks of items and other variables mentioned above. We have no basis for predicting a range of reliability coefficients for the group Priority Sort, since there are no empirical data available on this subject.

DATA ANALYSIS

In this section, some of the major issues concerned with statistical analysis of data resulting from the Priority Sort are discussed. Perhaps the most fundamental issue to be considered is the fact that the Priority Sort (and the Q-sort) technique are ipsative rather than normative measures. These two types of measurement were compared by Cattell[7] in a paper describing a categorization scheme for behavioral measures. With a normative measure, each score by an individual can be compared with a mean score from a group of subjects. An IQ test is an example of a normative procedure, and differences between mean IQ scores for two or more groups of subjects can be analyzed statistically.

With an ipsative measure, however, a score has meaning only in terms of other scores by the individual. Ranking is an illustration of ipsative measurement. For example, when asked to rank order five colors on the basis of preference, subjects may differ from one another in the ranks they assign to each color; however, the sum of the ranks (e.g., $5 + 4 + 3 + 2 + 1$) across the five colors will always be 15, regardless of who the subject is; likewise, the mean will always be 3, and the standard deviation 1.414.

In general if the researcher is interested in comparing ranks assigned to a single item (e.g., the color blue) or a subset of items, then ipsative data can be treated as normative, and such comparisons can be made. If, however, there is interest in comparing ranks across *all* of the items (e.g., across all five colors in the example given above), then the ipsative form of measurement is meaningless since the means and variances are identical from person to person and group to group.

Since the Priority Sort is basically a ranking technique that results in ipsative data, the following guidelines should be considered in planning statistical analysis:

1) If the purpose of the analysis is to compare the similarity between subjects on the basis of all of the items (e.g., N = 160 items), a correlational technique such as a Spearman rank order correlation coefficient is appropriate.
2) If the interest is in exploratory questions, then a multivariate correlation approach such as factor analysis can be used with data from a Priority Sort. A factor analysis of Priority Sort (and Q-sort) data begins with an intercorrelational matrix. Until the development of the Q-sort method, this matrix was based on correlations between variables; however, with the Q-sort, it became possible to correlate persons (sorters), and this additional possibility created a controversy in the psychometric literature. Initially, Cronbach[8] argued that questions about correlations between variables (R approach) differed substantially from questions about correlations between persons (Q approach); subsequently, however, the Q and R approaches came to be regarded as useful and valid for exploratory research.

Using the example of five colors mentioned above, an illustration of the difference between correlation of variables (R approach) and correlation of subjects (Q approach) might be the following: An investigator is interested in exploring the relationships within and between color preference and nationality. Using the Priority Sort (or Q-sort), 10 subjects from each of four countries (N = 40 subjects) are asked to sort a deck of 100 colors (20 shades each of five colors). With factor analysis, at least two kinds of questions can be asked of the data depending on whether an R approach or a Q approach is used in setting up the initial intercorrelation matrix.

If the focus is on colors, an R approach would be used and a 100 × 100 intercorrelation matrix of the colors would be generated. In this case, the cell data in the matrix would be the pairwise correlation coefficient between two colors. Note that the correlation coefficient is computed across all 40 subjects for each pair of colors.

If, however, the interest is in a comparison of subjects (perhaps with the intention of seeing if nationality accounts for four major factors corresponding to the four countries), then a Q approach would be used and a 40 × 40 subjects matrix would be generated with the cell data being the pairwise correlation of two subjects across all of the 100 colors.

When applied to data collected by the Q-sort method (or the Priority Sort), the Q approach permits the researcher to consider types of persons, for example, in empirically developing a typology of schizophrenics,[9] of psychiatric patients in general,[10] or of Air Force officers.[11] Block[12] has clarified the conditions under which Q and R are equivalent and

when they are different. The interested reader is also referred to other discussions about Q and R techniques (e.g., Nunnally[13]), and for a historical perspective, to Burt[14] and Stephenson.[2]

3) If the issue under consideration is one of differences (between subjects), the ipsative scores from a Priority Sort can be treated as normative data, and an analysis of variance or a similar technique is appropriate. Ipsative data can be treated as normative if a subset of the items rather than all of the items in the deck is the basis for the analysis. For example, given a deck of 160 educational objectives in mental health, a statistical analysis of the differences in priorities between a group of social workers and a group of psychiatrists is *not* possible if all 160 items constitutes the data set, but *is* possible if a subset of those 160 items is used. In other words, if two subsets of 80 items each are used, an analysis of variance for each can be calculated.

Thus the basic problem in running statistical tests of differences such as an analysis of variance with ipsative data is one of defining one or more subsets of items that are meaningful, and this in turn is directly related to an issue discussed at length in the Q-sort literature, that of structured versus unstructured sets of items.

A structured set is defined as one in which the items are based on some theoretical or *a priori* classification; whereas, with an unstructured set, the items have been assembled without regard to underlying variables or dimensions.[4,15] An example of a structured set of items in psychiatric education might be one in which different content areas are identified (e.g., child development and pathology, psychopharmacology, psychotherapy), and a representative sample of educational objectives generated within each of these content areas. Subjects engaged in the Priority Sort (and Q-sort) are not specifically told of the underlying structure of the deck. In this case, a separate t-test or analysis of variance can be used separately with each content area, adjusting the level of statistical significance to compensate for repeated tests with the same group of subjects.

A more general example of a structured set of items might be the following: An evaluator is asked to examine priorities for planning in a large organization that consists of eight departments, such as production, advertising, and personnel. In generating the items to be considered (and in consultation with the decision maker who requested the data), 20 items are identified within each of the eight departments. These 160 items are arranged randomly in a deck and subjects (e.g., the Board of Directors, central management, staff within the departments) complete a Priority Sort on an individual basis. The resulting data can then be analyzed separately for each of the eight departments.

COMPARISONS WITH OTHER TECHNIQUES

In developing the Priority Sort other techniques were considered but none satisfied the multiple criteria established initially, namely, an individual and/or group task applicable to decision making about a large number of items that would result in quantitative data about the relative importance of the items. Several of these other approaches can be described briefly.

Ranking

Perhaps the most obvious alternative, whether used individually or in groups, is that of ranking (e.g., given 20 items, rank one to 20 from lowest to highest priority). The problem with this approach is the limited number of items that can be ranked. Previous psychometric research has documented the finding that up to 20 points on a scale can be reliably discriminated by humans;[1] beyond that number, however, the reliability dwindles to the point that rankings of the items in the middle become meaningless. Since the number of educational objectives would need to be far more than 20 if the deck of items is to be representative of a course or curriculum, the use of a simple ranking technique would not be useful.

Rating

A similar approach, rating, was also considered but rejected because the data would not be appropriate to the questions being asked. Rating differs from ranking in that a scale of 1-10 (for example) can be used, where 1 = highest priority and 10 = lowest, and subjects assign a number to each item. This approach solves the problem of volume since there is no limit (within reason) to the number of items that can be considered. However, the use of rating creates another problem in that the items are not systematically compared with one another. It is possible for subjects to assign the same rating to all items, e.g., all rated "1". With no requirement for discrimination, there is no decision making about the relative merit of the items, and this defeats the purpose of the task.

Delphi Technique

A more sophisticated alternative is the Delphi approach which is a survey forecasting technique developed at the Rand Corporation in the 1960s.[16] This method consists of having experts, individually and independently, identify items about a topic and their level of importance. The experts are anonymous to one another, and feedback is provided in the form of a statistical analysis of the expert's own items and their relationship to those generated by the group. Each expert is given the opportunity to reconsider his/her own items and to adjust these in light of the group's position. The Delphi technique provides for several successive rounds of feedback and potential change by each expert; however, the experts never meet as a group or even know the identity of other raters.

There are two major problems with the Delphi technique in light of the criteria described above: The requirement that decision making be carried out individually, without possibility of discussion, and the relatively limited number of statements that can be considered. With an emphasis on collaboration and group decision making, an approach that prohibits interaction is simply not appropriate. Furthermore, most studies in which the Delphi technique is used report the consideration of approximately 50-75 items or statements. Such a limit on the number of items would present a major impediment to decision making that involved a large number of items (N = 120-200).

Multi-Attribute Utilities Method

A fourth methodology with which the Priority Sort can be compared is the multi-attribute utilities method described by Guttentag[17] and by Edwards, Guttentag and Snapper.[18] In general, the multi-attribute utilities method is an approach to quantifying values in order to choose among a number of outcome possibilities (or decisions). This method is similar to the Priority Sort in the identification of the decision maker(s), the use of an individual and/or group approach, and the identification of a potentially large number of items or entities. The multi-attribute utilities method requires the identification of a small ($N \leq 8$-15) number of value dimensions and the scaling of all items with respect to each value dimension. Although our work with the Priority Sort has not explicitly addressed the issue of different value dimensions, such an application would be feasible. For example, a deck of educational objectives could be sorted from the standpoint of the teacher, the student, the administrator, the cost analyst, etc.

The multi-attribute utility method also includes the assignment of items to a scale for each value dimension, the standardization of the measurement scales across value dimensions in order to permit the calculation of utilities for entities, and finally, the choice of one or more entities on the basis of the resulting utilities. When used for purposes of evaluation, the multi-attribute utilities method includes the use of Bayesian statistics.

The Priority Sort differs from the multi-attribute utilities method in several ways:

1) The Priority Sort is designed for ranking items which are a representative sample of a larger domain or population (e.g., a domain of educational objectives); therefore, content validation is emphasized in the development of the set of items for the Priority Sort.

2) The Priority Sort requires subjects to assign items to a predetermined distribution of categories in the ranking procedure. Previous research[19] has shown that a rectangular distribution, i.e., equal number of items in each category, produces the maximum discrimination in a Q-sort situation.

3) The Priority Sort requires subjects to discriminate among 10 categories of priority and, in the use of 200 items, within each category it is necessary to only discriminate among 20 items. These choices were made because of Gilford's research[1] concerning the maximum number of items among which human subjects can reliably discriminate. While the Priority Sort eventually results in discriminations across a maximum of 200 items, the results would not be reliable if the task was not systematically broken down into subtasks that are consistent with what is known about the information processing capabilities of humans. To reiterate, these subtasks consist of (a) the assignment of items to 10 categories, and then (b) the discrimination of up to 20 items within each category.

4) The Priority Sort is technically less complex than the multiple-attribute utilities approach in terms of the ranking task and the required psychometric procedures.

With the Priority Sort, the ranking task and the results of this approach are understandable to decision makers who do not have a statistical background.

Since the Priority Sort does not address the issue of multivalued dimensions, the standardization of the measurement scales across different value dimensions and the establishment of the reliability of this standardization of scales is therefore not necessary. Also, standard Fisherian statistics, rather than Baysian statistics, can be used in the analysis of Priority Sort data.

In summary, the Priority Sort was developed to assess the values of decision making across a large number of items taking into account the research literature and the information processing capabilities of humans, psychometric issues in the measurement of values and attributes, and the psychosocial dynamics of groups and/or individual decision making.

APPLICATIONS TO PLANNING AND EVALUATION

Although the emphasis throughout this paper has been on the use of the Priority Sort for planning, the method can also be applied in evaluation studies. For example, in assessing change in the faculty's priorities over time, an individual Priority Sort by all faculty administered on a pre-post basis would be appropriate. Note that the individuals doing the sorting task may change from the pre- to the postsession. However, if the focus is on the faculty collectively, this change would not appear to interfere with the validity of the results. Another example might be that of a question about differences between various groups within a program. Data from individual Priority Sorts by faculty, students, and administrators could be gathered and analyzed by group means. Such data could be examined in greater detail by looking at differences between groups with respect to different categories within the deck of objectives. (This strategy assumes that the deck of objectives has an a priori structure.) If the intent is in having members within each group—faculty, students, administrators—reach some consensus about their priorities, then a group priority sort could be used with the groups formed on a homogeneous basis (e.g., one group would be composed entirely of faculty, another entirely of administrators). In general, an individual sort is useful when there is interest in individual differences or when an estimate of variance is needed, and a group sort is appropriate when the purpose of the exercise is to encourage discussion about each of a large number of items and to reach a collective decision about each. Under some circumstances data can be collected on the basis of both individual and group sorts from the same subjects. This was the case in a recent research project where there was interest in examining the relative power or influence of individual teachers on decisions made by the group.[3]

In summary, the Priority Sort is a viable approach to systematically identifying priorities of a large number of items. The practicality of the technique together with the quantifiable nature of the data that result from its use make it a useful addition to the methodological repertoire of the planner, evaluator, or researcher.

For purposes of educational development the Priority Sort begins where most other approaches end: With a well-defined set of objectives. Consider the following possibility: A number of long-term projects at the national level in different disciplines are beginning to reach closure in generating domains of objectives. If the results of these efforts could be consolidated and a standardized domain produced for each discipline, educators at each school could use these domains to concentrate on establishing priorities of objectives rather than repeating the unnecessary task of generating a set of objectives de novo. Other possibilities for the use of the Priority Sort come to mind with regard to research and evaluation. For example, with the availability of a standardized domain of objectives, the technique could be used to ask questions about the core content of a field at local and national levels, or about differences about content within and between schools, or about changes in priorities within an educational program over time, or about similarities and differences between different levels of training within the same department. In general, the Priority Sort technique makes possible quantifiable data in an area that heretofore has been lost in a maze of oversimplification or subjectivity or both.

REFERENCES

1. Guilford JP: *Psychometric methods*. New York, McGraw-Hill, 1954.
2. Stephenson W: Some observations on Q technique. *Psychol Bull 49*:483–498, 1952.
3. Garrard J, Hausman W, Prosen H, Bebchuk W: An empirical approach to faculty decision-making about educational objectives. *J Psychiat Ed 5*(1):6–19, 1981.
4. Kerlinger FN: Q methodology. In FN Kerlinger (ed), *Foundations of behavioral research*, 1964, rev ed 1973.
5. Frank GH: Note on the reliability of Q-sort data. *Psychol Rep 2*:182, 1956.
6. Morsh JE: The Q-sort technique as a group measure. *Educ Psychol Meas 15*:390–395, 1955.
7. Cattell RB: Psychological measurement: Normative, ipsative, interaction. *Psychol Rev 51*:292–303, 1944.
8. Cronbach LJ: Correlations between persons as a research tool. In OH Mowrer (ed), *Psychotherapy: Theory and research*. New York, Ronald, 1953, pp. 376–388.
9. Beck SJ: The six schizophrenias. *Reg Monogr Amer Orthopsychiat Assn 6*, 1954.
10. Monro AB: Psychiatric types: A Q-technique study of 200 patients. *J Men Sci 101*:330–343, 1955.
11. Block J: A differentiated approach to the officer selection problem. *IPAR Res Rep.* Prepared under contract no. AF 18 (600) -8, 1954.
12. Block J: The difference between Q and R. *Psychol Rev 62*(5): 356–358, 1955.
13. Nunnally, JC: *Psychometric theory*. New York, McGraw-Hill, 1967, pp. 361–364.
14. Burt C, Stephenson W: Alternative views in correlations between persons. *Psychometrika 4*:269–281, 1939.
15. Wittenborn JR: Contributions and current status of Q methodology. *Psychol Bull 58*(2):132–142, 1961.
16. Gordon TJ, Helmer O: Report on a long-range forecasting study. Report No. P 2982. Santa Monica, CA, The Rand Corporation, 1964.
17. Guttentag M: Subjectivity and its use in evaluation research. *Evaluation 1*(2), 1973.
18. Edwards W, Guttentag M, Snapper K: A decision-theoretic approach to evaluation research. In EL Struening, M Guttentag (eds), *Handbook of evaluation research*, vol. 1. Beverly Hills, Sage, 1975.
19. Livson NH, Nichols TF: Discrimination and reliability in Q-sort personality descriptions. *J Abn Soc Psychol, 52*:159–165, 1956.

15

The Delphi:
Education and Assessment
in Institutional Goal Setting

Linda S. Fazio

ABSTRACT

This paper describes and analysies the use of a delphi research methodology to assess faculty perceptions of institutional needs and goals in an osteopathic medical education program. Use of the delphi to educate faculty in the administrative and political functioning of the institution as well as to involve all faculty in the refinement of specific needs and goals is discussed. Full-time clinical and basic science faculty of the New Jersey School of Osteopathic Medicine provided an example of the varied uses of the delphi research methodology in higher education and specifically in profesiional higher education. The three rounds of the delphi procedure produced faculty consensus on the following institutional variable items: (a) the philosophical and functional orientation of the curriculum; (b) location and design of the physical campus facilities and environment; (c) faculty issues of tenure, promotion, salary and merit; (d) teaching, and the evaluation of teaching; (e) student characteristics and admissions policies; and (f) administrative structure and communication networks.

INTRODUCTION

Almost all observers of higher education agree that the time has arrived for higher education to take a close, careful and critical look at itself. While it is true that there has always been the need for institutions to conduct ongoing programs of self-evaluation, the external pressures for evaluation and accountability are greater now than ever before.

Many educational theorists have argued for some time that any evaluation of an institution's effectiveness must take into consideration the institution's goals.[1] The problem is that too few institutions have seriously considered what their goals are, and those that have often find that the various members of the college community disagree over what should be the purposes of the institution.

Further complications in goal setting are likely when colleges and universities are combined into networks of interdependent institutions. An inevitable conflict is produced between the competing interests of the total network and those of its component parts, which is a phenomenon educators describe as the tension between central authority and local campus autonomy.[2] The point is also made that all networks of institutions share a common set of planning problems about which critical decisions need to be made: namely, the determination of general, shared goals for higher education; the establishment of patterns of cooperation among institutions; the allocation of resources consistent with long-range plans; and the promotion of innovation and change throughout a system.

The primary factor in the development of organisational goals is planning. The concept of planning appears to have no precise meaning. Albeit simplistic, perhaps it is best described as a three step process of (1) determining where you are, (2) where you want to go, and (3) how you are going to get there!

A successful planning process depends upon a clear sense of institutional identity. Of increasing importance are institutional purpose, or mission, and the perceived correlation between this mission and the operating goals of the institution.

As any organisation grows, many persons may influence its goals. It is necessary to offer all individuals in the organisation an opportunity to participate in goal setting so that they may have the opportunity to attain personal goals through the group goal of an organisation.[3] The more widely the faculty can become involved in goal setting, the more they will be committed to innovation and its success.[4]

The self-study process is perhaps the most significant vehicle for institutional planning through faculty involvement. Although procedures vary, all are designed to help institutions reassess their objectives, measure success in attaining objectives, explore ways and means by which educational efficiency may be improved, and prepare for the ever-increasing demands of a changing society.

Parekh[5] defines the components of an educational institution's goal structure as (a) instruction, (b) research, (c) public service, (d) academic support, (e) student support, and (f) institutional support. These components then offer useful guidelines for the broad structural areas of the self-study process.

Educational goal setting and accompanying concerns are, of course, shared by those institutions engaged in the education of physicians, the focus of this study. More and more, the future of quality health care depends on institutional goal setting. It is an age of "participation". This has provoked an increased need for skills and new techniques that can be used to increase rationality, creativity, and participation in the group process. While the group process has not been shown to be the most efficient method of arriving at decisions, it has been shown to greatly increase possibilities for implementation and success. When people feel part of a process, they are more willing to work toward a goal.

This study was conducted by using a data collection technique called the Delphi method. The Delphi survey technique, as we know it today, was developed by Dalkey and Helmer, a physicist and a futurist, respectively.[6] According to Dalkey, Delphi was the site of the oracle of Apollo in ancient Greece. It is believed that people came to the temple where priests divined from the entrails of animals what was to come. Centuries later, the future remains a mystery and foretelling events continues to be fraught with difficulties. Although the Delphi survey method of futures forecasting is still less than precise, it is believed to be somewhat removed from its primitive beginnings.

The Delphi research technique is designed to "elicit opinions with the goal of obtaining a group response from an initial panel of expert topic selection".[6, p.2] Delphi replaces direct confrontation and debate with a carefully planned, orderly program of sequential individual interrogations, most often conducted by a conventional questionnaire format. The series of questionnaires is interspersed with feedback derived from the responses. The technique emphasises informed judgment. It attempts to improve the panel or committee approach by subjecting the views of individual experts to the criticism of fellow experts without face-to-face confrontation, and by providing anonymity for the opinions and arguments that are advanced in defense of those opinions. The respondents are not identified in most Delphi studies.

The Delphi technique was originated by the RAND corporation as a means for obtaining greater consensus among experts about urgent defense problems without face-to-face discussion. A number of studies that employ the Delphi technique have been performed by the RAND corporation.

Generally the Delphi process focuses on collating the aggregate judgments of a number of individuals who speculate on the present and the future and who have either similar or diverse backgrounds. It has become not only a forecasting tool but also a procedure through which to assemble current thought and practice in defined areas. The Delphi, which has been used in many different settings and in many different ways, is an appropriate research tool wherever anonymous individual opinion is desired in an effort to reach agreement for future planning.

The Delphi has been used on university campuses in a number of ways, often as a means of involving faculty in the planning and decision-making processes for the future of the institution. A number of researchers[7,8,9] report that the Delphi technique lends itself well to use by faculty members in establishing the goals and objectives of a new or revised curriculum. The particular advantages of the Delphi technique in this context are that it minimises the biasing effects of dominant individuals and the amount of irrelevant communication. Each faculty member contributes freely and independently to the original statement of goals. At a later stage, the faculty member is able to benefit from the contribution of his or her colleagues in setting priorities among the objectives expressed by the entire group. It has been found that regardless of how divergent the original positions, opinions tend to converge and synthesise when the Delphi technique is used.

The nature of the Delphi technique, as described by Dalkey[6] and his associates has a number of objectives. Among these are:

(a)   to determine and develop a range of possible program alternatives,

(b)   to explore or expose underlying assumptions or information leading to different judgments,

(c)   to seek out information which may generate a consensus on the part of the respondent group,

(d)   to correlate informed judgments on a topic spanning a wide range of disciplines, and

(e)   to educate the respondent group as to the diverse and interrelated aspects of the topic.

In practice, the Delphi technique takes on diverse formats in different institutions and settings for different objectives and goals. The exact form of the Delphi is usually governed by the nature of the problem, resources, and the people implementing the program. The three critical conditions which are necessary for a successful Delphi are (a) sufficient time for the three rounds, (b) skills in written communication, and (c) motivation among the respondents.

There are, of course, criticisms of the Delphi research technique that focus on several areas of its technical construction and overall philosophical design.

Linstone and Turoff[10] believe that some respondents may allow their true opinions to be influenced by what they must assume is expert opinion reported through the rounds; a halo effect may therefore contaminate the results, inhibiting creativity and innovation. Other criticisms focus on the basic goal of forced consensus, the encouragement of conforming answers, weaknesses in questionnaire construction, the possibility of snap judgments and responses, and the lack of experimental support for the validity and reliability of the method.

One of the most significant contributions of the Delphi technique is its function as an 'educational' device. It is an excellent tool to alert faculties to those areas of importance identified by administrators, or others responsible for planning and development. Further, it allows participants to benefit from the contributions of his or her colleagues in setting priorities among the expressed objectives. It may also act to modify the awareness, assumptions, and skill of the participants. It serves to acquaint the faculty with the existing goal structure through efforts to solicit their individual concerns.

Purpose of this Investigation:
The purpose of this study was to determine faculty and administrator's perceptions of institutional needs and goals at one institution of medical education. The Delphi research technique was used to achieve the purpose of this investigation.

Procedures of the Study:
The University of Medicine and Dentistry of New Jersey (UMDNJ) is the state-wide health sciences university for the State of New Jersey. UMDNJ operates three medical schools, The New Jersey Medical School, the Rutgers Medical School, and the New Jersey School of Osteopathic Medicine.

This structure represents a consolidated system where many aspects of administration, physical facilities, budget and curriculum are shared. Goal setting at any one institution must be cognisant of all institutions.

Further, the professional and political tenor between allopathic and osteopathic medicine prompted concerns for independent goal structuring by the osteopathic administrators and faculty. Participatory self-study, and consensus regarding the direction of the instution was critical.

The initial panel for this study was comprised of upper level administrators from all of the colleges of osteopathic medicine in the United States. General areas of concern were identified through program emphasis at two national meetings. These areas of concern were then presented to the administrators and Self-Study Committee at the New Jersey School of Osteopathic Medicine. These areas of concern were reviewed and refined to reflect specific issues of importance in New Jersey; however, none of these more comprehensive areas was deleted.

The Round I Delphi instrument consisted of open-ended questions in keeping with the aforementioned areas of concern. This Round I instrument was distributed to all full-time faculty. Seventy-two questionnaires were distributed. Approximately 72% of the full-time faculty responded, agreeing to participate in all three rounds of the study. The results of the Round I instrument were categorised, the frequency of items was tabulated, and similar items were grouped. Efforts were made to reflect all Round I responses categorically in the Round II instrument. The Round II instrument consisted of three hundred and forty-one items. The length of this instrument was not typical of most Delphis; however, it was felt that a more comprehensive instrument would encourage a feeling of participation and solidarity, particularly where controversial issues were involved. The length of the instrument prevents it from being reproduced in total here; however, Figure 1 provides an example of the Round I statements.

DELPHI I

TEACHING AND EVALUATION:

a. How do you measure your teaching effectiveness?

b. How does the institution measure your teaching effectiveness?

c. Who decides what you teach?
    Are you in agreement with this procedure? Suggestions?

d. Do you have sufficient, and efficient secretarial support for preparing course materials, teaching aids etc.?

e. Do you have ready access to audio-visual materials, simulation models, computer-assisted instruction?

    If not, what are your needs?

f. Do you have adequate information and expertise in the following teaching skills:

    1) writing behavioural objectives
    2) test construction
    3) developing self-instructional materials
    4) lecture
    5) laboratory instruction
    6) individualised learning
    7) seminar
    8) other

FIGURE 1
Excerpt from Round I Delphi

The Round II instrument represented a categorical-item breakdown as follows: (a) physical campus and facilities (items 1–102); (b) future growth, missions and goals (items 103–144); (c) osteopathic perspective and philosophy (items 145–181); (d) curriculum (items 182–196); (e) administration (items 197–216); (f) teaching, and evaluation of teaching (items 217–242); (g) tenure, promotion, salary and merit (items 243–324); and (h) students and admissions (items 325–341).

The format of the Round II instrument was designed to elicit responses on a scale from one to seven. The respondents were asked to indicate degrees of agreement (1) or disagreement (7) for each statement. Space was provided so that respondents could comment on each item or add items if they wished. (See Figure 2 for an example of the Round II instrument statements.)

Fifty Round II questionnaires were returned (approximately 97% of the Round I respondents, and 69.4% of the total faculty). Computerized statistical analyses of the Round II data produced mean, median, mode, standard deviation, variance, value counts, and interquartile range for each of the individual items (341) on the Round II Delphi survey instrument. (See Table 1 for an example of the item by item statistical analyses.)

TABLE 1
Excerpt from Round II Delphi Statistical Table

ITEM NUMBER	MEAN	MEDIAN	MODE	STANDARD DEVIATION	VARIANCE	VALUES COUNTED	VALUES NOT COUNTED	(Q1)	(Q2)
223	2.77	3.00	2.00	1.51	2.30	49	1	2.0	3.0
224	4.15	4.00	4.00	1.71	2.93	46	4	3.0	6.0
225	2.30	2.00	1.00	1.86	3.46	49	1	1.0	3.0
226	2.54	2.00	1.00	1.96	3.87	48	2	1.0	3.0
227	2.33	2.00	2.00	1.50	2.26	48	2	1.0	3.0
228	4.29	5.00	5.00	2.02	4.08	48	2	3.0	6.0
229	3.67	4.00	4.00	1.89	3.59	49	1	2.0	5.0
230	2.91	3.00	n/u*	1.61	2.61	49	1	1.0	4.0
231	2.93	2.00	1.00	1.84	3.40	47	3	1.0	4.0
232	5.06	5.00	7.00	1.77	3.14	49	1	4.0	7.0

* not unique.

DELPHI II

TEACHING AND EVALUATION	Agree						Disagree
223. All faculty should have more input into their individual course selection and content	1	2	3	4	5	6	7
224. The institution makes a fair and accurate evaluation of my teaching skills	1	2	3	4	5	6	7
225. I would like information on the use of computer-assisted instruction	1	2	3	4	5	6	7
226. My teaching would benefit from a workshop on aspects of instructional preparation such as writing objectives, developing self-instructional materials, etc.	1	2	3	4	5	6	7
227. Peer review of teaching is a good idea	1	2	3	4	5	6	7
228. Student's test performance is the best measure of teaching effectiveness	1	2	3	4	5	6	7
229. Administrative review of teaching is generally biased and of no real value	1	2	3	4	5	6	7
230. There is no consistent system for student evaluation of teaching	1	2	3	4	5	6	7
231. I am encouraged by my department head to try innovative course design and implementation	1	2	3	4	5	6	7
232. On-site evaluation of teaching by peers and administration is a violation of academic freedom	1	2	3	4	5	6	7

FIGURE 2
Excerpt from Round II Delphi

The group median and interquartile range were printed above each item for Round III. Of the available statistics, the group median and interquartile range are most appropriate to help the respondent identify his or her response relative to other respondents. The quartile interval (Q) contains the middle 50% of the total responses; its size gives some indication of how widely the responses differed from one another. The median (M) reflects the mid point of all responses to each statement. Additional items for response were added to Round III from the Round II responses. Forty-seven additions were made.

DELPHI III

TEACHING AND EVALUATION	Agree Disagree
223. All faculty should have more input into their individual course selection and content	Q1 = 2.0 Q3 = 3.0 1 2 3 4 5 6 7 M = 3.0
224. The institution makes a fair and accurate evaluation of my teaching skills	Q1 = 3.0 Q3 = 6.0 1 2 3 4 5 6 7 M = 4.0
225. I would like information on the use of computer-assisted instruction	Q1 = 1.0 Q3 = 3.0 1 2 3 4 5 6 7 M = 2.0
226. My teaching would benefit from a workshop on aspects of instructional preparation such as writing objectives, developing self-instructional materials, etc.	Q1 = 1.0 Q3 = 3.0 1 2 3 4 5 6 7 M = 2.0
227. Peer review of teaching is a good idea	Q1 = 1.0/Q3 = 3.0 1 2 3 4 5 6 7 M = 2.0
228. Student's test performance is the best measure of teaching effectiveness	Q1 = 3.0/Q3 = 6.0 1 2 3 4 5 6 7 M = 5.0
229. Administrative review of teaching is generally biased and of no real use	Q1 = 2.0 Q3 = 5.0 1 2 3 4 5 6 7 M = 4.0
230. There is no consistent system for student evaluation of teaching	Q1 = 1.0/Q3 = 4.0 1 2 3 4 5 6 7 M = 3.0
231. I am encouraged by my department head to try innovative course design and implementation	Q1 = 1.0/Q3 = 4.0 1 2 3 4 5 6 7 M = 2.0
232. On-site evaluation of teaching by peers and administration is a violation of academic freedom	Q1 = 4.0/Q3 = 7.0 1 2 3 4 5 6 7 M = 5.0

FIGURE 3
Excerpt from Round III Delphi

Round III was returned to respondents with instructions to re-evaluate their responses in consideration of the group consensus. (See Figure 3 for an example of the Round III instrument.)

If the participant's Round III response remained outside the interquartile range of agreement, the participant was asked to provide explanation. (See Figure 4 for an example of individual respondents who remained outside the range of consensus.)

**NARRATIVE RESPONSES TO ROUND III DELPHI
INDICATING CONSENSUS WAS NOT OBTAINED ON ITEMS**

TEACHING AND EVALUATION

Item 224	The institution makes a fair and accurate evaluation of my teaching skills.
	$Q1 = 3.0/Q3 = 6.0$
	$M = 4.0$
	Six respondents remained in strong disagreement (outside the range) indicating that virtually no evaluation was made, and efforts were poor at best.
Item 238	The present system of student course evaluation is adequate.
	$Q1 = 2.0/Q3 = 6.0$
	$M = 4.0$
	Four respondents remained in strong disagreement (outside the range) indicating inconsistencies in current course evaluation procedures.

FIGURE 4
Excerpt from Narrative Responses to Round III Delphi
(Consensus Not Obtained)

Respondents were also asked to respond to the additional items added to Round III. Forty-seven Round III questionnaires were returned to the researcher (approximately 90% of the Round I respondents, and 65% of the total faculty).

Respondents were able to reach consensus by reporting within the group range of agreement on 372 of the 388 items of Round III.

SUMMARY

Results of this study would indicate that administrators and faculty at NJSOM are in fairly close agreement where concerns of the institution and broad goals are involved. All Round I responses in this study were readily grouped into the pre-selected variable categories; and no categories were without response.

There are several factors that are critical to the success of the Delphi when used as an implement of self-study. When faculty respond as enthusiastically as they did in this investigation, there are obviously concerns, both positive and negative, that must be addressed. The New Jersey School of Osteopathic Medicine, following results of this study have organised retreats and other study groups to discuss issues where faculty are dissatisfied or uninformed. The administration has also initiated changes where strong needs were reflected by the participants, particularly in the areas of a systematic practice plan for clinical faculty, student admission standards, and evaluation of teaching. The study also reflected faculty interest in learning new teaching methods, and pursuing clinical research; and efforts toward institutional workshops and seminars in these areas are being made.

The Delphi is recognised as one of the most comprehensive methods to elicit wide administrative and faculty participation in establishing a unified goal structure for an institution. Considering the diversity, and autonomous functioning of most medical school faculties, the success of this study is seen as a positive reflection on the flexibility of the Delphi method.

REFERENCES

(1)   HARTNETT, R. T., *Accountability in Higher Education*, Princeton, College Entrance Examination Board, 1971.

(2)   KEETON, M. (1971), *Shared Authority on Campus*, Washington, American Association for Higher Education.

(3)   ETZIONI, A. (1964) *Modern Organisations*, Englewood Cliffs, Prentice-Hall.

(4)   COOPER, R. (1966), "Initiating Education Change", *Innovations in Higher Education*, ed. HALLAM, K. J., pp. 72--93, Towson State College Press, Baltimore.

(5)   PAREKH. S. B. (1977), *Long-Range Planning*, New Rochelle, Change Magazine Press.

(6)   DALKEY, N. C., (1967), *Delphi*, Santa Monica, Rand Corporation.

(7)   McMANIS, G. L., and HARVEY, L. J., (1978), *Planning, Management and Evaluation Systems in Higher Education*, Littleton, Ireland Educational Corporation.

(8)   DOWELL, P. E. Jr., (1975), "Delphi Forecasting in Higher Education," unpublished doctoral dissertation, George Peabody College for Teachers, Nashville, Tennessee.

(9)   WOOD, L., and DAVIS, B. G. (1978), "Designing and Evaluating Higher Education Curricula", ERIC Document No. 8.

(10) LINSTONE, H. A., and TUROFF, M. (1975), *The Delphi Method: Techniques and Applications*, Reading, Addison-Wesley.

First version of paper received: June 1984
Final version received: October 1984

Further details from:
    Dr. Linda Fazio,
    Associate Professor of Occupational Therapy.
    Institute of Health Sciences,
    Texas Woman's University.
    Denton,
    Texas.

Dr. Fazio is associate professor of Occupational Therapy in the Institute of Health Sciences, Texas Woman's University, Denton, Texas, USA, and a consultant in Medical Higher Education.

16

A Sample Methodology
for Site-Specific Instrument Selection

Janice E. Williams

Craft Reports

Evaluators are often concerned with selecting the best possible test instrument for a site-specific application. These instruments should be selected on the basis of both theoretical and psychometric criteria. A small scale, site-specific field test was completed to illustrate some of the psychometric procedures that might be used in assessing the applicability of two different test instruments. The mathematical procedures used in this study illustrate the procedures that an evaluator might use in determining an empirical basis for subsequent instrument selection.

*W*hen an evaluator is called into a project, the design of the study has usually been determined. It may even appear that test instrument selection has been made without regard to the requirements of the particular site in which that instrument will be applied. As a consequence, part of the conscientious evaluator's job will be to aid in determining the best test for the specific situation. The current article is intended to present one possible methodology available to the serious evaluator who wishes to determine the best possible instrument for a particular site-specific application.

The current study provides a demonstration of one method for selecting the most appropriate instrument, given the preliminary theoretical work has reduced the number of tenable tests to a reasonable number. This example is oriented towards job satisfaction. Prior research of the available literature reduced the potential number of instruments used in the assessment of job satisfaction (O'Connor et al., 1978). Two possible candidates for selection were located for use in the current illustrative study.

Job satisfaction provides management with an index of the emotional well-being of employees (Lawler, 1980). The quality of the scales used

From Janice E. Williams, "A Sample Methodology for Site-Specific Instrument Selection," *Evaluation Review*, 1984, 8(5), 726-733. Copyright 1984 by Sage Publications, Inc.

for this assessment, however, has varied considerably. For example, most measures that view job satisfaction as a multidimensional construct have not been subjected to rigorous validation procedures (Locke, 1969, 1976; Wanous and Lawler, 1972). Soutar and Weaver (1978) and Evans (1969) indicate that indices based on satisfaction constructs are partially dependent upon the specific satisfaction measure chosen. Given these findings, it is apparent that the selection of an instrument for measuring job satisfaction at a particular site is not a simple task.

It seems apparent that the instrument selected for use in a specific situation should satisfy theoretical criteria for appropriateness of development and field-tested psychometric criteria for usability. The theoretical criteria may be determined from the literature. In this study the theoretical criteria includes the appropriateness of the construct, assumed factor structure, operational definitions, and their inter-relationships (Clegg and Wall, 1981; Warr et al., 1979; Gillet and Schwab, 1975).

Specific psychometric qualities of the selected instrument should include such data as internal consistency within each scale, factorial independence of scales, and scale sensitivity to group differences. However, published reports of such criteria are often based on populations that differ from one's target population and thus, a small scale field test is often required to establish these values. It is the purpose of this study to illustrate, with an example, some of the procedures that might be used in such a field testing of the relative appropriateness of two different instruments.

The two instruments selected for this demonstration are the carefully developed, well-validated Job Descriptive Index (JDI; Smith et al., 1969) widely used in the private sector and the Quality of Employment Survey (QES) developed for and used extensively in the public sector by the U.S. government (Quinn and Shepard, 1974; Staines and Quinn, 1979). These instruments reflect a common view of the operational and theoretical definitions of the construct. Both relate job satisfaction to a collection of affective responses associated with the job environment, and both contain five factor analytically distinct areas of job satisfaction. The definitional and theoretical similarities of these two instruments provide little basis for the selection of an instrument in a situation where the job site is neither clearly in the private sector nor in the Federal sector (i.e., a state-supported institution). Information collected on the selected psychometric criteria should, as a consequence, provide the evaluator with a rational and empirical basis for subsequent instrument selection for this site specific application.

METHOD

Sample. Small numbers in the target population are to be expected in most site-specific applications. In the present illustration, only 68 full-time state workers employed at the Meriam Library at California State University—Chico were available for the study. Given that a portion of these were to be retained for possible cross-validation or other instrument testing, the target sample consisted of 34 employees selected in alternating alphabetical order. The final sample (N = 30) is approximately 85% of the originally targeted sample.

Instruments. The JDI taps five facets of job satisfaction: the work itself, supervision, co-workers, pay, and promotions. Each facet is measured with either 9 or 18 adjectives that have been shown to differentiate between job conditions. Responses are scored on a three-point scale, yes = 3, ? = 1, no = 0 for positively discriminating items, and yes = 0, ? = 1 and no = 3 for negatively discriminating items. Depending on the number of items or phrases, the JDI subscale scores can range from 0 to 54 with higher respondent scores on the JDI scale indicating a greater satisfaction.

The QES measures employee attitudes towards: work challenge, resource adequacy, relations with co-workers, financial rewards, and promotions. Each QES facet contains from 3 to 11 phrases and is measured with Likert scales that range from "very true" to "not at all true." The QES subscale values can range from 3 to 44, with lower scores indicating greater employee satisfaction. Note that negative JDI-QES correlations between similar scales would be anticipated as a consequence of scale measurement directionality.

Demographic data was obtained from a series of questions added to the end of the combined survey instruments. Responses provided information on educational background, sex, age, income, and length of time at present job.

Procedure. Two versions of the basic questionnaire were prepared, differing only in the order in which the JDI and QES were administered. A brief instruction sheet was followed by the two satisfaction scales that were, in turn, followed by the demographic data sheet. Each of these two versions were administered randomly to half of the target sample on the work site, with the project being identified as a confidential research study. Its voluntary nature was stressed. Employees typically spent between twenty and thirty minutes completing the entire survey.

RESULTS

In any low-N site-specific study a first consideration must involve questions of the representativeness of the target sample and the presence of possible contaminating influences on the data collected. In the present study, the sample demographic data was compared visually with employee records from the personnel office to insure that the sample truly represented the targeted population. No marked discrepancies were apparent in this analysis.

The presence of low sample sizes in a site-specific application will constrain the types of analyses that can be made. Thus, with the exception of estimates of internal consistency, all present analyses were conducted on the 5 unit-weight factor scores for each instrument. The decision to generate unit-weight factors rather than regressed factors was based on pragmatic considerations of the normal "user circumstance." Very few survey users refer back to original factor analyses in an effort to generate regressed factor scores, and thus it is more realistic to use unit-weight factor scores. Although the resulting six subjects per variable falls somewhat short of the desired ten or more subjects per variable, the exploratory nature of the design was felt to justify this approach.

The group that answered the JDI first was compared with the group who answered the QES first. Because subjects were assigned randomly to the two groups, any differences found in the scale responses would suggest an order bias that may have affected the study's results. In this test for possible order effects, each questionnaire was analyzed separately by an ANOVA with subjects nested in order grouping but crossed with subscale. The nonsignificant main effect of order and the scale x order interaction in both analyses indicated any administration order effect was irrelevant. At this point, the sample had been judged to be representative and no contaminating influences on the data were detected. The remainder of the analyses could then be directed towards the assessment of possible instrument differences with some degree of confidence.

Reliability is a precursor to validity and without internal reliability, validity is questionable. The five subscales for each instrument were first examined for internal reliability using Cronbach's (1951) alpha. The mean alpha coefficients across each of the subscales were computed, and they are presented in Table 1. Both scales appear to meet the minimal criteria for reliability. Although the mean z-adjusted alphas are approximately the same (JDI a = 0.834; QES a = 0.803), it should be noted that

TABLE 1
Alpha Coefficients for JDI and QES Subscales

| | Factor Scale Number | | | | |
	1	2	3	4	5
JDI	0.84	0.86	0.85	0.81	0.80
QES	0.88	0.89	0.75	0.66	0.74

in this example the JDI is much more consistent from scale to scale (a range of z from 1.110 to 1.282) than the QES (a range of z from 0.798 to 1.437). The JDI's lower scale to scale variability would be a point in favor of its selection as a job satisfaction instrument for this particular application.

In theory, at least, factors represent independent measurement dimensions and thus should exhibit no intercorrelations. In practice, unit-weight factor scores typically exhibit some degree of dependence, although this should be minimal. To assess this aspect of the two scales, separate correlation matrices between factor scores on each subscale were computed. Two of the ten unique correlations on the JDI scale showed significant bivariate correlation at $p < .05$. In situations where an evaluator is comparing correlations it is helpful to use Fisher's r to z transformation, given that differences between z's represent differences as they appear in the real world—linearly. R-values do not represent differences in a linear manner. The mean z-adjusted r for the JDI scale was .196. For the QES, however, four of the ten unique correlation coefficients showed significant bivariate correlations at $p < .05$, and two additional variables were at $p < .10$. The mean z-adjusted r for this scale was .312. It is apparent that, for this study, the JDI more closely meets the psychometric criteria for independent factor scores than the QES.

Internal consistency is a necessary but not a sufficient condition to ensure one has selected the best instrument. It is apparent that an instrument that reveals overall group differences is preferable to one that is unable to detect such differences. Similarly, an instrument that is capable of detecting subgroup patterns of response has greater power than one that detects only overall group differences. When predefined groups exist, one may proceed directly to the ANOVA phase of the assessment, which is necessary to evaluate these criteria.

However, when groups have not been previously established (as in the present study), an additional step is necessary: determination of subgroup structure. In the real world, subgroups are often predefined from the sample. In many cases, however, predefined groups are not

TABLE 2
Factor Scores Analyses of Variance

Source	JDI MS	JDI df	JDI F	QES MS	QES df	QES F
Groups	8.72	2	26.13*	30.74	1	77.62*
Factors	7.09	4	23.89*	7.46	4	15.94*
G x F	1.27	8	4.27*	0.32	4	0.68
S/G	0.33	27		0.40	28	
F x S/G	0.30	108		0.47	112	

*p < .01

available for analysis. In the present illustrative study, groups were not defined. Cluster analysis was used to find the groups (Everitt, 1974; Friedman and Rubin, 1967) and thus aid instrument selection. A Q-type Ward (1963) hierarchical cluster analysis, using factor scores, was then completed for both the JDI and QES. A Scree test (Gorsuch, 1974; Catell, 1978) revealed three JDI cluster groups but only two QES cluster groups.

When preexisting groups exist, the ANOVA will aid the evaluator as an a priori test. In this particular study, the ANOVA is post hoc, in that the groups have been defined by the cluster analysis (i.e., group differences were known to exist). To determine the structure of the group differences in this illustration, confirmatory ANOVAs with subjects nested in cluster group but crossed with factor scores were computed for each scale. Although both analyses indicated significant differences owing to factors, this finding was of little interest to the current study (i.e., these individuals rated their relationships with co-workers more positively than they rated pay and advancement). Of particular interest were overall group differences and the groups × factors source of variance for detecting patterns of differences between groups. The results of these analyses are shown in Table 2. As noted there, both primary sources of interest are significant for the JDI, but only the overall group source was significant for the QES. These results indicate that, although both scales were sensitive to gross overall group differences, only the JDI was capable of picking up subtle subgroup pattern differences.

Finally, correlations between the corresponding factor scores for each of the five scales on the two instruments were determined. These correlations were computed in order to determine whether or not these two instruments were measuring the same underlying dimensions of the construct, in this case job satisfaction. Significant correlations (ranging from -0.56 to -0.77) were located for three of the pairs, but two other pairs showed nonsignificant relationships. It is apparent that, at least to some extent, the two instruments measure different construct dimensions and that different results might be obtained solely because of instrument selection.

DISCUSSION

The results cited above illustrate what one might expect when comparing instruments for selection and use in site-specific situations. The general structure of the data provide information for scale reliability assessment, measures of scale independence, overall and subgroup pattern difference measures and underlying construct dimension assessment.

For this specific testing situation, the JDI seems to exhibit superior psychometric qualities to the QES: It exhibits less scale to scale variability in reliability coefficients, the factor scores are more independent, and it more sensitively detects subgroup patterns of response. For this site-specific application, then, the JDI appears to be the appropriate choice as an instrument for measuring job satisfaction.

This research has examined the performance of two measurement scales that have general applicability in assessing job satisfaction. Both scales currently enjoy wide use. The face validity of these two instruments would lead one to believe that both are able to measure similar underlying dimensions of the construct. The results from this illustration, however, revealed that, although basic similarities existed between the scales, it was not safe to assume that these two measures are highly correlated. It should be reemphasized that different results at some other site might yield quite different results and, consequently, different instrument selection and would be more valid for that evaluation procedure. If, however, the approach advocated here is followed, achieving a site-specific "best fit" by these mathematical procedures would be possible.

REFERENCES

CATELL, R. B. (1978) The Scientific Use of Factor Analysis. New York: Plenum.
CRONBACH, L. J. (1951) "Coefficient alpha and the internal structure of tests." Psychometrika 16: 297-334.

CLEGG, C. W. and T. D. WALL (1981) "A note of some new scales for measuring aspects of psychological well-being at work." J. of Occupational Psychology 54: 221-225.

EVANS, M. G. (1969) "Conceptual and operational problems in the measurement of various aspects of job satisfaction." J. of Applied Psychology 53(2), 93-101.

EVERITT, B. (1974) Cluster Analysis. New York: John Wiley.

FRIEDMAN, H. P. and J. RUBIN (1967) "On some invariant criteria for grouping data." Amer. Stat. Assn. J. 62: 1159-1178.

GILLET, B. and D. P. SCHWAB (1975) "Convergent and discriminantalidities of corresponding Job Descriptive Index and Minnesota Satisfaction Questionnaire scales." J. of Applied Psychology 60(3): 313-327.

GORSUCH, R. L. (1974) Factor Analysis. Philadelphia: W. B. Sauders.

LAWLER, III, E. E. (1980) Organizational Assessment: Perspectives on the Measurement of the Organizational Behavior and the Quality of Work Life. New York: John Wiley.

LOCKE, E. A. (1976) "The nature and causes of job satisfaction," pp. 1297-1350 in M. D. Dunnette (ed.) Handbook of Industrial and Organizational Psychology. Chicago: Rand McNally.

————(1969) What is job satisfaction? Organizational Behavior and Human Performance 4: 309-336.

————, P. C. SMITH, L. M. KENDALL, C. L. HULIN and A. M. MILLER (1964) "Convergent and discriminant validity for areas and methods of rating job satisfaction." J. of Applied Psychology 48(5) 313-319.

O'CONNOR, E. J., L. H. PETERS and S. M. GORDON (1978) "The measurement of job satisfaction: Current practices and future considerations." J. of Management 4(2): 17-26.

QUINN, R. P. and L. J. SHEPARD (1974) The 1972-73 Quality of Employment Survey: Report to the Employment Standards Administration, U.S. Department of Labor. Michigan: Survey Research Center of the Institute for Social Research.

SMITH, P.C., L. M. KENDALL and C. L. HULIN (1969) The Measurement of Satisfaction in Work and Retirement. Chicago: Rand McNally.

SOUTAR, G. N. and J. R. WEAVER (1982) "The measurement of shop-floor job satisfaction: The convergent and discriminant validity of the Worker Opinion Survey." J. of Occupational Psychology 55: 27-33.

STAINES, G. and R. P. QUINN (1979) "American workers evaluate the quality of their jobs." Monthly Labor Rev. 102(1): 3-12.

WANOUS, J. P. and E. E. LAWLER, III (1972) Measurement and meaning of job satisfaction. J. Of Applied Psychology 56(2): 95-105.

WARD, J. H. (1963) "Hierarchical grouping to optimize an objective function. " Amer. Stat. Assn. J. 58: 236-244.

WARR, P. B., J. COOK and T. D. WALL "Scales for the measurement of some work attitudes and respects of psychological well-being. J. of Occupational Psychology 52: 120-148.

Janice E. Williams has a B.A. from Frostburg State College, an M.P.A. from California State University, Chico, and has been a member of the staff of the California State University at Chico Meriam Library since 1980. She recently resigned this position to continue her graduate studies at the University of California at Los Angeles.

17

The Feedback Research Approach to Evaluation
A Method to Increase Evaluation Utility
Debra J. Rog and Leonard Bickman

ABSTRACT

The utilization of evaluation results continues to be a great concern among professionals in the field. To increase the potential usefulness of evaluation, the feedback research approach is proposed as a method that is especially helpful in studies that fail to find program effectiveness. Going beyond the bounds of the evaluation framework and studying the problem for which the program was designed to ameliorate, evaluations that incorporate a feedback research component can provide clients with valuable information to guide further program development.

This paper provides a description of the approach and an illustration of its use in an evaluation of a major international corporation's health improvement/stress management program.

Within the last 2 decades, the field of program evaluation has grown and prospered. Sparked by a substantial federal investment, which by 1976 had reached an estimated level of over a quarter of a billion dollars (Kimmel, 1981), evaluation has become a frequently mandated component in federally-funded programs at the national, state, and local levels. Moreover, organizations in the private sector have begun to employ evaluation as a tool to assess the effectiveness and efficiency of their programs.

Despite this growth, the *direct* impact of evaluation results on policy and program development has been minimal (Alkin, Daillak, & White, 1979; Patton, Grimes, Guthrie, Brennan, French, & Blyth, 1977). A number of reasons have been offered for the apparent lack of use of evaluation results in making decisions about programs and services. One perspective is that the frequent finding of negative and null evaluation results has dampened their use. Failure to find effectiveness has left program administrators with little information on which to base program modifications.

Several approaches have been proposed for increasing the sensitivity of evaluation to program effects and to policy needs. Two approaches that have attempted to broaden the scope of the experimental method are Scriven's goal-free evaluation approach (1972, 1973)

and Chen and Rossi's theory driven approach (1980, 1983). Goal-free evaluation focuses on effects achieved rather than on stated goals or objectives. To conduct such an evaluation, one must compare the effects with a profile of the needs addressed by the program. Scriven's goal-free model, however, is procedurally vague and does not provide guidance in deciding what effects to examine or in deciding how to assess program needs.

Chen and Rossi (1980) have attempted to modify and improve upon goal-free evaluation with a multi-goal, theory driven approach. This method entails collecting data on a set of outcomes that are derived from social science knowledge and theory as well as from the stated goals of the program. By collecting data on a number of outcome variables, the possibility of finding some non-trivial program effects is maximized and decision makers are provided with information on a wide range of potential program effects (Chen & Rossi, 1980).

Both of these approaches are predicated on the assumption that programs do have effects and that these effects can be anticipated. Although this is an optimistic assumption, it may not be totally realistic. There may be situations in which negative or null findings appropriately represent a program's lack of effectiveness. If a program has addressed a problem that has not been adequately defined or if a program is directed at an inappropriate client population, it is highly probable that an evaluation will find little, if any, effect for the program. In fact, in some cases, the program may even be found to be having deleterious consequences.

The approach proposed in this paper, unlike the approaches previously mentioned (Chen & Rossi, 1980; Scriven, 1972), is designed to increase the sensitivity of evaluation in instances where null or negative findings may reflect the true state of affairs. The *feedback research approach,* incorporating a problem and needs assessment within the evaluation, allows the evaluator to go beyond the bounds of the traditional evaluation framework and to more thoroughly investigate the problem that the program or intervention is addressing. The approach is designed primarily for situations in which it is suspected that the lack of positive program effects is an indication that the progam is inappropriate either for the problem or for the needs of a specific client population. It is predicated on the belief that feedback on the nature of the problem and on clients' needs may increase the utility of an otherwise apparently useless evaluation for program development and redirection.

The feedback research approach is particularly relevant for evaluations of programs that have been developed and implemented without a problem or needs assessment component. Although it is better to determine both the extent of a problem in a specific environment and the needs of the target population as a preliminary step to the development of an intervention, limitations on time, money, and other resources frequently prevent any systematic data collection efforts prior to the impact evaluation. In addition, program administrators and sponsors often feel they have adequate information on the problem and either do not give thought to these activities or are not convinced of their necessity. Thus, while studying the problem before designing and implementing an intervention is desirable, it is often not possible.

The major emphasis of the feedback research approach is on increasing the usefulness of an evaluation's products by providing information that may explain "why" the program has not had the anticipated effects. Clearly, for evaluations in which a prior needs or problem assessment has been conducted or in which a well defined and studied issue has been covered, the feedback research approach may offer little additional information. In other cases, however, the approach may offer information that will not only aid program sponsors, but will also add to the findings of the basic research community. By contributing information about the nature of the problem, the approach can help in establishing a closer relationship between the applied and more traditional research communities.

The remainder of this article provides a more detailed description of the feedback research approach, supported by an example of its application in an evaluation of a health improvement/stress management program. As the approach appears to be tailor-made for some evaluative situations and inappropriate for others, the closing of this article will provide some general guidelines for determining whether or not the approach would be worthwhile in an evaluation.

The Feedback Research Approach

The feedback research approach is primarily designed to supplement evaluations in which prior examination of needs and the dynamics of the problem is not possible. Most appropriate for evaluations in which positive program effects have not been found, the approach is proposed to be conducted following outcome analyses and, to some degree, is modeled after the internal analysis method used in basic research.

In traditional experimental laboratory research, findings of null or negative effects often direct the researcher to an internal analysis of the research data. In this re-analysis, the distinction between the treatment and control groups is ignored; a new independent variable, typically some measure related to the treatment, is examined. For example, if an experimenter has designed a study to examine the effects of anxiety on performance, the primary analysis will involve a comparison of the performance of subjects randomly assigned to high and low anxiety conditions. Finding no difference between these conditions, the investigator may move to a weaker correlational design where some measure of anxiety is compared with performance, regardless of group membership. Thus, the phenomenon under study is re-examined and questions regarding the accuracy of its operationalization are posed. In addition, the characteristics of the subject population are examined to determine if they may have mediated the effects of the experimental manipulation. The information gained from this internal analysis is often then used to redesign the study.

In program evaluation, the feedback research approach can simulate traditional internal analysis by directing analysis efforts away from the program and concentrating on an assessment of the problem addressed by the program. This approach supplements impact analyses by providing an in-depth analysis of the specific problem as it operates within the study population. Like Chen and Rossi's (1980) approach, the proposed approach is similar to basic research and can contribute to the development of social science theory. The focus of the theory-driven approach, however, is on developing models that can help to elucidate the relations between program variables and outcomes, whereas the feedback research approach concentrates on studying the actual nature of the problem and the degree to which the program has adequately addressed the problem.

In the feedback research approach, the role of the evaluator changes from one who judges the merit or worth of a program to that of a more traditional researcher who attempts to obtain a better understanding of the phenomenon under study. Thus, sufficient data must be collected during the evaluation that will allow the evaluator to address research questions about the problem being investigated.

Although the proposed approach may appear to be similar to process or formative evaluation, the emphasis is quite different. In a process evaluation, the evaluator is concerned primarily with describing how the program operates and produces the intended effect; the focus is still on the program. In contrast, the feedback research approach concentrates on understanding the problem and not on understanding how the program operates. Although formative in nature, instead of providing continuous feedback on the program, the approach provides information on the nature of the problem to assist in better program development.

The feedback research approach was developed while evaluating a major international corporation's health program. Highlights of this evaluation are provided as an illustration of the approach's application.

FEEDBACK RESEARCH – AN APPLICATION FROM AN EVALUATION OF A HEALTH IMPROVEMENT/STRESS MANAGEMENT PROGRAM

Program Description
In line with its ongoing concern for employee health and well-being, a Fortune 500 corporation initiated a multiphase health improvement/stress management program for managers and their spouses. The program was designed to increase participants' awareness of stress and its effects and to provide instruction on techniques to prevent or cope with stressful situations. The program consisted of a 4-day workshop of seminars, skills sessions, and learning group sessions that emphasized the personal strategies one could use to deal with stress. In addition, several activities concerning relaxation training, nutrition, and stress carriers were offered to program participants during the months following the workshop's completion.

Evaluation Design
Having invested considerable resources in the development and implementation of the program, the corporation was interested in learning the degree to which the program had had an effect on participants' health attitudes and behaviors. Therefore, an evaluation was commissioned and conducted. The evaluation involved a pretest-posttest, nonequivalent group design. The participant group consisted of managers and their spouses who volunteered to attend the workshops. Those who agreed to participate in the comparison group were selected to be as similar as possible to those who participated in the program.

Both program and comparison group participants received questionnaires 1 month prior and 6 months following the workshops. The assessment consisted of a variety of measures of attitudes, behaviors, and beliefs concerning stress and physiological, physical, and mental health status. The majority of the measures were standard scales used in their original or adapted forms and included:

- Health Belief Model (e.g., Hochbaum, 1958; Rosenstock, 1966), consisting of a series of questions related to perceived susceptibility, perceived severity, perceived personal instrumentation, and perceived doctor's instrumentation regarding health and illness;
- Type A Behavior (e.g., Jenkins, Rosenman, & Friedman, 1967), measuring coronary-prone behaviors;
- General Well-Being (NCHS, 1973), assessing psychological health and well-being;
- Life Events (e.g., Holmes & Rahe, 1967), measuring the number of undesirable and desirable events that have occurred during the past year;
- Stressful Events (Kiev & Kohn, 1979), assessing the frequency with which stressful situations are experienced at work; and
- Stress Level (Kiev & Kohn, 1979), measuring the frequency with which stress symptoms are experienced.

In addition, several measures were used to assess the use of coping techniques and self-reported physiological indices of health. Only scales that were considered to have at least a fair degree of internal consistency (i.e., having a .60 or higher Cronbach's alpha coefficient) were included in the analyses.

Impact Analyses
Program participation did not appear to have any effects on the health status of either managers or their spouses. Analysis of covariance in a multiple regression system was performed on each posttest measure, controlling for the effects of the pretest score. Due to the differences in composition, employee and spouse respondent populations were analyzed separately.

The results of both sets of analyses indicated that program participation did not appear to have an effect on the health status of managers and their spouses. Although group participation explained a statistically significant amount of the variance in employees' beliefs of personal susceptibility to illness and in their use of exertion as a stress coping strategy (i.e., program participants reportedly feeling more susceptible to illness and reportedly exercising more than comparison group participants after completion of the program), the amount of variance explained in each analysis was minimal. Moreover, the nonsignificance of the majority of differences suggest these two findings may be spurious and thus, viewed with considerable caution.

Further analyses were conducted to investigate the role of other variables (e.g., age, number of years in the corporation) as possible mediators of the program's effects. These analyses, however, yielded no additional evidence of positive findings.

Feedback Analysis

Having employed primarily standard and demonstrably reliable measures, the evaluators felt reasonably confident that the lack of significant group differences was not due to the inadequacy of the measurement. In addition, there were some indications that the null evaluation outcomes may have been due more to a mistargeting of the program than to an insensitivity of the evaluation to positive effects. Specifically, the relatively low frequency of stressful events that were reportedly experienced and the low scores on the Stress Level scale suggested that the program may not have been appropriate to the needs of the management population. Thus, feedback research was conducted to explore the nature of the stress and health problems affecting the management population and to determine if the program was appropriate for the corporation's managers. Although intended for an evaluation of outcomes, the data collected offered valuable information for an investigation into the nature of stress in these populations. Taking a broader research perspective than is typically employed in evaluation, the evaluators dropped the group distinction and concentrated further analysis efforts on the pretest measures.

Examination of the bivariate correlations among the pretest variables for all employees and for all spouses led to the discovery of a pattern of results that provided rich descriptive information regarding the nature of the stress experience. Among managers, the level of general stress experienced (i.e., irritability, restlessness, inability to sleep) appeared to be a central variable. The strongest correlations with general stress variables included general well-being ($r = -.75$), Type A behavior ($r = .50$), perceived susceptibility to illness ($r = .46$), perceived personal instrumentation in illness ($r = -.44$), the number of physical ailments reported ($r = .47$), use of stress coping techniques that allow for venting anger ($r = .41$), and contact with relatives and friends ($r = -.31$). Thus, this measure of general stress appears to be a useful tool

for identifying managers who may be experiencing both psychological and physical negative effects of stress and who are prone to using maladaptive coping strategies.

For spouses, both general stress level and general well-being appeared to be significant variables. Spouses who reported experiencing higher general stress levels were more likely to report lower levels of general well-being ($r = -.53$), more physical ailments ($r = .40$), and more reliance on venting anger ($r = .37$) to cope with stress than spouses who reported lower levels of stress. Positive general well-being among spouses appears to be related to better physical health, measured by their self-ratings of their global health status ($r = .39$), the number of physical ailments suffered ($r = -.43$), and more use of vigorous exercises (e.g., calisthenics, swimming) ($r = .37$). These findings suggest that among spouses, the level of stress experienced and the mental health state are important correlates of physical health and health behaviors. In addition, the convergent validity demonstrated in the correlational analyses for both employees and spouses further supported the evaluators' confidence in the adequacy of the measures employed.

The information gained from the correlations was shared with the program administrators. It was then decided by both the evaluators and administrators that an additional set of analyses should be conducted to determine if the program had any differential effects. That is, was the program effective for certain types of employees? It was suggested that the program's emphasis on personal coping strategies may be successful only with a subset of the management population—those who are experiencing higher levels of general stress. Thus, a low-stress group, comprised of those who were in the bottom third of the frequency distribution of general stress pretest scale and a high stress group, comprised of the top third, were subject to a discriminant analysis to first determine if those who report to be experiencing low stress could be discriminated from those who report to be experiencing relatively higher levels of stress on the basis of other dimensions.

The stepwise discriminant analysis, using Wilk's lambda as the selection criterion, demonstrated that high and low stress individuals could be reliably discriminated on the basis of a subset of pretest variables (Table 1). Although the results of the bivariate correlations (discussed above) indicated various variables that were related to the general stress level among individuals in the employee population, the discriminant analysis allowed the evaluators to extend their power of explanation by discovering a set of variables that operate together to adequately discriminate individuals who experience extreme levels of stress.

Having defined two subsamples within the larger

TABLE 1
DISCRIMINANT ANALYSIS OF HIGH- AND
LOW-STRESS EMPLOYEES

Posttest Variable	Standardized Discriminant Function Coefficient
General well-being	−.79
Coping by use of "escapes"	.42
Type A	.31
Number of physical ailments	.23

Canonical Correlation = .86
Wilk's λ = .25, χ^2 = 35.70; $p < .00001$

sample of employees with respect to stress and its correlates, the evaluators were interested in determining whether these groups of individuals have been differentially affected by the health improvement/stress management program. Although the impact analyses conducted for the evaluation found no effect for the program as compared to a control condition when all participants were considered, analyses conducted with only a subset of the population may reveal program effects. Restricting the analyses to include only low stress and high stress individuals may yield results that "wash-out" in analyses that include individuals of intermediate stress levels. Therefore, two-way analyses of variance (Group × Stress Level) were conducted on three major posttest outcome measures: general stress level, personal instrumentation, and general well-being.

The analysis indicated that high-stress and low-stress employees did not appear to be differentially affected by the program. The main effects for program versus comparison group participation were nonsignificant as were the two-way interactions between group participation and stress level.

Two analytic issues must be considered, however, before accepting these results as definitive findings. First, the stress scores on the pretest were not normally distributed across the possible range of values. Few individuals had scores greater than 20 and the preponderance of individuals scored at the low end of the scale. Therefore, although two stress groups could be identified, the discrimination was not extreme. The high-stress group in the sample was "high" only relative to the sample and was not high with respect to the absolute values of the scale. Second, the number of individuals involved in the analysis was very small, with cell sizes as small as 6 when two-way interactions were examined. Thus, the analyses were not powerful enough to detect small differences between subgroups.

The feedback research approach also included an examination of responses to open-ended questions that had been added to the pretest questionnaire. Although these questions were concerned with the types of stressful events experienced and were originally intended to aid in the refinement of future evaluation assessments, they were used in the feedback research component to further our understanding of the nature of the managements' stressful experiences. Because there had not been any attempt to assess the needs of managers (or their spouses) prior to the development of the program, it was not known if the management had a need for this program or for any type of stress/health intervention. The results of the quantitative analyses had suggested that, overall, the level of stress experienced was low and that relatively few stressful situations occurred in the work setting (refer to Table 2).

Content analyses of 83 managers' responses revealed that the *nature* of the stress, rather than the *frequency* of stressful experiences appeared to be a problem among the management population. Asked to give a

TABLE 2
PRETEST MEANS FOR EMPLOYEES AND SPOUSES ON STRESS MEASURES

	Possible[a] Range	Employees (n)	Spouses (n)
Stress Level			
General stress	8–32	13.94 (66)	13.16 (51)
[b]Work stress	3–12	5.11 (66)	—
Stress-Producing Factors			
Changes in work routine	2–8	3.13 (65)	3.44 (22)
Anxiety & frustration on the job	4–16	7.78 (64)	6.72 (25)
Organizational factors	3–12	6.16 (66)	5.00 (23)
Life Events			
Number of undesirable life events	0–33	2.45 (64)	1.71 (55)
Number of desirable life events	0–33	3.19 (64)	2.83 (55)

[a]For each of the stress measures, the higher the value, the greater the amount of the variable.
[b]The work stress variable is omitted from the spouse analyses as it did not reach the criterion level of .60 Cronbach's α.

brief account of a recent stressful experience, the majority of managers reported an experience involving the strain of having to deal with subordinates without the support of supervisors and lacking sufficient authority to make final decisions on their own. Thus, the nature of the job stress experienced by employee program participants may have been different from the type of stress for which the program was targeted; that is, the program's emphasis on personal coping strategies may not have been appropriate for the communication problems managers were confronting. Rather, the types of stressful situations that were reported implied the need for some organizational changes and interventions.

All the information obtained through these additional analyses was fed back to the program developers with recommendations for redevelopment and reformulation. The developers were given a description of the needs of the "high-stress" management population and a listing of the measurement scales that were most useful in diagnosing the level of stress and coping skills. Recommendations included:

- developing interventions tailored to the specific needs of the "high stress" group as well as to the management population in general (i.e., focusing on the job setting and employing organizational interventions to target the "middle-person" situations that provoke stress among managers); and
- developing more sensitive quantitative assessments for evaluations of future interventions that focus on the types of stressors that operate within the corporation.

Thus, although the impact analyses had yielded nonsignificant results, the feedback research approach increased the utility of the overall evaluation by providing recommendations for program redevelopment based upon objective analysis of the problem. Program administrators felt they had been provided with rich descriptive information about their management population that had led to changes in their thinking about the types of stress reduction programs to offer in the future.

STEPS TO INCORPORATING A FEEDBACK RESEARCH APPROACH WITHIN EVALUATION: ADVANTAGES AND DRAWBACKS

In order to include a research component within an evaluation, the evaluator must obtain the cooperation and commitment from the program administrators at the onset of the evaluation. Conducting an internal problem analysis requires the collection of additional data, often from more respondents than would be required in an evaluation. This extra effort calls for an increase in the budget for increased data collection and analysis efforts, and an extended time frame. Although the expenditures are less than those required for preliminary assessments, they will undoubtedly increase the costs of an evaluation.

Furthermore, the evaluator who chooses to incorporate a feedback research component within an evaluation must decide if he or she has the necessary expertise to conduct research on the identified problem. That is, if the evaluator has methodological training but lacks sufficient knowledge of the area under study, additional research consultants may be needed to guide the internal analysis. The addition of consultants will also increase the total costs of the evaluation; therefore, the evaluator must weigh the potential benefits of incorporating the feedback research component into the evaluation against the costs it will entail.

A feedback research component can be worthwhile if:

- the program is a prototype;
- the problem has received little attention by the research community or the problem has not been clearly identified;
- the program sponsor has invested a considerable amount of resources in the program and is eager to learn of its effectiveness or reasons why it may have failed to have impact; or
- the program has been designed and developed without a problem or needs assessment component.

There are situations, however, in which a feedback research approach may *not* be appropriate. Some of the situations are:

- the program is a "one-shot" attempt to ameliorate a problem;
- the costs of the evaluation would be disproportionate to the costs of the program;
- systematic efforts to assess the needs of the population and to define the problem have been conducted prior to the design of the intervention; or
- the evaluator has little or no substantive expertise in the program area.

CONCLUSION

The feedback research approach has been proposed as one way to increase the usefulness of evaluation for program development. By providing an explication of the problem and an analysis of the program population, the feedback research approach can increase the utility of the evaluation for program development and reformulation. Rather than providing only a statement of failure of program effectiveness, the evaluator can provide recommendations for new program directions based upon a systematic analysis. This approach not

only guides the future efforts of program administrators, but also ties evaluation more closely to traditional research. This relationship between traditional and applied orientations should contribute to basic research findings and help to soften the "technician" image of evaluators.

REFERENCES

ALKIN, M. C., DAILLAK, R., & WHITE, P. (1979). *Using evaluations: Does evaluation make a difference?* Beverly Hills, CA: Sage Publications.

CHEN, H. T., & ROSSI, P. H. (1980). The multi-goal, theory driven approach to evaluation: A model linking basic and applied science. *Social Forces, 59,* 106–122.

CHEN, H. T., & ROSSI, P. H. (1983). Evaluating with sense: The theory-driven approach. *Evaluation Review, 7,* 283–302.

HOCHBAUM, G. (1958). *Public participation in medical screening programs: A socio-psychological study* (Public Health Service Publication No. 572). Washington, DC: Superintendent of Public Documents.

HOLMES, T. H., & RAHE, R. H. (1967). The social readjustment rating scale. *Journal of Psychosomatic Research, 11,* 213–218.

JENKINS, C. D., ROSENMAN, R. H., & FRIEDMAN, M. (1967). Development of an objective psychological test for the determination of the coronary-prone behavior pattern in employed men. *Journal of Chronic Diseases, 20,* 371–379.

KIEV, A., & KOHN, V. (1979). *Executive stress.* New York: AMACOM.

KIMMEL, W. A. (1981, April). Putting program evaluation in perspective for state and local government. *Human Services Monograph Series* (Serial No. 18).

NATIONAL CENTER FOR HEALTH STATISTICS. (1973). The psychological section of the current health and nutrition examination survey. *Proceedings of the Public Health Conference on Records and Statistics* (DHEW Pub. No. (HRA) 74-1214). Washington, DC: Government Accounting Office, 1973.

PATTON, M. Q., GRIMES, P. S., GUTHRIE, K. M., BRENNAN, N. J., FRENCH, B. D., & BLYTH, D. A. (1977). In search of impact: An analysis of the utilization of federal health research. In C. H. Weiss (Ed.), *Using social research in public policy making.* Lexington, MA: Lexington Books.

ROSENSTOCK, I. M. (1966). Why people use health services. *Milbank Memorial Fund Quarterly, 44,* 94ff.

SCRIVEN, M. (1972). Pros and cons about goal-free evaluation. *Evaluation Comment, 3,* 1–4.

SCRIVEN, M. (1973). Goal-free evaluation. In E.R. House (Ed.), *School evaluation: The politics and process.* Berkeley, CA: McCutchan.

SECTION 4
Assessing Benefits and Costs

An essential aspect of what we have called the program evaluation orientation is the judging or valuing of the nature and effects of the programs studied. The most fully developed framework available for this purpose is valuation in monetary terms, that is, cost-effectiveness or cost-benefit analysis (Catterall, 1985). Despite their apparent relevance, cost-benefit analysis and related techniques have not been used extensively in evaluation studies (see Smith & Smith, 1985, for an informative survey of educational use and reasons for lack of use). The chapters in this section explore the applicability of cost analysis to evaluation and its shortcomings, especially with regard to the persistent difficulty of valuing the benefits of human service programs.

In the first chapter, Yates provides a useful primer on the family of procedures that make up cost-effectiveness and cost-benefit analysis. He gives a clear and succinct description of the steps involved, the various approaches to assessing costs and outcomes, the choices to be made among alternate approaches, and the meaning of such concepts as discount rate, present value, and opportunity cost. Yate's presentation is highly informative but also somewhat troubling. Cost analysis permits various approaches and procedures from which the evaluation must at each step choose and there are no firm guidelines to follow for selecting among the alternatives.

It is just this latitude of choices that is the basis for the penetrating critique of cost-benefit analysis presented by Joglekar in the second chapter in this section. Using examples from health care programs, Joglekar argues that cost-benefit analysis is so dependent on the analyst's choice of assumptions and methods that its results are subject to bias, even manipulation. When different reasonable assumption can produce diametrically opposed results, the credibility of the entire approach is undermined. At a minimum, Joglekar argues, several analyses of a cost-benefit problem must be conducted from different perspectives and assumptions before the results are used for decision making. At worst, this chapter suggests that the benefits of cost-benefit analysis for assessing human service programs do not justify its considerable costs.

An especially problematic area in any analysis of human service programs is how to value their benefits when these are frequently intangible and rarely lend themselves to quantification in monetary terms. One recent interesting approach to this problem has been the combination of cost analysis and meta-analysis, the latter contributing quantitative effect size estimates for comparing the outcomes of alternate programs (Levin, Glass, & Meister, 1984).

The third chapter in this section takes a considerably different approach to this problem. In this chapter, Shapiro constructs a framework for analyzing program benefits based on models of social justice rather than economic models. Shapiro uses a published interchange between Strike and House about the moral values implicit in evaluation practice as a springboard for launching an analysis of different criteria of social justice. This chapter makes several valuable points, all of which warrant considerably more discussion than they have received in the evaluation literature. First, Shapiro reminds us that evaluation requires the use of criteria for comparing alternate social states and that we have an obligation to make explicit the critera used in any comparison. Second, and more important, he demonstrates what it means to be explicit about these matters. Shapiro does not offer abstract philosophy about values and morals but instead focuses close attention on the single issue of how program benefits are distributed and six defensible criteria by which that distribution might be judged. Each criterion links the practical level (e.g., a distribution of pretest and posttest scores) with a distinct model of social justice (e.g., utilitarianism, equality).

Within such a framework, the evaluator can be very explicit about what program outcomes are valued, how they are recognized, and what is at stake in selecting one criterion instead of another. This explicitness does not, in itself, indicate which is the "correct" criterion to use (indeed, no procedure could do that), but it does permit an informed negotiation in which the respective positions and values can be examined and debated, not simply assumed or, worse, imposed uncritically.

Shapiro's probing analysis of the distribution of benefits challenges the evaluation profession to develop the same sort of careful analysis of other relevant dimensions of program valuation. What, in careful distinctions, might be meant by "benefit" (or utility)? Social progress? Quality of life (e.g., see Olsen, Canan, & Hennessy, 1985)? An evaluation profession worthy of the name must be explicit about such things.

REFERENCES

Catterall, J. S. (Ed.). (1985) *Economic evaluation of public programs. New Directions for Program Evaluation, 26.*

Levin, H. M., Glass, G. V., & Meister, G. R. (1984). *Cost-effectiveness of four educational interventions.* Project Report No. 84-111, Institute for Research on Educational Finance and Governance, School of Education, Stanford University, CA.

Olsen, M. E., Canan, P., & Hennessy, M. (1985). A value-based community assessment process: Integrating quality of life and social impact studies. *Sociological Methods and Research, 13*(3), 325-361.

Smith, N. L., & Smith, J. K. (1985). State-level evaluation uses of cost analysis: A national descriptive survey. In J. S. Catterall (Ed.). *Economic evaluation of public programs. New Directions for Program Evaluation, 26.*

18

Cost-Effectiveness Analysis
and Cost-Benefit Analysis
An Introduction
Brian T. Yates

Cost-effectiveness analysis and cost-benefit analysis can combine information about the costs and outcomes of one or more techniques, providers, programs, or other manipulable variables to facilitate decisions about how to provide the best service with limited resources. This article describes several ways to assess costs, monetary benefits, and effectiveness. Also outlined are alternative procedures for quantifying relationships between cost and effectiveness and between cost and benefit. Methods are described for assessing personnel, facilities, and other costs from operations, societal, and client perspectives, and for adjusting costs for temporal distortions such as inflation and present value. Use of different perspectives for assessing effectiveness, and four different ways to quantify monetary benefits also are explained. Methods of comparing costs, effectiveness, and benefits are explored and the advantages and disadvantages of each are examined. Recommendations are made for conducting and reporting cost-effectiveness and cost-benefit analyses.

To make decisions about program design and program funding, it is not always enough to know the effectiveness of alternative treatments. Today's scientist-manager-practitioner often needs reliable and valid data on the costs and benefits, as well as the effectiveness, of different variables that he or she can influence (DeMuth, Yates, & Coates, 1984). If we ignore costs, we not only do our clients a disservice but we also put funding of our and others' services in jeopardy (McGuire & Frishman, 1983). Private insurers and government agencies, which fund an increasing proportion of human services, base their funding decisions on whatever effectiveness, cost, and benefit data are available. Without objective data our legislators' and competitors' typically low impressions of the effectiveness and benefits of our services, coupled with their high estimates of the costs of our services, may be used to justify low or no funding of our work.

Reprinted with permission from *Behavioral Assessment*, vol. 7, Brian T. Yates, "Cost-Effectiveness Analysis and Cost-Benefit Analysis: An Introduction." Copyright 1985, Pergamon Press, Ltd.

Decisions about service provision can be facilitated even more when relationships between cost and effectiveness or cost and benefit are understood. Several ways of understanding how cost and effectiveness covary are subsumed under *cost-effectiveness analysis.* Quantifying cost-effectiveness relationships still may not give decision-makers all the information they need, however. Third party funders and government agencies often are more interested in a program's monetary products—the program's *benefits*—and in the relationship between these benefits and program costs. Effectiveness measures such as enhanced behavior frequencies may not be easily understood by potential funders and may be difficult to incorporate into major funding decisions. Benefit measures such as dollars saved in court costs by residential programs for delinquents are more readily grasped and may be more influential measures of service outcomes.

Just as there are many ways to measure the effectiveness of a program, so there are a variety of procedures for measuring the monetary benefits of a program. There even are several methods of comparing benefits to costs. These procedures for quantifying benefits and describing cost-benefit relationships are subsumed under *cost-benefit analysis.*

ORIGINS OF, AND DIFFERENCES BETWEEN, COST-EFFECTIVENESS ANALYSIS AND COST-BENEFIT ANALYSIS

Cost-Benefit Analysis

Cost-effectiveness analysis and cost-benefit analysis are related methods of taking into account the value of resources consumed in an endeavor as well as the value of outcomes produced by the endeavor. Cost-benefit analysis has been practiced formally or intuitively by businesspeople for millennia, when they ask whether the money produced by an exchange or manufacturing process exceeds the money required to implement the exchange or process. Cost-benefit analysis has become so much a part of decision-making that in some cases it is required by law. For example, the Harbor Act of 1902 and the Flood Control Act of 1936 allow the Army Corps of Engineers to build only those dams or other water control projects that can be shown to generate more money (i.e., more benefits) than they consume (i.e., than they cost; cf. Thompson, 1980).

As might be imagined, when funding of desired activities is made contingent on certain outcomes of an evaluation (such as positive findings for a cost-benefit analysis), those outcomes become more likely. In particular, a variety of ways of estimating benefits have been developed. Cost-benefit analysis has evolved not into a succinct set of well-defined procedures, but into many alternative procedures, which can be applied to the same data with occasionally different results. Krapfl (1974) describes, for example, how three different cost-benefit analyses of the Jobs

Corps program found benefit-to-cost ratios of 4.0 to 1, 1.5 to 1, and 0.3 to 1 (Rossi, 1972). Although the individual procedures for assessing and comparing effectiveness, benefits, and costs may be well-defined, the rules for choosing among the procedures available are only beginning to receive attention.

Cost-Effectiveness Analysis

Cost-*effectiveness* analysis was developed to allow some comparison of the costs to the outcomes of an endeavor when the outcomes are not monetary and cannot be readily converted into monetary units (Levin, 1975; Quade, 1967). As with cost-benefit analysis, informal cost-effectiveness analyses have been conducted since people first began making decisions, for instance, comparing restaurants in terms of quality versus the cost of the food served. An early application of formal cost-effectiveness analyses was the justification and comparison of weapons systems, for which the outcome label "benefits" did not seem appropriate but "bang for the buck" did. Another early application of cost-effectiveness analysis was to education programs, which generate outcomes that often are measurable but rarely are monetizable (Levin, 1975; Thomas, 1971). As with cost-benefit analysis, cost-effectiveness analysis is sometimes required by law. California law, for example, requires regular cost-effectiveness analysis of certain programs (California Welfare and Institutions Code, Sections 5656 and 5660).

Cost-Effectiveness Analysis versus Cost-Benefit Analysis: Advantages and Disadvantages

Although cost-benefit analysis continues to be applied to behavioral medicine as well as to behavioral solutions for social problems (Rufener, Rachal, & Cruze, 1977; Weinstein & Stason, 1977), cost-effectiveness analysis seems to be gaining favor as a more socially acceptable means of evaluating treatment programs that have primarily nonmonetary goals (Kaplan, 1984).

Cost-effectiveness analysis has several advantages and disadvantages, relative to cost-benefit analysis. By removing part of the analysis from the realm of money, additional objectivity may be gained by using more objective measures of the results of human services. The monetary benefits generated by human services usually have to be estimated; they are difficult to observe directly. Monetary benefits of human services typically are transformations of effectiveness data into dollars, which removes the findings used in decisions further from the original data. Also, cost-effectiveness analysis can study outcomes of human services that are not monetary and for which no monetary equivalent can be found. In cost-effectiveness analysis, too, there is not the pressure to identify and monetize benefits so they exceed the identified costs (Joglekar, 1982).

One disadvantage of cost-effectiveness analysis relative to cost-benefit analysis is that the ratio of effectiveness to costs is not as informative as the ratio of benefits to costs. (Benefit/cost ratios are a common although sometimes misleading method of quantifying cost-benefit relationships, as explained later.) Also, while the difference between benefit and cost figures quantifies in another way the relative worth or "social profit" of different programs, the difference between effectiveness and cost provides no useful information. Finally, programs that measure effectiveness in different units are difficult to compare in terms of effectiveness or cost-effectiveness. Consider how you would compare two programs when one measures its effectiveness as years of life added while the other measures its effectiveness as number of thefts prevented. In contrast, programs that measure or transform their products into monetary benefits can be compared directly in terms of both benefits and cost-benefit.

Because each type of analysis provides unique information about program outcomes, perhaps it is best to conduct cost-effectiveness analysis *and* cost-benefit analysis whenever possible. The combined analysis might be termed *cost-outcome analysis*. To this end, we describe alternatives for measuring and comparing costs and outcomes, recognizing that no one measurement or comparison procedure presently is standard.

STEPS IN COST-OUTCOME ANALYSIS

The basic steps in cost-effectiveness and cost-benefit analysis are the same, and are similar to the steps in most evaluation research:

1. Decide which program or programs, or which technique or techniques, to analyze and which to exclude.

2. When comparing different programs, techniques, or other variables, try to use an experimental or quasiexperimental design and random assignment. Clients in the different conditions should be as similar as possible (except for any client variables being investigated), and programs should have equal access to resources such as personnel, facilities, equipment, and materials.

3. Decide in advance how to assess the costs, effectiveness, and benefits of the programs. Involve clients, staff, and funders in decisions to use particular procedures. If cost, effectiveness, and benefit data are collected over several years, adjust the data for changes in value over time.

4. Assess cost, effectiveness, and benefit variables using at least two different procedures, and report the findings of all assessments. This *multiple operationism* (Kazdin, 1980) may generate a more externally valid picture of the different techniques or programs than limiting one's analysis to a single viewpoint.

5. Compare cost to effectiveness and to benefit using two or more comparison procedures (detailed later). Again report the findings from all comparisons.

For example, Siegert and Yates (1980) decided to compare the effectiveness of ways to help troubled families by teaching parents child-management skills. The same skills were to be taught to all parents, except those in a measurement control condition. Three different systems for delivering training to parents were tested. The delivery systems were designed to approximate programs that could be adopted by local human services: training parents individually in professional offices, training parents in groups in an office, or training parents individually in their own homes. Parents volunteering for child-management training were randomly assigned to one of the three training systems or to a measurement control condition. Only a cost-effectiveness, and not a cost-benefit, analysis was attempted, because the monetary benefit of child-management training seems too remote and variable for reliable or valid assessment.

ASSESSING COSTS

Some of the above steps are familiar to most behavior analysts, but the assessment of costs and benefits probably are not. In a way analogous to the assessment of effectiveness, costs can be assessed by defining *variables* that characterize different resources consumed in a treatment, and then finding values for those variables. Unlike effectiveness, a small set of cost variables can be used to measure the cost of almost any technique or program, including personnel, facilities, equipment, and materials. These variables can be defined in several ways, however. Different interest groups may have different views or *perspectives* (Hawkins, Fremouw, & Reitz, 1982; Hiebert, 1974; Rothenberg, 1975) on how cost variables should be defined and on the importance of including certain cost variables (for example, psychological costs). These different perspectives will produce conflicting cost findings in some cases. The following sections briefly discuss different perspectives for cost assessment, and then describe how the perspectives can be translated into measurement procedures for specific costs.

Alternative Perspectives for Assessing Costs

The most common method used by economists to assess the costs of services—simply summing what is charged and trusting that the free market has kept the price near the cost—may be the least accurate for human services. The notion that prices reflect costs is difficult to maintain for most psychological services, because fees are often charged on sliding scales according to clients' incomes and insurance coverage. This *willingness to pay* perspective on costs also assumes that payers are well-informed and rational decision-makers. The clients of human services often are not, and neither are third-party funders who lack accurate data on costs and outcomes. For these reasons, data on costs need to be collected with the same diligence usually reserved for collecting data on effectiveness.

Operations Perspective. The operations perspective, as it has been called (Yates, Haven, & Thoresen, 1979), defines personnel, facilities, equipment, and materials costs as the expenditures listed in accounting ledgers.

An advantage of the accounting perspective is that procedures for assessing costs already may be incorporated in the accounting procedures used in a service system. Different programs may use different accounting practices, however, and those procedures may lump together costs that cost-outcome analysts wish to separate, such as the cost of services for different clients. Furthermore, some accounting procedures hide certain costs, and this could contribute to measurement error.

The operations perspective also ignores volunteers' time, facilities for which the program does not pay, and donated equipment and materials. The operations costing perspective also assumes that individuals are paid what their time is worth, which often is not the case. In many programs, therapists are underpaid or are not paid at all. Yates et al. (1979), for example, found that staff in one residential program were paid an average $686 per month even though their services were worth $3156 per month in terms of time spent in treatment-related activities. Thus, although the operations perspective provides readily used and occasionally reliable data on some costs, the data gleaned from this perspective often are not sufficiently valid to be the sole measure of cost.

Societal Perspective. The societal perspective (Conley, Conwell, & Arrill, 1967) on costs attempts to measure more truthfully the value of all resources used in delivering a service. Resources consumed in treatment are valued from the societal perspective according to their *opportunity value* (Bowman, 1966): how much they would have been worth if they had been put to the best alternative use. From the societal perspective, costs usually are measured in whatever units best describe them. The goal is to measure the value of resources consumed by the service system. Personnel time might be measured in hours, facilities in square feet (or square feet months), and equipment or materials in dollars.

Client Perspective. The client perspective includes money the *client* pays for the service and the time the client is required to invest in it. The client cost may be considerably less than the operations cost of therapy, given the prevalence of partial to full third-party coverage of many human services. The client perspective includes cost variables not assessed by most other perspectives, though, such as income that may be forfeited while going to, attending, and returning from sessions. The *psychological* costs of treatment that are borne by the client—and often by significant others such as the client's spouse and children—also would be tabulated if there was reason to suspect that psychological costs were affected considerably by different treatment variables. The resources of client time and client tolerance for the psychological disturbances sometimes introduced by counseling seem trivial to many practitioners and researchers. Consider, however, the possibility that a client's decision to continue or terminate therapy may be largely a function of these less tangible costs.

Other perspectives may be important to consider in some cost assessments. Erroneous conclusions about the cost and cost savings of deinstitu-

TABLE 1
PERSONNEL COSTS FROM DIFFERENT PERSPECTIVES (TOTAL COST PER PROGRAM)

Cost Variable	Cost Assessment Perspective (in Dollars)		
	Operations	Societal	Client
Therapist/trainer/data collector			
Individual, office training	310	310	0
Group, office training	240	240	0
Individual, home training	320	320	0
Measurement control	256	256	0
Supervisor			
Individual, office training	0	274	0
Group, office training	0	274	0
Individual, home training	0	274	0
Measurement control	0	274	0
Therapist babysitters			
Individual, office training	0	0	0
Group, office training	0	0	0
Individual, home training	32	32	0
Measurement control	0	0	0
Client			
Individual, office training	0	0	296
Group, office training	0	0	551
Individual, home training	0	0	368
Measurement control	0	0	138

tionalization can be made, for example, if the costs that released patients can impose on local community services are ignored and only the costs to the state or federal hospital are tallied. Assessing costs from the perspective of the community, as well as of the hospital, can produce more accurate information about the costs and cost-savings of deinstitutionalization (Foreyt, Rockwood, Davis, Desvousges, & Hollingsworth, 1975).

Assessing Specific Cost Variables from Different Perspectives

Siegert and Yates (1980) decided to use the operations, societal, and client perspectives in the cost assessment portion of their research, to see whether the different perspectives would result in different findings.

Personnel. Personnel costs can be assessed from the operations perspective by tallying salaries paid. Benefits such as medical services or insurance, pension plans, and room and board should be added for operations costing of personnel unless those benefits are withheld from salary. Siegert and Yates had modest personnel costs, as shown in Table 1. This was partly because the personnel held master's rather than advanced degrees and because they were participating partially in return for supervision. The program was temporary, too, so it did not have to pay health benefits and avoided many overhead costs. The operations cost of personnel time might be more meaningful in established programs with permanent, professional staff.

From the societal perspective, the value of the *time* of each staff member and each volunteer should be assessed. One way to measure the value of volunteer time is to calculate what it would cost the program if the volunteer had to be replaced by paid staff. The standard salary (perhaps the state or union salary) for the job description filled by the volunteer would be calculated as an hourly payrate and multiplied by the number of hours worked. For example, if a lawyer volunteered as a paraprofessional therapist for 5 hours a week and paraprofessional therapists were paid $20 per hour by the state, the societal cost of the lawyer's volunteered time would be $100 per week. Daily time logs and salaries of $35/hour for PhD's, $7/hour for MA's, and $3/hour for BA's were used by Siegert and Yates to measure this societal *replacement cost* of their personnel (Table 1). Time spent by the principal investigator in supervision of therapists was included in the cost estimate, as well as costs required to make therapists available such as babysitting costs for therapists' children.

Another way to quantify the value of volunteer time is according to its opportunity value. Persons who donated time that could have been spent in other activities would have their time valued at the best payrate they could have received elsewhere. Societal personnel costs are then calculated by multiplying the time spent by a person in all treatment-related activities by an hourly version of their best pay rate. That pay rate could be calculated in a replicable manner from the average salary that a person with that level of education, training, and experience receives in that locale according to government statistics.

If, for example, the typical lawyer practicing in the area earns $100,000 annually but volunteers as a paraprofessional counselor for 5 hours a week although she could have obtained enough work to spend that time working as a lawyer, that volunteer's time is worth $100,000 / (40 hours/ week × 48 working weeks/year) = $52.08/hour. If the same lawyer works a full day and then volunteers as a therapist instead of watching the sun set, there would be no opportunity value for the lawyer's time. The arbitrariness thus possible in assessing societal costs according to this second procedure makes the former, replacement costing procedure more desirable.

The client perspective on personnel costs includes both the fraction of personnel costs paid for by the client and time spent by the client receiving treatment and getting to and from the place of treatment. Time invested by significant others, employers, associates, and referral agents also would be measured as costs from the client perspective, using weekly time logs or periodic questionnaires. Practically, of course, there is a limit to the time that can be included in a personnel cost assessment. A minimum of, say, five hours might be imposed before a person's time would be included. Siegert and Yates restricted their client personnel costs to client time (Table 1), because clients did not have to pay for the child-management training. Client time was valued at the hourly equivalent of their annual income, or, if they were a homemaker, $5 per hour (the average of salaries offered in local want-ads for housework).

Assessing the Costs of Facilities

From the operations perspective, facilities costs are the rental or mortgage payment or other fee arranged for space used in therapy. If a facility is donated, or is being paid for by some other agency as is the case with many state and federal facilities, the operations costs could be nil but the societal costs might be substantial. Societal valuing of facilities is accomplished by multiplying the number of square feet in the area used by the average cost per square foot for space of similar quality. Some effort should be made to report the quality and surroundings of the office space, because facilities can differ greatly in cost depending on location. The average cost for space can be obtained by surveying several local office building managers by phone. Societal facilities costs would include tax exemptions granted some nonprofit services and interest paid by the program or other organizations on bonds that enabled construction of service facilities (Thomas, 1971).

Just as administrators and others who do not provide actual treatment should still be included in personnel costs, so should storage rooms, reception areas, closets, and administrative offices be included in square-foot sums. For facilities costing, the client perspective would include only that fraction of facilities costs for which clients paid.

Siegert and Yates (1980) estimated social costs by surveying the average square-foot costs for comparable office space and dividing monthly square-foot costs by the number of working hours in a month to arrive at a square-foot per hour cost. This was then multiplied by the number of hours the office space was used. Siegert and Yates paid a very modest amount for the offices in which they saw individual clients, so there was a difference between the operations and societal costs for that space (Table 2). They paid a more reasonable sum for the group office. Use of client facilities—their homes—was not deemed a societal cost because there was no opportunity cost for client facilities. (Most clients would not have

TABLE 2
FACILITIES COSTS FROM DIFFERENT PERSPECTIVES (TOTAL COST PER PROGRAM)

	Cost Assessment Perspective (in Dollars)		
Cost Variable	Operations	Societal	Client
Office Space			
Individual, office training	120	356	0
Group, office training	96	96	0
Individual, home training	0	0	0
Measurement control	0	0	0

TABLE 3
EQUIPMENT AND MATERIALS COSTS FROM DIFFERENT PERSPECTIVES (TOTAL COST PER PROGRAM)

Cost Variable	Cost Assessment Perspective (in Dollars)		
	Operations	Societal	Client
Telephone and paper			
Individual, office training	0	60	0
Group, office training	0	55	0
Individual, home training	0	55	0
Measurement control	0	55	0
Transportation			
Individual, office training	0	0	0
Group, office training	0	0	0
Individual, home training	64	0	0
Measurement control	0	67	0

received money for alternative uses of the same space.) Office space used for supervision was not tallied in this cost assessment, but should have been.

Equipment, Materials, and Other Costs

Donated or borrowed equipment and materials would not be valued from the operations perspective, although the societal perspective would assess equipment at the average local rental rate and materials at normal purchase prices. Equipment and materials usually do not differ in value when assessed from the operations or societal perspectives, because these resources usually are the least likely to be donated or loaned at below market rates to human services. The client perspective on equipment, materials, and other costs can differ greatly, however, depending on the share of total cost borne by the client and any equipment or other materials that the client is expected to purchase. Some services, such as certain weight control programs, may emphasize the purchase of particular foods while others may encourage use of exercise equipment. These requirements can make a considerable difference in the cost of treatment from the clients' perspective.

As shown in Table 3, Siegert and Yates paid for brief use of a telephone in the office delivery system so that was included as an operations cost. The therapists who trained clients in their homes also were reimbursed at $.12 per mile (a reasonable and common rate at the time). Societal costs for equipment and materials included donated paper and telephone services that were used for all delivery systems to coordinate meetings and data collection. In addition, the estimated cost of transportation to homes of subjects in the measurement control condition was added to the mileage reimbursement given to the therapist-trainer for the individual in-home delivery system (Table 3).

Psychological and other costs are rarely considered when assessing costs from the operations perspective, which may be one of the reasons that some mental health professionals abhor cost-effectiveness and cost-benefit analysis. The societal and client perspectives on cost assessment can, however, encompass psychological costs—to the client, to significant others, and to third parties such as community residents whose new neighbors turn out to have been recently deinstitutionalized. Psychological costs can be measured with rating scales. The validity of ratings for measuring subjective reactions to different techniques has been demonstrated (Kazdin & Cole, 1981). Choices between pairs of alternatives (going to a therapy session or having a tooth drilled, for example) also can be converted into interval scales with conjoint measurement techniques (Green & Carmone, 1970).

Siegert and Yates did not assess psychological costs of the different delivery systems, primarily because they did not think that application of the same technique in different ways would yield different psychological costs. This probably was not correct. Different delivery systems could exact different psychological costs, such as different degrees of stigma or different amounts of subjective discomfort or "hassle," just as different techniques can. For example, the stigma experienced when a mental health professional visits one's home might have been more, or less, than the stigma experienced when one visits a professional's office. The hassles of cleaning up a home for a visit by a professional may be more, or less, than the hassles of traveling to a professional office. Only a formal assessment of these psychological costs can determine whether such differences exist.

Issues in, and Suggestions for, Cost Assessment

Full Reporting of Data Collection Procedures and Analyses. To help other researchers replicate findings and to aid decision-makers in applying published findings to their own situations, the "raw" data of number of hours worked, payrates, square feet of office space, cost per square foot, and types and costs of equipment and materials used, should be reported. Just reporting all costs lumped into a single figure not only is difficult to understand and belittles the value of cost data, but also encourages exclusion of cost variables and underreporting of the value of costs included. When it is awkward to report cost data in the main body of an article, an appendix could be used.

Even reporting specific cost figures for salaries, but excluding information on hours spent by personnel, makes costs less useful if human service salaries change in the future or if salaries differ across regions or countries. Specific procedures used in collecting cost data, such as the time sheets and collection procedure used, also should be described by investigators. Essentially, cost data collection procedures and findings should be reported in the same detail that is devoted to effectiveness data collection procedures. This should take only a few more paragraphs in the *Method* and *Results* sections, and may encourage development of a standardized set of cost assessment procedures.

Using Actual Instead of Estimated Costs. Throughout this discussion an *empirical* rather than an *estimative* approach has been used for cost assessment. The value of the *actual* resources consumed, rather than the value of the minimum resources that the investigator believes are necessary to implement the treatment or program, was tabulated. Assessing the costs of the actual therapist and administrative services provided, of the facilities actually used, and so on may sometimes result in higher cost assessments than what is deemed necessary to implement the program or techniques being examined. However, relying solely on estimates of the minimum necessary cost (such as the cost of paraprofessional therapists and storefront offices) when using other resources (such as professional therapists and hospital offices) ignores the possible contributions of those particular resources to outcomes.

Statistical Analysis of Cost Data. Cost data often are worthy of the statistical analyses that outcome data typically undergo. If the cost is exactly the same for each subject in a condition, of course, statistical analyses seem unnecessary since the variance is zero within conditions and almost any difference would be statistically (if not socially or clinically) significant. The problem often is that the researcher collects cost data from the operations perspective only by looking up what the cost "should" be according to billing standards or averages from client billing records. A more acceptable approach is to assess costs for each client separately. Then variance will usually be found within as well as between conditions, and statistical analyses can be applied to cost as well as outcome data.

Adjusting Costs for Inflation. If costs have been assessed over a year or more and are in monetary units, the data collected later may be distorted by inflation. A common method for adjusting costs for different years is to divide the cost for a year by an inflation factor available from government offices for that year and region. This way, cost data will be in the same "base year" units, that is, " . . . in 1970 dollars." If inflation has been high since the base year, though, costs adjusted to base-year units may seem ridiculously low when they are published years later. A better method is to multiply cost data from earlier years by inflation factors, so that the *last* year of cost data collection is the base year for all costs. Even if costs are collected during a single year, the year of data collection might be reported so readers can properly adjust the costs reported in comparisons of costs reported for other years for other treatments.

Adjusting Costs for Present Value. When comparing techniques or programs that require resources over several years, there is one distortion that needs to be introduced into monetary cost data: the distortion that delayed costs are less than immediate costs. Most people would agree that, in terms of their personal finances, paying $2,000 to a creditor 4 years from now is not as bad as having $2,000 due tomorrow. This valid distortion of time on costs reflects the value of being able to invest the money in other activities in the meantime (and, perhaps, some uncertainty that the payment contingency will remain in effect). The value of delayed costs at the start of a program (their *present value*) is: (cost in year *i*) / $[(1 + d)^i]$, where *d* is the *discount rate*.

The discount rate is expressed as a proportion and is similar to the interest rate. Commonly, a discount rate of .08, .10, or .12 is used (Thomas, 1971). Because there is disagreement about how to determine the discount rate, and because the discount rate chosen can make a substantial difference in total present value costs (Thomas, 1971), several rates are often used and the results of applying each rate are reported. If a single criterion is needed, the prime interest rate might be used (Foreyt et al., 1975).

Present-value costing is used primarily when comparing a program that postpones some costs against a program that requires large initial costs. For example, a program that costs $900,000 in the first year and $500,000 in each of the 4 subsequent years has a present value of $2,483,541 (using a discount rate of .10), whereas a program that costs $500,000 in each of the first 4 years and $900,000 in the fifth has a present value of $2,405,085: $78,456 less. The same sort of present value adjustment should be performed on monetary *benefits* that accrue over several years (e.g., Foreyt et al., 1975). This reduces the apparent value of the benefits, but is more accurate.

Whether to Assess and Report Research Costs. Research, including the assessment of costs, effectiveness, and benefits, adds to the costs of many treatment programs. Some might argue that research costs such as time spent collecting outcome data should not be figured into treatment costs. That position ignores, however, the potential beneficial effects that conducting research in a program can have on program outcomes. Specifying treatment goals and regularly monitoring goal attainment can improve treatment effectiveness (Kiresuk & Lund, 1978). Personal experience with keeping one's checking account balance up to date suggests that monitoring costs can reduce them as well.

Unless it can be maintained that the research conducted in a program could not affect the program in any way, at least some research costs should be included in cost data because the benefits of conducting research probably are included in the outcome data. At least the cost of basic data collection should be included, as that probably is the most positively reactive aspect of the research. These costs could be itemized separately from other costs, allowing readers to add or exclude them from total costs. The costs of research supervision probably should not be included in cost assessments because these costs might vary greatly according to the previous research training of the principal investigator and associates.

Siegert and Yates included the research costs of therapist supervision and data collection in their study, but failed to itemize it separately from other costs. The extensive costs of writing research proposals and research supervision and training by a professor were excluded from the study.

Preparing Cost Data for Combination with Outcome Data. Because outcome data typically are collected for each client but cost data usually are collected for the program as a whole (especially if the operations perspective is used), either outcome data must be aggregated across individuals or cost data must be disaggregated to the level of individuals. The latter type of analysis is preferable for research, since it allows cost and outcome data to be analyzed with traditional statistical procedures while preserving the most detailed information available about outcomes.

Finding these values is more involved than might first be thought. The total cost of treatment, computed from whatever perspective, cannot simply be divided by the number of clients to estimate the cost per client. That procedure assumes that each client required exactly the same amount of therapist time, space, equipment, materials, and administrative "overhead" time. Instead, it would be ideal to continually monitor the actual amount of personnel time, facilities, and other resources spent on a given client, just as treatment outcomes such as behavior change are often tracked from week to week.

If this is not possible, the proportion of personnel and other costs consumed by a client can be estimated by first calculating the total number of "client hours" or "patient days" of service delivered by the program to all its clients. The total personnel and other costs of the program can then be divided by the total client hours or patient days for the period of cost assessment. The resulting cost per client hour or patient day would be multiplied by the number of hours or days of service received by the client to arrive at an estimate of treatment cost for that client (Sorensen & Phipps, 1975).

In the Siegert and Yates study, the cost per client was calculated in the latter manner, using session attendance records and estimates of the time clients spent in sessions, in travel to and from sessions, and in training-related activities outside of sessions. Analyses of variance and contrasts performed on the sum of personnel, facilities, and equipment and materials costs for individual clients showed that each of the four delivery systems differed significantly from each other when assessed from each of the costing perspectives. From the operations perspective, training groups in an office was least expensive, followed by training individuals in their homes and finally by training individuals in offices. From the societal perspective, however, training individuals in their homes was less expensive than training them in groups in an office. Individual training in office remained the most expensive. From the client perspective, training in the office was least expensive, followed by training in the home and then in groups (see Siegert & Yates, 1980, for details).

Defining Costs as Expenditures versus Defining Costs as Outcomes. Costs have been previously discussed as resources consumed to make treatment possible, but costs also can be defined as the outcomes of a treatment. Generally, these *outcome costs* are better viewed as a type of benefit, to avoid confusing them with what might be called *expenditure costs.*

One treatment, say, for alcohol abuse, might generate lower relapse rates than another and hence would probably cause smaller expenditures for additional treatment and alcohol-induced accidents. These outcomes certainly are costs, but usually are viewed in terms of the relative *savings* in costs produced by one treatment versus another. Suppose treatment A was found to require posttreatment outlays totaling $2,500 on the average for clients receiving the treatment, but treatment B requires $3,000 on the average. Assuming that these mean outlays are significantly different (an important test to perform), the overall cost savings is $500. That cost savings is best termed a benefit, as detailed below, not a cost.

ASSESSING OUTCOMES: EFFECTIVENESS AND MONETARY BENEFITS

Assessing Effectiveness

Methods for assessing the *effectiveness* of treatment have been developed for some time, are well-known to readers, and need not be reviewed here (see Hersen & Bellack, 1981; Kazdin, 1980). Most effectiveness assessments compare client behavior, cognition, or affect at different times such as before, during, or after treatment. Occasionally, effectiveness is defined as the approximation of client behavior to behavior goals or to normal frequencies of the behavior.

Some of the ideas used in assessing costs can be generalized to assessing effectiveness and benefits. The previously mentioned concept of alternative perspectives can be applied to the assessment of outcomes. Clients as well as therapists, third-party funders, taxpayers, and researchers have potentially different views on which outcomes should be included in the assessment and how they should be operationalized. There do not, however, appear to be a small set of outcome variables analogous to the common cost variables of personnel, facilities, equipment, and materials. Instead, outcome variables often are specific to the treatment or program being assessed. For effectiveness assessments, one usually can choose from numerous variables. The number of variables used to describe treatment benefits, however, is more limited and may be easier to standardize.

Siegert and Yates (1980) assessed the effectiveness of child-management training provided by the three delivery systems by calculating the percent reduction in daily parent reports of negative child behaviors before versus during interventions designed to decrease those behaviors. The results of this assessment are shown in Figure 1 for each week of training. The reduction in negative target behaviors was substantial and

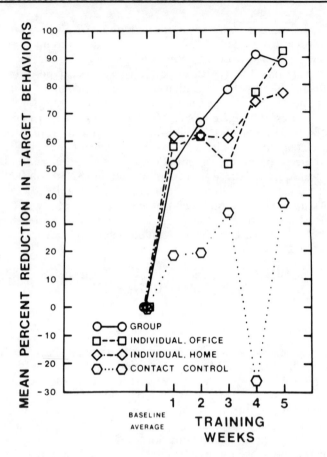

FIG. 1. Effectiveness versus sessions for three alternative systems for delivering behavioral child-management training to parents. From Siegert and Yates (1980). Copyright 1980 by Sage Publishing, Inc. Reprinted by permission.

was statistically significant for all but the measurement control condition. No differences were found in the effectiveness of the three delivery systems according to parent reports or a therapist report rating taken each session. A 4-month follow-up showed maintenance of improved child behavior. A standardized questionnaire completed by parents showed improvement for subjects on "behavioral issues," too, but on this measure control subjects improved as much as subjects who received child-management training.

Assessing Benefits: Four Major Types

A *benefit* is a measure of an outcome of treatment, just as is effectiveness, but measuring outcomes as "benefits" implies that outcomes and costs have been measured in the same units, such as dollars. The same units are used for benefits and costs so that the value to society of a technique or program can be calculated as the cost divided into, or subtracted from, benefits. Usually, benefits are expressed in monetary units because costs are. (Benefits and costs could be assessed in other units such as hours, as when comparing the time saved by time management training to the time consumed in training.)

Benefits often are assessed either as increments in income or as savings in expected expenditures. These income increments or cost savings are either measured directly from accounting records or are estimated from other data. The incremental and savings benefits of human services often are inferred from effectiveness data, because the actual savings or benefits are too difficult to measure or too delayed. For example, the money that a city saves when successfully treating 100 cases of heroin addiction is distributed over many agencies and private citizens. Given effectiveness data on the number of successful treatments for heroin addiction and estimates of the costs to agencies and citizens of heroin addiction and related crime, the monetary benefits of a heroin treatment program can be estimated (Rufener, Rachal, & Cruze, 1977).

Income actually generated for a client, company, or community would be an *actual income benefit*. An example of an actual income benefit is the income received by a client who had returned to employment as a result of treatment or of participating in a reemployment program. This benefit could be measured directly as the money earned by the client plus health benefits and tax payments contributed by the employer (Silkman, Kelley, & Wolf, 1983). An actual income benefit of employee counseling programs may be increased earnings for a corporation due to fewer absences and higher productivity (Jones & Vischi, 1979). An actual income benefit of health maintenance programs could be improved company profits produced by stress management training (Manuso, 1978).

The *actual cost-savings benefit* of preventive health programs can be measured over long periods by comparing outlays required of health insurers for persons randomly assigned to different programs. For short-term assessments, an *inferred cost-saving benefit* could be deduced from data on trends in medical service utilization and health-risk behaviors for comparison groups receiving different health maintenance programs. Rufener et al. (1977) began calculating the inferred cost-savings benefit of a heroin treatment program by measuring the many costs attributable to heroin abuse and transforming these into daily rates. Next, Rufener and associates assessed the effectiveness of the program as the decrease in days of heroin use. The inferred cost savings benefit was the reduction in heroin use days attributable to the program, times the estimated daily cost of heroin abuse to the community and legal system. Schnelle et al. (1978) have used related procedures to measure the cost-savings benefits of helicopter patrols in terms of theft reduction.

Finally, *inferred income benefits* can be deduced from data on non-monetary measures of employee productivity, such as speed and accuracy of claim processing at an insurance company. Hunter and Schmidt (1983) review how the improved job performance and productivity produced by various industrial/organizational interventions and personnel selection procedures can be translated by *utility analysis* into income produced (see also Hunter & Hunter, 1984). Another example of an inferred income benefit is increased lifetime income, estimated from changes in ratings of client functioning (see Potter, Binner, & Halpern, 1975, for details). Methods for transforming effectiveness data into benefits have become sophisticated enough that outcomes such as quality of life can be incorporated into more objective measures, such as years of life added by treatment (e.g., quality adjusted life years or QALYs; see Kaplan & Bush, 1982; Weinstein & Stason, 1977).

Because procedures for calculating these different benefits have not been agreed upon, researchers should report their benefit assessment procedures fully. Given the potential reinforcement for overestimating benefits and underestimating costs, it might be best to err slightly on the side of *under*estimating benefits and *over*estimating costs. If the cost-benefit findings are positive under these conditions, one can be confident that they really *are* positive. On the other hand, there are risks to excluding real benefits or outcomes, or including unrealistic costs, from cost-benefit calculations. In particular, an alternative program that actually is less beneficial may be chosen. A thorough cost-effectiveness or cost-benefit analysis might include a *sensitivity analysis* (Thompson, 1980) to examine how findings change if different cost or benefit variables or assessment procedures are used. If the same findings are produced under a variety of assumptions, more confidence can be placed in the finding that one program is more cost-effective or cost-beneficial.

COMBINING DATA ON COSTS AND OUTCOMES TO MAKE DECISIONS

Statistical Comparisons and Tables

There are several ways in which to analyze cost, benefit, and effectiveness data once they are obtained. If two or more programs or techniques are being compared on cost and outcome with the purpose of choosing one, the traditional method of statistically testing for significant differences in outcomes can be buttressed by additional, separate statistical tests for differences in costs. Often the findings are straightforward enough to make more sophisticated cost-outcome analyses unnecessary. Knowing that the outcomes of two techniques are not significantly different but that the costs are, for example, recommends selection of the less costly technique (Fishman, 1975; Weinrott, Jones, & Howard, 1982). This was what Siegert and Yates found: Effectiveness was high and not significantly different for all delivery systems, but cost was. Depending on whether the operations, societal, or client costing perspective was adopted for the decision, either group in-office, individual in-home, or individual in-office delivery of child-management training would be chosen, respectively. When costs are not significantly different for the alternatives but outcomes are, the choice also is simple.

When one alternative is significantly less costly but also significantly less effective, it is not clear which alternative should be selected until the maximum or minimum limits or *constraints* on costs and outcomes are considered. If cost or outcome constraints can be arrived at objectively before other data have been analyzed (such as by looking up budget limits or establishing minimum levels of acceptable treatment outcomes) constraint data still make the statistical difference method of cost-outcome analysis feasible. If the cost of one alternative exceeds the maximum tolerable cost, that alternative is infeasible and another will have to be used. If the outcome of an alternative is less than the minimum acceptable, that alternative also must be rejected.

The statistical difference approach to cost-outcome analysis can become more complicated if more than two programs or techniques are examined at once, or if multiple measures of costs and outcomes produce different findings about cost and outcome differences. In these instances, other methods of conducting cost-outcome analysis may better aid decisions.

Cost Outcome Matrices

Sometimes a cost-outcome analysis is conducted as a type of internal program review or self-initiated effort at program evaluation and improvement. The statistical difference procedure can be used within single programs to contrast the cost and outcome of using different techniques or practitioners to treat similar problems, or of treating different types of clients or problems (Fishman, 1975). Another way in which to examine the costs and outcomes of a single program is to categorize clients as receiving positive, neutral, or negative outcomes, and then to calculate the cost of treating clients in each outcome category.

Developed and promulgated by Newman and associates (Carter & Newman, 1976; Newman & Sorensen, in press), these *cost outcome matrices* typically categorize level of client functioning as reported by clinicians on rating scales. Functioning before treatment is shown in the rows of the matrix, and functioning after treatment is shown in the columns (Table 4). Behavior frequency groupings or skill levels could be used instead of these ratings, of course.

The cells of the matrix show the number of clients who began treatment at the row level and ended treatment at the column level. The average or total cost of treatment for these clients is entered in the cell, showing the viewer what it cost to produce that change in functioning (Table 4). The number of clients who experienced the neutral outcome of no substantial change in functioning is shown in the diagonal cells, running from the lower left to the upper right of the matrix. These 39 clients

TABLE 4
Cost-Outcome Matrix: Number of Clients Experiencing Changes
in Functioning and Mean Cost

Pretreatment Composite Level of Functioning	Posttreatment Composite Rating of Level of Functioning			
	Severe, major impairment	Serious impairment	Moderate impairment	Mild or no impairment
Mild or no impairment				3 $320
Moderate impairment	1 $650	1 $163	15 $549	10 $422
Serious impairment	1 $618	17 $533	19 $539	
Severe, Major impairment	4 $265	4 $339		

From Yates and Newman (1980a). Copyright 1980 by Sage Publishing, Inc. Reprinted by permission.

(52% of a total of 75) cost an average $495.28 ({[4 × $265] + [17 × $533] + [15 × $549] + [3 × $320]} / [4 + 17 + 15 + 3]) to treat. Given the importance of maintaining functioning that could deteriorate, this neutral outcome could be viewed as being somewhat positive, naturally. The positive outcome of improved functioning is shown in the cells below the diagonal: 33 or 44% of the clients moved up at least one level of functioning, at a mean cost per client of $479.30. Only 3 of the clients (4%) deteriorated in functioning, at an average cost of $477 per client.

These cost outcome matrices can alert therapists, administrators, and evaluators to problems in program operations and can lead to more detailed cost-outcome analyses. For example, upon seeing the data in Table 4, an administrator might request records for the three clients who deteriorated and for a random sample from the clients who improved. The administrator then could compare client background, diagnosis, and treatment techniques used to find probable reasons for the deterioration or improvement (Carter & Newman, 1976).

Ratios and Net Benefits

Separate significance tests for outcome and cost variables, and cost outcome matrices, can yield detailed pictures of relationships between costs and outcomes. Many researchers and policy makers are attracted to the even simpler cost/effectiveness or benefit/cost *ratio*, perhaps because it provides a single number on which to make difficult decisions about program funding. Dividing costs by effectiveness does generate an index that is easily understood and intuitively appealing for a variety of decisions (e.g., cost per pound lost, cost per nonreceded client, cost per additional year of life). Dividing benefits by costs seems even more useful, because a sort of "profit" index results (e.g., $2.13 of income generated for every dollar spent).

Although these ratios simplify findings, they discard important information, too. For example, one might think that two programs with cost-benefit ratios of 5.03 and 5.08 are similar. However, one program might cost $100,000 per client (and yield an average $500,000 benefit per client), while the other might cost $1,000 (and yield an average $5,000 benefit) per client. An alternative program might also have a superior benefit/cost ratio, but could have a benefit so low in absolute value that it did not meet minimum outcome criteria (Joglekar, 1982; Yates, 1982).

In the same way, the difference between benefits and costs (*net benefit*) provides a summary that can be valuable or misleading. Net benefit is potentially misleading because the same $50,000 net benefit could be found for a program that costs $500,000 and generates $550,000, and one that costs $5,000,000 and generates $5,050,000. To avoid misleading conclusions, researchers should report the raw cost and outcome figures as well as the cost/effectiveness or benefit/cost ratio and the net benefit. Reporting these indices also should facilitate secondary analyses such as meta-analysis. The sort of distortions noted above are less important, too, if costs and benefits are all within the same order of magnitude, for example, all between $100,000 and $900,000.

An additional problem with ratio and net difference methods of understanding cost-outcome relationships is that the *scale* of service provision is not indicated. Cost-benefit or cost-effectiveness can vary with client load in a single program. If one program is seeing just the right number of clients, it may have superior cost-effectiveness or cost-benefit indices when compared to other programs, even though the programs are otherwise the same. Assigning more (or fewer) clients to the program might well decrease cost-effectiveness or cost-benefit for the program, but cost-effectiveness and cost-benefit ratios do not suggest that possibility. Ratios also do not allow prediction of how the cost-outcome relationship would change as client load was altered within a program. A more complete model of the relationship between costs, outcomes, and other variables such as client load is needed—one that can be provided only by mathematical models or equations. These equations may be considerably more generalizable than single ratios. Graphs of cost and outcome data can make the equations almost as easily understood as a ratio or net benefits.

Mathematical Modeling of Cost-Outcome Relationships

It is tempting to assume that a simple linear equation can describe cost-outcome relationships adequately. In fact, if one assumes an intercept of zero (no cost, no outcome) and a positive straight-line function, the ratio of outcome to cost is the slope of the line and contains all the information one needs. Supposing that a linear, zero-intercept relationship always exists between costs and outcomes appears incorrect, however. Even the assumption often adopted in economics—that there will be diminishing returns in outcome for increments in costs, and thus a logarithmic cost-outcome function—does not hold when comparing different treatments.

For example, two obesity programs did not differ significantly in outcome, but did differ significantly in cost (an average $36 vs. $295 per client; Yates, 1978). For many problems and techniques, however, the cost of different techniques is directly related to effectiveness. Yates (1980a), for example, found that estimates of the effectiveness of obesity treatment techniques were directly related to estimates of the cost of those techniques, and that effectiveness seemed to rise more rapidly than costs. An exponential, rather than logarithmic, cost-outcome function was found in this study.

For other behavior problems or techniques, cost may be related *inversely* to outcome. Bandura, Blanchard, and Ritter (1969), for example, found that the *most* effective technique of three tested for snake phobia also was the *least* expensive in terms of client and therapist time. I have found, too, that as more resources were devoted to an obesity treatment through the addition of more techniques and more goals, *less* weight loss was produced. This is not just the typical logarithmic relationship of diminishing returns in outcome improvements for additional costs, but *negative* returns as more components (and costs) are added over the maximum that clients can tolerate.

There are several ways to develop mathematical models of cost-outcome relationships (Hillier & Lieberman, 1974), but perhaps the most easily applied are multiple regressions. Logarithmic and exponential transformations, plus the introduction of interaction terms, allow nonlinear cost-outcome relationships to be examined by multivariate analyses, too. Simple graphs of effectiveness or benefit against cost can yield a wealth of information about cost-outcome relationships (Fox & Kuldau, 1968), especially when contrasted to traditional graphs of outcomes against sessions. Compare, for instance, the graph of outcomes versus sessions presented earlier for Siegert and Yates's effectiveness data (Figure 1) to a graph of outcomes versus costs (Figure 2).

Siegert and Yates found that the cost-effectiveness relationships shown in Figure 2 could be characterized by simple logarithmic equations. These equations describe the diminishing returns on effectiveness increments for each additional session (and the resulting increment in costs).

This mathematical modeling of cost-outcome relationships seems to provide the most detailed analysis of the alternatives reviewed here, and seems more comprehensive than the ratio and net benefit methods. Those methods are more commonly used, however. Until there is some agreement on which forms of cost-outcome analysis are best for which situations, researchers should at least report the ratio and the more sophisticated and informative equation models for cost-outcome relationships.

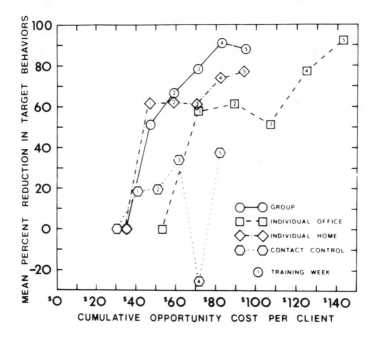

Fig. 2. Effectiveness versus costs for three alternative delivery systems. From Siegert and Yates (1980). Copyright 1980 by Sage Publishing. Inc. Reprinted by permission.

SYSTEMATIC IMPROVEMENT OF COST-EFFECTIVENESS AND COST-BENEFIT

Differences between programs on cost and outcome, equations, ratios, matrices, tables of cost and outcome statistics, and cost-outcome functions often suggest ways to improve effectiveness or reduce costs or both. Sometimes one can simply compare the costs and outcomes of different treatments and choose the most cost-effective or cost-beneficial one. The costs and outcomes of treating different problems and different client populations can be compared, too, perhaps resulting in more economically viable treatments that better meet community needs. There also are more systematic methods of improving cost-effectiveness and cost-benefit *within* a program. These methods can take into account numerous constraints on different costs and discover how to implement program components to maximize effectiveness or benefit within cost constraints. These procedures are part of *operations research* and are now being used in health and other human service systems (Hillier & Lieberman, 1974) to get the most out of current behavior change technologies.

Essentially, operations research uses the findings of cost and outcome assessments, plus information about cost constraints, to construct a multidimensional model of the problem. For example, the contribution of each component of a treatment to effectiveness might be added to an equation that modeled program outcome. Other equations would include the amount of personnel time, facilities, and so on needed by each component and the total amount of time, space, and other resources available. Operations research then uses mathematical techniques to find the best possible solution. Hillier and Lieberman (1974) show how operations research can use data on costs and outcomes to maximize outcomes, minimize the costs of achieving criterion levels of outcome, and anticipate how changes in procedures will affect demand for, use of, and the cost and outcomes of treatment. In this way, cost-outcome analyses can help human service systems do the most possible with the limited resources available. Cost-effectiveness and cost-benefit analysis thus can move from being just a summative "diagnosis" of the present performance of a human service system to an improvement-oriented "therapy" for a service system (Yates, 1982).

SUMMARY AND RECOMMENDATIONS

Before reading this article the reader undoubtedly was aware of the "political" nature of cost-outcome analyses. It is easily anticipated that saying one technique or program is more cost-effective or more cost-beneficial than another will generate more attention from more interest groups than simply declaring the superior effectiveness of a technique or program. By now the reader has recognized that cost-effectiveness and cost-benefit analyses are two related types of data analysis that are by no means standardized, leaving considerable room for variability in the analyses, which may in turn allow different findings to emerge from the same data.

This article has suggested some procedures for assessing costs, effectiveness, and benefits that are common and that show signs of becoming standard according to the cost-effectiveness and cost-benefit analysis literature in psychology, medicine, and education. More detailed accounts are provided by Levin (1983), Thompson (1980), and Yates (1980b). A review of cost-effectiveness and cost-benefit analyses performed in the behavior sciences is provided by Yates and Newman (1980a, 1980b). Recommendations about how to conduct cost-outcome analysis are made below to prompt discussion of research issues that are more acute when costs as well as outcomes are assessed.

Selecting Cost-Outcome Analysts

Ideally, a person or organization that will not benefit more from adoption of one program or another should conduct the analyses, because there is ample opportunity in current procedures for cost-outcome analysis to bias the findings toward one's favorite. The temptation is especially acute when the purpose of the analysis is to judge whether a single program is worth funding and that program happens to be one's own. If a developer, administrator, or employee of the program does conduct the analysis, measures and procedures for comparing costs to effectiveness or benefits at least should be made public well before the data are in. That may mitigate charges that costs and outcomes were defined and measured so that the findings of the analysis would be as positive as possible. Similar cautions apply to those who might benefit from finding that a program was *not* particularly cost-beneficial or cost-effective.

Selection of Cost and Outcome Variables

Because cost-effectiveness and cost-benefit analyses typically have more repercussions than outcome or cost assessments alone, it may be advantageous to incorporate the viewpoints of concerned interest groups in the analyses from the beginning. We should question the common practice of including and excluding whatever effectiveness measures we wish in our research and generally operating as autonomous agents. Because cost-outcome findings may affect funding for programs, all interested parties should be invited to suggest measures of effectiveness, benefit, and cost. The differences in conclusions that are possible when different perspectives on costs and outcomes are adopted make multiple variables obligatory.

A standard variable selection procedure might involve a series of meetings with representatives of clients, funders, therapists, and the community. Successive meetings could reduce the many variables that were first suggested to a manageable list and could operationalize those variables. The result could be a set of cost and outcome variables with more external validity, especially for decisions to be made about the program, than might be produced by the researcher alone. I have tried this procedure and it not only is less trouble than might be feared, but it is often enlightening. These meetings bring to the fore the concerns of different people involved in the analysis and usually end up eliciting their support in data collection rather than their wrath.

Reporting Findings

At this point in the development of cost-effectiveness and cost-benefit analysis for human services, it seems important to report procedures used for selecting and measuring variables and the "raw" data for each major variable. The methods used for comparing costs to outcomes, and for calculating cost-outcome indices, also should be related in detail. This will help reviewers translate the findings of individual studies that use different measurement and different comparison procedures into a coherent picture of the outcomes produced and costs required by different programs and techniques. In addition, a variety of cost-outcome analyses should be performed and reported, given the possibilities described above that different analyses will produce different findings. Performing different cost-outcome analyses will advance our knowledge, hopefully, and should promote standardization of procedures for cost-outcome analysis.

The Purpose of Cost-Outcome Analyses

Although researchers do their work for many reasons, the program-axing stigma that has been acquired by program evaluation in general and cost-outcome analyses in particular needs to be fought by efforts to make cost-outcome analysis *improve* rather than terminate programs. This constructive orientation should engender cooperation with data collection and utilization of findings, resulting in improvement rather than just assessment of the worth of human services to society.

REFERENCES

Bandura, A., Blanchard, E. B., & Ritter, B. (1969). Relative efficacy of desensitization and modeling approaches for inducing behavioral affective, and attitudinal changes. *Journal of Personality and Social Psychology*, **13**, 173–199

Bowman, M. J. (1966). The cost of human resource development. In E. A. Robinson & J. E. Vaizey (Eds.), *The economics of education.* New York: St. Martin's Press.

Carter, D. E., & Newman, F. L. (1976). *A client-oriented system of mental health service delivery and program management: A workbook and guide* (DHEW Publication No. ADM 76–307). Washington, DC: U. S. Government Printing Office.

Conley, R. W., Conwell, M., & Arrill, M. B. (1967). An approach to measuring the cost of mental illness. *American Journal of Psychiatry*, **124**, 63–70.

DeMuth, N. M., Yates, B. T., & Coates, T. (1984). Psychologists as managers: Old guilts, innovative applications, and pathways to being an effective managerial psychologist. *Professional Psychology*, **15**, 758–768.

Fishman, D. B. (1975). Development of a generic cost-effectiveness methodology for evaluating the patient services of a community mental health center. In J. Zusman & C. R. Wurster (Eds.), *Evaluation in alcohol, drug abuse, and mental health service programs.* Lexington, MA: D. C. Health.

Foreyt, J. P., Rockwood, C. E., Davis, J. C., Desvousges, W. H. & Hollingsworth, R. (1975). Benefit-cost analysis of a token economy program. *Professional Psychologist*, **6**, 26–33.

Fox, P. D., & Kuldau, J. M. (1968). Expanding the framework for mental health program evaluation. *Archives of General Psychiatry*, **19**, 538–544.

Green, P. E., & Carmone, F. J. (1970). *Multidimensional scaling and related techniques in marketing analysis.* Boston: Allyn & Bacon.

Hawkins, R. P., Fremouw, W. J., & Reitz, A. L. (1982). A model useful in designing or describing evaluations of planned interventions in mental health. In A. J. McSweeny, W. J. Fremouw, & R. P. Hawkins (Eds.), *Practical program evaluation in youth treatment.* Springfield, IL: Thomas.

Hersen, M., & Bellack, A. S. (1981). *Behavioral assessment: A practical handbook* (2nd ed.). New York: Pergamon.

Hiebert, S. (1974). Who benefits from the program? Criteria selection. In P. O. Davidson, F. W. Clark, & L. A. Hamerlynck (Eds.), *Evaluation of behavioral programs in community, residential, and school settings.* Champaign, IL: Research Press.

Hillier, F. S., & Lieberman, G. J. (1974). *Operations research* (2nd ed.). San Francisco: Holden-Day.

Hunter, J. E., & Hunter, R. F. (1984). Validity and utility of alternative predictors of job performance. *Psychological Bulletin*, **96**, 72–98.

Hunter, J. E., & Schmidt, F. L. (1983). Quantifying the effects of psychological interventions on employee job performance and work-force productivity. *American Psychologist*, **38**, 473–478.

Joglekar, P. (1982). Advocacy through convenient definition of societal objectives: Cost-benefit analyses in health care. *Evaluation and the Health Profession*, **5**, 363–379.

Jones, K. R., & Vischi, T. R. (1979). Impact of alcohol, drug abuse, and mental health treatment on medical care utilization: A review of the research literature. *Medical Care* (Supp.), **17**, 1–82.

Kaplan, R. M. (1984). The connection between clinical health promotion and health status: A critical overview. *American Psychologist*, **39**, 755–765.

Kaplan, R. M., & Bush, J. W. (1982). Health-related quality of life measurement for evaluation research and policy analysis. *Health Psychology*, **1**, 61–80.

Kazdin, A. E. (1980). *Research design in clinical psychology*. New York: Harper & Row.

Kazdin, A. E., & Cole, P. M. (1981). Attitudes and labeling biases toward behavior modification: The effects of labels, content, and jargon. *Behavior Therapy*, **12**, 56–68.

Kiresuk, T. J., & Lund, S. H. (1978). Goal attainment scaling. In C. C. Attkisson, W. A. Hargreaves, & M. J. Horowitz, (Eds.), *Evaluation of human service programs*. New York: Academic Press.

Krapfl, J. E. (1974). Accountability through cost-benefit analysis. In D. Harshbarger & R. F. Maley (Eds.), *Behavior analysis and systems analysis: An integrative approach to mental health programs*. Kalamazoo, MI: Behaviordelia.

Levin, H. M. (1975). Cost-effectiveness analysis in evaluation research. In M. Guttentag & E. L. Struening (Eds.), *Handbook of evaluation research* (Vol. 2). Beverly Hills, CA: Sage.

Levin, H. M. (1983). *Cost-effectiveness: A primer*. Beverly Hills, CA: Sage.

Manuso, J. (1978). Testimony to the President's Commission on Mental Health. Panel on Cost and Financing. *Report of the President's Commission on Mental Health: Appendix* (Vol. 2, p. 512). Washington, DC: U. S. Government Printing Office.

McGuire, T. G., & Frishman, L. K. (1983). Reimbursement policy and cost-effective mental health care. *American Psychologist*, **38**, 935–940.

Newman, F. L., & Sorensen, J. E. (in press). *Design and use of client-oriented cost outcome systems for program analysis and management*. Belmont, CA: Wadsworth.

Potter, A., Binner, P. R., & Halpern, J. (1975). Readmission discount factors in program evaluation: An output value analysis of an adult psychiatry program. *American Journal of Community Psychology*, **3**, 303–314.

Quade, E. S. (1967). Introduction and overview. In T. A. Goldman (Ed.), *Cost-effectiveness analysis: New approaches in decision-making*. New York: Praeger.

Rossi, P. H. (1972). Testing for success and failure in social action. In P. H. Rossi & W. Williams (Eds.), *Evaluating social programs*. New York: Seminar Press.

Rothenberg, J. (1975). Cost-benefit analysis: A methological exposition. In M. Guttentag & E. L. Struening (Eds.), *Handbook of evaluation research* (Vol. 2). Beverly Hills, CA: Sage.

Rufener, B. L., Rachal, J. V., & Cruze, A. M. (1977). *Management effectiveness measures for NIDA drug abuse treatment programs* (GPO Stock No. 017–024–00577–1). Washington, DC: U. S. Government Printing Office.

Schnelle, J. F., Kirchner, R. E., Macrae, J. W., McNees, M. P., Eck, R. H., Snodgrass, S., Casey, J. D., & Uselton, P. H., Jr. (1978). Police evaluation research: An experimental and cost-benefit analysis of a helicopter patrol in a high crime area. *Journal of Applied Behavior Analysis*, **11**, 11–21.

Siegert, F. A., & Yates, B. T. (1980). Cost-effectiveness of individual in-office, individual in-home, and group delivery systems for behavioral child-management. *Evaluation and the Health Professions*, **3**, 123-152.

Silkman, R., Kelley, J. M., & Wolf, W. C. (1983). An evaluation of two preemployment services: Impact on employment and earnings of disadvantaged youths. *Evaluation Review*, **7**, 467-496.

Sorensen, J. E., & Phipps, D. W. (1975). *Cost-finding and rate-setting for community mental health centers* (DHEW Publication No. ADM 76-291). Washington, DC: U. S. Government Printing Office.

Thomas, J. A. (1971). *The productive school: A systems analysis approach to educational administration.* New York: Wiley.

Thompson, M. S. (1980). *Benefit-cost analysis for program evaluation.* Beverly Hills, CA: Sage.

Weinrott, M. R., Jones, R. R., & Howard, J. R. (1982). Cost-effectiveness of Teaching Family programs for delinquents. *Evaluation Review*, **6**, 173-201.

Weinstein, M. C., & Stason, W. B. (1977). Foundations of cost-effectiveness analysis for health and medical practices. *New England Journal of Medicine*, **296**, 716-721.

Yates, B. T. (1978). Improving the cost-effectiveness of obesity programs: Reducing the cost per pound. *International Journal of Obesity*, **2**, 377-387.

Yates, B. T. (1980a). The theory and practice of cost-utility, cost-effectiveness, and cost-benefit analysis in behavioral medicine: Toward delivering more health care for less money. In J. Ferguson & C. B. Taylor (Eds.), *The comprehensive handbook of behavioral medicine* (Vol. 3). New York: SP Medical & Scientific.

Yates, B. T. (1980b). *Improving effectiveness and reducing costs in mental health.* Springfield, IL: Thomas.

Yates, B. T. (1982). Therapy for human service systems: Five basic steps for measuring and improving cost-effectiveness. In A. J. McSweeny, W. J. Fremouw, & R. P. Hawkins (Eds.), *Practical program evaluation in youth treatment.* Springfield, IL: Thomas.

Yates, B. T., Haven, W. G., & Thoresen, C. E. (1979). Cost-effectiveness analysis at Learning House: How much change for how much money? In J. S. Stumphauzer (Ed.), *Progress in behavior therapy with delinquents.* Springfield, IL: Thomas.

Yates, B. T., & Newman, F. L. (1980a). Approaches to cost-effectiveness and cost-benefit analysis of psychotherapy. In G. VandenBos (Ed.), *Psychotherapy: Practice, research, policy.* Beverly Hills, CA: Sage.

Yates, B. T., & Newman, F. L. (1980b). Findings of cost-effectiveness and cost-benefit analysis of psychotherapy. In G. VandenBos (Ed.), *Psychotherapy: Practice, research, policy.* Beverly Hills, CA: Sage.

RECEIVED: 3-19-84   FINAL ACCEPTANCE: 10-13-84

19

Cost-Benefit Studies of Health Care Programs
Choosing Methods for Desired Results
Prafulla N. Joglekar

This article summarizes the results of a critical review of several cost-benefit analyses (CBA) of health care programs. With pertinent examples, it is demonstrated that the results and conclusions of a study depend upon the assumptions and methods underlying the measurement of costs and benefits in a CBA. Given the incentives for an analyst to comply with desires of his sponsor, and given the scope of the choice available to an analyst among alternative assumptions and methods, it seems quite possible that desired results often dictate the assumptions and methods chosen. It is recommended that a policy maker should suspect an advocacy in the results and conclusions of every CBA. If CBAs are to be a true decision aid, a policy maker ought to obtain several of them, each of which assesses the costs and benefits of a given action plan using assumptions and methods substantially different from the other.

AUTHOR'S NOTE: This study was partially funded by the SmithKline Corporation. The author is indebted to Dr. Morton L. Paterson, Manager of Cost-Benefit Studies at SmithKline for his encouragement and guidance. An earlier version of this paper was presented at the ORSA/TIMS meeting in Washington, D.C., May 1980.

From Prafulla N. Joglekar, "Cost-Benefit Studies of Health Care Programs: Choosing Methods for Desired Results," *Evaluation & the Health Professions*, 1984, 7(3), 285-303. Copyright 1984 by Sage Publications, Inc.

The need for prudent use of scarce national resources in health care dictates that social costs and social benefits of alternative programs be measured carefully. It is encouraging, therefore, that recent years have seen a growing number of such cost-benefit or cost-effectiveness analyses (CBA).[1] Analysts have attempted to answer a wide variety of questions pertaining to prudent allocation of resources to and among health care programs. For example, what is the best age for administering rubella vaccination (Schoenbaum et al., 1976)? Do the benefits of BCG vaccinations in school justify their costs (Stilwell, 1976)? What are the social costs and benefits of surgeries (Bunker et al., 1977)? Do the benefits of methadone maintenance programs outweigh their costs (Hannan, 1976)? Can we evaluate the cost-effectiveness of drugs such as antidepressants (Brand et al., 1975), l-dopa (Brungger, 1972), cimetidine (Robinson Associates, 1978)? Do benefits of medical research justify their costs (Weisbrod, 1971)? What are the benefits and costs of certain government regulations (Peltzmen, 1974; Dworkin, 1980) and restrictive formularies (Hefner, 1979)?

Such efforts in conscious and explicit accounting of social costs and benefits of various programs are commendable and represent the first step towards improved societal decision making. However, detailed examination of these and other CBAs fails to prove that CBAs are worth their costs. This article argues that, although the theoretical concepts underlying CBA are rich and insightful, their practical application depends upon a series of assumptions an analyst must make. There is no universally acceptable set of assumptions. Often there are many equally reasonable sets of assumptions. The results and recommendations of an analysis could be diametrically opposite when different sets of equally reasonable assumptions are employed. Often methods and assumptions chosen by an analyst may be determined by the vested interests and/or the foregone conclusions of the analyst and his clients.

THE PROMISE OF CBA

Theoretically, one cannot but applaud the basic approach of CBA, which is to account for *all* social costs and social benefits of a proposed program. The conceptual foundations of CBA[2] are indeed very rich as can be seen from their partial enumeration below:

1. The CBA approach recognizes that resources are scarce and they deserve to be allocated prudently among alternative social programs in order to maximize their benefits for the society. On the other hand, many other types of analyses, particularly in the health care sector, often ignore the scarcity of resources. For example, a typical so-called medical evaluation of alternative therapies may concentrate only on the *health outcomes* of alternative therapies and may ignore the resource inputs required for the alternative therapies.

2. CBA has taught us to account for *indirect* as well as direct costs. For example, CBA tells us to account for the different time commitments imposed upon a patient and his family by the different therapeutic modes. Such costs are called indirect costs because the provider of care does not incur them. Economic analyses of profit-motivated providers are likely to ignore such indirect costs, although they are, in fact, costs to the society as a whole.

3. CBA also tells us to account for the externalities of a program, that is, to account for the benefits and costs of a program accruing to persons other than the doctor (or medical team/hospital), the patient, and the insurance agency. For example, when a communicable disease is prevented in a specific patient, the beneficiaries may include his neighbors and colleagues.

4. CBA methodology emphasizes that one must account for the incremental costs and benefits of a program, or its components, rather than using the current average costs to estimate the realizable benefits of a program. For example, an ulcer patient who abstained from work for ten days per year because of ulcers may not report any work loss owing to ulcers once they are healed by surgery. However, the worker may continue to abstain from

work for as many sick days as are allowed by the union contract, attributing that work loss to other real or fictitious diseases. In such a case, the incremental saving in work loss may be negligible, if any. CBA correctly tells us not to account for such hypothetical savings to that surgery.

5. CBA emphasizes that resources should be valued at their *opportunity cost*, that is, at the value of the benefits foregone by not being able to use the resources required by a program in their best possible alternative use. Thus, a surgery scheduled in an otherwise idle operating room may be valued at only the incremental cost of the surgical procedure, whereas a surgery scheduled in an overbooked surgical ward must be valued at the price another patient (or the insurance company) may be willing to pay if he or she did not have to forego surgery because this one was scheduled.

6. CBA recognizes that costs and benefits accruing in different years are not comparable unless they are *discounted to their equivalent values in a specific reference year*. Thus, avoiding $1000 in medical treatment costs five years from now may be worth saving only $621 in today's treatment costs, assuming a discount rate of 10% per year.

It is clear that CBA promises important insights for rational resource allocation and cost control in the health care sector. Furthermore, insofar as CBA requires the measurement of *all* costs and benefits of a program, it has the potential to encourage the systematic recordkeeping and tracing of the primary, secondary, and tertiary, direct and indirect, internal and external, as well as medical and nonmedical effects of a program. Of course, any analysis is based on some axioms or assumptions. CBA methodology requires that these assumptions be made explicit so that they can be critically examined and the effects of alternative assumptions can be assessed. Such an assessment is called sensitivity analysis. The potential for systematic recordkeeping, for detailed and explicit analysis, and for verification of results through sensitivity analysis accentuates the theoretical promise of CBA's value in rational decision-making.

Unfortunately, a review of available applications of the CBA methodology in the health care sector suggests that this promise actually has not been realized.

REASONS WHY THE PROMISE FAILED

There are many reasons why the promise of CBA approach is not adequately realized by available empirical studies. The most important of these reasons are detailed below:

1. Choosing among Societal Objectives. An attempt at measuring the social costs and benefits of a program assumes that societal objectives are known and defined precisely. Unless these objectives are known, one cannot determine as to what specific consequences constitute "costs" (because they are undesired), and what consequences constitute "benefits" (because they are desired). In democratic societies, societal objectives are plural, everchanging, and, often, mutually conflicting. A truly scientific analysis that recognizes the multiplicity, the dynamism, and the conflict among objectives can, at best, only *describe* the various consequences of a given program without attaching any values to these consequences. Such a description would leave it up to the policymakers to assign values to these consequences, aggregate the sum total of these values and arrive at the desired course of action. Yet, policy makers are not likely to accept such descriptions as "analyses." Policy makers often desire that the analyst should carry the process further and assist their decision making by imputing values to the various consequences, aggregating these values and providing definitive recommendations. Available CBA studies indicate that analysts are quite willing to comply with these desires of the policy maker, which is exactly where the process of choosing values, assumptions, and methods for desired conclusions may begin. Analysts who are willing so to comply, may be inclined particularly to arrive at conclusions that the policy maker (i.e., their client) may want to hear. Consciously or unconsciously, these analysts may choose among alternative societal objectives such that the chosen objectives are best fulfilled by the program the client favors. In specific cases, it is difficult to prove such a bias in the choice of societal objectives. But, certainly there is considerable scope for such a bias. In the health care sector an analyst may choose among a number of societal objectives including (a) maximization of equitable access to health care, (b) maximization of gross national produce of a nation state, (C) maximization of per capita income, (d) maximization of number of lives (or life-years) saved per dollar of health care expenditure, (e) the most beneficial allocation of a given health care budget, (f) the most beneficial allocation of the national budget, and so on. Depending upon the choice among these alternative objectives, the values attached to specific consequences of a program can be substantially different. For example, saving the life of an individual whose contribution to GNP is likely to be only marginal (i.e., below average) may be seen as a "cost" under objective (c), as a slight benefit under objective (b), as a substantial benefit under objective (d), and as an unavoidable activity in the pursuit of objective (a). Thus, if a client's health care program is aimed at saving the lives of the poor, the blacks, the women, or the elderly, the analyst could choose objectives (a) or (d) rather than (c) or (b). Perhaps this is why Riddiough (1979), whose study justifies pneumococcal vaccination for the elderly, uses objective (d); whereas, Barlow (1968), whose study questions the value of malaria eradication in underdeveloped countries, uses objective (c). Of course, one would never know if these analysts chose their objectives first and then arrived at their conclusions or vice versa. However, the existence of the potential for selective definition of societal objectives has been demonstrated by Joglekar (1982).

2. Identifying "Significant" Costs and Benefits. Although the foundation of CBA lies in the determination to account for *all* (meaning each and every) of the costs and benefits, in practice such a task is impossible considering the inevitable constraints on time and resources any study must face. Consequently, analysts must compromise and attempt to meaure only the most significant costs and benefits. Unfortunately, an analyst's judgment as to what consequences are "significant" and what are not, may be incorrect—deliberately or otherwise. For example, Steiner and Smith (1976), justify a program for administering PKU screening to each one of the 46,714 live-born babies each year in Mississippi so that an expected number of 1.76 cases of PKU could be detected and cured. Steiner and Smith (1976) can do this primarily because they ignore one significant social cost associated with such a screening program. They ignore the expected cost of the time, the money spent, the work lost, and the anxiety experienced by parents of the 46,714 babies that must be screened. In another study, Stilwell (1976) concludes that British schools' BCG vaccination program will be uneconomical by the mid-1980's, primarily because he assumes that a BCG vaccination protects only the child vaccinated. Insofar as TB is a contagious disease, the externalities associated with the BCG vaccination may be significant and ought to be accounted for. To repeat, one cannot be sure whether these analysts ignored such significant costs only out of innocence or because ignoring them made it easier to arrive at the specific conclusions. It may be noted further that in their decisions about what to measure and what not to, analysts may be tempted to include what is conveniently measurable and exclude what is not—even when what is excluded may be socially significant. For example in health care-related CBA's, pain, human suffering, and quality of life considerations are invariably excluded. Stilwell's (1976) study may have resulted in a different conclusion had he considered such nonquantifiable costs for the TB cases caused by a discontinuation of the BCG program. In a sense, this inclination to consider only what is quantifiable, also influences the analyst's choice of societal objectives mentioned earlier. Most CBAs avoid objectives such as the "maximization of equitable access to health care," because a quantitative determination of what is equitable may be difficult. Thus, CBAs focus on economic efficiency questions (which can be analyzed quantitatively with relative ease), although the history of social decisions pertaining to health care suggests that concerns of equitable access and of patients' rights in and to health care are the more dominant considerations.[3] Consequently, most of the available cost-benefit studies can be challenged on the grounds that they violate the true objectives of the society. The controversy generated by Schoenbaum's (1976) analysis of rubella vaccination policy may be a case in point. His recommendation to vaccinate all females at age 12 has been considered discriminatory because black females may be far more likely to be pregnant before being protected by this rubella vaccination policy than are white females (McBride et al., 1976).

3. Quantifying the Nonquantifiable. Another issue of concern is the analyst's tendency to force quantification on what may not be basically quantifiable. The value of a human life may not be quantifiable unless one wishes to restrict oneself to such quantifiable aspects of that life as expected years of survival, expected earnings in the future, or expected health care expenditures in the future. An individual's innovative potential or ethical and moral contributions must be downplayed, for such are not quantifiable. Thus, forcing the valuation of a human life is to account for only a *few* of the attributes of human life. No matter which attributes are chosen, such an account is partial and subject to controversy. Proponents of cost-effectiveness analysis often question analyses that put a dollar value on human lives (typically using the human capital approach).[4] Instead, they recommend the measurement of the quality-adjusted life years (QALY) as the measure of the value of that life.[5] This "quality adjustment" is typically in terms of the physical health of the human being. The fact is that a healthy year of life in poverty and slavery may not be as socially desirable as a healthy year of life in freedom and prosperity. In sum, regardless of the attributes chosen for quantification, a forced quantification of what is basically nonquantifiable will be misleading. More importantly, insofar as there are alternative methods of quantification, there is a scope for choosing suitable methods for desired conclusions. As pointed out earlier, analysts who want to justify programs for the poor, the minorities, or the elderly may use the QALY method of valuing human life; whereas, analysts who want to justify health care programs that benefit primarily white, young, adult males may insist upon the use of the human capital approach.[6]

4. Choosing the Discount Rate. Although there is a general consensus among CBA analysts that costs and benefits accruing in different years are not comparable unless they are adjusted to corresponding discounted values in a specific reference year, experts disagree on the proper numerical value of the discount rate to be used. Some argue for the social rate of time preference as the conceptual foundation for determining the appropriate discount rate. Such analysts use a rate that is lower than prevalent market rates of interest. Others espouse the social opportunity cost of capital as the conceptual basis and consequently use a higher discount. This controversy has manifested itself in the health care related CBAs in widely divergent choices of discount rates.[7] What is curious is that the chosen discount rates often seem to favor the conclusions of the studies. For example, Stilwell (1976) uses a 10% discount rate (which discounts future benefits heavily) in a study that concludes that BCG vaccinations may not be economical, whereas Brungger (1972) uses a –6% discount rate (which inflates future savings) in a study that concludes the l-dopa is a cost-beneficial treatment for Parkinson's disease insofar as it reduces future use of long-term hospitals and nursing homes. Of course, outsiders cannot tell whether an analyst chose a discount rate first and simply spelled out the consequent results, but clearly there is considerable scope for the analyst first to choose the results he or she desires and then the discount rate suitable for those results.

5. *Using Available Information Selectively.* In carrying out a cost-benefit analysis, information is required on a variety of pertinent factors, such as the current incidence rate, mortality rate, hospitalization rate, and medical care costs of a disease. Data on such factors are available through numerous sources. The methods employed by different data collection agencies are seldom consistent with each other. Consequently, estimates based on different sources vary widely, and an analyst can choose the source and the data he or she would use. Again, this situation presents an opportunity for the analyst to justify his or her desired conclusions by using sources and data which are most suitable for such a justification. For example, Robinson Associates (1978) projected substantial economic savings resulting from the intro-

duction of cimetidine for the treatment of duodenal ulcers. However, as Fineberg and Pearlman (1979) have pointed out, at the time Robinson Associates conducted their study, two independent estimates of the national costs of ulcer disease (in the absence of cimetidine) were available, the lower one prepared by the National Commission on Digestive Diseases (NCDD) and the higher one prepared by Stanford Research Institute (SRI). Robinson Associates based their study on the SRI estimate. Although the relative soundness of methods underlying the two studies may have justified the choice in this specific case, the fact is a higher estimate of costs without cimetidine enables one to attribute greater savings to cimetidine. Again, the purpose here is not to indict Robinson Associates. The purpose is to demonstrate the existence of the scope for CBA analysts to use available information, data, or estimates selectively.[8]

6. Interpreting Data and Analysis Conveniently. Perhaps the most fertile method of supporting desired conclusions is to interpret data and analysis conveniently. The literature on health care related CBAs is abundant with examples of such convenient interpretations, including:

(a) In his often quoted study of the costs and benefits of regulation of pharmaceutical innovation, Peltzman (1974) considers two distinct relationships between the prices of new drugs in a particular therapeutic category and the ratio of the number of new drug prescriptions to the number of all prescriptions in that category. In his equation E2, he considers the latter as a dependent variable and comes up with an R^2 value (i.e., the coefficient of correlation, which expresses the percent of variation explained by the assumed dependence) of 0.2885. In his equation E3, Peltzman (1974) entertains the hypothesis that the prices of new drugs are dependent on the quantity marketed. E3 results in an R^2 value of 0.8360. Given the R^2 values of the two dependencies hypothesized, a statistician would accept E3 as the "more explanatory" relationship. Yet, Peltzman (1974: 98) argues that "since E3 contains the implausible implicit assumption that sellers of new drugs predetermine output and then find a price which clears the

market of this output: E2 is probably closer to the truth than E3."
The truth is that the relationship implied by E3 may not only be
plausible but may be very realistic in the pharmaceutical context.
For any new drug, the number of prospective users (probably a
percentage of total number suffering from an illness) may, indeed,
be predetermined—not necessarily by the seller of the drug but by
the circumstances (i.e., the average incidence of the disease, the
availability and effectiveness of alternative drugs—so that the
only controllable variable for the producer of the new drug may
be its price. Nevertheless, one would not mind it very much if
Peltzman (1974) had instead used his equation E2 as the explanatory
relationship, for R^2 values do not *prove* causalities, they only
express a degree of association between two variables, and
causality is a matter of one's belief. However, Peltzman (1974)
transgresses fundamental principles of the theory of statistics
when he attempts to construct a new equation (E4) that takes an
average of the coefficients determined by E2 and E3. It can be
shown that the use of E4 biases the results *in favor* of Peltzman's
(1974) conclusions, contrary to his claim that he has deliberately
biased them against his conclusions.

(b) Bickley et al. (1978), in a paper aimed at seeking the addition of
the drug Keflex to Medi-Cal formulary, use an imaginative
approach to claim that Keflex would provide a net saving to
Medi-Cal. Their data show that the average episode costs using
alternative anti-infective therapies are smaller than the episode
costs using Keflex in almost every disease-code category. However, Bickley et al. (1978) argue that such a comparison (of
average episode costs) would obscure the key therapeutic and
economic basis for Keflex use: namely, that Keflex therapy may
reduce episode costs for *some* patients in a specified diagnosis
code. Consequently, Bickley et al. (1978) look at the distribution
of episode costs under alternative anti-infective therapy and
assume that all matched cases of episodes that involved a cost
higher than the episode cost with Keflex could have saved these
extra costs by using Keflex. Bickley et al. (1978) simply ignore the
fact that, at present, physicians have no basis to identify specific
patients whose episode costs with Keflex will be smaller. Consequently, once on the formulary, Keflex would be prescribed to
any "average patient". It follows that average cost comparison is
the only relevant comparison.

(c) In evaluating a multiemployer alcoholism treatment program, Schramm (1977) finds that the costs of treating a referred alcoholic in the first year are $2462, but the average savings from reduced absenteeism during the first year (calculated as the employee's hourly wage rate times the reduction in hours absent) are only $586.42. Although he points out that the second and third-year treatment costs will be almost one half of those for the first year, the data presented suggest that the program may not be cost-efficient even in the second or the third year. Yet, in his conclusion, Schramm claims that the program is cost-effective.

Although these types of convenient interpretations may be detected by a careful analyst, casual readers, and policy makers may be misled easily by them. It is this potential of CBA studies to mislead policy makers that makes one wonder whether CBA studies are worth their costs.

SOME POSITIVE TRENDS . . .
WITH THEIR OWN LIMITATIONS

A number of analysts seem to have recognized the arbitrariness of the chosen objectives, assumptions, and methods in a CBA. Consequently, they have attempted to overcome the limitations of CBA through a series of steps. Unfortunately, these steps have their own limitations. For example:

1. An increasing number of analysts seem to warn their readers of the potential indecisiveness of their conclusions. For examples, see Brungger (1972), Bunker (1977), Haunalter (1977), Conley (1975), Robinson Associates (1978), Weinstein and Stason (1977), Weisbrod et al. (1978), among others. Unfortunately, these warnings are rarely repeated in the abstracts of the CBAs and hardly imprinted upon the policy makers.[9] As Fein (1977) points out, numbers have the danger of implying false precision. Although analysts are more careful about the use of their numbers and often point out the limitations of certain assumptions upon which their numbers are based, outsiders may

impute greater certainty and authority to these numbers. There is
a danger that a study's conclusions will be remembered, but the
fact that they are derived from a narrow perspective (e.g., the
neglect of consideration of equity and distribution) will be
forgotten.

2. An increasing number of analysts are also including sensitivity
analysis (that is, a presentation of the effects of alternative
assumptions upon the results of a study) in their reports. For
examples, see Geiser and Menz (1976), Hannan (1976), NEI
(1977), Riddiough (1979), Rufener et al. (1977), Stason and
Weinstein (1977), Weisbrod (1978), among others. Unfortunately,
this sensitivity analysis is invariably carried out on assumptions
(about discount rates, incidence rates, drug penetration rates,
etc.) that are of lesser importance than assumptions about the
pertinent societal objectives, such as the choice between the
human capital approach and the QALY method of valuing a life.
Furthermore, sensitivity analysis cannot really be extended to
anything more than a few parameters. This difficulty can be
appreciated from the following quotation from Sassone and
Schaffer (1978):

For concreteness, let us suppose that the calculations for each of
two alternative projects involve 10 parameters, each a candidate
for sensitivity analysis. A selective sensitivity analysis on the 10
parameters would produce 20 NPVs (Net Present Values) for each
project, in addition to the initial 'best' estimate. The analyst must
present to the decision maker a total of 42 NPVs when comparing
two alternative projects. Such a large number of figures may not
aid the decision maker at all. In fact, the presentation of all NPV
estimates might even violate the analyst's charge to present the
decision maker with results in a format convenient for use (1978:
142).

3. This reviewer has come across at least one CBA that incorporates
the concept that a purely economic view does not fully reveal the
pros and cons of a therapy. Brand et al. (1972) present a
multidimensional study (including a medical analysis and a social
analysis, in addition to the economic analysis) of the benefits and
costs of antidepressants in Switzerland. In principle, the multidimensional approach is very commendable. However, in this
particular study, the use of the multidimensional approach has

left the economic analysis rather incomplete, if not biased. Some of the disadvantages of the antidepressant therapy mentioned in the medical and social analyses could have been quantified easily in economic terms (with about as much accuracy as that of the advantages and disadvantages that are quantified) but were not. In view of that omission, one wonders whether Brand's study may also represent one case of choosing suitable methods for desired conclusions.

4.   Lastly, there is a growing number of critiques of empirical CBAs. For examples, see Conley (1975), Churchman (1971), Fein (1977), Feinberg and Pearlman (1979), Gross (1976), Hatry (1970), Hoos (1972), Joglekar (1979), Jonsson (1976), Levine (1975), Self (1975), among others.[10] Although one of the basic principles of CBA methodology is to make the study's assumptions explicit and open for criticism, it is only human on the part of proponents of CBA to be alienated by such critiques. Consequently, these critiques have received a cold shoulder from those whose admittedly courageous and perhaps well-intentioned works have been criticized. Instead of adding a value, available critiques seem to have generated only conflicting emotions among analysts. Clearly, there is an urgent need for an attitudinal change among analysts as well as their critics.

In short, although there are few positive trends in the practice of CBA, at present, these trends cannot realize their full potential because of several limitations mentioned above.

CONCLUSION

The need for prudent use of scarce national resources in health care dictates that social costs and social benefits of alternative programs be measured carefully. The literature on cost-benefit methodology provides a rich conceptual base for the conduct of such studies. Unfortunately, in practice, analysts have considerable leverage for choosing objectives, assumptions, data, analytical methods, and interpretations that would yield desired conclusions. Given the current state of the art and the actual practice,

CBA's value in rational allocation of societal resources seems dubious.

In all fairness to the CBA methodology, however, it must be recognized that if the value of CBA is dubious, so is the value of the profit and loss (P & L) statement of a company for an outsider. Time and again, analysts have pointed out the scope available to the comptroller of a company in choosing depreciation and inventory valuation methods (among other more subtle methods) so as to dramatically alter a company's profitability picture. The validity of such indices as the gross national product (GNP) in measuring national productivity or the consumer price index (CPI) in measuring inflation has also been frequently questioned. Yet, P & L statements or CPIs have proved to be valuable information sources in a majority of circumstances. The reason is, there is a degree of standardization and year-to-year consistency in the P & L statements or CPIs. More significantly, the preparation and use of such statements and indices have reached a level of maturity. It is hoped that CBA will also reach a level of maturity in the coming decade or two. This process of maturity would necessitate, among other things:

(a) some explicit or implicit agreement among policymakers and analysts on the appropriate societal objectives,
(b) some standardization in the use of alternative methods of valuing human life,
(c) standardization in the range of discount rates to be used,
(d) availability of more complete and consistent data,
(e) simultaneous conduct of several CBAs using alternative objectives, alternative assumptions and alternative methods,
(f) a recognition of the value of independent critiques of CBAs,
(g) an attitude of tolerance towards the critics,
(h) an education of the policymakers in the value and the limitations of CBAs,
and, above all,
(i) a code of ethics to guide the choice of societal objectives, data, assumptions, methods, and interpretations.

In the meantime, every available CBA ought to be approached with care and caution to detect any elements of the types of biases suggested by this article. At present, CBAs are more likely to choose suitable methods to rationalize their desired conclusions than they are to be impartial aids for policy decisions.

NOTES

1. Available literature distinguishes between two basic types of studies. One type, called the cost-effectiveness (CE) study attempts to measure health consequences (e.g., morbidity, mortality) of a program in a stardardized but nonmonetary unit such as quality-adjusted-life years (QALY), but other consequences are measured in dollar terms. In CE studies, the objective is to minimize the cost per QALY. The other type, called the cost-benefit (CB) study attempts to measure all (health and nonhealth) consequences of a program in dollar terms. It aims at maximizing net benefits of a program, and at times net benefits per dollar of investment. In this article, both of these types are included in the general term cost-benefit analysis (CBA).

2. For a better understanding of the foundations of CBA, see Bunker et al. (1977), Churchman (1971), Drummond (1978), Gross (1976), Hatry (1970), Jonsson (1976), Levine (1975), Quade (1975), Rothenberg (1975), Sasson and Schaffer (1978).

3. For an elaboration of this point, see Churchman (1971), Drummond (1978), Fein (1977), Fried (1975), Hoos (1972), Self (1975).

4. For discussions of alternative approaches to valuing human lives in dollar terms, see Card and Mooney (1977), Gross (1976), Jonsson (1976), Mishan (1971), Mushkin (1962), Rothenberg (1975). The human capital approach uses lifetime earnings of an individual as the the basis for valuing his or her life. Other approaches include a measure of the willingness to pay to avoid a death on the part of the individual or the society (imputed by using expenditures per life saved resulting from past decisions). Card and Mooney (1977) discuss the limitations and controversies surrounding several approaches. Their discussion indicates that the estimated value of a life using one method may be as much as a thousandfold different than the estimated value using another method.

5. On the surface of it, the QALY method seems to circumvent the equity questions surrounding the human capital approach, which imputes considerably smaller dollar value to the life of a black or a woman compared to a white male. But, the QALY method is not really free of value judgments and questions of equity as some of its proponents have implied. For example, the QALY method places a substantially higher value on the life of a child than on the life of a sixty-year-old person. It also values the life of a female higher than the life of a male of the same age. In any case, the use of alternative quality adjustment methods and/ or alternative discount rates can make one estimated QALY value of a life severalfold different than another estimated QALY value of the same life.

6. For example, a rough computation (using simple but reasonable assumptions) indicates that a user of the human capital approach would rather save one 20-year-old man than eight 65-year-old men, but a user of the QALY method would rather save two 65-year-old men than one 20-year-old man.

7. For a better understanding of the discount rate controversy, see Baumol (1968).

8. Boden (1979) has made a similar point in the context of CBAs in pollution control.

9. In fact, these warnings rarely are resounded even by the technical reviewers of these reports. For examples, see the review by Bootman et al. (1979), Jonsson (1976), Levine (1975), Rothenberg (1975), Sasson and Schaffer (1978).

10. Not many of these critiques treat a large number of studies in adequate depth. Except for Joglekar (1979), they do a marginal job by either being too specific to a few studies (e.g., Fineberg and Pearlman, 1979) or being too general (e.g., Hoos, 1972). Joglekar (1979) presents detailed reviews of approximately twenty CBAs along with an integrative structure for the review.

REFERENCES

BARLOW, R. (1968) The Economic Effects of Malaria Eradication. Research Series 5. Bureau of Public Health Economics. Ann Arbor: University of Michigan.

BAUMOL, W. J. (1968) "On the social rate of discount." Amer. Economic Rev. 58, 4. (September): 788-802.

BICKLEY, J. H., D. C. CAVANDER, and J. C. MADDOX (1978) Estimating Potential and Realizable Cost Savings from Medi-cal Formularly Additions: A Pilot Study of Keflex Use in Eight Diagnosis Codes. Eli Lilly & Company (July). (unpublished)

BODEN, L. I. (1979) "Cost-benefit analysis: caveat emptor." Amer. J. of Public Health 69, 12: 1210-1211.

BRAND, M., A. MENZL, M. ESCHER, and B. HORISBERGER (1975) From Electroshock Therapy to Antidepressants: A Cost-Benefit Study. Pharma Information. Basle, Switzerland.

BRUNGGER, H. (1972) "Health in cost-benefit analyses: the case of the new drug l-dopa." Schwiz Zeitechur Fur Volkswirtshaft and Statisik: 347-375.

BUNKER, J. P., B. BARNES, and F. MOSTELLER (1977) Costs, Risks, and Benefits of Surgery. New York: Oxford Univ. Press.

CARD, W. J. and G. H. MOONEY (1977) "What is the monetary value of human life." British Medical J. (December): 1627-1629.

CHURCHMAN, C. (1971) "On the facility, felicity and morality of measuring social change." Accounting Rev. (January): 30-35.

CONLEY, R. W. (1975) "Issues in benefit-cost analysis of the vocational rehabilitation program." Amer. Rehabilitation (November/December): 19-24.

COOPER, B. S. and D. P. RICE (1976) "The economic cost of illness revisited." Social Security Bull. 31, 2 (February).

CUSANO, P. P., J. MAYO, and R. A. O'CONNEL (1977) "The medical economics of lithium treatment for manic depressives." Hospital and Community Psychiatry 28, 3 (March): 169-173.

DRUMMOND, M. F. (1978) "Evaluation and the National Health Service." In A. J. Culyer and K. G. Wright (ed.) Economic Aspects of Health Services. London: Martin Robertson.

DWORKIN, F. (1980) "On estimating the economic impact of regulations: a case study on trade secrets disclosure." Managerial and Decision Economics 1, 4 (December): 197-200.

FEIN, R. (1977) "But, on the other hand: high blood pressure, economics and equity." New England J. of Medicine 296, 13 (March): 751-753.

FINEBERG, V. H. and L. A. PEARLMAN (1979) "Benefit and cost analysis of medical interventions: the case of cimentidine and peptic ulcer disease." Harvard School of Public Health. (unpublished)

FRIED, C. (1975) "Rights and health care—beyond equity and efficiency." New England J. of Medicine 293, 5 (July): 241-245.

GEISER, E. G. and F. C. MENZ (1976) "The effectiveness of public dental care programs." Medical Care XIV, e: 189-198.

GROSS, A. M. (1976) Is Cost-Benefit Analysis Beneficial? Is Cost-Effectiveness Analysis Effective? F. Heller School for Advanced Studies in Social Welfare. Waltham, MA: Brandis University National Technical Information Service and U. S. Department of Commerce.

HANNAN, T. H. (1976) "The benefits and costs of methadone maintenance." Public Policy 24, 2 (Spring).

HATRY, H. P. (1970) "Measuring the effectiveness of nondefense public programs." Operational Research Q. (October): 772-784.

HAUNALTER, G. V. and V. V. CHANDLER (1977) Cost of Ulcer Disease in the United States. Menlo Park, CA: Stanford Research Institute.

HEFNER, D. L. (1979) A Study to Determine the Cost-effectiveness of a Restrictive Formulary: The Louisianna Experience. Washington, D.C.: National Pharmaceutical Council.

HOOS, I. R. (1972) "Systems Analysis in Public Policy: A Critique." Los Angeles: Univ. of California Press.

JOGLEKAR, P. N. (1982) "Advocacy through convenient definition of societal objectives: the case of cost-benefit analysis in health care." Evaluation & the Health Professions 5: 363-379.

———(1979) "Cost-Benefits of Health Care Programs: A Review of Methodologies Used." Presented at Operations Research Society of America, National Conference.

JONSSON, B. (1976) Cost-Benefit Analysis in Public Health and Medical Care. Lund, Sweden: Printlab.

LEVINE, H. M. (1975) "Cost-effectiveness analysis in evaluation research," pp. 89-112 in M. Gettentag and E. L. Struening (ed.) Handbook of Evaluation Research. Volume II. Beverly Hills, CA: Sage Publications.

MCBRIDE, A. D., J. L. BOOZER, and G. J. MERTZ (1976) "Rubella vaccination policies." New England J. of Medicine 294, 20: 1126.

MISHAN, E. J. (1971) "Evaluation of life and limb: a theoretical approach." J. of Political Economy 79, 4.

MUSHKIN, S. J. (1962) "Health as an investment." J. of Political Economy 70.

Netherlands Economic Institute (1977) Present Cost of Peptic Ulceration to Dutch Economy and Possible Impact of Cimetidine on This Cost. Rotterdam.

PELTZMAN, S. (1974) Regulation of Pharmaceutical Innovation: The 1962 Amendments. American Enterprise Institute for Public Policy Research. Washington, DC.

QUADE, E. S. (1975) Analysis for Public Decisions. New York: Elsevier North-Holland.

RIDDIOUGH, M. (1979) "Cost-Effectiveness Analysis of Vaccination." Office of Technology Assessment Report 4.

Robinson Associates Inc. (1978) The Impact of Cimetidine on the National Cost of Duodenal Ulcers. Bryn Mawr, PA.

ROTHENBERG, J. (1975) "Cost-benefit analysis: a methodological exposition." In M. Gettentag and E. L. Struening (ed.) Handbook of Evaluation Research. Beverly Hills, CA: Sage Publications.

RUFENER, B. L., V. J. RACHAL, and A. M. CRUZE (1977) Management Effectiveness Measure for NIDA Drug Abuse Treatment Programs. Volumes I and II. National Institute on Drug Abuse. Washington, DC: Government Printing Office.

SASSONE, P. G. and W. A. SCHAFFER (1978) Cost-Benefit Analysis—A Handbook. New York: Academic Press.

SCHOENBAUM, S. C., J. N. HYDE, Jr., L. BARTODHESKY, and K. CRAMPTON (1976) "Benefit-cost analysis of rubella vaccination policy." New England J. of Medicine 294, 6 (February): 306-310.

SCHRAMM, C. J. (1977) "Measuring the return on program costs: evaluation of a multi-employer alcoholism treatment program." Amer. J. of Public Health 67, 1. (January): 50-51.

SELF, P. (1975) Econocrats and the Policy Process: The Politics and Philosophy of Cost-Benefit Analysis. London: Macmillan.

STASON, W. B. and M. C. WEINSTEIN (1977) "Allocation of resources to manage hypertension." New England J. of Medicine 296, 13: 732-739.

STEINER, K. C. and H. A. SMITH (1976) "Application of cost-benefit analysis to a PKU screening program." Inquiry X, 4: 34-40.

STILWELL, J. A. (1976) "Benefits and costs to school's BCG vaccination programs." British Medical J.: 1002-1004.

WEINSTEIN, M. C. and W. B. STASON (1977) "Foundations of cost-effectiveness analysis for health and medical practices." New England J. of Medicine 296, 13: 716-721.

WEISBROD, B. A. (1971) "Costs and benefits of medical research: a case study of poliomyelitis." J. of Political Economy 79, 3. (May-June): 527-544.

WEISBROD, B. A., M. A. TEST, and L. T. STEIN (1978) An alternative to mental hospital treatment: III. economic benefit-cost analysis. (unpublished)

20

Social Justice and Educational Evaluation
Normative Implications of Alternative Critera for Program Assessment

Jonathan Z. Shapiro

In an interchange carried out in recent issues of the journal *Educational Theory,* Ernest R. House[1] and Kenneth A. Strike[2] debate the extent to which educational evaluation practice is, and ought to be, guided by principles of distributive justice. Strike's initial response[3] is to an earlier article by House[4] in which it is asserted that the structure of educational evaluation is predicated upon utilitarian notions of social justice. House argues that the hidden value message underlying the "classical" approach to education, student-gain-by-testing, promotes a utilitarian orientation toward the assessment of educational programs.[5]

Utilitarianism, as defined by Bentham, has as its goal the maximization of the "greatest happiness principle,"[6] often expressed as the greatest good for the greatest number. To aggregate the good, utilitarianism assumes that there exists an interpersonal comparability index (utility) such that quantitative calculations can be executed. Maximization of the aggregate utility function is performed by the "impartial spectator." Thus the rights, needs, and conditions of individuals are necessarily ignored, leading Rawls to observe that "utilitarianism does not take seriously the distinction between persons."[7] House suggests that most of the components of the evaluation process — for example, standardized tests, net gain scores, and other quantitative data — and modes of research such as needs assessment, social policy analysis, and management analysis reflect utilitarian values.

House proposes that this utilitarian orientation and consequent evaluation practice should be replaced by evaluation models predicated upon Rawls's theory of justice as fairness.[8] Rawls offers justice as fairness as a more rational model of social justice than that proposed by utilitarians. He bases his system on two principles.[9] They are:

First Principle:
Each person is to have an equal right to the most extensive system of basic liberties compatible with a similar system of liberty for all.

Second Principle:
Social and economic inequalities are to be arranged so that they are both:

---

1. E. R. House, "The Role of Theories of Justice in Evaluation — Justice on Strike," *Educational Theory* 30, no. 1 (1980): 67-72.
2. K. A. Strike, "The Role of Theories of Justice in Evaluation: Why a House Is Not a Home," *Educational Theory* 29, no. 1 (1979): 1-9; and "Justice in Evaluation: Homecoming Rejoinder to House," *Educational Theory* 30, no. 1 (1980): 73-76.
3. Strike, "The Role of Theories of Justice."
4. E. R. House, "Justice in Evaluation," in *Evaluation Studies Review Annual*, vol. 1, ed. G. V. Glass (Beverly Hills, Calif.: Sage, 1976).
5. Ibid., 76.
6. J. Bentham, *An Introduction to the Principles of Morals and Legislation* (New York: Hafner, 1948), 1.
7. House, "Justice in Evaluation . . . Justice on Strike," 79.
8. J. A. Rawls, *A Theory of Justice* (Cambridge, Mass.: Belknap, 1971).
9. House, "Justice in Evaluation," 84.

From Jonathan Z. Shapiro, "Social Justice and Educational Evaluation: Normative Implications of Alternative Criteria for Program Assessment," *Educational Theory*, 1984, 34(2), 137-149. Copyright 1984, American Educational Research Association, Washington, DC.

(a) to the benefit of the least advantaged, consistent with the just savings principle, and
(b) attached to offices and positions open to all under conditions of fair equality of opportunity.

Rawls justifies these principles, and his model of social justice, by arguing that rational individuals would be led to accept them if called upon to formulate basic norms of social life under the condition that none knew his relative standing in society when the norms are created.[10] The justification is based on the analogy of the creation of social norms to an n-person game under risk and to the conditions under which the individual minimax regret strategy would dominate all other individual approaches.[11] The minimax strategy is based on the notion that when rational individuals cannot be sure of the true state of nature such that the consequences of choice are risky, they will adopt behaviors that minimize possible negative consequences. In Rawls's model, if individuals are worst off, then change will benefit them. If they are not worst off, then they already are located at a social position which is at least somewhat advantaged relative to the individuals below. Thus the principles allow individuals to avoid the most negative situation where they may be worst off in society and would not benefit from social change.

House contends that the two principles can serve as the basis for educational evaluation practice and that such an enterprise would be clearly superior to utilitarian evaluation.[12] Elsewhere he suggests that this superiority is due to the fact that Rawls's original-ignorance position yields objective rather than subjective ethical development.[13] House concludes that in conducting ethically superior evaluation, researchers would not infringe upon individual liberties, would be pluralistic in orientation, and would primarily attend to the needs of the most disadvantaged members of society.[14]

Strike finds House's assertion that standard evaluation practice is based on utilitarian principles to be mistaken on two counts.[15] He argues that the reliance on published achievement tests, the assessment of unitary program criteria, and the analysis of group means is not necessarily standard evaluation practice and offers Coleman's study on equality of educational opportunity[16] and Cook's evaluation of Sesame Street[17] as counterexamples. More importantly, Strike argues that even if House's description of evaluation practice does constitute a standard evaluation model, there are no grounds for claiming that such practice stems from utilitarian notions of justice. He proposes that "evaluation practices can not be organized according to the principles of justice they presuppose. Evaluation practices are not per se utilitarian or 'Rawlsian.' I do not, however, conclude that philosophy is irrelevant to evaluation practice. I hold that its relevance is in the sharpening of the sensitivity and intuitions of evaluators to justice, not its ability to justify method."[18]

The problem is that utilitarianism and Rawlsian justice as fairness represent alternative normative positions concerning the structure of society and the complex interrelationship among social institutions, social policy, and individual circumstances in order to achieve a desired social state. To posit that specific characteristics of

---

10. C. W. Anderson, "The Place of Principles in Policy Analysis," *American Political Science Review* 73 (1979): 711-23.

11. See, for example, A. Rapoport, *Two Person Game Theory* (Ann Arbor, Mich.: University of Michigan Press, 1973); and S. J. Brams, *Game Theory and Politics* (New York: The Free Press, 1975).

12. House, "Justice in Evaluation," 98.

13. E. R. House, "Assumptions Underlying Evaluation Models," *Educational Researcher* 7, no. 3 (1978): 12.

14. House, "Justice in Evaluation."

15. Strike, "The Role of Theories of Justice."

16. J. S. Coleman et al., *Equality of Educational Opportunity* (Washington, D.C.: Government Printing Office, 1966).

17. T. D. Cook et al., *Sesame Street Revisited* (New York: Russell Sage Foundation, 1975).

18. Strike, "The Role of Theories of Justice," 1.

evaluation practice reveal an underlying, necessarily complex, conceptual world view is too simplistic and facile to be valid. If principles of social justice truly determined evaluation practice, the enterprise would consist of a more global approach than the narrow question of how programs are to be examined. An authentic utilitarian or Rawlsian evaluation would require evaluators to assess a program in terms of its impact upon society at large, for example, by examining how achievement translates into social welfare, by determining which stratum of society is most directly affected by the program, and by inferring how the expansion, continuation, or termination of the program would impact upon the social welfare distribution. Since the scope of the referent structure for models of distributive justice encompasses the social order, evaluation predicated upon principles of justice must examine the impact of programs upon the social order, and such concerns go beyond the procedural issues raised by House in his article.

Strike concludes that while evaluators have good reason to think seriously about justice and fairness, it is

> . . . very unlikely that issues of technique can be settled by trying to sort them in philosophical clubs such as utilitarianism and "Rawlsianism." Few evaluation techniques will clearly reflect the assumption of one club rather than another. . . . If the abstractions of political philosophy are to serve evaluators, it is more likely that they will do so by sharpening their intuitions and broadening their concerns than because some practices are clearly required or excluded by such considerations.[19]

In his reply to Strike, House modifies his argument in significant ways.[20] He acknowledges that his original "Justice" paper[21] contained applications that were too simple and heavy-handed and that if it were rewritten, he would be more critical of Rawls and less pejorative of utilitarianism.[22] While continuing to maintain that conceptions of social justice exert an impact upon evaluation practice, he agrees with Strike that the influence is complex and far from direct. He suggests that "the dominant conception of justice limits the approaches one takes, what activities one finds legitimate, what arguments count as significant. Conceptions of justice act more as broad frameworks of consideration rather than as internally consistent machines for deducing conclusions. They distribute the burdens of arguments in different ways."[23]

House reasserts his belief that a prominent, if not dominant, set of evaluation practices exist in the field and that these practices can be traced to utilitarian assumptions. He describes this prominent school of evaluation, sometimes labelled systems analysis, as consisting of defining a limited number of outcome measures and attempting to establish causal links between the measures and the program by appropriate experimental design. He argues that a utilitarian perspective underlies systems analyses, because the historical origins of the approach are in microeconomic theory,[24] an analytic structure explicitly founded upon utilitarian assumptions. Thus, House continues to advance the relationship between conceptions of social justice and general evaluation principles, if not practice, as significant. He concludes by arguing that evaluators ought to attend to the philosophical bases of evaluation, because "the evaluation profession needs philosophic analysis against which to check its institutions and social directions both to police and protect the evaluators."[25]

In his rejoinder to House's reply, Strike finds less to disagree with.[26] He concurs with House that a prominent, if not dominant, evaluation approach does exist and that

19. Ibid., 9.
20. House, "The Role of Theories . . . Justice on Strike."
21. House, "Justice in Evaluation."
22. House, "The Role of Theories . . . Justice on Strike," 72.
23. Ibid., 67.
24. Ibid., 68.
25. Ibid., 72.
26. Strike, "Justice in Evaluation."

systems analysis does exhibit aspects of utilitarianism. His acceptance of House's modified position is based on the greater persuasive power of an argument that demonstrates the systematic connection between the evaluation enterprise and viewpoints that are utilitarian in their commitment rather than depending upon superficial analysis between something in evaluation and something in utilitarianism.[27] Given that utilitarianism has been subjected to a persuasive and powerful critique in recent years, Strike agrees these practices and ideologies are rendered suspect.

However, Strike argues that a more useful application of philosophic analysis should focus on the consequences of evaluation activity rather than on the motivation of evaluators. He suggests that House's call for a central role for formal models of social justice in the process of deciding how a particular evaluation should be conducted is unnecessary. Where the commitments to justice are minimal, the intuitions of just and humane evaluators would suffice. Rather, because evaluation is a political activity that creates its own, often unintended, consequences, formal models of social justice should be used to "discover, analyze and critique the implicit and explicit moral commitments of evaluation practice."[28]

The aim of this paper is to extend Strike's notion of utilizing models of social justice to analyze models of evaluation. A rationale for the connection between the two types of models is offered. Based on this rationale, an analysis is presented of the relationship between six traditional criteria of distributive justice and general evaluation approaches. Finally, it is argued that the relationship between social justice and evaluation practice has methodological as well as ethical implications such that failure to explicate the conception of social justice associated with a chosen evaluation model may yield invalid data results. For evaluators who would argue that educational evaluation is only a methodological and not a social and ethical enterprise, the conclusions in this paper suggest that they still must concern themselves with the role of social justice in educational evaluation practice.

ON THE RELEVANCE OF SOCIAL JUSTICE TO EVALUATION RESEARCH

It is argued in this paper that Strike's notion of utilizing models of social justice to interpret evaluation practice is preferred to House's argument that conceptions of social justice determine valuation practice. In his reply to Strike, House contends that one of the factors that influence the design and conduct of particular evaluation is the conception of social justice maintained by the evaluator.[29] House perceives the relationship between conceptions of social justice and evaluation practice to be a "causal behavioral" relationship, in that a priori attitudes of social justice will influence subsequent evaluation behavior, or at least subsequent attitudes toward evaluation behavior.

In this paper it is asserted that it is more useful to conceive of models of social justice and models of evaluation as being parallel but independent rather than causally related. The parallelism stems from the fact that models of social justice and models of evaluation serve the same purpose: they provide decision makers with a means to compare and choose among alternative social situations, that is, they facilitate value judgments.

The function of the "greatest happiness" principle of utilitarianism or the minimax principle underlying Rawls's theory of justice is to provide ethical criteria by which alternative social states can be compared. For example, in utilizing a criterion of distributive justice to assess the impact of a legislative proposal, one compares the social welfare distribution of two social states. Social state T_0 would present the social utility distribution prior to the enactment of the proposed policy. Social state T_1 would represent the social welfare distribution if the social policy were in effect. To judge whether the policy should be enacted, say, from a utilitarian perspective, one would

---

27. Ibid., 73.
28. Ibid., 76.
29. House, "The Role of Theories . . . Justice on Strike," 67.

compare the aggregate utility level across social situations, while to employ the minimax criterion, one would compare the utility payoffs to the least advantaged individuals across the social situations. If the utility distribution in T_1 were preferred to that in T_0 by the designated criterion of distributive justice, it would be recommended that the legislation be enacted. Principles of social justice constitute criteria which a decision maker can utilize to compare social states on an ethical basis.

Evaluation models serve exactly the same purpose for decision makers. Evaluators (or evaluation clients who utilize the data) judge whether or not programs attained their goals by comparing across microsocial situations. When an evaluator pretests and posttests a treatment group or utilizes a treatment and control group, the two social states are T_0, containing the distribution of a variable of interest in the absence of treatment, and state T_1, containing the relevant distribution when the treatment is in effect. Program assessment is based on whether T_0 or T_1 exhibits the preferred distribution of the variable of interest. Evaluation models provide decision makers with criteria by which the social states can be compared and the preferred social state can be identified. Thus, principles of evaluation are criteria which a decision maker can utilize to compare social states on a methodological or statistical basis. Consequently, models of social justice and models of evaluation are parallel in that they both provide criteria to facilitate value judgments. They are independent, however, because models of social justice provide ethical criteria while models of evaluation provide methodological criteria upon which judgments can be based.

The independence of the ethical criteria of social justice and the methodological criteria of evaluation suggests that the causal behavioral hypothesis advanced by House is unlikely to be useful in explaining evaluation conduct. The prominence of the systems analysis evaluation model is more likely a function of methodological rather than ethical concerns. It is the psychometric rather than the social justice properties of standardized tests that account for their popularity in educational evaluation. Experimental designs are idealized in evaluation because of the desire to maximize internal validity rather than utilitarian principles. The causal determinants of evaluation conduct are methodological rather than ethical. In general, evaluators take their cues not from Bentham and Rawls but from Campbell and Stanley.[30]

Nonetheless, because models of social justice and models of evaluation provide mechanisms for the same behavior, namely, making value judgments, the same behavior can be assessed by both ethical and methodological criteria. This suggests that while the form of evaluation practice is not due to conceptions of social justice, evaluation models can be interpreted as implicitly being based on conceptions of social justice. For example, when an evaluator assesses a program by comparing treatment and control group means, it is not likely that the assessment is due to the evaluator's utilitarian world view. The motivation for such a comparison stems from the desirable statistical and inferential properties of sample means as estimators of population parameters and from the explanatory power of the general linear model, which is based upon the analysis of conditional means. However, when an evaluator compares group means, it is as if he or she were motivated by utilitarian principles, because the criterion by which a utilitarian would compare social states would probably involve the average values of a variable taken to represent utility.

Therefore, it is suggested that Strike's notion of the use of models of social justice to analyze evaluation conduct is more pertinent than House's argument that models of social justice should be used to explain evaluation conduct. Evaluation behavior does not reflect the underlying conception of justice maintained by an evaluator, because the motivation for behavior is methodological rather than ethical. However, one can interpret evaluation conduct by the use of models of social justice, because the methodological behavior has ethical implications. In the following section, the implicit

---

30. D. T. Campbell and J. C. Stanley, *Experimental and Quasi-Experimental Designs for Research* (Chicago: Rand McNally, 1966).

relationship between six traditional principles of distributive justice and various evaluation approaches is discussed.

SIX CRITERIA OF DISTRIBUTIVE JUSTICE IMPLIED BY ALTERNATIVE EVALUATION APPROACHES

In this section, six criteria of distributive justice are presented. For each criterion, the evaluation approach which would imply the criterion is considered. To illustrate the implicit relationships, an appropriate evaluation strategy for a hypothetical educational program is discussed, as well as actual educational situations in which the criterion would be implied.

Utilitarianism

As discussed above, the goal of utilitarianism is maximization of the greatest happiness principle, that is, the greatest good for the greatest number. Utilitarians would distinguish social states by the aggregate utility level in each state. Because of the intractability of maximizing both the good and the number, Barry and Rae note that the principle is often reformulated as the greatest good for a fixed number.[31] This suggests that social states can be compared in terms of average utility. The distributive principle in utilitarianism asserts that the preferred social state is that in which expected (average) utility is maximized. To determine that one social state is preferred to another is to indicate that the preferred social state yields a higher level of expected utility.

It is not difficult to interpret the application of statistical significance tests as implying a utilitarian distribution principle. If the treatment and control group are taken to be microsocial states and the variable of interest is assumed to represent a measure of utility, then a test of difference between conditional means is an assessment of which social state yields the greater average utility. (In fact, all the analogies in this section require the assumption that the variable of interest is a utility measure. Since in evaluation the outcome variables generally stand for program *goals*, the argument that the distribution of the variable represents the distribution of goodness or utility in a microsocial situation would seem reasonable.)

The important implication of utilitarianism with respect to educational evaluation is suggested by Rawls's comment that no distinction between persons is made. In assessing educational programs by the criterion, individual academic performance or progress is irrelevant to the analysis of group means. Some students may regress in "successful" programs provided that, on the average, posttest scores are greater than pretest scores. House[32] points out that since the sample variance is a component of an F- or t-test but the utilitarian focus on average utility is without regard to the form of the utility distribution,[33] the analogy between the utilitarian distribution criterion and significance testing is dubious. However, the sample variance pertains to the sampling distribution of the mean; it is an estimate of the variance of the sampling distribution, not of the distribution of individual scores in the population. The magnitude of the sample variance relates to the precision of the sample mean as an estimate of the population mean. Factoring the sample variance into the significance test indicates that the comparison is not between the numerical mean values of the alternative conditions, but rather is a comparison of the best estimates of the populations means from which the conditional samples are drawn. When comparison groups are populations rather than samples, the test of mean difference would simply be the numerical difference between the conditional means.

If a society consisted of three people, then by the utilitarian distribution criterion the following social states would be equally valued:

---

31. B. Barry and D. W. Rae, "Political Evaluation," in *Handbook of Political Science*, vol. 1, ed. F. Greenstein and N. Polsby (Reading, Mass.: Addison-Wesley, 1975), 360.
32. E. R. House, personal communication, 29 March 1982.
33. Strike, "The Role of Theories," 3.

		Social State		
		A	B	C
	1	10	20	30
Individual	2	10	10	0
	3	10	0	0

Equivalently, if the states represented reading achievement scores generated by alternative programs and the three individuals constituted a population rather than a sample, an analysis of the conditional means would reveal the programs to be equally effective. The extensive use of the general linear model to assess programs means that education evaluators often operate as if they maintained a utilitarian view of program assessment. Nonetheless, at times evaluators abandon the general linear model, either by choice or circumstance. In the remainder of this section, evaluation approaches which imply distributive criteria other than the utilitarian principle are examined. The alternative ethical criteria are equality, Pareto optimality, majority, minimax, and dominance.

Equality

The distribution criterion of equality has a different focus than utilitarianism. The criterion pertains to how evenly utility is distributed across individuals, and the preferred social state would be that which minimizes utility differences across individuals. Contrary to utilitarianism, where the relevant factor is average utility, the focus of equality is on the magnitude of the dispersion around some mean level, although the value of the mean is irrelevant.

If utilitarian principles are implied by statistical tests of significant mean differences, the egalitarian criterion would be implied by tests of significant difference in variance.[34] A program would be considered successful if the treatment group posttest exhibited a significantly smaller variance than the pretest on some relevant outcome measure. Consider the following scores from three reading programs:

		Program A	Program B	Program C
	1	100	100	10
Individual	2	100	100	10
	3	99	10	10

Although Program A is preferred to Program B, Program C would be most preferred with respect to minimum utility variance. When the intent of policymakers is to provide treatment such that outcomes are equalized, only Program C strictly meets the equality criterion.

The equality criterion would apply in situations where group homogeneity is an issue. Brown and Saks examined the effectiveness of various teaching strategies under homogeneous and heterogenous ability conditions.[35] They conclude that most teaching strategies are maximally effective when classes are homogeneous. The evaluation of programs designed to maintain homogeneity as instruction is delivered would implicitly maintain the equality principle of distributive justice.

Pareto Optimality

The distribution criterion of Pareto optimality requires that the transformation of a society of individuals from one state to another should only occur if no individual is

---

34. See, for example, T. Yamane, *Statistics: An Introductory Analysis*, 3rd ed. (New York: Harper & Row, 1973).

35. B. W. Brown and D. H. Saks, "Production Technologies and Resource Allocations within Classrooms and Schools: Theory and Measurement," in *The Analysis of Education Productivity*, ed. R. Dreeben and J. A. Thomas (Cambridge, Mass.: Ballinger, 1980).

worse off in the second state. One state is Pareto optimal to another if and only if no individual utility losses would result from a state shift. This is a more rigorous distribution criterion than utilitarianism, where individual utility losses would be tolerated in social change provided the gains offset the losses on a net basis. Pareto optimality requires ordinal assessments; therefore, absolute values of utility are irrelevant.

The Pareto optimality distribution criterion would be implied when educational policymakers would not condone programs that might have negative effects on individuals regardless of overall impact. For single programs, an analysis of individuals' gain scores would enable an evaluator to implement the Pareto optimality criterion. The presence of a single negative score would constitute sufficient grounds for rejection of the program. Several implications of Pareto optimality are illustrated by the following set of data:

		Pretest	Program A	Program B	Program C
	1	40	100	40	40
Individual	2	50	100	50	50
	3	55	50	55	60

Program A, despite the overall gains, would not be considered a successful program due to a utility loss on the part of individual 3. Program B would be assessed positively, since the utility distribution meets the distribution criterion of no individual utility loss. To avoid this situation, the strict Pareto optimality criterion has been defined as a state shift where no individual utility losses occur and some gain is made. Only Program C would meet the *strict* Pareto criterion.

One type of program which could be evaluated as if the Pareto optimality principle were maintained is mastery learning. Block states that the primary assumption underlying mastery learning is that all students should evidence academic progression, albeit at different rates.[36] Since, by its own rigorous assumption, all participants in a mastery learning program should move forward, the presence of negative gain scores would indicate an unsuccessful mastery learning program.

Majority

The distribution principle of majority is similar to, but less rigorous than, Pareto optimality. The criterion asserts that the social state should be preferred which advances the interest of more people rather than fewer.[37] Evaluation under the majority criterion would proceed by the analysis of gain scores. For a program to be successful, the majority of scores would need to be positive. This is to be distinguished from utilitarianism, where many small utility losses can be offset by a few very large gains. Similar to Pareto optimality, it is only the ordinal direction of change, rather than actual utility levels, on which the analysis focuses. One weakness of the majority criterion, when alternative programs are being considered, is that it is susceptible to Arrow's General Impossibility Theorem.[38] Consider the following data:

		Pretest	Program A	Program B
	1	99	100	10
Individual	2	99	100	101
	3	99	10	11

Starting from the pretest, the majority criterion would lead one to select program A, since two individuals gain and one loses, while in B only one would gain. However, once A becomes the existing social state program, B would actually be preferred, since

36. J. H. Block, *Mastery Learning* (Chicago: Holt, Rinehart and Winston, 1971).
37. Barry and Rae, "Political Evaluation," 363.
38. K. J. Arrow, *Social Choice and Individual Values*, 2nd ed. (New Haven, Conn.: Yale University Press, 1963).

two individuals would gain, while one would lose in moving from A to B. If the shift to B was made, the pretest would become the preferred social state, since again two individuals would gain and only one would lose. Thus, the use of the majority criterion to select among alternative programs may result in an indeterminate choice.

The majority criterion would be implied in situations where the number of people manifesting some program effect, rather than the magnitude of that effect, is the evaluation focus. It is more likely, for example, that a driver's education program would be assessed in terms of the proportion of program participants who gain a driver's license than by measuring the quality of their driving. Similarly, drug reeducation or rehabilitation programs are assessed by the percentage of nonrecidivism of participants rather than by measuring the quality of their lifestyles.

Minimax

The minimax distribution criterion is utilized by Rawls in his theory of justice.[39] The minimax criterion says that a comparison of alternative social states should be accomplished by comparing the utility levels of the worst-off individual in each state. The preferred state would be that which contained the best-off last-place individual. Unlike utilitarianism, which ignores individuals and equality, Pareto optimality and majority, which treat all individuals equally, the minimax criterion contains a normative assumption which says society must pay the most attention to those who have the least. The implication for evaluation is that program designers and evaluators should focus on those individuals in the treatment group who benefit the least. For a single program, one relevant indicator would be the score of the worst-off individuals in the program.

A variant of this criterion, the strong minimax criterion,[40] declares that if the worst-off person has the same score in the alternative social state, then the next-to-worst-off person should become the object of the analysis. Consider the following data from alternative programs:

		Pretest	Program A	Program B
	1	110	150	11
Individual	2	100	150	11
	3	10	10	11

In this case Program B yields the preferred outcome distribution. Although Program A is preferred to the pretest by the strong minimax criterion, where the second-worst-off individual is utilized, the worst-off individual is better off in Program B, and the other comparison is irrelevant.

The minimax criterion is generally applicable to the evaluation of programs for disadvantaged students. Title I funds, for example, are allocated on the basis of academic need and utilized to improve the abilities of those students in a school district who are at the bottom of the ability distribution. Evaluation of a Title I program is essentially the measurement of the degree to which the worst-off students in a school district have progressed.

Evaluation of minimal competency programs has a similar underlying perspective. Since the purpose of competency-based education is to ensure minimal competencies, the focus of such programs is on those who are not yet minimally competent. Evaluation of a minimal competency program is the assessment of the degree to which the worst-off students in a school or district have been elevated over some minimal level.

---

39. Rawls, *A Theory of Justice*.
40. Barry and Rae, "Political Evaluation," 364.

Dominance

The final distribution criterion is dominance. Barry and Rae note that dominance includes notions of minimax and utilitarianism, as well as a kind of anonymous version of Pareto optimality.[41] The dominance criterion states that if two social states have the same number of people, one state would be preferred to the other if and only if each person in the preferred state could be paired off with a person in the other state such that the person in the preferred state is at least as well off as the other. For evaluation, the simplest way to use the criterion would be by rank-ordering the individuals in the pretest and program states and comparing across individuals of the same rank within state ranking. An interesting aspect of the dominance criterion is revealed by the following data:

		Pretest	Program A	Program B
	1	100	100	101
Individual	2	11	12	12
	3	11	11	12

Given the condition of anonymous individuals, Program B, which dominates Program A and the pretest, would also be the preferred program by the criteria of utilitarianism, Pareto optimality, majority, minimax, and strong minimax. Thus, the dominance criterion would be the most rigorous of the alternative criteria discussed above. It would also be possible to construct an anonymous majority rather than an anonymous Pareto optimality criterion by requiring only a majority of the rank-ordered comparisons to be in favor of the preferred social state. However, a major weakness of the dominance criterion requires articulation. Similar to majority, the alternative social distributions may be such that no social state is dominant, suggesting a bias toward the status quo or, in terms of educational evaluation, a bias toward rejecting the outcomes of new programs.

Dominance is based on the logic of minimax applied to the entire societal structure rather than the relatively worst-off members of society. It is the analysis of the difference in absolute values of the same relative positions across social states. Such a criterion may be implied whenever an evaluator constructs treatment and control groups by matching and then comparing outcome scores of the groups. The Ohio-Westinghouse evaluation of Head Start[42] may exemplify the use of this criterion, for the analysis of matched samples implies a form of the dominance notion of social justice.

SOCIAL JUSTICE AND EVALUATION RESEARCH: IMPLICATIONS FOR PRACTICE

The implication of the preceding analysis, which suggests that evaluation models imply particular ethical distribution criteria, is that an evaluator acts as if a maintained conception of social justice underlies evaluation practice. Given that the conception of social justice is implicit, it may often be the case that the client's maintained conception of social justice may differ from that implied by the chosen evaluation model, and when such differences are not identified, bias is introduced into the evaluation process.

The detection and elimination of bias in evaluation has been an important area of concern for both evaluation theorists and practitioners. With respect to the evaluation process, two notions of bias are pertinent. The first concerns the institutional biases assimilated by an evaluator (or any professional) during the course of professional training. Such biases represent ingrained tendencies such as the evaluation questions a researcher is predisposed to examine, the analytic procedures a researcher prefers to utilize, and the philosophy of science to which a researcher subscribes. In this

41. Ibid., 365.
42. M. Smith and J. Bissell, "Report Analysis: The Impact of Head Start," *Harvard Educational Review* 40 (1970): 51-104.

sense, bias refers to the a priori, discipline-based value orientations that influence the conduct of evaluation.

The second type of bias relevant to evaluation may be labelled methodological bias and corresponds to the validity of the evaluation findings, in the sense of whether the data reflect the true state of the program. This bias occurs when errors in the evaluation process taint the results. An example of this sort of bias[43] would arise when evaluators misperceive the goals of a program and then assess the program against standards which are irrelevant to the true program intent. When clients utilize these data, their decisions are based upon invalid indicators of program performance and are unlikely to be appropriate to the true merit of the program.

It is argued in this paper that there exists a causal connection between institutional and methodological bias. The misperception of program intents by an evaluator may be a function of the a priori set of institutional biases that impact upon the conduct of the evaluation. A classic example of the influence of institutional bias on methodological bias was identified by Bachrach and Baratz in their comparison of two studies of the structure of the urban policy-making process,[44] one conducted by Robert A. Dahl, a political scientist,[45] and the other by Floyd Hunter, a sociologist.[46] Hunter concluded that the policy process was best described by the interactions among policymakers occupying different strata in the structure, with policy suggestions flowing up and policy decisions flowing down. Dahl, on the other hand, concluded that the actors in the policy process were not embedded in a fixed, stratified structure, but that different political configurations crystallized around various policy issues. In discussing the contradictory findings, Bachrach and Baratz observe:

> Sociologically oriented researchers have consistently found that power is highly centralized, while scholars trained in political science have just as regularly concluded that in "their" communities power is widely diffused. Presumably, this explains why the latter group styles itself "pluralist," its counterpart "elitist." There seems to be no room for doubt that the sharply divergent findings are the product, not of sheer coincidence, but of fundamental differences in both underlying assumptions and research methodology.[47]

It is an institutional bias common to sociologists — that social situations are necessarily stratified — that led Hunter to search for the strata involved in policy-making. He identifies four distinct strata and suggests that policy decisions are finalized at the highest level and that "the omnipresent threat of power sanctions used against recalcitrant underlings is recognized by lower echelons of power and they generally go along with most decisions."[48] An institutional bias common to political science — that policy-making is a pluralist enterprise — led Dahl to search for the various "issue publics" involved in the policy process, and he concludes that the influence of the economic notables of New Haven is not fixed, such that there is "little room for doubt that the Economic Notables, far from being a ruling group, are simply one of the many groups out of which individuals sporadically emerge to influence the policies and acts of city officials. Almost anything one might say about the influence of the Economic Notables could be said with equal justice about a half dozen other groups in the New Haven community."[49]

---

43. M. Scriven, "Evaluation Bias and Its Control," in *Evaluation Studies Review Annual*, vol. 1.

44. P. Bachrach and M. S. Baratz, "Two Faces of Power," *American Political Science Review* 16 (1962): 947-52.

45. R. A. Dahl, *Who Governs? Democracy and Power in an American City* (New Haven, Conn.: Yale University Press, 1961).

46. F. Hunter, *Community Power Structure: A Study of Decision Makers* (Chapel Hill: University of North Carolina Press, 1953).

47. Bachrach and Baratz, "Two Faces of Power," 947.

48. Hunter, *Community Power Structure*, 112.

49. Dahl, *Who Governs?*, 72.

Bachratz and Baratz note that political scientists have explained the differences in findings by pointing out the faulty approach and presuppositions of the sociologists. However, "The pluralists themselves have not grasped the whole truth of the matter; that while the criticisms of the elitists are sound, they, like the elitists, utilize an approach and assumptions which predetermine their conclusions."[50]

While the situation described by Bachrach and Baratz is admittedly an instance of institutional bias "overkill," it does suggest the relationship between institutional and methodological bias. In fact, research settings in which the institutional biases are not pronounced may be more problematic, for the resulting methodological bias may be subtle and imperceptible. A significant implication of the causal link between institutional and methodological bias is that one can moderate the latter by controlling the former, a position adopted by Scriven.[51]

However, Cherryholmes demonstrates that Scriven is mistaken in assuming that evaluators can control bias and, in effect, conduct objective evaluations.[52] Evaluators cannot be objective, because evaluation is an institutional rather than a brute activity. The statement is based upon Searle's distinction between brute and institutional facts.[53] Cherryholmes exemplifies the distinction by suggesting brute facts such as "This table is made of wood," "Window glass is transparent," or "That brick is on top of another brick." An institutional fact is of the order of "She was driving over the speed limit," "He caught the pass for a touchdown," or "The committee voted three to two to look for a new chairman." Institutional facts, Cherryholmes states, are of the form "X counts as Y in context C."[54]

Evaluation qua evaluation can only be undertaken from some institutional perspective. Just as Searle observes that it is only because of the institution of baseball that a man can be said to hit a home run when otherwise he would only hit a sphere with a stick,[55] so it can be argued that it is only within the institutions of education, research methodology, statistics, measurement, and normative analysis that one can be said to evaluate the effectiveness of a teacher's instructional style on student motivation and that without them one would only stand in a room, putting marks on a piece of paper as an adult speaks to a group of children. The point is that there is no such thing as brute or relatively objective evaluation conduct; there are only alternative institutional perspectives on how evaluation should be conducted. At best, Cherryholmes suggests, evaluators need to make their institutional commitments explicit, although it is acknowledged that this proposal is not unproblematic. The advantage of this approach is that the interpretation of findings would become more understandable and accessible to sponsors as well as critics.[56]

It is argued in this paper that the relevance of the models of social justice to the conduct of evaluation is based on the relationship between institutional and methodological bias. When an evaluator chooses an evaluation model, the conception of social justice implied by the model functions as an institutional bias, because the evaluator acts as if an a priori social justice criterion is maintained. The institutional bias will lead to methodological bias when the social justice criterion implied by the evaluation approach is at odds with the actual conception of justice underlying a program, and the bias is most consequential when the client's conception of social justice is strongly maintained, as it is likely to be in ameliorative educational and social action programs.

The invalidity of the data gathered under an implied social justice criterion different

50. Bachrach and Baratz, "Two Faces of Power," 948.
51. Scriven, "Evaluation Bias."
52. C. H. Cherryholmes, "Evaluation Research as a Linguistic Activity: An Exploration of Bias" (Paper presented at the conference "Political Science and the Study of Public Policy," Michigan State University Kellogg Center — Manor House, Hickory Corners, Michigan, May, 1978).
53. J. R. Searle, Speech Acts: An Essay in the Philosophy of Language (London: Cambridge University Press, 1969).
54. Cherryholmes, "Evaluation Research," 12.
55. Searle, Speech Acts, 54.
56. Cherryholmes, "Evaluation Research," 25.

from that actually underlying the program is analogous to the invalidity due to the misperception of goals on the part of the evaluator. When clients utilize the data, their decisions are based upon an irrelevant ethical standard, and therefore the decisions are unlikely to be appropriate to the true ethical merit of the program. To avoid this situation, Cherryholmes's suggestion can be invoked, namely, that in negotiating the intended evaluation, an evaluator needs to inform the client that underlying the methodological strategy is an implicit conception of social justice. The evaluator must explicate this conception such that it can be determined whether it is appropriate to the client's social justice concerns. If it is discovered that the evaluator and client hold conflicting notions, adjustments must be made, probably in the evaluation strategy, so that the data will reflect the actual conception of social justice underlying the program.

Summary

In an interchange conducted with Ernest House, Kenneth Strike advances the argument that models of social justice can be used to discover the implicit moral commitments associated with evaluation practice. The purpose of this paper was to extend that argument. It was suggested that six criteria of distributive justice can be implied by alternative evaluation assessments. It was further argued that the implicit relationship has methodological as well as ethical consequences and that evaluators need to explicate the implicit conceptions of social justice to avoid introducing methodological bias into evaluation findings.

SECTION 5
Qualitative Inquiry

An emphasis on what we have called the program evaluation approach puts a premium on relevance and responsiveness to the perceptions and concerns of program stakeholders, timely "formative" input to program decision makers, and evaluative results that reflect explicit judgment as well as detailed description. These are functions that are difficult to accomplish under the experimental research paradigm with its structured measures and prolonged data collection and analysis phases. Under these circumstances, qualitative inquiry techniques offer an attractive alternative. They have the advantages of maintaining close contact with stakeholders and participants, providing rich detail about program functioning, and yielding prompt results for use by decisionmakers.

It is not surprising, therefore, that interest in qualitative inquiry has burgeoned in recent years with a spate of books and articles promoting its use and describing its methodology. In many ways, advocacy of qualitative inquiry has outstripped actual practice. Despite the recent volume of literature, relatively few fully documented reports of completed qualitative evaluations have been available and much of the methodological discussion has been rather too general to provide useful guidelines for actual application. Discourse on qualitative inquiry for program evaluation has been long on advocacy and philosophy, short on example and practical detail.

Our sense is that qualitative inquiry for program evaluation has now reached a turning point in its development and is entering a more mature phase. The beginning of this phase was heralded by publication of Guba and Lincoln's book (1981), noteworthy for its treatment of the practical techniques and methods useful in qualitative evaluation. Recent literature shows a new depth of concern for the coherence of theory and method in qualitative evaluation, for careful explication of what validity means and how it can be established in this form of inquiry, and for the practical design and management of a qualitative study—documentation, sampling, synthesis of field notes, and so forth.

The four chapters in this section provide excellent examples of the thoughtfulness and quality of recent work on qualitative evaluation. In the first of these chapters, Dorr-Bremme provides a useful overview of "ethnographic evaluation," an adaptation of the theory and method of anthropological ethnography to the evaluation task. The strength of this chapter is its application of the theory of social organization inherent in ethnography and the linkage of that theory with ethnographic methodology. The concluding portion of this chapter develops five implications for the design and conduct of evaluation fieldwork that provide an excellent short lesson on how to get started in ethnographic evaluation.

Miles and Huberman, in the second chapter of this section, turn attention to a subject that has attracted more criticism to qualitative evaluation than any other—the validity and reproducibility of results. Their approach is to emphasize systematic and openly documented procedures for data collection, data display, data reduction, and the drawing and verification of conclusions. They identify literally dozens of useful tactics and techniques for accomplishing the necessary steps in this process. Committed qualitative evaluators will find much good practical advice in this chapter. More quantitatively oriented researchers may be surprised to discover that, at root, the issues of validity and verification are much the same in qualitative as in quantitative inquiry.

Central to validity and verification of qualitative results, and also to the evaluator's accountability for proper conduct of the evaluation, is careful and complete documentation at every stage of the research process. The third chapter of this section, by Levine, makes a penetrating analysis of qualitative data storage and retrieval. Drawing on developments in information and library science, he constructs a set of general principles for handling field-based data. His advice not only provides a set of excellent guidelines and practical suggestions for the qualitative evaluator, but offers many useful ideas for any researcher working in field settings.

The final chapter in this section offers a case study of a qualitative investigation that illustrates a distinctive point—the role of a priori theory in guiding inquiry toward certain crucial features of the program situation. Weinholtz and Friedman report a "preassessment study" of the effectiveness of teaching by attending physicians in a teaching hospital. Because observation is necessarily selective, an important initial question is what aspects of the teaching process most merit attention. The authors show how existing theory and prior empirical research on leadership can be put to good use in focusing and guiding the qualitative inquiry. Moreover, the initial theoretical framing put on the study enabled them to organize their diverse field observations into a relatively coherent set of results. An additional important function of this approach is its ability to transcend the specific site of investigation with some broader generalizations. The qualitative investigation Weinholtz and Friedman report not only provided context-specific testing of some of the original theoretical propositions, it became a source of theoretical refinement and development of additional propositions. Thus, although maintaining responsiveness to the demands of the appointed task and context, a contribution was made to "grounded theory" on teaching effectiveness.

We think this latter function is important and worth an additional comment. The intimate first-hand involvement of qualitative evaluation with programs as they are experienced by participants, which is the source of its responsiveness and relevance to stakeholder concerns, can also be a powerful source of theoretical insight. What is required for this purpose is awareness by the researcher of the state of existing applicable theory and an alertness to relationships that may have generality beyond the immediate context. An attractive scenario for improved theoretical understanding of social intervention within the program evaluation field is a collaboration between those focusing on "evaluation" and those focusing on "research." In this scenario, responsive practical evaluation with its heavier qualitative orientation would be a source for discovery of relationships and insights of possible generality. Systematic investigation of such propositions would be the task of those researchers with more theoretical interests using the usual methods of social science.

However attractive this scenario, there can be little doubt that work on qualitative evaluation is in an exceptionally vigorous phase. The combination of growing interest in the topic and movement beyond the advocacy stage to substantive probing of methods and theory has made this one of the bright spots in the recent evaluation literature. The chapters presented in this section show just how promising some of this work is.

REFERENCES

Guba, E. G., & Lincoln, Y. S. (1981). *Effective evaluation.* San Francisco: Jossey-Bass.

21

Ethnographic Evaluation
A Theory and Method
Donald W. Dorr-Bremme

Through the last decade or so, naturalistic or qualitative inquiry has won wide acceptance in the field of evaluation. This kind of evaluation inquiry has been borrowed or derived from ethnography, the fieldwork method long associated with anthropology. But in borrowing anthropology's inquiry techniques, most evaluators have left anthropological theory and concepts behind. Thus, as described in methods texts and as most often practiced to date, naturalistic-qualitative evaluation has had no theory appropriate to one of its central research goals: to "get inside" the world of program participants and to understand, describe, and explain the program and its effects from participants' points of view. Ethnography—defined here as a particular type of naturalistic-qualitative method that is guided by anthropological theory—can enable evaluation to achieve this goal.

This article briefly elaborates these points, demonstrating the importance of theory in evaluation fieldwork. Then, drawing on sources in current educational anthropology, the article (a) outlines a general theory that is relevant to evaluation fieldwork's goals and (b) details five key principles of inquiry design

that follow from it, showing how each can contribute to the greater validity and greater utility of fieldwork in evaluation. In so doing, the article establishes a general framework for an ethnographic approach to evaluation inquiry, one that is informed by a comprehensive, research-supported theory of how educational and other social service programs and their results are socially constructed and organized.

The Importance of Theory in Evaluation Fieldwork

The general inquiry goals and methods of anthropological ethnography and naturalistic-qualitative inquiry in evaluation have much in common; and the terms *ethnographic*, *naturalistic*, and *qualitative* have come to be used among evaluators as interchangeable, generic labels for fieldwork techniques. Nevertheless, ethnography and naturalistic-qualitative evaluation inquiry are not one and the same. In ethnography, anthropological theory and concepts link the goals of inquiry with the fieldwork method, contributing to "reality control," and (thus) to quality control, in research and reporting. Most naturalistic-qualitative evaluation, in contrast, lacks an appropriate theory to link its goals and methods. This section explains why this jeopardizes both the validity and usefulness of evaluation fieldwork.

The general inquiry goal in naturalistic-qualitative evaluation derives in part from the philosophical orientation known as phenomenology (Guba, 1978; Harris,

A longer version of this article was developed under a grant by the National Institute of Education (NIE-G-83-0001) to the Center for the Study of Evaluation. The author is especially indebted to Frederick Erickson, whose work has contributed substantially to the ideas presented here. Adrianne Bank, Aimee Dorr, and Harold Levine offered invaluable comments on earlier drafts. Any oversights or errors in these pages, however, are the author's own.

From Donald W. Dorr-Bremme, "Ethnographic Evaluation: A Theory and Method," *Educational Evaluation and Policy Analysis* 1985, 7(1), 65-83. Copyright 1985, American Educational Research Association, Washington, DC.

1968; Patton, 1980). In brief, phenomenology emphasizes that groups of people can and often do have systematically different views of reality and consistently different ways of interpreting what actions, words, objects, and so forth mean. Furthermore, the phenomenologist assumes that people take action in the world based on their ideas and beliefs about the way the world "really" is, in light of their notions of what things mean, regardless of what is verifiable "scientifically" as "fact."

Proceeding from the phenomenological viewpoint, most proponents of naturalistic-qualitative evaluation maintain that its goal is to do more than examine a program on site and close up. Ideally, they maintain, it should also "get inside" the program and its context to describe and explain that program and its consequences in terms of participants' realities and meaning systems (Guba, 1978, pp. 11–15; Parlett & Hamilton, 1976, pp. 144ff.; Patton, 1980, pp. 44–45). As Guba and Lincoln (1981, p. 133) have put it, quoting sociologist Erving Goffman (1961), "'any group of persons . . . develops a social life of their own that becomes meaningful, reasonable, and normal once you get close to it.'" And in a naturalistic-qualitative evaluation, they add, "It is the totality of this meaning, reasonableness, and normalcy in each context and setting that the naturalistic inquirer seeks to understand, to explain, and to describe" (p. 133).

Taken as stated, this is a goal that most modern anthropologists share in doing ethnography. Proceeding from a phenomenological perspective, they too take a primary interest in how human groups routinely make sense of their world and act sensibly in it. Indeed, for most anthropological ethnographers, description and interpretation are only valid to the extent that they take into account and clarify the views of reality and notions of meaning that participants in the activities under study are actually using as they enact those activities (e.g., Erickson, 1979a; Hymes, 1982; Mehan, 1982).

Like ethnography, too, naturalistic-qualitative evaluation inquiry is a holistic, inductive, responsive-adaptive method for studying human social activities (such as educational programs) in their naturally occurring circumstances. Given these characteristics, many evaluators have come to think that inquiry of this type is "theory-free," exclusively oriented by or based in the data that emerge as on-site investigation proceeds. With Guba (1978), they have in mind that "the naturalistic investigator . . . begins as an anthropologist might begin learning about a strange culture, by immersing himself in the investigation with as open a mind as possible, and permitting impressions to emerge" (p. 13).

It is quite true that naturalistic-qualitative evaluators and ethnographers do not begin inquiry with formal hypotheses, explicit conceptual models of the activity to be studied, or prespecified sets of variables such as those that guide inquiry in the experimental and other "quantitative" paradigms. They do shape and reshape the specific themes, issues, and questions of their inquiry in a recurrent cycle of on-site data gathering, data review and analysis, and reflection (Dorr-Bremme, 1985). But fieldwork and the description it finally yields always entail, always are shaped by, some theory of social organization. As Erickson (1979a) has convincingly argued,

> The theory entailed in a description of a connected sequence of events across time is in essence a theory of its social organization. . . . While descriptions may or may not entail theories of psychic processes within individuals—theories of motivation, temperament, learning or cognitive stage—descriptions of events involving the actions of more than one individual, I maintain, *always* entail theory about the organization of social relations. (p. 5)

This holds true even when the description emerges from naturalistic-qualitative inquiry or ethnography. It holds true because in doing fieldwork investigators cannot escape choices about how to focus inquiry, what to include as data, and how to describe what they have seen. They must decide, for example, what sites to visit, which settings within each site to focus on, when to be there, and how often and for how long. Wherever they choose to go, myriad phenomena are taking place each moment from one moment to the next; they must decide which of these phenomena are worth attending to and noting down. Similarly, ethnographers or naturalistic-qualitative evaluators must repeatedly make choices throughout the course of inquiry about whom to interview formally and whom to talk to informally, what questions to ask, and how and when to ask them. Then they have to decide which words and other behaviors, of all those that occur each moment in each conversation, deserve a place in the study record. Furthermore, as inquiry proceeds, they must constantly determine which terms, behaviors, and so forth that they encounter on site can safely be treated as unproblematic, their purposes and meanings sufficiently clear, and which should be treated as problematic, their purposes and meanings requiring further inquiry and explanation. As noted earlier, in naturalistic-qualitative evaluation inquiry and ethnography these and other such decisions should eventually be informed by the accumulating data and the issues and questions these data progressively suggest. *But from the very outset of inquiry, these decisions are also made constantly on the basis of, and so the accumulating data always reflect, the investigator's perspective on what is important:* his or her explicit or implicit ideas about how the social activity (the program, etc.) under study works, of what influences its workings, and (therefore) of what is important to pay attention to and document in studying and describing it. Finally, these ideas, which constitute the investigator's theory, influence his or her choices of how to label and describe the cast of characters, the actions they have taken, and the relationships among those actions (cf., Erickson, 1979a, p. 4). Thus, the investigator's theory—whether it was chosen deliberately in advance or evolved unself-consciously and ad hoc throughout the inquiry process—plays a critical role in fieldwork. It functions to shape the vision of reality that evolves in the data and appears in the findings. It is in this sense that theory is a reality control, and thus a quality (or validity) control, in fieldwork.

It follows from all this that in ethnography and in the naturalistic-qualitative evaluation approaches that are based on it, as in other modes of inquiry,

> the problem is not the elimination of "bias" in description, for all description [and the inquiry which yields it] is done in terms of a point of view. Rather, the problem is the *selection of "bias"*—or theoretical frame—appropriate to the research problem at hand. (Erickson, 1979a, p. 4)

Now, as we have seen, a central research problem at hand in evaluation that purports to be naturalistic or qualitative is generally (a) to identify activities that are, from participants' point(s) of view, routinely related in some way to the program to be evaluated and/or its results; and (b) to understand, describe, and explain those activities in terms of participants' socially shared notions of reality, meaning, and appropriate action. The evaluator can and often should go on to provide an analysis of the program and program "outcomes" from other frames of reference that suggest themselves as relevant. First and foremost, however, his or her account should show its audiences how participants have constructed the program and its effects in light of their social realities and meaning systems, since it is in terms of those (and not the evaluator's concepts of reality and meaning) that program participants routinely take action.

A theory appropriate to this problem or goal would be a general theory of how human endeavors such as educational and other programs are socially assembled and organized by participants as they use their particular ideas and beliefs about what is real and true, their values and notions of what behaviors and things mean. Such theory would serve to link the general phenomenological stance of naturalistic-qualitative evaluation inquiry with its fieldwork method, indicating where and how to shape fieldwork in order to identify the "realities" and systems of meaning that program participants are using as they enact the program from day to day.

As noted earlier, ethnography has traditionally drawn such theory from anthropological and related research on culture and social organization and from the generalizations and constructs that such research supports. But in borrowing the phenomenological stance and inquiry method of ethnography, naturalistic-qualitative evaluation has set aside these theoretical foundations. As described by most methodologists and as usually practiced, naturalistic-qualitative evaluation is a generic approach: a set of philosophical assumptions and data-collection techniques which, like the experimental paradigm, is independent of any disciplinary conceptual structure. (See, e.g., the methodological texts of Guba, 1978; Guba & Lincoln, 1981; Hamilton et al., 1978; Patton, 1980. On major evaluations, refer to Firestone & Herriott, 1984.) *Thus, in going into the field, the naturalistic or qualitative evaluator has no formal, recognized and recognizable system for defining and locating participants' realities or meanings: for determining what they are, where they are manifested or displayed, or how they function in relation to the daily, program-relevant activities to be described and explicated.*

In this situation, the naturalistic evaluator can only fall back on some other theory in deciding how to shape his or her inquiry, what to include as data, and how to describe and explain the program in reporting. Many have chosen the traditional quantitative inquiry tactic, selecting a theory in advance from one or several academic disciplines or from a set of research findings they deem relevant (cf. Firestone & Herriott, 1984). Others, attempting to maintain the open-endedness and flexibleness of the naturalistic-qualitative approach, have inadvertently and unself-consciously allowed their intuitive notions of "how this kind of program works" to serve as their theory. But whichever the case, the evaluator's inquiry and reports become structured by the premises of his or her theory—his or her vision of reality, of how the program and the world in which it is embedded work—rather than in terms of the realities known to and experienced by program participants. Then, the phenomenological foundations and goals of naturalistic-qualitative evaluation are undercut, jeopardizing not only the evaluation's validity, but also its practical utility. If the account of the program or other activity under study does not accurately portray reality as participants know and experience it, participants can easily reject the evaluation as a useful basis for decision and action. Moreover, if such an account is used by decisionmakers who are not participants at the sites studied (e.g., central program managers or administrators in sponsoring agencies), it can lead them to decisions and policies that local site participants find ill suited to their circumstances and needs.

As we have seen, none of these problems is eliminated by an effort to enter the study setting(s) without preconception or bias; choices must be made about how to shape the inquiry, what to count as data, and how to describe people and events. Nor can an evaluator ascertain participants' realities and notions of what things mean simply by asking rigorously open-ended questions and observing in formally unstructured ways. The social meanings and social functions that kinds of actions, words, things, and so forth routinely have for participants do not leap out of interview responses or from the stream of observed behavior. They *are* discernible in naturally occurring talk and action, but only through an appropriate set of data collection and analysis strategies, strategies that are predicated on a theory of how organized social life unfolds. Since the literature on naturalistic-qualitative evaluation has yet to offer such a theory, it makes sense to look for one in anthropological ethnography.

A Constitutive-Ethnographic Theory of Social Organization

The theory presented here is most closely associated with what has come to be called "constitutive ethnography" (Mehan, 1978, 1979, 1982), an orientation that has evolved during the last 10 years especially within educational anthropology. It is based on theoretical constructs and a good deal of research from anthropology, sociolinguistics (or the ethnography of communication), and ethnomethodology (the study of practical reasoning in everyday life). As indicated earlier, it is a theory of how group members generate and sustain organized social relations and of the role that members' perceptions and interpretations of phenomena (their "realities") play in that process. As such, it includes a number of interrelated premises which elaborate the fundamental phenomenological axiom that persons act in terms of their ideas and beliefs about the nature of reality, in terms of the meaning that phenomena have for them. The most important of these premises are explained below, and then they are drawn together in a model of how endeavors such as educational programs are socially organized.

Basic Theoretical Premises

A first, fundamental supposition of this theory is that some body of sociocultural knowledge lies at the foundation of and facilitates social life. In general this knowledge can be conceptualized as a series of principles for making sense of the world and acting sensibly in it. From the perspective of some "cognitive" anthropologists, these more-or-less shared operating principles constitute a group's culture. In Goodenough's (1964) terms, "a society's culture consists of whatever one has to know or believe in order to operate in a manner acceptable to its members, and to do so in any role that they accept for any one of themselves" (p. 36). More recently, Goodenough (1981) has defined culture more succinctly as a "system of standards for perceiving, believing, evaluating and acting" (p. 110). Other anthropologists (e.g., Spradley, 1972), as well as sociolinguists (e.g., Gumperz, 1972; Hymes, 1972, 1974) and many ethnomethodologists (e.g., Cicourel, 1974; Garfinkel, 1967; Mehan & Wood, 1975, pp. 98–115), begin their theories with very similar constructs. They too assume that the interaction of human groups is socially organized according to some set of operating principles for determining what behaviors and things mean and when particular kinds of actions are appropriate.

This initial premise begins to flesh out the notions of "reality" and "meaning" which are so important to phenomenologically based inquiry but so incompletely explained in works on naturalistic-qualitative evaluation. It should be apparent that the "realities" of primary interest to ethnographers are not those which abide idiosyncratically in particular individuals, but those of societal groups. Furthermore, these realities are not random or

isolated bits of perception and interpretation; rather they are systemic in nature—coherent bodies of perception and belief, sets of standards for interpreting and acting in ways the group deems appropriate.

To refer to the bodies of systematic sociocultural knowledge that members of a particular group use to organize their perceptions, interpretations, and actions, many anthropological ethnographers use the term emic, which they contrast with the term etic. In this dichotomy etic constructs or accounts consider phenomena from the point of view of standardized measurement "or if not in terms of measurement at least in terms of systematic ways in which scientists as external observors define units" (Erickson, 1977, p. 60). Emic constructs and accounts, on the other hand, are those of the ordinary actor in the setting under study. Erickson (1977) uses the concepts "stature" and "height" to illustrate the etic-emic distinction. At the same time, his remarks indicate the kinds of "systems of standards for perceiving, believing, evaluating and acting" in which ethnographers are typically interested.

In everyday interaction, for example, people may treat the phenomenally continuous variable of height as if it were discontinuous, categorizing people as short, average, and tall in stature. Units of stature, then, would be social facts [i.e., emic categories], defined in terms of people's discriminations of thresholds and the actions they take toward each other on the basis of those discriminations. The continuous variable height could also be measured formally [i.e., etically] by an arbitrarily defined unit such as the inch or the millimeter, capable of reliable use by observors in making low-inference judgments. These units of description could be used in valid and reliable ways within a system of technical [etic] categorization independent from functional categories or discontinuous [emic] "chunks" used by people in thinking of stature. (p. 60)

Put another way, anthropological ethnographers' interest in how people in a group systematically order their social lives directs ethnographers' attention to the emic categories (and ways of distinguishing among categories, e.g., of stature) that group members routinely employ and to the actions that members routinely take based on these categories. Thus, the "meaning" in which most ethnographers are primarily interested is *social meaning*—the functional significance that kinds of persons (statuses), actions, and things recurrently and routinely have for group members, as manifested in the kinds of actions they routinely take with respect to them.

A second theoretical premise further elaborates the fundamental concepts of culture (or social reality) and social meaning described above. This is the premise that a social group's standards for sensibly and appropriately interpreting phenomena, ascribing meaning and value, and choosing actions can vary with features of the social context or situation. Texts on naturalistic or qualitative evaluation always emphasize that context is important, but they rarely define the term. The definition of *social context* (or *social situation*) intended here is a very specific one. As construed by ethnographers, especially constitutive ethnographers, *context* refers to an interpretation of "who we are and what we are doing now," which circumscribes or frames the set of alternatives from which participants in a social scene choose what to do socially "now" and "next" (Bateson, 1972; Cicourel, 1974). As such, contexts or situations may be nested one within another at various levels of interpretive generality. For example, a person in interaction may interpret the situation now as "a moment of misunderstanding *in* a casual social conversation with a colleague *during* a break between classes *while* at school *during* the period when we first began to try out the new curriculum"—if he or she were to articulate an interpretation in so many words.

When one joins this view of social context with the definition of culture given earlier, it follows that "culture ceases to refer to a generic phenomenon of study and refers instead only to some level of that phenomenon" (Goodenough, 1975, p. 4). That is, the culture of any society as a whole—its "macroculture"—is a broad level of organization integrating numerous situation-bound cultures.

Every human being, then, lives in what is for him a multicultural world, in which he is aware of different sets of others to whom different cultural attributions must be made and different contexts in which the different cultures of which he is aware are operative. His competence in any one of these is indicated by his ability to interact effectively in its terms with others who are acknowledged as already competent. (Goodenough, 1975, p. 4)

Notice, then, that from the perspective presented here many types of social groups (teachers, program administrators, etc.) may have their own culture; culture is not something associated exclusively with ethnicity or national boundaries.

In summary, culture (or social reality) is multilayered. A society's system of standards for perceiving, believing, evaluating, and acting varies with features of the social context or situation—features that are themselves interpreted by group members at various hierarchical levels.

Implicit in the theoretical tenets presented thus far is another that deserves explicit mention: In the view taken here, the culture (or social reality) and behavior of a social group are in constant, dialectical relationship. In a process that goes on continuously in real time as group members conduct their everyday affairs, culture informs action, and, simultaneously, action embodies and manifests culture. That is, as persons interact with one another, they draw upon and use their sociocultural knowledge—their ideas of kinds of contexts, people, actions, and things; their systems of beliefs, ideas, and values; their standards for interpreting others' behavior appropriately and choosing appropriate actions in context. As they use this knowledge, their behavior becomes patterned in certain routine ways. Thus, patterns of behavior are constructed in interaction; and in the behavioral patternings that they routinely construct, group members display their sociocultural knowledge, projecting it (and the social meanings and views of reality that it entails) onto and into the world, making it available to others.

It follows that culture (or a group's reality) is not purely subjective, not solely a cognitive or mental state existing only in persons' heads, as proponents of naturalistic-qualitative evaluation sometimes suggest (e.g., Guba, 1978, p. 15). Nor is culture exclusively objective in nature; it is not only "patterns of behavior" existing "out there" in the world. Rather, from the perspective of the constitutive-ethnographic theory presented here, culture (or social reality) is *intersubjective*: a *social* phenomenon not only in the sense that it is *of* or pertaining to society, but also in the sense that it is *by* society, that is, produced and maintained conjointly by group members in interaction. From this theoretical perspective then,

> the objective facts and subjective states associated with education, like those associated with other cultural domains, are interactional accomplishments. "Classroom organization," "curricular programs," "teacher effectiveness," and other so-called "objective" aspects of schooling are intersubjective phenomenon, constructed in interaction. Similarly, "students' abilities," "students' intelligence," "teachers' styles," and other seemingly subjective states of individuals are intersubjective phenomena, displayed in interaction. (Mehan, 1982, p. 64)

A Theory of Social Organizational Process

Inherent in the premises outlined above is a theoretical model of social organizational process. The model explains how educational and other programs are constructed in interaction as participants draw upon and use their notions of reality and meaning (or, in terms of this theory, their systems of standards for perceiving, believing, evaluating, and acting). This model is now described.

Participants in face-to-face interaction perpetually scan the scene, taking in countless perceptual "data" (Spradley, 1972). They routinely gather information on the time, location, and personnel present (Erickson, 1971), and they attend to one another's actions. As McDermott (1976) has put it, persons in interaction become environments for each other. The behavior of all participants in the scene, enacted through many behavioral modes simultaneously, bears information for

each other participant about the evolving definition and direction of the social situation at hand. Lexical, syntactical, and paralinguistic behaviors can carry meaning. So, too, can gaze direction, body orientation and posture, interpersonal distance, gestures, and so on. At any given moment, a person's behavior in all these channels can contribute to the total "message" he or she is seen as sending at that moment. (See Dorr-Bremme, 1982, for a comprehensive review of research supporting these points.)

Drawing on sociocultural systems of standards of the type described in the last section, participants in the interaction encode, organize, and interpret the perceptual data they are constantly receiving; they make sense of "who we are and what we are doing now" (Cicourel, 1974; Mehan & Wood, 1975, pp. 102–106). But even if participants have an adequate practical knowledge of sociocultural standards, what particular behaviors, objects, and so forth mean in context remains problematic for them. Why? Because "all symbolic forms [written statements, vocal utterances, gestures, other actions, things in the setting] carry a fringe of incompleteness that must be filled in, and filled in differently every time" (Mehan & Wood, 1975, p. 90).

For example, in speech we never say all that would be necessary and sufficient in order to be understood by a person who knew nothing about our social world. We assume knowledge on the part of others in our society; we expect them to be able to fill in around what we literally say in order to understand what we mean. To do this filling in, persons draw on their sociocultural knowledge, knowledge that includes conceptualizations of how the social world is routinely organized (e.g., of "who" people are, of how they are related, of how various types of social activities are routinely carried out, etc.), as well as rules for behaving and making sense in interaction. But each individual has had experiences in the world that are at least slightly different from others'; sociocultural knowledge is differentially distributed among members of a society (Gearing & Sangree, 1978; Wallace, 1970). Each participant, therefore, may fill in around the very same words in different ways and in ways different from what the speaker intends. (See Garfinkel, 1967, pp. 38ff., for additional explanation; for an illustration refer to Erickson, 1975.)

Thus, sociocultural standards (or rules) do not "tell" participants in social interaction how to make sense of others' behavior or what the situation is now; they do not "give" persons interpretations of social phenomena. Rather, sociocultural standards serve as a body of resources on which people creatively draw in interpreting what others mean by their words and actions.

Simultaneously, of course, as participants engage in the work of interpreting—attending to and making sense of the scene and others' emerging behavior—they themselves are also acting. (Participants in social life may take turns at speaking, but everyone is always engaged in behaving.) As they interpret "who we are and what we are doing now" from moment to moment, they are perpetually determining how to act appropriately given their interpretations and given their social intents at the moment, that is, what they hope to achieve through their actions. Just as sociocultural standards do not tell persons the correct interpretation of others' behavior, they do not mandate what, specifically, is appropriate for a person to do at a particular moment in interaction. Rather, they guide people toward a range of options, deemed situationally appropriate in their group's culture, for realizing their social intents (cf. Cazden, 1974). Choosing among these options in ways that will communicate the subtleties of their social perceptions and intentions at the moment is part of the creative work in which participants in social exchanges routinely engage.

To summarize the theory of social organization presented here, participants actively and creatively construct social events. Drawing on sociocultural rules, maps, and plans, each participant perpetually interprets "what is going on now" as new perceptual data are generated through others' actions. And each participant continuously and simultaneously acts on the basis of his or her interpretations, selecting among the options for behaving that his or her interpretations of the situation and of the relevant situa-

tional rules suggest are appropriate, given his or her personal social intents. In this way, through their successive, collective interpretations and actions, participants collaboratively assemble everyday social events.

How does all this relate to a program that one might want to evaluate? Very simply, any educational or other program and the results it produces are actually an interdependent network of social events, each of which is constructed through the very processes just described.

Five Implications for the Design and Conduct of Evaluation Fieldwork

As suggested earlier, this research-based, constitutive-ethnographic theory of social organization provides a link between the phenomenological perspective of naturalistic-qualitative evaluation inquiry and its fieldwork method—a link that has been missing in methods texts and in most evaluations. The linkage takes the form of theory-based principles for determining where to look, what to look for, and how to structure looking in order to identify and gain data on those local systems of meaning, belief, value, and action that are constitutive of and/or functionally relevant to the particular program to be evaluated and the results that it generates. Five of the most fundamental of these principles are spelled out below. Collectively, they form the foundation for an ethnographic approach to evaluation fieldwork.

A First Principle: Treat the Program's Definition and Boundaries as Problematic

Oriented by the constitutive theory presented above, evaluation fieldwork should treat the definition and boundaries of the program to be studied as problematic. It should consider participants' interpretations of "the program" as a central matter during inquiry.

It is true that nearly every program is defined and explained in a variety of documents: enabling legislation, administrative guidelines, "how-to" booklets, curriculum objectives and materials, and/or others. In addition, participants at local sites can usually gain information on particular programs in face-to-face briefings with various experts. But as is the case with all symbols, the language of these sources is indexical, inherently incomplete. None of them is, nor are all collectively, a complete script for assembling and maintaining the program from moment to moment. Those who are to enact the program as part of their daily lives, therefore, must draw upon their sociocultural knowledge and personal experiences in order to determine, first, which available documents and which briefings merit greatest attention and, next, exactly what the words they contain mean for action "here and now."

Ethnographic evaluators, then, should treat definitions of the program inherent in documents, in briefings by program experts, and in the interview accounts of participants as open to interpretation as part of the normal, natural course of social affairs. They should approach these accounts as data. In so doing, their primary interest should not be in whether participants at a particular site have arrived at a "correct" understanding of the program. Instead, evaluators interested in participants' realities should be concerned with how the interpretation(s) apparent at this site have been achieved and how these interpretations function in the program's enactment. Furthermore (for reasons to be elaborated later), evaluation fieldwork should seek local interpretations of the program in naturally occurring interaction, turning to interviews only as a way of obtaining elaboration on what was observed. And recognizing the perpetual interdependence between participants' ongoing interpretations and actions, ethnographic evaluators should consider participants' interpretations of the program as likely to be dynamic rather than static. They should keep an eye out for evolution in participants' conceptualization and performance of the program over time.

A Second Principle: Focus Inquiry on Central Interactional Events

As evaluation fieldworkers begin inquiry, they are faced with two fundamental questions: (1) What level of social organization should we concentrate on in conducting observation, interviewing, and so forth? (2) Aside from participants' interpretations of the program itself, what elements of participants' culture(s) (or social realities) should we include in our inquiry?

Constitutive ethnographers usually resolve these questions by centering initial inquiry on whole events that routinely recur and compose the central scenes in which the social endeavor under study is played out. This tactic has two distinct advantages. Both facilitate the more economical use of inquiry resources.

First, participants can readily and relatively reliably direct evaluators to the events that they see as central to their program effort. Chunks of social life at this intermediate organizational level are especially salient for participants. They most often agree on names for events— PTA meeting, staff development session, legislative briefing, reading lesson, and so on. They can roughly define when events begin and end (Erickson & Shultz, 1981). They can usually tell the evaluator what, in general, each type of event is for and about. The boundaries, labels, and meanings of larger and (especially) smaller units of social life tend to be much more difficult for participants to identify and/ or agree upon.

Second and more important, concentrating on routinely recurring, central program events helps to focus inquiry on those elements of participants' culture(s) and social organization that are functionally relevant to the program's enactment, that is, those that participants are actually using as they construct and maintain the program from day to day. Using techniques described in the following sections, evaluators can begin to locate these program-relevant features of culture and social organization as they are displayed in participants' naturally occurring interactional behavior. Then, future inquiry steps can be designed and directed toward understanding and describing them more fully, ascertaining whether they do indeed function to influence the program, and if so how—through what chains of events, through what networks of social thought and action. Meanwhile, other aspects of participants' culture and social organization can be set in the background, unless and until they too appear relevant to the program or its effects.

An example will help clarify this process. In one evaluation of a California education program (Dorr-Bremme, 1979), initial observation focused on formal, school-site planning meetings and informal decisionmaking encounters that routinely occurred during the school day between meetings. Participants' judgments, confirmed by observation, indicated that these were key program events. Parents were allocated seats on the site council at each school by law, and everyone concerned with the program interpreted parent involvement as a main program goal. Nevertheless, parents were rarely present during the informal encounters in which program decisions were substantially made, and they played only a minor role in formal planning meetings. All this suggested the need to explore the general social organization of parent-school relationships, that is, at a broader hierarchical level. It also suggested the need to examine the social organization of discourse in the meetings, that is, at a lower or more fine-grained level, in order to understand how the roles that parents and others routinely played in the meetings were socially produced. Findings from the former line of inquiry illuminated how parents' and staff members' beliefs about societal roles became enacted in some broad institutional arrangements, arrangements that inadvertently but systematically deterred parent involvement in the program. The latter line of sociolinguistic inquiry uncovered ways in which staff members' jargon and interactional strategies during meetings functioned systematically (but again inadvertently) to discourage and subordinate the participation of those parents who did turn out for them. Each set of findings had clear implications for program management and the delivery of program support services by the state education agency.

In summary, the general tactic in evaluation fieldwork following the constitutive theory should be to center initial inquiry on routinely recurring, interactional events that are central to the program and then to direct inquiry "outward" and/or "inward" in order to identify and trace relationships of functional relevance.

A Third Principle: Emphasize Ethnographic Observation

Evaluation fieldwork designed in light of the constitutive theory should allocate resources such that ethnographic observation takes precedence over interviewing. This is a departure from what advocates of naturalistic-qualitative evaluation generally recommend in that (a) they place equal emphasis on interviewing and observing, suggesting that interviewing is especially important for getting at program participants' realities and notions of meaning (this follows from their tendency to treat realities and meaning as subjective states that lie only in the minds of participants); and (b) they generally overlook the importance of explicitly seeking participants' realities and meanings in their naturally occurring, everyday talk and actions. Ethnographic observation, especially when based in the constitutive theory, emphasizes this. Let us see why.

The constitutive theory of social organization posits that as people proceed through their daily social lives, they interpret the context from moment to moment: They continually make sense of who we are and what we are doing now. As they do so, they routinely select their current and next actions in light of the context as they have interpreted it, within the parameters of their sociocultural standards of appropriateness.

This process goes on during interviews as it does during other social occasions. Interview respondents make sense of the situation or context. The respondent draws on his or her sociocultural knowledge and the interviewer's behavior to arrive at interpretations of matters such as the social identity of the interviewer (what kind of a person she or he is), the interviewer's reasons for coming here now, why the interviewer wants to interview him or her, what social rights and obligations the interviewer and respondent have with regard to one another in general and in this specific situation, and so on. As the interview itself unfolds, these and similar features of the context are the subject of continual, implicit, interactional negotiation between researcher and respondent as they read one another's evolving behavior (Cicourel, 1974, pp. 11–41; Erickson & Schultz, 1982).

Furthermore, the respondent is in the position of having to interpret what exactly, in the situation of the moment, the interviewer wants to know. There are a great many ways of organizing and describing any part of one's personal experience or knowledge, even in response to a question that appears on the surface to be very simple and straightforward. What is more, the interviewer's language, along with other symbolic forms, is indexical. Interviewers cannot possibly say all that they mean in so many words; they must count on respondents' abilities as culture members to fill in sensible meanings around what they literally say. Thus, from moment to moment throughout an interview, respondents need to interpret what aspects of their knowledge and experience the questions seem to call for. They must also decide which ways of approaching the topic and wording their account seem best: where to start, how to sequence the explanation or description, how much detail to give, what to emphasize, what terminology to use, and so on. These and other communicative decisions are based on the respondent's evolving interpretations of what the researchers' project is about, what kind of a person the interviewer is, why he or she was chosen to be interviewed, and so forth, as well as in view of the wording of the particular query the interviewer has just posed.

In short, the interview places the respondent in a social context outside the flow of everyday life. It presents him or her with the task of producing, *in this situation* (as he or she is interpreting it), talk about some aspect(s) of the program or other feature(s) of his or her daily affairs. What the interviewer receives, then, is not "facts" or even the respondent's perceptions of the facts. What the interviewer receives is a jointly produced and situated account of some actions, thinking, or emotions. It is a jointly produced account in that it is generated by the successive interactional moves of both respondent and interviewer. And it is a situated, or context-specific, account in that it is produced "here and now" within the successive frames of the respondent's moment-to-moment interpretations of what is going on and what that implies for his or her action choices. Whether the beliefs and values and feelings, the perceptions and interpretations, described in this sit-

uation are in any way functionally relevant to the program is uncertain. Whether they are depends on whether the interviewee holds, experiences, and uses them in taking action in one or another of a variety of naturally occurring, everyday contexts. And all of this remains true regardless of how carefully worded and sequenced the interview questions are, how much affective "rapport" is established, and how "truthful" the respondent strives to be. As anthropologist Charles O. Frake (1980) has summarized it, "The problem with [respondents'] verbalized interpretations is not a difficulty in eliciting them, but in locating what cues are being responded to [by the respondent] in formulating an interpretation" (p. 50).

This does not mean that an evaluator operating from a constitutive theory of social organization would reject interviewing or would relegate interview accounts to the status of "mere talk." (The role that interviewing can appropriately play will be discussed a bit later.) Rather, as Frake (1980) points out, it means that

perhaps instead of trying to devise provocative questions and other instruments to persuade people to talk about things they do not ordinarily talk about in that way, we should take as a serious topic of investigation what people in fact talk about, or, better, what they are in fact doing when they talk. When we look at talk, we find that people do not so much ask and answer inquiries; they propose, defend, and negotiate interpretations of what is happening. Because what is happening is what we are interested in explicating, these interpretations provide the key to understanding. (p. 50)

Evaluators operating from the constitutive theory, then, should place heavy emphasis on observation and, in observing and documenting, on what program participants say in naturally occurring circumstances. They should do so not because seeing what is going on is more important than people's ideas and beliefs, values and interpretations. Rather, they should do so because the ideas, beliefs, values, and interpretations that people are using to generate what is going on, as well as their moment-to-moment sense of what is going on, are displayed in their everyday talk and actions. This follows from the premise that culture is intersubjective in nature. As Erickson (1979a) has explained,

> The assumption is that people engaged in face-to-face interaction are constantly engaged in telling each other verbally and nonverbally what is going on, what the "rules" are, and what the context is—and that careful analysis of their "telling" can elucidate their underlying purposes and rules of procedure. Statements of such regularities, then, would not be just an arbitrary construction of the researcher, but would actually make contact with the points of view of those involved in the action. (p. 6)

Observing with this assumption in mind is what was intended by the term *ethnographic observation* used in introducing this section. Observing ethnographically means keeping a weather eye (and ear) out for what people in interaction are "telling" one another about their sociocultural systems of standards for perceiving, believing, evaluating, and acting; about their notions of kinds of people, things, and social contexts; and about the situation-specific social meanings of actions. (Principle #5 below, on using ethnographic rules of evidence, elaborates on how to do this.)

Observing in this way entails a very different kind of noticing or attending than most naturalistic or qualitative evaluation methodologists usually recommend. It also entails a different way of thinking about what one has observed. And to reiterate: This kind of ethnographic observation would be the fundamental data-collection method in an evaluation oriented by the constitutive theory presented earlier.

A Fourth Principle: Use Interviews To Guide and Explicate Observation

For the reasons set forth above, interviewing should play a supplemental role in an evaluation oriented by the constitutive ethnographic theory of social organization. Most important, it should help to guide observation and to explicate what is observed.

Interviews as a guide to observation. Interviews can guide the evaluator's observations in two ways: (1) They can suggest where and when to observe; and (2) they can suggest issues and dynamics to attend to in observing.

Especially during the early stages of inquiry, interviewing can help the evaluator to locate the interactional events in which, from participants' points of view, the program is routinely enacted. They can also help indicate which of these scenes participants construe as most central to their program efforts. Similarly, when interview respondents describe connections between program elements and other phenomena in their world, their remarks can direct observation to settings, scenes, and activities that might otherwise be deemed irrelevant to the program and its results.

That interviewing can help indicate where and when to observe, as well as what to attend to in observing, is hardly a unique idea. The point here, however, is that from a constitutive-ethnographic perspective interview information can only serve as a guide—it cannot be treated as primary study data—unless and until it is tied to phenomena that are observed in naturally occurring events and related functionally to the program. This follows from the ethnographer's primary interest in functional relationships and social meaning, as well as from the view of interview remarks as jointly produced, situated accounts.

Interviews to explicate what is observed. This second major role for interviewing in an ethnographic evaluation is by far the more important. The constitutive theory, as noted earlier, posits that group members display their sociocultural standards (or social realities) in interaction: They continually inform one another through their verbal and nonverbal behavior about their situation-specific social purposes and about "what is going on now, what the 'rules' are, and what the context is" (Erickson, 1979a, p. 6). Nevertheless, everything that is going on for participants cannot be taken as unequivocally apparent in their interaction. In developing an emic description of the action observed, evaluators should check their behavior-based analysis of the action with the participants who were involved in it. Thus, the greatest part of the ethnographic evaluator's interviewing should be undertaken to elicit participants' descriptions and explanations of the program-relevant interactions in which they routinely engage. One good strategy for obtaining such information is to ask people to describe what they are doing as they are doing it or as soon thereafter as possible. Another is to use a videotape or audiotape record of an event to help participants recall during interviews what they were doing and thinking during the interaction recorded (e.g., Dorr-Bremme, 1982; Erickson & Shultz, 1982). Bringing the interview to the naturally occurring interactional scene (or, in the latter case, bringing the interactional scene to the interview with a recording) helps provide access to the beliefs, values, and ideas, the context-specific rules for interpretation and action, and so forth, that participants were actually using to construct the observed event. The goal, then, is not only to capture participants' interpretations and intents while they are still fresh in participants' minds. More important, it is to help the respondent sustain the naturally occurring context as the salient interpretive frame—to facilitate respondents' ability to report on their actions and thoughts in terms of the everyday interactional scene, rather than in terms of the interview context.

A Fifth Principle: Use Ethnographic Rules of Evidence

Most works on naturalistic/qualitative evaluation enjoin investigators to search inductively for "patterns, themes, and categories" in their data (Patton, 1980, p. 306). In the naturalistic or qualitative paradigm, these "recurring regularities in sources" (Guba & Lincoln, 1981, p. 93) indicate directions for ongoing inquiry; in final data analysis, they constitute findings. The nature of the patterns that evaluators should seek, however, is described rather incompletely in most writing on naturalistic-qualitative evaluation. Usually, examples of patterns and categories from actual evaluation data are given, and the investigator is advised to look for ideas, actions, words, and phrases that recur and seem logically connected.

Ethnographers also seek patterns in this way as they conduct inquiry and review their data, but they are usually more specific about the kinds of patterns that count as evidence. Fundamentally, they seek *patterns of co-occurrence among phenomena*—patterns that display the system(s) of standards for perceiving, believing, evaluating, and acting which group members are using in situ to organize their affairs.

Phenomena can co-occur in two ways. When they routinely occur at a particular moment in time and function conjointly, they are described as in vertical co-occurrence. When they recur consistently together in sequence and function in relation to one another, they are described as in horizontal co-occurrence (see Ervin-Tripp, 1972).

Co-occurrence patterns can be found at various levels of social organization. Some display the very small or brief contexts that participants recognize, the social meanings that particular behaviors have in those contexts, and the rules for selecting and interpreting actions appropriately that are applicable in context. While evaluators have seldom had time to examine co-occurrence patterns at this fine-grained level, they should be aware of them. The social meanings and interactional "rules" that they reveal can be tremendously important to the quality of social service programs and their outcomes, and some highly focused evaluations could profit by taking this into account. Furthermore, patterns at this level of social organization illustrate the principle of co-occurrence in its truest, most elegant form. One example should serve to demonstrate all of this.

Working in Chicago in the late 1960s, Erickson (1975, 1979b; Erickson & Shultz, 1982) noticed that blacks often reported that they had been "talked down to" in encounters with white organizational "gate-keepers." Erickson's research traced this experience, in part, to differences in black and white communicational styles. Among white conversationalists, he discovered, a speaker's simultaneous production of a clause terminal juncture, moderately falling intonation, and a glance toward the listener routinely meant, "I want to know if you are attending and following what I am saying." In other words, the vertical co-occurrence of these behaviors meant that the listener was expected to provide some listening response more or less immediately. This social meaning was demonstrated in the routine (horizontal or sequential) co-occurrence of such a response in the form of a vocalized "Mmmhmm," "yeah," a head nod, and so forth. That forms of behavior such as these in fact functioned as listening responses (i.e., meant socially, "I'm following what you're saying") was revealed in what the speakers regularly did next (another pattern of horizontal co-occurrence). Recognizing a listening response in the behavior of listeners, speakers routinely went on to their next speaking point. Failing to receive such a response, speakers consistently persisted at the same point, reiterating it in progressively simplified and concrete ways until the listener performed some form of listening behavior.

Erickson found, however, that among black conversationalists the implicit rules for signaling when listening responses were relevant and the rules for appropriately showing listening were quite different from those routinely used by whites. Thus, while white listeners consistently supplied listening responses to white speakers at appropriate moments with the white conversational system, black listeners routinely did not. It followed that white speakers (assuming that their black conversational partners weren't listening or understanding) regularly "overexplained" and simplified the points they were trying to make. This left blacks feeling demeaned; they often experienced the "talking down" as an instance of racism (e.g., Erickson, 1975, pp. 54–55). Furthermore, this pattern of interactional dissonance had other consequences. In the junior college counseling encounters studied by Erickson, it was one factor that contributed to black students routinely receiving less "special help" from white counselors than white students received.

While such subtle patterns as these can clearly be very important to social outcomes, patterns of co-occurrence can readily be found among larger, more enduring and obvious phenomena—phenomena that most evaluations can readily

examine. A short-term, exploratory, school district evaluation of compensatory education reading programs in elementary schools (Dorr-Bremme, 1981) offers some examples. At the broadest level of social organization examined, the study discovered the following pattern of co-occurrence: (a) consistently high reading test scores + (b) schoolwide emphasis on "reading for understanding" + (c) high standards and expectations for students' performance + (d) organizational strategies that reduced the number of reading-ability groups per teacher + (e) curriculum and staff stability over time. That is, program features (b) through (e) were routinely copresent in schools with consistently higher test scores in reading, and they were routinely absent in comparable schools with comparable students but median or low test scores in reading. (See Keesling, Dorr-Bremme, & King, 1981–82, for the contrastive analysis of schools with median and low scores.) These two, contrasting co-occurrence patterns— (higher scores) + (b) + (c) + (d) + (e) and (median or low scores) + (not b) + (not c) + (not d) + (not e)—strongly suggested that higher scores and the four program features listed were functionally interdependent.

It is important to recognize that each of the features labeled (b) through (e) was in itself a co-occurrence pattern, a pattern which was in turn made up of and displayed in a number of more specific patterns of co-occurrence among phenomena. It is impossible, of course, to recount all of these here; but consider (c), high standards and expectations for students' performance, as an example. At an intermediate level of social organization (the instructional unit), high standards were regularly manifest in the following sequential pattern: (introduction of concept or skill X) + (in-class assignment on X) + (homework assignment on X) + (lesson to elaborate concept or skill X_1) + (in-class assignment on X_1) + (homework assignment on X_1), and so on. In other words, reading homework was given daily in higher scoring schools, and it served to provide added practice with skills and concepts introduced in class. In schools with median and low test scores, by contrast, reading homework was rarely given;

when it was, it did not consistently connect with the day's classroom instruction. At lower levels of social organization, for example, in certain situations in daily lessons, still other co-occurrence patterns demonstrated teachers' high standards and expectations. Figure 1 illustrates one of these. It shows what routinely happened in higher scoring schools in a daily context we can call "collecting last night's homework." Summarized, Figure 1 indicates that teachers consistently held students accountable for not doing their homework and for not putting forth their best effort. Under these conditions, observations suggested, nearly all students turned in their homework on time and few had to redo assignments. A very different pattern, however, appeared in the same context in comparable schools with median or low reading test scores. Teachers there simply accepted whatever homework was turned in; they did not require those who had not done their homework to complete it. They also omitted the review cycle shown in Figure 1; they did not routinely require students to redo work that was less than their best. Under these circumstances, many students routinely failed to turn in the few homework assignments that were given.

Coming full circle, these and similar co-occurrence patterns reflected abiding differences in teachers' beliefs about students. Teachers in higher scoring schools consistently labeled the behaviors described above as instances of "high standards" and/or "high expectations." Furthermore, they explained that such expectations were reasonable because (as one teacher put it in a characteristic remark) "these youngsters can learn despite the kinds of problems they face in their home and community." In contrast, teachers in schools with low and median scores in reading recurrently cited community socioeconomic conditions as explanations for their instructional choices and for students' lower reading achievement.

These examples illustrate how contrasting patterns of co-occurrence at various, nested levels of social organization can reveal the social meanings, beliefs, and practices that program participants routinely use to organize their program activities and (thus) to generate program effects.

Ethnographers can establish co-occurrence relationships of the types described above in three ways.

First and most basically, they can identify them in patterns of the copresence and contrastive relevance of particular phenomena. This should be evident from the preceding discussion. Note that in

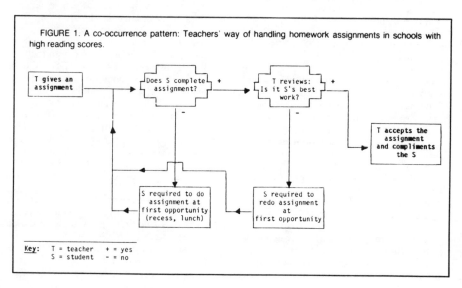

FIGURE 1. A co-occurrence pattern: Teachers' way of handling homework assignments in schools with high reading scores.

each case the mere copresence of a particular set of phenomena was not enough to establish co-occurrence. Rather, the phenomena had to be copresent *and* functionally relevant to some other phenomena of interest. Contrastive analysis established the functional relevance of each item in the pattern and (thus) of the pattern as a whole. That is, when a given set of phenomena was present together in a particular context, one thing routinely followed (speakers continued to their next point, test scores were higher, etc.). When one or more of those same phenomena was absent, in contrast, something else routinely occurred (speakers reiterated the same point, test scores were lower, etc.).

Second, co-occurrence relationships are also evident when participants in interaction make the absence of some behavior explicitly accountable, that is, when one participant calls for another to explain why he or she did not perform some specific behavior, or when a participant offers an account of another's "missing" behavior. When this happens, the observer can infer that there is a "rule" for the occurrence of the expected behavior in the place where it is missed (Mehan & Wood, 1975, pp. 132–134; Schegloff, 1972). This principle is apparent in everyday remarks such as, "I called you; why didn't you answer? Are you mad at me?" Similarly, in Figure 1 the recurrent teacher behaviors that follow missing or low-quality student homework demonstrate the following rule: When homework is assigned, each student should have it done the next day, and it should reflect his or her best effort.

Third, co-occurrence relationships can be located in participants' positive and negative sanctions of one another's behavior. When participants routinely sanction particular types of behavior, they are telling others in the scene (and the investigator as well) what the rules for appropriate action are here and now. Classroom scenes are replete with instances of positive and negative sanctions, many of which include explicit formulations of appropriateness rules, for example, "I like the way Juan and Charlene are working quietly." Instances are also readily available in routine program interactions: "We can't approve this plan; once again, it

wasn't discussed with the entire staff." "The state is pleased to commend the following district reading programs for their excellence in attending to bilingual issues . . . "

In summary, patterns of co-occurrence are the main evidentiary base of ethnographic accounts and should serve as such in evaluations oriented by the theory presented earlier. Co-occurrence patterns are recognizable in the behaviors that routinely "go together" at particular kinds of moments and those that routinely follow one another in sequence through time and which are functionally relevant to one another and (thus) to the social event in question and the program as a whole. Once again, the functional relevance proviso is a key one. It differentiates the constitutive ethnographer's concept of co-occurrence from the statistician's concept of correlation. The functional relevance of a specific behavior or set of behaviors is apparent interactionally: What happens next when the behavior is present is systematically different from what happens next when the action is absent. From this perspective, "deviant" or "discrepant" cases—cases that do not fit the pattern apparent in most comparable instances— are not treated as "unexplained variance" as they are when statistical methods are employed. Rather, as Mehan (1979) notes, "When action takes place that seems to violate the rules, but participants do not mark the violations, it means the data have not been described adequately" (p. 105).

Summary and Conclusions

The investigator's theory of social organization inevitably structures fieldwork inquiry and the reality portrayed in the description it yields. In naturalistic-qualitative evaluation, therefore, theory selection is an issue of "reality control" and (thus) of quality control.

Drawing on contemporary constitutive ethnography, this article has provided a research-based theory and five inquiry principles that follow from it. Together these can give naturalistic-qualitative evaluation access to social realities it purports to seek: those that program participants experience and act in terms of each day as they generate and sustain the program and program effects under study. To date, such theory has not been part of naturalistic or qualitative evaluation. Using the theory and design principles provided here brings evaluation fieldwork closer to the phenomenological orientation and research paradigm of its ethnographic roots and to ethnographic criteria for validity. There are, however, also good, practical reasons for naturalistic-qualitative evaluation to follow the guidelines laid out here, reasons that go beyond validity to assuring acceptance and utility.

Evaluators generally think of naturalistic-qualitative approaches as especially useful for gaining close-up, holistic, richly detailed information on programs, innovations, and routine institutional operations as they occur in the complexity of real-world contexts. Thus, they usually recommend them for types of evaluations that can best utilize these strengths. Among these are formative evaluation, implementation evaluation, process evaluation, and evaluations that follow "responsive" (Stake, 1975), "illuminative" (Parlett & Hamilton, 1976), and other "transactional" evaluation models (e.g., Guba, 1978, pp. 38ff; Guba & Lincoln, 1981; Patton, 1980, pp. 49ff). But note that these kinds of evaluation tend generally to be oriented toward program management, fine-tuning, or improvement. They tend to emphasize meeting evaluation audiences' information needs and responding to multiple value perspectives. For these purposes, more than richly detailed, holistic information is needed. Information is needed that accurately shows how participants have assembled the program and its "outcomes" using their ideas and beliefs about what is real and true, using their values and interpretations of meaning.

Such information puts local-site participants and other audiences in touch with "what is going on" in a compelling way. When participants find that an evaluation portrays the social meanings and social realities that they know and experience, they are more likely to accept that evaluation as valid and useful. Moreover, an evaluation that makes contact with participants' realities in its description and analysis can actually be more useful than one that does not. It can enable program sponsors, administrators, and local managers to better understand how things have come to be as they are. More specifically, it can detail how participants—acting in terms of their particular understandings of how the world operates, what the program is for and about, and so forth—have come to enact the program as they have. It can also show how their enactments have come to produce the effects that they have. With this kind of diagnosis in hand, decisionmakers can make more appropriate prescriptions. They can make decisions that take into account more fully and respond more sensitively to the needs, concerns, and viewpoints of participants in local settings. This, in turn, can increase the chances that the program or innovation will be carried out locally with enthusiasm and with goals and procedures in line with those intended by sponsors and central administrators. In other words, evaluation findings that make contact with participants' realities can facilitate a process of mutual adaptation: the modification of overall program goals and methods in light of local realities and the exigencies they entail, and the adjustment of local goals and operations in the direction of the larger program's goals. There is good evidence to suggest that mutual adaptation along these lines is important to successful program implementation as well as to program longevity (McLaughlin, 1976).

A final point: The kind of ethnographic inquiry outlined here can be more time consuming and expensive than some of the quick, interview-dominated site visits that have come to be labeled as naturalistic or qualitative evaluation. This theory-based ethnographic approach, however, is completely compatible with the scope and resources of many on-site evaluations and policy studies that have been conducted. Furthermore, with careful focusing on central program events as recommended here, this approach can play a significant role even in modest evaluation efforts.

References

BATESON, G. (1972). *Steps to an ecology of mind.* New York: Ballantine Books.

CAZDEN, C. (1974). Functions of language in the classroom; Two reviews and a reply. *Research in the Teaching of English, 8*, 60-65.

CICOUREL, A. V. (1974). *Cognitive sociology.* New York: Free Press.

DORR-BREMME, D. W. (1979). *Study of the California school improvement program* (Vol. 2: Case Studies). Los Angeles: Center for the Study of Evaluation, University of California, Los Angeles.

DORR-BREMME, D. W. (1981). *Higher reading achievement in Los Angeles Title I elementary schools: An exploratory study of underlying factors* (CSE Report No. 190). Los Angeles: Center for the Study of Evaluation, University of California, Los Angeles. (ERIC Document Reproduction Service No. ED 219 728)

DORR-BREMME, D. W. (1982). Behaving and making sense: Creating social organization in the classroom. *Dissertation Abstracts International, 43,* 1945A-1946A. (University Microfilms No. 82-23, 203)

DORR-BREMME, D. W. (1985). Naturalistic evaluation. In T. Husen & T. N. Postlethwaite (Eds.), *The international encyclopedia of education: Research and studies.* Oxford, England: Pergamon Press.

ERICKSON, F. (1971). *The cycle of situational frames: A model for microethnography in urban anthropology.* Paper presented at the annual meeting of the Midwest Anthropological Association, Detroit, Michigan.

ERICKSON, F. (1975). Gatekeeping and the melting pot. *Harvard Educational Review, 45*(1), 44-70.

ERICKSON, F. (1977). Some approaches to inquiry in school-community ethnography. *Anthropology and Education Quarterly, 8*(2), 58-69.

ERICKSON, F. (1979a). *On standards of descriptive validity in studies of classroom activity* (Institute for Research on Teaching Occasional Paper #16). East Lansing: Institute for Research on Teaching, College of Education, Michigan State University.

ERICKSON, F. (1979b). Talking down: Some cultural sources of miscommunication in inter-racial interviews. In A. Wolfgang (Ed.), *Research in nonverbal communication.* New York: Academic Press.

ERICKSON, F., & SHULTZ, J. (1981). When is a context? Some issues and methods in the analysis of social competence. In J. Green & C. Wallat (Eds.), *Ethnography and language in education settings* (pp. 147-160). Norwood, NJ: Ablex.

ERICKSON, F., & SHULTZ, J. (1982). *The counselor as gatekeeper: Social interaction in interviews.* New York: Academic Press.

ERVIN-TRIPP, S. (1972). On sociolinguistic rules: Alteration and co-occurrence. In D. Hymes & J. Gumperz (Eds.), *Directions in sociolinguistics: The ethnography of communication* (pp. 213-250). New York: Holt, Rinehart and Winston.

FIRESTONE, W. A., & HERRIOTT, R. E. (1984). Multisite qualitative policy research: Some design and implementation issues. In D. M. Fetterman (Ed.), *Ethnography in educational evaluation* (pp. 63-88). Beverly Hills, CA: Sage.

FRAKE, C. O. (1980). Plying frames can be dangerous: Some reflections on methodology in cultural anthropology. In C. O. Frake, *Language and cultural description: Essays by Charles O. Frake* (pp. 45-60). Stanford, CA: Stanford University Press.

GARFINKEL, H. (1967). *Studies in ethnomethodology.* Englewood Cliffs, NJ: Prentice-Hall.

GEARING, F., & SANGREE, L. (1978). *Toward a general cultural theory of education and schooling.* Chicago: Aldine.

GOFFMAN, E. (1961). *Asylums.* New York: Doubleday.

GOODENOUGH, W. H. (1964). Cultural anthropology and linguistics. In D. Hymes (Ed.), *Language in culture and society: A reader in linguistics and anthropology* (pp. 36-39). New York: Harper & Row.

GOODENOUGH, W. H. (1975). Multiculturalism as the normal human experience. *Anthropology and Education Quarterly, 7*(4), 4-7.

GOODENOUGH, W. H. (1981). *Culture, language, and society* (2d ed.). Menlo Park, CA: Benjamin/Cummings.

GUBA, E. G. (1978). *Toward a methodology of naturalistic inquiry in educational evaluation* (CSE Monograph Series in Evaluation No. 8). Los Angeles: Center for the Study of Evaluation, University of California, Los Angeles.

GUBA, E. G., & LINCOLN, Y. S. (1981). *Effective evaluation: Improving the usefulness of evaluation results through responsive and naturalistic approaches.* San Francisco: Jossey-Bass.

GUMPERZ, J. (1972). The speech community. In P. P. Giglioli (Ed.), *Language and social context* (pp. 219-230). Harmondsworth, Middlesex, England: Penguin Education.

HAMILTON, D., et al. (Eds.). (1978). *Beyond the numbers game.* Berkeley, CA: McCutchan.

HARRIS, M. (1968). *The rise of anthropological theory.* New York: Thomas Y. Crowell.

HYMES D. (1972). Introduction. In C. B. Cazden, V. P. John, & D. Hymes (Eds.), *Functions of language in the classroom* (pp. xi-lvii). New York: Teachers College Press.

HYMES, D. (1974). *Foundations of sociolinguistics: An ethnographic approach.* Philadelphia: University of Pennsylvania Press.

HYMES, D. (1982). What is ethnography? In P. Gilmore & A. A. Greenblatt (Eds.), *Children in and out of school* (pp. 21-32). Washington, DC: Center for Applied Linguistics.

KEESLING, W., DORR-BREMME, D. W., & KING, N. (1981-82). *Final report from the first year of a three-year study of effective practices in Title I schools.* Los Angeles: Los Angeles Unified School District Research and Evaluation Branch.

McDERMOTT, R. P. (1976). Kids make sense: An ethnographic account of the interactional management of success and failure in one first grade classroom. *Dissertation Abstracts International, 38,* 1505A. (University Microfilms No. 77-18, 265)

McLAUGHLIN, M. (1976). Implementation as mutual adaptation. In W. Williams & R. F. Elmore (Eds.), *Social program implementation.* New York: Academic Press.

MEHAN, H. (1978). Structuring school structure. *Harvard Educational Review, 48*(1), 32-64.

MEHAN, H. (1979). *Learning lessons: Social organization in the classroom.* Cambridge, MA: Harvard University Press.

MEHAN, H. (1982). The structure of classroom events and their consequences for student performance. In P. Gilmore & A. A. Greenblatt (Eds.), Children in and out of school (pp. 59–87). Washington, DC: Center for Applied Linguistics.

MEHAN, H., & WOOD, H. (1975). The reality of ethnomethodology. New York: Wiley Interscience.

PARLETT, M., & HAMILTON, D. (1976). Evaluation as illumination: A new approach to the study of innovatory programs. In G. V Glass (Ed.), Evaluation studies annual review (Vol. 1, pp. 140–157). Beverly Hills, CA: Sage.

PATTON, M. Q. (1980). Qualitative evaluation methods. Beverly Hills, CA: Sage.

SCHEGLOFF, E. (1972). Sequencing in conversational openings. In D. Hymes & J. Gumperz (Eds.), Directions in sociolinguistics: The ethnography of communication (pp. 346–380). New York: Holt, Rinehart and Winston.

SPRADLEY, J. P. (1972). Foundations of cultural knowledge. In J. P. Spradley (Ed.), Culture and cognition: Rules, maps and plans (pp. 3–38). San Francisco: Chandler.

STAKE, R. E. (1975). Evaluating the arts in education: A responsive approach. Columbus, OH: Charles E. Merrill.

WALLACE, A. F. G. (1970). Culture and personality (2d ed.). New York: Random House.

Author

DONALD W. DORR-BREMME, Senior Research Associate, Center for the Study of Evaluation, Graduate School of Education, University of California, Los Angeles, CA 90024. Specializations: Educational anthropology, classroom and school social organization, naturalistic research and evaluation.

22

Drawing Valid Meaning from Qualitative Data
Toward a Shared Craft
Matthew B. Miles and A. Michael Huberman

Most researchers would agree that, to know what you're doing, you need to know how your model of knowing affects what you are doing. Your model, however, may not be the same as your colleague's. Thus, it is not surprising that the *Educational Researcher* over the past year has contained a good deal of impassioned argument at the paradigmatic level (Eisner, 1983; Phillips, 1983; Smith, 1983b; Tuthill & Ashton, 1983).

The debate turns around the claim that epistemologies and procedures such as logical empiricism, scientism, the hypothetico-deductive method, realism, experimentalism, and instrumentalism all go together and are inherently different from—in fact, incompatible with—contrasting epistemologies and procedures of phenomenology, hermeneutics, critical theory, verstehen approaches, and artistic modes of knowing. It is argued (e.g., Norris, 1983, Smith, 1983b), that the quantitative and interpretive perspectives are irreconcilable; that claims of their complementary characteristics are unfounded; and that blending the two approaches will result in equivocal conclusions.

Matthew B. Miles is Senior Research Associate at the Center for Policy Research, Inc., 475 Riverside Drive, New York, New York 10115. His specializations are social psychology of education and the assessment of planned change.

A. Michael Huberman is Professor of Education at the University of Geneva, 6 ch. des Mouilleuses, 1287 Laconnex (GE), Switzerland. His specializations are adult learning, knowledge dissemination and utilization, and educational innovation.

This is a nontrivial battle, because it challenges the very foundations of the research enterprise, and particularly any given empirical study. But we are inclined to leave the battle to others, for several reasons. First, we continue to need working canons and procedures to judge the validity and usefulness of research in progress. Second, no one reasonably expects the dispute to be settled in any satisfactory way because it has come to rest on crystallized stances, each with its faithful, eager pack of recently-socialized disciples. Finally, if one looks carefully at the research actually conducted in the name of one or another epistemology, it seems that few working researchers are *not* blending the two perspectives.

One consequence of such blending is that more and more studies include not only quantitative but also qualitative data. Yet there is an Achilles heel here: As we shall show, there are few agreed-on canons for analysis of qualitative data, and therefore such work are uncertain. In the remainder of this article, after exploring the general paradigmatic debate a bit further, we place the need for clearer canons and methods of qualitative analysis in context, outline a conception of qualitative data analysis, and list a series of practical methods that seem promising for doing it. We conclude with a call for widespread experimentation, documentation, and sharing of methodological advances among qualitative researchers.

Epistemological Ecumenism

We contend that researchers should pursue their work, be open to an ecumenical blend of epistemol-

ogies and procedures, and leave the grand debate to those who care most about it. On what grounds?

The first answer is perhaps naive: If the debate is unlikely to be resolved during your working lifetime, it is probably best to get on with your work, clarifying for yourself and your readers in which camp you are nestled. It may turn out that no one is nestled firmly in any camp. A look at the evolution of leading neo-positivist methodologists (e.g., Cook & Campbell, 1979, Cronbach, 1975; Snow, 1974), shows that the more hard-nosed, quantitatively-oriented approaches to construct and external validity have shifted substantially toward the endorsement of context-embedded, qualitative, more interpretative inquiry. Similarly, as Mishler (1979) and others have shown, virtually no action theorist, social phenomenologist, ethnomethodologist or interpretive sociologist is actually conducting research fully consonant with the epistemological stance underlying the approach. Furthermore, much social phenomenological work derived from Husserl and Schutz has involved systematic, inferential, sometimes outright "etic" procedures—often needed to establish the validity of such constructs as typification or reflexivity—that would make some neo-positivists feel right at home.

Moreover, a close look at the actual practice of educational criticism and connoisseurship suggests that it is not a question of an "artist's" giving shape to seamless, inchoate material, but of an intense observer's scrupulous recording of naturally-occurring social interactions from which patterns are inferred and interpreted by many of the

From Matthew B. Miles and A. Michael Huberman, "Drawing Valid Meaning from Qualitative Data: Toward a Shared Craft," *Educational Researcher*, 1984, 20-30. Copyright 1984, American Educational Research Association, Washington, DC.

same algorithms that inductivist researchers use in a more clearly defined, logical-empiricist paradigm. The "artistry" (Eisner, 1981) is a sort of simile; there are no actual poems or dramas being produced here. Rather, there is a license to amplify or interpret the results of observations at a higher level of inference than might be warranted under the classical canons of inductive, Bayesian, or statistical inference. The results are expected to be taken seriously, to be accepted as plausible, even valid, beyond the corps of people using the critical perspective. Otherwise, no one beyond the observer would be illuminated, and no serious claims of connoisseurship could be made that other publics could acknowledge.

From the positivistic end, we should note that it is typical for the hardest of hypothetico-deductive noses to engage in inductive sniffing in data sets; to acknowledge the imposition of the researcher's vision on a messy world; to launch into flights of inspired intuition when it comes to giving names to objectively-found factors; and to give as much weight to what the subjects said after the experiment as to the type and frequency of the buttons they pushed. Epistemological purity doesn't get research done.

We might also note that many qualitative researchers are turning to more systematic methods of data storage, retrieval and analysis with the aid of micro-computers; see the articles in Conrad and Reinharz (1984). It is important not to confuse the systematic use of tools with one's epistemological position. Idealists can be structured, and realists can be loose.

A second, perhaps more widely accepted, reason for staying in the field and out of the debating forum is that both neo-positivism and neo-idealism constitute an epistemological continuum, not a dichotomy. Schools of thought are opposing at the conceptual extremes, but to unbundle each set is to release tremendous variability.

In this vein, Halfpenny (1982) has pointed out that positivism is not monolithic: There are at least 12 varieties. Several authors have shown that phenomenology and critical theory don't belong together

(McCutcheon, 1981), that ethnographic studies and ethnomethodology are different species, and that much current inquiry represents paradigmatic blends (see Norris, 1983, who deplores this in construct validation theory). It looks as if the research community is groping its way painfully to new paradigms, those that will be more ecumenical and probably more congruent with the data being collected and interpreted.

The history of research in many fields shows shifts from "either-or" to "both-and" formulations. Perhaps the most familiar shift is the accommodation between the supposedly incompatible wave and particle theories of light. Closer to home, we can invoke the long-standing polarization between behaviorists and cognitivists, which has softened enough that Piagetian constructivists can easily acknowledge environmental determinants, and the phrase "cognitive behaviorism" is not seen as absurd. Or the situationalism-dispositionalism debate that pitted personologists against social psychologists (e.g., Bem & Allen, 1974; Mischel, 1969) has settled cleanly into the recognition that, in Lewinian terms, B is indeed a function of both P and E (Bowers, 1973). Even at the philosophical level, we note epistemologies such as transcendental realism (Bhaskar, 1975, 1982; Harré, 1972; Manicas & Secord, 1983) that acknowledge both personal cognizing experience and durable social phenomena, and discard such positivistic baggage as the correspondence theory of truth and probabilistic prediction. In Churchman's (1971) terms, we may be moving toward a commensurable, complementary, Kantian inquiry system and away from a traditionally dialectical one.

But hard-bitten dichotomizers still exist. Perhaps the most questionable dichotomy appears when the claim is made (e.g., Smith, 1983a, 1983b) that positivism and its associated companions are essentially focused on a certain kind of data—namely, quantitative—and that the interpretive-idealist views of the world necessarily emphasize qualitative data. This link has been roundly debunked by Cook and Reichardt (1979), but it tends to per-

sist. Meanwhile, in the real research world, we see more and more of what Smith and Louis (1982) call multisite, multimethod studies linking qualitative and quantitative data, using both confirmatory and exploratory approaches. More and more researchers in fields with a traditional quantitative emphasis (not only educational research, but psychology, sociology, linguistics, public administration, organizational studies, urban planning, program evaluation, and policy analysis) have shifted to an interest in qualitative data.

We are not saying that paradigmatic issues are trivial, or that those who wish to clarify them should cease to do so. Rather, our belief is that wholesale devotion to paradigmatic disputation diverts the audience's attention from a critical aspect of educational research: Despite a growing interest in qualitative studies, we lack a body of clearly-defined methods for drawing valid meaning from qualitative data. We need methods that are practical, communicable, and not self-deluding: scientific in the positivist's sense of the word, and aimed toward interpretive understanding in the best sense of that term.

Qualitative Methods: The Context and the Need

If working researchers are, as we argue, operating as if there were an epistemological middle ground, integrating positivist and idealist perspectives, we must take this discussion down a peg, to the methodological level. Just how is this work being done?

For the qualitative researcher—whether positivist or phenomenologist or at heart—who ventures into psychometrics and statistics, the terrain is well-marked. There are measurement theories, decision rules, confidence levels, error terms, computing algorithms, and analysis conventions. The real complications come later. But the move in the other direction, which we focus on in the remainder of this article, is more perilous.

Qualitative data are attractive. They are a source of well-grounded, rich description and explanation of processes occuring in local contexts.

With qualitative data, one can preserve chronological flow, assess local causality, and derive fruitful explanations. Serendipitous findings and new theoretical integrations can appear. Finally, qualitative findings have a certain undeniability (Smith, 1978) that is often far more convincing to a reader than pages of numbers.

But that very plausibility has its problems. If we genuinely want an ecumenical epistemology to be accompanied by appropriate research procedures, we need canons to assure ourselves and our readers that the sample of cases at hand is reasonably representative of some universe the reader has in mind, and that the conclusions were reached through some reasonably communicable set of procedures. Note: It is not a question of replicability, narrowly and positivistically defined. In the world of "wicked problems" (Churchman, 1971) where qualitative researchers are struggling, no single conclusion or explanation can be unequivocally established. On the other hand, some conclusions are better than others, and not everything is acceptable. We need to be confident that the conclusions are not unreasonable, that another researcher facing the data would reach a conclusion that falls in the same general "truth space."

The problem is that there is an insufficient corpus of reliable, valid, or even minimally agreed-on working analysis procedures for qualitative data (Miles, 1979). Worse still, there appears to be little sharing of experience, even at the rudimentary level of recipe exchanges. We don't know much about what other qualitative researchers are actually doing when they reduce, analyze, and interpret data.

For example, Sieber (1976) examined seven well-respected textbooks on field methods and found that less than 5-10% of their pages was devoted to analysis. Recent textbooks (e.g., Bogdan & Biklen, 1982; Dobbert, 1982; Guba & Lincoln, 1981; Patton, 1980; Spradley, 1979) have redressed the balance somewhat, but many qualitative researchers still consider analysis an art and stress intuitive approaches to it. So-called bracketing of one's interpretations to mark off and clarify the analyst's personal frames and meanings does not seem to be clearly formulated; beyond this, the actual paths followed by the analyst who progressively discerns clear classifications and overarching patterns from the welter of field data are only rarely discussed (cf. LeCompte & Goetz, 1983).

To be fair, we should note that some researchers have hesitated to focus on analysis issues on the grounds that unequivocal determination of the validity of findings is not really possible (Becker, 1958; Bruyn, 1966; Lofland, 1971). More fundamentally, for some phenomenological researchers, there is no social reality to be accounted for; hence, there is no need to evolve a robust set of methodological canons to help explicate its laws (cf. Dreitzel, 1970). In this view, social processes are ephemeral, fluid phenomena with no existence independent of social actors' ways of construing and describing them. Still, such a view leaves phenomenologists fully accountable to readers for their data-gathering and interpretive procedures.

It is fair to say that although most published qualitative reports provide detailed descriptions of the settings, people, events, and processes that were studied, they say little about how the researcher got the information, and almost nothing about the specific analysis procedures used. One cannot ordinarily follow how a researcher got from 3,600 pages of field notes to the final conclusions. Thus, internal validity issues become primary (Dawson, 1979, 1982; LeCompte & Goetz, 1982). How, for example, did Stearns et al. (1980) get from dozens of cases to a small set of propositions or to a series of site factor matrices, and what kind of matrix are we talking about? How did Stake and Easley (1978) boil down a gargantuan data set to a small number of issues and problems, and what is the veridical status of those issues and problems?

It seems that we are in a double bind: The status of conclusions from qualitative studies is uncertain because researchers don't report on their methodology, and researchers don't report on their methodology because there are no established conventions for doing that. Yet the studies are conducted, and researchers do fill up hundreds of pages of field notes, then somehow aggregate, partition, reduce, analyze, and interpret those data. In publishing the results, they must assume that theirs is not a solipsistic vision: that people at the field sites or an independent researcher would acknowledge the core findings as plausible. Thus, qualitative researchers do have a set of assumptions, criteria, decision rules, and operations for working with data to decide when a given finding is established and meaningful. The problem is that these crucial underpinnings of analysis remain mostly implicit, explained only allusively.

For example, terms such as plausibility, coherence, compellingness, and referential adequacy are all evocative, but ultimately somewhat hollow. For one thing, they need to be defined specifically and concretely. For another, we believe that a researcher can always provide a plausible account, and with careful editing and vivid vignettes may assure coherence and undeniability. But this result might well be the product of selective data collection, unacknowledged bias, and/or impressionistic analysis. We simply don't know, partly because the researcher hasn't left adequate tracks enabling us to make such an assessment, and partly because we are insecure about which validation criteria to apply if the tracks were in fact there.

Setting an agenda. The first order of business, then, is reasonably clear: We need to make explicit the procedures and thought processes that qualitative researchers actually use in their work. For that to happen, we need a minimal set of reporting conventions documenting successive moves through data collection, analysis, and interpretation.

Such conventions are familiar for quantitative studies; the authors can almost fill in the blanks when drafting sections on sampling, methods, and data analysis. These conventions serve two important functions. First, they are a verification device by which the reader can track down the procedures used to arrive at the findings. Second, the reporting procedures furnish details (e.g., means, standard deviations, error terms) that secondary analysts can use to doublecheck the findings using other analytic techniques, to integrate these findings into another study, or to synthesize several studies on the same topic.

In other words, a more or less clear technology is in use here, but it is confined to statistical studies. Most qualitative researchers are uncomfortable in the reporting straitjacket we have just decribed, but they have no alternative. As Lofland (1974) said, they are lacking "a public, shared and codified conception of how what they do is done and how what they report should be formulated (p. 101)."

Were we to have more documentation in hand, we could compare the various assumptions and procedures in use to see whether there is any common terrain to build on. We could also gauge with more precision whether that terrain is similar in some aspects, for example, to the assumptions and procedures of quasi-experimental research (Cook & Campbell, 1979), or of analytic induction (Swinburne, 1974).

There are some useful efforts under way to develop working validation criteria, for example, Guba and Lincoln's (1981) criteria for determining the trustworthiness of qualitative data. But with the exception of some preliminary work by Halpern (1983), to our knowledge none of the proposed desiderata has actually been applied to a datum. Perhaps these conventions are inapplicable, redundant, or operationally ambiguous—we don't know. The crucial question is this: How does one actually proceed, step by step, through analysis to produce and document findings that other qualitative analysts would regard as dependable and trustworthy?

A Conception of Qualitative Analysis

First, a general remark on our epistemological stance. The concerns we have expressed about validity and verifiability will make some readers identify us with the positivist camp. We see ourselves closer to the middle ground. We are interested in the idiosyncratic meanings people (including ourselves) develop, *and* we believe in the existence

of lawful yet historically evolving relationships to be discovered in the social world. As a result, we consider it important to evolve a set of valid and verifiable methods for capturing those social relationships and their causes. Thus, like typical causal realists and fallibilists, we want to interpret and explain (though not predict) these phenomena, *and* have confidence that others, using the same tools, would arrive at analogous conclusions. With middle-range epistemologists such as Bhaskar (1982) and Manicas and Secord (1983), we believe that full determination and closure on explanations is not possible, but that some explanations are more powerful, more fully saturated, than others. This stance does not exclude verstehen or intersubjective resonance, nor does it demand that we draw an arbitrary conceptual line between idiographic and nomothetic approaches to research. No social phenomenon, we believe, is wholly idiosyncratic, nor is any overarching social pattern uncontingent.

Even with this middle-range commitment, we should acknowledge some biases, or at least those of which we are aware. We do tilt somewhat toward the realist/positivist side. We strongly believe in being systematic about inquiry and favor the development of substantive and methodological consensus among researchers. Perhaps we are right-wing qualitative researchers, or only "soft-nosed positivists." We offer our ideas to qualitative researchers of all persuasions, including the mostly resolutely interpretive, and believe they can be useful. One reader of this article understood us as "advising idealists to be more like realists." That may be true, but we also encourage realists to attend to the importance of their own personal visions in constructing meaning in data, or in deciding what to consider "data" in the first place, and to remember that understanding and portraying the unique individual case may be more important than "generalizations" and "variables."

Next, we turn to our general conception of qualitative data analysis.[1] First, the data concerned appear in words rather than in numbers. They may have been collected in a variety of ways (observation, interviews, extracts from documents, tape recordings), and are usually processed somewhat before they are ready for use via dictation, typing up, editing, or transcription, but they remain words, usually organized into extended text.

We consider that analysis consists of three concurrent flows of activity: data reduction, data display, and conclusion-drawing/verification. These flows of activity are illustrated in Figure 1.

Data reduction. This term refers to the process of selecting, focusing, simplifying, abstracting, and transforming the raw data that appear in edited field notes. As we see it, data reduction occurs continuously throughout the life of any qualitatively-oriented project, in forms ranging from sampling decisions to data coding and summaries.

Data reduction is not something

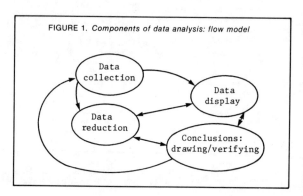

FIGURE 1. *Components of data analysis: flow model*

separate from analysis. It is a *part* of analysis that sharpens, sorts, focuses, discards, and organizes data in such a way that final conclusions can be drawn and verified.

We should clarify one thing: By data reduction we do not necessarily mean quantification. Qualitative data can be reduced and transformed in many ways—through sheer selection, through summary or paraphrase, through being subsumed in a larger pattern or metaphor, and so on. We do not rule out converting the data into numbers or ranks, provided that the numbers, and the words used to derive the numbers, remain *together* in the ensuing analysis. That way one never strips the data at hand from the contexts in which they occur.

Data display. The second major flow of analysis activity is data display, defined as an organized assembly of information that permits conclusion-drawing and action-taking. Displays in daily life include gasoline gauges, newspapers, and computer screens. Looking at displays helps us understand what is happening, and to conduct further analysis or take action based on that understanding. In the course of our work, we became convinced that better displays—alternatives to cumbersome narrative text—are a major avenue to valid qualitative analysis, and we developed a wide range of matrices, graphs, networks, and charts (Miles & Huberman, 1984).

As with data reduction, the creation and use of displays is not something separate from analysis; it is a *part* of analysis. Designing the rows and columns of a matrix for qualitative data and deciding which data, in which form, should be entered in the cells are analytic activities. In short, the dictum "You are what you eat" might be transposed to "You know what you display."

Conclusion-drawing and verification. The third stream of analysis activity involves drawing meaning from displayed, reduced data—noting regularities, patterns, explanations, possible configurations, causal flows, propositions. These conclusions are also verified, tested for their plausibility, robustness, sturdiness, and validity.

We have presented these three streams—data reduction, data display, and conclusion-drawing/verification—as interwoven before, during, and after data collection in parallel form, to make up the general domain called analysis. The three streams can also be represented as in Figure 2.

In this view, the three types of analysis activity and the activity of data collection form an interactive, cyclical process. The researcher steadily moves among these four "nodes" during data collection, then shuttles among reduction, display, and conclusion-drawing/verification for the remainder of the study. The coding of data, for example (data reduction) leads to new ideas on what should go into a matrix (data display). Entering the data requires further data reduction. As the matrix fills up, preliminary conclusions are drawn, but they lead to the decision (for example) to add another column to the matrix to test the conclusion.

Such a process is actually no more complex, conceptually speaking, than the analysis modes used by quantitative researchers. They, too, must be preoccupied with data reduction (computing means, standard deviations, indexes), with display (correlation tables, regression print-outs), and with conclusion-drawing/verification (significance levels, experimental-control differences). The point is that these activities are carried out through well-defined, familiar methods, they have canons guiding them, and they are usually more sequential than iterative or cyclical. Qualitative researchers, on the other hand, are in a more fluid, and a more pioneering, position. Hence the need for experimentation, documentation, and sharing.

Illustrative Analysis Methods

We have pointed to the need for more sharing of analysis methods. We can list some examples, drawn from our own and others' work. Where we offer our own, rather than others' techniques, we do so in a nonimperialistic, colleaguely mode. A list of this sort cannot be convincing or clearly understood; we supply it mainly as a matter of record, with sources, for the interested reader. For full detail, see Huberman and Miles (1983a, 1983b) and Miles and Huberman (1984).

Data Reduction Methods. "Data" and "reduction" appear to be dirty words in some circles. Rather, one "compiles information," or "focuses progressively." Data are taken to mean numbers, and reduction implies context-stripping. The question is not whether qualitative research entails data reduction, but rather when and how the reduction cycles occur. As Figure 1 suggests, we believe that data reduction can profitably occur before and during, as well as after data collection.

Anticipatory data reduction. This reduction usually occurs in the form of methods for focusing and bounding the collection of data.

1. *Conceptual frameworks.* What orienting ideas does the researcher—even one with a strongly inductive or hermeneutical bent—bring to the inquiry? We have found that making such initial frames explicit, usually in the form of a simple

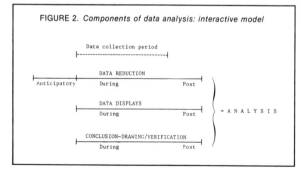

FIGURE 2. *Components of data analysis: interactive model*

Data collection period

DATA REDUCTION

Anticipatory   During   Post

DATA DISPLAYS

During   Post   } = A N A L Y S I S

CONCLUSION-DRAWING/VERIFICATION

During   Post

graphic structure of major variables with arrows showing relationships between them, substantially aids focus.

2. *Research questions.* By the same token, qualitative researchers usually have general or specific questions in mind that derive from the conceptual framework. Making explicit what one really wants to know is a further bounding device.

3. *Sampling.* Qualitative researchers typically engage in purposive rather than random sampling. What quantitative researchers do not fully appreciate when they dismiss "$N = 1$" studies is that a qualitative researcher must make a wide range of sampling decisions, even within one case, let alone several (see Campbell, 1975). There may be, for example, samples of actors, settings, events, time periods, and processes. Lofland (1971) and Bogdan and Biklen (1982) have carefully reviewed these and other options.

4. *Instrumentation.* Decisions about how data will be collected and recorded are a further form of anticipatory data reduction. Generally speaking, should the instrumentation—interviews, observation, document collection, field note-taking, tape recording—be minimal (thus emphasizing construct and contextual validity), or actively preplanned (thus emphasizing internal validity, generalizability, and manageability of the data)?

In general, our talks with many qualitative researchers and students, and consideration of case studies of qualitative research (Hammond, 1964; Herriott & Firestone, 1983) lead us to believe that anticipatory data reduction is important: It leads to data that are radically more analysis-rich.

Interim data reduction. A second cluster of methods is perhaps the main corrective for the potential blinders of excessive prefocusing and bounding. Essentially, the field worker cycles back and forth between thinking about the existing data set and generating strategies for collecting new data (Glaser, 1978; Glaser & Strauss, 1967). Data collection and analysis are interwoven from the outset.

How can interim data reduction be accomplished without butchering

the data or absorbing time badly needed for field work? Below are some methods that have been tried.

1. *Contact summary sheets.* The researcher summarizes a site visit on a single sheet containing information about the people and events involved, main themes or issues, the research questions addressed, new hypotheses or speculations, and target issues for the next visit.

2. *Coding.* Coding schemes, developed inductively or driven by research questions, are a critical data-reduction tool. They may include descriptive codes, as well as second-level explanatory (pattern) codes. They are intimately related to the storage and retrieval system used to manage qualitative data (see Levine, 1983) for a thoughtful explication).

3. *Memoing.* The memo is a brief conceptual look at some aspect of the accumulating data set: an insight, a puzzle, a category, an emerging explanation, a striking event. For illustrations and advice, see Smith and Keith (1971) and Glaser (1978).

4. *Site analysis meetings.* In multiple-site studies, or single-site studies with multiple researchers, these are well-structured occasions to step back from the flood of fieldwork and take interim stock. A typical agenda (and recording form) covers main themes, emerging hypotheses, alternative explanations, disagreements, next steps for data collection, and coding scheme revisions. (See also Stiegelbauer, Goldstein, and Huling, 1982).

5. *Interim site summaries.* These are short (10-20 pp.) provisional syntheses of what the researcher knows about the site and what is still to be pursued. The summary reviews findings, looks carefully at the robustness of the data supporting them, and sets the next data collection agenda.

6. *Post data collection reduction.* The methods used after data collection are integrally related to methods of data display, conclusion-drawing, and verification. These methods are discussed in the following sections.

Data Display

Narrative text in the form of field notes is an awkward form of data display: It is bulky, dispersed (thus

hard to remember), sequential, not simultaneous (thus making it hard to look at several variables at once), only vaguely ordered or structured, and often monotonous and overloading. These difficulties apply with equal force to narrative text as the form of the final report to readers (see Mulhauser, 1975).

A quantitative comparison may help. One often overlooks the fact that statistical packages such as SPSS or BMD are widely used not only because of their computational speed, but because: (a) They display the (reduced) data in one place, (b) they allow the analyst to plan further analyses, (c) they make it easier to compare different data sets, and (d) they permit direct use of the results in a report. Quantitative researchers take these virtues for granted, and simply expect to see computed data appear in histograms, correlation matrices, scatterplots, vectors, and so on. Qualitative researchers, at the moment, have to hand-craft their displays.

We suggest that spatially-compressed, organized display modes are a major avenue to improving qualitative data analysis. Below is a brief listing.

Descriptive figures. Qualitative data lend themselves well to graphic representation. Two types are:

1. *Context charts.* These map the relationships among roles, groups, settings, or organizations making up the context of individual behavior. Symbols can be used to show actor attributes (e.g., attitude to an innovation, advocacy effort). The flows of information, assistance or influence between actors can be mapped and coded. (See Huberman, 1981.)

2. *Growth gradients.* The increase over time of some critical variable (e.g., number of users of an innovation) can be shown graphically in line form; critical events or actions relevant to the variable can be mapped on to the line.

Explanatory figures. Once it is clear what happened, an analyst often wants to go on to explanations at some level. There are several ways to do this.

1. *Scatterplots.* In multiple-site studies, displaying sites according to two (or more) variables often is illuminating; one can begin to infer

co-variation and to note clusters of sites in the space defined by the axes.

2. *Event-state flow charts.* These charts assemble the key events during a particular time period in the setting being studied, and the system-state effects of these events. Using a left-to-right time flow, events, states, and their relationships are connected in an overall diagram.

3. *Causal networks.* These display the most important independent and dependent variables in a study, and the deterministic relationships among them. An accompanying narrative text is usually needed for full explication. Such networks are, in effect, the qualitative researcher's analogue to path-analytical causal modeling. For exemplars, see Smith and Keith (1971) and the extended discussion in Miles and Huberman (1984).

Descriptive matrices. Matrices for quantitative data are familiar, whether for raw data (e.,g., spreadsheet displays) or aggregated data (e.g., cross-tabs). We have found systematic matrix displays for words to be uncommonly fruitful. Form naturally follows function: Is one aiming to "eyeball" data; to do detailed analyses; to set data up for next-step analysis in a more reduced (or more differentiated) form for next analyses; to combine parallel data from a single site or multiple sites; or to report findings?

The rows and columns of the matrix can include almost any aspect of the data: time periods, persons, groups, roles, event classes, settings, processes, key variables, researcher or respondent explanations. The cell entries can be equally diverse, ranging from direct-quote raw data excerpts to key phrases, summaries, or quasi-scaled judgments. Such matrices both force and support analysis; rows and columns can be reordered, combined, or separated as new avenues of significance open up. Local contexts are seen holistically, not lost in dispersed narrative. Too, one is forced to look at all the relevant data in drawing conclusions, not just those on page 236 of the field notes, or those sharing a single code.

There is a catch, of course. One is limited to the data in the display.

Thus a great deal depends on the care with which data have been selected from the field notes, and how far they are aggregated or abstracted. More generally, it is crucial for the analyst to keep a record of and announce the decision rules used for data entry (e.g., include an instance if given by one informant, confirmed by another, and disconfirmed nowhere in the data).

The range of descriptive matrix types is broad. In addition to the *checklist matrix* (with indicators of a single underlying variable), qualitative analysts have begun to explore *time-ordered matrices* displaying phenomena as they occurred chronologically; *role-ordered matrices* distributing data according to their sources (and/or targets) of attention; and *conceptually-clustered matrices* bringing together variables connected by theoretical ideas (e.g., a set of motives and attitudes relevant to innovation adoption).

Descriptive matrices can also be used at the multiple-site level: First-level matrices can be reduced and aggregated to *descriptive meta-matrices* displaying common information across sites. For deeper understanding, these can be site-ordered by some key variable such as student impact or degree of institutionalization. (cf. Huberman & Miles, 1983a).

Explanatory matrices. Matrices can also aid in sorting out explanations, reasons, and causes for observed phenomena. Examples include the *effects matrix*, which displays the results or outcomes of a process (such as assistance provided to users of an innovation); the *site dynamics matrix*, which examines, at a more inferential level, the strains, dilemmas or other forces for change in a setting, and their resolution; the *process-outcome matrix* (Patton, 1980) tracing the outcomes of different processes; and, more concretely, the *event listing*, which displays a series of critical events in a system over time, using rows to delineate different system levels or actors. At the multiple-site, explanatory level, there is the *site-ordered predictor-outcome matrix* that arrays sites by a general variable such as smoothness of implementation, then displays each site's standing on a number of predictors of that outcome.

Matrix formulation is, in our experience, a simple, enjoyable and creative process, as anyone who has ever constructed a dummy table knows. It is also decisive: Matrix formats set boundaries on the types of conclusions that can be drawn. Many different formats can be generated for the same research question, each with differing emphases and tradeoffs. Hence the importance of format iteration, bending, and improvement before settling in. As we've noted, the decision rules for data entry must be explicit. Finally, many matrices can be part of the final report, either in direct or reduced/abstracted form. Just as readers of quantitative studies need to see the correlation matrix or the factor loadings, so qualitative report readers need the displays to verify, disconfirm, or illuminate the conclusions offered.

Conclusion-Drawing and Verification

From the beginning of data collection, the qualitative analyst is beginning to draw conclusions, to decide what things mean, and to note regularities, patterns, explanations, possible configurations, causal flows, and propositions. The competent researcher holds these conclusions lightly, maintaining openness and skepticism, but the conclusions are still there, inchoate and vague at first, then increasingly explicit and grounded, to use the classic term of Glaser and Strauss (1967).

Conclusion-drawing, in our view, is only half of a Gemini configuration. Conclusions are also verified as the analyst proceeds. That verification may be as brief as a fleeting second thought crossing the analyst's mind during writing, with a short excursion back to the field notes, or it may be thorough and elaborate, with lengthy argumentation and review among colleagues to develop intersubjective consensus, or with extensive efforts to replicate a finding in another data set.

Tactics of conclusion-drawing. The display types described above usually involve a strategy, a general approach to finding (and/or creating) meaning in a set of data. But general strategies are not enough. There will always be a flow of specific analysis tactics operating in, through, and around the displays. For example, *particulars are subsumed into the general.* Several instances of angry confrontation between school district personnel translate into, let us say, "between-role conflict." We could stop there, or we could go on. The policy issues and conflicts might fit into a general pattern that includes groupings of other instances and actors—for example, an inter-institutional bargaining pattern, which itself is conceptually coherent with conflict theories of organizational behavior. Thus we have moved via a successively more astringent clustering procedure from multiple empirical instances to a single conceptualization of the basic social processes (Glaser, 1978) underlying those instances. Most conclusion-drawing tactics amount to doing two things: reducing the bulk of data and bringing a pattern to them. Such tactics are sometimes rationally trackable, sometimes not.

We can illustrate with *making metaphors,* a frequent and productive tactic for moving interpretively from the denotive to the connotive, much as a novelist or poet does. One steps back from the welter of observations and conversations in the field notes and says to oneself, "What's going on here? What's the image that describes this?" Using a metaphor moves you past sheer description of a phenomenon, up a notch to a slightly more inferential—and personal—level. Dozens of dispersed pages, or data in a display, are subsumed into one generalizing descriptor. In one of our studies (Huberman & Miles, 1983b, 1984), we found at one site that the remedial learning room felt like an oasis for the pupils sent there for part of each day. Generating the metaphor immediately pulled a mountain of fragmented observations together—the quality of the materials in the remedial lab, the nurturant interactions there, the attitude of teachers sending pupils there, the starkness of the corridors and classrooms surrounding the lab. This metaphor then suggested another image at a similar level of generality: the ascetic, resource-thin school (desert) housing the remedial lab.

With these illustrations as a backdrop, the following is a general list of 12 conclusion-drawing tactics assembled from the literature and our experience. (For more detail, see Miles & Huberman, 1984). *Counting* is a familiar way to see "what's there" in a qualitative data set; there is a long content-analytic tradition for qualitative researchers to draw on (e.g., Berelson, 1971; Holsti, 1968, 1969; Pool, 1973). *Noting patterns or themes* (cf. Stearns, Greene, & David, 1980), *seeing plausibility,* and *clustering* (Krippendorff, 1980) are all tactics that help the analyst see what goes with what. As we've noted, *making metaphors* (cf. Lakoff & Johnson, 1980; Ortony, 1979) is still another way to achieve integration among diverse pieces of data. Differentiation is sometimes needed too, as in *splitting variables.* We also need tactics for viewing things and their relationships more abstractly. These include *subsuming particulars into the general* (Glaser, 1978; LeCompte, 1983); *factoring,* a qualitative analogue of the familiar quantitative technique for representing many specific variables in terms of a few hypothesized ones (Huberman, 1981); *noting relations between variables;* and *finding intervening variables.* Finally, how can we assemble coherent understandings of data? Two tactics for doing this are *building a logical chain of evidence,* and *making conceptual/theoretical coherence.*

Conclusion verification. We cannot avoid the question of verification. Conclusions drawn from any of the preceding tactics can be evocative, illuminating, masterful, and yet still unjustified. Looked at more scrupulously, the data may not support the conclusions. Researchers doublechecking the site come up with discrepant findings. Site informants, asked to report on the findings, plausibly contest some or all of them. The phenomenologist chuckles, reinforced by the idea that there is no single reality out there to "get right." The psychometrician concludes that nonstatistical research is an albatross.

How do we know whether a conclusion is surreal or real? By "real" we mean that another competent researcher, working independently at the same site, would not come up with wholly contradictory findings.

It is meaningful here to draw from research on information-processing by individuals. Humans are not very powerful as processors of large amounts of information; the cognitive tendency is to reduce complex information into selective, simplified, personally-congruent Gestalts. A long tradition of studies (Dawes, 1971; Goldberg, 1970; Meehl, 1954, 1965) shows that human judgments are consistently less accurate than statistical/actuarial ones—even that "expert" judges can be worse than untrained ones (Taft, 1955). Oskamp (1965) showed how clinicians felt increasingly confident of their initially *erroneous* judgments as they got more *accurate* information. The mechanics of information seeking and processing entail our seeing confirming instances of original beliefs or perceptions, rather than seeing disconfirming instances, even when the latter are more frequent (cf. Edwards, 1968). Still more ominously, Tversky and Kahneman (1971) were easily able to catch mathematical psychologists in the act of making biased inferences from samples to populations. What does this suggest about the lone field worker, operating with home-made instrumentation in an area in which he or she is likely easier prey to deception and bias than are many of the local actors?

In our recent research, we have chipped away at this problem, deciding to reframe it in terms of working out operationalized tactics for verifying conclusions in qualitative research. For example, in dealing with the confirming instances problem mentioned above, we believe that the field worker should assume he or she is drawing inferences from a weak or nonrepresentative sample of "cases," whether they are people, events, or processes, and *check for representativeness.* This can be done by: (a) increasing the number of cases; (b) looking purposively for contrasting (i.e., negative, extreme, countervailing) cases; (c) sorting the cases systematically and filling out weakly-sampled case types; and (d) sampling randomly within the universe of people and phenomena under study. The last two procedures are familiar to quantitative researchers, who use them early, as anticipatory controls against sampling and measurement error. The qualitative researcher uses them later, as verification devices, allowing all the candidate people and data in, so that the most influential ones will have an equal chance of emerging. But the researcher still has to carry the burden of proof that the patterns found are representative, and not merely personal choices.

Again we offer a listing of 12 verification tactics. The first set deals with assuring the basic quality of the data at hand. *Checking for representativeness* has just been reviewed. *Checking for researcher effects* on the site and vice versa is especially important in qualitative studies, and has received much attention (Adams & Preiss, 1960; Douglas, 1976; Lofland, 1971; Pelto & Pelto, 1978; Wax, 1971). *Triangulating* across data sources and methods (Jick, 1979) is also a well-known tactic, but tends to be preached more often than practiced. Checks like these may also involve *weighting the evidence*, or deciding which kinds of data are most trustworthy (Becker, 1970; Bogdan & Taylor, 1975; Dawson, 1979, 1982; Sieber, 1976; Van Maanen, 1979).

Conclusions also can be verified by looking carefully at differences within the data set. *Making contrasts/comparisons, checking the meaning of outliers*, and *using extreme cases* (Sieber, 1976) are all tactics that test a conclusion about a pattern by saying what it does not resemble.

There are also well-developed tactics for pushing a conclusion hard to see if it holds up. These include *ruling out spurious relations; replicating a finding* in another part of the data, or a new data source or set; *checking out rival explanations* (Huck & Sandler, 1979; Platt, 1964) and *looking for negative evidence* (Kidder, 1981).

Finally, a good explanation deserves attention from the people whose behavior it is about; informants who supplied the original data. *Getting feedback from informants* (Bronfenbrenner, 1976; Becker, Geer, Hughes, & Strauss, 1961; Guba, 1981; Stake, 1976) though it is rife with difficulties, has particular confirmatory power.

Need for Documentation and Sharing of Analysis Methods

We have already stressed the fact that there are few canons for doing good qualitative analysis, and few methods that have general currency In this article and in the sourcebook (Miles & Huberman, 1984), we have begun the task of assembling both. We believe that qualitative data analysis processes, while at times demanding and complex, are not arcane, obscure, or ineffable. They will be even less so when when we know more about what qualitative researchers really do. To echo Mills (1959):

Only by conversations in which experienced thinkers exchange information about their actual ways of working can a useful sense of method and theory be imparted...

Thus we support the idea of the audit trail proposed by Guba (1981) and Guba and Lincoln (1981), and encourage its further operation (see Halpern, 1983; Miles and Huberman, 1984). We also urge that qualitative researchers use some regular log or diary that tracks what was actually done during the operations of data reduction, display, conclusion-drawing, and verification.

We have argued for a systematic approach to analysis methods. However, there is a danger: As one reader said, "Overly rigorous approaches can lead to rigor mortis... to easily confirmable but inane analyses." We might add the dangers of overpreoccupation with method rather than substance and the development of a crippling, mechanical orthodoxy. If we can keep our collective sense of humor and our wits about us, perhaps these traps can be avoided. Our own experience over the past 5 years has repeatedly shown us that trusting our own personal visions during the analysis process was crucial, that creativity was central in the design of display modes, and that sharing the results of both with our colleagues was most important of all.

Note

[1] This view and the many different detailed analysis methods resulting from it, were developed during. the past 5 years in a qualitative study of innovation implementation in schools (Huberman & Miles, 1983a, 1983b, 1984) and an extended methodological study of analysis methods culminating in a practical sourcebook (Miles & Huberman, 1984). We are grateful to the Office of Planning, Budget and Evaluation of the Department of Education (Contract 300-78-0527) through The Network, Inc., and to the National Institute of Education (Grant G-81-0018). No agency endorsement is implied.

References

Adams, R., & Preiss, J. (1960). (Eds.) *Human organization research.* Homewood, IL: Dorsey Press.

Becker, H.S. (1958). Problems of inference and proof in participant observation. *American Sociological Review, 23,* 652-660.

Becker, H.S. (1970). *Sociological work.* Chicago: Aldine.

Becker, H.S., Geer, B., Hughes, E.C., & Strauss, A.L. (1961). *Boys in white.* Chicago: University of Chicago Press.

Bem, D., & Allen, A., (1974). On predicting some of the people some of the time: The search for cross-situational consistencies in behavior. *Psychological Review, 81,* 506-520.

Berelson, B. (1971). *Content analysis in communication research.* New York: Hafner.

Bhaskar, R. (1975). *A realist theory of science.* Leeds, U.K: Leeds Books.

Bhaskar, R., (1982). Emergence, explanation and emancipation. In P.F. Secord (Ed.), *Explaining social behavior: Consciousness, behavior and social structure.* Beverly Hills, CA.: Sage.

Bogdan, R.C., & Biklen, S.K. (1982). *Qualitative research in education.* Boston: Allyn & Bacon.

Bogdan, R., & Taylor, S. J. (1975). *Introduction to qualitative research methods.* New York: Wiley.

Bowers, K. (1973). Situationalism in psychology: An analysis and a critique. *Psychological Review, 80,* 307-336.

Bronfenbrenner, U. (1976). The experimental ecology of education. *Teachers College Record, 78* (2), 157-178.

Bruyn, S. (1966). *Human perspective in sociology.* Englewood Cliffs, N.J.: Prentice-Hall.

Campbell, D.T. (1975). Degrees of freedom and the case study. *Comparative Political Studies, 8* (2), 178-193.

Churchman, C.W. (1971). *The design of inquiring systems: Basic concepts of systems and organization.* New York: Basic Books.

Conrad, P., & Reinharz, S. (1984). Computers and qualitative data. *Qualitative Sociology, 7,* (1,2), Entire double issue.

Cook, T.D., & Campbell, D.T. (1979).

Quasi-experimentation: Design and analysis issues for field settings. Chicago: Rand McNally.

Cook, T.D., & Reichardt, C.S. (1979). *Qualitative and quantitative methods in evaluation research.* Beverly Hills CA: Sage.

Cronbach, L. (1975). Beyond the two disciplines of scientific psychology. *American Psychologist, 30,* 116-127.

Dawes, R. (1971). A case study of graduate admissions: Applications of three principles of human decision-making. *American Psychologist, 26* (2), 180-188.

Dawson, J.A. (1979, April). *Validity in qualitative inquiry.* Paper presented at the annual meeting of the American Educational Research Association, San Francisco.

Dawson, J.A. (1982, April). *Qualitative research findings: What do we do to improve and estimate their validity?* Paper presented at the annual meeting of the American Educational Research Association, New York.

Dobbert, M.L. (1982). *Ethnographic research: Theory and application for modern schools and societies.* New York: Praeger.

Douglas, J. (1976) *Investigative social research.* Beverly Hills, CA: Sage.

Dreitzel, H. (1970). Introduction. In H. Dreitzel (Ed.) *Recent Sociology,* Vol 2. London: Macmillan.

Edwards, W. (1968). Conservatism in human information processing. In K.B. Kleinmuntz (Ed.), *Formal representation of human judgment.* New York: Wiley.

Eisner, E.W. (1983). Anastasia might be alive, but the monarchy is dead. *Educational Researcher, 12* (5), 13-14; 23-24.

Eisner, E. (1981). On the differences between scientific and artistic approaches to qualitative research. *Educational Researcher, 10* (4), 5-9.

Glaser, B. (1978). *Theoretical sensitivity.* Mill Valley, CA: Sociology Press.

Glaser, B., & Strauss, A.L. (1967). *The discovery of grounded theory: Strategies for qualitative research.* Chicago: Aldine.

Goldberg, L. (1970). Man versus model of man: A rationale, plus some evidence, for a method of improving on clinical inferences. *Psychological Bulletin, 73* (4), 422-432.

Guba, E.G. (1981). Criteria for assessing the trustworthiness of naturalistic inquiries. *Educational Communication and Technology Journal, 29,* 75-92.

Guba, E.G., & Lincoln, Y.S. (1981). *Effective evaluation.* San Francisco, CA: Jossey-Bass.

Halfpenny, P. (1982). *Positivism and sociology: Explaining social life.* Edison, NJ: Allen & Unwin.

Halpern, E.S. (1983, April). *Auditing naturalistic inquiries: Some preliminary applications. Part I: Development of the process. Part 2: Case study application.* Paper presented at the annual meeting of the American Educational Research Association, Montreal, Canada.

Hammond, P.E. (Ed.) (1964). *Sociologists at work.* New York: Basic Books.

Harré, R. (1972). *Philosophies of science.* Oxford, U.K.: Oxford University Press.

Herriott, R.E., & Firestone, W.A. (1983). Multisite qualitative policy research: Optimizing description and generalizability. *Educational Researcher, 12*(2), 14-19.

Holsti, O.R. (1968). Content analysis. In G. Lindzey & E. Aronson (Eds.) *Handbook of social psychology.* Vol. 2: *Research methods.* (2d ed.) Reading, MA: Addison-Wesley.

Holsti, O.R. (1969). *Content analysis for the social sciences and the humanities.* Reading, MA: Addison-Wesley.

Huberman, A.M. (1981). *School-university collaboration supporting school improvement. Vol. 1, The midwestern state case.* Washington, DC: American University, Knowledge Transfer Institute.

Huberman A.M., & Miles, M.B. (1983 a). Drawing valid meaning from qualitative data: Some techniques of data reduction and display. *Quality and Quantity, 17,* 281-339.

Huberman, A.M., & Miles, M.B. (1983b). *Innovation up close: A field study in 12 school settings.* Vol. IV of D.P. Crandall and associates, *People, policies and practices: Examining the chain of school improvement.* Andover, MA: The Network.

Huberman, A.M., & Miles, M.B. (1984). *Innovation up close: How school improvement works.* New York: Plenum.

Huck, S.W., & Sandler, H.M. (1979). *Rival hypotheses: "minute mysteries" for the critical thinker.* London: Harper & Row.

Jick, T.D. (1979). Mixing qualitative and quantitative methods: Triangulation in action. *Administrative Science Quarterly, 24,* 602-611.

Kidder, L.H. (1981). *Selltiz, Wrightsman & Cook's research methods in social relations* (4th ed.). New York: Holt, Rinehart, & Winston.

Krippendorff, K. (1980). *Content analysis: An introduction to its methodology.* Beverly Hills, CA: Sage.

Lakoff, G., & Johnson, M. (1980). *Metaphors we live by.* Chicago: University of Chicago Press.

LeCompte, M.D., & Goetz, J.P. (1982) Problems of reliability and validity in ethnographic research. *Review of Educational Research, 52,* 31-60.

LeCompte, M.D., & Goetz, J.P. (1983, April). *Playing with ideas: Analysis of qualitative data.* Paper presented at the annual meeting of the American Educational Research Association, Montreal, Canada.

Levine, H.G. (1983, April). *Principles of data storage and retrieval for use in qualitative evaluations.* Paper presented at the annual meeting of the American Educational Research Association, Montreal, Canada.

Lofland, J., (1971). *Analyzing social settings: A guide to qualitative observation and analysis.* Belmont, CA: Wadsworth.

Lofland, J. (1974). Styles of reporting qualitative field research. *American Sociologist, 9,* 101-111.

Manicas, P., & Secord, P. (1983). Implications for psychology of the new philosophy of science. *American Psychologist, 38* (4), 399-413.

McCutcheon, G. (1981). On the interpretation of classroom observations. *Educational Researcher, 10* (5), 5-10.

Meehl, P. (1954). *Clinical versus statistical prediction.* Minneapolis: University of Minnesota Press.

Meehl, P. (1965). Clinical versus statistical prediction. *Journal of Experimental Research in Personality, 63* (1), 81-97.

Miles, M.B. (1979). Qualitative data as an attractive nuisance: the problem of analysis. *Administrative Science Quarterly, 24,* 590-601.

Miles, M.B., & Huberman, A.M. (1984). *Qualitative data analysis: A sourcebook of new methods.* Beverly Hills, CA: Sage.

Mills, C.W. (1959). On intellectual craftsmanship. Appendix to Mills, C.W., *The sociological imagination.* New York: Oxford University Press.

Mischel, W., (1969). Continuity and change in personality. *American Psychologist, 24*(11), 1012-1018.

Mishler, E. (1979). Meaning in context: Is there any other kind? *Harvard Educational Review, 49* (1), 1-19.

Mulhauser, F. (1975). Ethnography and policy-making: The case of education. *Human Organization, 34,* 311-315.

Norris, S.P. (1983). The inconsistencies at the foundation of construct validation theory. In E.R. House (Ed.) *Philosophy of evaluation* (New Directions for Program Evaluation, No. 19). San Francisco: Jossey-Bass.

Ortony, A. (Ed.) (1979). *Metaphor and thought.* Cambridge, U.K.: Cambridge University Press.

Oskamp, S. (1965). Overconfidence in case-study judgments. *Journal of Counseling Psychology, 29* (3), 261-265.

Patton, M.Q. (1980). *Qualitative evaluation methods.* Beverly Hills: Sage.

Pelto, P.J., & Pelto, G.H. (1978). *Anthropological research: The structure of inquiry* (2d. ed.). Cambridge University Press.

Phillips, D.C. (1983). After the wake: Postpositivistic educational thought. *Educational Researcher, 12* (5), 4-12.

Platt, J.R. (1964). Strong inference. *Science, 146,* 347-353.

Pool, I. de S. (1973). *Handbook of communication.* Chicago: Rand McNally.

Sieber, S.D. (1976). *A synopsis and critique of guidelines for qualitative analysis contained in selected textbooks.* New York: Center for Policy Research, Project on Social Architecture in Education.

Smith, A.G., & Louis, K.S. (1982). Multimethod policy research: Issues and applications. *American Behavioral Scientist, 26* (1).

Smith, J.K. (1983 a). Quantitative vs. interpretive: The problem of conducting social inquiry. In E.R. House (Ed.) *Philosophy of evaluation.* (New Directions for Program Evaluation, No. 19). San Francisco: Jossey-Bass.

Smith, J.K. (1983 b). Quantitative vs. qualitative research: An attempt to clarify the issue. *Educational Researcher, 12* (3), 6-13.

Smith, L.M. (1978). An evolving logic of participant observation, educational ethnography and other case studies. In L. Shulman (Ed.) *Review of Research in Education* (Vol. 6). Itasca, IL: F.E. Peacock.

Smith, L.M., & Keith, P. (1971). *The anatomy of educational innovation.* New York: Wiley.

Snow, R. (1974). Representative and quasi-representative designs for research in teaching. *Review of Educational Research, 1974, 44,* 265-292.

Spradley, J. (1979). *The ethnographic interview.* New York: Holt, Rinehart, & Winston.

Stake, R. (1976). *Evaluating educational programs: The need and the response.* Washington, D.C.: OECD Publications Center.

Stake, R., & Easley, J. (Eds.) (1978). *Case studies in science education.* Urbana, IL: Center for Instructional Research and Curriculum Evaluation.

Stearns, M.S., Greene, D., & David, J.L. (1980) *Local implementation of PL 94-142: First year report of a longitudinal study.* Menlo Park, CA: SRI International, SRI Project 7124.

Stiegelbauer, S., Goldstein, M., & Hul-

ing L.L. (1982). Through the eye of the beholder: On the use of qualitative methods in data analysis. In Rutherford, W.L., *Quantitative and qualitative procedures for studying interventions influencing the outcomes of school improvement.* (R & D Report 3140). Austin, TX: University of Texas, R & D Center for Teacher Education.

Swinburne, R. (Ed.) (1974). *The justification of induction.* London: Oxford University Press.

Taft, R. (1955). The ability to judge people. *Psychological Bulletin, 52* (1), 1-23.

Tuthill, D., & Ashton, P. (1983). Improving educational research through the development of educational paradigms. *Educational Researcher, 12* (10), 6-14.

Tversky, A., & Kahneman, D. (1971). The belief in the law of small numbers. *Psychological Bulletin, 76* (2), 105-110.

Van Maanen, J. (1979). The fact of fiction in organizational ethnography. *Administrative Science Quarterly, 24,* 539-611.

Wax, R. (1971). *Doing fieldwork: Warnings and advice.* Chicago: University of Chicago Press.

23

Principles of Data Storage and Retrieval for Use in Qualitative Evaluations

Harold G. Levine

In spite of increased interest in recent years in the mechanics of
qualitative evaluation, few evaluators or other qualitative researchers
have addressed the related issues of qualitative data storage-retrieval
and data reduction-analysis. Generalized procedures for these tasks,
which are generally known within the field of anthropology, have
never been systematically examined or codified. This paper borrows
from developments in information and library science to construct
general principles of data storage and retrieval for the field-based
investigator. The five principles that are examined are formatting,
cross-referral, indexing (including thesauri design and cross-referencing), abstracting, and pagination. The principles are illustrated
with examples from evaluations of school-based programs in the
United States. Although the emphasis is on techniques for
manual data manipulation, the paper also explores the advantages
of, and considerations for, computerized data storage and search.
Finally, the paper also includes a discussion of the more obvious
implications of decisions about data storage and retrieval for data
reduction and analysis.

Qualitative and ethnographic evaluation has become an increasingly common
form of programmatic assessment. Typically, such evaluations involve an on-site
evaluator making long-term, in-depth observations which are written up as narrative field notes. These notes, in turn,
form the data base from which the subsequent evaluation is to be written. During the last dozen years there has been

new interest within anthropology and al-
lied disciplines in writing about how to
do fieldwork, including discussions of
how to collect and write up field notes,
and in providing models of fieldwork
through candid, first-person accounts
(e.g., Agar, 1980; Bogdan, 1972; Bogdan &
Taylor, 1975; Bruyn, 1966; Filstead, 1970;
Freilich, 1970; Georges & Jones, 1980;
Golde, 1970; Rabinow, 1977; Schatzman
& Strauss, 1973; Spradley, 1980; Wax,
1971). Given this interest in the fieldwork
process and, more particularly, in the generation of field notes, it is surprising how
few of these sources present schemes for
qualitative data storage-retrieval (e.g.,
Lofland, 1971; Smalley, 1960; Williams,

I would like to thank Professors Harold Borko,
Ronald Gallimore, Jim Turner, and Thomas Weisner
for their comments and help in the preparation of
this manuscript.
   An earlier version of this paper was presented at
the annual meeting of the American Educational
Research Association, Montreal, Canada, April 1983.

From Harold G. Levine, "Principles of Data Storage and Retrieval for Use in Qualitative Evaluations," *Educational Evaluation and Policy Analysis*, 1985, 7(2), 169-186. Copyright 1985, American
Educational Research Association, Washington, DC.

1967; Wolff, 1960; see also Chambers & Bolton, n.d.[1]), and how infrequently they systematically address the related issue of qualitative data reduction and analysis (e.g., Becker, 1958; Glaser & Strauss, 1967; Goetz & LeCompte, 1981; Miles & Huberman, n.d.; Robinson, 1951). While there is a vast lore and some published accounts within anthropology and related fields on how data storage-retrieval and data reduction-analysis are best achieved, generalized principles for such tasks remain noncodified. The materials that are available, however, seem to have had only limited impact on the practice of evaluation.

There are a number of important reasons for systematically addressing data storage-retrieval and data reduction-analysis. First, a field investigator may produce hundreds of pages of field notes so that some technique of readily accessing pertinent data becomes crucial. The problem is exacerbated if the fieldwork, as is particularly common today in qualitative evaluation (e.g., Herriott, 1982; Herriott & Firestone, 1982; Miles & Huberman, 1984; Patton, 1980), involves multiple investigators at diverse sites. Some method of coordinating their data collection and data storage is necessary for the field site monitor or project director to later trace, combine, and compare data sets. Second, fieldwork data are typically recorded in a sequence related to the social interaction of investigator and informant rather than linearly to the (often numerous) topics under investigation. One must be able to record, block, file, and index these data so that they can later be retrieved in a way that aids the analysis of the topics being investigated. Third, a rationale for data storage and retrieval must be developed if one investigator is to build effectively on the work of another. Finally, because data storage involves the definition and aggregation of salient categories of information within a data set, first-stage data reduction is, ipso

facto, accomplished. This process may place serious constraints on later data analysis or reanalysis.

The only widely available, systematic model for qualitative data classification, storage, and retrieval occurs within anthropology and was developed by scholars at the Human Relations Area Files (HRAF). The HRAF approach offers a comprehensive thesaurus (*The Outline of Cultural Materials*, Murdock et al., 1982), an extensive cross-referencing system, and indexing procedures. One of its chief virtues is its wide acceptance and use by anthropologists, thereby enhancing comparability of data sets produced by different investigators in different parts of the world. It is limited in that it was not developed explicitly for use by evaluators or researchers in the field and therefore is not really appropriate for day-to-day use. More important, it represents only one among many options of data storage and retrieval, and not necessarily the most appropriate approach given a particular investigator's research goals and data base. That is, it is most suited to a "typical" ethnographic study in which all major domains of cultural behavior (e.g., religion, death ritual, economics) may be touched upon or to hologeistic studies where hypotheses about behavior are tested cross-culturally. The index offers an array of terms/concepts independently created and intended to be of universal application. However, a researcher may actually need index items that are *derived* from his or her data set and that are more analytic in nature.

To find more general models of data storage and retrieval for the field-based investigator one must turn to the fields of information and library science. Although there are special problems associated with qualitative data bases not addressed by writers in these fields, they remain the only scholars who have carefully investigated the crucial problems connected with data storage and retrieval: abstracting, syndetic index systems, thesaurus design, file creation, semantic textual analysis, and the like. As one might expect given increasingly sophisticated computer technology, the literature on information processing/retrieval is voluminous (see, e.g., Borko, 1967; Borko & Bernier, 1975, 1978; Garvin, 1963; Kochen, 1967, 1974; Lancaster, 1968; Salton, 1975; Saracevic, 1970; Sparck, Jones & Kay, 1973; van Rijsbergen, 1979; Vickery, 1970, 1973). For our purposes, this literature offers basic principles for the creation of information storage and retrieval systems by which users may be efficiently guided to interconnected and coordinated data sources.

There are five principles by which fully coordinated file systems are created: formatting, cross-referral, indexing (including thesauri and cross-references), abstracting, and pagination. In this paper I systematically explicate these five principles and illustrate them with examples taken from actual qualitative evaluations and educational research projects. Although the emphasis in this discussion is on manual data storage and retrieval systems, I wish also to indicate some of the general considerations for, and advantages of, computerized data storage and search. The latter is still in its infancy within anthropology and other social science disciplines, but is almost certain to become of increasing importance in the years to come (see, e.g., Dow, 1982; Kirk, 1981; Sproull & Sproull, 1982; Weinberg & Weinberg, 1972). Finally, even though I wish to reserve for elsewhere a full discussion of how decisions made by an investigator about qualitative data storage and retrieval affect data reduction and analysis, I do wish to point out some of the more obvious implications in the conclusion.

Principles of Data Storage and Retrieval

Formatting

Format refers to both the physical forms and layouts field notes can take and any file structures set up within a given form. Layout refers to any pre-set categories of information that are routinely included with a field note, such as name of evaluator, date when field observations were made or recorded, bio-demographic information on site members, and the like. A file structure is an aggregation of data pertaining to a given topic, type of event, individual actor (or class of actors), or other narrowly delimited evaluation goal. Ideally, all files are uniform in physical

characteristics, although this is crucial only when computerized searches are to be undertaken. Further discussion of the way in which file structures can be used for computerized *document* retrieval can be found in van Rijsbergen, 1979.)

In their physical form most noncomputer-based field notes are entered in hard-bound volumes or loose-leaf notebooks. Some investigators use different forms within a single project: a hardbound volume with perforated "tear sheets" for observational data, a loose-leaf notebook for a daily log, and a small, pocketsize notebook for use as a diary. Others use 5 × 8 inch (or other size) cards or one of several punched cards (e.g., Hollerith; edge-notched) that are available (see Chambers & Bolton, n.d.). For computerized data management, behavioral records are entered and stored as text files. File creation and manipulation, data coding, file duplication, and other "clerical" tasks can then be managed by using the word processing capacities of computer software (see Sproull & Sproull, 1982).

The use of particular file structures depends exclusively on the data storage and retrieval needs of the investigator. The chief virtue of a file structure is that salient data (of whatever sort chosen by the investigator) is physically organized in the same place, simplifying later retrieval and analysis. In terms of general content (and the organizational logic of the overall project) there are three types of files most likely to be of widespread use: (a) event centered, (b) topic focused, and (c) person centered.

There are two subtypes of *event-centered files*. The first is of a more general nature and includes information about how the investigator spent his or her fieldwork time, the major events of a period (usually a single day), and other information relevant to a particular evaluation. Such files are usually ordered chronologically and represent a fieldwork *log*.

An example of a general event file is found in Figure 1. This represents the evaluator's log for an ethnographic evaluation of a child and family (primary prevention) mental health program (CFMH) in Headstart. It includes entries for each data collection activity relevant to each

FIGURE 1. General event file (Log).

Day/date	Classroom/teacher/child observation	Time of day	File page number	Comment	Mental health session type	Time of day	File page number	Comment	Interview	Time of day	File page number	Abstract	Miscellaneous	File page number

evaluation goal, including classroom observations, observations of mandated mental health activities (e.g., counseling, consultation), and interviews on primary prevention activities, as well as space for brief comments or abstracts of these observed events. A more specific event file is also possible. In this case, accounts of certain narrowly defined, but relatively frequent, events are serially ordered in a single file. For each subfile, informational queries may be made of the investigator, including "Page Code" (see below under Pagination), "Entry No.," "Names of Participants and Positions," "Place," and the like. Both the subfiles and these informational queries aid in data organization and cross-site comparison, and help give a context to both the fieldwork ("Names of Participants" and "Place") and the field note write-up ("Date of Observation," "Date of Write-up").

Topic-centered files can also be subdivided into general and specific types. General topic files are characteristic of most ethnographic or participant-observation fieldwork. These are narrative accounts of cultural knowledge, beliefs, and practices as observed by the investigator or recounted to him or her by an informant. Typically these accounts are on a wide range of topics. In all cases the field investigator should specify in the notes themselves the date of observation and of write-up and the name(s) of the primary informant(s). In specific topic files, only data pertinent to a single, narrowly delimited issue are recorded.

Thus, in the CFMH evaluation, field researchers aggregated in one subfile all interview data bearing on the attitudes, beliefs, and knowledge held by informants regarding mental health. They established a separate subfile on attitudes, beliefs, and knowledge of this same set of informants on primary prevention, and established a third subfile on interview material relating to specific classroom techniques mentioned by informants for achieving mental health and primary prevention as well as any behaviors of children by which mental health and primary prevention could be recognized. These subfiles were created to more readily assess attitudinal change in staff over time (and as a presumed function of the CFMH program), to gauge the degree to which the knowledge and attitudes held by program participants overlapped, and to construct behavioral inventories as a prelude to the construction of a formal observational protocol of teacher and child classroom behaviors related to "mental wellness." Given that these evaluation goals were explicitly defined before actual field work began, it was possible to systematically plan for the appropriate subfiles. In some instances, however, the mere exercise of defining the content for the subfiles may force the investigator to more sharply define the topics of inquiry.

Person-centered files collect information on single individuals, on groups of individuals (e.g., the governing board or PTA), or on social roles or positions (e.g., school principal). As with event- and topic-focused files, these too depend on particular evaluation goals, as does any internal subdivision of the file. In life history research, for example, a file on the individual(s) of concern seems obvious, with perhaps chronological subdivisions (e.g., early years, adolescence, middle years, etc.), important life events (e.g., high school, marriage, child birth, etc.), or the use of some other organizing concept. Information collected on individuals can also be quite specific, for example, instances of sick leave or tardiness by site personnel or the verbal behavior of key individuals at public meetings. These latter are examples of topic- or event-files suborganized by individuals. One of the important uses of such files is in the development of case histories in which "discrete items of information, culled from various sources, are ordered first chronologically and then by topic until an internally coherent process appears in which the subject's decisions and attitudes are demonstrably related to his current situation and past experience" (Wallace, 1961, p. 280).

Whether one defines a file as event-, topic-, or person-centered is relatively inconsequential. Indeed, whether a set of observed behaviors is best conceptualized as, say, an event or as a topic may result in unnecessary confusion. Most fieldworkers, rather, are better served by having "general purpose" field notes that include event-focused accounts of behav-

iors on-site as well as topic-focused accounts. Often, investigators add a limited number of specialized files. An educational evaluator, for example, might typically include information on the funding of a program and the "cast of characters" responsible for it. The central concern is that the investigator make some preliminary decisions about the internal structure of the data and organize his or her materials accordingly.

In summary, while the exact form of a complete file structure may vary widely, it is important that the evaluator:

(1) Make as many decisions as possible before entering the field about his or her specific data collection or data analysis needs (Kirk, 1981; Sonquist, 1977). Ordinarily, any focal point in the project that can be even broadly conceptualized and delimited should be given a separate file for ease of later access.

(2) Examine the total file structure to make sure that all potential data types are classifiable in one or more files and that unwanted redundancy and omission are kept to a minimum. Data that appropriately belong in two files may be recopied or photocopied. It may also be subjected to cross-referral (see below). In its entirety, the file structure should be a kind of map for the field evaluator for his or her data, and its use as a guidepost should be kept in mind. An example of a complete file structure, with the significant categories by which it should be evaluated and ordered, is given in Figure 2.

Cross-Referral

To aid the data search process, it is usually advantageous to make notations in one file or subfile of identical or related data in another file (or elsewhere in the same subfile). This notation process is termed cross-referral (and is distinguished from cross-referencing discussed below under "Thesauri"). A typical example of this can be found in Figure 1 in which a brief, abstracted version of an event relevant to the evaluation is entered in a log with a notation of which event- or topic-centered file the full account may be found. One can also cross-refer from

FIGURE 2. *Complete file structure (multisite evaluation of Child and Family Mental Health Program).*

File/Purpose	Reality to be approximated	Format	Internal organization
I. General			
A. An ongoing, sequentially ordered account of all events and background information at a site (particularly notes on school "norms," "rules," history of program, etc.)	Everyday life and special events, actual and hypothetical; volunteered and elicited informant statements; occasional or isolated events	Longhand or typed accounts in journal form (page codes)	1. Independent and derived sets of index terms; integration of terms 2. Integration with B. and C. below through cross-referral
B. A quick guide to all major events with cross-referral to A. above and to specialized files below where details are located; possible correlation of events with each other	Capsule account of major events, interviews, and observations relevant to evaluation goals	Daily entries in journal form (as above)	Standardized format
C. Personal reactions to daily events; literary emotional outlet; musings; a mnemonic device	Subjective experience; experiential "wholeness"	Diary	Written almost daily; largely unstructured; stream of consciousness, but usually grounded in the events of the day
II. Specialized			
D. Interview information on mental health and social adjustment from program participants	Attitudes, beliefs, and knowledge (1) about mental health, (2) about primary prevention, and (3) about specific classroom techniques for achieving mental health and primary prevention and behaviors of children by which mental health and primary prevention can be recognized	Longhand or typed accounts in journal form (page codes)	Name of interviewee, position in the school, date interviewed, date of write-up
E. Classroom observations	Actual classroom implementation of mental health and social adjustment practices	As in D. above.	As in D. above. Additional context provided: adults present, classroom period, background activity
F. Observations of CFMH mandated activities	(1) Training, (2) orientation, (3) counseling, (4) consultation, (5) site specific events	As in D. above.	Names of participants and positions, place, date of observation, date of write-up. Sample of all possible events used.
G. Focused child observations	Observable aspects of mental "wellness" and "social adjustment" in children	As in D. above.	Time-sampled observations of selected subsample of children with coding of transcripts
H. Follow-up and notation of ideas to be used in data interpretation	Errors or inconsistencies in observations; important leads toward which further observations should be conducted; intellectual concerns	Bracketed inserts or occasional paragraphs in A.-G. above, and a journal form "Ideas" page	Flexible

one account to additional, follow-up material in the same source. This would most likely occur when events transpire over several days and intervening material is entered into the file interrupting the serial continuity of the account. Finally, one might also want to cross-refer when data entered in one file are pertinent to a second file or subfile. Rather than copy the information in its entirety, one can note in the second file its existence in the first file, perhaps giving a brief, abstracted version of the contents of the data, omitting the full context. Sometimes, in complex retrieval systems the researcher may wish to create a cross-referral file. An example of this is included in Figure 3.

In this evaluation of four Headstart bilingual education programs, the evaluators were primarily interested in classroom events and the speech and classroom behavior of each of the young children being studied. Hence, event and individual files were created. However, project officers recognized that valuable information relating to other aspects of the study, such as classroom organization and curricular content, would also be included in these files. Consequently, they established a cross-referral file to monitor

these topics (listed under the "Category number" column) and the files and page numbers within the files where the data were stored.

Indexing

Indexing in qualitative data storage and retrieval refers to a three-part process for identifying/defining categories of relevant information, organizing these in a uniform manner, and physically pairing these categories (or coded numerical representations of them) with the actual written data set. The identification/definition phase is ultimately an arbitrary one, since obviously any data set can be classified in an infinite number of ways. The keys to a successful indexing system, therefore, are consistency, cross-referencing among index categories (see below under "Thesauri"), and continuous updating (see below). For most investigators the central goal in the design of an indexing system will be ease and accuracy of retrieval (to be discussed below in terms of "Precision" and "Recall").

Index Language. Every index has an index *language*, the set of terms and their modifiers used to describe field notes and to make information retrieval requests for

FIGURE 3. *Example of a cross-referral file.*

```
                                                    page _____
                         CROSS-REFERRAL FILE
                              (Topics)
                                        Fieldworker: _____
                                        Site:        _____
```

Category number	Event	Individual/source	Page
1.0			
1.1			
1.2			
1.3			
1.3.1			
1.3.2			
1.3.3			
1.3.4			
1.3.5			
2.0			
2.1			
2.2			
2.3			
2.3.1			
2.3.2			
2.3.3			
2.3.4			
2.3.5			

categories of information. The index terms can themselves be described along five interrelated dimensions.

1. *Independent vs. derived* (see also Wooster, as cited in Borko & Bernier, 1978, pp. 94–95). This distinction parallels the etic-emic dichotomy commonly found in anthropology and other social science disciplines. An independent set of terms is based on the deliberations, experiences, and accumulated wisdom of experts in a field who have developed a set of descriptors intended to have universal applicability for that field. The most widely used independent index in anthropology is in the *Outline of Cultural Materials* (OCM) with its 888 two-tiered category list. Independent index terms such as these allow cross-site comparability. However, their universalist orientation is also their major limitation: The terms may be too general to be of meaningful use. A cultural event or topic may be fully defined only by the simultaneous use of several of these categories (thereby necessitating extra indexing time), or the category domain of scientific interest may be so specialized that the OCM (or any other set of independent terms) is simply not detailed enough. For educational evaluators interested in classroom processes, for example, they must rely on a mere six categories (Educational System, Elementary Education, Liberal Arts Education, Vocational Education, Teachers, Educational Theory and Methods) in the OCM which treat formal education. The solution to this dilemma, of course, is to *derive* one's set of terms from the data themselves. The terms which then represent salient concepts, institutions, belief systems, and the like are thus more likely to be expressed in the *natural* language of informants. This adds to indexical validity of content. However, it also means that compatibility with data sets generated by other investigators suffers (without an overarching concordance of some sort), as well as the data analytic phase of fieldwork since *scientific* categories need to be constructed and then linked with the natural language categories already produced. In spite of these shortcomings, however, derived terms are often preferred by fieldworkers since that is inevitably how they are most likely to think about their data set when

searches are to be made later. In addition, if the technology for automatic indexing of qualitative data by computer becomes sophisticated enough, it will most likely use natural language procedures.

There are three basic approaches to combining derived and independent terms. One can develop two separate sets of terms and index the data in terms of both. While a cumbersome technique, it enhances retrievability without sacrificing compatibility. It has another advantage as well. An independent set of terms can function as a kind of subject index or table of contents for a body of material. Materials may even be physically filed according to such an index. The set of derived terms, in this scheme, can then be used to provide a further perspective on the data set since there is no one-to-one correspondence between the terms in the two index languages.

A second approach to combining independent and derived terms is to mix the two. This would be particularly appropriate if the focus of the research were relatively narrowly delimited. In this way the set of independent terms can be used for coverage of the nonessential field materials with a set of derived terms fully indexing the subject(s) of interest. Finally, one can use a set of independent terms as higher order boundary setters, which give a previously established form to the index with subcategories of derived terms being used to do most of the actual work of the indexing.

2. *Descriptive versus analytic.* Independent terms may be either descriptive or analytic. While this distinction is really one of degree rather than an absolute difference, descriptive terms are intentionally neutral; their intent is to "indicate" some information in or about the data set. Thus, a teacher complimenting a student during a lesson and all other such behavioral episodes might be indexed as "Compliments" or "Praises." It might also be rendered more *specifically* as "Teacher-to-Student Praises" or more *generally* as "Classroom Interaction." Analytic terms, on the other hand, depend on a body of theory for which the terms represent concepts or constructs in the theory. In the above example teacher compliments might be rendered as "Posi-

tive Reinforcement" if the investigator were trying to study classroom behaviors with traditional behaviorist theory. Analytic terms are clearly not possible with a derived term set unless the latter are themselves theoretical by nature.

3. *Precoordinate versus postcoordinate.* With precoordinate terms the exact categories of interest are constructed prior to any actual data search. With postcoordinate terms specific categories for information retrieval are constructed at the time of the search. An example will make this clear. In a precoordinate system one might define "Code-switching by students during academic lesson" as an appropriate category and index the field data accordingly. One might also, for example, have a second category defined as "Code-switching by students during nonacademic periods" and a third category defined as "Code-switching by aides during academic lessons." One would similarly index the data as appropriate to these two categories. At the time of search the evaluator would merely go to the index, find the categories, and look for the file and page number where the material is to be found. In a postcoordinate system, however, the index terms would be five in number ("Code-Switching," "Students," "Aides," "Academic Lessons," and "Nonacademic Periods"), and the data would be indexed accordingly. When the search was initiated, any *combination* of these five terms would be possible. Thus, the Boolean product (AND) would be used to construct a search category "Code-Switching" + "Students" + "Academic Lessons," or any other product. (Other kinds of computer-based search strategies are described in van Rijsbergen, 1979.) When the search revealed a locator that was identical for all three terms, the searcher would be led to their interaction in the data set.

When precoordinate systems are used specificity is normally achieved by the modification of the main term either with additional descriptors (e.g., lower order abstractions), syntactical devices (e.g., prepositional phrases), or cross-referencing (see below under "Thesauri"). When making modifications they can either be derived for the entry or selected from a standard (independent) list. Such modifi-

cations are normally not used for postcoordinate systems. In these, specificity is achieved, as mentioned, by the use of Boolean products as well as the addition of adjectives to the noun or gerund heading and by the use of "weights" to indicate the importance (as seen by the investigator) of a heading in indexing a given content (Borko & Bernier, 1978, p. 24).

Typically, precoordinate indexes are the rule in qualitative fieldwork, although this may be less a function of their appropriateness than of lack of investigator familiarity with postcoordinate types. The greatest benefit to be realized from postcoordinate systems is when the data set, or its representation in the form of index terms and locators, is computer based. Under such conditions Boolean searches are extremely easy. Of course, even a precoordinate system can still be subject to some degree of postcoordination. In general, however, postcoordinate systems are employed when the data set is large and multidimensional and when the analysis is apt to proceed in unanticipated directions.

4. *Controlled versus uncontrolled.* Index languages must, of course, serve as a kind of description of the content of a document or set of field notes. The lexical items of the language are used to do this. However, it is usually the case that some way must be provided for expansion or contraction of index classes as well as any change in directionality to meet the actual search needs of the user. Thus, index languages are often *controlled* by a set of logical devices (see Cleverdon, Mills, & Keen 1966; Vickery, 1965).

In controlled systems there are various rules that limit the number or types of terms (single or multiword phrases) to be used and their relationships with one another (including respective levels of abstraction). At the broadest conceptual level such rules include exclusionary principles (e.g., "A" is not authorized; see "B" instead), affinitive principles (e.g., "A" is permitted; "B" may be used as well), and hierarchical principles ("A" is permitted; "B" may be used instead) (Angell, as cited in Borko & Bernier, 1978, p. 99; see also Vickery, 1973). (For a full discussion of how hierarchies vary and how this variability affects search strategies, see Cleverdon et al., 1966.) The Outline of Cultural Materials (OCM) is, in effect, characterized by rules of affinity in which synonyms for various index terms are offered to the searcher—for example, the entry "Elementary Education" contains the "See also" terms "Arithmetic," "Books and writing materials," "civics," and so on. At the same time, the various terms are ordered in a limited hierarchy. "Elementary Education," as an example, is a subheading under "Education" and is commensurate with other terms such as "Educational System," "Liberal Arts Education," "Teachers," and so on. (The structure of the OCM is also limiting in that, given the numbering system, only nine subheadings are possible—e.g., under 76 only 761–769 can be included.) When fieldworkers use hierarchial relations to order term sets they most frequently make use of both generic and nongeneric elements. That is, they develop a hierarchy that "subordinates some terms to others regardless of the relation involved, so long as the subordinated term can be seen to belong to some category or facet of the 'containing class'" (Cleverdon et al., 1966, p. 69). As an example, the term "bilingual education" may subsume such diverse facets as times when it is practiced, content areas of interaction in one language over another, school solutions to problems connected with bilingual instruction, and so forth.[2] The advantages of this type of hierarchy are that context helps provide definition to the term set and that the ambiguities of natural language (and the underlying reality that such ambiguities partially reflect) are not oversimplified and artificially constrained by having to strictly define any term by a single one of its facets.

As distinct from controlled languages employing hierarchical or other devices, uncontrolled languages have no such rules and are usually characterized by a proliferation of terms in the natural language of the data set. While such a system

would seem to be undesirable, it is often characteristic of a set of derived terms. In addition, research under experimental conditions shows that uncontrolled vocabularies based on the natural language of the documents attain retrieval effectiveness comparable to vocabularies with more elaborate controls (van Rijsbergen, 1979, p. 23).

5. Exhaustive versus specific. Indexing exhaustivity refers to the number of different topics the investigator has indexed. Index language specificity, on the other hand, refers to the ability of the language to describe and therefore pinpoint information types with precision. Experimental findings show that a high level of exhaustivity of indexing leads to high recall (defined as the ratio of the number of relevant documents retrieved to the total number of relevant documents, whether retrieved or not retrieved) and to low precision (defined as the ratio of the number of relevant documents retrieved to the total number of documents retrieved). Systems with high specificity, on the other hand, have low recall but high precision. Thus recall and precision appear to be, with qualifications, inversely related (Cleverdon et al., 1966).

In practice, investigators typically try to balance exhaustivity and specificity. In fact, experimental findings seem to suggest that there is an optimum level of index exhaustivity. To transcend this level appears to do little to significantly improve recall ratio but may seriously jeopardize the precision ratio (Cleverdon et al., 1966). Of course, with relatively small data sets field evaluators may essentially be able to optimize both recall and precision. With larger data sets the evaluator's goals must define how exhaustive or how specific the term sets will be. For exploratory research, research into "whole" cultures (as would be typical for many ethnographic studies), formative evaluations, and the like, exhaustivity might likely be emphasized. For highly focused studies or summative evaluations, specificity would most likely be preferred. This is an area where further empirical research, in the context of actual ongoing field studies, will benefit the field in important ways.

Thesauri. Index terms are ordered

---

[2] In constructing such classification hierarchies, one must be cognizant of the underlying theory one has by which the hierarchy is constructed. The theory has important implications for concept development and data analysis (see Levine, in press).

through a thesaurus, which is defined as "an organized list of terms from a specialized vocabulary arranged to facilitate the selection of synonyms and of words that are otherwise related" (Borko & Bernier, 1978, p. 92). For qualitative data storage and retrieval systems, the thesaurus identifies the total set of index terms to be used (derived or independent, descriptive or analytic, exhaustive or specific), defines them, pairs them with any code equivalents that are used, connects words that are intersubstitutable, specifies any control rules to be used, and in essence gives the rules for making queries of the data set (see Soergel, 1974; Wessel, 1975). It also, of course, provides a permanent record of retrieval options exercised by the investigator.

The OCM (Murdock et al., 1982) provides the most widely used example of a thesaurus in field research. Figure 4 shows an example from the OCM of a typical index term entry—"Elementary Education." It contains a series of glosses (e.g., "tutorial education," "primary schools [e.g., private, parochial, public]," "periods of instruction [e.g., terms, vacations; hours per day, days per week, weeks per year, years required for graduation]") which tell the user what has been included under the heading and, in effect, how the heading is organized. Although the OCM does not do so, one can also note exceptions to the indexing and, through the use of parenthetical expressions, denote synonyms for the index label actually used. In effect, as with all materials included in a thesaurus, these specifications help bring the user's terminology in line with the indexer's. Following the synonyms (or intersubstitutable words and phrases, with "Elementary Education" accepted by the indexer as the representative of the class), there are "see also" cross-references, which tell the user the related index categories where additional pertinent information may be found. In addition to "see also" cross-references one can use "see" cross-references, which refer the searcher to a higher order heading (if the terms are hierarchically controlled), or "see under" cross-references, which refer the searcher to other terms under other headings. In an information retrieval device such cross-references obviously lead searchers to correct subheadings and to additional information. They also help eliminate, or at least control, what is known as "scattering," by which index terms related to the same general construct or behavior pattern proliferate and become haphazardly distributed throughout the thesaurus, resulting in reduced system efficiency.

Another feature of the OCM is that all terms are listed and their hierarchic relations specified. At a glance the searcher is able to achieve some understanding of the range and depth of the entire set of terms and the underlying logic that the index developer adopted in constructing the set of terms. However, the index terms of a thesaurus do not necessarily have to be organized hierarchically or in terms of some conventional order (in the OCM, demographic descriptors precede material culture descriptors, which precede economic descriptors, which precede religious ones, etc., revealing the logic of the traditional presentation of ethnographic

FIGURE 4. Index term entries from Outline of Cultural Materials (from Murdock et al., 1982, p. 172).

872 ELEMENTARY EDUCATION—tutorial education; primary schools (e.g., private, parochial, public); periods of instruction (e.g., terms, vacations, hours per day, days per week, weeks per year, years required for graduation); compulsory or voluntary attendance; objectives (e.g., universal literacy); curriculum (e.g., subjects and their progression); grading and advancement; educational aids (e.g., textbooks, stationery, blackboards); ceremonial (e.g., graduation); special institutions for very young children (e.g., nursery schools, kindergartens); etc. See also:

Arithmetic	803	Music	533
Books and writing materials	21*	Reading, writing, and spelling	212
Civics	641	Religious beliefs	77*
Ethical ideals	577	School buildings	346
Ethnogeography	823	Teachers	875
Informal transmission of social norms	867	Traditional history	173

data). One can merely organize an index alphabetically as in a book index.

In any index the terms must be paired with the locators where the data are to be found. This is usually done manually by most field investigators by placing the locator after the index term and by entering the index term (or a numerical representation of it) in the margin of the field note source or as a heading to a fieldnote (see Figure 5). If computer technology is available to the investigator, other procedures are available. Sproull and Sproull (1982), for example, describe a system by which descriptors or category labels are assigned to discrete items of data in the behavioral record, and word processing procedures are used to interline these labels with the items. Labels and associated data can then be located by developing a computer program that reads through each data file looking for each occurrence of the particular label(s) sought. The resulting list and data set are then printed out as necessary.

FIGURE 5. Pairing numerical representations of index terms with field notes.

Time Context: Snack-time

5.7.2/5.7.10,5.2/5.7.10	9:54 Diana—playing with paper
5.7.2/5.7.10	cups says "I got it, I got. . ."
	then sings, "I got more than
	you." (2x). She looks at
	Armacela who asks T where the
	aide is in Sp. The teacher ig-
	nores the question while asking
5.4	the group one of her own, "Quienes
	son los que quieren leche?" Diana
5.1	responds "Yo." The teacher asks a
	question of another child in Spanish
	while Diana looks on. She then
	looks at Herbert at the next table
5.7.2/5.7.10	and sings "I got milk, I got milk"
9.57	showing her glass to Herbert.
Large Group	Felipe 11:33 Sits on the rug,
	glances at (Obs) and brushes back
	his hair with a brush while mouth-
	ing a few words. Angie says to
5.4/8.2	him, "Felipe, tu tambien canta."
5.1/7.14	He then sings loudly. When the
5.1	song changes to "La Casita" he
	sings and forces his index fin-
	gers into eaves as called for.
6.5.1	Similarly he makes the motions
	of waves with his hands togeth-
	er with the other children while
	singing "suben y bajan las olas
	del mar." Felipe questions Angie
5.7.1/5.7.7/5.7.13	"Todavia van a hacer verdad?"
	He then moves forward with the
6.5.3	other children imitating a frog
	or playing in the sand in re-
	sponse to a new song. He says
	something to Angie which begins
5.3	"Miss Yo. . .". One of the kids
	asks for "Elena la ballena,"
	which is put on. Felipe
	doesn't take part actively but
7.16	simply mouths a few of the
	words while scratching his
	chest and looking around.
5.4/8.2 11:38	Teacher says "Felipe canta."

Questions related to updating the thesaurus must constantly be addressed, unless one has adopted an independent, controlled thesaurus, such as the OCM, which can be used from the first day in the field without modification. Derived systems, however, need constant revising and, in fact, often cannot even be started until some time (weeks or even months) has elapsed during which field observations are being made and recorded. Although an investigator will generate index terms, cross-references, modifications, and the like, there will inevitably be changes in these as time progresses. Old headings may no longer have the meaning the investigator once thought they did, and a new alternative may be deemed better. What was once thought to be a shading of the original meaning may turn out to be an important new organizing category or one of two alternatives to an even higher order category, and so forth. When such changes occur, two options are possible using manual procedures. One can recode all the data according to the new scheme, a time-consuming and tedious process; or one can make note of the change and the data. This is usually done on file cards with a separate color-coded set for the index terms, a set for index term modifications, and a third set for any cross-reference cards. When the investigator later wants to access these data, he or she simply makes two searches, one for the data collected *since* the change to the new index items (and using these as markers) and one for the data *prior to* the change using the *old* distinctions. Updates such as this may have to be made numerous times.

Updating and recording procedures are, of course, less tediously accomplished when data files and codes are computerized. Sproull and Sproull (1982), as one example, developed a "frequency analysis" program to scan a data set and list all descriptors of a particular type. The list was then scrutinized to reveal a set of general order descriptors which subsumed more specific ones. The latter were then replaced by the former with text editing procedures. Subsequently, a new list of both general and specific descriptors was generated and the process repeated. Not only does such a process allow

convenient updating of index terms, it also facilitates coding when derived term sets are to be used. Salient attributes of behavior do not have to be identified ahead of time, nor do all of the nuances of an attribute have to be specified (Sproull & Sproull, 1982, p. 286).

Abstracting

An abstract is one type of document surrogate offering a condensed version of the information to be found in the original without (normally) added interpretation or criticism (Borko & Bernier, 1975; Maizell, Smith, & Singer, 1971). Abstracts may serve a largely *informative* purpose by giving the user thoroughgoing data summaries from the parent document, thereby often obviating the need to consult the original. Abstracts may also be *indicative* or *descriptive*. Since this type of abstract merely indicates what is to be found in the parent materials, it does not normally save the user the time and trouble of consulting the latter. Indicative abstracts are particularly suited for describing lengthy or discursive texts such as would be characteristic of qualitative data sets. Abstracts differ from *extractions* in that the former paraphrase and the latter represent word-for-word reproductions from the original. In some abstracts for qualitative data, extracted material may also be appropriately included.

Abstracts, which should be used to preface any lengthy field note, are most useful in enhancing field note retrieval rather than information retrieval *within* a field note (for which the indexing system is designed). To do this an abstract of qualitative data must include two essential features: a reference section and body section. The reference section offers precise guidance from the abstract to the original. While the field investigator must decide what kinds of information will allow him or her to perform this locator function, typical items include the dates of the observations, the fieldworker(s) involved, and a duplication of the field note page code (see "Pagination" section below). Proper identification becomes particularly crucial if the abstracts are to be filed separately from the notes themselves (though most investigators typically use a copy of the abstract page as the covering page for the field note).

While the body of the abstract contains the paraphrased or extracted material, the function of an abstract is enhanced if descriptors or index terms are also included. These key the user on the content of the abstract (and, hence, the original field note). If tied together through a subject index, descriptors can be used in a postcoordinate abstract search procedure.

Figure 6 shows an example of an abstract with accompanying descriptors in a research project concerned with everyday cognition among mildly mentally re-

tarded adults. The abstract highlights both the observations themselves and the fieldworker's personal reactions to the events. Two of the descriptors ("laundry," "N") allow efficient retrieval of all field note abstracts related to laundry expeditions by the research participants (other daily domains were studied for contrastive purposes) and all notes on research subject "N." The two remaining descriptors ("cultural knowledge," "other regulation"), which are actually rather more specific than any of the terms used in the abstract, allow aggregation of abstracts by domain of theoretical concern. In even

---

FIGURE 6. Field note cover sheet with abstract.

Contact/Cover Sheet

I.D. # 555.13.40.01

Name of contact ___N___	Field researcher ___D.T.___
Date of contact ___10-6-82___	Field ___X___ Phone ___

If other than participant:

Participant with whom affiliated ___

Relationship to participant/Agency ___

Address ___   Phone ___

Initiated by ___D.T.___	Reason ___Observe her doing laundry___

Setting(s) ___Public laundry near her apartment___

Others present ___Other customers___

Duration ___1-3/4 hr.___

Taped? ___No___	Number of tapes ___

Field notes to follow? ___Yes___

Descriptors: Laundry; N; Cultural	Date of write-up ___10-12-82___
Knowledge; Other regulation	Date turned in ___10-14-82___

Summary: The original plan was to do the laundry at the apartment building where "N" lives. But when she discovered that the machines were out of order (the first time this has been the case) she decided to go to a laundry near her place. It later came out that she had done this mostly to be nice to me since "you came all this way." If it wasn't for this courtesy she said that she probably would have waited until the machine was fixed by the manager (such optimism). "N" had no real problems with any part of the laundry process in terms of knowledge of sequences, etc.—she did have some difficulty lifting the basket, conceptualizing amounts of soap and taking things out of the washer and transferring them to the dryer, though. It was very possible though that at a certain point I was being coopted into helping her to do things that she was very capable of doing herself—this suggests the need to repeat this observation at least one more time.

Comments:

more sophisticated systems the investigator might also provide a set of *identifiers* with each abstract. These tend to be even more specific than descriptors, and even though they are excluded from the subject index they are typically used to formulate a computer search (Borko & Bernier, 1975, p. 67). In qualitative data bases typical identifiers might be the names of participants, organizations, characteristic events, and the like. Occasionally, words that were initially used as identifiers may qualify as descriptors.

A fieldworker's retrieval interests are best served if at least the abstract and its descriptors and identifiers are rendered in machine readable form. This makes computerized Boolean searches possible. This also allows highly efficient access to aspects of the fieldwork. For the project director of a multisite qualitative evaluation, for example, it permits quick monitoring of the content of stored field notes as well as the progress/direction of the fieldworkers themselves.

Pagination

Retrieval depends not only on a thorough index but also on a set of mutually exclusive page numbers (locators) by which the data can actually be pinpointed. Pagination here refers to the process of assigning unique page numbers (or other locators) to every page (or other subunit) of field notes. Pagination may be simple and descriptive, merely distinguishing "page 1" from "page 2" and the like. In projects where two investigators are doing research, a letter might be used before the numeral to indicate whose data set is being paginated. The index would then contain the letter and the page number as the full locator.

Beyond description, page codes may be informational as well. In this case variables of concern in the project, or other information that in some way characterizes or identifies the notes (e.g., the date on which they were collected), are embedded in the page code. An example will make this clear. In a project to study the everyday problem-solving demands placed on moderately mentally retarded learners, two field observers ("B" and "K") were employed. The observations were of 12 students (each student was given a number from 1–12), across 36 different school-day "activity periods" (each period given a number from 1–36), and in three different periods (each period given a number from 1–3). To uniquely identify each page, however, two additional numbers had to be added. The first of these was a number representing the 1 ...nth time that the student was observed since, given field exigencies, it might take an observer two or more visits to complete the observations for a single activity period. Finally, the page number for that "nth" visit was recorded. As a result of these considerations, each page code consisted of a letter with a five-digit sequence following. Thus, as an example, the page number K.2.10.2.3.4 indicated that the page includes observations by field observer "K" on student 2, during activity period 10 ("Recess"), during the second observation period, and that this was the third observation of student 2, and the fourth page of the third observation.

Overview of Data Storage and Retrieval Principles and Consequences for Data Reduction and Analysis

The principles for data storage and retrieval discussed here are fundamental tools for the field investigator to better manage the "information explosion" that has always characterized qualitative research and evaluation. However, for such principles to be used effectively, the field researcher/evaluator must take the time to *design* the information retrieval system he or she is to use (even if it is only borrowing a data retrieval plan from elsewhere and adapting it). This design, in turn, is dependent on one's answer to the question of what specific uses are intended for the system's output. Without an objectivized plan the evaluator may be wasting valuable time and money: The system may only haphazardly fit the investigator's planned data retrieval needs; it may overlook or misclassify important sources of data; or it may be incompatible with the systems of other evaluators working in similar geographical or theoretical areas with which the investigator might ideally interface.

Researchers in the fields of library and information science have long been interested in indexing, thesauri, abstracting, file formatting, and the like. Now, with the availability of high speed computers and a concomitant rise in interest in information retrieval, a great deal of sophisticated research is directed toward comparing the utility of various index languages, assessing the effectiveness of different computerized file structures and search strategies, evaluating existing systems and deciding on the appropriate criteria for evaluation, and understanding the intricacies of automatic (i.e., computer-based) text analysis and classification. Other research is in progress as well, and while future work in these areas may prove to be of benefit to qualitative evaluators, some previous findings are suggestive. It has been argued, for example, that the decisionmaker is the most important variable affecting all components of an information retrieval system (Saracevic, as cited in Vickery, 1973, p. 123). As another example, the *length* of indexes seems more important in determining system performance than the *version* of the actual indexing language used (Saracevic, as cited in Vickery, 1973, p. 124). As a last example, it has become increasingly clear that no one structural feature (or set of features) in a document representation will adequately solve every search problem posed, or that any single system can be developed to meet all user needs (Vickery, 1973). Whether or not, or to what degree, these findings will also apply to qualitative data sets and their storage and retrieval remains to be seen, but the implications for the future use of such systems by qualitative evaluators under field conditions are potentially great. In spite of the difficulties, it may yet be possible to formulate some quite specific rules for the development of qualitative information and retrieval systems which have been shown empirically to enhance their overall effectiveness.

Finally, a few comments about qualitative data reduction and analysis are appropriate. Given that formatting, indexing, abstracting, and the like are the primary tools for data storage and retrieval—whether computer based, manual, or both—they are necessarily also important tools in data analysis. In fact, they are but an update of the strategies for organizing and manipulating ideas and data advocated by the sociologist C. Wright Mills in his 1959 "personal" essay, "On Intellectual Craftsmanship." Mills recommended that scientists set up a file (or journal) which would encourage self-reflection and idea generation and serve as a repository for notes on future studies, books read, observations made, experiences encountered, and so forth. These could be used to spur the "sociological imagination" by such techniques as rearranging the files in new ways, establishing new classifications, and cross-classifying. In this essay I have tried to show that a data storage and retrieval system offers an efficient and systematic way to achieve the same purposes.

However, beyond data manipulation and planned serendipity, a properly designed and used data storage and retrieval system has other important advantages in data analysis. The indexing language, for example, through successive modifications and updating as more information is collected and conceptualized, may become the language within which the final study may be cast, as theoretical constructs to be explicated and/or as actual section or subsection headings within the report. Eliminating index terms in favor of appropriately focused files achieves similar results with the added benefit of having all the relevant information in a single place. One can also alter the number of index terms to enhance certain kinds of retrieval, opting either for broader (more exhaustive) or more precise (higher specificity) coverage. Thus, the meaningfulness or applicability of a concept or construct can be tested against the data at hand. Also, with the proper coordination of the data set, classifications can be developed and competing models of events and behaviors (e.g., temporal models or structural models) attempted. As a last possibility, properly indexed/coded behavioral data are easily rendered as frequency data allowing quantitative analysis where appropriate.

There are thus many uses to which a fully coordinated information storage and retrieval system can be put in qualitative evaluation. However, it must also be recognized that *any* formalization of data storage and retrieval procedures places some constraints on data analysis. This is especially true for retrieval systems that employ sets of terms that are analytic, independent, or highly ordered. The use of a second term set which is derived, or a term set which is also postcoordinate, are two ways of reordering the data categories and examining their fit with the actual data. Thus, the technology of information storage and retrieval is not without its problems; but it is also not without possible solutions. It is probable that as information management continues to be of concern in social science research and as new technologies develop and become available (as, for example, microcomputers), qualitative evaluators and others will encounter these problems and search for their solutions with increasing frequency.

References

AGAR, M. H. (1980). *The professional stranger: An informal introduction to ethnography.* New York: Academic Press.

BECKER, H. S. (1958). Problems of inference and proof in participant observation. *American Sociological Review, 23,* 652–660.

BOGDAN, R. (1972). *Participant observation in organizational settings.* Syracuse, NY: Syracuse University.

BOGDAN, R., & TAYLOR, S. J. (1975). *Introduction to qualitative research methods.* New York: John Wiley.

BORKO, H. (Ed.). (1967). *Automated language processing.* New York: John Wiley.

BORKO, H., & BERNIER, C. L. (1975). *Abstracting concepts and methods.* New York: Academic Press.

BORKO, H., & BERNIER, C. L. (1978). *Indexing concepts and methods.* New York: Academic Press.

BRUYN, S. T. (1966). *The human perspective in sociology: The methodology of participant observation.* Englewood Cliffs, NJ: Prentice-Hall.

CHAMBERS, A., & BOLTON, R. (n.d.). *We all do it, but how? A survey of contemporary field note procedure.* Unpublished manuscript, Pomona College, Claremont, CA.

CLEVERDON, C., MILLS, J., & KEEN, M. (1966). *Factors determining the performance of indexing systems, Vol. I: Design.* London: Aslib Cranfield Research Project.

DOW, J. (1982, December). The combined use of computers and audio tape recorders in storing, managing, and using qualitative verbal ethnographic data. Paper presented at the 81st annual meeting of the American Anthropological Association, Washington, DC.

FILSTEAD, W. J. (Ed.). (1970). *Qualitative methodology: Firsthand involvement with the social world.* Chicago: Markham.

FREILICH, M. (Ed.). (1970). *Marginal natives: Anthropologists at work.* New York: Harper and Row.

GARVIN, P. L. (1963). *National language and the computer.* New York: McGraw-Hill.

GEORGES, R. A., & JONES, M. O. (1980). *People studying people: The human element in fieldwork.* Berkeley: University of California Press.

GLASER, B. G., & STRAUSS, A. L. (1967). *The discovery of grounded theory: Strategies for qualitative research.* Chicago: Aldine.

GOETZ, G. P., & LE COMPTE, M. D. (1981). Ethnographic research and the problem of data reduction. *Anthropology and Education Quarterly, 12,* 51–70.

GOLDE, P. (Ed.). (1970). *Women in the field.* Chicago: Aldine.

HERRIOTT, R. E. (1982). Tensions in research design and implementation. *American Behavioral Scientist, 26,* 23–44.

HERRIOTT, R. E., & FIRESTONE, W. A. (1982). *Multisite qualitative policy research in education: A study of recent federal experience.* Final report. Washington, DC: National Institute of Education.

KIRK, R. C. (1981). Microcomputers in anthropological research. *Sociological Methods and Research, 9,* 473–492.

KOCHEN, M. (1967). *The growth of knowledge; readings on organization and retrieval of information.* New York: John Wiley.

KOCHEN, M. (1974). *Principles of information retrieval.* Los Angeles: Melville.

LANCASTER, F. W. (1968). *Information retrieval systems: Characteristics, testing and evaluation.* New York: John Wiley.

LEVINE, H. G. (in press). "Taboos" and statements about taboos: Issues in the taxonomic analysis of behavioral restrictions among the New Guinea Kafe. In L. L. Langness & T. E. Hays (Eds.), *Anthropology in the high valleys: Essays in honor of Kenneth E. Read.* Novato, CA: Chandler and Sharp.

LOFLAND, J. (1971). *Analyzing social settings: A guide to qualitative observation and analysis.* Belmont, CA: Wadsworth.

MAIZELL, R. E., SMITH, J. F., & SINGER, T. E. R. (1971). *Abstracting scientific and technical literature.* New York: Wiley-Interscience.

MILES, M., & HUBERMAN, M. (1984). *Analyzing qualitative data: A sourcebook of new methods.* Beverly Hills, CA: Sage.

MILLS, C. W. (1959). On intellectual craftsmanship. In *The sociological imagination.* New York: Oxford University Press.

MURDOCK, G. P., FORD, C. S., HUDSEN, A. E., KENNEDY, R., SIMMONS, L. W., WHITING, J. W. M. (1982). *Outline of cultural materials* (5th rev. ed.). New Haven, CT: Human Relations Area Files.

PATTON, M. Q. (1980). *Qualitative evaluation methods.* Beverly Hills, CA: Sage.

RABINOW, P. (1977). *Reflections on fieldwork in Morocco.* Berkeley: University of California Press.

ROBINSON, W. S. (1951). The logical structure of analytic induction. *American Sociological Review, 16,* 812–818.

SALTON, G. (1975). *Dynamic information and library processing.* Englewood Cliffs, NJ: Prentice-Hall.

SARACEVIC, T. (1970). *Introduction to information science.* New York: R. R. Bowker.

SCHATZMAN, L., & STRAUSS, A. L. (1973). *Field research: Strategies for a natural sociology.* Englewood Cliffs, NJ: Prentice-Hall.

SMALLEY, W. A. (1960). Making and keeping anthropological field notes. *Practical Anthropology, 7,* 145–152.

SOERGEL, D. (1974). *Indexing languages and thesauri: Construction and maintenance.* Los Angeles: Melville.

SONQUIST, J. A. (1977). Computers and the social sciences. *American Behavioral Scientist, 20,* 295–318.

SPARCK JONES, K., & KAY, M. (1973). *Linguistics and information science.* New York: Academic Press.

SPRADLEY, J. P. (1980). *Participant observation.* New York: Holt, Rinehart and Winston.

SPROULL, L. S., & SPROULL, R. F. (1982). Managing and analyzing behavioral records: Explorations in nonnumeric data analysis. *Human Organization, 41,* 283–290.

VAN RIJSBERGEN, C. J. (1979). *Information retrieval.* London: Butterworths.

VICKERY, B. C. (1965). *On retrieval system theory* (2nd ed.). London: Butterworths.

VICKERY, B. C. (1970). *Techniques of information retrieval.* London: Butterworths.

VICKERY, B. C. (1973). *Information systems.* London: Butterworths.

WALLACE, A. F. C. (1961). Mental illness, biology and culture. In F. L. K. Hsu (Ed.), *Psychological an-*

thropology: Approaches to culture and personality (pp. 255–295). Homewood, IL: Dorsey Press.

WAX, R. H. (1971). *Doing fieldwork: Warnings and advice.* Chicago: University of Chicago.

WEINBERG, D., & WEINBERG, G. M. (1972). Using a computer in the field: Kinship information. *Social Science Information, 11,* 37–59.

WESSEL, A. E. (1975). *Computer-aided information retrieval.* Los Angeles: Melville.

WILLIAMS, T. R. (1967). *Field methods in the study of culture.* New York: Holt, Rinehart and Winston.

WOLFF, K. H. (1960). The collection and organization of field materials: A research report. In R. Adams & J. Preiss (Eds.), *Human organization research.* Homewood, IL: Dorsey Press.

Author

HAROLD G. LEVINE, Assistant Professor, Graduate School of Education, University of California, Los Angeles, 405 Hilgard Avenue, Los Angeles, CA 90024. *Specializations:* Qualitative methods, cognition and culture.

24

Conducting Qualitative Studies
Using Theory and Previous Research
A Study Reexamined
Donn Weinholtz and Charles P. Friedman

Interpreting qualitative data in the context of existing theories is a process frequently alluded to, but rarely discussed in detail. This article is a case study illustrating how existing theories and research findings were used to enrich a qualitative, preassessment study examining effective teaching by attending physicians. The investigators advocate an approach in which preliminary theoretical assumptions and orienting concepts are explicitly stated prior to conducting fieldwork. These assumptions and concepts are then modified during an initial pilot phase of study from which more focused theoretical perspectives and key orienting principles emerge. The remainder of the field experience is used for refinement of these perspectives and principles, which serve as the final results of the study.

AUTHORS' NOTE: We would like to acknowledge the substantial contribution of Dr. William D. Mattern to the study described in this article.

Qualitative investigation techniques can be applied to the full range of evaluation needs, from preassessments to formative and summative studies. This article focuses on how qualitative techniques were used in a study to identify teaching effectiveness criteria among attending physicians in a department of internal medicine. This preassessment study was the initial phase of an ongoing effort to improve the department's instructional program through evaluation. Our intent here is not to focus in depth on the criteria that emerged from the pressessment study, as these results have been reported elsewhere (Weinholtz, 1981; Mattern et al, 1983). For researchers in health professions education, this narrative will be a methodological case study in depth, highlighting how we addressed an important methodological issue: the role of existing theory and empirical studies in qualitative or naturalistic studies.

Recently, Engel et al. (1984) argued that investigators of clinical education should begin generating grounded theory from qualitative studies. Generating such theory is desirable because it could play a valuable role in guiding future educational development and evaluation efforts. We believe that if a comprehensive theory of clinical education is going to evolve, it will likely emerge from attempts to interpret phenomena observed in natural settings in light of existing theories and empirical findings, but without this existing knowledge biasing or preordaining the results. Our focus will be on how this can be done, how to resolve the inevitable tension between the already known and the newly observed. Following a description of the setting and methods of the study, we will explain how a set of orienting concepts and principles emerged and were gradually refined from a priori assumptions and interpretations of subsequent observed events. By intent, we have not included in this narrative a description of the time, effort, and tension involved in reaching virtually every key decision of study procedure. In so doing, we do not mean to imply that qualitative research, using this model or any other, can be reduced to an algorithm that removes the researchers' judgment from the process or somehow uncouple the value of the results from the quality of the effort expended. Our general procedure is as follows:

(1) Prospectively determine the framework of the study: goals, setting, sample procedures, and data collection techniques.
(2) Prior to initiating the study, review the theoretical and empirical literature assumed to be most pertinent to the interpretation of the phenomena under investigation. State broad, preliminary assumptions derived from this review and any orienting concepts that seem useful to structure the study.
(3) Conduct a pilot phase of the study, using the techniques chosen for the fieldwork. Follow the pilot phase with a several-week respite from fieldwork during which theoretical perspectives and focused assumptions emerging from the pilot phase are stated.
(4) Complete the fieldwork, refining interpretations incrementally, and prepare a final report asserting the key results from the study.

At this surface level of articulation, our process seems conventional. However, use of the process to capitalize on theory and past research without constraining the results required specific procedures, which will be described in detail, each step addressed in turn.

STEP 1: DETERMINE THE
STUDY FRAMEWORK

A major feature of this first step of the study process is its full delineation in advance. Although we were prepared to alter the plan in any aspect to conform to unforeseen developments during the field research, any such changes could be considered with respect to a complete methodological blueprint.

GOALS AND RATIONALE

Our study represented an initial step in developing criteria for distinguishing effective from ineffective teaching by attending physicians during attending rounds. Such criteria appeared essential to developing well-conceived programs to evaluate and improve instruction by attending physicians. Because the previous literature (Daggett, 1977; Daggett et al., 1979) offered only a vague picture of how instruction actually occurred in attending rounds, a qualitative study appeared appropriate to this first step. The decision to undertake such a study was rooted in the complexity of the clinical teaching environment; particularly, how the group dynamics of the ward team affects an attending physician's teaching effectiveness. In recognition of this complexity and the fact that the study was mapping out an area for future investigators, we set as our goal the formulation of a set of initial propositions for exploration in further qualitative or quantitative studies. Homans (1964: 959) cited the value of deriving such propositions:

> Many sociological propositions, particularly those made by induction from observations in the field where the effects of "third variables" are uncontrolled, are tendency statement. Some people claim that tendency propositions from field research should not even be stated. They are quite wrong, for a proposition not stated is a proposition that can not be retested, and unless it is tested and retested, the conditions in which it holds good or fails to do so can not be discovered.

Such propositions would lend coherence to the findings, at the same time making the inevitably tentative nature of these findings apparent to those who might put them to immediate practical use and to those wishing to initiate further studies.

SETTING OF THE STUDY

The study was conducted within the Department of Internal Medicine in the School of Medicine of the University of North Carolina at Chapel Hill, where interest in development of explicit evaluation criteria for attendings had been expressed. All ward teams observed were within the North Carolina Memorial Hospital (NCMH), which is the primary teaching hospital of the school. The hospital's staff consisted of more than 400 attending physicians, all of whom were faculty members of the School of Medicine.

At the time our study was conducted (1980) the Department of Internal Medicine selected seven faculty members per month (from a pool of approximately 80) to serve as attending physicians on the department's general medicine wards. These attending physicians were ultimately responsible for all medical care on the service; their focal teaching activities were daily attending rounds for teams of houseofficers and medical students. The teams participating in these rounds varied somewhat in size according to the requirements of the particular ward services. All services received at least one ward resident and several had a second resident. Each had two or three interns and three or four medical students in their third year of training.

SAMPLING PROCEDURES

Sampling procedures for the study required attention to issues of chronology, as well as individual differences among attending physicians. Choice of specific months to conduct field observations was linked to the July 1 start of the hospital year. Beginning with this date, all houseofficers mature in their fixed roles as the year progresses. For third-year medical students, on the other hand, May is the first month of the academic year. By beginning field observations in the spring and continuing through July, the study included rotations with housestaff and students, in combination, at both extremes of experience. The particular months selected generated three distinct combinations of experience levels between housestaff and students: (1) March, experienced-experienced, (2) May, experienced-inexperienced, and (3) July, inexperienced-experienced. Inclusion of these different experience levels assured us that our findings would not be biased by any particular developmental stages of the attending physicians' teams. A redundancy of experience levels in April and June suggested that field work during these months could be omitted from the study, while providing time for the review and analysis of findings from the previous month to inform the work yet to come.

The optimal number of medical service teams to include in the sample was linked to the issue of individual differences among attending physicians. Because the purpose of the study was to deepen understanding of effective teaching approaches in attending rounds, it was necessary to capture the full range of teaching behaviors of each attending observed, and to capture the variation among attendings. To observe attending rounds conducted by all 21 attending physicians in the three months selected for fieldwork would not permit adequate time for thorough observation, and would render the results potentially superficial. Observing one attending per month would generate too small a sample.

A compromise decision was made to observe two teams per month—a total of six teams over the course of the study—to provide ample time for the participant observation of each team chosen, thereby providing the depth critical in ethnographic studies (Zelditch, 1969). This choice enabled observation of teams in both the early and later phases of each rotation, providing an opportunity to examine the teams for maturational effects. Six teams were viewed as sufficient for obtaining a representative spread of behaviors, while keeping the accumulated amount of field materials at a manageable level.

During each of three months of fieldwork, two of seven attending physicians—and implicitly, the housestaff and students assigned to their teams—were randomly chosen, observed, and interviewed. One team was observed during the first and third weeks of the month; the other was observed during the second and fourth weeks. Each attending physician selected agreed in advance to participate, based on a full description of proposed data collection and reporting methods.

DATA COLLECTION TECHNIQUES

The data collection phase of the study was designed to yield the qualitative data and depth of insight necessary to develop a view of effective clinical teaching formulated as propositions suitable for further testing in future studies. Participant observation was chosen as the primary data collection technique because it is well suited for exploring group processes at work in a field setting (Dean et al., 1969). To lend perspective to inferences from these observations and to allow exploration of certain issues in greater depth, audiotaped interviews were conducted with all of the attending physicians and residents on ward teams participating in the study.

During attending rounds, a single observer functioned as a passive participant in seminar rooms, hallways, and at patients' bedsides. At other times of the day, the observer engaged in either informal interviewing of team members at all levels, or in document analysis. Documents reviewed included departmental guidelines governing the conduct of attending rounds, and the formal expectations of attendings, housestaff, and students. The evaluation forms used by some team members to rate the performance of other team members were also reviewed.

In addition to observations of attending rounds, the participant observer attended the orientation session provided by the Department of Internal Medicine for medical students entering the Department's clerkship, and the director of the clerkship was informally interviewed. Throughout the study the observer relied on an unobserved attending physician as a sounding board to assist in interpretation of the events encountered. To minimize the influence of the investigative process on events encountered, the observer adopted procedural guidelines outlined by Lofland (1971).

Following each day's observations, the observer typed a full set of field notes from the day's jotted notes. The jotted notes served as cues that enabled the researcher to produce an expanded running description of each day's events. Analytic inferences were included in the full field notes, but were clearly differentiated from descriptive materials.

The study plan included an in-depth interview following the two weeks of observation with each of the six attending physicians and the ward residents on the teams observed. As recommended by Strauss et al. (1969), these interviews were open-ended to provide the respondents with the opportunity to expand upon their personal perspectives. All in-depth interviews with attending physicians and ward residents were audiotaped and transcribed.

A critical aspect of the field research was organizing and filing of the information collected by the researcher. As recommended by Lofland (1971), three carbon copies were made of field notes typed at the end of each day's interview and observations. This allowed creation of several sets of files. A chronological file was maintained to ensure existence of one complete data archive. Mundane files were kept on key people and settings (e.g., wards). Finally a set of analytic files was maintained to provide for the categorization and convenient retrieval of materials related to key variables within the study.

The creation and maintenance of the analytic files required reviewing all field notes at the end of each week, and categorizing portions of the field notes in relation to our evolving set of perspectives and principles. Carbons of the field notes were then cut up, and the coded portions of the notes were filed. The availability of several carbon copies was essential, as many notes were coded as evidence in two or three categorical areas. To provide a means of judging the relative validity of different pieces of evidence, a practice recommended by Becker (1958) was adopted. The items of evidence were classified according to whether they were volunteered or directed statements, statements or observed activities, or statements and observed activities witnessed personally by the researcher or witnessed by others.

STEP 2: DERIVE PRELIMINARY ASSUMPTIONS AND ORIENTING CONCEPTS FROM THE LITERATURE

THE VALUE OF PRELIMINARY ASSUMPTIONS

A fundamental problem facing the evaluator or researcher using a qualitative approach is how thoroughly to address and make explicit his or her prior assumptions regarding the phenomena under study. The cumulative character of scientific investigation suggests that field research will be enriched through conscious application of past experience. We therefore advocate explicit articulation of assumptions and theoretical predispositions, prior to the beginning of fieldwork, as long as the observer does not adopt such a narrow perspective that the exploratory benefits of qualitative research are neutralized. We further suggest that the structured methodological plan offered previously makes possible such a theoretically informed approach to qualitative research. The specific theories selected to guide interpretation of results will inevitably emphasize some aspects of the phenomena studied; however, explicit articulation will place this entire process "in the sunlight," open to review by the scientific community as a whole.

In implementing this approach informed by theory and past research, we were not running counter to any basic precepts of qualitative research. For example, Patton (1980: 276-278) suggests:

> First, evaluation researchers have a responsibility to reflect on, bring into consciousness, and make explicit whatever theoretical predispositions they may have with regard to the focus of a particular study.... This will allow them to consider the extent to which their observations and analyses have been distorted by conscious or unconscious predispositions. Furthermore, by making such predispositions explicit, decision makers and information users can judge for themselves the extent to which some subtle bias on the part of the evaluator has intruded in the data analysis.

This posture is, in fact, consistent with the "goal free" posture advocated by Scriven (1972). Scriven's assertion that the evaluator be unbiased, and not bound by the manifest intended outcomes of a program, should not be equated with a dictum that the evaluator disconnect himself or herself from the past. No investigator is, or can be, a tabula rasa. Similarly, when Parlett and Hamilton (1972) argue that the initial step in an "illuminative" study should be observation, they are supporting a broad exploration of the "learning milieu."

The challenge to qualitative researchers, who inevitably have strong predispositions, is how to put these consistent dicta into effective practice, so that as the study progresses, observed events can be interpreted in the context of stated assumptions. At times observation may be quite consistent with preexisting views; at other times the data may subtly conflict with these views, or even conflict quite dramatically, making some assumptions appear absurd. When such modest or extreme contradictions occur the investigator must tackle the intriguing task of searching for new ways to understand events encountered in the field. This search may lead to the consideration of alternative theoretical perspectives and lines of past empirical research or may even lead to the suggestion of new theory to account for what is observed.

We found further support for a theoretically informed approach to the study of attending rounds in the state of previous work in this area. The literature consisted primarily of opinions and of empirical findings lacking clear theoretical underpinnings

(Daggett, et al., 1979). Consequently, efforts to understand the findings, as well as efforts to suggest alternative approaches had been hampered. After considerable review, it appeared that small group leadership theory would provide a means of organizing past empirical findings and aid in formulating testable propositions addressing the critical dimensions of current teaching practices.

SELECTION OF SMALL GROUP LEADERSHIP THEORY

We based the study on small group leadership theory after considering three critical assumptions derived from features of the study determined in Step 1. First, attending rounds are a small group learning experience, because,—if for no other reason,—6 to 12 individuals typically participate. Second, the instructor-centered nature of attending rounds as reported in previous literature (Daggett et al., 1979) suggested that the leadership behavior of the attending physician substantially affects the quality and quantity of education. Third, general leadership principles are applicable across various small group instructional settings (Hare, 1976).

Again, the study was not designed explicitly as a test of any single theory. Instead, insights provided by various theories were used to promote interpretation of the phenomena observed. Although several particular leadership theories were reviewed prior to initiating the fieldwork, none was presumed to be most appropriate for interpreting events likely to be encountered in the study. Indeed, we were't sure exactly what to expect.

ORIENTING CONCEPTS

Prior to the initial fieldwork, we purposefully limited digestion of theory and past research to that required to determine "orienting" concepts capable of establishing some initial, flexible parameters on the field of inquiry. Having selected small group leadership theory as a primary theoretical basis for the initial phase, we drew on this perspective for orienting concepts. Although several were reviewed, three ("leadership," "headship," and "emergent leadership") emerged as broad enough to provide some necessary direction to the study without unduly inhibiting the free interpretation of daily events. A brief explanation of each of the three concepts follows.

Shaw (1976: 274) proposed that leadership is demonstrated by any group member "who exerts positive influence over other group members, or . . . who exerts more positive influence over others than they exert over him." Because the focus of the study was on clinical instruction, an emphasis of the study became one of identifying and describing leadership behaviors used by attending physicians to promote the instructional aspects of attending rounds, rather than routine clinical work.

Insko and Schopler (1972: 411) offer a distinction between leadership and headship:

> In general, the leader's influence potential is spontaneously granted to him, or is legitimized, by the members. Instances of domination or *headship,* on the other hand, involve deriving influence from some power external to the group. Such influence is maintained through an organized system.

In this study, we viewed both attending physicians and ward residents as holding headship positions. Attending physicians were recognized as having formal authority, or position power, over ward residents, interns, and students. Similarly, residents maintained position power over interns and students. Interns were considered to possess position power over medical students, but were not viewed as holding positions of headship with regard to the entire team. Juxtaposing "leadership" and "headship" as orienting concepts, we were led to speculate whether some attending physicians, although serving as heads of their teams, would show little or no leadership in the area of instruction— maintaining control, but doing little teaching as such.

In the event that the appointed head of a group does not exhibit leadership in a particular area (e.g., instruction), to the extent that leadership is provided it must be exhibited by another group member. Such a group member may be called an emergent leader (Hollander, 1978). Possible role variability in attending physicians' instructional leadership made emergent leadership a third concept of interest. Because ward residents possessed experience and positional power over all team members excepting the attending physician, we viewed the ward resident role as that most likely to embody emergent leadership.

STEP 3: IDENTIFY THEORETICAL
PERSPECTIVES AND FOCUSED ASSUMPTIONS
FOLLOWING PILOT PHASE

In order to obtain familiarity with the field setting we designated the first of the three months of fieldwork as a pilot phase. We followed this with a month's respite from fieldwork for analysis of pilot field materials. During the pilot phase of the study and the month that followed, we moved beyond our orienting concepts and began deriving a set of principles for synthesis and organization of the study's results. The pilot phase suggested that leadership perspective that we had adopted was too limited to explain significant features of the dynamics of the ward teams and that additional theoretical perspectives might prove helpful as we formulated the initial findings from the field research into a set of focused assumptions providing more precise direction to the study.

These focused assumptions were developed from a synthesis of four perspectives on leadership and small groups. The first perspective was based on Hare's (1976) stages of development among classroom groups which was modified to fit experiential learning in clinical settings. In light of the findings of the field research, this perspective ultimately provided the study's main theoretical focus. The other three perspectives clustered around the notion of leadership, including Hersey and Blanchard's (1977) situational leadership theory, Fiedler's (1967) contingency theory, and as a group, the findings of a number of unassimilated empirical studies of group leadership.

MODIFYING HARE'S GROUP DEVELOPMENT MODEL

The literature on small group dynamics has frequently dealt with the interplay between group and individual development (Cartwright and Lippitt, 1957). From the pilot field observations in this study, it was apparent that team development and individual development could not be treated as separate issues.

As individual team members learned, they were better able to contribute to their teams; and as teams developed their abilities to work together, the resulting cohesiveness appeared to promote learning among individual members. Thus, a theoretical perspective merging individual and team development seemed most promising to explain behavior on a medical service team.

Because it focuses primarily on therapy and training groups, much of the literature on small group development deals with psychosocial interactions not characteristic of task-oriented learning groups such as the medical service team (Shambaugh, 1978). However, Hare's (1976) theoretical treatise explored groups in educational settings. Hare drew on the functional theory of groups developed by Parsons et al. (1953), to suggest that groups realize maximum educational benefit if they progress sequentially through five developmental phases, and complete fully the activities associated with each phase. During these phases, members (1) define the purpose of their efforts, (2) acquire the necessary knowledge and skills for task accomplishment, (3) reorganize in order for members to practice the skills without being too dependent on the teacher, (4) work to accomplish their tasks, and (5) redefine the relationships between members as the group disbands. In the interest of brevity, these phases are labeled (1) orientation, (2) acquisition, (3) practice, (4) work, and (5) termination.

Impressed by the potential relevance of Hare's insights, we modified the model he described to fit the context of a small group in a hospital service. Figure 1 illustrates the Experiential Development Model that we devised.

The model delineates five distinct but interrelated instructional phases potentially entered into by a group. The ongoing "work" requirements of the team provide an encompassing phase affecting each of the four other phases. Rather than being stable, discrete, and sequential, as in Hare's model, these other phases fluctuate in emphasis and overlap in occurrence. To the extent that there is a developmental sequence, it is cyclical or iterative in nature. Thus, the phases are demarcated using broken lines and connected by a feedback loop. During the team's working life, there is a net flow from orientation to termination, but the daily encounters with work demands generate a recurring cycle of opportunities for acquiring knowledge and skills and for practice

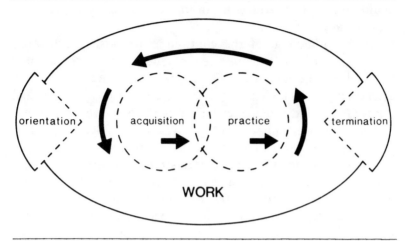

Figure 1 : Experiential Development Model

opportunities when such knowledge and skills can be demonstrated under the watchful eye of the instructor.

From this model we speculated whether, in order to teach effectively, an attending physician must take full advantage of the opportunities inherent in all five phases of the model. We further speculated that the ongoing work demands of the medical ward as an experiential learning setting would place an extreme demand on the instructional leadership abilities of the attending physician. Although some sort of orientation and termination phases would naturally occur, the intrusion of work demands would make scheduling and control of content so difficult that specific knowledge aquisition and practice activities might result only from a tenacious effort on the part of the instructor.

These considerations led to the postulation of an instruction continuum bounded on one end by attending physicians who, while serving as heads of their clincial teams, demonstrate little in the way of instructional leadership. We assumed such physicians might not find their teaching roles congenial, or might be unaware of instructional possiblities that they miss. For whatever reasons, we suspected that these attending physicians do not transcend the role of head of the medical service team to provide leadership in the area of instruction. Such attending physicians could still provide leadership in matters exclusively related to patient care.

At the other end of the continuum we posited attending physicians who more aggressively pursue strategies deliberately to develop team members' clinical knowledge and skills. These attending physicians transcend the role of head of the medical service team, and provide leadership in the area of instruction.

These suppositions do not imply a lack of learning when attending physicians function solely as instructional heads of medical service teams. A purported strength of the experiential learning format is that participants continually encounter useful learning opportunities in the course of their daily work responsibilities. As part of a medical service, students have ample opportunities to acquire knowledge and develop skills (e.g., procedures and tests) under the supervision of interns and residents. The interns, likewise, can learn in a similar fashion from the residents, whereas the residents are able to develop new skills through execution of their teaching responsibilities—all within the work milieu of patient care. The focal issue raised by this perspective was not whether learning would occur on the service, but rather the type and extent of additional learning that could be promoted by the attending physician, and the leadership behaviors that bring about this learning.

The Experiential Development Model provided a normative theoretical basis for analyzing the headship and leadership behavior of attending physicians regarding instruction. In turn, this normative basis suggested two focused assumptions useful in guiding the interpretation of our field data.

(1) Instructional leadership behaviors demonstrated by attending physicians may be specified and organized according to their occurrence during the phases of the experiential development model.

(2) Those attending physicians whose attending rounds address all phases of the experiential development model provide instructional leadership to the maximum possible extent.

A third assumption was stimulated by our recognition that the work demands of the ward service might intrude upon instructional opportunities and from repeated reports from houseofficers interviewed during the pilot phase that they ignored attending physicians whose clinical credibility they doubted.

(3) Attending physicians must establish their own clinical credibility within the medical service team in order to transcend the role of head of the team, and lead the team for purposes of instruction.

SITUATIONAL LEADERSHIP THEORY

We drew upon situational leadership theory (Hersey and Blanchard, 1977) to provide a more complete picture of attending round leadership than could be obtained from the experiential development model alone. In many ways, situational leadership theory reinforced the assumptions derived from the experiential development model, as it also suggested a normative scenario in which group members develop their skills maximally under the guidance of a leader who progressively withdraws from a dominating position within the group. Hersey and Blanchard (1977) have argued for the applicability of their theory to learning settings, and have indicated that high levels of learner enthusiasm, morale, and motivation might be associated with the movement from highly directive to nonparticipatory behaviors by the formal "teacher."

Situational leadership theory provided additional insight into what might constitute instructional leadership among attending physicians, emphasizing the need for leaders to accurately assess the demands confronting their groups at any given time. Based on our pilot observations, this suggested an important leadership behavior wherein attending physicians would spend time, outside of attending rounds, collecting information on the condition of the patients on the service. Such behavior would not only ensure that patients receive proper care, but also would allow the attending physician to assess the learning possibilities for team members inherent in the patients' conditions. The attending physician could then use this knowledge to allocate time during attending rounds.

Based on situational leadership theory we were also able to derive a leadership scenario appropriate for the overall management of attending rounds. The scenario suggested the following progression:

(i) During the first few attending rounds of the month, the orientation phase, the attending physician clearly asserts (tells) his or her views regarding the key guidelines for individual and group behavior during the team's length of the time on the service.

(ii) The attending physician initiates (sells) a series of instructional opportunities aimed at developing the knowledge and skills of the team members. The attending physician plays a very focal role by closely determining the team's tasks, but assigns some duties to others and maintains a high level of relationship behavior by acknowledging the successful completion of learning activities.

(iii) As the team's experience on the service grows, the attending physician increasingly limits the team's dependence on him or her. The attending physician decreases his or her level of dictation of learning activities, while remaining available as a technical resource and source of emotional support to the team. Group members actively practice their skills within rounds, and begin to rely on each other for feedback, rather than looking strictly to the attending physician for evaluation.

(iv) Near the end of the team's time together, members are capable of conducting rounds with very little reliance on the attending physician, who has delegated responsibilities and assumed the role of an observer, assessing group member performance in prepartion for completing written evaluations on each member.

Underlying these guidelines was a critical assumption that the team would not continually be confronted by new patient care demands beyond the members' capabilities. Under these circumstances, situational leadership theory suggests that, in order to ensure proper care, the attending physician must maintain a high level of direction and control in attending rounds.

To summarize, consideration of situational leadership theory led to two more focused assumptions

(4) Attending physicians demonstrating instructional leadership are likely to spend a large amount of time outside of attending rounds (work phase) collecting information on the conditions of the

patients on the service. In addition to ensuring the proper care of the patients, this behavior enables them to determine instructional possibilities of the service, and to set priorities for the use of time during attending rounds.

(5) Learning and team satisfaction might be maximized by attending physicians following a leadership progression approximating the "telling-selling-participating-delegating" sequence advocated by situational leadership theory. Under conditions where their teams' abilities to cope with the patient care demands of their services are low, the attending physician will need to reinstate directive behaviors in order to ensure instruction and proper patient care.

CONTINGENCY THEORY

Consideration of Fiedler's (1967) contingency theory presented us with an alternative perspective suggesting why some attending physicians' might not demonstrate the type of leadership flexibility prescribed by both the experiential group development model and situational leadership theory. Fiedler (1967) argues strongly that leadership style is a relatively fixed phenomenon, as unlikely to change as basic personality structure. Fiedler's adamant stance suggested a phenomenon worth exploring.

As a consequence of limited leadership flexibility, most attendings observed might rely heavily on a single instructional approach, which might be described as a basic instructional style. This assumption, although derived directly from Fiedler's assertions regarding leadership flexibility, was not totally inconsistent with situational leadership theory. Hersey and Blanchard (1977) emphasize, less adamantly than Fiedler (1967), that leaders often rely on a single leadership style. Hersey and Blanchard veer substantially from Fiedler in their belief that leaders can be trained to vary their styles; thus indicating their greater faith in the flexibility of the individual. If not for Fiedler's more forceful presentation on leadership inflexibility, we might possibly have overlooked it as a variable of interest.

A second emphasis of contingency theory indicates three variables identified by Fiedler (1967) as pertinent in determining leader effectiveness. These variables are (1) warmth of leader-member relations, (2) task structure, and (3) leader position power. Fiedler's (1977) later research indicated that leaders can advantageously manipulate only these three variables to influence group behavior. Drawing on Fiedler's (1967) assertion that these variables interact with leadership style to influence task accomplishment (in this case learning), we assumed that attending physicians demonstrating instructional leadership might intuitively adopt strategies for manipulating any or all of the three variables to their advantage in their teaching efforts.

In summary, consideration of contingency theory led to formulation of two additional focused assumptions keying us to potential behavior by attending physicians.

(6) Most attending physicians will show little flexibility in leadership style, relying on a basic style that is indicative of their fundamental orientation toward group leadership.

(7) Attending physicians will vary in their uses of the warmth of their relationships with team members, the task structure of attending rounds, and positional power to promote their instructional efforts.

PERTINENT EMPIRICAL STUDIES

Some additional studies in leadership raised important issues not inherent in the previously cited theoretical frameworks. These studies helped us to generate the remaining focused assumptions.

Leavitt's (1951) discovery that the central figures in communications networks tend to become the leaders suggested that attending physicians might be intuitively aware of this phenomenon and might consequently maintain a focal position during attending rounds to perpetuate their positions as leaders. Because leadership in the experiential setting is not "automatic," there is a counterincentive for attending physicians to provide active practice opportunities for their teams by withdrawing from the focal directing position in attending rounds.

A number of studies reviewed by Stogdill (1974) indicated that groups experiencing frequent changes in leadership or high rates of personnel turnover suffer declining performance. Thus, the rotation of personnel on the medical service team might inhibit the ability of attending physicians to initiate acquisition and practice activities. The transient nature of the medical service teams might inhibit candid evaluation of trainees by attending physicians.

Hemphill (1950) found that larger groups tend to make greater demands upon the leader for strength, reliability, predictability, job competence, coordination, impartial enforcement of rules, and structure. These findings projected on this study suggested that attending physicians in larger teams might be more likely to maintain a focal position than in smaller teams. Given that the practice opportunities indicated by the experiential development model require the attending physician to adopt a lower profile, smaller teams might be more likely to experience such opportunities in attending rounds.

Finally, both Greening (1973) and Stinson and Robertson (1973) found that group members' satisfaction with leader style varies with the members' expectations. To the effect that different team members might have dramatically varying expectations in accord with their roles on the team, the instructional skills of attending physicians might be judged differently by students, interns, and residents. Attending physicians perceived as highly influential instructional leaders by certain team members might be viewed as less influential by others.

Consideration of the empirical studies, as described above, led to four remaining focused assumptions.

(8)   Attending physicians will be reluctant to withdraw from a focal position during attending rounds, and therefore will promote few practice opportunities.

(9)   The transient nature of the medical service team membership will tend to inhibit the full expression of instructional leadership by attending physicians for all phases of the experiential development model.

(10) The fullest expression of instructional leadership by attending physicians for all phases of the experiential development model will most likely occur in smaller medical service teams.

(11) Satisfaction with the instructional leadership demonstrated by attending physicians will vary somewhat across the subgroups of the medical service team.

STEP 4: COMPLETE FIELDWORK AND
PREPARE FINAL REPORT

After stating our theoretical perspectives and focused assumptions we resumed our fieldwork; punctuating it with a second hiatus to allow further reflection on the field materials. During the remainder of the fieldwork, we repeatedly examined our field materials in light of the orienting concepts and principles.

Following the completion of the fieldwork we assembled the final report. This itself was a critical part of the study process. The act of writing enhanced our focus on the interplay of theory and data. While writing, new interpretations emerged and final assumptions were forged.

The refinement of the focused assumptions into a set of propositions for further study was a painstaking process during which the investigators regularly challenged each other's interpretations. Similarly, a faculty member from the department of internal medicine who had sponsored our study challenged our concensus opinions. Not himself one of the observed attendings, this faculty member played a vital role as a sounding board and devil's advocate as we honed our insights. His depth of experience as an attending physician enabled him to point out our misconceptions. As nonphysicians we had a distinct advantage because we were unhampered by years of socialization within the system under study, but ultimately the insider's perspective was a crucial validity check.

A key difference between the focused assumptions and the final propositions was their level of abstraction. The final propositions were substantially more concrete because the propositions constituted the product of our effort to ground the theoretical insights using empirical observations. The challenge of formulating the final propositions came in the process of merging the insights of the espoused assumptions with the evidence accumulated within the coding scheme used for filing the field materials. The categories of this coding system were not limited to the variables specified in the focused assumptions. Instead they constituted an account of virtually all events perceived as significant and recurring often enough to form natural clusters. These categories emerged much as do clusters of incidents in a critical incident study, or clusters of similar responses when open-ended questionnaire items are analyzed.

The questions asked during the interpretative process were, "How do these principles help us to make sense of these data?" and "Does this principle or coding category still seem relevant?" If not for the fact that we specified that our propositions were tentative hypotheses best suited for future research, we might never have felt comfortable terminating our questioning. Nevertheless, after many revisions, we did terminate the process with a final product we deemed a satisfactory set of causal inferences about teaching and learning in the attending round setting.

McCall and Simmons (1969) have pointed out the difficulties facing qualitative investigators in reporting their results. Among the most common is the challenge of minimizing the sheer bulk of evidence to permit easy summarization and comparison with other studies. To meet this requirement, the preparation of the final report involved a conscious effort to weave tabular summaries and illuminating incidents in a manner concisely and effectively presenting the major findings. This necessarily entailed several stages of revision. Again, these revisions were vital to our interpretive process.

Finally, in the presentation of the qualitative findings, it was essential to take precautions to preserve the anonymity of the participants, as guaranteed to them prior to observation and interview. In the report, fictitious names were assigned to each participant. Furthermore, explicit references to the subspecialties of the attending physicians and descriptions that would identify specific ward services were deleted.

RESULTS

To illustrate the nature of the final synthesis, a brief synopsis of the results included in the final report follows. We concluded that a wide variety of instructional behaviors employed by attending physicians could be keyed to the phases of the experiential development model. Furthermore, our observations revealed substantial variation in teaching behaviors among attending physicians. For further detail regarding these findings, consult Weinholtz (1981) and Mattern et al. (1983).

We concluded that two generic behaviors transcended the phases of the experiential development model and played important roles in attending physicians' instructional efforts throughout their tenure on the medical service teams. First, attending physicians' methods of allocating time influenced all else accomplished during attending rounds. Second, the general tone set by attending physicians had a substantial impact on instruction. Regarding allocation of time, attending physicians were differentiated by their willingness to schedule separate instructional sessions solely for medical students. They also varied substantially in their allocation of time to discussion topics during attending rounds.[1] Concerning tone, substantial variation was observed in the nature of the attending physicians' interpersonal relations with team members. We found that several interpersonal styles were described by housestaff and medical students as effective.

In addition to the generic leadership behaviors, each phase of the experiential development model seemed associated with specific leadership behaviors affecting instruction. During the orientation phase, setting expectations for the performances of team members and establishing clinical credibility with team members were found to influence the instructional impact of the attending physicians.

The knowledge and skill acquisition of team members were affected by the manner in which the attendings (1) directed case presentations, (2) directed diagnostic and management discussions, (3) gave didactic presentations, (4) modeled consideration of the psychosocial aspects of patient care, and (5) modeled bedside interactions with patients.

Evidence indicated that a practice phase as suggested by the Experiential Development Model may be introduced by attending physicians adopting a lower profile within the team and allowing team members to perform the skills emphasized in the attendings' skill development efforts. Nevertheless, such practice opportunities were observed infrequently. Contributing to this trend were pressures of time and perceptions among attendings that delegation of control of attending rounds is not feasible.

Concerning the work phase of the Experiential Development Model, and behaviors of the attending physicians outside of attending rounds had an impact upon instruction during rounds. By closely monitoring the status of the patients on the service, certain attending physicians minimized the time in rounds allocated to provision of basic information, thereby creating greater opportunities for skill development and practice activities. By performing the liaison functions expected by the housestaff, various attending physicians ensured that clinical work progressed smoothly and that their teams had adequate information for education during attending rounds.

Regarding the termination phase, only one attending physician of the set observed discussed with team members his evaluations of their individual performances. Although the Department of Internal Medicine guidelines for attending physicians indicated that such discussions are required, other discussions of this sort were not observed. Similarly, although all attending physicians expressed their desire for feedback concerning their teaching, they rarely solicited such feedback from team members.

PROPOSITIONS FOR FURTHER STUDY

Toward the end of the report we offered fifteen propositions informative to ongoing study. These propositions focused on behaviors distinguishing attending physicians who clearly establish their leadership by demonstrating influence as instructors from those who serve as the heads of their teams for purposes of patient care, but have little influence as instructors. For further elaboration see Weinholtz (1981).

(1) Instructional activities, other than routine work activities, occur in attending rounds to the extent that the attending physician allocates time for these activities in advance.

(2) The attending physician's ability to establish instructional influence is not systematically affected by the nature of the working relationships established between the attending and the team members. However, immediate satisfaction with the

attending may vary by level of training, as a function of the working relations established.

(3) The degree of confusion and anxiety experienced by housestaff and students at the start of their service on a team is inversely proportional to the comprehensiveness of the attending physician's orientation sessions.

(4) The attending physician's ability to establish instructional influence varies directly with the clinical credibility of the attending physician among the team members.

(5) The attending physician most readily obtains an indication of a team member's ability to present a patient by adopting a low-frequency/clarifying questioning style during the presentation.

(6) Systematic clinical problem solving is modeled and diagnostic and management discussions remain clearly focused to the extent that the attending physician makes a graphic list of problems, diagnoses, tests or treatments.

(7) The attending physician's influence as an instructor is heightened by sharing clinical knowledge and "wisdom" through didactic presentations pertinent to cases on the service, as long as such presentations do not repeatedly dominate attending rounds.

(8) Psychosocial issues of patient care are discussed by the team to the extent that the attending physician actively models concern for such issues and focuses discussions on their consideration.

(9) Interaction of bedside visits with conference room discussion is favorably evaluated by team members to the extent that the attending models specific techniques for discovering physical findings or communicating with patients.

(10a) Team members' comprehension of what constitutes a good presentation is enhanced to the extent that the attending physician requires the team members to present cases to each other.

(10b) The attending physician's ability to assess team members' presenting skills is enhanced to the extent that the attending requires the team members to present cases to each other.

(11a) The attending physician's ability to assess the team's problem-solving skills is enhanced by the attending occasionally adopting a low profile during diagnostic and management discussions.

(11b) Team member's feelings of inclusion and team cohesion are enhanced by the attending physician occasionally adopting a low profile during diagnostic and management discussions.

(12a) Medical students will demonstrate increased learning and report feelings of inclusion to the extent that the attending physician assigns them didactic presentations on topics related to the care of the students' patients.

(12b) Residents will report increased feelings of inclusion to the extent that the attending physician assigns them didactic presentations on topics of their own selection.

(13) The attending physician's ability to assess students' clinical skills is enhanced by observing students performing case workups at the bedside.

(14) The attending physicians' ability to provide instructional activities during attending rounds is related to the attending physician's use of time outside of attending rounds to visit patients, review charts, and perform liaison functions for the team.

(15) Team members acknowledge learning from their experiences on the medical service team to the extent that the attending physician conducts discussions with the individual team members concerning the attending's final evaluation of their performance.

CONCLUSION

In this article we have explained the procedures adopted while attempting to base a previous qualitative study in existing theory and empirical findings. Although the results of our study are idiosyncratic to a particular domain of investigation, we believe that the specific steps we followed merit attention by other investigators conducting either evaluation or research studies. We were able to apply general theoretical perspectives to generate "grounded" theoretical insights tailored to the setting of the study. This in turn enabled us to organize our findings from the field into a set of coherent results. In this manner, the goal of seeking "grounded theory" can be addressed.

NOTE

1. For example, one attending physician routinely devoted 30-40 minutes to a review of all of the patients on the ward, whereas two other attending physicians gathered similar information outside of attending rounds so as to conserve time for instruction.

REFERENCES

BECKER, H. S. (1958) "Problems of inference and proof in participant observation." Amer. Soc. Rev. 23: 625-660.

CARTWRIGHT, D. P. and R. LIPPITT (1978) "Group dynamics and the individual," in L. P. Bradford (ed.) Group Development (2nd ed.). LaJolla, CA: University Associates.

DAGGETT, C. J. (1977) "A study to determine the role of attending physicians in clinical training of medical students and resident physicians." Ph.D. dissertation, University of Massachusetts.

———J. M. CASSIE, and G. F. COLLINS (1979) "Research in clinical teaching." Rev. of Educ. Research 49: 151-169.

DEAN, J. P., R. L. EICHHORN, and L. R. DEAN (1969) "Limitations and advantages of unstructured methods," in G. J. McCall and J. L. Simmons (eds.) Issues in Participant Observation. Reading, MA: Addison-Wesley.

ENGEL, J. D., C. FILLING, L. R. LAPALIO, and P. O. WAYS (1984) "Requirements for generating theories of clinical education." Professions Education Researcher Notes 6, 1: 15-16.

FIEDLER, F. E. (1967) A Theory of Leadership Effectiveness. New York: McGraw-Hill.

———,M. M. CHEMERS, and L. MAHAR (1977) Improving Leadership Effectiveness (2nd ed.). New York: John Wiley.

GREENING, T. C. (1973) "When a group rejects its leader." Small Group Behavior 4: 245-248.

HARE, A. P. (1976) Handbook of Small Group Research (2nd ed.). New York: Free Press.

HEMPHILL, J. K. (1950) "Relations between the size of the group and the behavior of 'superior' leaders." J. of Social Psychology 32: 11-22.

HERSEY, P. and K. BLANCHARD (1977) Management of Organizational Behavior: Utilizing Human Resources (3rd ed.). Englewood Cliffs, NJ: Prentice-Hall.

HOLLANDER, E. P. (1978) Leadership Dynamics. New York: Free Press.

HOMANS, G. C. (1964) "Contemporary theory in sociology," In R.E.L. Faris (ed.) Handbook of Modern Sociology. Chicago: Rand McNally.

INSKO, C. A. and J. SCHOPLER (1972) Experimental Social Psychology. New York: Academic.

LEAVITT, H. J. (1951) "Some effects of certain communication patterns on group performance." J. of Abnormal Psychology 46: 38-50.

LOFLAND, J. (1971) Analyzing Social Settings. Belmont, CA. Wadsworth.

MATTERN, W. D., D. WEINHOLTZ, and C. P. FRIEDMAN (1983) "The attending physician as teacher." New England J. of Medicine 308: 1129-1132.

McCALL, G. J. and J. L. SIMMONS (1969) Issues in Participant Observation. Reading, MA: Addison-Wesley.

PARLETT, M. and D. HAMILTON (1972) Evaluation as Illumination. Occasional Paper #9, Center for Research in the Educational Sciences, University of Edinburgh.

PARSONS, T., R. F. BALES, and E. A. SHILS (1953) Working Papers in the Theory of Action. New York: Free Press.

PATTON, M. Q. (1980) Qualitative Evaluation. Beverly Hills, CA: Sage.

SCRIVEN, M. (1972) "Prose and cons about goal free evaluation." J. of Educ. Evaluation 3, 4: 1-4

SHAMBAUGH, P. W. (1978) "The development of the small group." Human Relations 31, 3: 283-295.

SHAW, M. E. (1976) Group Dynamics: The Psychology of Small Group Behavior. New York: McGraw-Hill.

STINSON, J. E. and J. H. ROBERTSON (1973) "Follower maturity and preference for leader-behavior style." Psych. Reports 32: 245-250.

STOGDILL, R. M. (1974) Handbook of Leadership Survey of Theory and Research. New York: Free Press.

STRAUSS, A., L. SCHATZMAN, R. BUCHER, D. EHRLICH, and M. SABSHIN (1969) "Field tactics," in G. J. McCall and J. L. Simmons (eds.) Issues in Participant Observation. Reading, MA: Addison-Wesley.

WEINHOLTZ, D. (1981) "A study of instructional leadership during medical attending rounds." Ph.D. dissertation, University of North Carolina—Chapel Hill.

ZELDITCH, M. (1969) "Some methodological problems of field studies," in G. J. McCall and J. L. Simmons (eds.) Issues in Participant Observation. Reading, MA: Addison-Wesley.

PART III

PROGRAM RESEARCH

Earlier in this volume we introduced the distinction between *program evaluation,* oriented toward evaluative judgment and practical service to stakeholders, and *program research,* a phrase we are using to designate a more analytic-descriptive investigation of social programs. Part II presented a selection primarily reflecting the practical program evaluation perspective. Here, in Part III, we present a selection reflecting some aspects of what we see as the program research perspective.

The short history of program evaluation research as a specialty area has been characterized by the dominance of the applied social science approach. This approach emphasizes measurement of program effects, formal research design, sampling, and statistical analysis. It is organized around the concept of relationships between variables and what is required to demonstrate such relationships. In particular, the shape of contemporary evaluation study has been heavily influenced by the experimental paradigm, enlarged to include quasi-experimentation, and the accompanying concern with cause and effect inferences and their validity.

Challenge to the applied social science orientation has come primarily from the "evaluation" perspective. The applied research orientation has been criticized as narrow, unresponsive, and misguided. It is charged as narrow for examining only defined program goals that can be quantitatively measured and for virtually ignoring the social and political context of a program. It is labeled unresponsive, first, because its methods are relatively inflexible in relation to the fluid and dynamic nature of social programs and, second, because it does not always answer the questions decision makers need to have answered or provide its answers timely to the decision schedule. It is judged misguided, perhaps even naive, in presuming that cause-and-effect relationships are central to social programs in contrast to the political values and purposes those programs embody. Above all, the implicitly value-neutral descriptive-analytic research orientation is criticized for evading the "evaluation" imperative to value and judge the program not merely measure and describe it.

Although acknowledging the validity of many of the criticisms of the research perspective, we think program research can be defended as a separable and justifiable endeavor. Within the program research category we wish to include that range of inquiries that focus less on the practical issues facing program managers and decision makers and more on the matter of understanding just how the program works (or fails to work). Although not the only thing in this category, we would explicitly include just that type of research that has been most heavily criticized from the "evaluation" perspective. We refer to the essentially academic investigation of relationships and effects in social programs that is, in the short run, relatively unresponsive to decision makers' needs, slow to produce results, and oriented more toward hypothesis testing, development of theory, and conceptual generalization than toward practical administration and evaluation. Over the longer run, these individual assessments can be synthesized to form a broader understanding of how programs work, when, for whom and how well. Such syntheses, drawing from carefully executed assessments, can often be conducted quickly, meeting the needs of decision makers in a timely fashion. To achieve this end, an investment in program research-oriented evaluation studies is necessary, regardless of the immediate needs of the policy decision makers. This perspective assumes that ultimately the question of program effects and differential effects will be asked. Adequate answers require sufficient time, resources, and careful research.

The primary, although not exclusive, focus of program research is on the cause-and-effect linkages that connect organized social action with social effects. Its underlying purpose is to provide a conceptual basis for understanding how social programs work and how effective social intervention can be planned and understood. Program research, then, is the study of organized social intervention and its effects based on a particular social program as the setting for the research.

The importance of program research is twofold. First, from a policymaking and social action perspective there is something very natural about cause-and effect thinking. Frequently, although not universally, social programs represent deliberate attempts to produce defined beneficial effects. Effective intervention requires some general understanding of what sorts of programs produce what sorts of effects and can profit from explicit study of such matters. Second, careful program research can contribute to a body of winnowed knowledge about the features of social situations, and the organizational, psychological, and sociological processes involved in intervention. This knowledge, in turn, will not only improve program planning and design but will improve the craft of program evaluation. With such background knowledge as a guide, program evaluators will know better what sorts of program features are likely to be most important, what might be expected from different types of treatments, how to diagnose the problems with a failing program, and how improvement might be brought about. Lewin's often quoted dictum of social action research—"There is nothing so practical as good theory"—might apply with special force to the inherent complexities of social problems and social intervention.

Program research can take a variety of forms. At the level of the primary study it is distinguished by explicit theorizing and theory testing about program process and effects or, at least, by some conceptual dimension that reaches for generalization beyond the particulars of the case at hand. A related aspect of program research is attention to identifying the mechanism or system of action by which treatments have their effects. Minimally, this may involve investigation of treatment as an independent variable in relationship to various dependent variables. In more powerful and differentiated form, however, it peers into the treatment black box and attempts to specify the psychosocial processes linking treatment to outcome. At the meta-analytic level, program research constitutes a broad, multiple study approach to understanding social interventions. Because of the salience of cause-and-effect issues in program research, the experimental paradigm provides a natural methodology for program research, though many other social science techniques are also relevant.

Program research can range from a focused, practical evaluation-oriented study that works in a bit of hypothesis testing, for example, about a variable that may mediate treatment effects, to an almost entirely academic study of organizational process or psychosocial treatment mechanisms much like basic research in social/organizational psychology and sociology. An especially interesting in-between category is research on demonstration programs set up explicitly to learn something general about the nature of a particular social intervention (e.g., the negative income tax experiments; see Rossi & Wright in Part I, of this volume).

As the program evaluation orientation, program research has a distinctive pattern of strengths and weaknesses that necessitates certain trade-offs. Not surprisingly, those trade-offs are the mirror images of the ones made by the program evaluation orientation. Whereas program evaluation is strong on responsiveness and usefulness, program research serves these practical concerns much less well. Program research, however, is potentially strong on generalizability and conventional notions of validity—just the areas that are problems for the practical evaluation orientation. There is thus a certain complementarity between program evaluation and program research that, in our view, indicates that they do not present a clash between incommensurate paradigms but rather approaches serving somewhat different purposes. We think program research and program evaluation should coexist, though not uncritically, recognizing that they are servants of different masters. Both are necessary to wed practice and theory in evaluation studies.

It is symptomatic of the lack of theoretical depth in contemporary program evaluation research that, despite the predominance of the experimental paradigm, there are few good exemplars of what we have described here as the program research orientation. The contributions selected for inclusion under that heading here in Part III of this volume, however, all touch on some aspect of that orientation. Some have a distinct theoretical dimension or include some overt theory testing. Some are included because of their scope, covering issues that transcend the particulars of individual programs. Others deal with aspects of applied social science methodology pertinent to conducting program research.

We have organized these chapters into five sections. The first includes a selection of chapters dealing broadly with our understanding of social problems and social intervention. Section Two collects chapters distinguished by attention to program theory, that is, the underlying causal rationale that links program activity with its intended effects. Section Three is devoted to an issue that has become increasingly salient in program evaluation research in recent years—program implementation, including interesting views on aspects of the client-treatment interaction so crucial to program effects. The fourth section focuses on social experimentation and its attendant methodological concerns, topics central to the program research orientation. The final deals with research synthesis, an endeavor that epitomizes the program research orientation in its attempt to fashion substantive and methodological knowledge from the particulars of individual studies.

SECTION 1
Social Problems and Social Intervention

One feature that should characterize an applied research perspective on social programs, though it may not always in fact do so, is application of a conceptual framework that connects those program particulars of interest to some more general propositions, hypotheses, or theories. In its minimal form, this may consist only of a cause-and-effect proposition linking the independent "program" variable with the dependent "outcome" variables. The generality of this proposition comes from the (at least implicit) assumption that other instances of the independent variable will have similar effects.

Other sorts of propositions and theoretical frameworks are, of course, also possible. Program research can draw on concepts from the various relevant disciplines (sociology, psychology, education, economics, etc.), from other program evaluation research, or from the researcher's own formulations. One of the current weaknesses of program evaluation research is the relatively slight use made of concepts from applicable theory and other research. The result is a largely idiosyncratic use of concepts and variables in most studies that provides little support for cumulative theory and understanding in the field.

In this section, we introduce the broad conceptual framework within which program research is located. It is convenient to divide that framework into three different parts having to do, respectively, with the processes and nature of social intervention, the nature of the social problems addressed by intervention, and the social system within which problems are defined and interventions are organized. Both program evaluators and program researchers function with at least intuitive knowledge of many features of this framework. We think more systematic study is warranted, not merely as a background to program evaluation and research but as an intrinsic part of it.

This task is made easier by the emergence, in recent years, of defined areas of social science study that focus on social and community interventions and social problems. An important conceptual and practical question is how (or if) the field of program evaluation research will relate to these emerging areas. That there are overlapping concerns is obvious; whether or not there will be exchange and collaboration between the areas remains to be seen.

The first chapter in this section is excerpted from a review by Iscoe and Harris of the area that is coming to be known as social and community intervention (SCI). This review follows on the heels of the publication of the massive *Handbook of Social Intervention* (Seidman, 1983), and together they signal the consolidation of diverse, but related, work into a defined area of study. Iscoe and

Harris address psychologists in their review and thus emphasize mental health issues, but much of their framework is quite general. The most noteworthy are their forays into "systems" thinking, from which perspective many social programs seem fragmented and overspecialized, prevention and unserved populations take on significance and the interconnectedness of social institutions (in which change in one affects the others) is paramount. Iscoe and Harris identify many issues on which research is needed and issue a call for psychologists and, by extension, other interested researchers to help in "unraveling the complex interactive phenomena to which SCIs address themselves."

In the second chapter of this section, Schneider reviews developments in the study of the other side of the social intervention coin—the social problems on which intervention is targeted. He reports on the development of a new specialty in sociology—the sociology of social problems. Of special interest is the constructionist theory he espouses. In this view, social problems are socially constructed, that is, they are the products of social definition rather than objective conditions. This perspective organizes otherwise diverse topics involving emergence of "problems," reactions to them by public institutions, the role of professionals, and the influence of the media. The constructionist analysis, with its phenomenological orientation, nicely parallels recent viewpoints in evaluation that emphasize the perceptions and values of program participants rather than objective program process (e.g., Guba & Lincoln, Part I of this volume; Dorr-Bremme, Part II of this volume).

Social intervention and social problem definition occur within a broader social and political system that has significant influence on both. The third chapter in this section vividly illustrates the importance of the values, interests, and ideologies that operate in that system. Shadish uses the case of deinstitutionalization of mental health patients to demonstrate that the policies that are actually implemented in the social system must not only respond to the perceived problem but must be compatible with existing social structure and ideology. In particular, intervention programs developed by researchers, even if demonstrably effective, may fail to gain widespread acceptance while virtually untested programs may experience rapid growth. Shadish illustrates this point by comparing the rapid expansion of the nursing home industry to serve deinstitutionalized mental patients to the very limited implementation of Fairweather's thoroughly designed and tested Lodge Society programs. To provide some theoretical framework for this case, Shadish sketches a model of change and strain in the social system and their relationship to the intervention selected for implementation.

With these three chapters, therefore, we get an overview of three major components of the conceptual framework within which program research is conducted. Each chapter identifies many topics that warrant further research if we are to have full understanding of the way in which social problems are defined, how interventions are designed and implemented, and what effects they have on the target problems. More specifically, these chapters raise the themes and concepts to which research on any given program must be linked if evaluation studies is to be a field in which knowledge cumulates and generalizes.

REFERENCES

Seidman, E. (Ed.). (1983). *Handbook of social intervention.* Beverly Hills, CA: Sage.

25

Social and Community Interventions

Ira Iscoe and Lorwen C. Harris

INTRODUCTION

Social and community interventions (SCIs) are part of the fabric of American
life. They range from federally funded, large-scale programs such as Welfare,
Food Stamps, and Medicare, to block and neighborhood organizations dealing
with problems and issues of local or national importance. The arena is usually
at the community (local) level and the targets are groups, institutions, and
organizations. The purpose is the betterment of the human condition with
efforts directed mainly toward assisting the poor, the underprivileged, and the
dependent to cope with problems and to improve or maintain a quality of life.
Recently there is an increasing number of SCIs directed toward neighborhood
and environmental concerns, of interest to middle class populations. Church
and voluntary philanthropic groups (e.g. United Way) also initiate and maintain a variety of SCIs. Existing and potential roles for psychologists in SCI
range from that of researcher, evaluator, and organizer through that of consultant, planner, and negotiator. The clients may include state and national
agencies, schools, hospitals, community-based institutions, minority populations and special groups, among others.

The priorities of a nation in many ways are a reflection of the amount, type,
and extent of its SCIs. Competition for resources is increasingly severe, and as
community and neighborhood organizations note, "the military do not have to
hold bake sales to buy a new airplane." Currently, we are in the midst of a
period of pessimism, reassessment, and retrenchment. Programs and strategies
for the improvement of the human condition are being questioned and many are
being reduced, altered, or terminated. It is not as if SCIs have failed completely
as much as they have not fulfilled their promise. An almost 40-year trend of
government activity in SCIs is being reversed by the New Federalism. The
election of 1980 overwhelmingly endorsed a platform of conservativism and
the need to reappraise the degree of involvement of the federal government in
SCIs. Other competing demands have arisen and alternatives, including greater
involvement of the private sector, are being proposed. The failure of a multibil-
lion dollar weapon system does not evoke the outcry generated when an SCI, of

much lesser financial magnitude but of equal or greater complexity, fails to meet its goal.

Symbolic of the changing climate is the concept of block grants to the states. Carried out appropriately, block grants could very well constitute one of the more important SCIs in the latter half of this century. They offer the potential for program implementation, administration, and consumer input at the local level. Whether all problems of national scope and importance can be better addressed at the state level remains to be seen. It is unclear how the maintenance of minimal standards and the allocation of appropriate resources for target populations will be safeguarded. Funds alone do not determine successful SCIs. Some of the most innovative SCIs are the results of departures from a "more of the same" philosophy.

The literature does not yet fully reflect the stress and reappraisal that is taking place in the entire fabric of American culture. Huge budget deficits raise questions of how increasingly scarce monies should be allocated. What proportion can be diverted from a casualty-deficit model to one that emphasizes competence and resource building? Will the humanistic, compassionate approach be underemphasized in the torrent of computer printouts?

SCI Literature and Research

The literature is widely scattered in behavioral science and human service journals. A relatively small percentage appears in publications labeled psychological and less in refereed prestigious journals. The complexities of SCIs are reflected by an increasing number of edited volumes. There are also many top quality government publications, some incorporating the proceedings of research symposia and clarifying the "state of the art" in a particular area. The catalog and reports from state departments of community affairs, health, and human services are also good sources of information. Many SCI reports and studies may not be Library of Congress referenced but are being increasingly included in data banks. Well-designed scientifically respectable studies, until quite recently, have been the exception. It seems that the more important the problem to human beings and communities, the less the rigor of the research. The movement from the laboratory to the community is admittedly difficult, but once having established credibility and obtained the cooperation of the neighborhood group or agency, the way is to open to gathering gold mines of data. Advances in qualitative and quantitative analyses allow for the overcoming of some of the limitations previously inherent in community-based research.

Fragmentation of Services and the Redefinition of Professionalism

Mental illness, delinquency, criminal justice, aging, unmarried teenage pregnancy, abortion, single parents, poverty, and unemployment, among others, are treated as separate entities despite their obvious communalities and interrelationships. There is a need for a dialogue and a systems approach in which SCIs cut across different aspects of the same problem. Related to this is an increasing emphasis on regionalism, ethnocentrism, and single purpose groups. Yet another trend is neighborhood and citizen groups rallying around threats to the immediate environment such as contamination and pollution or the defense of open space.

The democraticization and wider dissemination of knowledge plus the inability of professionals to meet the increasing needs of consumers has resulted in a blurring of boundaries and an emergence of new personnel. The paraprofessionals of yesteryear are now the new professionals. There has been a huge increase in the number of nontraditionally trained personnel (and sometimes untrained) in the human service fields (Riessman 1980). There is concomitantly a decline in the number and degree of involvement of persons from the traditional mental health and human service disciplines (Fink & Weinstein 1979). We turn now to topics covered in the present review.

SOCIAL POLICY, RESEARCH, AND THEORY

Seidman (1983) has produced a handbook of social interventions which makes a valuable contribution to theory, research, and practice of SCIs. There are other evidences of growing maturity. Muñoz et al (1979) have rendered a singular service to research-oriented interventions by addressing the processes involved in bringing about change in nonlaboratory community settings. Mechanic (1980) deals with major issues and questions that mental health planners, practitioners, and researchers face in implementing programs in the private and public sectors. Another mark of maturity is the important and oft neglected question of ethics and responsibility. Bermant et al (1978) examine the ethics of social interventions and point out the dilemmas in gaining consent of target populations, assessing unforeseen negative consequences of SCIs, and ascribing responsibility when social experiments fail. The implications for research are enormous.

Some major theoretical advances have appeared which directly relate to SCIs. Cowen (1980) clarifies the crucial parameters of primary prevention and opens the way for the development and testing of genuine primary prevention endeavors. Brickman et al (1982) present a social psychological framework for the assignment of responsibility and the planning of remediation in SCIs. Their framework, derived from attribution theory, clarifies the underlying assumptions of responsibility in traditional help-giving perspectives (e.g. the medical model) and sheds light on the assumptions underlying less well-defined perspectives (e.g. the compensatory model). Rappaport (1981) advances a theory of empowerment of individuals and communities and argues for the recognition of the paradoxical nature of community intervention. Once a particular type of SCI becomes institutionalized, efforts are then made to divert persons or groups away from its services. He recommends the study of how communities cope with various problems on a local level. The impending changes in sources and patterns of funding for SCIs may very well be a reflection of Rappaport's contentions (e.g. the movement to divert youth away from the juvenile justice system).

Failure to consider humanistic variables in SCIs is voiced by several writers. Taber (1980), in a review of 38 appropriate journals, concludes that the social sciences "have not studied and analyzed the helping situation to any significant degree" (p. 5). He also asserts that we have neglected to study the social environments in which persons are receiving help and care. Shore (1981) notes that in the human services there is a movement away from a compassionate approach toward a managerial, bureaucratic one. M. Levine (1979) goes further and states that

> the exclusive emphasis on hard-headed realities, to the exclusion of equally careful consideration of how we can guide and monitor the implementation of our ideals, has resulted in a betrayal of our ideals. As social scientists and evaluators, we need to learn how to be as sophisticated about theory, the philosophy, the operationalization, and the measurement of actions that meet our ideals as we are about fiscal matters, head counts, and other hard data (pp. 15–16).

The work of a number of researchers indicates increasing sensivitiy to the valid criticisms voiced above. Changes in patterns and utilization of mental health services between 1955 and 1975 have been carefully studied by Veroff et al (1981a), and in a companion volume, Veroff et al (1981b) present a rich and detailed picture of Americans' attitudes toward themselves, their work, their troubles, and the remedies they seek. Both of these volumes are abundant in data and possess enormous implications for the design, delivery, and evaluation of SCIs. The careful sampling and methodological rigor make these findings especially important.

On the community level, A. Levine (1982), working with the residents of Love Canal, provides an outstanding example of onsite scientific research. She details the problems of citizens struggling for the recognition of the legitimacy of their complaints in the face of bureaucratic obstacles, chicanery, and denial. Gibbs (1982) presents a resident's view of Love Canal and identifies many of the factors affecting a community's response to an environmental problem. As more and more "Love Canals," both nuclear and chemical, are discovered the importance of these two publications will be enhanced.

The need for more sophisticated research methodologies and evaluations in community settings is being increasingly recognized. For example, Dooley & Catalano (1980) report that changes in economic climate expose existing and *untreated behavior disorders* in contrast to the prevailing theory of provoking symptoms in previously normal persons. This finding has important ramifications for the nature and type of community interventions related to unemployment. Price & Polister (1980) present new paradigms for social research and practice with special emphasis on community and human service fields. Stahler & Tash (1982) deal with innovative approaches to the complex field of mental health evaluation.

On a social policy level, Albee (1982a) explores the politics of nature and nurture and emphasizes the need for sophistication on the part of psychologists. Zigler & Gordon (1981) discuss provisions of youth services in relation to social policy. Kiesler (1981, 1982) and Kiesler & Sibulkin (1982), in a series of ground-breaking papers, deal with the social policy implications of mental health research, the problems and issues in the identification of the mentally ill, and community implications of de jure vs de facto treatment approaches. In 1981, in recognition of changing political realities, APA set up an Institute of Policy Analysis and, beginning in 1982, the *American Psychologist* incorporated a continuing section called "Psychology in the Public Forum" which deals with policy-related issues. A rich variety of public interest and policy topics are presented on an almost monthly basis. The APA Congressional Fellows program and the Bush Foundation Fellowships in Child Development and Social Policy are examples of efforts to produce knowledgeable younger psychologists to add to an increasing cadre of psychologists in the public policy area. The link between research, theory, and social policy will undoubtedly be strengthened by these new developments.

COMMUNITY MENTAL HEALTH AND COMMUNITY PSYCHOLOGY: DEVELOPMENTS AND PROSPECTS

The Community Mental Health Centers (CMHCs) Act of 1965 laid the basis for SCIs in the area of mental health and mental illness. CMHCs were to deliver services to a wide variety of needy populations, in particular those formerly treated in state hospitals. Boards of citizens rather than professionals were to determine policy and exercise control of these centers. By the 1980s, CMHCs became the third largest component of the mental health service delivery system (Thompson et al 1982). Seven hundred and sixty CMHCs (composed of catchment areas of approximately 100,000 persons) are presently operational, serving an average of 54% of the population in each state and averaging approximately 3.1 million patient episodes yearly (Klerman 1981). These centers receive about 25% of state mental health dollars and are involved in approximately 75% of all psychiatric episodes (Andrulis & Mazade 1983). The Mental Health Systems Act of 1980 embodied changes which would have greatly improved the scope and quality of CMHCs as well as secured a continual financial support. Unfortunately, the Act was not funded and it is unclear how different funding sources will be combined to meet programs such as those involving the chronically mentally ill, children, the elderly, and ethnic minorities. It does seem likely that as financial support shrinks, we are going to see more conflict and competition among CMHC program sectors (e.g. preventive vs treatment services) as well as between CMHCs and other human service facilities (e.g. State Hospitals; Tarail 1980).

Changing Perspectives in Community Mental Health

An examination of the community mental health literature between 1979 and 1982 reveals the following major issues, that: (*a*) there is a movement toward marketing CMHC services more competitively to consumers in the private sector; (*b*) CMHCs are becoming more dependent on the need for third party payments (D'Augelli 1982a); (*c*) a marked exodus of mental health professionals is occurring as a result of an ideological split in what the priorities are in meeting the mental health needs of the community (Fink & Weinstein 1979); and (*d*) CMHCs are not meeting the needs of the chronically mentally ill (Rose 1979).

With the loosening of federal guidelines, each state has the opportunity to define community mental health in its own way. Some states may reinforce community-based programs which serve needy populations such as the chronically mentally ill while others may continue to support inpatient facilities. By examining the historical antecedents of the present mental health system, Levine (1981) and Sarason (1981) shed light on the overarching social and political processes which shape our current notions of community mental health. In addition, Schulberg & Killilea (1982), in an edited volume honoring Gerald Caplan, provide a valuable overview of the past, present, and future status of practically every aspect of community mental health as we know it today. Bloom's (1983) second edition of *Community Mental Health* adds to this knowledge, and we particularly note his timely contribution to the area of mental health education.

COMMUNITY PSYCHOLOGY'S MOVEMENT AWAY FROM COMMUNITY MENTAL HEALTH   At its origins in 1965, community psychology was closely identified with clinical and community mental health. The failure of community psychology to separate from these concerns was discussed by Novaco & Monahan (1980), McClure et al (1980), and Lounsbury et al (1980). We now note a decided turn toward environmental issues and activities involving target populations which have not previously been identified as mentally ill or in need of treatment. For example, there are now articles in the *American Journal of Community Psychology* on neighborhood groups and urban environments (Unger & Wandersman 1982), interventions promoting safety-belt use (Geller et al 1982), and the training of natural helpers in rural communities (D'Augelli & Ehrlich 1982). Additionally, a number of books and articles have emerged which reflect community psychologists' growing interest in and application of social psychological, cognitive, and behavioral theories. O'Neill (1981) approaches community psychology from a cognitive perspective, Jeger & Slotnick (1982) take a behavioral-ecological approach, and Glenwick & Jason (1980) present the first book on behavioral community psychology. O'Neill & Trickett (1982) combine the areas of social cognition and biological-ecology to analyze consultation from a systems perspective. Gibbs et al (1980), in a basic text, explore the contributions to community psychology from a number of fields primarily within psychology (e.g. labeling theory, learned helplessness, and environmental stress).

ECONOMICS AND MENTAL HEALTH SYSTEMS   The inclusion of economic research into the mental health field is heralded by McGuire & Weisbrod (1981). Mental health will be viewed increasingly as a commodity rather than a humanitarian endeavor. Cost benefit analysis and other economic terminology will be heard of more frequently. Broskowski et al (1981), in a very important edited volume, note the advantages of delivering health and mental health services in one setting. CMHCs could very well be combined with health centers which already have a long tradition of serving needy populations. Although there is a threat to the autonomy of mental health personnel, a more holistic approach to health (physical and mental) would be welcome.

MENTAL HEALTH ADMINISTRATION AND PERSONNEL   Mental health administration has come into its own as a discipline and must be recognized as a reality in SCIs. Austin & Hershey (1982) give a general survey of this area, and a source book for governing and advisory boards of CMHCs has appeared (Silverman 1981). The journal *Administration and Mental Health* (Saul Feldman, general editor) has been in existence for a decade and offers valuable information on management and leadership issues, particularly for CMHCs. In addition, the recommendations of a conference on ethical issues on mental health administration and an annotated bibliography were published by Bayer et al (1981).

In the personnel realm, PhD level psychologists and psychiatrists are having less and less to do with the severely mentally ill and comprise a decreasing percentage of CMHC staff (Berlin et al 1981). The so-called paraprofessionals have moved into what is called the "new" professional status and have taken over more and more aspects of care and treatment for the mentally ill. This trend is decried by some professionals who recommend a return to a medical model as opposed to a socioenvironmental model (Langsley 1980, Winslow 1982).

PRIMARY PREVENTION AND HEALTH PROMOTION

We attempt a brief "state of the art" description. The public health areas related to life-style problems (e.g. smoking, eating, and drinking) are focusing more on prevention. NIMH in 1982 established the Prevention Research Branch (PRB) with a National Office of Prevention Policy. Prevention Intervention Centers are currently being funded, and it is anticipated that three or four regional centers will be started up nationally each year for the next 3 years. ADAMHA (Klerman 1981) addresses issues in prevention policy including funding and joint programming. In terms of total budget, prevention expenditures are miniscule indeed.

The Journal of Primary Prevention was founded in 1980 and its "Clearing House" section for primary prevention programs is especially valuable. The *Prevention in Human Service Series* (1981) is also evidence of mounting interest in prevention. Issues dealing with the preventive impact of television (Sprafkin et al 1982) and early intervention programs for infants (Moss et al 1982) are excellent contributions. Moreover, Felner & Jason's (1983) edited volume on preventive psychology, the recommendations of the Task Force on Prevention of the President's Committee on Mental Health and the seven volumes contaning the papers delivered at the Vermont Conferences on Primary Prevention of Psychopathology (G. W. Albee and J. M. Joffe, General Editors) singly and collectively have made significant contributions to the area of primary prevention. The *Wellness Resource Bulletin*, published by the California State Department of Mental Health (1981), and the monograph by Aronowitz (1982) on state prevention programs are welcome additions. New York and Michigan have developed prevention components in their state departments of mental health.

Prevention Research and Theory

Much of the verbiage, rhetoric, and methodological underbrush are being cleared away in primary prevention (Cowen 1980). In discussing policy guidelines for primary prevention, Cowen (1980), Iscoe (1980), and Bloom (1981) extend the base of prevention knowledge so that new research questions can be generated. Lorion (1983) offers a set of research principles for systematically analyzing preventive interventions, and Lorion & Lounsbury (1982) present conceptual and methodological guidelines for evaluating such programs. In addition, Cowen (1980) and D'Augelli (1982b) have contributed to the understanding of the differences between C & E and primary prevention. Albee (1982b) has presented a formula for determining the incidence of mental illness. Price et al (1980) make a distinct contribution to the area of prevention by discussing critical research concerns. This volume marks the first in a series of Sage annual reviews of mental health, and the field is well served. A "special number" of the *American Journal of Community Psychology* (Cowen 1982) is comprised of nine studies specifically selected to meet rigorous criteria of primary prevention research. A "compleat roadmap," offered by Cowen (1982), synthesizes each of the studies from the point of view of the target group, objectives, major methodologies, and variables affected.

To investors and investigators primary prevention activities and research must indeed appear as a "hi risk" endeavor. While the findings of Shure & Spivack (1981), Bloom et al (1982), Tableman et al (1982) suggest that primary prevention programs can have significant short-term effects, these interventions have not been subjected to long-term scrutiny. Evaluation of whether these effects are lasting or not necessitates complex costly longitudinal research. Therefore, support for evaluation of primary prevention programs is not a major policy priority.

SELF-HELP GROUPS, SOCIAL SUPPORT, AND SOCIAL NETWORK SYSTEMS

There are at least 500,000 self-help groups in the U.S. embracing a total membership of about 23,000,000 (Katz 1981). Gartner & Riessman (1980) have compiled a working guide of many of these groups, cross-referenced by problem and location. They range from those groups involving persons experiencing similar circumstances or misfortunes (e.g. single parents groups, Parents Without Partners, Alcoholics Anonymous) to those involving organizations of persons designed to deal with a national problem at the local level [e.g. Mothers Against Drunk Driving (MADD)]. Characteristic of self-help groups is that the initiators and members perceive existing social institutions or agencies as not meeting their needs (Knight et al 1980). Typically there is a shared belief system and, in some instances, the focus is on the social origins of problems rather than the individualistic, introspective origins espoused by clinicians. Additionally, nonprofessional involvement is a common factor in many self-help groups.

Self-help Groups: Sociopolitical Aspects and Professionalism

Self-help groups partially reflect a reaction to political and economic changes in the past two decades. There is an emphasis on closely tied small groups and the development of new strategies for dealing with human or environmental concerns against which a single individual feels powerless. In many ways self-help groups can be a source of community empowerment (Gartner & Riessman 1982). The joining of forces by like-minded people leads to a singleness of purpose which can effect policy changes at the local, state, or national levels. Taking a cross-cultural perspective, Weber & Cohen (1982) examine the unique ways in which ethnicity and beliefs structure and define self-help groups. In this same volume, Schensul & Schensul (1982) deal with the distinction between social advocacy and mutual assistance in relation to ethnicity, socialization, beliefs and group organization.

   Voluntary grass roots involvement is a key to successful community action and the basis of citizen groups of all types. The fact that they exist and are increasing indicates continued need. Spiegel (1982) notes that groups are more likely to be found in areas where there are few professionals or the individual lacks access to professional services. Many self-help groups function as an information source or a psychological support. For example, Spiegel notes that "Ostomy Clubs" deal with an aspect of postsurgical care, working with patients and their families on important problems rarely dealt with by physicians. He outlines the main types of self-help groups and discusses self-help in relation to deviance theory, professionalism, and transition phases in life.

Warren (1981) notes that a majority (72%) of middle class Americans enter and leave helping pathways and resources at frequent intervals and present problems which are well over the capacity of any agency or group of professionals to deal with effectively. Cowen et al (1981) emphasize the growing importance of informal help-giving processes and how effective they are with different types of helper groups. Rodolfa & Hungerford (1982), expressing the concern of many mental health professionals, contend that the self-help approach encourages individuals to neglect mental health care and rely exclusively on the group where symptoms rather than the underlying problem are treated. A two-way referral (and possibly screening process) has yet to be developed. A genuine collaborative relationship between professionals and various self-help and social support groups would be a constructive step in meeting the diverse needs of individuals in the community. To this end, Jeger & Slotnick (1982) develop a "self-help-professional collaborative" perspective within an ecological context.

Research Issues in Self-help

Evaluating the effectiveness of self-help groups poses considerable challenge. Little is known about how members are recruited, the extent of their dependence on group support, how they evolve and change within the group, and on a macro level, the social forces which have given birth to such a movement (Knight et al 1980). Lieberman & Bond (1978) contend, and we agree, that it is still uncertain who is served, what problems are highlighted, and the process by which needs are met in self-help groups. To answer such questions one needs to examine systems level criteria as outcome measures as well as individual level criteria involving the lifestyles and values of the clients. This research entails a compilation of methodological techniques from a number of disciplinary perspectives such as sociology, anthropology, and psychology. Until a multidisciplinary perspective is implemented, the boundary and domain of self-help groups will remain unclear.

Developments in Social Network Analysis and Social Support

Wellman & Leighton (1979) advance the notion of networks in examining social linkages within communities. Subsequently a number of conceptual, methodological, and program advances in the area of social networks have appeared (Wellman 1980, Connections 1982). Gottlieb & Hall (1980) provide a model by which to conceptualize the referral pattern and utilization of individuals into social support networks. In addition, Gottlieb (1981) discusses the functions of social networks as positive additions to the professional sector and as support in times of crisis. Sarason & Lorentz (1979) address the complexities of resource exchange networks in a complex setting and furnish some cogent observations on the negative role of professionalism in our society.

Definitions of social support range from extensive, close interpersonal ties to those involving only key individuals or groups (Heller 1979). In a factor analysis of the social support construct, Heller & Swindle (1983) report four main elements: the structure and function of support networks, personal attributes of individuals that keep the network open, cognitive appraisal that discerns if support is available, and support-seeking behavior (usually generated from the cognitive appraisal component). Recent reviews of the buffering hypothesis of social support were conducted by Thoits (1982) and Heller & Swindle (1983). Wilcox (1981) found that quality of support rather than quantity was a significant factor in buffering stress. In addition, Porritt (1979) reports a relationship between the source and quality of social support in a crisis situation and favorableness of outcome.

DEINSTITUTIONALIZATION: MORE APPARENT THAN REAL?

Deinstitutionalization (DE) helped to change the organizational structure of the mental health service delivery system and modified policies and practices in institutions. It also highlighted the importance of social support systems programs, family involvement, and alternative living situations to maintain the chronically mentally ill in the community. It has served to reemphasize the complexity of problems faced by the chronically mentally ill and severely questioned the sufficiency of the medical model. While state hospital census has markedly decreased, there is an increased concern about whether the deinstitutionalized are better off in terms of quality of life and health status. DE as a concept rests on a set of assumptions about the needs of the chronically mentally ill in relation to institutional vs community-based care and treatment. These assumptions are now becoming increasingly questioned (Goldman et al 1983). There is a high proportion of mentally disabled persons in institution-like community-based facilities. In addition, Weinstein (1982) points out that there have been only a few studies which have asked deinstitutionalized patients about their perceptions of the institution. He suggests that many ex-mental patients view the institution in more favorable terms than was previously supposed.

At least 60 major publications have appeared since 1979, ranging from anecdotal accounts (Sheehan 1982) to scholarly works documenting the impact of program and systems level interventions (Levine 1980, Talbott 1981, Krauss & Slavinsky 1982, Tessler & Goldman 1982). Some of these are focused on the planning of alternative care facilities (Rutman 1981) such as nursing homes (Vladeck 1980), and others are more concerned with specific research issues such as public attitudes toward the chronically mentally ill in the community (Rabkin et al 1980), the pioneering work of Gordon Paul on treatment modalities (Rhoades 1981) and cross-disciplinary perspectives (Lerman 1981). In addition, several journals have published special issues on DE. These journals include the *Journal of Social Issues* (1981), *Archives of General Psychiatry* (1980), *Milbank Memorial Fund Quarterly* (1979), and *Hospital & Community Psychiatry* (1982, 1983). Topics such as community support systems for chronic patients (Stein 1979), longitudinal follow-up of the Fairweather Lodge (Fairweather 1980), community residential treatment (Budson 1981), and the young adult chronic patient (Pepper & Ryglewicz 1982) have appeared in a series entitled *New Directions in Mental Health* (R. Lamb, editor).

Alternative Treatment and the Chronic Mental Patient

Except for a few well-conceptualized and supported programs, DE has not lived up to its humanitarian goals. Discharge from the institution, in many cases, has resulted in increased exposure to a hostile environment, lack of health care, and deterioration of living conditions (Gruenberg & Archer 1979, Rose 1979, Lamb 1981, G. E. Miller 1981). Fifteen years after DE was formally launched as an intervention policy, NIMH, responding to mounting criticism, began the Community Support Program (CSP). As a demonstration program, the CSP was to facilitate planning and coordination of program services for the chronically mentally ill. Highlights on the CSP federal initiative are covered in *A Network for Caring* (Turner & Stockdill 1982), and Tessler & Goldman (1982) present the evaluation results of various CSP programs. There are some encouraging signs. Rightly, the dissemination of these findings would be aided if they appeared in journals or as an NIMH report. Presently, CSP efforts are stifled by a limited federal funding, and it is still unknown whether, in the reduction of funding, the CSP philosophy will be taken up and acted upon by the states.

Braun et al. (1981), in a critical review of outcome studies on DE, conclude that satisfactory DE appears to depend on the availability of appropriate programs for care in the community—a finding that applies to virtually all types of chronic conditions. While Test (1981) offers some laudable conditions regarding effective treatment of the chronic patient in a minimally restrictive environment, it is unrealistic to suppose such approaches can be implemented given the scarce resources presently available. The extensive work by Stein & Test (1980) involves issues of continuity of care and the provision of appropriate resources for the DE patient. They contend that in the long run high direct costs will reduce overall patient costs and will yield a richer quality of life. Promising alternative treatment, programs such as Horizon House in Philadelphia and Fountain House in New York City utilize a variety of resources, including inexpensive apartments, job training, psychiatric coverage, and numerous social and recreational activities. It is to be hoped that these promising programs will be able to articulate the factors that contribute to their success, thus permitting replication in other settings. Of particular concern is whether these programs meet the needs of long-term chronic patients who have limited education and manifest little or no job and social skills before hospitalization. There are, however, still a number of methodological difficulties in assessing quality of life variables and relating these in a causal fashion to the DE movement (Schulberg & Bromet 1981, Morrissey 1982, Tessler & Goldman 1982).

Apropos of quality, the literature suggests that approximately 50% of the deinstitutionalized live in settings that provide little or no supervision: private homes, single room occupancy hotels (SROs), boarding houses, or unsupervised cooperative apartments (Tessler et al 1982); are uneployed or, if working, hold low-paying service jobs; and, on the average, are hospitalized for approximately one month every 3 to 5 years (Estroff 1981).

An emerging population of young adult chronic patients has recently come to the attention of investigators (Schwartz & Goldfinger 1981, Lamb 1982, Sheets et al 1982). This group evidences a unique combination of problems involving violence, a lack of control, and management in community settings (Stelovich 1979), thus placing considerable challenges on service delivery systems (Bachrach 1982b, Lamb 1982, Pepper & Ryglewicz 1982). To date, little research has documented the plight of the young adult chronic patient and few programs have been developed to address their special needs (Spivack et al 1982). Further, little is known of patients who do not participate in community aftercare treatment programs.

Research and Evaluation Issues

Research on DE and the fate of the DE patient is hampered by the frequent failure to recognize that there are degrees of institutionalization ranging from traditional restrictions of freedom and lack of treatment (the warehouse concept) to benign regimes which impose a minimum of restrictions and have a treatment program. Also, there has been a failure of middle class planners to comprehend fully the life-styles and priorities of the poor. The literature is lacking sound evaluations accounting for differential adjustment patterns (Talbott 1981) and, we note, has not substantially advanced beyond the descriptive level. This bottleneck in research activity appears to be due partly to a lack of standardized measures and comparable definitional terms. A host of evaluation studies have been published on various model programs and alternative treatment packages; however, an assessment of the totality of treatment effects has yet to be done. Additionally, little attention has been paid to impact evaluation research and a systems theory approach to examining DE (Bachrach & Lamb 1982).

The current status of DE is an example of failing to consider the framework presented at the beginning of this chapter. Until the contending forces of genuine humanistic motivation, political and economic realities, plus legitimate community concerns are equitably resolved, DE will remain a vexing and troublesome SCI. Any reappraisal should certainly include a consideration of the definitions and purposes of asylum and sanctuary.

UNDERSERVED AND UNSERVED POPULATIONS

Reasonably accurate estimation of what groups are unserved, underserved, or badly served is difficult and fraught with value judgments at all levels. Many individuals, young and old, singly and collectively, need some form of assistance; however, it is a formidable problem to ascertain genuine needs and assign priorities for this diverse group of individuals. For example, on all fronts (e.g. mental health, education, etc) the persons within the age range 10 to 14 years remain particularly underserved or badly served. If indeed 10% of the population at any one time are in need of mental health services, then only about one-third come to the attention of any sort of mental health treatment facility. The fate (good or bad) of the rest of this population is as yet undetermined.

Snowden (1982) has compiled a timely volume which addresses the complex issues facing the underserved (e.g. minorities, women, children, and the elderly). Gonzales et al (1983) provide a review of the current status of underserved and badly served groups and note that the impending takeover by the states of such programs as AFDC, Medicare, and Food Stamps is unlikely to result in an ideological advance. The Manpower Demonstration Research Corporation (MDRC) (1980) has designed, implemented, and evaluated a number of interventive projects addressing the needs of underserved populations. The national work support project, for example, demonstrated that welfare recipients (females on AFDC) could acquire and maintain employment after work skills training, counseling, and general supportive environments. Additionally, a significant proportion of the exaddict population obtained jobs with adequate earnings and were less likely subsequently to be involved in drug-related or other types of crime. It was, however, only marginally effective with exconvicts (nondrug-related offenses) and had little or no effect on adults who were early school dropouts. Auletta (1982) details the human aspects of the MDRC programs and coins the term "underclass" to cover some 9,000,000 Americans who have not assimilated the dominant American culture.

Rural Mental Health, Ethnic Minorities, and Women

In rural mental health a welcome handbook has appeared (Keller & Murray 1982). This volume addresses recent changes in rural life, the mental health of rural populations, and the critical factors that influence service delivery. There are generally few health/mental health resources in these areas and very few rural mental health training programs (Solomon 1980). At the same time, there is a high proportion of the elderly, migrant workers and persons in poor physical health, all needing such services. Certainly appropriate SCIs, meeting the unique needs of rural populations, deserve high priority.

A number of research developments have occurred for ethnic minority populations. Jones & Korchin (1982), in a sophisticated edited volume on minority mental health, examine change-oriented community interventions and organizational structures designed to empower particular ethnic groups such as Japanese Americans, Chinese, Blacks, Hispanics, and Cubans. An exhaustive annotated bibliography of American Indian research is now available (Kelso & Attneave 1981), and the *Hispanic Journal of Behavioral Sciences*, first published in 1980, clearly marks a movement toward more rigorous experimental research on the Hispanic cultures. Barón (1981) has edited a volume rich in foundation work for Chicano psychology, and M. Ramirez (1983) advances the theoretical base by including a bicultural/bicognitive perspective. In terms of mental health service utilization, more clarity is being achieved (Acosta 1979). D. G. Ramirez (1982), in an extensive study on the underutilization of mental health services by Mexican Americans in Texas, suggests that the relative youth (median age 17 years) of the Mexican American population is a major factor in their underutilization of services. D. G. Ramirez predicts increased utilization of mental health services as the Hispanic population grows older. This parsimonious explanation is a welcome replacement for the rhetoric which has accumulated in the area of Mexican American underutilization of mental health facilities. Hopefully, similar findings will be obtained with other Hispanic populations.

Methodological problems in studying women in the midst of economic, social, and environmental changes have recently been addressed (Stewart & Platt 1982). Contrary to popular notions of service utilization, women are still underserved, especially when the problem runs counter to societal stereotypes (Gonzales et al 1983). For example, seldom are the needs of the female alcoholic taken into account by program designers and service providers (Russo & Sobel 1981). Clearly much remains to be done. The rapid increase in centers for battered women and counseling devoted to women's problems testify that the needs of this group are not being met within the existing context of community services. Paradoxically, the involvement of women's organizations in the fabric of American life has increased as well. Clearly, research in this area could expand our knowledge base by including information on the vast array of organized women's groups and more informal systems of mutual support for women.

Concern for the Elderly and Children

By the year 2000 one out of every six Americans will be over the age of 65. We are witnessing increased political activism of the elderly population at the local level (e.g. the Gray Panthers) and a rise in policy-related literature such as *Ageing and Society* (Johnson 1982). The American Psychological Associations' Boulder Conference in 1981 is a benchmark for psychology's involvement in older populations (Santos & VandenBos 1982). In addition, The White House Conference on Aging produced a series of volumes on national policy issues and proceedings (Armitage 1981). These hopeful developments should not obscure the myriad problems that need to be dealt with at national and community levels. The developing political "clout" of the elderly is an avenue for influencing policy.

Somewhat in contrast, Grubb & Lazerson (1982) carefully detail the lack of equitable distribution of resources and services for children in proportion to the entire population. Gabarino (1981) asserts that the utilization and dissemination of research-based knowledge about children has low priority in the activities of social scientists, policymakers and practitioners, while Garduque & Peters (1982) note the gap between information needs of child care program personnel and developmental research. Two out of three seriously disturbed children in the U.S. are not receiving the mental health services they need, and only 17% of CMHC funds are spent on children. Under the new mental health block grant program, not a cent is required to be spent on disturbed children (Children's Defense Fund 1982). The assault on children is all-pervasive. Reduction in support for nutrition, education, day care, safety, and AFDC typify the low priority to SCIs for children. If the priorities of a nation are mirrored in its SCIs, the welfare of children and youth are clearly not uppermost in the minds and intentions of policymakers.

Encouragingly, Zigler & Valentine (1979) detail the clear gains to children and families in the Head Start Program, and Lazar & Darlington (1982) present the highly significant combined results of 11 studies demonstrating the beneficial long-lasting effects of day care. Clearly some SCIs work. However, the failure to commit adequate resources for children is particularly disheartening when, for example, single-parent families (mostly mothers) today comprise the largest poverty group in America. We hope that the present reality will give way to more optimistic findings in the future.

Suggestions for Research Directions

Our review of the burgeoning and scattered literature in the "underserved" section strongly suggests the need for a more precise definition of the populations covered. For example, the comparison of Hispanics and Anglos without careful specification leads to understandably vague and nonreplicable findings. Generalities such as the underclass, the underserved, single parent families, rural mental health, the needs of women, although valuable for preliminary identification of groups or areas, must eventually undergo refinement if research is to be advanced in the area of SCIs. Such refinements, in our opinion, are best forthcoming through the development of an expanded psychology of individual differences.

CONCLUSIONS

Our review has touched on only a small portion of the programs and activities under the title of SCIs. The many diciplines and belief systems involved in SCIs raise the question of the optimum role for psychologists and psychology. Although we note an encouraging increase in published research, we also note a clear need for more methodological and procedural sophistication to produce the knowledge required for the planning and execution of effective SCIs. This calls for a movement from the laboratory of the university to the laboratory of the community, using data often already in the possession of an agency, group, or neighborhood or by "piggy-backing" onto an ongoing SCI or one in the planning stage. This holds for more traditional as well as newer SCIs, the "hard" as well as the "soft" areas of psychology. The necessary cognitive reorientations for SCI research can be facilitated by open and continued dialogue between those who fund and administer programs and those who wish to research and evaluate them.

It is in the research and consultant areas that psychologists can make unique contributions. Existing fragmentations can be reduced, ambiguities clarified, and more unified concepts and paradigms can be advanced. Many of the conditions to which SCIs presently address themselves can be prevented or reduced were valid knowledge available about causality and the collaborative efforts of communities and investigators harnessed. We urge a social and research policy which encourages psychologists to adopt appropriate ecological and system approaches to unraveling the complex interactive phenomena to which SCIs address themselves. The potential contributions and benefits to psychology are enormous, the challenge formidable indeed.

ACKNOWLEDGMENTS

Our gratitude to Jerry B. Harvey, Brian Wilcox, Brian Rasmussen, and Jeffrey Anderson for helpful comments about the manuscript; to Shannon Minter and Terry Foster for locating library materials; to Karen Bordelon, Patricia Britton, and Nadea Gizelbach for compilation of the bibliography. A special note to Ms. Bertha Shanblum for putting up with all of us while typing many drafts of this manuscript.

Literature Cited

Acosta, F. X. 1979. Barriers between mental health services and Mexican Americans: An examination of a paradox. *Am. J. Community Psychol.* 7:503–20

Adler, P. T. 1982. An analysis of the concept of competence in individuals and social systems. *Community Ment. Health J.* 18:34–45

Albee, G. W. 1982a. The politics of nature and nurture. *Am. J. Community Psychol.* 10:1–36

Albee, G. W. 1982b. Preventing psychopathology and promoting human potential. *Am. Psychol.* 37:1043–50

Alpert, J. L., ed. 1982. *Psychological Consultation in Educational Settings.* San Francisco: Jossey-Bass

Alpert, J. L., Meyers, J. 1983. *Training in Consultation.* Springfield, Ill: Thomas

Anchor Mental Health Association. 1982. *Community Guidebook.* Washington DC

Andrulis, D. P., Mazade, N. A. 1983. American mental health policy: Changing directions in the 80s. *Hosp. Community Psychiatry* 34:601-6

Armitage, C. C., Chairman. 1981. *Final Report on the 1981 White House Conference on Aging*. Vols. 1-3. Washington DC: GPO

Aronowitz, E., ed. 1982. *Prevention Strategies for Mental Health*. New York: Prodist

Ashbaugh, J. W., Bradley, V. J. 1979. Linking deinstitutionalization of patients with hospital phase-down: The difference between success and failure. *Hosp. Community Psychiatry* 30:105-10

Auletta, K. 1982. *The Underclass*. New York: Random House

Austin, M. J., Hershey, W. E., eds. 1982. *Handbook on Mental Health Administration*. San Francisco: Jossey-Bass

Bachrach, L. L. 1980. Is the least restrictive environment always the best? Sociological and semantic implications. *Hosp. Community Psychiatry* 31:97-102

Bachrach, L. L. 1982a. Assessment of outcomes in community support systems: Results, problems, and limitations. *Schizophr. Bull.* 8:39-61

Bachrach, L. L. 1982b. Young adult chronic patients: An analytical review of the literature. *Hosp. Community Psychiatry* 33:189-97

Bachrach, L. L., Lamb, R. 1982. Conceptual issues in the evaluaton of the deinstitutionalization movement. See Stahler & Tash 1982

Barón, A. Jr., ed. 1981. *Explorations in Chicano Psychology*. New York: Praeger

Bayer, R., Feldman, S., Reich, W. 1981. *Ethical Issues in Mental Health Policy and Administration*. DHHS Publ. (ADM) 81-1116

Berkowitz, W. R. 1982. *Community Impact: Creating Grass Roots Change*. Cambridge, Mass: Schenkman

Berlin, R. M., Kales, J. D., Humphrey, F. J. II, Kales, A. 1981. The patient care crises in community mental health centers: A need for more psychiatric involvement. *Am. J. Psychiatry* 138:450-54

Bermant, G., Kelman, H. C., Warwick, D. P., eds. 1978. *The Ethics of Social Intervention*. Washington: Hemisphere

Biegel, D. E., Naparstek, A. J. 1982. *Community Support Systems and Mental Health*. New York: Springer

Bloom, B. L. 1979. Prevention of mental disorders: Recent advances in theory and practice. *Community Ment. Health J.* 15:179-91

Bloom, B. L. 1980. Social and community interventions. *Ann. Rev. Psychol.* 31:111-42

Bloom, B. L. 1981. The logic and urgency of primary prevention. *Hosp. Community Psychiatry* 32:839-43

Bloom, B. L. 1983. *Community Mental Health: A General Introduction*. Monterey: Brooks/Cole. 2nd ed.

Bloom, B. L., Asher, S. J., eds. 1982. *Psychiatric Patient Rights and Patient Advocacy*. New York: Human Sci. Press

Bloom, B. L., Hodges, W. F., Caldwell, R. A. 1982. A preventive program for the newly separated: Initial evaluation. *Am. J. Community Psychol.* 10:251-64

Braun, P., Kochansky, G., Shapiro, R., Greenberg, S., Gudeman, J., et al. 1981. Overview: Deinstitutionalization of psychiatric patients, a critical review of outcome studies. *Am. J. Psychiatry* 138:736-49

Brickman, P., Rabinowitz, V. C., Karuza, J., Coates, D., Cohn, E., et al. 1982. Models of helping and coping. *Am. Psychol.* 37:368-84

Broskowski, A., Marks, J., Budman, S., eds. 1981. *Linking Health and Mental Health*. Vol. 2. Beverly Hills: Sage

Budson, R. D. 1981. *New Directions for Mental Health Services. Issues in Community Residential Care*. No. 11. San Francisco: Jossey-Bass

California Department of Mental Health, Mental Health Promotion Branch. 1981. *Wellness Resource Bulletin*

Children's Defense Fund. 1982. *Unclaimed Children, the Failure of Public Responsibility to Children and Adolescents in Need of Mental Health Services*. Washington DC: GPO

Connections: Bulletin of the International Network for Social Network Analysis. 1982 Vol. 5: Structural Analysis Programme, Univ. Toronto, Canada

Cowen, E. L. 1973. Social and community interventions. *Ann. Rev. Psychol.* 24:423-72

Cowen, E. L. 1980. The wooing of primary prevention. *Am. J. Community Psychol.* 8:258-84

Cowen, E. L. 1982. The special number: A compleat roadmap. *Am. J. Community Psychol.* 10:239-49

Cowen, E. L., issue ed. 1982. *Special issue: Research in Primary Prevention in Mental Health. Am. J. Community Psychol.* 10:239-67

Cowen, E. L., Gesten, E., Davidson, E., Wilson, A. 1981. Hairdressers as caregivers II: Relationships between helper characteristics and helping behaviors and feelings. *J. Prev.* 1:225-39

Curtis, M. J., Zins, J. E., eds. 1981. *The Theory and Practice of School Consultation*. Springfield, Ill: Thomas

D'Augelli, A. R. 1982a. A funny thing happened on the way to the community: Consultation and education in community mental health centers, or how I learned to stop worrying about prevention and love third-party payments. *J. Primary Prev.* 2:235-39

D'Augelli A. R. 1982b. Historical synthesis of consultation and education. See Ritter 1982. pp. 3-50

D'Augelli, A. R., Ehrlich, R. P. 1982. Evaluation of a community-based system for training natural helpers. II. Effects on informal helping activities. *Am. J. Community Psychol.* 10:447-56

Davis, D. Z., Osborne, G. E., Dahn, A. J., Conyne, R. K., Matice, K. L. 1981. Caveats in the consultation process. *Adm. Ment. Health* 2:137-48

Dooley, D., Catalano, R. 1980. Economic change as a cause of behavioral disorder. *Psychol. Bull.* 87:450-68

Dorwart, R. A. 1980. Deinstitutionalization: Who is left behind? *Hosp. Community Psychiatry* 31:336-38

Estroff, S. E. 1981. Psychiatric deinstitutionalization: A sociocultural analysis. *J. Soc. Issues* 37:116-31

Fairweather, G. W. 1980. *New Directions for Mental Health Services: The Fairweather Lodge: A Twenty-Five Year Retrospective.* No. 7. San Francisco: Jossey-Bass

Felner, R. D., Jason, L. A., eds. 1983. *Preventive Psychology: Theory, Research and Practice.* New York: Pergamon

Fink, P., Weinstein, S. 1979. Whatever happened to psychiatry? The deprofessionalization of community mental health centers. *Am. J. Psychiatry* 136:406-9

Gabarino, J. 1981. Knowledge in the service of children and youth. *Child. Youth Serv. Rev.* 3:269-75

Gallessich, J. 1982. *The Profession and Practice of Consultation.* San Francisco: Jossey-Bass

Garduque, L., Peters, D. 1982. Toward reapproachment in child care research: An optimistic view. *Child Care Q.* 2:12-21

Gartner, A., Riessman, F. 1980. *Help: A Working Guide to Self Help Groups.* New York: Viewpoint, Franklin Watts

Gartner, A., Riessman, F. 1982. Self-help and mental health. *Hosp. Community Psychol.* 33:631-35

Geller, E. S., Johnson, R. P., Pelton, S. L. 1982. Community-based interventions for encouraging safety belt use. *Am. J. Community Psychol.* 10:183-95

Gibbs, L. M. 1982. *Love Canal: My Story.* New York: Grove

Gibbs, M. S, Lachenmeyer, J. R., Sigal, J., eds. 1980. *Community Psychology.* New York: Gardner

Glasscote, R. M., Chief. 1980. *Preventing Mental Illness: Efforts and Attitudes.* Washington DC: Joint Inf. Serv. Am. Psychiatric Assoc.

Glenwick, D., Jason, L., eds. 1980. *Behavioral Community Psychology.* New York: Praeger

Goldman, H. H., Adams, N. H., Taube, C. A. 1983. Deinstitutionalization: The data demythologized. *Hosp. Community Psychiatry* 34:129-34

Gonzales, L. R., Hays, R. B., Bond, M. A., Kelly, J. G. 1983. Community mental health. In *The Clinical Psychology Handbook,* ed. M. Hersen, A. E. Kazdin, A. S. Bellack. New York: Pergamon

Gottlieb, B. H. 1981. *Social Networks and Social Support.* Beverly Hills: Sage

Gottlieb, B. H., Hall, A. 1980. Social networks and the utilization of preventive mental health services. See Price et al 1980, pp. 167-94

Grady, M. A., Gibson, J. S., Trickett, E. J. 1981. *Mental Health Consultation: Theory, Practice, and Research 1973-1978.* DHHS Publ. (ADM) 81-948

Greenblatt, M., Becerra, R. M., Serafetinides, E. A. 1982. Social networks and mental health: An overview. *Am. J. Psychiatry* 139:977-84

Grubb, W. N., Lazerson, M. 1982. *Broken Promises.* New York: Basic Books

Gruenberg, E. M., Archer, J. 1979 Abandonment of responsibility for the seriously mentally ill. *Milbank Mem. Fund Q./Health Soc.* 57:485-506

Hammer, M. 1981. Social supports, social networks, and schizophrenia. *Schizophr. Bull.* 7:45-56

Hatfield, A. B. 1981. Self-help groups for families of the mentally ill. *Soc. Work.* 26:408-13

Heller, K. 1979. The effects of social support: Prevention and treatment implications. In *Maximizing Treatment Gains: Transfer Enhancement in Psychotherapy,* ed. A. P. Goldstein, F. H. Kanfer, pp. 353-82. New York: Academic

Heller, K., Swindle, R. W. 1983. Social networks, perceived social support and coping with stress. In *Preventive Psychology: Theory, Research and Practice in Community Intervention,* ed. R. D. Felner, L. A. Jason, pp. 87-103. New York: Pergammon

Holahan, C. J., Moos, R. H. 1981. Social support and psychological distress: A longitudinal analysis. *J. Abnorm. Psychol.* 90: 365-70

Insel, P. M., ed. 1980. *Environmental Variables and the Prevention of Mental Illness.* Lexington, Mass: Lexington Books

Iscoe, I. 1980. Conceptual barriers to training for the primary prevention of psychopathology. In *Prevention Through Political Action and Social Change,* ed. J. M. Joffe, G. W. Albee. Hanover, NH: Univ. Press New England

Jeger, A. M., Slotnick, R. S., eds. 1982. *Community Mental Health and Behavioral-Ecology.* New York: Plenum

Johnson, M. L., ed. 1982. *Ageing and Society. J. Cent. Policy Ageing and Br. Soc. Gerontol.,* Vol. 2. Cambridge, Mass: Cambridge Univ. Press

Jones, E. E., Korchin, S. J. 1982. *Minority Mental Health.* New York: Praeger

Katz, A. H. 1981. Self-help and mutual aid: An emerging social movement. *Ann. Rev. Sociol.* 7:129-55

Keller, P. A., Murray, J. D. 1982. *Handbook of Rural Community Mental Health*. New York: Human Sci. Press

Kelly, J. G., Snowden, L. R., Muñoz, R. F. 1977. Social and community interventions. *Ann. Rev. Psychol.* 28:323–61

Kelso, D. R., Attneave, C. L., eds. 1981. *Bibliography of North American Indian Mental Health*. Conn: Greenwood

Ketterer, R. 1981. *Consultation and Education in Mental Health: Problems and Prospects*, Vol. 3, Sage Studies in Community Mental Health Ser. Beverly Hills: Sage

Kiesler, C. A. 1981. Barriers to effective knowledge use in national mental health policy. *Health Policy Q.* 1:201–15

Kiesler, C. A. 1982. Mental hospitals and alternative care. *Am. Psychol.* 37:349–60

Kiesler, C. A., Sibulkin, A. E. 1982. People, clinical episodes, and mental hospitalization: A multiple-source method of estimation. In *Advances in Applied Social Psychology*, ed. R. F. Kidd, M. J. Saks, 2:131–61. Hillsdale, NJ: Erlbaum

Klerman, G. 1981. *Report of the Administrator: Alcohol, Drug Abuse and Mental Health Administration, 1980*. DHHS Publ. 81–1165

Knight, B., Wollert, R., Levy, L., Frame, C., Padgett, V. 1980. Self-help groups: The members' perspectives. *Am. J. Community Psychol.* 8:53–65

Krauss, J. B., Slavinsky, A. T. 1982. *The Chronically Ill Psychiatric Patient and the Community*. Boston: Blackwell

Lamb, H. R. 1981. What did we really expect from deinstitutionalization? *Hosp. Community Psychiatry* 32:105–9

Lamb, H. R. 1982. Young adult chronic patients: The new drifters. *Hosp. Community Psychiatry* 33:465–68

Lamb, H. R., Zusman, J. 1979. Primary prevention in perspective. *Am. J. Psychiatry* 136:12–17

Lamb, H. R. Zusman, J. 1981. A new look at primary prevention. *Hosp. Community Psychiatry* 32:839–43

Langsley, D. G. 1980. The community mental health center: Does it treat patients? *Hosp. Community Psychiatry* 31:815–19

Lazar, I., Darlington, R. B. 1982. Lasting effects of early education. *Monogr. Soc. Res. Child Dev.* 47:1–151

Lerman, P. 1981. *Deinstitutionalization: A Cross-Problem Analysis*. DHHS Publ. (ADM) 81–987

Levine, A. 1982. *Love Canal: Science, Politics, and People*. Lexington, Mass: Lexington Books

Levine, M. 1979. Congress (and evaluators) ought to pay more attention to history. *Am. J. Community Psychol.* 7:1–17

Levine, M. 1980. *From State Hospital to*

Psychiatric Center: The Implementation of Planned Organizational Change. Lexington, Mass: Lexington Books

Levine, M. 1981. *The History and Politics of Community Mental Health*. New York: Oxford Univ. Press

Lieberman, M. A., Bond, G. R. 1978. Self-help groups: Problems of measuring outcome. *Small Group Behav.* 9:221–41

Lorion, R. P. 1983. Evaluating preventive interventions: Guidelines for the serious social change agent. See Felner & Jason 1983, pp. 251–68

Lorion, R. P., Lounsbury, J. W. 1982. Conceptual and methodological considerations in evaluating preventive interventions. See Stahler & Tash 1982, pp. 23–57

Lounsbury, J. W., Leader, D. S., Meares, E. P., Cook, M. P. 1980. An analytic review of research in community psychology. *Am. J. Community Psychol.* 8:415–41

Mannino, F. V. 1981. Empirical perspectives in mental health consultation. *J. Prev.* 1:147–55

Manpower Demonstration Research Corporation, N. Y. 1980. *Summary and Findings of the National Supported Work Demonstration*. Cambridge: Ballinger

McClure, L., Cannon, D., Allen, S., Belton, E., Connor, P., et al. 1980. Community psychology concepts and research base: Promise and product. *Am. Psychol.* 35:1000–11

McGuire, T. G., Weisbrod, B. A. 1981. *Economics and Mental Health*. DHHS Publ. (ADM) 81–1114

Mechanic, D. 1980. *Mental Health and Social Policy*. New Jersey: Prentice Hall

Meyers, J., Parsons, R. C., Martin, R. 1979. *Mental Health Consultation in the Schools*. San Francisco: Jossey-Bass

Miller, G. E. 1981. Barriers to serving the chronically mentally ill. *Psychiatric Q.* 53:118–31

Miller, R. D. 1982. The least restrictive alternative: Hidden meanings and agendas. *Community Ment. Health J.* 18:46–54

Monahan, J. 1982. Three lingering issues in patient rights. See Bloom and Asher 1982, pp. 263–77

Morrissey, J. P. 1982. Deinstitutionalizing the mentally ill: Processes, outcomes, and new directions. In *Deviance and Mental Illness*, ed. W. R. Gove, Beverly Hills: Sage

Morrissey, J. P., Goldman, H. H., Klerman, L. V., et al. eds. 1980. *The Enduring Asylum: Cycles of Institutional Reform at Worcester State Hospital*. New York: Grune & Stratton

Moss, H. A., Hess, R., Swift, C., eds. 1982. *Prevention in Human Services. Early Intervention Programs for Infants*, Vol. 1. New York: Haworth

Munóz, R. F., Snowden, L. R., Kelly, J. G., eds. 1979. *Social Psychological Research in Community Settings*. San Francisco: Jossey-Bass

Murray, J. D., Keller, P. A., eds. 1982. *Innovations in Rural Mental Health*. New York: Human Sci. Press

Novaco, R. W., Monahan, J. 1980. Research in community psychology: An analysis of work published in the first 6 years of the *American Journal of Community Psychology*. *Am. J. Community Psychol.* 8:131–45

O'Neill, P. 1981. Cognitive community psychology. *Am. Psychol.* 36:457–69

O'Neill, P., Trickett, E. J. 1982. *Community Consultation*. San Francisco: Jossey-Bass

Pepper, B., Ryglewicz, H., eds. 1982. *New Directions for Mental Health Services: The Young Adult Chronic Patient*. No. 14. San Francisco: Jossey-Bass

Porritt, D. 1979. Social support in crisis: Quantity or quality. *Soc. Sci. Med.* 13A:715–21

Price, R. H., Ketterer, R., Bader, B., Monahan, J., eds. 1980. *Prevention in Mental Health: Research, Policy and Practice*. Beverly Hills: Sage

Price, R. H., Polister, P. E., eds. 1980. *Evaluation and Action in the Social Environment*. New York: Academic

Rabkin, J., Gelb, L., Lazar, J. B., eds. 1980. *Attitudes Toward the Mentally Ill: Research Prospectives*. Rep. NIMH workshop. Rockville, Md: NIMH

Ramirez, D. G. 1982. *An empirical assessment of the concept of Mexican Americans' underutilization of mental health services*. PhD thesis. Univ. Texas, Austin, DAI 43:3-B

Ramirez, M. 1983. *Psychology of the Americas: Mestizo Perspectives on Personality and Mental Health*. New York: Pergamon

Rappaport, J. 1981. In praise of paradox: A social policy of empowerment over prevention. *Am. J. Community Psychol.* 9:1–25

Rhoades, L. J. 1981. *Treating and Assessing the Chronically Mentally Ill: The Pioneering Research of Gordon L. Paul*. DHHS Publ. (ADM) 81-1100

Riessman, F. 1980. The role of the paraprofessional in the mental health crisis. *Paraprof. J.* 1:1–3

Ritter, D. R., ed. 1982. *Consultation, Education and Prevention in Community Mental Health*. Springfield: Thomas

Rodolfa, E., R., Hungerford, L. 1982. Self-help groups: A referral resource for professional therapists. *Prof. Psychol.* 13:334–53

Rogawski, A. S., ed. 1979. *New Directions for Mental Health Services: Mental Health Consultation and Community Setting*, No. 3. San Francisco: Jossey-Bass

Rose, S. M. 1979. Deciphering and deinstitu-

tionalization: complexities in policy and program analysis. *Milbank Mem. Fund Q./ Health Soc.* 57:429–57

Russo, N. P., Sobel, S. D. 1981. Sex preference in the utilization of mental health facilities. *Prof. Psychol.* 12:7–19

Rutman, I. D., ed. 1981 *Planning for Deinstitutionalization*. *Hum. Serv. Monogr. Ser. 28*. DHEW Publ. (OS) 76–130

Santos, J. D., VandenBos, G. R., eds. 1982. *Psychology and the Older Adult: Challenges for Training in the 1980's*. Washington DC: Am. Psychol. Assoc.

Sarason, S. B. 1981. *Psychology Misdirected*. New York: Free Press

Sarason, S. B., Lorentz, E. 1979. *The Challenge of the Resource Exchange Network*. San Francisco: Jossey-Bass

Schensul, S. L., Schensul, J. J. 1982. Self-help groups and advocacy. See Weber & Cohen 1982, pp. 298–336

Schulberg, H. C., Bromet, E. 1981. Strategies for evaluating the outcome of community services for the chronically mentally ill. *Am J. Psychiatry* 138:930–35

Schulberg, H. C., Killilea, M., eds. 1982. *The Modern Practice of Community Mental Health: A Volume in Honor of Gerald Caplan*. San Francisco: Jossey-Bass

Schwartz, S. R., Goldfinger, S. M. 1981. The new chronic patient: Clinical characteristics of an emerging group. *Hosp. Community Psychiatry* 32:470–74

Seidman, E., ed. 1983. *Handbook of Social Intervention*. Beverly Hills: Sage

Sheehan, S. 1982. *Is There No Place on Earth For Me?* Boston: Houghton Mifflin

Sheets, J. L., Prevost, J. A., Reihman, J. 1982. The young adult chronic patient: Three hypothesized subgroups. See Pepper & Ryglewicz 1982, pp. 15–24

Shore, M. F. 1981. Marking time in the land of plenty: Reflections on mental health in the United States. *Am. J Orthopsychiatry* 51:391–402

Shore, M. F., Shapiro, R. 1979. The effect of deinstitutionalization on the state hospital. *Hosp. Community Psychiatry* 30:605–8

Shure, M. B., Spivack, G. 1981. The problem solving approach to adjustment: a competency-building model of primary prevention. *Prev. Hum. Serv.* 1:87–103.

Silverman, W. H. 1981. *Community Mental Health: A Sourcebook for Professionals and Advisory Board Members*. New York: Praeger

Snow, D., Swift, C. 1981. *Recommended Policies and Procedures for Consultation and Education Services Within Community Mental Health Systems/Agencies*. Washington DC: Natl. Counc. Community Ment. Health Cent.

Snowden, L., ed. 1982. *Reaching the Under-

served: Mental Health Needs of Neglected Populations. Beverly Hills: Sage

Solomon, G. 1980. *Problems and Issues in Rural Community Mental Health: A Review.* ERIC Doc. Reprod. No. 182101. Lubbock. Texas Tech

Spiegel, D. 1982. Self-help and mutual support groups; A synthesis of the recent literature. See Biegel & Naparstek 1982, pp. 98–117

Spivack, G., Siegel, J., Sklaver, D., Deuschle, L., Garrett, L. 1982. The long-term patient in the community: Life style patterns and treatment implications. *Hosp. Community Psychiatry* 33:291–95

Sprafkin, J., Swift, C., Hess, R., eds. 1982. *Prevention in Human Services: Rx Televi sion: Enhancing the Preventive Impact of TV,* Vol 2. New York: Haworth

Stahler, G. J., Tash, W. R., eds. 1982. *Innovative Approaches to Mental Health Evaluation.* New York: Academic

Stein, L. I., ed. 1979. *New Directions for Mental Health Services: Community Support Systems for the Long-Term Patient,* No. 2. San Francisco: Jossey-Bass

Stein, L. I., Test, M. A. 1980. Alternative to mental hospital treatment. *Arch. Gen. Psychiatry* 37:392–97

Stelovich, S. 1979. From the hospital to the prison: A step forward in deinstitutionalization? *Hosp. Community Psychiatry* 30:618–20

Stewart, A. J., Platt, M. B. 1982. Studying women in a changing world. *J. Soc. Issues* 38:1–16

Stockdill, J. W. 1982. ADM block grants: Political context, implementation philosophy, and issues related to consultation in mental health. *Consultation* 1:20–24

Taber, M. A. 1980. *The Social Context of Helping: A Review of the Literature on Alternative Care for the Physically and Mentally Handicapped.* NIMH Stud. Soc. Change. DHHS Publ. (ADM) 80–842

Tableman, B., Marciniak, D., Johnson, D., Rodgers, R. 1982. Stress management training for women on public assistance. *Am. J. Community Psychol.* 10:357–67

Talbott, J. A., ed. 1981. *The Chronic Mentally Ill: Treatment, Programs and Systems.* New York: Human Sci. Press

Tarail, M. 1980. Current and future issues in community mental health. *Psychiatric Q.* 52:27–38

Tessler, R. C., Bernstein, A. G., Rosen, B. M., Goldman, H. H. 1982. The chronically mentally ill in community support systems. *Hosp. Community Psychiatry* 33:208–11

Tessler, R. C., Goldman, H. H. 1982. *The Chronically Mentally Ill: Assessing Com munity Support Programs.* Cambridge: Ballinger

Test, M. A. 1981. Effective community treatment of the chronically mental ill: What is necessary? *J. Soc. Issues* 37:71 86

Thoits, P. A. 1982. Conceptual methodological and theoretical problems in studying social support as a buffer against life stress. *J. Health Soc. Behav.* 23:145 59

Thompson, J. W., Bass, R. D., Witkin, M. J. 1982. Fifty years of psychiatric services: 1940–1990. *Hosp. Community Psychiatry* 33:711 21

Turner, J. C., Stockdill, J. W. 1982. *A Network for Caring: The Community Support Program of the National Institute of Mental Health.* Proc. 4 natl. conf., 1978 79. DHHS Publ. (ADM) 81- 1063

Unger, D. G., Wandersman, A. 1982. Neighboring in an urban environment. *Am. J. Community Psychol.* 10:493 509

Veroff, J., Douvan, E., Kulka, R. A. 1981a. *The Inner American.* New York: Basic Books

Veroff, J., Kulka, R., Douvan, E. 1981b. *Mental Health In America: Patterns of Help-Seeking from 1957–1976.* New York: Basic Books

Vladeck, B. C. 1980. *Unloving Care; The Nursing Home Tragedy.* New York: Basic Books

Warren, D. I. 1981. *Helping Networks: How People Cope with Problems in the Urban Community.* Notre Dame, Ind: Univ. Notre Dame Press

Weber, G. H., Cohen, L. M., eds. 1982. *Beliefs and Self-Help.* New York: Hum. Sci. Press

Weinstein, R. M. 1982. The mental hospital from the patient's point of view. In *Deviance and Mental Illness,* ed. W. R. Gove. Beverly Hills: Sage

Wellman, B. 1980. *A Guide to Network Analysis.* Univ. Toronto, Dep. Sociol.: Work. Pap. Ser.

Wellman, B., Leighton, B. 1979. Networks, neighborhood, and communities. *Urban Affairs Q.* 14:363–90

Wilcox, B. L. 1981. Social support, life stress, and psychological adjustment: A test of the buffering hypothesis. *Am. J. Community Psychol.* 9:371–85

Winslow, W. W. 1982. Changing trends in CMHCs: Keys to survival in the eighties. *Hosp. Community Psychiatry* 33:273–77

Zigler, E. F., Gordon, E. W., eds. 1981. *Day Care: Scientific and Social Policy Issues.* Boston: Auburn House

Zigler, E. F., Valentine, J., eds. 1979. *Project Head Start: A Legacy of the War on Poverty.* New York: Free Press

26

Social Problems Theory
The Constructionist View
Joseph W. Schneider

Abstract

This paper reviews and critiques the origin and development of a new specialty in sociology, the sociology of social problems. While social problems long has been a topic of sociological attention, it is only since the work of Blumer and, most especially, Spector & Kitsuse in the early 1970s, that a theoretically integrated and empirically viable tradition of writing and research has developed. The central proposition of this tradition is that social problems are the definitional activities of people around conditions and conduct they find troublesome, including others' definitional activities. In short, social problems are socially constructed, both in terms of the particular acts and interactions problem participants pursue, and in terms of the process of such activities through time. The founding theoretical statements are reviewed and the research is discussed in terms of the following categories: containing trouble and avoiding problems; the creation, ownership, and processing of problems; public regulatory bureaucracies and legal institutions; medicalizing problems and troubles; and social problems and the media. The paper closes with an overview of problems and insights of the perspective. There is a bibliography of 105 items.

INTRODUCTION

The social constructionist perspective offers a way to define, understand, and study social problems that is decidedly distinct from previous perspectives. The past decade has witnessed considerable research that, in varying degree, uses or is relevant to the social constructionist or definitional view. In this essay, I review the core statements of this perspective, describe selected research relevant to it, and discuss some of the problems with and insights from using the perspective in research.

Reproduced, with permission, from the Annual Review of Sociology, Volume 11, © 1985 by Annual Reviews, Inc.

PROGRAMMATIC STATEMENTS: MAJOR THEMES

The possibility of a research-based sociology of social problems integrated around a distinct theoretical perspective is not new. More than forty years ago, Waller (1936), Fuller & Myers (1941a, 1941b), and others pursued this goal under the banner of value-conflict theory. A renewed interest in this goal has developed in the past fifteen years (see Tallman & McGee 1971) along with a detailed critique of previous theory and a sharpened conceptualization of what such a sociology of social problems might look like.

While constructionist research and writing has not been the only sociological work on social problems, it arguably constitutes the only serious and sustained recent discussion of social problems theory—a theory *of* social problems distinct from sociological theory used *in* research on undesirable conditions. This latter accurately describes most previous sociological writing and research on social problems, whether it was guided by functionalist, Marxist, conflict theory, or other perspectives. While these latter constitute legitimate sociological work, none informs the question of whether a distinct theory of social problems is possible, what its subject matter might be, or how it might be developed in empirical research. These are precisely the questions Blumer (1971) and particularly Spector & Kitsuse (1973, 1977; Kitsuse & Spector 1973) address.

The question of just what "social problems" means as a sociological concept and how we might study such phenomena has been at the center of the dilemma surrounding this topic since its emergence in the last century. Given this long-lived confusion, Blumer (1971:298) called for a fundamental change in conceptualization to reflect a definition of social problems as "products of a process of collective definition" rather than "objective conditions and social arrangements." Traditional work, he says, reflects a "gross misunderstanding of the nature of social problems" and is virtually useless as a basis for policy since it defines social problems as objective conditions harmful to society. Moreover, sociologists have identified such conditions based on public concern. This is problematic, Blumer says, since many ostensibly "harmful conditions" are not recognized as such by the public, and thus are ignored by sociologists.

Concepts such as "deviance," "dysfunction," and "structural strain" have been "impotent" as guides for research to identify social problems. They can not account for why some conditions fail to become social problems while others do. Sociologists instead "ought to study the process by which a society comes to recognize its social problems" (Blumer 1971:300).

Spector & Kitsuse have called for a similar change, claiming: "There is no adequate definition of social problems within sociology, and there is not and never has been a sociology of social problems" (1977:1). They, like Blumer, critique the familiar functionalist perspective (e.g. Merton & Nisbet 1971) that concentrates on dysfunctional conditions and turns on abstractions such as "latent problems," "collective purposes," society as an "integrated social system," and so on. The sociologist here is a technical expert whose moral vision supersedes that of the people studied. Kitsuse & Spector say this view is empirically problematic, morally infused, and grossly presumptuous. It provides no distinctive subject matter for the sociology of social problems and no effective direction for research.

Kitsuse & Spector endorse the early value-conflict emphasis on the "subjective component" of social problems, but argue that these authors compromised a distinct theory of social problems by their continued attention to objective conditions as a necessary part of the conceptualization. This dualism and confusion as to what social problems are is also found in Blumer's essay, when he speaks of social problems as "products" of collective definitional process, as outcomes, and of objective conditions as a "corrective for ignorance and misinformation" about the "objective makeup of social problems" (Blumer 1971:305). Even Becker's (1966) view of social problems endorses this dualism. This is precisely what Spector & Kitsuse reject. Blumer also cites policy relevance as a criterion to evaluate theory, and implies that public definitions of social problems are somehow inadequate bases for sociological theory (cf. Manis 1984, on "public" definitions). Spector & Kitsuse say that these differences confound the value-conflict approach and thus make it a poor guide for empirical research.

Conventional usage of the term social problems makes it difficult to distinguish what Spector & Kitsuse see as crucial, namely, that it refers to a social process of definition and to the activities that move this process along. For Kitsuse & Spector, participants' definitional activities *constitute* the social problem (Rains 1975, Woolgar 1983), rather than leading to social problems as a product or outcome (cf. Mauss 1975).

Social problems are "*the activities of groups making assertions of grievances and claims with respect to some putative conditions*" (Kitsuse & Spector 1973:415, emphasis in original). Social problems sociology, so defined, should "account for the *emergence and maintenance of claim-making and responding activities*" (Kitsuse & Spector, 1973:415, emphasis in original). Claims making includes: "demanding services, filling out forms, lodging complaints, filing lawsuits, calling press conferences, writing letters of protest, passing resolutions, publishing exposes, placing ads in newspapers, supporting or opposing some governmental practice or policy, setting up picket lines or boycotts. . . ." (Spector & Kitsuse 1977:79). To study the causes of social problems is to examine how such activities come about and how they have been sustained. Toward this end, Spector & Kitsuse, like Fuller & Myers, Blumer, and others, suggest an heuristic, four-stage natural history model.

Stage one comprises "collective attempts to remedy a condition that some group perceives and judges offensive and undesirable. . . . Initial social problems activities consist of attempts to transform private troubles into public issues . . . and . . . the contingencies of this transformation process" (Spector & Kitsuse 1973:148). How claims and grievances are formed and presented, the varieties and nature of the claims and grievances, strategies to press these claims and gain wider attention and support, the power of the group(s) making claims, and the creation of a public controversy are important issues.

Stage two begins with recognition of these claims by "governmental agencies or other official and influential institutions." To continue beyond stage two a social problem must involve "an institution . . . to deal with the claims and complaints concerning the condition in question" (Spector & Kitsuse 1973:154). Social problems thus become routinized in an organization charged with doing something about the putative conditions.

Spector & Kitsuse say that whereas past natural history models end with legitimation and implementation, theirs is open-ended and takes official acceptance as possible grounds for a "new generation" of definitional activities around this official response. When participants claim such response is problematic, *stage three* begins. *Stage four* is marked by claimants' "contention that it is no longer possible to 'work within the system' . . ." and their attempts to develop alternative institutions (Spector & Kitsuse 1973:156).

In their view, sociologists who act as experts on problematic conditions are social problems participants. They become part of the problem rather than analysts of it. Whether he or she "will be treated as a scientist by other participants in the process and accorded the special status of a disinterested and unbiased expert is a problematic empirical question" (Spector & Kitsuse 1977:70). This means sociologists of social problems should not concern themselves with the validity of participants' (their colleagues included) claims about conditions, but with how such claims and definitions are created, documented, pressed, and kept alive. Documenting claims or definitions about conditions constitutes participation. The point is to account for the viability of these claims, not to judge whether they are true. And while social problems participants attribute values to their own and others' activities, sociologists of social problems should not. Gusfield (1984) has characterized this stance as being "on the side" or neutral, rather than choosing "whose side" we are on (Becker 1967).

Besides crediting Fuller & Myers, Becker, and Blumer as important resources in developing their constructionist view, Spector & Kitsuse cite Mauss (1975) and his attention to definitions in his analysis of social problems as social movements. They endorse Ross & Staines's (1971) emphasis on the politics of the definitional process, and they cite as particularly relevant the Hewitt & Hall (1973) analysis of how participants use "quasi-theories" to order problematic situations.

RELEVANT RESEARCH
Containing Trouble and Avoiding Problems

Logically prior to but thus far relatively ignored in research are those diverse definitional activities that occur before professional, bureaucratic, and media categories and personnel become involved. Emerson & Messinger (1977) see such informal reactions as "trouble" and as forerunners of official labeling.

Most research on this informal activity examines how normal others use vernacular categories of mental illness to define troublesome persons. Before Emerson & Messinger (1977) are the well-known studies by Yarrow et al (1955), Sampson et al (1962), Lemert (1962), and Goffman (1959.1969). Goldner (1982) continues this tradition in a study of how others react to "pronoids" in various bureaucratic settings, and Lynch (1983) studied how normals respond to and manage "crazies" in everyday settings.

Research on the origins and development of trouble is not limited to craziness and mental illness. Shearing & Stenning's (1983) study of private security in Canada and the United States shows how owners of mass private property (e.g. shopping malls, apartment complexes, college campuses) define threats to security in precisely such a prebureaucratic, prepublic (in this case precrime) way. Public labeling and processing is something owners usually want to avoid. Private security agents are hired to control anything the owners do not like. This can include behaviors not in violation of the law (e.g. absenteeism, breaches of confidentiality), as well as those that are in violation but not troublesome to owners (e.g. victimless crimes are ignored). By making prevention more important than retribution or restitution, owners and their security forces create a new kind of offender—the employee who allows the theft, damage, or breach to occur. The ultimate wrong is to be nonvigilant in loyalty to owners' interests (see also, Ghezzi 1983, on private control of insurance fraud).

Ball & Lilly (1984) analyze data from a study of a motel used for clandestine sexual encounters to see how motel owners and their staff work to deflect problem-defining activities by three relevant publics: the morally concerned citizenry, the police, and the patrons. The authors show how motel staff attempt to take the role of these three others toward their operations so as to prevent or modify conditions that might become grounds for claims making. They demonstrate that just as conditions are not inherently problematic, neither are they inherently normal. The staff worked hard to create and sustain definitions of the motel as a tolerated and even desirable part of what they saw as a potentially critical environment.

Schneider (1984) studied moral vocabularies used by antismoking and smoking respondents to see how they defined and dealt with trouble around smoking in various public and private settings. He details how antismoke people made claims (or did not) against smokers. While respondents used many negative words to describe smoking and smokers in the interviews, they found confronting bothersome smokers considerably more difficult. The best values to ground their claims were their own health interests and their rights. These claimants and responders were sensitive to the importance of the words they used. Personal dislike alone was considered insufficient grounds for claims.

The language of claims is also important in a study by Cohn & Gallagher (1984) of a social problem involving a gay student group at the University of Maine, a proposed gay conference, a local newspaper, and a group of fundamentalist ministers. Initial claims by the ministers against the University and the gay student group were couched in Biblical terms of sin and immorality. They claimed that the University was condoning such conduct. The University defended itself with a Constitutional and civil rights vocabulary, without mentioning homosexuality or gays. This was strategic. The University thus assured that the issue would not be joined, that they and their critics would not communicate in the ministers' more perilous moral rhetoric. Various sympathetic yet conventional audiences could then support the University while leaving their private opinions about homosexuality unspoken. The case demonstrates how responses are contingent upon, but not determined by initial claims. It also shows that respondents may want not to debate the issue as framed by those initiating claims, particularly if these claims are in unfriendly or difficult vocabularies. Smokers, for instance, felt there was virtually no effective defense against others' health claims.

The Creation, Ownership, and Processing of Problems

The most popular topic for constructionist research has been the creation of bureaucratic and professional categories for problematic conditions, conduct, and persons. Coincidental to Spector & Kitsuse's work, Gusfield (1975,1976,1981), pursuing past interests in the nature of symbolic action (Gusfield 1963,1967), has raised these questions in research on public definitions and policy toward drinking, driving, and accidents in the United States.

Gusfield begins by noting the dominance of one view of this problem: accidents are caused by a category of drivers, "the drunk driver," and their careless and dangerous conduct. Much official data that detail characteristics of the driver, the presence of alcohol, and degree of intoxication have been produced to support this view (cf Kitsuse & Cicourel 1963). Policy has followed accordingly: make drunk drivers control themselves and/or keep them from driving. The laws and public programs that reflect this dominant view, Gusfield argues, contribute to our sense of social order.

To underscore the selective quality of this construction, he details some of what the dominant view omits. Where are such systematic data on vehicle design, the roadway, age and condition of the car, weather, and available emergency assistance as related to "accidents involving alcohol"? How different would definitions and solutions of the problem be were they built on these data?

Gusfield emphasizes connections between the organizational ownership of the problem—a concept he aligns with Becker's (1963) concept, "moral entrepreneur," the construction of supportive scientific facts and causal explanations—and the attribution of political responsibility to "do something about" the problematic condition. This affirms the sociology of knowledge theme in the constructionist approach (see also Aronson 1984) and shows how scientists and experts participate in social problems they purport to analyze. Champions and owners of this favored view of drinking and driving have been The National Safety Council, major auto and life insurance companies, the legal system, the alcoholism industry, and the National Institute on Alcohol Abuse and Alcoholism (NIAAA). Only recently have they been challenged by other groups offering alternate definitions, explanations, and interventions.

Gusfield shows how social context—an important element in constructionist analysis (Woolgar & Pawluch 1985)—facilitates these drunk driver–centered definitions and claims. These favored definitions and explanations allow social drinkers to continue to drive unperturbed and are resources for the alcohol and alcoholism industries to portray the problem of drinking as due to certain sick drinkers rather than the drink. Wiener (1981) examines this social world of alcoholism treatment, policy, and research, and the connections between its participants and their diverse, shifting definitions and claims.

The study of organizational ownership and management of social problems directs attention to how people do this work, to how they handle various kinds of problems and troubles. This parallels earlier work on the organizational processing of deviants and deviance. Recent studies examine how various workers, clients, and others negotiate these definitions. Schwartz & Kahne (1983, Kahne & Schwartz 1978) studied how professionals and clients in a college psychiatric unit negotiated the nature and treatment of students' troubles. Maynard (1982) studied plea bargaining sessions to uncover how court officials use defendants' personal attributes to make sentencing decisions. Miller (1983) examined how workers in a work incentive program used conciliation sessions to reaffirm program morality about responsibility and encourage conformity among troublesome clients. Spencer (1983) examined the familiar probation officer–client relationship and how probation officers negotiate a moral character for their clients to fit the sentencing recommendations they make.

Some studies have focused on how workers, clients, and others use official categories or rules so work can proceed. Joffe (1978) studied how lay abortion counselors balance their ideological support of abortion services with their revulsion at clients who refuse to acknowledge the moral aspects of abortion. McCleary et al (1982) examined how workers in police departments code officers' observations using Uniform Crime Report codes. Pontell et al (1982) studied how California State government reviewed possible fraud and abuse by physicians who used the public medical insurance program. Lynxwiler et al (1983) show how mine inspectors, working for the Office of Surface Mining Reclamation and Enforcement, use discretion in making and processing claims against mining companies. Peyrot (1982) analyzed how community mental health workers used discretion to categorize clients so as to make the best use of scarce resources.

Routinizing and managing people's problems is the essence of the "public interest state"—that complex of federal and state administrative rules, regulations, and personnel that define eligibility for various public endorsements and support (Reich 1964). Spector (1981) says that personnel in these public bureaucracies and programs define troublesome people as "ineligible" to receive benefits (rather than criminal, deviant, or sick) and manage them accordingly.

Public Regulatory Bureaucracies and Legal Institutions

Public regulatory bureaucracies both initiate and receive social problems claims (Chauncey 1980, Randall & Short 1983). Several studies show government agencies as social problems entrepreneurs. Becker's (1963) analysis of how the Treasury Department's Bureau of Narcotics defined the "marijuana problem" is well known (see also Galliher & Walker 1977). Gusfield (1981) and Wiener (1981) point to the NIAAA as a central participant in the world of alcoholism. Nuehring & Markle (1974) and Troyer & Markle (1983, Markle & Troyer 1979) identify the Public Health Service, the Federal Trade Commission, the Civil Aeronautics Board, the Surgeon General, and former Health Education and Welfare Secretary Joseph Califano as important entrepreneurs against smoking.

Chauncey (1980) studied how NIAAA officials tried to convince the nation of the seriousness of teenage drinking. These attempts largely failed because NIAAA was unable to secure endorsement from various private and nonofficial public groups. Public reception ranged from minimal to confused. Specific local teenage drinking programs were few, parents did not buy the definition, doctors did not support it, it had to compete with the drug problem, school officials did not see the problem, and it was rarely reported to police, who, in any case, had little access to special programs. Troyer & Markle (1983) show that antismoking claims made by government agencies have fared considerably better in terms of such grass roots and organization support (see also Ball & Lilly 1982, on the shifting fate of margarine).

When bureaucracies receive citizens' complaints, these claims are transformed by a language that is created and controlled by experts or bureaucrats (cf Latour 1983). Citizens' complaints become part of a system of proper procedures. Murray's (1982) study of the abolition of the short-handled hoe in California farm work makes this clear. While workers and their attorney won the case against managers and the hoe, Murray asks what they did not and could not win, namely, attention to the hazards of all corporate production and to power differences between workers and management. Where claims are made, that is, to whom, can constrain subsequent definitional activities in loosely predictable ways—if one has detailed and current knowledge of the bureaucracy (see also Randall & Short 1983). Without the counsel of legal experts, claimants usually do not possess this knowledge. Murray describes how these experts can control and even change the problem.

Randall & Short (1983) studied a controversy over an Idaho mining company's policy requiring women workers to be sterilized to continue work in an area declared a risk for genetic damage. OSHA initiated claims against the company's policy on behalf of these women. OSHA ultimately lost this case because it could not marshall the necessary external power resources. A court rejected its claims to jurisdiction in such cases, and the Ford Administration was explicitly hostile to all OSHA actions (see also Calavita 1983, and Murray 1982 for similar views of the larger political context and such agencies' claims). The company's claims, definitions, and policy remained intact.

Calavita's (1983) study of the dismantling of OSHA, especially by the Reagan Administration, uncovers the paradox of one part of government making claims against another. By replacing the heads of OSHA (and the FTC) with antiregulators, the Administration was able not only to undermine these agencies and their claims, but to discredit the agency's past work publicly through media stories. Randall & Short say such public agencies are able to make claims, propose general remedies, and gain legitimacy all in one set of activities, effectively collapsing Spector & Kitsuse's first and second stages.

Kitsuse et al (1984) studied the *kikokushijo mondai*—returning student problem—in Japan. In contrast to the Randall & Short case, their study shows how a receptive context—the highly stratified educational system that is considered an essential prerequisite to career success in Japan as a Japanese—can be used to enhance the viability of claims made to a government bureaucracy. This problem consisted of definitional activities by diplomatic, academic, and corporate parents about the educational deficiencies they felt their school-age children experienced upon returning to Japan from foreign residence and education. The authors detail the many and varied ways this problem has become institutionalized, both in the Japanese educational system and in the larger society, while alternative, positive definitions of the returning students' situation (they are "broadened" and "internationalized") have foundered.

Filing a law suit is a common form of claims making today. People, groups, and institutions, including the state, attempt to transform various troubles into legal issues. Such claims making allows us to observe how social problems participants use social structure as a resource.

One topic of study is how various devalued people and their lawyers have challenged owners by invoking the Constitution. Kitsuse (1980) describes how these people have "come out" to demand their civil rights and integrity. Spector (1981) describes these claims as demands to government for "entitlements." These deviants have gone beyond deviance to create new social problems, sometimes with radical social and political implications (see Weitz 1984).

Civil rights, public interest, and consumer law have grown apace. The law here becomes a set of official symbolic categories for making claims to effect social change (cf Gusfield 1981). Using this law, attorneys for black people, the poor, consumers, juveniles, mental patients, prisoners, and others, have attacked a variety of traditional definitions and practices in our public life.

Feminists have been one such challenging group, and rape a particularly important object of their attention. Rose (1977) calls the social problem of rape "a by-product of the feminist movement" and details how women's groups have attacked traditional rape laws and police and court treatment of rape victims. These feminist criticisms offer new definitions of rape (e.g. Brownmiller 1975) and an analysis of its source in traditional gender roles. Alternate institutions run for women by women, some who are themselves rape victims, have grown. As with gay activists and reformed alcoholics, these claimants have taken ownership of the problem away from traditional experts and bureaucrats and made it the object of their and others' routine work (see also Tierney 1982, on the battered women problem).

Spector (1981) and Spector & Batt (1983) compare criminal and civil court procedures concerning rape. These two legal institutions offer victims distinct experiences and opportunities. To define rape as a crime makes the conflict one between the state and the accused. Rape victims sometimes do not even participate in the state's case, which is controlled by lawyers and the judge. If they do, they act as witnesses for the state rather than in their own interests. Spector & Batt use Christie's (1977) idea of conflicts as property to argue that criminal categories, procedures, and professionals steal this conflict from rape victims and transform it into a legal case that seems little related to the victim's experience. By contrast, civil law defines rape as a wrong done to an individual. The state provides the formal setting, judge, and rules to guide the claims-making process. Lawyers (ideally) advise rather than manipulate clients. Rape victims can own their conflicts and express moral outrage against offenders. Spector & Batt examined 31 civil rape cases since the turn of the century and found evidence that rape victims' experiences, compared with those of victims in criminal proceedings, support their analysis.

In another study of legal change, Frank (1983) shows how civil law has replaced criminal law in problems of health and safety in the workplace and the environment since the turn of the century. Through detailed attention to major participants, definitions, and contests in this history, Frank effectively challenges "'knee-jerk' applications of conflict theory" that portray this change as a simple function of corporate capitalist power (see also Donnelly's 1982 study of the origins of the Occupational Safety and Health Act of 1970).

Medicalizing Problems and Troubles

Much recent research on the medicalization of deviance draws on the constructionist perspective. This work examines the implications of these new medical meanings and personnel for participants and the society, and the ownership struggles between professional and lay claims makers. In an early paper, Conrad (1975) draws on Becker (1963), Freidson (1970), and Zola (1972) to describe the origins, rise, and legitimacy of the medical diagnosis hyperkinesis at the hands of a small number of medical researchers, two drug companies, a Congressional Subcommittee on Privacy, and the Association for Children with Learning Disabilities. Conrad contrasts the implications of these medical definitions and interventions around children's troublesome behavior with those contained in the deviant labels "bad" or "problem" child. These new definitions solve problems for teachers and parents responsible for children's difficult behavior, and displace social contextual explanations potentially critical of the educational status quo.

Pfohl's (1977) analysis of child abuse also identifies professional moral entrepreneurs: a few pediatric radiologists who created the new diagnosis, "Battered Child Syndrome." Context is again important in that these radiologists saw this "discovery," says Pfohl, as a welcome opportunity to do significant, career-enhancing work.

The Conrad and Pfohl studies highlight an important kind of professional claims making: scientific publication in a respected professional journal. Such publication is usually not seen as relevant social problems data. These studies also show that those outside medicine can use medical definitions to their own ends, which experts may see as contrary to their own. When professionals become social problems participants, they often must share definitional prerogatives with diverse individuals and groups (see Wiener 1981). Ownership does not always ensure complete control.

Schneider (1978) studied the viability of the "humanitarian" disease concept of alcoholism and found that medical experts in fact were not the primary entrepreneuers. Alcoholics Anonymous, a few scientists and "recovered alcoholics," research centers at Yale and Rutgers Universities, the National Council on Alcoholism, and the NIAAA were the most active political champions of this disease definition (cf Wiener 1981). Similarly, Johnson & Hufbauer (1982) found parents of Sudden Infant Death Syndrome (SIDS) victims were the most active claimants behind new scientific and Congressional awareness and research support for SIDS. These lay champions used scientific research, official medical statements, and public sympathy as important contextual resources to establish the viability of their claims. Troyer & Markle (1983, 1984) reiterate this kind of lay participation around problems of smoking and coffee drinking.

Conrad & Schneider (1980; Schneider & Conrad 1980) studied mental illness, alcoholism, opiate addiction, children's deviant behavior, and homosexuality as prime cases where medical definitions and technology have been championed over sin and crime designations. They used medical journals, professional speeches, editorials, news stories, popular magazines, autobiographies, historical studies, and court cases as sources of data. They identified the actors behind these historic changes and how this definitional work was done. Those who could establish their prerogatives to define the problem and designate who should be responsible for it were powerful figures in these social dramas (cf Gusfield 1975, Latour 1983, Peyrot 1984).

Lay persons can be critics as well as champions of professional owners' definitions and can even win this ownership. The demedicalization of homosexuality illustrates this. Following Spector (1977), Conrad & Schneider (1980) show how gay liberation advocates, with the support of a few insider psychiatrists, challenged the medical disease diagnosis of homosexuality. Using the psychiatrists' own medical, scientific culture, these lay challengers scored a definitional victory that led ultimately to gays themselves becoming the new owner-experts of homosexuality as a "lifestyle." McCrea (1983) studied how a few doctors championed the "deficiency disease" of menopause and a treatment of estrogen replacement. They were effectively challenged by feminists, who used independent scientific research on the link between cancer and estrogen therapy, who defined menopause as a natural part of women's lives, and who claimed that the disease view was sexist. Troyer & Markle's (1984) study of the definition of coffee reiterates the importance of sympathetic professionals and/or supportive research for such challenge. This research enlightens us about how stage three claims are made and successfully pursued.

Studies of the medicalization of deviance also illustrate how professionals create the problems they own and treat (see Hughes 1971, Freidson 1970). In doing this, they make moral judgments both in the technical language of the profession and in the popular moral meanings so far as this language often incorporates popular moral meanings. This second kind of morality seems to be a useful resource for critics, as McCrea's (1983) study demonstrates. Billings & Urban's (1982) analysis of the medical construction of transsexualism and the transsexual shows how doctors became dupes of well-schooled patients who effected key diagnostic criteria to gain treatment, which they later criticized. Loseke & Cahill (1984) describe and criticize—that is, participate in the social problem of—the way experts on battered women label the women who remain in such relationships as unable to control their lives and in need of experts' counsel.

Pawluch's (1983) analysis of the history of pediatrics shifts attention from problematic individuals to how some pediatricians responded to a declining professional market. As childhood diseases and problems of baby feeding were controlled, pediatricians had both less work and less medically worthwhile work to do. Some began to champion new definitions of the baby doctor's role to include, as one advocate said, "shades of difference between health and disease, conditions whereby the child is not invalided, but his social and individual efficacy is decreased" (Pawluch 1983:457; see also Riessman 1983, on women as vulnerable to such medical definitions).

Such professional claims making about problematic conditions in the society is found in science more generally. Aronson's (1982) study of the origins and institutionalization of nutrition research shows how conditions outside science that were seen to threaten powerful interests provided an opportunity for scientist-entrepreneurs to gain financial support and legitimacy by defining themselves and their science as a solution to those "problems." Nutrition's leading late nineteenth-century advocate, Wilbur Atwater, argued he could solve the problem of labor unrest over wages by teaching workers to buy and prepare food in a more economical and healthy way. Such claims appealed to capitalist owners, who sought a productive and cooperative workforce without raising wages. Nutrition advocates finally won official endorsement from Congress, with an appropriation to support their research in US Agricultural Experiment Stations.

Aronson says this case shows some of the conditions under which scientists will make such activist, "social problems interpretive claims" (Aronson 1984) to groups and organizations outside science. When resources to support research are scarce and the opportunity for public funding exists, such enterprising activities might be expected. Johnson & Hufbauer's (1982) study of SIDS shows a contrasting situation in which demands from parents for more research were important as both a direct and indirect impetus to a new medical research community (see also Wiener 1981, on alcoholism research). Latour (1983) makes the most bold argument here, citing the history of Pasteur's capture of the anthrax problem in late nineteenth century France to show how distinctions between science and society, upon close scrutiny, virtually disappeared in the face of compelling scientific facts. Clearly, problems in the larger society and problems in science are often linked, with significant consequences for social organization.

Social Problems and the News Media

Social problems participants usually hope the news media will help them publicize claims and thus enhance their legitimacy. Research shows, however, that the media do not function simply as mirrors claimants can use to reflect "what is really going on." Rather, they decidedly shape the images they convey. Newsworkers are, in short, the true "newsmakers" (Glasgow University Media Group 1980, Fishman 1980), and relevant questions include the following: What happens to claims and definitions that go to media organizations? How do they emerge? What is the place of the media in the social problems process? Do media communicate claims and definitions of their own, quite aside from what other claims makers say?

Fishman (1978) shows that a crime wave against the elderly reported by three New York City media organizations was, in fact, a growing, overlapping media coverage. He details how editors created this news theme to solve routine problems of news work. The theme became a media wave when it was reiterated in other news reports. Fishman calls crime news ideological because it reports crime as the police see it (e.g. street crimes and violent crimes) and because routine newswork produces stories that convey meanings all their own. For instance, news workers recognize good and newsworthy stories by using criteria that systematically filter out things that are not (see also Wiener, 1981:207–211, discussion of media coverage of the Rand Report).

News reporters' routine dependence for information on official owners of problems effectively discourages interpretations foreign to or in conflict with those interpretations on which owner organizations rest. This is what Randall & Short (1983) suggest about the link between OSHA and other official bureaucracies and the media. These agencies are a news beat; they regularly provide the information reporters use to do their work.

Gitlin's (1980) study of how the media covered the New Left and the antiwar movement of the 1960s describes how claims makers who challenge dominant institutions fare in encounters with the media. He studied coverage of antiwar activity by the *New York Times* and CBS News in 1965. When movement spokespersons sought to use the media to convey their views of American society and the war, they found to their dismay that what came out usually gave short shrift to important ideas, but gave full play to conflict, the dramatic, and the bizarre. Individuals in action were important to reporters, who are taught that objectivity and balance are produced by quoting spokespersons for various sides. Gitlin shows how the media created these spokespersons, how they made them "movement leaders" and then celebrities who, overwhelmed by the spotlight, became less concerned with conveying movement claims. The agendas that shape rudimentary news work, then, augur poorly for seriously conveying protest arguments.

Tierney's (1982) research on wife beating reiterates Gitlin's point about what media cover. Wife beating was a topic that was new and controversial, contained violence, was timely and serious, and touched on the familiar themes of feminism, equality, and family life; all of these could still be handled in an entertaining way. Tierney argues that as definitions of wife beating were publicized, social service agencies responded to the conditions described.

Cohn & Gallagher (1984), in the study noted above, detail an incident in which a "conservative" Maine newspaper was involved in a social problem concerning a homosexual group and a planned gay conference at the University of Maine. Fundamentalist ministers attacked the University for allowing the student group on campus and for hosting the conference, after they read about it in the paper (one wonders if a Regents' board meeting was a news beat). The newspaper became a forum for and reporter of the controversy. The editors pursued a delicate balance between their sense of the paper's responsibility to the community, good journalism, and local definitions of the kind of paper theirs was (it did not cause news or stir up trouble). Once the problem developed, it had to be covered, but in a way that would not harm the University and its elite trustees—important figures in the community. By reporting the University's Constitutional defense and the ministers' demands that the University be punished by a legislative budget cut, the paper helped channel the problem. The ministers became the threat against whom the University and community had to be protected.

It is particularly revealing, Cohn & Gallagher say, that, coincidental to this controversy, a major revision of the Maine Criminal Code that decriminalized homosexual intercourse was being voted into law. A second gay conference was planned at the University for a year later. There was no coverage of and virtually no public attention directed to either. Asked about this lack of coverage, editors said that good news stories were about conflict and controversy. There were none around either event; they were not newsworthy. By using these journalistic criteria and their sense of being a responsible paper, editors precluded more social problems concerning homosexuality.

PROBLEMS WITH AND INSIGHTS OF THE PERSPECTIVE

Problems

CONDITIONS AND SOCIAL PROBLEMS   An important source of both confusion and disagreement among those using the constructionist perspective is the question of how conditions should figure in social problems analysis. As Rains (1975) focused attention on the "deviant behavior" that societal reaction theory keeps in the background, there has been much comment on Spector & Kitsuse's argument that conditions, as regarded by the sociologist, are irrelevant to a definitional analysis. That these difficulties beset both the labeling and constructionist perspectives suggests that the confusion is perhaps in part a product of the perspective's requirements.

Woolgar (1983), and Woolgar & Pawluch (1985) appropriately note the tension in some constructionist research between a view that sees the natural world, especially in the form of social context, giving rise to various or alternative accounts of what *is* (the "mediative" position), and the view that these accounts, definitions, and claims are "constitutive" of reality (cf Berger & Luckmann 1966). This is the same tension Rains (1975) identifies in labeling work. The criticism is justified for many of the studies identified as constructionist and discussed here.

Sociologists are members of the society they study. The perspective requires them as analysts to suspend both commonsense commitments about what social problems are—e.g. undesirable conditions—and their own scientific judgments about which claims and definitions about these putative conditions are true. The latter proves to be especially difficult (see Gusfield 1984; Aronson 1984). Moreover, as Gusfield (1984) notes, being on the side (that is, standing aside) in the study of social controversies (especially involving differentially powerful participants) has become professionally unpopular as well as personally unsatisfying.

Social problems participants, however, typically neither treat conditions as putative nor suspend their moral convictions, although the perspective does not preclude this possibility. Instead, they see social problems definitions as reflective of the objective reality (Woolgar 1983) in which the problem resides. The sociologist's problem is to avoid participation and, especially, to avoid defending or challenging claims and definitions about putative conditions. This includes avoiding an ironic stance toward some participants' definitions. Few of the authors considered here maintain this distinction consistently in their research. Some make no attempt to do so, even though they call their work definitional.

CLAIMS, DEFINITIONS, AND VIABILITY   Spector & Kitsuse's emphasis on claims and claims making has been broadened. They encourage this in their examples (how "floods" and "morons" are products of the social problems process) and by use of the word definitional. Clearly, some of the activities studied fit the definition of claim the authors cite (Spector & Kitsuse 1977:78), but much is described more accurately as definitional. Researchers should consider as data all verbal and nonverbal behavior that conveys meaning about the problematic condition or object of attention. The import of language and how it shapes interpretations and conduct is here enormous. Definitional activities should be treated as an inclusive but carefully grounded concept.

The concept *viability*, important to judging social problems development, should be clarified. Spector & Kitsuse say that viable claims and definitions are those that "live" and that claimants can "get away with." A clear definition of viability is necessary for accurate data collection and to compare the development of various problems. Viability is evident when participants give credibility to claims and definitions, when they treat them as valid. Viability is often produced by media coverage. It is produced when officials and professionals warrant definitions, implement them, and accept responsibility for problematic conditions. We need a clearer understanding of precisely how participants' activities affect the viability of claims and definitions.

NATURAL HISTORY   The concept *natural history* is heuristic and directs attention to loose similarities across cases. It leads easily, however, to premature generalization and prediction (R. J. Troyer 1983, unpublished manuscript). Since generalizing is an essential part of scientific work, a cautious strategy would be to examine case studies from similar settings (see Peyrot 1984). One might study problems involving public regulatory bureaucracies. What generalizations might be made about how the news media figure in social problems? What casts of characters emerge at various points in this process? One pitfall to avoid here is the ad hoc, overly topical quality of so much past social problems writing. By using comparative, analytic categories defined by their effects on viability, or examining how the definitional process is moved along by the activities in question (J. I. Kitsuse 1984, personal communication), this might be avoided.

Wiener (1981), in her study of the politics of alcoholism, argues that the sequential aspect of natural history models probably misleads us about the definitional process. She believes a more accurate view is one of "overlapping," simultaneous, "continuously ricocheting interaction" (Wiener 1981:7). A natural history model may encourages us to overstate the extent to which kinds of activities occur only at certain points. This seems likely for Spector & Kitsuse's stage one and stage three activities. Wiener's view reinforces Spector & Kitsuse's argument that the social problems process is open-ended rather than moving to some logical end point (see also Peyrot 1984).

SOCIAL MOVEMENTS SOCIOLOGY VS SOCIAL PROBLEMS SOCIOLOGY?   A recent question is whether or not the definitional perspective on social problems is sufficiently distinct from social movements theory to warrant continued attention. Mauss (1984 and unpublished observations) argues it is not, and that social problems are always outcomes of social movements. To study the latter is to study the former.

R. Troyer (1984, unpublished manuscript) uses both definitional and social movements theory and notes the similarities and differences between the definitional approach, the standard structural social movements view, and the more recent resource mobilization perspective on social movements. A traditional social movements approach (e.g. Smelser 1963), with its emphasis on structural strain (to explain grievances) and on organizational considerations and membership recruitment, is contrasted by Troyer with the constructionist view of social problems. Troyer sees the differences as substantial. He also compares the latter with the resource mobilization view (Oberschall 1973, McCarthy & Zald 1973, 1977). While there are general similarities, resource

mobilization's emphasis on structural conditions, social movement organizations, and successful outcomes, and its neglect of meaning lead to research
agendas quite distinct from those described here. Rather than argue, as Mauss
does, that social problems theory should be subsumed by social movements
theory, we might better argue that social movements are an example of the
social problems process. Moreover, the topics and data of the research cited
here seem to challenge the conclusion that the definitional view simply reproduces social movements research.

Insights

The insights of the constructionist perspective as detailed by Spector & Kitsuse
appear intact, criticisms notwithstanding. We can still ask, where is a theoretically integrated, empirically based, original research tradition in social problems sociology prior to the work cited here? Have researchers used the core
statements and subsequent research to form new and promising questions, as a
sociology of social problems? The work described here seems to support an
affirmative reply—quite aside from how this or that study could be improved,
or whether elements of the core statements are vague or undeveloped. On the
other hand, research based ostensibly on a condition-focused approach, or even
on a subjective/objective elements approach to social problems has given us
few distinct insights. Like the modest claims made by the founders of labeling
theory, the definitional view should be judged more by what it has called for
and stimulated than what it ignores. Unlike the labeling tradition, Spector &
Kitsuse have proposed bold changes. Rather than offering merely another view
of social problems sociology, they and others have launched a new speciality
and stimulated a sizeable body of work. Whether or not this work would have
been done as social movements, Marxist, or conflict sociology we cannot say.

New questions have been asked about what social problems are and how they
should be studied. This approach avoids, moreover, some of the major criticisms of labeling by giving attention to the political and historical quality of
collective definitional process, and by rejecting an oversocialized view of
deviants as "helpless, hapless" victims (see Conrad & Schneider 1980, Kitsuse
1980; Spector 1981). One who carefully reviews this and similar work can
hardly reiterate these familiar criticisms (but see Piven 1981).

The perspective and much of the research reaffirms a major strength of
labeling, namely, the independence of meaning from the objects to which it is
or may be attached by sentient actors as they create, recreate, and are created by
social life (cf Matza, 1969, Giddens 1976). Quite contrary to Piven's critique
(1981), actors' agency is the source of social action in the constructionist's
world.

Finally, this and future work may breathe new life into deviance sociology, particularly as it breaks down old divisions and creates new, more theoretically coherent ones. What might a sociology of trouble or a sociology of morality look like, distinct from theory and research that concentrate on why people behave in ways that happen to break rules or on the social distribution of this behavior and how to control and punish it? I do not say this pejoratively but rather on the assumption that success in these diverse endeavors might be enhanced if we concentrate on the questions our theories ask and on where these theories are incomplete rather than attacking each other because we pursue different questions.

ACKNOWLEDGMENTS:

This review benefited from conversations with John Kitsuse, Malcolm Spector, and Ronald Troyer. Thanks to them. They of course bear no responsibility for my interpretations.

Literature Cited

Aronson, N. 1982. Nutrition as a social problem: A case study of entrepreneurial strategy in science. *Soc. Probl.* 29:474–86

Aronson, N. 1984. Science as a claims-making activity: Implications for social problems research. In *Studies in the Sociology of Social Problems*, ed. J. W. Schneider, J. I. Kitsuse, pp. 1–30. Norwood, NJ: Ablex

Ball, R. A., Lilly, J. R. 1982. The menace of margarine: The rise and fall of a social problem. *Soc. Probl.* 29:488–98

Ball, R. A., Lilly, J. R. 1984. When is a 'problem' not a problem?: deflection activities in a clandestine motel. See Schneider and Kitsuse 1984, pp. 114–39

Becker, H. S. 1963. *Outsiders.* New York: Free

Becker, H. S., ed. 1966. *Social Problems: A Modern Approach.* New York: Wiley

Becker, H. S. 1967. Whose side are we on? *Soc. Probl.* 14:239–47

Berger, P., Luckmann, T. 1966. *The Social Construction of Reality.* New York: Doubleday

Billings, D. B., Urban, T. 1982. The sociomedical construction of transsexualism: An interpretation and critique. *Soc. Probl.* 29:266–82

Blumer, H. 1971. Social problems as collective behavior. *Soc. Probl.* 18:298–306

Brownmiller, S. 1975. *Against Our Will: Men, Women and Rape.* New York: Simon & Schuster

Calavita, K. 1983. The demise of the Occupational Safety and Health Administration: A case study in symbolic action. *Soc. Probl.* 30:437–48

Chauncey, R. L. 1980. New careers for moral entrepreneurs: Teenage drinking. *J. Drug Issues* 10:45–70

Christie, N. 1977. Conflicts as property. *Br. J. Criminol.* 17:1–15

Cohn, S. F., Gallagher, J. E. 1984. Gay movements and legal change: Some aspects of the dynamics of a social problem. *Soc. Probl.* 32:72–86

Conrad, P. 1975. The discovery of hyperkinesis: Notes on the medicalization of deviant behavior. *Soc. Probl.* 23:12–21

Conrad, P., Schneider, J. W. 1980. *Deviance and Medicalization: From Badness to Sickness.* St. Louis: Mosby

Donnelly, P. G. 1982. The origins of the Occupational Safety and Health Act of 1970. *Soc. Probl.* 30:13–25

Emerson, R. M., Messinger, S. L. 1977. The micro-politics of trouble. *Soc. Probl.* 25:121–35

Fishman, M. 1978. Crime waves as ideology. *Soc. Probl.* 25:531–43

Fishman, M. 1980. *Manufacturing the News.* Austin, Texas: Univ. of Texas Press

Frank, N. 1983. From criminal to civil penalties in the history of health and safety laws. *Soc. Probl.* 30:532–44

Freidson, E. 1970. *Profession of Medicine* New York: Dodd Mead

Fuller, R., Myers, R. 1941a. Some aspects of a theory of social problems. *Am. Sociol. Rev.* 6:24–32

Fuller, R., Myers, R. 1942b. The natural history of a social problem. *Am. Sociol. Rev.* 6:320–28

Galliher, J. F., Walker, A. 1977. The puzzle of the social origins of the Marijuana Tax Act of 1937. *Soc. Probl.* 24:367–76

Ghezzi, S. G. 1983. A private network of social control: Insurance investigation units. *Soc. Probl.* 30:521–31

Giddens, A. 1976. *New Rules of Sociological Method: A Positive Critique of Interpretive Sociologies.* New York: Basic

Gitlin, T. 1980. *The Whole World Is Watching: Mass Media in the Making and Unmaking of the New Left.* Berkeley, Calif: Univ. of Calif. Press

Glasgow University Media Group. 1980. *More Bad News.* London: Routledge & Kegan Paul

Goffman, E. 1959. The moral career of a mental patient. *Psychiatry* 22:123–42

Goffman, E. 1969. The insanity of place. *Psychiatry* 32:357–388

Goldner, F. H. 1982. Pronoia. *Soc. Probl.* 30:82–91

Gusfield, J. 1963. *Symbolic Crusade.* Urbana, Ill: University of Ill. Press

Gusfield, J. 1967. Moral passage: The symbolic process in the public designations of deviance. *Soc. Probl.* 15:175–88

Gusfield, J. 1975. Categories of ownership and responsibility in social issues: Alcohol abuse and automobile use. *J. Drug Issues* 5:285–303

Gusfield, J. 1976. The literary rhetoric of science: Comedy and pathos in drinking driver research. *Am. Sociol. Rev.* 41:16–34

Gusfield, J. 1981. *The Culture of Public Problems: Drinking Driving and the Symbolic Order.* Chicago: Univ. of Chicago Press

Gusfield, J. 1984. On the side: Practical action and social constructivism in social problems theory. See Schneider & Kitsuse pp. 31–51

Hewitt, J. P., Hall, P. M. 1973. Social problems, problematic situations, and quasi-theories. *Am. Sociol. Rev.* 38:367–74

Hughes, E. C. 1971. *The Sociological Eye.* Chicago: Aldine

Joffe, C. 1978. What abortion counselors want from their clients. *Soc. Probl.* 26:112–21

Johnson, M. P., Hufbauer, K. 1982. Sudden infant death syndrome as a medical research problem since 1945. *Soc. Probl.* 30:65–81

Kahne, M. J., Schwartz, C. G. 1978. Negotiating trouble: The social construction and management of trouble in a college psychiatric context. *Soc. Probl.* 25:461–75

Kitsuse, J. I. 1980. Coming out all over: Deviants and the politics of social problems. *Soc. Probl.* 28:1–13

Kitsuse, J. I., Cicourel, A. V. 1963. A note of the uses of official statistics. *Soc. Probl.* 12:131–9

Kitsuse, J. I., Spector, M. 1973. Toward a sociology of social problems: Social conditions, value-judgments, and social problems. *Soc. Probl.* 20:407–19

Kitsuse, J. I., Murase, A. E., Yamamura, Y. 1984. *Kikokushijo:* The emergence and insti-

tutionalization of an educational problem in Japan. See Schneider & Kitsuse 1984, pp. 162–79

Latour, B. 1983. Give me a laboratory and I will raise the world. In *Science Observed: Perspectives on the Social Study of Science.* ed. K. D. Knorr-Cetina, M. Mulkay, pp. 141–70. Beverly Hills, Calif.: Sage

Lemert, E. M. 1962. Paranoia and the dynamics of exclusion. *Sociometry* 25:2–20

Loseke, D. L., Cahill, S. E. 1984. The social construction of deviance: Experts on battered women. *Soc. Probl.* 31:296–310

Lynch, M. 1983. Accommodation practices: Vernacular treatments of madness. *Soc. Probl.* 31:152–64

Lynxwiler, J., Shover, N., Clelland, D. A. 1983. The organization and impact of inspector discretion in a regulatory bureaucracy. *Soc. Probl.* 30:425–36

Manis, J. G. 1984. *Serious Social Problems.* Boston: Allyn & Bacon

Markle, G. E., Troyer, R. J. 1979. Smoke gets in your eyes: Cigarette smoking as deviant behavior. *Soc. Probl.* 26:611–25

Matza, D. 1969. *Becoming Deviant.* Englewood Cliffs, NJ: Prentice-Hall

Mauss, A. L. 1975. *Social Problems as Social Movements.* Philadelphia: Lippincott

Mauss, A. L. 1984. The myth of social problems theory. *Social Problems Theory Division Newsletter.* Summer, 1984. Buffalo, NY: Society for the Study of Social Problems

Maynard, D. W. 1982. Defendant attributes in plea bargaining: Notes on the modeling of sentencing decisions. *Soc. Probl.* 29:347–60

McCarthy, J. D. Zald, M. N. 1973. *The Trend of Social Movements in America: Professionalization and Resource Mobilization.* Morristown, NJ: General Learning Press

McCarthy, J. D. Zald, M. N. 1977. Resource mobilization and social movements: A partial theory. *Am. J. Sociol.* 82:1212–41

McCleary, R., Nienstedt, B. C., Erven, J. M. 1982. Uniform crime reports as organizational outcomes: Three time series experiments. *Soc. Probl.* 29:361–72

McCrea, F. B. 1983. The politics of menopause: The "discovery" of a deficiency disease. *Soc. Probl.* 31:111–23

Merton, R. K., Nisbet, eds. 1971. *Contemporary Social Problems.* New York: Harcourt Brace Jovanovich

Miller, G. 1983. Holding clients accountable: The micro-politics of trouble in a work incentive program. *Soc. Probl.* 31:139–51

Murray, G. L. 1982. The abolition of *el cortito,* the short-handled hoe: A case study in social conflict and state policy in California agriculture. *Soc. Probl.* 30:26–39

Nuehring, E., Markle, G. E. 1974. Nicotine and norms: The re-emergence of a deviant behavior. *Soc. Probl.* 21:513–26

Oberschall, A. 1973. *Social Conflicts and Social Movements.* Englewood Cliffs, NJ: Prentice-Hall

Pawluch, D. 1983. Transitions in pediatrics: A segmental analysis. *Soc. Probl.* 30:449–65

Peyrot, M. 1982. Caseload management: Choosing suitable clients in a community mental health agency. *Soc. Probl.* 30:157–67

Peyrot, M. 1984. Cycles of social problem development: The case of drug abuse. *Sociol. Q.* 25:83–96

Pfohl, S. J. 1977. The "discovery" of child abuse. *Soc. Probl.* 24:310–23

Piven, F. F. 1981. Deviant behavior and the remaking of the world. *Soc. Probl.* 28:489–508

Pontell, H. N., Jesilow, P. D., Geis, G. 1982. Policing physicians: Practitioner fraud and abuse in a government medical program. *Soc. Probl.* 30:117–25

Rains, P. 1975. Imputations of deviance: A retrospective essay on the labeling perspective. *Soc. Probl.* 23:1–11

Randall, D. M., Short, J. F. 1983. Women in toxic work environments: A case study of social problem development. *Soc. Probl.* 30:410–24

Reich, C. A. 1964. The new property. *Yale Law J.* 73:733–87

Riessman, C. K. 1983. Women and medicalization: A new perspective. *Soc. Policy* 14:3–18

Rose, V. M. 1977. Rape as a social problem: A byproduct of the feminist movement. *Soc. Probl.* 25:75–89

Ross, R., Staines, G. L. 1971. The politics of analyzing social problems. *Soc. Probl.* 18:18–40

Sampson, H., Messinger, S. L., Towne, R. D. 1962. Family processes and becoming a mental patient. *Am. J. Sociol.* 68:88–96

Schneider, J. W. 1978. Deviant drinking as disease: Alcoholism as a social accomplishment. *Soc. Probl.* 25:361–72

Schneider, J. W. 1984. Morality, social problems, and everyday life. See Schneider & Kitsuse 1984, pp. 180–205

Schneider, J. W., Conrad, P. 1980. The medical control of deviance: Contests and consequences. *Research in the Sociology of Health Care* 1:1–53. Greenwich, Conn: JAI

Schneider, J. W., Kitsuse, J. I., eds. 1984. *Studies in the Sociology of Social Problems.* Norwood, NJ: Ablex

Schwartz, C. G., Kahne, M. J. 1983. Medical help as negotiated achievement. *Psychiatry* 46:333–50

Shearing, C. D., Stenning, P. C. 1983. Private security: Implications for social control. *Soc. Probl.* 30:493–506

Smelser, N. J. 1963. *Theory of Collective Behavior.* New York: Free

Spector, M. 1977. Legitimizing homosexuality. *Society* 14:20–24

Spector, M. 1981. Beyond crime: Seven methods to control troublesome rascals. In *Law and Deviance,* H. L. Ross, ed., pp. 127–157. Beverly Hills, Calif: Sage.

Spector, M., Batt, S. 1983. *Toward a more active victim.* Unpublished manuscript. Department of Sociology, McGill University, Montreal, Quebec, Canada

Spector, M., Kitsuse, J. I. 1973. Social problems: A reformulation. *Soc. Probl.* 20:145–59

Spector, M., Kitsuse, J. I. 1977. *Constructing Social Problems.* Menlo Park, Calif: Cummings

Spencer, J. W. 1983. Accounts, attitudes, and solutions: Probation officer-defendant negotiations of subjective orientations. *Soc. Probl.* 30:570–81

Tallman, I., McGee, R. 1971. Definition of a social problem. In *Handbook of the Study of Social Problems,* E. Smigel, ed., pp. 19–59. Chicago: Rand McNally

Tierney, K. J. 1982. The battered women movement and the creation of the wife beating problem. *Soc. Probl.* 29:207–20

Troyer, R. J., Markle, G. E. 1983. *Cigarettes: The Battle Over Smoking.* New Brunswick, NJ: Rutgers University Press

Troyer, R. J., Markle, G. E. 1984. Coffee drinking: An emerging social problem? *Soc. Probl.* 31:403–16

Waller, W. 1936. Social problems and the mores. *Am. Sociol. Rev.* 1:922–34

Weitz, R. 1984. From accommodation to rebellion: Tertiary deviance and the radical redefinition of lesbianism. See Schneider & Kitsuse 1984, pp. 140–61

Wiener, C. 1981. *The Politics of Alcoholism: Building an Arena Around a Social Problem.* New Brunswick: Transaction

Woolgar, S. 1983. Irony in the social study of science. In *Science Observed: Perspectives on the Social Study of Science.* K. D. Knorr-Cetina, M. Mulkay (eds.), pp. 239–66. Beverly Hills, Calif: Sage

Woolgar, S., Pawluch, D. 1985. Ontological gerrymandering: The anatomy of social problems explanations. *Soc. Probl.* 32: (forthcoming)

Yarrow, M. R., Schwartz, C. G., Murphy, H. S., Deasy, L. C. 1955. The psychological meaning of mental illness in the family. *J. Soc. Issues* 11:12–24

Zola, I. K. 1972. Medicine as an institution of social control. *Sociol. Rev.* 20:487–504

27

Policy Research
Lessons from the Implementation of Deinstitutionalization

William R. Shadish, Jr.

ABSTRACT: Deinstitutionalization has created problems in treating mental patients in the community. The solutions that researchers have proposed have rarely affected policy significantly. Society has attempted to solve these problems satisfactorily (but not optimally) through social, political, and economic transactions that are under no particular rational control—for example, by treating mental patients in general hospitals and nursing homes. Policy researchers have rarely acknowledged the legitimacy of these solutions and have contributed little to them. Policy researchers have failed to understand the ideologies implicit in their own work and in policy. As a result, they have proposed solutions that are inconsistent with the social system that must implement them.

Deinstitutionalization emerged in the 1950s as a mental health policy to accommodate the needs and intentions of diverse groups in American society. State governments, for example, projected that the costs of state mental hospital systems would soon exceed acceptable levels, and some cheaper alternative was needed (Bloom, 1973; U.S. Senate Special Committee on Aging, 1976). Social critics noted that mental hospitals fostered patients' dependence on total institutions and hindered their return to productive roles in society (Goffman, 1961). These critics advocated policies that would provide care closer to the patient's home and that would minimize institutional dependence. Simultaneously, the newly developed psychotropic medications allowed for care of many mental patients in noninstitutional settings (Baldessarini, 1977; Crider, 1979). Advocates of deinstitutionalization in the 1950s, therefore, looked forward to significant benefits to the patient and to society as a result of this new policy.

Indeed, deinstitutionalization has benefited both mental patients and society. Alternatives to hospitalization have been developed that may be as cheap and effective as hospitalization (Kiesler, 1982a; Stein & Test, 1978). Major shifts in the location of mental health care did occur (Kramer, 1977). Psychotropic medications have enabled many patients to live in noninstitutional community settings (Greenblatt, 1978). Continued optimism about community care seemed warranted.

Tempering this optimism, however, are increasing signs of a discrepancy between the intentions and the consequences of deinstitutionalization. Kiesler (1980), for example, noted that, despite the intentions of deinstitutionalization, more patients are now treated in institutions than before, and more mental health dollars still go to institutions than not (see also Kramer, 1977). In another article, Kiesler also noted that inpatient care in general hospitals without psychiatric units is now the single largest source of episodes of mental health care (Kiesler, 1982b). Bardach (1977) studied the implementation of deinstitutionalization legislation in California and concluded that, despite its noble intentions, it "has probably done more harm than good" (p. 295). Bachrach (1980) noted that innovative model programs have not proven practical for widespread use in treating deinstitutionalized mental patients.

Such observations bespeak growing recognition of a discrepancy between the ideology that allegedly guided deinstitutionalization and the practices that policy actually spawned (Felton & Shinn, 1981; Institute for Social Research, 1980). A number of authors have already documented this discrepancy, so the evidence of it will not be detailed here. Rather, this article will suggest a way of analyzing and understanding this discrepancy, how policy researchers have contributed to this discrepancy, and what kinds of policy research might be more likely to impact on practice.

The dichotomy between intents and consequences is generally understandable and predictable: Policies are implemented to the extent that they are consistent with extant social structures and ideologies. The remainder of this article will elaborate that theme. But first, an example is presented that vividly highlights this dichotomy.

The Lodge Society and the Nursing Home Industry

Twenty-five years ago, Fairweather developed an innovative project for treating released mental patients—the Lodge society (Fairweather et al., 1960; Fairweather, 1980). Although it is one of many innovative projects for mental patients (Stein & Test, 1978), the Lodge is worth studying for several reasons.

From William R. Shadish, Jr., "Policy Research: Lessons from the Implementation of Deinstitutionalization," *American Psychologist*, 1984, 39(7), 725-738. Copyright 1984 by the American Psychological Association. Reprinted (or Adapted) by permission of the publisher and author.

First, of course, it helps patients. The Lodge reduces patients' dependence on mental institutions and professionals, it helps patients to compete for scarce resources such as employment, and it reduces society's exposure to deviant behavior without depriving patients of access to the community—all this without exploiting mental patients.

Second, the Lodge society has existed for about 25 years (Fairweather, 1980); many practitioners and policymakers know about it. Third, many lodges become self-supporting (Fairweather, 1980), and lodges are often less costly than alternatives (Norwood & Mason, 1982). Finally, Fairweather, Sanders, and Tornatzky (1974) describe several major efforts to disseminate the Lodge program to 255 hospitals through persuasion and attempts to activate interest. Thus, the Lodge program has probably had a fair chance to be used in mental health policy.

Was it used? Not much, apparently. Even by optimistic estimates, the Lodge society probably serves a few thousand mental patients at most. In fact, this paradoxical difficulty in implementing the Lodge in policy was apparent to the original researchers from the start:

It was a matter of some surprise to the researchers who had created and evaluated the lodge program to find that though the hospital management was sympathetic to the new program and readily perceived its merits, it was unable or unwilling to establish the lodge project as an integral part of the hospital treatment program. *Apparently, experimenting with a new social treatment program is one process; incorporating it into ongoing treatment programs is quite another.* (Fairweather, et al., 1974, p. 10; italics in original text)

In fact, of the 255 hospitals contacted in the Lodge society dissemination study (Fairweather et al., 1974), less than 10% made any move at all to adopt the Lodge, and these moves were often left incomplete. Of course, the Lodge program is used in policy occasionally. Local practitioners sometimes do start a lodge (Fairweather, 1980); similarly, the State of Texas recently compared local projects for chronic mental patients and found that the Lodge program could play a role in policy (Norwood & Mason, 1982), though probably a relatively small one compared to nursing homes (Dittmar & Franklin, 1980a, 1980b).

All in all, then, the Lodge society is not used much in policy even though in many respects it is an ideal project to fund. Other model projects (Bach-

The author would like to thank Leona Bachrach, Michael Berger, Richard Bootzin, Thomas D. Cook, George W. Fairweather, Arthur Houts, Laura Leviton, Kenneth Lichstein, Charles Kiesler, Amy Sibulkin, and an anonymous reviewer for comments on previous drafts of this manuscript.

Requests for reprints should be sent to William R. Shadish, Jr., Department of Psychology, Memphis State University, Memphis, Tennessee 38152.

rach, 1980; Stein & Test, 1978) for deinstitutionalized mental patients suffered a similar fate. Why? This article suggests they are not widely used because they tend to be inconsistent with existing social structures and ideologies. For example, the Lodge society eschews dependence on mental health professionals, but professionals control resources that the Lodge needs. The Lodge says society causes many of the problems of mental patients, a view that conflicts with society's beliefs that individuals are responsible for their own problems. Although lodges may be cheaper than hospitalization, they are not widely reimbursable or profitable under existing mechanisms, and so it is difficult to find start-up and maintenance funds for such lodges. This list could be elaborated (and will be later). However, the point is clear and can be made sharper by comparing the failures of the Lodge society to the successes of the nursing home industry.

Concurrent with development of the Lodge society significant changes occurred in the American nursing home industry, including an increased supply of nursing home beds and a changed fiscal structure. Vladeck (1980) suggested that these changes were intended to foster use of nursing home care for recuperating patients at less cost than general hospitals. Medicare, and later Medicaid, incentives generated a nursing home industry with the bed capacity to fill this function. Unfortunately, general hospitals had too many empty beds themselves and could not afford the loss of revenue caused by transferring patients to nursing homes (Vladeck, 1980). So nursing homes, in turn, had to look elsewhere for patients to fill their beds, and (among other patients) they found deinstitutionalized mental patients (Shadish & Bootzin, 1981a).

Nursing homes now serve an enormous number of (primarily chronic) mental patients in the United States, although there is considerable state-to-state variation. By one estimate (Goldman, Gattozzi, & Taube, 1981), fully 350,000 nursing home residents had mental disorders and another 400,000 had diagnoses of senility with psychosis. These figures include geriatric patients, of course, but a surprisingly large percentage are young (Bootzin & Shadish, 1983). This massive role makes Medicaid the largest single mental health program in the country (Kiesler, 1982a). With few exceptions (Stotsky, 1967), researchers have studiously avoided recognizing or examining the role of the nursing home in mental health policy. The crowning irony, of course, is that the nursing home resembles the total institutions that previously cared for mental patients (Shadish & Bootzin, 1981b)—exactly the kind of placement that deinstitutionalization was designed to avoid.

Nursing homes assumed this role in deinstitutionalization because, unlike the lodges, they reflected

American social structures and ideologies. Nursing homes yield private sector profits; their institutional walls and lower class neighborhood locations (Shadish, Straw, McSweeny, Koller, & Bootzin, 1981) protect middle-class sensibilities from deviant behavior; and they rely on professionals to provide care, rather than seeing professionals as part of the problem. The contrasting fates of the lodges and nursing homes are consistent with the following analysis.

Policy and Social Structure

Lindblom and Cohen (1979) argued that social systems routinely solve their problems through social interactions—endless economic, political, and social transactions under no particular rational control, with little or no input from social scientists (see also Johnson, 1978). In this article, these will be called "social system solutions." Scientists and policymakers, of course, have little control over the interactions that produce these solutions (Bevan, 1982), and science lacks the social authority to impose its own solutions. Therefore, science must take advantage of ordinary social interactions if it wants to contribute in the short term to solving social problems. (Excluded from this argument, therefore, is basic research that claims not to contribute to short-term social problem solving—although such research can benefit from the present discussion.) Problematically, many social scientists fail to study or acknowledge such social interactions. The ensuing paucity of knowledge handicaps scientists who seek to construct social science solutions to problems.

Social system solutions, moreover, tend to be economically, socially, and politically compatible with the social system from which they emerged (why this should be the case is a topic in a later section). Social science solutions, on the other hand, often have been constructed with little concern for compatibility with extant social systems. When an attempt is made to implement these solutions, powerful social networks are activated whose interests have been ignored and who are, therefore, often hostile to implementing the solution (Sarason, 1976; VandenBos, 1983).

To solve social problems, therefore, the social scientist must not only produce solutions, but study how the solution fits into the social system in which it is to be implemented:

If you purport that your theories and findings have significance for social practice, it is incumbent upon you to demonstrate that the conditions of research from which your findings derive approximate the conditions of actual social living. (Sarason, 1981, pp. 134–135)

Those conditions of social living include financial aspects (e.g., How will funding be obtained? Will the service be financially competitive with alternatives?); political aspects (Will powerful networks perceive their interests to be threatened? What networks will be affected?); organizational aspects (How will contact be made with clients? How will temporal, spatial, and physical arrangements be organized?); social aspects (Will existing service providers want to do the job?); and demographic aspects (Do sufficient numbers of clients exist to ensure demand?). This list is tentative and no doubt incomplete, though it resembles similar lists by other authors (Cline & Sinnott, 1981; Tornatzky & Johnson, 1982; Weiss & Fuller, 1983), and warrants elaboration if structural compatibility is to be anticipated in research.

Many examples exist of scientifically good innovations that resist implementation due to structural incompatibility. Witness, for example, the fate of an innovative behavioral treatment project for autistic children reported by Graziano (1969). When proposed, the project drew resistance from psychoanalysts who opposed behavioral approaches and who politically and economically thwarted the project's implementation in their mental health settings. Resistance also came from external funders with ties to other mental health networks that also opposed the new project. Years passed, and the project remained unfunded. When funding finally arrived, the innovative nature of the project had apparently been compromised.

Another example comes from Paul and Lentz's (1977) behavioral treatment project for chronic schizophrenic inpatients. Their behavioral interventions were demonstrably effective, both absolutely and compared to alternatives such as psychotropic medications or milieu therapy. Yet some of these effective interventions encountered difficulty due to incompatibility with the social system. Their use of "time-out" to control highly dangerous patient behavior was dramatically curtailed by state policy. Several aspects of their token economy were potentially in conflict with legal opinion that patients could not be forced to perform labor for privileges, or without minimum wage compensation.

A number of other examples could be cited that lead to the same conclusion, including of course the Lodge society and the nursing home industry, but also drawing from experience with hospices (Aiken & Marx, 1982), HMOs (Bauman, 1976), welfare for the elderly (Frankfather, 1982), preventive mental health (Iscoe, 1982), psychotherapy (Karon & VandenBos, 1981), community mental health centers (CMHCs; Naierman, Haskins, & Robinson, 1978), and prevention of alcoholism and drug abuse (Nathan, 1983). All show that social interventions are implemented to the extent that they are consistent with extant social structures. Social system solutions usually have little trouble meeting this requirement; social science solutions usually have a great deal of trouble. Notably, however, structural inconsistency signals another problem—the consistency of a solution with the public values and ideologies that those structures facilitate.

Policy and Ideology

In evaluating deinstitutionalization, the temptation is to deplore its supposed negative consequences and to assert good intentions to improve the lot of mental patients. Barring further contemplation, however, it is also tempting to assume that those negative consequences were just unfortunate happenstance, not the result of intentional acts, important social values, or public ideology—particularly not those of policymakers, mental health professionals, or other socially responsible people. In such reasoning, the solution is to begin with noble intentions to reshape policy toward better consequences.

Presume, however, that the opposite is true: that social system solutions are not random, but reflect the pluralistic self-interests of a policy-shaping community, and only policies consistent with these self-interests are implemented. Then policy as implemented reveals the ideologies that guide mental health policy (Cameron, 1978). Social science solutions, on the other hand, are at best orthogonal to public values, and at worst assume that the public holds the same "rational" ideology held by the scientific community. By implication, then, social science solutions, like the Lodge society, are inconsistent not only with social structures but also with the ideologies those structures facilitate. The following public ideologies could be inferred from policy, as implemented, if we take such social system solutions as nursing homes and general hospitals to be reasonably representative of that policy.

First, social system solutions in the United States reflect "professionalism" (Lenrow & Cowden, 1980). Care-giving professions have evolved over the last century to give social services formerly given by extended families, neighbors, and other sources of support that became less available during industrialization. The public expects mental health care from professionals—physicians, clergy, and especially, mental health professionals—and existing social structures facilitate such care. Medical care is particularly valued; innovations to be implemented in medical settings must reflect this. Clinical psychologists working in psychiatrically dominated settings know this well (Fox, 1982; Pertschuk & Correia, 1983; Wiggins, Bennett, Batchelor, & West, 1983). A similar example is evident in the drift of health maintenance organizations (HMOs) toward serving medical interests that were not present in the original Kaiser-Permanenté model (Cummings & VandenBos, 1981).

Second, social system solutions reflect "individualism" (Hall, 1983; James, 1972). The needs and rights of individuals are valued over those of the state; conversely, individuals are thought to be the cause of their own problems. The state only intervenes when individuals cannot compete fairly with others. Even then, such interventions only maintain the individual at a subsistence level, as is historically evident in policies toward the chronically indigent (Levine, 1979). This ideology reflects not just particular conservative presidential administrations (Fishman & Neigher, 1982), but also large segments of American society that support those administrations. A proposed policy innovation that runs counter to individualism is often, for example, fought on the "ground that it is a step toward socialism" (Bevan, 1982, p. 1129), as evidenced in much of the rhetoric against national health insurance.

Third, public attitudes toward mental illness reflect intolerance and stigmatization (Bevan, 1982; Heller & Monahan, 1977; Kiesler, 1981), which social system solutions mirror. Bachrach (1976), for example, noted that one reason mental institutions exist is to prevent exposure of society to deviant behavior. Goffman (1961), whose work was an influential rationale in deinstitutionalization, noted that doing away with mental hospitals would not do away with the public's intolerance for mental deviance. Segal and Aviram (1978) found that neighbors of board-and-care homes for the mentally ill were intolerant of patients as a group: "When neighbors' response is directed at the whole group of residents in a facility, . . . the impact of this response is negative and leads to a reduction in level of social integration" (p. 171).

Fourth, social system solutions reflect a public valuing of what Schorr (1971) called greed and pragmatism. According to Schorr, greed refers to the American propensity to accumulate material goods and the means to obtain them. Pragmatism means implementing policy options that are feasible given contending political and economic forces, despite compromises over ideals. Nursing homes, consistent with these values, give a profit to the private sector (Vladeck, 1980), minimize costs to states (U.S. Senate Special Committee on Aging, 1976), and compromise the ideal with the feasible in American mental health care. The Lodge program, however, only minimally profits anyone and can add costs to state mental health systems. Because the Lodge competes for limited aftercare resources that are already claimed by other institutions such as CMHCs, new resources often have to be added for the Lodge. Similarly, greed and pragmatism partly account for limited health insurance coverage of mental health services. Because consumers do not demand it, no profit is seen in offering it, even if it is cost effective (VandenBos, 1983).

The role of ideology in policy is also seen in cross-cultural comparisons. Italy's emerging socialist perspective approaches mental health policy as "part of the larger leftist struggle against oppression" (McNett, 1981, p. 9). As one result, in 1977 Italy banned compulsory institutionalization, with apparently positive results (Mosher, 1982). In communist China (Turkington, 1982), community care reflects an ideology that mental patients should stay in their community to contribute toward the common social good. All this is not, of course, to praise socialist systems for *better* mental health care; the previous article, for example, reported that some Chinese patients had frozen to death in mental hospitals. Moreover, noncommunist systems also foster community care (Stein & Test, 1978). For example, in Geel, Belgium, mental patients have been placed in local family homes for 800 years (Roosens, 1979). Rather, these examples all show how mental health systems reflect the local or national ideology.

The preceding paragraphs demonstrate that policy as implemented reveals public ideologies. But similarly, science as implemented reveals the values held by scientists. Characteristically, scientists overlook public values that will impede implementation of their solutions, perhaps believing their work is value free (Scriven, 1983). But this belief is just an ideology, as numerous philosophers of science are fond of showing (Feyerabend, 1975, 1978; Hesse, 1980). The structure of particular social science solutions necessarily facilitates particular values, just as the structure of social system solutions facilitates values. Even when values do not directly conflict, the need to divide limited social resources requires giving some values priority over others. Scientists are engaged in activities that foster particular values; the argument here is that they should explicitly recognize this and systematically study it as part of their work.

Second, social science solutions are designed to provide care in the patients' best interests. Scientists (and mental health professionals) like to think this ideology is also central to mental health policy. But if the preceding analysis of ideology in American mental health policy is accurate, then care in the patients' best interests may not be the highest priority. Of course, some scientists (and local mental health professionals) do intend to act in the patients' best interests. But they do so within the political, economic, and social constraints set by extant social structures. They often serve patients' interests in spite of the system rather than because of it, and because their own ideals overcome the inertia of policy as implemented.

However, these scientists (and professionals) sometimes underestimate their support for the ideologies facilitated by extant social structures. After all, the use of social resources to provide salaries for scientists and professionals probably favors them as much or more than mental patients. These scientists and professionals probably prefer to invest in profit-generating enterprises like nursing homes more than in relatively profitless enterprises like lodges, and they

might resist a rezoning that allowed a group of mental patients to live next door. They probably do wish to foster patient care, but not always at the expense of other values.

Change and the Conservative Nature of Policy

If innovations are implementable in policy to the extent that they are consistent with existing social structures and ideologies, then a logical implication is that policy is conservative, change is difficult to accomplish, and existing social systems foster the status quo (Klein, 1982). The more an innovation departs from the status quo, the more networks will mobilize against it. Practices that already function in extant political, social, and economic systems are not easily displaced by practices of unknown compatibility with those systems (Rich, 1981), even if the new practices are best for patients. So new practices must fight for legitimacy, often with few resources for the fight. Beneficiaries of current policies rarely sacrifice those benefits to advocates of a new policy. How, then, do we innovate in society?

Change and Strain

A concept such as "strain" is often used to explain the driving force behind social change. Heller and Monahan (1977) define strain for the individual citizen "as a discrepancy between expected and perceived reality" (p. 374). Mayer (1979) says institutions are strained when their structures and ideologies cannot adequately reduce environmental pressures.

Strain creates pressure to change. The goal is not elimination of strain, but its reduction to a less disturbing level. Borrowing from Simon's (1960) terminology, the goal is to find a "satisficing" solution to strain, not an "optimizing" solution. But this task is complicated because strain is not uniformly experienced by all groups in a social system and because particular solutions create strain as well as reduce it between and within groups in a social system. Consider this example of the potential strain created by a proposed solution to rising health care costs:

You can save several billion dollars annually by applying the hospital cost-containment program and imposing it only on the public sector. You would not get as much opposition from the hospitals as you would otherwise. It is a very attractive strategy. The problem is that it will probably lead to a dual system of medicine—one for the poor and another for everyone else. It also will simply shift costs from Medicaid and Medicare to the private sector, and hospitals are going to have to make up those costs somewhere, so they will need to shift the burden as well. (Bevan, 1982, p. 1129)

Solutions to strain emerge from interactions between interest groups, each working within the limits of its power and resources. In health insurance, for example, these groups include consumers, providers, insurers, federal reimbursers, hospitals, unions, and employers (VandenBos, 1983). Each successive change creates new strain to which other groups may respond, creating another solution and modifying the old one. The process continues until a satisfycing equilibrium is reached. Of course, some strain is always present in a social system, and incremental changes constantly occur with little effect on the system as a whole.

Consistent with the ideologies outlined previously, strain reduction in mental health policy emphasizes individual competition among solutions, dominated by a professional ethic and consistent with intolerance for deviance and with the profit making and pragmatic orientations of the public:

Although a policy has to be seen as consistent with the society's traditions and picture of the public welfare, its adoption (or rejection) always reflects (in our society) the activities of competing self-interest groups varying in political and economic power. Public policy is forged in a marketplace of power and influence, and if you are not in that marketplace your future and self-interests are determined by others. (Sarason, 1981, p. 9)

Psychologists learned this in battles with psychiatry, where policy reflects medical power (Pertschuk & Correia, 1983; Wiggins et al., 1983). Conversely, mental patients are politically, socially, and economically impotent, with little power to use in the policy marketplace (Heller & Monahan, 1977). So mental health policies probably reflect their input least of all.

In the 1950s, state mental health systems experienced considerable strain. Projections were that demand for state mental hospitals would soon exceed what states could afford to pay (U.S. Senate Special Committee on Aging, 1976). Deinstitutionalization was an attempt to reduce this strain—a search for satisfycing solutions. Nursing homes satisfactorily reduced strain on state mental health systems by transferring costs to the federal government (U.S. Senate Special Committee on Aging, 1976), and possibly also by losing as many patients as possible in the confusion of the transfer (Segal, Baumohl, & Johnson, 1977). Also, recall that a satisfycing solution creates as little new strain in the system as possible. Nursing homes were consistent with the structure and ideology of the existing mental health system and created less new strain than inconsistent solutions such as the lodge.

Strain is usually not of the magnitude that prompted deinstitutionalization in the 1950s. Small strains foster incremental, technical changes that leave the basic system untouched. An example is the strain caused by tardive dyskinesia—a negative, permanent physical side effect of a satisfycing solution, the phenothiazine medications (Berger & Rexroth, 1980). The physical sequelae cause strain for mental patients; the ethics of harming a patient with a treatment cause

physicians strain; and increased treatment costs cause economic strain. One could stop using phenothiazines. But that solution might create more strain than it reduced by increasing displays of symptomatology and costs for inpatient care and by reducing patient productivity and profits to drug manufacturers. Satisfycing solutions to tardive dyskinesia, then, are more likely to include medication vacations, decreased dosage levels, and a long-term search for drugs that do not cause the side effect or that reverse it.

Ideological Change

Although strain can result from environmental pressures on social systems, it also results from changes in expectations about reality—from changes in ideologies (Mayer, 1979). For example, Italy's 1977 ban on compulsory institutionalization (McNett, 1981) resulted partly from drifts toward socialist ideologies that viewed institutions as a form of political repression. Rarely, such ideological change can cause rapid social change; more commonly, social changes of this kind are a matter of decades, at least.

When an innovation is ideologically and structurally inconsistent with a social system, one option is to spread information about it anyway, to effect a slow, grass-roots change in the system toward a more compatible ideology. Such a shift creates a strain between ideology and social reality. If enough citizens adopt the new ideology, they may advocate new social structures that would allow adoption of the change. Fairweather et al. (1974), for example, seem to have taken this approach to disseminating the Lodge society.

Similarly, over the last 30 years, many mental health professionals grew to believe that institutional care was bad, and they tried to change mental health systems toward noninstitutional structures of care. Problematically, however, these professionals often acted as if mental health systems were isolated entities that could be changed without affecting other social systems (DeLeon, O'Keefe, VandenBos, & Kraut, 1982). This false premise is a key reason why deinstitutionalization failed to accomplish many of its goals. Mental health systems participate in networks for health reimbursement, social control, welfare, and tax, to name a few. Changing the mental health system potentially changes all these networks, impinging on their ideologies and structures. Moreover, mental health professionals participate not just in mental health networks but also in the others, and they may find these other interests threatened by a mental health change.

Strain and Problem Definition

Social system problems are the sum of all the strains of each interest group, probably weighted by the power of each group, and adjusted for redundancy and for the mutual incompatibility of some strains. Social science problems tend to focus on a limited part of the social system problem. In deinstitutionalization, for example, the social system problem is *not* how to care best for patients because, other than the patients themselves, very few groups experience this issue as a strain. Rather, the social system problem is how to accommodate the strains of deinstitutionalization with the least new strain possible. Although these strains are too numerous to list here, they include how to save state money without laying off too many union workers and how to determine where patients should live in communities that dislike mental patients. They have little to do with treatment outcome. Social scientists who define the problem as providing effective patient care, therefore, produce solutions that are at best orthogonal to the social system problem.

In defining problems, policy researchers tend to overlook many important interest groups, and they are also in a poor position to understand the particular strains on each group:

It is conceited to assume that one has solutions for people whose lives one does not share and whose problems one does not know. It is foolish to assume that such an exercise in distant humanitarianism will have effects pleasing to the people concerned. (Feyerabend, 1978, p. 121)

To be understood, social system problems need comprehensive investigation. This probably requires more attention to needs assessments (Hagedorn, Beck, Neubert, & Werlin, 1976; Kamis-Gould & Piasecki, 1981; Scriven, 1980), stakeholder surveys (Shadish, Thomas, & Bootzin, 1982), and such methodologies as participant observation and case studies (Guba & Lincoln, 1981) than is typically the case in social science.

Mental health researchers, unfortunately, seldom take this comprehensive look at policy, even though looking at small pieces of it can foster misleading recommendations. Kiesler (1983) shows how discussions of psychotherapy can change in the context of total mental health policy. In that context, the problem is not only the effectiveness of psychotherapy but also its practicality given a demand that overwhelms any conceivable supply of therapists, its marginal utility in the context of other services, and the worth of trained therapists when cheaper, untrained ones do well. Advocating therapy in policy simply because it is effective, or even cost effective, ignores the complexity of policy implementation.

Exceptions, Integrations

Some readers will take exception to the present analysis. For example, it could be argued that social science solutions are not widely implemented due to poor communication with policymakers with the power to implement them, rather than because of any inconsistency with social systems. This alternative, however, is only partly valid and, if remedied, would still not solve the fundamental problem. Improved communication of social science solutions might increase their chances of being implemented (Leviton & Hughes, 1981; Storandt, 1983; Swensen, 1983). Problematically, however, isolated policymakers with power to implement social innovations are quite rare; most social policy "emerges" from the interactions of pluralistic interest groups (Cronbach et al., 1980). Also, if this alternative held, then the extensive attempts to disseminate the Lodge Society (Fairweather et al., 1974) should have met with more success.

Another objection has more merit. This objection does not challenge the idea that innovations must be consistent with the structures and ideologies of the system in which they are to be implemented, but rather challenges whether all such systems are characterized by greed, pragmatism, and so forth. One example is the work of volunteers in such settings as hospitals or crisis centers, which appears incompatible with ideologies like professionalism or greed. Self-help groups like Alcoholics Anonymous are a similar challenge (President's Commission on Mental Health, 1978), as are other forms of social support (Gottlieb, 1981). The characteristics of volunteerism in mental health policy probably include pragmatism and individualism, but also some other new characteristics. The main difficulty with volunteerism is likely to be with the kind and magnitude of the role that it can play in policy: Can it cope with the magnitude of the problem, and will volunteers simply refuse to deal with some important problems?

Another exception concerns large-scale federal intervention, which can bypass extant structures and ideologies somewhat. Examples include the CMHC program (Chiles, 1982), the Community Action Program (CAP; Heller & Monahan, 1977), and the Community Support Program (CSP; Turner & TenHoor, 1978). At first glance, these interventions seem to foster major social change. But careful study of their limitations is needed—such alternative institutions often conflict with existing systems and either terminate or adapt. CMHCs adapted to the larger mental health system once federal funding waned (Naierman et al., 1978). CAPs either adapted or had their funds shut off (Heller & Monahan, 1977). The CSP has apparently been funded at a low level and was proposed for elimination in the federal budget for several years running. It was saved only by the joint lobbying of the National Mental Health Association, a State Mental Health Directors group, the American Psychological Association, and several others. The changes brought about by such programs are sometimes just incremental, and at other times they dissipate over time.

These exceptions do suggest that finer distinctions among the avenues for implementing policy should be made (e.g., private sector, public sector, private nonprofit, and volunteer). Ideological and structural characteristics of each need delineation, and the potential of each for solving social problems needs study. Characteristics of policy innovations could then be compared to those needed for implementation within each avenue, fostering prediction of the likely extent of implementation and problem solving. Argyris (1983) presented an example of such an analysis in organizational development.

These exceptions also suggest that trade-offs among the ideologies listed in the previous sections often occur. One example is cooperation between mental health professionals and volunteer crisis centers. Professionals are willing to cooperate with the nonprofessional helpers in those settings because it is pragmatic to do so. Crisis centers often handle late-night and weekend calls from the clients of those professionals. Professionalism is traded for pragmatism. Is there a hierarchy of ideologies that dictates the form of such trade-offs? If there is, it has not been convincingly articulated. At any rate, such a hierarchy would probably vary across situations, with some values accorded higher status in, say, volunteer settings than in proprietary ones.

In contrast to such exceptions, the concepts in this article integrate emerging literature on the role of research in social problem solving. For example, the idea that ordinary social interactions solve social problems is consistent with Campbell's evolutionary epistemology (Brewer & Collins, 1981), which posits that various solutions to social problems evolve naturally in society and the scientist's task is to find the solutions. But an added caution here concerns evaluating *planned* variations (Rhine, 1983). Such planning too easily overlooks structural and ideological characteristics that the variation must have to be implementable. Maybe *unplanned* variations should be the starting point. Perhaps this is partly why Sarason (1976, 1981), Cronbach (1982), and Rhine (1983) exhorted social scientists to conduct policy research under conditions of actual social living—it presumably fosters the implementability of a solution by increasing its consistency with social interactions.

The importance of compatibility with extant social systems receives similar support (Argyris, 1983). Cross and Guyer (1980), for example, studied the consistency of social action with social system reinforcers in their book on "social traps"—situations characterized by multiple but conflicting rewards that induce victims toward behavior that is rewarded in the short term but is socially deleterious in the long term. Examples include steel mill executives who pollute towns where they live, diplomats who destroy the peace and security of those they represent, and

commuters who willingly engage in behaviors that create traffic jams. They might have included policymakers who write deinstitutionalization legislation that does more harm than good (Bardach, 1977). Cross and Guyer's (1980) thesis is consistent with the present one—behavior follows the reinforcers in the social system.

The need to complement existing social change processes is also increasingly recognized. Cook (1981), for example, noted that most change in social policy ordinarily occurs in local projects, or elements within local projects. Cook saw a trade-off between these two points; projects like the lodge can affect more people in more ways than can elements within projects, but elements such as the phenothiazines may be changed more quickly and with less resistance. Watzlawick, Weakland, and Fisch (1974) discussed the process of change and problem resolution in psychotherapy and developed principles about change of all sorts. For example, some solutions generate new social interactions that maintain the problem, as was the case with Prohibition as a solution to alcoholism.

Many of the present arguments also illuminate the rapidly developing field of knowledge use in policy (Horowitz & Katz, 1975; Rich, 1981; Weiss, 1977). One finding is that social science knowledge is seldom used instrumentally, although it is valued by policymakers in the abstract (Weiss & Weiss, 1981) and can influence their thinking (Leviton & Hughes, 1981). This article simply notes that usable information must be consistent with the structures and ideologies of the user, whether that user is a policymaker, a local practitioner, or a large social system consisting of many interest groups with many ideologies and structures. The more networks are affected by the proposed change, the harder it will be to achieve use.

As the above discussion illustrates, the analysis of policy outlined in this article is unlikely to hold perfectly and needs considerable attention and development. But its consistency with an array of theory and research does suggest its promise. Significantly, however, most of the work just cited resembles the present analysis. These works also involve retrospective, theoretical analyses that attempt to explain the relationship between science and social change. Prospective, empirical studies of these matters are far rarer and are needed.

Reconsidering Policy Research

Policy research must systematically attend to the strains in existing systems, the solutions that might reduce strain, and the implementability of those solutions. This research should not be piecemeal, addressing pet areas with little concern for how those areas fit into the entire mental health policy picture. Top-down policy analysis (Kiesler, 1983) is needed that considers discrete areas in their larger policy context. The following areas illustrate the kinds of research that might be done, for example, in mental health policy.

Describing the System

Time and time again, mental health policy researchers stumble over their ignorance of what "mental health policy" is. It comes as a surprise to most researchers, for instance, that more chronic mental patients may reside in, and more mental health dollars go to, nursing homes than to any other single mental health setting (Kramer, 1977; Kiesler, 1982a). Myths about the mental health system abound, with little evidence supporting their validity (Kiesler, 1982b). Such simple descriptive ignorance is due partly, of course, to the fragmented nature of the system itself. For example, the National Institute of Mental Health (NIMH) may consistently ignore nursing homes in most of its work because it has little regulatory or fiscal jurisdiction over them—the latter tasks fall to the Health Care Financing Administration (HCFA).

One need, then, is for a comprehensive description of mental health policies, programs, projects, and elements (Cook, Leviton, & Shadish, in press). This includes not only CMHCs, hospitals of all sorts, freestanding clinics, and private practices, but also nursing homes, clergy, HMOs, physician offices, schools, self-help groups, and emergency rooms (Kiesler, 1983). The description should allow comparison of settings and practices on common grounds such as number of patient episodes and dollars (e.g., Kiesler, 1982b). The description ought to be thorough, describing who is served, what services are provided, at what costs, and with what effects (Cook et al., in press), as well as the political, economic, social, organizational, and demographic conditions that surround the intervention.

Such descriptions will stimulate questions about why patients and dollars go where they do: What functions does the mental health system serve? Whose interests does the system foster? Who would be affected by changing the system, in addition to patients and professionals? Such questions are being asked and answered (Bachrach, 1976; Shadish & Bootzin, 1981a, 1981b) but not often enough. Such descriptions also expose new opportunities for research. For example, nursing home care for mental patients occurs in many major cities, but little research addresses that topic. Similarly, little is known about the care of mental patients in general hospitals without psychiatric units, even though more episodes of care may occur there than in any other setting (Kiesler, 1982b).

Making Innovations Implementable

Many policy researchers see their sole responsibility as identifying treatments that help patients. However,

considering that many treatments have failed to be put into practice, such research is not enough. The innovation must also be implementable to be useful in practice. When researchers want to produce findings that might be of some immediate use in policy, little reason exists to study an innovation if its implementability is anticipated to be low, even if it is good for patients. Policy researchers must study an innovation's structural and ideological characteristics as much as its effects.

An option, of course, is to improve the implementability of an intervention. For example, Levine (1980) reported on the transition of a state hospital to a psychiatric center in New York, a transition that encountered stiff resistance from the existing hospital. Levine's (1980) report was a marvelous case study of how to make a change implementable in a stubborn system. For example, the change agents manipulated social prestige and power to entice mental health professionals to leave comfortable old roles for new ones. More such studies would contribute to our knowledge about how to increase the implementability of policy innovations.

Another example approaches implementability as a problem of marketing. Fox (1982) described organizational structures that clinical psychologists can adopt to sell their products in a marketplace dominated by medicine. Others market alcohol and drug abuse treatment programs to employers (see, for example, the *EAP Digest*, which advertises employee assistance programs to industry). Marketing is making a treatment implementable by finding a way for someone to make a profit from it. Carried to an extreme, of course, marketing can ignore questions about the social needs for the treatment and can tip the balance between need and implementability too far away from the former in the service of the latter (Bryk & Raudenbush, 1983). But the opposite also holds. Attending entirely to needs will obscure the practicality of an innovation, as efforts to control health care costs are now revealing (VandenBos, 1983).

An example at the national level is provided in Vladeck's (1980) discussion of economic and regulatory mechanisms to shift health policy away from nursing homes toward large, cooperative apartment complexes. Vladeck recommended tightening eligibility for nursing home admission to create competition for eligible patients and demand from previously eligible patients for a new system and giving reimbursements to cooperative apartments for taking former nursing home patients. Since the publication of Vladeck's book, high interest rates have virtually halted nursing home construction, so that his recommendations have partially come true (VandenBos & Buchanan, 1983). This offers a natural experiment for studying the implementability of his approach.

Psychologists might object that such work is for economists or health service researchers. But policy research is multidisciplinary and requires that economics be considered; and mental health policy researchers *are* health services researchers who must be catholic in their work.

Identifying Strains in the System

Heller and Monahan (1977) advise community psychologists to assess the nature and sources of strain in communities. So, too, the mental health policy researcher ought to anticipate strains in the mental health system. Doing so provides an opportunity to anticipate needed change, to find and assess the value of possible changes, and thus to help shift policy toward a more constructive and predictable course. The following examples are illustrative.

Increased mental health system costs. A major cause of deinstitutionalization was states' anticipation of intolerable system cost increases (U.S. Senate Special Committee on Aging, 1976). States encouraged nursing home care for mental patients partly to lower their mental health system costs. Today, however, nursing home costs strain the system. Medicaid and Medicare costs have burgeoned dramatically (Neugarten, 1983), partly due to an increasingly aged society (Eisdorfer, 1983). But Medicaid also funds mental health care (DeLeon & VandenBos, 1980; Fisher, 1983) to the tune of $4 billion in 1977 (Kiesler, 1981), with more than half this amount going to nursing home care for mental patients (Kiesler, 1980).

Such costs could be controlled by limiting reimbursement for mental health care. Such pressures have already appeared ("50% rule," 1982). In California, Connecticut, Georgia, Illinois, and Minnesota, nursing homes were said to violate a Medicaid regulation prohibiting more than 50% of a nursing home's patients from having a primary mental diagnosis. In each state, millions of dollars were at stake. Other dissatisfactions with nursing home care for mental patients are evident (Recktenwald, 1980; U.S. Senate Special Committee on Aging, 1976). Growing strains could cause policymakers to discourage nursing home care for mental patients. Policy researchers need to anticipate where those patients will go—to the lodge, board-and-care homes, the street, families? Which option holds the future of the mental health system, and why? Similarly, Kiesler (1982b) documents an increased use of general hospitals without psychiatric units as primary care sites for mental patients. What strains will this form of care produce—increased health care costs, for example?

A fundamental challenge in this task is to find solutions that do not create more strain than they reduce. Recall, for example, the recent attempt to implement a National Plan for the Chronically Mentally Ill (Public Health Service, 1980). The plan dealt

usefully with the needs of those patients. But its potential costs were so great that the Health Care Financing Administration was reluctant to support it, and so the plan remained an unrealized contribution (Shadish & Bootzin, 1981b). Contrast this with NIMH's Community Support Program (CSP; Turner & TenHoor, 1978), a small program that works with existing resources rather than requiring extensive new ones. Although it is still too early to judge the value of the CSP as policy, its focus on existing structures is more realistic than the National Plan's more grandiose scope.

Estimating demand for services. Mental health policy has always been stymied with problems in estimating demand for mental health care. In the 19th and early 20th centuries, efforts at hospital reform, for example, succeeded modestly until demand for reformed hospitals overwhelmed resources (Bell, 1980). State mental hospitals of the mid-20th century met demand until costs in the 1950s again overwhelmed the system. The National Plan for the Chronically Mentally Ill (Public Health Service, 1980) is viewed cautiously because the potential demand for its services is unknown but is feared to be high (Shadish & Bootzin, 1981b). Demand for nursing home care of mental patients has increased in recent years, potentially overwhelming the supply of Medicaid dollars (VandenBos & Buchanan, 1983). Insurance companies are unenthusiastic about funding mental health benefits partly because they fear "it might attract large numbers of people" (VandenBos, 1983, p. 952) and undermine the company's competitive position in relation to other companies not offering the benefit.

All this suggests a need to study potential demand for mental health services of all kinds. Some research, for example, suggests that mental patients enjoy institutions (Braginsky, Braginsky, & Ring, 1969) and may use such places if available. Generally, however, we know little about why patients use services or how many patients might use different kinds of services if offered. Without this knowledge, policymakers risk implementing solutions that will create more strain than their budgets can bear. If they perceive this risk, they may opt to cancel the program entirely (Bevan, 1982).

Legal concerns of mental patients. The legal system intervenes slowly in social systems. But when it does, its decisions are long lasting. State mental hospital systems already have felt the effects of cases like *O'Connor v. Donaldson* (1975) on patient treatments, rights, and activities (Bernard, 1977). Effects of such cases spread slowly, but inexorably, across mental health systems, as seen in extensions of such arguments to nursing home care for mental patients (Barnett, 1978). They will eventually affect the rest of the "de facto" (Kiesler, 1980) mental health system as well. Strain in the system will increase from these sources as courts and researchers better define concepts such as dangerousness and treatment (Bernard, 1977; Stone, 1976).

Conclusions

If policy research is more instrumentally usable to the extent that it is consistent with extant social structures and ideologies, then a new problem surfaces: Implementable policy research must avoid social problems caused by flaws in those basic social structures and ideologies. However, some of these problems are undoubtedly important. How can the policy researcher be optimistic about contributing to their solution?

The answer is that the policy researcher should be pessimistic, at least in the short term. For two reasons, of course, this pessimism will not be absolute. First, grass-roots changes in ideology do occur, creating system strains over decades that can encourage change. Second, unanticipated major changes in implemented policies do occur occasionally; varied innovations are worth retaining so they can be used in such change as opportunity permits. The implementation of health maintenance organizations (HMOs) illustrates this opportunistic approach—HMOs entered policy subsequent to several unpredicted political and economic events that resulted in the necessary social structures and ideologies in which an HMO could work (Bauman, 1976). If the strains that give rise to such opportunities could be anticipated, the study of currently nonimplementable innovations would have a better rationale.

In the meantime, however, researchers who want to produce implementable findings are constrained to work within the flaws of existing structures and ideologies, searching mostly for incremental, technical changes (DeLeon et al., 1982; Kiesler, 1982c; Rich, 1981). Although such changes generally produce small reductions in strain, they can occasionally be major—the phenothiazines, for example, are consistent with extant structures and ideologies, but they reduce a great deal of strain in the mental health system. But all in all, the set of implementable solutions must be smaller than the set of all possible solutions. So policy researchers who want their research to be implementable face a critical constraint in identifying the smaller set of solutions from the larger one.

This constraint, of course, leads to a final, fundamental question: Should policy researchers aim to produce implementable findings? Consider some implications of that choice. The policy researcher who answers yes to this question assumes the role of servant to a policy system that is conservative in redressing grievances against its basic structure and ideology. This makes the policy researcher similarly conservative, which may conflict with the political values

of social scientists, who tend to "cluster on the left-liberal end of the political spectrum" (Weiss, 1978, p. 25). Also, if the scientist's role is to be a critic of society (Dye, 1972; Gouldner, 1970), then serving the existing system may conflict with that goal. So the policy researcher must choose the servant role carefully, when an assessment of social needs and an estimate of the maximum potential of the program to meet those needs suggest that incremental changes are defensible approaches to a problem.

Many scientists, however, will decide that such changes are not marginally defensible. Evaluator Carol Weiss (1973), looking back on the failure of many of the social policies and programming of the 1960s, suggested exactly this about evaluation research, a field that is closely aligned to the kind of research discussed in the present article:

For the social scientist who wants to contribute to the improvement of social programming, there may be more effective routes at this point than through evaluation research. There may be greater potential in doing research on the processes that give rise to social problems, the institutional structures that contribute to their origin and persistence, the social arrangements that overwhelm efforts to eradicate them, and the points at which they are vulnerable to societal intervention. (pp. 44–45)

This "back to the drawing board" approach sacrifices immediate implementability, but only after an informed judgment that more fine-tuning of existing programs cannot succeed in an important way. Also, notice that Weiss did not advise the scientist simply to invent one more model program and see how it does. As does the present article, she called for study of institutional structures and of the process of change itself, to understand why current change efforts have failed and to suggest ways that might bypass these failures to produce more significant, important, or larger change.

Weiss's experiences, of course, were not unique. Many social science specialties emerged or blossomed during the social reform fervor of the 1960s, often with an avowed purpose of applying social science knowledge to important social problems, including community psychology (Heller & Monahan, 1977), evaluation research (Weiss, 1973) and policy analysis (Wildavsky, 1979). Through different routes, each arrived at a similar point—they repeatedly found many of their change efforts stymied by a social system that resisted change. These experiences may suggest that the best one can hope for is incremental change. But only a few policy researchers are seriously studying the alternative (Seidman, 1983). In this regard, if the present analysis of change is at all informative, then applied social scientists have much to learn about the relationship of their work to social change. If not, then at least it will prevent social scientists from being surprised that their good intentions do not lead to good effects in social policy. In either case, however, the study of social structures, ideologies, and change and the study of the relation of science to them is a legitimate—indeed essential—part of social science.

REFERENCES

Aiken, L. H., & Marx, M. M. (1982). Hospices: Perspectives on the public policy debate. *American Psychologist, 37,* 1271–1279.

Argyris, C. (1983). Action science and intervention. *Journal of Applied Behavioral Science, 19,* 115–140.

Bachrach, L. L. (1976). *Deinstitutionalization: An analytic review and sociological perspective* (DHEW Publication No. ADM 79-351). Washington, DC: U.S. Government Printing Office.

Bachrach, L. L. (1980). Overview: Model programs for chronic mental patients. *American Journal of Psychiatry, 137,* 1023–1031.

Baldessarini, R. J. (1977). *Chemotherapy in psychiatry.* Cambridge, MA: Harvard University Press.

Bardach, E. (1977). *The implementation game: What happens after a bill becomes a law.* Cambridge, MA: MIT Press.

Barnett, C. F. (1978). Treatment rights of mentally ill nursing home residents. *University of Pennsylvania Law Review, 126,* 578–629.

Bauman, P. (1976). The formulation and evolution of health maintenance organization policy, 1970–1973. *Social Science and Medicine, 10,* 129–142.

Bell, L. V. (1980). *Treating the mentally ill: From colonial times to the present.* New York: Praeger.

Berger, P. A., & Rexroth, K. (1980). Tardive dyskinesia: Clinical, biological, and pharmacological perspectives. *Schizophrenia Bulletin, 6,* 102–116.

Bernard, J. L. (1977). The significance for psychology of O'Connor v. Donaldson. *American Psychologist, 37,* 1085–1088.

Bevan, W. (1982). Human welfare and national policy: A conversation with Stuart Eisenstat. *American Psychologist, 37,* 1128–1135.

Bloom, B. L. (1973). *Community mental health: A historical and critical analysis.* Morristown, NJ: General Learning Press.

Bootzin, R. R., & Shadish, W. R. (1983, January). *Evaluation of mental health long term care facilities* (Final report for Grants Numbers 908-13 and 8209-21). Chicago, IL: State of Illinois Department of Mental Health and Developmental Disabilities.

Braginsky, V. M., Braginsky, D. D., & Ring, K. (1969). *Methods of madness: The mental hospital as a last resort.* New York: Holt, Rinehart, & Winston.

Brewer, M. B., & Collins, B. E. (Eds.). (1981). *Scientific inquiry and the social sciences: A volume in honor of Donald T. Campbell.* San Francisco: Jossey-Bass.

Bryk, A. S., & Raudenbush, S. W. (1983). The potential contribution of program evaluation to social problem solving: A view based on the CIS and Puch/Excel experiences. In A. S. Bryk (Ed.), *Stakeholder-based evaluation.* San Francisco: Jossey-Bass.

Cameron, J. M. (1978). Ideology and policy termination: Restructuring California's mental health system. In J. V. May & A. B. Wildavsky (Eds.), *The policy cycle* (pp. 301–328). Beverly Hills, CA: Sage Publications.

Chiles, L. M. (1982). The federal budget and the new federalism: Trends affecting mental health. *American Psychologist, 37,* 835–842.

Cline, H. F., & Sinnott, L. T. (1981). What can we learn about change in organizations? In S. Ball (Ed.), *Assessing and interpreting outcomes* (pp. 1–19). San Francisco: Jossey-Bass.

Cook, T. D. (1981). Dilemmas in evaluations of social programs. In M. B. Brewer & B. E. Collins (Eds.), *Scientific inquiry and the social sciences: A volume in honor of Donald T. Campbell* (pp. 257–287). San Francisco: Jossey-Bass.

Cook, T. D., Leviton, L. C., & Shadish, W. R. (in press). Program evaluation. In G. Lindzey & E. Aronson (Eds.), *Handbook of social psychology* (3rd ed.). Reading, MA: Addison-Wesley.

Crider, A. (1979). *Schizophrenia: A biopsychological perspective.* Hillsdale, NJ: Erlbaum.

Cronbach, L. J. (1982). *Designing evaluations of educational and social programs.* San Francisco: Jossey-Bass.

Cronbach, L. J., Ambron, S. R., Dornbusch, S. M., Hess, R. D., Hornick, R. C., Phillips, D. C., Walker, D. F., & Weiner, S. S. (1980). *Toward reform of program evaluation.* San Francisco: Jossey-Bass.

Cross, J. G., & Guyer, M. J. (1980). *Social traps.* Ann Arbor, MI: University of Michigan Press.

Cummings, N. A., & VandenBos, G. R. (1981). The twenty year Kaiser-Permanenté experience with psychotherapy and medical utilization: Implications for national health policy and national health insurance. *Health Policy Quarterly, 2,* 159–174.

DeLeon, P. H., O'Keefe, A. M., VandenBos, G. R., & Kraut, A. G. (1982). How to influence public policy: A blueprint for activism. *American Psychologist, 37,* 476–486.

DeLeon, P. H., & VandenBos, G. R. (1980). Psychotherapy reimbursement in federal programs: Political factors. In G. R. VandenBos (Ed.), *Psychotherapy: Practice, research, policy* (pp. 247–285). Beverly Hills, CA: Sage Publications.

Dittman, N. D., & Franklin, J. L. (1980a). State hospital patients discharged to nursing homes: Are hospitals dumping their more difficult patients? *Hospital and Community Psychiatry, 31,* 251–254.

Dittman, N. D., & Franklin, J. L. (1980b). State hospital patients discharged to nursing homes: How are they doing? *Hospital and Community Psychiatry, 31,* 255–258.

Dye, T. R. (1972). Policy analysis and political science: Some problems at the interface. *Policy Studies Journal, 1,* 104.

Eisdorfer, C. (1983). Conceptual models of aging: The challenge of a new frontier. *American Psychologist, 38,* 197–202.

Fairweather, G. W. (Ed.). (1980). *The Fairweather lodge: A twenty-five year retrospective.* San Francisco: Jossey-Bass.

Fairweather, G. W., Sanders, D. H., & Tornatzky, L. G. (1974). *Creating change in mental health organizations.* Elmsford, NY: Pergamon Press.

Fairweather, G. W., Simon, R., Gebhard, M. E., Weingarten, E., Holland, J. L., Sanders, R., Stone, G. B., & Reahl, G. E. (1960). Relative effectiveness of psychotherapeutic programs: A multicriteria comparison of four programs for three different groups. *Psychological Monographs, 74* (5, Whole No. 492).

Felton, B. J., & Shinn, M. (1981). Ideology and practice of deinstitutionalization. *Journal of Social Issues, 37,* 158–172.

Feyerabend, P. (1975). *Against method: Outline of an anarchistic theory of knowledge.* London, England: Redwood Burn Limited.

Feyerabend, P. (1978). *Science in a free society.* London, England: NLB.

"50% rule" triggers state suits. (1982, April). *APA Monitor,* p. 2.

Fisher, K. (1983, April). Mentally ill bear brunt of crackdown. *APA Monitor,* pp. 20–21.

Fishman, D. B., & Neigher, W. D. (1982). American psychology in the eighties: Who will buy? *American Psychologist, 37,* 533–546.

Fox, R. E. (1982). The need for a reorientation of clinical psychology. *American Psychologist, 37,* 1051–1057.

Frankfather, D. L. (1982). Welfare entrepreneurialism and the politics of innovation. In E. R. House, S. Mathison, J. A. Pearsol, & H. Preskill (Eds.), *Evaluation Studies Review Annual* (Vol. 7, pp. 603–620). Beverly Hills, CA: Sage Publications.

Goffman, E. (1961). *Asylums: Essays on the social situation of mental patients and other inmates.* New York: Doubleday Anchor.

Goldman, H. H., Gattozzi, A. A., & Taube, C. A. (1981). Defining and counting the chronically mentally ill. *Hospital and Community Psychiatry, 32,* 21–27.

Gottlieb, B. H. (Ed.). (1981). *Social networks and social support.* Beverly Hills, CA: Sage Publications.

Gouldner, A. W. (1970). *The coming crisis of Western sociology.* New York: Basic Books.

Graziano, A. M. (1969). Clinical innovation and the mental health power structure. *American Psychologist, 24,* 10–18.

Greenblatt, M. (1978). Drugs, schizophrenia and the third revolution. In M. A. Lipton, A. DiMascio, & K. F. Killam (Eds.), *Psychopharmacology: A generation of progress* (pp. 1179–1184). New York: Avon Books.

Guba, E. G., & Lincoln, Y. S. (1981). *Effective evaluation: Improving the usefulness of evaluation results through responsive and naturalistic approaches.* San Francisco: Jossey-Bass.

Hagedorn, H. J., Beck, K. J., Neubert, S. F., & Werlin, S. H. (1976). *A working manual of simple program evaluation techniques for community mental health centers* (DHEW Publication No. ADM 79-404). Washington, DC: U.S. Government Printing Office.

Hall, P. M. (1983). Individualism and social problems: A critique and an alternative. *Journal of Applied Behavioral Science. 19,* 85–94.

Heller, K., & Monahan, J. (1977). *Psychology and community change.* Homewood, IL: Dorsey Press.

Hesse, M. B. (1980). *Revolutions and reconstructions in the philosophy of science.* Bloomington, IN: Indiana University Press.

Horowitz, I. L., & Katz, J. E. (1975). *Social science and public policy in the United States.* New York: Praeger.

Institute for Social Research. (1980). Mental health programs in trouble. *ISR Newsletter, 8,* 5–6.

Iscoe, I. (1982). Toward a viable community health psychology: Caveats from the experiences of the community mental health movement. *American Psychologist, 37,* 961–965.

James, D. B. (1972). *Poverty, politics, and change.* Englewood Cliffs, NJ: Prentice-Hall.

Johnson, D. W. (1978). Social policy planning in a federal structure: A social learning strategy. *Evaluation and Program Planning. 1,* 259–264.

Kamis-Gould, E., & Piasecki, J. R. (Eds.). (1981). Needs assessment. [Special issue]. *Evaluation and Program Planning, 4.*

Karon, B. P., & VandenBos, G. R. (1981). *Psychotherapy of schizophrenia: The treatment of choice.* New York: Aronson, Jason.

Kiesler, C. A. (1980). Mental health policy as a field of inquiry for psychology. *American Psychologist, 35,* 1066–1080.

Kiesler, C. A. (1981). Barriers to effective knowledge use in mental health policy. *Health Policy Quarterly, 1,* 201–215.

Kiesler, C. A. (1982a). Mental hospitals and alternative care: Non-institutionalization as a potential public policy for mental patients. *American Psychologist, 37,* 349–360.

Kiesler, C. A. (1982b). Public and professional myths about mental hospitalization: An empirical assessment of policy-related beliefs. *American Psychologist, 37,* 1323–1339.

Kiesler, C. A. (1982c). A rich analysis of a failure [Review of *Social science information and public policy making*]. *Contemporary Psychology, 27,* 697–698.

Kiesler, C. A. (1983, March). *Psychotherapy research and top-down policy analysis.* Paper presented at the meeting of the American Psychopathological Association, New York City.

Klein, R. (1982). Evaluation and social policy: Some reflections on ideas and institutions. *Evaluation and Program Planning, 5,* 133–140.

Kramer, M. (1977). *Psychiatric services and the changing institutional scene, 1950–1985* (DHEW Publication No. ADM 77-433). Washington, DC: U.S. Government Printing Office.

Lenrow, P., & Cowden, P. (1980). Human services, professionals, and the paradox of institutional reform. *American Journal of Community Psychology, 8,* 463–484.

Levine, M. (1979). Congress (and evaluators) ought to pay more attention to history. *American Journal of Community Psychology, 7,* 1–17.

Levine, M. (1980). *From state hospital to psychiatric center.* Lexington, MA: Lexington Books.

Leviton, L. C., & Hughes, E. F. X. (1981). Research on the utilization

of evaluations: A review and synthesis. *Evaluation Review, 5,* 525–548.

Lindblom, C. E., & Cohen, D. K. (1979). *Usable knowledge: Social science and social problem solving.* New Haven, CT: Yale University Press.

Mayer, R. R. (1979). *Social science and institutional change* (DHEW Publication No. ADM 78-627). Washington, DC: U.S. Government Printing Office.

McNett, I. (1981, January). Deinstitutionalization in Italy: More politics than economics. *APA Monitor, 12,* 9.

Mosher, L. R. (1982). Italy's revolutionary mental health law: An assessment. *American Journal of Psychiatry, 139,* 199–203.

Naierman, N., Haskins, B., & Robinson, G. (1978). *Community mental health centers—A decade later.* Cambridge, MA: Abt Associates.

Nathan, P. E. (1983). Failures in prevention: Why we can't prevent the devastating effect of alcoholism and drug abuse. *American Psychologist, 38,* 459–467.

Neugarten, B. L. (1983). Health care, Medicare, and health policy for older people: A conversation with Arthur Flemming. *American Psychologist, 38,* 311–315.

Norwood, L., & Mason, M. (1982, September). *Evaluation of community support programs in Texas* (Contract No. 2 H84 MH 35825-02). Washington, DC: National Institute of Mental Health.

O'Connor v. Donaldson, 422 U.S. 563 (1975).

Paul, G. L., & Lentz, R. J. (1977). *Psychological treatment of chronic mental patients: Milieu versus social-learning programs.* Cambridge, MA: Harvard University Press.

Pertschuk, M., & Correia, E. (1983). The AMA versus competition. *American Psychologist, 38,* 607–610.

President's Commission on Mental Health. (1978). *Report to the President* (Vols. 1–4). Washington, DC: U.S. Government Printing Office.

Public Health Service. (1980). *Towards a national plan for the chronically mentally ill.* Washington, DC: Department of Health and Human Services.

Recktenwald, W. (1980, July 27). U.S. blasts state on nursing homes. *Chicago Tribune,* Section 1, p. 3.

Rhine, W. R. (1983). The role of psychologists in the national Follow Through Project. *American Psychologist, 38,* 288–297.

Rich, R. F. (1981). *Social science information and public policy making.* San Francisco: Jossey-Bass.

Roosens, E. (1979). *Mental patients in town life: Geel—Europe's first therapeutic community.* Beverly Hills, CA: Sage Publications.

Sarason, S. B. (1976). Community psychology, networks, and Mr. Everyman. *American Psychologist, 31,* 317–328.

Sarason, S. B. (1981). *Psychology misdirected.* New York: The Free Press.

Schorr, A. L. (1971). Public policy and private interest. In I. L. Horowitz (Ed.), *The use and abuse of social science* (pp. 155–169). New Brunswick, NJ: Transaction Books.

Scriven, M. (1980). *The logic of evaluation.* Inverness, CA: Edgepress.

Scriven, M. (1983). Evaluation ideologies. In G. F. Madaus, M. Scriven, & D. L. Stufflebeam (Eds.), *Evaluation models: Viewpoints on educational and human services evaluation.* Boston: Kluwer-Nijhoff.

Segal, S. P., & Aviram, U. (1978). *The mentally ill in community-based sheltered care.* New York: Wiley.

Segal, S. P., Baumohl, J., & Johnson, E. (1977). Falling through the cracks: Mental disorder and social margin in a young vagrant population. *Social Problems, 24,* 387–400.

Seidman, E. (Ed.). (1983). *Handbook of social interventions.* Beverly Hills, CA: Sage Publications.

Shadish, W. R., & Bootzin, R. R. (1981a). Long-term community care: Mental health policy in the face of reality. *Schizophrenia Bulletin, 7,* 580–585.

Shadish, W. R., & Bootzin, R. R. (1981b). Nursing homes and chronic mental patients. *Schizophrenia Bulletin, 7,* 488–498.

Shadish, W. R., Straw, R. B., McSweeny, A. J., Koller, D. L., &

Bootzin, R. R. (1981). Nursing home care for mental patients: Descriptive data and some propositions. *American Journal of Community Psychology, 9,* 617–633.

Shadish, W. R., Thomas, S., & Bootzin, R. R. (1982). Criteria for success in deinstitutionalization: Perceptions of nursing homes by different interest groups. *American Journal of Community Psychology, 10,* 553–566.

Simon, H. A. (1960). *The new science of management decision.* New York: Harper and Row.

Stein, L. I., & Test, M. A. (Eds.). (1978). *Alternatives to mental hospital treatment.* New York: Plenum Press.

Stone, A. A. (1976). *Mental health and law: A system in transition* (DHEW Publication No. ADM 76-176). Washington, DC: U.S. Government Printing Office.

Storandt, M. (1983). Psychology's response to the graying of America. *American Psychologist, 38,* 323–326.

Stotsky, G. A. (1967). Nursing home or mental hospital: Which is better for the geriatric mental patient? *Journal of Genetic Psychology, 111,* 113–117.

Swensen, C. H. (1983). A respectable old age. *American Psychologist, 38,* 327–334.

Tornatzky, L. G., & Johnson, E. C. (1982). Research on implementation: Implications for evaluation practice and evaluation policy. *Evaluation and Program Planning, 5,* 193–198.

Turkington, C. (1982, June). Chinese culture facilities care for mentally ill. *APA Monitor, 13,* 32.

Turner, J. C., & TenHoor, W. J. (1978). The NIMH Community Support Program: Pilot approach to a needed social reform. *Schizophrenia Bulletin, 4,* 319–349.

U.S. Senate Special Committee on Aging, Subcommittee on Long-Term Care. (1976). *Nursing home care in the United States: Failure of public policy: Supporting Paper No. 7. The role of* nursing homes in caring for discharged mental patients (and the birth of a for-profit boarding home industry). Washington, DC: U.S. Government Printing Office.

VandenBos, G. R. (1983). Health financing, service utilization, and national policy: A conversation with Stan Jones. *American Psychologist, 38,* 948–955.

VandenBos, G. R., & Buchanan, J. (1983). Aging, research on aging, and national policy: A conversation with Robert Butler. *American Psychologist, 38,* 300–307.

Vladeck, B. C. (1980). *Unloving care: The nursing home tragedy.* New York: Basic Books.

Watzlawick, P., Weakland, J., & Fisch, R. (1974). *Change: Principles of problem formation and problem resolution.* New York: Norton.

Weiss, C. H. (1973). Where politics and evaluation research meet. *Evaluation, 1,* 37–45.

Weiss, C. H. (Ed.). (1977). *Using social research in public policy making.* Lexington, MA: Lexington Books.

Weiss, C. H. (1978). Improving the linkage between social research and public policy. In L. E. Lynn (Ed.), *Knowledge and policy: The uncertain connection* (pp. 23–81). Washington, DC: National Academy of Sciences.

Weiss, C. H., & Fuller, T. D. (1983). On evaluating development assistance projects: Some innovations. *Evaluation Review, 7,* 175–190.

Weiss, J. A., & Weiss, C. H. (1981). Social scientists and decision makers look at the usefulness of mental health research. *American Psychologist, 38,* 837–847.

Wiggins, J. G., Bennett, B. E., Batchelor, W. F., & West, P. R. (1983). Psychologists in defense of the Federal Trade Commission. *American Psychologist, 38,* 602–606.

Wildavsky, A. (1979). *Speaking truth to power: The art and craft of policy analysis.* Boston: Little, Brown.

SECTION 2
The Role of Program Theory

One of the characteristic features of a program research orientation to evaluation study, as we have described it, is attention to theory, that is, some level of conceptual generalization, especially causal analysis. The four chapters in this section of the volume exemplify this feature of program research quite well. All are explicitly concerned with program theory—the assumptions and concepts embodied in the program that explain how it is to have its intended effects. Additionally, such theory is quite naturally structured in the form of causal chains, sets of cause-and-effect propositions connecting controllable program activities with expected outcomes.

Following from this broad concern with theory and causality, we find another common feature of these four chapters. All advocate or apply a relatively comprehensive approach to program study. That is, they attend to organizational features of the program, the actual implementation of intended program activities and delivery of intended services, the characteristics and responses of program recipients, and the eventual effects of the program on those recipients. Among these studies, programs are represented as something more than undifferentiated "black boxes" with categorical effects; they have a complexity that must be mirrored in the concepts and design of the program research study.

With this differentiation and complexity comes a necessary enlarging and prolonging of the research process. All of these chapters reflect evaluation studies that have a multifaceted, programmatic, sequential character; none report quick "one-shot" studies. Such differentiated, theory-sensitive studies require ample time, labor, and technical expertise to be done well. The fact that the recent literature contains numerous good examples of studies taking an explicitly theoretical orientation constitutes, we think, a sign of the potential and vigor of the program research orientation.

The first of the chapters in this section is, in some ways, the most ambitious. Gottfredson describes what he calls the "program development evaluation" approach as an integration of theory and theory testing not only into the evaluation but also into the original design and planning of the program itself. The result, he argues, is a stronger program, a more responsive evaluation, and enhanced theory testing. This approach thus aspires to increase both the theoretical and the practical relevance of evaluation research.

In the second chapter, Wang and Walberg present a case example of a theory-driven approach to evaluation that shares much in spirit with Gottfredson's approach. Their most distinctive emphasis is on adapting research and theory from relevant disciplines, for example, psychology, sociology, and education, for use in designing the intervention and structuring the evaluation. (See Silberman, 1984, for a similar approach applying social learning theory to vocational education; also, Bell, 1985, regarding design and evaluation of educational technology.)

The dual role played by research is especially interesting in the Wang and Walberg study. Developmental research was first used to test elements of proposed program design; then evaluation research was conducted on implementation and outcome once all the components were assembled into an operative program.

In this section, the third chapter by Shapiro represents something of a contrast. Although the first two chapters report attempts to build theory into program design, Shapiro examines a case where it is necessary to extract the theory implicit in the program design. He shares the view of evaluation research as a theory-testing activity and dramatizes the point by describing a program that failed because its implicit theory was in error. By representing the program as a cause-and-effect relationship, Shapiro is able to distinguish between a program failure (lack of implementation of the assumed causal process) and a program theory failure (inability of that process to produce the expected outcome). We might add that a program theory could be wrong for some circumstances and right for others, a point made nicely in a recent article by Fuller and Rapoport (1984).

Finney and Moos, in the fourth chapter of this section, use mental health and substance abuse programs to illustrate that inclusion of social-environmental measures can be used to assess treatment implementation, analyze treatment process, identify extratreatment factors that mediate treatment effects, and define outcome variables. Their contribution to program theory is to argue for the inclusion of environmental variables and not solely person-centered variables when unpacking the black-box representing treatment processes.

Our characterization of the program research orientation stresses its conceptual aspects and potential contribution to generalizable knowledge and theory regarding social intervention. This emphasis may mislead both critics and sympathizers into believing that we expect studies done with a program research orientation to serve exclusively theoretical purposes and necessarily have limited practical value to program managers and decision makers. The chapters in this section show just how misleading such an impression would be. All of the projects they present provide a wealth of detailed and practical information that could be used for program improvement and effective program management. Indeed, we would expect all competently executed program research studies to have considerable practical value. What distinguishes the program research orientation is that the evaluation design is framed in terms of concepts, variables, and relationships of potential generality. The chapters in this section illustrate various ways in which that can be done.

REFERENCES

Bell, M. E. (1985). The role of instructional theories in the evaluation of microcomputer courseware. *Educational Technology, 25*(3), 36-39.

Fuller, B., & Rapoport, T. (1984). Indigenous evaluation: Distinguishing the formal and informal organizational structures of youth programs. *Evaluation Review, 8*(1), 25-44.

Silberman, H. F. (1984). Evaluating intrinsic goals. *Studies in Educational Evaluation, 10,* 27-38.

28

A Theory-Ridden Approach to Program Evaluation

A Method for Stimulating Researcher-Implementer Collaboration

Gary D. Gottfredson

ABSTRACT: Social programs are often based on unarticulated or vague theoretical rationales. The typical evaluations of such programs are theory free, and therefore the evaluations make limited contributions to theory. A program development evaluation (PDE) approach, planned to integrate theory testing with the development and evaluation of action programs, is described and illustrated. This approach is intended to (a) develop stronger programs and achieve the implementation of more relevant and useful evaluations through collaboration with project implementers, (b) increase the clarity of projects' theoretical rationales, (c) identify and measure the most appropriate variables, and (d) increase the strength and fidelity of interventions. As an adaptation of the action research paradigm, the PDE approach is a method to increase the theoretical and practical relevance of evaluation research.

This article is about a critical task facing psychologists—how to design research that advances both theory and practice in community, mental health, and organizational psychology. Social programs, like programs in other areas, are often based on unarticulated or unclearly articulated theoretical rationales. The evaluations of these programs are typically theory free, and therefore make limited contributions to theory (Chen & Rossi, 1980; Martin, Sechrest, & Redner, 1981). In addition, theory is seldom used as a guide to program implementation. Too often what is implemented is unknown, or is not what was intended (Dixon & Wright, 1975; Sarason, 1971). Many attempts to demonstrate the effectiveness of specifiable social programs may have failed because plausible interventions were not implemented or their implementation was not documented (Hall & Loucks, 1977; Quay, 1977; Sechrest, White, & Brown, 1979), or the plan for the innovation was not clearly articulated at the outset. Evaluations are therefore evaluations of weak or unknown programs.

My colleagues and I (G. D. Gottfredson, 1982;

G. D. Gottfredson, D. C. Gottfredson, & Cook, 1983; G. D. Gottfredson, Rickert, D. C. Gottfredson, & Advani, in press) have created a program development evaluation (PDE) method to facilitate the design, implementation, and testing of stronger programs. The method provides a structure to merge the roles and activities of organization developer, theoretician, and evaluation researcher. An elaboration of action research (Chein, Cook, & Harding, 1948; Lewin, 1947; Sanford, 1970), the PDE method is an approach to knowledge generation and organizational growth derived from a tradition of concern for practical theory, useful research, and organizational change and development.

Guiding Principles

The evolution and use of the PDE structure is guided by seven principles. They are used to make decisions about the conduct of the evaluation research and to resolve ambiguities about appropriate next steps. The guiding principles form a theory about doing theory-relevant research while increasing organizational effectiveness. We assume that evaluation research conducted in accordance with these principles will be more productive. Similarly, organizations that implement programs using these principles should be more effective than organizations that ignore them.

1. Projects guided by explicit theories that can be translated into practice will be most effective. Not all theories can be translated into action by any given project, and all theories are not created equal. Science progresses by creating ideas and eventually rejecting the unproductive ones; some ideas have shown utility, and other things being equal, ideas that have survived previous empirical tests should have considerable precedence. The theory guiding a project should be a template for it, with decisions and interventions judged against it at the same time that the theory is judged by the effectiveness of the interventions. Projects will be implemented with most enthusiasm, be strongest, and contribute most

to knowledge if (a) the theory is generated by or regarded as sensible by the project implementers and (b) the theory is consistent with evidence from research and evaluation.

2. Effective *adoption* of an innovation is more likely when explicit plans for adoption are available and perceived obstacles to organizational change are seen as likely to be overcome by a conceivable plan.

3. Effective *implementation* of an intervention or innovation is more likely if (a) blueprints for the intervention (manuals, protocols, etc.) are available, or the intervention is structured by forms, rules, or operating procedures, and (b) implementation is subject to data guidance, or observation and feedback of information to workers about the degree to which their behavior accords with the behavior specified by the blueprints for the intervention. Effective blueprints include plans for the data guidance and provide for documentation of the implementation of interventions.

4. Projects will increase in effectiveness under evaluation pressure (Tharp & Gallimore, 1979). This pressure or influence takes many forms, the most important of which are (a) pressure to focus on theory in examining organizational behavior and the behavior of the organization's inhabitants; (b) pressure from potentially useful knowledge or information of relevance to the organization; (c) pressure from "personal knowledge" based on many sources, including direct observation or experience; (d) pressure from the rigorous, theory-based evaluation of intervention components; (e) pressure from the rigorous, theory-based evaluation of projects as a whole; (f) pressure from feedback about steps taken to adopt an innovation; and (g) pressure from feedback about steps taken to implement an intervention.

5. Projects internalizing these principles will behave in accordance with them more often than projects that simply comply with the application of them, and the former will therefore ultimately be more effective.

6. The more directly project implementers

An earlier version of this report was presented at the meeting of the American Society of Criminology, Toronto, November 1982. The development of this report was supported in part by Grant 80-JN-AX-0005 from the National Institute for Juvenile Justice and Delinquency Prevention, U.S. Department of Justice, and in part by Grant NIE-G-80-0113 from the National Institute of Education, U.S. Department of Education. The opinions expressed do not necessarily reflect the position or policy of either institute. I am grateful for advice from Michael S. Cook, Deborah Daniels, Denise C. Gottfredson, John L. Holland, John Hollifield, Robert Slavin, and Jane St. John on a draft of this article and for discussions with LaMar Empey, J. Douglas Grant, Lee Sechrest, and Carol Yamasaki.
Requests for reprints should be sent to Gary D. Gottfredson, Center for Social Organization of Schools, Johns Hopkins University, 3505 North Charles Street, Baltimore, Maryland 21218.

benefit from evaluation, the more evaluation will be integrated with project operations.

7. The interests of project implementers and evaluators coincide because one of the best ways to create communicable knowledge is through the rigorous, theory-guided evaluation of well-implemented interventions that can be described so well that others can understand what was done and therefore replicate them. In short, both implementers and researchers need rigorous evaluation, the adoption of innovations, well-implemented interventions, thorough description, and theory.

These guiding principles appear consonant with sound organization development practice (French & Bell, 1978), useful field research practices (Empey, 1980), practical wisdom in evaluation research (Tharp & Gallimore, 1979) and the calling of evaluation research (Patton, 1981). They were used to create the PDE method.

Organization Development as an Antecedent of PDE

One of the roots of program development evaluation is the practice of organization development (OD). French and Bell (1978) characterize OD as a process involving action research that emphasizes normative change, is based on behavioral science, involves experience-based learning of intact work teams, and emphasizes goals and objectives. By characterizing OD as a process, French and Bell mean that OD is "not to be regarded as a one-shot solution to organizational problems, but more as a 'growing toward' greater effectiveness through a *series* of intervention activities over a period of time. . . . Changing the *culture* of . . . an entire organization is a long-term, involved process" (p. 69). In addition, they see OD as a process involving rational, empirical strategies, but one that is even more dependent on normative–reeducative strategies: "The *client* defines what changes and improvements he or she wants to make, rather than the change agent; the change agent attempts to intervene in a mutual, collaborative way with the client as they together define problems and seek solutions; anything hindering effective problem solving is brought to light and publicly examined" (pp. 75–76). The emphasis on normative education is based on the assumption that behaviors are rooted in norms, values, or beliefs as well as in rationality and self-interest. Typically, OD emphasizes concrete goal setting through the shared experience of group planning. The on-the-job learning experience of an intact group is presumed to promote organizational and individual effectiveness.

The interactive, collaborative, participative approach, often used by behavioral scientists serving as consultants or facilitators of organizational planning and decision making, has much to offer in overcoming some of the difficulties a research effort may expect to face. First, increasing the effectiveness of an organization's decision-making process should increase the likelihood that it will succeed in implementing interventions with a possibility of being shown to be effective when subjected to summative evaluation. Second, in the OD process, the scientist approaches an organization in a manner that may decrease the extent to which he or she is perceived as an alien invader. By helping an organization clarify its goals and objectives, by assisting in creating more open communication, and by fostering the expectation that projects will change and develop over time, the researcher may come to be considered a person to be trusted to convey useful news. And, the perspective that information, even uncomfortable information, is valuable in confronting important problems may decrease the organization's usual fear of evaluation. Finally, the links between OD and action research make the interjection of formal research possible.

The program development evaluation method is in part a descendant of an OD method previously used by the Social Action Research Center (Blanton & Alley, 1976, 1978, 1981) in projects to manage and study social change. This predecessor, called the program development (PD) model, involves examining a project's environment, creating implementation strategies, and focusing on goals. In practice, the PD specialist focuses on interaction with project implementers to assist in assessing needs, in articulating goals and more specific objectives, in analyzing a project's environmental constraints and resources, and in developing strategies for change or implementation. Like other forms of organizational development, PD emphasizes participatory planning to increase organizational and individual competencies in decision making and planning.

Action Research as an Antecedent of PDE

PDE also has roots in action research. The modern origins of action research lie in the work of Dewey (1933) and Lewin (1946). The roots of action research are, however, deeper than this. They can be traced back to the Baconian formulation of the scientific method, which specified three steps: (a) the formation of hypotheses, (b) the empirical testing of the hypotheses, and (c) the acceptance or rejection of the hypotheses (Deese, 1972). Since Bacon, science has been more active than speculative, historical, or reflective. Dewey translated the scientific method of problem solving for laypersons, and Lewin applied the scientific method to solving practical social problems.

Broad attention was called to action research by Lewin (1947), who saw that collaboration between the change agent (or field worker) and the researcher is important for both planning and management:

Planning starts usually with something like a general idea. For one reason or another it seems desirable to reach a certain objective. . . . The first step, then, is to examine the idea carefully in the light of the means available. Frequently more fact-finding about the situation is required. If the first period of planning is successful, two items emerge: an "overall plan" of how to reach the objective and a decision in regard to the first step of the action. Usually this planning has also somewhat modified the original idea. The next period is devoted to executing the first step of the overall plan . . . [and] by certain fact-findings. . . . This . . . fact-finding has four functions. It should evaluate the action by showing whether what has been achieved is above or below expectation. It should serve as a basis for correctly planning the next step, [and for] modifying the "overall plan." Finally, it gives the planners a chance to learn, that is, to gather new general insight . . . regarding the strength or weakness of certain . . . techniques of action. . . .

Rational social management, therefore, proceeds in a spiral of steps each of which is composed of a circle of planning, action, and fact-finding about the result of the action. (pp. 333–334)

This sequential and spiraling method of problem solving is now widely used in organizational development efforts and has been applied in a variety of industrial, human service, and educational action research projects; and it appears to be at the heart of Tharp and Gallimore's (1979) evaluation succession model.

Several varieties of activity are often called action research (Chein, Cook, & Harding, 1948). Sometimes the effort is limited to diagnosis and recommendations; sometimes organizations or project implementers carry out the entire process; sometimes records or diaries of actions taken and their perceived effects are maintained. Tharp and Gallimore (1979) describe several ways of "knowing," each appropriate to different stages in the development of a program. What they call "experimentation," "qualitative/personal knowing," "data guidance," and "program evaluation" are all useful in program development and research. But the variety of action research most productive of trustworthy knowledge is experimental action research. Unfortunately, experimental action research is also the most difficult to perform, because it requires the conditions necessary for confident inference (Cook & Campbell, 1979; G. D. Gottfredson, 1982, Ch. 3) and a stable set of interventions that the organization knows how to and can implement in testable form. Because of the pace of organizational change, rigorous examination of the consequences of actions may not always be timely, and less rigorous ways of knowing about the effects of innovations are often necessary. But research must be coordinate rather than subordinate to problem solving; solving problems without learning how or why they were solved will contribute little in the long run to organizational effectiveness or to theory.

The PDE Method

The PDE method emphasizes (a) theory, (b) measurement, and (c) experimental or quasi-experimental design to a greater extent than do many approaches to organizational change and development. In addition, some commonly used terms (most notably *objectives*) are defined in a special way. (The use of the term *objectives* is different from the way this term is used by Rossi and Freeman, 1982, for example.) Mastery of the practical meanings of the terms in the PDE structure will provide change agents and researchers with a language for thinking about, facilitating, managing, and studying change efforts.

The program development evaluation method, illustrated in Figure 1, incorporates theory as an explicit component, gives *measurable* goals and objectives a central place, and incorporates planning for implementing the evaluation in the same way that planning for any other aspect of a project is incorporated. It allows project implementers and evaluators to monitor critical benchmarks in the adoption of a strategy to create change, and it allows them to monitor implementation standards in the implementation of interventions. The principal concepts involved in the PDE structure are elaborated below.

Problems and Goals

Within the PDE structure, an overarching aim is called a goal. A goal is the obverse of a problem; it specifies how the level of the problem may be measured and, therefore, how one may know if progress is being made. Several secondary questions are important when discussing goals. The first question serves to reduce ambiguity and enable evaluation; it asks how each goal may be measured. The second question serves to promote realistic research designs; it asks when a project can expect to make a substantial difference and therefore specifies the duration of intervention and the timing of measurement. And the third question, essential in experimental or quasi-experimental action research, asks how one may know that the project itself is responsible for progress toward the goal. These questions are, of course, steps toward involving project implementers in the design of the research, and they serve to make explicit what the organization expects to accomplish.

Theory

Actions are taken for reasons that are either articulated or unarticulated. The PDE method is a vehicle for making theory explicit. Theory helps to organize knowledge and to communicate, it provides a guide for action, and it assists in developing and assessing interventions. "Once a basic problem is stated in theoretical terms, planners have an explicit foundation on which to build an intervention strategy and from which to derive a research strategy in conjunction with the intervention" (Martin et al., 1981, p. 34; cf. Glaser, 1980). In short, an explicit theory provides a template for project implementers' use in building their interventions, as well as a template by which both implementers and researchers can assess those interventions. Therefore, the PDE method calls for deliberate consideration of the question "Why do these problems exist?" When an intervention is designed using theory, its evaluation tests the theory undergirding the intervention.

Objectives

In the language of PDE, an objective is an intermediate outcome that a project's theory of action implies is important. Like goals, objectives must be stated in measurable terms. Some examples may help make the distinction between goals and objectives clear.

Suppose that a change agent wishes to decrease the death rate due to gastroenteritis in a rural society. The change agent theorizes that the deaths are due to the contamination of village water supplies

Figure 1
The Program Development Evaluation Method

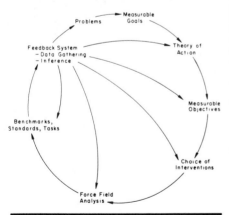

with the cholera microorganism. This theory might suggest a campaign to chlorinate wells, with the objective of decreasing this contamination. The *objective* would be measured by laboratory analyses of well-water samples to determine the levels of microbial contamination, and attainment of the *goal* might be measured by counts of deaths per 100,000 population due to gastroenteritis.

Another change agent might see the problem somewhat differently. This second change agent might theorize that the suffering and death are due to poor environmental sanitation: Because few villagers use sanitary latrines, well water is easily contaminated, and the cholera microorganism spreads from infected to uninfected persons. This theory might suggest a campaign directed at persuading villagers to construct sanitary latrines and sanitary wells. The objective now involves villager behavior and might be measured by the proportion of households using sanitary latrines and water from protected wells.

A theory can, of course, suggest multiple interventions and multiple objectives. The second change agent's theory would also reasonably imply chlorination of wells and assessment of well water. The more comprehensive a theory, the more complex the array of interventions and objectives it is likely to suggest.

Change agents could develop theories at many levels to explain the problem of cholera deaths, and each level might suggest different interventions. To continue the examples, change agents might attribute the problem to (a) beliefs in village societies that current standards of environmental sanitation are adequate; (b) the poverty and segregation of the rural people, which deprive them of the resources to build sanitary devices and concentrate them so that they are at high risk; (c) social stratification that allows only an elite merchant class access to sufficient resources to enjoy a sanitary environment; or (d) stratification in the world system that enables capitalist countries to keep countries with rural rubber-tapping populations impoverished and the cost of raw materials low. Each of these theories may have considerable validity. Yet each would imply different interventions to solve the problem, ranging from dumping chlorine in wells to world economic reorganization. No single cholera prevention project is likely to attempt interventions at all of these levels, and so will not have objectives at each level. A project's theory of action—the theory that drives its interventions—is the theory that is relevant in specifying objectives.

Again, answers to several key questions—how objectives may be measured, when effects are to be expected, and how one may know that the intervention caused the effects—serve to create the evaluation or research design. In addition, the explicit statement of objectives serves to make clear to the organization what it expects to happen as a result of its efforts.

Intervention

An intervention is an action taken to achieve an objective or set of objectives. Ordinarily, it is a major component of a project. The term is often synonymous with *change, treatment,* or *component.* Some interventions are aimed at changing the behavior, attitudes, or status of individual people; others are aimed at changing the behavior of an organization or collectivity. An intervention is a process, action, structure, rule, or substance that is applied or put in place to achieve an objective or set of objectives, and therefore to move closer to achieving a goal. An intervention may be chemical, physical, biological, behavioral, social, political, or structural. The interventions employed should be aimed at the objectives an organization's theory of action implies must be achieved.

Force Field

A force field (Lewin, 1951) is the social–psychological field that immediately surrounds a decision or action. It includes the forces that compel or restrain against alternative actions as they are perceived by an individual or corporate actor. An examination or analysis of an organization's force field, especially one that focuses on the resources available and the obstacles to action, is frequently useful for four reasons: (a) By focusing on the organization's perceptions of environmental influences, the nature of these perceptions becomes explicit and open to scrutiny, revision, supplementation, and test; (b) a complete account of obstacles and resources decreases the likelihood that pitfalls or potentials will be overlooked in the development of a project; (c) using knowledge of the influences in the project's environment helps to capitalize on opportunities or arrangements that go beyond the resources under a project's direct control; and (d) alternative strategies or plans to implement any intervention can be created and assessed in the context of the force field. Attention to the force field surrounding a research project increases the likelihood that both interventions and research designs will be implemented as intended.

Because initial analyses of a force field may be objectively incorrect, because perceptions change over time, and because the action of a project may alter its force field, the field should be viewed as dynamic. A sensible practice, therefore, is to perform force field analysis periodically, especially when any strategy being executed on the basis of an initial force field analysis is not working well. Breakdowns in experimental design or in the implementation of an intervention would require a new analysis. Examples of force field analysis are provided by Hersey and Blanchard (1982, pp. 115–119, 269–272), and practical guidance on working with an organization to analyze its force field is offered by Blanton and Alley (1976, pp. 103–113).

Strategies

Strategies are plans. According to the PDE method, strategies are developed from a force field analysis, just as objectives and interventions derive from a theory of action about a problem. Several possible strategies for implementing a research project or one of its component interventions are likely to exist. The task for project implementers and researchers is to create a plan that is perceived as feasible and attractive. If a critical path in some plan is blocked and no way around the obstacle is perceived, the plan is not a good one. Alternative paths that objectively exist but have not been perceived will not be followed. A workable strategy makes use of an organization's resources to overcome obstacles to implementation and research. Such a strategy may involve (a) moving around an obstacle, (b) decreasing the strength of the forces working against implementation, (c) turning an obstacle into a resource, or (d) using a strategy in which the obstacle is irrelevant and need not be overcome.

A fully articulated strategy is composed of three kinds of elements: critical benchmarks, implementation standards, and tasks.

Critical benchmarks. A critical benchmark is a key decision, agreement, action, or arrangement necessary to move forward with a plan. A benchmark is much like a gate that must be opened to move along a path. If the gate does not open, progress in executing the strategy is blocked. The locations and nature of these benchmarks are made clear in the process of analyzing the force field around an intervention. For example, the force field analysis about a project's efforts to provide in-service training for teachers might imply that an obstacle lies in teacher unwillingness to participate in training outside of normal working hours and that a resource is the authority of the deputy superintendent of schools to grant release time and to allocate funds for substitute instructors. The deputy superintendent's agreement to grant release time and to authorize the expenditure is a critical benchmark. The deputy superintendent is a gatekeeper (Lewin, 1947, p. 333).

Specifying when a critical benchmark is to be accomplished facilitates management. Any strategy requires a temporal or logical sequence of milestones that must be met. In the foregoing example, a failure to accomplish the critical benchmark would signal the need to devise a new strategy for getting the training done or the need to seek an alternative to training.

Implementation standards. The second part of a strategy for the implementation of both intervention and research involves developing a set of implementation standards. Sound research practice involves attention to survey response rates, the measurement of independent and dependent variables, and the procedures used to induce experimental manipulations. Researchers in experimental social psychology and physiology routinely conduct manipulation checks to determine that implementation standards have been met. In research on the effects of dietary supplementation or deficiencies, investigators do not assume that an artificial diet has been composed as intended, but they perform quantitative analyses on samples of the actual food to determine that the diet consumed *was* the diet intended (e.g., Vohra, Gottfredson, & Kratzer, 1968). And, careful researchers on labeling effects perform manipulation checks to see that interpersonal expectancies have been experimentally modified as intended (e.g., Eden & Shani, 1982).

Implementation standards in a prevention research project might include the specification of such intervention characteristics as (a) the skills, knowledge, and numbers of staff members; (b) the frequency, duration, and content of interactions of workers with clients, families, or community organizations; (c) the specific actions to be taken in a range of specified situations; and (d) guidelines for the nature and value of reinforcers to be applied for specific kinds of performance. Implementation standards should be sufficiently concrete to allow for a comparison of what is being done with what is intended.

Tasks. The third part of a strategy is the set of tasks required to execute it. A task statement specifies who will do what by when. Specifying a person responsible for executing a particular task, even when a group will be involved, promotes clarity. And specifying when a task is expected to be completed is an additional management tool.

Critical benchmarks, implementation standards, and tasks all serve important functions in project management and worker reinforcement: They serve to guide an organization's efforts; and they provide one kind of objective standard of achievement. A lack of such objective standards "deprives the workers . . . of their legitimate desire for satisfaction on a realistic basis. Under these circumstances, satisfaction or dissatisfaction with [one's] own achievement becomes mainly a question of temperament" (Lewin, 1946, p. 35).

Development

Project development and research are ongoing processes, and projects are embedded in dynamic environments. Tension, reassessment, and revision are characteristic of vigorous projects as group members interact with influential environments and gain experience. Consequently, PDE is a cyclical process as progress is made toward achieving goals and objectives (or as goals and objectives are redefined), as new information becomes available, as the environment changes, and as new research questions emerge.

Development occurs largely through the use of information. Information about the achievement of or failure to reach critical benchmarks signals that the force field has been usefully understood or that new effort is required to reassess the organization's force field. Information that an objective is being achieved signals that an intervention is effective; information that an objective is not being achieved signals a reconsideration of the appropriateness, strength, or fidelity of the intervention, and it prompts new planning. Information that there is progress toward a goal signals that the organization is on the right track. Information that there is no progress may signal several things. If interventions are being implemented as intended and are achieving their objectives, the theory is called into question. If objectives are not being met, either the theory or the integrity of the intervention, or both, should be scrutinized. Success in bringing about elusive objectives and solving serious problems is not to be expected at once. But the PDE structure is intended to provide interim feedback on progress to enable a strengthening of the project. Evidence of project effectiveness lends support to the theory guiding the project.

Evaluation

The PDE structure is intended to facilitate several kinds of evaluation. The explication of a theory of action allows an assessment of the theory's plausibility and an assessment of the plausibility or strength of the project's planned interventions in light of the theory (cf. Chen & Rossi, 1983).

By tracking the achievement of critical benchmarks, the structure allows assessment of progress toward implementing an intervention. Monitoring implementation standards provides for the assessment of how well interventions are being executed; it provides manipulation checks for both researchers and project managers. These are key elements of formative evaluation and the conduct of research.

The PDE method is also intended to facilitate rigorous summative evaluation. It repeatedly asks the question "How do we know the intervention made the difference?" The implementation of an evaluation design is treated in the same way as the implementation of any other intervention. The PDE method assumes that evaluation is an essential component of effective project development and should receive coordinate effort with other aspects of project implementation. Therefore, force field analysis is

performed for design and data collection issues just as it is for any other project component. Because project implementers are involved in the research design and in the specification of the research questions, their commitment to strong evaluation is expected to increase. Because the force field analysis focuses on the project implementers' own perceptions of the possible, the immediate environment of the evaluation is taken into account when the evaluation is designed, perhaps mitigating some of the resistance to evaluation activities commonly encountered among implementers.

Strength and Fidelity

The PDE method makes possible the assessment of the strength and fidelity of planned interventions through judgments about theoretical plausibility and benchmark monitoring. This assessment can occur in two ways. First, project implementers can assess the consistency of their interventions and objectives with the theory of action underlying their project. That is, a project implementer can determine whether the objectives sought are in accord with theory, and whether the interventions planned will likely achieve the project's objectives. In short, theory is a template for making judgments about the appropriateness of interventions and objectives that project implementers can use to control the quality of their own projects. Second, observers of a project, including researchers, can assess the project's a priori strength by determining whether the planned interventions will plausibly lead to the objectives or goals of the project by assessing them in comparison to state-of-the-art theories in the field and the history of similar projects.

As a project develops, the focus of concern shifts. Early in a project's development, major issues have to do with ideas for interventions or with strategies for getting an innovation adopted. Later, important issues involve the integrity of the intervention's implementation and the assessment of effectiveness. In the early stages of movement toward the adoption of an innovation, critical benchmarks involve events related to the decision to adopt a change. Later, implementation standards or quality control checks on the faithfulness of the implementation increase in importance.

The documentation and assessment of interventions as implemented may involve detailed manuals for the administration of treatments; descriptions of the characteristics of staff and target groups; and accounts of the duration and scheduling of treatments or events, treatment protocols, or proportion of the population served. Therefore, as projects develop, PDE increasingly focuses on the development of manuals to guide service delivery, make diagnoses, and train the staff. Projects using this model will develop strategies to monitor staff performance, provide incentives to keep performance according to specifications, and the like. The implementation of those strategies is expected to have two consequences: (a) The plans and their execution will *increase* the integrity of the intervention; and (b) the information generated by the implementation of these plans will *describe* the integrity of interventions. Manuals developed in the course of carefully implementing a project will allow for subsequent close replications in future research or application.

Some Examples

Two examples of projects underway provide some insights into the way the PDE method enables the translation of practitioner ideas into theoretical terms and promotes project development. First, consider a delinquency prevention project involving a peer group intervention. Basically, the project implementers assumed that delinquent behavior is supported by a normative subculture. To prevent delinquency the project intended to compose groups of delinquent and nondelinquent youths and to structure group interaction so that delinquent behavior and expressions of beliefs counter to traditional moral beliefs were confronted in the group. Promoting conventional beliefs was an important objective. This project's theoretical rationale and statement of intervention standards evolved during a period of over two years in which a field worker for the evaluation (Jane St. John) and project implementers (Geantry Luster and William Kottman) used the PDE method (St. John, 1982, 1983). Early research results for this project implied that theoretically important objectives were not always being met. Early research results implied that treatment decreased belief in conventional social rules for nondelinquent group participants. This research outcome was used by the project implementers to revise their treatment specifications and to devise ways to monitor group process more closely. Specifically, group leaders were provided additional training, more attention was given to the composition of the group, and monitoring of group interaction using the Hill (1965, 1977) interaction matrix was initiated. Although the development and evaluation of this project are still underway, the early negative result has disappeared in subsequent evaluations.

A second example is a project being conducted by a Southern urban school system. This project's theory assumes that assistance and pressure to improve academic performance, combined with the opportunity to develop attachments to prosocial others, will result in more rewarding experiences in school, greater attachment, and less truancy and delinquent behavior among high-risk youths. This theory suggests that students who experience academic difficulties and who are disruptive in school should receive special attention from project personnel in the form of tutoring and advocacy on behalf of the student with teachers, parents, and others. The evaluation field worker (Denise Gottfredson) and project staff (Doris Coaxum, Barbara Dilligard, Ann Birdseye, and Martha Stewart) used the PDE method. Early implementation monitoring (D. C. Gottfredson, 1982) showed that the intervention was not being implemented as intended, with project personnel interacting mostly with students who did not fall within the target group, and interacting only to a limited extent with target students. Clearer implementation standards were specified for the workers to follow, and monitoring of these standards increased. Subsequent research results (D. C. Gottfredson, 1983a, 1983b) show improved implementation, increased academic performance as measured by both standardized test scores and school grades, and some evidence of decreased school disruptiveness and misconduct when randomly equivalent treatment and control students are compared. Some intermediate outcomes, notably attachment to school, were not affected as expected, suggesting that the program can be strengthened further.

Limitations and Virtues

The PDE method has some limitations. The most important appear to be that it is complex, time and expertise intensive, and is unable completely to resolve the tensions that summative evaluation causes for project implementers.

Time and Talent

The human behavior required to implement the PDE method is complex, and the method's implementation calls for a marked investment of human resources. Use of the PDE structure calls for high levels of interpersonal competency, communication skill, and understanding of group relations in organizations. In addition, it calls for a thorough understanding of measurement, social science theory, and experimental and quasi-experimental methods. Ironically, this combination of competencies is rarely found in one person, so that a team of workers may be required. Furthermore, the cyclical or developmental nature of PDE requires periodic attention, monitoring, updating, and information communication. This taxing process goes beyond the effort typically expended in research.

Because staff with the requisite skills are hard to find, training will be required. Experience implies that social scientists trained primarily in research methods and theory can implement the method, but that they require additional training in organization development.

Tensions

Tension is endemic in evaluation research. Too often in the past, evaluation has been used as a tool for canceling a project—even when positive evaluations could not reasonably be expected at an early stage of project development. Tension is also created by the inherently political environment of action projects and by environments where the successful project does not rock the boat. The development of sound programs usually requires the expenditure of time and money, and often implies the need for disruptive arrangements.

Values

Program development evaluation is value laden. The pursuit of the goals of the implementing organization is generally assumed to be desirable (although open to question), and an aim of PDE is to develop the implementing organization's capacity to accomplish its goals. Therefore, researchers and implementers collaborate in evaluation design, question formulation, and planning. As a result, researchers extensively intervene in project development—indeed they become a part of the project. Some evaluators (Perloff, 1979) see this as undesirable in a summative evaluation because it raises questions about the generalizability of the results to situations where researchers are absent. In addition, just as research needs sometimes intrude in project operations by creating new tasks or structural arrangements, the pursuit of a project's programmatic activities can result in compromises in research design. As Deutsch (1968) said, "The danger that confronts the research worker in such situations is the possibility that his research design or methodology will be sacrificed to the achievement of the social-action objective" (p. 466). This danger may account in part for the reluctance academic social scientists have shown to participate in action research, but it seems a small price to pay in exchange for the opportunity action research creates to contribute to theory testing and the solution of human problems. In short, the PDE method is no panacea for this tough problem.

Complexity

The PDE method is complex, but each component of the method is useful and desirable in action research efforts. For brief organization development interventions without a research purpose, the selective use of those portions of the PDE structure that seem to be the most relevant to the problem at hand is more appropriate than attempting to use all parts of the method. Researchers should not abandon any part of the method.

Practical Application

Our experience implies that parts of this process are useful to project implementers in defining their own jobs, in formulating plans, and in clarifying their intentions. Experience also implies that the entire process is sometimes viewed as burdensome. On balance, this structure seems a clear improvement over some more traditional research methods because it involves implementers in research planning, creates arrangements for evaluation based on an organization's force field, and focuses on goals and objectives of concern to implementers.

My colleagues and I have used the PDE method in the evaluation of delinquency projects conducted by 17 different organizations. In an area where true experiments are almost unknown (Dixon & Wright, 1975; G. D. Gottfredson, 1981), six of these projects have implemented true experiments. The quasi-experimental designs of most of the remaining projects are substantially better than they would have been had the PDE method not been applied. Even where the original research design has broken down, project implementers have usually shared with the researchers the tasks of creating alternative designs and developing plans to prevent subsequent breakdowns.

Researchers will gain knowledge useful in applying the PDE method effectively if they approach their own research effectiveness as a topic of inquiry. For example, M. S. Cook (1983) examined the ways project implementers generate and revise theories of action for their projects. He suggested that project implementers who are already committed to an intervention or other course of action tend to generate theories congruent with their interventions, and that those theories provide limited guidance in the choice or development of interventions. This research suggests that the method may be most effective if used to structure program development from the outset and provides an additional reason for involving evaluators in the design of demonstration projects at the earliest possible stage.

Expense

A perceptive anonymous reviewer of an earlier version of this article noted, "The model is extremely expensive to implement. . . . It is difficult to conceive of many agencies in the public sector wanting to spend the dollars and years it takes to evaluate, revise the theory, reevaluate, reimplement, reimprove." Partly true. It is not difficult to conceive of enlightened agencies *wanting* to do these things, but examples of such developmental spirals of activity are hard to find. Rare examples include the Kamehameha Early Education Project (T. D. Cook, 1983; Tharp & Gallimore, 1979), which developed effective educational interventions for native Hawaiian children, and Project Follow Through (Rhine, 1983), which was an extensive and productive educational research and development program. A distinguishing characteristic of the Kamehameha program of research and development is instructive. Myron Thompson, a trustee of the Kamehameha Schools/ Bishop Estate, reported (T. D. Cook, 1983, p. 1017) that when school officials presented a one-year budget for the school the treasurer refused to look at it until a plan or goal for the next 10 to 15 years was also presented. A lesson to be drawn from this example is that we must allocate development and research resources to meet our long-range goals (and we must be clear about what these goals are). Distinguishing features of both the Kamehameha project and Follow Through were their commitments to an iterative research process resembling that entailed in the PDE method. According to Rhine (1983), $740 million was directly allocated to development and research activities in Follow Through between 1967 and 1982, and a key decision in the operation of the program was an allocation of 20% of the budget to knowledge production activities. That it is difficult to conceive of such behavior on the part of many agencies at present is a sign of limited vision and a failure to approach the development of social programs realistically.

Many persons now in a position to make public policy seem to have drawn the wrong conclusion from the experience of the Great Society. How often do we hear, "You cannot solve a problem by throwing money at it." The conclusion should have been: You cannot solve a problem *simply* by throwing money at it. Developing programs to solve some of our most intractable problems will seldom be easy or inexpensive. Just as the expenditure of great sums of money, programmatic research over an extended period of time, and the dedication of talented persons with suitably lengthy time perspectives are required to develop and test an effective new drug or a space shuttle, so also are these features likely to be required to develop effective programs to better educate the children of the urban poor, to reduce crime, and to increase industrial efficiency. I share the reviewer's difficulty in conceiving of many agencies' implementing programs requiring such an expenditure of time and money, but this is the kind of commitment we must make to solve some of our society's greatest problems.

One review of the state of the art of organizational development in schools (Fullan, Miles, & Taylor, 1980) implied that brief interventions in organizations may actually cause more harm than good, and it suggested that developmental efforts may require about five years before planful development becomes an integral and ongoing part of an agency's activities. This review also suggested, however, one approach to reducing the *apparent* costs of program development and evaluation. It appears that program development activities may be effective

if they involve personnel internal to the organization as developmental specialists, with guidance from and collaboration with external change agents. If one views PDE as the kind of activity managers of programs, professionals, and other members of an organization should be pursuing as an integral part of their roles in organizations, then the *additional* cost of the external developer-evaluator becomes less formidable.

Inside Versus Outside Evaluation

Having argued that integrating PDE into the operations of programs is desirable if not essential, I will discuss some reasons for organizations to collaborate with *outside* program developers and evaluators. Researchers following the PDE method behave in many respects as consultants to an organization, and they are therefore useful much as other consultants are. Outside researchers provide critical information to guide organizational decision making, but they do not make the decisions. Outside researchers are more able to maintain an arm's-length relationship with factions within an organization than are insiders. They can bring skills in organizational analysis, development, and research that are lacking in particular organizations. And, they are much freer to bring news—good or bad—than are organizational insiders. For these reasons and because of the practical constraints that are likely to be placed on the costs of program development and evaluation activities in the near future, collaboration between outside researchers and inside program implementers using the PDE method may be a desirable arrangement.

Virtues

The greatest virtues of the PDE method appear to be (a) its ability to make theoretical tests possible in research on action projects; (b) its ability to elaborate clear, measurable intermediate outcomes useful in assessing the effectiveness of interventions in theoretical terms; (c) its ability to generate creative strategies perceived as feasible to implementers based on the divergent and then convergent thinking that takes place in force field analysis; (d) its ability to involve project implementers in the research enterprise by engaging them in the specification of measurable goals and objectives and in the creation of evaluation designs; (e) its ability to provide short-term assessments of progress through the monitoring of critical benchmarks, implementation standards, and tasks; and (f) its ability to enable researchers to understand the nature of a project by translating implementers' ideas into a structured language of theoretical research.

PDE makes serious organizational change and rigorous research somewhat more attractive to organizations. Ideally, practice and research would be merged into a single enterprise in which rigorous theoretical research becomes an integral component of program operation. It is unrealistic to think that most practitioners will ever acquire the technical skills required to systematically conduct rigorous research on their activities (just as it is unrealistic to expect all researchers to become adroit practitioners). In addition, rigorous research is not always called for in the development of a project, and not all action projects test theoretically interesting ideas. When rigorous evaluation is called for, however, the PDE structure is helpful. Program development evaluation does not successfully resolve many of the sources of tension in merging action with research, but it is progress.

REFERENCES

Blanton, J., & Alley, S. (1976). Program development: A manual for organizational self-study. *JSAS Catalog of Selected Documents in Psychology, 6,* 26. (Ms. No. 1216)
Blanton, J., & Alley, S. (1978). Clinical and nonclinical aspects of program development consultation. *Professional Psychology, 9,* 315–321.
Blanton, J., & Alley, S. (1981). Evaluation of paraprofessional programs in the human services. In S. S. Robin & M. O. Wagenfeld (Eds.), *Paraprofessionals in the human services* (pp. 237–257). New York: Human Sciences Press.
Chein, I., Cook, S., & Harding, J. (1948). The field of action research. *American Psychologist, 3,* 43–50.
Chen, H.-T., & Rossi, P. H. (1980). The multi-goal, theory-driven approach to evaluation: A model linking basic and applied social science. *Social Forces, 59,* 106–122.
Chen, H.-T., & Rossi, P. H. (1983). Evaluating with sense: The theory-driven approach. *Evaluation Review, 7,* 283–302.
Cook, M. S. (1983, August). *Delinquency prevention program managers' theories of action: A content analysis.* Paper presented at the meeting of the American Psychological Association, Anaheim, CA.
Cook, T. D. (1983). Research, program development, and the education of native Hawaiians: A conversation with Myron Thompson. *American Psychologist, 38,* 1015–1021.
Cook, T. D., & Campbell, D. T. (1979). *Quasi-experimentation: Design and analysis issues for field settings.* Chicago: Rand McNally.
Deese, J. (1972). *Psychology as science and art.* New York: Harcourt Brace Jovanovich.
Deutsch, M. (1968). Field theory in social psychology. In G. Lindzey & E. Aronson (Eds.), *The handbook of social psychology: Vol. 1* (2nd ed., pp. 412–487). Reading, MA: Addison-Wesley.
Dewey, J. (1933). *How we think* (rev. ed.). New York: Heath.
Dixon, M. C., & Wright, W. E. (1975). *Juvenile delinquency prevention programs: An evaluation of policy related research on the effectiveness of prevention programs.* Washington, DC: National Science Foundation.
Eden, D., & Shani, A. B. (1982). Pygmalion goes to boot camp: Expectancy, leadership, and trainee performance. *Journal of Applied Psychology, 67,* 194–199.
Empey, L. T. (1980). Field experimentation in criminal justice: Rationale and design. In M. W. Klein & K. S. Teilmann (Eds.), *Handbook of criminal justice evaluation* (pp. 143–176). Beverly Hills, CA: Sage.
French, W. L., & Bell, C. H., Jr. (1978). *Organization development: Behavioral science interventions for organization improvement* (2nd ed.). Englewood Cliffs, NJ: Prentice-Hall.

Fullan, M., Miles, M. B., & Taylor, G. (1980). Organization development in schools: The state of the art. *Review of Educational Research, 50,* 121–183.
Glaser, D. (1980). The interplay of theory, issues, policy, and data. In M. W. Klein & K. S. Teilmann (Eds.), *Handbook of criminal justice evaluation* (pp. 123–142). Beverly Hills, CA: Sage.
Gottfredson, D. C. (1982). *Project PATHE: First interim report.* Unpublished manuscript. The Johns Hopkins University, Center for Social Organization of Schools, Baltimore.
Gottfredson, D. C. (1983a, August). *Implementing a theory in a large-scale educational intervention.* Paper presented at the meeting of the American Psychological Association, Anaheim, CA.
Gottfredson, D. C. (1983b). *Project PATHE: Second interim report.* Unpublished manuscript, The Johns Hopkins University, Center for Social Organization of Schools, Baltimore.
Gottfredson, G. D. (1981). Schooling and delinquency. In S. E. Martin, L. B. Sechrest, & R. Redner (Eds.), *New directions in the rehabilitation of criminal offenders* (pp. 424–469). Washington, DC: National Academy Press.
Gottfredson, G. D. (1982). *The School Action Effectiveness Study: First interim report* (Report No. 325). Baltimore: The Johns Hopkins University, Center for Social Organization of Schools. (ERIC Document Reproduction Service No. ED 222 835)
Gottfredson, G. D., Gottfredson, D. C., & Cook, M. S. (Eds.). (1983). *The School Action Effectiveness Study: Second interim report* (Report No. 342). Baltimore: The Johns Hopkins University, Center for Social Organization of Schools.
Gottfredson, G. D., Rickert, D. E., Jr., Gottfredson, D. C., & Advani, N. (in press). Standards for program development evaluation. *Psychological Documents.*
Hall, G. E., & Loucks, S. F. (1977). A developmental model for determining whether the treatment is actually implemented. *American Educational Research Journal, 14,* 263–276.
Hersey, P., & Blanchard, K. (1982). *Management of organizational behavior* (4th ed.). Englewood Cliffs, NJ: Prentice-Hall.
Hill, W. F. (1965). *Hill interaction matrix* (rev. ed.). Los Angeles: University of Southern California, Youth Study Center.
Hill, W. F. (1977). Hill interaction matrix (HIM): The conceptual framework, derived rating scales, and an updated bibliography. *Small Group Behavior, 8,* 251–268.
Lewin, K. (1946). Action research and minority problems. *Journal of Social Issues, 2,* 34–46.
Lewin, K. (1947). Group decision and social change. In T. M. Newcomb & E. L. Hartley (Eds.), *Readings in social psychology* (pp. 330–344). New York: Holt.
Lewin, K. (1951). *Field theory in social science.* New York: Harper.
Martin, S. E., Sechrest, L. B., & Redner, R. (Eds.). (1981). *New directions in the rehabilitation of criminal offenders.* Washington, DC: National Academy Press.
Patton, M. Q. (1981). *Creative evaluation.* Beverly Hills, CA: Sage.
Perloff, R. (Ed.). (1979). *Evaluator interventions: Pros and cons.* Beverly Hills, CA: Sage.
Quay, H. (1977). Three faces of evaluation: What can be expected to work. *Criminal Justice and Behavior, 4,* 341–354.
Rhine, W. R. (1983). The role of psychologists in the national Follow Through project. *American Psychologist, 38,* 288–297.
Rossi, P. H., & Freeman, H. E. (1982). *Evaluation: A systematic approach* (2nd ed.). Beverly Hills, CA: Sage.
Sanford, N. (1970). Whatever happened to action research? *Journal of Social Issues, 26,* 3–23.
Sarason, S. B. (1971). *The culture of the school and the problem of change.* Boston: Allyn & Bacon.
Sechrest, L., White, S. O., & Brown, E. D. (Eds.). (1979). *The rehabilitation of criminal offenders: Problems and prospects.* Washington, DC: National Academy of Sciences.
St. John, J. (1982). *Peer culture development (PCD), Chicago.*

Unpublished manuscript, Johns Hopkins University, Center for Social Organization of Schools, Baltimore.

St. John, J. (1983). *Peer culture development: Second interim report.* Unpublished manuscript. The Johns Hopkins University, Center for Social Organization of Schools, Baltimore.

Tharp, R. G., & Gallimore, R. (1979). The ecology of program research and evaluation: A model of evaluation succession. *Evaluation Studies Review Annual, 4,* 39–60.

Vohra, P., Gottfredson, G. D., & Kratzer, F. H. (1968). The effects of high levels of dietary EDTA, zinc or copper on the mineral contents of some tissue of turkey poults. *Poultry Science, 47,* 1334–1343.

29

Evaluating Educational Programs
An Integrative, Causal-Modeling Approach
Margaret C. Wang and Herbert J. Walberg

This paper presents a case for the use of causal models derived from a substantive knowledge base of theory and research in the evaluation of educational programs. Such evaluation can be based on a synthesis of theory, empirical research, and program evaluations that are often considered disparate and unrelated. Included among the inquiries on which evaluation can be based are substantive research in academic disciplines such as anthropology, psychology, and sociology; case, correlational, and experimental studies; and needs assessment, implementation, process, and outcome evaluations.

Current Approaches to Evaluation

Eight post-1975 typologies of evaluation are outlined in Figure 1. As the figure shows, these representative typologies include a total of 47 different categories: two forms of inquiry, seven types, eight

The authors wish to thank Rita Catalano for her editorial assistance in the preparation of this manuscript.

The research reported herein was supported by the Learning Research and Development Center, supported in part as a research development center by funds from the National Follow Through Program, and the Special Education Program of the U.S. Department of Education. The opinions expressed do not necessarily reflect the positions or policies of these agencies, and no official endorsements should be inferred.

models, five philosophical questions, 13 alternative approaches, four groups of standards, four basic questions, and four methodologies. Examination of these sets of categories reveals that, although they are useful in pointing out important distinctions and trends in the field of evaluation, little consensus can be found among recent major efforts at classification. For example, the jurisprudence and adversary models, which appear to be similar, are subsumed by the Glass and Ellett (1980) and House (1980) typologies, yet they are excluded from the six other classifications. Similarly, what might be called "qualitative inquiry" constitutes a category in the Guba (1978), Glass and Ellett (1980), and Talmage (1982) classifications but not in the others.

The descriptions of each category within the typologies yield many useful insights but only somewhat discursive or illustrative, rather than explicit, definitions. Because the typologies include different, implicit criteria for similarly labeled categories, it can be argued that each category is unique and that the typologies must be completely cross-classified for a comprehensive analysis of the field. Multiplying the numbers of categories by one another in such an exercise yields 465,920 unique cells—obviously too large a number for useful analysis and understanding.

From Margaret C. Wang and Herbert J. Walberg, "Evaluating Educational Programs: An Integrative, Causal-Modeling Approach," *Educational Evaluation and Policy Analysis*, 1983, 5(3), 347-366. Copyright 1983, American Educational Research Association, Washington, DC.

Forms of Inquiry (Guba, 1978)	Types of Evaluation (Glass & Ellett, 1980)	Evaluation Models (House, 1980)
Conventional logical positivism Naturalistic phenomenology	Applied science Systems management Decision theory Assessment of progress toward goals Jurisprudence Description or portrayal Rational empiricism	Systems Behavioral objectives Decision making Goal free Criticism Accreditation Adversary Transaction

Philosophical Value Questions (Gowin & Green, 1980)	Alternative Approaches (Stufflebeam & Webster, 1980)	Evaluation Standards (Joint Committee, 1981)

Is this thing good (instrinsic)?
What is it good for (instrumental)?
Is it better than something else (comparative)?
Can I make it better (idealization)?
Is this the right thing to do (decision)?
	Politically oriented
	  Politically controlled
	  Public-relations inspired
	Questions oriented
	  Objectives based
	  Accountability
	  Experimental research
	  Testing programs
	  Management information
	Values oriented
	  Accreditation or certification
	  Policy studies
	  Decision oriented
	  Consumer oriented
	  Client centered
	  Connoisseur based
		Utility or responsiveness to clients
		Feasibility or practicality
		Propriety or ethics and morals
		Accuracy or information soundness

Basic Questions (Cronbach, 1982)	Methodologies (Talmage, 1982)
Causal conclusions? Conservative influence? Targeted inquiry? Standardized conditions?	Experimentation Eclecticism Description Benefit/cost

FIGURE 1. *Eight post-1975 typologies of evaluation*

A major problem with the classification schemes represented in Figure 1 lies in their interpretation or application, rather than their conception. As Talmage (1982) points out, varying the emphases on evaluation purposes, methods, and questions yields a number of classifications that are useful for different purposes. In practice, however, the various distinctions sometimes harden and produce confusing points of view among antagonistic camps of evaluators. Qualitative and quantitative methods, for example, need not be contradictory and might be made mutually enriching; yet tensions and rivalry between what are viewed as two major forms of evaluation inquiry (Guba, 1978) can be readily felt (e.g., see Hamilton, MacDonald, King, Jenkins, & Parlett's *Beyond the Numbers Game*, 1977). Similar competitive, if not imperial, ambitions may be found in the advocates of the eight categories identified by House (1980; see Figure 1). Such controversy is to be expected in a young and growing field. In fact, some tension may be constructive in bringing about greater maturity and usefulness of evaluation, if mutual dialogue can be maintained.

An Integrative, Causal-modeling Approach

The kind of detached, bird's-eye view of the field represented in Figure 1 suggests a number of considerations for the planning and execution of program evaluations. The primary literature cited by the classifiers in Figure 1, moreover, encompasses numerous positions and procedures, none of which appears to be without merit and utility. Two features in particular seem worthy of stronger integration, or reintegration, into the field of evaluation: causal modeling and substantive research from disciplines such as psychology and sociology. These are explicitly represented in three (about 6%) of the 47 categories in Figure 1: Glass and Ellett's (1980) first and last categories, applied science and rational empiricism, and Cronbach's (1982) first category, causal conclusions.

The link between evaluation and substantive research in academic disciplines may have been weakened in the late 1960s and early 1970s by influential writings that emphasized their different purposes. Hemphill (1969), for example, distinguished evaluation and research with respect to the type of problem selected and how it is defined, the use of hypotheses, the role of value judgments, the replicability of findings, the specification of data to be collected, and the randomization of study samples. Worthen and Sanders (1973) added other distinguishing features: laws versus description, autonomy of inquiry, criteria for judging activities, disciplinary base, and training. Suchman (1967) also cited many of these distinctions in earlier writing.

Removing evaluation from the mainstream of substantive research, however, may weaken both fields. Without theory, parsimony, generalizability, and other research canons, evaluation would lose its substantive validity and practical utility. Uninformed of current developments in educational and disciplinary research, evaluation also would tend to overlook new constructs from topics such as motivation, time-on-task, and teaching that have important bearings on the success of educational innovations. Conversely, substantive research in psychology and other disciplines stands to lose its relevance to educational policy and practice, unless it is stimulated by the puzzles and findings of needs assessments as well as by evaluations of program implementation, processes, and outcomes.

Several have pointed out the need for a close connection between substantive theory and methodological and utilitarian research (e.g., Anastasi, 1967; Glaser, 1973). In an analysis of the relationship between psychological science and testing, Anastasi (1967) concluded that "psychological testing today places too much emphasis on testing and too little on psychology. As a result, outdated interpretations of test performance may remain insulated from the impact of subsequent behavior research" (p. 297). She further pointed out the tendency of "test theory" to focus on the psychometric property, or the mechanics, of test construction rather than psychological theory about behavior.

A widely recognized prerequisite for maintaining the theoretical and practical utility of research is sufficient concern for causal relations among means and ends. Perhaps because many believe that causality can only be inferred from experiments, which may be difficult to execute in natural settings, recent evaluations and commentaries have tended to give short shrift to causal questions. Nevertheless, the most obvious question about new programs from both the scientific and practical perspectives is, "Do they work?" (Florio, Behrmann, Masson, & Goltz, 1979). Cook and Campbell (1979) described many practical ways to execute experiments, pointing out that a reasonable indication of causality may be inferred from quasi-experiments and correlational studies, particularly if they are repeated in varying circumstances. The statisticians Mosteller and Tukey (1977) insisted that an approximate answer to the right question is more valuable than an exact answer to the wrong question, and they offered reasonable hope that regression and related correlational techniques can be helpful in coming closer to answering the right questions.

In further consideration of this issue, Murray and Smith (1979) argued that, even in cases where relatively few units, occasions, and variables are observed, simple correlations, particularly across time intervals, can be informative about the results of training and other programs. They recommended that evaluators work with program developers and practitioners to make their implicit or latent causal models of the program explicit and testable. According to the authors, such models should include identification of program components, depiction of the presumed chains of causality, measurement of the components, and calculation of the correlations among them. Correlations that are small, insignificant, or wrong in hypothesized sign may yield formative insights and clues about areas in which a program is less efficient, encountering difficulties, or contrary to expectations. On the other hand, correlations that are large and in the hypothesized direction hardly prove causality, but they do lend some degree of confidence and plausibility to the validity of the presumed and portrayed causal model of the program.

Both simple and elaborate causal models of evaluation may be derived from disciplines such as psychology and from research on teaching and learning (e.g., Bentler, 1980; Maruyama & Walberg, 1982; Wang, 1983a). Program evaluations guided by a combination of substantive research findings and practitioners' wisdom are likely to lead to findings that remain robust across settings, conditions, and subjects. Accumulation and synthesis of evidence from extensive or multiple evaluations can yield useful generalizations that extend beyond the immediate programs and studies. Because subsequent evaluations may merely check, rather than exhaustively probe, the efficacy of local implementation, such smaller scale evaluations can be less critical and demanding of educational and evaluation resources.

Thus, an integrative, causal-modeling approach can build on theory and research from academic disciplines such as psychology; from educational research findings; from the wisdom and experience of practitioners and program developers; and from various research methodologies such as quasi-experiments, correlational analyses, and case studies. Rather than oppose existing models and techniques of evaluation like those outlined in Figure 1, this approach attempts to incorporate more fully and explicitly the standards and procedures of the mainstream research on education, particularly those related to causal questions of means and ends, into the emerging evaluation canon.

An Illustration of an Integrative, Causal-modeling Approach: Purpose and Overview

This section will exemplify and illustrate an integrative, causal-modeling approach to program evaluation. Included are (a) a discussion of the objectives and overall program design and evaluation research conducted in conjunction with the implementation and development of an innovative educational program known as the Adaptive Learning Environments Model (ALEM); (b) a summary of substantive developments in psychology and research on cognition and teaching that have influenced the design and evaluation of the ALEM; and (c) selected illustrations from a program of research and evaluation of the ALEM. Summary descriptions are provided of an evaluation of implementation procedures and classroom processes aimed at making teaching and learning more student-centered and efficient with respect to time; a randomized field trial of the ALEM's accommodation of individual differences among students classified as gifted, regular, and handicapped; and a correlational study of the hypothesized relationships among assessed training needs of teachers, training plans, training as actually executed, and classroom behavior change.

Adaptive Learning Environments Model

The ALEM is an educational program designed with the overall goal of ensuring that most, if not all, students experience learning success in regular school settings. In the program, students are expected to acquire academic skills while becoming confident of their abilities to learn and cope with their classroom social and physical surroundings. To this end, a major design focus has been the development of alternative approaches to maximizing each student's learning. Among these approaches are those that incorporate optimal use of school resources, including student and teacher time, and provision of the programming and classroom organizational supports required to accommodate students' individual learning needs. The basic program design of the ALEM can be characterized as a combination of prescriptive instruction that has been shown to be effective in ensuring academic skills mastery (Bloom, 1976; Glaser, 1977; Rosenshine, 1979) and aspects of informal or open education that are considered to be conducive to generating attitudes and processes of inquiry, independence, and social cooperation (Johnson, Maruyama, Johnson, Nelson, &

Skon, 1981; Marshall, 1981; Peterson, 1979).

Figure 2 shows the overall framework that provided the basis for a decade of research related to the development, implementation, and evaluation of the ALEM (Wang, Note 1). Two lines of supporting research were conducted: empirical studies related to program design, and program evaluation studies of implementation and outcomes (see the bottom box in Figure 2).

The first line of research consisted of instructional experiments concerning the design of program components for providing adaptive instruction in school settings.

FIGURE 2. A model of program development and instructional design/program evaluation research for adaptive instruction

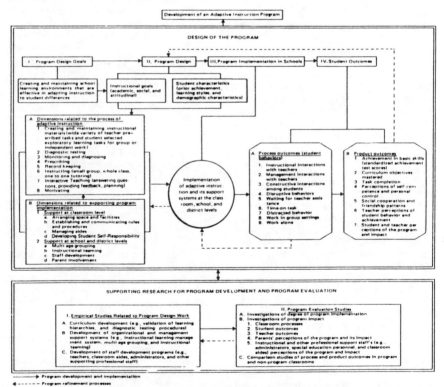

The main tasks were operationalization and integration of what is known from psychological theories of learning, instructional methods, and effective schooling practices in the design of educational environments that successfully accommodate students' diverse needs. Examples of this work include development and validation of curriculum hierarchies in the various basic skills areas (Resnick, Wang, & Kaplan, 1973; Wang, Resnick, & Boozer, 1971); development of diagnostic tests and student progress monitoring procedures (Glaser, 1967; Wang & Fitzhugh, 1978; Lindvall & Cox, Note 2); development and study of specific instructional program components, in terms of the "how" of teaching and learning (Glaser, 1977; Resnick, Wang, & Rosner, 1977); development and study of a student self-management training program (Smith, 1976; Stone & Vaughn, 1976; Wang, 1983a); and design and study of the efficacy of a data-based, individually adaptive, staff development program (Wang & Gennari, in press).

The second line of research addressed two sets of questions related to program implementation and evaluation. Specifically, this research dealt with the practicalities of implementing adaptive instruction in school settings. The focus was on studying what it takes to implement and maintain an adaptive instruction program, and whether or not it is feasible to implement such a program widely in different school settings. The main objective was to examine the manner and extent to which various components can be put together in complementary ways to form a cohesive and comprehensive program for school implementation. Thus, this work involved studies of the operationalization of program components in schools (Resnick & Wang, 1974; Wang, in press; Wang, Nojan, Strom, & Walberg, in press). Essentially, the studies were designed to characterize the program as it actually was operated and to use the results from analyses of degree of implementation data to answer the question, "How can we do it better?" (see the dotted arrows in Figure 2).

Evaluation studies of the type described above were concerned with program efficacy, particularly "for whom" and "under what conditions" the program was effective. Studies were aimed at investigating (a) the extent to which implementation of various program components led to the presence of those specific classroom processes (teacher and student behaviors) that are hypothesized to be supportive of the provision of adaptive instruction; and (b) the extent to which the presence of those classroom processes led to student achievement, or success, in school. Examples of such studies include analysis of program impact on teachers' and students' use of time (Wang & Walberg, in press) and evaluation of learning processes and outcomes in a variety of school sites (Wang, 1983b; Wang, Leinhardt, & Boston, 1980; Wang, Resnick, & Scheutz, 1974).

Development of the ALEM consisted of four tasks. As shown in Figure 2, they are (a) identification of program goals for providing adaptive instruction in school settings, (b) design of program components on the basis of instructional objectives and student characteristics, (c) development of systems to support program implementation in schools, and (d) identification and documentation of student process and product outcomes.

The design of the ALEM incorporates specific program dimensions related to the process of adaptive instruction, as well as dimensions related to the provision of support for the implementation process. The "process" dimensions concern "how" the program is taught. Included among these dimensions is the development of instructional-learning materials and instructional strategies. Examples of such strategies are diagnostic testing and prescription, instructional grouping, physical design of the learning environment, and scheduling of classroom activities. The "implementation" dimensions, on the other hand, include an instructional-learning management system, a supportive school organizational pattern, a personnel support system, and staff development and parent involvement programs.

Listed in Figure 2 among the expected student outcomes are process outcomes (e.g., instructional interactions between teachers and students, time-on-task, constructive interactions among students) and product outcomes (e.g., achievement in basic skills and perceptions of self-competence and personal control). As reflected in the direction of the arrows in Figure 2, certain classroom processes have been hypothesized to be consequences of the implementation of various program dimensions. In turn, these classroom processes also are viewed as mediating variables that contribute to achievement of the program's expected product outcomes.

Although the early design and evaluation objective was to establish the validity of individual components of the ALEM in accomplishing specific program goals, subsequent evaluation was aimed at investigating the interrelationships among the program components as they were implemented in school settings. Later evaluation was influenced particularly by psychological research on constraints in cognitive processing that have considerable implications for the design and evaluation of educational programs aimed at accommodating student differences and for the efficient use of resources such as human energy and time. Some of the relevant research is discussed in the next section.

Cognitive Psychology and the Teaching Effectiveness Research

To a great extent, recent developments in cognitive psychology and the research on teaching have provided the substantive base for the design and evaluation of the ALEM. This section consists of a discussion of the contributions of some of these developments.

Cognitive Psychology and Educational Productivity. Following several decades of perhaps excessive preoccupation with behaviorism, psychologists' interest in cognition was renewed during the 1950s and 1960s. In the second edition of *The Sciences of the Artificial*, Herbert Simon (1981) summarized important findings from several decades of fruitful efforts in cognitive psychology. He concluded that, aside from motivation and external opportunities and incentives, the major constraints on knowledge acquisition and other demanding cognitive activities are the few items of information that can be held in immediate, conscious memory and the time required to store an item in long-term memory. Thus, "bounded rationality" and the scarcity of human attention and time are the limiting factors in most human activities, including teachers' mastery of a complex system of adaptive instruction such as the ALEM.

Basic psychological studies of "experts" and "novices" in science, chess, and other fields have shown differences not only in the amount of information in permanent memory, but more significantly, in the ability to process the information efficiently. Experts index information more thoroughly and bring it to conscious memory more rapidly; they also represent information in large abstract chunks for more efficient processing. Experts, moreover, elaborately associate chunks, thereby recovering information by alternative associations when direct indexing is lost; thus, they can conduct rapid trial-and-error and means-ends searches to solve problems in their fields quickly and efficiently (Simon, 1981).

Although experts clearly have great advantages over novices and the relatively less skilled, it is possible to understand and promote expertise dramatically. Leibenstein (1976), for example, reviewed literature on organizational and industrial productivity and reported immense ratios in the ranges of worker output across 14 studies. He concluded that most managers and workers ordinarily operate within the bounds of considerable intellectual slack, and that consultants routinely can raise output 30 percent to 70 percent and, occasionally, much more. The costs of increased productivity, however, include the search for and testing of new methods, the difficulty of new learning and the exercise of independent judgment, the breaking and forming of social relationships, and the nondeferral of decisions and action. Thus, both expertise and improved productivity depend on new learning, resources, and support. Such findings in cognitive psychology and economics regarding expertise and productivity have stimulated research on teaching (e.g., Peterson & Walberg, 1979).

These findings also have significant implications for the design of adaptive instruction programs (Fogarty & Wang, Note

3). They have come into play in the planning and implementation of instruction as well as in the identification of the substantive and psychological factors that affect effective processing of the wide array of information involved in adapting instruction to differences among individual students. Adaptive instruction requires ongoing processing of information on each student's learning progress as teachers evaluate, and make alternative plans to facilitate, the student's mastery of learning objectives. Hence, teachers must make instructional decisions based not only on student cues, but also on information about the availability of alternative strategies and materials as well as the nature of the tasks to be learned. Furthermore, the ways in which such information is put to use in the provision of adaptive instruction also are influenced by each teacher's own beliefs about education and about the potential of particular strategies in working with specific students. Thus, teachers face immense cognitive complexity in the implementation of adaptive instruction in classroom settings (Borko, Cone, Russo, & Shavelson, 1979; Clark & Yinger, 1979; Fogarty & Wang, Note 3). Consequently, one major agenda for research on the provision of adaptive instruction is to further understand and develop ways to promote the kind of efficiency in information processing that enables teachers to make on-the-spot decisions during the ongoing instructional-learning process.

Classroom Teaching and Learning. Jackson (1968) found that teachers in ordinary classrooms engage in 200 to 300 interpersonal exchanges an hour and that their language reveals "an uncomplicated view of causality; an intuitive, rather than rational approach to classroom events; an opinionated, as opposed to an open-minded stance when confronted with alternative teaching practices; and a narrowness in working definitions assigned to abstract terms" (p. 144). Rosenshine (Note 4) argues that expert teachers can go far beyond these kinds of simple expressions, but that such expertise may be rare and may take years, if not decades, to acquire.

As a consequence, students in conventional classroom settings often receive inconsistent or vague information about learning goals and uninformative mass-processed feedback about their performance (Doyle, 1977). They also are made to wait. Jackson (1968) found that delay, denial, interruption, and distraction typify classroom life; patience seems to be the greatest virtue. On the other hand, Shimron's (1976) research, for example, has shown that students who were allowed to work at their own pace on individualized materials spent twice as much time on-task, completed three times as many units, and found the experience of a faster pace more varied and interesting. Similarly, synthesis of research on open education, in which some authority for planning and conducting learning is delegated to students, has shown nearly equal gains on standardized achievement tests, but higher levels of creativity, positive attitudes toward school, independence, freedom from anxiety, cooperation, and other socialization outcomes that educators, parents, and students hold more valuable than conventional test results (Peterson, 1979; Raven, 1981; Wang, 1983b; Wang & Stiles, 1976).

Thus, developments over the past few decades in cognitive psychology and the research on classroom teaching and learning suggest the importance of organizational support and effective classroom teaching and management practices in the implementation of new programs, as well as the need for more effective matching of program components that are unique yet must be integrated in the operationalization of complex systems such as adaptive school learning environments. Research points to the cognitive complexity of teaching, the difficulty of suitably accommodating individual differences, and the need to attain efficient time use by students and teachers while increasing the overall efficiency and productivity in education. Discussion in the next section is aimed at illustrating how such considerations are incorporated in the design of the ALEM and how the resulting design features are evaluated.

Illustrations of an Integrative, Causal-modeling Approach to Evaluation

In this section, three examples of an integrative, causal-modeling approach to evaluation of the ALEM are summarized. These examples of evaluation are concerned with (a) degree of implementation and engaged time, (b) accommodation of handicapped and gifted students, and (c) needs assessment and staff development. The findings summarized here are from large-scale field studies designed to address the following sets of questions.

1. Can a high degree of implementation of adaptive instruction programs, like the ALEM, be attained in classroom settings across a variety of school sites with differing needs and contextual characteristics? In other words, is there evidence of program implementability?

2. When the critical dimensions for the implementation of adaptive instruction programs are in place, do the hypothesized patterns of classroom processes occur? To what extent do the classroom process patterns differ from, or concur with, the predicted trends? Are the findings on classroom process patterns in classrooms where adaptive instruction is implemented compatible with findings in the effective schooling research literature?

3. Do the provision of adaptive instruction (as characterized by degree of implementation data) and the resulting classroom process patterns lead to expected student outcomes, particularly in terms of improved student achievement, positive social behavior, and positive attitudes?

Three sets of data were analyzed to answer these questions: data on the degree of program implementation, classroom process data, and student outcomes data. Ten collaborating, field-demonstration school sites where the ALEM is implemented were the settings for the studies. The samples were 138 teachers in 156 classrooms that are located in schools where the majority of students are from poor families and schools where the ALEM is implemented as a full-time mainstreaming program for handicapped and gifted students. The schools are spread across a wide geographic region that varies considerably in ethno-cultural characteristics.

Implementation and Engaged Time. To test the effectiveness and efficiency of classroom time use under the ALEM, degree of implementation and classroom

process outcomes were evaluated. It was anticipated that, with the support of a data-based, individualized staff development program (Wang, Note 5), teachers would be able to establish and maintain a high degree of implementation of the ALEM and, furthermore, that the degree of implementation would predict the constructive use of classroom time.

The causal model illustrated in Figure 3 incorporates hypothesized relationships between critical program dimensions and teachers' and students' time use. It was hypothesized that program design features such as diagnosis and prescription, a wide range of learning options, a supportive management system, multiage grouping, and instructional teaming are likely to lead to reduced amounts of time needed for learning basic skills, increased time available for exploratory learning, and increased time spent on-task. As shown in Figure 3, these changes in the time needed for, and the time spent on, learning are expected to result in attainment of desired process and product outcomes such as engaged learning time and academic and attitudinal achievement.

Analysis of the degree of implementation: Although the importance of assessing the degree of implementation of new programs before evaluating their outcomes has been suggested by many (e.g., Alkin, 1969; Fullan & Pomfret, 1977; Stake, 1967; Loucks & Hall, Note 6), published implementation studies are comparatively rare. Very few program evaluations actually have included systematic assessments of the degree of implementation as an integral step. Wang and Ellett (1982) point out, for example, that of 74 early childhood and special education programs recently approved by the U.S. Department of Education-sponsored Joint Dissemination Review Panel and listed as exemplary, none included direct empirical measures of implementability or implementation as evidence of effectiveness.

Two recent articles in this journal (*EEPA*) illustrate the value of implementation assessment and offer frameworks similar to the one illustrated in Figure 3. In the first article, Leithwood and Montgomery (1982) describe a framework for planned educational change, and they apply the framework to an assessment of

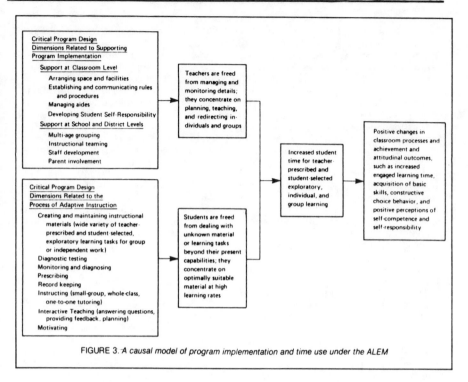

FIGURE 3. A causal model of program implementation and time use under the ALEM

program implementation, which included student entry behaviors, instructional objectives, classroom resources, and assessment instruments and procedures. In the second *EEPA* article, Rubin, Stuck, and Revicki (1982) describe the evaluation of a school-based, home-stimulation program, in which performance criteria were assessed with respect to the numbers of home visits made by staff, classroom instructional activities performed by paraprofessional staff, and school meetings attended by parents.

In the context of business innovation and consultation, where results can be measured accurately, Leibenstein (1976) showed that both initial assessment and continued monitoring of implementation or performance are essential, because productivity often increases greatly as the result of new activities but nearly as often reverts to prior levels unless assessment and correction continue. In evaluating the

implementation of the ALEM. it was hypothesized not only that teachers are able to establish and maintain a high degree of program implementation. but also that program implementation leads to effective use of teacher and student time and achievement of expected outcomes.

Evaluation results and discussion: Evaluation of the degree of program implementation at the sites participating in the field studies suggested many significant results (Wang, 1983b; Wang & Walberg. in press). Although teachers differed significantly ($p < .05$) across the 10 school districts in terms of their degree of program implementation, the site averages in observed degree of implementation for the 12 critical program dimensions (see the Appendix) all were at or near 85 percent, the recommended criterion for a high degree of implementation. This result suggests that the ALEM can be implemented with a high degree of treatment fidelity in a large number of classes that include poor and handicapped students and are located in schools with varying characteristics and constraints.

The higher the degree of implementation, moreover, the greater the percentages of observed time spent on teacher-student interactions for instructional rather than management purposes, peer interactions for idea sharing rather than disruption, cooperative group work rather than individual seat work, exploratory rather than prescriptive activity, and learning tasks rather than waiting and distraction. More on-task time also was associated with instruction-related, teacher-student interactions; exploratory activities; cooperative group efforts; and self-initiated activities (Wang & Walberg, in press).

Although a positive but nonsignificant relationship was observed between the degree of program implementation and student learning outcomes, the students' performance on standardized achievement tests in reading and math is noteworthy. On the average, they scored about 25 to 55 percentile points above the national norms for poor and handicapped students. Because students in ALEM classrooms are encouraged to work on exploratory activities as well as master prescriptive tasks, and because most of the teachers in the study were found to implement the program at a uniformly high degree, the positive but nonsignificant relation of the degree of implementation to curricular objectives completed and standardized achievement scores was expected.

The results from the study do not indicate which critical dimensions and performance indicators included in the ALEM's design led to the encouraging findings on the use of classroom time. However, they do indicate that the program as a whole can succeed in accomplishing its process goals if it is implemented with a reasonable degree of fidelity. As pointed out earlier, instructional design studies of the ALEM were aimed at discovering and developing those program features that were likely to prove effective, and the task of the evaluation described here was to test the combined effectiveness of those features in the field. While the results support the psychological and pedagogical conceptions on which the ALEM was founded, they also yield ideas that are relevant to educational treatments other than the ALEM and to populations beyond the particular sites in the sample.

Accommodation of Handicapped and Gifted Students. Current definitions of mainstreaming (e.g., Birch, 1974) emphasize the integration of regular and exceptional students in educational settings so that they might share the same resources and opportunities. In this context, the ultimate purpose can be said to be the provision of "special" education for all students, and mainstreaming could be interpreted to mean the elimination of many remedial and tracking programs for students in segregated special education classrooms. As indicated by substantive research, however, varying student abilities and interests are not accommodated easily by conventional, whole-group teaching; much time can be wasted when all students are expected to follow the same course of study at the same pace (Jackson, 1968).

The programming goals and design features of the ALEM, on the other hand,

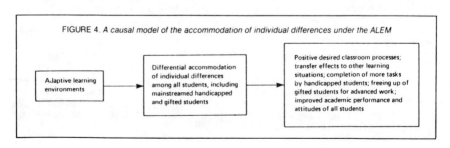

FIGURE 4. *A causal model of the accommodation of individual differences under the ALEM*

| Adaptive learning environments | Differential accommodation of individual differences among all students, including mainstreamed handicapped and gifted students | Positive desired classroom processes; transfer effects to other learning situations; completion of more tasks by handicapped students; freeing up of gifted students for advanced work; improved academic performance and attitudes of all students |

seem to be particularly suited to operationalizing mainstreaming in regular classroom settings. These features include a diagnostic-prescriptive monitoring system for identifying learning problems; instruction-related descriptions of students' learning needs, rather than the use of categorical labels; an instructional-learning, self-management component that enables students to take increased responsibility for planning and carrying out their own learning; and an organizational and staffing support system for maximizing the use of classroom time and other school resources. Figure 4 illustrates the causal links involved in accommodating student differences through the creation of adaptive school learning environments. As shown in the figure, the effects of this approach to mainstreaming are expected to include desired classroom processes and transfer effects to other learning situations, increased task completion rates for handicapped students, availability of time for advanced work by gifted students, and improved academic performance and attitudes for all students.

Analysis of program efficacy: To test the feasibility of accommodating individual differences in exceptional students under the ALEM, a randomized experiment was planned and conducted (Wang, in press; Wang, Thompson, & Meece, Note 7). A total of 357 students classified as regular, gifted, and handicapped (i.e., educable mentally retarded, socially and emotionally disturbed, learning disabled) by their two school districts were randomly assigned to ALEM and non-ALEM classes. Handicapped students in the non-ALEM classrooms received basic skills instruction in a part-time resource room. They attended the resource room in the morning and returned to their regular classrooms in the afternoon. By contrast, mainstreamed handicapped students spent the entire school day in the ALEM classrooms, receiving basic skills instruction through the program's components in the morning and participating in the same school district program as the non-ALEM handicapped students in the afternoon. Thus, it was possible to assess not only the differences in processes and outcomes between the two groups of handicapped students in the morning, when they were

in different programs, but also the transfer effects in the afternoon, when both groups participated in the same program.

Evaluation results and discussion: As reported above, the degree of implementation measures showed a high degree of treatment fidelity in the ALEM classes. In addition, large and significant differences in classroom interactions and processes were found for the ALEM and non-ALEM students. For example, 40 percent of the student-teacher interactions in the ALEM classes were student-initiated, in contrast to 8 percent in the non-ALEM classes. ALEM students interacted with their teachers more often for instructional than management and discipline purposes; they spent more time on-task; and they engaged more frequently in exploratory, self-selected learning activities than did the non-ALEM students (Wang, in press).

Comparisons of students in the ALEM classes showed that teachers prescribed more basic skills work for handicapped students, and they allocated more time for these students to complete the work. Accordingly, the handicapped students spent significantly more time working on individualized tasks, and the regular and gifted students spent more time in interactive groups. All three groups of ALEM students, had high rates of time-on-task (82%, 88%, and 79%, respectively, for handicapped, regular, and gifted students), compared to the usual rates of below 50 percent reported in the literature (Rosenshine, 1980; Berliner, Fisher, Filby, & Marliave, Note 8). The handicapped students completed more prescribed tasks than did the other two groups. Although all three groups of ALEM students, on the average, scored considerably above the respective national norms on standardized achievement tests, the handicapped and gifted students made greater gains during the school year than did the regular students. This finding suggests that exceptionality can be accommodated more productively in regular classroom settings by differential treatments than by conventional whole-group instruction and/or "pullout" special education services.

Needs Assessment and Staff Development. The final evaluation example shows how staff training that is geared to specific needs can be causally traced from needs assessment, to written staff development plans, to actual implementation of the plans and, finally, to improvements in targeted classroom practices (see Figure 5). Evaluation of the ALEM's systematic needs assessment and staff development procedures is based on the assumption that, although initial program implementation and treatment fidelity are obviously important in field trials, sustained delivery is required if educational innovations are to remain effective (Leithwood & Montgomery, 1982; Rubin, Stuck, & Revicki, 1982).

Evaluating staff development efforts: Because of professional and social pressures, as well as the difficulties of sustaining demanding new programs, teachers may slacken in their efforts to maintain program implementation. Evidence of deterioration in treatment fidelity and declining productivity is cited and discussed in earlier sections of this paper. In addition, the history of educational innovation is full of examples of promising and apparently successful programs started by charismatic leaders or "master developers" (Rosenshine, Note 4) that faded from view because they were described in insufficient operational detail and had neither instrumentation nor explicit training materials and procedures to make them "transportable" beyond the original developers and sites. Indeed, programs similar to the ALEM in purpose and method, such as the Winnetka and Dalton plans of the 1920s, ungraded schools of the 1960s, and open education of the 1970s, seemed insufficiently specified to be generalized or sustained (Joncich-Clifford, 1973). In view of such difficulties, the design of the ALEM represents considerable effort in the development and testing of a data-based, adaptive system of materials and procedures for initial train-

ing, diagnosis, and retraining (Wang, Note 5).

The components of the ALEM's Data-Based Staff Development Program are outlined in Figure 6. As shown in the figure, the program consists of three training levels ranging in focus from initial awareness training to ongoing in-service training. Level I of the staff development program provides basic working knowledge of curricular content and procedures. In Level II, more intensive training is provided in specific staff functions. Level III is a clinical training component tailored to the needs of individual staff. Training at Level III is ongoing in-service training designed to help school staff continually improve and upgrade their classroom implementation. It is primarily at the third level of the staff development program that the iterative process of assessment, feedback, planning, and training occurs. This process is operationalized through the design of staff development plans that specify training objectives for the 12 critical dimensions (see Figure 2); dates by which training is be completed; persons responsible for training; specific training activities; expected outcomes; and evidence to be sought to reveal the effectiveness of training activities.

Evaluation results and discussion: The evaluation data permitted a statistical assessment of the hypothesized causal links shown in Figure 6 (Wang & Gennari, in press). It should be noted that some of the classrooms included in the study sample were half-day, kindergarten classes. Thus, the results reported here are for 138 teachers as units rather than 156 classrooms. Specifically, the first link assessed was the degree to which the written staff development plans reflected a needs assessment that was based on degree of implementation scores for the critical dimensions from October 1981. An unu-

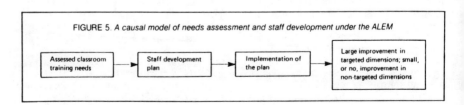

FIGURE 5. *A causal model of needs assessment and staff development under the ALEM*

| Assessed classroom training needs | → | Staff development plan | → | Implementation of the plan | → | Large improvement in targeted dimensions; small, or no, improvement in non-targeted dimensions |

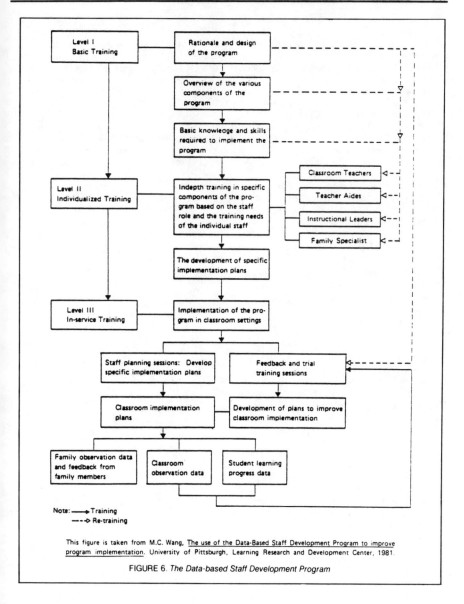

Note: ——▶ Training
      ——-▷ Re-training

This figure is taken from M.C. Wang, The use of the Data-Based Staff Development Program to improve
program implementation. University of Pittsburgh, Learning Research and Development Center, 1981.

FIGURE 6. The Data-based Staff Development Program

sually close correspondence was found: The plans excluded 98 percent of the dimensions with scores above the 85 percent criterion level, and included 86 percent of the dimensions with scores below the 85 percent criterion level.

To assess the next link, correlations were calculated between critical dimensions listed in the staff development plans and the number of times training related to these dimensions was listed in the training specialists' logs. The correlations were all positive and ranged from .05 to .59, with a median of .31 for the available training logs on 119 teachers.

Finally, to assess the specificity of targeted training, changes in the degree of implementation scores from fall to spring of the 1980–81 school year were analyzed. Although the overall average change from 83 percent to 93 percent was significant for the 138 teachers, 80 percent of the dimensions included in training showed observed improvement, and only 40 percent of those not included in training showed improvement. In short, the evaluation suggests that, with explicit specifications and careful monitoring, staff development plans can productively address training needs; action can follow the targeted plans; and classroom results can be expected from specific training or retraining action.

Conclusion

One of the underlying assumptions of this paper is that evaluation that is not connected closely with substantive research in the disciplines tends to drift away from the scientific canons of generalizability, parsimony, and theory. Such evaluation risks captivation by purely definitional, methodological, practical, political, and polemical considerations. Thus, to maintain scientific alliances, useful evaluation must address the causal questions of means-ends sequences that are of great concern to educators.

This paper illustrates several efforts to build a fruitful coalition of educational evaluation and current substantive developments in psychological and educational research, particularly research on cognitive processing and time use in teaching and learning. Such developments can offer theory, findings, and methods for guiding causal evaluations of complex, innovative programs in field settings. The illustrations in the present paper show how substantive research can enrich evaluations of implementation, time use, accommodation of individual differences, and retraining in the case of adaptive education. However, the integrative, causal-modeling approach to evaluation obviously is generalizable to many other programs, populations, and conditions and deserves further exploration and testing.

The nation can hardly afford evaluations of all educational programs and each of their specific components under all possible circumstances. Thus, evaluations with the greatest generalizability are likely to be the most useful and cost-efficient in the long run. Those that are grounded in the enduring findings of psychology and other disciplines, operationally based on effective instructional practices, and implemented with ongoing monitoring are likely to remain robust in field settings.

To these ends, evaluation must strengthen its connection with substantive research. Philosophy of science students have long maintained that both the natural and social sciences are emotion- and value-laden (e.g., see Kuhn, 1970; Weber, 1949). To the extent that it is even more committed to values questions, evaluation must yet aspire to objectivity and disinterestedness if it is to be credible. Educational evaluation and research, if that distinction is admitted, differ in degree rather than in kind: They might be considered adjacent parts of the overlap between the social sciences and professional education. Insofar as both aim for scientific rigor and relevance to practice, their contributions to education will be greater if based on a firm alliance.

Reference Notes

1. Wang, M. C. *The design and study of the Adaptive Learning Environments Model: Interactive roles in program design and supporting research.* Symposium paper presented at the annual meeting of the American Psychological Association. Washington, D.C., August 1982.
2. Lindvall, C. M., & Cox, R. C. *A rationale and plan for the evaluation of the individually prescribed instruction project.* Paper presented at the annual meeting of the American Educational Research Association. New York, February 1967.
3. Fogarty, J., & Wang, M. C. *A descriptive study of experienced and novice teachers' interactive instructional thoughts and actions.* Pittsburgh, Pa.: University of Pittsburgh, Learning Research and Development Center, 1982.
4. Rosenshine, B. V. *The master teacher and the master developer.* Unpublished paper. University of Illinois at Champaign-Urbana, 1982.
5. Wang, M. C. *The use of the Data-Based Staff Development Program to improve program implementation.* Pittsburgh, Pa.: University of Pittsburgh, Learning Research and Development Center, 1981.
6. Loucks, S. F., & Hall, G. E. *Investigating program implementation: A field perspective.* Paper presented at a conference entitled "Documenta-

tion of School Improvement Efforts: Some Technical Issues and Future Research Agenda." Pittsburgh, Pa.: Learning Research and Development Center, March 1981.

7. WANG, M. C., THOMPSON, M. D., & MEECE, J. L. Provision of effective learning experiences for mainstreamed mildly handicapped and gifted students. Paper presented at the annual meeting of the American Educational Research Association, New York, March 1982.

8. BERLINER, D. C., FISHER, C. W., FILBY, N. N., & MARLIAVE, R. Executive summary of Beginning Teacher Evaluation Study. San Francisco: Far West Laboratory for Educational Research and Development, 1978.

9. WANG, M. C. The degree of implementation assessment measures for the Adaptive Learning Environments Model. Pittsburgh, Pa.: University of Pittsburgh, Learning Research and Development Center, 1980.

10. SCHMIDHAMMER, J. A computer program for the analysis and reporting of degree of implementation data. Pittsburgh, Pa.: University of Pittsburgh, Learning Research and Development Center, 1980.

11. WANG, M. C. The use of degree of program implementation information in the evaluation and improvement of innovative educational programs. Paper presented at the annual meeting of the Northeastern Educational Research Association, Ellenville, New York, October 1981.

References

ALKIN, M. C. Evaluation theory development. Evaluation Comment, 1969, 2(1), 2–7.

ANASTASI, A. Psychology, psychologists, and psychological testing. American Psychologist, 1967, 22, 297–306.

BENTLER, P. M. Multivariate analysis with latent variables: Causal modeling. Annual Review of Psychology, 1980, 31, 419–456.

BIRCH, J. W. Mainstreaming: Educable mentally retarded children in regular classes. Reston, Va.: Council for Exceptional Children, 1974.

BLOOM, B. S. Human characteristics and school learning. New York: McGraw-Hill, 1976.

BORKO, H., CONE, R., RUSSO, N., & SHAVELSON, R. J. Teachers' decision making. In P. L. Peterson & H. J. Walberg (Eds.), Research on teaching. Berkeley, Calif.: McCutchan, 1979.

CLARK, C. M., & YINGER, R. J. Teachers' thinking. In P. L. Peterson & H. J. Walberg (Eds.), Research on teaching. Berkeley, Calif.: McCutchan, 1979.

COOK, T. D., & CAMPBELL, D. T. Quasi-experimentation: Design and analysis issues for field settings. Chicago: Rand-McNally, 1979.

CRONBACH, L. J. Designing evaluations of educational and social programs. San Francisco: Jossey-Bass, 1982.

DOYLE, W. Paradigms for research on teaching. In L. S. Shulman (Ed.), Review of research on teaching (Vol. 5). Itasca, Ill.: F. E. Peacock, 1977.

FLORIO, D. H., BEHRMANN, M. M., MASON, G., & GOLTZ, D. L. What do policy makers think of educational research and evaluation? Or do they? Educational Evaluation and Policy Analysis, 1979, 1, 61–87.

FULLAN, M., & POMFRET, A. Research on curriculum and instruction implementation. Review of Educational Research, 1977, 47, 335–397.

GLASER, R. Criterion-referenced testing for measurement (LRDC Publications Series R41). Pittsburgh, Pa.: University of Pittsburgh, Learning Research and Development Center, 1967.

GLASER, R. Educational psychology and education. American Psychologist, 1973, 28(7), 557–566.

GLASER, R. Adaptive instruction: Individual diversity and learning. New York: Holt, Rinehart and Winston, 1977.

GLASS, G. V., & ELLETT, F. S. Evaluation research. Annual Review of Psychology, 1980, 31, 211–228.

GOWIN, D. B., & GREEN, T. F. Two philosophers view education. Educational Evaluation and Policy Analysis, 1980, 2, 67–70.

GUBA, E. G. Toward a methodology of naturalistic inquiry in educational evaluation. Los Angeles: Center for the Study of Evaluation, 1978.

HAMILTON, D., MACDONALD, G., KING, C., JENKINS, D., & PARLETT, M. (Eds.). Beyond the numbers game. Berkeley, Calif.: McCutchan, 1977.

HEMPHILL, J. K. The relationships between research and evaluation studies. In R. W. Tyler (Ed.), Educational evaluation: New roles, new means. Chicago: University of Chicago Press, 1969.

HOUSE, E. R. Evaluation with validity. Beverly Hills, Calif.: Sage, 1980.

JACKSON, P. W. Life in classrooms. New York: Holt, Rinehart and Winston, 1968.

JOHNSON, D. W., MARUYAMA, G., JOHNSON, R., NELSON, D., & SKON, L. Effects of cooperative, competitive, and individualistic goal structures on achievement: A meta-analysis. Psychological Bulletin, 1981, 89, 47–62.

JOINT COMMITTEE ON STANDARDS FOR EDUCATIONAL EVALUATION. Standards for evaluation of educational programs, projects, and materials. New York: McGraw-Hill, 1981.

JONCICH-CLIFFORD, G. The history of research on teaching. In R. M. W. Travers (Ed.), Second handbook of research on teaching. Chicago: Rand McNally, 1973.

KUHN, T. S. The structure of scientific revolutions (2nd ed.). Chicago: The University of Chicago Press, 1970.

LEIBENSTEIN, H. Beyond economic man. Cambridge, Mass.: Harvard University Press, 1976.

LEITHWOOD, K. A., & MONTGOMERY, D. J. A framework for planned educational change: Application to the assessment of program implementation. Educational Evaluation and Policy Analysis, 1982, 4, 157–167.

MARSHALL, H. H. Open classrooms: Has the term outlived its usefulness? Review of Educational Research, 1981, 51, 181–192.

MARUYAMA, G., & WALBERG, H. J. Causal modeling. In H. M. Mitzel (Ed.), Encyclopedia of educational research. New York: Macmillan, 1982.

MOSTELLER, F., & TUKEY, J. W. Data analysis and regression: A second course in statistics. Reading, Mass.: Addison-Wesley, 1977.

MURRAY, S. L., & SMITH, N. L. Causal research on teacher training. In H. J. Walberg (Ed.), Educational environments and effects. Berkeley, Calif.: McCutchan, 1979.

PETERSON, P. L. Direct instruction reconsidered. In P. L. Peterson & H. J. Walberg (Eds.), *Research on teaching: Concepts, findings, and implications.* Berkeley, Calif.: McCutchan, 1979.

PETERSON, P. L., & WALBERG, H. J. (Eds.). *Research on teaching: Concepts, findings, and implications.* Berkeley, Calif.: McCutchan, 1979.

RAVEN, J. The most important problem in education is to come to terms with values. *Oxford Review of Education,* 1981, 7(3), 253–272.

RESNICK, L. B., & WANG, M. C. Improvement of academic performance of poor-prognosis children through the use of an individualized instructional program (*LRDC Publications Series* 1974/2). Pittsburgh, Pa.: University of Pittsburgh, Learning Research and Development Center, 1974.

RESNICK, L. B., WANG, M. C., & KAPLAN, J. Behavior analysis in curriculum design: A hierarchically sequenced introductory mathematics curriculum. *Journal of Applied Behavior Analysis,* 1973, 6(4), 679–710.

RESNICK, L. B., WANG, M. C., & ROSNER, J. Adaptive education for young children: The Primary Education Project. In M. C. Day (Ed.), *Pre-school in action.* Boston: Allyn & Bacon, 1977.

ROSENSHINE, B. V. Content, time, and direct instruction. In P. L. Peterson & H. J. Walberg (Eds.), *Research on teaching: Concepts, findings, and implications.* Berkeley, Calif.: McCutchan, 1979.

ROSENSHINE, B. V. How time is spent in elementary classrooms. In C. Denham & A. Lieberman (Eds.), *Time to learn.* Washington, D.C.: National Institute of Education, 1980.

RUBIN, R., STUCK, G., & REVICKI, D. A model of assessing the degree of implementation in field-based educational programs. *Educational Evaluation and Policy Analysis,* 4, 189–196.

SHIMRON, J. Learning activities in IPI. *Instructional Science,* 1976, 5, 391–401.

SIMON, H. A. *The sciences of the artificial.* Cambridge, Mass.: MIT Press, 1981.

SMITH, E. Implementation of the Self-Schedule System: The teacher's perspective. In M. C. Wang (Ed.), *The Self-Schedule System for instructional-learning management in adaptive school learning environments* (*LRDC Publications Series* 1976/9). Pittsburgh, Pa.: University of Pittsburgh, Learning Research and Development Center, 1976.

STAKE, R. Toward a technology for the evaluation of educational programs. In R. W. Tyler, R. M. Gagne, & M. Scriven (Eds.), *Perspectives of curriculum evaluation: AERA monograph series on curriculum evaluation.* Chicago: Rand-McNally, 1967.

STONE, R., & VAUGHN, L. Implementation evaluation of the Self-Schedule System in an adaptive school learning environment. In M. C. Wang (Ed.), *The Self-Schedule System for instructional-learning management in adaptive school learning environments* (*LRDC Publications Series* 1976/9). Pittsburgh, Pa.: University of Pittsburgh, Learning Research and Development Center, 1976.

STUFFLEBEAM, D. L., & WEBSTER, W. J. An analysis of alternative approaches to evaluation. *Educational Evaluation and Policy Analysis,* 1980, 2, 5–20.

SUCHMAN, E. A. *Evaluative research.* New York: Russell Sage Foundation, 1967.

TALMAGE, H. Evaluation of programs. In H. M. Mitzel (Ed.), *Encyclopedia of educational research.* New York: Macmillan, 1982.

WANG, M. C. Development and consequences of students' sense of personal control. In J. Levine & M. C. Wang (Eds.), *Teacher and student perceptions: Implications for learning.* Hillsdale, N.J.: Erlbaum, 1983. (a)

WANG, M. C. Provision of adaptive instruction: Implementation and effects (*LRDC Publications Series*). Pittsburgh, Pa.: University of Pittsburgh, Learning Research and Development Center, 1983. (b)

WANG, M. C. Effective mainstreaming is possible—Provided that . . . *Analysis and Intervention in Developmental Disabilities,* in press.

WANG, M. C., & ELLETT, C. D. Program validation: The state of the art. *Topics in Early Childhood Special Education,* 1982, 1(4), 35–49.

WANG, M. C., & FITZHUGH, R. J. Planning instruction and monitoring classroom processes with computer assistance. *Educational Technology,* February, 1978, 7–12.

WANG, M. C., & GENNARI, P. Analysis of the design, implementation, and effects of the Data-Based Staff Development Program. *Teacher Education and Special Education,* in press.

WANG, M. C., LEINHARDT, G., & BOSTON, E. *The Individualized Early Learning Program* (*LRDC Publications Series* 1980/2). Pittsburgh, Pa.: University of Pittsburgh, Learning Research and Development Center, 1980.

WANG, M. C., NOLAN, M., STROM, C. D., & WALBERG, H. J. The utility of degree of implementation measures in program evaluation and implementation research: A case study. *Curriculum Inquiry,* in press.

WANG, M. C., RESNICK, L. B., & BOOZER, R. The sequence of development of some early mathematics behaviors. *Child Development,* 1971, 41, 1,767–1,778.

WANG, M. C., RESNICK, L. B., & SCHEUTZ, P. R. PEP in the Frick elementary school: Interim evaluation report 1969–70 (*LRDC Publications Series* 1974/13). Pittsburgh, Pa.: University of Pittsburgh, Learning Research and Development Center, 1974.

WANG, M. C., & STILES, B. An investigation of children's concept of self-responsibility for their school learning. *American Educational Research Journal,* 1976, 13, 159–179.

WANG, M. C., & WALBERG, H. J. Adaptive instruction and classroom time. *American Educational Research Journal,* in press.

WEBER, M. *The methodology of the social sciences.* New York: Free Press, 1949.

WORTHEN, B. R., & SANDERS, J. R. *Educational evaluation: Theory and practice.* Worthington, Ohio: Charles A. Jones, 1973.

Appendix

Instrumentation and Procedures for
Collecting and Analyzing Degree of
Implementation Data on the Adaptive
Learning Environments Model

Margaret C. Wang

A systematic set of instruments and procedures has been developed to collect and analyze data on the degree of implementation of the Adaptive Learning Environments Model (ALEM) in school settings. Included in this appendix are brief descriptions of the Implementation Assessment Battery for Adaptive Instruction and the procedures for analyzing and reporting degree of implementation data.

Implementation Assessment Battery for Adaptive Instruction. Development of the battery of degree of implementation instruments was based on the 12 critical program dimensions (features) identified through analysis of the ALEM's structural and action domains. These dimensions are Arranging Space and Facilities (AS&F); Creating and Maintaining Instructional Materials (CMIM); Establishing and Communicating Rules and Procedures (ECRP); Managing Aides (MA); Diagnostic Testing (TEST); Record Keeping (RCRD); Monitoring and Diagnosing (M&D); Prescribing (PRES); Interactive Teaching (IT); Instructing (INST); Motivating (MOTI); and Developing Student Self-Responsibility (DSSR). The critical dimensions incorporate 106 performance indicators for assessing the presence or absence of the critical dimensions in ALEM classrooms. The performance indicators, in turn, are grouped into the six instruments that comprise the Implementation Assessment Battery for Adaptive Instruction (Wang, Note 9).

Two of the instruments are used in observing dynamic aspects of program implementation: the Teacher Instructional Roles and Interactions Observation Form, and the Student Learning Process and Behaviors Observation Form. Both are administered during class time. Two instruments, the Checklist for Physical Design of the Classroom and the Checklist for Classroom Records, focus on nondynamic observables and are administered when students and teachers are not present in the classroom. The final two instruments, the Student Interview and the Teacher

Interview, are interview questionnaires designed to elicit comments from students and teachers on various aspects of program implementation. The Teacher Interview is administered before or after class time; the Student Interview, during class time.

The Battery is used by school personnel on a regular basis to collect information for staff development purposes (i.e., the design of in-service training) and to monitor the overall degree of implementation of the ALEM in their classrooms. Degree of implementation data also are collected three times during the school year (usually in October, February, and April) specifically for program evaluation purposes. It generally takes about 2 hours per classroom to administer the entire Battery.

Analysis and Reporting of the Degree of Implementation Data. A computer program has been developed to analyze and report degree of implementation data in a form that can be used by site personnel to design and monitor site-specific staff development plans for improving program implementation (Schmidhammer, Note 10). Figure A-1 illustrates the format for reporting the data. As shown in the figure, which simulates a computer printout of the results of the analysis of degree of implementation data from School District X, the data are analyzed in three different levels or units: school, grade level, and class (teacher). The mean scores for the critical dimensions of the ALEM are reported in 12 separate columns. The names and acronyms for the dimensions are listed at the top of the printout. The number in parentheses under the acronym for each dimension indicates the total number of performance indicators included in the six degree of implementation instruments for that dimension. For example, under CMIM, shown in the second column of Figure A-1, 12 performance indicators are included in the instruments to assess the implementation of that aspect of the ALEM's design. The printout also includes information on each teacher's degree of implementation of the 12 critical dimensions, as well as mean percentages of the degree of implementation for each grade within a particular school, for a given school, and for specific grade levels across an entire school district.

The kind of summary analysis shown

	Critical Dimension Codes		
AS&F	Arranging Space & Facilities	PRES	Prescribing
CMIM	Creating and Maintaining Instructional Materials	M&D	Monitoring & Diagnosing
ECRP	Establishing and Communicating Rules & Procedures	IT	Interactive Teaching
MA	Managing Aides	INST	Instructing
RK	Record Keeping	MOTI	Motivating
TEST	Diagnostic Testing	DSSR	Developing Student Self-Responsibility

District X   Fall, 1982

School/Grade		AS&F (15)*	CMIM (12)	ECRP (15)	MA (3)	RK (3)	TEST (4)	PRES (7)	M&D (10)	IT (6)	INST (13)	MOTI (5)	DSSR (13)
School A													
Grade 1	Teacher A	87	67	73	67	33	50	71	70	67	77	60	77
Grade 2	Teacher B	93	83	87	67	100	25	57	90	50	69	60	69
Grade 3	Teacher C	87	67	80	67	67	75	86	70	83	92	80	62
Kindergarten	Teacher D	73	58	93	100	67	75	86	80	83	85	80	92
Average for School		85	69	83	75	67	56	75	77	71	81	70	75
School B													
Grade 1	Teacher E	67	75	73	67	67	75	71	80	50	77	40	54
Grade 2	Teacher F	80	67	73	33	67	25	14	60	50	62	20	46
Grade 3	Teacher G	87	83	87	67	100	75	86	90	67	85	80	85
Kindergarten	Teacher H	93	83	93	67	67	50	71	70	83	92	60	77
Average for School		82	77	82	59	75	56	61	75	63	79	50	66
Average for Site													
Grade 1		77	71	73	67	50	63	71	75	59	77	50	65
Grade 2		87	75	80	50	83	25	36	75	50	66	40	58
Grade 3		87	75	83	67	83	75	86	80	75	88	80	74
Kindergarten		83	71	93	83	67	63	79	75	83	88	70	85
Overall Average		83	73	82	67	71	56	68	76	67	90	60	71

*Numbers in parentheses indicate numbers of items (Performance Indicators) included in the Implementation Assessment Battery.

Figure A-1. A sample computer printout of a summary of degree of Implementation data.

TEACHER L

TEACHER CONTACTS PER UNIT OF OBSERVATION/STUDENT BEHAVIOR

TOTAL NUMBER OF STUDENTS IS 22
AVERAGE NUMBER OF CHILD CONTACTS (PER OBSERVATION INTERVAL) IS 7
AVERAGE NUMBER OF CHILDREN WAITING (PER OBSERVATION INTERVAL) IS 7
AVERAGE NUMBER OF CHILDREN ON-TASK (PER OBSERVATION INTERVAL) IS 14
AVERAGE NUMBER OF CHILDREN OFF-TASK (PER OBSERVATION INTERVAL) IS 5
NUMBER OF ADULTS (OTHER THAN TEACHER) IN CLASSROOM IS 2
PRIMARY TRAVELER IS TEACHER

CATEGORY	INSTRUMENT	ITEM	AREAS NEEDING IMPROVEMENT
AS&F	CLASSROOM DESIGN	3	Storage/display areas—marked and accessible
		11	Materials labeled for students' understanding
CMIM	CLASSROOM DESIGN	14	Current listing of teacher-constructed tasks
		18	Teacher-made materials—accompanied by teacher scripts
		19	Scripts—related to task objective
ECRP	STUDENT OBSERVATION	1	Students distribute themselves among areas
		7	Students use materials/equipment appropriately
		11	Students have and use own prescription appropriately
		12	Students have and use own self-schedule form appropriately
	STUDENT INTERVIEW	1	Students have knowledge of number of assignments to finish today
		2	Students have knowledge of number of tasks remaining
		4	Students have knowledge of time for prescriptive work
		7	Students have knowledge of time restrictions on activity areas
		9	Students have knowledge of consequences of work not completed
TEST	TEACHER INTERVIEW	8	Pre-tests administered (beginning of unit)
M&D	TEACHER INTERVIEW	1	Teacher has knowledge of students' levels in each area
		2	Knowledge of preferred curriculum area
		11	Teacher changes prescription while traveling
IT	TEACHER OBSERVATION	16	Travel route includes all areas
INST	TEACHER INTERVIEW	6	Students are grouped for supplementary instruction
	TEACHER OBSERVATION	4	Teacher helps students understand purpose of work
		17	Teacher acknowledges requests for help
		18	Teacher uses appropriate questioning techniques to extend responses
		21	Teacher restructures learning tasks
		22	Teacher's interaction concerns specific area
MOTI	TEACHER OBSERVATION	19	Teacher shows interest in students' work
DSSR	TEACHER OBSERVATION	6	Teacher helps students discuss work plans/progress toward completion

Figure A-2.   A sample computer printout indicating specific areas needing further training, based on degree of Implementation data.

in Figure A-1 is used by school personnel to determine areas where improvements in program implementation or program refinement are needed. Analysis of changes in degree of implementation from one assessment period to the next, for example, provides information to teachers about their implementation progress, as well as the data base for designing and evaluating the effectiveness of schools' staff development efforts aimed at improving and maintaining their degree of program implementation. In addition, the overall degree of implementation across a variety of schools for an extended period of time provides evidence of the program's "implementability." That is, the proportion of classrooms at an overall high degree of implementation level across a variety of schools and over a reasonable period of time serves as an index for assessing the extent to which program implementation can be established and maintained consistently by teachers with different characteristics, on a wide-scale basis, and in different school settings (Wang, Note 11).

To further investigate the exact nature of the difficulty causing low degree of implementation scores in a given dimension for a teacher/school/district, more detailed analysis is needed. Figure A-2 shows an example of such an analysis, whereby a computerized summary is provided of the specific areas (performance indicators within the critical dimensions) in which improvement is needed for a given teacher. The summary in Figure A-2 includes a list of the critical dimensions for which the degree of implementation scores were found to be below the criterion level, as well as the specific items (performance indicators) needing further improvement. The list provides the basic information for designing staff development plans for individual teachers.

Authors

MARGARET C. WANG, Professor, Educational Psychology, Director, The Design and Study of Adaptive Learning Environments Unit, Learning Research and Development Center, 3939 O'Hara Street, Pittsburgh, PA 15260. *Specializations:* Design and study of adaptive learning environments, research on effective schooling practices, program evaluation methodology, student motivation.

HERBERT J. WALBERG, Professor of Urban Educational Research, University of Illinois at Chicago, College of Education, Box 4348, Chicago, IL 60680. *Specializations:* Educational theory and productivity; measurement, evaluation, and statistical analysis.

30

Evaluation of a Worksite Program in Health Science and Medicine

Jonathan Z. Shapiro

This paper reports the results of an evaluation of a worksite program in health science and medicine. The evaluation design was based on an approach suggested by Stake (1976), which requires the assessment of theoretical and empirical aspects of program structure and operation. The significance of Stake's model is that establishing the logical contingency of program conceptualization and the congruence between the conceptual model and empirical data constitute the necessary and sufficient conditions for validating the evaluative inference that the program's goals were successfully attained due to the intended treatment.

The effect of meeting the contingency and congruence conditions is to minimize the likelihood of accepting a spurious relationship as causal. Suchman (1976) illustrates the potential problem of considering indicators of program impact only:

> The challenge [is] not only to demonstrate that effect B follows program A but also to "prove" that effect B was really due to program A. Some administrators may argue that so long as B occurs, it does not really matter whether A was the actual cause. This will be legitimate insofar as A is not a spurious cause of B. However, if A is spurious, one may institute an expensive, broad program based on A only to find (or, even worse, not to find because the evaluation is not continuous) that the desired effect no longer occurs because of a change in the "true" cause which may have been only momentarily related to A. (pp. 86–87)

Assessing the contingency and congruence of an educational program is also useful when the program fails to attain the desired goals. Using Stake's approach, one can distinguish failure due to lack of logical contingency in the conceptual model from failure due to lack of congruence between the program model and actual operation. Suchman (1976) labels the lack of logical contingency "theory failure" and the lack of congruence "program failure." Theory failure occurs when the program is based on an invalid theory of operation. Program failure occurs when the implemented program does not reflect the underlying theoretical model.

The implication of the distinction between theory failure and program failure concerns the appropriate administrative response to each situation. Given fixed goals, theory failure indicates that a program based on the particular conceptual model could never attain those goals, for success is predicated on an invalid set of hypothesized relationships. A policymaker would either have to develop a new program (i.e., conceptual model) to attain the given goals or modify the goals in terms of feasible outcomes for a given conceptual program model.

From Jonathan Z. Shapiro, "Evaluation of a Worksite Program in Health Science and Medicine: An Application of Stake's Model of Contingency and Congruence," *Educational Evaluation and Policy Analysis*, 1985, 7(1), 47-56. Copyright 1985, American Educational Research Association, Washington, DC.

Program failure, in contrast, does not imply the need to modify program conceptualization or goals. Rather, the problem is one of implementation. The program as implemented deviates from the underlying conceptual model, thus a test of the conceptual model did not take place. The appropriate administrative response would be to refine and restructure program implementation such that the program could constitute an operationalization of the conceptual model. Only then could the model be verified with empirical program data. Unlike theory failure, an inference of program failure does not constitute a conclusive disconfirmation of the underlying conceptual model.

Suchman (1976) notes that the process of designing program treatment necessarily implies some level of theoretical consideration, since there must be some logical reason for believing that the program of activities as the independent or stimulus variable has some causal connection to the desired goal as the dependent or effect variable. There must be some theoretical basis for linking the program to the objectives. Consequently, there is always an element of theoretical analysis underlying program evaluation. The implication of Suchman's distinction between program failure and theory failure, and Stake's notion of assessing logical contingency and congruence, is that it is useful to explicate the necessarily present, usually implicit theory. The explication yields important evaluation information. In the case of the worksite program analyzed in this paper, it will be shown that explicating the conceptual structure was not just useful, but it was a necessary step to evaluate the program with validity.

Background and Description of the Worksite Program

The worksite program in health science and medicine was a component of two larger enrichment programs administered by the College of Education and Office of Early Outreach of the Medical Center of the University of Illinois at Chicago. The programs, one entitled Career Awareness in Health Professions, and the other, Biomedical Sciences, maintain the same

major goal: to prepare academically talented, economically disadvantaged minority high school students to enter professions in health science and medicine, fields where minorities are currently underrepresented. In each program, components exist for developing student achievement, student affect, and student perceptions of the health science and medicine work world. Each of these aspects of student development is related to career aspiration. The curriculum of each program includes instruction in English, mathematics, and science; personal, academic, and career counseling; and work experiences in health science and medical settings.

Because Career Awareness began operation before Biomedical Sciences, the initial implementation of the worksite program was with Career Awareness students in the spring of 1981. It is the evaluation of the logical contingency and congruence of that program that is the major focus of this paper. Based on the results of that evaluation, changes were instituted prior to the subsequent implementation of the worksite program with Biomedical Sciences students.

The notion of work experiences in health science and medical settings was part of the proposed Career Awareness curriculum. Program designers hypothesized that these work experiences would contribute toward achieving the major program goals, particularly that of expanding the students' horizons in available health science and medical occupations. The program designers planned to have Career Awareness students work in various departments of the University of Illinois Hospital. The following were expected program outcomes:

(1) increased aspiration for careers in health science and medicine;
(2) student contact with, and increased sensitivity to, clients and patients;
(3) increased awareness of job opportunities in health science and medicine;
(4) acquisition of job-related skills; and
(5) increased appreciation for the responsibilities of, and satisfaction derived from, working.

As a step toward implementing the

worksite program, department supervisors at the University of Illinois Hospital were contacted, and several agreed to take on Career Awareness students. However, perhaps reflecting the organizational control wielded by hospital department heads, each supervisor indicated that he or she alone would determine the activities in which the students would engage. No input was requested or accepted from Career Awareness staff members.

The implication of being excluded from the design of the worksite program, as suggested by Stake and Suchman, was that the intended program might not be evident to the Career Awareness evaluators. Problems of spurious inference would be uncontrolled because theory failure could not be distinguished from program failure. To avoid this, Stake's evaluation model was employed to assess the worksite program because, as part of the assessment, the conceptual model underlying the program is explicated.

Stake's Model of Contingency and Congruence

Stake's approach to the evaluation of educational programs is described in his well-known article, "The Countenance of Education Evaluation" (1976). Stake represented the components of the empirical analysis of a program in a 3 × 2 data matrix as described in Figure 1.

The matrix is read and data are col-

FIGURE 1. *Stake's program description matrix (1976, p. 38).*

lected from top to bottom and left to right. It is within the Intents column that the program conceptualization is explicated. The three cells are time ordered from top to bottom, with cell 1 describing the relevant prior conditions, cell 2 describing the transactions, that is, the intended treatment, and cell 3 describing the intended program outcomes.

Logical contingency refers to the relationship among the three time-ordered cells in the Intents column. The column can be viewed as a deductive theoretical argument where the outcomes must logically and necessarily follow from the interaction of antecedent conditions and program transactions. According to Stake, in the search for "relationships that permit the improvement of education, the evaluators' task is one of the identifying outcomes that are contingent upon particular antecedent conditions and instructional transactions" (p. 42).

Congruence refers to the symmetry between what is intended and what is observed. Stake suggests that congruence is a continuous, rather than discrete, variable and therefore within each row of the data matrix "the evaluator should be able to compare the cells containing intents and observations, to note the discrepancies and to describe the amount of congruence for that row" (p. 42). The horizontal analysis between cells 1 and 4, 2 and 5, and 3 and 6 corresponds to Suchman's notion of the assessment of program failure, that is, the degree to which the implemented program reflects the intended program model.

Taken together, logical contingency and congruence yield "empirical contingency," that is, the evaluative inference that the observed outcomes are due to the interaction of the observed antecedent conditions and observed transactions. Should the intended outcomes fail to materialize (in cell 6) the evaluator must retrace the steps in the matrix to determine whether the failure is due to a lack of logical contingency or congruence. The distinction is necessary in order to focus the administrative response toward reconceptualization or reimplementation.

The process of evaluation, as depicted by Stake, is a theory-testing activity. It begins with the explication of a conceptual model, a theoretical argument which asserts that the intended outcome is a logical consequence of the antecedent conditions and transactions. The analysis of logical contingency is the assessment of the logic and plausibility of the theoretical argument. If the program theory is logically correct, evaluation data are collected to determine the degree of correspondence between the program and the theory. This was the approach adopted by the evaluators in assessing the worksite program in Career Awareness.

Evaluation Design for the Career Awareness Worksite Program

The evaluation of the worksite program proceeded according to Stake's description matrix. The major problem, as indicated earlier, was that Career Awareness program planners controlled the contents of cells 1 and 3 in the Intents column, but the hospital supervisors developed the intended transactions. The intended antecedent conditions primarily referred to characteristics of the Career Awareness students. The intention was for the program to be filled with educationally talented, economically deprived, minority students. While the students would have minimal work experience of this sort, they would have expressed interest in pursuing careers in health science and medicine. The intended outcomes cell contained the five expected program outcomes previously described.

To explicate the intended transaction, survey questionnaires were sent to each site supervisor requesting a list of the activities students would engage in once the program commenced. Appendix A contains descriptions of the intended transactions for the worksites analyzed in the evaluation. For each of the worksites, X-ray, Escort, Orthoclinic, and Admissions, a description of the nature of the site and a set of seven to eight activities were provided. Upon return of the questionnaires, the Intents column was completed.

During the course of the worksite program, data were collected to fill in the Observations column. The antecedent conditions cell contained data that had been collected on the students when they applied for the Career Awareness pro-

gram. The Career Awareness selection procedure was based on a regression discontinuity design (Cook & Campbell, 1979) using a criterion score, which was a function of a standardized achievement test in science, mathematics, and reading, high school attendance, and an interview with a Career Awareness counselor. One hundred and five students applied for the program, and the top 70 scorers, stratified by sex and ethnicity, were admitted to the program. The statistical descriptions of the program students (Lourenco, Eash, & Bardwell, 1981) were located in cell 4. The data indicated that they were educationally talented, economically deprived, minority students who were interested in careers in health science and medicine.

The major effort in the worksite evaluation focused on the collection of data for the observed transactions cell. Since the entire program consisted of work activities, a plan was developed for on-site observation of students at work. The observations were conducted by graduate students enrolled in an advanced evaluation research seminar in the College of Education. Each student was required to observe at one of the four worksites. For each site, an observation instrument was constructed based on the statement of intended activities for the site. Each instrument contained the list of intended activities with space to indicate whether or not the activity was observed and with what frequency. The instrument also had space to record observed activities that were not part of the statement of intents. Consequently, the observations could reflect three possible situations. The graduate student could observe (a) intended activities being carried out, (b) intended activities not taking place, and/or (c) unintended activities occurring. In this way, the degree of correspondence between the intended and observed transactions could be assessed.

Data for the observed outcomes cell were collected through the administration of two evaluation instruments. The first was the Strong Vocational Interest Blank (Strong & Campbell, 1974). Because it had been hypothesized that the program would increase aspiration for careers in science and medicine, pretest and posttest data on attitudes toward careers in health science, mathematics, medical service, and medical science were collected.

The second evaluation instrument was a survey questionnaire administered to the students at the end of the program. The students were asked to respond to statements about their worksite experience by selecting a number from 1 to 4 (extremely negative, somewhat negative, somewhat positive, extremely positive) that indicated their feelings toward each statement. The statements were constructed to reflect the expected program outcomes hypothesized by the Career Awareness program staff.

With the collection of the postprogram data, the evaluators completed the description matrix. Its contents are summarized below:

Cell 1 (Intended Antecedent Conditions): It was intended that the worksite program participants would be educationally talented, economically disadvantaged, minority high school students. It was presumed that the students would enter the program with no prior work experience of this sort, but would have expressed interest in pursuing careers in health science and medicine.

Cell 2 (Intended Transactions): The intended transactions cell contained the lists of intended activities for each worksite as described in Appendix A. Since the only program activity was work (there was no classroom instruction) it was asserted that the descriptions of the intended activities constituted the entire set of intended transactions.

Cell 3 (Intended Outcomes): The intended outcomes cell contained the five expected outcomes previously discussed. The primary program goal was increased aspiration for careers in health science and medicine because this is an expressed goal of the larger Career Awareness program. Furthermore, aspiration was viewed as a global concept, likely to be a function of (a) contact with patients, (b) increased awareness of job opportunities, (c) acquisition of job-related skills, and (d) increased appreciation for work.

Cell 4 (Observed Antecedent Conditions): The observed antecedent condi-

tions cell contained the statistical descriptions of the students based on the data collected during the Career Awareness application process.

Cell 5 (Observed Transactions): The observed transactions cell contained the observation data collected by the graduate students who visited the worksites over the course of the program.

Cell 6 (Observed Outcomes): The observed outcomes cell contained the pretest/posttest Strong Vocational Interest Blank data on aspirations for careers in mathematics, science, medical science, and medical service, as well as the survey data on students' attitudes toward their worksite experience.

Results of the Worksite Program Evaluation

Because the basic question addressed in an evaluation concerns program impact, analysis of the worksite program data began with an inspection of cell 6. Tables I and II report the data from the Strong Vocational Interest Blank and the survey of worksite experience.

The data suggest that the worksite program exerted only moderate influence on the students. Table I indicates that none of the aspiration differences approach statistical significance. The dimensions are conceptually very general; however, it was hypothesized that given the nature of the worksite activities, program impact would most likely be reflected by an increase in aspiration for medical service careers. No such change was indicated.

The survey data also reflect only moderate student responses to their worksite experiences, although the interpretation of point estimates of ordinal measures is necessarily tenuous. The students responded most positively to the "acquisition of new skills" and "derived satisfaction from work" dimensions. These findings are intuitively reasonable since students had little prior work experience, particularly in a hospital setting. However, the program is perceived more negatively on the remaining dimensions. The data depict a situation where the students acquired new skills, from which they derived satisfaction, but the worksite experience was not enjoyable, suggesting why attitudes toward careers in health science

TABLE I

Career Awareness Pretest/Posttest Strong Vocational Interest Blank (N = 36)

	Pretest		Posttest		
Dimension	$\bar{X}$	SD	$\bar{X}$	SD	Significance
Science	52.8	9.3	54.6	9.2	.57
Mathematics	53.0	7.5	56.2	7.0	.19
Medical science	55.7	10.1	58.3	8.2	.40
Medical service	61.7	9.8	63.5	9.5	.57

TABLE II

Career Awareness Student Attitudes Toward the Worksite Experience (N = 36, Scaled 1-4)

Dimension	$\bar{X}$	SD
Derived satisfaction from work	3.47	1.17
Desire health science career	3.19	1.02
Acquired useful skills	3.43	.93
Had contact with patients	2.77	1.15
Enjoyed the worksite activities	2.43	1.07

and medicine did not change. Taken together, the Strong Vocational Interest Blank and survey data suggest a program of minimal effectiveness. Since the expectation was that the students involved in the program, given their background, would be predisposed to responding positively to this sort of treatment, the evaluators concluded that the Career Awareness worksite program basically failed to attain the expected program outcomes.

Having designed the evaluation according to Stake's description matrix, the evaluators were able to investigate the cause of the failure in terms of logical contingency and congruence. The distinction (Suchman, 1976) is between the failure of the theory on which the program is based and the failure of the program as implemented to reflect the underlying theory. Because it is common for the lack of program impact to be a function of faulty implementation (Charters & Jones, 1973; Leinhardt, 1980), the evaluators began by assessing the congruence between the columns of intents and observations.

Congruence between the intended and observed antecedent conditions was rather simple to establish since the participants were Career Awareness students of known characteristics. Of greater significance was the congruence between the intended and observed transactions. An inference of high congruence between cells 2 and 5 was based on the observation

data gathered by the graduate students. For each worksite, the mean proportion of activities observed over time and over raters was calculated. The results were extremely consistent across the sites. As indicated in the evaluation report (Lourenco & Eash, 1981), the mean proportion of intended activities that were observed across the sites was 93% with no site assessed under 90%. Furthermore, there was no observation of any unintended activities, reflecting the control the supervisors exert over their areas of responsibility. Thus, the program as intended was almost fully implemented.

In sum, high congruence was established across the first two rows of the description matrix, breaking down across the outcome row. This suggested that the problem was a lack of logical contingency in the column of intents. An inspection of the contingency in the Intents column was conducted to identify where the theoretical problems existed.

For the worksite program, the intended sequence, or program model, was as follows:

A. Given academically talented, economically disadvantaged students with no work experience in health science or medical settings, but an expressed interest in pursuing careers in those fields, and

B. having them engaged in activities such as
1. filing x-ray reports
2. processing request slips for x-ray films
3. filing x-ray films
4. moving patients in wheelchairs
5. delivering patient reports
6. delivering x-rays
7. cleaning up examination areas
8. running messages between labs
9. filing records on patients, and
10. helping to keep daily reports on admissions, should lead to
C. the following outcomes:
1. increased aspiration for careers in health science and medicine;
2. student contact with, and increased sensitivity to, clients and patients;
3. increased awareness of job opportunities in health science and medicine;
4. acquisition of job-related skills;
5. increased appreciation for the responsibilities of and satisfaction derived from working.

Examining the explicit program theory in this manner leads to a suggestion as to why C does not follow from A and B. Since the antecedent conditions are not manipulable, the only possibilities are that the transactions are not appropriate to the given outcomes, or that the outcomes are not appropriate to the given transactions. As discussed in the first section, in a theory failure situation, a policymaker either has to develop a new program to attain the given goals or modify the goals in terms of feasible outcomes for a given program model.

Because the goals postulated for the worksite program were derived from the Career Awareness program it was decided that they should be maintained. Therefore, the evaluative inference was that the intended transactions were not appropriate to the intended program outcomes. That is, the sets of activities developed by the site supervisors were not sufficiently interesting, stimulating, informative, or important to achieve the program goals, particularly those pertaining to student attitudes and aspirations. It had been assumed that placing the students in a hos-

pital environment would lead to the desired outcomes. The evaluation data indicated that this was not the case, but rather that the sorts of activities the students performed in the work environment was a critical factor.

Based on the evaluation data and inferences, the recommendation of the evaluators with respect to future applications of the worksite program was that the set of intended activities must be more clearly articulated with the maintained program goals. This, in turn, would require better communication between Early Outreach program staff and worksite supervisors in order for the supervisors to understand clearly the aims of the worksite program and to specify an intended treatment appropriate to these aims. These recommendations were incorporated in the design of the succeeding worksite program involving Biomedical Sciences students.

The Biomedical Sciences Worksite Program

The subsequent application of the worksite program was with Biomedical Sciences students. The students were drawn from the same population as those in Career Awareness; that is, they were also educationally talented, economically disadvantaged high school students interested in pursuing careers in health science and medicine. Some differences between the programs exist: Each is funded by a separate agency, and the Biomedical Science students began the program as freshmen rather than sophomores. The goals of the Biomedical Sciences worksite program were identical to those of the Career Awareness program. In fact, in designing the evaluation of the Biomedical Sciences program, cells 1 and 3 were the same as those in the previous evaluation. However, in response to the recommendations from the previous evaluation, a conscious attempt was made to upgrade the conceptual level of the intended transactions.

Because Biomedical Sciences used the services of various community organizations, the program was moved to sites across the city, including community hospitals, clinics, and health science organizations. Again, site supervisors made all decisions concerning the intended activities for the students. Learning from the previous program, the Biomedical Sciences staff invested greater time and effort in explaining to site supervisors the caliber of the students as well as the set of rather rigorous program outcomes that were expected. (In effect, the staff was describing the contents of cells 1 and 3 to the site supervisors to enable the supervisors to develop appropriate contents for cell 2.)

Appendix B contains the descriptions from five Biomedical Sciences worksites. The descriptions suggest that the intended transactions had been enriched substantially because activities such as (a) interpreting between Spanish-speaking patients and their doctors and nurses, (b) assisting mothers with children who come into the clinic, (c) participating in basic training on perinatal visits, (d) accompanying staff on postpartum home visits, (e) administering basic medical tests, and (f) assisting on intake procedures with emergency patients, are likely to create a more salient and meaningful experience for the students than the activities of the Career Awareness program. The evaluators concluded that the intended Biomedical Sciences worksite program was qualitatively superior to the Career Awareness program, and it was hypothesized that the new program would lead to more positive outcomes. The evaluation results appeared to confirm this expectation.

Evaluation of the Biomedical Sciences Worksite Program

The evaluation of the Biomedical Sciences worksite program also was based on Stake's model of contingency and congruence. As indicated above, cells 1 and 3 of the Intents column were identical to those in the Career Awareness description matrix. The contents of cell 2 were based on the response of the site supervisors to a survey questionnaire. The data collected during the application process were placed in cell 4. Data for the observed transactions cell were collected as before by a new group of students in the same advanced evaluation research seminar. The Strong Vocational Interest Blank and the survey of worksite experiences were employed to collect data for cell 6. A high level of congruence was obtained across all three rows of the description matrix (Lourenco & Eash, 1982).

The data from cell 6 are reported in Tables III and IV. Table III contains the results of the pretest and posttest Strong Vocational Interest Blank. A statistically significant increase is indicated for the medical service aspiration dimension. This suggests that the service activities engaged in by the students exerted an impact on their career orientations.

The survey data in Table IV support the inference that the Biomedical Sciences worksite program was effective. The table reports students' attitudes toward the worksite experience and compares the responses with those of the Career Awareness students. In each instance, not only are the attitudes expressed by the Biomedical Sciences students more positive, but the smaller dispersions suggest a more uniform program impact. Statistically significant differences are indicated for the "had contact with patients" and "enjoyed the worksite activities" dimensions.

Taken together, the data suggest that upgrading the intended transactions resulted in a significantly more effective worksite program. The use of Stake's description matrix provided a framework for interpreting the failure of the initial work-

TABLE III

Biomedical Sciences Pretest/Posttest Strong Vocational Interest Blank (N = 80)

Dimension	Pretest $\bar{X}$	SD	Posttest $\bar{X}$	SD	Significance
Science	54.0	7.3	53.8	8.6	.88
Mathematics	52.9	7.7	53.8	8.0	.61
Medical science	54.7	9.6	55.0	8.8	.88
Medical service	52.0	9.4	60.2	10.4	.00

TABLE IV

Career Awareness and Biomedical Sciences Student Attitudes Toward the Worksite Experience

Dimension	Career Awareness			Biomedical Sciences			Significance
	$\bar{X}$	SD	N	$\bar{X}$	SD	N	
Derived satisfaction from work	3.47	1.17	36	3.80	.43	80	.18
Desire health science career	3.19	1.02	36	3.55	.82	80	.21
Acquired useful skills	3.43	.93	36	3 60	.65	80	.44
Had contact with patients	2.77	1.15	36	3.60	.51	80	.00
Enjoyed the worksite activities	2.43	1.07	36	3.15	.95	87	.01

site program and a direction for modifying the subsequent, more successful program. The benefits that obtained from using Stake's model of contingency and congruence should encourage evaluators to employ this theory testing approach to evaluation research when it is feasible to do so.

APPENDIX A

A Description of Intended Worksite Activities in Career Awareness

Worksite: X-ray, Room 345, Old Hospital. Supervisor: Miss Demeres.

X-ray is an important, extremely busy department oriented to accurate record keeping and filing. This is the place where all patient x-ray film is recorded, filed, and dispersed to doctors when called for. There is also a viewing area where doctors can view multiple sets of large x-ray films.

Duties of Career Awareness students:

(1) learn and do the coding system for filing x-ray film,
(2) file reports,
(3) pull x-ray film from files,
(4) process request slips for films,
(5) file x-ray films, and
(6) receive requests for film over the telephone.

Worksite: Escort, Room C-515, New Hospital. Supervisor: Mr. Grant.

This department delivers hospital patients to their proper treatment center. Department also delivers x-ray film to doctors or departments as well as other items, such as reports or patient records.

Duties of Career Awareness students:

(1) move patients in wheelchairs,
(2) transport patients on wheeled carts (sometimes two students are needed),
(3) deliver x-rays to clinic and departments,
(4) deliver reports.

(5) deliver charts and specimens,
(6) fill out forms to check proper delivery (trip books),
(7) complete reports of activities, and
(8) secure proper signatures on all deliveries.

Worksite: Clinic (Orth), First Floor, Old Hospital. Supervisor: Liz Stewart.

This is an out-patient clinic for children and maladies characteristic of children. There is a particularly high patient load (in the hundreds each day) with limited staff and space. The most busy time of this clinic is from 2:00 pm to 5:00 pm when our students are present.

Duties of Career Awareness Students:

(1) transport patients to correct examining station,
(2) go and get x-ray films,
(3) assist in supplying examination areas with materials,
(4) under limitation, help to supervise children but not care for children (this is parents' responsibility as per supervisor),
(5) clean up the examination areas, and
(6) run messages between labs.

Worksite: Admissions, Main Floor, New Hospital. Supervisor: Mr. Kahn.

Responsible for the proper admission of all patients to the hospital. Open 24 hours a day. All records are initiated as part of admissions process.

Duties of Career Awareness students:

(1) escort patient to proper room,
(2) work with computer to process data on patients,
(3) file records on patients,
(4) help complete patient assessment cards,
(5) help collect pertinent data,
(6) help keep daily reports on activity of admissions office, and
(7) help assemble data for reports on statistics about department.

APPENDIX B

A Description of Intended Worksite Activities in
Biomedical Sciences

Worksite: Lower West Side H.C., 1713 S. Ashland
Ave., Chicago, IL 60608. Supervisor: Lucy Gutierrez.
Neighborhood Health Care Services; the need to
help others and themselves to care and remain in
good health.
Duties of Biomedical Sciences students:
(1) interpret for doctors and nurses with Spanish-
speaking patients,
(2) file lab reports and call patients for appointments,
(3) carry out health programs in the neighborhood
communities for special programs,
(4) file all statistical pr records,
(5) help clients fill out school physical forms,
(6) help patients find the rooms for their service,
and
(7) assist mothers who come into the clinic with
their children.

Worksite: South Chicago Community Hospital,
2320 E. 93rd St., Chicago, IL 60617. Supervisor: N.
Ajose.
Students will work in the emergency medicine
department and the 24-hour emergency out-patient
facility.
Duties of Biomedical Sciences students:
(1) assist in intake procedures with emergency
patients,
(2) assist in medical research survey project,
(3) assist in emergency out-patient medical procedures, and
(4) obtain vital signs from patients.

Worksite: Latina Infant Mother Program, "Dar-A-
Luz," 1823 W. 17th St., Chicago, IL 60608. Supervisor: Patty Sorrondeguy.
The Latina Mother Infant Program "Dar-A-Luz"
is a program of Pilsen-Little Village Community
Mental Health Center, provides community health
education in perinatal health, and conducts workshops on sex education for high school students and
other community groups. A series of nine prenatal
classes is offered covering topics such as pregnancy,
prepared childbirth, breastfeeding, family planning,
infant development, and nutrition. The staff also
provides counseling, advocacy, and postpartum
home visits for clients.
Duties of Biomedical Sciences students:
(1) receive and make phone calls to prospective
clients. Give accurate information,
(2) fill registration form for contacted clients,
(3) send out program flyers and other materials
requested by organizations and hospitals,

(4) be familiar with the different forms and filing
system used in the program,
(5) participate in basic training on perinatal topics
and presentation of films,
(6) observe prenatal classes,
(7) go with staff on postpartum home visits to
clients, and
(8) explore literature and learn to use resources
in the community.

Worksite: Hyde Home Health Agency, 1525 E.
53rd St., Chicago, IL 60625. Supervisor: Ms. Kay
Macky.
Students participate in southside home visitations
accompanying nurses, occupational therapists,
speech therapists, and physical therapists.
Duties of Biomedical Sciences students:
(1) observe and assist with patient intake procedures,
(2) develop and use home nursing skills,'and
(3) learn to administer basic medical tests.

References

CHARTERS, W. W., JR., & JONES, J. E. (1973). On the
risk of appraising non-events in program evaluation. Educational Researcher, 2(11), 5–7.
COOK, T. D., & CAMPBELL, D. T. (1979). Quasi-experimentation: Design and analysis issues for field
settings. Chicago: Rand McNally.
LEINHARDT, G. (1980). Modeling and measuring educational treatment in evaluation. Review of Educational Research, 3, 393–420.
LOURENCO, S., & EASH, M. (1981). Career awareness
in health professions (Tech. Rep. submitted to
the State of Illinois, Department of Commerce
and Community Affairs). Chicago: University of
Illinois at Chicago.
LOURENCO, S., & EASH, M. (1982). Biomedical sciences
annual report (Tech. Rep. submitted to the U.S.
Department of Education, Division of Student
Services). Chicago: University of Illinois at Chi-
cago.
STAKE, R. (1976). The countenance of educational
evaluation. In C. Weiss (Ed.), Evaluating action
programs. Boston: Allyn and Bacon.
STRONG, E. K., JR., & CAMPBELL, D. P. (1974). The
Strong-Campbell interest inventory merged form
of the Strong vocational interest blank. Stanford,
CA: Stanford University Press.
SUCHMAN, E. (1976). Evaluative research. New York:
Russell Sage Foundation.

Author

JONATHAN Z. SHAPIRO, Associate Pro-
fessor of Educational Administration,
College of Education, Louisiana State
University, Baton Rouge, LA 70803.
Specializations: Evaluation research,
policy analysis.

31

Environmental Assessment and Evaluation Research
Examples from Mental Health and Substance Abuse Programs
John W. Finney and Rudolf H. Moos

ABSTRACT

Evaluation researchers have been broadening the traditional client input—"black box" treatment—client outcome paradigm that has guided many evaluations of mental health, substance abuse treatment, and other intervention programs. The points of expansion are in the areas of treatment implementation and treatment processes, as well as "extratreatment" influences on treatment selection, duration, and, especially, outcome. This review illustrates the application of environmental assessment procedures—particularly social climate measures—in four aspects of evaluation research suggested by the more comprehensive model: (a) evaluating treatment implementation; (b) exploring treatment processes; (c) identifying extratreatment influences on client posttreatment functioning; and (d) operationalizing outcome variables. Conceptual and methodological issues raised by these applications are discussed, and the benefits to be derived from an expanded model of evaluation research—especially the greater potential for program improvement—are considered.

Two areas that have captured the attention of social and behavioral scientists over the past decade are evaluation research and environmental influences on behavior. For the most part, work in these two areas has proceeded independently. Our objective here is to illustrate the utility of environmental measures (with a special focus on the social environment) in evaluation research. To do so, we review relevant literature using an expanded model of evaluation research as a guide. More specifically, we show how environmental measures may be used to (a) document treatment implementation and delivery; (b) assess treatment processes; (c) tap extratreatment factors that affect individual or system functioning outside of treatment; and (d) operationalize outcome criteria. Many of the examples are drawn from our own research on alcoholism and psychiatric treatment programs, but the issues raised are general ones and research by other investigators is incorporated when appropriate.

The Expanding Paradigm of Evaluation Research
Until recently, a client input—"black box" treatment—client outcome paradigm guided many evaluations of

mental health and substance abuse treatment programs. This approach systematically minimized the role of environmental factors. The treatment program was the sole environmental determinant of client functioning examined, and it usually was assessed in terms of gross categories (such as treatment versus no or an alternate treatment, or only a few levels of treatment). Not surprisingly, the treatment variable often was found to exert only a weak influence on posttreatment client functioning in comparison to client social background characteristics and intake functioning variables; moreover, only a small proportion of the variance (often less than 20%) in posttreatment functioning usually was accounted for by patient and treatment variables combined (e.g., Luborsky & McLellan, 1978; Polich, Armor, & Braiker, 1981). In short, relatively little was learned in such evaluations about either the treatment program or the underlying problem to which it was directed (Cronbach & Associates, 1980).

This "summative" paradigm has been broadened in several ways. As evaluators have come to realize that intervention programs tend not to be implemented

The preparation of this paper was supported by National Institute on Alcohol Abuse and Alcoholism Grant AA02863 and by Veterans Administration Medical Research funds. We thank Andrew Billings, Ruth Cronkite, and Roger Mitchell for their comments on an earlier draft.

Requests for reprints should be sent to John Finney, Social Ecology Laboratory, Department of Psychiatry and Behavioral Sciences, Stanford University School of Medicine, Stanford, CA 94305.

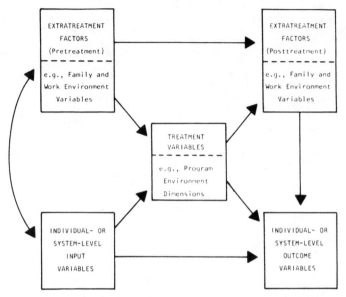

Figure 1. An expanded conceptual model of evaluation research (with emphasis on social environment factors).

precisely according to plan, and are not delivered to clients in a fixed or standard manner, they have focused greater attention on the implementation of treatment (Sechrest, West, Phillips, Redner, & Yeaton, 1979). Given that treatment delivery often varies across individual recipients, evaluators have begun to look within the "black box" and explore treatment processes, or the relationship between specific aspects of treatment and treatment outcome. Evaluators have also recognized that powerful extratreatment or life context factors can affect the benefits derived from an intervention program. Consequently, they have begun to embed treatment evaluations in more comprehensive conceptual frameworks that take into account personal and environmental factors which influence the focal problem or disorder (for an overview of these developments, see Cronbach & Associates, 1980; Cronbach, 1982).

The model of evaluation research diagrammed in Figure 1 embodies these trends in two ways. First, it incorporates a more intensive examination of treatment variables, including aspects of the program's social environment. Second, it considers extratreatment factors, such as the psychosocial characteristics of clients' family and work settings, as additional determinants of treatment entry, duration, and of particular interest here, outcome.[1] The model helps to clarify the fact that treatment is only one of many sets of influences on client posttreatment functioning, that the traditional summative paradigm does not adequately capture the complexity of the treatment/rehabilitation process, and that there are important interrelationships among the sets of factors that influence treatment outcome.

To use this approach, an evaluator must function as a social scientist familiar with theory and empirical findings relevant to the targeted problem and to the intervention applied, rather than merely as a technician routinely applying a particular (usually experimental or quasi-experimental) research design (Chen & Rossi, 1980). Although the demands on the evaluator are greater, the increased information yield from conceptually-based evaluations should justify the effort. Using

[1] A comprehensive approach to treatment and extratreatment factors encompasses more than social climate dimensions. In the treatment domain of our alcoholism project, for example, we also have focused on specific components of treatment, such as the number of therapy sessions a patient attended (see Finney, Moos, & Chan, 1981). Similarly, we have examined a variety of extratreatment factors, including negative life change events, spouse drinking, and personal coping styles (Cronkite & Moos, 1980; Finney, Moos, & Mewborn, 1980).

the expanded paradigm enables investigators to suggest multiple options for program improvement; to better estimate and understand the effects of the intervention program; to more accurately determine the extent to which program impact will generalize to new situations in which the program may be implemented; and to learn more about the problem that required the intervention in the first place. We particularly stress the program improvement function here.

The Social Climate Approach to Environmental Assessment

In this review, we concentrate on social climate variables as examples of the environmental domain. One reason for doing so is to provide a consistent focus and hopefully a more coherent presentation. Another reason for restricting our environmental focus to social climate dimensions is that few (if any) evaluation studies have examined other domains of environmental factors. We assume, however, that social climate dimensions, representing the psychosocial characteristics of a setting, constitute "proximal" (Jessor, 1981) environmental influences on individual functioning. The effects of other types of environmental factors (e.g., physical design features, organizational policies) are likely to be mediated, at least in part, by the social climate they facilitate. For example, an inpatient alcoholism treatment facility with a number of small communal lounges (a physical design feature) may be more involving and cohesive than one with only a single

large lounge, and thus provide greater benefits to its clients. Although social climate dimensions appear to be more strongly related to individual behavior and functioning than are other types of environmental variables, they may not represent the most "proximal" points of leverage for environmental change efforts. Such aspects as organizational policies or physical environment factors may be more accessible to intervention. We return to this point later.

The social climate approach is based on the assumption that environments, like people, have "personalities." Some people are more supportive than others; similarly, some social environments are more supportive than others. Some people are dominating; likewise, some social milieus are rigid, autocratic, and controlling. The conceptual/methodological orientation is to assess these environmental "personalities" as they are *perceived* by the persons within a particular setting, *a la* Murray's (1938) concept of "beta press." MacLeod (1951) pointed out that the perceived environment can be thought of in both personal and consensual terms. Not only does each individual have his or her own perception of the characteristics of a setting (*private* beta press), but perceptions of the environment may be shared by the persons in a setting (*common* or *consensual* beta press; see also James & Jones, 1974). This latter, system-level construct typically has been operationalized by aggregating the individual perceptions of the participants in a given environment.

Based on work in a variety of settings, Moos (1974a)

TABLE 1
DIMENSIONS OF THE SOCIAL CLIMATE SCALES

Scale	Relationship Dimensions	Personal Development Dimensions	System Maintenance and System Change Dimensions
Treatment Environment			
Ward Atmosphere Scale (WAS)	Involvement	Autonomy	Order & organization
Community Oriented Programs Environment Scale (COPES)	Support Spontaneity	Practical orientation Personal problem orientation Anger & aggression	Program clarity Staff control
Extratreatment Environment			
Family Environment Scale (FES)	Cohesiveness Expressiveness Conflict	Independence Achievement orientation Intellectual-cultural orientation Active recreational orientation Moral-religious orientation	Organization Control
Work Environment Scale (WES)	Involvement Peer cohesion Staff support	Autonomy Task orientation	Work pressure Clarity Control Innovation Physical comfort

has developed a conceptualization of three major sets of dimensions thought to underlie social environments. *Relationship* dimensions focus on the nature and intensity of interpersonal relationships within environments. *Personal growth* or *goal orientation* dimensions focus on the basic directions along which personal growth or self-enhancement are encouraged in a setting. The exact nature of these dimensions varies somewhat across different contexts depending on their underlying purposes and goals. *System maintenance and change* dimensions, which are relatively similar across settings, assess the extent to which an en-

vironment is orderly, clear in its expectations, maintains control, and is responsive to change.

Here, we will focus primarily on two social climate measures that have been used to assess *treatment* environments: the Ward Atmosphere Scale (WAS; Moos, 1974b) and the Community-Oriented Programs Environment Scale (COPES; Moos, 1974b); and two measures of community or *extratreatment* settings: the Family Environment Scale (FES; Moos & Moos, 1981) and the Work Environment Scale (WES; Moos, 1981). Table 1 gives the dimensions within the three domains just described for each of these measures.

UTILIZING ENVIRONMENTAL MEASURES IN EVALUATION RESEARCH

The next four sections constitute the heart of the present review. In them we attempt to show how environmental assessment may be incorporated in four aspects of program evaluation.

Treatment Implementation Assessment and Standards of Comparison

We have noted that in many evaluations the treatment program has had the status of a "black box." The key to illuminating the black box is assessment of treatment implementation, or what Quay (1977) has labeled the "third face of evaluation" (his first two were outcome assessment and research design). It is crucial that information on the treatment as actually delivered be collected. Without this form of "manipulation check," evaluators run "the risk of appraising non-events" (Charter & Jones, 1973, p. 5), or, more likely, of evaluating a program that has been only partially implemented, or operationalized in a form different from that intended. In this regard, Patton (1978) has argued that "failure at the implementation stage is a major reason for the human service shortfall and ineffective social programs" (p. 175), while, on the research side, failure to assess treatment implementation has been pointed to as "*the* crucial impediment to improving program operations, policy analysis, and experimentation in social policy areas" (Williams, 1975, p. 531, emphasis in the original; for a discussion of several methods for assessing program implementation, see Scheirer & Rezmovic, 1983).

To assess treatment implementation, an evaluator must determine the discrepancy between the program as actually carried out and perceived versus the program as it was intended to be applied and experienced (Provus, 1971). The problem is to formulate appropriate standards of comparison. Sechrest, West, Phillips, Redner, and Yeaton (1979) suggest three sources of information that can be used to develop such standards: (a) normative data on conditions in other programs; (b) specification of an "ideal" treatment; and (c) theoretical analysis/expert judgment. We have discussed elsewhere how these standards have been used to assess

the implementation of specific treatment components or activities (e.g., group therapy sessions, social skills training) in alcoholism treatment programs (Moos & Finney, 1983); here we indicate how social environment data can be evaluated against each of these standards.

Normative Data. The normative approach to implementation analysis can be illustrated by the two COPES profiles in Figure 2, which are based on data provided by 15 residents and six staff members from a county-funded halfway house for alcoholic persons. At the time these data were collected, the facility was a newly established 16-bed long-term recovery home that had a modified therapeutic community orientation and offered various types of therapy groups and activities, individual counseling, and films and lectures on alcoholism (Bliss, Moos, & Bromet, 1976). To generate the profiles, average raw scores on the COPES dimensions were converted to standard scores to make it possible to compare the social climate of the halfway house with normative data ($M = 50$, $SD = 10$) from a sample of 54 community-oriented treatment programs (Moos, 1974b).

Overall, the picture portrayed by both staff and patient perceptions is one of a program that was relatively well-implemented in the relationship and personal growth domains (at least in comparison to conditions in other programs). Both groups saw an above average emphasis on involvement, support, and, at different levels, spontaneity. Both perceived above average stress on autonomy, concern for personal problems, and the expression of anger and aggression. On the other hand, partial normative implementation in some of the system maintenance areas is evident from their low scores — an indicator, apparently, of the "newness" of the program. Indeed, when the facility was reassessed 7 months later, these dimensions were rated more in line with the program's philosophy of establishing a clear and well-organized treatment milieu. If the program's fate was to have been determined by the results of an ensuing impact evaluation, the administrator would have been

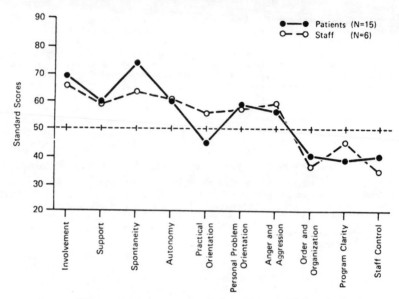

Figure 2. COPES Form R profiles for patients and staff from a halfway house alcoholism program.
Note. From "Monitoring change in community-oriented treatment programs" by F. R. Bliss, R. H.
Moos, and E. J. Bromet, 1976, *Journal of Community Psychology, 4,* p. 318. Copyright 1976 by the
Clinical Psychology Publishing Company. Reprinted by permission.

wise to insist that the outcome assessment phase not begin until the program was "up to speed" in the system maintenance area.

"Ideal" Program. A second, more "tailored" or program-specific method for generating an implementation standard is to specify an "ideal" form of the intervention. Provus (1971) recommends that such ideals be "derived from the values of program staff and the client population it serves" (p. 12). Form I (Ideal) of the treatment environment scales allows patients and staff to indicate their treatment goals and values.

Figure 3 displays the degree of change in program environment desired by residents and staff of the halfway house. The real-ideal discrepancy scores were calculated by subtracting the average score participants gave the actual program (Form R for "Real" subscale scores) from the average score they gave an ideal program (Form I of the COPES). The profile shows the amount and direction of change needed in each area to match the current ideals of patients and staff. The line marked zero in the center of the profile indicates no change is desired, or no discrepancy between real and ideal subscale means.

The real-ideal discrepancies show that both halfway house residents and staff saw a need for greater emphasis on all program dimensions (see Figure 3). Overall, staff wanted a clear and orderly program in which involvement, support, spontaneity, practical orientation, and personal problem orientation would be high, and in which they would not be faced with the "management" problems that might ensue from a strong emphasis on resident autonomy and the open expression of anger and aggression. The data illustrate that dimensions that might be judged sufficiently implemented on the basis of normative data (e.g., involvement and spontaneity), may still be found wanting when compared with the desires of patients and/or staff.

Theoretical Analysis/Expert Judgment. Standards for program implementation evaluation can also be formulated by consulting theoretical works and utilizing expert judgments regarding the social environment implications of a particular treatment theory or philosophy. For example, after reviewing the relevant literature, Price and Moos (1975) concluded that one of the six profiles they identified in a cluster analysis of treatment program climates constituted a "therapeutic community" type. Subsequently, as part of their

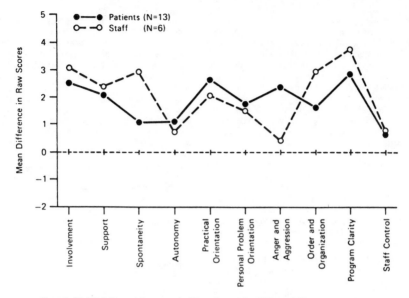

Figure 3. Real-ideal discrepancies as perceived by patients and staff from a halfway house alcoholism program. *Note.* From "Monitoring change in community-oriented treatment programs" by F. R. Bliss, R. H. Moos, and E. J. Bromet, 1976, *Journal of Community Psychology, 4,* p. 318. Copyright 1976 by the Clinical Psychology Publishing Company. Reprinted by permission.

evaluations, Steiner, Haldipur, and Stack (1982) and Bell (in press) carried out implementation assessments by examining the "goodness of fit" between the COPES profiles of their therapeutic community (TC) treatment units and the TC type of Price and Moos (1975). One potential consequence of inadequate treatment implementation is illustrated in the study by Bell (in press) in which the program whose profile failed to measure up most consistently to the TC type had the highest dropout rate.

Comment. Several social climate scales (e.g., Ellsworth & Maroney, 1972; Moos, 1974b) have been used to assess the implementation—specifically, the quality of the social environment—of a number of psychiatric treatment programs: e.g., hospital- and community-based partial care programs (Luft & Fakhouri, 1979); an alternative treatment (Soteria House) for schizophrenia (Mosher & Menn, 1978); a token economy program (Gripp & Magaro, 1971); and a drug abuse treatment unit (Penk & Robinowitz, 1978). In addition, such scales have been employed in implementation evaluations of other types of intervention programs, e.g., secondary school classrooms, a rehabilitation center, and correctional facilities (see Fraser,

1981; Greenwood, Marr, Roessler, & Rowland, 1980; Wexler, 1979). As our example of the halfway house for alcoholics illustrates, such information can be used to aid in the implementation of new programs—to help bring them up to the desired social environment specifications—as well as to check on the level of implementation of established programs. If the environment of either a new or an established program is judged to be inadequately implemented, efforts can be mounted to modify the setting, as we discuss later.

Process Analyses:
Linking Treatment Environment with Outcome
Treatment process analyses focus on the causal chain between treatment and outcome (Judd & Kenny, 1981). One overarching linkage in that chain is the relationship between the treatment as actually implemented and outcome.[2] It is generally assumed that the psychosocial

---

[2]Elsewhere (Moos & Finney, 1983) we have described forms of process analysis in addition to the correlational approach focused on here. In particular, we reviewed experimental and meta-analytic approaches for examining the relationship between specific components of alcoholism treatment programs and various outcome variables.

characteristics of the treatment setting play an important role in determining the effectiveness of the intervention. Although this orientation was initially most apparent in milieu therapy and therapeutic community models of treatment for psychiatric disorders and substance abuse, it is present in most other treatment approaches as well (e.g., Gripp & Magaro, 1971).

Some researchers have focused on program-level relationships between the consensual beta press (average social climate perception) and aggregate treatment outcome, whereas others have examined individual patients' perceptions of treatment environments in relation to their posttreatment functioning. With each approach, there is some evidence of patient-treatment environment interaction effects, i.e., that different treatment environments may be beneficial for different types of patients. We review studies at both levels of analysis here, and also consider two factors that may mediate the linkage between treatment climate and outcome: dropout from treatment and patient participation in aftercare services.

Aggregate Climate and Outcome. Therapeutic environments for more disturbed, chronic psychiatric patients tend to be well-organized and structured, and not to emphasize self-understanding or the open expression of anger. For example, Klass, Growe, and Strizich (1977) examined the relationship between treatment climate and both in-treatment behavior and longer-term outcome (length of time out of hospital following discharge) across 14 programs for chronic patients. During treatment, the number of violent episodes resulting in injuries was greater in programs that emphasized the expression of anger and aggression, and lower in those that were characterized by higher levels of organization. Moreover, patients who received treatment in programs that stressed organization and the suppression of anger and aggression remained out of the hospital longer, on average. Moos and Schwartz (1972) also found that psychiatric programs that emphasized structure and staff control were the most successful in promoting community retention among chronic, schizophrenic patients.

In contrast, programs that seem most successful with less seriously disturbed patients emphasize the discussion of personal problems and the open expression of anger in a well-organized and moderately structured context that is also oriented toward patient autonomy and preparation for release back to the community (Moos, 1974b). Consistent with these findings, Bale, Zarcone, Van Stone, Kuldau, and Engelsing (in press) found that substance abusers were most likely to have their impulsive behavior successfully challenged in a program that stressed dealing with personal problems in a context in which expectations and social contracts were clear and well-defined. Treatment outcome was more negative among patients treated in a program that had a heavy emphasis on involvement and patient participation, but which lacked organization and clarity of expectations. These findings support Penk and Robinowitz's (1978) view that successful treatment programs must deal with drug abusers' contradictory desire for both freedom (spontaneity) and structure.

Overall, the results suggest that more disturbed patients who are treated in well-organized programs that emphasize impulse control may internalize some of the socially structured norms of the program and consequently remain in the community longer after discharge. Thus, a therapeutic community may provide a growth-enhancing milieu for less disturbed individuals, but it may lead to an exacerbation of symptoms and relapse among more disturbed or long-term patients. Persons who are functioning marginally (such as chronic schizophrenic patients) need a more structured setting that insulates them from too much interpersonal stimulation, whereas less impaired individuals are more likely to benefit from a program that emphasizes autonomy and self-understanding (see also Cronkite, Moos, & Finney, in press).

Individual Patients' Perceptions and Posttreatment Functioning. Turning to the individual level of analysis, the psychosocial dimensions of alcoholism programs that have been linked with improved patient functioning are similar to those that were identified in program-level analyses of data from less seriously disturbed psychiatric patients. For example, Kogutek (1977) found that patients who saw their inpatient alcoholism treatment unit as encouraging more spontaneity, self-sufficiency, self-understanding, and the expression of anger, while maintaining an emphasis on organization, experienced a better outcome. Similarly, in a study of inpatient (WAS) and outpatient (COPES) alcoholics' perceptions of their treatment environments, Fischer (1979) noted that patients who reported a greater stress on personal problem orientation, open expression of anger, and clarity of rules and expectations for patient behavior more often reported improved posttreatment functioning (see also Slater & Linn, 1982–83).

In another individual-level analysis (Cronkite & Moos, 1978), perceptions of alcoholism treatment programs (COPES) were among the strongest predictors of 6-month outcome, relative to patient variables (demographic characteristics and intake symptoms) and other treatment variables (type of program and actual treatment experiences such as the number of therapy sessions attended). Because the direct effects for the treatment environment perceptions were independent of the effects for treatment experiences, this finding suggests that such perceptions tap more than just the quantity of treatment received; they may also be indicators of the psychotherapeutic *quality* of treatment.

Treatment Environment, Attrition, and Aftercare. The foregoing studies identify relationships between the social climates of treatment settings and treatment outcome. The mechanisms underlying these relationships may be clarified by examining the links between the psychosocial characteristics of treatment settings and such potential mediating variables as patient dropout and participation in aftercare services.

In a program-level analysis, Moos and Schwartz (1972) linked the social climates of seven large psychiatric wards to their dropout rates. Attrition rates were higher on wards that patients collectively perceived as less orderly and organized ($p < .10$), and those on which staff perceived less involvement, support, and program clarity, and more expression of anger and aggression.

Individual perceptions of treatment environments have also been related to patient dropout. For example, although residents at a Salvation Army alcoholism program who terminated treatment early did not differ from the rest of the treated group in personal resources at intake, they did perceive the treatment milieu (COPES) more negatively than those who remained longer. Specifically, the dropouts saw less involvement, support, organization, and clarity in the treatment setting (Moos, Mehren, & Moos, 1978; for other examples, see Doherty, 1976; Linn, Shane, Webb, & Pratt, 1979).

Only one study of the association between treatment environment and aftercare was located. Using an older version of the WAS, Pratt, Linn, Carmichael, and Webb (1977) found that alcoholic patients who attended aftercare (a reentry group that focused on outpatients' achievements and problems in adjusting to community life) had perceived greater emphasis on autonomy on the inpatient ward in which they were initially treated. There were also trends ($p < .10$) for attenders to have seen more emphasis on the expression of anger and aggression and achieving insight. Taken together, the results indicate that alcoholic patients who see a treatment program as encouraging independence, insight, and the open expression of personal feelings (including hostility) are more likely to participate in aftercare services offered by that same facility. However, studies reviewed earlier suggest that such findings may be specific to less seriously disturbed individuals. More dysfunctional patients might find such an inpatient program overstimulating, and thus be less likely to attend aftercare sessions offered by it.

Comment. Although they fall short of establishing causal linkages (see Edelson & Paul, 1977; Ellsworth & Maroney, 1972), the studies we have reviewed indicate significant associations between treatment climate dimensions—in terms of both personal and consensual beta press—and individual and collective outcomes. Some of the findings also suggest that different types of psychiatric patients and substance abusers—individually or in aggregate—respond more or less favorably depending on the characteristics of the treatment environment. Finally, some data—again at both levels—imply that the relationship between the social climates of treatment settings and outcome may be mediated by treatment environment effects on client attrition, and at the individual level, on aftercare attendance.

To date, the relationship between treatment environments and outcome has been explored in separate analyses at either the individual or aggregate level. What is needed in future studies are "multilevel" analyses (Burstein, 1980a; 1980b). Applied to data gathered from patients across multiple treatment settings, multilevels analyses can partition treatment environment impact into between-program (system level) and within-program ("individual" level) effects. Among the studies reviewed, the program-level analyses carried out with psychiatric treatment data did not control for individual level processes and thus mixed both between- and within-program effects. "Specific" within-group effects of a sort were explored in Kogutek's (1977) study of the perceived treatment environment-outcome relationship within a single alcoholism program, whereas Cronkite and Moos (1978), by controlling for program, explored a variant of "pooled" within-facility effects (specifically, an ANCOVA model). The analyses of individual perceptions of patients from multiple treatment settings reported by Fischer (1979) were between-patient analyses, and, as such, mixed between- and within-program effects (for more details, see Boyd & Iversen, 1979).

A fundamental principle in the multilevel literature is that measures at different levels of aggregation are likely to assess different constructs (Cronbach, 1976). To see this in relation to social climate data, it is necessary to decompose an individual's score on a social climate dimension into its component sources of variance. When asked to report on the psychosocial characteristics of a treatment setting, an individual's response is likely to be influenced by the setting's "true" climate (a system-level property), random measurement error, and several within-setting effects. In other words, an individual's score on a social climate dimension can deviate from the group consensus or average for several reasons in addition to measurement error: (a) an individual could differ from the group (average) in his or her attention to and interpretation of events in the environment (filtering effect); (b) an individual's behavior could evoke atypical responses from others in the setting (eliciting effect); and (c) an individual could have an unusual pattern of contact with different aspects of the overall environment, e.g., associate only with a subset of other patients or receive treatment from only one of several staff teams (exposure effect).

In statistical terms, these within-program influences are individual-level effects, but in fact they represent a mixture of personal and (sub)environment influences, not merely the impact of the individual's personality characteristics (cf. Capell, 1979). One implication of this conceptual analysis (specifically, that portion on exposure effects) is that aggregate analyses should be conducted at the level at which pattern interactions (statistical dependencies; see Burstein, 1980a) occur between clients and staff or among clients—for example, at the treatment team or patient clique level—in addition to the program level. Complicating this approach is the fact that there are likely to be multiple, partially overlapping subenvironments (patterns of social interaction) within any treatment setting.

To further pinpoint the meaning of social climate dimensions at the program and individual levels, these constructs need to be more deeply embedded in nomological nets. The meaning of aggregate-level climate variables will become clearer as they are linked with "global" properties of treatment units such as size, organizational policies, and physical design features that cannot be disaggregated, as well as with other aggregate characteristics such as patient and/or staff composition, i.e., "suprapersonal" environment variables (see Moos & Igra, 1980). At the individual level, the deviations of patients' perceptions from their program mean need to be linked to subenvironment variables, as well as to patient personality and behavior characteristics.

Multilevel analyses of the relationship between treatment program social climate and outcome should provide a more comprehensive view of the therapeutic processes operating between and within programs. Consequently, such analyses will suggest two broad types of intervention strategies—those that can be applied at the treatment unit level and those that can be implemented within units for individual patients (see Burstein, Fischer, & Miller, 1980). Program-level interventions could result from the broad policy mandates of a state legislature or commission. For example, a state mental health agency might require changes in the selection processes of publicly-funded programs to counteract the negative effects of aggregate patient characteristics (suprapersonal environment) on aggregate treatment outcome. Such a body might also mandate physical design or organizational innovations in both private and public programs to reduce negative aggregate social climate effects not associated with selection processes.

A considerable portion of the total variance in patient outcome is likely to be related to within-facility differences, however. For this reason, analyses also are

needed that inform more clinical or individually-oriented interventions. Staff must be able to identify (e.g., from discrepant social climate perceptions) and intervene effectively with patients who are more likely to drop out of treatment and/or experience negative outcome. Multilevel analyses of treatment environment processes can help to create a broad-based armamentarium with which to attempt to effect positive changes in patients within and across treatment settings.

Extratreatment Environmental Factors

The summative research paradigm that has been employed in many evaluations implicitly assumes a "closed system" in which patients are exposed only to a treatment program. In reality, of course, a treatment program is but one (indeed, a temporary one) of the multiple environmental "microsystems" (Bronfenbrenner, 1979) or specific settings in which the client is enmeshed. During treatment, and even more directly afterward, the client is exposed to a myriad of influences emanating from other, more enduring microsystems such as family and work environments. Thus, long-term outcome indices assess "*both* the residue of a program's initial impact *and* the effects of any postprogram experiences" (Cook, Appleton, Connor, Shaffer, Tomkin, & Weber, 1975, p. 55, emphasis in the original).

This line of reasoning is not new; it often emerges after data analyses have indicated little or no long-term effect of an intervention. Evaluators and service providers, confronted with negative results, frequently point to the deleterious effects of patients' extratreatment environments—environments that presumably contributed to the initial development of the patients' problem—as possible sources of decay in treatment benefits. In order to develop more effective interventions that consider clients' normal life situations, data on extratreatment factors need to be collected routinely in evaluations of intervention programs. We now review several studies in which extratreatment circumstances, as assessed by social climate scales, have been related to treatment outcome criteria.

Family Environment and Treatment Outcome. Spiegel and Wissler (in press) examined the relationship between posttreatment family environment and the global adjustment of a diagnostically mixed group of psychiatric patients (e.g., 18% schizophrenic, 33% depressive). Family Environment Scales were completed by 60 men who had received inpatient treatment at a Veterans Administration Medical Center, and by their wives. Patients who returned to families that were more cohesive and expressive, and that had a greater emphasis on recreational pursuits and a stronger moral-religious orientation tended to be better adjusted. In addition, adjustment was positively related to greater congruence or similarity in husband-wife perceptions of the family environment.

In a series of studies (Bromet & Moos, 1977; Moos, Bromet, Tsu, & Moos, 1979; Finney et al., 1980), we explored the relationships between characteristics of patients' family settings and the outcome of residential treatment for alcoholism. In cross-sectional analyses of 6-month follow-up data, we found that patients located in families that were more cohesive, less conflict-ridden, more involved in recreational pursuits, and less controlling, functioned better after treatment. These relationships were significant after considering the effects of background characteristics and the intake functioning of patients, and many held when family environment dimensions assessed 6 months after treatment were used to predict patient functioning at a 2-year follow-up (see also Ward, 1981).

Work Environment and Treatment Outcome. An individual's work environment may also affect the outcome of an intervention effort. Such an impact was suggested in an evaluation of a 2-week training/orientation program for "hard-core unemployed" persons (HCUs) by Friedlander and Greenberg (1971), which included a measure of the social climate of the work setting to which participants were subsequently assigned. Whereas none of nine measures of personality and attitudes toward work assessed at program admission was predictive of employee effectiveness and behavior as rated by supervisors 6 months after training, participants in work environments they saw as more supportive were rated as more competent, congenial, friendly, and conscientious than were those in settings perceived as less supportive. Friedlander and Greenberg (1971) concluded that manpower programs for the unemployed should focus, in part, on improving the social climates of the settings in which participants work.

In our alcoholism study, the relationships between psychosocial characteristics of patients' work settings and 6-month follow-up functioning were generally weak and nonsignificant among individuals returning to families after treatment. However, for working individuals who were not living in families, those who saw their work milieus as higher in involvement, peer cohesion, supervisor support, and physical comfort, experienced better outcome on two or more of the criteria examined (self-rating of drinking problem, behavioral impairment, psychological impairment, and social activities). One interpretation of these data is that location in family settings may help to cushion the adverse impact of stressful conditions in the workplace (see Bromet & Moos, 1977).

Comment. Although, again, they do not establish causal relationships, the studies reviewed suggest that

extratreatment environments play a significant role in affecting the outcome of various interventions. Researchers contributing to this literature, however, need to be sensitive to correlated measurement error as a likely source of inflated relationships between posttreatment factors and outcome. For example, when extratreatment environment perceptions and functioning measures are obtained in the course of the same interview, the respondent's mood may affect scores on both measures. Therefore, to the extent possible, investigators should attempt to assess extratreatment variables and functioning criteria at different times and by different means.

We have concentrated on the "direct effects" of extratreatment environments on the outcome of intervention efforts. We should point out, however, that family and work environments may exert an indirect effect on patient posttreatment functioning in the same manner as that described for treatment environments—by influencing a patient's length of treatment and/or participation in aftercare. In regard to treatment attrition, patients undoubtedly weigh the perceived costs and benefits of dropping out versus remaining in treatment. One consideration for patients in residential treatment would be the quality of their family and work milieus. If these settings are viewed as attractive relative to the treatment setting, patients may be more likely to drop out. Consistent with this hypothesis, Reynolds, O'Leary, and Walker (1982) reported that patients who did not complete a treatment regimen (consisting of both inpatient treatment and aftercare) perceived their families as more cohesive and organized, and as having a greater emphasis on recreational activities and moral-religious issues than did completers. Thus, knowledge of patients' extratreatment circumstances allows program evaluators to better model and predict the outcome of patients' decision-making processes with respect to treatment attrition. Eventually, such knowledge also may make it possible to differentiate between those individuals for whom early treatment termination does or does not signal a poor prognosis.

Evaluations that include assessment of extratreatment factors may yield information that can be used to generate new, and potentially more effective, intervention strategies. The value of comprehensive environmental assessment in suggesting appropriate interventions was noted by Spiegel (1983). He points out that empirical findings relating "expressed emotion" to patient decompensation (e.g., Vaughn & Leff, 1976) have led to recommendations that the posttreatment contact of schizophrenic patients with family members be curtailed. In his research, however, the supportive features of family environment (cohesion, expressiveness, recreational orientation) were more strongly associated with the adjustment of schizophrenic patients than was family conflict.

Spiegel's finding that treatment outcome may be negatively affected by posttreatment conflict in the family milieu mirrors that discussed earlier with respect to the negative impact of anger and aggression in the treatment environment on outcome for severely disturbed psychiatric patients. As such, it suggests a continuity in the beneficial aspects of treatment and extratreatment environments, and point to the value of thinking of "treatment" in broader terms. In this regard, Tuchfeld (1977) has suggested that "we can increase the likelihood of specifying optimal (and thus more economically efficient) strategies" for alcoholism treatment if we focus on the integration of "informal treatment resources with formal modalities" (p. 1812). Efforts to identify congruent cross-setting effects may be facilitated by measures of treatment and extratreatment environments that share the same conceptual underpinnings (e.g., relationship, personal growth, and system maintenance and change dimensions).

Environmental Measures as Outcome Indices

Environmental systems, like individuals, can be the object of intervention programs. When this situation arises, environmental dimensions assume the conceptual status of outcome variables. One criterion for judging the adequacy of any outcome assessment instrument, whether individual- or system-focused, is that it captures multiple aspects of functioning. With such an instrument, a range of intended consequences of the intervention may be tapped, as well as some of its unintended side effects. Comprehensive assessment of environmental dimensions across varied domains allows evaluators to explore multiple environmental outcomes.

Both community and treatment environments may be the object of intervention efforts. We describe how measures of social climate can be used to assess the impact of "independently derived" change efforts, that is, interventions not informed by prior measurement of the social environment; we also consider the dual use of such measures to shape or facilitate and then to monitor the impact of environmental innovations. Because a major thrust of this review is on the development of program improvement strategies, our discussion of the latter, "formative" use of social climate data is more detailed.

Family Environment as the Object of Change. Karoly and Rosenthal (1977) used the FES to assess the effects of an "independently derived" family therapy program — 10 weekly training sessions in which parents of "problem" children received instruction in behavior modification. Nine families were randomly assigned to receive Parent Group Training, while eight families were relegated to a wait-control group. At a 1-month follow-up, treated parents reported a significant increase in family cohesion and a trend ($p < .10$) to-

ward reduced conflict, as compared with perceived family climate at treatment entry. In addition, target children in the experimental group showed decreases in deviant behaviors as observed by parents and, to an even greater degree, by "blind" outside observers. No changes in either family climate or child behavior were observed among the controls.

The use of family climate data to shape treatment delivery, as well as to assess its impact, is illustrated in a case study by Fuhr, Moos, and Dishotsky (1981). A married couple entered therapy to discuss the wife's drinking problem and to explore a lack of warmth and cohesion in their relationship. Each partner completed the FES with respect to the current and to an ideal family environment. With feedback on the actual family environment, the husband realized that his failure to assist with housework, compounded by the poor planning of family activities, contributed to family tension and conflict. Several changes were made during the ensuing 3 months (such as hiring part-time household help). Substantial improvements were shown when the FES was readministered, as would be expected from the relatively high initial agreement between spouses on therapeutic goals. Family cohesion and organization were seen as higher, whereas conflict was reduced. In addition, cultural and recreational activities had increased, although both partners felt that more change was needed in these areas.

Treatment Environment as the Object of Change. The WAS and COPES have been used to evaluate the impact of a number of independently derived innovations in psychiatric and substance abuse treatment programs (see Moos & Spinrad, in press). For example, Ryan, Bell, and Metcalf (1982) reported changes that occurred in the treatment milieu as a psychoanalytically oriented inpatient treatment program was being modified into a social rehabilitation and work training unit. Thirteen separate administrations of the COPES at 4-month intervals revealed significant and predictable changes in the quality of the perceived treatment environment, including increases in autonomy, practical orientation, and staff support, and decreases in staff control. It was felt that these changes mirrored the conceptual shift in treatment orientation.

Facilitating treatment environment change: Initial assessment. A methodology for using treatment environment data to facilitate and monitor program change has been outlined by Moos (1973). This process consists of four stages: (a) systematic assessment of the environment; (b) feedback and discussion of the resulting information; (c) program change planning and implementation; and (d) reassessment of the environment. The first step (assessment of the environment) was discussed earlier under the heading of program implementation analysis; therefore, we describe only the final three stages of the process here (an "ideal" program standard as the basis of comparison is assumed). For examples of the actual use of the procedure, see Moos (1974b), Shinn (1980), and Verinis and Flaherty (1978).

Feedback and discussion. Once initial responses to the environmental measure have been scored and the discrepancies between real and ideal perceptions calculated, a meeting is held to present and discuss these data. The 10 dimensions of the social climate scales provide a systematic framework that allows participants to conceptualize and articulate their concerns about a treatment environment. This structure may be especially valuable in eliciting comments from persons who previously have voiced few opinions about the operation of the treatment program. In the feedback process, particular attention can be paid to similarities and differences in the perceptions and values of different groups, such as clients and staff, as exemplified by the data presented in Figure 3. When relatively large disagreements occur (e.g., more than one standard deviation), item-by-item feedback on real and ideal scores may be warranted to identify the reasons for the discrepancies.

Program change planning and implementation. After areas of shared concern and dissatisfaction have been clarified, the discussion can turn to planning innovations to bring about the desired social climate. Three broad classes of social climate determinants—organizational policies and characteristics, physical design features, and suprapersonal factors—constitute the most obvious foci for change efforts. Specific strategies for program improvement within each of these categories may come from a variety of sources. Clients and staff will provide some ideas for program innovations. In addition, the content of the environmental measure's items may suggest change targets. Data on the relationship between patients' participation in different aspects of the treatment program and their perceptions of the global treatment milieu can also indicate avenues for program reorientation. If, for instance, patients who participated in more group therapy sessions had more positive perceptions of the treatment environment, strategies for increasing the involvement of patients in group therapy might be devised.

Reassessment. After the innovations have been implemented, the social climate is reassessed as one measure of the impact of change efforts. This assessment should take place after the program changes have been in operation for a reasonable period of time (e.g., 6 weeks). When the setting is reevaluated while innovations are still in the early stages of implementation, one may well find a decrease in program clarity. Similarly, if for some reason patients have not been involved in the planning process, an "early" reassessment may detect increases in system maintenance dimensions (e.g., staff control) from the patients' perspective, and perhaps a decrease in the relationship dimension of involvement. By scheduling a series of environmental assessments following program change, participants may be able to "fine tune" the innovative program elements; longer-term assessments will allow participants to discriminate between stable environmental impact and temporary fluctuations that represent transitory reactions to the introduction of the change process.[1] (For an example of the use of these procedures in changing staff work environments, see Koran, Moos, Moos, & Zasslow, 1983.)

Comment. The data-based feedback process we have described is the essence of formative program evaluation. The procedure is most efficient in relatively small, stable settings in which participants interact frequently and have "local" control over at least some relevant aspects of the intervention program. The methodology is well-suited for use as a routine quality control inventory because the measures are easy to administer and the process does not require technically-trained evaluators. The approach allows participants to disentangle and analyze the multiple dimensions of their setting's functioning; thus, important characteristics of the environment that are often overlooked can be systematically called into awareness. If the process is continued over time, involvement in the setting may increase simply because people are engaged in the common task of changing their own social environment. Finally, after first-hand experience with the application of formative evaluation findings, clients and program personnel may be much more receptive to subsequent research efforts, including an assessment of the program's impact on client posttreatment functioning.

DISCUSSION

We have described four applications of environmental measures (assessing treatment implementation, treatment processes, extratreatment factors, and outcome variables) within an expanded conceptual model of evaluation research. For each application, we have stressed how research findings can be used to improve program operations and treatment delivery. Our review has focused on social climate measures, but we

[1]The data-based feedback process outlined here assumes relative stability of social climates in the absence of program innovations. There is considerable evidence of such stability (e.g., Moos, 1974b; Ryan et al., 1982). In addition, program innovation projects employing comparison (no-innovation) programs have found significant innovation effects on social climate dimensions (e.g., Crisler & Settles, 1979).

recognize that other types of environmental factors may influence individual functioning during and after treatment.

Guided by a conceptualization of four classes of environmental variables, Moos and his colleagues (e.g., Moos & Lemke, 1982) have recently developed a Multiphasic Environmental Assessment Procedure (MEAP) to assess the environments of sheltered care settings (skilled nursing facilities, residential care centers, and apartment complexes) for older persons in terms of physical design features, organizational policies and characteristics, human aggregate variables (suprapersonal environment), and social climate dimensions. The MEAP can be applied, with minor modifications, to sheltered care facilities for mentally retarded persons, and plans have been made to adapt it for use in mental health settings. Comprehensive assessment of environmental characteristics not only affords a more complete account of individual adaptation within a given setting, but it also allows researchers to explore the determinants of what usually constitute the most proximal environmental influences on functioning— social climate dimensions (Moos & Igra, 1980). Increased knowledge about the relationship of other environmental variables to social climate factors will provide more points of leverage for effecting social environment change.

Most efforts to bring about change in social climates currently involve organizational innovations (Moos & Lemke, 1982). The importance of physical and suprapersonal environment features should not be overlooked, however. For example, removing televisions from individual rooms and setting up a common viewing area (a physical design innovation) can increase cohesion in a treatment setting (Bliss et al., 1976). Moreover, selection policies can be changed to alter the "mix" of individuals in a setting (suprapersonal environment) and thereby create a more therapeutic social environment. Kahana and Kahana (1970) randomly assigned elderly psychiatric patients to an age-integrated custodial ward, an age-segregated custodial ward, or an intensive therapy ward. The patients on the age-heterogeneous unit showed significant increases on measures of cognitive functioning over a 3-week period (increases equal to those found in the intensive therapy ward), while the individuals assigned to the age-homogeneous ward exhibited no improvement. The suprapersonal environment in the age-integrated unit apparently provided a more cognitively complex and involving milieu for older patients; in addition, some of the younger patients were able to achieve a greater sense of purpose and involvment by providing assistance to the older patients.

Throughout this paper, we have emphasized the "formative" use of evaluation research findings in improving intervention programs. As noted earlier, however, there are several other benefits to be derived from the inclusion of environmental variables in an expanded paradigm of evaluation research: (a) better estimates and understanding of the effects of treatment; (b) more accurate estimates of the generalizability of research findings; and (c) greater understanding of the disorder or problem that required the intervention.

Estimating and Understanding the Effects of Treatment
In theory, either of two approaches can be used to achieve unbiased estimates of treatment effects in nonexperimental studies (Cronbach, Rogosa, Floden, & Price, 1977): accurately specifying a causal model of the process of selection into treatment (as is done in experimental studies via random assignment) or specifying a complete causal model of posttreatment functioning. When the variables that determine either treatment selection or posttreatment functioning are controlled, the effects of treatment can be gauged without bias. Our review has presented evidence of significant relationships between environmental variables and both treatment selection (length of treatment, aftercare participation) and client posttreatment functioning. Taking into account environment factors should reduce some of the "specification error" in causal models of either treatment selection or posttreatment functioning and foster better understanding of the causal mechanisms through which the treatment exerts an influence on client posttreatment functioning. In this latter regard, Cronkite and Moos (1980) combined patient, treatment, and extratreatment variables in a causal model of alcholism treatment outcome. Although the direct effects of treatment on outcome were relatively weak, the total causal effect of treatment was more substantial, due to cumulative indirect effects via extratreatment factors. Specifically, there was some evidence that treatment affected individual functioning at follow-up by helping patients reduce posttreatment stressors and to develop more effective coping strategies.

Determining the Generalizability of Findings
Much of the literature on evaluation research design has emphasized "internal validity," or "the approximate validity with which we infer that a relationship between two variables [e.g., treatment and outcome] is causal or that the absence of a relationship implies the absence of cause" (Cook & Campbell, 1979, p. 37). On the other hand, Cronbach and his colleagues (1980) have argued that "'external validity'—the validity of inferences that go beyond the data—is the crux in social action, not 'internal validity'" (p. 231). Decision makers need to know to what extent the results of a particular evaluation can be expected to generalize to new situations in which the program may be implemented. They will be better able to make such extrapolations if the evaluation has provided information on the causal mechanisms through which the treatment exerts its effects (Judd & Kenny, 1981), including the environmental

factors that enhance or impede positive outcomes. If, for example, an alcoholism treatment program was found to be effective primarily among persons located in cohesive family situations, program planners could concentrate its implementation in catchment areas in which many families resided.

Learning More About the Problem
Requiring Intervention

Evaluations are used in a variety of ways, e.g., to decide the fate of a program, or to indicate methods by which the program could be augmented to achieve a greater impact. Another use (see Weiss, 1977) is in shaping or reorienting the thinking of policymakers and program developers about the problem or behavior that required the intervention in the first place. As an exam-

ple, the Rand study of alcoholism treatment (Polich et al., 1981) provided new descriptive information on the natural course of alcoholism. Consistent with earlier findings on problem drinkers (Clark & Cahalan, 1976), it was discovered that the drinking behavior of many severely symptomatic alcoholics fluctuated widely over time between high and low levels of alcohol consumption. As we have argued elsewhere (Moos & Finney, 1980), it is possible to go a step further and to offer a better explanation of within-individual variability in drinking behavior by linking these behavioral changes with intraindividual variation in exposure to such extratreatment factors as social pressure to drink, social controls over drinking, environmental stress, and social support.

CONCLUSION

Over the past decade and a half, the inadequacy of explanations of human behavior that rely solely on person-centered constructs has (once again) become apparent. Contemporary theorists emphasize the role of both personal and environmental factors in influencing individual functioning (Endler & Magnusson, 1976). We hope that the present review will facilitate the extension of this trend into the field of evaluation research, so that the systematic assessment of treatment and extratreatment environment characteristics

becomes a routine part of program evaluations. By using environmental measures to document treatment implementation and delivery, assess treatment process variables, tap extratreatment factors, and shape and/or monitor change efforts, program evaluators should be able to contribute to the development of more effective intervention programs, as well as to the advancement of basic knowledge concerning determinants of environmental factors and their effects on client health and adaptation.

REFERENCES

BALE, R., ZARCONE, V., VAN STONE, W., KULDAU, J., & ENGELSING, T. (in press). Three therapeutic communities: Process and outcome in a prospective controlled study of narcotic addiction treatment. *Archives of General Psychiatry.*

BELL, M. (in press). The perceived environments of three therapeutic communities with the same treatment model for drug abusers. *International Journal of Alcohol and Drug Abuse.*

BLISS, F. H., MOOS, R. H., & BROMET, E. J. (1976). Monitoring change in community-oriented treatment programs. *Journal of Community Psychology, 4,* 315–326.

BOYD, L. H., & IVERSEN, G. R. (1979). *Contextual analysis: Concepts and statistical techniques.* Belmont, CA: Wadsworth.

BROMET, E., & MOOS, R. H. (1977). Environmental resources and the posttreatment functioning of alcoholic patients. *Journal of Health and Social Behavior, 18,* 326–338.

BRONFENBRENNER, U. (1979). *Th ecology of human development: Experiments by nature and design.* Cambridge, MA: Harvard University Press.

BURSTEIN, L. (1980a). The role of levels of analysis in the specification of educational effects. In R. Dreeben & J. A. Thomas (Eds.), *Analysis of educational productivity. Vol. 1: Issues in microanalysis.* Cambridge, MA: Ballinger.

BURSTEIN, L. (1980b). The analysis of multilevel data in educa-

tional research and evaluation. In D. E. Berliner (Ed.), *Review of research in education.* Vol. 8. Washington, DC: American Educational Research Association.

BURSTEIN, L., FISCHER, K. B., & MILLER, M. D. (1980). Multilevel effects of background on science achievement: A cross-national comparison. *Sociology of Education, 53,* 215–225.

CAPELL, F. J. (1979), April). *Interpreting multilevel data from program evaluations.* Paper presented at the annual meeting of the American Educational Research Association, San Francisco.

CHARTER, W. W., Jr., & JONES, J. E. (1973). On the risk of appraising non-events in program evaluation. *Educational Researcher, 2*(11), 5–7.

CHEN, H., & ROSSI, P. H. (1980). The multi-goal, theory-driven approach to evaluation: A model of linking basic and applied social science. *Social Forces, 59,* 106–122.

CLARK, W. B., & CAHALAN, D. (1976). Changes in problem drinking over a 4-year span. *Addictive Behaviors, 1,* 251–259.

COOK, T. D., APPLETON, H., CONNOR, R. F., SHAFFER, A., TOMKIN, G., & WEBER, S. J. (1975). *"Sesame Street" revisited.* New York: Russell Sage Foundation.

COOK, T. D., & CAMPBELL, D. T. (1979). *Quasi-experimentation: Design and analysis issues for field settings.* Chicago: Rand McNally.

CRISLER, J., & SETTLES, R. (1979). An integrated rehabilitation team effort in providing services for multiple disability clients. *Journal of Rehabilitation, 45*, 344-38.

CRONBACH, L. J. (1976, July). (with the assistance of J. E. Deken & N. Webb) *Research on classrooms and schools: Formulation of questions, design, and analysis.* Occasional paper, Stanford Evaluation Consortium, Stanford, CA.

CRONBACH, L. J. (1982). *Designing evaluations of educational and social programs.* San Francisco: Jossey-Bass.

CRONBACH, L. J. and associates. (1980). *Toward reform of program evaluation: Aims, methods, and institutional arrangements.* San Francisco: Jossey-Bass.

CRONBACH, L. J., ROGOSA, D. R., FLODEN, R. E., & PRICE, G. G. (1977). *Analysis of covariance in nonrandomized experiments: Parameters affecting bias.* Occasional paper, Stanford Evaluation Consortium, Stanford University, Stanford CA.

CRONKITE, R. C., & MOOS, R. H. (1978). Evaluating alcoholism treatment programs: An integrated approach. *Journal of Consulting and Clinical Psychology, 46*, 1105-1119.

CRONKITE, R. C., & MOOS, R. H. (1980). Determinants of the posttreatment functioning of alcoholic patients: A conceptual framework. *Journal of Consulting and Clinical Psychology, 48*, 305-316.

CRONKITE, R. C., MOOS, R. H., & FINNEY, J. W. (in press). Contexts of adaptation: An integrative perspective on community and treatment settings. In W. A. O'Connor & B. Lubin (Eds.), *Ecological models in clinical and community mental health.* New York: Wiley.

DOHERTY, E. (1976). Length of hospitalization in a short-term therapeutic community: A multivariate study by sex across time. *Archives of General Psychiatry, 33*, 87-92.

EDELSON, R., & PAUL, G. (1977). Staff "attitude" and "atmosphere" scores as a function of ward size and patient chronicity. *Journal of Consulting and Clinical Psychology, 45*, 874-884.

ELLSWORTH, R., & MARONEY, R. (1972). Characteristics of psychiatric programs and their effects on patients' adjustment. *Journal of Consulting and Clinical Psychology, 39*, 436-447.

ENDLER, N. S., & MAGNUSSON, D. (1976). Toward an interactional psychology of personality. *Psychological Bulletin, 83*, 956-974.

FINNEY, J. W., MOOS, R. H., & CHAN, D. A. (1981). Length of stay and program component effects in the treatment of alcoholism: A comparison of two techniques for process analyses. *Journal of Consulting and Clinical Psychology, 49*, 120-131.

FINNEY, J. W., MOOS, R. H., & MEWBORN, C. R. (1980). Posttreatment experiences and treatment outcome of alcoholic patients 6 months and 2 years after hospitalization. *Journal of Consulting and Clinical Psychology, 48*, 17-29.

FISCHER, J. (1979). The relationship between alcoholic patients' milieu perception and measures of their drinking during a brief follow-up period. *International Journal of the Addictions, 14*, 1151-1156.

FRASER, B. J. (1981). Learning environment in curriculum evaluation: A review. *Evaluation in Education, 5*, 1-93.

FRIEDLANDER, F., & GREENBERG, S. (1971). Effect of job attitudes, training, and organization climate on performance of the hard-core unemployed. *Journal of Applied Psychology, 55*, 287-295.

FUHR, R., MOOS, R., & DISHOTSKY, N. (1981). The use of family assessment and feedback on ongoing family therapy. *American Journal of Family Therapy, 9*, 24-36.

GREENWOOD, R., MARR, J., ROESSLER, R., & ROWLAND, P. (1980). The social climate of a rehabilitation center: Implications for organizational development. *Journal of Rehabilitation Administration, 4*, 20-24.

GRIPP, R., & MAGARO, P. (1971). A token economy program evaluation with untreated control ward comparison. *Behaviour Research and Therapy, 9*, 137-139.

JAMES, L. R., & JONES, A. P. (1974). Organizational climate: A review of theory and research. *Psychological Bulletin, 81*, 1096-1112.

JESSOR, R. (1981). The perceived environment in psychological theory and research. In D. Magnusson (Ed.), *Toward a psychology of situations: An interactional perspective.* Hillsdale, NJ: Lawrence Erlbaum Associates.

JUDD, C. M., & KENNY, D. A. (1981). Process analysis: Estimating mediation in treatment evaluations. *Evaluation Review, 5*, 602-619.

KAHANA, E., & KAHANA, B. (1970). Therapeutic potential of age integration. *Archives of General Psychiatry, 23*, 20-29.

KAROLY, P., & ROSENTHAL, M. (1977). Training parents in behavior modification: Effects on perceptions of family interaction and deviant child behavior. *Behavior Therapy, 8*, 406-410.

KLASS, D. B., GROWE, G. A., & STRIZICH, M. (1977). Ward treatment milieu and post-hospital functioning. *Archives of General Psychiatry, 34*, 1047-1052.

KOGUTEK, M. (1977). The assessment of an alcoholism rehabilitation program treatment environment as related to treatment outcome. *Dissertation Abstracts International, 38*(2-B), 907.

KORAN, L. M., MOOS, R. H., MOOS, B. & ZASSLOW, M. (1983). Changing hospital work environments: An example of a burn unit. *General Hospital Psychiatry, 5*, 7-13

LINN, M., SHANE, R., WEBB, N., & PRATT, T. (1979). Cultural factors and attribution in drug abuse treatment. *International Journal of the Addictions, 14*, 259-280.

LUBORSKY, L., & McLELLAN, A. T. (1978). Our surprising inability to predict the outcomes of psychological treatments—with special reference to treatments for drug abuse. *American Journal of Drug and Alcohol Abuse, 5*, 387-398.

LUFT, L., & FAKHOURI, J. (1979). A model for a comparative cost-effectiveness evaluation of two mental health partial care programs. *Evaluation and Program Planning, 2*, 33-40.

MacLEOD, R. B. (1951). The place of phenomenological analysis in social psychological theory. In J. H. Rohrer & M. Sherif (Eds.), *Social psychology at the crossroads.* New York: Harper.

MOOS, R. H. (1973). Changing the social milieus of psychiatric treatment settings. *Journal of Applied Behavioral Science, 9,* 575–593.

MOOS, R. H. (1974a). *The social climate scales: An overview.* Palo Alto, CA: Consulting Psychologists Press.

MOOS, R. H. (1974b). *Evaluating treatment environments: A social ecological approach.* New York: Wiley.

MOOS R. H. (1981). *Work environment scale manual.* Palo Alto, CA: Consulting Psychologists Press.

MOOS, R. H., BROMET, E., TSU, V., & MOOS, B. (1979). Family characteristics and the outcome of treatment for alcoholism. *Journal of Studies on Alcohol, 40,* 78–88.

MOOS, R. H., & FINNEY, J. W. (1980). Alcoholism and its vicissitudes: A comment on the Rand research. *Journal of Studies on Alcohol, 41,* 769–777.

MOOS, R. H., & FINNEY, J. W. (1983). The expanding scope of alcoholism treatment evaluation. *American Psychologist, 38,* 1036–1044.

MOOS, R. H., & IGRA, A. (1980). Determinants of the social environments of sheltered care settings. *Journal of Health and Social Behavior, 21,* 88–98.

MOOS, R. H., & LEMKE, S. (1982). Assessing and improving social-ecological settings. In E. Seidman (ed.), *Handbook of social and community intervention.* Beverly Hills, CA: Sage.

MOOS, R. H., MEHREN, B., & MOOS, B. S. (1978). Evaluation of a Salvation Army alcoholism treatment program. *Journal of Studies on Alcohol, 39,* 1267–1275.

MOOS, R. H., & MOOS, B. S. (1981). *Family environment scale manual.* Palo Alto, CA: Consulting Psychologists Press.

MOOS, R. H., & SCHWARTZ, J. (1972). Treatment environment and treatment outcome. *Journal of Nervous and Mental Disease, 154,* 264–275.

MOOS, R. H., & SPINRAD, S. (in press). *Social Climate Scales annotated bibliography update.* Palo Alto, CA: Consulting Psychologists Press.

MOSHER, L., & MENN, A. (1978). Lower barriers in the community: The Soteria model. In L. I. Stein & M. A. Test (Eds.), *Alternatives to mental hospital treatment.* New York: Plenum.

MURRAY, H. (1938). *Explorations in personality.* New York: Oxford University Press.

PATTON, M. Q. (1978). *Utilization-focused evaluation.* Beverly Hills, CA: Sage.

PENK, W., & ROBINOWITZ, R. (1978). Drug users' views of psychosocial aspects of their treatment environment. *Drug Forum, 7,* 129–143.

POLICH, J. M., ARMOR, D. J., & BRAIKER, H. B. (1981). *The course of alcoholism: Four years after treatment.* New York: Wiley.

PRATT, R., LINN, M., CARMICHAEL, J., & WEBB, N. (1977).

The alcoholic's perception of the ward as predictor of aftercare attendance. *Journal of Clinical Psychology, 33,* 915–918.

PRICE, R. H., & MOOS, R. H. (1975). Toward a taxonomy of inpatient treatment environments. *Journal of Abnormal Psychology, 84,* 181–188.

PROVUS, M. (1971). *Discrepancy evaluation for educational program improvement and assessment.* Berkeley, CA: McCutchan.

QUAY, H. C. (1977). The three faces of evaluation: What can be expected to work? *Criminal Justice and Behavior, 4,* 341–354.

REYNOLDS, F. D., O'LEARY, M., & WALKER, R. D. (1982). Family environment as a predictor of alcoholism treatment outcome. *International Journal of the Addictions, 17,* 505–512.

RYAN, E., BELL, M., & METCALF, J. (1982). The development of a rehabilitation psychology program for schizophrenics: Changes in the treatment environment. *Journal of Rehabilitative Psychology, 27,* 67–85.

SCHEIRER, M. A., & REZMOVIC, E. L. (1983). Measuring degree of program implementation: A methodological review. *Evaluation Review, 7,* 599–633.

SECHREST, L., WEST, S. G., PHILLIPS, M. A., REDNER, R., & YEATON, W. (1979). Some neglected problems in evaluation research: Strength and integrity of treatments. In L. Sechrest, S. G. West, M. A. Phillips, R. Redner, & W. Yeaton (Eds.), *Evaluation studies review annual* (Vol. 4). Beverly Hills, CA: Sage.

SHINN, M. (1980). Assessing program characteristics and social climate. In A. J. McSweeny, R. Hawkins, & W. Fremouw (Eds.), *Practical program evaluation.* New York: Charles Thomas.

SLATER, E., & LINN, M. (1982-83). Predictors of rehospitalization in a male alcoholic population. *American Journal of Drug and Alcohol Abuse, 9,* 211–220.

SPIEGEL, D. (1983). *Family environment as a predictor of rehospitalization among schizophrenics.* Unpublished manuscript, Department of Psychiatry and Behavioral Sciences, Stanford University, Stanford, California.

SPIEGEL, D., & WISSLER, T. (in press). Perceptions of family environment among psychiatric patients and their wives. *Family Process.*

STEINER, H., HALDIPUR, C., & STACK, L. (1982). The acute admission ward as a therapeutic community. *American Journal of Psychiatry, 139,* 897–901.

TUCHFELD, B. A. (1977). Comments on "Alcoholism: A controlled trial of 'treatment' and 'advice'." *Journal of Studies on Alcohol, 38,* 1808–1813.

VAUGHN, C. E., & LEFF, J. P. (1976). The influence of family and social factors on the course of psychiatric illness: A comparison of schizophrenic and depressed neurotic patients. *British Journal of Psychiatry, 29,* 238–240.

VERINIS, J., & FLAHERTY, J. (1978). Using the Ward Atmosphere Scale to help change the treatment environment. *Hospital and Community Psychiatry, 29,* 238–240.

WARD, D. A. (1981). The influence of family relationships on social and psychological functioning: A follow-up study. *Journal of Marriage and the Family, 43*, 807–815.

WEISS, C. H. (Ed.). (1977). *Using social research in public policy making.* Lexington, MA: Lexington Books.

WEXLER, H. K. (1979). Program implementation: An environmental approach *Eastern Evaluation Research Society Newsletter, 1*(2).

WILLIAMS, W. (1975). Implementation analysis and assessment. *Policy Analysis, 1*, 531–566.

SECTION 3
Client-Treatment Interaction

In the simplest experimental paradigm for evaluation research, treatment is represented categorically as something either present or absent (treatment versus control group) and, when present, is assumed to have the same effect on each recipient (i.e., to add a constant to each score). Any departure from these conditions is treated as experimental "error" that obscures treatment effects— not as an actual component of those effects. In recent years, there has been increased recognition of the possibility of variation in the treatment provided different recipients and of the possibility that recipients will respond differently to similar treatment. It remains as a challenge to methodologists to find sensitive ways to handle these variations and interactions within the experimental paradigm. More developed in certain program areas is the evidence of such variability and analysis of its sources.

The two contributions presented in this section stand as representatives of current empirical and conceptual work on this topic. Other equally capable and provocative work is also available in recent literature, some of which we will cite here as a guide to the interested reader.

In the first of the chapters in this section, Rezmovic examines the issue of treatment implementation in the context of a counseling program for exoffenders. This chapter illustrates two important aspects of the implementation issue. One is the simple recognition that a program that is not implemented cannot have effects. It therefore follows that the evaluation researcher should document the level of implementation as a preliminary to testing for program effects. Rezmovic persuasively discusses the need for such documentation and the difficulty of obtaining it for relatively unstructured programs. The second aspect of implementation highlighted in this chapter is the great variability possible in the treatment delivered to clients who are ostensibly in the same treatment condition. In Rezmovic's example, a small proportion of clients were provided the full treatment, more or less as planned, others were provided virtually no treatment, and most were provided with various degrees of partial treatment.

Although the nature of social service programs may make treatment variation especially likely, it is by no means confined to that program area. An interesting comparison is provided by Wennberg (1984) who discusses variability in the relatively more structured area of surgical and medical services. He reports persisting differences among physician's varying styles of practice. Treatment variability therefore may be endemic to any system in which professionals exercise discretion in the provision of service.

Turning now to the receiving end of treatment, we find a small spate of recent articles commenting on recipients' differential response to treatment. Alcabes and Jones (1985), for example, provide a probing analysis of the nature of "clienthood" in social work. They conclude that not every program applicant or recipient of service is a "true" client and that treatment benefits cannot reasonably be expected for those in other roles. Powell (1985) takes a more empirical approach to examining the participation of parents in an educational support program. He discovered at least four distinct patterns of program participation and wide differences in the rapidity with which program services were used by different clients. He concludes that treatment is multidimensional and that analysis of the relationship of participants to the program is best undertaken in terms of the interpersonal structure of the intervention setting.

Most compelling, of course, are those cases where it can be shown that client differences interact with treatment to produce differential program effects. Two recent reports make just that case. Crano and Messe (1985) provide close analysis of the extent to which recipients of an energy conservation program comprehended the contingencies to which they were subjected and the appropriate behavioral responses for them to make. The researchers were able to show that the program had considerable impact on those who understood it and negligible impact on the remainder. Bronson, Pierson, and Tivnan (1984) show a similar relationship in an early education program with a more conventional demographic variable playing the role of mediator. They found that children with highly educated mothers showed gains at all program service levels; children with less educated mothers showed gains only at intensive service levels.

The second chapter in this section reviews available research on a client variable that is especially potent in affecting treatment outcome in many programs. Focusing on alcoholism treatment, Miller summarizes the research relating motivational variables to treatment entry, compliance, and outcome. Miller identifies a number of practical strategies that might be effective to increase the likelihood of a favorable treatment outcome. Most important, however, he comes to the conclusion that motivation should not be conceptualized as a unidimensional trait along which individuals vary. Rather, he argues that it is a facet of a dynamic interpersonal process involving client, therapist, and social environment. It will be a considerable challenge for program evaluation researchers to represent that fluid process and its influence on treatment outcome within their research designs.

REFERENCES

Alcabes, A., & Jones, J. A. (1985). Structural determinants of "clienthood." *Social Work, 30*(1), 49-53.

Bronson, M. B., Pierson, D. E., & Tivnan, T. (1984). The effects of early education on children's competence in elementary school. *Evaluation Review, 8*(5), 615-629.

Crano, W. D., & Messe, L. A. (1985). Assessing and redressing comprehension artifacts in social intervention research. *Evaluation Review,9*(2), 144-172.

Powell, D. R. (1985). Stability and change in patterns of participation in a parent-child program. *Professional Psychology: Research and Practice, 16*(2), 172-180.

Wennberg, J. E. (1984). Dealing with medical practice variations: A proposal for action. *Health Affairs, 3*(2), 6-32.

32

Assessing Treatment Implementation Amid the Slings and Arrows of Reality

Eva Lantos Rezmovic

Increasing numbers of evaluators are cognizant of the need to observe treatment systematically. To date, however, little headway has been made toward operationalizing and executing the required effort. In the context of an experiment in criminal justice, a number of "real world" constraints on documenting, monitoring, and measuring treatment implementation are discussed. The contract researcher who is hired to conduct an impact evaluation of a black box intervention cannot readily divert the study's focus and funds to an examination of process. By incorporating provisions for gathering implementation data into their funding criteria, evaluation funders would help to advance the meaningfulness and social value of outcome studies.

*T*hrough painful experience, social researchers have come to recognize the importance of describing, monitoring, and measuring treatment delivery. The experience has been painful because evaluators have too often found themselves at a loss to explain why a particular intervention did or did not produce the expected effects. Even among the most rigorously designed studies in criminal justice, examples of this state of affairs are not difficult to find. Berger et al.'s (1975) experimental study of a volunteer program for juvenile court probationers, for example, devoted only a few paragraphs, in a report exceeding 400 pages, to describing program events. Consequently, despite an 18-month evaluation effort, the reasons for the program's inability to reduce delinquent behavior could not be discerned. It was reported, however, that the treatment was not administered to everyone in the experimental group. "From a quarter to a third of the probationers who were supposed to receive some service never did. For various reasons, they were never contacted by a volunteer probation officer, they got no

From Eva Lantos Rezmovic, "Assessing Treatment Implementation Amid the Slings and Arrows of Reality," *Evaluation Review*, 1984, 8(2), 187-204. Copyright 1984 by Sage Publications, Inc.

tutoring, or they never participated in counseling" (Berger et al., 1975: VII-2). Even among those who did receive service, some youths met with their volunteers immediately after referral, while others met up to 4 months later.

Reckless and Dintz's (1972) experimental evaluation of a delinquency prevention program was also confronted with the problem of how to interpret treatment outcome as a function of treatment input. One hypothesis about the null findings suggested that the treatment program may not have been intensive enough to impel attitude or behavior changes in the youths. With no monitoring or measurement of treatment delivery, the program's inability to produce the expected changes could not be well understood.

As a final example, the "nothing works" doctrine in corrections (Adams, 1976; Martinson, 1974) has been well buttressed by Kassebaum et al.'s (1971) no-effect findings on prison group counseling. This controlled study found no differences in parole outcome between inmates receiving up to two years of counseling by specially trained counselors and controls not given the group treatment. When the study report was scrutinized by Quay (1979), the following program characteristics were revealed: Counseling sessions were often superficial and ineptly handled; the sessions bored a segment of participants; staff and client turnover was high; offenders were less interested in the program than in impressing the parole board with their participation; and offenders mistrusted the motives of the program and considered group leaders to be incompetent. Given these types of conditions, which Kassebaum et al. were singularly insightful and diligent in documenting, failure to achieve significant treatment effects is not surprising. Nevertheless, in the many discussions of this highly regarded experiment, emphasis generally has been placed on the study's outcome and rarely on the reasons for it.

Reviews of the literature bear out the discrete findings that suggest insufficient attention has been given to program operations and their implications. Slaikeu's (1973) review of 23 evaluation studies on group treatment of offenders found that all of them lacked adequate descriptions of treatment practices. Furthermore, "beyond labeling the treatment as psychotherapy or counseling, few researchers go on to say precisely what this means to them. The studies are notably lacking in clear definition of treatment" (p. 89). Cook and Scioli's (1975) review of 43 studies on volunteer programs in courts and corrections found essentially the same thing. They stated that "failure to specify program activities was one of the most pronounced shortcomings of the research we evaluated" (p. 17). In looking at 236 federally funded evaluations, Bernstein and Freeman (1975) found that 22% of the studies took no steps to determine whether program specification and program implementation corresponded with one another. Sechrest and Redner (1979) found that 23 out of 29 studies in criminal justice (71%) did not describe the treatment adequately or assess its integrity. In education, Thomas's (1980) review of 61 experiments found no mention of treatment implementation in 61% of the studies.

TREATMENT INTEGRITY
AND DECISION MAKING

Treatment integrity refers to how well treatment practice conforms to treatment plan. When treatment integrity is lacking in a program under evaluation, the implications for policymaking can be considerable. The potentially harmful effects of this situation can be illustrated via the four-fold table in Figure I. Cells A and D represent the fulfilled assumptions of conventional experimental methodology. If a treatment that has been implemented is found to be superior to a comparison treatment (A), then the decision to adopt the innovation is valid. Conversely, an implemented treatment that fails to demonstrate its superiority (C) can be discarded validly. Call A, then, represents a treatment well conceptualized in design, while cell C represents a poorly conceptualized treatment. It is decisions stemming from cells B and D that can confound the validity of policy decisions. When a treatment is not implemented according to design, then decisions to adopt the new treatment (B) or to retain the old one (D) may or may not be valid. Given that the program is not harmful, decisions based on cell B merely may imply a wasteful expenditure of money. The cumulative effect of decisions based on cell D, however, may have retarded the progress of corrections considerably. It is impossible to know how often studies have concluded that treatments were ineffective when they should have concluded that shortcomings in treatment implementation precluded the drawing of conclusions about their value as rehabilitative techniques. If evaluations have been performed on poorly implemented correctional treatments, as increasing evidence seems to suggest (Sechrest et al., 1979), then the current "nothing works" dilemma is not well founded. Quite likely, innovative rehabilitative methods have not been fully tested, and

Experimental Program

	Implemented	Not Implemented
Reject H_0	A	B
Fail to reject H_0	C	D

Decision

Figure 1:   Decision Alternatives in Hypothesis Testing

worthwhile programs have not been detected. According to Yeaton (1980), "When next to nothing is implemented in a watered down way, it doesn't work."

TREATMENT MEASUREMENT
AND EVALUATION ORGANIZATION:
A CONDITIONAL BALANCE

In response to prior neglect of documenting and measuring what took place during the treatment period, writers on evaluation issues are becoming increasingly vocal in calling for studies that focus on program components as well as outcomes. They cite the need for details on intended versus actual program operations; duration, frequency, and intensity of treatment; training and qualifications of treatment deliverers; character of the target population; external events affecting study variables; and so forth (Bernstein and Cardascia, 1975; Leithwood and Montgomery, 1980; Patton, 1978; Quay, 1979; Riecken and Boruch, 1974). To collect such implementation data, several methodologies have been suggested. These include personal interviews, questionnaires, videotaping, record analysis, participant observation, anecdotal reporting, and task analysis. Seldom discussed, however, are issues concerning the feasibility and appropriateness of such methodologies and the practical problems of obtaining process data in impact evaluations.

The task of collecting process data is most easily dealt with when the evaluator is also the treatment administrator and thus has maximum control over experimental conditions (Fairweather and Tornatzky, 1977). In such situations, the evaluator can personally formulate experimental hypotheses, develop the evaluation plan, operationalize treatment components in measurable terms, manipulate experimental variables so they correspond to the treatment as conceptualized, and document exactly what took place, for how long, with whom, and at what level of intensity.

The task of documenting and measuring treatment delivery becomes more difficult when the roles of evaluator and treatment administrator are handled by different individuals. Nevertheless, very satisfactory attempts at assaying treatment strength may be made if treatment delivery takes place in a closed setting (e.g., prison, hospital, school). For example, the evaluator may directly determine how many clients receive treatment and how long the sessions last simply by being an inconspicuous onlooker. It also may be possible for the evaluator to observe treatment sessions through a one-way mirror, to listen to sessions from an adjacent room, or to record sessions by discreetly placing a taping device in the treatment delivery area. Such unobtrusive monitoring of treatment implementation can provide strong evidence on magnitude and integrity of treatment.

The least tractable situation for monitoring treatment—the one that presented itself in the Challenge experiment described below—arises when the intervention is of human service nature and is delivered in the community by nonresearch personnel. In two of the experimental conditions, counseling staff from the agency met with clients in the clients' homes; in the third condition, counselors met with clients on "neutral ground" (e.g., restaurants, parks, museums) in the community. Such decentralized treatment delivery posed substantial problems for assessing implementation.

THE EXPERIMENT:
A BRIEF OVERVIEW

Between 1977 and 1979, an experiment was conducted in Chicago in which the relative effects of two social service programs for exoffenders were evaluated. Funded by the Law Enforcement Assistance Administration, it was perhaps the first true experiment in the area of exoffender volunteerism. The study took place at the Safer Foundation, a nonprofit corporation that provides employment and personal counseling services to former prisoners released to the Chicago metropolitan area.

The study design involved random assignment of 367 exoffenders to one of the following treatment programs:

(a) Operation DARE—clients assigned to DARE received employment counseling and referral services, only. This program served as the control condition in the experiment.

(b) Staff Associate program—Staff Associates were private citizens who voluntarily worked with an exoffender for one year. During that year, the Staff Associate was to serve as a resource person, ombudsman, and "ear" to the exoffender.

(c) VISTA program—VISTA counselors were volunteers of the national ACTION program who were placed with the Safer Foundation. They were themselves exoffenders, who were purportedly in a good position to serve as role models and offer empathic guidance to parolees. The functions of the VISTA counselors were similar to those of Staff Associates, but they worked with caseloads of 15-20 clients for 3 months.

(d) Paraprofessional program—Paraprofessionals were employees of the Safer Foundation who handled caseloads of 25-30 clients for 6 months. In general, Paraprofessionals were also exoffenders, and they provided services similar to those of Staff Associates and VISTA counselors.

The Staff Associate, VISTA, and Paraprofessional treatment programs were all aimed at aiding the social reintegration of exoffenders into mainstream community life. Collectively, these three treatments comprised a program called Challenge. Since the counseling and support services of Challenge were supplemental to the employment services of DARE, the experiment was actually an evaluation of the relative effectiveness of DARE versus Staff Associate + DARE versus VISTA + DARE versus Paraprofessional + DARE programs.

The study results were disappointing: No significant differences were found between the Challenge programs and Operation DARE on any of the recidivism, employment, program stability, or goal achievement measures utilized. Data limitations precluded adequate testing of the remaining two impact dimensions: residential stability and utilization of community resources. The interested reader is referred to Cook et al. (1980), Dobson and Cook (1979), Rezmovic (1982a, 1982b), and Rezmovic et al. (1981) for a fuller discussion of the study, its findings, and attendant evaluation issues.

In an effort to determine whether the overall analyses may have masked a relationship between extent of service delivery and program outcome, additional analyses were performed on the data. However, such post hoc analyses on the effects of degree of implementation are vulnerable to many validity threats, and the results have been subject to differential interpretation (Cook and Dobson, 1982; Dobson and Cook, 1980; Rezmovic, 1982b). Clearly, a priori planning for the collection of implementation data is a preferable alternative, since the researcher's knowledge of and control over experimental variables is enhanced. This is no simple task, however. As described below, the "real world" just may not be conducive to fulfilling such ideal methodological aspirations.

OBSTACLES TO IMPLEMENTATION ANALYSIS IN THE CHALLENGE EXPERIMENT

As a first step toward identifying the contents of treatment, an attempt was made to document the treatment practices of each Challenge program. I spent considerable time reviewing agency documents and interviewing program heads and counselors prior to the onset of the experiment. The difficulties encountered in trying to ascertain the specifics of program operations cannot be overstated. The programs were found to have no formal structure; rather, they operated on the premise that they could best respond to individual client needs by being maximally flexible. "Treatment specifications" detailing program activities as explicitly and completely as possible were prepared for each of the three experimental programs. However, they were riddled with caveats concerning interpretation of the programs as organized, systematir entities. It is noteworthy that the Staff Associate program was described as "vague" with respect to specific behavioral expectations of counselors, that the VISTA counseling sessions were described as "lack[ing] an identifiable design and direction," and that "the flexibility and lack of structure which characterize[d] the client-VISTA meetings also characterize[d] the client-Paraprofessional meetings." It also should be noted that upon reviewing these reports, program heads found no inaccuracies in the descriptions of their programs.

Given that none of the programs could be well articulated, our limitation to conducting a black box evaluation may well have been inevitable. Other problems were also present, however, further delimiting opportunities to clarify the processes of treatment imposition. These included the following:

(a) If treatment implementation even nominally conformed with treatment plan (i.e., if all Challenge clients were assigned to counselors and the intended client-counselor meetings took place), there should have been over 3,500 meetings between 120 counselors and 261 clients during the 2-year evaluation period. Moreover, these meetings were to be held on a one-to-one basis in diverse community settings. Given this decentralized form of treatment delivery, tremendous logistical problems would have arisen from trying to observe treatment directly. The Staff Associates, private citizens who volunteered their personal time for working with an exoffender, were primarily in telephone contact with the agency. Aside from initially agreeing to meet with their clients twice a month, they had no prescribed schedule for meeting, and there were no agency controls to ensure that meetings did take place. Similarly, there was little direct oversight by program managers of the activities of VISTA and Paraprofessional counselors. Since line staff were rarely able to predict when, where, and for how long they would meet with clients, the evaluators could not formulate an effective, practical plan for observing counseling sessions. Such a plan would have required greater order and predictability of the treatment delivery process than existed.

(b) In point of fact, of the 3,500 client-counselor meetings called for in the treatment plan, fewer than 450 meetings (13%) took place. There were two major reasons for this: (1) Failure to make a match between clients and counselors. This occurred in 107 cases (Cook et al., 1980) and reduced by 1,500 the number of meetings that could be expected. (2) Inability to contact clients. The 70 counselors who were matched with 154 Challenge clients should have met with them roughly 2,000 times. Instead, only 450 meetings (22%) were known to have taken place. Both program managers and counselors cited the mobility of the exoffender sample and their unreliability in keeping appointments as reasons for lack of contact. In the case of VISTA and Paraprofessional counselors, unsuccessful attempts to reach the client by telephone would generally result in a home visit. Such unarranged visits, however, did not often find the client at home. Had evaluation staff accompanied counselors on these trips, much staff time would have been expended on unproductive efforts to simply make contact with clients.

(c) Most counselors hired by the Safer Foundation are themselves exoffenders, native Chicagoans, and fairly unhesitant about visiting poor, black, high-crime neighborhoods in Chicago. Because most newly released prisoners reside in such neighborhoods, this is where meetings between clients and their VISTA and Paraprofessional counselors took place. By contrast, the evaluation staff was not as "street wise" as the agency counselors and would not have easily fit into their milieu. This served as a further obstacle to treatment monitoring. While a street wise evaluator would be the ideal resource person for studies involving community treatment of offender samples, this type of individual remains a relative rarity.

(d) Because counseling sessions were held individually in private homes, restaurant booths, and so forth, it would have been awkward and intrusive for evaluation staff to be present. In fact, VISTA and Paraprofessional counselors were not permitted to fill out the necessary agency forms—or even to take notes—during counseling sessions for fear that this would distract from the rapport-building purpose of the meetings. It was made clear to the evaluation staff that our presence in meetings with clients would be threatening to both clients and counselors and detrimental to maintaining a trusting relationship between them. In effect, we were not welcome to observe the contents of the black box.

(e) We also could not listen to the contents of the black box. Counselors claimed that recorders would be threatening to clients and bias the nature of client-counselor interactions. Whether this contention was correct was not verified by the evaluators. Perhaps interviews should have been held with agency clients to assess their aversity to recorded counseling sessions. Perhaps a small pilot study should have been undertaken to examine whether the substance or style of recorded and unrecorded meetings would differ. Perhaps a literature review on the use of recorders in research studies should have been conducted. Since some researchers have reported no deleterious effects of recorders in psychotherapy sessions (Redlich et al., 1950) or in marriage counseling (Harper and Hudson, 1952), evidence from a literature search may have helped to alter the subjective views of program personnel.

A further look at the literature might also have suggested to program managers that relying on counselors' written reports may be problematic. For example, comparing written reports with tape recordings,

Covner (1944) and Symonds and Dietrich (1941) found that over 60% of the ideas contained in counseling interviews were omitted from counselor's reports. When time and personnel are available, there is much to recommend such procedures. Indeed, hindsight suggests that—given the lack of specificity of treatment activities and the many program management problems evidenced—tape recorded counseling sessions might have been the key to understanding why and where program outcomes fell so short of expectation. Such a procedure would have been most productive in the case of the VISTA and Paraprofessional treatment groups. Since 60% of the experimental clients were treated by a total of 10 VISTA and Paraprofessional counselors, 10 tape recorders might have gathered useful information on treatment content while containing research costs within practical limits. At the time that the issue arose, however, there were compelling reasons for not pressing for the taping of treatment activities: Funds had not been allocated for that purpose, and the program found the suggestion unacceptable.

In an effort to assess the components of Challenge treatment, clients were asked in research interviews how often they met with their counselors, what kinds of topics were discussed, whether and how the counselors were helpful to them, and whether they felt that the counselors cared about them. Such questions provided only crude information on treatment delivery. Responses were subject to the distorting effects of recall errors, which is a drawback in any type of retrospective reporting. In addition, our ability to uncover the various dimensions of treatment through specific description of the counseling sessions was curtailed by the clients' inarticulateness. Hence, only general information was obtained from these indirect attempts to appraise treatment integrity.

The situation was more serious than portrayed above. Not only were there major problems with monitoring the contents of the treatment, but the extent to which services were delivered at all was also suspect. While we knew that variations existed in service delivery—and repeatedly voiced our concern to program managers—we were not in a position to remedy the situation. Our role was to evaluate, not to intrude on normal program operations. Not until the data were analyzed were the differences in levels of treatment delivery revealed: Based on 145 initial reports submitted by Challenge counselors, 32% of clients were contacted within the first 20 days following program entry, 32% were contacted during the second 20 days, and 35% required over 40 days to contact. Based on 151 final reports, working relationships between

EVALUATION STUDIES REVIEW ANNUAL

Challenge counselors and clients terminated within 20 days of their formation in 25% of the cases. Finally, when all 261 exoffenders the 3 experimental groups were considered, there was no report of counselor-client contact in fully 41% of the cases. It was ultimately determined that only 5% of the experimental group participants worked with a counselor at least 5 hours per month for the full period of time designated by the treatment model (Cook et al., 1980). The finding that there were no significant between group differences on any of the impact measures is understandable in view of the massive degradation of treatment.

THE NONINDEPENDENT STATUS OF
IMPLEMENTATION ASSESSMENT PROBLEMS

The problem of black box interventions is not independent of other problem areas within evaluation. In the corrections field, for instance, the atheoretical orientation of rehabilitation research has often been lamented (Adams, 1975; Cressey, 1958; Glaser, 1975, 1974a, 1974b, 1973; Gottfredson, 1972; Lejins, 1971; Lejins and Courtless, 1973; Lipton et al., 1975; Nelson and Richardson, 1971; Reed, 1974; Schulman, 1961; Wilkins, 1964). Little has changed since Cressey's (1958) observation that the labeling of a program as rehabilitative is less grounded in theoretical expectations of effective practices than in the tautological belief that rehabilitation is whatever it is that the program does. Whether due to insufficient theory development or to the failure of researchers and practitioners to capitalize on existing theories, tapping the black box of treatment intervention suffers on its account. A theoretical basis for conducting evaluation studies could assist the evaluator in identifying the intermediary steps involved in achieving program goals and subgoals. With this knowledge, program activities or characteristics predicted to be associated with each step could be monitored, and the fidelity of treatment to program design could be more readily verified. Such causal sequencing of program events and the concomitant concern with short-term objectives could provide the substantive basis for specifying and measuring treatment implementation.

Ability to measure treatment imposition also interfaces with type of study population. Exoffenders, for example, are generally more difficult to track than captive populations such as inmates, patients, or students. Therefore, uncovering the nature of treatment delivered via observation, questionnaire, or interview methods depends on the characteristics and stability of the subject sample and should be so recognized.

Finally, subject attrition and failure to implement treatment need not be independent methodological problems. For example, it was reported above that, for practical purposes, 41% of Challenge clients received no treatment. While there is no argument that treatment was not delivered to these clients, discerning the origins of the problem is important to proper understanding of the program. That is, if clients were not treated because of counselor negligence, then the problem is one of deficient service delivery system. If, on the other hand, clients either refused to participate (after volunteering initially) or could not be contacted, the problem is one of subject attrition. The Safer data suggest that both conditions were present, although attribution of causation in the majority of the cases could not be established. Of 57 Challenge clients who reported no contact with their counselors, 11 clients (19%) cited health problems, working, moving, or lack of interest as reasons for noncontact. These answers suggest that subject attrition was a factor in failure to receive the intended treatment. Difficulties in contacting counselors were cited by 4 (7%) of the untreated respondents. For this subgroup, then, unresponsiveness of the program was the main perceived factor in treatment implementation failures. The responses of 31 clients (54%) were unrevealing as to the source of treatment implementation breakdown. These responses stated merely that no match or no communication by the program had taken place. In these cases, it might have been useful to make further inquiry into the reasons for noncontact. Was the client interested in program participation, did he have a permanent residence, was he accessible by phone? A parallel inquiry into agency efforts to reach clients could have helped to assay the extent to which clients as opposed to program staff—defaulted in their commitment to treatment. In terms of providing useful feedback to program managers, such efforts to disentangle the components of treatment failure can be as important as specifying the components of treatment delivered.

CONCLUSIONS

The extent to which program organization and operations were not conducive to a satisfactory assessment of treatment implementation have been described. Service deliverers were given such latitude in executing their jobs that uncontrolled treatment variation was very high, a problem common to many human service delivery systems (Rossi, 1978). Thus the situation was one in which program management chose to exercise little control over service content and in which evaluation personnel had no direct control over any aspect of program activity. Although the design of the Challenge study was founded on measurable goals, a delineation of causal consequences was missing. Since program activities were not articulated clearly (and therefore not linked to program objectives), the evaluation could not develop a focused approach to implementation assessment. Whether the resultant finding that treatment imposition was incomplete or nonexistent is an indictment of the experiment is debatable. Certainly, it detracts from the study's power, meaningfulness, and social value. On the other hand, the best was done in a difficult situation. Under the conditions presented to the evaluators once the study was funded, there was little opportunity to investigate alternative implementation assessment strategies. Such is the reality of contract research work

What can external evaluators do to ensure that the treatments they set out to evaluate will actually function as stated? This is a vastly neglected area in which prescriptions are lacking. Emergent theories have discussed ways in which the adoption of new programs is affected by program characteristics and by social, political, and organizational forces (Fullan and Pomfret, 1977; Scheirer, 1980). When evaluators are called on to evaluate an established program, however, the context of evaluation is likely to be quite different. Obstacles to program implementation are less likely to be environmental and more likely to be internal in nature. Resistance may be encountered in altering what has come to be conventional (and in this case, weak and vague) service delivery procedures. In the Challenge study, the evaluation staff attempted to stimulate increased levels of treatment delivery by bringing the problem to the attention of program managers. While program managers in turn emphasized the need for full programmatic effort to their staff, there were few controls or feedback mechanisms (particularly in the case of the Challenge program) for ensuring the implementation of their directives. Hence, assistance to exoffender clients was very much subject to individual counselor's conscientiousness in fulfilling their job functions. Defying expectation, treatment strength and integrity need not be well maintained even when administrator and researcher work together compatibly for common purposes. Even in such administrative experiments as the Challenge study, tandem efforts to promote treatment implementation may fail without a corresponding framework for skillfully selecting and training service deliverers, supervising their work, airing problems, providing support and assistance, and maintaining quality control over actual program operations.

A related question concerns whether the evaluator should become involved with the program's implementation activities. On the one hand, the accumulation of scientific knowledge requires experimental testing of fully implemented treatment models. On the other hand, alterations in treatment imposition for the purpose of program evaluation may result in findings that are impractical, unresponsive, or irrelevant to program needs. A similar dilemma applies to the specification and analysis of treatment contents. As stated by Mann (1971: 178):

> Unfortunately, the greater the scientific precision in demonstrating the effectiveness of a given method, the greater the likelihood that the experiment bears little resemblance to the method as it is normally employed by practitioners. On the other hand, when a procedure is tested as it is used by practitioners, it is almost impossible to describe the change process in a precise and scientific manner.

Practical advice on how to monitor treatment implementation in field settings and evidence on the effects of monitoring on evaluation results are lacking. As applied researchers, we found the problem of gathering process data an intractable one. For example, it was logistically impossible to keep tabs on client-counselor meetings. Even if this could have been done, our attendance would have subjected the research results to the common criticism that "the presence of outsiders disturb[ed] the normal conduct of the session" (Ward and Kassebaum, 1976: 302).

It may be argued that black box interventions should not be implemented (Rossi, 1979), that if implemented they should not be evaluated (Rossi, 1979), and that if evaluated and found to be ineffective, their results should be ignored (Sechrest and Redner, 1979). While these suggestions may have some merit, there should be available more pragmatic advice on how to handle problems of activating, monitoring, and measuring treatment imposition. In addition, more information is needed on the extent to which intuitions are correct: Are evaluation results biased by treatment monitoring? If yes, what types of monitoring produce bias? In what settings and under what conditions? What is the magnitude and direction of bias? Boruch and Gomez (1977) have offered some theory on the drop in statistical power when the treatment delivered in the field is a degraded version of the treatment administered under laboratory conditions. Obtaining data on the effects of different types of treatment monitoring, under varying degrees of experimenter control over treatment delivery, would at least enable the evaluator to make some reasoned decisions about the tradeoffs involved in monitoring treatment and risking biased results versus not monitoring and risking low power results.

Funding of evaluation studies should also be made contingent on the inclusion in proposals of an outline that details procedures to be used for gathering process data on actual program operations. The purpose of such an outline would be twofold: (a) The mandating of treatment monitoring by the funding agency would reduce opportunities for conflict between program and evaluation staff. With this type of reduction in degrees of freedom, program personnel would be less likely to resist scrutiny of the treatment. (b) If funding agencies required an assessment of treatment strength, they would be more aware of the need to provide sufficient funds for such an effort. We do not know how often the treatment in a black box evaluation could have been specified clearly and monitored had there been sufficient funds to do so. Funds spent on implementation analysis might even have been more useful than funds spent on impact analysis (Patton, 1978). If a program or policy is not even feasible, it is pointless to conduct an outcome evaluation. In this direction, studies focusing on evaluation of program implementation are now emerging (Hall and Loucks, 1977; Leithwood and Montgomery, 1980).

REFERENCES

ADAMS, S. (1976) "Evaluation: a way out of rhetoric," in Rehabilitation, Recidivism, and Research. Hackensack, NJ: National Council on Crime and Delinquency.
——(1975) Evaluative Research in Corrections: A Practical Guide. Law Enforcement Assistance Administration: National Institute for Law Enforcement and Criminal Justice.
BERGER, R. J., J. E. CROWLEY, M. GOLD, and J. GRAY with M. S. ARNOLD (1975) Experiment in a Juvenile Court: A Study of a Program of Volunteers Working with Juvenile Probationers. Ann Arbor: Institute for Social Research, University of Michigan.

BERSTEIN, I. N., and J. CARDASCIA (1975) "Strategies and designs for criminal justice evaluation." Presented at the meeting of the American Sociological Association, San Francisco.

——— and H. E. FREEMAN (1975) Academic and Entrepreneurial Research. New York: Russell Sage.

BORUCH, R. F., and H. GOMEZ' (1977) "Sensitivity, bias, and theory in impact evaluations." Professional Psychology 8: 411-434.

COOK, T. J., and L. D. DOBSON (1982) "Reaction to reexamination: more on Type III error in program evaluation." Evaluation and Program Planning 5: 119-121.

COOK, T. J., L. D. DOBSON, and E. L. REZMOVIC (1980) Working with Ex-Offenders: The Challenge Experiment. Research Triangle Park, NC: Research Triangle Institute.

COOK, T. J., and F. P. SCIOLI (1975) The Effectiveness of Volunteer Programs in Courts and Corrections: An Evaluation of Policy Related Research. Washington, DC: National Science Foundation.

COVNER, B. J. (1944) "Studies in phonographic recordings of verbal material: III. The completeness and accuracy of counseling interview reports." J. of General Psychology 30: 181-203.

CRESSEY, D. R. (1958) "The nature and effectiveness of correctional techniques." Law and Contemporary Problems 23: 754-771.

DOBSON, L. D. and T. J. COOK (1980) "Avoiding Type III error in program evaluation: results from a field experiment." Evaluation and Program Planning 3: 269-276.

———(1979) "Implementing random assignment: a computer-based approach in a field experimental setting." Evaluation Q. 3: 472-489.

FAIRWEATHER, G. and L. TORNATZKY (1977) Experimental Methods for Social Policy Research. New York: Pergamon.

FULLAN, M. and A. POMFRET (1977) "Research on curriculum and instruction implementation." Rev. of Educ. Research 47: 335-397.

GLASER, D. (1974a) "Remedies for the key deficiency in criminal justice evaluation research." J. of Research in Crime and Delinquency 11: 144-154.

———(1974b) "The state of the art of criminal justice evaluation." Presented at the Second Annual Meeting of the Association for Criminal Justice Research, Los Angeles.

———(1973) Routinizing Evaluation: Getting Feedback on effectiveness of Crime and Delinquency Programs. Rockville, MD: Department of Health, Education, and Welfare.

GOTTFREDSON, D. M. (1972) "Five challenges." J. of Research in Crime and Delinquency 9: 68-86.

HALL, G. E. and S. F. LOUCKS (1977) "A developmental model for determining whether the treatment is actually implemented." Amer. Educ. Research J. 14: 263-276.

HARPER, R. A. and J. W. HUDSON (1952) "The use of recordings in marriage counseling: a preliminary empirical investigation." Marriage and Family Living 14: 332-334.

KASSEBAUM, G., D. A. WARD, and D. M. WILNER (1971) Prison Treatment and Parole Survival. New York: John Wiley.

LEITHWOOD, K. A. and D. J. MONTGOMERY (1980) "Evaluating program implementation." Evaluation Rev. 4: 193-214.

LEJINS, P. P. (1971) "Methodologies in the evaluation of correctional programs," in Proceedings of the 101st Congress of Correction of the American Correctional Association. College Park, MD: American Correctional Association.

——— and T. F. COURTLESS (1973) "A general model for justification and evaluation of correctional programs," in Proceedings of the 103rd Congress of Correction of the American Correctional Association. College Park, MD: American Correctional Association.

LIPTON, D., R. MARTINSON, and J. WILKS (1975) The Effectiveness of Correctional Treatment: A Survey of Treatment Evaluation Studies. New York: Praeger.

MANN, J. (1971) "Technical and social difficulties in the conduct of evaluative research," in F. G. Caro (ed.) Readings in Evaluation Research. New York: Russell Sage.

MARTINSON, R. (1974) "What works—questions and answers about prison reform." The Public Interest 35: 22-54.

NELSON, E. K., JR. and F. RICHARDSON (1971) "Perennial problems in criminological research." Crime and Delinquency 17: 23-31.

PATTON, M. Q. (1978) Utilization-Focused Evaluation. Beverly Hills, CA: Sage.

QUAY, H. C. (1979) "The three faces of evaluation: what can be expected to work," in L. Sechrest, S. G. West, M. A. Phillips, R. Redner, and W. Yeaton (eds.) Evaluation Studies Review Annual, Vol. 4. Beverly Hills, CA: Sage.

RECKLESS, W. and S. DINITZ (1972) The Prevention of Juvenile Delinquency: An Experiment. Columbus, OH: State Univ. Press.

REDLICH, F. C., J. DOLLARD, and R. NEWMAN (1950) "High fidelity recordings of psychotherapeutic interviews." Amer. J. of Psychiatry 107: 42-47.

REED, J. A. (1974) "Program evaluation research." Federal Probation 38: 37-42.

REZMOVIC, E. L. (1982a) "Evaluation practice: determinants of quality in social experimentation." Unpublished Ph.D. dissertation, Northwestern University.

———(1982b) "Program implementation and evaluation results: a reexamination of Type III error in a field experiment." Evaluation and Program Planning 5: 111-118.

———T. J. COOK, and L. D. DOBSON (1981) "Beyond random assignment: factors affecting evaluation integrity." Evaluation Rev. 5: 51-67.

RIECKEN, H. W. and R. F. BORUCH [eds.] (1974) Social Experimentation: A Method for Planning and Evaluating Social Intervention. New York: Academic.

ROSSI, P. H. (1979) "Critical decisions in evaluation studies," in W. B. Schrader (ed.) Measurement and Educational Policy Proceedings of the 1978 ETS Invitational Conference. Washington, DC: Jossey-Bass.

———(1978) "Issues in the evaluation of human services delivery." Evaluation Q. 2: 573-599.

SCHEIRER, M. A. (1980) "An organizational framework for implementation analysis." Presented at the Special National Workshop on Research Methodology and Criminal Justice Program Evaluation, Baltimore, Maryland.

SCHULMAN, H. M. (1961) Juvenile Delinquency in American Society. New York: Harper.

SECHREST, L. and R. REDNER (1979) "Strength and integrity of treatments in evaluation studies," in How Well Does It Work? Review of Criminal Justice Evaluation, 1978. Washington, DC: National Institute of Law Enforcement and Criminal Justice, Law Enforcement Assistance Administration, U.S. Department of Justice.

SECHREST, L., S. O. WHITE, and E. D. BROWN (1979) The Rehabilitation of Criminal Offenders: Problems and Prospects. Washington, DC: National Academy of Sciences.

SLAIKEU, K. A. (1973) "Evaluation studies on group treatment of juvenile and adult offenders in correctional institutions: a review of the literature." J. of Research in Crime and Delinquency 10: 87-100.

SYMONDS, P. M. and D. H. DIETRICH (1941) "The effect of variations in the time interval between an interview and its recording." J. of Abnormal and Social Psychology 36: 593-598.

THOMAS, S. (1980) "Numerical indicators of program implementation in field tests: Education" (working paper). Division of Methodology and Evaluation Research, Northwestern University.

WARD, D. A. and G. G. KASSEBAUM (1976) "On biting the hand that feeds: some implications of sociological evaluations of correctional effectiveness," in C. H. Weiss (ed.) Evaluating Action Programs: Readings in Social Action and Education. Boston: Allyn and Bacon.

WILKINS, L. T. (1964) Social Deviance. London: Tavistock.

YEATON, W. (1980) "Strength and integrity of treatments in evaluations. Presented at the Meeting of the Evaluation Research Society, Washington, DC.

Eva Lantos Rezmovic is an evaluator with the Program Evaluation and Methodology Division, U.S. General Accounting Office. Her research interests include applied methodology, field research management, and factors affecting the quality of evaluation results.

33

Motivation for Treatment
A Review With
Special Emphasis on Alcoholism

William R. Miller

Motivation is often regarded as a client attribute related to maladaptive defense mechanisms, and it is used to explain unfavorable treatment outcome. This article provides an integrative review of research relating motivational variables and interventions to treatment entry, compliance, and outcome; special focus is on alcoholism and other addictive behaviors. Empirical evidence is considered regarding motivational interventions including advice, feedback, goal setting, role playing, modeling, contingencies, continuity of care, voluntary choice, and modification of behavior attractiveness. Beyond these specific interventions, nonspecific aspects of motivation are reviewed including client characteristics (distress, self-esteem, locus of control, severity, conceptual level), environmental variables, and therapist characteristics (hostility, expectancy, empathy). A dynamic conceptualization of treatment motivation is proposed as an alternative to a trait model.

Why does treatment fail? A common attribution, especially in the treatment of addictive behaviors, is to client deficits, in particular poor motivation. Lack of proper motivation has been used to explain failure to enter, continue in, comply with, and succeed as a result of treatment since the early days of psychoanalysis (Appelbaum, 1972). Often this lack of motivation is, in turn, attributed to client characteristics: personality traits, resistance, and overuse of defense mechanisms such as denial. Motivation has long been regarded as an important nonspecific factor in treatment (Karoly, 1980).

This review is a survey of theory and research on motivation for treatment, using alcoholism as the heuristic focus. It is intended to be a contribution toward specifying this often-discussed nonspecific factor. I first address descriptive and conceptual issues, including determinants of therapists' perceptions of client motivation. I then review evaluations of specific motivational strategies, with an emphasis on experimental studies. Finally, I discuss correlational and experimental data bearing on nonspecific determinants of treatment compliance.

Emphasis on the role of client motivation has been particularly strong in the treatment of alcoholism. Surveying alcoholism treatment personnel, Sterne and Pittman (1965) found that 75% believed patient motivation to be important to recovery, and 50% viewed it as essential. Indeed motivation is frequently described as a prerequisite and a *sine qua non* for treatment, without which the therapist can do nothing (Beckman, 1980; Dean, 1958; Deaton, 1975). Alcoholics tend to be viewed as poorly motivated, resistant, denying, and having poor prognosis, a view shared both by therapists (Nir & Cutler, 1978; Tamerin, Tolor, Holson, & Neumann, 1974) and by alcoholics themselves (Coney, 1977). However, the latter tend to be more optimistic than the former (Mogar, Helm, Snedeker, Snedeker, & Wilson, 1969; Reinehr, 1969). New trainees in alcoholism counseling may be viewed by more seasoned staff as overoptimistic (Manohar, 1973).

Treatment failures are commonly explained as deriving from negative dispositional characteristics of clients. Accounting for its own unsuccessful cases, Alcoholics Anonymous (1955) stated: "Rarely have we seen a person fail who has thoroughly followed our path. Those who do not recover are people who cannot or will not completely give themselves to this simple program, usually men and women who are constitutionally incapable of

Requests for reprints should be sent to William R. Miller, Department of Psychology, University of New Mexico, Albuquerque, New Mexico 87131.

From William R. Miller, "Motivation for Treatment: A Review With Special Emphasis on Alcoholism," *Psychological Bulletin*, 1985, 98(1), 84-107. Copyright 1985 by the American Psychological Association. Reprinted (or Adapted) by permission of the publisher and author.

being honest with themselves" (p. 58). In a national survey of hospitals treating alcoholics, Moore (1971) found that 72% blamed the patient for negative outcomes, whereas only 11% acknowledged partial responsibility of the program itself. A similar attributional pattern has been observed in Britain (Orford & Hawker, 1974).

The most common explanation of the poor prognosis of alcoholics is that it is due to virulent defense mechanisms, particularly denial (Clancy, 1961; DiCicco, Unterberger, & Mack, 1978; Moore & Murphy, 1961). Fox (1967) asserted that "most patients are not motivated to stop drinking. . . . Most patients refuse to face their alcoholism for many years, using the defense mechanisms of denial, rationalization, regression, and projection" (p. 772). Elaborating on denial, she stated that the alcoholic "builds up an elaborate defense system in which he denies that he is alcoholic and ill, rationalizes that he needs to drink for business or health or social reasons, and projects the blame for the trouble he is in" (p. 771). These patterns are viewed as universal to alcoholics and part of their character structure (Clancy, 1961). Recovery is seen as beginning when the alcoholic finally "hits bottom" (Bateson, 1971), accepts the illness (Clancy, 1964), admits personal powerlessness over alcohol, and undergoes the processes of surrender and reduction of ego (Cavaiola, 1984; Tiebout, 1953, 1954; Wilson, 1977).

According to such thinking, the one hope to accelerate recovery lies in helping the alcoholic hit bottom through confrontational techniques (DiCicco et al., 1978). Greenberger (1983) described a representative confrontational intervention from an employee assistance program: "They called a surprise meeting, surrounded him with colleagues critical of his work and threatened to fire him if he didn't seek help quickly. When the executive tried to deny that he had a drinking problem, the medical director . . . came down hard. 'Shut up and listen,' he said. 'Alcoholics are liars, so we don't want to hear what you have to say.' " (p. 1). The use of such coercive techniques is regarded as necessary because "the layers of denial in alcoholism run deep and present an almost impenetrable wall" (DiCicco et al., 1978, p. 600).

Disadvantages of a Trait Model of Motivation

This trait model is not without its drawbacks. Numerous writers have observed that this conception of motivation is a thinly veiled resurrection of the much older moral-blame model of psychopathology: that clients could overcome the problem if they really wanted to and tried hard enough (Appelbaum, 1972; Chafetz, 1968a; Davies, 1979; Peters, 1960; Saslow, 1969). The concepts of sufficient motivation and "really trying" (Alcoholics Anonymous, 1955) quickly reduce to the notion of will power (Sterne & Pittman, 1965), and the client is left with moral culpability for treatment failure.

The alternative to this within a trait model is to view poor motivation as a constitutional deficit beyond the individual's control. However, this view fosters the previously mentioned expectancy of poor prognosis in both therapist and client, and such views are readily translated into self-fulfilling prophecies (R. A. Jones, 1977; Rosenthal, 1976). In an experimental replication of the familiar Pygmalion effect (Rosenthal & Jacobson, 1968), Leake and King (1977) informed counselors that certain alcoholics were likely to show remarkable recovery during counseling on the basis of their personality test profiles. These clients, who actually had been selected at random, were subsequently rated by counselors as being more motivated to accept treatment, more punctual and cooperative, and showing better appearance and more effort. Peer clients also rated them as more likable and improved. Indeed they showed significantly fewer absences and premature terminations from the program, had more sober days and fewer slips at 1-year follow-up, and were more likely than their comparable peers to have had and held a job.

Another shortcoming of the trait model has been the failure of measures of motivation to account for client behavior. Stated willingness or intention to participate in treatment has been found to be unrelated to actual participation in or outcome from treatment (Aharan, Ogilvie, & Partington, 1967; Finlay, 1977; Orford & Hawker, 1974). With a few exceptions (e.g., Adamson, Fostakowsky, & Chebib, 1974), other attempted measures of client motivation have likewise shown poor predictive power (Marcus, 1967; Orford & Hawker, 1974; Siegel & Fink, 1962). This is consistent with the more general social–psychological literature indicating that verbal intentions and overt behavior may be controlled by different determinants (Kanfer, 1980; Leventhal, 1971). In addition, it should not be surprising that verbal intentions and outcomes do not always correspond (Fishbein, 1980).

By contrast, therapist perceptions of client motivation and prognosis have been found to be related to client compliance and outcome (Gillis & Keet, 1969; Schorer, 1965; Wanberg & Jones, 1973), particularly when the same therapists judge the outcome (Finlay, 1977). This correlation could be attributed to the therapists' accurate perception of client motivational characteristics, but it might equally be accounted for by self-fulfilling properties of therapist expectancies.

Other central tenets of the trait model of motivation have failed to find support in the empirical literature. Extensive searches for "the alcoholic personality" have revealed few definitive traits or patterns typical of alcoholics beyond those directly attributable to the effects of overdrinking (W. R. Miller, 1976). The character defense mechanism of denial has been found to be no more frequent among alcoholics than among nonalcoholics (Chess, Neuringer, & Goldstein, 1971; Donovan, Rohsenow, Schau, & O'Leary, 1977; Skinner & Allen, 1983). Perhaps owing to differing operational definitions, denial has shown no consistent relation to outcome in research to date. Whereas Moore and Murphy (1961) found denial to be inversely related to improvement, O'Leary, Rohsenow, Schau, and Donovan (1977) found high levels of trait denial to be predictive of long-term success, and other investigators have found either no relation (Lemere, O'Hollaren, & Maxwell, 1958; Trice, 1957) or a negative relation (Orford, 1973) between acceptance of the self-label "alcoholic" and treatment acceptance and outcome. Baumann, Obitz, and Reich (1982), using a semantic differential measure of self-labeling, reported less denial among alcoholic clients before treatment than afterward. Further, self-labeling as "alcoholic" has been found to be unrelated to degree

of problem recognition (Shaw, Cartwright, & Harwin, 1978), and alcohol abusers in general have been found to be able and willing to acknowledge abnormal and problematic consequences of their drinking (Landeen, 1979; Orford, 1973; Richard & Burley, 1978; Tamerin et al., 1974). Nor is problem recognition sufficient for recovery (Blanc, 1968; Moore & Murphy, 1961). Polich, Armor, and Braiker (1981) found a high level of problem recognition among alcoholics showing poor outcome. Thus, research to date has not found denial to be predictive of treatment outcome.

A further disadvantage of the trait model is that is discourages intervention. Although it is comfortable and understandable for therapists to engage in defensive attribution of failures to client traits (Babow, 1975; Holt, 1967) or to make dispositional attributions because of their observer (vs. actor) perspective (E. E. Jones & Nisbett, 1972), such explanations from the client's perspective attribute failure to an internal stable source and diminish hope of future success (Kopel & Arkowitz, 1975; W. R. Miller, 1983b). The perception of client denial may dissuade a therapist from attempting to instill motivation (Davies, 1981). Indeed a trait model minimizes the importance of therapist behavior: "When the patient willingly admits his problem and is sincerely motivated to change, the battle is largely won, irrespective of the treatment technique" (Moore & Murphy, 1961, p. 605). The resulting negative perceptions of unmotivated clients may in turn evoke counterproductive therapist patterns such as suspiciousness, hostility, moralizing, low empathy, and power struggles (Bateson, 1971; Mann, 1950; Miller, 1983b; Milmoe, Rosenthal, Blane, Chafetz, & Wolf, 1967; Tamerin et al., 1974).

Perceptions of Motivation

If motivation is not a static trait, what factors influence a therapist's perceptions of client motivation? In clinical writing *motivation* is often used as an antonym for terms such as *denial* and *resistance* and a synonym for constructs such as *acceptance* and *surrender* (Brunner-Orne, 1959; Kilpatrick et al., 1978; Nir & Cutler, 1978). An examination of the literature on how professionals have used these constructs suggests several determinants of perceptions of motivation.

Agreement

With great consistency, denial has been attributed when a client disagrees with the therapist regarding certain realities. Questionnaires and procedures devised to assess degree of motivation often have consisted largely of an evaluation of the extent to which the client accepts the authors' views as reality (Bell, Weingold, & Lachin, 1969; Canter, 1966; Weinberg, 1973). A belief to which particular importance has been attached is the concept of powerlessness—that the alcoholic is totally unable to exercise volitional control over alcohol consumption. A client's refusal to endorse this doctrine is frequently labeled *denial* (Blane, 1968; Canter, 1966; Hoff, 1974; Paredes, 1974; Tiebout, 1953; Wolff, 1968). Disagreement may even override stated intent in determining perceptions of motivation. Holser (1979) described a group of patients perceived by therapists as unmotivated and terminated from treatment despite the patients' clear stated desire to continue.

Self-Label

Faia and Shean (1976) noted that a client may not disagree with the ideology of alcoholism, but only with its applicability in client's particular case. Thus, a second issue of denial versus motivation regards client acceptance of the self-label *alcoholic* (Alcoholics Anonymous, 1955; Blane, 1968; Mann, 1950; Paredes, 1974; Wolff, 1968). Viewed at a broader level, this represents the individual's willingness to acquiesce to the "sick role" (Parsons, 1951) and its central assumptions of need for external help and inability to overcome the problem by volitional control (Paredes, 1974; Stunkard, 1961).

Desire for Help

This in turn raises a third dimension determining perceptions of motivation: the client's expressed desire for external help. Problem recognition may be an important determinant (Hingson, Mangione, Meyers, & Scotch, 1982; Smith-Moorehouse, 1971), although Shaw et al. (1978) found desire for help to be unrelated to perceived problems with drinking. It should be noted that an absence of desire for help is called denial only when an external agent perceives a problem (Nir & Cutler, 1978).

Distress

Studying the determinants of staff judgments of patient motivation, Kilpatrick et al. (1978) found that those judged to be motivated showed higher levels of subjective distress, neuroticism on the Minnesota Multiphasic Personality Inventory (MMPI), anxiety, and depression on a mood scale. Wolff (1968) found that all patients judged genuinely motivated were also rated as neurotic. Thus, higher levels of distress are perceived as contributing to motivation for treatment.

Compliance/Dependence

Sterne and Pittman (1965) found that staff frequently judge motivation retrospectively, postdicting from degree of compliance with and success in treatment. Koumans (1969) suggested that the motivated client is one who does not challenge the authority and prescriptions of the treatment agent and who plays by the rules. Nonmotivation and denial have been equated with nonacceptance of the particular treatment prescriptions offered (Canter, 1966; Sterne & Pittman, 1965). O'Leary, Speltz, and Walker (1980) found that patients scoring high on a scale measuring perceptions of helplessness were rated by staff as more enjoyable to work with and more likable. Blane and Meyers (1963) reported that patients rated as dependent (overt asking for help, compliance to requests, demands for caretaking) were four times as likely to remain in and respond to treatment relative to those judged to be contradependent. Davies (1981) found that therapists work more readily at inducing motivation in dependent patients.

Summary

A client tends to be judged as motivated if he or she accepts the therapist's view of the problem (including the need for help and the diagnosis), is distressed, and complies with treatment prescriptions. A client showing the opposite behaviors—disagreement, refusal to accept diagnosis, lack of distress, and rejection of treatment prescriptions—is likely to be perceived as unmotivated, denying, and resistant. Commenting on the concept of readiness for treatment, Karoly (1980) observed: "Unfortunately, readiness is often interpreted to mean only the individual's willingness to place himself or herself in the hands of an authoritative therapist or nurturant institution" (p. 212).

Motivational Interventions

If therapist judgments of client motivation represent indirect measures of compliance behavior, a more straightforward approach might be to ask what processes influence the probability that an individual will take certain recovery related actions (Council for Philosophical Studies, 1981). The dependent variable to be influenced is engaging in such actions (which may or may not be related to favorable outcome). A *motivational intervention*, then, is defined as an operation that increases the probability of entering, continuing, and complying with an active change strategy. Although it is recognized that parallel processes operate within self-directed change (Prochaska & DiClemente, 1982; Saunders & Kershaw, 1979; Tough, 1982; Vaillant, 1983), the following review focuses on interventions relevant to the context of treatment and helping agents. Included here are studies identified as evaluating interventions intended to increase the likelihood of entering into, continuing in, or complying with treatments or other actions to reduce drinking behavior. Where they are illustrative, a few studies of motivational interventions for other addictive behaviors are included.

Giving Advice

Perhaps the simplest intervention is advice to make a change in behavior. Burnum (1974) reported that at an average follow-up of 5 years patients who had been advised by a physician to alter addictive behaviors showed varying compliance: 31 of 124 smokers, 5 of 58 alcohol abusers, and 4 of 32 drug abusers practiced the advised abstinence, whereas 19 of 61 overweight patients lost at least 20 pounds. This study was uncontrolled, however, and the improvement data resemble spontaneous remission rates for these problems. Burnum noted that those who complied did so following 1.3 occasions of advice, and that further exhortation was ineffective in increasing compliance.

Russell, Wilson, Taylor, and Baker (1979) conducted a random assignment controlled evaluation of advice to stop smoking. Patients advised by a general practitioner to abstain reported increased motivation (desire) to stop and intention to stop relative to nonadvised controls; the largest effect was in the month following advice. At 12 months, the non-smoking rate in the control group was 0.3%, whereas 3.3% of those advised to stop did so. Another group receiving both advice and a pamphlet with recommendations on how to stop smoking showed a 5.1% abstinence rate at 1 year. Although the overall compliance rates in these two studies are low, the advice interventions are economical and, at least in the latter study, they increased motivation and abstinence relative to controls. The addition of advice on how to stop brought a slight increment in effectiveness, although none of Russell's interventions had an impact on the self-efficacy of clients to achieve the goal.

A similar controlled evaluation of advice compared a minimal persuasive intervention with the full state-of-the-art alcoholism treatment program of the Maudsley Hospital (Edwards et al., 1977). Socially stable alcoholics applying for treatment were assigned at random to receive either the advice program or the full treatment package including Alcoholics Anonymous, medications, outpatient counseling, and inpatient care as needed. Advice consisted of 3 hr of assessment followed by a 1-hr counseling session in which patients "were told that responsibility for attaining of the stated goals lay in their own hands rather than it being anything which could be taken over by others, and this message was given in sympathetic and constructive terms" (Edwards et al., 1977, p. 1006). The stated goal was total abstinence from alcohol. At both 12- and 24-month follow-up, the groups showed equal and significant improvement in alcohol consumption and symptom severity as well as in social adjustment (Orford, Oppenheimer, & Edwards, 1976). Improvement in the advice group was not attributable to treatment received elsewhere. In three controlled evaluations, Miller et al. found that problem drinkers receiving a minimal "bibliotherapy" intervention showed significant improvement compared with clients randomly chosen for therapist-directed treatment (W. R. Miller, Gribskov, & Mortell, 1981; W. R. Miller & Taylor, 1980; W. R. Miller, Taylor, & West, 1980). The bibliotherapy intervention in these studies was quite comparable with Edwards's advice condition—3 to 4 hr of assessment plus minimal advice—except that the goal in these studies was moderation. A subsequent study used a dismantling design, comparing bibliotherapy with still more minimal controls: an untreated group on the waiting list and a self-monitoring group not receiving information on how to modify drinking. Neither control group showed improvement, whereas the bibliotherapy group again showed marked reduction in alcohol consumption similar to that of a therapist-treated group (Buck & Miller, 1984). From these studies, it appears that the sufficient conditions for change can be contained, at least for some individuals and problems, in a minimal intervention including advice elements (cf. Davies, 1979, 1981; Glasgow & Rosen, 1978).

Providing Feedback

A common element of Edwards et al.'s (1977) and Miller et al.'s (1980) advice interventions is extensive individual assessment, which provides the client with feedback regarding the status and severity of drinking-related problems. Numerous writers have commented on the motivational and preventive potential inherent in objective feedback of personal health measures such as serum tests of liver function (P. Davies, 1981; Henningsen, Hood, Mattiasson, Trell, & Kristenson, 1981; Hertzman, 1979; Peterson et al., 1980), neuropsychological impairment (Brewer, 1974; W. R. Miller & Saucedo, 1983), and other indexes of severity of alcohol problems and dependence (Miller, 1983b).

A presumed mechanism underlying the motivational properties of feedback is the establishment of a discrepancy between one's present state and the desired or ideal state, resulting in self-dissatisfaction (Bandura & Cervone, 1983; Finlay, 1966; Gergen, 1969; Kanfer, 1970a). Studying exercise behavior, Bandura and Cervone (1983) found that self-dissatisfaction is predictive of effort expended to reduce discrepancy, but only in the presence of feedback. Richards, Anderson, and Baker (1978) demonstrated that feedback is a key element mediating the reactivity of observational procedures: change in verbal behavior resulting from observation occurred only in the presence of feedback. Feedback need not be accurate in order to modify behavior (Nelson & Hayes, 1981).

Kristenson (1983) studied the effects of a simple motivational feedback intervention in a sample of Swedish men who were identified during routine health screening as showing abnormal elevations on a blood test sensitive to alcohol-related liver damage. A subgroup was selected at random to receive an intervention including feedback of the results of the blood test and advice to alter drinking habits. Five years after intervention, the group receiving feedback and advice showed significantly reduced sick days, absence from work, and rates of hospitalization and mortality.

One particularly salient type of feedback that has been used as a motivational intervention with alcoholics is videotape self-confrontation (VSC). In the typical VSC procedure, the client is filmed during a period of peak inebriety, either during routine detoxification (S. D. Thomas & Lowe, 1978) or experimentally induced intoxication (Paredes, Ludwig, Hassenfeld, & Cornelison, 1969). The client then views this tape on a later day while sober, reviewing it with the therapist with the intent that this experience will increase motivation for treatment (S. D. Thomas & Lowe, 1978). In clinical reports, the emotional impact has consistently been described to be substantial; VSC resulted in negative self-perception, decreased self-esteem, distress, depression, and decreased denial of problems (Bailey & Sowder, 1970; Baker, Udin, & Vogler, 1975; Faia & Shean, 1976; Feinstein & Tamerin, 1972; Paredes et al., 1969, 1971). Weiss and Summers (1983) reported similar negative affect resulting from VSC by distressed couples before marital therapy. The effect appears to be one of broadening the discrepancy between observed self and ideal self (Bailey & Sowder, 1970). Rothbaum, Weisz, and Snyder (1982) provided a general review of research on self-observation, suggesting that when a negative image is perceived, self-esteem and perceived choice are decreased and submissiveness is increased. Videotape feedback of positive behavior, in contrast, can increase self-esteem and decrease anxiety and self/ideal discrepancy (cf. Boyd & Sisney, 1967; Gergen, 1969; Hosford, Moss, & Morrell, 1976). This suggests two possible uses of feedback: initial feedback of negative information to instill motivation for change and later feedback of positive improvement information to consolidate change.

The effects of VSC in alcoholism treatment have been evaluated in several studies. The typical result has been proximal dropout and relapse to drinking (Faia & Shean, 1976; Feinstein & Tamerin, 1972). Schaefer, Sobell, and Mills (1971) found that 100% of alcoholics exposed to VSC relapsed (vs. 83% and 75% in two randomly assigned control groups), and that there was also a tendency toward more rapid relapse among VSC subjects. Dropout from the VSC group was also high (56%) relative to the same treatment without VSC (10%). At 12 months, the groups receiving VSC had begun to show more frequent use of treatment resources, and the authors interpreted this as a delayed motivational effect (Schaefer, Sobell, & Sobell, 1972), although no statistically significant differences in outcome were found. Baker et al. (1975) reported greater improvement in a VSC group at 6 weeks relative to three comparison groups, but this difference had disappeared by 6 months. The effect of VSC appears to be brief and transitory and consists primarily of the induction of a self/ideal discrepancy with accompanying negative affect. It is noteworthy that these effects diminish with repeated VSC viewings, suggesting a desensitization process (Paredes et al., 1971; Weiss & Summers, 1983). The maximal impact, as with advice (Burnum, 1974), appears to be experienced with the first occasion.

Lanyon, Primo, Terrell, and Wener (1972) similarly found no benefit from a VSC intervention with alcoholics, relative to a nonrandom comparison group not receiving VSC. When VSC was combined with training in

systematic desensitization, however, five of eight clients retained abstinence, whereas only one each abstained in the comparison and VSC-only groups. Thus, combining feedback with training in an active coping skill may enhance effectiveness. Providing negative feedback in the absence of such coping skills may prove ineffective or even detrimental (Bandura & Simon, 1977; Buck & Miller, 1984; Schaefer et al., 1971).

Goal Setting

Feedback must be considered in relation to a goal or standard of performance (Kanfer, 1980). Bandura and Cervone (1983) found that feedback in the absence of a provided goal was ineffective in increasing effortful exercise behavior, whereas the combination of goal plus feedback induced marked behavior change. Interestingly, within the feedback-only group those subjects who selected goals for themselves (without being told to do so) showed a 40% behavior change if the goal was demanding and a 27% change if it was more modest, compared with a 0.4% change among those setting no goal. Similarly, Bandura and Simon (1977) found that feedback alone was ineffective as a weight-reduction strategy, resulting in a slight weight gain. The addition of a clear weight goal, however, resulted in significant weight loss.

This is consistent with Buck and Miller's (1984) finding of a slight increase in drinking among those using self-monitoring alone, but a significant reduction among clients using self-monitoring plus a behavioral self-control program in which the first step is goal setting (Miller & Muñoz, 1982). Feedback alone had little impact, although subjects undergoing this program frequently reported in retrospect that feedback was the most important element of the intervention (cf. Glasgow, Klesges, Godding, & Gegelman, 1983).

Goal setting has been found to produce robust effects on performance across a broad range of behavior domains (Locke, Shaw, Saari, & Latham, 1981). The motivational impact of goals seems to be optimal when they are specific rather than vague, more demanding rather than easy, and are perceived as attainable (Latham & Baldes, 1975; Locke et al., 1981). Goals are also clearly more likely to influence behavior when they are accompanied by feedback (Bandura, 1982b; Bandura & Cervone, 1983; Kolb, Winter, & Berlew, 1968; Locke et al., 1981; P. M. Miller, Hersen, & Eisler, 1974). Intrinsic motivation (Deci, 1975) and self-efficacy may be enhanced by the setting of proximal and attainable goals rather than distal ones, even though the long-term objective remains the same (Bandura & Schunk, 1981; Miller & Muñoz, 1982).

Thus, goals and feedback appear to enhance each other as motivational interventions. Feedback regarding present negative state may induce a discrepancy and an intention to change. Progress toward a clear goal then proceeds, influenced and reinforced by continuing feedback regarding the remaining degree of discrepancy (Kanfer, 1970b).

Role Playing and Modeling

Role-playing interventions have been used to enhance goal commitment. Janis and Mann (1965) attempted to induce fear regarding the negative consequences of smoking by having subjects play the role of a patient informed of terminal lung cancer. The subjects were encouraged to express aloud their worries, thoughts, and feelings about having cancer and the effects of smoking. At 2-week follow-up, 10 of 14 experimental subjects showed reduction of smoking ($M = 10.5$ fewer cigarettes per day) as compared with 5 of 12 controls who had heard a tape-recorded role play ($M = 4.8$ cigarette reduction). At 18-month follow-up, Mann and Janis (1968) reported that the difference in reduction between groups remained significant, although modest in absolute terms. Two interesting parallels to videotape self-confrontation are noteworthy: The role play resulted in a high level of distress, and the maximal impact appears to have been proximal to the role play. The impact of role play on additive behaviors, however, appears to be small, and has proved difficult to replicate. Mausner and Platt (1971), for example, failed to find smoking reductions among role-play "patients," although subjects playing the role of the doctor or an observer did evidence modest decrements in smoking.

One explanation of a motivational effect of role-play behavior is that it induces dissonance or discrepancy between present and ideal behavior (Fishbein & Ajzen, 1975). Relatedly, self-observation theory (Kopel & Arkowitz, 1975) hypothesizes a synergistic effect of performing discrepant behavior and observing oneself doing so, such that in the absence of obvious extrinsic motivation the new behavior is attributed to intrinsic motivation. Leventhal (1971) found that even imaginal rehearsal of a new health-related behavior increases the probability of performing the action. This is consistent with the larger literature on counterattitudinal role play (Zimbardo, 1969) and may account for the reported beneficial effects of being a recovering model for others (Alcoholics Anonymous, 1955; Christensen, Miller, & Muñoz, 1978; Slaughter & Torno, 1968).

The effects of being exposed to appropriate models have been evaluated less frequently within the addictive behaviors. S. D. Thomas and Lowe (1978) described a motivational intervention package, including meetings between prospective treatment candidates and patients already involved in treatment, but provided no outcome data. Discussing therapy in general, Goldstein (1980; Goldstein, Heller, & Sechrest, 1966) has recommended use of videotaped models to create appropriate expectancies regarding treatment and the patient's role in it. That this may be of value in treating addictive behaviors is suggested by studies finding that accurate pretreatment expectations regarding the therapeutic process are associated with continuation in treatment (Corrigan, 1974; Epperson, Bushway, & Warman, 1983; Prochaska & DiClemente, 1982; Trice, 1957). Models may be particularly persuasive when perceived as being similar to the client (Bandura, 1982a).

Maintaining Contact

Some of the most successful motivational interventions reported to date have been relatively simple, involving continuity of contact between client and treatment agent. Tarleton and Tarnower (1960) suggested that personal handwritten letters might be used to enhance therapeutic relationships. Applying this idea within an alcoholism-screening setting, Koumans and Muller (1965) randomly assigned

100 cases either to receive or not to receive a personal follow-up letter expressing concern for the individual's welfare and inviting further consultation. This simple intervention boosted the self-referral rate from 31% to 50%, and those receiving the letter came sooner and were more likely to come sober. The authors concluded that "the inability of alcoholics to accept treatment pertains to traditional referral practices" (Koumans & Muller, 1965, p. 1152). Panepinto and Higgins (1969) reported that subjects assigned a primary care worker who wrote letters when an appointment was missed were much less likely (28%) to drop out of treatment than were control clients (51%) who received no such letters during a baseline period before the procedure was instituted. Nirenberg, Sobell, and Sobell (1980) found that a telephone call or a personal letter expressing interest in the client increased the probability of return following a missed appointment, although a more impersonal letter had no effect.

Similarly, Koumans, Muller, and Miller (1967) randomly assigned 100 clients to receive or not receive a follow-up telephone call after an initial visit. Of those called, 44% returned for treatment within 1 week, whereas only 8% of the uncalled group returned. Intagliata (1976) found that a group of posttreatment patients assigned at random to receive or not receive six telephone contacts over 10 weeks differed in their participation in after-care activities. Those called showed significantly more use of outpatient services, which in turn was associated with better maintenance of abstinence (cf. Catanzaro & Green, 1970). Wedel (1965) found that continuation in treatment was significantly increased in an experimental group receiving personal letters and telephone calls when an appointment was missed. However, this intervention had no long-term effect on treatment outcome relative to a control group.

Other minimal continuity procedures may increase compliance. Kogan (1957) reported that referrals were more likely to be completed when the counselor took initiative for placing the referral call (82%) than when this responsibility was left to the client (37%). Gerrein, Rosenberg, and Manohar (1973) found that an increase in frequency of counseling contact from once to twice weekly improved the chances of remaining in treatment for 8 weeks from 39% to 85%, and continuous abstinence (8 weeks) was more frequent in the twice-weekly group. Panepinto, Galanter, Bender, and Strochlic (1980) found that 15 hr of orientation to outpatient after-care, when given to inpatients, increased after-care attendance to 71% relative to 53% in the year before orientation was instituted. Two experimental evaluations of brief orientation meetings for outpatients, however, found no significant increase in attendance at subsequent sessions (Gallant, Bishop, Stoy, Faulkner, & Paternostro, 1966; Olkin & Lemle, 1984).

Another issue of continuity of care involves waiting lists. It has been suggested that asking clients to wait before treatment decreases motivation (Chafetz, 1961; Davis & Ditman, 1963; Kanfer & Grimm, 1980). Two studies have confirmed this, finding a negative relation between the length of time a caller is asked to wait and the probability of returning for treatment (Mayer, Needham, & Myerson, 1965; Wanberg & Jones, 1973). Mayer et al. (1965) found that length of assigned wait was influenced by the client's sex, employment, and legal status, but that the length of wait alone predicted probability of return, whereas these demographic variables did not. Buck and Miller (1984) observed that clients receiving treatment after a 10-week wait improved less than did those receiving the same treatment but assigned at random to begin immediately.

Manipulating External Contingencies

It is quite common for individuals seeking alcoholism treatment to report one or more sources of coercion involved in their motivation for change (Lemere et al., 1958; Shaw et al., 1978). The advisability of such external pressure is a source of considerable confusion in the alcoholism field. Whereas the trait model maintains that intrinsic motivation is essential to treatment (Deaton, 1975), constructive-coercion policies are becoming increasingly common in industry and the courts (Greenberger, 1983; Smart, 1974; Trice & Beyer, 1983). Three general conclusions can be drawn at present. First, the mere external initiation of treatment is not associated with favorable compliance. Individuals voluntarily seeking help are more likely to enter and comply with treatment than are those brought or referred by others (Chafetz, Blane, & Hill, 1970; Corrigan, 1974; Kogan, 1957). If, alternatively, the extrinsic pressure includes a contingency such that participating versus not participating has differential consequences, the coerced client may be more likely to enter and comply with treatment (Freedberg & Johnston, 1978; Gallant et al., 1973; Rosenberg & Liftik, 1976), although this is not always the case (Davis & Ditman, 1963). If the contingency is in effect for a limited period of time, compliance characteristically ends at its termination (Rosenberg & Liftik, 1976). Nor is increased compliance that is motivated by extrinsic pressure necessarily reflected in superior outcome (Martinson, 1974). This relates to the third overall conclusion: that coerced versus voluntary clients show approximately equal rates of successful outcome within the same program (Freedberg & Johnston, 1978, 1980; Gallant et al., 1973; Miller, 1978; Sedmak & Dordevic-Bankovic, 1978; Smart, 1974).

Contingencies can be incorporated within an intervention itself. Rosenberg, Gerrein, and Schnell (1978) unsuccessfully attempted to increase treatment participation of alcoholics by dispensing marijuana cigarettes contingent upon attendance. Other strategies have proved more effective. With the drug disulfiram, which induces violent illness if the person later consumes alcohol, compliance is a particular problem (Serebro, 1979). Although clients volunteering to take disulfiram appear to benefit little from receiving it (Aharan et al., 1967; W. R. Miller & Hester, 1980), less voluntary populations are sometimes subjected to coercive contingencies to increase disulfiram-enforced sobriety (Bigelow, Strickler, Liebson, & Griffiths, 1976; Haynes, 1972). In two well-designed studies, Azrin (1976; Azrin, Sisson, Meyers, & Godley, 1982) succeeded in increasing disulfiram compliance (and consequently number of days sober) by collateral monitoring of self-administration within a larger community-reinforcement treatment program. Liebson, Bigelow, and Flamer (1973) likewise suppressed drinking behavior in clients under treatment for heroin addiction by making methadone administration contingent on disulfiram dos-

age. Maintenance of contingency-induced change would be anticipated to be best either when the contingency is ongoing (e.g., threat of job loss; Heyman, 1976, 1978) or when the reinforcing aspects of drinking have been replaced by new reinforcement contingencies (Azrin, 1976; Azrin et al., 1982).

Providing Choice

Another intervention dimension with apparent motivational properties is the degree of choice afforded to clients regarding the goal and mode of treatment. Some programs adhere dogmatically to one intervention mode, providing neither choice among alternative change strategies nor differential matching of clients with optimal approaches (Boscarino, 1980; Bromet, Moos, Wuthmann, & Bliss, 1977). Intrinsic motivation theory (Deci, 1975) would predict that when clients choose (or at least perceive that they have chosen) a particular change strategy they will be more likely to comply with it voluntarily than when perceived choice is low.

The first requirement for perceived choice is the availability of alternatives, a condition not often met within alcoholism-treatment programs (Orford & Hawker, 1974). In reviews of the literature on treatment choice, Costello (1975) and Parker, Winstead, and Willi (1979) concluded that providing clients with a selection of intervention alternatives decreases drop out and resistance, increases compliance, and improves overall effectiveness of the treatment program. Kissin, Platz, and Su (1971), offering patients (on a random basis) one, two, or three treatment choices, found that treatment acceptance and overall success rate increased with the number of choices offered, whereas patient characteristics were poor predictors of compliance and outcome.

Such choices can apply not only to change strategies but to treatment goals as well. Orford and Hawker (1974) commented that a "decision-making model rests upon the availability of a number of alternative courses of action . . . whilst in practice alcoholism rehabilitation facilities . . . restrict the alternative courses of action to two, stopping altogether or continuing as before" (p. 332). The feasibility of a moderate drinking goal has been well established (Heather & Robertson, 1983; Miller, 1983a; Miller & Hester, 1980) and the choice of treatment goal is a viable and important one (Carroll, 1980; Gottheil, 1978; Miller & Caddy, 1977). Thornton, Gottheil, Gellens, and Alterman (1977) found that patients voluntarily choosing an abstinence goal were more likely to attain it than those required to pursue an abstinence goal. This design, however, was confounded by nonrandom assignment based on problem severity. Lemere et al. (1958) reported that their abstinence-oriented treatment was effective with 68% of those desiring abstinence as a goal and with only 37% of those not wanting abstinence. Sanchez-Craig (1980) found that among clients applying to and eligible for a treatment program including controlled drinking as an option those randomly assigned to a goal of moderation were more likely to comply with an assigned period of abstinence than were those assigned to a goal of permanent abstinence.

From the studies, it appears that clients benefit more when offered a choice among various intervention alternatives, which could also include self-directed versus therapist-administered options (Miller & Hester, 1980).

Decreasing Attractiveness of
Problem Behavior

It has been observed that motivation for change is often highest immediately following a period of acute intoxication, when the negative consequences of drinking are both proximal and salient (Pediaditakis, 1962). Clancy (1964) recommended that interventions that "keep alive in actual or symbolic form the circumstances which initiated the abstinence" (p. 516) would have motivational properties, and Karoly (1980) observed that psychologists have neglected methods for helping clients recognize the adverse consequences of their behavior. Marlatt suggested that positive perceptions and expectancies of substance use during a period of abstinence are likely to increase the probability of relapse (Cummings, Gordon, & Marlatt, 1980; Marlatt & Gordon, 1985).

At present, aversive counterconditioning is the only well-researched intervention for decreasing the attractiveness of a stimulus

(Kanfer, 1980). Aversion therapies have a promising record of success in treating alcohol abuse, although the mechanism for effectiveness is less than clear (Miller & Hester, 1980). Thimann (1968) observed that the long-term effects of chemical aversion therapy resemble an indifference to alcohol, not a conditioned avoidance response. In one of the most successful reports to date on covert sensitization with alcoholics, Elkins (1980) found a relation between the establishment of a conditioned response to alcohol and long-term success. His successful cases included, however, a number of individuals drinking in moderate fashion, an outcome consistent with learned indifference but not with a conditioned-avoidance explanation.

Interventions that decrease the perceived attractiveness and increase the salience and immediacy of negative consequences of a behavior should in theory increase motivation for change. Although relevant data exist (e.g., Janis & Mann, 1968), direct testing of this hypothesis remains for future research.

Nonspecific Determinants of Motivation

Motivational variables and interventions are defined here as those that increase the probability of initiating, complying with, and continuing behaviors intended to promote recovery. The preceding section has focused on specific interventions—specifiable operations with motivational properties. There remain a variety of variables often subsumed under the title nonspecific: characteristics of the client, environment, and therapist that influence the probability of treatment compliance behaviors and thus can be considered motivational. Again, this review focuses primarily on studies of variables relevant to alcoholism treatment.

Client Characteristics

Distress. As noted earlier, when therapists judge the level of a client's motivation, the degree of apparent distress is often an important determinant (Kilpatrick et al., 1978; Wolff, 1968). The relation between measured distress and motivation, however, appears to be complex. Janis and Feshbach (1953) reported that a strong fear induction approach, which succeeded in increasing worry, also was most likely to result in denial strategies such as risk minimizing and ignoring and was less likely to result in an actual increase in positive coping behaviors than a low-fear approach. McArdle (1973) likewise found that high fear was associated with a lower rate of signing up for alcoholism treatment and an undermining of perceived potential benefit from treatment. Baekeland, Lundwall, and Shanahan (1973) found high anxiety to be predictive of rapid dropout from treatment.

Alternatively, Leventhal (1971) reported high fear to be associated with a more positive attitude and intention to change, and Rogers, Deckner, and Mewborn (1978) found high fear to be predictive of sustained abstinence from smoking. High arousal has been associated with perceived inability to cope, need for help, and concern for personal health (Bandura, 1982b; Partington & Johnson, 1969). Individuals may be more influenceable under conditions of psychological distress (Bandura & Rosenthal, 1966), and thus more amenable to setting goals (Pervin, 1983) and accepting treatment (Pediaditakis, 1962).

It appears that client distress is a two-edged sword. Although it may inspire the search for a change strategy, the strategy chosen may be one of fear reduction rather than adaptive behavior change. Rogers (1975) hypothesized that self-efficacy mediates the choice of fear- versus behavior-change strategies.

Self-esteem. The maintenance of self-esteem emerges as one of the most common general goals mentioned by individuals as a motivating factor in their behavior (Pervin, 1983). In an excellent review of determinants of help seeking and help acceptance, Fisher, Nadler, and Whitcher-Alagna (1982) concluded that threat to self-esteem is a reliable predictor of an individual's response to offered aid.

Measured self-esteem has been found to interact in several ways with alcoholism-treatment compliance. Low self-esteem may increase help-seeking and dependent-compliant behavior (Allen, 1969; Blane & Meyers, 1963; Charalampous, Ford, & Skinner, 1976), but poor self-regard can also influence motivation in detrimental ways. Those low in self-esteem respond to threat with a decreased desire for self-protection (Beck & Frankel, 1981). In-

volvement in an active change intervention may be undermined by a desire to avoid failure or disappointment (Mozdzierz & Semyck, 1980; Rothbaum et al., 1982). Leventhal (1970, 1971) reported that low self-esteem is generally associated with a decreased probability of adaptive responding to threat and an increased use of fear-reducing denial strategies. Low self-esteem individuals require a higher degree of extrinsic motivation to sustain effort (Locke et al., 1981). High self-esteem, by contrast, has been found to be associated with an increased probability of adaptive behavior change among drinkers (Carpenter, Lyons, & Miller, 1985). The process of treatment may itself influence self-esteem, inducing positive or negative outcome spirals. Self-esteem is promoted by clear goals and perceived efficacy for achieving them (Seligman, 1975). In contrast, interventions that increase self/ideal discrepancy or encourage perceptions of helplessness and uncontrollability may diminish self-esteem (Canter, 1969; Ends & Page, 1957). Treatment failures may damage self-esteem and self-efficacy and decrease motivation for future change efforts, particularly if the failure is attributed to static qualities of the client (Donovan & O'Leary, 1979; Matkom, 1969; Mindlin, 1964; Mottin, 1973; Thimann, 1968). Richman and Smart (1981) reported that the probability of entering treatment decreases with each subsequent admission to detoxification.

Locus of control. Internal versus external locus of control has been studied extensively among alcoholics. An external orientation is associated with higher anxiety and distress, which may in turn influence motivation for treatment (Donovan & O'Leary, 1979; O'Leary, Donovan, & Hague, 1975). Clients with a more internal orientation may more readily accept and succeed in self-directed and nondirective approaches and be less likely to participate in structured and directive change strategies (Abramowitz, Abramowitz, Roback, & Jackson, 1974; DiClemente & Prochaska, 1982; O'Leary, Rohsenow, & Donovan, 1976; Wallston, Wallston, Kaplan, & Maides, 1976).

Severity. Although it is generally agreed that more severely deteriorated alcoholics have a poorer overall prognosis (Miller & Hester,

1980), current data are less than consistent (Gibbs & Flanagan, 1977). Compliance patterns may account for this in part. Individuals with poorer adjustment and more severe problems have been found to be likely to accept help (Corotto, 1963), but data on remaining in treatment are mixed. Some studies have found that higher problem severity is associated with drop out (Corrigan, 1974), whereas others have found the opposite (Baekeland et al., 1973; Miller, 1978). Orford et al. (1976) found that problem severity interacted with treatment approach such that less impaired drinkers were more likely to benefit from minimal intervention, whereas more impaired individuals showed better outcomes following more structured and extensive treatment. Severity is likely to be confounded with an increased number of prior unsuccessful treatment attempts, which may hinder motivation to participate in further treatment. Impaired health, another common correlate of long-term substance abuse, has been associated with poorer treatment outcomes in alcoholism (Moos, Bromet, Tso, & Moos, 1979) and smoking (Hansen, 1983). Perceived severity of problem may be more crucial to motivation for treatment than is actual symptom severity (Rogers, 1975; Rogers & Mewborn, 1976). Hingson et al. (1982) reported that clients' perceptions of negative consequences of their own drinking were significant correlates of help seeking.

Conceptual level. Research on conceptual level likewise suggests that a client's motivation level cannot be assessed in general but must be considered in relation to the particular treatment being offered. Conceptual level (CL) is a measure of interpersonal development: low CL is associated with cognitive simplicity, dependence on authority, and concern with rules; high CL is characterized by cognitive complexity and independence or interdependence. Studying the interaction of client CL with method of alcoholism treatment, McLachlan (1972, 1974) found no main effect of either treatment approach (nondirective vs. directive) or client CL, but a significant interaction emerged. Alcoholics well matched to treatment (low CL in directive and high CL in nondirective) differed from those mismatched (low CL in nondirec-

tive and high CL in directive) in rate of recovery as well as in subjective measures of satisfaction and benefit from treatment. Canter (1971) found authoritarianism to be associated with preference for structured versus unstructured therapy. Alcoholics Anonymous (1955), a low-CL, rule-oriented system, has been found to be most attractive and successful with clients high in authoritarianism, field dependence, and affiliative and dependency needs but lower in education (Canter, 1966; Ditman, Crawford, Forgy, Moskowitz, & MacAndrew, 1967; Ogborne & Glaser, 1981; Trice & Roman, 1970). Locke et al. (1981) reported that individuals high in need for achievement fare better in work settings when they set their own goals, whereas low-achievement individuals function better when goals are set for them.

Environmental Characteristics

Client traits account for only a small proportion of the variance in treatment compliance and outcome, and investigators have also looked to situational determinants of motivation. Both Mayer et al. (1965) and Wanberg and Jones (1973) found that treatment entry was predictable from the amount of time the client was asked to wait before consultation, whereas client attributes were not predictive of contact. Similarly Gallant et al. (1966) found that individuals who were given intake interviews within 48 hr of their initial contact with an alcoholism clinic were significantly more likely to keep their appointments than individuals asked to wait longer for intake. Prue, Keane, Cornell, and Foy (1979) found that whereas client differences were unhelpful in differentiation, attendance at after-care meetings could be predicted from the distance a client had to travel to attend. Bigelow et al. (1976) suggested that "motivation may be characteristic of environmental contingencies rather than of individuals" (p. 378). Social support variables have been found to influence the probability of entering, continuing, and succeeding in certain types of treatment (Adamson et al., 1974; Adinolfi, DiDario, & Kelso, 1981; Finlay, 1977; Moos et al., 1979; Strug & Hyman, 1981; Trice, 1957).

Therapist Characteristics

Perhaps the most underestimated and least investigated determinants of motivation (at least within the additive behaviors) are therapist characteristics (Goldstein, 1980; Hoff, 1957; Pattison, 1966; Shaw et al., 1978). Cartwright (1981) averred: "The repeated failure of studies . . . to find differences between experimental group and control group has usually been interpreted to indicate that treatments are themselves ineffective, and that patient characteristics are the most important determinant of outcome in the treatment of alcoholism. Few researchers considered the alternative . . . that it is not the patient's characteristics which are of key importance, but factors concerned with the therapeutic perspective" (pp. 351–353).

An early clue as to the importance of therapist behavior lay in studies of drop out from alcoholism treatment. With great consistency, such studies reported that client characteristics differentiated minimally between those leaving versus those remaining in treatment, but that dropouts were disproportionately distributed among staff with whom clients had had contact (Greenwald & Bartmeier, 1963; Raynes & Patch, 1971; Rosenberg, Gerrein, Manohar, & Liftik, 1976; Rosenberg & Raynes, 1973). Greenwald and Bartmeier (1963) found that supervisor ratings of therapeutic effectiveness were significantly correlated ($r = .65$) with rate of irregular discharge, although it is unclear whether the ratings were contaminated by knowledge of dropouts. Schorer (1965) found no difference in supervisor ratings of doctors with no irregular discharges versus those with the highest rates of dropout, but personality variables did differentiate these two groups. Doctors with high client-attrition rates scored higher on need for abasement, achievement, and aggression, whereas low-attrition doctors peaked on deference, introspection, and nurturance needs. Those successful in retaining patients also showed stronger resemblance to "psychiatrist" and "minister" profiles on the Strong Vocational Interest Blank. Davies (1979, 1981) studied therapist behavior during early sessions of alcoholism treatment and suggested that these are important determi-

nants of client motivation (cf. Sapir, 1953). Three specific therapist attributes—hostility, expectancy, and empathy—are considered.

Hostility. The detrimental impact of therapist hostility and moralizing has been recognized for decades (Mann, 1950; Selzer, 1957). In studying the attributes of encounter group leaders, Lieberman, Yalom, and Miles (1973) found that treatment casualties were differentially associated with therapists adopting a hostile–confrontational style, and that survivors of such groups had coped via withdrawal, lower involvement, and distancing. A confrontational style (not uncommon in alcoholism treatment) may also elicit reactance and resistance from clients (Jacobs, 1981; W. R. Miller, 1983b; Parker et al., 1979).

Selzer (1957) commented that hostility is not always overt, but may be unconscious and unintentional. That this may be so was illustrated by Milmoe et al. (1967), who interviewed nine doctors about their experiences wtih alcoholics and then compared coded interview data with treatment success rates of each physician. Verbal content of interviews (coded from transcripts) bore no relation to outcome, nor did coders' ratings of audiotapes. However, when the taped speech was passed through a filter to obscure content and leave only verbal tone, coders' ratings of anger in the voice predicted treatment success ($r = .65$).

Expectancy. Motivation and outcome can be affected by the therapist's view of a client and the prognosis (Parker et al., 1979). In an analogue study unrelated to alcoholism E. Thomas, Polansky, and Kounin (1955) found that client perception of the therapist wanting to help increased commitment to continue treatment and willingness to be influenced. Leake and King (1977), in a study reviewed earlier, reported that random designation of certain clients as good prognosis cases influenced counselor views of those clients and their subsequent outcome. Gunne (1958), summarizing eight studies of procedures for treating delirium tremens, noted that the implementation of any new technique resulted in a drop in mortality rate regardless of content of the old (average 10% mortality; range: 5% to 32%) and new methods (average 2% mortality; range: 0 to 5%). Gunne suggested that the decreased fatality rate might be attributable to increased interest and enthusiasm from personnel rather than from specific effects of these diverse procedures.

Empathy. A crucial aspect of therapist deportment in alcoholism treatment has been variously described as respect (Chavigny, 1976), warmth (Chafetz, 1959), sympathetic understanding (Mann, 1950), supportiveness (Malcolm, 1968), caring, concern, commitment, and active interest (Swenson, 1971). The term *empathy* is used here because it has been operationally defined by Rogers and his students (Truax & Carkhuff, 1967) and because empathy is often an intended goal and outcome in counselor training (Manohar, 1973; W. R. Miller, Hedrick, & Orlofsky, 1983; Wehmer, Cooke, & Gruber, 1974). Care must be taken, however, to specify the phenomenon being considered. Stewart (1954), for example, described an empathy intervention for alcoholics and included transcripts of interviews in which therapist responses would be rated as *poor* in empathy according to the Truax and Carkhuff (1967) system.

Several studies provide data relevant to the importance of empathy in motivation and treatment of alcoholics. Chafetz (1961; Chafetz et al., 1962) observed that of over 1,200 emergency room patients diagnosed as alcoholic each year fewer than 1% had sought treatment. A motivational intervention was devised by which a primary care team undertook a more thorough evaluation of the patient, attempting to communicate respect and consideration and a desire to help. The control condition was standard emergency-room advice, and 200 patients were assigned at random to receive motivational versus standard intervention. Of the 100 controls, 5 made an initial outpatient visit but only 1 made more than four visits. By contrast, 65 of the motivated patients made an initial visit, and 42 of these continued beyond four sessions. A replication with 100 patients (Chafetz, 1968b; Chafetz et al., 1964) found that 39 of 50 patients who received the motivational intervention initiated treatment, and 28 had more than four visits, whereas 3 initiated treatment, and none followed through among the controls. In three further uncontrolled replications with correctional samples, about half of the subjects became involved in treatment following supportive interviewing (Demone, 1963). These findings are consistent with one more general conclusion of Locke et al. (1981): that a supportive style increases goal acceptance and the setting of more challenging goals (cf. Erez & Kanfer, 1983).

Ends and Page (1957) assigned 16 groups of six patients each to receive one of four interventions: client-centered therapy, psychoanalytic psychotherapy, a learning-based discussion group, and a social discussion control condition. All were equated for length at 15 sessions over 5 weeks. The highest percentage of improvement with regard to drinking was observed in the client-centered condition, which also showed increased self-acceptance.

Valle (1981) assigned alcoholics at random to eight counselors differing on levels of interpersonal functioning, including empathy as defined by Truax and Carkhuff (1967). Ratings of therapist skill were based on written responses to simulated client statements on a paper and pencil test. Valle found that level of therapist skill was predictive of the rate and number of client relapses at 6, 12, 18, and 24 months following treatment.

Finally, in a study of behavioral self-control training (W. R. Miller et al., 1980), three supervisors rank ordered nine therapists on the degree of empathy shown in sessions. Ratings were independent and based on observation of therapy via one-way mirrors, using the Truax and Carkhuff (1967) definition of accurate empathy. Ratings were completed without knowledge of client outcome. At 6-month follow-up, therapist empathy was predictive of percentage of the therapist's cases rated as successful according to objective data collected by an independent assessment team ($r = .82$). At later follow-up (Miller & Baca, 1983), this relation remained but had diminished by 12 months ($r = .71$) and 24 months after treatment ($r = .51$). This is consistent with Ford's (1978) report that therapeutic relation variables predict immediate gains following behavior therapy, but are less predictive of long-term maintenance of gains. Nevertheless, therapist empathy accounted for more variance than did differences in amount and content of treatment (Miller et al., 1980). Empathy may, in turn, interact with other therapist characteristics. Low-empathy therapists tend to confront client weaknesses and pathology, whereas high-empathy therapists are more likely to focus on discrepancies, objective feedback, and client strengths (Truax & Mitchell, 1971). Manohar (1973) found that counselors who were themselves recovering alcoholics and who had had less than 12 months of sobriety showed lower levels of nonpossessive warmth after training and were less able to detach themselves, more likely to become overinvested in patient behavior and choices. Studying trainees for community crisis-intervention services, Miller et al. (1983) found that posttraining degree of improvement in empathic communication was directly related to the counselor's pretraining level of self-esteem; low self-esteem trainees showed less acquisition and lower levels of empathy.

Conclusions

Trait models viewing motivation as a client attribute have not improved our ability to predict or influence compliance, but rather have favored moralistic blame attributions when treatment fails. When motivation is conceptualized as a probability of behavior occurring within an interpersonal context, however, psychological interventions can be developed and evaluated for increasing the likelihood of entering, continuing in, and complying with recovery-relevant actions.

Several types of interventions show promise in augmenting motivation for change. Clear advice to change (particularly when accompanied by recommended strategies for how to change) appears to be superior to no advice, but advice alone is insufficient for modifying addictive behaviors in the majority of cases. Successful advice interventions have incorporated additional motivational strategies such as feedback and goal setting. Interventions that increase discrepancy—including feedback of adverse consequences, self-confrontation, and role playing—can elevate client distress. In the absence of goals

and apparent efficacious responses, however, such distress may trigger avoidant fear-reducing strategies (denial) instead of adaptive behavior change (Leventhal, 1970, 1971; Rogers & Mewborn, 1976). The setting of specific and demanding but attainable goals has a facilitating effect on behavior, particularly when supplemented by feedback. Simple therapist initiations in maintaining contact, such as letters and telephone calls, have been shown to increase treatment participation. Compliance can be encouraged via operant contingencies at least while consequences remain in effect, although the undermining of intrinsic motivation is a risk (Deci, 1975; Kopel & Arkowitz, 1975). Providing apparent voluntary choices, alternatively, can enhance intrinsic motivation and has been found to improve compliance and outcome. Finally, respondent procedures that decrease attractiveness of the problem behavior may amplify motivation for change. Here motivational strategies begin to blend with direct behavioral intervention.

Client characteristics appear to play a modest and inconsistent role in predicting treatment participation and adherence. Distress, low self-esteem, locus of control, and problem severity seem to activate offsetting influences, both encouraging and discouraging adaptive changes. Matching of intervention to client characteristics such as severity and conceptual level may improve motivation and outcome.

Environmental and therapist attributes have been greatly underestimated and underinvestigated as determinants of motivation. Accessibility and social support encourage change and persistence. Therapist characteristics such as hostility, expectancy, and empathy powerfully influence whether a client will enter, continue, comply with, and succeed in treatment.

An enduring conceptual problem is the separation of motivation from treatment outcome. Both are defined in reference to observable behavior change. Motivation has been conceived here as the probability of engaging in behaviors that are intended to lead to positive outcomes. This conception of motivation is proximal to traditional operational definitions of behavioral self-control as the performance of controlling responses to alter other (controlled) responses (Kanfer, 1970b). This review has focused primarily on variables and operations that influence the probability of performing controlling responses. Nevertheless, it must be recognized, in discussing the controlling of controlling responses to control controlled responses, that one necessarily encounters nested chains of behaviors, that common processes influence the occurrence of both controlling and controlled behaviors, and that the distinctions between controlling and controlled responses blur at times.

The reconceptualization of motivation for treatment as a dynamic interpersonal process involving therapist and environmental as well as client determinants is an optimistic one. In this view, one is encouraged to seek interventions for influencing the motivation that was once hopelessly and helplessly attributed to intrapsychic determinism. The data to date provide encouraging evidence that entry, continuation, and compliance are behaviors highly influenced by what the therapist does during the early phases of treatment. There is still much to be learned, but promising progress has been made to begin redressing the error of omission noted by Dean (1958) in the *American Psychologist* more than a quarter century ago:

Graduate schools do not offer courses on the treatment of the reluctant client, probably because little study has gone into the problem. Psychotherapy proceeds from the assumption of a motivated client; instructors may point out that some cases will require extra effort to motivate. But what are the techniques most likely to produce motivation in what kinds of reluctant client? (p. 630)

References

Abramowitz, C. V., Abramowitz, S. F., Roback, H. B., & Jackson, C. (1974). Differential effectiveness of directive and nondirective group therapies as a function of client internal-external control. *Journal of Consulting and Clinical Psychology, 42*, 849–853.

Adamson, J. D., Fostakowsky, R. T., & Chebib, F. S. (1974). Measures associated with outcome on one year follow-up of male alcoholics. *British Journal of Addiction, 69*, 325–337.

Adinolfi, A. A., DiDario, B., & Kelso, F. W. (1981). The relationship between drinking patterns at therapy termination and intake and termination status on social variables: A replication study. *International Journal of the Addictions, 16*, 555–565.

Aharan, C. H., Ogilvie, R. D., & Partington, J. T. (1967).

Clinical indications of motivation in alcoholic patients. *Quarterly Journal of Studies on Alcohol, 28*, 486–492.

Alcoholics Anonymous. (1955). *Alcoholics Anonymous: The story of how many thousands of men and women have recovered from alcoholism.* (rev. ed.) New York: Author.

Allen, L. R. (1969). Self-esteem of male alcoholics. *Psychological Record, 19*, 381–389.

Appelbaum, A. (1972). A critical re-examination of the concept of "motivation for change" in psychoanalytic treatment. *International Journal of Psychoanalysis, 53*, 51–59.

Azrin, N. H. (1976). Improvements in the community-reinforcement approach to alcoholism. *Behaviour Research and Therapy, 14*, 339–348.

Azrin, N. H., Sisson, R. W., Meyers, R., & Godley, M. (1982). Alcoholism treatment by disulfiram and community reinforcement therapy. *Journal of Behavior Therapy and Experimental Psychiatry, 13*, 105–112.

Babow, I. (1975). The treatment monopoly in alcoholism and drug dependence: A sociological critique. *Journal of Drug Issues, 5*, 120–128.

Baekeland, F., Lundwall, L., & Shanahan, T. J. (1973). Correlates of patient attrition in the outpatient treatment of alcoholism. *Journal of Nervous and Mental Disease, 157*, 99–107.

Bailey, K. G., & Sowder, W. T. (1970). Audiotape and videotape self-confrontation in psychotherapy. *Psychological Bulletin, 74*, 127–137.

Baker, T. B., Udin, H., & Vogler, R. E. (1975). The effects of videotaped modeling and self-confrontation on the drinking behavior of alcoholics. *International Journal of the Addictions, 10*, 779–793.

Bandura, A. (1982a). The self and mechanisms of agency. In J. Suls (Ed.), *Psychological perspectives on the self* (pp. 3–39). New York: Erlbaum.

Bandura, A. (1982b). Self-efficacy mechanism in human agency. *American Psychologist, 37*, 122–147.

Bandura, A., & Cervone, D. (1983). Self-evaluative and self-efficacy mechanisms governing the motivational effects of goal systems. *Journal of Personality and Social Psychology, 45*, 1017–1028.

Bandura, A., & Rosenthal, T. L. (1966). Vicarious classical conditioning as a function of arousal level. *Journal of Personality and Social Psychology, 3*, 54–62.

Bandura, A., & Schunk, D. H. (1981). Cultivating competence, self-efficacy, and intrinsic interest through proximal self-motivation. *Journal of Personality and Social Psychology, 41*, 586–598.

Bandura, A., & Simon, K. M. (1977). The role of proximal intentions in self-regulation of refractory behavior. *Cognitive Research and Therapy, 1*, 177–193.

Bateson, G. (1971). The cybernetics of "self": A theory of alcoholism. *Psychiatry, 34*, 1–18.

Baumann, D. J., Obitz, F. W., & Reich, J. W. (1982). Attribution theory: A fit with substance abuse problems. *International Journal of the Addictions, 17*, 295–303.

Beck, K. H., & Frankel, A. (1981). A conceptualization of threat communications and protective health behavior. *Social Psychology Quarterly, 44*, 204–217.

Beckman, L. J. (1980). An attributional analysis of Alcoholics Anonymous. *Journal of Studies on Alcohol, 41*, 714–726.

Bell, A. H., Weingold, H. P., & Lachin, J. M. (1969).

Measuring adjustment in patients disabled with alcoholism. *Quarterly Journal of Studies on Alcohol, 30,* 634–639.

Bigelow, G., Strickler, D., Liebson, I., & Griffiths, R. (1976). Maintaining disulfiram ingestion among outpatient alcoholics: A security-deposit contingency contracting procedure. *Behaviour Research and Therapy, 14,* 378–381.

Blane, H. T. (1968). *The personality of the alcoholic.* New York: Harper & Row.

Blane, H. T., & Meyers, W. R. (1963). Behavioral dependence and length of stay in psychotherapy among alcoholics. *Quarterly Journal of Studies on Alcohol, 24,* 503–510.

Boscarino, J. (1980). AA ideology among alcohol treatment directors. *British Journal of Addiction, 75,* 65–71.

Boyd, H. S., & Sisney, V. V. (1967). Immediate confrontation and changes in self-concept. *Journal of Consulting Psychology, 31,* 291–294.

Brewer, C. (1974). Alcoholic brain damage: Implications for sentencing policy. *Medical Science and the Law, 14,* 40–43.

Bromet, E., Moos, R., Wuthmann, C., & Bliss, F. (1977). Treatment experiences of alcoholic patients: An analysis of five residential alcoholism programs. *International Journal of the Addictions, 12,* 953–958.

Brunner-Orne, M. (1959). Ward group sessions with hospitalized alcoholics as motivation for psychotherapy. *International Journal of Group Psychotherapy, 9,* 219–224.

Buck, K., & Miller, W. R. (1984). *Behavioral self-control training for problem drinkers: Components of effectiveness.* Manuscript submitted for publication.

Burnum, J. F. (1974). Outlook for treating patients with self-destructive habits. *Annals of Internal Medicine, 81,* 387–393.

Canter, F. M. (1966). Personality factors related to participation in treatment of hospitalized male alcoholics. *Journal of Clinical Psychology, 22,* 114–116.

Canter, F. M. (1969). A self-help project with hospitalized alcoholics. *International Journal of Group Psychotherapy, 19,* 16–27.

Canter, F. M. (1971). Authoritarian attitudes, degree of pathology and preference for structured versus unstructured psychotherapy in hospitalized mental patients. *Psychological Reports, 28,* 231–234.

Carpenter, R. A., Lyons, C. A., & Miller, W. R. (1985). Peer-managed self-control program for prevention of alcohol abuse in American Indian high school students: A pilot evaluation study. *International Journal of the Addictions, 20,* 303–314.

Carroll, J. F. X. (1980). Does sobriety and self-fulfilment always necessitate total and permanent abstinence? *British Journal of Addiction, 75,* 55–63.

Cartwright, A. K. J. (1981). Are different therapeutic perspectives important in the treatment of alcoholism? *British Journal of Addiction, 76,* 347–361.

Catanzaro, R. J., & Green, W. G. (1970). WATS telephone therapy: New follow-up technique for alcoholics. *American Journal of Psychiatry, 126,* 1024–1027.

Cavaiola, A. A. (1984). Resistance issues in the treatment of the DWI offender. *Alcoholism Treatment Quarterly, 1,* 87–100.

Chafetz, M. E. (1959). Practical and theoretical considerations in the psychotherapy of alcoholism. *Quarterly Journal of Studies on Alcohol, 20,* 281–291.

Chafetz, M. E. (1961). A procedure for establishing therapeutic contact with the alcoholic. *Quarterly Journal of Studies on Alcohol, 22,* 325–328.

Chafetz, M. E. (1968a). The past revisited. *International Journal of Psychiatry, 5,* 47–48.

Chafetz, M. E. (1968b). Research in the alcohol clinic an around-the-clock psychiatric service of the Massachusetts General Hospital. *American Journal of Psychiatry, 124,* 1674–1679.

Chafetz, M. E., Blane, H. T., Abram, H. S., Clark, E., Golner, J. H., Hastie, E. I., & McCourt, W. F. (1964). Establishing treatment relations with alcoholics: A supplementary report. *Journal of Nervous and Mental Disease, 138,* 390–393.

Chafetz, M. E., Blane, H. T., Abram, H. S., Golner, J., Lacy, E., McCourt, W. F., Clark, E., & Meyers, W. (1962). Establishing treatment relations with alcoholics. *Journal of Nervous and Mental Disease, 134,* 395–409.

Chafetz, M. E., Blane, H. T., & Hill, M. J. (1970). *Frontiers of alcoholism.* New York: Science House.

Charalampous, K. D., Ford, B. K., & Skinner, T. J. (1976). Self-esteem in alcoholics and nonalcoholics. *Journal of Studies on Alcohol, 37,* 990–994.

Chavigny, K. (1976). Self-esteem for the alcoholic: An epidemiologic approach. *Nursing Outlook, 24,* 636–639.

Chess, S. B., Neuringer, C., & Goldstein, G. (1971). Arousal and field dependence in alcoholics. *Journal of General Psychology, 85,* 93–102.

Christensen, A., Miller, W. R., & Muñoz, R. F. (1978). Paraprofessionals, partners, peers, paraphernalia, and print: Expanding mental health service delivery. *Professional Psychology, 9,* 249–270.

Clancy, J. (1961). Procrastination: A defense against sobriety. *Quarterly Journal of Studies on Alcohol, 22,* 269–276.

Clancy, J. (1964). Motivation conflicts of the alcohol addict. *Quarterly Journal of Studies on Alcohol, 25,* 511–520.

Coney, J. C. (1977). *The precipitating factors in the use of alcoholic treatment services: A comparative study of black and white alcoholics.* San Francisco: Rand.

Corotto, L. V. (1963). An exploratory study of the personality characteristics of alcoholic patients who volunteer for continued treatment. *Quarterly Journal of Studies on Alcohol, 24,* 432–442.

Corrigan, E. M. (1974). *Problem drinkers seeking treatment.* New Brunswick, NJ: Rutgers Center of Alcohol Studies.

Costello, R. M. (1975). Alcoholism treatment and evaluation: In search of methods. *International Journal of the Addictions, 10,* 251–275.

Council for Philosophical Studies (1981). *Psychology and the philosophy of mind in the philosophy curriculum.* San Francisco: San Francisco State University.

Cummings, C., Gordon, J. R., & Marlatt, G. A. (1980). Relapse: Prevention and prediction. In W. R. Miller (Ed.), *The addictive behaviors: Treatment of alcoholism, drug abuse, smoking, and obesity.* Oxford, England: Pergamon.

Psychotherapy and the psychology of behavior change. New York: Wiley.

Gottheil, E. (1978). The rationale and range of treatment objectives in alcoholism. *American Journal of Drug and Alcohol Abuse, 5,* 315–320.

Greenberger, R. S. (1983, January 13). Sobering method: Firms are confronting alcoholic executives with threat of firing. *The Wall Street Journal,* pp. 1, 26.

Greenwald, A. F., & Bartmeier, L. H. (1963). Psychiatric discharges against medical advice. *Archives of General Psychiatry, 8,* 117–119.

Gunne, L. M. (1958). Mortaliteten vid delirium tremens. *Nordisk Medicin, 60,* 1021–1024.

Hansen, B. (1983, April). *Relapse among ex-smokers who report smoking-related illness.* Paper presented at the meeting of the Western Psychological Association, San Francisco, CA.

Haynes, S. N. (1972). Contingency management in a municipally administered Antabuse program for alcoholics. *Journal of Behavior Therapy and Experimental Psychiatry, 4,* 31–32.

Heather, N., & Robertson, I. (1983). *Controlled drinking* (rev. ed.). London: Methuen.

Henningsen, N. C., Hood, B., Mattiasson, I., Trell, E. V., & Kristenson, H. (1981). Alcohol and hypertension. *Lancet, 2,* 992–993.

Hertzman, M. (1979). Getting alcoholics out of your office, into treatment, and back to your office. *Primary Care, 6,* 403–416.

Heyman, M. M. (1976). Referral to alcoholism programs in industry: Coercion, confrontation and choice. *Journal of Studies on Alcohol, 37,* 900–907.

Heyman, M. M. (1978). *Alcoholism programs in industry: The patient's view.* New Brunswick, NJ: Rutgers Center of Alcohol Studies.

Hingson, R., Mangione, T., Meyers, A., & Scotch, N. (1982). Seeking help for drinking problems: A study in the Boston metropolitan area. *Journal of Studies on Alcohol, 43,* 273–288.

Hoff, E. C. (1957). Some principles of therapy for alcoholics. In H. E. Himwich (Ed.), *Alcoholism: Basic aspects and treatment* (pp. 181–189). Washington, DC: American Association for the Advancement of Science.

Hoff, E. C. (1974). *Alcoholism: The hidden addiction.* New York: Seabury.

Holser, M. A. (1979). A socialization program for chronic alcoholics. *International Journal of the Addictions, 14,* 657–674.

Holt, W. E. (1967). The concept of motivation for treatment. *American Journal of Psychiatry, 123,* 1388–1394.

Hosford, R. E., Moss, C. S., & Morrell, G. (1976). The self-as-model technique: Helping prison inmates change. In J. D. Krumboltz & C. E. Thoresen (Eds.), *Counseling methods* (pp. 487–495). New York: Holt, Rinehart & Winston.

Intagliata, J. (1976). A telephone follow-up procedure for increasing the effectiveness of a treatment program for alcoholics. *Journal of Studies on Alcohol, 37,* 1330–1335.

Jacobs, M. R. (1981). *Problems presented by alcoholic clients: A handbook of counseling stategies.* Toronto: Addiction Research Foundation.

Janis, I. L., & Feshbach, S. (1953). Effects of fear-arousing communications. *Journal of Abnormal and Social Psychology, 48,* 78–92.

Janis, I. I., & Mann, L. (1968). A conflict-theory approach to attitude change and decision making. In A. G. Greenwald, T. C. Brock, & T. M. Ostrom (Eds.), *Psychological foundations of attitudes* (pp. 327–360). New York: Academic.

Jones, E. E., & Nisbett, R. E. (1972). The actor and the observer: Divergent perceptions of the causes of behavior. In E. E. Jones, D. E. Kanouse, H. H. Kelly, R. E. Nisbett, S. Valins, & B. Weiner (Eds.), *Perceiving the causes of behavior* (pp. 79–94). Morristown, NJ: General Learning.

Jones, R. A. (1977). *Self-fulfilling prophecies: Social, psychological, and physiological effects of expectancies.* Hillsdale, NJ: Erlbaum.

Kanfer, F. H. (1970a). Self-monitoring: Methodological limitations and clinical applications. *Journal of Consulting and Clinical Psychology, 35,* 148–152.

Kanfer, F. H. (1970b). Self-regulation: Research, issues, and speculations. In C. Neuringer & J. L. Michael (Eds.), *Behavior modification in clinical psychology* (pp. 178–220). New York: Appleton-Century-Crofts.

Kanfer, F. H. (1980). Self-management methods. In F. H. Kanfer & A. P. Goldstein (Eds.), *Helping people change* (2nd ed., pp. 334–389). New York: Pergamon.

Kanfer, F. H., & Grimm, L. G. (1980). Managing clinical change: A process model of therapy. *Behavior Modification, 4,* 419–444.

Karoly, P. (1980). Person variables in therapeutic change and development. In P. Karoly & J. J. Steffen (Eds.), *Improving the long-term effects of psychotherapy* (pp. 195–261). New York: Gardner.

Kilpatrick, D. G., Roitzsch, J. C., Best, C. L., McAlhany, D. A., Sturgis, E. T., & Miller, W. C. (1978). Treatment goal preference and problem perception of chronic alcoholics: Behavioral and personality correlates. *Addictive Behaviors, 3,* 107–116.

Kissin, B., Platz, A., & Su, W. H. (1971). Selective factors in treatment choice and outcome in alcoholics. In N. K. Mello & J. H. Mendelson (Eds.), *Recent advances in studies of alcoholism* (pp. 781–802). Washington, DC: U.S. Government Printing Office.

Kogan, L. S. (1957). The short-term case in a family agency: Part II. Results of study. *Social Casework, 38,* 296–302.

Kolb, D. A., Winter, S. K., & Berlew, D. E. (1968). Self-directed change: Two studies. *Journal of Applied Behavioral Science, 4,* 453–471.

Kopel, S., & Arkowitz, H. (1975). The role of attribution and self-perception in behavior change: Implications for behavior therapy. *Genetic Psychology Monographs, 92,* 175–212.

Koumans, A. J. R. (1969). Reaching the unmotivated patient. *Mental Hygiene, 53,* 298–300.

Koumans, A. J. R., & Muller, J. J. (1965). Use of letters to increase motivation in alcoholics. *Psychological Reports, 16,* 1152.

Koumans, A. J. R., Muller, J. J., & Miller, C. F. (1967). Use of telephone calls to increase motivation for treatment in alcoholics. *Psychological Reports, 21,* 327–328.

Kristenson, H. (1983). *Studies on alcohol related dis-*

Davies, P. (1979). Motivation, responsibility and sickness in the psychiatric treatment of alcoholism. *British Journal of Psychiatry, 134,* 449–458.

Davies, P. (1981). Expectations and therapeutic practices in outpatient clinics for alcohol problems. *British Journal of Addiction, 76,* 159–173.

Davis, F. M., & Ditman, K. S. (1963). The effect of court referral and disulfiram on motivation of alcoholics: A preliminary report. *Quarterly Journal of Studies on Alcohol, 24,* 276–279.

Dean, S. I. (1958). Treatment of the reluctant client. *American Psychologist, 13,* 627–630.

Deaton, J. G. (1975). Alcoholism a disease? *Annals of Internal Medicine, 82,* 117–118.

Deci, E. L. (1975). *Intrinsic motivation.* New York: Plenum.

Demone, H. W. (1963). Experiments in referral to alcoholism clinics. *Quarterly Journal of Studies of Alcohol, 24,* 495–502.

DiCicco, L., Unterberger, H., & Mack, J. E. (1978). Confronting denial: An alcoholism intervention strategy. *Psychiatric Annals, 8,* 596–606.

DiClemente, C. A., & Prochaska, J. O. (1982). Self-change and therapy change of smoking behavior: A comparison of processes of change in cessation and maintenance. *Addictive Behaviors, 7,* 133–142.

Ditman, K. S., Crawford, G. D., Forgy, E. W., Moskowitz, H., & MacAndrew, C. (1967). A controlled experiment on the use of court probation for drunk arrests. *American Journal of Psychiatry, 124,* 160–163.

Donovan, D. M., & O'Leary, M. R. (1979). Control orientation among alcoholics: A cognitive social learning perspective. *American Journal of Drug and Alcohol Abuse, 6,* 487–499.

Donovan, D. M., Rohsenow, D. J., Schau, E. J., & O'Leary, M. R. (1977). Defensive style in alcoholics and nonalcoholics. *Journal of Studies on Alcohol, 38,* 465–470.

Edwards, G., Orford, J., Egert, S., Guthrie, S., Hawker, A., Hensman, C., Mitcheson, M., Oppenheimer, E., & Taylor, C. (1977). Alcoholism: A controlled trial of "treatment" and "advice." *Journal of Studies on Alcohol, 38,* 1004–1031.

Elkins, R. L. (1980). Covert sensitization treatment of alcoholism: Contributions of successful conditioning to subsequent abstinence maintenance. *Addictive Behaviors, 5,* 67–89.

Ends, E. J., & Page, C. W. (1957). A study of three types of group psychotherapy with hospitalized male inebriates. *Quarterly Journal of Studies on Alcohol, 18,* 263–277.

Epperson, D. L., Bushway, D. J., & Warman, R. E. (1983). Client self-terminations after one counseling session: Effects of problem recognition, counselor gender, and counselor experience. *Journal of Counseling Psychology, 30,* 307–315.

Erez, M., & Kanfer, F. H. (1983). The role of goal acceptance in goal setting and task performance. *Academy of Management Review, 8,* 454–463.

Faia, C., & Shean, G. (1976). Using videotapes and group discussion in the treatment of male chronic alcoholics. *Hospital and Community Psychiatry, 27,* 847–851.

Feinstein, C., & Tamerin, J. S. (1972). Induced intoxi-
cation and videotape feedback in alcoholism treatment. *Quarterly Journal of Studies on Alcohol, 33,* 408–416.

Finlay, D. G. (1966). Effect of role network pressure on an alcoholic's approach to treatment. *Social Work, 11*(4), 71–77.

Finlay, D. G. (1977). Changing problem drinkers. *Social Work Research and Abstracts, 13*(4), 30–37.

Fishbein, M. (1980). A theory of reasoned action: Some applications and implications. In M. M. Page (Ed.), *Beliefs, attitudes, and values* (pp. 65–116). Lincoln: University of Nebraska Press.

Fishbein, M., & Ajzen, I. (1975). *Belief, attitude, intention, and behavior: An introduction to theory and research.* Reading, MA: Addison-Wesley.

Fisher, J. D., Nadler, A., & Whitcher-Alagna, S. (1982). Recipient reactions to aid. *Psychological Bulletin, 91,* 27–54.

Ford, J. D. (1978). Therapeutic relationship in behavior therapy: An empirical analysis. *Journal of Consulting and Clinical Psychology, 46,* 1302–1314.

Fox, R. (1967). A multidisciplinary approach to the treatment of alcoholism. *American Journal of Psychotherapy, 123,* 769–778.

Freedberg, E. J., & Johnston, W. E. (1978). Effects of various sources of coercion on outcome of treatment of alcoholism. *Psychological Reports, 43,* 1271–1278.

Freedberg, E. J., & Johnston, W. E. (1980). Outcome with alcoholics seeking treatment voluntarily or after confrontation by their employer. *Journal of Occupational Medicine, 22,* 83–86.

Gallant, D. M., Bishop, M. P., Mouledoux, A., Faulkner, M. A., Brisolara, A., & Swanson, W. A. (1973). The revolving door alcoholic. *Archives of General Psychiatry, 28,* 633–635.

Gallant, D. M., Bishop, M. P., Stoy, B., Faulkner, M. A., & Paternostro, L. (1966). The value of a "first contact" group intake session in an alcoholism outpatient clinic: Statistical confirmation. *Psychosomatics, 7,* 349–352.

Gergen, K. J. (1969). Self theory and the process of self-observation. *Journal of Nervous and Mental Disease, 148,* 437–448.

Gerrein, J. R., Rosenberg, C. M., & Manohar, V. (1973). Disulfiram maintenance in outpatient treatment of alcoholism. *Archives of General Psychiatry, 28,* 798–802.

Gibbs, L., & Flanagan, J. (1977). Prognostic indicators of alcoholism treatment outcome. *International Journal of the Addictions, 12,* 1097–1141.

Gillis, L. S., & Keet, M. (1969). Prognostic factors and treatment results in hospitalized alcoholics. *Quarterly Journal of Studies on Alcohol, 30,* 426–437.

Glasgow, R. E., Klesges, R. C., Godding, P. R., & Gegelman, R. (1983). Controlled smoking with or without carbon monoxide feedback as an alternative for chronic smokers. *Behavior Therapy, 14,* 386–397.

Glasgow, R. E., & Rosen, G. M. (1978). Behavioral bibliotherapy: A review of self-help behavior therapy manuals. *Psychological Bulletin, 85,* 1–23.

Goldstein, A. P. (1980). Relationship-enhancement methods. In F. H. Kanfer & A. P. Goldstein (Eds.), *Helping people change* (pp. 18–57). New York: Pergamon.

Goldstein, A. P., Heller, K., & Sechrest, L. B. (1966).

abilities in a medical intervention (2nd ed.). Malmo, Sweden: University of Lund.

Landeen, R. H. (1979). Will power and denial, clinical findings about these pervasive concepts. In M. Galanter (Ed.), *Currents in alcoholism* (Vol. 5, pp. 301–307). New York: Grune & Stratton.

Lanyon, R. I., Primo, R. V., Terrell, F., & Wener, A. (1972). An aversion-desensitization treatment for alcoholism. *Journal of Consulting and Clinical Psychology, 38,* 394–398.

Latham, G. P., & Baldes. J. J. (1975). The "practical significance" of Locke's theory of goal setting. *Journal of Applied Psychology, 60,* 122–124.

Leake, G. J., & King. A. S. (1977). Effect of counselor expectations on alcoholic recovery. *Alcohol Health and Research World, 11*(3), 16–22.

Lemere, F., O'Hollaren, P., & Maxwell, M. A. (1958). Motivation in the treatment of alcoholism. *Quarterly Journal of Studies on Alcohol, 19,* 428–431.

Leventhal, H. (1970). Findings and theory in the study of fear communications. *Advances in Experimental Social Psychology, 5,* 119–186.

Leventhal, H. (1971). Fear appeals and persuasion: The differentiation of a motivational construct. *American Journal of Public Health, 61,* 1208–1224.

Lieberman, M. A., Yalom, I. D., & Miles, M. B. (1973). *Encounter groups: First facts.* New York: Basic.

Liebson, I., Bigelow, G., & Flamer, R. (1973). Alcoholism among methadone patients: A specific treatment method. *American Journal of Psychiatry, 130,* 483–485.

Locke, E. A., Shaw, K. N., Saari, L. M., & Latham, G. P. (1981). Goal setting and task performance: 1969–1980. *Psychological Bulletin, 90,* 125–152.

Malcolm, A. I. (1968). On the psychotherapy of alcoholism. *Addictions, 15*(1), 25–40.

Mann, L., & Janis, I. L. (1968). A follow-up study on the long-term effects of emotional role playing. *Journal of Personality and Social Psychology, 8,* 339–342.

Mann, M. (1950). *Primer on alcoholism.* New York: Rinehart.

Manohar, V. (1973). Training volunteers as alcoholism treatment counselors. *Quarterly Journal of Studies on Alcohol, 34,* 869–877.

Marcus, S. (1967). The motivational patterns of remitted and unremitted alcoholics: An exploration into the motivation-hygiene theory. *Dissertation Abstracts, 28,* 1203B–1204B.

Marlatt, G. A., & Gordon, J. R. (1985). *Relapse prevention: Maintenance strategies in the treatment of addictive behaviors.* New York: Guilford.

Martinson, R. (1974). What works? Questions and answers about prison reform. *The Public Interest, 35,* 22–54.

Matkom, A. J. (1969). An alcoholic treatment center in a general hospital. *Quarterly Journal of Studies on Alcohol, 30,* 453–456.

Mausner, B., & Platt, E. S. (1971). *Smoking: A behavioral analysis.* New York: Pergamon.

Mayer, J., Needham, M. A., & Myerson, D. J. (1965). Contact and initial attendance at an alcoholism clinic. *Quarterly Journal of Studies on Alcohol, 26,* 480–485.

McArdle, J. A. (1973). Positive and negative communications and subsequent attitude and behavior change

in alcoholics. *Dissertation Abstracts International, 34,* 844B. (University Microfilms No. 73-17, 317)

McLachlan, J. F. C. (1972). Benefit from group therapy as a function of patient-therapist match on conceptual level. *Psychotherapy: Theory, Research and Practice, 9,* 317–323.

McLachlan, J. F. C. (1974). Therapy strategies, personality orientation and recovery from alcoholism. *Canadian Psychiatric Association Journal, 19,* 25–30.

Miller, P. M., Hersen, M., & Eisler, R. M. (1974). Relative effectiveness of instructions, agreements, and reinforcement in behavioral contracts with alcoholics. *Journal of Abnormal Psychology, 83,* 548–553.

Miller, W. R. (1976). Alcoholism scales and objective assessment methods: A review. *Psychological Bulletin, 83,* 649–674.

Miller, W. R. (1978). Behavioral treatment of problem drinkers: A comparative outcome study of three controlled drinking therapies. *Journal of Consulting and Clinical Psychology, 46,* 74–86.

Miller, W. R. (1983a). Controlled drinking: A history and critical review. *Journal of Studies on Alcohol, 44,* 68–83.

Miller, W. R. (1983b). Motivational interviewing with problem drinkers. *Behavioural Psychotherapy, 11,* 147–172.

Miller, W. R., & Baca, L. M. (1983). Two-year follow-up of bibliotherapy and therapist-directed controlled drinking training for problem drinkers. *Behavior Therapy, 14,* 441–448.

Miller, W. R., & Caddy, G. R. (1977). Abstinence and controlled drinking in the treatment of problem drinkers. *Journal of Studies on Alcohol, 38,* 986–1003.

Miller, W. R., Gribskov, C. J., & Mortell, R. L. (1981). Effectiveness of self-control manual for problem drinkers with and without therapist contact. *International Journal of the Addictions, 16,* 1247–1254.

Miller, W. R., Hedrick, K. E., & Orlofsky, D. O. (1983). *The Helpful Responses Questionnaire: An objective instrument for measuring accurate empathy.* Unpublished manuscript.

Miller, W. R., & Hester, R. K. (1980). Treating the problem drinker: Modern approaches. In W. R. Miller (Ed.), *The addictive behaviors: Treatment of alcoholism, drug abuse, smoking, and obesity* (pp. 11–141). Oxford, England: Pergamon.

Miller, W. R., & Muñoz, R. F. (1982). *How to control your drinking* (2nd ed.). Albuquerque: University of New Mexico Press.

Miller, W. R., & Saucedo, C. F. (1983). Assessment of neuropsychological impairment and brain damage in problem drinkers. In C. J. Golden, J. A. Moses, Jr., J. A. Coffman, W. R. Miller, & F. D. Strider (Eds.), *Clinical neuropsychology: Interface with neurologic and psychiatric disorders* (pp. 141–195). New York: Grune & Stratton.

Miller, W. R., & Taylor, C. A. (1980). Relative effectiveness of bibliotherapy, individual and group self-control training in the treatment of problem drinkers. *Addictive Behaviors, 15,* 13–24.

Miller, W. R., Taylor, C. A., & West, J. C. (1980). Focused versus broad-spectrum behavior therapy for problem drinkers. *Journal of Consulting and Clinical Psychology, 48,* 590–601.

Milmoe, S., Rosenthal, R., Blane, H. T., Chafetz, M. E., & Wolf, I. (1967). The doctor's voice: Postdictor of successful referral of alcoholic patients. *Journal of Abnormal Psychology, 72,* 78–84.

Mindlin, D. F. (1964). Attitudes toward alcoholism and toward self: Differences between three alcoholic groups. *Quarterly Journal of Studies on Alcohol, 25,* 136–141.

Mogar, R. E., Helm, S. T., Snedeker, M. R., Snedeker, M. H., & Wilson, W. M. (1969). Staff attitudes toward the alcoholic patient. *Archives of General Psychiatry, 21,* 449–454.

Moore, R. A. (1971). Alcoholism treatment in private psychiatric hospitals: A national survey. *Quarterly Journal of Studies on Alcohol, 32,* 1083–1085.

Moore, R. C., & Murphy, T. C. (1961). Denial of alcoholism as an obstacle to recovery. *Quarterly Journal Studies on Alcohol, 22,* 597–609.

Moos, R. H., Bromet, E., Tso, V., & Moos, B. (1979). Family characteristics and the outcome of treatment for alcoholism. *Journal of Studies on Alcohol, 40,* 78–88.

Mottin, J. L. (1973). Drug-induced attenuation of alcohol consumption: A review and evaluation of claimed, potential or current therapies. *Quarterly Journal of Studies on Alcohol, 34,* 444–472.

Mozdzierz, G. J., & Semyck, R. W. (1980). Relationship between alcoholics' social interest and attitude toward success and failure. *Journal of Individual Psychology, 36,* 61–65.

Nelson, R. O., & Hayes, S. C. (1981). Theoretical explanations for reactivity in self-monitoring. *Behavior Modification, 5,* 3–14.

Nir, Y., & Cutler, R. (1978). The unmotivated patient syndrome: Survey of therapeutic interventions. *American Journal of Psychiatry, 135,* 442–447.

Nirenberg, T. D., Sobell, L. C., & Sobell, M. B. (1980). Effective and inexpensive procedures for decreasing client attrition in an outpatient alcohol treatment program. *American Journal of Drug and Alcohol Abuse, 7,* 73–82.

Ogborne, A. C., & Glaser, F. B. (1981). Characteristics of affiliates of Alcoholics Anonymous: A review of the literature. *Journal of Studies on Alcohol, 42,* 661–675.

O'Leary, M. R., Donovan, D. M., & Hague, W. H. (1975). Relationship between locus of control and defensive style among alcoholics. *Journal of Clinical Psychology, 31,* 362–363.

O'Leary, M. R., Roshenow, D. J., & Donovan, D. M. (1976). Locus of control and attrition from an alcoholism treatment program. *Journal of Consulting and Clinical Psychology, 44,* 686–687.

O'Leary, M. R., Rohsenow, D. J., Schau, E. J., & Donovan, D. M. (1977). Defensive style and treatment outcome among men alcoholics. *Journal of Studies on Alcohol, 38,* 1036–1040.

O'Leary, M. R., Speltz, M. L., & Walker, R. D. (1980). Influence of reported helplessness on client-clinician relationships in an alcoholism program. *Hospital and Community Psychiatry, 31,* 783–784.

Olkin, R., & Lemle, R. (1984). Increasing attendance in an outpatient alcoholism clinic: A comparison of two intake procedures. *Journal of Studies on Alcohol, 45,* 465–468.

Orford, J. (1973). A comparison of alcoholics whose drinking is totally uncontrolled and those whose drinking is mainly controlled. *Behaviour Research and Therapy, 11,* 565–576.

Orford, J., & Hawker, A. (1974). An investigation of an alcoholism rehabilitation halfway house: II. The complex question of client motivation. *British Journal of Addiction, 69,* 315–323.

Orford, J., Oppenheimer, E., & Edwards, G. (1976). Abstinence or control: The outcome for excessive drinkers two years after consultation. *Behaviour Research and Therapy, 14,* 409–418.

Panepinto, W., Galanter, M., Bender, S. H., & Strochlic. M. (1980). Alcoholics' trnasition from ward to clinic: Group orientation improves retention. *Journal of Studies on Alcohol, 41,* 940–945.

Panepinto, W. C., & Higgins, M. J. (1969). Keeping alcoholics in treatment: Effective follow-through procedures. *Quarterly Journal of Studies on Alcohol, 30,* 414–419.

Paredes, A. (1974). Denial, deceptive maneuvers, and consistency in the behavior of alcoholics. *Annals of the New York Academy of Sciences, 233,* 23–33.

Paredes, A., Ludwig, K. D., Hassenfeld, I. N., & Cornelison, F. S., Jr. (1969). A clinical study of alcoholics using audiovisual self-image feedback. *Journal of Nervous and Mental Disease, 148,* 449–456.

Paredes, A., Ludwig, K. D., Hassenfeld, I. N., & Cornelison, F. S., Jr. (1971). Filmed representations of behavior and responses to self-observation in alcoholics. In N. K. Mello & J. H. Mendelson (Eds.), *Recent advances in studies of alcoholism* (pp. 709–729). Washington, DC: U.S. Government Printing Office.

Parker, M. W., Winstead, D. K., & Willi, F. J. P. (1979). Patient autonomy in alcohol rehabilitation: I. Literature review. *Internatinal Journal of the Addictions, 14,* 1015–1022.

Parsons, T. (1951). *The social system.* Glencoe, IL: Free Press.

Partington, J. R., & Johnson, F. G. (1969). Personality types among alcoholics. *Quarterly Journal of Studies on Alcohol, 30,* 21–34.

Pattison, E. M. (1966). A critique of alcoholism treatment concepts: With special reference to abstinence. *Quarterly Journal of Studies on Alcohol, 27,* 49–71.

Pediaditakis, N. (1962). Motivating the acutely intoxicated alcoholic patient to obtain further treatment. *North Carolina Medical Journal, 23,* 11–12.

Pervin, L. A. (1983). The stasis and flow of behavior: Toward a theory of goals. In M. M. Page (Ed.), *Personality: Current theory and research* (pp. 1–53). Lincoln: University of Nebraska Press.

Peters, R. S. (1960). *The concept of motivation* (2nd. ed.). London: Routledge & Kegan Paul.

Peterson, B., Kristenson, H., Sterby, N. H., Trell, E., Fex, G., & Hood, B. (1980). Alcohol consumption and premature death in middle-aged men. *British Medical Journal, 280,* 1403–1406.

Polich, J. M., Armor, D. J., & Braiker, H. B. (1981). *The course of alcoholism: Four years after treatment.* New York: Wiley.

Prochaska, J. O., & DiClemente, C. C. (1982). Transtheoretical therapy: Toward a more integrative model of change. *Psychotherapy: Theory, Research and Practice, 19,* 276–288.

Prue, D. M., Keane, T. M., Cornell, J. E., & Foy, D. W. (1979). An analysis of distance variables that affect aftercare attendance. *Community Mental Health Journal, 15*, 149-154.

Raynes, A. E., & Patch, V. D. (1971). Distinguishing features of patients who discharge themselves from psychiatric ward. *Comprehensive Psychiatry, 12*, 473-479.

Reinehr, R. C. (1969). Therapist and patient perception of hospitalized alcoholics. *Journal of Clinical Psychology, 25*, 443-445.

Richard, G. P., & Burley, P. M. (1978). Alcoholics' beliefs about and attitudes to controlled drinking and total abstinence. *British Journal of Social and Clinical Psychology, 17*, 159-163.

Richards, C. S., Anderson, D. C., & Baker, R. B. (1978). The role of information feedback in the relative reactivity of self-monitoring and external observations. *Behavior Therapy, 9*, 687.

Richman, A., & Smart, R. G. (1981). After how many detoxications is rehabilitation possible? *Drug and Alcohol Dependence, 7*, 233-238.

Rogers, R. W. (1975). A protection motivation theory of fear appeals and attitude change. *Journal of Psychology, 91*, 93-114.

Rogers, R. W., Deckner, C. W., & Mewborn, C. R. (1978). An expectancy-value theory approach to the long-term modification of smoking behavior. *Journal of Clinical Psychology, 34*, 562-566.

Rogers, R. W., & Mewborn, C. R. (1976). Fear appeals and attitude change: Effects of a threat's noxiousness, probability of occurrence, and the efficacy of coping responses. *Journal of Personality and Social Psychology, 34*, 54-61.

Rosenberg, C. M., Gerrein, J. R., Manohar, V., & Liftik, J. (1976). Evaluation of training of alcoholism counselors. *Journal of Studies on Alcohol, 37*, 1236-1246.

Rosenberg, C. M., Gerrein, J. R., & Schnell, C. (1978). Cannabis in the treatment of alcoholism. *Journal of Studies on Alcohol, 39*, 1955-1958.

Rosenberg, C. M., & Liftik, J. (1976). Use of coercion in the outpatient treatment of alcoholism. *Journal of Studies on Alcohol, 37*, 58-65.

Rosenberg, C. M., & Raynes, A. E. (1973). Dropouts from treatment. *Canadian Psychiatric Association Journal, 18*, 229-233.

Rosenthal, R. (1976). *Experimenter effects in behavioral research* (rev. ed.). New York: Irvington.

Rosenthal, R., & Jacobson, L. (1968). *Pygmalion in the classroom.* New York: Holt, Rinehart & Winston.

Rothbaum, R., Weisz, J. R., & Snyder, S. S. (1982). Changing the world and changing the self: A two-process model of perceived control. *Journal of Personality and Social Psychology, 42*, 5-37.

Russell, M. A. H., Wilson, C., Taylor, C., & Baker, C. D. (1979). Effect of general practitioners' advice against smoking. *British Medical Journal, 2*, 231-235.

Sanchez-Craig, M. (1980). Random assignment to abstinence or controlled drinking in a cognitive-behavioral program: Effects on drinking behavior. *Addictive Behaviors, 5*, 35-39.

Sapir, J. V. (1953). Relationship factors in the treatment of the alcoholic. *Social Casework, 34*, 297-303.

Saslow, G. (1969). New views of the alcoholic. *Rehabilitation Record, 10*(1), 22-26.

Saunders, W. M., & Kershaw, P. W. (1979). Spontaneous remission from alcoholism: A community study. *British Journal of Addiction, 74*, 251-265.

Schaefer, H. H., Sobell, M. B., & Mills, K. C. (1971). Some sobering data on the use of self-confrontation with alcoholics. *Behavior Therapy, 2*, 28-39.

Schaefer, H. H., Sobell, M. B., & Sobell, L. C. (1972). Twelve month follow-up of hospitalized alcoholics given self-confrontation experiences by videotape. *Behavior Therapy, 3*, 283-285.

Schorer, C. G. (1965). Defiance and healing. *Comprehensive Psychiatry, 6*, 184-190.

Sedmak, T., & Dordevic-Bankovic, V. (1978). Motivacija za lecenje u alkoholicare [Motivation for treatment of alcoholics]. *Alkoholizam, 18*(3-4), 13-17. (From *Journal of Studies on Alcohol, 1980, 41*. Abstract No. 929)

Seligman, M. E. D. (1975). *Helplessness.* San Francisco: Freeman.

Selzer, M. L. (1957). Hostility as a barrier to therapy in alcoholism. *Psychiatric Quarterly, 31*, 301-305.

Serebro, B. (1979). Compliance in the treatment of alcohol-dependent individuals (alcoholics). *Journal of International Medical Research, 7*, 165-167.

Shaw, S., Cartwright, A., Spratley, T., & Harwin, J. (1978). *Responding to drinking problems.* Baltimore, MD: University Park Press.

Siegel, N., & Fink, M. (1962). Motivation for psychotherapy. *Comprehensive Psychiatry, 3*, 170-173.

Skinner, H. A., & Allen, B. A. (1983). Differential assessment of alcoholism. *Journal of Studies on Alcohol, 44*, 852-862.

Slaughter, L. D., & Torno, K. (1968). Hospitalized alcoholic patients: IV. The role of patient-counselors. *Hospital and Community Psychiatry, 19*, 209-210.

Smart, R. G. (1974). Employed alcoholics treated voluntarily and under constructive coercion: A follow-up study. *Quarterly Journal of Studies on Alcohol, 35*, 196-209.

Smith-Moorehouse, P. M. (1971). An insight giving technique which assists in diagnosing alcoholics. *Journal of Alcoholism, 6*, 84-89.

Sterne, M. W., & Pittman, D. J. (1965). The concept of motivation: A source of institutional and professional blockage in the treatment of alcoholics. *Quarterly Journal of Studies on Alcohol, 26*, 41-57.

Stewart, D. A. (1954). Empathy in the group therapy of alcoholism. *Quarterly Journal of Studies on Alcohol, 15*, 74-110.

Strug, D. L., & Hyman, M. M. (1981). Social networks of alcoholics. *Journal of Studies on Alcohol, 42*, 855-884.

Stunkard, A. J. (1961). Motivation for treatment. *Comprehensive Psychiatry, 2*, 140-147.

Swenson, C. H. (1971). Commitment and the personality of the successful therapist. *Psychotherapy: Theory, Research and Practice, 8*, 31-36.

Tamerin, J. S., Tolor, A., Holson, P., & Neumann, C. P. (1974). The alcoholic's perception of self: A retrospective comparison of mood and behavior during states of sobriety and intoxication. *Annals of the New York Academy of Sciences, 233*, 48-60.

Tarleton, G. H., & Tarnower, S. M. (1960). The use of letters as part of the psychotherapeutic relationship: Experiences in a clinic for alcoholism. *Quarterly Journal of Studies on Alcohol, 21*, 82-89.

Thimann, J., (1968). Reflections on Dr. Fox's paper. *International Journal of Psychiatry, 5,* 56–59.

Thomas, E., Polansky, N., & Kounin, J. (1955). The expected behavior of a potentially helpful person. *Human Relations, 8,* 165–174.

Thomas, S. D., & Lowe, W. C. (1978). Acute treatment as motivation for rehabilitation. *Alcohol Health and Research World, 2*(3), 38–40.

Thornton, C. C., Gottheil, E., Gellens, H. K., & Alterman, A. I. (1977). Voluntary versus involuntary abstinence in the treatment of alcoholics. *Journal of Studies on Alcohol, 38,* 1740–1748.

Tiebout, H. M. (1953). Surrender vs. compliance in therapy: With special reference to alcoholism. *Quarterly Journal of Studies on Alcohol, 14,* 58–68.

Tiebout, H. M. (1954). The ego factors in surrender in alcoholism. *Quarterly Journal of Studies on Alcohol, 15,* 610–621.

Tough, A. (1982). *Intentional changes: A fresh approach to helping people change.* Chicago: Follett.

Trice, H. M. (1957). A study of the process of affiliation with Alcoholics Anonymous. *Quarterly Journal of Studies on Alcohol, 18,* 39–54.

Trice, H. M., & Beyer, J. M. (1983). Social control in worksettings: Using the constructive confrontation strategy with problem-drinking employees. In D. A. Ward (Ed.), *Alcoholism: Introduction to theory and treatment* (rev. ed., pp. 314–339). Dubuque, IA: Kendall/Hunt.

Trice, H. M., & Roman, P. M. (1970). Sociopsychological predictors of affiliation with Alcoholics Anonymous: A longitudinal study of "treatment success." *Social Psychiatry, 5,* 51–59.

Truax, C. B., & Carkhuff, R. R. (1967). *Toward effective counseling and psychotherapy.* Chicago: Aldine.

Truax, C. B., & Mitchell, K. M. (1971). Research on certain therapist interpersonal skills in relation to process and outcome. In A. E. Bergin & S. L. Garfield (Eds.). *Handbook of psychotherapy and behavior change* (pp. 299–344). New York: Wiley.

Vaillant, G. M. (1983). *The natural history of alcoholism: Causes, patterns, and paths to recovery.* Cambridge, MA: Harvard University Press.

Valle, S. K. (1981). Interpersonal functioning of alcoholism counselors and treatment outcome. *Journal of Studies on Alcohol, 42,* 783–790.

Wallston, B. S., Wallston, K. A., Kaplan, G. D., & Maides, S. A. (1976). Development and validation of the Health Locus of Control (HLC) Scale. *Journal of Consulting and Clinical Psychology, 44,* 580–585.

Wanberg, K. W., & Jones, E. (1973). Initial contact and admission of persons requesting treatment for alcohol problems. *British Journal of Addiction, 68,* 281–285.

Wedel, H. I. (1965). Involving alcoholics in treatment. *Quarterly Journal of Studies on Alcohol, 26,* 468–479.

Wehmer, G., Cooke, G., & Gruber, J. (1974). Evaluation of the effects of training of paraprofessionals in the treatment of alcoholism: A pilot study. *British Journal of Addiction, 69,* 25–32.

Weinberg, J. (1973). Counseling recovering alcoholics. *Social Work, 18,* 84–93.

Weiss, R. L., & Summers, K. J. (1983, April). *Effects of video playback on spouses' mood and home interactions.* Paper presented at the meeting of the Western Psychological Association, San Francisco, CA.

Wilson, W. H. (1977). Sobriety: Conversion and beyond. *Maryland State Medical Journal, 26*(4), 85–91.

Wolff, K. (1968). Hospitalized alcoholic patients: III. Motivating alcoholics through group psychotherapy. *Hospital and Community Psychiatry, 19,* 206–209.

Zimbardo, P. G. (1969). *The cognitive control of motivation: The consequences of choice and dissonance.* Glenview, IL: Scott, Foresman.

Received December 17, 1983
Revision received December 16, 1984 ∎

SECTION 4
Social Experimentation

A central feature of the program research perspective is its emphasis on examining cause-and-effect linkages connecting organized social action with social effects. The term ascribed to this perspective is *social experimentation.* At the heart of this perspective are two distinct processes: (1) deliberate staging of a reform; and (2) rigorous experimental assessment of the consequences of the reform. To be successful, both processes have to be initiated simulanteously. This requires a joint venture between the experimenters and the reformers (e.g., policymakers and program personnel). As witnessed throughout this volume, the "marriage" has had a rocky history. Although recent federal legislative actions (e.g., the Omnibus Budget Reconciliation Act of 1981; the Deficit Reduction Act of 1984; and Gramm-Rudman-Hollings Balanced-Budget Act of 1985) by policymakers have threatened to breakup the partnership, conciliatory behavior by proponents of experimentation have kept the possibility of an "experimenting society" alive. The selections in this section reiterate and expand on the concepts associated with experimentation and provide practical advice for avoiding the many statistical and design pitfalls encountered while trying to launch, keep afloat, and moor an experiment.

The first chapter by Berk, Boruch, Chambers, Rossi, and Witte, represents the latest incarnation of social experimentation as proposed 15 years ago by Donald T. Campbell. In contrast with Campbell's original conception, their model has several new features and many old ones have been given greater emphasis. First, the name has been changed to "social policy experimentation"—a modification intended to make explicit the linkage between the policymaking process and experimentation. Second, the position offered by Berk et al. argues for a process that entails a series of investigations, not simply an assessment of an isolated policy action. Whereas Campbell suggested that the experimenters limit their role to that of methodological servants to the experimenting society, Berk et al. break us out of that bondage by defining into their scheme explicit reliance on social science theory and research and emphasize inquiry directed at description of underlying causal mechanisms. Further, they make explicit the need for sufficient resources to do the job correctly.

There are a number of key issues that are conspicuously absent from their discussion. Most notable is the absence of any mention of the term *evaluation* (despite the fact that it appeared in *Evaluation Review*). The process they describe is exclusively referred to as *assessment* of programs or interventions. Whether or not this was deliberate, we take it as additional justification for separating program research and program evaluation into distinct activities. By inference, the role of social policy experimentation is to provide evidence to policymakers to aid their deliberations (and value judgments)—both at the front end, as courses of action are planned, and later, when the evidence is available from the experiments. The cycle begins anew as the results of the experiments suggest additional questions.

Social policy experimentation is clearly a long-term perspective for improving social conditions. As such, it needs institutionalized mechanisms to assure resources, formulation of policy options to be tested, and so on. Berk et al. also detail some plausible mechanisms to ensure this critical, long-term support.

On conceptual and statistical grounds, experimentation has not been difficult to justify as a superior (relative to weaker designs) means of understanding causal relationships. The practical aspects of planning, research implementation, and analysis have been the source of much concern. The remaining chapters in this section summarize many of these critical issues, and, more important, offer concrete advice on minimizing their adverse consequences.

Experimentation is not simply limited to the assignment of individuals to deliberately manipulated treatments. In the second selection, Kramer and Shapiro enumerate six aspects of randomized clinical trials that warrant special attention, especially when experimentation is conducted in field settings that entail the delivery of services. Challenges to internal validity—the sine qua non of experimentation—that are explictly addressed include selective participation, treatment compliance, and mode of assignment. As for generalization, their focus is on the distinctive aspects of the evaluative/assessment situation that limit inference. Although Berk et al. make a case for relatively inexpensive experiments, as the situation becomes more vulnerable to the uncontrolled factors outlined by Kramer and Shapiro, additional time, controls, and expense will be necessary.

The third chapter by Olejnik provides a concise summary of one major planning step in the research process—determining the necessary sample size. Many introductory and intermediate statistics books offer extended discussions of factors (level of Type I error, size of the effect, desired level of power, directionality of the hypothesis, and so on) to be considered in determining the requisite sample size to test a given hypothesis or achieve a prespecified level of statistical precision. The review by Lipsey et al. (section 3, Part I) suggests that either we have skipped those pages, the message was not sufficiently clear, the kind of situations that program researchers find themselves in do not fit these conditions, or the planner has insufficient information. The lack of statistical power, in many assessments, appears to be a persistent problem.

Olejnik shows how aggregate meta-analysis findings can refine estimates of likely effect sizes, yielding more realistic estimates of sample size and, in turn, more realistic estimates of power. Further, he shows how alternative designs (e.g., ANCOVA and matching prior to random assignment) can increase precision of estimates when natural constraints (fiscal resources, limited program recipient pool) are encountered. Closer attention to sample size determination and analytic strategies may avoid the "parade of null effects" witnessed in the past.

Fortune and Hutson, the final chapter in this section, enumerate five classes of statistical models of changes and the conditions under which they apply. The emphasis here is on selecting a model of analysis that meets the conditions surrounding the data collection process. The unique feature of this presentation is its deliberate specification of four fundamental questions that can be used to guide the choice of a statistical model or models. Of course, to be maximally useful, working through these questions, options, and decision points as part of the planning process—*before* data collection is completed—may avoid the uncomfortable position of knowing that a superior analysis strategy could have been used if the relevant data had been collected.

The chapters in this section represent one critical component of a program research perspective—the machinery for establishing the presence and magnitude of causal relationships. Berk et al. remind us of the uncertainties that are likely to accompany any single assessment. They call for planning a package of studies, each of which builds from prior research, theory, and the preceding assessment. A supplement to this perspective is presented in the next section. Research synthesis can facilitate the planning process as described by Berk et al., *and* it can serve as a means of accumulating the results of the individual assessments that make up the package of studies they describe.

34

Social Policy Experimentation
A Position Paper

Richard A. Berk, Robert F. Boruch, David L. Chambers,
Peter H. Rossi, and Ann D. Witte

We review the arguments for and against randomized field experiments design to address important questions of social policy. Based on this review, we make a number of recommendations about how the use of randomized field experiments might be fostered.

I: INTRODUCTION

In Donald T. Campbell's justly famous article, "Reforms as Experiments" (1969), an explicit link was proposed between rigorous experimental methods and social reforms:

The United States and other modern nations should be ready for an experimental approach to social reform, an approach in which we try out new programs designed

AUTHORS' NOTE: *Funding for this position paper was provided by the John D. and Catherine T. MacArthur Foundation. We are also indebted to Lawrence J. Hubert, Otis*

From Berk et al., "Social Policy Experimentation: A Position Paper," *Evaluation Review*, 1985, 9(4), 387-429. Copyright 1985 by Sage Publications, Inc.

to cure specific social problems, in which we learn whether or not these programs
are effective, and in which we retain, imitate, modify, or discard them on the basis
of apparent effectiveness [Campbell, 1969: 409].

Experimental methods had, of course, long been popular in those
natural and social sciences with laboratory traditions. And the technical
advances made by Gosset, Fisher, Yates, and others had permitted
rigorous experimentation to be undertaken outside of laboratory
settings. Likewise, the notion of social reform was hardly new. There
had even been a number of earlier attempts to apply experimental
methods to estimate the effect of changes in public policy.

Campbell's contribution was the argument that social reforms and
experimental methods should be *routinely* adjoined. A commitment to
an experimental *philosophy* would make it possible to be innovative and
cautious at the same ti. ie; it would be possible to try new things in
overtly tentative manner. A commitment to the experimental *method*
would allow *factual* questions abo 11 the impact of the social reforms to
be addressed within the best scientific traditions. Thus, whether
interventions such as Head Start, peak-load pricing, Job Corps, or
CETA "worked" was an empirical question to be explored with the most
demanding of scientific procedures. The same logic applied in principle
to any change in policy: Revisions of a penal code, deregulation of
particular industries, alterations in school curricula, the implementation
of environmental legislation, and many others.

Since Campbell's statement 15 years ago, the experimental approach
to social reform has had an uneven history. A number of major
experiments were launched, and much was learned. For instances, we
now know that residential consumers of water and electricity can be
induced to "conserve" when the price per unit is increased to more
closely approximate the true marginal cost. We also know that prison
rehabilitation programs operating in the 1960s did not on the average
demonstrably reform criminals.

However, meaningful experiments also proved harder to implement
than many had expected: one could not simply move laboratory

*Dudley Duncan, and Sarah Fenstermaker Berk for their comments on an earlier draft of
this report. Finally, some of the better ideas in the article were formulated in general
discussions the senior author had with members of the Social Science Research Council's
Advisory Committee on Social Indicators.*

technique into the field. For example, it was often difficult in practice to maintain tight control over implementation of a research design. In one large study (Rossi and Lyall, 1976), for instance, the experimental treatment involved providing income subsidies to randomly selected households, at the same time providing no support for another set of randomly selected, comparison households. These comparison households were also not eligible for other kinds of public assistance. Unfortunately, midway through the experiment, local officials changed the eligibility rules for AFDC payments so that many of the comparison households now qualified for AFDC support. Consequently, the experimental subsidies no longer effectively distinguished the experimental households from many of these comparison households; both were often receiving approximately the same level of income.

The use of experimental results by policymakers has also been uneven. Some experiments have had a clear and direct impact on important decisions. For example, a recent experiment on police responses to domestic violence incidents has already affected law enforcement practices in a number of major departments (Sherman and Berk, 1984). More commonly, experimental results have been ignored or sometimes even misused. No doubt one major obstacle has been poor communication between the scientific community and public officials. Another obstacle has been a lack of incentives for both researchers and policymakers to invest heavily in experimental approaches to social reform.

In our view, these and other difficulties can be attributed significantly to the growing pains of a new endeavor. Researchers have gradually learned to promise less and deliver more. Policymakers are gradually learning what experiments can and cannot accomplish. The more general point is that reforms *can* be introduced as experiments, and we have learned a great deal about when experimental procedures make sense, how laboratory methods should be altered when moved into the field, and experimental results can be made more responsive to the needs of policymakers. However, we are still a very long way from an effective marriage between experimental methods and assessments of public policy.

In this position paper, therefore, we argue for a concerted effort to facilitate social policy experimentation. By social policy experiments, we have in mind the application of rigorous research designs to determine the impact of changes in social policy.[1] Thus, a social policy experiment is *an effort to introduce social change in a way that allows one to effectively discern the net effect of the change on important social outcomes.* We require, as a result, that the "treatment" be a legitimate and manipulable instrument of public policy. Changes in our tax laws would qualify whereas altering the age mix of our population would not (because it is not manipulable in practice). We also require that resources be provided "up front" for estimating the impact of the policy change. One cannot have a social policy experiment without the resources to conduct the research. Finally, we require that existing theory and knowledge be exploited; we leave to others undirected "tinkering" with the system. Thus, we would favor in principle an experimental treatment of transfer payments designed from micro-economic theory, but within the context of social policy experiments disapprove of transfer payments justified solely as a means of making poor people less poor.

In summary, we believe that the time is right to launch a major *and* coordinated effort in social policy experimentation. We try to make the case in this position paper that social policy experiments can produce good science and good social policy; it is possible to do good and do it well.

The rest of our position paper is organized into four sections: section II provides some general background on the nature of social policy experiments; section III addresses social policy experiments in more depth through three experiments on a single topic; and section IV provides a definition of social policy experiments and elaborates on that definition. Finally, section V describes a number of concrete proposals that may further social policy experimentation.

II: SOME BACKGROUND ON SOCIAL POLICY EXPERIMENTS

The term "social policy experiment" can connote a variety of activities from seat-of-the-pants innovations in public policy to scientific experiments on social policy tested in the field. Although we will shortly be far more specific, it will be apparent that we are concerned with the use of experimental procedures to determine the impact of social interventions having significant implications for public policy. We begin with four examples.

EXAMPLES OF SOCIAL POLICY EXPERIMENTS

In the early 1960s, there was a growing concern that proposals to provide even modest income subsidies to the poor would reduce motivation to find and keep jobs. One charge was that "handouts" undermined the "work ethic." In response, several experiments were launched to determine if members of households that were given monthly cash grants at various levels (including no payments) varied as a consequence in their labor force participation. A second intervention involved the rate at which these payments were reduced in response to earnings from employment. In order to ensure that households in the different groups were as comparable as possible, households were assigned at random to the experimental (e.g., payment) and control (e.g., nonpayment) conditions. In fact, the work disincentives produced by the payments were on the average rather modest, and most of the labor force reductions came from households' "secondary workers" such as teenagers or women with small children (Rossi and Lyall, 1976). That is, work effort was reduced especially for those household members who presumably had other pressing demands on their time (i.e., school and child care, respectively). One implication was that a "negative income tax" to assist the poor and near poor was arguably less problematic (in terms of work disincentives) than many had predicted.[2]

At about the same time, prison rehabilitation programs were coming under attack as ineffective or worse. Criticisms from the right focused on administrators and programs that "coddled" prisoners. Criticisms from the left centered on civil liberties violations that rehabilitation programs necessarily engendered (e.g., the lack of due process in decisions about when "rehabilitation" was complete). As a step toward moving beyond impressionistic evidence, Kassbaum et al. (1971) compared the postprison behavior of convicts randomly assigned to group therapy with the postprison behavior of convicts randomly assigned to the usual prison programs. Arrests for new crimes were of particular concern. Parole records revealed no significant difference between the two groups, suggesting that nothing was gained from exposure to the group therapy, at least as delivered in this study. Part of the problem was the difficulty of delivering meaningful therapy using prison personnel operating behind bars. In any case, the study allowed both the Right and the Left to continue their assault on rehabilitation, fueled by the idea that "nothing works."

A bit more recently, there was interest in developing a Spanish version of *Sesame Street* for use in Mexico and other Lation American countries. It was not clear, however, whether the television program would have beneficial effects sufficient to justify its costs. It was also not clear whether all children would benefit about the same amount, or whether children who were already better equipped for school would benefit more than children who were less well equipped. Such differential responsiveness to the program might or might not improve school performance averaged over all children, but it would certainly increase the *gap* between the fast and slow learners. There was some debate about whether programs that fostered inequality between groups of school children were a good idea and deserving of support with taxpayer's money. To answer these and other questions, an experiment was launched in Mexico City to determine if children randomly assigned to watch over 100 episodes of *Plaza Sesamo* scored higher on a variety of achievement tests than children randomly assigned to watch an equivalent number of cartoon shows and other noneducational programs. On the average, the children exposed to *Plaza Sesamo* did better than the children exposed to other kinds of programs, especially on those tests most closely related to the stated goals of *Plaza Sesamo*. Apparently, all children benefited on the average, but as more talented children gained greater amounts than less talented children, the gap between fast and slow learners was increased (Diaz-Guerrero et al., 1976).

In the middle 1970s, utility companies were becoming increasingly worried about the "peak load" problem. They found that the demand for electricity varied enormously over the course of the day and over the course of the year. Providing for high-demand periods meant building new power plants costing hundreds of millions of dollars. The alternative was potential blackouts during periods of especially high demand. But even if such capacity were built, there would be many slack periods when the new capacity would go unused. Consequently, an experiment was initiated to determine if by raising the residential price of electricity during the peak load hours, consumers would shift substantial amounts of their demand for electricity to other times of the day. Households were assigned at random to different price structures, and on the average, consumption dropped by about 5% for a 10% increase in price, (Aigner and Hausman, 1980). In other words, it seemed possible to overcome at least part of the peak load problem by altering the price structure. One implication was that perhaps pricing strategies should be tried before commitments for new power plants were made.

The four studies just described represent "social policy experiments" as we will use the term. Our primary aim in the pages ahead is to argue the case for social policy experiments and suggest ways in which foundations, government agencies, and even private enterprise might make a larger commitment to scientifically sound social experiments designed to inform public policy. Thus, we have written something far closer to a position paper than a literature review. Readers interested in the latter can find excellent treatments in any of a number of accessible sources (e.g., Reiken and Boruch, 1974; Cook and Campbell, 1979; Rossi and Freeman, 1983; Ferber and Hirsch, 1983; Tanur, 1983; Fienberg et al., 1984).

A FIRST PASS OVER
SOME IMPORTANT ISSUES

People experiment all the time. Common sense quite properly counsels that in order to determine the consequences of some action, trying it out can be a pretty good idea. Implicit are three important notions: (1) speculations about how the world works can be meaningfully informed by reference to observable phenomena, (2) one must intervene in "business as usual" in order to get a clear fix on cause and effect, and (3) any measures of effect are inherently comparative. Whether anything is different after an intervention requires a benchmark of how things would have been in the absence of the intervention. Thus, we test-drive cars before making a purchase, grant tenure at universities only after a lengthy probationary period, and date before deciding whether or not to marry.

Over the past two centuries, common-sense views of experimentation have been substantially clarified and expanded. We now know, for example, that inferences about the relationship between cause and effect must take into account the full range of possible explanations for why a particular outcome materialized. Whether "New Math," for instance, really improves mathematical reasoning requires that the impact of New Math be separated from the impact of normal maturation in students' mathematical aptitudes. Likewise, whether psychotherapy really works requires that the impact of the therapy be distinguished from a remission of symptoms that would have occurred without intervention. Or, whether the current economic recovery can be attributed to supply side economics requires that the independent impetus of changes in consumer spending (among other things) first be factored out.

There is now a widespread consensus among statisticians that for questions of causal inference some research strategies are more illuminating than others. In particular, experiments in which subjects are assigned at random to various treatments are the procedure of choice when causal inference is the dominating concern.[3] Random assignment ensures that experimental and control groups are on the average equivalent before the treatments are introduced. Hence, fair comparisons between the outcomes of the experimental and control conditions can be made. Moreover, under random assignment in "factorial" designs, it is possible to test the impact of several different kinds of treatments. One might explore, for instance, whether conservation appeals and price increases each made independent contributions to reductions in the use of electricity during peak hours and whether one was more effective when the other was already in place. That is, the price effects might be enhanced once customers were sensitized by appeals to conserve.

In similar fashion, it is now widely recognized that generalizations from a particular experiment to other settings, subjects, and times are often problematic. Thus, New Math might work for students in small classes, but not for students in large classes. Similarly psychotherapy might be effective for individuals who volunteer for treatment, but not for individuals who are coerced into treatment by court order. Supply side economics might have worked in the 1920s, but not now. And just as with current views on causal inference, there is a virtual consensus that some research strategies are stronger than others. In particular, sound generalizations follow more readily from samples drawn at random from known populations coupled with packages of experiments in which one can determine the degree to which initial findings are routinely replicated.

Finally, it is now generally accepted that all experiments are subject to chance forces. That is, an apparent tendency for one or more interventions to work better than others may reflect nothing more than the "luck of the draw." For example, student performance on standardized mathematics tests can fluctuate from day to day in an unpredictable fashion due to a host of small effects unrelated to what is taught in the classroom (e.g., the amount of sleep the student had the night before). Consequently, it is possible that superior performance by students learning New Math may be a fluke. Likewise, psychopathology and economic indicators are well known to respond to random perturbations that may be confused with genuine responses to experimental interventions.

The role of chance substantially complicates inferences from experiments because one must try to account for the possibility that the effects one interprets as "real" are actually happenstance. And it is here that notions such as "statistical significance" take on special import; one must formally be able to assess the probability that a given finding (or set of findings) is a chance outcome. Note that there are two kinds of chance errors: One may falsely find that an intervention does not work or one may falsely find that an intervention does work.

These and other considerations lead naturally to a definition of social policy experiments that will suffice until later, when we shall be more complete. By a social policy experiment we shall initially mean a *planned effort to produce unbiased, reasonably precise estimates of the effect of a social intervention or change. The plan involves identification or construction of a control condition that will yield, compared to other procedures, substantially less equivocal, quantifiable statements about the effect.* This definition excludes many kinds of applied social research (more on that later, as well) such as political polling, census enumerations in different political jurisdictions, and monthly surveys on labor force participation. None of these addresses the effects of a particular social intervention or includes a control condition to provide a baseline.

Our point more generally is that common-sense experimental methods have been practiced throughout recorded history, and in the recent past, experimental methods have been dramatically improved. Among those who believe that scientific methods can make a useful contribution to policy formation and testing, there is little debate about the overall merits of these procedures. Yet, modern experimental methods are used very selectively. They are of course, important tools for basic research, especially in the natural sciences. They are also used routinely by social scientists working in laboratory settings. In addition, modern experimental methods are from time to time used in applied research, especially in biomedical research. Recall, for example, the massive trials of the Salk vaccine 30 years ago and the recent and highly publicized experiment on cholesterol and heart disease. However, alternative social policies are rarely subjected to rigorous experimental scrutiny. For example, there are no rigorous experimental studies on the impact of the minimum wage, the deterrent value of longer prison terms, how microcomputers affect worker productivity, whether the price mechanism might be widely used to discourage water and air pollution, whether entitlement programs really engender "welfare dependency," how private education compares to public education, how lowering the speed limit affects automobile fatalities, and many others. Rigorous experiments in social policy are the exception, not the rule.

There are several probable reasons why experimental methods have not become more central to the policy-making process. First, there are few incentives for public officials to undertake experiments today. Launching an experiment is an admission of ignorance, and there is little political mileage to be made in the search for answers. We expect our leaders to have the answers. Moreover, the political process too often settles questions of fact by ideological fiat. Can an old-fashioned liberal dare to find out whether unions really improve the worker's lot? Can an old-fashioned conservative dare to find out whether deregulation really leads to greater efficiency? Finally, experiments take time, a very scarce commodity in the political process. The recent cholesterol study, for instance, took 10 years to complete. Ten years can cross four presidential administrations.

For these and other reasons, rigorous experiments in social policy are rarely embraced (let alone funded) by public officials. This does not prevent these officials from routinely making statements of fact as if they were based on sound scientific knowledge. This also does not mean that social experiments are necessarily incompatible with the political process; indeed, among our goals is to suggest ways in which a better relationship might be forged between politicians and social experimenters.

Second, although much of the necessary technical expertise can be found in universities and other research institutions, there are few academic incentives to engage in social policy experiments (or applied research more generally). As we have argued elsewhere at some length (Berk, 1981), applied research is typically viewed as a second-class undertaking and rewards such as tenure are reserved primarily for those who do not soil their hands with practical concerns. For example, it is almost impossible to publish applied sociological research in any of the major sociological journals. But, these and other obstacles need not prevent academics from becoming more involved in social policy experiments; indeed, later we will suggest some ways in which this might be accomplished.

Third, the social policy experiments undertaken over the past two decades have been of uneven quality, relevance and cost-effectiveness

(Ferber and Hirsch, 1983). The record of research actually conducted does not provide a basis for a ringing endorsement of all social experiments. Part of the problem has been unrealistic expectations about the ease with which sound experiments could be undertaken. We now know that the implementation of proper experimental procedures is at least as important as the design of experiments. Both the randomization and the treatment itself must be successfully put in place.

Another part of the problem has been naiveté about how compelling the results of any empirical research could be to political decision makers. We now understand that there cannot be a single definitive experiment in social policy studies. All beliefs about what works are held tentatively and subject to many caveats. The findings from social policy experiments are certainly no different in principle. The advantage of rigorous experiments is that the caveats are usually fewer and far less damning. Hence, the proper benchmark for social experiments is not unassailable knowledge, but the information that would have *otherwise been available*. Alternatively put, is the policy process now substantially *better* informed with the experimental results in hand?

And yet another part of the problem has been that many of the earlier social policy experiments addressed questions that were in retrospect not easily answered within an experimental context. We are more humble now; we have a better sense about *when* to experiment. In short, one might conclude from the experience of the past two decades that social experiments are too often of questionable value. We believe that this overlooks the many successes of social experimentation and fails to take account of the enterprise's growing pains.[4]

Fourth, the nature of social policy experiments is often misunderstood. There are claims, for instance, that rigorous experimentation is typically unethical. Of course, serious ethical problems can and do arise, yet many experiments of great utility can be conducted that will meet strict ethical standards (Bennet and Lumsdaine, 1975; Boruch et al., 1978; Boruch et al., 1979; Boruch and Shadish, 1982). There are also claims that on grounds of cost-effectiveness, rigorous experimentation is too dear. However, such conclusions are not based on a careful assessment of the record (e.g., Spencer, 1980; Mosteller and Weinstein, 1984). For example, a *nonexperimental* study on the effectiveness of New York State's gun control laws is currently budgeted by the National Institute of Justice (NIJ) for over $400,000. Yet, another NIJ project involving a *true experiment* on police practices in incidents of domestic violence has cost less than $200,000, and instructive, rigorous experiments can often be undertaken for under $50,000 (a typical award by the National Science Foundation, Division of Biological and Social Sciences).

One must also not forget that even very expensive social policy experiments may be cost-effective when millions of tax dollars are at stake. For example, in 1980, the health-care budget in the United States was approximately $200 billion (Mosteller and Weinstein, 1984). Consequently, experiments totaling $1 billion per year might well be cost-effective if health-care costs were reduced by only .5%. This is hardly a demanding criterion. For example, experiments on increasing the competition among health-care providers (e.g., allowing nurse practitioners and paramedics to provide more services previously requiring a physician) might easily pay for themselves.[5]

It is also very expensive to keep people in prison. In California, for instance, a year of incarceration in the State's crowded and understaffed prisons costs about $15,000 per prisoner. With approximately 30,000 inmates, the annual bill is around $450 million. This implies that social experiments in California costing $450,0000 yearly would probably pay for themselves if they led to savings of only .1% of the annual prison budget. Again, this is hardly an unreasonable target. For example, if it could be shown that prisoners who were released only 30 days before the end of their effective sentences presented no greater danger to the public than those who served their full sentences, hundreds of thousands of tax dollars could be saved.

Finally, consider social problems on a far smaller scale. In the Southwest, the average residental consumer pays about $25 a month for water. For a town of 100,000, therefore, the annual residential water bill would amount to approximately $2.5 million. Local experiments costing the community $125,000 a year would pay for themselves, if they reduced each residential consumer's budget by only 5%. For example, if an experiment costing under $125,000 could show that local ordinances prohibiting watering of lawns in the heat of the day were typically followed without expensive enforcement mechanisms, the benefit-cost ratio might be very favorable.

In summary, the idea of experimenting in a generic sense seems to be part of human nature and formal experimental methods are now well developed. There is also ample evidence that rigorous experiments in social policy are often feasible, ethical, and cost-effective. Yet, social policy experiments are rarely initiated in order to determine what works. We believe that as a result, a very important policymaking tool is being underutilized. In the pages ahead, we will consider more deeply the nature of social policy experiments, how they might enhance the policymaking process, and what public agencies, private foundations, and private enterprise might do to improve matters.

III: A CASE STUDY OF THREE
SOCIAL POLICY EXPERIMENTS—
POSTRELEASE BENEFITS
FOR PRISONERS

The previous two sections of this article have considered social policy experiments in rather general terms. As we turn to a more detailed treatment, it will perhaps be instructive to begin with a more lengthy treatment of some examples. Consequently, we proceed to a description of three social policy experiments related to one another in the problems addressed, the interventions tried, and the outcomes explored.

STAGE 1: THE LIFE EXPERIMENT

The Manpower Development and Training act was passed in 1962. Amendments to the act in subsequent years added provisions for vocational training and other job-related services for individuals incarcerated in state and federal prisons. It was hoped that these programs would increase the chances of employment after release from prison. Evaluation of these programs, however, could find no impact on either employment or recidivism (e.g., Taggart, 1972).

Meanwhile, the Manpower Administration had commissioned a study of the postrelease experiences of federal prisoners. There were no surprises: ex-prisoners were typically released with very little "gate money" (often less than $50) and had great difficulty finding jobs. One conclusion was that economic hardship contributed to the commission of new crime.

The failure of prison vocational training programs, the high unemployment rates of ex-prisoners, and the meager financial resources available at release led the Manpower Administration (later renamed the Employment and Training Administration) to consider new programs built around the idea of providing ex-prisoners with some sort of financial assistance to aid in the transition to life on the outside. It was hoped that such assistance would serve as a cushion, allowing exoffenders to search more effectively for a steady job and in the meantime, directly reduce the economic motivation for crime. The perspective was also explicitly experimental; a rigorous evaluation was contemplated.

After a very small and successful pilot study to determine the feasibility of a particular social policy experiment, the LIFE (Living Insurance for Ex-Offenders) experiment was designed. An initial step was the development of a rationale and a research design with which to deliver financial aid to ex-prisoners. In brief, because eligibility for unemployment benefits was (and is) determined from employment in the four to six quarters prior to an application for benefits, the vast majority of ex-prisoners necessarily were losing whatever eligibility they had. Hence, prisoners sentenced for felonies, who typically serve a year or more behind bars, could not possibly establish eligibility—irrespective of their employment prior to incarceration.

In response, one of the experimental conditions was to be an approximation of unemployment benefits. Individuals who could not find jobs would be eligible for $60 a week for 13 weeks. A second experimental condition was job-placement services, much like those routinely provided by the U.S. Employment Service. A third experimental condition was a combination of the two "main" conditions. The fourth experimental (or control) condition was neither the benefits eligibility nor job counseling. Finally, approximately 400 prisoners were to be *randomly* assigned to each of the four conditions, and then followed for two years through interviews and official records (e.g., arrest reports) to measure any effects on postrelease behavior.

With the design in hand, the next step was to find a site to implement the experiment. For reasons that need not concern us here, the Maryland Department of Corrections agreed to cooperate, and the experiment was to be fielded in Baltimore. More important than the site were the criteria used to select prisoners to participate in the study. "High-risk" subjects were selected primarily because of a need to avoid floor effects; one could not determine which treatment most reduced the number of new crimes if very few crimes were committed overall. High risk was operationalized as males under 45 years of age with multiple convictions and at least one arrest for property crimes. No one addicted to alcohol or heroin was included, in part because the problems of addiction were assumed to be somewhat different from those of the "garden-variety" felon. There were other, less important, restrictions on participation that are described in Lenihan (1977) and Rossi et al. (1980).

Each of several analyses of the LIFE data revealed that financial aid reduced arrests on charges for property crimes. Approximately 30% of the individuals who did not receive benefits committed property crimes, compared to about 22% of those who received the benefits. The 8% difference was not a chance outcome by conventional criteria. On the other hand, no treatment effects were found for other kinds for crimes.

It was also believed by some that individuals receiving payments would be less likely to find and hold jobs. However, no such effects surfaced, in part because of a generous tax rate on earnings; it was possible to earn as much as $150 a week and still receive some portion of the benefits.

Finally, when all of the findings were subjected to a benefit-cost analysis, it was estimated conservatively that were LIFE's findings to hold up in a regular program, 4 dollars would be saved for every dollar invested in the unemployment benefits. Clearly, the program would be cost-effective.

The LIFE results were certainly encouraging, but required at least three caveats. First, although the experimental effects were statistically significant by conventional standards, they were just barely so; chance effects were just barely being ruled out. Second, the experiment was administered by an energetic and dedicated research team. It was unlikely that should LIFE-like payments be administered by the personnel of state unemployment agencies, that the same level of effort would be forthcoming. Hence, it was possible that benefitical effects would fail to appear. Finally, the high-risk sample of ex-offenders was certainly not representative of all persons who might be eligible for the payments. Consequently, it was difficult to determine what might happen were unemployment benefits eligibility routinely made available to ex-prisoners. Clearly there was a need for more research.

STAGE 2: THE TARP EXPERIMENT

More research was also the recommendation of two gatherings of social scientists, government officials, and criminal justice professionals. This led to a larger and more realistic experiment dubbed TARP (Transitional Aid for Released Prisoners; see Rossi et al., 1980). Again there was to be random assignment to payment and nonpayment groups. Again there was to be a two-year follow-up. However, the unemployment benefits were to be administered by personnel from state unemployment offices, not specially recruited research staff. In addition, there was to be on the average a substantially larger tax on earnings so that the payments would be dramatically reduced by rather modest earnings from employment. Finally, there were to be two experiments, one in Texas and one in Georgia, with about 1000 ex-prisoners in each, and virtually no restrictions on which ex-prisoners participated.

In contrast to the findings from the LIFE experiment, the TARP payments did *not* reduce overall property arrests or arrests for person crimes. As described in great detail in Rossi et al. (1980), a structural equation analysis of the experiment suggested that potential reductions in crime were swamped by an *increase* in new crimes stemming from unemployment *created* by the payments. In other words, there was apparently a tendency among those who received the benefits to reduce their labor force participation, at least in the short run.[6] These individuals, in turn, were more likely to get into trouble. And the crimes committed by these individuals obscured the otherwise benefical consequences of the payments. Recall that under LIFE, generous tax rates on earnings virtually eliminated any work disincentives. Under TARP, the work disincentives were substantial, and this led to what the TARP researchers called a "counterbalancing model": the payments had two *opposing* effects. (For another perspective, see Zeisel, 1982.)

The TARP study suggested that unemployment benefits could reduce both property and person crimes only if the work disincentives produced by the benefits could be affectively eliminated. And it was not clear precisely how that could be done, as the tolerance for error might not be very large. To complicate matters further, the inferences about appropriate levels of payments and the rate at which earnings would be taxed rested on findings from structural equations (i.e., statistical adjustments) that could not fully capitalize on the assets of random assignment to treatment and control groups. Hence, any causal inferences about the counterbalancing effects of unemployment benefits were more easily challenged than the overall conclusions that *as administered*, the payments did not reduce crime.

The content and timing of the TARP findings (corresponding with the beginning of the Reagan Administration) effectively ended any chance of federal initiative on transfer payments and crime. The LIFE and TARP experiments certainly did not show that providing unemployment eligibility to ex-offenders increased crime; the payments clearly did not make matters worse. There was also evidence that some form of transfer payments might well reduce crime. However, a clear mandate for a specific kind of program was not to be found. At least as important, the values and premises that lay beneath the LIFE and TARP studies for other reasons fell out of fashion in Washington circles. Put a bit too simply, the stick replaced the carrot and interest turned to deterrence through punishment and incapacitation through imprisonment.

STAGE 3: CALIFORNIA SENATE BILL 224

At about the time that the TARP study was being designed, Peter Behr, a California state senator (Republican, Beverly Hills), heard about the LIFE experiment. He had long been associated with a number of moderate to liberal legislative programs and saw in the LIFE experiment the opportunity to reduce crime and save taxpayers a lot of money. He had read that programs built on the principles underlying LIFE could save at least 4 dollars for every dollar invested. (At that time, it cost about $12,000 a year to keep a person in California incarcerated in a state facility.)

Drawing heavily on the LIFE experiment, Senate Bill 224 was introduced. The basic idea was to allow prisoners to establish eligibility for unemployment benefits from jobs held while doing time. Individuals working in prison jobs would be assumed to be earning the minimum wage of $2.30 an hour (although they were actually earning about 20 cents an hour), and individuals who "earned" at least $1500 over a 12-month interval would be eligible for unemployment benefits upon release. The size of the payments would depend on the level of earnings, but in practice, payments were likely to be a bit smaller than the $60 per week provided by LIFE. In addition, all of the usual rules for receiving unemployment benefits were supposed to apply. For example, to receive the payments, and ex-prisoner had to be actively seeking work.

Despite Behr's claims that the legislation would reduce crime and save tax dollars, it was opposed by conservative interests (e.g., professional law enforcement organizations, the California Chamber of Commerce). And not surprisingly, it was supported by liberal groups (e.g., the American Friends Service Committee). Clearly, ideology was carrying the day.

Eventually the bill became law, but in part to mollify the opposition, the legislation had two unusual features: There was a "sunset" clause giving the program a five-year life, and the program was to be subjected to a rigorous evaluation.[7] In other words, the program was clearly experimental and based on the evaluation results, would be completely reassessed at the end of five years. If the findings were favorable, the legislature presumably would be moved to introduce a *new* bill resurrecting the program.

All of this was far easier said than done. First, the legislature did not appropriate any funds to pay for the required evaluation. The California Department of Corrections was supposed to finance the research. In fact, the kind of evaluation demanded by the language of Senate Bill 224 was far more expensive than the Department of Corrections could afford.[8] Second, at the time there was no technical expertise within the Department of Corrections to ensure a credible evaluation. And third, the need for technical sophistication was made more important by legislative language that all but precluded random assignment to experimental and control groups. It is now widely recognized by individuals experienced in social experimentation that the weaker the research design, the greater the need for elaborate statistical models.

The U.S. Department of Labor's Employment and Training Administration saved the day by providing the necessary funding. They too were interested in testing a program based on the LIFE experiment. Experienced researchers were recruited from the University of California, solving the technical expertise problem. However, a randomized experiment could not be implemented. It became necessary, therefore, to settle for a quasi-experimental approach resting on a regression-discontinuity design. For present purposes, the major point is that although the regression-discontinuity design is quite powerful, it is far more easily challenged than "true" experiments resting on random assignment to experimental and control groups.

The evaluation was to be finished and the results released to the legislature at the end of the program's fourth year. Six months earlier, however, an effort was made to scuttle the program before the fifth year could begin. The real motivations were primarily ideological; there was a genuine hostility toward ex-prisoners and a deep-seated feeling that they did not deserve any help from the state. The explicit rationale, however, was economic. The program was expensive, and there was alleged to be no evidence of effectiveness. Fortunately, the state senator who was carrying the bill said publicly that he was prepared to withdraw the legislation if there was any evidence that the program was working as promised. And preliminary analyses (rather dramatically) introduced during committee hearings shortly thereafter were optimistic. The legislation was withdrawn.

Six months later, the final report was available. It showed reductions in crime much like those found in the LIFE experiment and consistent with the TARP counterbalancing model. A conservative benefit-cost analysis suggested that the program saved California taxpayers about $2000 per participant. (For more details, see Rauma and Berk, 1982; Berk and Rauma, 1983.) Based on these findings, an assembly bill was introduced to reinstitute the program, and it easily cleared the liberal-dominated committee in which it was initially heard. It foundered in the conservative-dominated assembly Ways and Means Committee (which reviews all spending measures). The argument was that the program perhaps saved money in the long run, but there was a fiscal crisis in California that could not wait for the long run to arrive. In all fairness, the state was facing a large deficit, which is prohibited by the California constitution. Times have again changed, however, and with the projected surplus California is now enjoying, it is likely that the bill will be reintroduced. Passage, of course, is another question.

SOME LESSONS

There are a number of lessons that might be extracted from the three studies just described. For our purposes, five stand out. First, the LIFE and TARP were exemplary applications of rigorous scientific methods to assess the impact of a social program (Cronbach, 1983). The evaluation of Senate Bill 224 was nearly as strong. Yet, none of the efforts produced social policy recommendations that were truly definitive; the general conclusion was that transfer payments might well reduce crime, but only if the work disincentives were not strong. Hence, although the information provided was far superior to the information that had earlier informed public policy, an ironclad case one way or the other was surely not made for extending unemployment benefits to ex-prisoners. In short, even exemplary social experiments can do no more than reduce uncertainty about the impact of various interventions. The reduction in uncertainty may be dramatic, but some uncertainty will always remain. In other words, experiments in social policy can be extremely instructive, especially when compared to the ignorance in which so many social programs are debated. But they are only helpful; they can never be truly conclusive.

Second, if exemplary true and quasi-experiments cannot produce definitive results, it follows that findings from studies using weaker designs may be worse than useless. On one hand, the research may be so obviously flawed that scientific methods themselves may inappropriately take the rap. The early evaluations of Head Start, for example, helped stimulate across the board skepticism of "positivist"[9] methods. On the other hand, misleading findings may be seized upon, perhaps for the wrong reasons, and influence social policy. A recent study claiming to show that parochial schools were more effective than public shools (Coleman et al., 1983), for instance, is both badly flawed (Rossi, 1984) and widely quoted. It follows, therefore, that powerful research designs and data analysis plans are essential and that in addition, resources must be provided to capitalize on them. A research design that founders for want of sufficient support would be better off left on the drawing board.

Third, even exemplary social policy experiments, however, do not necessarily lead to appropriate social policy. Despite state-of-the-art research methods, the findings may be wrong, misconstrued, or simply ignored. For example, there is no credible evidence for the deterrent effect of capital punishment (Blumstein et al., 1980), but that has not kept public officials from claiming that the death penalty deters. Likewise, strong evidence that price is an effective water conservation tool (Berk et al., 1981) has had little impact on continuing low prices for agricultural users, clearly encouraging waste (and, incidently acting as a subsidy to argibusiness). We raise these difficulties in part to provide a realistic picture of the current scene, but also to support later arguments for efforts that might improve matters.

Fourth, political fashions come and go and witn them concerns for particular social problems. One result is haphazard social policy research programs. Social policy experiments need to be planned carefully with an eye toward *packages* of studies. Single experiments hastily initiated to answer the questions of the moment may on occasion provide useful information, but are unlikely to produce the *cumulative* body of knowledge required for sound policy decisions. For example, a recent experiment showing that under certain conditions, arrests deter incidents of wife battery (Sherman and Berk, 1984) should really have been undertaken as part of a general research program on law enforcement responses to family problems. We have an isolated finding when we should have a growing body of knowledge. In response, means will be suggested later to provide some coherence to social policy experiments.

Finally, all three experiments made little use of social science theory and in turn have been essentially ignored by the basic research community. It is likely that each study would have been significantly enriched and strengthened had the treatments been more directly based on what social science has to say about the impact of monetary incentives and employment. It is also likely that basic research on crime is all the poorer as a consequence of ignoring what was found.

IV: SOCIAL POLICY EXPERIMENTS
MORE FORMALLY DEFINED

WHAT IS SOCIAL POLICY EXPERIMENTATION?

A social policy experiment is here defined as *a theoretically based effort to introduce social change in a way that permits discerning the net effect of the change on social outcomes.* Thus, an explicit and clearly articulated alteration in policy or practice is expressly linked to the need to determine what consequences follow, after taking into account other things that might affect those consequences.

We envision two major purposes for social policy experiments: first and foremost to inform policy decisions and, second, to advance social science theory and knowledge. In the past, these two enterprises have been artificially separated to the detriment of both. It is, in fact, hard to imagine good social policy not capitalizing on the accumulated wisdom of the social sciences, and equally hard to imagine changes in social policy from which social scientists could not learn. But our point here is that both the applied and basic research audiences can benefit from social policy experiments. The TARP experiment, for instance, had important implications for microeconomic theory and for whether transfer payments delivered to ex-offenders under different taxing schemes were an effective way to reduce crime.

The form of social policy experimentation that we advocate here has three distinctive features. First, it must exploit social science theory. Many policy interventions that are seriously proposed may seem sensible on their face, but are rarely thought out carefully, and rarely capitalize on theories from psychology, economics, sociology, and political science. This is no small loss, because social science theory could make important contributions when an intervention and research design are formulated. A serious scrutiny of social science theory would also alert researchers to potential implementation problems. For example, in developing a water conservation program and an appropriate evaluation design, it would be essential to capitalize on microeconomic theory, asserting that for water to be used efficiently, the price (per unit) must equal the marginal cost. Efficient allocations will not follow, in contrast, if the price consumers pay per unit is equal to the average cost (which is common practice).

At the same time, what we mean by theory is quite elastic. It ranges from the lay "let's try this," to propositions deductively derived from first principles. We take this broad stance in part because we could not agree (and we are hardly alone) about what constitutes a theory, and in part because it seems silly to exclude lay understandings of how things work simply because social science certification is lacking. The key point is that social theories are meant to explain *how* a particular social process works, and we are stressing the need to think things through carefully, exploiting all available information. In any case, we certainly do not want to get bogged down in a long and abstract discussion of the nature of theory, especially when it is unnecessary for our purposes.

Our requirement that existing theory be exploited excludes ad hoc efforts to "tinker with the system," and policy changes that fail to recognize existing knowledge. So, for example, we regard tinkering as a legitimate and important activity for public program managers and program staff. We could easily imagine, for instance, a teacher intuitively altering his or her classroom technique in response to the mix of pupils. But such efforts fall outside our purview unless the intervention is carefully considered, bringing extant knowledge to bear.

We also exclude all forecasts if they are not backed by a description of the underlying causal mechanisms. One could easily imagine, for example, a company forecasting demand for its products by simple extrapolation from past demand. Likewise, one might forecast the unemployment rate by extrapolating from historical (e.g., seasonal) patterns. Although both forecasts may be quite accurate and useful, they are not theoretical statements; they fail to address how things work. On a more subtle level, a forecast might draw on "leading indicators." Yet, unless there is an accompanying explanation of how the leading indicators are causally linked to the outcome, no theoretical statements are being made.

A second distinctive feature of our perspective on social policy experimentation is that the social changes or interventions of interest are necessarily policy mutable. They include changes in law (e.g., from indeterminant to determinant prison sentences), corporate policy (e.g., the introduction of workers councils), administrative regulations (e.g., certification requirements for food stamps), and other instruments important enough to justify a planned effort to understand their effects in the least equivocal manner. They would exclude changes that for all practical purposes were not subject to manipulation: natural disasters (e.g., earthquakes), charismatic social movements (e.g., the rise of the New Right), historical events (e.g., the election of Ronald Reagan), and the like.

To illustrate more thoroughly, the age mix of the population surely has an impact on crime, school crowding, and the demand for certain kinds of consumer goods, but in the short run at least, and under current social arrangements in the United States, the mix of young to old people in the population is not subject to manipulation. Likewise, one might be interested in the impact of race on income, but it is not possible to alter someone's race to determine whether, for example, people assigned to "black" do worse than people assigned to "white."[10]

It is possible, of course, to explore the relationships between age mix and crime, school crowding, or consumer demand with nonexperimental methods. Similarly, one could examine the relationship between race and income with nonexperimental methods. Much, in principle, could be learned. However, we are advocating experimental approaches because of a general consensus that causal inferences from non-experimental methods are typically inferior to those obtained from experimental methods (Boruch and Reiken, 1974; Cook and Campbell, 1979; Holland and Rubin, 1984, Rosenbaum and Rubin, 1983; Rossi and Freeman, 1982; Pratt and Schlaifer, 1984; Dawid, 1984; Rosenbaum and Rubin, 1984). Indeed, Holland and Rubin would consign all nonexperimental social research to mere description.[11]

Lest we be misunderstood, we are *not* arguing that the only useful applied social research is based on experimentation. There are times when causal inferences are not at issue, such as when we try to estimate the number of families in the United States living below the poverty level. We are then only interested in some quite important "mere description."

There will be other times when causal inferences are desirable, but when experimentation is impractical. One might then settle for nonexperimental studies as a second best alternative. Many would argue, for instance, that it would be unethical to undertake an experiment on the psychological effects of having an abortion. Even if a group of pregnant women could be found who would volunteer for random assignment to treatment and control groups, the fetus' interests are not considered. Under these circumstances, one might proceed with a nonexperimental design in which women who had an abortion were first matched with women who had not had an abortion (see for example, Rosenbaum and Rosen, 1983, for a discussion of matching). Insofar as the experimentals and controls were matched on all of the important variables that might otherwise explain any differences in psychological functioning (e.g., age, religion, martial status, income), plausible causal inferences about the *net* impact of an abortion might be made. These might serve as the best policy-relevant results available on which programmatic decisions could be made or as formal hypotheses from which more powerful studies could be designed.

Finally, there will be still other times when alternative attributes of sound, applied research are more important than making the most credible causal inferences. Suppose, for example, that one were interested in the impact of avoidance conditioning on alcohol abuse. However, the individuals who are available for random assignment to avoidance conditioning (i.e., punishing instances of the undesirable behavior) are under a court order to undergo immediate treatment (e.g., because of a drunk-driving conviction). It would be very difficult, therefore, to generalize one's findings to other kinds of persons in need, and one might choose to undertake a study based on matching (or statistical adjustments) if a more representative sample could be obtained.

We also do not mean to ignore that role of applied research that *supports* good social experiments. Thus, it often is essential to do applied studies determining the nature and extent of a particular social problem before a program is designed (i.e., "needs assessments"). A recent instance is investigations into whether there are a large number of Americans who were malnourished. Similarly, it is often desirable to determine whether a given social program is operating as designed. Here, under the label of "monitoring," *ethnographic methods* are essential. Even a casual inspection of many of the projects launched under the Model Cities Program of the 1960s, for instance, revealed that a number of programs for which funds were allocated were never actually implemented. Hence, a failure to find any program impact could often be explained by an absence of a program rather than by program ineffectiveness. And in a similar fashion, analyses of cost-effectiveness are typically helpful, because so many programs should be justified in monetary terms. For example, given the costs of incarceration, it is not at all clear that recent legislation requiring longer prison terms is cost-effective, even if (and this has not been demonstrated) longer prison terms reduce crime. In short, there is nothing in our perspective that denies the importance of such activities as needs assessments, monitoring, or benefit-cost analysis. We view them, however, as being in service of determining the net impact of policy innovations; we do not see them as ends in themselves.

The third distinctive characteristic of our approach is that we regard as crucial the requirement that when experiments are attempted, the government or others provide resources for estimating the impact of the changes in the program or policy, before the changes are introduced. This prior commitment distinguishes social policy experiments from ex post facto analyses. It also permits the design of research that leads to less debatable, more precise, and more reliable information about the outcomes of the intervention.

We briefly mentioned earlier, for example, an experiment undertaken to determine which of three police responses to wife battery most reduced the number of postintervention wife-battery incidents. In the experiment, arresting the offender proved more effective than ordering the offender from the premises for several hours, or trying to mediate the dispute. Although the study relied on random assignment of households to one of the three treatments, allowance had to be made for instances in which the separation and mediation interventions had to be "upgraded" to an arrest (on a nonrandom basis). If an offender refused to leave the premises when ordered to do so, for instance, the officer had to be given the option of making an arrest. This in turn meant that data had to be collected on (1) the assigned treatment, (2) the treatment actually delivered, and (3) variables that might affect the shift from separation or mediation to arrest. It is extremely unlikely that such information would have been recorded had not adequate resources for the study been provided; police do not typically indicate in much detail (if at all) why a particular action is taken. And under those circumstance, a far weaker analysis of the data would have resulted. In short, we envision social policy experiments as requiring a commitment to research backed by the necessary resources. This excludes from our definition such programs as Jesse Jackson's Push for Excellence, because meaningful resources have not been allocated in advance to determine the program's impact. Excluded for the same reason are activities such as "scientific jury selection" (which uses social science technology to help in the selection of jury panels).

WHY SHOULD WE DO
SOCIAL POLICY EXPERIMENTS?

The principal beneficiary of social policy experiments is society itself. It should not have to be argued that with more reliable information about the impact of policy alternatives, the opportunity exists for more effective public policy. We are well aware that the opportunity may not translate into real benefits; the information may be ignored or even misused. Better information is surely a necessary prerequisite for improved responses to social problems.

To illustrate, educational foundations have relied on randomized field experiments to discover the beneficial effects of *Sesame Street*, *The Electric Company*, and other programs, and to justify continued support. Yet, randomized tests of the television show *Feeling Good* revealed that despite good intentions and glowing rhetoric, some forms of television-based health education for poor families simply do not work. The negative findings were used to terminate a program whose costs would have far exceeded any benefits, and to reallocate scarce resources to more effective approaches to health education.

In addition, there are often costs involved in *not* experimenting. Clearly, early Comprehensive Employment and Training Act (CETA) programs produced no credible evidence about their impact, and as a consequence, public debate was confused, money was poorly spent, and human expectations were dreadfully misdirected. To take a more recent example, many millions of dollars are now being spent introducing "computer literacy" into schools. All kinds of grand claims are being made. We are told by some, for instance, that learning how to program will teach the kind of conceptual skills that children need to master algebra. Or, we are told that with computer literacy will come better coping abilities needed in the world of the twenty-first century, or that people comfortable with computers will more easily find employment. But none of these claims has been subjected to randomized field experiments. It may be that most of the claims are false, in which case a lot of expectations have been inappropriately raised and enormous amounts of money wasted. It may be that there are some benefits from the introduction of computers into schools, but that the same money spent in more traditional ways would be at least as effective. Or it may be that a number of benefits follow, but as a result, students from less richly endowed schools will fall still farther behind their more fortunate peers. Perhaps some ways of using computers are effective although others are not. In short, it may be very costly not to know; a failure to experiment may well incur substantial costs.

There are also a number of somewhat more subtle benefits from social policy experimentation. First, there may be high political costs in launching untested programs that fail. If a substantial investment is made in responses to a particular social problem, and the social problem persists, political leaders may throw up their hands and conclude that the problem is intractable. An excellent recent example is unemployment. Over the last decade, as the unemployment rate has grown in the face of many remedial efforts, politicians have gradually redefined to higher and higher levels what is called the "natural" rate of unemployment. Alternatively, one might argue that the remedial efforts were not properly designed, tested, and implemented. The CETA program, for instance, was at best terribly administered.

Second, social policy experiments can serve as inspiration. An experiment can be undertaken before there is a full political commitment even to seeking a cure for the problem. Finding that something works may inspire a legislator to "discover" the problem by providing a particular course of action to pursue; a legislator with a hammer will likely look for a nail. For example, the experiment described earlier on police interventions in wife-battery incidents (which was very widely publicized) has led legislators in a number of states to discover the problem of law enforcement responses to family violence

Third, experiments catch the eye. They seem to speak for themselves as a self-contained and comprehensible response to a particular social problem. They give the appearance that someone is trying to do something. Other forms of applied social research are less readily interpreted in this manner. There were a great many correlational studies of the relationship between cholesterol and heart disease before the recent experiment; it was the experiment that made the cover of *Time* magazine.

Fourth, social policy experiment that are done well will give increased legitimacy to the scientific enterprise at a time of considerable public skepticism. From the Fundamentalist attacks on the theory of evolution to quite proper concerns about the environmental implications of genetic engineering, science has been on the defensive for a number of years. Good social policy experiments may help to counter this trend.

Fifth, good social experiments educate the public about the scientific method and increase public understanding about the sorts of issues that must be addressed to provide compelling answers to factual questions. The senior author of this report, for example, was recently presenting some nonexperimental results on the causes of prison crowding to a meeting of a local Optimists Club, and was quite properly grilled about the credibility of his causal inferences. Indeed, one of the members (an owner of a nursery) developed an argument that basically captured the ideas behind regression to the mean. Visible social policy experiments may well foster such sophistication.

Finally, social policy experiments permit adventurousness tempered with caution. Properly presented, social policy experiments should appeal to both the audacious and the deliberate. Creative innovations of all kinds can be implemented on a small scale, and their effects examined. Social policy experiments can be progressive in the interventions tried and yet conservative in the speed with which full implementation may be undertaken.

In the face of these and other benefits, the case against social policy experimentation seems quite weak. Most of the criticism addresses much larger issues beyond social policy experimentation per se. Thus, claims remain unchallenged that social policy experiments are inherently "conservative" in that the innovations tried are modest in scope and impact, leaving the basic "system" intact. By and large, this is an accurate portrayal of social policy experiments, but it also describes virtually all social change mechanisms available within "democratic" societies. No one is claiming that social policy experimentation is a ready means to social revolution.

Others claim that because social policy experiments are typically initiated by those in power, social experiments will only heip the powerful at the expense of the powerless. Whether or not this is true, it is not an inherent feature of social policy experiments. To run social policy experiments does require access to funding and enough political power to secure cooperation from public officials, but large numbers of diverse groups have succeeded in the past. For example, effective applied research has been undertaken by labor unions, consumer groups, environmental groups, and—perhaps most recently and visibly—by an informal coalition of scientists who demonstrated that a "nuclear winter" might well result from a nuclear exchange. There is no reason why social policy experiments cannot in a similar fashion respond to concerns raised by a wide variety of interests.

Still others claim that social policy experiments undermine the democratic process by putting political and value questions in the hands of technocrats. Although we certainly do not claim that there is any simple distinction between fact and value, social policy experiments are meant to produce knowledge based on scientific methods. And there is nothing in those methods that need imperialize activities in the political arena. For example, the decision about what sorts of social problems are important enough to address through experiments is primarily a political question. Likewise, decisions about what sorts of experimental effects are important enough to measure is primarily a political decision. Social policy experiments do not inform such judgments.

In the end, the major objections to social policy experiments are practical and particular: Is a given experiment too costly? Does a given experiment violate important ethical principles? Can a given experiment deliver the information required in the time available? Can a given experiment be properly implemented in the field? These are all important concerns, and occasionally there will be insurmountable problems, but by and large, the usefulness and feasibility of social policy experiments has been amply demonstrated. What is needed, therefore, are means to capitalize on the promise of social policy experiments. In the pages ahead we will suggest some ways in which this might be done.

V: A PROGRAM FOR
SOCIAL POLICY EXPERIMENTATION—
AN ORGANIZING STRUCTURE FOR
SOCIAL POLICY EXPERIMENTATION

We believe that wise social experimentation is most likely to occur if an organization is created to serve as orchestrator. Such an organization can help promote experiments and help avoid a piecemeal approach that will waste scarce resources. A possible organizing structure would be one or more centers for social policy experimentation. There are excellent examples in other disciplines of centers on which to draw. The Salk Institute, National Center for Atmoshperic Research, and the Institute for Theoretical Physics are three instances with which we are acquainted.

At this point, however, we do *not* for several reasons favor establishing any centers for social policy experimentation. First, centers are typically very costly to start and maintain. Second, even if money were available to start a center, that money might well be better spent in other ways; the opportunity costs would be great. Third, centers too often ossify, as researchers, administrators, and staff become invested in the center per se and not its activities. Fourth, centers concentrate massive resources in a few locations and in a small number of hands. The possibility of large and relatively *indivisible* resources almost inevitably triggers a fierce and often self-destructive scramble among prospective suitors. In the end, a few win big and most lose big. This is not the atmosphere in which cooperative scientific endeavors thrive. In short, all-or-nothing competitions are sometimes useful, but we see no compelling advantages for them here. Fifth and finally, we think that there is an alternative structure that will accomplish much the same goal at less cost and with fewer liabilities.

We propose the establishment of a committee on social policy experimentation (or some similar name) whose main purpose would be to stimulate the use of social policy experiments addressing pressing social problems. The committee would have about 15 members knowledgeable in experimentation who would meet frequently and regularly; perhaps once a month for two days year round. Appointments to be committee would be for terms of 3 to 5 years.

The committee would have an executive officer in charge of administration on a day-to-day basis: providing agendas for the monthly meetings, overseeing support services, and the like. The appointment would be for a maximum of five years. There would also be associates of the committee who would be more junior persons, serving essentially as committee staff. Finally, there would be support personnel for clerical work and bookkeeping.

At the monthly meetings, three broad tasks would be addressed. First, the committee would *develop and advocate policy-fostering experiments and other related research activities, programs and projects.* These would include such actions as (1) identifying and suggesting needed technical improvement in research methods, (2) identifying and suggesting measures needed to augment the supply of social scientists and others trained in the requisite skills for social policy experiments, and (3) identifying and suggesting enabling legislation needed to support experimental approaches to social problem solutions. For example, the committee might decide that experimental approaches developed by engineers to evaluate the reliability of complicated pieces of machinery had potential applications in the evaluation of social programs. One action might be to outline and then "peddle" to funders a postdoctoral program for social scientist who wanted to learn about engineering quality control techniques.

Second, drawing on a variety of sources, the committee *would identify and suggest social issues needing new policies and programs.* When such problem areas were found—and assuming they were sufficiently serious, well defined, and tractable—a special, *ad hoc subcommittee would be formed (recruited from outside the national committee) to explore experimental and other research opportunities.* For example, responding to recent publicity, a subcommittee might be formed around the problem drunk driving. That subcommittee might develop a set of experimental designs to evaluate the impact of recent drunk-driving laws and then "shop" for funding with which to get the research done. Alternatively, they might first seek funders and then in collaboration, design and implement the study.

Finally, the committee would *recommend to foundations, government agencies, and private enterprise substantive areas in which programs of experimentation offer promise.* Examples might include tax compliance, incentives systems to reduce acid rain, the needs of the homeless, and the deterrent effect of incarceration.

To make the functioning of the committee more concrete, consider the following example. Technological obsolescence is a recurrent problem in certain industries. Companies such as Exxon, DuPont, and Boeing as well as service industries and government agencies are routinely affected. Suppose that technical obsolescence is selected by the committee as one of several problems that need to be pursued. It would be apparent that a number of different consequences are involved: productivity, plant closings, structural unemployment, worker safety, balance of trade with foreign countries, and many others.

A subcommittee would then be constituted to address macrolevel issues (e.g., balance of trade) and microlevel issues (e.g., worker retraining), pulling together what was known about the causes and consequences of technological obsolescence. At this point, the abilities of an expert and ecumenical subcommittee would be critical as the subcommittee would have to decide what kinds of experiments at what level (micro or macro) would best advance the policy-formulation process (as well as scientific progress).

Assuming that such experiments could be described, the next step would be to facilitate the desired field research. Options might include the following (other possible activities are described more generally later):

(1) contract or grant-funded experiments to assay effectiveness of theory-based "solutions" to one or more of the most pressing problems;

(2) contract or grant-funded experiments *adjoined* to federal/state demonstration projects to generate theory-related evidence about whether particular projects work, why they work, and whether a positve benefit-cost ratio results;

(3) contract or grant-funded reanalyses of data from earlier experiments for what could be learned about responses to technical obsolescence;

(4) contract or grant-funded efforts to solve methodological problems preventing sound experimentation on the problem; and

(5) "seed money" and "matching funds," efforts to get any of the four options funded by other private or public sources.

AVOIDING PITFALLS

Given the activities and structure proposed for the committee, there are clearly a number of pitfalls to be avoided. First, the danger of ossification exists; long-term participation may make committee members stale, tired, or even lazy. In response, we recommend that no committee appointments be for more than three years, with each appointment made for one year at a time.

Second, there is the risk of special pleading by committee members. In response, we recommend that no committee members can apply for or receive grants during their tenure on the committee from funding sources used by the committee for social policy experiments; basically they must not be permitted to use the committee to line their own research pockets.

Third, committees of this general type can founder on lack of commitment; members just go through the motions. In response, we recommend that a reasonable stipend be paid to committee members for their work. Alternatively, released time from teaching or administration might be purchased.

Fourth, it is possible for such committees to become dominated by their staffs. Committee meetings may be little more than rubber stamps for work done by full-time, paid staff members. In partial response, we recommend that staff appointments be for a single term of perhaps no more than five years or treated as fellowships of even shorter duration.

Fifth, there is the risk of the committee becoming too cozy with a particular discipline or point of view. To encourage heterogeniety, we recommend that "slots" for different disciplines be established. There should also be a good mix of individuals from different professional settings (academe, government agencies, private research firms, etc.), who are at different stages of their careers.

Sixth, there is a danger that the committee will become too "political" and lose its credibility. That is, the committee is surely a vehicle for enhancing social policy experimentation, but must be seen as reasonably evenhanded on a variety of other dimensions. It must try to avoid, for example, being identified with either liberal or conservative camps (e.g., The Brookings Institute and the Hoover Institute). We recommend, therefore, that the committee not function as a lobbying group with Congress or other official decision-making bodies and that the committee avoid making public pronouncements on the issues of the day, except issues relating to research and scientific methods themselves. We are not suggesting, of course, that social policy experiments or the committee could ever be "value free." Values of various sorts must necessarily be embodied in whatever actions are taken. We are arguing however, that the committee avoid traditional political activities and that the committee respond fairly to a wide range of value positions.

Finally, there is the possibility that the committee will not function as planned and either gradually take on a less desirable agenda or simply perform in an ineffective manner (compared to other ways to facilitate social policy experimentation). Hence, we recommend that in addition to yearly auditing and substantive reviews, there be every five years a thorough assessment by an outside panel of academics, public officials, and others knowledgeable in social policy experimentation. The committee itself is an experiment and needs to be evaluated.

In summary, we are proposing the establishment of a committee to facilitate and shape at a national level the use of field experiments to inform public policy. In general terms, therefore, there are ample precedents; the Social Science Research Council and various committees of the National Academy of Sciences are examples. However, our proposed committee is in many ways unique.

To begin, it has a relatively narrow mission. There is no intent to directly influence a wide variety of social science activity, much as the Social Science Research Council does. The more specific focus will prevent the committee's overriding agenda from becoming diluted in a host of other concerns about the social sciences or science more generally. Likewise, the committee is not an appendage to some larger collection of scientists. Hence, the committee is free to establish its own agenda unencumbered by unrelated issues, historical baggage, or ongoing commitments. This freedom is all the more important given the unusual mandate explicitly combining scientific and policy concerns.

ACTIVITIES THE COMMITTEE
MIGHT FOSTER OR UNDERTAKE

With the committee's structure described, we can turn in more detail to the kinds of activities that might be undertaken by the committee or with its encouragement and support. What follows is a list of possibilities varying in size, likely impact, and cost.

Direct Involvement in Social Policy Experiments

(1) *Funding particular social policy experiments.* We have already tried to make the case for social policy experiments and hope that nothing of major importance still needs to be said.

(2) *Funding replications of social policy experiments.* Over the past 20 years social policy experiments have been funded from time to time, and many of these have been very instructive. Replications are much less commonly supported. Yet, replication lies at the heart of generalized knowledge.

(3) *Funding for particular secondary analyses.* Social policy experiments often produce large data sets that are incompletely analyzed by the original investigators. In addition, there are often alternative data analytic approaches, occasionally leading to alternative results, not all of which are explored by the original investigators. It is often useful, therefore, to support a set of analyses of the same data undertaken by several independent groups of researchers.

(4) *Funding particular meta-analyses.* A meta-analysis is basically an attempt to draw some overall conclusions from a series of social policy experiments on a given topic (e.g., the impact of deinstitutionalization on mental patients). Summaries of the literature have been undertaken as long as there have been literatures to summarize. Recent work in meta-analysis has tried to apply more rigorous, statistical procedures for formally aggregating results over the set of experiments, and has advanced understanding about what works and the extent to which it works.

Providing Resources for
Social Policy Experiments

(5) *Support for field laboratories in social policy experimentation*. In the environmental sciences, the National Science Foundation supports the maintenance of several large research sites (e.g, a desert setting, a coastal setting) in which environmental scientists can conduct observational studies and experiments. In such sites, it is possible, for example, to dam a stream and see what ecological consequences follow. One could imagine establishing ongoing research sites for social policy experimentation. These might be designated as individuals, households, geographical areas (e.g., neighborhoods), or institutions (e.g., a particular police department, a particular school system), *voluntarily* making a relatively long-term commitment to participation in a series of social policy experiments. There are a number of advantages to this approach, including the prospect of reduced costs, better quality control, and especially rich data sets.

(6) *Endowed chairs in social policy experimentation*. Endowed chairs would give added stature to social policy experimentation and applied social science research more generally. As noted earlier, applied social science research typically carries low prestige activity in academic circles. As a result, talented social scientists often avoid applied work and their students primarily pursue basic research. The prestige of endowed chairs may help to right the balance. In addition, endowed chairs will allow energetic applied researchers to be devoted full time to social policy experiments.

(7) *Subsidized publications in social policy experimentation*. Many important reports of social policy experiments go unpublished because they are thought by publishers to be unprofitable. Whether they are or not, a series of subsidized publications (e.g., a monograph series) would help to give stature to the field and disseminate important findings.

(8) *"MacArthur awards" for particular social policy experiments*. One might designate several "MacArthur awards" per year for someone active in social policy experimentation. Besides allowing that individual to pursue full-time experimentation, the award would add legitimacy to the field.

(9) *"Blank check" research awards for some period of time.* These would be much like the "MacArthur award" but would be given solely to support research activities in social policy experimentation (of the recipient's choosing.)

(10) *Support for making social policy experiments a greater part of the political process.* Examples include funding trips to testify at legislative hearings, funding a newsletter on social policy experiments, holding conferences on social policy experimentation for the news media, funding meetings between social policy experimenters and legislative aides and others. It includes establishing special, ongoing seminars to enhance *regular productive exchanges between experimenters and legislators willing to test their ideas.*

(11) *Conferences for academics on social policy experimentation.* There may be too much "conferencing" among academics already, but maybe not.

(12) *Annual awards for outstanding work on social policy experimentation.* One might support something like an R.A. Fisher Award to be given each year by the American Statistical Association or the Evaluation Research Society for outstanding contributions to social policy experimentation. The award might well include a substantial honorarium.

Training and Retooling

(13) *Paid leaves or sabbaticals for university faculty who want to train or retool in social policy experimentation.* The recent flurry of interest in applied social research has demonstrated that there are a number of academics who might pursue more applied careers if they could obtain the necessary technical skills. One might, for example, have a postdoctoral program for academics five years or more beyond the Ph.D.

(14) *Paid leaves or sabbaticals for government officials, business executives, and others who want to train or retool in social policy experimentation.* Many government employees, among others, would seek training in social policy experimentation if they could afford to do so. Several years ago, summer training programs in evaluation research

at Northwestern University and the University of Massachusetts routinely drew a considerable number of government employees.

(15) *Postdoctoral training programs.* Although no labor market surveys have been done, impressionistic evidence suggests that there are many jobs for individuals trained in social policy experimentation. For example, postdoctoral programs in evaluation research at UCLA and Northwestern University always place their students. We also have had success placing our students, many of whom have applied interests. In addition, it is entirely possible that with more people trained in social policy experimentation, interest in social policy experimentation will grow (a kind of supply-side effect), and grow in a productive manner. At the very least, the legitimacy of the social policy experimentation would be enhanced.

(16) *Pre-doctoral training programs.* The arguments for pre-doctoral training programs are much the same as those for post-doctoral training programs, except that one is likely to be educating not just individuals who will do social policy experiments, but individuals who will have to understand them and put their findings into practice. That is, "consumers" of social policy experiments will be trained as well: corporate executives, elected officials, government administrators, and others.

(17) *Retooling programs for government personnel.* There is no reason why training programs in social policy experimentation should exclude people who already have established careers. One could imagine a range of retooling efforts lasting from a weekend to several years. It is entirely conceivable that many government agencies would pay for such training programs. Summer programs on applied research have in fact been reasonably successful in the past.

(18) *Retooling programs for business personnel.* The arguments for retooling that apply to government personnel apply equally to business personnel. Many firms have active applied research programs and in fact undertake social policy experiments as we have defined them (e.g., on worker productivity). They also have to know how to interpret social policy experiments undertaken by others (e.g., on vocational training programs). Like government agencies, businesses might well pay for training programs in social policy experimentation.

(19) *Support for the development of curricula for colleges in social policy experimentation.* To the best of our knowledge, there are very few courses in social policy experimentation currently being offered to

undergraduates. There has not even been very much systematic thought about what such courses should contain. One might support individuals or groups (or hold a conference or two) wanting to improve existing curricula (e.g., by "buying back" release time from their other duties).

In short, there are clearly a number of activities in support of social policy experimentation that our proposed committee could undertake or directly encourage. The problem will not be finding useful things to do. The problem will be to select among a rich menu of opportunities.

SOME BRIEF OBSERVATIONS ON
GETTING FROM HERE TO THERE

Even if the views expressed in this position paper are persuasive, many steps remain before our committee on social policy experimentation could be launched. Perhaps most important, we have not considered the various ways one might get from the current situation to a more organized and visible presence for social policy experiments.

On the surface, the best approach might be from the top down. One or more funding organizations could provide the necessary support, and within a relatively short time the national committee would in principle be functioning. Certainly, the costs of the committee is not a significant obstacle relative to other investments in the social and natural sciences.

However, it seems to us that such a scenario is unlikely. As a practical matter, there is fierce competition for existing resources, and the game is sometimes very close to zero sum. In addition, there is in applied social research—just as in any enterprise—a considerable commitment to the status quo. We are proposing substantial change. Finally, for reasons discussed earlier, social experimentation has been viewed with some hostility by the basic research community and with some skepticism by policymakers. In short, whatever the merits of our national committee, there will no doubt be significant opposition.

Therefore, a bottom-up strategy may be more productive, and several complementary approaches are possible. Thus, if the national scale is too grand, significant progress might be made at the state or even local level. Likewise, one might begin within a particular policy area or in concert with a single government agency. For example, the Attorney General of California recently proposed collaborative undertaking in applied social research between the state's Bureau of Criminal Statistics and the University of California. Central to this effort would be a governing committee much like our proposed national committee. And perhaps most important, social policy experiments would figure significantly in the collaboration. Should this effort prove productive, similar arrangements might be established in a number of agencies and ultimately at the national level.

Another bottom-up approach might begin with one or more of the specific initiatives briefly described above, with the goal of fostering a community of interest in social policy experiments. For example, a foundation or government agency might be persuaded to fund a package of social policy experiments to be initiated over a five-year period. These experiments would be billed as exemplary efforts tackling important social problems using state-of-the art methods and theory. The key element, however, would be regular meetings among individuals associated with the experiments to exchange views and experiences. A wide variety of disciplines and substantive interests would be represented, and over time an influential constituency for social policy experiments could develop. It might then be a short step to a national committee on social policy experimentation.

A CLOSING EXHORTATION

The scientific arguments for social policy experiments are well-known and widely accepted when causal inferences are essential to the policy formation process. It is also apparent, that the practical and ethical obstacles to social policy experiments have been vastly overrated. Finally, useful social policy experiments can be funded for modest sums and even rather dear social policy experiments can be highly cost-effective. Thus, an intellectual case against social policy experiments is difficult to construct. It is time to get on with the operational problem of integrating social policy experiments into the policy formation process.

NOTES

1. We use the term "social policy experiments" rather than "social experiments" to emphasize the explicit links to the policymaking process and to negate some of the "Strangelovean" connotations associated with the term "social experiments."

2. This rendering of the income maintenance experiments is vastly simplified for purposes of exposition. The same holds for the other experiments summarized in this section. In each case, a full discussion can be found in cited material. Nevertheless, it is perhaps worth mentioning that the later income maintenance experiments undertaken in Denver and Seattle found modest work disincentive effects across the board.

3. One does not have to randomly assign subjects. If one has a longitudinal design, one can also randomly assigned *when* the intervention occurs.

4. For example, the *Evaluation Review*, which is the journal most widely subscribed to in the field of evaluation research (which is built around social experimentation), is only 7 years old. The Evaluation Research Society is about the same age.

5. In practice, anticipating whether an experiment will be cost-effective is very complicated (Mosteller and Weinstein, 1981). For example, whether an experiment will be cost-effective depends in part on what the findings will be. But if these were known, there would be no need to do the research.

6. However, there was evidence that the unemployment benefits helped ex-offenders find better (i.e., higher-paying) jobs, just as anticipated.

7. The legislation required, for example, both an impact assessment on a number of outcomes and monitoring of how the program was implemented. Such specificity is very rare and shows how social policy experimentation as a method was already affecting legislative thinking (at least in some circles).

8. It is not clear whether the failure to pass an appropriation was due to an oversight, a belief that the Department of Corrections had the necessary resources, or political opposition. One could imagine, for example, a decision not to push for an appropriation when much of the bill's justification rested on saving tax dollars.

9. For those who care, positivism is an outdated philosophy of science that no one familiar with the issues takes seriously any longer. Yet, positivism has been adopted as a rallying cry by many of those who object to quantification, statistics, or scientific methods more generally. Although quantification, statistics, and scientific methods are hardly flawless and do overlook or fail to capitalize on other ways of "knowing," no one has yet proposed in any detail what the alternative might be. Serious statements that have appeared are either broadly philosophical (and, therefore, offer little on how concretely to proceed) or are more properly thought of as complements to experimental approaches.

10. And it is not clear what one learns from cross-sectional comparisons. It is hard to accept that comparing the incomes of white and black people, other things equal, will tell you much about what would happen if race were manipulated at random; imagine waking up one morning with your race changed.

11. According to Holland and Rubin, unless the treatment can be manipulated, there can be no experiment; indeed, the notion of cause does not apply. Thus, one cannot meaningfully ask, as do Pratt and Schlaifer (1984), whether there would be more snow in Denver if the Rocky Mountains were lower. However, we are *not* limiting experiments to instances in which treatments are assigned randomly. We *include* quasi-experiments.

REFERENCES

AIGNER, D. J. and J. A. HAUSMAN (1980) "Correcting for truncation bias in the analysis of experiments in time-of-day pricing of electricity." Bell Journal 35: 405.

BENNETT, C. A. and A. A. LUMSDAINE (1975) Evaluation and Experimentation. New York: Academic.

BERK, R. A. (1981) "On the compatibility of applied and basic research: an effort in marriage counseling." Amer. Sociologist 4: 204.

———R. A. and D. RAUMA (1983) "Capitalizing on nonrandom assignment to treatments: a regression discontinuity evaluation of a crime-control program." J. of the Amer. Statistical Assn. 78: 21.

BERK, R. A., C. J. LaCIVITA K. SREDL, and T. F. COOLEY (1981) Water Shortage: Lessons in Conservation from the Great California Drought, 1976-1977. Cambridge: Abt.

BLUMSTEIN, A., J. COHEN, and D. NAGIN [Eds.] (1978) Deterrence and Incapacitation: Estimating the Effects of Criminal Sanctions on Crime Rates. Washington, DC: National Research Council.

BORUCH, R. F. and W. SHADISH (1982) "Design issues in community intervention research," in E. Seidman (ed.) Handbook of Community Intervention Research. Beverly Hills, CA: Sage.

BORUCH, R. F., A. J. McSWEENEY, and E. J. SODERSTROM (1978) "Randomized field experiments for program planning, development and evaluation: an illustrative bibliography." Evaluation Q. 2: 655.

BORUCH, R. F., P. ANDERSON, D. RINDSKOPF, I. AMIDJAYA, and D. JANSON (1979) "Randomized experiments for planning and evaluating local programs: a summary on appropriateness and feasibility." Public Administration Rev. 39: 36.

CAMPBELL, D. T. (1969) "Reforms as experiments." Amer. Psychologist 24: 409.

COLEMAN, J. S., T. HOFFER, and S. KILGORE (1982) High School Achievement: Public, Catholic, and Private Schools Compared. New York: Basic Books.

COOK, T. D. and D. T. CAMPBELL (1979) Quasi-Experimentation: Design and Analysis in Field Settings. Skokie, IL:; Rand McNally.

CRONBACH, L. J. (1983) Designing Evaluations of Educational and Social Programs. San Francisco: Jossey-Bass.

DAWID, A. P. (1984) "Comment on the nature and discovery of structure." J. of the Amer. Statistical Assn. 79: 22.

DIAZ-GUERRERO, R., I. REYES-LAGUNES, D. B. WITZE, and W. H. HOLTZMAN (1976) "Plaza Sesamo in Mexico." J. of Communications 26: 145.

FERBER, R. and W. Z. HIRSCH (1982) Social Experiments and Social Policy. Cambridge: Cambridge Univ. Press.

FEINBERG, S. E., B. SINGER, and J. M. TANUR (1984) "Large scale social experimentation in the U.S.A.," Working paper, Department of Statistics, Carnegie-Mellon University.

HOLLAND, P. W. and D. B. RUBIN (1983) "On Lord's paradox," in H. Wainer and S. Messick (eds.) Principles of Modern Psychological Measurement: Festschrift for Frederic M. Lord. Hillsdale, NJ: Lawrence Erlbaum.

KASSBAUM, G., D. WARD, and D. WILNER (1971) Prison Treatment and Parole Survival. New York: John Wiley.

LENIHAN, K. (1977) Unlocking the Second Gate. Washington, DC: Government Printing Office.

MOSTELLER, F. and M. C. WEINSTEIN (1984) "Toward evaluating the cost-effectiveness of medical and social experiments," in J. A. Hausman and D. A. Wise (eds.) Social Experimentation. Chicago: University of Chicago Press.

PRATT, J. W. and R. SCHLAIFER (1984) "On the nature and discovery of structure." J. of the Amer. Statistical Assn 79: 9.

RAUMA, D. and R. A. BERK (1982) "Crime and poverty in California: some quasi-experimental evidence." Social Sci. Research 11: 318.

RIECKEN, H. W. and R. F. BORUCH (1974) Social Experimentation: A Method for Planning and Evaluating Social Invervention. New York: Academic.

ROSENBAUM, P. R., and D. B. RUBIN (1984) "Comment on the nature and discovery of structure." J. of the Amer. Statistical Assn 79: 26.

———(1983) "The central role of propensity score in observational studies of causal effects." Biometrics 70: 41.

ROSSI, P. H. (1982) "High School achievement: Public, Catholic, and private schools compared," Amer. J. of Education 91: 78-89.

ROSSI, P. H. and K. LYALL (1976) Reforming Public Welfare. New York: Russell Sage.

ROSSI, P. H. and H. E. FREEMAN (1982) Evaluation: A Systematic Approach. Beverly Hills, CA: Sage.

ROSSI, P. H., R. A. BERK, and K. J. LENIHAN (1980) Money, Work and Crime: Experimental Evidence. New York: Academic.

SHERMAN, L. W. and R. A. BERK (1984) "The specific deterrent effects of arrest for domestic assault." Amer. Soc. Rev. 49: 261.

SPENCER, B. D. (1980) Benefit-Cost Analysis of Data used to Allocate Funds. New York: Springer-Verlag.

TAGGART, R. (1972) The Prison and Unemployment: Manpower Programs for Offenders. Baltimore MD: Johns Hopkins Press.

TANUR, J. M. (1983) "Methods for large-scale surveys and experiments," in S. Leinhardt (ed.) Sociological Methodology 1983-1984. San Francisco: Jossey-Bass.

ZEISEL, H. (1982) "Disagreement over the evaluation of a controlled experiment." Amer. J. of Sociology 88: 378.

35

Scientific Challenges in
the Application of Randomized Trials

Michael S. Kramer, M.D. and Stanley H. Shapiro, Ph.D.

● In recent years, scientific challenges in the application of randomized trials have become more apparent, especially with the extension of such trials to the assessment of nondrug treatments, such as health education, psychotherapy, and health care provision. Six issues (individual v group randomization, blinding and unblinding, the effect of trial participation on outcome, selective subject participation, treatment compliance, and standardized v individualized treatment) are discussed in terms of their impact on internal validity, generalizability (external validity), and clinical relevance. Specific design strategies may be necessary to enhance these methodological and clinical desiderata. Attention to these challenges should lead to improvements in future randomized trials.

(*JAMA* 1984;252:2739-2745)

THE RANDOMIZED controlled trial (RCT) is generally regarded as the most potent scientific tool for evaluating medical treatments.[1,3] Its appeal stems from its apparent similarity to the laboratory experimental setting, where two or more groups of genetically identical animals (or tissue cultures, cells, or cellular extracts) are subjected to different maneuvers or manipulations, and some outcome of interest is then measured. Although human beings do not share the homogeneity usually achievable with mice or fibroblasts, randomization into treatment groups is generally relied on to account for known or unknown

From the Departments of Epidemiology and Health (Drs Kramer and Shapiro) and Pediatrics (Dr Kramer), McGill University Faculty of Medicine, Montreal.

Reprint requests to Department of Epidemiology and Health, McGill University, Purvis Hall, 1020 Pine Ave W, Montreal, Quebec, Canada H3A 1A2 (Dr Kramer).

baseline attributes, also called confounding factors, which might otherwise predispose to or protect from the outcome of interest, independent of treatment.

Randomized trials have contributed greatly to the evolution of more effective treatments and preventive measures for a variety of medical conditions. Randomized controlled trials represent an increasing proportion of the articles published in leading medical journals[4] and have become the sine qua non for the proof of efficacy the Food and Drug Administration requires for marketing new drugs. Despite the obvious advantages and impressive track record of RCTs, clinical investigators have become increasingly aware of certain difficulties in their interpretation,[5-7] feasibility,[8,9] and ethics.[10,11] Some of these difficulties have become overcome; others await resolution. None, however, has challenged the scientific

validity of the method itself. In recent years, especially with the extension of RCT methodology to assessments of nondrug treatments, including health education, psychotherapy, and health care provision, new concerns have emerged that challenge our uncritical reliance upon the RCT as an automatic scientific "gold standard" in clinical research.

It seems timely, therefore, to consider a critical reappraisal of some of the scientific issues involved in randomized trials. Our purpose here is not to discredit the method but rather to emphasize difficulties and challenges inherent in its application, especially in studying behavioral outcomes or outcomes that might be influenced by behavior (eg, cardiovascular mortality). When such difficulties arise, specific design strategies may be necessary to enhance scientific validity and clinical relevance. Some of the issues we raise have already surfaced in previous clinical trials; others remain theoretical and await empirical demonstration. We shall focus on six aspects of RCT design: (1) individual v group randomization, (2) blinding and unblinding, (3) the effect of trial participation on outcome, (4) selective subject participation, (5) treatment compliance, and (6) standardized v individualized treatment.

The first two of these issues threaten the internal validity of a trial, ie, the extent to which the treatment

From *Journal of the American Medical Association*, 252, 2739-2745. Copyright 1984, American Medical Association.

comparison is unbiased. The next three affect the generalizability, or external validity, of the trial's findings. The last issue concerns the clinical relevance and utility of the treatment comparison.

Individual v Group Randomization

Random allocation of treatment to each subject maximizes the chance that treatment assignment remains unpredictable by either the subject or the clinician-investigator. It also tends to result in groups that are similar for both known and unknown susceptibility factors that could otherwise confound the treatment effect, and provides a basis for statistical inference. Thus, randomization of individual subjects has become firmly ensconced as a sine qua non of a methodologically sound clinical trial. This is entirely appropriate for the classic drug efficacy trial. In such a trial, patients are treated individually, treatment groups remain distinct, and an unbiased comparison of drug v placebo, or drug A v drug B, is thus likely. For some types of maneuvers, however, random assignment by individuals can actually be detrimental, because interaction among subjects may lead to consequent "contamination" of the treatment, and hence a biased comparison. Such bias directly threatens the internal validity of a trial. Psychosocial, educational, and health care provision interventions are particularly prone to this problem because subjects are likely to interact with one another between the administration of the treatment and the measurement of the outcome. For such trials, treatment allocation by hospital room, ward, or geographic region may be preferable to randomization of individuals.

For example, of the dozen or so controlled clinical trials assessing the effect of early maternal-infant contact on subsequent maternal attachment behavior ("bonding"), most randomized individual women, rather than entire postpartum wards. Thus, mothers receiving different treatments (early contact v usual "routine") were housed in the same ward, and often in the same room. The interaction between these new mothers might well be expected to contaminate the treatments under compari-

son, and such contamination would tend to reduce true treatment differences.[12] Analogously, a hypothetical trial studying the effects of a high school sex education program on subsequent rates of adolescent pregnancy would do better to randomize by geographically distinct schools or even by regions, rather than individually within a given school or region. En bloc randomization appears preferable whenever relatively closed, naturally formed groups are capable of modifying the treatment allocated to individuals within those groups. Thus, water fluoridation trials usually randomize by community, while in dietary prevention trials, the family is the logical unit of randomization.

It is important to emphasize, however, that en bloc allocation carries some hazards not inherent in the individual approach. Unless sample sizes are very small, balanced distribution of potential confounders is likely when individual subjects are randomly assigned to treatment groups. When only two groups are assigned en bloc, however, "randomization" reduces to a single toss of the coin. The risk that important prognostic differences between the groups could confound the observed treatment effect is thus considerable, even when group assignment is truly random. This is because individuals within a group cannot necessarily be regarded as independent, and effective sample size is reduced by the extent of within-group dependence.[13,14] The investigator thus needs either to demonstrate substantial independence of individuals within the groups or to include a sufficient number of groups to ensure adequate statistical power.

When closed, natural groupings do not already exist, investigators should attempt to randomize individual subjects to treatment groups, while keeping the groups geographically separate and eliminating or severely limiting any opportunities for their interaction. When such individual randomization is infeasible, the trial design needs to incorporate procedures that protect against confounding while preserving the advantages of en bloc allocation. One such procedure is the use of a crossover design, in which treatment assignment is reversed in the two

study groups after an appropriate period of time. This is analogous to the individual crossover trial, in which individuals are changed from one study treatment to another within the course of the trial.[15] With the group crossover design, each group is "paired" to itself, theoretically eliminating any confounding effect due to group differences, while increasing the effective sample size. With psychosocial or health care maneuvers, however, contamination may occur during a crossover, owing to learning effects or behavioral changes in either the subjects or their caregivers. This is often a serious enough problem to discourage use of the crossover approach.

Another approach involves the use of a pretrial study period to demonstrate that individuals in different groups experience similar outcomes when exposed to the same treatment. Equivalent pretrial results increase the plausibility that any differences in outcome that occur when the same groups are exposed to different treatments during the actual trial are attributable to the treatments, rather than to potentially confounding differences between the groups. Such a design was utilized in a recent trial examining the effect of restricting in-hospital supplementation on duration of breast-feeding.[16] Before the trial, two well-baby nurseries followed similar supplementation practices and experienced similar outcomes (their "graduates" were breast-fed for equivalent durations). The trial began when one of the nurseries changed its practice by restricting supplementation.

Blinding and Unblinding

Blinding may be infeasible for some treatment maneuvers. This is obviously true for most surgical procedures, but also pertains to many behavioral (eg, exercise v no exercise in a trial to prevent coronary events) or health care (eg, care by nurse practitioner v physician) maneuvers. Depending on the type of outcome assessed, observers involved in this assessment usually can be kept blind, but the subjects themselves (the other half of the "double blind"), of course, cannot. The subject's knowledge of which group he has been randomized to can then lead to a biased treatment comparison. This is especially true when the comparison is one of intervention v no intervention. Those who receive the intervention will obviously be aware that they are among the "chosen," and this awareness may create a feeling of specialness that can exert a profound (and uncontrolled) placebo effect.

An opposite bias can arise if subjects are aware of their randomization to a no intervention group, and then attempt to compensate by changing their behavior in beneficial ways. This may have occurred in the recent Multiple Risk Factor Intervention Trial (MRFIT),[17] in which cardiovascular mortality was compared in two groups, one of which was randomized to receive a complex set of interventions, including increased exercise, improved diet, and reduced smoking. Pretrial calculations of required sample sizes were based on cardiovascular mortality predictions from the Framingham studies. Fortunately for the subjects randomized to the nonintervention control group (but unfortunately for the investigators), the control group experienced a cardiovascular death rate lower than predicted, and differences favoring the intervention group were not statistically significant.

Although several hypotheses could be offered to explain the controls' better-than-predicted survival, the most likely appears to stem from nonblinding. The nature of the MRFIT interventions made blinding infeasible, and nonblind control subjects, who were obviously aware of the interventions, may have attempted similar behavioral changes (exercise, diet, or smoking) that lowered their risk for cardiovascular mortality.

Even when an RCT involves lookalike, taste-alike treatments, these treatments may not feel alike, and true blinding may be difficult to maintain. Side effects may be more common with active treatments than placebos and may differ between two or more active treatments.[18] The occurrence of such side effects may end up unblinding the subjects, their physicians, or both. Although firm data are scarce (the issue is rarely even broached in most published reports of trials), such unblinding probably occurs in a large number of RCTs, including the standard phase 3 drug trials required for demonstration of efficacy.

The potential for bias due to unblinding is even greater when the control treatment involves a placebo. If the active treatment leads to improvement in the patient's symptoms or signs, he or his physician may become unblinded and subsequently exaggerate the treatment's beneficial effects. Although such a bias cannot create an efficacious effect, it can lead to positive feedback (amplification) that overestimates true treatment efficacy. Furthermore, the occurrence of side effects in the group receiving the active treatment may result in an enhanced "placebo effect" that is inadequately controlled for by a placebo treatment that does not lead to these side effects. The magnitude of the bias probably depends on the severity and specificity of the side effects, as well as on the type of outcome, ie, the extent to which the outcome can be influenced by a placebo effect.

One strategy for measuring potential bias due to unblinding involves asking subjects, after the trial is completed, to guess whether they received the active treatment or placebo. (We recommend this strategy solely as a means of assessing possible bias due to unblinding. We do not advocate stratification by blinding status for the statistical analysis of the trial's results, which should be based on a comparison of the groups created by the randomization, irrespective of whether subjects remained blinded.) Bias should be suspected whenever differences in outcome appear only in subjects who are unblinded. This can occur if, among active treatment recipients, those who correctly identify their treatment have better outcomes than those who either are unsure or believe they received the active treatment. It can also occur if unblinded subjects receiving the placebo have worse outcomes than placebo recipients who remained blind. A good example of the use of this bias assessment strategy was one of the RCTs of vitamin C in the prevention and treatment of the common cold.[19] The shorter duration and lesser severity of cold experienced by the vitamin C group were confined to subjects who were un-

blinded; in those who remained blind, no such differences were found.

Effect of Participation on Outcome

Participation in a study can change behavior, even in the control group, and the behavioral change itself may affect the outcome under study. Since most such behavioral changes would be expected to be beneficial (improved self-esteem, better self-care, more appropriate utilization of the health care system), results in the control group may be significantly better than expected from an otherwise similar nonparticipant group in the population. This is the well-known Hawthorne effect. Randomized controlled trials carry with them the sense of uncertainty and risk (randomization), which may be more potent behavior modifiers than merely being followed up or interviewed about a self-selected or physician-selected treatment. Thus the potential for a Hawthorne effect may be enhanced.

A considerable body of research has documented the effect of psychological factors on physical health.[20,21] It seems likely that the feeling of specialness attendant upon participation in an RCT might have a beneficial effect on certain outcomes. Trial participation might also serve as a social network or social support and thus help mitigate the effects of stress.[22-24] These effects seem most likely to occur in trials concerned with behavioral outcomes or outcomes that can be influenced by behavioral changes (eg, coronary events).

An excellent example of the Hawthorne effect occurred in an RCT of two strategies (chart review and financial incentives) to reduce the number of laboratory and radiologic tests ordered by first-year medical residents.[25] Residents were aware of the existence of the study as well as its principal outcome: "It was widely known in the hospital . . . that some type of study to reduce the ordering of tests would be carried out."[25] Compared with the baseline period, all residents, including those in the control group, showed statistically significant reductions in testing during the intervention period.

If participation affects outcome equally in the experimental and control groups, no bias is introduced into the treatment comparison, and internal validity is maintained. A marked benefit of treatment should thus be detectable despite the presence of a Hawthorne effect. In the test-ordering trial cited previously,[25] for example, the group of residents randomized to the chart review strategy ordered significantly fewer tests than those in the control group, despite the participation-mediated reduction evident in the latter.

Theoretically, however, situations may arise in which the benefit of active treatment is diluted, or even eliminated, by the effect of participation. Because the potential magnitude of the benefit may be limited (the so-called ceiling effect), the end result may be either a smaller treatment difference or no significant difference, and thus a false (externally invalid) inference concerning the effectiveness of the active treatment in the general population. As a hypothetical example, imagine a trial of an educational intervention to reduce medication errors by nurses. If the study nurses were aware of the existence and purpose of the trial, their participation alone might eliminate most of the pretrial errors, and thus remove the potential for showing any benefit of the educational intervention. The intervention might, in fact, be an effective strategy for reducing nursing medication errors, but a potent Hawthorne effect in the trial renders its benefit undetectable.

What can be done to minimize the Hawthorne effect? Trial subjects can be kept unaware that they are being studied, or at least unaware of the precise treatment comparison or the research hypothesis. Such was the approach taken in a recently published trial that assessed the effect of distributing free infant formula samples among new, breast-feeding mothers on the subsequent duration of breast-feeding.[26] For many types of treatments, however, keeping trial participants "in the dark" may not be ethically defensible. In such cases, the possibility of a Hawthorne effect should be acknowledged by the trial's investigators, and inferences should be modified accordingly.

Selective Subject Participation

Subjects (or their advocates) are generally less willing to participate in randomized trials than in nonexperimental (observational) studies. For example, in our current studies of adverse drug reactions in a general pediatric group practice, we asked the parents of 3,316 children visiting the practice to participate in an observational cohort study of all children receiving prescription or nonprescription drug therapy during one calendar year. Parents of 3,181 (96%) agreed to participate. In a roughly contemporaneous placebo-controlled RCT of acetaminophen in febrile children, however, 132 of the same parents who agreed to enroll their children in the cohort study were asked to participate in the RCT; 39 (34%) of them refused (M. S. Kramer, MD; L. Naimarle; and D. G. Leduc, MD, unpublished data, August 1982 to December 1983).

Physicians can undoubtedly influence participation rates by the manner in which they describe the trial and solicit enrollment. If a physician supports the need for a trial, however, he should be uncertain as to which of the studied treatment is best for a given patient. Some patients may find this uncertainty unacceptable, even if adequately and fairly explained, and thus may decline participation.

That participation rates are lower in RCTs than in other types of clinical epidemiologic studies poses, in itself, no problem insofar as internal validity is concerned. Lower participation rates can be overcome by approaching additional subjects. Desired sample sizes can thus be attained, as long as sufficient numbers of potential subjects exist.

The issue here, however, is not statistical power, but rather generalizability, or external validity, of the study results. It is not just that many people decline participation, but that those who participate may be quite different from those who do not. Most clinicians and investigators will wish to generalize the findings from an RCT to the entire population of subjects or patients who might benefit from the treatment under study in the trial. Unfortunately, selective participation in an RCT entails the risk that the trial's findings may not be generalizable. Because of the complex psychological motives that lead people to accept or decline participation, readers of reports of such trials

will be unable to know to whom the results may be applied.

A common example of this type of problem arises whenever low-risk or high-risk patients are preferentially enrolled in a trial. A treatment comparison in one of these risk strata may not be generalizable to the other. For example, in an RCT of medical v surgical (portacaval shunt) treatment of patients with cirrhosis and esophageal varices,[27] no difference in survival was detected between the two treatments, but study patients survived significantly longer than eligible patients not participating in the trial. Since the latter group received the same treatment as participants who were randomized to the medical-treatment group of the trial, they appear to represent patients with more advanced disease and hence with a higher risk for death. It is thus not clear whether the finding of no treatment difference in the trial can be generalized to the higher-risk group who did not participate.

For the portacaval shunt trial, the main difference between participants and nonparticipants seems clear, and generalizations can be restricted accordingly. If a reliable method existed for stratifying cirrhotic patients into high v low risk, we would at least be reasonably confident that surgery was of no benefit in the latter group. In trials involving outcomes sensitive to behavioral or motivational differences the problem is more insidious, because the nature of these differences may not be known, and even if appreciated qualitatively, no instrument may exist to measure them adequately. Motivational differences among potential subjects are very likely to affect their decision to accept or decline participation in a trial. If motivation can affect (usually improve) the outcome under study, those who participate may show no difference according to treatment, but experience significantly better outcomes than the nonparticipants. The study treatment might be of benefit to the lesser-motivated, poorer-prognosis group, but this effect is masked by their low rate of participation. Unlike risk in cirrhotic patients, motivation is often difficult to assess. Thus the negative results obtained from a trial in which participants are unusually highly motivated may not be usefully extrapolated to any known population.

The best that can and should be done about selective participation in randomized trials is to keep track of, and include in all resulting publications, both the numbers and relevant characteristics of all subjects who accept and decline. *Relevant characteristics* here can be taken to mean any factors that, independent of the treatment under study, can affect the susceptibility to develop the outcome of interest. Sociodemographic variables, disease severity, and comorbidity are the kinds of easily measurable factors that should be considered. New instruments may need to be developed to measure motivational and behavioral factors that can both lead to selective participation and affect the outcome. When participation rates are exceptionally high (80% to 90%), the results can usually be considered externally valid. In the more usual case, however, investigators should compare participants and nonparticipants, and indicate characteristics of the population to whom the results appear to apply.

Treatment Compliance

Just as the uncertainty engendered by randomization can reduce subject participation in a trial, so too can it reduce compliance once the subject is enrolled. In a two-group comparison with equal rates of allocation to each treatment, a patient's knowledge that he has only a 50-50 chance of receiving the active treatment in a placebo-controlled RCT, or the new, experimental treatment in an RCT comparison with the existing, standard treatment, might well be expected to reduce compliance below that achieved when the patient receives a prescription for a treatment the physician deems best for him. The reduced compliance could then bias the trial toward finding no benefit of treatment and lead to an erroneous failure to reject the null hypothesis.

As with participation, compliance is probably influenced by the manner in which the physician explains the reason for the trial. Even in a placebo-controlled trial, if the physician explains that he is genuinely uncertain as to whether the active treatment will do more good than harm, the patient will realize that his chances of receiving the better therapy are as good under randomization as they would be if either of the choices was specifically prescribed for him. Nonetheless, many people do not appear to react favorably to the double uncertainty of treatment efficacy, on the one hand, and blind, randomized choice of treatment, on the other.

Selective subject participation in a trial can in itself lead to another, opposite effect on compliance. Among the population of eligible subjects to whom an investigator may wish to generalize the findings of a trial, those who agree are, by definition, more highly motivated, and thus may be more likely to comply with the assigned treatment. In fact, some trials have used a pretrial test period to "weed out" poor compliers before randomization.[28,29] The trial then becomes an *explanatory* trial (efficacy) rather than a *pragmatic*[5] or *management*[6] trial (effectiveness). The enhanced compliance achieved by selective enrollment in a trial may or may not compensate for the decrement expected as a result of the subjects' knowledge of the 50-50 chance of receiving either treatment.

On occasion, high motivation and prior beliefs can, paradoxically, lead to poor compliance with an assigned treatment. In the previously mentioned placebo-controlled RCT of acetaminophen in febrile children, for example, some mothers who agreed to participate were so convinced that acetaminophen may do more harm than good that they withheld the study medication to avoid the "risk" of their child's receiving the active agent!

Because of these complex and often unpredictable effects on treatment compliance, compliance in the "real world" may differ considerably from that attained in a randomized trial. Furthermore, good compliance may be associated with a better outcome, regardless of treatment.[30] The external validity of a trial's findings, therefore, may be difficult or impossible to assess. Although measurement of compliance can be helpful and should be incorporated into the trial protocol, the trial's investigators may still be unable to gauge the generalizability of their results, since compliance with treatment as prescribed in the usual clinical setting is rarely measured. Nonetheless, measurement of compliance can be of use later on in interpreting the results of future trials, or in explaining the treatment's subsequent success or failure if and when it achieves general clinical usage.

Standardized v Individualized Treatment

In an attempt to standardize treatment comparisons and maintain blinding, many clinical trials have employed a rigid, fixed-dose treatment schedule. Neither lack of apparent clinical effect nor the occurrence of side effects is used to adjust the regimen. Unless the anticipated treatment benefit is a qualitative change in clinical status totally unrelated to the administered dose, such trials run the risk of masking an overall benefit in the group by failing to optimize treatment in each individual.[9] Even if the treatment comparison is internally valid and the results are generalizable (externally valid), the treatments administered may have little relevance for the usual clinical setting of flexible individualized therapy.

Good clinicians usually adjust the dosage regimen of a given treatment in individual patients in order to maximize benefits and minimize side effects. Dosages are often increased gradually until some threshold clinical end point is achieved or until adverse effects prevent further increases. When fixed regimens dictated by trial protocol prevent this flexibility, treatment potency may be insufficient to result in clinical benefit. For example, in the University Group Diabetes Program clinical trial comparing various treatments for diabetes,[31] the two oral hypoglycemic agents, tolbutamide and phenformin hydrochloride, were given in standardized dosage regimens. Critics have suggested that the failure to benefit patients randomized to this regimen might be explained by the fact that dosage was not optimized, ie, not tied to attempts to control hyperglycemia or glycosuria.[32]

Conversely, the potency of a standardized treatment could be excessive and, even if efficacious, lead to such adverse side effects that patients stop taking their treatment, or even drop out of the trial altogether. Whether potency is insufficient or excessive, inability to individualize the therapy under investigation can lead to false inferences about treatment efficacy by reducing observed differences between treatment groups. The null hypothesis is not rejected, and the end result is a kind of "biological type II error."

One of the arguments usually offered in favor of standardized, rather than individualized, treatment is that the latter makes blinding difficult or impossible to maintain. The clinician administering the therapy in the trial must know the identity and dosage of the treatment to optimize its administration. One way to retain individualized treatment without sacrificing blind assessment of outcome is to have the persons administering the treatment be different from those observing the outcome. The former need not be blinded, while blinding the latter ensures an unbiased outcome assessment. This kind of combination mechanism was used in one of the RCTs of anticoagulant prophylaxis in patients experiencing myocardial infarction.[11] For some trials, however, this kind of design may create as many difficulties as it resolves. Unblinding of physicians, while encouraging the flexibility of individualized therapy, may permit the physician to introduce subtle, even unconscious, cointerventions that could contaminate the treatment under study and invalidate the treatment comparison. A better format for such a combination mechanism, if practicable, would involve direct patient care by an appropriately blinded physician, while a second, nonblinded physician would adjust the dosage based on clinical or paraclinical measurements of treatment effects.

When one of the individualized treatments is a placebo, however, keeping the trial subjects blinded may be more problematic. Unless "dummy" (artificial) dosage adjustments are similarly made in subjects assigned to the placebo group, the placebo effect of the experimental (active) treatment may be enhanced by the subjects' feeling of individualized care, and thus be inadequately controlled for in the placebo group. One successful approach to this problem was that taken by the Veterans

Administration Cooperative Study Group in their RCT of antihypertensive therapy.[3] The therapy assessed was a combination of three antihypertensive agents (reserpine, hydrochlorothiazide, and hydralazine hydrochloride) v a placebo. To facilitate adjustment of its hypotensive effect, hydralazine was available in both 25-mg and 50-mg tablets, as was its corresponding placebo. Minimization of side effects was accomplished using special formulations (in both active and placebo forms) of the combination reserpine-hydrochlorothiazide tablets in which either one or the other drug had been removed. This innovative, if complex, approach permitted flexible, individualized therapy while maintaining adequate blinding.

Conclusions

Although the RCT design appears to come closest to approximating the laboratory experiment, the complexities of the human psyche can affect participation, compliance, blinding, and outcome in a trial. This is especially true when the outcome is either itself an observed behavior (eg, maternal-infant bonding) or an event that is known to be etiologically linked to behavior (eg, cardiovascular mortality). These human psychological factors can affect the internal validity of the treatment comparison, the generalizability (external validity) of the results to a larger population, or the clinical relevance of the conclusions.

These same factors also operate in observational, nonexperimental research studies. In fact, they can also influence treatment selection, and thus lead to selection bias in such studies. In an RCT, randomization usually occurs after the decision to participate, and selection bias is thereby eliminated. This is a strong argument in favor of the RCT, since selection bias affects the internal validity of a treatment comparison. Internal validity is a necessary prerequisite for external validity and should always, therefore, receive highest methodological priority.

When selective participation seriously threatens external validity, trade-offs will occur between higher participation and a risk of selection bias in observational studies, com-

pared with an unbiased (internally valid), but possibly less generally applicable, result in randomized trials. This kind of trade-off arises, for example, in studying putative health effects of breast-feeding. If an RCT were attempted, women agreeing to be randomly assigned to breast-feed or formula-feed their infant would be so few and so atypical that the results would have little meaning for mothers and infants in general.

For most questions involving treatment efficacy, the RCT remains the research methodology of choice whenever randomization is feasible, but a study's use of this methodology does not necessarily confer certainty on its conclusions. In the majority of cases in which scientific challenges arise, implementation of specific design strategies should enhance internal and external validity. In other cases, a trial's conclusions may have to be tempered by inescapable methodological limitations.

Our purpose here has not been to denigrate the value of the RCT, but rather to discuss some scientific difficulties and challenges inherent in its application. As has been noted, the model of methodological rigor represented by the RCT invites close scrutiny for any departures from the ideal.[14] We hope that a critical reappraisal of some of the scientific underpinnings of the randomized trial may help bring about changes in attitudes and practice. The interests of medical research and the public it is intended to benefit may not be best served by an unquestioning acceptance of the results of a study merely because it uses an RCT design that can, in certain circumstances, lead to scientifically invalid or clinically irrelevant inferences. Most importantly, we hope that attention to these challenges may facilitate improvements in future RCTs.

Dr Kramer is a National Health Research Scholar of the National Health Research and Development Program, Health and Welfare, Canada.

Tom Hutchinson, MB; Jean-François Boivin, MD, ScD; James Hanley, PhD; Abby Lippman, PhD; and Mary Ellen Thomson, MSc, gave helpful suggestions in the preparation of the manuscript.

References

1. Fisher RA: *The Design of Experiments*, ed 8. New York, Hafner, 1966.

2. Hill AB: *Statistical Methods in Clinical and Preventive Medicine*. Edinburgh, Churchill Livingstone, 1962.

3. Shapiro SH, Louis TA (eds): *Clinical Trials: Issues and Approaches*. New York, Marcel Dekker Inc, 1983.

4. Fletcher RH, Fletcher SW: Clinical research in general medical journals. *N Engl J Med* 1979;301:180-183.

5. Schwartz D, Lellouch J: Explanatory and pragmatic attitudes in therapeutic trials. *J Chronic Dis* 1967;20:637-648.

6. Sackett DL, Gent M: Controversy in counting and attributing events in clinical trials. *N Engl J Med* 1979;301:1410-1412.

7. Louis TA, Shapiro SH: Critical issues in the conduct and interpretation of clinical trials. *Annu Rev Public Health* 1983;43:25-46.

8. Ederer F: Practical problems in collaborative clinical trials. *Am J Epidemiol* 1975;102:111-118.

9. Feinstein AR: Clinical biostatistics XXIV: The role of randomization in sampling, testing, allocation, and credulous idolatry (conclusion). *Clin Pharmacol Ther* 1973;14:1035-1051.

10. Schafer A: The ethics of the randomized clinical trial. *N Engl J Med* 1982;307:719-724.

11. Lebacqz K: Ethical aspects of clinical trials, in Shapiro SH, Louis TA (eds): *Clinical Trials: Issues and Approaches*. New York, Marcel Dekker Inc, 1983, pp 81-98.

12. Thomson ME, Kramer MS: Methodological standards for controlled clinical trials of early contact and maternal-infant behavior. *Pediatrics* 1984;73:294-300.

13. Cornfield J, Mitchell S: Selected risk factors in coronary disease: Possible intervention effects. *Arch Environ Health* 1969;19:382-394.

14. Buck C, Donner A: The design of controlled experiments in the evaluation of nontherapeutic interventions. *J Chronic Dis* 1982;

35:531-538.

15. Louis TA, Lavori PW, Bailar JC, et al: Crossover and self-controlled designs in clinical research. *N Engl J Med* 1984;310:24-31.

16. Gray-Donald K, Kramer MS, Munday S, et al: Effect of in-hospital formula supplementation on the duration of breast feeding: A controlled clinical trial. *Pediatrics*, in press.

17. Multiple Risk Factor Intervention Trial Research Group: Multiple risk factor intervention trial: Risk factor changes and mortality results. *JAMA* 1982;248:1465-1477.

18. Rickels K, Downing RW: Side reactions in neurotics: II. Can patients judge which symptoms are caused by their medication? *J Clin Pharmacol* 1970;10:298-305.

19. Karlowski TR, Chalmers TC, Frenkel LD, et al: Ascorbic acid for the common cold: A prophylactic and therapeutic trial. *JAMA* 1975;231:1038-1042.

20. Jenkins CD: Recent evidence supporting psychological and social risk factors for coronary disease. *N Engl J Med* 1976;294:987-994, 1033-1038.

21. Vaillant GE: Natural history of male psychological health: Effects of mental health on physical health. *N Engl J Med* 1979;301:1249-1254.

22. Cassell J: The contribution of the social environment to host resistance. *Am J Epidemiol* 1976;104:107-123.

23. Cobb S: Social support as a moderator of life stress. *Psychosom Med* 1976;38:300-314.

24. Kaplan BH, Cassel JC, Gore S: Social support and health. *Med Care* 1977;15(suppl 5):47-57.

25. Martin AR, Wolf MA, Thibodeau LA, et al: A trial of two strategies to modify the test-ordering behavior of medical residents. *N Engl J Med* 1980;303:1330-1336.

26. Bergevin Y, Dougherty C, Kramer MS: Do

infant formula samples shorten the duration of breast-feeding? *Lancet* 1983;1:1148-1151.

27. Garceau AJ, Donaldson RM, O'Hara ET, et al: A controlled trial of prophylactic portacaval-shunt surgery. *N Engl J Med* 1964;270:496-500.

28. Veterans Administration Cooperative Study Group on Antihypertensive Agents: Effects of treatment on morbidity in hypertension: Results in patients with diastolic blood pressures averaging 115 through 128 mm Hg. *JAMA* 1967;202:1028-1034.

29. The Coronary Drug Project Research Group: The Coronary Drug Project: Design, methods, and baseline results. *Circulation* 1973; 47(suppl 1):I1-I50.

30. The Coronary Drug Project Research Group: Influence of adherence to treatment and response of cholesterol on mortality in the Coronary Drug Project. *N Engl J Med* 1980; 303:1038-1041.

31. University Group Diabetes Program: A study of the effects of hypoglycemic agents on vascular complications in patients with adult-onset diabetes: I. Design, methods, and baseline results. II. Mortality results. *Diabetes* 1970; 19(suppl 2):747-830.

32. Feinstein AR: Clinical biostatistics VIII: An analytic appraisal of the University Group Diabetes Program (UGDP) study. *Clin Pharmacol Ther* 1971;12:167-191.

33. Seaman AJ, Griswold HE, Reaume R, et al: Long-term anticoagulant prophylaxis after myocardial infarction: Final report. *N Engl J Med* 1969;281:115-119.

34. Mosteller F, Gilbert JP, McPeek B: Controversies in design and analysis of clinical trials, in Shapiro SH, Louis TA (eds): *Clinical Trials: Issues and Approaches*. New York, Marcel Dekker Inc, 1983, pp 13-64.

36

Selecting Models for Measuring Change When True Experimental Conditions Do Not Exist

Jim C. Fortune and Barbara A. Hutson

Action researchers seek to instigate change in process and practice through the systematization of instructional methods. Trainers seek to change the skills and abilities of their trainees through presentation and guided practice. Teachers seek to change students' knowledge and understanding of a given body of content through instruction, classroom activities and assignments, and interaction. Social reform programs are directed toward change of certain aspects of a selected target group or specific institutional practices. Compensatory education and remedial programs seek to induce change which has previously failed to occur. Almost all intervention programs attempt to induce change—change in reading skills, in language proficiency, in job skills, in functional literacy, in attitudes, etc.

The measurement of change undergirds the application and utilization of program evaluation in education. Intuitively, the measurement of change is simple. The discrepancy between criterion measures administered before and after program participation should represent the change due to the program. But this relationship is true only in ideal conditions where perfectly reliable criterion measures and pure experimental design are used.

Several factors, including the purpose of measurement, the criteria used, measurement instrumentation, and availability and nature of controls, confound the relationship and make the measurement of change a difficult and highly technical operation. This paper will attempt to review the artifacts occurring in the process of measuring change in evaluations and quasi-experimental designs, delineate considerations in choosing a model to measure change under these conditions, and suggest ways to organize the existing models so as to facilitate the selection process.

The first section describes several types of data artifacts potentially present in the measurement of change

under less than ideal conditions. The second section contains the classification of models of change. The third section analyzes the relationship of data artifacts to models for the analysis of change data. The fourth section illustrates factors that should be considered in the selection of one or more of these models. The final section describes briefly a strategy for the development of "confidence bounds" for decision making based on evaluation results when none of the models appears clearly appropriate.

The Nature of Artifacts in Measuring Change

Artifacts in the measurement of change differ from statistical assumptions in that they represent phenomena due to the combined effects of measurement and design conditions, while statistical assumptions concern the appropriateness of the data and the design groupings for a particular probability model upon which a test is based.

Artifacts can be grouped in several ways, but for our purpose it is useful to think in terms of three primary conditions, the artifacts arising directly from these conditions and from the interactions of these conditions. The three primary conditions are: 1) the effects of outside influences which change the base of comparison; 2) a priori differences in the groups being compared; and 3) the fallibility of the measurement. Each of these three conditions can act directly or in concert with another to cause artifacts (See Figure 1).

The absence of random equivalence between two groups makes the assumption of equal group experiences untenable, suggesting that uncontrolled and unmeasured external influences can combine with the

Address correspondence to Jim C. Fortune, College of Education, Virginia Polytechnic Institute and State University, Blacksburg, VA 24061.

From *Journal of Educational Research*, 1984, 77, 187-206. Copyright 1984 by Heldref Publications.

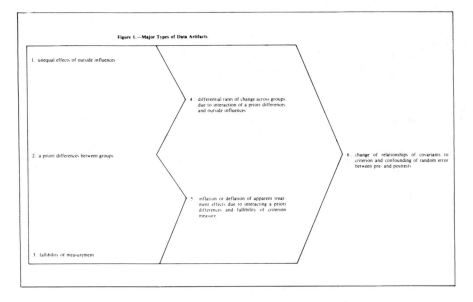

Figure 1.—Major Types of Data Artifacts

1. unequal effects of outside influences

4. differential rates of change across groups due to interaction of a priori differences and outside influences

2. a priori differences between groups

6. change of relationships of covariants to criterion and confounding of random error between pre- and posttests

5. inflation or deflation of apparent treatment effects due to interacting a priori differences and fallibility of criterion measure

3. fallibility of measurement

treatment effect to reduce or enhance its visibility. A priori differences in the two groups which are being compared on a mediating variable correlated with the criterion variable may result in an observable differential rate of change of the criterion measure across groups. The fallibility or absence of total reliability of the criterion measure results in the negative correlation between pretest scores and raw gain score ratios. The interaction of outside influences and a priori differences in comparison groups can result in an unpredictable differential rate of change across groups attributable to observed differences in the correlation of the mediating variable to the criterion variable across groups. The interaction of a priori group differences and fallibility of measurement can result in differential levels of measurement within groups across testing periods resulting in a spurious increase or decrease of observable criterion variable differences in the comparison. The interaction of outside influences and fallibility of measurement can result in differential errors of measurement within groups across testing periods confounding the effects of random error on group differences. In any given situation, one of these major types of artifacts can be more of a problem than the others and may require a data adjustment strategy utilized in a specific model or model classification for appropriate analysis. Each of these types of artifacts will be discussed briefly.

Several artifacts of measuring change prevent the simple gain-score or discrepancy between pretest and posttest criterion assessment from being an accurate representation of change attributable to a program or treatment. The first artifact arises from the nature of the program being assessed. No educational program is all-encompassing and free from either the facilitative or detrimental influence of outside forces. Hence, in order to measure change that is attributable to a given program, control for the effects of outside influences is necessary. Without controls, change caused by outside influences can be mistaken for change due to program, or change attributable to program can be overlooked due to confounding with outside influences.

The nature of the controls attempted establishes the next artifact. Program evaluation usually does not allow the control or random assignment required in experimental studies. Randomly equivalent control groups are usually not available. The lack of the ideal control generates two conditions which confound the measurement of change. These conditions are: a) differences between the program group and the control group on one or more unmeasured correlates of the criterion measure; or b) differences between the program group and the control group on the pretest measure of the criterion. When group differences on pretest means exist, attempts to adjust data for fair comparisons may result in adjusting out part of the program effects. Differences in relationship of covariants to criterion measures may result in differential adjustment of the comparison groups.

A third source of artifacts exists in the measure itself. Practically no criterion measure of educational programs is totally reliable. Even when groups are equivalent, fallibility of criterion measurements gives rise to measurement error which confounds the measurement of change in two ways: a) measurement error can interact with attempts to adjust the data; and b) measurement error in the pretest can combine with measurement error in the posttest to diminish reliability of any estimate of gain. The resulting artifact produced is that estimated gains based upon pretest-posttest differences are negatively correlated with pretest scores, diminishing the ability to see program effects on persons with high pretest scores. This phenomenon is a product of regression toward the mean of the two tests which are both fallible, and contributes to differences in interpretation of the measurements of subjects at the extremes of the test distribution.

When two or more of these phenomena are present in the measurement of change, additional confounding artifacts are produced. One such artifact occurs when the groups have unequal pretest means and are different on a mediating variable which is correlated with the criterion measure. In this case group differences attributable to program are confounded with observed original group differences and with differential group growth rates. For instance, if the comparison group to a group receiving a compensatory education program begins a study scoring higher on a pretest, and has more academic ability and motivation, then simple adjustments of pretest scores are not adequate, as the control group will continue to progress at a more rapid rate than will the treatment group because of their superior capability. Other illustrations of the presence of confounding conditions can be found when the metric of measure across groups is different in interpretation because of group differences in the beginning of the study and because of the nearness of one of the groups to either the floor or ceiling of the criterion measure. Still a third example exists when the mediating variables differ in their combined relationships to the criterion variable. These differences can be a result of either group composition, nature of the criterion measure, or beginning status of the two groups.

The above phenomena are confounded additionally by the violation of statistical assumptions. Most specifically, these violations result in erroneous estimates of group differences or change. This may occur through either biased comparisons or differential data adjustment. For this paper, the statistical assumptions will not be addressed directly, but will be treated indirectly through discussion of the proposed selection process.

Types of Change Models

Over 50 variations of 5 generic types of statistical models have been devised to make estimates of change by adjusting or estimating data in some way. Generally, these models differ in the ways they address the different artifacts, statistical assumptions, and measurement requirements. All of the models have been designed to be used with ratio, interval or quasi-interval data. For some of these models there are non-parametric procedures which allow the use of nominal and ordinal data. Although much of the content of this paper is pertinent to these parallel nonparametric models, discussion will be limited to the more frequently used parametric models. For this discussion the many models of change may be grouped into five categories, each especially useful for some purposes (more fully described in Fortune & Hutson, 1982) and under some conditions.

The four major purposes for evaluation of change are: 1) the identification of individuals who achieved specific levels of change, such as high gainers or low- or no-gainers; 2) identification of correlates of change such as factors associated with high gain; 3) estimation of magnitude of change; and 4) comparison of amount of change across groups or ascertainment of relative group change. Research reported in Linn and Slinde (1977) suggests that adjusted gain score models are adequate for addressing the first purpose. Models which do not alter the covariant structure of the data appear more appropriate for addressing the second purpose. These models are usually found in either the adjusted gain score or true score models. To address the third purpose, models from classifications three, four, and five are more appropriate, and the choice of particular models from these three classifications depends upon other information about the specific situation. The fifth classification of models (structural equations) is recommended if precise comparisons of gain are needed.

If an evaluation has more than one major purpose, it might be wise to select a model comprehensive enough to serve both needs, though no more complex than necessary.

As discussed later, there are situations in which it may be desirable to select two appropriate but contrasting models. It should be pointed out that the selection processes suggested here will identify the least complex appropriate model; some more complex models may also be totally appropriate.

Relationships Between Data Artifacts and Models of Change

If groups to be compared were initially equal (on the criteria and on the level and relationship of various covariants), were not differentially affected by outside effects, and were not differentially subject to fallibility

Table 1.—Categories of Change Models

Classification Type	Primary Purpose	Examples
1. Adjusted gain score models	identification of high and low gainers identification of correlates of change	DuBois, Manning and DuBois simple gain score
2. True score models	identification of high and low gainers identification of correlates of change	Lord, Kenny, Porter ANCOVA
3. Group equating models	group comparisons, estimation of magnitude of change	Myers, Rubin, Campbell and Erlebacher, Rubin and Cochran
4. Growth analysis	group comparisons, estimation of magnitude of change	Dyer, Forbes, Bryk and Weisberg Ball and Bogatz, Hibbs, Potholf and Roy, Box and Jenkins
5. Structural equations models	group comparison, identification of correlates of change	Cronbach et al. Magidson Joreskog

of measurement, there would be no need for adjustment or estimation models. These conditions are often approximated in pure experimental design where random assignment of subjects is possible. Since, however, these problems are real and pervasive in intervention situations, many models have been developed over the last two decades to deal with one or more of these data artifact problems.

The proliferation of models can be explained in part by the complexity of the problem, in part by individuals' preferences for a specific approach to statistics, and in part by the fact that no one model does it all. Even models as comprehensive as the structural equation approach suffer both from the lack of understanding by potential users and from greater than average data requirements. Each model attempts to address one or more of the shortcomings in analysis that exist when simple gain scores are used. The models differ in what they attempt to address primarily and in the statistical approach they adopt in making that attempt.

Table 2 outlines for each type of model the principal data artifact problem addressed, the data adjustment strategies typically employed by such models, and the potential problems created by such adjustments.

It should be noted here that all of the models except perhaps those in the first classification assume the existence of a control group as the basis of comparison. Studies of intervention which seek to measure change by using subjects as their own control or by using test norms as the standard of comparison are not advocated by these authors and do not lend themselves to the models addressed in this paper. A simple t-test for correlated distributions is perhaps the most appropriate analytical model for studies which use their subjects as their own control. Those studies, however, are subject

to erroneous assumptions about the characteristics of the subjects and about the influence of external forces. The procedures for the completion of Model A evaluation reporting for Title I of the Elementary and Secondary Education Act provide instructions and a few needed caveats for the use of norms to discern change due to intervention.

The first category of models for the measurement of change, adjusted gain score models, is perhaps the simplest and least thorough in addressing confounding artifacts. This group of models basically addresses the lack of reliability of gain scores and attempts to reduce the negative correlation between estimates of individual gain and pretest scores. Models in this category generate estimates of gain by individual participants, using regression adjustments or Bayesian probability estimates. Among these solutions are the raw gain score, covariant-adjusted posttest scores, the residual gain-score models of DuBois (1957) and of Manning and DuBois (1962) and the Bayesian solutions of Novick and Jackson (1974). For the most part these models fail to account for any between group differences, allowing differential group aptitude or experience to foil comparisons. These models also assume that the measurement metric means the same for subjects who are near either the floor or the ceiling of the criterion measure.

A second classification of proposed solutions, true score models, can be generated from attempts to deal directly with the elimination or equating of measurement errors in both the pretest and posttest. Three models of this type are: the standardized gain score model of Kenny (1975), the true score adjustment models of Lord (1969), and Porter (1968).

A third set of solutions, group equating models, approaches the measurement of change by addressing

Table 2.—Relationships of Models of Change to Data Artifacts

Classification of Measurement of Change Model	Problem Addressed[a]	Data Adjustment Strategy Used	Potential Problem Created
I. Adjusted gain score models	(3) lack of reliability of gain scores; (5) negative correlation between estimates of gain and pretest scores	generates estimates of gain by individuals	fails to take into account (2) initial group differences, which are correlated with performances on criterion measures; (4) differential rates of change across groups due to outside influences; (6) differences in relationship of covariant to criterion
II. True score models	(2) initial group differences on pretest; (3) lack of reliability of gain scores; (5) negative correlation between estimates of gain and pretest scores	eliminates or adjusts measurement errors	(5) negative correlation of gain with pretest; group differences that are correlated with criterion; (6) change of relationships of covariant to criterion confounding random error between pretest and posttest
III. Growth equating models	(2) differential beginning points on criterion measure; and (5) inflation or deflation of apparent treatment effects (negative correlation between estimates of gain and pretest)	adjusts posttest scores by pretest differences	(3) fallibility of pretest or posttest or (6) change of relationship of covariant to criterion and confounding of random error between pretest and posttest
IV. Growth analysis models	(2) differential beginning points on criterion measures; (3) fallibility of pretest and posttest; (4) differential rates of growth; and (5) inflation or deflation of apparent treatment effects	estimates what growth would have been without treatment	avoids these artifacts by making assumptions about equality of comparison groups due to interaction of a priori differences and outside influences; (6) change of relationships of covariants to criterion and confounding of random error between pre- and posttests due to interaction of outside influences and fallibility of measurement
V. Structural equations models	all of the above can be addressed by these models, though it is difficult to judge how well	uses covariant relationships of additional measures to define pretest-posttest relationships more precisely	addresses all data artifacts but models are complex and have strictest data requirements

[a]Number in parentheses refers to type of artifacts (see Figure 1).

two factors in the problem, average initial group differences on the criterion score and the fallibility of the criterion measure. This third classification of models seeks to adjust either the data or the design so as to gain a fair comparison between groups. Three strategies of adjustments exist in this classification. The randomized block model of Myers (1972) uses blocking on levels of pretest scoring (i.e., high pretest scores, average, etc.) to estimate differences of effect for students showing initial differences on the criterion pretest. This model, however, requires a reasonable number of subjects in each group scoring at each pretest level and does little to address the fallibility problem except through sample size. The direct matching and bias calibration model of Rubin (1973) adjusts for initial group differences and fallibility of criterion measure by choosing matched subsamples of each group for the comparison and estimating the design bias. This model also requires a medium to large sample size and a substantial number of subjects across groups scoring similarly on the pretest. The third adjustment strategy utilizes combined group regression upon which to base between group comparisons. The best known example of this strategy is

the regression discontinuity model of Campbell and Erlebacher (1970).

None of the models in the third classification provides adjusted individual scores. All of these models provide more precise comparisons when there are large sample sizes and are subject to erroneous estimation in small sample studies due to a priori group differences.

A fourth type of solution, growth analysis models, addresses the problems of initial group differences, fallibility of criterion measures, differential rates of growth, and confounding of treatment effect by not making a head-on statistical comparison. These models attempt to predict what the posttest scores of participants would have been if they had had no program intervention. Two strategies are used to estimate growth without treatment. One strategy compares waves of cohort groups in a naturalistic setting such that one wave includes the treatment or intervention of concern. A second strategy uses a control group to generate a prediction equation with which estimates of gain without treatment can be made for the treatment group. This strategy is often referred to as the "value-added" model. Models falling in this classification and using the first strategy include: the accountability model of Dyer (1970), the National Assessment Model of Forbes (1977), the cohort model of Ball and Bogatz (1970), the MANOVA model of Potthoff and Roy (1964), the least squares model of Hibbs (1974), and the interrupted time series of Box and Jenkins (1976). A model exemplifying the second strategy is the growth model of Bryk and Weisberg (1977).

Although these models avoid directly facing the artifacts due to initial group differences and fallibility of measure, they still are subject to bias due to external influences which tend to confound treatment with setting characteristics. The first strategy of comparing undifferentiated waves of subjects across time is weak if a major proportion of the second wave of subjects have not received the intervention. Seasonal effects which can be controlled for most easily in time series can be a threat to valid comparisons in the other models if timing is not considered in the schedule of assessments. Models in this classification using the second strategy require the availability of an array of mediating variables that possess the collective capability of accurately predicting the criterion variable. A general criticism of this strategy is the questioning of the degree to which one believes that the mediating variables relate to the criterion variable in the same manner across groups.

The final classification, structural equations models, addresses all of the data artifact problems discussed. These models utilize covariant relationships of additional measures to explicate more definitively the pretest-posttest relationships. Models included in this classification are: the ideal covariant and complete discriminant model of Cronbach, Rogosa, Floden and Price (1977), the extended ANOVA model of Magidson (1977), and the structural equation solutions of Joreskog (1977). Such models, however, are complex, hard to interpret, require the availability of an array of mediating variables related to the criterion measure, and

need a priori research on these variables to generate a theoretical order of expected interrelationships.

The potential problems created or left unresolved by the data adjustment strategies used in various model types are not always problems in actuality. A given blind spot will not matter if the problem to which a given model type is susceptible is not present in the situation to be evaluated. Even a real problem may be outweighed by other considerations. The procedure outlined in the next section takes into account the most troublesome data artifact problems (as well as design considerations and purpose) in selecting models for measuring change.

A Procedure for Selecting Models for Evaluating Change

The appropriate selection of a given model or even a type of model for a particular change measurement task is part art and part science. There is at present inadequate research comparing the performance of models across different situations. A series of considerations and some supportive research that facilitates model selection can be organized, but this thin body of systematic research must be supplemented by analysis of statistical and measurement issues, a wide acquaintance with the field as it has developed, and broad experience with use of various models in large scale evaluations in which model effects are most clearly displayed. These combined sources have led to the pragmatic suggestions posed in this paper and in previous discussions (Fortune & Hutson, 1981, 1982). At present we recommend that the selection of a single model be made through an elimination process. Table 3 illustrates the two-phase elimination process which takes the user to a point in the selection process where factors other than data artifacts and design concerns determine the final model selection. The first phase identifies the appropriate model type;

Table 3.—Diagram of the Model Selection Process—Phase I

Question	Response	Action
1. What is the purpose for measuring change?	a. identify high and low gainers b. identify correlates of change c. estimate magnitude of change d. compare change across two groups	a. eliminate classifications 3,5 b. eliminate classification 3 c. eliminate classifications 1,5 d. eliminate classification 1
2. How reliable is the criterion measure in the population?	a. greater than .95 b. less than .95	a. eliminate classification 2 b. eliminate classification 1
3. Are there known mediating variables which predict pretest scores?	a. yes b. no	a. eliminate classifications 1,2,3 b. eliminate classifications 4,5
4. If you are not now in a single classification, does each group contain 30 or more subjects?	a. yes b. no	a. eliminate classifications 2,4 b. eliminate classifications 3,5

the second phase aids in selecting an appropriate specific model within a category.

Selecting a Model Type

As can be seen in Table 3, the rough sorting process using only a few questions is sufficient to determine the general classificaton of models most appropriate for a given situation.

The first question concerns the purpose for a given evaluation, with the model types matched to purpose as discussed earlier. The second question concerns the precision of the criterion measure. This question tends to make a choice between models which address the fallibility issues directly and at an individual subject level and models which address this issue indirectly. The third question concerns the presence or absence of supportive information concerning the criterion measure beyond that provided by the pretest and posttest. If none is available, growth analysis and structural equations cannot be used to ascertain change. Question four concerns the number of subjects used in the analysis. The procedures which offer the potential for more precise adjustments usually require larger sample sizes.

The utilization of the four questions delineated in Table 3 will determine which model classification is most appropriate and efficient for a specific problem situation.

This is not to suggest that no other model type is suitable (though some are ruled out), but that the model types recommended in this phase of the selection process are the least complex feasible approaches for a given purpose and set of conditions. The next step in the process is to select a specific change model from within a category. Figure 2 illustrates by way of a tree diagram the selection or elimination process.

Selecting a Specific Model From a Classification

Each proposed classification of models includes two or more different strategies through which a given artifact is addressed. To complete the model selection process, the basis of selection within classifications must be established. Since each classification of models can be associated with a unique set of questions for model selection from within the classification, each classification will be treated separately. The within classification selection process is not as clear in terms of objective decision dimensions as is the selection process for classifications. Hence, some choices within a classification may be more a product of the authors' preferences than a product of established practice. The suggestions made here, though, may provoke further research.

Model Selection Within Classification 1

Classification 1 contains three basic types of gain-score estimates: 1) an estimate based upon direct sub-

traction, the raw gain score; 2) an estimate based upon regression-based prediction, the residual gain-score; and 3) an estimate based upon Bayesian prediction, the expected gain score. There are five questions which will, when used sequentially, determine by elimination a single model for a majority of the design circumstances. These questions and their recommended actions are: 1) Is the reliability of the criterion test unknown? If the answer is yes, you should avoid the use of raw gain scores; 2) Are there subjects in the data near either the floor or ceiling of the criterion test? If there are, then use of raw gain scores should be avoided; 3) Are there data from a previous study or assessment upon which to build expectations of change? If the previous data is not available, then the expected gain-score model must be rejected; 4) Are there 60 or more subjects in the study? If not, then residual gain scores should be avoided; and 5) Is there supportive information in addition to the pretest that will contribute to the prediction of the posttest? If the answer is no, then residual gain scores should not be used.

These five questions will identify a single model within classification 1 for a majority of conditions. For those conditions in which a single model is not identified, the choice is usually narrowed down to two models except in an unusual set of circumstances. If the selection process has not eliminated any of the three models, raw gain scores are preferred on the basis of simplicity. For the same reason, raw gain scores are preferred over expected gain scores using Bayesian procedures. Either raw gain scores or expected gain scores are recommended over residual gain scores due to the bias which can be produced in the prediction process.

Model Selection Within Classification 2

In the second classification there also exist three different models from which to choose. These are: 1) covariant adjustments of the data; 2) standardized gain-score conversions of the data; and 3) true-score adjustment of the data. Again, five questions used sequentially will eliminate a majority of the cases, leaving a single model or a choice between two models. The questions and their recommended actions include: 1) Is the reliability of the criterion measure known for the subjects being studied? If not, then the true-score adjustment must be eliminated; 2) Is there equality of covariant relationships to the criterion measure across groups? If not, ANCOVA adjustments should not be used; 3) Are the subjects distributed similarly in regard to pretest scores across groups? If not, standard score adjustments should not be used; 4) Are the sample sizes across groups approximately equal? If not, ANCOVA adjustments should not be used; and 5) Is the reliability of the criterion test above .90 for the sample being studied? If not, then the standardized gain score correlation test should not be employed.

Figure 2.—A Decision Tree Illustration of the Selection of a Type of Measurement of Change Model

Q.1. What is the purpose for measuring change?

Q.2. How reliable is the criterion measure?

Q.3. Are there known mediating variables which predict the criterion measure?

Q.4. Are the sample sizes of each group greater than 30?

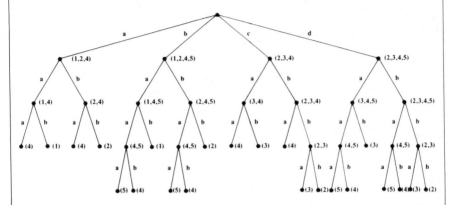

*Limbs of diagram represent responses to questions corresponding to Table 3; numbers in parentheses represent model classifications which have not been eliminated.

If the elimination process has not singled out one model, the true-score adjustment is preferred over the other two adjustments due to the benefits of error reduction and the ANCOVA adjustment is favored over the standard score adjustment only on the basis of frequency of use and availability of computer packages.

Model Selection Within Classification 3

Three strategies of adjustment make up the choice of models in the third classification of models. They are: 1) blocking of pretest scores; 2) direct matching and bias calibration; and 3) the regression discontinuity model. The decision between models in the third classification does not lend itself to sequential questioning and elimination. In fact, the choice between models is usually made through compromise. Each of the three model options should, however, pass a single test of appropriateness prior to application of two questions which establish the conditions of the compromise. If reliability is low or unknown for the criterion test and if the distribution of the pretest scores does not contain any natural breaking points, the blocking strategy should not be used. If there is not a substantial overlap of pretest scores across groups, the direct matching and bias calibration is not recommended. If there is not a similar or continuous range of pretest scores for the combined groups, the regression discontinuity model is not recommended. All three of the strategies are more efficient and precise for large samples. For sample sizes of less than 60 subjects the blocking strategy is preferred, provided there is high reliability on the criterion measure. Otherwise, the regression discontinuity approach is recommended.

Model Selection Within Classification 4

Two strategies of growth analysis exist in the fourth classification. One strategy involves the comparison of two or more successive assessments where the later assessments include treated subjects. The second strategy attempts to utilize characteristics of untreated subjects to predict where treated subjects would progress had there been no intervention. There are two distinct models which utilize the first strategy: the cohort wave model and the interrupted time series model. Basically, the suggested questions will be directed toward selection between the cohort wave models, the interrupted time series models, and the projected growth without treatment or value-added model. No attempt will be made to select among the variations of these models suggested by various model developers.

Several questions appear useful in eliminating some models for given conditions. These questions and their recommended actions include: 1) Are change scores on individuals needed? If so, then the value-added model appears the most useful. The cohort wave model should be eliminated in this case especially if the waves are cross sectional; 2) Have the points of assessment been coordinated at similar calendar times before and after the intervention? If this is not true, the cohort wave model should be eliminated. However, if an adequate number of assessments has occurred before the intervention the interrupted time-series models will allow the discernment of seasonal variations; 3) Does a majority of the assessed sample receive the intervention at approximately the same point in time? If not, use of the cohort wave model is not recommended; 4) Is there more than one intervention which may influence posttest criterion scores occurring within the sample over the elapsed period of time between assessments? If so, neither the cohort wave model nor the interrupted time series model is recommended; 5) Are these multiple points of assessment before and after the intervention? If the answer is no, then the interrupted time series should not be used; 6) Are there enough available data on mediating variables to predict the pretest with a multiple correlation greater than or equal to .90? If not, the use of the value-added model is questionable; 7) Is there any reason to suspect unmeasured differences which possess potential to influence the criterion variable between groups? If so, use of the value-added model is again questionable; 8) Are there sufficient similarities in group characteristics to generate expected posttest scores with adequate precision across groups? If not, then the value-added model is not recommended; and 9) Does each assessment sample equally represent the population for which the intervention is directed? If not, then the cohort wave model is not recommended.

Model Selection Within Classification 5

In classification 5 all of the proposed models are similar in structure and the choice between these models is arbitrary in regard to the content discussed in this paper. The Magidson model tends to be more nearly analogous to regression analysis. The Joreskog model is available as a packaged computer program.

Developing Confidence Bounds for Evaluation Results

Ideally, the responses to the questions previously discussed will eliminate most inappropriate models and will allow the selection of a change model which can easily be administered and interpreted. However, if the elimination process fails to narrow choices altogether the selection of two or more competing models is recommended, where both are suitable for the purpose but one tends to produce higher estimates than the other. The resulting change estimates can be treated like magnitudes within confidence bounds; that is, the true gain is likely to lie between the two estimates. This strategy is especially appealing when the alternative models within a classification can be divided into two groups, where one group is expected to provide a conservative estimate of change and the other group is expected to provide a liberal estimate of change. The strategy of using estimates as confidence bounds can be repeated until the user feels that the true gain has been adequately described, that is, until the user has reached the precision level required for the impending decision.

As it appears now, no model or classification of models appears superior across all cases. Research systematically comparing the estimation capabilities of the models across varying conditions is needed. Until those results give a firm base for selecting evaluation models, the pragmatic suggestions offered here may help in selecting the model(s) least riddled with troublesome artifacts and most appropriate for a given situation.

REFERENCES

Ball, S., & Bogatz, G. A. *The first year of Sesame Street: An evaluation.* Princeton, NJ: Educational Testing Service, 1970.

Box, G. E. P., & Jenkins, G. M. *Time-series analysis: Forecasting and control.* San Francisco: Holden-Day, 1976.

Bryk, A. S., & Weisberg, H. I. Use of the nonequivalent control group design when subjects are growing. *Psychological Bulletin,* 1977, *85,* 950-962.

Campbell, D. T., & Erlebacher, A. E. How regression artifacts in quasi-experimental evaluations can mistakenly make compensatory education look harmful. In J. Hellmuth (Ed.), *Compensatory education: A national debate (Vol. 3): The Disadvantaged Child.* New York: Brunner/Mazel, 1970.

Cronbach, L. J., Rogosa, D. R., Floden, R. E., & Price, G. G. *Analysis of co-variance in non-randomized experiments: Parameters affecting bias* (Occasional paper). Berkeley, CA: Stanford University, Stanford Evaluation Consortium, 1977.

DuBois, P. H. *Multivariate correlational analysis.* New York: Harper & Row, 1957.

Dyer, H. S. Toward objective criteria of professional accountability in the schools of New York City. *Phi Delta Kappan,* 1970, *52,* 206-211.

Forbes, R. NAEP: One tool to improve instruction. *Educational Leadership,* 1977, *34,* 276-281.

Fortune, J. C., & Hutson, B. A. Does your program work? Strategies for measuring change. *Educational Technology,* Spring, 1981.

Fortune, J. C., & Hutson, B. A. *Selecting models for measuring change: Sensitivity to several kinds of data artifacts.* Paper presented at the meeting of the American Educational Research Association, New York, March 1982.

Hibbs, D. A., Jr. Programs of statistical estimation and causal inference in time-series regression models. In H. L. Costner (Ed.), *Sociological methodology, 1973-1974.* San Francisco: Jossey-Bass, 1974.

Joreskog, K. G. Structural equation models in the social sciences: Specification, estimation and testing. In P. R. Krishnaiah (Ed.), *Application of statistics.* Amsterdam: North Holland, 1977.

Kenny, D. A. A quasi-experimental approach to assessing treatment effects in the nonequivalent control group design. *Psychological Bulletin,* 1975, *82,* 345-362.

Linn, R. L., & Slinde, J. A. The determination of the significance of change between pre- and posttesting periods. *Review of Educational Research,* 1977, *47*(1), 121-150.

Lord, F. M. Statistical adjustments when comparing pre-existing groups. *Psychological Bulletin,* 1969, *72,* 336-337.

Magidson, J. Toward a causal model approach for adjusting the pre-existing differences in the nonequivalent control group situation: A general alternative to ANCOVA. *Evaluation Quarterly,* 1977, *1,* 399-420.

Manning, W. H., & DuBois, P. H. Correlational methods in research on human subjects. *Perceptual Motor Skills,* 1962, *15,* 287-321.

Myers, J. L. *Fundamentals of experimental design* (2nd ed.). Boston: Allyn & Bacon, 1972.

Novick, M. R., & Jackson, P. H. *Statistical methods for educational and psycholgical research.* New York: McGraw-Hill, 1974.

Porter, A. C. The effects of using fallible variables in the analysis of covariance (Doctoral dissertation, University of Wisconsin, 1967). *Dissertation Abstracts International,* 1968, *51,* 313-325.

Potthoff, R. F., & Roy, S. N. A generalized multivariate analysis of variance model useful especially for growth curve problems. *Biometrika,* 1964, *51,* 313-325.

Rubin, D. B. The use of matched sampling and regression adjustment to remove bias in observational studies. *Biometrics,* 1973, *29,* 185-203.

37

Planning Educational Research
Determining the Necessary Sample Size
Stephen F. Olejnik

ABSTRACT

In planning a research study, investigators are frequently uncertain regarding the minimal number of subjects needed to adequately test a hypothesis of interest. The present paper discusses the sample size problem and four factors which affect its solution: significance level, statistical power, analysis procedure, and effect size. The interrelationship between these factors is discussed and demonstrated by calculating minimal sample size requirements for a variety of research conditions.

THOUGHTFUL PLANNING and careful implementation are two basic characteristics of all good quantitative research studies. The quality of experimental research studies depends to a great degree on the extent to which the investigator has "thought through" the research plan. In the planning stage of the research process, special emphasis is often given to instrumentation, research design, and statistical analysis procedures. Research methods courses and textbooks discuss these issues extensively and researchers are continually reminded to select instruments having high reliability and validity coefficients, to choose designs which minimize threats to internal and external validity, and to select analysis procedures appropriate for testing hypotheses of interest.

Another critical concern in the planning of a quantitative research study in which hypothesis testing is of interest is the determination of the number of experimental units which should be involved in the research study. While sample size can influence the choice of instrumentation, design, and analysis, very little, if any,

attention is given to this topic in research methods and introductory statistics textbooks. Several advanced analysis of variance textbooks (i.e., Glass & Stanley, 1970; Kirk, 1982; Myers, 1979) do discuss sample size as a factor affecting statistical power, but the discussions are limited to one-way ANOVA designs. Furthermore, textbooks on correlational and regression techniques generally avoid the sample size issue completely (Draper & Smith, 1966; Kerlinger & Pedhazur, 1973; Kleinbaum & Kupper, 1978; Pedhazur, 1982). As a result, many researchers in psychology and education are frequently uncertain how many subjects are needed for their research study. A common solution to this problem is to rely on the following rule of thumb: "Use as many subjects as you can get and you can afford." This is poor advice because all of the available subjects may still be insufficient for an adequate test of a hypothesis and the inclusion of all available subjects can produce statistically significant differences or relationships even though the differences are trivial. Evidence indicating that many researchers do not have a sound rationale for the sample size included in their studies is provided in noting that it is a rare research paper that discusses how the sample size was determined as part of the description of the sample in the methodological section of research papers.

The purpose of the present paper is to discuss the issue of sample size determination for a hypothesis testing research study and to provide some general guidelines regarding minimal sample size requirements for several popular research designs and analysis procedures. The primary reference source used in this paper is Cohen's (1977) text, *Statistical Power Analysis for the Behavioral Sciences*. Cohen's text has been used as a reference in the review of statistical power of unpublished research from several disciplines (Brewer, 1972; Chase

From the *Journal of Experimental Education*, Vol. 53, 40-48, 1984. A publication of the Helen Dwight Educational Foundation.

& Baran, 1976; Katzer & Sodt, 1973; Kroll & Chase, 1975). Rather than analyze past research, the present paper focuses on the planning stage of the research process as it relates to the determination of an adequate sample size.

In a previous discussion of sample size requirements, Feldt (1973) considered single factor ANOVA and ANCOVA analysis strategies when the outcome of interest was measured with a standardized achievement test. The results of his analysis showed the insensitivity of standardized achievement measures to identify treatment effects and the need to collect and analyze pretreatment data to be used in an ANCOVA model rather than to rely on an ANOVA analysis. More recently, Levin (1975) presented a general model for determining the sample size needed for ANOVA models and for planned contrasts.

The present paper differs from the previous discussions of sample size determination in three ways. First, sample size requirements for additional analysis procedures are considered. Specifically, sample sizes for tests of interaction effects, Pearson correlation, partial correlation, and the chi-square test of independence are considered in addition to the ANOVA and ANCOVA models. A second distinction between the past papers and the present report is the latter considers sample size requirements for several effect sizes. The previous papers avoided this issue by ignoring it completely (Levin, 1975) or by limiting the discussion to standardized achievement tests (Feldt, 1973). A third distinction between the present and previous papers is the current paper focuses on the interrelationship between factors which affect the sample size problem.

Four Factors Influencing Sample Size Determination

To determine the necessary sample size for a hypothesis testing research study, four factors must be taken into consideration. These four factors are: criterion for statistical significance, level of statistical power, statistical analysis strategy, and the size of an effect judged to be meaningful. In the sections that follow, the first three factors are discussed briefly as they are generally well known and understood by researchers. The size of an effect is less well known and is, therefore, discussed in some detail. Following this discussion, calculations for minimal sample sizes for a variety of situations are summarized in two tables and used to demonstrate how the four factors affect sample size as well as to show the interrelationship between the four factors.

Statistical Criteria of Significance

One factor which directly influences sample size requirements for a research study is the criterion chosen by the researcher for statistical significance when the null hypothesis of interest is tested. In any hypothesis test based on sample data, it is possible, due to sampling errors, to conclude that a relationship exists between the variables studied, even though such a relationship does not exist in the total population. The level of significance chosen by the researcher is the probability that this type of error (Type I) will be made. Generally, researchers consider the Type I error as a serious mistake and, therefore, attempt to minimize the probability of its occurrence. Given that other factors (power, analysis strategy, and effect size) are unchanged, the necessary sample size is inversely related to significance level. That is, a large sample size will be required if the probability of a Type I error is to be minimized, but if an increased probability of a Type I error is acceptable, then a smaller sample size may be sufficient. Most hypotheses in the social sciences are tested at a .05 level of significance. While this criterion of significance is arbitrary, it has gained wide acceptance to the point where any hypothesis tested at a higher probability of a Type I error is viewed with considerable reservation. In the discussion which follows, the rigid adherence to the 5% criterion for significance is questioned based on its implication for a minimal sample size.

Level of Statistical Power

A second consideration that affects the number of subjects needed for a hypothesis testing research study is statistical power. In the converse of the situation described in the previous section on significance level, it is possible that in the population a relationship may exist between the variables being studied, but in testing the hypothesis using sample data, a relationship may not be observed. Errors of this second type (Type II) are generally of less concern to researchers; however, the probability that such an error is *not* made cannot be totally ignored. If a relationship between the variables does exist in the population, researchers should expect a reasonable probability of identifying that relationship in their investigation. The probability of rejecting the null hypothesis when the null hypothesis is false is referred to as statistical power. Without sufficient statistical power, conducting the research study is likely to be an inefficient use of time and resources. Guidelines for defining adequate statistical power are not as rigidly established as the criteria for statistical significance. However, statistical power ranging between .70 and .85 might generally be viewed as acceptable. The number of subjects needed for testing a hypothesis is directly related to the issue of statistical power. Given that significance level, statistical analysis, and effect size remain unchanged, an increase in the level of statistical power will increase the sample size needed. On the other hand, a reduction in sample size will reduce statistical power.

Data Analysis Procedure

The number of subjects needed for an adequate test of a hypothesis is also affected by the statistical analysis strategy chosen by the researcher. The choice of an appropriate statistical test depends on the research question of interest, the research design adopted, and the nature or type of variables studied. These three considerations are not totally independent of each other and for any combination of these factors several analysis procedures could be chosen. General analysis strategies, which take into consideration more information about the subjects, tend to require fewer subjects. Thus, research studies involving quantitative independent variables require fewer subjects than studies using qualitative independent variables and investigations with data collected both pretreatment and posttreatment require fewer subjects than studies based on posttreatment data alone. An exception to this generalization, however, is provided in analyzing factorial designs. The more independent variables included in the study, the more subjects that are needed to adequately test all of the hypotheses generated in the design.

Effect Size

A fourth and final consideration that affects the decision on how many subjects are needed to test a hypothesis of interest is the degree to which the null hypothesis is false. Specifically, for a given level of significance, statistical power, and analysis strategy, sample size is inversely related to the falseness of the null hypothesis. For example, in a research study comparing two population means, the null hypothesis states that the two population means are equal. If there is, in fact, a large difference between the population means, only a few subjects from each population are needed to detect that difference. On the other hand, if the two populations differ but the difference is slight, then the number of subjects needed from each population will be considerably larger.

At the planning stage of a research study, many investigators find it difficult to state the degree to which the null hypothesis is false. It is, after all, the purpose of the research study to provide an estimate of the relationship or the difference between population means. If these parameters were known, there would be no point in conducting the study. To answer the question concerning the necessary sample size, however, researchers must specify the minimal relationship or minimal difference in population means that the investigator believes would be important to detect from a practical perspective. Another way of considering this point is to state what difference between population means or what relationship between variables would be considered trivial by the researcher. A statement on the practical difference between groups requires the researcher to interpret an anticipated effect in terms of the instrumentation used in the study. This, in turn, requires the researcher to be totally familiar with the instrument used in the study and to be able to translate observable scores into meaningful behavior. Unfortunately, too many investigators lack the necessary familiarity with their assessment tools. As a result, it is difficult for them to distinguish between a meaningful and a trivial difference or relationship. This problem with instrument unfamiliarity also explains why many researchers become disappointed when the data analysis indicates a nonsignificant difference even though a large program effect was anticipated. It is not sufficient to anticipate a large or medium size effect, but rather the effect size must be considered in relation to the assessment tools used. The use of new or infrequently used instruments makes the determination of effect size especially difficult. However, the development of any new instrument requires a considerable number of pilot studies and the results of these investigations should provide some guidance regarding the meaning of the observed scores.

Even with considerable familiarity with an instrument, distinguishing between a trivial and meaningful relationship is difficult because the judgment is so subjective. Choosing a significance level for a hypothesis test is also subjective, but because of wide acceptance of the .10, .05, and .01 levels, the arbitrariness of the choice is somewhat limited. In the case of effect size, however, widely accepted guidelines do not exist because what might be considered a small or large effect depends on the population studied, the nature of the variables investigated, and the procedures used to measure the variables. One attempt, however, to define a large effect was provided by Feldt (1973) when he considered the problem of minimal sample size requirements for studies comparing group means using an achievement measure. In terms of a standardized norm referenced achievement test, Feldt suggested that a large effect be defined as one in which subjects increased their test scores from the fiftieth to the seventy-fifth percentile. In the case of the Iowa Test of Basic Skills (Lindquist & Hieronymus, 1964), such a change amounted to between .246 and .372 standard deviation units across six types of scales and four grade levels.

A second source of guidance for providing a reasonable definition of an effect size for a particular variable might be found in the publication of meta-analytic studies. Meta-analysis is a methodological procedure suggested by Glass (1978) to integrate the findings of several independent research studies whose only source of commonality lies with the theoretical constructs being investigated. The procedure requires the transformation of reported test statistics in terms of a metric-free unit. Such a scale is provided when the results are reported in terms of the dependent variable's standard deviation units. After all studies investigating a construct have been standardized, the average effect size is computed and interpreted as the overall typical effect. Mantzana and Fry (1983) have recently compiled a bibliography of publications addressing the issue of research integration. In that report, the authors cite 172 references to meta-analytic studies. By identifying a meta-analytic study involving factors similar to those the researcher intends to study, the typical size of an effect can be specified and used in the estimation of the necessary sample size. Table 1 presents the results of 11 meta-analytic studies which were reported over the past five years in the *Journal of Educational Psychology*, *Review of Educational Research*, *American Educational Research Journal*, and *Educational Evaluation and Policy Analysis*. The purpose of this table is to provide some indication of the typical effect size obtained in many research studies in the social sciences. While the effect size obtained varied greatly, about half (45% of those reported in the table) were greater than .3 standard deviation units. This result provides some evidence

that Feldt's definition of a large effect size may be appropriate for an achievement measure, but it should not be generalized to all social science variables.

A final source of guidance for defining an effect size that is considered here was suggested by Cohen (1977). In his text on statistical power, Cohen considered several hypothesis testing procedures and for each approach he suggested a definition for a large, medium, and small effect size. For hypothesis tests comparing sample means, Cohen suggested differences of .2, .5, and .8 standard deviation units as being small, medium, and large effects, respectively. For analysis of variance problems comparing several treatment groups, effect sizes were defined in terms of eta squared (η^2). Specifically, sources of variation which explained 13%, 6%, and 1% of variability in the dependent variable were considered as large, medium, and small effects, respectively. Hypothesis tests using the Pearson product moment correlation were defined as small, medium, and large if the coefficient of determination equaled 1%,

Table 1—Average Effect Size (ES) Reported in Recent Meta-Analytic Studies on a Variety of Variables of Interest to Social Scientists

Authors	Variables	ES
Kulik, C., & Kulik, J. A. (1982)	Ability grouping	
	Standardized test	.10
	Local test	.11
	Published research	.19
Cohen, P. A., Kulik, J. A., & Kulik, C. (1982)	Tutoring	
	Tutees—Achievement	.40
	—Attitude	.29
	—Self-concept	.09
	Tutors—Achievement	.33
	—Attitude	.42
	—Self-concept	.18
Luiten, J., Ames, W., & Ackerman, G. (1980)	Advance organizers	
	Learning	.21
	Retention	.25
Smith, M. L., & Glass, G. V. (1980)	Class size	.49
Uguroglu, M. E., & Walberg, H. (1979)	Motivation and achievement	.70
Redfield, D. L., & Rousseau, E. W. (1981)	Teacher questioning	.73
Kulik, J. A., Kulik, C. C., & Cohen, P. A. (1980)	Computer-based college teaching	
	Achievement	.25
	Attitude	.24
Kulik, J. A., Cohen, P. A., & Ebeling, B. J. (1980)	Programmed instruction	
	Higher education	.28
Kulik, J. A., Bangert, R. C., & Williams G. W. (1983)	Computer-based teaching	
	Secondary	.32
Dusek, J. B., & Joseph, G. (1983)	Teacher expectation	
	Physical attractiveness	
	Achievement	.30
	Social	.19
	Gender	
	Achievement	.20
	Social	.07
	Cumulative folder	.85
	Social class	.47
	Race	.11
Rosenthal, R., & Rubin, D. (1982)	Cognitive gender differences	
	Verbal	.30
	Quantitative	.35
	Visual-spatial	.50
	Field articulation	.51

6%, or 13%, respectively. Finally, for the analysis of contingency tables using the chi-square test statistic, contingency coefficients equaling .1, .207, and .447 were considered as small, medium, and large effects, respectively. In the special case of a 2 × 2 table which could be analyzed using the Pearson correlation coefficient, the definition of a small, medium, and large effect correspond to coefficients of determination of .01, .09, and .25. While discussing these various effect sizes, Cohen stressed that his suggestions were only recommendations which should be used as guidelines only when other sources of information (i.e., pilot studies, previous research findings) were not available. Cohen strongly encouraged researchers to provide their own definition of a reasonable effect size depending on the subjects and variables under investigation. In spite of these cautionary notes, Cohen's definitions of effect sizes are probably the best known and widely accepted guidelines currently used by researchers.

Examples of Sample Size Solutions

In the previous sections, the four factors which influence the decision regarding the number of subjects needed for an adequate test of a hypothesis were discussed and the general effect of each of these considera-

tions was indicated. While this general information is useful in providing some indication of the complexity of the sample size question, it does not provide a satisfactory answer to the question: "How many subjects do I need?" nor does it adequately provide the researcher with a "feel" for the approximate number of subjects needed. Furthermore, by discussing one factor at a time, an inadequate understanding of the interrelationship between the four factors is provided. The four factors interact in such a way that changes in one factor can be compensated for by changes in one or more of the remaining considerations.

The exact answer to the sample size question can be given only when the specific parameters of the problem are provided and power curves such as those provided in advanced statistics textbooks (Glass & Stanley, 1970; Kirk, 1982) or sample size tables (Cohen, 1977) are consulted. However, the nature of the interrelationship between significance level, statistical power, effect size, and analysis procedures can be demonstrated through a series of sample size calculations in which each factor is varied sytematically. Tables 2 and 3 report the results of these calculations for two levels of significance (.05, .10); two levels of statistical power (.7, .5); fourteen statistical analysis procedures; and three levels of effect size (small, medium, and large). The results of all com-

Table 2—Minimal Sample Sizes for Fourteen Hypothesis Tests at the .05 and .10 Levels of Significance with Power of .7 for Detecting Small, Medium, and Large Effect Sizes

		Effect Size					
		Small		Medium		Large	
α	Hypothesis Test	n	N	n	N	n	N
.05	Independent samples t test	310	620	50	100	20	40
	Related samples t test ($\varrho = .7$)	94	188	16	32	7	14
	Related samples t test ($\varrho = .5$)	155	310	26	52	11	22
	ANOVA $k = 3$	288	774	42	126	17	51
	ANOVA $k = 4$	221	884	36	144	15	60
	ANCOVA $k = 3$, $\varrho = .7$	132	396	22	66	9	27
	ANCOVA $k = 3$, $\varrho = .5$	193	579	32	96	13	39
	3 × 4 Factorial main effect $k = 3$	65	780	11	132	5	60
	main effect $k = 4$	74	888	13	156	6	72
	interaction	94	1128	16	192	7	84
	Pearson correlation		616		66		23
	Partial correlation ($r_{yx \cdot z}$)		312		44		21
	Chi-square contingency analysis (2 × 4)		879		98		35
	(3 × 4)		1114		124		45
.10	Independent samples t test	236	472	38	76	15	30
	Related samples t test ($\varrho = .7$)	72	144	12	24	5	10
	Related samples t test ($\varrho = .5$)	119	238	20	40	8	16
	ANOVA $k = 3$	200	600	32	96	13	39
	ANOVA $k = 4$	173	692	28	112	11	44
	ANCOVA $k = 3$, $\varrho = .7$	103	309	17	51	7	21
	ANCOVA $k = 3$, $\varrho = .5$	150	450	25	75	10	30
	3 × 4 Factorial main effect $k = 3$	51	612	9	72	4	48
	main effect $k = 4$	58	696	10	120	5	60
	interaction	75	900	13	156	6	72
	Pearson correlation		470		51		18
	Partial correlation ($r_{yx \cdot z}$)		238		33		15
	Chi-square contingency analysis (2 × 4)		688		76		28
	(3 × 4)		884		98		35

Table 3—Minimal Sample Sizes for Fourteen Hypothesis Tests at the .05 and .10 Levels of Significance with Power of .5 for Detecting Small, Medium, and Large Effect Sizes

		Small		Medium		Large	
α	Hypothesis Test	n	N	n	N	n	N
.05	Independent samples t test	193	386	32	64	13	26
	Related samples t test ($\varrho = .7$)	59	118	11	22	5	10
	Related samples t test ($\varrho = .5$)	97	194	16	32	7	14
	ANOVA $k = 3$	166	498	27	81	11	33
	ANOVA $k = 4$	145	580	24	96	10	40
	ANCOVA $k = 3$, $\varrho = .7$	85	255	15	45	7	21
	ANCOVA $k = 3$, $\varrho = .5$	125	375	21	63	9	27
	3 × 4 Factorial main effect $k = 3$	42	504	8	96	3	36
	main effect $k = 4$	49	588	9	108	4	48
	interaction	63	756	11	121	5	60
	Pearson correlation		384		42		15
	Partial correlation ($r_{yx \cdot z}$)		195		29		14
	Chi-square contingency analysis (2 × 4)		576		64		23
	(3 × 4)		750		83		30
.10	Independent samples t test	136	272	22	44	9	18
	Related samples t test ($\varrho = .7$)	42	84	8	16	4	8
	Related samples t test ($\varrho = .5$)	69	138	12	24	5	10
	ANOVA $k = 3$	119	357	20	60	8	24
	ANOVA $k = 4$	105	420	18	72	7	28
	ANCOVA $k = 3$, $\varrho = .7$	62	186	11	33	5	15
	ANCOVA $k = 3$, $\varrho = .5$	90	270	15	45	7	21
	3 × 4 Factorial main effect $k = 3$	31	372	6	72	2	24
	main effect $k = 4$	36	432	7	84	3	36
	interaction	47	564	8	96	4	48
	Pearson correlation		277		30		11
	Partial correlation ($r_{yx \cdot z}$)		138		21		11
	Chi-square contingency analysis (2 × 4)		418		46		17
	(3 × 4)		553		61		22

binations of these four factors can be represented as a completely crossed 2 × 2 × 14 × 3 factorial design. Cohen's definitions of small, medium, and large effect sizes were adopted for this demonstration. The rationale behind this choice was the fact that different analysis procedures report results using different metrics which raises some difficulties if comparisons between analysis procedures were of interest. An attractive feature of Cohen's work is that his definitions of effect sizes are relatively consistent in terms of the proportion of variation in the dependent measure which is explained. Thus, a fairly accurate comparison between procedures in terms of sample size requirements can be made for a given significance level, power, and effect size.

A close examination of Tables 2 and 3 identifies some interesting relationships between the four factors and minimal sample size for an adequate hypothesis test. One of the most striking results reported in these tables is the number of subjects needed when the size of a meaningful effect is classified as being small. Regardless of the analysis procedure, the detection of a small effect requires a large number of subjects and this is true even when the significance level is set at .10 and statistical power of .5 is judged acceptable. For example, to identify a small effect with an independent samples t test with the significance level set at .10 and the power at .5

(Table 3), a sample of 272 subjects would be needed. If the significance level was set at .05 and power at .7 (Table 2), 620 subjects would be needed to identify a small effect with the independent samples t test. These calculations assume that an equal number of subjects would be assigned to each group. Given these results and the results of the meta-analytic studies discussed earlier, which showed a high percentage (55%) of the average effect sizes as being small, it is not surprising that the results of many research studies do not show statistical significance. On the other hand, when a meaningful effect is classified as large, the necessary sample size is much more manageable. Only 18 subjects (equal n) are needed to test a hypothesis with an independent samples t test if the significance level is set at .10, power of .5 is acceptable, and a large effect is judged as meaningful. Researchers must be cautioned against justifying a small sample size in the planning stage of investigations by suggesting only large effects are meaningful. If the researcher is wrong or changes his/her mind about a meaningful effect size, then the hypothesis test based on a sample size calculated for a large effect will be greatly inadequate for detecting a medium effect size. For example, with a sample of 18 subjects using an independent samples t test at a .10 level of significance, the power to detect a medium effect would only be .27.

Thus, when deciding a meaningful effect, it is much better to underestimate the size of the effect than to overestimate it. It should also be recalled that very few results of the meta-analytic studies could be judged as being large. For researchers to anticipate a large effect size may only, in many situations, be wishful thinking.

Another interesting, but not surprising, fact which is clearly demonstrated in the results reported in Tables 2 and 3 is that considerably fewer subjects are needed in research studies in which investigators have more information on the subjects besides scores on the dependent measure. Hypothesis tests for a comparison of group means using an independent samples t test or analysis of variance requires a relatively large sample unless the effect size is large. If additional information such as a pretest is available to either match subjects or to use as a covariate, sample size requirements can be reduced considerably. Furthermore, the amount of the reduction in sample size depends on the strength of the relationship between the additional information and the dependent variable. For example, a total sample of 126 subjects would be needed in an ANOVA model $k = 3$ to detect a medium effect when the significance level is set equal to .05 and power is set at .7. For the same set of conditions, only 66 subjects would be needed if pretest data were available to be used as a covariate in an ANCOVA model and the relationship between the measures was equal to .7. On the other hand, if the relationship between the pretest and dependent measure equaled .5, then 96 subjects would be needed. Researchers often consider the analysis of covariance model only in non-experimental research studies and use the procedure to attempt to adjust for initial group differences. Analysis of covariance is extremely useful in experimental research, however, to reduce error variance and thus reduce the number of subjects needed while maintaining statistical power.

The calculations of sample size reported in Tables 2 and 3 for analysis of covariance assume an experimental research study. In non-experimental research, larger sample sizes than those reported in these tables for ANCOVA would be needed. Without random assignment to treatment conditions, it is likely that the populations from which the samples were selected differ in terms of the pretest means. These initial differences increase the standard errors for contrast between adjusted posttest means and, therefore, reduce statistical power. To maintain acceptable statistical power, an increase in sample size is needed. The greater the initial differences between groups, the more subjects that are needed.

A third interesting relationship demonstrated in Tables 2 and 3 involves the effect on sample size when the level of statistical power is increased from .5 to .7. Statistical power equal to .5 means that the researcher had only a 50–50 chance of detecting a statistically significant effect. For many researchers, this probability is

unacceptably low. But by increasing statistical power to .7, the number of subjects needed increases substantially. If the significance level is set at .05, an average of 34% more subjects is needed. This result was relatively consistent across analysis procedures and effect size with a standard deviation of .04. Within each effect size, the average increase in sample size across analysis procedures was 36% ($SD = .016$), 34% ($SD = .04$), and 32% ($SD = .046$) for small, medium, and large effect sizes, respectively. When statistical significance is set at .10, an average of 39% more subjects is needed when power is increased from .5 to .7. Again, this estimate is relatively stable with a standard deviation of .06 across analysis strategies and effect sizes. For small, medium, and large effect sizes, the average increases in sample sizes across the statistical procedures were 41% ($SD = .014$), 38% ($SD = .026$), and 37% ($SD = .098$), respectively.

A similar analysis can be made when the acceptable level for the probability of a Type I error is increased from .05 to .10. When statistical power is set at .7, an average of 23.5% fewer subjects is needed across analysis procedures and effect size. This estimate is again relatively stable with a standard deviation of .02. Within each effect size, the average reduction in sample size across the analysis procedures was 23% ($SD = .009$), 23% ($SD = .012$), and 24% ($SD = .032$) for small, medium, and large effects, respectively. If statistical power set at .5 was acceptable, then the probability of a Type I error is increased from .05 to .10, an average of 28% fewer subjects is required. This result is consistent across effect sizes and analysis strategies with the standard deviation equal to .02. For small, medium, and large effects, the average reduction in sample size across statistical strategies was 28% ($SD = .01$), 28% ($SD = .017$), and 28% ($SD = .05$), respectively.

A final noteworthy relationship demonstrated in Tables 2 and 3 involves sample size requirements in factorial designs. The necessary sample size needed to adequately test the hypotheses for the two main effects and the interaction effect in a 3×4 factorial design are reported in these tables. Two points can be made regarding the results. First, the hypothesis tests for the main effects in a factorial design require only slightly more subjects than would be required if each factor were analyzed separately in single factors ANOVAs. Cohen (1977) pointed out that the increase in sample size is needed to compensate for the loss of degrees of freedom for the mean square error in the factorial design. These results assume that a reduction in the within-cell variability does not occur. This assumption is valid if both independent variables are manipulated by the researcher but it probably is not valid if one independent variable was a blocking variable (i.e., ability groups). Under the latter condition, a reduction in error variance might be expected and as a result fewer subjects would be needed to test the main effect. The reduction in sample size would depend on the relationship between the blocking variable and the dependent variable.

The second and more important result demonstrated in Tables 2 and 3 is the total number of subjects needed in a factorial design when the test of the interaction is of interest. Across effect sizes, significance levels, and power, the difference in sample size between the main effect with $k = 3$ and the interaction effect is an average of 33% more subjects. With $k = 4$, the difference in sample size required is an average of 19.8% more subjects. Both of these estimates are relatively stable with standard deviations equal to .065 and .038 for $k = 3$ and $k = 4$, respectively. The difference in sample size requirements presented here is applicable only to 3 × 4 factorial designs. Factorial designs of other dimensions would reflect different relationships. Only in 2 × 2 factorial designs are the sample size requirements the same for both main effects and the interaction term.

The results of the sample size requirements for interaction effects indicate that when an interactive effect is expected and is of interest, researchers need to plan to involve a large number of subjects in the study. An alternate strategy might be to test the interaction hypothesis at a higher level of significance. That is, researchers might accept an increase in the probability of a Type I error to compensate for an inadequate sample size. For example, in the 3 × 4 factorial design, a total sample size of 156 subjects is needed to test the interaction with $k = 4$ when the significance level is set at .05, power is equal to .7, and a medium effect size is judged to be meaningful. The same sample size would provide an adequate test of the interaction hypothesis for a medium effect size and power of .7 if the significance level of .10 is acceptable.

The results of the analysis of sample size requirements for the interaction effect has a futher implication for analyzing factorial designs. Occasionally, researchers will recommend that if an interactive effect is nonsignificant, then the sums of squares for that effect be pooled with the sums of squares error to produce a new error term referred to as a residual (Kirk, 1982). The advantage of pooling sources of variation is to increase degrees of freedom for the residual and, therefore, produce a more powerful analysis. However, the results of the present analysis indicates that the test for an interaction may lack sufficient statistical power unless the sample size is large. As a result, a Type II error may be made in the conclusion for the interaction hypothesis. Pooling the sums of squares after a Type II error would result in inappropriate tests of the main effects when the mean square residual is used as the denominator of the F ratio. Researchers should, therefore, be advised not to pool sum of squares for the interaction with the sum of squares error unless the sample size is sufficiently large to provide an adequate test of the interaction. However, if a sufficient sample size was available to adequately test the interaction hypothesis, then there probably would be no need for pooling sum of squares since adequate power would also be available to test the main effects without the pooling.

Conclusion

The above discussion has demonstrated that the answer to the question "How many subjects do I need?" is not a simple matter. Four factors influence the determination of the number of subjects needed in a research study to adequately test hypotheses of interest: significance level, statistical power, analysis strategy, and effect size. The complexity of the problem is, to some extent, a function of the subjectivity involved in selecting specific levels of each of these four factors. General guidelines have been suggested regarding significance level, statistical power, and, to some extent, the appropriate analysis procedure. Unlike the other considerations, however, a widely accepted definition of an effect size does not seem to exist. In addition, many researchers seem to hesitate in suggesting a meaningful effect size. The hesitation is the result of a lack of familiarity with assessment tools as well as the feeling that any definition might be difficult to defend. As a result, providing an answer to the sample size question cannot be provided in many situations. Researchers need to be more aware of the role effect size plays in the planning of a research study. Furthermore, investigators should be encouraged to report in the results section of journal articles the magnitude of the observed effect to assist future researchers in solving the sample size problem.

Examining the interrelationship between significance level, statistical power, analysis strategy, and effect size has provided some indication of the sample size requirements for a variety of situations. These calculations have demonstrated the insensitivity of the independent samples t test and analysis of variance to detect effect sizes commonly observed in social science research. The importance of considering research designs that use both pretreatment and posttreatment data such as a randomized block design or the randomized pretest-posttest design, has been discussed. The reduced sample size requirements for these designs should provide a convincing argument supporting their use. The results also indicate that it is perhaps time to reevaluate the criteria chosen for statistical significance. While it is desirable to minimize the probability of a Type I error, it is also important to have a reasonable probability of identifying a meaningful effect. Since effect sizes in the social sciences tend to be small and sample sizes often cannot be increased greatly, a reasonable alternative for maintaining statistical power is to accept an increased chance of a Type I error. Over replications of the study, true effects would be separated from Type I errors.

Finally, the results of the calculations determining minimal sample size provides some indication of the importance of selecting instruments sensitive to the effects of the independent variables being studied. A possible explanation for the small effects found in meta-analytic studies is that these investigations have used assessment tools which were not sensitive to factors under investigation. It is necessary, therefore, for researchers to become totally familiar with their instruments and to make accurate judgments on whether the tests measure the intended outcomes. To achieve larger effects, it may be necessary for researchers to rely more on locally developed assessment tools than standardized instruments.

REFERENCES

Brewer, J. K. (1972). On the power of statistical tests in the *American Educational Research Journal. American Educational Research Journal, 9*, 381–401.
Chase, L. J., & Baran, S. J. (1976). An assessment of quantitative research in mass communication. *Journalism Quarterly, 53*, 308–311.
Cohen, J. (1977). *Statistical power analysis for the behavioral sciences.* New York: Academic Press.
Cohen, P. A., Kulik, J. A., & Kulik, C. (1982). Educational outcomes of tutoring: A meta-analysis of findings. *American Educational Research Journal, 19*, 237–248.
Draper, N., & Smith, H. (1966). *Applied regression analysis.* New York: Wiley.
Dusek, J. B., & Joseph, G. (1983). The bases of teacher expectancies: A meta-analysis. *Journal of Educational Psychology, 75*, 327–346.
Feldt, L. S. (1973). What size samples for methods/materials experiments? *Journal of Educational Measurement, 10*, 221–226.
Glass, G. V. (1978). Integrating findings: The meta-analysis of research. In L. S. Shulman (Ed.), *Review of research in education* (Vol. 5). Itasca, IL: Peacock.
Glass, G. V., & Stanley, J. C. (1970). *Statistical methods in education and psychology.* Englewood Cliffs, NJ: Prentice-Hall.
Katzer, J., & Sodt, J. (1973). An analysis of the use of statistical testing in communication research. *Journal of Communication,* 251–265.
Kerlinger, F. N., & Pedhazur, E. J. (1973). *Multiple regression in behavioral research.* New York: Holt, Rinehart & Winston.

Kirk, R. E. (1982). *Experimental design: Procedures for the behavioral sciences,* (2nd ed.). Belmont, CA: Brooks/Cole.
Kleinbaum, D. G., & Kupper, L. L. (1978). *Applied regression analysis and other multivariate methods.* North Scituate, MA: Duxbury Press.
Kroll, R. M., & Chase, L. J. (1975). Communication disorders: A power analytic assessment of recent research. *Journal of Communication Disorders, 8*, 237–247.
Kulik, C., & Kulik, J. A. (1982). Effects of ability grouping on secondary school students: A meta-analysis of evaluation findings. *American Educational Research Journal, 19*, 415–428
Kulik, J. A., Bangert, R. L., & William, G. W. (1983). Effects of computer-based teaching on secondary school students. *Journal of Educational Psychology, 75*, 19–26.
Kulik, J. A., Cohen, P. A., & Cohen, P. A. (1980). Effectiveness of programmed instruction in higher education: A meta-analysis of findings. *Educational Evaluation and Policy Analysis, 2*, 51–64.
Kulik, J. A., Kulik, C. C., & Cohen, P. A. (1980). Effectiveness of computer-based college teaching: A meta-analysis of findings. *Review of Educational Research, 50*, 525–544.
Levin, J. R. (1975). Determining sample size for planned and post hoc analysis of variance comparisons. *Journal of Educational Measurement, 12*, 99–107.
Lindquist, E. F., & Hieronymus, A. L. N. (1964). *Iowa Test of Basic Skills.* Boston: Houghton Mifflin.
Luiten, J., Ames, W., & Ackerson, G. (1980). A meta-analysis of the effects of advance organizers on learning and retention. *American Educational Research Journal, 17*, 211–218.
Mantzana, T., & Fry, B. (1983). *Meta-analysis: A working bibliography of research integration.* Occasional paper of the University of Florida Bilingual Education Service Center, 343 Norman Hall, Gainesville, Florida.
Myers, J. L. (1979). *Fundamentals of experimental design* (3rd ed.). Boston: Allyn & Bacon.
Pedhazur, E. J. (1982). *Multiple regression in behavioral research* (2nd ed.). New York: Holt, Rinehart & Winston.
Redfield, D. L., & Rousseau, E. W. (1981). A meta-analysis of experimental research on teacher questioning behavior. *Review of Educational Research, 51*, 237–246.
Rosenthal, R., & Rubin, D. (1982). Further meta-analytic procedures for assessing cognitive gender differences. *Journal of Educational Psychology, 74*, 708–712.
Smith, M. L., & Glass, G. V. (1980). Meta-analysis of research on class size and its relationship to attitudes and instruction. *American Educational Research Journal, 17*, 419–434.
Uguroglu, M. E., & Walberg, H. (1979). Motivation and achievement: A quantitative synthesis. *American Educational Research Journal, 16*, 375–390.

SECTION 5
Research Synthesis

A core component of program research is a collection of activities referred to as *research synthesis*. Here, the primary function is to ascertain if, how, how well, for whom, and under what conditions interventions work from the cumulative results of previously completed studies. These issues can be addressed before a new intervention is planned and, in a retrospective fashion, once a series of investigations have been completed. Indeed, a systematic review of prior research is a natural starting point for framing questions to be addressed by future studies. Not only does it facilitate identification of successful practices and generates testable hypotheses about potentially useful treatments, gaps in substantive and methodological knowledge become evident.

Research syntheses can take a variety of forms. They can range from conventional literature reviews to highly technical, quantitative manipulation of original data from several primary studies followed by statistical aggregation of results across these independent investigations. The chapters in this section emphasize the quantitative side of research synthesis, but they do not advocate ignoring the rich contextual information that can be gleaned from the written accounts. In fact, one chapter is devoted to synthesizing the evidence from diverse case studies.

In the first chapter of this section, Light identifies six issues that research synthesis is potentially better able to address than single studies. That is, when studies differ in context, clients, treatment arrangements, strength, or fidelity of the treatment, and so forth, Light argues that a broader understanding of program effects can often be achieved. For example, research synthesis can uncover client by treatment interactions (e.g., program A works for client-type X but not for client-type Y and the reverse is true for program B) and features of treatments (e.g., counseling) that make a difference and those that do not (e.g., awareness training). For policy purposes, this may be exactly the type of evidence that can influence where to target limited resources effectively.

Shapiro (1985) provides a particularly useful summary of how research synthesis (in this case meta-analysis) can be used to examine the relative effectiveness of different treatment modalities, heterogeneous intervention strategies, and types of disorders in the psychotherapy context. The selection by Light and the illustrations provided by Shapiro (1985) exemplify how research synthesis fits into the program research perspective we would like to see emphasized in the future.

To date, the majority of research synthesis has been fashioned after the work of Glass and his associates within a "meta-analysis" framework. All independent assessments are collected, results are converted into a common metric (e.g., Cohen's d statistic), attributes of the study are coded in an effort to account for differences among studies, and these separate assessments are then aggregated to form a composite summary of all the evidence on a particular program or topical area. In practice, the nature of the questions to be addressed by the research synthesis limit the synthesis to comparative studies. Such a limitation is, of course, not necessary.

In the second chapter of this section, Berger details how the meta-analytic perspective can be applied to noncomparative, heterogeneous case studies. As Berger notes, in shifting from comparative studies to case studies, several adjustments in procedures and conceptualizations are necessary. For example, the unit of analysis for case studies is the "case," whereas the unit for the conventional analysis is the between-group analysis. The diversity of methods used within case studies also poses new challenges. In a technical report not reprinted here, Finsterbusch (1984) provides an illustration of this method. In this instance, he shows how some of the influence of macrocontextual and microcontextual factors (see section 1 of this Part of the volume) can be synthesized for effectiveness-oriented studies that do not have a methodologically sophisticated comparative design.

The interesting aspect of both of these selections is that they pave the way for improved linkages between the practical program evaluations described in Part II of this volume and the program research perspective espoused here. That is, the collection of individual assessments that do not attempt to come to generalizable conclusions about relationships or constructs can serve as the "data" for a research synthesis that does focus on more abstract levels of inference about why programs or interventions work or fail to work.

Research synthesis is also appealing from a methodological perspective. Specifically, when research synthesis is focused on the methodological character-istics of the studies, it can assist planning decisions, thereby reducing the likelihood of repeating previous errors and increasing the overall sensitivity of the design. For example, Andrews (1984) reanalyzed six different surveys to estimate the influence of specific survey design characteristics. Subsequent researchers can use this synthesis as a basis for selecting the least error-prone design configurations. Similarly, Cordray and Sonnefeld (1985) demonstrate how the results of meta-analysis can be used to obtain probabilistic ranges of several parameters needed in designing impact evaluations.

As with each of the other methods described in this volume, there are practical constraints that detract from the overall technical adequacy and ultimate utility of many syntheses. Since its introduction, debates on these issues have been vigorous, leading to refinements in theory and practice. It is now generally accepted as a useful form of inquiry. The two remaining chapters in this section highlight progress, promise, and needed corrective actions within research synthesis.

One of the most fundamental aspects of research synthesis is the theory underlying the statistical aggregation of results. The third chapter by Hedges, summarizes several key advances in statistical methods for meta-analysis. These include better specification of the following: (1) the statistical properties of the effect sizes—the basic "data" for the synthesis; (2) methods for assessing the influence of treatment by study interactions; and (3) general analytic procedures for combining studies. The latter is essential to Light's point of view.

The final contribution in this section examines the procedural aspects of research synthesis. The chapter by Bullock and Svyantek begins as an attempt to replicate a meta-analysis study. From their experience, they educe a list of general evaluative criteria that could be used to gauge the adequacy of current and future syntheses. This chapter represents one of a number of assessments of the practical strengths, limitations, and needed improvements in research synthesis. Others (e.g., Orwin & Cordray, 1985; Shapiro, 1985; Slavin, 1984 and Strube, Gardner, & Hartmann, 1985) address subsets of these issues in somewhat more detail.

Strube et al. (1985), for example, examine three problematic features of the synthesis process: reporting deficiencies (e.g., finding studies, unavailability of information within studies); statistical difficulties (e.g., independence, models for effect size analysis); and unresolved conceptual concerns. Solving, or at least reducing the influence of, these problems is likely to require changes in practices at all levels of research and evaluation. The meta-analyst can provide critical feedback to primary researchers on stereotypical difficulties they encounter while trying to synthesize a primary study. Our emphasis on documentation (section 2 and 5, Part II) has been guided by a need to routinize clear, complete, and accurate reporting of evidence in primary studies. The meta-analyst is also in a good position to provide helpful feedback to editors on the type of information that is desirable but conspicuously absent in published papers. To date, these types of feedback have not been formalized except in isolated cases (e.g., Mosteller, Gilbert, & McPeek, 1980).

The prospects for research synthesis in coming years seem very promising. Recent federal legislation has decentralized the evaluation process (e.g., the conversion of 77 federal categorical grants into 9 block grants to states). As such, research and evaluation synthesis will undoubtedly play a greater role in efforts to understand if, how, for whom, and under what conditions organized interventions work. The credibility of the answers that are generated depend heavily on following sound synthesis practices, accessibility of primary studies, and adequate reporting of evidence at all levels of analysis.

REFERENCES

Andrews, F. M. (1984). Construct validity and error components of survey measures: A structural modeling approach. *Public Opinion Quarterly, 48,* 409-442.

Cordray, D. S., & Sonnefeld, L. J. (1985). Quantitative synthesis: An actuarial base for planning evaluations. In D. S. Cordray (Ed.). *New directions for program evaluation, No. 27* (pp. 29-48) San Francisco, CA: Jossey-Bass.

Finsterbusch, K. (1984) *Statistical summary of 52 AID projects: Lessons on project effectiveness.* Unpublished report, Sociology Department, University of Maryland.

Orwin, R. G., & Cordray, D. S. (1985). Effects of deficient reporting on meta-analysis: A conceptual framework and reanalysis. *Psychological Bulletin, 97*(1), 134-147.

Mosteller, F., Gilbert, J. P., & McPeek, B. (1980). Reporting standards and research strategies for controlled trials: Agenda for the editor. *Controlled Clinical Trials, 1,* 37-58.

Shapiro, D. A. (1985). Recent applications of meta-analysis in clinical research. *Clinical Psychology Review, 5*(1), 13-34.

Slavin, R. E. (1984). Meta-analysis in education: How has it been used? *Educational Research, 13*(8), 6-15.

Strube, M. J., Gardner, W., & Hartmann, D. P. (1985). Limitations, liabilities, and objectives in review of the literature: The current status of meta-analysis. *Clinical Psychology Review, 5*(1), 63-78.

38

Six Evaluation Issues That Synthesis
Can Resolve Better Than Single Studies

Richard J. Light

*Syntheses of research studies identify important interactions
that any one study rarely finds.*

What can a synthesis of evaluation studies do that a single study cannot? In
this chapter, I will discuss six issues that synthesis helps us to resolve. The
most frequently cited virtue of synthesis is that the increased sample size can
increase statistical power. This virtue has been discussed widely (Glass, 1977;
Glass and others, 1981; Hunter and others, 1982; Light and Smith, 1971).
The six properties of synthesis that I want to emphasize here have little to do
with sample size. What they have in common is that they help us to say *when* a
social, medical, or educational program works, not just whether or not it
works on the average.

One way we can identify when a program works is by focusing on interaction. What do I mean by *interaction?* Statisticians often use this word to indicate nonlinearity. That is how I interpret the word here. In a program evaluation context, we can ask two questions: First, does the program work well for
certain kinds of people and less well for others? Second, does the program work
well in certain settings and less well in others? Both these questions are about
interactions. A single study can find certain kinds of interactions, but synthesis
of several studies can turn up much richer, more useful information.

From Richard J. Light, "Six Evaluation Issues That Synthesis Can Resolve Better Than Single
Studies," pp. 57-73 in W. H. Yeaton, P. M. Wortman (Eds.), *Issues in Data Synthesis.* New
Directions for Program Evaluation, No. 24. Copyright 1984, Jossey-Bass. Reprinted by permission.

Why Are Interaction Effects Important?

Usually, social, educational, and health programs are evaluated to see how well they work. Good evaluations also examine how changes in program format could incrementally help to improve them. One way of asking whether a program works is to ask whether it works *on the average.* Another way is to ask whether it works for a subgroup of people or in special settings.

For policy purposes, the interaction question can be as important as the main effects question. For example, when a physician considers what anesthesia to give a patient prior to surgery and has a choice between two drugs, it is useful to learn which of the two is better on the average. However, it is even more valuable to learn which of the two is preferable for the precise surgery the patient will have. Or which of the two has a better track record for the particular kind of patient, such as a young male in excellent health. It would not be surprising to find, for example, that the anesthesia best suited for a twenty-year-old in excellent general health is different from the anesthesia best suited for a seventy-year-old in poor health.

Finding such interactions is important not only when making decisions for individuals but also when assessing the effectiveness of large-scale programs. Suppose that Head Start works generally well for children under four but far less well for children five years or older. That would be worth knowing. If resources for the program were limited, such knowledge could tell us where to concentrate them. Or, if substantial resources were available, this interaction finding would suggest that the Head Start curriculum should be modified for older children. So, whether the main purpose of an evaluation is to target resources or to change a program incrementally, finding an interaction can guide decisions.

Why Is Synthesis So Useful in Identifying Interactions?

Let us recall how a single research study can identify an interaction effect. Basically, there are two ways. One way is to build a search for the interaction directly into the study design. For example, let us hypothesize that job training program A works better for high school dropouts than it does for high school graduates and that the reverse is true for training program B. Then, if we have control over treatment assignments, we can test this hypothesis by making sure that all four combinations of people and program type are represented. Ideally, randomization will be used to develop the four groups— dropouts given A, dropouts given B, graduates given A, and graduates given B. Then, comparisons of the four effect sizes will give a clear indication of what program type works best, on the average, for what type of person. These findings will either refute or strengthen the initial hypothesis.

The other way of identifying interaction effects in a single study involves the use of post hoc procedures. Suppose that a search for interaction has not been formally designed into a study. In that case, such procedures as regression analysis and other applications of the general linear model can be applied retrospectively. The dilemmas and caveats involved in this process are well known (Anderson and others, 1980). If people were free to choose their own treatment, there may be self-selection. There may be confounding of background variables. For example, most of the high school dropouts may come from poor families in cities, while most of the graduates may come from middle-income families in rural areas. Suppose that a single study of this type did not assign people to training programs at random. Then, because the study was not designed to examine interaction, its findings could well be confounded by graduation status, setting, and family type.

Against this background, we can now address the central theme of this chapter—that research synthesis can be far more effective in identifying interactions than any single study. (For a discussion of the statistical procedure for detecting interactions, see Chapter Two in this volume.) Any one study is conducted in a particular context, under a particular set of constraints. Unless the study is extraordinarily large in scope, it has a limited group of participants who are assigned to treatments in a certain way. Each of these facts is good for a single study. It is important to know exactly what population is in and what population is out. It is important to know how people chose, or were assigned to, a treatment.

The advantage of looking at a group of evaluation studies is that the individual studies often take place in different contexts. And, we can learn much about interactions from noticing how findings relate to context. To illustrate this idea concretely, we can now address the six evaluation issues that synthesis can resolve better than any single study.

Synthesis Can Help to Match Treatment Type with Recipient Type

The Head Start program was created in the early 1960s in response to a growing belief that something had to be done to help poor children start school on a stronger footing. In 1964, Sargent Shriver, director of the Office of Economic Opportunity (OEO), formed a committee chaired by the pediatrician Robert Cooke. Its charge was to develop a program for reducing the effects of poverty on children. These efforts led to the creation of Head Start, which had seven concrete goals, including improving the child's mental processes and skills, with particular attention to conceptual and verbal skills.

The program was formally authorized to begin in summer 1965. Between 50,000 and 100,000 children were expected to participate in the first summer program. In fact, 560,000 did. By 1967, Head Start funding had grown to $349 million. OEO decided to evaluate its performance and contracted in 1968 with Westinghouse Learning Corporation and Ohio State University to conduct a formal evaluation. The findings were released in 1969, and they stunned the education community.

The key sentence in the Westinghouse final report (Cicirelli, 1969, p. 43) says: "Although this study indicates that full-year Head Start appears to be a more effective compensatory program than summer Head Start, its benefits cannot be described as satisfactory." According to Datta (1976, p. 134), "children who participated in Head Start summer programs did not score higher at the beginning of first, second, and third grades in such programs on all measures of academic achievement, linguistic development, and personal/social development than children who had not participated. Children who had attended the full-year programs and were tested in the first grade achieved higher scores on the Metropolitan Reading Test and some subtests of the Illinois Test of Psycholinguistic Abilities. Scores of children who had attended full-year programs and were tested in the second and third grade were not different from the scores of comparison children."

The disappointing findings of this evaluation generated great controversy. Smith and Bissell (1970), Campbell and Erlebacher (1970), and others criticized the methodology severely. Supporters of preschool education found many problems with the study's design and implementation. Yet, despite the criticism, the study had a large impact on policy. Supporters of Head Start were placed on the defensive. For example, both Alice Rivlin and Christopher Jencks, who supported such remedial programs as Head Start in the late 1960s, became more cautious after the Westinghouse-Ohio study. Rivlin (1971, p. 32) notes that "Jencks and his associates dismiss the whole preschool child development movement in a few skeptical paragraphs, citing the Westinghouse-Ohio study's findings that, on the average, Head Start children showed no long-term cognitive gains over non–Head Start children" (Datta, 1983).

How should we interpret the findings of this single, large study, which had such a large impact? A synthesis of early education programs conducted by Bissell (1970) throws much light on Head Start and related preschool programs. Her review emphasizes a search for interactions. Bissell reanalyzes data collected by three researchers: Karnes in Urbana, Illinois; DiLorenzo in New York state; and Weikart in Ypsilanti, Michigan. She chooses these three data sets because each author compared two or more specific curricula, each project had well-formulated goals, and each project was conducted and documented carefully.

Taken together, these three data sets compare five types of curriculum, each of which has supporters in the preschool community: the Karnes Ameliorative curriculum, a highly structured cognitive curriculum; the Bereiter-Engelmann curriculum, a highly structured informational program; a traditional enrichment program emphasizing language development, with a relatively permissive low-structure environment; a traditional enrichment program emphasizing psychosocial development, with a relatively permissive low-structure environment; and a Montessori program with a structured environment.

Bissell finds small main effects. For example, programs with strong quality control, well-trained staff, a high degree of staff supervision, and a low pupil-to-teacher ratio produce bigger cognitive gains than other programs. Her big finding involves interaction. To quote her (Bissell, 1970, p. 62): "Directive, highly structured preschool programs tend to be more effective with the *more* disadvantaged of poor children. . . . In contrast, nondirective, less-structured programs tend to be more effective with the *less* disadvantaged of poor children."

Bissell's data make her point sharply. The reanalyses of scores on three standardized tests—the Binet, the Peabody Picture Vocabulary Test, and the Illinois Test of Psycholinguistic Abilities—show that when a child is well matched with the optimal program (for example, exceptionally down-and-out children and highly structured programs), the average difference between experimental and control groups is between two thirds and three quarters of a standard deviation. If the match is poor (as when down-and-out children from poor backgrounds are exposed to a relatively open curriculum), the comparative gains are minimal. A few of the comparisons even find a marginally negative program effect.

A synthesis such as Bissell's has at least three virtues. First, since the individual evaluations examined projects organized to serve different children in different places with different programs, we get a broad panorama of findings. Second, since the data collected by several independent investigators display similar interaction patterns—that highly structured programs are better for the poorest children—the credibility of this overall finding is enhanced. Third, the synthesis of several evaluations puts the results of the single, big Westinghouse study in a new light. Most of the early Head Start sites, such as those examined by Westinghouse, had clearly open and permissive styles. They offered relatively little formal cognitive work. To quote Bissell (1970, p. 81), "directors favor supportive, unstructured, socialization programs rather than structured informational programs for poor children." Knowing this about the early Head Start centers that Westinghouse and Ohio State University examined and combining this fact with Bissell's review findings, we can see why the study found little success. There is also reason for optimism that student performance should improve as more structure is introduced at local Head Start sites.

Synthesis Can Explain Which Features of a Treatment Matter

In 1968, Rosenthal and Jacobson wrote: "As teaching training institutions begin to teach the possibility that teachers' expectations of their pupils' performance may serve as self-fulfilling prophecies, there may be new expectancy created. The new expectancy may be that children can learn more than had been believed possible, an expectation held by many educational theorists, though for quite different reasons" (p. 141).

Three years later, Baker and Crist (1971, p. 56) asserted the opposite:

"Teacher expectancy probably does not affect pupil IQ. This conclusion is supported by a background of decades of research suggesting the stability of human intelligence and its resistance to alterations by environmental manipulation, by the reanalysis of the Rosenthal and Jacobson (1968) study . . . , and by the failure of all replication studies to demonstrate effects on IQ."

So, here we find arguments from distinguished scholars that disagree sharply. The expectancy hypothesis is central to classroom conduct in education, because it has both substantive and ideological components. Suppose that teachers' expectations for a particular student's performance actually play a role in determining the student's performance. Some people see schools as perpetuating or even exacerbating inequality among children's life achievement. For these people, the expectancy argument offers a strong explanation for why poor children do less well in school than other children. Educators have vigorously debated the importance of teachers' expectations. Ryan (1971) and Kohl (1971) both argue that teachers expect less from poor children and therefore receive less. Elashoff and Snow (1971) argue the reverse — that methodological flaws in the study by Rosenthal and Jacobson (1968) undercut their findings.

To assess the importance of teacher expectancy on student IQs, Raudenbush (forthcoming) synthesized eighteen such experimental studies. Seventeen of these studies had a strong research design, in which children were assigned at random to treatments. While the eighteen studies include children of different ages and income groups, they all used IQ as an outcome measure. Raudenbush uses several different methods for combining studies in a quantitative meta-analysis (Fisher, 1973; Edgington, 1972; Winer, 1971; Mosteller and Bush, 1954). He emphasizes the effort to explain variation among outcomes (Pillemer and Light, 1980). His conclusion is not at all obvious for someone simply looking at the findings of eighteen studies: "The effect sizes of the studies, in standard deviation units, range from .55 down to − .13. Five of the eighteen achieved statistical significance, three at the .05 level and two at the .01 level. For the thirteen other studies, in five the experimental children scored higher than the controls, while in the other eight the control children scored higher" (Raudenbush, forthcoming).

Raudenbush's findings are clear and important. He finds a small average effect size across the eighteen studies of .11. But, as he reports, this main effect summary "certainly conceals more than it clarifies." That is because the studies can be divided into two broad groups. In one group, teachers were given information about each student (the "treatment") *after* a few weeks of initial contact. In the other group, teachers got information *before* they met students.

This difference between the two subgroups proved to be the key finding. Teachers who obtain information before they meet students show a strong expectancy effect. Teachers who obtain information after knowing students for several weeks show essentially no expectancy effect. To quantify this difference, the correlation between timing of the treatment induction and outcomes is $r = .68$. Raudenbush summarizes: "When no teacher-student contact preceded the experiment, the average probability level was .06. After the second week of teacher-student contact, only one reported a probability of less than .50."

So, this synthesis sheds light on a controversy that has raged for fifteen years. All these years, the debate focused on main effects: Does expectancy have a big effect or not? There seems to be a main effect, but it is very small. The synthesis tells us that the important treatment component lies in when the induction is given. It would be impossible to learn this from any one of the eighteen studies alone. In fact, one major finding of this synthesis is the consistency of treatment effect in studies where there was no prior teacher-student contact. Similarly, outcomes of studies where expectancy induction took place two weeks or more into the school year show very little variance. Raudenbush found that the big news in these studies is that when the treatment is implemented matters a lot. Knowing this enables us to understand how teacher expectancy works.

Synthesis Can Explain Conflicting Results

In the late 1970s, discussions of job training emphasized the importance of "integrated services." Evaluations of the Comprehensive Employment and Training Act, the broad umbrella jobs program budgeted at several billion dollars a year, were finding marginal success at best. Some of these evaluations (National Academy of Sciences, 1978, 1979) suggested that job training alone, when narrowly defined, could not break a family's cycle of poverty and unemployment. These assessments found that integrated services, which included matching a family's needs for education, health services, and job training with a well-coordinated group of "helpers," offered far more promise than a stand-alone jobs program.

To assess this idea, the U.S. Department of Labor initiated several studies of integrated services programs. The key idea was to coordinate a series of services for poor families in which job training was an important component but not the only component. Several demonstration programs took place at several different sites. Yet, the results were conflicting. While these conflicting findings about the value of integrated services were discouraging, the investigators ultimately capitalized on the varying outcomes to learn a great deal about the contexts in which integrated services worked well and worked badly and about how to organize a good matching plan between services and recipients.

The broad question, then, is, How can a synthesis harness different findings from several studies to enhance our understanding about a program's effectiveness? It is not rare in an effort to pull together information about a program's effects across studies to find that the studies provide severely conflicting information. These conflicts can be frustrating. Yet, it is precisely such conflicts that may give evaluators some insights into the matching problem. The job training example shows this. Let us look at some data, rounded off for illustrative purposes. Weeks of employment are the outcome measure.

Take the case of two studies conducted in different states by different investigators. Each compares an integrated service program with a single-service job training program. The study in one state looks at eighty men. Forty receive one program and forty receive the other. This study finds that the integrated services group has an average of eighty weeks of employment, while the single-service group has seventy weeks. Integrated services seem to be more effective. Yet, the study in the other state finds precisely the opposite. It also examines eighty men. Again, forty receive one program, and forty receive the other. Yet, this second study finds that the integrated services men work only sixty weeks, while the single-service men in the comparison group work an average of seventy weeks.

The results conflict. This is not unusual for evaluation studies, but it is frustrating. What can be done? An effort can be made to see if we can discover from this conflict something about matching people's needs to the services that are offered in an integrated plan. Here is how synthesis could explain the conflict: Categorize the eighty men in each study by their "problem" constellation. Such categorization can be difficult when the people or families served have multiple problems, but let us simplify here and assume that there are two broad types of problem sets, problem set A and problem set B. First, look at the *allocation* of people with each type of problem to each program in the two studies, then separate that allocation from the average *effect* found for those people in each program. Table 1 displays some results. The numbers in the cells are the effects — the average number of weeks employed for the men in each cell. The numbers between parentheses are the allocations — the number of men in that cell.

We can learn surprisingly much from this simple table. We see that although the grand means of the two studies caused the results to conflict, the two studies had identical effects for the groups of men receiving each treatment. Both studies found that men with problem set A who received integrated services were employed an average of ninety weeks, while men with problem

Table 1. Comparing Studies with Conflicting Outcomes

	Problem Set A	Problem Set B	Overall Means
Study One			
Integrated Services	90 (30)	50 (10)	80 (40)
Single Service	50 (20)	90 (20)	70 (40)
Study Two			
Integrated Services	90 (10)	50 (30)	60 (40)
Single Service	50 (20)	90 (20)	70 (40)

Source: Light, 1979.

set A who received the single service worked an average of only fifty weeks. And, both studies found that the reverse was true for men with problem set B. Why, then, was there a conflict? The conflict was caused by different allocations of problem types across the two service types in the two studies. In the first study, more A men than B men received integrated services. In the second study, the reverse was true. This difference in allocations, combined with the consistent finding of both studies that integrated services were more effective for men with problem set A and less effective for men with problem set B, created the conflict.

What policy implications can be drawn from this synthesis? If these data are in fact a good description of reality, we learn how integrated services should be targeted to a subgroup of people whose needs best match those services. And, the inkling that this might be the case emerged from an observation that two studies comparing integrated with single services reached opposite findings. It would not have emerged from either of the studies alone. We learn here that by examining program effects and allocations of people across studies, we can improve the matching process and target integrated services to those who will benefit the most.

Synthesis Can Determine Whether Relative or Absolute Performance Is the Critical Outcome

Most programs can be looked at in two different ways. One way is to see whether an intervention has taken hold as intended. For example, does the child really know how to count better? Does the drug for hypertension actually lower the patient's blood pressure? Is the prisoner who is about to be released actually a competent carpenter? The other way of assessing a program is to see what happens in the end. Does the child who now counts better get higher marks in school? Do the patients who now have lower blood pressure also have a lower incidence of heart attacks? Does the newly released carpenter earn a reasonable income with his new skills?

A synthesis of evaluation findings that is well done usually looks at the studies that it examines in both ways. But, it is worth noticing that synthesis has a special comparative advantage over any single study in answering the second question. This is because, while some programs can confer benefits or inculcate skills that indeed take hold, it is not always the case that these skills or benefits can be translated into concrete positive outcomes in the end. In particular, some benefits are valuable only in a comparative sense, because of the limited number of opportunities in which certain skills are useful. If too many others have the same skills, they become less valuable to any particular person who has them.

Job training can illustrate both points — the point about the comparative benefits and the point about the special value of synthesis. Suppose that a job skills program undertaken in one city is evaluated. The research design is excellent. One hundred applicants are divided at random into two groups. One group receives training to become carpenters, while the other group does not. If this evaluation finds that two years after the job program the trainees clearly earn more than the control group, what can we conclude? We would probably conclude that the job training works—and well we should, since the one available study has positive findings, and they come from a randomized experimental design allowing causal inferences.

Let us assume that this positive finding is noticed and that the same program is offered at ten other sites around the country. Learning from the excellent example set in the initial evaluation, each of the ten new sites organizes its own randomized trial. The results become available two years later, and they are difficult to interpret: At three sites, the training is a clear success; the trainees have good jobs. At two sites, it is at best marginal; only some trainees have jobs. At the other five sites, it didn't work at all.

Efforts to organize these ten findings into an evaluation synthesis can move forward in two quite different ways. One way is to emphasize the skills question—did the trainees at all ten sites become reasonably good carpenters? The other way is to emphasize the outcome question—why did the findings differ so much across the ten sites? By tackling both questions, synthesis can generate valuable insights. For example, a finding that sites varied enormously in their trainees' knowledge of carpentry provides management information. Clearly, the substantive training component needs to be improved across sites, and it needs to be strengthened in certain weak places. However, a finding that trainees learned carpentry quite well at all ten sites would be even more informative, because it would force us to ask why trainees differed so substantially across the ten sites in their ability to get jobs.

One possible explanation is that the benefit of the carpentry training for any one recipient depends on the number of other people who receive the training. Synthesis could support this explanation by examining the correlation across sites between the fraction of trainees who got jobs and the opportunity for success as measured by, say, the total population at each site. If the correlation is clearly positive, we learn three things. First, we learn that training works in a predictable way. Trainees in bigger cities have better prospects than trainees in smaller towns. Second, we learn two important things about the training itself—that it indeed confers skills on participants and that when relative performance is not a constraint on any one trainee—that is, when the trainee lives in a big city—the program succeeds. Third, we learn how to organize and manage such training programs better in the future: They are best targeted to settings in which there are opportunities for trainees to put their training to use.

To summarize, synthesis can identify programs whose value depends not only on their substantive features but also on the number of people who participate. That is, synthesis can point out when programs are constrained by limited opportunities for success. A single study cannot answer these questions.

Synthesis Can Assess the Stability of Treatment Effectiveness

Usually, any single study is organized by a single investigator or a small group of investigators, and it takes place in one or a very few sites. A single study at a single site allows us to assess whether a treatment worked. A single study at several sites allows us to assess whether the treatment worked overall. We can even examine the variance among outcomes at the several sites. But we cannot tell how robust the treatment is when it is provided by several different investigators or organizations. Only a synthesis of results across several studies allows us to answer this question. When each of several organizations implements the same program in different places, the variation in outcomes offers a good signal of the program's robustness. If it works extraordinarily well in a few places and poorly in others, we must try to explain why. But, whatever the explanation, we will have discovered that the program is not robust. We learn that it is sometimes effective but that its strength is easy to undercut. At some sites, the poor performance may be explained by weak implementation or by a poor match between recipients and program. The only way to assess the stability of a program in different settings is to see how it functions in different settings.

Special Supplemental Program for Women, Infants, and Children, known as the WIC program, illustrates these points. The U.S. Senate Committee on Agriculture, Nutrition, and Forestry asked the U.S. General Accounting Office (GAO) to synthesize all available evidence about WIC (U.S. GAO, 1984; Chapter Five in this volume provides detailed information about synthesis at the GAO). This program, funded at over $1.1 billion a year, provides nutrition supplements to approximately three million people each year. These people are pregnant women from low-income families and children from birth to age five in low-income families who are considered at high nutritional risk. The Senate Committee's request to the GAO was motivated by the sharply conflicting testimony that it received about WIC's effectiveness. Some witnesses argued that it was a highly effective program and that it had clear positive effects in increasing children's birthweight, reducing fetal and neonatal mortality, improving nutrition in mothers and children, and reducing mental retardation in children. Other witnesses argued that there was no concrete evidence for these positive assertions. They testified that while it seemed hardhearted to oppose the distribution of food vouchers to low-income mothers, the facts did not support assertions that women or their children benefited in any concrete way.

To resolve these conflicting claims, the GAO identified sixty-one evaluations of the WIC program. Using both internal staff and outside advisers, the agency asked several readers to examine each study independently and rate it for methodological quality. The findings about WIC's effect on birthweights illustrate how such a synthesis can provide useful information about the robustness of a given program. Only six of the sixty-one studies of WIC's overall effectiveness were rated by GAO and its advisers as reasonably high in quality. These six were then carefully examined for specific data about birthweights. Table 2 presents these data.

It seems clear from Table 2 that both sides in the debate about WIC's effectiveness are overstating their case. Those who argue that WIC has major positive effects on birthweight are not supported by the empirical evidence. Among the six studies, the single most positive finding is a 3.9 percent increase in average birthweight. Yet, the case of those who argue that there is no concrete evidence for WIC's effectiveness is also weakened by this synthesis, because five of the six studies showed gains in birthweight, although the gains were small. The one study that showed a small loss in birthweight is based on a tiny sample—thirty-seven WIC participants and forty-two comparison children—while in the five other studies samples numbered in the several hundreds or several thousands. Moreover, the outlier is not statistically significant.

This GAO summary is instructive, because it tells us a lot about the impact that WIC is having on birthweights among participants. First, it is clear that the impact is never very great—a gain of perhaps 2 percent. Second, the small gain seems reasonably consistent, as the GAO (1984, p. 15) concluded: "On the average, there appears to be a positive benefit from WIC participation; a reasonable estimate is that the average birthweight of WIC infants is higher by somewhere between thirty and fifty grams." The robustness of this finding would not have been apparent from any single study—it took a review of six studies to identify the reasonably consistent, if small, effect.

Synthesis Can Assess the Importance of Research Design

Some scholars spend a large fraction of their time arguing that research design matters. Riecken and others (1974), Gilbert and others (1975), Chalmers (1982), and Hoaglin and others (1982) have worked hard to convince the evaluation community that randomization is a crucial ingredient for evaluations, since it underlies our ability to make causal inferences. The efforts of these investigators have made some headway. Yet, sometimes randomization is difficult or impossible, so we must turn to alternatives and do the best that we can despite their imperfections. Alternatives include case studies, quasi-experiments, observational designs, studies of management records, and computer simulations when appropriate (Hoaglin and others, 1982).

None of this is news. But, when a researcher or policy maker faces a concrete problem, such as whether a certain nutrition program is effective or whether a new surgical procedure is worth using, any single study is almost certain to have a single research design. There are a few exceptions, but they are rare (Ruopp and others, 1979). The reader of this one study must then ask two questions: First, does the study stand well on its own merit—is it well done? Second, does the research design introduce any constraints, limitations, or biases? It is difficult to answer this second question with evidence from only

Table 2. Mean Birthweight Quantitative Summary

Study	Year and Location	Reported Birthweight (grams)[a]			Quantitative Indicators		
		WIC	Non-WIC	Raw Difference	Percent Difference[b]	Statistical Significance
Kotelchuck	1978 Massachusetts	3,281 (4,126)	3,260 (4,126)	21.0	0.6	Marginal
Metcoff	1980–82 Oklahoma City	3,254 (238)	3,163 (172)	91.0[c]	2.9	Yes
Stockbauer	1979–81 Missouri	3,254 (6,657)	3,238 (6,657)	16.0	0.5	Yes
Silverman	1971–77 Allegheny County, Pennsylvania	3,189 (1,047)	3,095 (1,361)	94.0	3.0	Yes
Bailey	1980 Two Florida counties	3,229 (37)	3,276 (42)	−47.0	−1.4	No
Kennedy	1973–78 Massachusetts	3,261.4	3,138.9	122.5	3.9	Yes
Summary						
Average		3,244.7	3,195.1	49.6	1.55[d]	
Weighted Average[e]		3,257.8	3,225.9	31.3	0.97[d]	
Range: Lowest		3,189.0	3,095.0	−47.0	−1.4	
Range: Highest		3,281.0	3,276.0	122.5	3.9	

[a]The numbers in parentheses are sample sizes.
[b]Raw difference divided by non-WIC birthweight.
[c]Adjusted.
[d]Average raw difference divided by average non-WIC birthweight.
[e]Each mean is weighted by the number of participants or controls in its group, and an overall average is obtained by dividing by the total number of participants and controls in the six studies. The raw difference is based on the total number of participants and controls.
Source: GAO 1984, p. 16.

715

one study, even one that is well done. But, a synthesis helps us a lot. It allows us to compare findings — and the research designs that lead to those findings — across a group of studies. Chapter Three in this volume provides a useful example. If there are correlations, we learn two things: First, we see what specific designs led to what specific outcomes. Second, we can organize future research knowing more about the consequences of specific designs.

Several concrete illustrations from recent syntheses show how research design can matter. One example comes from surgery. Chalmers (1982) reviews the findings from ninety-five studies of portacaval shunt surgery. These ninety-five reports were published over a period of many years by different investigators who worked at different hospitals. Chalmers asks two questions about each study: First, did its research design have adequate controls, poor controls, or no controls at all? Second, what did the investigator say about the surgery; was there marked enthusiasm, moderate enthusiasm, or no enthusiasm? The results of Chalmers's review are presented in Table 3. The conclusion here is clear: Poorly controlled studies of this surgery are far more likely than well-controlled studies to make investigators happy. Perhaps Table 3 illustrates Hugo Muench's law of clinical studies: Results can always be improved by omitting controls (Bearman and others, 1974).

A second example comes from the dilemma of how best to control spiraling health care costs. In 1982, the Committee on Labor and Human Resources of the U.S. Senate asked the General Accounting Office to examine all available evidence about the effects on medical costs of increasing the amount of health care provided at home for elderly citizens (U.S. GAO, 1982). It was proposed in Senate debate that by providing more health care at home, total service costs would drop, because the chronically ill would make less use of hospitals. To assess the cost implications of increased home care, the GAO reviewed more than thirty studies. About half were nonquantitative case studies, while the other half were comparative and used either an experimentally developed control group or an existing comparison group. The GAO's findings were striking. The case studies, mostly small-sample narrative reports, almost unanimously suggested that costs would decline. But, the quantitative studies found the opposite — that total costs would not decline; indeed, they might even increase slightly. The quantitative studies turned up

Table 3. Synthesis of Evidence on Portacaval Shunt Surgery

| | Degree of Enthusiasm | | | |
Controls	Marked	Moderate	None	Totals
Adequate	0	3	4	7
Poor	8	2	1	21
None	50	14	3	67
Totals	68	19	8	95

Source: Chalmers, 1982.

a clear reason for this surprising result. Rather than leading some elderly recipients of service to change the site from hospital to home, the new opportunity for home care considerably expanded the total number of people requesting care. People not receiving services began to request them. So, while the offering of reimbursable home care as an alternative to hospitalization can reduce the cost per recipient for those who accept the alternative, it seems also to create a substantial new group of service recipients, and total service costs do not drop.

I do not include this example to argue for or against home care. Some people argue that the home care option is a good idea even if costs are higher. Others disagree. But whatever one's values about the trade-offs between hospital and home care, the point is that a study's design is closely related to its outcome. A reviewer could examine every published case study and conclude that the evidence for lower costs with home care was overwhelming. Meanwhile, another reviewer who examined only studies with comparison or control groups would find overwhelming evidence in the other direction. Knowing that different types of studies generally lead to different sorts of findings offers guidance for the future. Whoever designs the next study to examine the costs of a home care program can try to incorporate the strengths of both types of designs.

Conclusion

Research synthesis is not a panacea. Each effort faces dilemmas. Perhaps because certain value judgments must be made, such as the weight that must be placed on findings from different research designs, some investigators may be tempted to fall back on traditional narrative reviews. I believe that this would be a mistake. Just because a synthesis turns up conflict or requires a judgment call is not good reason to shoot the messenger. The messenger gives us information that is vital in two ways. First, synthesis points to the features of a treatment or program that seem to matter. Is there a crucial background variable? Does research design matter much? How stable are the findings across a group of studies? Second, synthesis helps us to design the next study. Examining the first ten studies and learning which program features are important and which are not help us to develop an effective research plan for the eleventh study. Findings from a synthesis help to make a study as powerful as possible in answering a specific question or resolving a dilemma. In a world of scarce resources, such targeting is valuable. While any one study is important, the great virtue of synthesis is that it helps to answer questions single studies cannot answer.

References

Anderson, S., Auquier, A., Hauck, W., Oakes, D., Vandaele, W., and Weisberg, H. *Statistical Methods for Comparative Studies.* New York: Wiley, 1980.
Baker, P. J., and Crist, U. L. "Teacher Expectancies: A Review of the Literature." In

R. E. Snow and J. D. Elashoff (Eds.), *Pygmalion Reconsidered.* Worthington, Ohio: Jones, 1971.

Bearman, J. E., Loewenson, R. B., and Gullen, W. H. *Muench's Postulates, Laws, and Corollaries, or Biometricians' Views on Clinical Studies.* Biometrics Note No. 4. Bethesda, Md.: Office of Biometry and Epidemiology, National Eye Institute, National Institute of Health, 1974.

Bissell, J. W. "The Effects of Preschool Programs for Disadvantaged Children." Unpublished doctoral dissertation, Harvard University, 1970.

Campbell, D. T., and Erlebacher, A. "How Regression Artifacts in Quasi-Experimental Evaluations Can Mistakenly Make Compensatory Education Look Harmless." In J. Hellmuth (Ed.), *The Disadvantaged Child.* Vol. 3: *Compensatory Education—A National Debate.* New York: Brunner/Mazel, 1970.

Chalmers, T. C. "The Randomized Controlled Trial as a Basis for Therapeutic Decisions." In J. M. Lachin, N. Tygstrup, and E. Juhl (Eds.), *The Randomized Clinical Trial and Therapeutic Decisions.* New York: Marcel Dekker, 1982.

Cicirelli, V. *The Impact of Head Start: An Evaluation of the Effects of Head Start on Children's Cognitive and Affective Development.* Washington, D.C.: Clearinghouse for Federal Scientific and Technical Information, 1969. (ED 036 321)

Datta, L. "The Impact of the Westinghouse/Ohio Evaluation on the Development of Project Head Start." In C. C. Abt (Ed.), *The Evaluation of Social Programs.* Beverly Hills, Calif.: Sage, 1976.

Datta, L. "A Tale of Two Studies: The Westinghouse/Ohio Evaluation of Head Start and the Consortium for Longitudinal Studies Report." *Studies in Educational Evaluation,* 1983, *3,* 271–280.

Edgington, E. S. "An Additive Model for Combining Probability Values from Independent Experiments." *Journal of Psychology,* 1972, *80,* 351–363.

Elashoff, J. D., and Snow, R. E. (Eds.). *Pygmalion Reconsidered.* Worthington, Ohio: Jones, 1971.

Fisher, R. A. *Statistical Methods for Research Workers.* London: Oliver & Boyd, 1973.

Gilbert, J. P., Light, R. J., and Mosteller, F. "Assessing Social Innovation: An Empirical Base for Policy." In C. A. Bennett and A. A. Lumsdaine (Eds.), *Evaluation and Experiment.* New York: Academic Press, 1975.

Glass, G. V. "Integrating Findings: The Meta-Analysis of Research." In L. S. Shulman (Ed.), *Review of Research in Education.* Vol. 5. Itasca, Ill.: Peacock, 1977.

Glass, G. V., McGaw, B., and Smith, M. L. *Meta-Analysis in Social Research.* Beverly Hills, Calif.: Sage, 1981.

Hoaglin, D. C., Light, R. J., McPeek, B., Mosteller, F., and Stoto, M. *Data for Decisions.* Cambridge, Mass.: Abt Books, 1982.

Hunter, J. E., Schmidt, F. L., and Jackson, G. B. *Meta-Analysis: Cumulating Research Findings Across Studies.* Beverly Hills, Calif.: Sage, 1982.

Kohl, H. "Great Expectations." In R. E. Snow and J. D. Elashoff (Eds.), *Pygmalion Reconsidered.* Worthington, Ohio: Jones, 1971.

Light, R. J. "Capitalizing on Variation: How Conflicting Research Findings Can Be Helpful for Policy." *Educational Researcher,* 1979, *8* (8), 3–8.

Light, R. J., and Smith, P. V. "Accumulating Evidence: Procedures for Resolving Contradictions Among Different Research Studies." *Harvard Educational Review,* 1971, *41,* 429–471.

Mosteller, F., and Bush, R. "Selecting Quantitative Techniques." In G. Lindzey (Ed.), *Handbook on Social Psychology.* Vol. 1: *Theory and Method.* Cambridge, Mass.: Addison-Wesley, 1954.

National Academy of Sciences. *Evaluation of the Comprehensive Employment and Training Act.* Washington, D.C.: National Academy Press, 1978.

National Academy of Sciences. *Case Studies of CETA.* Washington, D.C.: National Academy Press, 1979.

Pillemer, D. B., and Light, R. J. "Synthesizing Outcomes: How to Use Research Evidence from Many Studies." *Harvard Educational Review,* 1980, *50,* 176–195.

Raudenbush, S. W. "Utilizing Controversy as a Source of Hypotheses for Meta-Analysis: The Case of Teacher Expectancy's Effects on Pupil IQ." *Journal of Educational Psychology,* forthcoming.

Riecken, H. W., and others. *Social Experimentation: A Method for Planning and Evaluating Social Intervention.* New York: Academic Press, 1974.

Rivlin, A. *Systematic Thinking for Social Action.* Washington, D.C.: Brookings Institution, 1971.

Rosenthal, R., and Jacobson, L. *Pygmalion in the Classroom.* New York: Holt, Rinehart and Winston, 1968.

Ruopp, R., Travers, J., Glantz, F., and Coelen, C. *Children at the Center: Report of the National Daycare Study.* Cambridge, Mass.: Abt Books, 1979.

Ryan, W. *Blaming the Victim.* New York: Pantheon, 1971.

Smith, M. S., and Bissell, J. "Report Analysis: The Impact of Head Start." *Harvard Eduational Review,* 1970, *40,* 51–104.

U.S. General Accounting Office. *The Elderly Should Benefit from Expanded Home Health Care but Increasing Those Services Will Not Ensure Cost Reductions.* Washington, D.C.: U.S. General Accounting Office, 1982.

U.S. General Accounting Office. *WIC Evaluations Provide Some Favorable but No Conclusive Evidence.* Washington, D.C.: U.S. General Accounting Office, 1984.

Winer, B. J. *Statistical Principles in Experimental Design.* New York: McGraw-Hill, 1971.

Richard J. Light is professor at the Graduate School of Education and the Kennedy School of Government at Harvard University, and chairman of the Evaluation Seminar at Harvard. His recent writings emphasize how different forms of statistical evidence can inform policy decisions.

39

Studying Enrollment Decline (and Other Timely Issues) via the Case Survey

Michael A. Berger

The subject of this paper is a technique to integrate several isolated case studies. It was created, almost by necessity, as a result of two problems which often plague educational researchers: constraints on data collection and the proliferation of one-shot case studies. Each problem will be discussed briefly.

If educational researchers want to study a controversial issue, the implementation of a new technique, or the impact of a new policy, they are often constrained by a number of factors. In school closings, for example, it is possible that the cost of collecting data over the duration of the decision making process will be prohibitive. Second, access to the various participants may be problematic. People move away, boards go into executive session, and subjects may refuse to cooperate. Finally, it is often difficult to conceive a quasi-experimental or experimental design. Imagine a researcher who wants to study the effects of a community involvement policy on the closure decision. The

researcher could not ask the school board to use a community task force in one part of the district to recommend schools for closure, and prohibit community involvement in another part of the district.

In light of these constraints, researchers often rely on the intensive case study. The method usually includes participant observation, open-ended interviews, and situation-specific documents to describe the events and to form qualitative conclusions about the policy phenomena in question. In the area of enrollment decline, for example, case studies proliferate (see Colton & Frelich, 1979; Duke & Meckel, 1980; Rogers & Nord, 1981; Wachtel & Powers, 1979; Yeager, 1979).

Case studies have several advantages over experiments. First, they offer detailed accounts of a particular phenomenon. Second, their longitudinal nature allows the description of events over time. Third, cases offer close-at-hand impressions of the case writer which may be more accurate than impersonal surveys which ask for a rating on a number of quantitative scales. Most important, case studies overcome the cost, access, and design constraints of quantitative research. Thus, for many policy questions, intensive case studies may be ideal and often become the dominant mode of research.

On the other hand, numerous case studies can be a curse (Wilson, 1979). The various "war stories" are too idiosyncratic. They describe what happened in one situation and generalization to other

This paper is based on research supported by the National Institute of Education (NIE-G-80-0170). Any opinions, conclusions, or recommendations are those of the author and do not necessarily reflect the views of the Institute.

I am grateful to Ned Reese, Carol Boone, Gayle Fox, Pam Henderson, and Dirk Lorenzen for their research assistance. I also want to acknowledge the helpful comments of Professors Raymond Norris, Leonard Bickman, and William Barkley.

An earlier version of this paper was presented at the Annual Meeting of the American Educational Research Association, New York, March 1982.

settings may be limited. While researchers know it is important to review and integrate previous research before they pursue a topic, the presence of diverse case studies makes it difficult to know exactly what the case study literature says. As the number of case studies on a certain topic grows, it becomes increasingly important, however difficult, to integrate their collective meaning.

In his presidential address at the American Educational Research Association's Annual Meeting in 1975, later published in the *Educational Researcher*, Glass (1976) underscored this very point:

> The literature of dozens of topics in education is growing at an astounding rate. In five years time, researchers can produce literally hundreds of studies on IQ and creativity, or impulsive vs. reflective cognitive styles, or any other topic. (p. 3)

> Our problem is to find the knowledge in the information. We need methods for the orderly summarization of studies so that knowledge can be extracted from the myriad of individual researches. (p. 4)

This is not to suggest that synthesis of multiple case studies does not occur. Qualitative syntheses in the area of enrollment decline were done by Rideout (1975), Burlingame (1979), and Boyd (1979). These scholars have taken an important step, and while the number of cases they analyzed was usually small (6–10), their efforts were critical to the integration of diverse case materials.

This paper describes a more extensive technique for dealing with the twin problems of constraints on data collection and the need to integrate many case studies. The technique is called the case survey and involves analyzing the content of case studies via a closed-ended questionnaire. This instrument enables the researcher to aggregate the various case experiences and, in turn, to make generalizations about the studies as a whole. After outlining the roots of this approach and its relationship to meta-analysis, the discussion turns to a description of the basic process with an application to the enrollment decline case literature and an evaluation of the case survey's strengths and weaknesses.

Roots of the Case Survey Method

The case survey method attempts to carry many isolated case studies several steps forward by systematic aggregation and analysis. The origins of the approach can be found in content analysis, and more recently, in the efforts of a handful of organization researchers.

The content analysis of published data is not new in social science research. It has been used in history, journalism, anthropology, and sociology for many decades (for several classic examples, see Berelson, 1954; Budd, Thorp, & Donohew, 1967; Carney, 1972; North, 1963; Pool, 1959). The technique involves coding, tabulating, and analyzing content. Coding categories may include (a) the number of occurrences of an event, (b) the presence or absence of a phenomenon, (c) the attitude toward an object, and (d) the intensity of feelings about a role.

Bend's study (1952) is an excellent example of content analysis. He investigated the spouse-wanted columns in a New York Yiddish newspaper called *The Day*. This paper regularly published a classified spouse-wanted column; interestingly, this form of spouse selection was considered quite acceptable until the early 1950s. A typical ad read, "Parents seek a physician for pretty daughter." Bend compared the ads from 1935 and 1950 to determine if the value preferences stated for spouses varied over time. He hypothesized that socioeconomic characteristics (as opposed to personal characteristics) would be more important in the period immediately following immigration than they would be at a later period. Following a systematic sampling and coding procedure, he searched each advertisement to determine the order in which various spouse characteristics were mentioned. The data showed that socioeconomic factors in spouse selection were indeed higher and personal traits were lower in the early year than in the later year.

During the last 9 years, a handful of organization researchers have been working with the method, calling it either the case survey or the structured content analysis of cases. The modern era began with a group of researchers at the Rand Corporation (see Lucas, 1974). Yin and

Yates (1975) content analyzed various cases to determine the attitudinal effects of urban decentralization. Gamson (1975) used the technique to study 53 protest organizations. Miller and Friesen (1977) investigated corporate decisionmaking in *Fortune* articles. Yin, Heald, and Vogel (1977) studied technological innovations. McDonnell and Zellman (1978) evaluated the effects of Emergency School Aid Act (ESAA) funded projects. Miller and Friesen (1980) researched 26 companies for structural and strategy change. Jauch, Osborn, and Martin (1980) studied executive succession, and Berger (1983b) studied community protests to school closing decisions.

The appeal of the case survey method is strong because it transforms qualitative evidence into quantitative statements. Until now, the main limitation of isolated, one-shot case studies was that the insights from the various cases could not be aggregated in any systematic manner. The case survey overcomes this problem by integrating the individual studies via conventional statistics. Moreover, because case studies are in the public domain, data collection constraints (cost, access, and design) are minimized. Finally, the method is based on the assumptions that: (a) the case study is a legitimate sampling unit, (b) there is a meaningful population of cases from which one might generalize, and (c) selected aspects of the cases can be quantified.

The Case Survey and Meta-analysis

By now, knowledgeable researchers have concluded that the case survey method sounds like secondary analysis, meta-evaluation, or meta-analysis. If it is true that secondary analysis is "the reanalysis of data for the purpose of answering the original research question with better statistical techniques or answering new questions with old data" (Glass, 1976, p. 3), then the case survey is secondary analysis. By the same token, if it is true that meta-evaluation involves Stufflebeam's (1975) notion of the evaluation of formative research and nonempirical evaluations, then the case survey is similar to meta-evaluation. Finally, if meta-analysis refers to "the analysis of analyses, in other words, the statistical

analysis of a large collection of results from individual studies for the purpose of integrating the findings" (Glass, 1976, p. 3), then the case survey is definitely a form of meta-analysis.

Despite these apparent definitional similarities, the case survey and meta-analysis do differ. To explore the differences, we need to specify the meaning of meta-analysis more precisely. Glass, McGaw, and Smith (1981) define meta-analysis as the "statistical analysis of the summary findings of many empirical studies" (p. 21). Cook and Leviton (1980) are more explicit. They see meta-analysis as a process where "studies relevant to a conceptual issue are collected, summary statistics from each study (e.g., means or correlations) are treated as the units of analysis, and the aggregate data are then analyzed in quantitative tests of the proposition under examination" (p. 445).

In both definitions, meta-analysis refers to a collection of experimental or correlational studies on a particular topic, where the quantitative findings of the various studies (differences in means, correlation coefficients and/or frequencies) are used as the dependent variable, and the substantive or methodological characteristics of the various studies are used as the independent variables. A classic example is the Smith and Glass (1977) study on the effects of psychotherapy. They found nearly 400 controlled evaluations on the effects of psychodynamic, client-centered, behavior modification, and rational-emotive psychotherapy. Eschewing the traditional narrative review and voting method of meta-analysis, they converted the various outcomes to a common metric, known as "effect size," and conducted a quantitative analysis on the study's attributes. Their major impression was that the four types of therapy were not significantly different in their average impact.

If we contrast the case survey method with this more precise meaning of meta-analysis, several differences emerge. First, where meta-analysis uses experimental or correlational studies, the case survey uses highly descriptive accounts of a phenomenon. Second, where meta-analysis attempts to account for study quality (although Glass et al., 1981, reject the conventional wisdom that findings are in part determined by the quality of design), the case survey does not account for traditional threats to internal validity (Campbell & Stanley, 1966).

Finally, where meta-analysis uses the statistical findings and methodological characteristics of the various studies, the case survey analyzes the content of the various cases according to the conceptual categories of the case survey researcher. Thus, the findings of the original case writer may or may not be relevant to the goals of the case survey. For example, it is possible the case survey researcher is interested in community opposition to a school closure policy. While the original case writer may have focused on leadership under conditions of enrollment decline, and mentioned only casually the community's initiation of a lawsuit to prevent a school closure, the case survey researcher would use that particular case because it contained data on the community's reaction.

These differences suggest that the case survey is like meta-analysis only when the meta-analysis concept is used in the most general way. If, however, meta-analysis is used to refer to the quantitative analysis of statistical findings, then the case survey is different. We now turn to a discussion of how the case survey is conducted, using the enrollment decline literature as a running example.

The Case Survey Process and Application

The case survey method requires a case analyst to answer the same set of questions for each case study. The various questions are closed-ended to permit easy quantification. The basis for the questions is derived from the policy literature and the researcher's own theoretical perspective.

The process can be conceptualized in six basic steps: (a) definition of the unit of analysis; (b) identification of the case search strategy and case sources; (c) actual case search and selection; (d) checklist development; (e) checklist application to the cases; and (f) data analysis and interpretation. This process is no different than the process of primary research (Jackson, 1978). Because the goals of both the case survey and primary research are the same, namely, to make generalizations about phenomena from diverse bits of information, it follows that these processes should be similar.

Step 1: Definition of the Unit of Analysis

The unit of analysis in a case survey is a site-specific description of the events surrounding a phenomenon. Careful definition of the unit of analysis is essential because it delineates the consistent set of decision rules whereby a certain type of case is included in the study and others are ruled out. Cases can vary in terms of when the case was written, what organizational events were described, what types of settings were studied, what constituted the level of analysis, and whether or not the case was published.

Beginning in the mid-1970's, enrollment decline case studies appeared in the educational research literature. These highly descriptive cases were written by superintendents, education professors, consultants, and government officials. They focused primarily on what happened in a particular district as the board of education, the community, and administration coped with the problems of enrollment decline. The nature of this literature was as follows: (a) the cases were virtually the only empirical information available on the topic; (b) with few exceptions, integration of the various cases was nonexistent; and (c) where synthesis did occur, it was usually based on a small number of cases. Thus, an application of the case survey method to this literature seemed to be the natural next step to advance the state of knowledge about responses to enrollment decline.

The study's unit of analysis was an enrollment decline experience in a case defined as "any report or reports, written between 1971 and 1980, which described the organizational responses to enrollment decline in a public elementary/secondary school district." This definition ruled "in" multiple case descriptions on a single district and fugitive documents, such as task force studies or consultant reports. It ruled "out" cases written after 1980, private school decline experiences, responses to enrollment decline in higher education, and nondistrict level responses (e.g., how one school within a district weathered a closing decision). Published and unpublished cases were considered acceptable.

Step 2: Identification of Case Search Strategy and Case Sources

One of the most critical tasks of the method is the discovery of case studies. These units constitute the data base for the checklist items. Like the sampling process in primary research, here is where bias can enter the study. It enters through the inclusion of cases that may be unrepresentative of the literature as a whole. Glass et al. (1981) argue that the best protection against this source of bias is a thorough description of the procedures used to locate studies so the reader can make an accurate assessment of the representativeness and completeness of the data base used in the integration. The sources of case studies, in turn, determine the search strategy.

To locate cases for the enrollment decline study, 10 sources were identified: journals, dissertations, government agencies, bibliographies (e.g., ERIC), papers from scholarly meetings, abstracts, professional associations, education commissioners in the various states, American Association of School Administrators (AASA) state presidents, and private research organizations (e.g., Institute for Responsive Education). These sources were searched systematically by the research team for case studies that fit the unit of analysis definition. In all, we reviewed 94 journals and contacted 140 agencies, associations, and professionals by letter and/or telephone. The search included not only case studies but theoretical papers as well. These papers and their bibliographies were used for possible leads to other case studies.

Step 3: Actual Case Search and Selection

Once the source of cases and search strategy have been determined, the actual process of search and selection can begin. Case search implies reading various case materials in light of the study's decision rules and applying the selection criteria. Based on the accumulation of cases and the explicit criteria defining the unit of analysis, the final set of cases is determined. This final set of cases becomes the study's population or, if a subset of this population is selected, the study's sample.

About 250 enrollment decline documents were read. A total of 208 cases met the original criteria for selection. However, we noticed that some cases reported on the same district. We also noted that case studies varied from 1 to 2 pages of description to elaborate discussions of 50 pages or more. Faced with the issues of district duplication and case variation, we developed more precise selection criteria.

To deal with the duplication issue, we decided to treat all documents on a particular district as one and only one case. Some districts (e.g., Skokie, Illinois, and Salt Lake City, Utah) have been described by several authors. This information was pooled for each district, thereby enriching the data base and providing a crude qualitative check on case validity.

To cope with the case variation issue, which implied missing data problems, the principal investigator read the 208 cases and distinguished those cases that had little descriptive data from those cases that had good or excellent data (based on a quality assessment scale of 0 to 3). The 138 documents (comprising 66.3% of the original cases discovered) receiving a 0 or 1 score were typically theoretical papers, prescriptive forecasting papers, aggregated state data or multidistrict surveys. Case studies receiving a score of 2 or 3 were descriptions with substantial data on the study's major variables. This latter set of 70 cases comprised 33.7 percent of the original cases discovered.

It is impossible to know whether the 208 total cases discovered comprise the entire enrollment decline case literature. Multiple references to cases on file and our comprehensive search process led us to believe we were highly inclusive. It is important to note that the sampling procedure was judgmental (or "convenient" as Jackson, 1978, states) rather than random. That is, we selected 70 cases on the presence of predetermined variables, rather than chance. Because it is unclear what portion of the literature was collected, and because the sampling procedure involved judgment, the hypothesis of no bias cannot be ruled out entirely.

Step 4: Checklist Development

The development of the checklist (i.e., the instrument used by the case analysts to survey each case) is usually begun concurrently with earlier steps, depending on the energy and resources of the researcher. Checklist development is similar to the construction of any instrument: Variables of interest are identified and scaled in a closed-ended fashion to permit quantitative analysis. To the extent that variables can be grouped in logical categories and scaled in realistic values, the subsequent application of the checklist to the individual cases is facilitated.

The process of checklist development in the enrollment decline study occurred in tandem with the case search activities. After consultation with several enrollment decline experts and a review of the theoretical literature, the research team generated about 300 variables and their operational definitions. These variables were reduced to 227 and placed in the checklist under the following conceptual categories: (a) nature of the district study; (b) community demographics; (c) district characteristics; (d) nature of the enrollment decline response; (e) school board role; (f) administration role; (g) professional staff role; and (h) community role. When the checklist was completed, it was ready for application to the final set of 70 cases (see the Appendix for checklist examples).

Step 5: Checklist Application to the Final Set of Cases

Checklist application requires two preliminary steps. First, case analysts need training on the content of the checklist, and second, they must practice the process by which the checklist is applied. Training is critical because multiple meanings and ambiguities are inevitable. This is especially true with items that call for case analyst judgment rather than the recording of numerical data.

Clarity and consistent interpretation of the various items are the goals of checklist training. In terms of the process of application, case analysts will vary in their style. Some analysts like to read an entire case several times and fill out the checklist at the end, whereas other analysts prefer to fill out the various questions as they read. Whatever the preference, case analysts should practice on several cases before actual coding begins. Once the case analysts are familiar with the checklist and comfortable with the process of application, the actual checklist application process can begin. It continues until one checklist is completed for each district.

During several sessions, the enrollment decline case analysts were instructed in the nature and uses of the checklist. The various items were explained and analysts were given an opportunity to clarify their understanding and to practice checklist application. Since the case analysts were graduate students knowledgeable about enrollment decline, training and practice were rather straightforward. When training was completed the 70 cases were distributed randomly among the analysts. The 70 checklists became the study's data base.

Step 6: Data Analysis and Interpretation

With the checklists completed, the researcher is now ready for data analysis and interpretation. Analysis is facilitated through the use of multivariate statistics. The main goal of the case survey is to transform isolated, qualitative judgments from disparate cases into quantitative statements about the case literature as a whole. It seems neither possible nor feasible to make such statements without the help of statistical methods (Glass et al., 1981). Typical statistical tests include univariate description, frequency analysis, correlation, regression analysis, factor analysis, analysis of covariance, and/or discriminant analysis.

While the case survey provides quantitative integration and increases the generalizability of isolated case studies, it is not without its methodological problems. Specifically three problems seem to be inherent in the method: establishing case validity and interanalyst reliability, evaluating case quality, and overcoming missing data problems.

The question of validity refers to the relationship between each checklist item and the concept it attempts to measure, and the case study and the reality it attempts to describe. On both counts, the case survey is particularly vulnerable. In terms of the former problem, items on the checklist rarely exceed face validity. In terms of the latter problem, the case survey fares no better. Jauch et al. (1980), for example, dismiss the issue entirely by stating that it awaits further investigations. The Miller and Friesen (1980) study is one notable exception. They surveyed 26 published corporate histories and attempted to correlate their checklists with responses on a separate questionnaire sent to 12 firms whose executives were knowledgeable about the events described in the cases.

Reliability is a concern in the case survey because the checklist quantifies, classifies, and codes the characteristics and descriptive accounts of various case studies. Jackson (1978) points out that when the number of studies and items is relatively small, coding can be done by a single investigator, and hence, remains fairly consistent. But if many cases are coded, and they are coded over time, serious threats to coding stability may occur. In more precise terms, measurement unreliability is likely to occur when different case analysts fail to see or fail to judge case events in the same way. The problem is usually resolved by having more than one analyst fill out a checklist on the same case. The amount of interanalyst agreement becomes the measure of reliability (Yin & Heald, 1975).

Variation in case quality is also a problem in case survey research. This usually comes from the meta-analysis notion that the findings of poorly designed studies are often combined with the findings of "good" studies, while aggregated conclusions should be based only on the findings of "good" studies (Cook & Leviton, 1980). Concern about quality may also occur if there is "selection bias" in the original collection of cases (e.g., cases chosen from only academically oriented journals).

In the enrollment decline study, validity of the various checklist items was not checked empirically. Experts did assert that the various items had face validity, but no further quantitative analysis was conducted. Reliability, on the other hand, was verified empirically. Reliability was defined as the degree of consistency between two checklists on the same district,

each completed by a different case analyst. This is similar to reliability on a psychological or educational instrument when the researcher is interested in the stability of a person's score under slightly different conditions.

To estimate reliability, researchers typically use a test-retest, equivalent forms, or split-half technique. A test-retest estimate is obtained by administering a test to a group of individuals, readministering the same test to the same group at a later date, and correlating the two sets of scores. In contrast, the equivalent forms estimate is obtained by giving two forms of a test to the same group on the same day and correlating these sets of scores. The split-half method is basically a variation of equivalent forms; instead of administering an alternate form, only one test is administered and an estimate of reliability is obtained by taking two halves of the test and correlating them. To estimate reliability for the entire test, a correction factor is applied using the Spearman-Brown prophecy formula (see Mehrens & Lehman, 1973, p. 114):

$$r_{xx} = \frac{2r_{\frac{1}{2}\frac{1}{2}}}{1 + r_{\frac{1}{2}\frac{1}{2}}},$$

where
r_{xx} = estimated reliability for the entire test
$r_{\frac{1}{2}\frac{1}{2}}$ = correlation coefficient for the half-test.

The present study used a variation of the split-half technique. The advantage of this procedure was that it required only one form of the checklist. A random sample of 36 of the 70 cases (51.4%) was chosen. Two analysts read each case independently and completed a checklist (for a similar procedure see Jauch et al., 1980; Miller & Friesen, 1980; Yin et al., 1977). After selecting a random sample of 50 checklist items for the reliability estimate, a Pearson's product moment correlation coefficient was calculated for the two raters across the 36 cases. The correlation was .64. To estimate reliability for the entire checklist, the Spearman-Brown prophecy formula was applied as follows:

$$r_{xx} = \frac{2\,(.64)}{1 + .64} = \frac{1.28}{1.64} = .78.$$

Thus, with an interanalyst correlation coefficient of .64, the estimated reliability for the entire checklist was .78. Jauch et al. (1980) suggest that a Spearman-Brown reliability coefficient of at least .67 is adequate for questionnaires, and hence, case survey research.

The issue of quality refers to the possibility that the final set of 70 cases was biased in some way. Bias may be present as a result of the sampling procedures. The cases in this study were selected if they contained the study's variables of interest. Thus, there is no way to estimate whether the final set of 70 cases was representative of the entire case literature or of school districts as a whole.

The missing data problem is also implied in the issue of quality. Despite attempts to select cases that contained most of the variables, the large number of variables on the checklist, and the disparate cases meant that this study suffered from missing data problems. At this point the researcher is faced with a decision: delete cases from the analysis that lack data, or pursue missing data in order to retain a high number of cases. For this study, we developed an elaborate follow-up procedure. We reasoned that missing data could be collected with a little detective work. Thus, we attempted to contact the original case writer, the education reporter for the local newspaper, and/or personnel in the district itself. This follow-up process was similar to the one used by Yin (1979) in his study of urban bureaucracies. When information could not be located, the checklist item was marked "Impossible to say" and deleted from the quantitative analysis.

Various analyses of the final set of 70 cases (see Table I for a breakdown by community type) were performed. Two recent examples are published elsewhere. They include community opposition to school closure decisions (Berger, 1983b) and the organizational effects of retrenchment policies (Berger, 1983a).

TABLE I

Community Distribution of the Final Set of Cases

Urban Districts (n = 25)	Suburban Districts (n = 34)	Rural Districts (n = 11)
California: Haywood, Palo Alto, Santa Barbara	California: Berkeley	Illinois: Champaign. Pawnee-Diver-non
Colorado: Englewood	Illinois: Alton,* Camden,* Deerfield, Elmhurst, Glencoe, La Grange,	Indiana: Monroe County
Connecticut: Hamden	Leland,* Mt. Prospect, North-view,* Oakton,* Oregon, Shab-	Iowa: Cal Community District, Lohrville
Illinois: North Chicago, Pekin	bona, Skokie, Trenton.* Weston*	Ohio: Bradford, Fairborn, Franklin
Massachusetts: Boston	Maryland: Montgomery County	Oklahoma: Blackwell
Michigan: Grand Rapids	Massachusetts:Lexington, Natick, Newton	Minnesota: #3, #4*
Minnesota: #2, #5*	Michigan: Birminghan, Livonia, Oakpark	
Missouri: Kansas City, St. Louis	Minnesota: #1*	
New York: East Syracuse, Yon-kers	New Jersey: Bridgeton	
Ohio: Berea, Euclid, Lakewood, Steubenville	New York: Arbutus,* Clarence, East Meadow, Great Neck, Kar-lin,* Mamaroneck, White Plains	
Oklahoma: Tulsa	Pennsylvania: South Allegheny	
Oregon: Eugene	Virginia: Arlington	
Tennessee: Nashville		
Utah: Salt Lake City		
Virginia: Richmond		
Washington: Seattle		

Note: The terms suburban and rural were at times applied based on proximity to urban centers rather than population. For example, some districts (e.g., Skokie, Illinois, and Montgomery County, Maryland) are large in size but are adjacent to urban centers. They were categorized as suburban. Other districts (e.g., Grand Rapids. Michigan, and Steubenville, Ohio) are smaller in size but are relatively industrialized and independent of any larger, nearby city and are categorized as urban.

* District names are pseudonyms used by the original case authors.

Discussion

The case survey approach involves placing data from descriptive case studies into a closed-ended checklist and analyzing the checklists from the cases via conventional statistical techniques. Clearly, the case survey method has many strengths. First, it is a systematic, explicit way to integrate a diverse set of case materials. Second, because it relies on existing knowledge, it may be less costly for some policy studies than the production of primary data for research. Third, because case materials are in the public domain, the method avoids troublesome access and data collection problems that often surround controversial policy decisions. Fourth, by using multivariate statistics, the case survey permits the investigation of relationships and differences when the nature and location of the data preclude an experimental or quasi-experimental design. Finally, because the case survey employs more than one case study, the results are more generalizable.

This is not to suggest that the method is without problems. In addition to the problems discussed above (establishing case validity and interanalyst reliability, evaluating case quality, and overcoming missing data problems), Jackson (1978) has argued that when multivariate statistics are used, the set of original cases should be sufficiently large because the standard errors of both the R^2 and partial regression coefficients are the inverse function of N-k-one, where N is the number of cases and k is the number of predictor variables. If the N is small, the standard errors of the partials will be large and possibly overestimate the population parameter (Kerlinger & Pedhazur, 1973).

Finally, generalizability may be problematic. While it is true that the case survey goes beyond the narrowness of one particular case study, generalization of the findings should be to the case study literature rather than to other organizations as a whole. The reason for this assertion is that there is no way to determine if the case study literature is representative of other organizations. Jauch et al. (1980) have argued that cases that appear in print are often the "exemplars" or "disasters." Thus, while the case survey

moves the state of knowledge several steps ahead, one should be cautious about generalizing any findings.

Conclusion

This paper described the case survey method as a technique to overcome data collection problems and the lack of integration of many case studies. More specifically, it outlined the roots of the method, distinguished it from meta-analysis, described the basic process with illustrations from a recent enrollment decline study, and analyzed its strengths and limitations.

The case survey should be viewed as one method for improving the quality and generalizability of one-shot case studies. It is not the only answer to the problems of conducting policy research. Rather, it is a tool and, as such, it has appropriate and inappropriate uses. Whether it will be useful, however, depends on more development and application. Hopefully, the method will be refined and improved to build on its strengths and minimize its limitations.

References

BEND, E. Marriage offers in a Yiddish newspaper. *American Journal of Sociology*, 1952, 58, 60–66.

BERELSON, B. *Content analysis in communication research*. Glencoe, Il.: Free Press, 1954.

BERGER, M. Retrenchment policies and their organizational consequences. *Peabody Journal of Education*, 1983, 60, 49–63. (a)

BERGER, M. Why communities protest school closings. *Education and Urban Society*, 1983, 15(2), 149–163. (b)

BOYD, W. Educational policy making in declining suburban school districts. *Education and Urban Society*, 1979, 11, 313–332.

BUDD, R., THORP, R., & DONOHEW, L. *Content analysis of communications*. New York: Macmillan, 1967.

BURLINGAME, M. Declining enrollment and small rural cities and districts. *Education and Urban Society*, 1979, 11, 313–332.

CAMPBELL, D., & STANLEY, J. *Experimental and quasi-experimental designs for research*. Chicago: Rand McNally, 1966.

CARNEY, T. *Content analysis: A technique for systematic inference from communications*. Winnepeg: University of Manitoba Press, 1972.

COLTON, D., & FRELICH, A. Enrollment decline and school closings in a large city. *Education and Urban Society*, 1979, 11, 396–417.

COOK, T., & LEVITON, L. Reviewing the literature: A comparison of traditional methods with meta-analysis. *Journal of Personality*, 1980, 48, 445–472.

DUKE, D., & MECKEL, A. The slow death of a public high school. *Phi Delta Kappan*, 1980(June), 674–677.

GAMSON, W. *The strategy of social protest*. Homewood, Il.: Dorsey Press, 1975.

GLASS, G. Primary, secondary, and meta-analysis of research. *Educational Researcher*, 1976, 5, 3–8.

GLASS, G., McGAW, B., & SMITH, M. *Meta-analysis in social research*. Beverly Hills, Calif.: Sage, 1981.

JACKSON, G. *Methods of reviewing and integrating research in the social sciences*. Washington, D.C.: National Science Foundation, 1978.

JAUCH, L., OSBORN, R., & MARTIN, T. Structured content analysis of cases. *Academy of Management Review*, 1980, 5, 517–525.

KERLINGER, F., & PEDHAZUR, E. *Multiple regression in behavioral research*. New York: Holt, Rinehart and Winston, 1973.

LUCAS, W. *The case survey method: Aggregating case experience*. Santa Monica, Calif.: Rand, 1974.

McDONNELL, L., & ZELLMAN, G. *An evaluation of the Emergency School Aid Act non-profit program*. Santa Monica, Calif.: Rand, 1978.

MEHRENS, W., & LEHMAN, I. *Measurement and evaluation in education and psychology*. New York: Holt, Rinehart and Winston, 1973.

MILLER, D., & FRIESEN, P. Strategy-making in context: Ten empirical archetypes. *Journal of Management Studies*, 1977, 14, 251–260.

MILLER, D., & FRIESEN, P. Momentum and revolution in organizational adaptation. *Academy of Management Journal*, 1980, 23, 591–614.

NORTH, R. C. *Content analysis: A handbook*. Evanston, Il.: Northwestern University Press, 1963.

POOL, J. *Trends in content analysis*. Urbana: University of Illinois Press, 1959.

RIDEOUT, E. B. *Meeting problems of declining enrollment*. Toronto: Ontario Institute for Studies in Education, 1975.

ROGERS, K., & NORD, W. *The effects of collaborative decision making on participants in a school dis-*trict facing organizational decline. Paper presented at the annual meeting of the American Educational Research Association, Los Angeles, April 1981.

SMITH, M., & GLASS, G. Meta-analysis of psychotherapy outcome studies. *American Psychologist*, 1977, 32, 752–760.

STUFFLEBEAM, D. L. *Meta-evaluation* (Occasional Paper #3). Unpublished manuscript. Michigan University Evaluation Center, 1975.

WACHTEL, B., & POWERS, B. *Rising above decline*. Boston: Institute for Responsive Education, 1979.

WILSON, S. Explorations of the usefulness of case evaluations. *Evaluation Quarterly*, 1979, 446–459.

YEAGER, R. Rationality and retrenchment. *Educational and Urban Society*, 1979, 11, 296–312.

YIN, R. *Changing urban bureaucracies*. Lexington, Mass.: D.C. Heath, 1979.

YIN, R. & HEALD, K. Using the case survey method to analyze policy studies. *Administrative Science Quarterly*, 1975, 20, 371–381.

YIN, R., HEALD, K., & VOGEL, M. *Tinkering with the system*. Lexington, Mass.: D.C. Heath, 1977.

YIN, R., & YATES, D. *Street-level governments: Assessing decentralization and urban services*. Lexington, Mass: D.C. Heath, 1975.

Author

MICHAEL A. BERGER, Assistant Professor of Education, Peabody College of Vanderbilt University, Nashville, TN 37203. *Specializations:* Organizational responses to decline; desegregation; educational and public administration.

APPENDIX
Case Survey Checklist
(Examples)

Case Analyst_____   District Name_____

Date_____   Sample Number (s)_____

Case Number (s)_____

CATEGORY	ITEM

Nature of the District Materials

1. The district enrollment decline experience described below appeared in:
   (1) a single case study   ☐
   (2) more than one document

Community Demographics

2. The district is the following community type:
   (1) urban   ☐
   (2) rural
   (3) suburban

District Characteristics

3. The total number of students (omit 000) in the district from peak enrollment year (PE) to PE+10 was:

PE	PE+2	PE+4	PE+6	PE+8	PE+10
☐☐☐	☐☐☐	☐☐☐	☐☐☐	☐☐☐	☐☐☐

Nature of the Response

4. The total number of schools closed for each period was:

PE	PE+2	PE+4	PE+6	PE+8	PE+10
☐☐	☐☐	☐☐	☐☐	☐☐	☐☐

School Board Role

5. The case materials mention that the total time from the establishment of a task force to final recommendations was:
   (1) 3 months   ☐
   (2) 6 months
   (3) 9 months
   (4) 12 months
   (5) more than 1 year
   (9) impossible to say

Administration Role

6. The case materials mention the district's superintendent left his or her post after the peak enrollment year.
   (1) yes   ☐
   (2) no
   (9) impossible to say

Professional Staff Role

7. The case materials mention the teachers went on strike.
   (1) yes, they went out on strike   ☐
   (2) no, they did not strike
   (9) impossible to say

Community Role

8. The case materials mention the community used the following opposition tactics to the closure decision (1 = yes, this was used; 2 = no, never used; 9 = impossible to say.)
   (1) letters to board members   ☐
   (2) petitions   ☐
   (3) alternative proposals to board   ☐
   (4) heated attacks at board meetings   ☐
   (5) demonstrations   ☐
   (6) voting down referenda/budgets   ☐
   (7) board member replacement   ☐
   (8) law suit   ☐

40

Advances in Statistical Methods
for Meta-Analysis

Larry V. Hedges

Recent advances in statistical methods for meta-analysis help reviewers to identify systematic variation in research results.

Meta-analysis makes use of statistical methods to describe the results of a number of research studies. Typically, the results of each study are summarized by an index of effect size. These indices can then be averaged to obtain an overall estimate of the magnitude of effects. Other statistical analyses can also be performed to study the variation of effect sizes across studies. Until recently, meta-analysis used such conventional statistical methods as multiple regression analysis and analysis of variance to analyze effect size data. Such use seemed at first to be an innocuous extension of statistical methods to a new situation. However, recent research has demonstrated that the use of such statistical procedures as analysis of variance and regression analysis cannot be justified for meta-analysis. Fortunately, some new statistical procedures have been designed specifically for meta-analysis. These new procedures exploit the properties of effect sizes to provide analyses that avoid the difficulties created for meta-analysis by conventional statistical procedures.

This chapter introduces some of the new statistical procedures that were recently developed for the analysis of effect size data. The first section analyzes the goals of statistical procedures for research synthesis. The next section shows that conventional statistical methods cannot accomplish some of

From Larry V. Hedges, "Advances in Statistical Methods for Meta-Analysis," pp. 25-42 in W. H. Yeaton, P. M. Wortman (Eds.), *Issues in Data Synthesis*. New Directions for Program Evaluation, No. 24. Copyright 1984, Jossey-Bass. Reprinted by permission.

these goals. The third section examines the basic statistical sampling properties of effect sizes, and develops some analogues to analysis of variance and multiple regression analysis for effect sizes. The fourth section discusses the importance of tests for the consistency of effect sizes in interpreting the results of meta-analysis. The fifth section discusses some of the problems in obtaining well-specified models for meta-analysis. Finally, an appendix provides detail on some statistical computations.

Goals of Statistical Procedures in Research Synthesis

Before addressing any specific statistical procedures for the quantitative synthesis of research, it will be useful to consider what can be expected of statistical analysis in the best possible situation. Perhaps the simplest situation for the synthesis of research results is one in which the raw data from several experiments can be pooled directly. For example, suppose that we have a series of k two-group experiments, each of which uses an experimental–control group design to investigate the effects of a given treatment. Let us assume that each study uses the same instrument and the same sampling plan to measure the normally distributed outcome variable, so that the within-group population variances of the outcome scores are identical. We can even arbitrarily set the common within-group variances to one, although it is not necessary to do so.

The situation just defined is one in which the raw data from all the individuals in all the studies are directly comparable. Consequently, the outcome scores of all the individuals can be combined and analyzed in one large statistical analysis. In this situation, most social scientists know how to proceed. Most investigators would use the data from all individuals in one large $2 \times k$ (two treatments $\times k$ studies) analysis of variance. In the idealized case just described, the assumptions of analysis of variance will be exactly met.

What will the investigator learn from the analysis of variance? There are three omnibus F tests in the textbook analysis. The F test for the main effect of studies is relatively uninteresting. It tests whether the value of the outcome variable averaged over both experimental and control groups differs across studies. The other two F tests are more interesting. The F test for the treatment factor tests whether the treatment group outperforms the control group on the average across all k experiments. The F test for the treatment-by-studies interaction tests whether the treatment effect is consistent across studies. The interpretation of the statistical analysis rests largely on the second and third tests. A large treatment effect with a negligible interaction is easy to interpret: The treatment produces a large consistent effect across studies. If the interaction is not negligible, then interpretation becomes more complicated, because interaction suggests that the treatment effect is larger in some studies than it is in others. Thus, any statements about the main effect must be qualified by the fact that treatment effects vary significantly across studies.

If a significant interaction is found, most investigators will probably begin to look for reasons why the treatment effect varies across studies. Variations in treatment, experimental procedure, conditions of measurement, or sample composition can all figure in explanations of variations in treatment effect. If a suitable explanatory variable can be found, it can be entered into the statistical analysis as a blocking factor. By an appropriate F test, further analysis could then reveal whether the new factor accounted for a significant amount of variation in the treatment effects and whether variations in the treatment effect remained substantial across studies within levels of the new factor. That is, we can test whether a proposed explanatory factor succeeds in "explaining" — that is, in removing — the variations in treatment effect across studies. This test is conceptually analogous to the original test for the treatment-by-studies interaction.

Thus, in the best possible case, where data from all studies can be combined directly, statistical analysis has four features: First, the average treatment effect can be estimated and tested across all studies. Second, the consistency of treatment effects can also be tested via the treatment-by-studies interaction. Third, if explanatory variables corresponding to differences among studies are used to explain variations in treatment effect, the effect of those explanatory variables can be tested. Fourth, the significance of variation in treatment effects across levels of the explanatory variables can be tested to determine whether all variations in treatment effect have been explained.

In evaluating statistical methods for research synthesis, it is useful to ask which features of the best-case analysis just described are available for the analysis that is proposed. Statistical methods now exist that provide all the advantages of best-case analysis for any meta-analysis. These methods allow the meta-analyst to answer essentially the same questions that he or she would ask if it were possible to combine the raw data from all the studies directly. Conventional statistical procedures fail to answer one or more of the questions of interest. Moreover, use of some conventional analyses for effect size data frequently involves serious violations of the assumptions of these techniques. Thus, use of conventional statistical procedures in meta-analysis is problematic for both statistical and conceptual reasons. Let us now turn to the specific problems of conventional statistical procedures in meta-analysis.

Conventional Analyses for Effect Size Data

The use of conventional analyses for research synthesis has been greatly influenced by the pioneering work of Glass (1976). He suggested combining the results of studies by first calculating an estimate of effect size g, which is the standardized difference between the experimental and control group means; that is,

$$g = (\bar{Y}_E - \bar{Y}_C)/S.$$

The estimates of effect size from different studies are standardized so that they exist in effect on the same scale. As a result, the meta-analyst can combine these estimates across studies or treat the effect sizes as raw data for analysis of variance or multiple linear regression that relate characteristics of studies to treatment effects (Glass and others, 1981).

Table 1 summarizes the results of six studies of the effects of open and traditional education on student cooperativeness (Hedges, 1982b). Conventional statistical analysis would calculate the average of the g values to obtain $\bar{g} = .168$. The investigator would probably conclude that the effect of open education on cooperativeness was not statistically significantly different from zero (the one-sample t test for $\bar{g}$ is $t(5) = .819$, $p > .25$). The investigator could also test for the existence of a relation between degree of treatment fidelity and effect size by using a t test or an analysis of variance to determine whether the average effect size for the studies where treatment fidelity was low differed from the average effect size of the studies where treatment fidelity was high. Conventional analysis of variance would show that the average effect sizes of the two groups did not differ significantly: $F(1,4) = 4.15$, $p > .10$. We shall see later that use of statistical procedures designed specifically for meta-analysis would cause all these conclusions to be modified.

Conceptual Problems with Conventional Analyses. Let us now compare the conventional analysis with the best-case analysis in which all the raw data can be directly combined. In our idealized best case, the treatment effect (mean difference) corresponds directly to the effect size for each study. In the conventional analysis, the effect sizes can be averaged to obtain an estimate of the average treatment effect. Similarly, the effect of any particular explanatory variable can be tested by using that variable as a blocking factor in an analysis of variance or as a predictor in a regression analysis in which the effect size is the dependent variable. Thus, the conventional effect size analysis has two features of the best-case analysis.

Table 1. Effect Sizes from Six Studies of the Effects of Open Education on Cooperativeness

Study	Treatment Fidelity	n^E	n^C	g	d	v	w	wd	wd^2
1	Low	30	30	.181	.179	.0669	14.940	2.669	.4768
2	Low	30	30	− .521	− .514	.0689	14.520	− 7.467	3.8396
3	Low	280	290	− .131	− .131	.0070	142.152	− 18.597	2.4330
4	High	6	11	.959	.910	.2819	3.547	3.228	2.9386
5	High	44	40	.097	.096	.0478	20.928	2.011	.1933
6	High	37	55	.425	.421	.0462	21.657	9.127	3.8467
				Totals			217.745	− 9.028	13.7282

Source: Hedges, 1982b.

At the same time, however, the conventional analysis lacks two important features of the best-case analysis. First, conventional analysis cannot test the consistency of effect sizes directly across studies. That is, there is no analogue in conventional effect size analysis to the test for treatment-by-study interactions. The conventional analysis for testing systematic variation among k effect sizes has $(k - 1)$ degrees of freedom for systematic variation among effect sizes and one degree of freedom for the grand mean. No degrees of freedom are left for estimation of error or nonsystematic variation. Consequently, it is impossible in the conventional framework to construct a test that can determine whether the systematic variation in k effect sizes is larger than the nonsystematic variation exhibited by those effect sizes.

It is possible in the conventional analysis to construct a test for differences among the average effect sizes of two or more groups of studies, as long as at least one of the groups contains two or more effect sizes. The multiple effect sizes within these groups serve as replicates from which an estimate of unsystematic variance can be obtained. The test itself is constructed by comparing systematic variance among group mean effect sizes with the unsystematic variance of effect sizes within groups. However, such a test is both conceptually and statistically perilous. How does the analyst know that the effect sizes vary nonsystematically within the groups? If the wrong groups are chosen, considerable systematic variance may be pooled into the estimate of error variance. This issue lay at the core of Presby's (1978) criticism of Smith and Glass's meta-analysis of psychotherapy outcome studies (1977). She argued that their analysis of differences among types of psychotherapy was flawed because the categories of therapy that they used were overly broad; they included considerable systematic variation. The effect of pooling systematic variation into estimates of error terms is well known to statisticians. It decreases the sensitivity of the statistical test for systematic variation. The conceptual problem that threatens the conventional analysis is that the analyst can never know how much of the variation among effect sizes is systematic.

Precisely the same problem plagues attempts to construct a test for the variation in effect sizes that remains after an explanatory variable has been applied. If the analyst tries to explain variation in effect sizes by grouping studies with similar characteristics or by using a linear predictor, he or she still has no way of assessing whether the remaining variation among effect sizes is systematic or random.

Statistical Problems with Conventional Analyses. Use of conventional statistical methods to analyze effect sizes or correlation coefficients is also problematic for purely statistical reasons. Conventional statistical procedures — t tests, analysis of variance, multiple regression analysis — rely on parametric assumptions about the data. All these procedures require the unsystematic variance associated with individual observations to be the same — the so-called homoscedasticity assumption. That is, if we think of each observation as composed of a systematic part and an error part, then the errors for all observations must be equally variable. In analysis of variance, we are accustomed to verifying that within-cell variances are reasonably similar in value for all cells in the design. In regression analysis, we can check this assumption by determining whether the residual variance about the regression line is reasonably constant for all values of the predictor variable.

In the case of estimates of effect magnitude (either correlation coefficients or effect sizes), the unsystematic variance of an observation can be calculated analytically. In fact, the unsystematic variance of estimates of effect size is proportional to $\frac{1}{n}$, where n is the sample size of the study on which the estimate is based. Thus, if studies have different sample sizes, which is usually the case, the effect size estimates will have different error variances. If the sample sizes of the studies subjected to meta-analysis vary widely, so will the error variances. In many meta-analyses, it is not unusual for the range of sample sizes to be on the order of fifty to one. In these cases, the error variances are substantially heterogeneous.

How can we deal with this problem? The effects of heterogeneity of variance on analysis of variance F tests have been studied extensively (for example, Glass and others, 1972). Heterogeneous variances have been shown to have very small effects on the validity of F tests in conventional analysis of variance. However, the situation in research synthesis is usually quite different. Studies of the effects of heterogeneity of variance in analysis of variance usually give a different variance to one or more groups in the design. Thus, every observation in the same group has the same variance, and there are at most two to three different variances in the entire experiment. In the case of research synthesis, the heterogeneity is usually more pronounced. Every observation — that is, every study — can have a different variance. Moreover, the range of variances studied in connection with the robustness of conventional F tests is usually rather limited, often less than five to one. The studies that have examined the effects of very wide ranges of variances have found that the F test is not necessarily robust to substantial heterogeneity of variance. For example, Glass and others (1972) note that when the ratio of variances is five to one and the sample sizes are unequal, then the actual significance level of an F test can be six times as large as the nominal significance level — .30 instead of .05.

Thus, the violation of the assumption of analysis of variance and regression analysis about homogeneity of variance is severe in research synthesis. Moreover, the particular nature of this violation has not been extensively studied. There is very little reason to believe that the usual robustness of the F test will somehow prevail. The statistical problem created by violation of the assumptions of conventional statistical procedures, combined with the potential problem of bias due to pooling of systematic variation in estimates of error variance, raises severe questions about the validity of conventional statistical procedures in meta-analysis. There does not appear to be any rigorously defensible argument for the use of conventional t tests, analysis of variance, or regression analysis to analyze effect sizes or correlations.

Modern Statistical Methods for Effect Sizes

Modern statistical methods for the analysis of effect sizes overcome both the conceptual and the statistical problems that plague conventional statistical analyses. The new methods are designed specifically for effect size data, but they can be calculated from standard packaged statistical programs, such as the Statistical Analysis System (SAS) or the Statistical Package for the Social Sciences (SPSS). In the remainder of this section, the basic properties of effect sizes on which these new methods are based are described, and the systematic and unsystematic components of sample effect sizes are distinguished. Properties of unsystematic sampling variation are used first to construct statistical tests for average effect size, then to develop an analogue to analysis of variance for effect sizes.

Properties of Effect Sizes. For meta-analysis, the effect size or standardized mean difference is the fundamental quantity in between-group studies. Let us begin by focusing on the effect size for a single study. Glass (1976) defined effect size as the difference between the experimental group mean and the control group mean, divided by the standard deviation of the control group:

$$g = (\overline{Y}E - \overline{Y}C)/S.$$

If there is no concrete reason to believe that the within-group variances differ, the standard deviation of the control group can be replaced by a pooled within-group standard deviation defined by

$$S^2 = [(n^E - 1)(S^E)^2 + (n^C - 1)(S^C)^2]/(n^E + n^C - 2)$$

The pooled standard deviation has desirable statistical properties such as small sampling error (Hedges, 1981), and when effect sizes must be derived from test statistics it is often the only standard deviation that is available.

The effect size estimate g can be decomposed into a systematic part, which reflects a true or population treatment effect, and an unsystematic part, which reflects sampling error of the individual scores used to calculate the effect size. The systematic part is called the *population effect size:*

(1) $$\delta = (\mu^E - \mu^C)/\sigma,$$

where μ^E and μ^C are the population means of scores in the experimental and the control group respectively, and σ is the population standard deviation within the groups of the study. I use the Greek letters δ, μ^E, μ^C, and σ to indicate that the population effect size δ is a population parameter defined by population parameters μE, μC, and σ of the observations in the study. The unsystematic part of the effect size estimate g is the sampling error $\epsilon = g - \delta$. Thus, the decomposition of g follows directly as

(2)
$$g = \delta + \epsilon$$

This decomposition is important, because it highlights an important feature of meta-analysis. That is, all systematic relationships in meta-analysis are relationships involving δ, the population effect size. The sampling error ϵ is nonsystematic by definition, and therefore it has no systematic relationship to anything. The estimate of effect size g is useful only because it provides information about δ. Thus, if the meta-analyst uses regression or analysis of variance to study the relationship between degree of treatment implementation and effect size, the systematic relationship is between degree of treatment implementation and population effect size. This fundamental decomposition of the sample estimate of effect size into systematic and unsystematic components is essential in statistical analysis for effect sizes.

The simplest statistical question in effect size analyses concerns the properties of g. Since g is of interest only because it provides information about δ, we need to ask whether g is a good estimator of δ. The answer is that g is a slightly biased estimator of δ that tends to overestimate δ for small samples. A simple correction gives an unbiased estimator of δ (Hedges, 1981). This unbiased estimator, d, is obtained by multiplying g by a constant that depends on the sample size in the study. That is,

(3)
$$d = c_n g = c_n(\overline{Y}E - \overline{Y}C)/S$$

where the values of c_n are given to a very good approximation by

(4)
$$c_n = 1 - \frac{3}{4nE + 4nC - 9}$$

Note that c_n is very close to one for all but very small values of nE and nC. Consequently, g is almost unbiased except in very small samples. However, the correction for bias is easy to apply, and the unbiased estimator has theoretical advantages. Consequently, there is little reason not to use the bias correction routinely. The remainder of this discussion uses the notation d for the estimator of effect size and assumes that the bias correction has been used. The correction for bias is analogous to the correction for the sample estimate of variance. The definition of the population variance has an n in the denominator. Using $n - 1$ in the denominator of the sample variance is equivalent to multiplying the population definition by the constant $\frac{n}{(n-1)}$ to obtain an unbiased estimate.

An understanding of the sampling properties of the estimator d of effect size is essential for the construction of statistical tests and estimation procedures for effect sizes. The sampling properties of d can be derived analytically for the case in which the assumptions of the t test are met by the observations in a study. That is, if the t or F test that the primary researcher has used is valid, then the properties of the sampling error ϵ of the effect size are completely determined. Hedges (1981) showed that d is approximately normally distributed with mean δ and variance

$$(5) \qquad v = \frac{nE + nC}{nEnC} + \frac{d^2}{2(nE + nC)}$$

Alternatively, we could say that $\epsilon = d - \delta$ is normally distributed with the mean zero and variance given in equation 5. If the experimental and control groups of a study are equal in size — that is, if $nE = nC = n$ — then the variance becomes

$$v = \frac{2}{n}\left(1 + \frac{d^2}{8}\right)$$

The variance of d is completely determined by the sample sizes and the value of d. Consequently, it is possible to determine the sampling variance of d from a single observation. The ability to determine the nonsystematic variance of d (the variance of ϵ) from a single observation of d is the key to modern statistical methods for meta-analysis. This relationship allows the meta-analyst to use all the degrees of freedom among different d values for estimating systematic effects while still providing a way of estimating the unsystematic variance needed to construct statistical tests.

Combining Estimates of Effect Sizes for a Set of Studies. One of the first statistical questions that arises is how to combine estimates of effect size. Suppose that a series of k studies with sample sizes $n_1^F, n_1^C, \ldots, n_k^F, n_k^C$ provides k independent effect size estimates (that is, effect size estimates based on independent samples) $d_1, \ldots, d_k$. One way of combining the estimates is simply to take the average $\bar{d}$. The most precise combination, however, is a weighted average that takes the variances $v_1, \ldots, v_k$ of $d_1, \ldots, d_k$ into account. This weighted average, denoted $d.$, is defined as follows:

$$(6) \qquad d. = \sum_{i=1}^{k} w_i d_i / \sum_{i=1}^{k} w_i$$

where

$$(7) \qquad w_i = 1/v_i = \frac{2(n_i^F + n_i^C)n_i^F n_i^C}{2(n_i^F + n_i^C)^2 + n_i^F n_i^C d_i^2}$$

If all k studies share a common population effect size δ, the weighted mean $d.$ is approximately normally distributed with a mean of δ and a variance of

$$(8) \qquad v. = 1/\sum_{i=1}^{k} w_i$$

Consequently, if it is reasonable to believe that a set of studies shares a common effect size δ, then a $100(1 - \alpha)$ percent confidence interval for δ is given by

$$d. - z_\alpha\sqrt{v.} < \delta < d. + z_\alpha\sqrt{v.}$$

where z_α is the 100α percent two-tailed critical value of the standard normal distribution. If the confidence interval does not include zero or, alternatively, if

$$|d. / \sqrt{v.}| > z_\alpha$$

then the hypothesis that $\delta = 0$ is rejected at significance level α.

In our example, the effect size estimates from $k = 6$ studies are given in Table 1. The variances v_i, the weights w_i, and $w_i d_i$ are also given for each study. Thus, $d.$ is calculated from the totals (sums) or w_i and $w_i d_i$ values as $d. = .041 = -9.028/217.745$. The variance $v.$ of $d.$ is calculated from the total of the w_i values as $v. = 1/217.745 = .004592$. To test that the average effect size is zero, compute $|d./\sqrt{v.}| = .41/.06776 = .605$, which is not significant.

Testing Homogeneity of Effect Size. Combining estimates of effect size across studies is reasonable if the studies have a common population effect size δ. In this case, the estimates of effect size differ only by unsystematic sampling error. However, if the studies do not share a common underlying effect size, it can be misleading to combine estimates of effect size across studies. For example, if half of the studies had a large positive population effect size and half of the studies had a negative population effect size of equal magnitude, then the average — zero — is not representative of the effect size in any of the studies. The obvious question at this point is, How do we determine whether population effect sizes are relatively constant across studies? That is, how do we test for treatment-by-study interactions?

A test for homogeneity of effect size has been given by Hedges (1982a) and independently by Rosenthal and Rubin (1982). The test involves computing

(9)
$$H_T = \sum_{i=1}^{k} w_i(d_i - d.)^2$$

where $w_i = 1/v_i$ is the weight given in equation 7 and $d.$ is the weighted mean given by equation 6. The H_T statistic is simply the weighted sum of squares of the estimates $d_1, \ldots, d_k$ of effect size about the weighted mean $d.$. If all studies share a common effect size δ, then the statistic H_T has approximately a chi square distribution with $(k-1)$ degrees of freedom. Thus, the test for treatment-by-study interaction rejects homogeneity of effect size at significance level α if H exceeds the $100(1 - \alpha)$ percent critical value of the chi square distribution with $(k-1)$ degrees of freedom.

Returning to our example, we can compute H_T to test whether the six studies summarized in Table 1 have homogeneous effect sizes. Using the totals (sums) of w_i, $w_i d_i^2$ from Table 1 and equation 12 from the appendix to this chapter, we compute H_T as $H_T = 13.728 - (-9.028)^2/217.745 = 13.384$. Because H_T exceeds 11.1 — the 95 percent critical value of the chi square distribution with five degrees of freedom — we can reject the hypothesis that the six studies share a common underlying effect size. Thus, there is systematic variation among these effect sizes that needs to be explained, and any attempt to summarize these studies by a single average effect size is likely to be misleading.

An Analogue to Analysis of Variance for Effect Sizes. When effect sizes are not homogeneous across studies — that is, when treatment-by-study interactions are present — the meta-analyst may want to explain variations in effect sizes by variations in characteristics of studies. One way of proceeding is to group studies that share characteristics that can influence effect size. Thus, the meta-analyst would seek to create groupings in which the variability of effect sizes was small. If the raw data from all studies could be combined directly, the grouping factor could be introduced into an analysis of variance, and an F test could be used to test the significance of between-group variation.

A statistical procedure that permits the same kind of analysis for effect sizes was introduced by Hedges (1982b). This analogue to analysis of variance for effect sizes permits the meta-analyst to test the significance of variations between groups of effect sizes. It also permits the investigator to test whether the remaining variation within groups of effect sizes is significant. Thus, it permits the meta-analyst to determine whether the explanatory grouping variable adequately explains the treatment-by-study interaction.

The analysis of variance for effect sizes involves a partitioning of the overall homogeneity statistic H_T given in equation 9 into two independent homogeneity statistics: H_B, reflecting between-group homogeneity, and H_W, reflecting within-group homogeneity. These homogeneity statistics are related by the algebraic identity $H_T = H_B + H_W$, which is analogous to the partitioning of sums of squares in analysis of variance.

The between-group homogeneity statistic H_B is a weighted sum of squares of weighted group mean effect size estimates about the overall weighted mean effect size. That is,

(10) $$H_B = \Sigma w_{j.}(d_{j.} - d_{..})^2$$

where $d_{..}$ is the overall weighted mean across all studies ignoring groupings, $d_{j.}$ is the weighted mean of effect size estimates in the jth group, and $w_{j.} = 1/v_{j.}$ is the reciprocal of the variance of $d_{j.}$. Here, the weighted means and their variances are calculated using equation 6 and equation 8. The between-group homogeneity statistic H_B is analogous to the F statistic used for testing between-group differences in the conventional analysis of variance.

When there are p groups, the statistic H_B has approximately a chi square distribution with $(p - 1)$ degrees of freedom when there is no variation between group mean effect sizes. Thus, the test for variation in effect sizes between groups compares H_B with the $100(1 - \alpha)$ percent critical value of the chi square distribution with $(p - 1)$ degrees of freedom. If H_B exceeds the critical value, the variation between group mean effect sizes is significant at level α.

The within-group homogeneity statistic is the sum of the homogeneity statistics (equation 9) calculated for each of the p groups separately. That is,

$$(11) \qquad H_W = H_{W1} + \ldots + H_{Wp}$$

where $H_{W1}, \ldots, H_{Wp}$ are the homogeneity statistics (equation 9) calculated as if each group were an entire collection of studies. Whenever a group contains more than one study, the within-group homogeneity statistic for the group can be used to test the homogeneity of effect sizes within that group. If there is only one effect size estimate in a group, then $H_{Wi} = 0$ for that group. The total H_W provides an overall test of homogeneity of effect size within the groups of studies.

If a total of k studies is divided into $p < k$ groups, then H_W has a chi square distribution with $(k - p)$ degrees of freedom when the effect sizes are homogeneous within groups. The test for homogeneity of effect size within groups at significance level α consists of comparing H_W with the $100(1 - \alpha)$ percent critical value of the chi square distribution with $(k - p)$ degrees of freedom. The homogeneity of effect sizes within groups is rejected if H_W exceeds the critical value.

Let us suppose that the meta-analyst "explains" the variations in effect sizes by finding that effect sizes are reasonably homogeneous within groups but that they differ between groups. If there are only two groups of studies, then a significant H_B statistic indicates that there is a significant difference between their population effect sizes. If there are more than two groups, then the meta-analyst may want to use comparisons or contrasts analogous to those in analysis of variance to explore the differences among effect sizes for the different groups. Procedures for testing comparisons among the effect sizes of different groups follow from the properties of $d_.$; they have been discussed by Hedges (1982b).

For the six studies summarized in Table 1, we calculated H_T and found that they did not share a single common effect size. If we now subdivide the studies into two groups — one with low treatment fidelity (studies one through three) and one with high treatment fidelity (studies four through six) — we calculate the within-class fit statistics $H_{W1} = 3.560$ for studies where treatment fidelity is low and $H_{W2} = 2.504$ for studies where treatment fidelity is high. Hence, the total within-class fit statistic is $H_W = H_{W1} + H_{W2} = 3.560 + 2.504 = 6.064$, which is much less than 9.49, the 95 percent critical value of the chi square distribution with four degrees of freedom. Hence, the effect sizes within the two groups are homogeneous. Calculating H_B, we obtain $H_B = H_T - H_W = 13.394 - 6.064 = 7.320$. Comparing 7.320 with 3.84, the 95 percent critical value of the chi square distribution with one degree of freedom, we see that the difference between the effect sizes in the two groups is statistically significant. The weighted average effect size for the low fidelity studies is $d_1. = -.136$, which is not statistically significant at the $\alpha = .05$ level. The weighted average effect size for the high fidelity studies is $d_2. = .311$, which is statistically significant at the $\alpha = .05$ level.

It is instructive to compare the results of the analysis described here with the results of conventional analysis. Conventional analysis found a small and nonsignificant average effect size for all studies. Conventional analysis also suggested that the effect sizes of studies where treatment fidelity was low did not differ from those of studies where treatment fidelity was high. Thus, conventional analysis concluded that the overall effect was small and that treatment fidelity had no effect on the results of the individual studies.

Analysis with the new methods described in this chapter reached different conclusions. First, the test of overall homogeneity of effect size showed that the studies did not produce consistent results. This suggested that no single estimate was adequate to describe the results of all six studies. The analysis of variance for effect sizes showed that the two groups of studies produced significantly different average effect sizes. Moreover, the analysis showed that the effect sizes were homogeneous within the two groups. Thus, the results of the analysis of variance for effect sizes suggest that there is a consistent but negligible effect among the studies with low treatment fidelity and a consistent, statistically significant positive effect among the studies with high treatment fidelity.

An Analogue to Multiple Regression Analysis for Effect Sizes. In many research reviews, it is desirable to investigate the relationship between variations in one or more quantitative explanatory variables and variations in effect size. For example, Smith and Glass (1977) used conventional multiple regression analysis in their meta-analysis of psychotherapy outcome studies to determine the relationship between several coded characteristics of studies, such as type of therapy, duration of therapy, and internal validity, and effect size. The same authors have used this method in other meta-analyses (Glass and Smith, 1979; Smith and Glass, 1980). Conventional multiple regression analysis cannot be used with effect sizes, but an analogue can. This analogue, which uses a weighted regression procedure, provides a way of estimating and testing the relationship between several predictor variables and effect size. It also provides a way of testing whether the regression model is adequately specified, that is, whether significant systematic variation in effect sizes remains unexplained by the data analysis model. A complete set of formulas, derivations, and computational procedures has been given by Hedges (1982c), but the computational procedure itself can be explained quite easily without recourse to complicated formulas.

Suppose that we have k independent effect size estimates $d_1, \ldots, d_k$ and p predictor variables $X_1, \ldots, X_p$ that we believe to be related to effect sizes. Under the data analysis model described here, the systematic part of the effect sizes (the population effect sizes) $\delta_1, \ldots, \delta_k$ is determined as a linear function of the values of the predictor variables $X_1, \ldots, X_p$. That is,

$$\delta_i = \beta_0 + \beta_1 x_{ip} + \ldots + \beta_p x_{ip},$$

where $\beta_0, \beta_1, \ldots, \beta_p$ are unknown regression coefficients, and x_{ij} is the value of the jth predictor variable for the ith study. One object of statistical analysis is to use the observed estimates of effect size $d_1, \ldots, d_k$ and the values of the predictor variables to estimate the relationship between $X_1, \ldots, X_p$ and the effect sizes, that is, to estimate the unknown regression coefficients. Another object of this analysis is to test whether the regression model is correctly specified, that is, whether significant systematic variation remains unexplained by the regression model.

The easiest way to compute the estimates of regression coefficients and the test for model misspecification is to use a packaged computer program, such as the Statistical Analysis System Procedure General Linear Model (SAS Proc GLM), that can perform weighted regression analyses. It can be proved that the best estimate of regression coefficients can be obtained by using a weighted multiple regression of effect size estimates on the predictor variables, weighting each effect size by $w_i = 1/v_i$ given in equation 7. This is accomplished by creating a variable W whose value for each effect size equals the reciprocal of the variance of that effect size. The multiple regression is then run in the usual way, except that the variable W is specified as the weighting variable.

The output of the weighted regression analysis gives the estimates $\hat{\beta}_0$, $\hat{\beta}_1, \ldots, \hat{\beta}_p$ of the regression coefficients directly. The standard errors and the t or F tests printed by the packaged computer program are incorrect, and they should be ignored. The correct standard errors for $\hat{\beta}_0, \ldots, \hat{\beta}_p$ are given by the square roots of the diagonal elements of the $X'WX$ inverse matrix printed by the weighted regression program. The correct test for the significance of β_j uses the fact that

$$z_j = \hat{\beta}_j / \sqrt{S_{jj}}$$

is approximately a standard normal variable if $\beta_j = 0$, where S_{jj} is the correct standard error of β_j (the jth diagonal element of the $X'WX$ inverse matrix). Consequently, if $|z_j|$ exceeds the 100α percent critical value of the standard normal distribution, the hypothesis that $\beta_\sigma = 0$ is rejected at the significance level α.

If the number k of studies exceeds $(p + 1)$, the number of predictors plus the intercept, then a test for model specification is possible. The test uses the weighted sum of squares H_E about the regression line. Computer printouts sometimes term this statistic the *residual* or *error sum of squares*. When the population effect sizes are completely determined by the predictor variables — that is, when the regression model is correctly specified — then the statistic H_E has a chi square distribution with $(k - p - 1)$ degrees of freedom. Thus, the test for model specification at significance level α compares the error sum of squares H_E to the $100(1 - \alpha)$ percent critical value of the chi square distribution with $(k - p - 1)$ degrees of freedom. The model specification is rejected if H_E exceeds the critical value. Thus, the test for model specification is a test for greater than expected residual variation.

The Importance of Tests for Homogeneity and Model Specification

Some critics have argued that meta-analysis can lead to oversimplified conclusions about the effects of treatment because it condenses the results of a set of studies into a few parameter estimates. For example, Presby (1978) argued that even when studies were grouped according to variations in treatment, reviewers could reasonably disagree on the appropriate groupings. Grouping studies into overly broad categories and calculating a mean effect size for each category could wash out real variations among treatments within the categories. As a result, variations in treatment would appear to be unrelated, because the mean effect sizes for the categories did not differ. One obvious extension of this argument is that reviewers can reasonably disagree on explanatory variables that can be related to effect sizes. Hence, the failure of conventional analyses to find variables that are systematically related to effect size does not imply that the effect sizes are consistent across studies, since it can also imply that the reviewer has examined the wrong explanatory variables.

A related criticism is that the artifacts of a multitude of design flaws can cause the studies within a given set to give fundamentally different answers, that is, to have different population effect sizes (Eysenck, 1978). Any analysis of the effect sizes is therefore an analysis of estimates that are influenced by factors other than the true magnitude of the effect of treatment. The argument underlying this criticism is that flaws in the design or execution of studies can influence effect sizes.

Both criticisms imply the existence of treatment-by-study interactions—interactions that make the average or main effect of treatment difficult to interpret. The failure of conventional analysis to provide general tests for treatment-by-study interactions makes it vulnerable to such criticisms as those of Eysenck (1978) and Presby (1978). Statistical tests of the homogeneity of within-group effect size and tests for misspecification of multiple regression models can provide answers to such criticisms. More significantly, such tests provide the meta-analyst with concrete guidelines that he or she can use to judge whether the data have been adequately explained. In the simplest case, the meta-analyst summarizes the results of a set of studies by the average effect size estimate. Does this oversimplify the results of the individual studies? The test of homogeneity of effect size provides a method of testing empirically whether the variation in effect size estimates exceeds the variation that could be expected from chance alone. If the hypothesis of homogeneity is not rejected, the meta-analyst is in a strong position to reject the argument that the real variability of the studies in question has been obscured by coarse grouping. If the model of a single population effect size fits the data adequately, then the criterion of parsimony suggests that this model should be considered seriously.

Failure to reject the homogeneity of effect sizes for a set of studies does not necessarily disarm the criticism that the results of the studies are artifacts of design flaws. For example, if the studies in a set all share the same flaw, consistent results across the studies may be an artifact of that one flaw. That is, the same design flaw in all the studies may act to make the effect sizes in the studies consistently wrong as an estimate of the treatment effect. However, the studies may not all have the same flaws. If different studies with different design flaws all yield consistent results, it may be implausible to explain the consistency of their results as the result of consistent bias. Thus, the meta-analyst who finds consistency in research results and who knows the limitations of the individual studies is in a strong position to reject the argument that results are only as good as the data. It should be emphasized that careful examination of the individual research studies and some scrutiny of the attendant design problems are essential. Without such examination and such scrutiny, a single source of bias is a very real and plausible rival explanation for empirical consistency in research results.

When the meta-analyst uses a model relying on explanatory variables (for example, effect size varies with grade level) to explain the effect sizes for a whole set of studies, tests of model specification play a role analogous to that of the test of homogeneity. It is difficult to argue that additional variables are needed to explain the variation in effect sizes if the specification test suggests that additional variables are not needed.

Evidence that the model is correctly specified does not necessarily mean that the artifacts of design flaws can be ignored. If all studies share a common design flaw, then the results of all the studies may be biased to an unknown extent. If design flaws correlate with explanatory variables, then the effects of the design flaws are confounded with the effects of the explanatory variables. It may be difficult or impossible to determine the real source of the effect. However, if several design flaws are uncorrelated with the explanatory variables and if simple models appear to be specified correctly, then it does not seem plausible that inferences about effect sizes are artifacts of bias created by design flaws.

Problems in Obtaining Well-Specified Models

It may seem unlikely that the messy data generally obtained by social science research would be amenable to serious modeling of the type described in this chapter. Cynics may believe that model specification will always be rejected. However, my own experience in reanalyzing several meta-analyses suggests that the data from research studies in education and psychology are often consistent with relatively simple models.

Nevertheless, it is rare that an entire collection of effect sizes is homogeneous. Effect sizes calculated on different metrics—for example, raw posttest scores and analysis of covariance–adjusted posttest scores—are rarely consistent with one another. Variations in experimental procedure must sometimes be used as explanatory variables. Even when all studies measure a common dependent variable, such as conformity, different measurement procedures can cause effect size to vary. Perhaps the most significant explanatory variable is the degree of preexisting difference between the experimental and the control groups. Well-controlled studies—for example, those with small pretest differences or those using random assignment—often provide effect sizes that are homogeneous or that conform to simple models. Poorly controlled studies rarely conform to simple models. Even when the average effect size for well-controlled studies agrees with that of poorly controlled studies, effect sizes for the poorly controlled studies often exhibit much greater variability.

Appendix: Computing H_T, H_B, and H_W

Although equation 9 helps to illustrate the intuitive nature of the H_T statistic, a computational formula is more useful in computing actual H_T values. It can be shown that equation 9 is algebraically equivalent to the computational formula

(12) $$H_T = \sum_{i=1}^{k} w_i d_i^2 - (\sum_{i=1}^{k} w_i d_i)^2 / (\sum_{i=1}^{k} w_i)$$

The advantage of equation 12 is that H_T can be computed from the sums across studies of three variables: w_i, $w_i d_i$, and $w_i d_i^2$. The weighted mean $d.$ and its variance $v.$ can also be computed from sums of w_i and $w_i d_i$. Consequently, any packaged computer program that computes sums or means can be used to obtain the components of H_T, $d.$, and $v.$ in a single run.

The easiest way of computing the statistics needed for the analysis of variance of effect sizes is to compute three additional variables for each study: w_i, given in equation 7, $w_i d_i$, and $w_i d_i^2$. The sums of these three variables across all studies can be used with equation 12 to compute H_T. Obtaining the sums of w_i, $w_i d_i$, and $w_i d_i^2$ for each group of studies separately permits H_{W_i} to be computed for each group. Then, H_W is calculated as $H_X = H_{W1} + \ldots + H_{Wp}$. It is easiest to compute H_B as $H_B = H_T - H_W$. Note that the sums of w_i and $w_i d_i$ for each group of studies also permit the weighted mean effect size d_i and its variance v_i to be computed.

References

Eysenck, H. J. "An Exercise in Mega-Silliness." *American Psychologist*, 1978, *33*, 517.
Glass, G. V. "Primary, Secondary, and Meta-Analysis of Research." *Educational Researcher*, 1976, *5*, 3-8.
Glass, G. V., McGaw, B., and Smith, M. L. *Meta-Analysis in Social Research.* Beverly Hills, Calif.: Sage, 1981.

Glass, G. V., Peckham, P. D., and Sanders, J. R. "Consequences of Failure to Meet Assumptions Underlying the Fixed Effects Analyses of Variance and Covariance." *Review of Educational Research*, 1972, *42*, 237–288.

Glass, G. V., and Smith, M. L. "Meta-Analysis of Research on the Relationship of Class Size and Achievement." *Educational Evaluation and Policy Analysis*, 1979, *1*, 2–16.

Hedges, L. V. "Distribution Theory for Glass's Estimator of Effect Size and Related Estimators." *Journal of Educational Statistics*, 1981, *6*, 107–128.

Hedges, L. V. "Estimation of Effect Size from a Series of Independent Experiments." *Psychological Bulletin*, 1982a, *92*, 490–499.

Hedges, L. V. "Fitting Categorical Models to Effect Sizes from a Series of Experiments." *Journal of Educational Statistics*, 1982b, *7*, 119–137.

Hedges, L. V. "Fitting Continuous Models to Effect Size Data." *Journal of Educational Statistics*, 1982c, *7*, 245–270.

Presby, S. "Overly Broad Categories Obscure Important Differences Between Therapies." *American Psychologist*, 1978, *33*, 514–515.

Rosenthal, R., and Rubin, D. B. "Comparing Effect Sizes of Independent Studies." *Psychological Bulletin*, 1982, *92*, 500–504.

Smith, M. L., and Glass, G. V. "Meta-Analysis of Psychotherapy Outcome Studies." *American Psychologist*, 1977, *32*, 752–760.

Smith, M. L., and Glass, G. V. "Meta-Analysis of Class Size and Its Relationship to Attitudes and Instruction." *American Educational Research Journal*, 1980, *17*, 419–433.

Larry V. Hedges is assistant professor of education at the University of Chicago. His current research interests include statistical methods in educational research and evaluation and methodology for the quantitative synthesis of research.

41

Analyzing Meta-Analysis
Potential Problems, an Unsuccessful Replication, and Evaluation Criteria

R. J. Bullock and Daniel J. Svyantek

This article identifies some potential problems in meta-analysis research and suggests 14 specific criteria for evaluating the quality of meta-analysis research. The analysis is based on a review and replication of a meta-analysis research study. Our replication of the Terpstra (1981) study on methodological rigor in OD research found no evidence of positive-findings bias in OD. Our review of that research study identified a series of methodological problems that are applicable to other meta-analysis studies. These general problems are discussed, and some solutions are offered.

Meta-analysis is a relatively new and increasingly important research approach to accumulating knowledge in the social sciences (Glass, McGaw, & Smith, 1981; Hunter, Schmidt, & Jackson, 1982). As a methodologically rigorous technique for integrating findings across studies, it has been useful in such diverse fields as education (Hedges, 1982; Johnson, Johnson, & Maruyama, 1983; Kulik & Kulik, 1982), psychotherapy (see the special section of *Journal of Consulting and Clinical Psychology,* February 1983), personnel selection and validity generalization (Callender & Osburn, 1980; Osburn, Callender, Greener, & Ashworth, 1983; Schmidt & Hunter, 1977), leadership (Strube & Garcia, 1981), role conflict and role ambiguity (Fisher & Gitelson, 1983), and organization development (Bullock & Tubbs, 1983). Because of the newness and widespread applicability of meta-analysis, it is critical at this early stage to identify and resolve problems and discrepancies arising in meta-analysis research (see Green and Hall, 1984).

This article attempts to provide such an interim assessment of meta-analysis. Potential problems in meta-analysis are identified, and recommendations for solutions are suggested. To show the background for these problems,

to underscore their importance, and to illustrate the issues, we use an extended example of a previous meta-analysis study. The research example used is the study on positive-findings bias in OD research reported by Terpstra (1981) and discussed by Bass (1983). Although the Terpstra study did not use the label "meta-analysis," the study was an example of meta-analysis in that it quantitatively pooled results across studies and statistically analyzed how study characteristics affected results. The review and replication of this study provides an excellent opportunity to closely examine potential problems and solutions in the meta-analysis style of research and to use the results of this analysis to further our understanding of potential bias in OD research.

Because a detailed inspection of this example is important for understanding the issues in meta-analysis, the first part of this paper reviews the Terpstra (1981) study and the Bass (1983) discussion, then replicates the meta-analysis. The second part presents potential problems and suggested solutions. The final section uses these resolutions as specific criteria for evaluating the quality of meta-analysis studies.

Review and Replication

Terpstra (1981)

Terpstra (1981) reported an inverse relationship between methodological rigor and reported outcomes of OD research. The *Jour-*

The authors are very grateful to Bob Pritchard, Allan Jones, Patti Bullock, and the journal reviewers for their suggestions on earlier drafts.

Requests for reprints should be sent to R. J. Bullock, Department of Psychology, University of Houston, Houston, Texas 77004.

nal of Applied Behavioral Science (*JABS*) was examined by Terpstra (1981) for the years 1965–1980. Fifty-two articles that (a) reported applications of four major OD techniques (laboratory training, survey feedback, team-building, and process consultation) and (b) analyzed and reported quantitative data were examined. Each study was assigned a rigor score on six dimensions (sampling strategy, sample size, control group utilization, random assignment, measurement strategy, and significance level used) using a 0-1 coding scheme (see Terpstra, 1981, for details). Interrater agreement was reported as 1.0 for all six dimensions. The total methodological rigor score (MRS) each study received was the sum of these six methodology dimensions (0 = *least rigorous*, 6 = *most rigorous*). The 52 studies were also classified on a seventh variable, success outcome, using a 3-point scale (*uniformly positive results, mixed or nonsignificant results,* or *uniformly negative results*). Interrater agreement was 1.0 on this variable as well. The mean MRS was found to be significantly different for the three outcome groups. Studies reporting uniformly negative results had higher MRSs than did those reporting mixed results. Studies reporting uniformly positive results were found to have lower MRSs than the other two groups. This finding was interpreted as evidence of positive findings bias in OD research.

Bass (1983)

Bass (1983) discussed this finding and proposed that the positive findings bias for OD research found by Terpstra might be explained by the philosophical background of the OD researchers, divided into two camps, the "softies" and "hardheads." According to Bass, the "hardheads" are convinced that rigorous methodological standards are the *sine qua non* of applied evaluation efforts. The "softies," on the other hand, are more liable to accept less rigorous evaluation efforts and use the data from such efforts as strong support of a philosophical (e.g., a humanistic orientation) position. Both camps, however, are seen as liable to response bias in their selection of data to support their explicit (or implicit) philosophical positions. Bass's (1983) discussion is based on the premise that Terpstra's

(1981) reporting of positive findings bias in OD research is a valid contention. The next section of the article presents our replication of the Terpstra (1981) study (see Bullock and Svyantek, 1983).

Method

Sample

The list of 52 studies used in the original study was not available, so the present authors used the criteria reported by Terpstra (1981) to select studies for inclusion. In all, 90 articles were found and used in the present analysis.

Measures

To insure maximum comparability between the current replication and the original study, we used the same measures and analyses published in the original study. The total study period of 1965–1980 was divided into halves in order to develop reliability estimates and resolve preliminary coding problems. Using the published coding scheme, the authors independently scored the first half period, or the years 1965–1972. This period yielded 56 different articles, slightly more than the total sample of the original study.

Interrater Reliability

We found the coding scheme to be ambiguous in many respects and used our best independent judgments in applying the scheme. Several alternatives are available for estimating interrater reliability of these judgments. Recent literature suggests that many of these statistics, such as Cohen's (1968) kappa, are misleading when the results are skewed, a common occurrence with 0-1 coding schemes (Burton, 1981; Green, 1981; Jones, Johnson, Butler, & Main, 1983; Uebersax, 1982). Percentage of agreement has thus been suggested as the most accurate statistic for use in such situations (Burton, 1981; Jones et al., 1983). This procedure was used to assess interrater reliability between the two raters in the study.

Results, shown in Table 1, indicate interrater reliability for the coding of the 90 studies on the six methodological dimensions and outcome variable. Interrater reliability was generally lower for the first half of the data set ($N = 56$). This half of the data set was coded independently by the two raters. We attempted to improve interrater reliability for the coding scheme by developing more explicit decision rules for the same coding scheme. We discussed each instance of rater disagreement and reanalyzed the 56 articles. Where the coding was ambiguous, we resolved the discrepancies by a consensus decision rule based on our best judgment of how the coding scheme should be applied in such a situation. These more explicit decision rules for the coding scheme were then applied to the 34 studies in the second half of the time period (1973–1980). Interrater reliability for the second half is also shown in Table 1. This strategy improved the percentage of agreement for all variables, with the exception of sampling strategy, where we contin-

Table 1

Interrater Agreement for All Variables in Current Study

Variable	First half (1965–1972)[a]	Second half (1973–1980)[b]	Total sample
Sampling strategy	76.8	64.7	72.2
Sample size	69.6	94.1	78.9
Control group	76.8	94.1	83.3
Random assignment	85.7	94.1	88.9
Pretest–posttest	80.4	88.2	83.3
Significance level	69.6	85.3	76.7
Success outcomes	75.0	94.1	82.2

Note. All figures are percentages.
[a] Using Terpstra's published coding scheme.
[b] Using Terpstra's published coding scheme with more explicit decision rules.

ued to find cases where the coding scheme was ambiguous. In all cases, we resolved the discrepancies between raters by reanalyzing each article and used the consensus judgment in the data analysis below. Decision rule documentation and the sample of studies are available from the first author.

Results

As in the Terpstra (1981) study, we used analysis of variance (ANOVA) between the three success outcome groups for the mean methodological rigor score. Assuming an eta of .27 as found in the Terpstra study, the power of the Terpstra (1981) study was .40 and the power of the current study is .65; the ANOVA reported here had greater power than the Terpstra study because of the larger sample. The probability of a Type II error (beta) was .6 and .35 for the Terpstra study and the current study, respectively. There was no significant difference, $F(2, 87) = 0.217$, $p = .805$, in the mean methodological score among the three outcome groups. There was no evidence in the current study that more rigorous evaluation studies found more positive findings. Thus, the positive-findings bias reported by Terpstra was not found in this replication.

The pattern reported by Terpstra (1981) for the relationship between MRS and OD outcome score was not found. Terpstra (1981) reported that, as the degree of rigor increased,

the outcome score decreased. In the current study, there was little difference between the mean MRS for uniformly positive ($M = 3.17$) and mixed outcome ($M = 3.26$) scores. The only uniformly negative study located by the current investigation had a MRS score of 4.0.

To further analyze the relationship between methodological rigor and outcome scores, a 7×7 correlation matrix of the six methodological variables and the outcome variable was calculated. The only significant correlation between a methodological rigor variable and outcome was for random assignment ($r = -.18$, $p = .04$). Significant but modest correlations between rigor variables were found between sample size and control groups ($r = .18$, $p = .045$), between random assignment and control groups ($r = .20$, $p = .03$), and between significance level and control groups ($r = .21$, $p = .02$).

Discussion

The present study failed to support Terpstra's (1981) conclusion that a positive findings bias exists in OD research. There are several differences between this study and the Terpstra (1981) study.

One discrepancy is the sample size. The present study was based on 90 studies fitting the published criteria, whereas the original study included only 52. The list of studies for the previous study is not available, so we were unable to reconcile this difference or to determine the degree of overlap. The larger sample of the current study provided greater power for the statistical tests and also greater external validity in generalizing to the domain sampled.

There were also difficulties in coding the variables. Terpstra's (1981) classification for determining the MRS for a study was found to be ambiguous. For example, it is not clear what measurement strategies are "at least a pretest–posttest measurement strategy" (p. 542) and which are not. Some studies assessed the impact of a T-group on its members by measuring behaviors at multiple points in the group's development. Although such studies did not measure behavior before and after the T-group, they used multiple waves of "posttest" measurement to empirically assess change in the group.

The total MRS is based on a simple addition of six variables coded 0-1. The rationale was ostensibly to use these six variables to assess the multiple facets of methodological rigor. The equal weighting of these six variables may produce the most valid measure of methodological rigor for research where the independent variables are under the control of the experimenter, but it is much less meaningful in field research where the individuals in the study plan and manage their own interventions. More relevant indicators of rigor and/or differential weighting of these indicators for OD field research may be necessary.

One major difference between the current study and Terpstra's (1981) study is the outcome-variable distribution. Terpstra (1981) found 35 studies to be uniformly positive, 12 to be mixed or nonsignificant, and 5 to be uniformly negative. The current study found 12, 77, and 1, respectively. Clearly, there is a large difference in the coding of this key variable.

The decision rule used in the current study to code the outcome variable was the following: If a study reported both significant and nonsignificant results, it was coded as "mixed." If the study reported all significant results, it was coded as "uniformly positive"; if the study reported all nonsignificant results, it was coded as "uniformly negative." This decision rule followed *Webster's* definition of "uniform": "having always the same form, manner, or degree: not varying or variable." Some studies coded as mixed in the current investigation may have been coded as uniformly positive or negative in the Terpstra study.

Without a clear distinction between mixed and uniform, the coding of the research outcome becomes a subjective judgment. Bass (1983) proposed that biases operating in OD "softies" and "hardheads" may have an effect on decisions made by investigators during a study. Two key decision areas of meta-analysis that may be affected by such biases are the coding of results and the decision rules used to code study characteristics (Green & Hall, 1984; Paul, in press). It is proposed that the system for coding OD results as presented by Terpstra (1981) and used in this replication is inadequate. One of several changes needed

by future meta-analysis of OD research is new outcome measures for coding results of OD studies. This measure should be stated in as objective manner as possible to minimize potential bias as presented by Bass (1983).

Terpstra asserted that bias occurred because "top management typically invests heavily in an OD program," because "evaluators frequently find that they have been knowingly or unknowingly in the role of defendant" and because "professional consultants and evaluators want to stay in business" (p. 541). One problem with this assertion is the failure to consider alternative explanations for the original results. Before accepting the cause of possible bias as being the impropriety of OD evaluators, other major alternative explanations need to be considered and ruled out.

One alternative explanation for the findings is the peer review process. Manuscripts reporting positive findings in new areas of research are more likely to be published even if they contain some methodological shortcoming, whereas a study finding nonsignificant or negative results needs to demonstrate a strong design to be considered for publication. Poorly designed studies finding negative results are not normally published; only well-designed studies are considered in such a case. Such an explanation is consistent with the a posteriori analysis done by Terpstra: The only significantly different group was the one that had presented negative results and had the most rigorous design. If this explanation is correct, the bias would exist in many areas of published literature and could be better described as "positive published findings bias." Such a bias would not be specific to OD evaluators; it could be considered consensus judgment of the profession regarding findings important enough to publish. The coding scheme used by Terpstra might incorrectly identify such a bias in short research notes briefly reporting positive results important to the profession: If an article did not explicitly provide enough information for coding, but did use quantitative data, it might be coded as not rigorous following the coding scheme rather than not being included in the data set.

Another alternative explanation for the results may have been the mixture of interventions studied. Although Terpstra generalized the results to the entire field, only four types of interventions were selected for study. One intervention, laboratory training, was the focus of much *JABS* research, particularly in the early years. It may be that this particular intervention leads to null or negative results and that the bias found by Terpstra resulted not from evaluator impropriety but from the predominance of laboratory training interventions in the data set. Such an explanation is congruent with the research of Bowers (1973), who found negative results for T-group interventions, but positive results for other types of interventions. More rigorous studies of OD evaluation research have compared results for different intervention types for precisely this reason (see Porras, 1979; Porras & Berg, 1978; Golembiewski, Proehl, & Sink, 1981; Margulies, Wright, & Scholl, 1977). Terpstra (1982) found such problems of validity and generalization in a recent report of an extension of the Terpstra (1981) data set. Terpstra (1982) reported that "it is quite evident that varying degrees of methodological rigor are associated with the four OD intervention types" and concluded: "Thus, it may not be advisable to lump the major OD variants together for the purposes of generalizing as to either their degree of methodological rigor or their degree of effectiveness" (p. 415).

To test this proposal, we coded the studies for the type of intervention used. The majority of the studies in the current investigation were laboratory training studies ($N = 66$; 73.3%). In the second study reported by Terpstra, about two thirds of the studies concerned laboratory training (Terpstra, 1982, p. 416). Clearly, the data set being analyzed here is not an adequate sample of OD research, and conclusions about the relationship between methodological rigor and outcome score cannot be made for the domain of OD research. Thus, any bias found by the Terpstra study can only be safely applied to laboratory training.

Bass (1983) has discussed the possible implications of Terpstra's (1981) results for OD research; however, Bass's (1983) discussion should be interpreted as a tentative conceptual explanation because at present, the relation, if any, between methodological rigor and research outcome is unresolved.

In summary, Terpstra (1981) reported a positive findings bias in OD research. The finding was not confirmed in this replication of that study. Although Terpstra reported perfect reliability for the coding scheme in his study, the present replication encountered many problems concerned with reliability and validity in the coding effort. Serious problems occurred in the coding of the only dependent variable used in the research (reported outcomes of the research), where coding required a great deal of subjectivity in rater judgment. Although the current effort differed somewhat from the Terpstra study in the sample used and the need for extensive interrater discussion to produce agreement on coding, it replicated the earlier effort in all other significant areas. In spite of such parallels, the present study found no evidence of bias.

Bass (1983) contended that the "hardheads," in regard to OD research, may be biased against the findings of OD research. It may be that Terpstra's (1981) findings struck a responsive chord. Because the Terpstra (1981) findings were not replicable, it may be better to focus attention on the problems in meta-analysis research so that future research can answer more adequately the question of the relationship between methodological rigor and reported outcomes in OD (see Woodman and Wayne, in press). The next section identifies potential problems and solutions in meta-analysis research as exemplified in the Terpstra (1981) study. The final section proposes some explicit criteria for evaluating future meta-analysis research.

Potential Meta-Analysis Problems

Public availability. One key characteristic of the scientific method is public availability of the data and the research process. This hallmark of objective scientific inquiry is particularly critical for meta-analysis because meta-analysis research is itself based on publicly available information. In fact, one of the major contributions meta-analysis research makes beyond traditional literature reviews is that meta-analysis research is objectively verifiable, using measured concepts, quantitative data, and statistical analyses, whereas literature reviews depend on the subjective integration of results across studies by the reviewer. Paul (in press) suggested that "meta-analytic reviews are subject to all the problems and potential biases of any other means of literature review, but they may at least be more explicit such that some of the problems are easier to identify." For meta-analysis, it is important that several aspects of the study be publicly available: the list of studies used in the analysis, the coding rules used to convert the research studies to measured variables (including documentation on how problems in applying the coding scheme were resolved), copies of the data set and possibly copies of the analyses performed. In the Terpstra (1981) example, none of these are available for reanalysis or further inspection. Fisher and Gitelson (1983), for example, published as an appendix the full list of 43 studies used in their meta-analysis.

Coding documentation. The results of the meta-analysis rely on the adequacy of the coding scheme. The application of any coding scheme is an attempt to convert some complex reality to a set of mutually exclusive and exhaustive numbers and will thus always encounter problems of fitting the phenomena to the numerical scheme. In meta-analysis, the differences in the studies are confounded with differences in reporting style and thoroughness, so coding is often a difficult process. Detailed decision rules are necessary for adapting the coding scheme to the many special situations encountered. Codes for combinations and codes for unreported or missing data are usually necessary. If estimates for variables are to be made based on the published information, the estimation procedures should be delineated. Thus, in meta-analysis research, it is critical that detailed documentation of coding decision rules be maintained and publicly available.

Domain of generalization. Meta-analysis research examines studies fitting certain inclusion criteria. It is the right of a meta-analysis researcher to identify the domain within which some hypothesis is to be tested; the exercise of that right also brings the responsibility to limit generalizations of results to that domain. Meta-analysis researchers have emphasized the need to define content domain theoretically, excluding publication criteria or rigor criteria, although not all meta-analyses study the complete domain.

For example, Fisher and Gitelson (1983) limited their search to an 11-year period and included two unpublished studies by the authors, but failed to search for the entire domain of studies. The Terpstra (1981) study limited the domain to articles published in a single journal, whereas other meta-analyses used all available studies (published and unpublished) fitting a well-defined conceptual domain. Literature reviews typically are limited to the most rigorous research in order to simplify the task of integrating subjectively the findings of the studies, but in meta-analysis, all studies fitting the content domain are included and any conjectures that rigor influences results are tested using variables coded by the meta-analysis, as was done in the Terpstra (1981) investigation. It is important to understand that these inclusion criteria define the domain to which generalizations are limited. In the Terpstra (1981) investigation, for example, the obtained results are limited to empirical studies of four intervention types published in one journal, not to the field of OD research in general.

Study characteristics. Literature reviews (e.g., Terpstra, 1982) often describe a research literature in terms of research designs used, sample sizes, sample demographics, authors' affiliation, and so forth as a guide to current research and as a stimulant for new research. Meta-analysis goes beyond a description of study characteristics to understand what the generalized results are and how the conduct of research affects those findings. Glass et al.'s (1981) approach to meta-analysis always codes descriptive characteristics of the studies analyzed, whereas Hunter et al. (1982) proposed that study characteristics should not be coded or analyzed unless and until the null hypothesis that the obtained variation of results could be explained by statistical artifacts was rejected. Our analysis of and replication of the Terpstra (1981) study indicates that study characteristics should be included in all meta-analysis research in order to understand fully the nature and limits of the research domain. Even if generalized validities are obtained following the Hunter et al. (1982) approach, it is still important to report study characteristics because they precisely define the domain over which the validities can be safely generalized. In the Terpstra (1981) investigation, the domain criteria allowed inclusion of four types of OD interventions, but a very unequal sampling of those interventions was actually obtained. As explained in a later report (Terpstra, 1982), the vast majority of studies analyzed were laboratory training studies, whereas the other three interventions were represented by only a handful of studies. Thus, although the domain criteria were broader, the obtained results can only be safely applied to laboratory training studies because the collection process failed to produce a representative mix of OD interventions. Domain limitations can only be known if descriptive characteristics are analyzed and reported.

Selective reporting. Meta-analysis is often a major undertaking involving detailed coding and analysis of dozens of variables. Simple probabilities will provide some statistically significant relationships in large-scale meta-analysis research. The selective reporting of results introduces a significant source of bias in the meta-analysis research process. This bias is particularly a problem in exploratory meta-analysis where variables are included based on convenience or ease of coding. Our suggestion for solving this potential problem is to develop the hypotheses to be tested in advance of the coding, code only those variables to be directly tested by the research, and fully report the results. Such a procedure will maintain meta-analysis as a vehicle for testing hypotheses of theoretical significance. The Terpstra (1981) study, for example, reported only one relationship excerpted from a large study of many variables described more fully by Terpstra (1982); thus, it is difficult to rule out the hypothesis that the reported finding was simply the result of chance.

Interpretation of results. As discussed by Bass (1983), human beings tend to confirm what we already believe to be the case, regardless of whether the position is hard-headed or soft. The problem is encountered in any line of research, but interpretation problems are particularly important in meta-analysis. Converting many varied research studies to a manageable set of coded variables is a process that potentially loses important meaning. The coded variables used in meta-analysis are often a relatively limited repre-

sentation of a complex reality of empirical studies, so interpretation of obtained results must be made very carefully (Green & Hall, 1984). In the Terpstra (1981) investigation, the results of one hypothesis test on four intervention types published in one journal were interpreted as adequate evidence that OD researchers were biased. In meta-analysis, it is particularly appropriate to differentiate data-based conclusions from extrapolations because of the potential for generalizing the results beyond the boundaries of the domain and overinterpreting the meaning of relatively simple coding schemes. It is also important to rule out competing explanations for whatever results are obtained in order to increase confidence in the interpretation of those results.

Criteria for Evaluating Meta-Analysis Research

Based on our consideration of these problems, we propose a series of criteria for evaluating meta-analysis research. Meta-analysis research meeting acceptable quality standards

1. Uses a theoretical model as the basis of the meta-analysis research and tests hypotheses from that model.
2. Identifies precisely the domain within which the hypotheses are to be tested.
3. Includes all publicly available studies in the defined content domain (not just published studies, or easily available studies).
4. Avoids selecting studies based on criteria of methodological rigor, age of study, or publication status.
5. Publishes or makes available the final list of studies used in the analysis.
6. Selects and codes variables on theoretical grounds rather than convenience.
7. Provides detailed documentation of the coding scheme and the resolution of problems in applying the coding scheme, including estimation procedures used for missing data.
8. Uses multiple raters to apply the coding scheme and provides a rigorous assessment of interrater reliability.
9. Reports all variables analyzed in order to avoid problems of capitalizing on chance relationships in a subset of variables.
10. Publishes or makes available the data set used in analysis.

11. Considers alternative explanations for the findings obtained.

12. Limits generalization of results to the domain specified by the research.

13. Reports study characteristics in order to understand the nature and limits of the domain actually analyzed.

14. Reports the entire study in sufficient detail to allow for direct replication.

The 14 criteria outlined above are concerned with the theoretical basis of a meta-analysis, with methodological issues of how the meta-analysis is conducted, and with the reporting and availability of data and documentation. The use of these or similar criteria will, we think, establish and maintain high quality standards for meta-analysis research as applied to organization development and to other fields as well.

References

Bass, B. M. (1983). Issues involved in relations between methodological rigor and reported outcomes in evaluations of organization development. *Journal of Applied Psychology, 68,* 197–199.

Bowers, D. G. (1973). OD techniques and their results in 23 organizations: The Michigan ICL Study. *Journal of Applied Behavioral Science, 9,* 21–43.

Bullock, R. J., & Svyantek, D. J. (1983). Positive-findings bias in positive-findings-bias research: An unsuccessful replication. In K. H. Chung (Ed.), *Academy of Management Proceedings* (pp. 221–224).

Bullock, R. J., & Tubbs, M. (1983). A meta-analysis of gainsharing plans as OD interventions. Paper presented to the OD division of the Academy of Management. Dallas TX.

Burton, N. W. (1981). Estimating scorer agreement for nominal categorization systems. *Educational and Psychological Measurement, 41,* 953–962.

Callender, J. C., & Osburn, H. G. (1980). Development and test of a new model for validity generalization. *Journal of Applied Psychology, 65,* 543–558.

Cohen, J. (1968). Weighted kappa: Nominal scale agreement with provision for scaled disagreement or partial credit. *Psychological Bulletin, 70,* 213–220.

Fisher, C. D., & Gitelson, R. (1983). A meta-analysis of the correlates of role conflict and ambiguity. *Journal of Applied Psychology, 68,* 320–333.

Glass, G. V., McGaw, B., & Smith, M. L. (1981). *Meta-analysis in social research.* Beverly Hills, CA: Sage Publications.

Golembiewski, R. T., Proehl, C. W., & Sink, D. (1981). Success of OD applications in the public sector. *Public Administration Review, 41,* 679–682.

Green, S. B. (1981). A comparison of three indexes of agreement between observers: Proportion of agreement, G-index, and kappa. *Educational and Psychological Measurement, 41,* 1069–1072.

Green, B. F., & Hall, J. A. (1984). Quantitative methods for literature reviews. *Annual Review of Psychology, 35,* 37–53.

Hedges, L. V. (1982). Fitting continuous models to effect size data. *Journal of Educational Statistics, 7,* 245–270.

Hunter, J. E., Schmidt, F. L., & Jackson, G. B. (1982). *Meta-analysis: Cumulating research findings across studies.* Beverly Hills, CA: Sage Publications.

Johnson, D. W., Johnson, R. T., & Maruyama, G. (1983). Interdependence and interpersonal attraction among heterogeneous and homogeneous individuals: A theoretical formulation and a meta-analysis of the research. *Review of Educational Research, 53,* 5–54.

Jones, A. P., Johnson, L. A., Butler, M. C., & Main, D. S. (1983). Apples and oranges: An empirical comparison of commonly used indices of interrater agreement. *Academy of Management Journal, 26,* 507–519.

Kulik, C. C., & Kulik, J. A. (1982). Effects of ability grouping on secondary school students: A meta-analysis of evaluation findings. *Journal of Consulting and Clinical Psychology, 19,* 415–428.

Margulies, N., Wright, P. L., & Scholl, R. W. (1977). Organization development techniques: Their impact on change, *Group & Organization Studies, 2,* 428–448.

Osburn, H. G., Callender, J. C., Greener, J. M., & Ashworth, S. (1983). Statistical power of tests of the situational specificity hypothesis in validity generalization studies: A cautionary note. *Journal of Applied Psychology, 68,* 115–122.

Paul, G. L. (in press). Can pregnancy be a placebo effect? Terminology, designs, and conclusions in the study of psychosocial and pharmocological treatments of behavioral disorders. In L. White, B. Tursky, & G. F. Schwartz (Eds.). *Placebo: Clinical phenomena and new insights.* New York: Guilford Press.

Porras, J. I. (1979). The comparative impact of different OD techniques and intervention intensities. *Journal of Applied Behavioral Science, 15,* 156–178.

Porras, J. I., & Berg, P. O. (1978). Evaluation methodology in organization development: Analysis and critique. *Journal of Applied Behavioral Science, 14,* 151–174.

Schmidt, F. L., & Hunter, J. E. (1977). Development of a general solution to the problem of validity generalization. *Journal of Applied Psychology, 62,* 529–540.

Strube, M. J., & Garcia, J. E. (1981). A meta-analytic investigation of Fiedler's contingency model of leadership effectiveness. *Psychological Bulletin, 90,* 307–321.

Terpstra, D. E. (1981). Relationship between methodological rigor and reported outcomes in organization development evaluation research. *Journal of Applied Psychology, 66,* 541–543.

Terpstra, D. E. (1982). Evaluating selected organization development interventions. The state of the art. *Group and Organization Studies, 7,* 402–417.

Uebersax, J. S. (1982). A generalized kappa coefficient. *Educational and Psychological Measurement, 42,* 181–185.

Woodman, R. W., & Wayne, S. J. (in press). An investigation of positive-findings bias in organization development evaluation. *Academy of Management Journal.*

Received March 1, 1983
Revision received April 30, 1984 ∎

About the Editors

DAVID S. CORDRAY is Group Director for public assistance and federal evaluation policy in the Program Evaluation and Methodology Division at the United States General Accounting Office, Washington, D.C. He is a member of the Board of Directors of the American Evaluation Association, and has served as Co-chair of the Ethics and Standards Committee, and Associate Professor of Psychology at Northwestern University. Dr. Cordray has published numerous articles on evaluation methodology and practices associated with primary studies, secondary analysis, and quantitative synthesis. He has coedited several books, serves as associate editor for *Evaluation Review,* and is on the editorial board of *New Directions for Program Evaluation.* The opinions expressed in this volume do not represent official policy of the United States General Accounting Office.

MARK W. LIPSEY is Professor of Psychology and Chair of the Psychology Department at Claremont Graduate School, California. Dr. Lipsey has published articles on evaluation and applied research methodology, is the Editor-in Chief for *New Directions for Program Evaluation,* and serves as associate editor for *Evaluation Review.* He has conducted evaluations of juvenile delinquency treatment and a variety of other human service programs. His recent work focuses on methodological issues in program evaluation, including design and measurement sensitivity, methods for representing program theory in program research, and technical and conceptual issues in primary evaluation studies. During this past academic year, Dr. Lipsey was awarded a Fulbright Fellowship to study and lecture in New Delhi, India.

NOTES